P9-CCA-661

OUT OF MANY

A History of the American People

Fourth Edition

John Mack Faragher
YALE UNIVERSITY

Mari Jo Buhle
BROWN UNIVERSITY

Daniel Czitrom
MOUNT HOLYOKE COLLEGE

Susan H. Armitage
WASHINGTON STATE UNIVERSITY

Prentice Hall

Upper Saddle River, New Jersey 07458

Library of Congress Cataloging–in–Publication Data

Out of many: a history of the American people / John Mack Faragher
   . . . [et al.]. — 4th ed.
     p.   cm.
   Includes bibliographical references and index.
   ISBN 0-13-097797-7
   1. United States—History.   I. Faragher, John Mack, 1945–
E178.1.0935   2003
973—dc21   2002016905

Editorial Director: Charlyce Jones Owen
Senior Acquisitions Editor: Charles Cavaliere
VP, Editor-in-Chief of Development: Susanna Lesan
Production Editor: Jean Lapidus
Creative Director: Leslie Osher
Art Director: Ximena Tamvakopoulos
Marketing Manager: Claire Rehwinkel
Interior and Cover Designer: C2K, Inc.
Scanning: Central Scanning Services
Cover Image Specialist: Karen Sanatar
AVP, Director of Production and Manufacturing: Barbara Kittle
Manufacturing Manager: Nick Sklitsis

Manufacturing Buyer: Sherry Lewis
Photo Researcher: Linda Sykes
Director, Image Resource Center: Melinda Reo
Copy Editor: Stephen C. Hopkins
Line Art Manager: Guy Ruggiero
Artist: Mirella Signoretto
Photo Permissions Coordinator: Carolyn Gauntt
Editorial Assistant: Adrienne Paul
Indexer: Murray Fisher
Text Permissions: The Permissions Group
Cartographers: Alice and William Thiede/CARTO-GRAPHICS;
Mirella Signoretto

Cover Art: Harvey Dinnerstein, *Underground, Together* 1996,
          oil on canvas, 90″ × 107″. Photograph courtesy of
          Gerold Wunderlich & Co., New York, NY.

Credits and acknowledgments for materials borrowed from
other sources and reproduced, with permission, in this textbook
appear on page C-1.

This book was set in 11/12 Weiss by the TSI Graphics
And was printed and bound by RR Donnelley & Sons Company.
The cover was printed by Phoenix Color Corp.

Printed in the United States of America
10 9 8 7 6 5 4 3 2 1

ISBN 0-13-097799-3

Prentice-Hall International (UK) Limited, *London*
Prentice-Hall of Australia Pty. Limited, *Sydney*
Prentice-Hall Canada Inc., *Toronto*
Prentice-Hall Hispanoamericana, S.A., *Mexico*
Prentice-Hall of India Private Limited, *New Delhi*
Prentice-Hall of Japan, Inc., *Tokyo*
Pearson Education Asia Pte. Ltd., *Singapore*
Editora Prentice-Hall do Brasil, Ltda., *Rio de Janeiro*

TO OUR STUDENTS,

OUR SISTERS,

AND OUR BROTHERS

Brief Contents

CONTENTS

18 Conquest and Survival: The Trans-Mississippi West, 1860–1900 529

19 The Incorporation of America, 1865–1900 564

Community & Memory: Representing Chicago's History 595

20 Commonwealth and Empire, 1870–1900 597

21 Urban America and the Progressive Era, 1900–1917 629

Community & Memory: Battle for the Lower East Side 663

22 World War I, 1914–1920 665

23 The Twenties, 1920–1929 696

Community & Memory:
Exhibiting the *Enola Gay* 805

26 The Cold War, 1945–1952   807

27 America at Midcentury, 1952–1963   838

28 The Civil Rights Movement, 1945–1966 869

**Community & Memory:
Flying the "Stars and Bars" 900**

29 War at Home, War Abroad, 1965–1974 902

30 The Conservative Ascendancy, 1974–1987 938

31 Toward a Transnational America, since 1988 974

Community & Memory: The World Trade Center and Ways of Remembering 1006

MAPS

CHARTS, GRAPHS, AND TABLES

PREFACE

*O*ut of Many: A History of the American People, fourth edition, offers a distinctive and timely approach to American history, highlighting the experiences of diverse communities of Americans in the unfolding story of our country. The stories of these communities offer a way of examining the complex historical forces shaping people's lives at various moments in our past. The debates and conflicts surrounding the most momentous issues in our national life—independence, emerging democracy, slavery, westward settlement, imperial expansion, economic depression, war, technological change—were largely worked out in the context of local communities. Through communities we focus on the persistent tensions between everyday life and those larger decisions and events that continually reshape the circumstances of local life. Each chapter opens with a description of a representative community. Some of these portraits feature American communities struggling with one another: African slaves and English masters on the rice plantations of colonial Georgia, or *Tejanos* and Americans during the Texas war of independence. Other chapters feature portraits of communities facing social change: the feminists of Seneca Falls, New York, in 1848, or the African Americans of Montgomery, Alabama, in 1955. As the story unfolds we find communities growing to include ever larger groups of Americans: the soldiers from every colony who forged the Continental Army into a patriotic national force at Valley Forge during the American Revolution, or the moviegoers who aspired to a collective dream of material prosperity and upward mobility during the 1920s.

Out of Many is also the only American history text with a truly continental perspective. With community vignettes from New England to the South, the Midwest to the far West, we encourage students to appreciate the great expanse of our nation. For example, a vignette of seventeenth-century Sante Fé , New Mexico, illustrates the founding of the first European settlements in the New World. We present territorial expansion into the American West from the viewpoint of the Mandan villagers of the upper Missouri River of North Dakota. We introduce the policies of the Reconstruction era through the experience of African Americans in Hale County, Alabama. A continental perspective drives home to students that American history has never been the preserve of any particular region.

In these ways *Out of Many* breaks new ground, but without compromising its coverage of the traditional turning points that we believe are critically important to an understanding of the American past. Among these watershed events are the Revolution and the struggle over the Constitution, the Civil War and Reconstruction, and the Great Depression and World War II. In *Out of Many*, however, we seek to integrate the narrative of national history with the story of the nation's many diverse communities. The Revolutionary and Constitutional period tested the ability of local communities to forge a new unity, and success depended on their ability to build a nation without compromising local identity. The Civil War and Reconstruction formed a second great test of the balance between the national ideas of the Revolution and the power of local and sectional communities. The Depression and the New Deal demonstrated the importance of local communities and the growing power of national institutions during the greatest economic challenge in our history. *Out of Many* also looks back in a new and comprehensive way—from the vantage point of the beginning of a new century and the end of the cold war—at the salient events of the last fifty years and their impact on American communities. The community focus of *Out of Many* weaves the stories of the people and the nation into a single compelling narrative.

Out of Many, fourth edition, includes expanded coverage of our diverse heritage. Our country is appropriately known as "a nation of immigrants," and the history of immigration to America, from the seventeenth to the twenty-first centuries, is fully integrated into the text. There is sustained and close attention to our place in the world, with special emphasis on our relations with the nations of the Western Hemisphere, especially our near neighbors, Canada and Mexico. In a completely new final chapter we consider the promises and the risks of American diversity in the new century. The statistical data has been completely updated with the results of the 2000 census. We have also incorporated new scholarship on the South, popular culture, science and technology, and the Cold War.

The fourth edition also includes an important new feature, Community & Memory, in which we examine the way American communities have attempted to commemorate and memorialize the past. Communities sometimes come to blows over different ways of looking at history. Arguments over the meaning of the past are not confined to the classroom.

SPECIAL FEATURES

With each edition of *Out of Many* we have sought to strengthen its unique integration of the best of traditional American history with its innovative community-based focus and strong continental perspective. A wealth of special features and pedagogical aids reinforces our narrative and helps students grasp key issues.

- **Community and Diversity.** *Out of Many*, fourth edition, opens with an introduction, titled "Community and Diversity," that acquaints students with the major themes of the book, providing them with a framework for understanding American history.

- **Community & Memory.** New to the fourth edition, this special illustrated feature, located at the end of Chapters 1, 4, 6, 9, 14, 19, 21, 25, 28, and 31, examines the ways in which American communities have attempted to commemorate the past and the conflicts that arise when the meaning of the past divides the members of a community. Discussion questions and annotated links to relevant Websites for each Community & Memory feature are found on the *Companion Website* for *Out of Many*.

- **Maps.** *Out of Many*, fourth edition, has more maps than any other American history textbook. Most maps include topographical detail that helps students appreciate the impact of geography on history. Many maps have been redrawn to better reflect a hemispheric perspective.

- **Web Explorations.** New to the fourth edition, Web explorations are tied directly up to two maps in each chapter and provide interactive exploration of key geographical, chronological, and thematic concepts in each chapter. Each Web exploration is found on the *Companion Website* for *Out of Many: www.prenhall.com/faragher*, and on the *Mapping American History CD-ROM*, which is packaged with each copy of the text.

- **Overview tables.** Overview tables provide students with a summary of complex issues.

- **Graphs, charts, and tables.** Every chapter includes one or more graphs, charts, or tables that help students understand important events and trends.

- **Photos and Illustrations.** The abundant illustrations in *Out of Many*, 30 percent of them new to the fourth edition, include many that have never before been used in an American history text. None of the images is anachronistic—each one dates from the historical period under discussion.

Extensive captions treat the images as visual primary source documents from the American past, describing their source and explaining their significance.

- **Chapter-opening outlines and key topics lists.** These pedagogical aids provide students with a succinct preview of the material covered in each chapter.

- **Chronologies.** A chronology at the end of each chapter helps students build a framework of key events.

- **Review Questions.** Review questions helps students review, reinforce, and retain the material in each chapter and encourage them to relate the material to broader issues in American history.

- **Recommended Reading and Additional Bibliography.** The works in the short, annotated Recommended Reading list at the end of each chapter have been selected with the interested introductory student in mind. The extensive Additional Bibliography provides a comprehensive overview of current scholarship on the subject of the chapter.

- **History on the Internet.** New to the fourth edition, sections in each chapter list useful Web resources related to the topics discussed, along with helpful comments describing the material on each site.

CLASSROOM ASSISTANCE PACKAGE

In classrooms across the country, many instructors encounter students who perceive history as merely a jumble of names, dates, and events. *Out of Many*, fourth edition, brings our dynamic past alive for these students with a text and accompanying print and multimedia classroom assistance package that combine sound scholarship, engaging narrative, and a rich array of cutting-edge pedagogical tools.

PRINT SUPPLEMENTS

Instructor's Resource Manual

A true time-saver in developing and preparing lecture presentations, the *Instructor's Resource Manual* contains chapter outlines, detailed chapter overviews, lecture topics, discussion questions, readings, and information about audio-visual resources.

Test Item File

The *Test Item File* offers a menu of more than 1,500 multiple-choice, identification, matching, true-false, and essay test questions and 10–15 questions per chapter on the maps found in each chapter. The guide includes a collection of blank maps that can be photocopied and used for map testing purposes or for other class exercises.

Prentice Hall Custom Test

This commercial-quality computerized test management program, available for Windows and Macintosh environments, allows instructors to select items from the *Test Item File* and design their own exams.

Transparency Pack

This collection of more than 160 full-color transparency acetates provides instructors with all the maps, charts, and graphs in the text for use in the classroom. Each transparency is accompanied by a page of descriptive material and discussion questions.

Study Guide, Volumes I and II

Each chapter in the *Study Guide* includes a chapter commentary and outline, identification terms, multiple-choice questions, short essay questions, map questions, and questions based on primary source extracts.

Documents Set, Volumes I and II

In revising the documents set for the fourth edition, the authors have selected and carefully edited more than 300 documents that relate directly to the themes and content of the text and organized them into five general categories: community, social history, government, culture, and politics. Each document is approximately two pages long and includes a brief introduction and study questions intended to encourage students to analyze the document critically and relate it to the content of the text. The *Documents Set* is available at a substantial discount when packaged with *Out of Many*.

Retrieving the American Past, 2003 Edition

Written and developed by leading historians and educators, this reader is an on-demand history database that offers 300 primary source documents (eight new to the 2003 edition) on key topics in American History, such as: Women on the Frontier, The Salem Witchcraft Scare, The Age of Industrial Violence, and Native American Societies, 1870–1995. Each module includes an introduction, several primary documents and secondary sources, follow-up questions, and recommendations for further reading. By deciding which modules to include

and the order in which they will appear, instructors can compile a custom reader to fit their needs. Contact your local Prentice Hall representative for more information about this exciting custom publishing option.

Many Lives, Many Stories: Biographies in American History

New to the fourth edition, this two-volume collection of sixty-two biographies in American history was written specifically to match the chapter sequence and themes of *Out of Many*.

Introductions, prereading questions, suggested readings, and a special prologue about the role of biography in the study of American history enrich this important new supplement. Available free when packaged with *Out of Many*. Annotated links to relevant Websites for each biography can be found on the *Companion Website* for *Out of Many*.

Understanding and Answering Essay Questions

Prepared by Mary L. Kelley, San Antonio College

This brief guide suggests helpful study techniques as well as specific analytical tools for understanding different types of essay questions and provides precise guidelines for preparing well-crafted essay answers. The guide is available free to students when packaged with *Out of Many*.

Reading Critically About History

Prepared by Rose Wassman and Lee Rinsky, both of DeAnza College.

This brief guide provides students with helpful strategies for reading a history textbook. It is available free when packaged with *Out of Many*.

Themes of the Times

Themes of the Times is a newspaper supplement prepared jointly by Prentice Hall and the premier news publication, the *New York Times*. Issued twice a year, it contains recent articles pertinent to American history. Contact your local Prentice Hall representative for details.

Prentice Hall and Penguin Bundle Program

Prentice Hall and Penguin are pleased to provide adopters of *Out of Many* with an opportunity to receive significant discounts when orders for *Out of Many* are bundled together with Penguin titles in American history. Please contact your local Prentice Hall representative for details.

MULTIMEDIA SUPPLEMENTS

Out of Many Companion Website™

Address: http://www.prenhall.com/faragher

With the *Out of Many* Companion Website™ students can take full advantage of the Web and use it in tandem with the text to enrich their study of American history. The Companion Website™ ties the text to related material available on the Internet. Its many instructional features include learning objectives and study questions organized by the primary subtopics of each chapter, map labeling exercises, annotated links, document questions, and Community & Memory resources.

Mapping American History CD-ROM

This innovative electronic supplement takes advantage of the interactive capabilities of multimedia technology to enrich students' understanding of the geographic dimensions of history with animated maps, time-lines, and related on-screen activities tied directly to key issues in each chapter of *Out of Many*.

Instructor CD-ROM for *Out of Many*

This new multimedia ancillary section contains a Power Point™ presentation directly linked to the text, as well as maps and graphs from *Out of Many*, lecture outlines, and other instructional materials.

History on the Internet: Evaluating Online Resources

This brief guide introduces students to the origin and innovations behind the Internet and provides clear strategies for navigating the Web to find historical materials. Exercises within and at the end of the chapters allow students to practice searching the wealth of resources available to the student of history. This 48-page supplementary book is free to students when packaged with *Out of Many*.

Course Management Systems

As the leader in course-management solutions for teachers and students of history, Prentice Hall provides a variety of online tools. Contact your local Prentice Hall representative for details or visit www.prenhall.com.

ACKNOWLEDGMENTS

In the years it has taken to bring *Out of Many* from idea to reality and to improve it in successive editions, we have often been reminded that although writing history sometimes feels like isolated work, it actually involves a collective effort. We want to thank the dozens of people whose efforts have made the publication of this book possible.

At Prentice Hall, Charles Cavaliere, Senior Acquisitions Editor, gave us his full support and oversaw the entire publication process. Susanna Lesan, Editor-in-Chief of Development, edited the first and fourth editions of the book; without her efforts this book would never have been published. Jean Lapidus, Production Editor, oversaw the entire complicated production process in an exemplary fashion. Linda Sykes, our photo researcher, expertly tracked down the many pertinent new images that appear in this edition.

Among our many other friends at Prentice Hall we also want to thank Yolanda de Rooy, President; Charlyce Jones Owen, Editorial Director; Claire Rehwinkel, Marketing Manager; Leslie Osher, Creative Design Director; Ximena Tamvakopoulos, Art Director; Stephen Hopkins, Copy Editor; and Adrienne Paul, Editorial Assistant.

Although we share joint responsibility for the entire book, the chapters were individually authored: John Mack Faragher wrote chapters 1–8; Susan Armitage wrote chapters 9–16; Mari Jo Buhle wrote chapters 18–20, 25–26, 29; and Daniel Czitrom wrote chapters 17, 21–24, 27–28. (For this edition Buhle and Czitrom co-authored Chapters 30–31.)

Historians around the country greatly assisted us by reading and commenting on our chapters for this and previous editions. We want to thank each of them for the commitment of their valuable time.

Donald Abbe, Texas Tech University, TX
Richard H. Abbott, Eastern Michigan University, MI
Guy Alchon, University of Delaware, DE
Don Barlow, Prestonburg Community College, KY
William Barney, University of North Carolina, NC
Alwyn Barr, Texas Tech University, TX
Debra Barth, San Jose City College, CA
Peter V. Bergstrom, Illinois State University, IL
William C. Billingsley, South Plains College, TX
Kevin Boyle, University of Massachusetts, MA
Peter H. Buckingham, Linfield College, OR
Bill Cecil-Fronsman, Washburn University of Topeka, KS
Victor W. Chen, Chabot College, CA
Jonathan M. Chu, University of Massachusetts, MA
P. Scott Corbett, Oxnard College, CA
Matther Coulter, Collin County Community College, TX
Virginia Crane, University of Wisconsin, Oshkosh, WI
Jim Cullen, Harvard University, MA
Thomas J. Curran, St. John's University, NY

Richard V. Damms, Ohio State University, OH

Elizabeth Dunn, Baylor University, TX

Emmett G. Essin, Eastern Tennessee State University, TN

Mark F. Fernandez, Loyola University, IL

Leon Fink, University of North Carolina, Chapel Hill, NC

Michael James Foret, University of Wisconsin, Stevens Point, WI

Joshua B. Freeman, Columbia University, NY

Glenda E. Gilmore, Yale University, CT

Don C. Glenn, Diablo Valley College, CA

Lawrence Glickman, University of South Carolina, SC

Kenneth Goings, Florida Atlantic University, FL

Mark Goldman, Tallahassee Community College, FL

Gregory L. Goodwin, Bakersfield College, CA

Gretchen Green, University of Missouri, Kansas City, MO

Emily Greenwald, University of Nebraska at Lincoln, NE

Mark W. T. Harvey, North Dakota State University, ND

Sally Hadden, Florida State University, FL

James A. Hijiya, University of Massachusetts at Dartmouth, MA

Jon Hunner, New Mexico State University, NM

Albert Hurtado, University of Oklahoma, OK

Raymond M. Hyser, James Madison University, VA

John Inscoe, University of Georgia, GA

Lesley Ann Kawaguchi, Santa Monica College, CA

John C. Kesler, Lakeland Community College, OH

Peter N. Kirstein, Saint Xavier University, IL

Frank Lambert, Purdue University, IN

Susan Rimby Leighow, Millersville University, PA

Janice M. Leone, Middle Tennessee University, TN

Glenn Linden, Southern Methodist University, Dallas, TX

George Lipsitz, University of California, San Diego, CA

Judy Barrett Litoff, Bryant College, RI

Jesus Luna, California State University, CA

Larry Madaras, Howard Community College, MD

Lynn Mapes, Grand Valley State University, MI

John F. Marszalek, Mississippi State University, MS

Scott C. Martin, Bowling Green State University, OH

Robert L. Matheny, Eastern New Mexico University, NM

Thomas Matijasic, Prestonburg Community College, KY

M. Delores McBroome, Humboldt State University, CA

Gerald McFarland, University of Massachusetts, Amherst, MA

Sam McSeveney, Vanderbilt University, TN

Warren Metcalf, Arizona State University, AZ

M. Catherine Miller, Texas State University, TX

Norman H. Murdoch, University of Cincinnati, OH

Gregory H. Nobles, Georgia Institute of Technology, GA

Ellen Nore, Southern Illinois University, Edwardsville, IL

Dale Odom, University of Texas at Denton, TX

Sean O'Neill, Grand Valley State University, MI

Edward Opper, Greenville Technical College, Greenville, SC

William A. Paquette, Tidewater Community College, VA

Charles K. Piehl, Mankato State University, MN

Carolyn Garrett Pool, University of Central Oklahoma, OK

Christie Farnham Pope, Iowa State University, IA

Susan Porter-Benson, University of Missouri, MO

Russell Posner, City College of San Francisco, CA

John Powell, Penn State University, Erie, PA

Sarah Purcell, Central Michigan University, MI

Joseph P. Reidy, Howard University, DC

Marilyn D. Rhinehart, North Harris College, TX

Leo P. Ribuffo, George Washington University, DC

Judy Ridner, California State University at Northridge, CA

Neal Salisbury, Smith College, MA

Roberto Salmon, University of Texas-Pan American, TX

Steven Schuster, Brookhaven Community College, TX

Megan Seahold, University of Texas, Austin, TX

Nigel Sellars, University of Oklahoma, Norman, OK

John David Smith, North Carolina State University, NC

Patrick Smith, Broward Community College, FL

Mark W. Summers, University of Kentucky, KY

John D. Tanner, Jr., Palomar College, CA

Robert R. Tomes, St. John's University, NY

Michael Miller Topp, University of Texas at El Paso, TX

John Trickel, Richland Community College, IL

Steve Tripp, Grand Valley State University, MI

Fred R. Van Hartesveldt, Fort Valley State University, GA

Philip H. Vaughan, Rose State College, OK

Robert C. Vitz, Northern Kentucky University, KY

Elliot West, University of Arkansas, AR

F. Michael Williams, Brevard Community College, FL

Charles Regan Wilson, University of Mississippi, MS

Harold Wilson, Old Dominion University, VA

Andrew Workman, Mills College, CA

William Woodward, Seattle Pacific University, WA

Loretta E. Zimmerman, University of Florida, FL

Each of us depended on a great deal of support and assistance with the research and writing that went into this book. We want to thank: Kathryn Abbott, Nan Boyd, Krista Comer, Jennifer Cote, Crista DeLuzio, Keith Edgerton, Carol Frost, Jesse Hoffnung Garskof, Pailin Gaither, Jane Gerhard, Todd Gernes, Mark Krasovic, Melani McAlister, Cristiane Mitchell, J. C. Mutchler, Keith Peterson, Alan Pinkham, Tricia Rose, Gina Rourke, Jessica Shubow, Gordon P. Utz, Jr., and Maura Young.

Our families and close friends have been supportive and ever so patient over the many years we have devoted to this project. But we want especially to thank Paul Buhle, Meryl Fingrutd, Bob Greene, and Michele Hoffnung.

ABOUT THE AUTHORS

Chris Freitag

JOHN MACK FARAGHER

John Mack Faragher is Arthur Unobskey Professor of American History and Director of the Howard R. Lamar Center for the Study of Frontiers and Borders at Yale University. Born in Arizona and raised in southern California, he received his B.A. at the University of California, Riverside, and his Ph.D. at Yale University. He is the author of *Women and Men on the Overland Trail* (1979), which won the Frederick Jackson Turner Award of the Organization of American Historians, *Sugar Creek: Life on the Illinois Prairie* (1986), *Daniel Boone: The Life and Legend of an American Pioneer* (1992), and (with Robert V. Hine) *The American West: A New Interpretive History* (2000).

MARI JO BUHLE

Mari Jo Buhle is William R. Kenan Jr. University Professor and Professor of American Civilization and History at Brown University, specializing in American women's history. She received her B.A. from the University of Illinois, Urbana–Champaign, and her Ph.D. from the University of Wisconsin, Madison. She is the author of *Women and American Socialism, 1870–1920* (1981) and *Feminism and Its Discontents: A Century of Struggle with Psychoanalysis* (1998). She is also coeditor of *Encyclopedia of the American Left,* second edition (1998). Professor Buhle held a fellowship (1991–1996) from the John D. and Catherine T. MacArthur Foundation.

DANIEL CZITROM

Daniel Czitrom is Professor of History at Mount Holyoke College. Born and raised in New York City, he received his B.A. from the State University of New York at Binghamton and his M.A. and Ph.D. from the University of Wisconsin, Madison. He is the author of *Media and the American Mind: From Morse to McLuhan* (1982), which won the First Books Award of the American Historical Association and has been translated into Spanish and Chinese. He has served as a historical consultant and a featured on-camera commentator for several documentary film projects, including two recent PBS series, *New York: A Documentary Film* and *American Photography: A Century of Images.*

SUSAN H. ARMITAGE

Susan H. Armitage is Claudius O. and Mary R. Johnson Distinguished Professor of History at Washington State University. She earned her Ph.D. from the London School of Economics and Political Science. Among her many publications on western women's history are three coedited books, *The Women's West* (1987), *So Much To Be Done: Women on the Mining and Ranching Frontier* (1991), and *Writing the Range: Race, Class, and Culture in the Women's West* (1997). She currently serves as an editor of a series of books on women and American history for the University of Illinois Press. She is the editor of *Frontiers: A Journal of Women's Studies.*

One of the most characteristic features of our country has always been its astounding variety. The American people include the descendants of native Indians, colonial Europeans, Africans, and migrants from virtually every country and continent. Indeed, as we enter a new century the United States is absorbing a flood of immigrants from Latin America and Asia that rivals the great tide of people from eastern and southern Europe one hundred years ago. What's more, our country is one of the world's most spacious, incorporating more than 3.6 million square miles of territory. The struggle to meld a single nation out of our many far-flung communities is what much of American history is all about. That is the story told in this book.

Every human society is made up of communities. A community is a set of relationships linking men, women, and their families to a coherent social whole that is more than the sum of its parts. In a community people develop the capacity for unified action. In a community people learn, often through trial and error, how to transform and adapt to their environment. The sentiment that binds the members of a community together is the mother of group identity and ethnic pride. In the making of history, communities are far more important than even the greatest of leaders, for the community is the institution most capable of passing a distinctive historical tradition to future generations.

Communities bind people together in multiple ways. They can be as small as local neighborhoods, in which people maintain face-to-face relations, or as large as the nation itself. This book examines American history from the perspective of community life—an ever-widening frame that has included larger and larger groups of Americans.

William Sidney Mount (1807–1868) *California News* 1850. Oil on canvas. The Long Island Museum of American Art, History and Carriages. Gift of Mr. and Mrs. Ward Melville, 1955.

Harvey Dinnerstein, *Underground, Together* 1996, oil on canvas, 90" × 107". Photograph courtesy of Gerold Wunderlich & Co., New York, NY.

Networks of kinship and friendship, and connections across generations and among families, establish the bonds essential to community life. Shared feelings about values and history establish the basis for common identity. In communities, people find the power to act collectively in their own interest. But American communities frequently took shape as a result of serious conflicts among groups, and within communities there has often been significant fighting among competing groups or classes. Thus the term *community*, as we use it here, includes tension and discord as well as harmony and agreement.

For years there have been persistent laments about the "loss of community" in modern America. But community has not disappeared—it is continually being reinvented. Until the late eighteenth century, community was defined primarily by space and local geography. But in the nineteenth century communities began to be reshaped by new and powerful historical forces such as the marketplace, industrialization, the corporation, mass immigration, mass media, and the growth of the nation-state. In the twentieth century, Americans have struggled to balance commitments to several communities simultaneously. These were defined not simply by local spatial arrangements, but by categories as varied as racial and ethnic groups, occupations, political affiliations, and consumer preferences.

The "American Communities" vignettes that open each chapter reflect this shift. Most of the vignettes in the pre–Civil War chapters focus on geographically defined communities, such as the ancient Indian city at Cahokia, or the experiment in industrial urban planning in early nineteenth-century Lowell, Massachusetts. In the post–Civil War chapters different and more modern kinds of communities make their appearance. In the 1920s, movies and radio offered a new kind of community—a community of identification with dreams of freedom, material success, upward mobility, youth and beauty. In the 1950s, rock 'n' roll music helped germinate a new national community of teenagers, with profound effects on the culture of the entire country in the second half of the twentieth century. In the late 1970s, fear of nuclear accidents like the one at Three Mile Island brought concerned citizens together in communities around the country and produced a national movement opposing nuclear power.

The title for our book was suggested by the Latin phrase selected by John Adams, Benjamin Franklin, and Thomas Jefferson for the Great Seal of the United States: *E Pluribus Unum*—"Out of Many Comes Unity." These men understood that unity could not be imposed by a powerful central authority but had to develop out of mutual respect among Americans of different backgrounds. The revolutionary leadership expressed the hope that such respect could grow on the basis of a remarkable proposition: "We hold these truths to be self-evident, that all men are created equal; that they are endowed by their Creator with certain unalienable rights; that among these are life, liberty, and the pursuit of happiness." The national government of the United States would preserve local and state authority but would guarantee individual rights. The nation would be strengthened by guarantees of difference.

"Out of Many"—that is the promise of America, and the premise of this book. The underlying dialectic of American history, we believe, is that as a people we need to locate our national unity in the celebration of the differences that exist among us; these differences can be our strength, as long as we affirm the promise of the Declaration. Protecting the "right to be different," in other words, is absolutely fundamental to the continued existence of democracy, and that right is best protected by the existence of strong and vital communities. We are bound together as a nation by the ideal of local and cultural differences protected by our common commitment to the values of our Revolution.

Today those values are endangered by terrorists using the tactics of mass terror. In the wake of the September 11, 2001, attack on the United States, and with the continuing threat of biological, chemical, or even nuclear assaults, Americans can not afford to lose faith in our historic vision. The United States is a multicultural and transnational society. The thousands of victims buried in the smoking ruins of the World Trade Center included people from dozens of different ethnic and national groups. We must fight to protect and defend the promise of our diverse nation

Our history shows that the promise of American unity has always been problematic. Centrifugal forces have been powerful in the American past, and at times

Thomas Satterwhite Noble, *Last Sale of Slaves on the Courthouse Steps*, 1860, oil on canvas, Missouri Historical Society.

the country has seemed about to fracture into its component parts. Our transformation from a collection of groups and regions into a nation has been marked by painful and often violent struggles. Our past is filled with conflicts between Indians and colonists, masters and slaves, Patriots and Loyalists, Northerners and Southerners, Easterners and Westerners, capitalists and workers, and sometimes the government and the people. War can bring out our best, but it can also bring out our worst. During World War II thousands of Japanese American citizens were deprived of their rights and locked up in isolated detention centers simply because of their ethnic background. Americans often appear to be little more than a contentious collection of peoples with conflicting interests, divided by region and background, race and class.

Our most influential leaders have also sometimes suffered a crisis of faith in the American project of "liberty and justice for all." Thomas Jefferson not only believed in the inferiority of African Americans, but he feared that immigrants from outside the Anglo-American tradition might "warp and bias" the development of the nation "and render it a heterogeneous, incoherent, distracted mass." We have not always lived up to the American promise, and there is a dark side to our history. It took the bloodiest war in American history to secure the human rights of African Americans, and the struggle for full equality for all our citizens has yet to be won. During the great influx of immigrants in the early twentieth century, fears much like Jefferson's led to movements to Americanize the foreign born by forcing them, in the words of one leader, "to give up the languages, customs, and methods of life which they have brought with them across the ocean, and adopt instead the language, habits, and customs of this country, and the general standards and ways of American living." Similar thinking motivated Congress at various times to bar the immigration of Africans, Asians, and other ethnic groups and people of color into the country, and to force assimilation on American Indians by denying them the freedom to practice their religion or even to speak their own language. Such calls for restrictive unity still resound in our own day.

But other Americans have argued for a more fulsome version of Americanization. "What is the American, this new man?" asked the French immigrant Michel Crèvecoeur in 1782. "A strange mixture of blood which you will find in no other country." In America, he wrote, "individuals of all nations are melted into a new race of men." A century later Crèvecoeur was echoed by historian Frederick Jackson Turner, who believed that "in the crucible of the frontier, the immigrants were Americanized, liberated, and fused into a mixed race, English in neither nationality nor characteristics. The process has gone on from the early days to our own."

The process by which diverse communities have come to share a set of common American values is one of the most fundamental aspects of our history. It did not occur, however, because of compulsory Americanization programs, but because of free public education, popular participation in democratic politics, and the impact of popular culture. Contemporary America does have a common culture: We share a commitment to freedom of thought and expression, we join in the aspirations to own our own homes and send our children to college, we laugh at the same television programs.

To a degree that too few Americans appreciate, this common culture resulted from a complicated process of mutual discovery that took place when different ethnic and regional groups encountered one another. Consider just one small and unique aspect of our culture: the barbecue. Americans have been barbecuing since before the beginning of written history. Early settlers adopted this technique of cooking from the Indians—the word itself comes from a native term for a framework of sticks over a fire on which meat was slowly cooked. Colonists typically barbecued pork, fed on Indian corn. African slaves lent their own touch by introducing the use of hot sauces. The ritual that is a part of nearly every American family's Fourth of July silently celebrates the heritage of diversity that went into making our common culture.

The American educator John Dewey recognized this diversity early in the last century. "The genuine American, the typical American, is himself a hyphenated character," he declared, "international and interracial in his make-up." The point about our "hyphenated character," Dewey believed, "is to see to it that the hyphen connects instead of separates." We, the authors of *Out of Many*, share Dewey's perspective on American history. "Creation comes from the impact of diversity," wrote the American philosopher Horace Kallen. We also endorse Kallen's vision of the American promise: "A democracy of nationalities, cooperating voluntarily and autonomously through common institutions, . . . a multiplicity in a unity, an orchestration of mankind." And now, let the music begin.

SEVENTEEN
RECONSTRUCTION

1863–1877

Theo Kaufmann, *On to Liberty*, 1867. Oil on canvas, 36″ × 56″. The Metropolitan Museum of Art, Gift of Erving and Joyce Wolf, 1982. (1982.443.3). Photograph © 1982 The Metropolitan Museum of Art.

AMERICAN COMMUNITIES

Hale County, Alabama:
From Slavery to Freedom
in a Black Belt Community

ON A BRIGHT SATURDAY MORNING IN MAY 1867, 4,000 FORMER slaves eagerly streamed into the town of Greensboro, bustling seat of Hale County in west-central Alabama. They came to hear speeches from two delegates to a recent freedmen's convention in Mobile and to find out about the political status of black people under the Reconstruction Act just passed by Congress. Tensions mounted in the days following this unprecedented gathering as military authorities began supervising voter registration for elections to the upcoming constitutional convention that would rewrite the laws of Alabama. On June 13, John Orrick, a local white, confronted Alex Webb, a politically active freedman, on the streets of Greensboro. Webb had recently been appointed a voter registrar for the district. Orrick swore he would never be registered by a black man, and shot Webb dead. Hundreds of armed and angry freedmen formed a posse to search for Orrick, but failed to find him. Galvanized by Webb's murder, 500 local freedmen formed a chapter of the Union League, the Republican Party's organizational arm in the South. The chapter functioned as both a militia company and a forum to agitate for political rights.

Violent political encounters between black people and white people were common in southern communities in the wake of the Civil War. The war had destroyed slavery and the Confederacy, but left the political and economic status of newly emancipated African Americans unresolved. Communities throughout the South struggled over the meaning of freedom in ways that reflected their particular circumstances. The 4 million freed people constituted roughly one-third of the total southern population, but the black–white ratio in individual communities varied enormously. In some places the Union army had been a strong presence during the war, hastening the collapse of the slave system and encouraging experiments in free labor. Other areas had remained relatively untouched by the fighting. In some areas small farms prevailed; in others, including Hale County, large plantations dominated economic and political life.

West-central Alabama had emerged as a fertile center of cotton production just two decades before the Civil War. There, African Americans, as throughout the South's black belt, constituted more than three-quarters of the population. The region was virtually untouched by fighting until the very end of the Civil War. But with the arrival of federal troops in the spring of 1865, African Americans in Hale County, like their counterparts elsewhere, began to challenge the traditional organization of plantation labor.

One owner, Henry Watson, found that his entire workforce had deserted him at the end of 1865. "I am in the midst of a large and fertile cotton growing country," Watson wrote to a partner. "Many plantations are entirely without labor, many plantations have insufficient labor, and upon none are the laborers doing their former accustomed work." Black women refused to work in the fields, preferring to stay home with their children and tend garden plots. Nor would male field hands do any work, such as caring for hogs, that did not directly increase their share of the cotton crop.

Above all, freed people wanted more autonomy. Overseers and owners thus grudgingly allowed them to work the land "in families," letting them choose their own supervisors and find their own provisions. The result was a shift from the gang labor characteristic of the antebellum period, in which large groups of slaves worked under the harsh and constant supervision of white overseers, to the sharecropping system, in which African American families worked small plots of land in exchange for a small share of the crop. This shift represented less of a victory for newly freed African Americans than a defeat for plantation owners, who resented even the limited economic independence it forced them to concede to their black workforce.

Only a small fraction—perhaps 15 percent—of African American families were fortunate enough to be able to buy land. The majority settled for some version of sharecropping, while others managed to rent land from owners, becoming tenant farmers. Still, planters throughout Hale County had to change the old routines of plantation labor. Local African Americans also organized politically. In 1866 Congress had passed the Civil Rights Act and sent the Fourteenth Amendment to the Constitution to the states for ratification; both promised full citizenship rights to former slaves. Hale County freedmen joined the Republican Party and local Union League chapters. They used their new political power to press for better labor contracts, demand greater autonomy for the black workforce, and agitate for the more radical goal of land confiscation and redistribution. "The colored people are very anxious to get land of their own to live upon independently; and they want money to buy stock to make crops,"

reported one black Union League organizer. "The only way to get these necessaries is to give our votes to the [Republican] party . . . making every effort possible to bring these blessings about by reconstructing the State." Two Hale County former slaves, Brister Reese and James K. Green, won election to the Alabama state legislature in 1869.

It was not long before these economic and political gains prompted a white counterattack. In the spring of 1868, the Ku Klux Klan—a secret organization devoted to terrorizing and intimidating African Americans and their white Republican allies—came to Hale County. Disguised in white sheets, armed with guns and whips, and making nighttime raids on horseback, Klansmen flogged, beat, and murdered freed people. They intimidated voters and silenced political activists. Planters used Klan terror to dissuade former slaves from leaving plantations or organizing for higher wages.

With the passage of the Ku Klux Klan Act in 1871, the federal government cracked down on the Klan, breaking its power temporarily in parts of the former Confederacy. But no serious effort was made to stop Klan terror in the west Alabama black belt, and planters there succeeded in reestablishing much of their social and political control.

The events in Hale County illustrate the struggles that beset communities throughout the South during the Reconstruction era after the Civil War. The destruction of slavery and the Confederacy forced African Americans and white people to renegotiate their old economic and political roles. These community battles both shaped and were shaped by the victorious and newly expansive federal government in Washington. In the end, Reconstruction was only partially successful. Not until the "Second Reconstruction" of the twentieth-century civil rights movement would the descendants of Hale County's African Americans begin to enjoy the full fruits of freedom—and even then not without challenge. ∎

Greensboro

─────────────── **KEY TOPICS** ───────────────

■ Competing political plans for reconstructing the defeated Confederacy

■ Difficult transition from slavery to freedom for African Americans

■ The political and social legacy of Reconstruction in the southern states

■ Post–Civil War transformations in the economic and political life of the North

---

THE POLITICS OF RECONSTRUCTION

When General Robert E. Lee's men stacked their guns at Appomattox, the bloodiest war in American history ended. More than 600,000 soldiers had died during the four years of fighting, 360,000 Union and 260,000 Confederate. Another 275,000 Union and 190,000 Confederate troops had been wounded. Although President Abraham Lincoln insisted early on that the purpose of the war was to preserve the Union, by 1863 it had evolved as well into a struggle for African American liberation. Indeed, the political, economic, and moral issues posed by slavery were the root cause of the Civil War, and the war ultimately destroyed slavery, although not racism, once and for all.

The Civil War also settled the Constitutional crisis provoked by the secession of the Confederacy and its justification in appeals to states' rights. The name "United States" would from now on be understood as a singular rather than a plural noun, signaling an important change in the meaning of American nationality. The old notion of the United States as a voluntary union of sovereign states gave way to the new reality of a single nation in which the federal government took precedence over the individual states. The key historical developments of the Reconstruction era revolved around precisely how the newly strengthened national government would define its relationship with the defeated Confederate states and the 4 million newly freed slaves.

The Defeated South

The white South paid an extremely high price for secession, war, and defeat. In addition to the battlefield casualties, the Confederate states sustained deep material and psychological wounds. Much of the best agricultural land lay waste, including the rich fields of northern Virginia, the Shenandoah Valley, and large sections of Tennessee, Mississippi, Georgia, and South Carolina. Many towns and cities—including Richmond, Atlanta, and Columbia, South Carolina—were in ruins. By 1865, the South's most precious commodities, cotton and African American slaves, no longer were measures of wealth and prestige. Retreating Confederates destroyed most of the South's cotton to prevent its capture by federal troops. What remained was confiscated by Union agents as contraband of war. The former slaves, many of whom had fled to Union lines during the latter stages of the war, were determined to chart their own course in the reconstructed South as free men and women.

It would take the South's economy a generation to overcome the severe blows dealt by the war. In 1860 the South held roughly 25 percent of the nation's wealth; a decade later it controlled only 12 percent. Many white Southerners resented their conquered status, and white notions of race, class, and "honor" died hard. A white North Carolinian, for example, who had lost almost everything dear to him in the war—his sons, home, and slaves—recalled in 1865 that in spite of all his tragedy he still retained one thing. "They've left me one inestimable privilege—to hate 'em. I git up at half-past four in the morning, and sit up till twelve at night, to hate 'em." As late as 1870 the Reverend Robert Lewis Dabney of Virginia wrote: "I do not forgive. I try not to forgive. What! forgive those people, who have invaded our country, burned our cities, destroyed our homes, slain our young men, and spread desolation and ruin over our land! No, I do not forgive them."

Emancipation proved the most bitter pill for white Southerners to swallow, especially the planter elite. Conquered and degraded, and in their view robbed of their slave property, white people responded by regarding African Americans more than ever as inferior to themselves. In the antebellum South, white skin had defined a social bond that transcended economic class. It gave even the lowliest poor white a badge of superiority over even the most skilled slave or prosperous free African American. Emancipation, however, forced

Decorating the Graves of Rebel Soldiers, *Harper's Weekly*, August 17, 1867. After the Civil War, both Southerners and Northerners created public mourning ceremonies honoring fallen soldiers. Women led the memorial movement in the South which, by establishing cemeteries and erecting monuments, offered the first cultural expression of the Confederate tradition. This engraving depicts citizens of Richmond, Virginia decorating thousands of Confederate graves with flowers at the Hollywood Memorial Cemetery on the James River. A local women's group raised enough funds to transfer over 16,000 Confederate dead from Northern cemeteries for reburial in Richmond.

SOURCE: The Granger Collection (4E1090.99).

white people to redefine their world. Many believed that without white direction, the freed people would languish, become wards of the state, or die off. Most white people believed that African Americans were too lazy to take care of themselves and survive. At the very least, whites reasoned, the South's agricultural economy would suffer at the hands of allegedly undisciplined and inefficient African Americans. The specter of political power and social equality for African Americans made racial order the consuming passion of most white Southerners during the Reconstruction years. In fact, racism can be seen as one of the major forces driving Reconstruction and, ultimately, undermining it.

Abraham Lincoln's Plan

By late 1863, Union military victories had convinced President Lincoln of the need to fashion a plan for the reconstruction of the South (see Chapter 16). Lincoln based his reconstruction program on bringing the seceded states back into the Union as quickly as possible. He was determined to respect private property (except in the case of slave property), and he opposed imposing harsh punishments for rebellion. His Proclamation of Amnesty and Reconstruction of December 1863 offered "full pardon" and the restoration of property, not including slaves, to white Southerners willing to swear an oath of allegiance to the United States and its laws, including the Emancipation Proclamation. Prominent Confederate military and civil leaders were excluded from Lincoln's offer, though he indicated that he would freely pardon them.

The president also proposed that when the number of any Confederate state's voters who took the oath of allegiance reached 10 percent of the number who had voted in the election of 1860, this group could establish a state government that Lincoln would recognize as legitimate. Fundamental to this Ten Percent Plan was acceptance by the reconstructed governments of the abolition of slavery. Lincoln's plan was designed less as a blueprint for Reconstruction than as a way to shorten the war and gain white people's support for emancipation. It angered those Republicans—known as Radical Republicans—who advocated not only equal rights for the freedmen but a tougher stance toward the white South. As a result, when Arkansas and Louisiana met the president's requirements for reentry into the Union, Congress refused to seat their representatives.

In July 1864, Senator Benjamin F. Wade of Ohio and Congressman Henry W. Davis of Maryland, both Radicals, proposed a harsher alternative to the Ten Percent Plan. The Wade-Davis bill required 50 percent of a seceding state's white male citizens to take a loyalty oath before elections could be held for a convention to rewrite the state's constitution. The bill also guaranteed equality before the law (although not suffrage) for former slaves. Unlike the president, the Radical Republicans saw Reconstruction as a chance to effect a fundamental transformation of southern society. They thus wanted to delay the process until war's end and to limit participation to a small number of southern Unionists. Lincoln viewed Reconstruction as part of the larger effort to win the war and abolish slavery. He wanted to weaken the Confederacy by creating new state governments that could win broad support from southern white people. The Wade-Davis bill threatened his efforts to build political consensus within the southern states, and Lincoln therefore pocket-vetoed it, by refusing to sign it within ten days of the adjournment of Congress.

Redistribution of southern land among former slaves posed another thorny issue for Lincoln, Congress, and federal military officers. As Union armies occupied parts of the South, commanders had improvised a variety of arrangements involving confiscated plantations and the African American labor force. For example, in 1862 General Benjamin F. Butler began a policy of transforming slaves on Louisiana sugar plantations into wage laborers under the close supervision of occupying federal troops. Butler's policy required slaves to remain on the estates of loyal planters, where they would receive wages according to a fixed schedule, as well as food and medical care for the aged and sick. Abandoned plantations would be leased to northern investors. Butler's successor, General Nathaniel P. Banks, extended this system throughout occupied Louisiana. By 1864, some 50,000 African American laborers on nearly 1,500 Louisiana estates worked either directly for the government or for individual planters under contracts supervised by the army.

In January 1865, General William T. Sherman issued Special Field Order 15, setting aside the Sea Islands off the Georgia coast and a portion of the South Carolina low-country rice fields for the exclusive settlement of freed people. Each family would receive forty acres of land and the loan of mules from the army—the origin, perhaps, of the famous call for "forty acres and a mule" that would soon capture the imagination of African Americans throughout the South. Sherman's intent was not to revolutionize southern society but to relieve the demands placed on his army by the thousands of impoverished African Americans who followed his march to the sea. By the summer of 1865 some 40,000 freed people, eager to take advantage of the general's order, had been settled on 400,000 acres of "Sherman land."

Conflicts within the Republican Party prevented the development of a systematic land distribution program. Still, Lincoln and the Republican Congress supported other measures to aid the emancipated slaves. In March 1865 Congress established the Freedmen's Bureau. Along with providing food, clothing, and fuel to destitute former slaves, the bureau was charged with supervising and managing "all the abandoned lands in the South and the control of all subjects relating to refugees and freedmen." The act that established the bureau also stated that forty acres of abandoned or confiscated land could be leased to freed slaves or white Unionists, who would have an option to purchase after three years and "such title thereto as the United States can convey." To guarantee the end of slavery once the war ended, Republicans drafted the Thirteenth Amendment, declaring that "neither slavery nor involuntary servitude, except as a punishment for crime . . . , shall exist within the United States." This amendment passed both houses of Congress by January 1865 and was ratified by the necessary three-fourths of the states on December 18, 1865—eight months after Lee's surrender.

At the time of Lincoln's assassination, his Reconstruction policy remained unsettled and incomplete. In its broad outlines the president's plans had seemed to favor a speedy restoration of the southern states to the Union and a minimum of federal intervention in their affairs. But with his death the specifics of postwar Reconstruction had to be hammered out by a new president, Andrew Johnson of Tennessee, a man whose personality, political background, and racist leanings put him at odds with the Republican-controlled Congress.

Andrew Johnson and Presidential Reconstruction

Andrew Johnson, a Democrat and former slaveholder, was a most unlikely successor to the martyred Lincoln. By trade a tailor, educated by his wife, Johnson overcame his impoverished background and served as state legislator, governor, and U.S. senator. Throughout his career Johnson had championed yeoman farmers and viewed the South's plantation aristocrats with contempt. He was the only southern member of the U.S. Senate to remain loyal to the Union, and he held the planter elite responsible for secession and defeat. In 1862 Lincoln appointed Johnson to the difficult post of military governor of Tennessee. There he successfully began wartime Reconstruction and cultivated Unionist support in the mountainous eastern districts of that state.

In 1864 the Republicans, in an appeal to northern and border state "War Democrats," nominated Johnson for vice president. But despite Johnson's success in Tennessee and in the 1864 campaign, many Radical Republicans distrusted him, and the hardscrabble Tennessean remained a political outsider in Republican circles. In the immediate aftermath of Lincoln's murder, however, Johnson appeared to side with those Radical Republicans who sought to treat the South as a conquered province. "Treason is a crime and must be made odious," Johnson declared. "Traitors must be impoverished. . . . They must not only be punished, but their social power must be destroyed." The new president also hinted at indicting prominent Confederate officials for treason, disfranchising them, and confiscating their property. Such tough talk appealed to Radical Republicans. But support for Johnson quickly faded as the new president's policies unfolded. Johnson defined Reconstruction as the province of the executive, not the legislative branch, and he planned to restore the Union as quickly as possible. He blamed individual Southerners—the planter elite—rather than entire states for leading the South down the disastrous road to secession. In line with this philosophy, Johnson outlined mild terms for reentry to the Union.

In the spring of 1865 Johnson granted amnesty and pardon, including restoration of property rights except slaves, to all Confederates who pledged loyalty to the Union and support for emancipation. Fourteen classes of Southerners, mostly major Confederate officials and wealthy landowners, were excluded. But these men could apply individually for presidential pardons. The power to pardon his former enemies—the Old South's planter elite—gratified Johnson and reinforced his class bias. It also helped win southern support for his lenient policies, for Johnson pardoned former Confederates liberally. In September 1865 Johnson granted an average of a hundred pardons a day, and during his tenure he pardoned roughly 90 percent of those who applied. Significantly, Johnson instituted this plan while Congress was not in session.

Johnson also appointed provisional governors for seven of the former Confederate states, requiring them to hold elections for state constitutional conventions. Participation in this political process was limited to white people who had been pardoned or who had taken a loyalty oath. Johnson also called on state conventions to repudiate secession, acknowledge the abolition of slavery, and void state debts incurred during the war. By the fall of 1865 ten of the eleven Confederate states claimed to have met Johnson's requirements to re-enter the Union. On December 6, 1865, in his first annual message to Congress, the president declared the "restoration" of the Union virtually complete. But a serious division within the federal government was taking shape, for the Congress was not about to allow the president free rein in determining the conditions of southern readmission.

Andrew Johnson used the term "restoration" rather than "reconstruction." A lifelong Democrat with ambitions to be elected president on his own in 1868, Johnson hoped to build a new political coalition composed of northern Democrats, conservative Republicans, and southern Unionists. Firmly committed to white supremacy, he opposed political rights for the freedmen. In 1866, after Frederick Douglass and other black leaders had met with him to discuss black suffrage, Johnson told an aide: "Those damned sons of bitches thought they had me in a trap! I know that damned Douglass; he's just like any nigger, and he would sooner cut a white man's throat than not." Johnson's open sympathy for his fellow white Southerners, his antiblack bias, and his determination to control the course of Reconstruction placed him on a collision course with the powerful Radical wing of the Republican Party.

The Radical Republican Vision

Most Radicals were men whose careers had been shaped by the slavery controversy. At the core of their thinking lay a deep belief in equal political rights and equal economic opportunity, both guaranteed by a powerful national government. They argued that once free labor, universal education, and equal rights were implanted in the South, that region would be able to share in the North's material wealth, progress, and fluid social mobility. Representative George W. Julian of Indiana typified the Radical vision for the South. He called for elimination of the region's "large estates, widely scattered settlements, wasteful agriculture, popular ignorance, social degradation, the decline of manufactures, contempt for honest labor, and a pampered oligarchy." This process would allow Republicans to develop "small farms, thrifty tillage, free schools, social independence, flourishing manufactures and the arts, respect for honest labor, and equality of political rights."

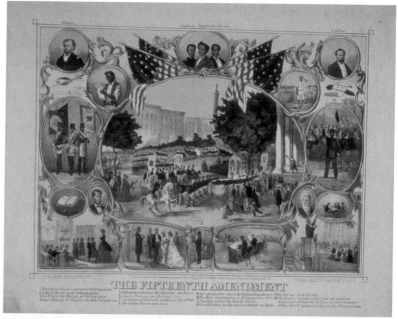

The Fifteenth Amendment, 1870. The Fifteenth Amendment, ratified in 1870, stipulated that the right to vote could not be denied "on account of race, color, or previous condition of servitude." This illustration expressed the optimism and hopes of African Americans generated by this Constitutional landmark aimed at protecting black political rights. Note the various political figures (Abraham Lincoln, John Brown, Frederick Douglass) and movements (abolitionism, black education) invoked here, providing a sense of how the amendment culminated a long historical struggle.

SOURCE: Courtesy of the Library of Congress.

In the Radicals' view, the power of the federal government would be central to the remaking of southern society, especially in guaranteeing civil rights and suffrage for freedmen. In the most far-reaching proposal, Representative Thaddeus Stevens of Pennsylvania called for the confiscation of 400 million acres belonging to the wealthiest 10 percent of Southerners, to be redistributed to black and white yeomen and northern land buyers. "The whole fabric of southern society must be changed," Stevens told Pennsylvania Republicans in September 1865, "and never can it be done if this opportunity is lost. How can republican institutions, free schools, free churches, free social intercourse exist in a mingled community of nabobs and serfs? If the South is ever to be made a safe republic let her lands be cultivated by the toil of the owners."

Northern Republicans were especially outraged by the stringent "black codes" passed by South Carolina, Mississippi, Louisiana, and other states. These were designed to restrict the freedom of the black labor force and keep freed people as close to slave status as possible. Laborers who left their jobs before contracts expired would forfeit wages already earned and be subject to arrest by any white citizen. Vagrancy, very broadly defined, was punishable by fines and involuntary plantation labor. Apprenticeship clauses obliged black children to work without pay for employers. Some states attempted to bar African Americans from land ownership. Other laws specifically denied African Americans equality with white people in civil rights, excluding them from juries and prohibiting interracial marriages.

The black codes underscored the unwillingness of white Southerners to accept the full meaning of freedom for African Americans. Mississippi's version contained a catchall section levying fines and possible imprisonment for any former slaves "committing riots, routs, affrays, trespasses, malicious mischief, cruel treatment to animals, seditious speeches, insulting gestures, language, or acts, or assaults on any person, disturbance of the peace, exercising the function of a minister of the Gospel without a license . . . vending spiritous or intoxicating liquors, or committing any other misdemeanor, the punishment of which is not specifically provided for by law."

The Radicals, although not a majority of their party, were joined by moderate Republicans as growing numbers of Northerners grew suspicious of white southern intransigence and the denial of political rights to freedmen. When the Thirty-ninth Congress convened in December 1865, the large Republican majority prevented the seating of the white Southerners elected to Congress under President Johnson's provisional state governments. Republicans also established the Joint Committee on Reconstruction. After hearing extensive testimony from a broad range of witnesses, it concluded that not only were old Confederates back in power in the South but that black codes and racial violence required increased protection for African Americans.

As a result, in the spring of 1866, Congress passed two important bills designed to aid African Americans. The landmark Civil Rights bill, which bestowed full citizenship on African Americans, overturned the 1857 *Dred Scott* decision and the black codes. It defined all persons born in the United States (except Indian peoples) as national citizens, and it enumerated various rights, including the rights to make and enforce contracts, to sue, to give evidence, and to buy and sell property. Under this bill, African Americans

Office of the Freedmen's Bureau, Memphis, Tennessee, *Harper's Weekly*, June 2, 1866. Established by Congress in 1865, the Freedmen's Bureau provided economic, educational, and legal assistance to former slaves in the post-Civil War years. Bureau agents were often called upon to settle disputes between black and white Southerners over wages, labor contracts, political rights, and violence. While most Southern whites only grudgingly acknowledged the Bureau's legitimacy, freed people gained important legal and psychological support through testimony at public hearings like this one.

SOURCE: Library of Congress.

acquired "full and equal benefit of all laws and proceedings for the security of person and property as is enjoyed by white citizens."

Congress also voted to enlarge the scope of the Freedmen's Bureau, empowering it to build schools and pay teachers, and also to establish courts to prosecute those charged with depriving African Americans of their civil rights. The bureau achieved important, if limited, success in aiding African Americans. Bureau-run schools helped lay the foundation for southern public education. The bureau's network of courts allowed freed people to bring suits against white people in disputes involving violence, nonpayment of wages, or unfair division of crops. The very existence of courts hearing public testimony by African Americans provided an important psychological challenge to traditional notions of white racial domination.

But an angry President Johnson vetoed both of these bills. In opposing the Civil Rights bill, Johnson denounced the assertion of national power to protect African American civil rights, claiming it was a "stride toward centralization, and the concentration of all legislative powers in the national Government." In the case of the Freedmen's Bureau, Johnson argued that Congress lacked jurisdiction over the eleven unrepresented southern states. But Johnson's intemperate attacks on the Radicals—he damned them as traitors unwilling to restore the Union—united moderate and Radical Republicans and they succeeded in overriding the vetoes. Congressional Republicans, led by the Radical faction, were now unified in challenging the president's power to direct Reconstruction and in using national authority to define and protect the rights of citizens.

In June 1866, fearful that the Civil Rights Act might be declared unconstitutional and eager to settle the basis for the seating of southern representatives, Congress passed the Fourteenth Amendment. The amendment defined national citizenship to include former slaves ("all persons born or naturalized in the United States") and prohibited the states from violating the privileges of citizens without due process of law. It also empowered Congress to reduce the representation of any state that denied the suffrage to males over twenty-one. Republicans adopted the Fourteenth Amendment as their platform for the 1866 congressional elections and suggested that southern states would have to ratify it as a condition of readmission. President Johnson, meanwhile, took to the stump in August to support conservative Democratic and Republican candidates. His unrestrained speeches often degenerated into harangues, alienating many voters and aiding the Republican cause.

For their part, the Republicans skillfully portrayed Johnson and northern Democrats as disloyal and white Southerners as unregenerate. Republicans began an effective campaign tradition known as "waving the bloody shirt"—reminding northern voters of the hundreds of thousands of Yankee soldiers left dead or maimed by the war. In the November 1866 elections, the Republicans increased their majority in both the House and the Senate and gained control of all the northern states. The stage was now set for a battle between the president and Congress. Was it to be Johnson's "restoration" or Congressional Reconstruction?

Congressional Reconstruction and the Impeachment Crisis

United against Johnson, Radical and moderate Republicans took control of Reconstruction early in 1867. In March, Congress passed the First Reconstruction Act over Johnson's veto. This act divided the South into five military districts subject to martial law. To achieve restoration, southern states were first required to call new constitutional conventions, elected by universal manhood suffrage. Once these states had drafted new

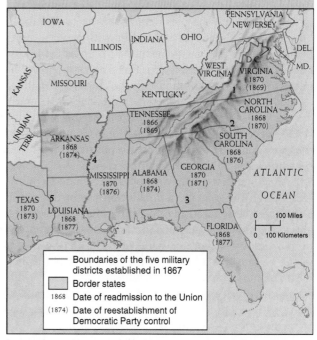

Web Exploration

In these interactive maps, consider the politics of Reconstruction in the South. What were the competing plans for reconstructing the southern states?
www.prenhall.com/faragher/map17.1

Reconstruction of the South, 1866–1877   Dates for the readmission of former Confederate states to the Union and the return of Democrats to power varied according to the specific political situations in those states.

constitutions, guaranteed African American voting rights, and ratified the Fourteenth Amendment, they were eligible for readmission to the Union. Supplementary legislation, also passed over the president's veto, invalidated the provisional governments established by Johnson, empowered the military to administer voter registration, and required an oath of loyalty to the United States.

Congress also passed several laws aimed at limiting Johnson's power. One of these, the Tenure of Office Act, stipulated that any officeholder appointed by the president with the Senate's advice and consent could not be removed until the Senate had approved a successor. In this way, congressional leaders could protect Republicans, such as Secretary of War Edwin M. Stanton, entrusted with implementing Congressional Reconstruction. In August 1867, with Congress adjourned, Johnson suspended Stanton and appointed General Ulysses S. Grant interim secretary of war. This move enabled the president to remove generals in the field that he judged to be too radical and replace them with men who were sympathetic to his own views. It also served as a challenge to the Tenure of Office Act. In January 1868, when the Senate overruled Stanton's suspension, Grant broke openly with Johnson and vacated the office. Stanton resumed his position and barricaded himself in his office when Johnson attempted to remove him once again.

Outraged by Johnson's relentless obstructionism, and seizing upon his violation of the Tenure of Office Act as a pretext, Radical and moderate Republicans in the House of Representatives again joined forces and voted to impeach the president by a vote of 126 to 47 on February 24, 1868, charging him with eleven counts of high crimes and misdemeanors. To ensure the support of moderate Republicans, the articles of impeachment focused on violations of the Tenure of Office Act. The case against Johnson would have to be made on the basis of willful violation of the law. Left unstated were the Republicans' real reasons for wanting the president removed: Johnson's political views and his opposition to the Reconstruction Acts.

An influential group of moderate Senate Republicans feared the damage a conviction might do to the constitutional separation of powers. They also worried about the political and economic policies that might be pursued by Benjamin Wade, the president pro tem of the Senate and a leader of the Radical Republicans, who, because there was no vice president, would succeed to the presidency if Johnson were removed from office. Behind the scenes during his Senate trial, Johnson agreed to abide by the Reconstruction Acts. In May, the Senate voted 35 for conviction, 19 for acquittal—one vote shy of the two-thirds necessary for removal from office. Johnson's narrow acquittal established the precedent that only criminal actions by a president—not political disagreements—warranted removal from office.

The Election of 1868

By the summer of 1868, seven former Confederate states (Alabama, Arkansas, Florida, Louisiana, North Carolina, South Carolina, and Tennessee) had ratified the revised constitutions, elected Republican governments, and ratified the Fourteenth Amendment. They had thereby earned readmission to the Union. Though Georgia, Mississippi, Texas, and Virginia still awaited readmission, the presidential election of 1868 offered some hope that the Civil War's legacy of sectional hate and racial tension might finally ease.

Republicans nominated Ulysses S. Grant, the North's foremost military hero. An Ohio native, Grant had graduated from West Point in 1843, served in the Mexican War, and resigned from the army in 1854. Unhappy in civilian life, Grant received a second chance during the Civil War. He rose quickly to become commander in the western theater, and he later destroyed Lee's army in Virginia. Although his armies suffered terrible losses, Grant enjoyed tremendous popularity after the war, especially when he broke with Johnson. Totally lacking in political experience, Grant admitted after receiving the nomination that he had been forced into it in spite of himself: "I could not back down without leaving the contest for power for the next four years between mere trading politicians, the elevation of whom, no matter which party won, would lose to us, largely, the results of the costly war which we have gone through."

Significantly, at the very moment that the South was being forced to enfranchise former slaves as a prerequisite for readmission to the Union, the Republicans rejected a campaign plank endorsing black suffrage in the North. Their platform left "the question of suffrage in all the loyal States . . . to the people of those States." State referendums calling for black suffrage failed in eight northern states between 1865 and 1868, succeeding only in Iowa and Minnesota. The Democrats, determined to reverse Congressional Reconstruction, nominated Horatio Seymour, former governor of New York and a long-time foe of emancipation and supporter of states' rights. Democrats North and South exploited the race question to garner votes. Their platform blasted the Republicans for subjecting the nation "in time of profound peace, to military despotism and negro supremacy." The party sought "the abolition of the Freedmen's Bureau; and all political instrumentalities designed to secure negro supremacy." Throughout the South, violence marked the electoral process. The Ku Klux Klan, founded as a Tennessee social club in 1866, emerged as a potent instrument of terror (see the opening of this chapter). In Louisiana, Arkansas, Georgia, and South Carolina the Klan threatened, whipped, and murdered black and white Republicans to prevent them from voting. This terrorism enabled the Democrats to carry Georgia and Louisiana, but it ultimately cost the Democrats votes in the North. In the final tally, Grant carried twenty-six of the thirty-four states for an electoral college victory of 214 to 80. But he received a popular majority of less than 53 percent, beating Seymour by only 306,000 votes. Significantly, more than 500,000 African American voters cast their ballots for Grant, demonstrating their overwhelming support for the Republican Party. The Republicans also retained large majorities in both houses of Congress.

In February 1869, Congress passed the Fifteenth Amendment, providing that "the right of citizens of the United States to vote shall not be denied or abridged . . . on account of race, color, or previous condition of servitude." Noticeably absent was language prohibiting the states from imposing educational, residential, or other qualifications for voting. Moderate Republicans feared that filling these discriminatory loopholes might make it difficult to obtain ratification for the amendment by the required three-quarters of

the states. To enhance the chances of ratification, Congress required the three remaining unreconstructed states—Mississippi, Texas, and Virginia—to ratify both the Fourteenth and Fifteenth Amendments before readmission. They did so and rejoined the Union in early 1870. The Fifteenth Amendment was ratified in February 1870. In the narrow sense of simply readmitting the former Confederate states to the Union, Reconstruction was complete.

Woman Suffrage and Reconstruction

The battles over the political status of African Americans proved an important turning point for women as well. The Fourteenth and Fifteenth Amendments, which granted citizenship and the vote to freedmen, both inspired and frustrated women's rights activists. Many of these women had long been active in the abolitionist movement. During the war, they had actively supported the Union cause through their work in the National Woman's Loyal League and the United States Sanitary Commission. Elizabeth Cady Stanton and Susan B. Anthony, two leaders with long involvement in both the antislavery and feminist movements, objected to the inclusion of the word "male" in the Fourteenth Amendment. "If that word 'male' be inserted," Stanton predicted

OVERVIEW

RECONSTRUCTION AMENDMENTS TO THE CONSTITUTION, 1865–1870

Amendment and Date Passed by Congress	Main Provisions	Ratification Process (3/4 of all states including ex-Confederate states required)
13 (January 1865)	Prohibited slavery in the United States	December 1865 (27 states, including 8 southern states
14 (June 1866)	• Conferred national citizenship on all persons born or naturalized in the United States • Reduced state representation in Congress proportionally for any state disfranchising male citizens • Denied former Confederates the right to hold state or national office • Repudiated Confederate debt	July 1868 (after Congress makes ratification a prerequisite for readmission of ex-Confederate states to the Union)
15 (February 1869)	Prohibited denial of suffrage because of race, color, or previous condition of servitude	March 1870 (ratification required for readmission of Virginia, Texas, Mississippi, and Georgia)

in 1866, "it will take us a century at least to get it out." Insisting that the causes of the African American vote and the women's vote were linked, Stanton, Anthony, and Lucy Stone founded the American Equal Rights Association in 1866. The group launched a series of lobbying and petition campaigns to remove racial and sexual restrictions on voting from state constitutions. In Kansas, for example, an old antislavery battlefield, the association vigorously supported two 1867 referendums that would have removed the words "male" and "white" from the state's constitution. But Kansas voters rejected both woman suffrage and black suffrage. Throughout the nation, the old abolitionist organizations and the Republican Party emphasized passage of the Fourteenth and Fifteenth Amendments and withdrew funds and support from the cause of woman suffrage. Disagreements over these amendments divided suffragists for decades.

The radical wing, led by Stanton and Anthony, opposed the Fifteenth Amendment, arguing that ratification would establish an "aristocracy of sex," enfranchising all men while leaving women without political privileges. In arguing for a Sixteenth Amendment that would secure the vote for women, they used racist and elitist appeals. They urged "American women of wealth, education, virtue, and refinement" to support the vote for women and oppose the Fifteenth Amendment "if you do not wish the lower orders of Chinese, Africans, Germans, and Irish, with their low ideas of womanhood to make laws for you and your daughters." Other women's rights activists, including Lucy Stone and Frederick Douglass, asserted that "this hour belongs to the Negro." They feared a debate over woman suffrage at the national level would jeopardize passage of the two amendments.

By 1869 woman suffragists had split into two competing organizations. The moderate American Woman Suffrage Association (AWSA), led by Lucy Stone, Julia Ward Howe, and Henry Blackwell, focused on achieving woman suffrage at the state level. It maintained close ties with the Republican Party and the old abolitionist networks, worked for the Fifteenth Amendment, and actively sought the support of men. The more radical wing founded the all-female National Woman Suffrage Association (NWSA). For the NWSA, the vote represented only one part of a broad spectrum of goals inherited from the Declaration of Sentiments manifesto adopted at the first women's rights convention held in 1848 at Seneca Falls, New York (see Chapter 13).

Although women did not win the vote in this period, they did establish an independent suffrage movement that eventually drew millions of women into political life. The NWSA in particular demonstrated that self-government and democratic participation in

Susan B. Anthony (1820–1906) and Elizabeth Cady Stanton (1815–1902), the two most influential leaders of the woman suffrage movement, ca. 1892. Anthony and Stanton broke with their longtime abolitionist allies after the Civil War when they opposed the Fifteenth Amendment. They argued that the doctrine of universal manhood suffrage it embodied would give constitutional authority to the claim that men were the social and political superiors of women. As founders of the militant National Woman Suffrage Association, Stanton and Anthony established an independent woman suffrage movement with a broader spectrum of goals for women's rights and drew millions of women into public life during the late nineteenth century.

SOURCE: The Susan B. Anthony House, Rochester, NY.

the public sphere were crucial for women's emancipation. Stanton and Anthony toured the country, speaking to women's audiences and inspiring the formation of suffrage societies. The NWSA's weekly magazine, *Revolution*, became a forum for feminist ideas on divorce laws, unequal pay, women's property rights, and marriage. The failure of woman suffrage after the Civil War was less a result of factional fighting than of the larger defeat of Radical Reconstruction and the ideal of expanded citizenship.

THE MEANING OF FREEDOM

For 4 million slaves, freedom arrived in various ways in different parts of the South. In many areas, slavery had collapsed long before Lee's surrender at Appomattox. In regions far removed from the presence of federal troops, African Americans did not learn of slavery's end until the spring of 1865. There were thousands of sharply contrasting stories, many of which revealed the need for freed slaves to confront their owners. One Virginia slave, hired out to another family during the war, had been working in the fields when a friend told her she was now free. "Is dat so?" she exclaimed. Dropping her hoe, she ran the seven miles to her old place, confronted her former mistress, and shouted, "I'se free! Yes, I'se free! Ain't got to work fo' you no mo'. You can't put me in yo' pocket now!" Her mistress burst into tears and ran into the house. That was all the former slave needed to see. But regardless of specific regional circumstances, the meaning of "freedom" would be contested for years to come. The deep desire for independence from white control formed the underlying aspiration of newly freed slaves. For their part, most southern white people sought to restrict the boundaries of that independence. As individuals and as members of communities transformed by emancipation, former slaves struggled to establish economic, political, and cultural autonomy. They built on the twin pillars of slave culture—the family and the church—to consolidate and expand African American institutions and thereby laid the foundation for the modern African American community.

Emancipation greatly expanded the choices available to African Americans. It helped build confidence in their ability to effect change without deferring to white people. Freedom also meant greater uncertainty and risk. But the vast majority of African Americans were more than willing to take their chances. Many years later, one former Texas slave pondered the question "What I likes bes, to be slave or free?" She answered: "Well, it's dis way. In slavery I owns nothin' and never owns nothin'. In freedom I's own de home and raise de family. All dat cause me worryment and in slavery I has no worryment, but I takes de freedom."

Moving About

The first impulse of many emancipated slaves was to test their freedom. The simplest, most obvious way to do this involved leaving home. By walking off a plantation, coming and going without restraint or fear of punishment, African Americans could savor freedom. Throughout the summer and fall of 1865, observers in the South noted enormous numbers of freed people on the move. One former slave squatting in an abandoned tent outside Selma, Alabama, explained his feeling to a northern journalist: "I's want to be free man, cum when I please, and nobody say nuffin to me, nor order me roun'." When urged to stay on with the South Carolina family she had served for years as a cook, a slave woman replied firmly: "No, Miss, I must go. If I stay here I'll never know I am free."

Yet many who left their old neighborhoods returned soon afterward to seek work in the general vicinity, or even on the plantation they had left. Many wanted to separate themselves from former owners, but not from familial ties and friendships. Others moved away altogether, seeking jobs in nearby towns and cities. Many former slaves left predominantly white counties, where they felt more vulnerable and isolated, for new lives in the relative comfort of predominantly black communities. In most southern states, there was a significant population shift toward black belt plantation counties and towns after the war. Many African Americans, attracted by schools, churches, and fraternal societies as well as the army, preferred the city. Between 1865 and 1870, the African American population of the South's ten largest cities doubled, while the white population increased by only 10 percent.

Disgruntled planters had difficulty accepting African American independence. During slavery, they had expected obedience, submission, and loyalty from African Americans. Now many could not understand why so many former slaves wanted to leave despite urgent pleas to continue working at the old place. The deference and humility white people expected from African Americans could no longer be taken for granted. Indeed, many freed people went out of their way to reject the old subservience. Moving about freely was one way of doing this, as was refusing to tip one's hat to white people, ignoring former masters or mistresses in the streets, and refusing to step aside on sidewalks. After encountering an African American who would not step aside, Eliza Andrews, a Georgia plantation mistress, complained, "It is the first time in my life that I have ever had to give up the sidewalk to a man, much less to negroes!" When freed people staged parades, dances, and picnics to celebrate their new freedom, as they did, for example, when commemorating the Emancipation Proclamation, white people invariably condemned them angrily for "insolence," "outrageous spectacles," or "putting on airs."

The African American Family

Emancipation allowed freed people to strengthen family ties. For many former slaves, freedom meant the opportunity to reunite with long-lost family members. To track down relatives, freed people trekked to faraway places, put ads in newspapers, sought the help of Freedmen's

Bureau agents, and questioned anyone who might have information about loved ones. Many thousands of family reunions, each with its own story, took place after the war. To William Curtis of Georgia, whose father had been sold to a Virginia planter, "that was the best thing about the war setting us free, he could come back to us." One North Carolina slave, who had seen his parents separated by sale, recalled many years later what for him had been the most significant aspect of freedom. "I has got thirteen great-gran' chilluns an' I know whar dey ever'one am. In slavery times dey'd have been on de block long time ago."

Thousands of African American couples who had lived together under slavery streamed to military and civilian authorities and demanded to be legally married. By 1870, the two-parent household was the norm for a large majority of African Americans. "In their eyes," a Freedmen's Bureau agent reported, "the work of emancipation was incomplete until the families which had been dispersed by slavery were reunited." For many freed people the attempt to find lost relatives dragged on for years. Searches often proved frustrating, exhausting, and ultimately disappointing. Some "reunions" ended painfully with the discovery that spouses had found new partners and started new families.

Emancipation brought changes to gender roles within the African American family as well. By serving in the Union army, African American men played a more direct role than women in the fight for freedom. In the political sphere, black men could now serve on juries, vote, and hold office; black women, like their white counterparts, could not. Freedmen's Bureau agents designated the husband as household head and established lower wage scales for women laborers. African American editors, preachers, and politicians regularly quoted the biblical injunction that wives submit to their husbands. African American men asserted their male authority, denied under slavery, by insisting their wives work at home instead of in the fields.

For years after 1865, southern planters complained about the scarcity of women and children available for fieldwork. African American women generally wanted to devote more time than they had under slavery to caring for their children and to performing such domestic chores as cooking, sewing, gardening, and laundering. Yet African American women continued to work outside the home, engaging in seasonal field labor for wages or working a family's rented plot. Most rural black families barely eked out a living, and thus the labor of every family member was essential to survival. The key difference from slave times was that African American families themselves, not white masters and overseers, decided when and where women and children worked.

An overflow congregation crowds into Richmond's First African Baptist Church in 1874. Despite their poverty, freed people struggled to save, buy land, and erect new buildings as they organized hundreds of new black churches during Reconstruction. As the most important African American institution outside the family, the black church, in addition to tending to spiritual needs, played a key role in the educational and political life of the community.

SOURCE: Wood engraving. The Granger Collection (4E1090.98).

African American Churches and Schools

The creation of separate African American churches proved the most lasting and important element of the energetic institution building that went on in post-emancipation years. Before the Civil War, southern Protestant churches had relegated slaves and free African Americans to second-class membership. Black worshipers were required to sit in the back during services, they were denied any role in church governance, and they were excluded from Sunday schools. Even in larger cities, where all-black congregations sometimes built their own churches, the law required white pastors. In rural areas, slaves preferred their own preachers to the sermons of local white ministers who quoted Scripture to justify slavery and white supremacy. "That old white preachin' wasn't nothin'," former slave Nancy Williams recalled. "Old white preachers used to talk with their tongues without sayin' nothin', but Jesus told us slaves to talk with our hearts."

In communities around the South, African Americans now pooled their resources to buy land and build their own churches. Before these structures were completed, they might hold services in a railroad boxcar, where Atlanta's First Baptist Church began, or in an outdoor arbor, the original site of the First Baptist Church of Memphis. By late 1866 Charleston's African American community could boast of eleven churches in the city—five Methodist, two Presbyterian, two Episcopalian, one Baptist, and one Congregational. In rural areas, different denominations frequently shared the same church building. Churches became the center not only for religious life but for many other activities that defined the African American community: schools, picnics, festivals, and political meetings. They also helped spawn a host of organizations devoted to benevolence and mutual aid, such as burial societies, Masonic lodges, temperance clubs, and trade associations.

The church became the first social institution fully controlled by African Americans. In nearly every community ministers, respected for their speaking and organizational skills, were among the most influential leaders. By 1877 the great majority of black Southerners had withdrawn from white-dominated churches. In South Carolina, for example, only a few hundred black Methodists attended biracial churches, down from over 40,000 in 1865. The various Protestant denominations competed for the allegiance of African American worshipers. Among Methodists, the African Methodist Episcopal Church, originally founded in 1816, gained ascendancy over white-dominated rivals. Black Baptist churches, with their decentralized and democratic structure and more emotional services, attracted the greatest number of freed people. By the end of Reconstruction the vast majority of African American Christians belonged to black Baptist or Methodist churches.

The rapid spread of schools reflected African Americans' thirst for self-improvement. Southern states had prohibited education for slaves. But many free black people managed to attend school, and a few slaves had been able to educate themselves. Still, over 90 percent of the South's adult African American population was illiterate in 1860. Access to education thus became a central part of the meaning of freedom. Freedmen's Bureau agents repeatedly expressed amazement at the number of makeshift classrooms organized by African Americans in rural areas. A bureau officer described these "wayside schools": "A negro riding on a loaded wagon, or sitting on a hack waiting for a train, or by the cabin door, is often seen, book in hand delving after the rudiments of knowledge. A group on the platform of a depot, after carefully conning an old spelling book, resolves itself into a class."

African American communities received important educational aid from outside organizations. By 1869 the Freedmen's Bureau was supervising nearly 3,000 schools serving over 150,000 students throughout the South. Over half the roughly 3,300 teachers in these schools were African Americans, many of whom had been free before the Civil War. Other teachers included dedicated northern white women, volunteers sponsored by the American Missionary Association (AMA). The bureau and the AMA also assisted in the founding of several black colleges, including Tougaloo, Hampton, and Fisk, designed to train black teachers. Black self-help proved crucial to the education effort. Throughout the South in 1865 and 1866, African Americans raised money to build schoolhouses, buy supplies, and pay teachers. Black artisans donated labor for construction, and black families offered room and board to teachers.

Land and Labor after Slavery

Most newly emancipated African Americans aspired to quit the plantations and to make new lives for themselves. Leaving the plantation was not as simple as walking off. Some freed people did find jobs in railroad building, mining, ranching, or construction work. Others raised subsistence crops and tended vegetable gardens as squatters. White planters, however, tried to retain African Americans as permanent agricultural laborers. Restricting the employment of former slaves was an important goal of the black codes. For example, South Carolina legislation in 1865 provided that "no person of color shall pursue or practice the art, trade, or business of an artisan, mechanic, or shopkeeper, or any other trade employment, or business, besides that of husbandry, or that of a servant under contract for service or labor" without a special and costly permit.

The majority of African Americans hoped to become self-sufficient farmers. As *DeBow's Review* observed in 1869, the freedman showed "great anxiety to have his little home, with his horse, cow, and hogs, separate and apart from others." Many former slaves believed they were entitled to the land they had worked throughout their lives. General Oliver O. Howard, chief commissioner of the Freedmen's Bureau, observed that many "supposed that the Government [would] divide among them the lands of the conquered owners, and furnish them with all that might be necessary to begin life as an independent farmer." This perception was not merely a wishful fantasy. The Freedmen's Bureau Act of 1865 specifically required that abandoned land be leased for three years in forty-acre lots, with an option to buy. Frequent reference in the Congress and the press to the question of land distribution made the idea of "forty acres and a mule" not just a pipe dream but a matter of serious public debate.

Above all, African Americans sought economic autonomy, and ownership of land promised the most independence. "Give us our own land and we take care of ourselves," was how one former slave saw it. "But widout land, de ole massas can hire us or starve us, as dey please." At the Colored Convention in Montgomery, Alabama, in May 1867, delegates argued that the property now owned by planters had been "nearly all earned by the sweat of our brows, not theirs. It has been forfeited to the government by the treason of its owners, and is liable to be confiscated whenever the Republican Party demands it." But by 1866 the federal government had already pulled back from the various wartime experiments involving the breaking up of large plantations and the leasing of small plots to individual families. President Johnson directed General Howard of the Freedmen's Bureau to evict tens of thousands of freed people settled on confiscated and abandoned land in southeastern Virginia, southern Louisiana, and the Georgia and South Carolina low country. These evictions created a deep sense of betrayal among African Americans. A former Mississippi slave, Merrimon Howard, bitterly noted that African Americans had been left with "no land, no house, not so much as a place to lay our head. . . . We were friends on the march, brothers on the battlefield, but in the peaceful pursuits of life it seems that we are strangers."

A variety of labor arrangements could be found in southern agriculture in the immediate postwar years. Each featured both advantages and disadvantages for planters and freed people. Writing in 1866, white planter Percy Roberts identified three distinct "systems of hire" for working the land: money wages, share wages, and sharecropping. Under both the money wage and share wage systems, planters contracted former slaves to work in large gangs, paying them either in cash (money wage) or with a share of the crop that the workers divided among themselves (share wage). Freedmen's Bureau agents, who generally advocated the money wage arrangement, would often help freedmen negotiate labor contracts with planters. Planters tended to prefer the money wage system because it clearly defined laborers as hirelings and gave planters more direct control over the labor force—for example, by enabling them to discharge the hands they thought inefficient. Yet most planters were forced to adopt share wages at the insistence of black laborers who were adamantly opposed to serving as mere hirelings.

But both the money wage and share wage systems were unsatisfactory from the perspective of freed people. Both systems relied on the gang labor approach so reminiscent of slavery. And both systems often left African Americans at the mercy of unscrupulous planters who cheated them of their wages or fair shares.

Above all, the deep desire for economic improvement and greater autonomy led many African Americans to press for an alternative. By the late 1860s, black people's resistance to working in gangs and their desire to establish independent homesteads forced planters into the compromise system of sharecropping, which emerged as the dominant form of working the land.

Under sharecropping arrangements, individual families contracted with landowners to be responsible for a specific plot. Large plantations were thus broken into family-sized farms. Generally, sharecropper families received one-third of the year's crop if the owner furnished implements, seed, and draft animals, or one-half if they provided their own supplies. African Americans preferred sharecropping to gang labor, as it allowed families to set their own hours and tasks and offered freedom from white supervision and control. For planters, the system stabilized the workforce by requiring sharecroppers to remain until the harvest and to employ all family members. It also offered a way around the chronic shortage of cash and credit that plagued the postwar South. But as the *Southern Argus* of Selma, Alabama, editorialized, sharecropping was "an unwilling concession to the freedmen's desire to become a proprietor. . . . It is not a voluntary association from similarity of aims and interests." Freed people did not aspire to sharecropping. Owning land outright or tenant farming (renting land) were both more desirable. But though black sharecroppers clearly enjoyed more autonomy than in the past, the vast majority never achieved economic independence or land ownership. They remained a largely subordinate agricultural labor force.

Sharecropping came to dominate the southern agricultural economy and African American life in particular. By 1880 about 80 percent of the land in the black belt states—Mississippi, Alabama, and Georgia—had been divided into family-sized farms. Nearly three-quarters of black Southerners were sharecroppers. Through much of the black belt, family and community were one. Often several families worked adjoining parcels of land in common, pooling their labor in order to get by. Men usually oversaw crop production. Women went to the fields seasonally during planting or harvesting, but they mainly tended to household chores and child care. In addition, women frequently held jobs that might bring in cash, such as raising chickens or taking in laundry. The cotton harvest engaged all members of the community, from the oldest to the youngest. Cotton picking remained a difficult, labor-intensive task that took priority over all other work.

The Origins of African American Politics

Although the desire for autonomy had led African Americans to pursue their economic and religious goals largely apart from white people, inclusion rather than

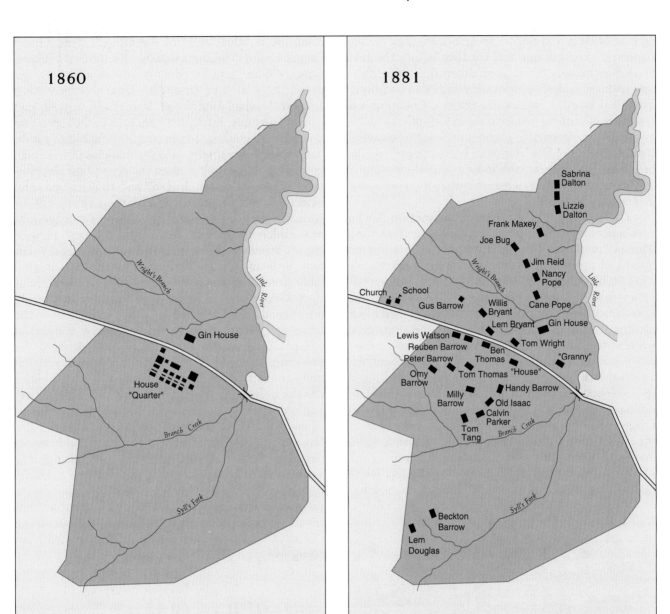

The Barrow Plantation, Oglethorpe County, Georgia, 1860 and 1881 (approx. 2,000 acres) These two maps, based on drawings from *Scribner's Monthly*, April 1881, show some of the changes brought by emancipation. In 1860 the plantation's entire black population lived in the communal slave quarters, right next to the white master's house. In 1881 black sharecropper and tenant families lived on individual plots, spread out across the land. The former slaves had also built their own school and church.

separation was the objective of early African American political activity. The greatest political activity by African Americans occurred in areas occupied by Union forces during the war. In 1865 and 1866, African Americans throughout the South organized scores of mass meetings, parades, and petitions that demanded civil equality and the right to vote. In the cities, the growing web of churches and fraternal societies helped bolster early efforts at political organization.

Hundreds of African American delegates, selected by local meetings or churches, attended statewide

political conventions held throughout the South in 1865 and 1866. Previously free African Americans, as well as black ministers, artisans, and veterans of the Union army, tended to dominate these proceedings, setting a pattern that would hold throughout Reconstruction. Convention debates sometimes reflected the tensions within African American communities, such as friction between poorer former slaves and better-off free black people, or between lighter- and darker-skinned African Americans. But most of these state gatherings concentrated on passing resolutions on issues that united all African Americans. The central concerns were suffrage and equality before the law. Black Southerners firmly proclaimed their identification with the nation's history and republican traditions. The 1865 North Carolina freedmen's convention was typical in describing universal manhood suffrage as "an essential and inseparable element of self-government." It also praised the Declaration of Independence as "the broadest, the deepest, the most comprehensive and truthful definition of human freedom that was ever given to the world."

The passage of the First Reconstruction Act in 1867 encouraged even more political activity among African Americans. The military started registering the South's electorate, ultimately enrolling approximately 735,000 black and 635,000 white voters in the ten unreconstructed states. Five states—Alabama, Florida, Louisiana, Mississippi, and South Carolina—had black electoral majorities. Fewer than half the registered white voters participated in the elections for state constitutional conventions in 1867 and 1868. In contrast, four-fifths of the registered black voters cast ballots in these elections. Much of this new African American political activism was channeled through local Union League chapters throughout the South. However, as the fate of Alex Webb in Hale County, Alabama, again makes clear, few whites welcomed this activism.

Begun during the war as a northern, largely white middle-class patriotic club, the Union League now became the political voice of the former slaves. Union League chapters brought together local African Americans, soldiers, and Freedmen's Bureau agents to demand the vote and an end to legal discrimination against African Americans. It brought out African American voters, instructed freedmen in the rights and duties of citizenship, and promoted Republican candidates. Not surprisingly, newly enfranchised freedmen voted Republican and formed the core of the Republican Party in the South. In 1867 and 1868, the promise of Radical Reconstruction enlarged the scope of African American political participation and brought new leaders to the fore. Many were teachers, preachers, or others with useful skills, such as literacy. For most ordinary African Americans, politics was inseparable from economic issues, especially the land question. Grass-roots political organizations frequently intervened in local disputes with planters over the terms of labor contracts. African American political groups closely followed the congressional debates over Reconstruction policy and agitated for land confiscation and distribution. Perhaps most important, politics was the only arena where black and white Southerners might engage each other on an equal basis. As the delegates to an Alabama convention asserted in 1867: "We claim exactly the same rights, privileges and immunities as are enjoyed by white men—we ask nothing more and will be content with nothing less. . . . The law no longer knows white nor black, but simply men, and consequently we are entitled to ride in public conveyances, hold office, sit on juries and do everything else which we have in the past been prevented from doing solely on the ground of color."

SOUTHERN POLITICS AND SOCIETY

By the summer of 1868, when the South had returned to the Union, the majority of Republicans believed the task of Reconstruction to be finished. Ultimately, they put their faith in a political solution to the problems facing the vanquished South. That meant nurturing a viable two-party system in the southern states, where no Republican Party had ever existed. If that could be accomplished, Republicans and Democrats would compete for votes, offices, and influence, just as they did in northern states. Most Republican congressmen were moderates, conceiving Reconstruction in limited terms. They rejected radical calls for confiscation and redistribution of land, as well as permanent military rule of the South. The Reconstruction Acts of 1867 and 1868 laid out the requirements for the readmission of southern states, along with the procedures for forming and electing new governments.

W. L. Sheppard, "Electioneering at the South," *Harper's Weekly*, July 25, 1868. Throughout the Reconstruction-era South, newly freed slaves took a keen interest in both local and national political affairs. The presence of women and children at these campaign gatherings illustrates the importance of contemporary political issues to the entire African American community.

SOURCE: Library of Congress.

Yet over the next decade the political structure created in the southern states proved too restricted and fragile to sustain itself. Republicans had to employ radical means to protect their essentially conservative goals. To most southern whites the active participation of African Americans in politics seemed extremely dangerous. Federal troops were needed to protect Republican governments and their supporters from violent opposition. Congressional action to monitor southern elections and protect black voting rights became routine. Despite initial successes, southern Republicanism proved an unstable coalition of often conflicting elements, unable to sustain effective power for very long. By 1877, Democrats had regained political control of all the former Confederate states.

Southern Republicans

Three major groups composed the fledgling Republican coalition in the postwar South. African American voters made up a large majority of southern Republicans throughout the Reconstruction era. Yet African Americans outnumbered whites in only three southern states—South Carolina, Mississippi, and Louisiana. They made up roughly one-quarter of the population in Texas, Tennessee, and Arkansas, and between 40 and 50 percent in Virginia, North Carolina, Alabama, Florida, and Georgia. Thus, Republicans would have to attract white support to win elections and sustain power.

A second group consisted of white Northerners, derisively called "carpetbaggers" by native white Southerners. One Democratic congressman in 1871 said the term "applied to the office seeker from the North who came here seeking office by the negroes, by arraying their political passions and prejudices against the white people of the community." In fact, most carpetbaggers combined a desire for personal gain with a commitment to reform the "unprogressive" South by developing its material resources and introducing Yankee institutions such as free labor and free public schools. Most were veterans of the Union army who stayed in the South after the war. Others included Freedmen's Bureau agents and businessmen who had invested capital in cotton plantations and other enterprises.

Carpetbaggers tended to be well educated and from the middle class. Albert Morgan, for example, was an army veteran from Ohio who settled in Mississippi after the war. When he and his brother failed at running a cotton plantation and sawmill, Morgan became active in Republican politics as a way to earn a living. He won election to the state constitutional convention, became a power in the state legislature, and risked his life to keep the Republican organization alive in the Mississippi Delta region. Although they made up a tiny percentage of the population, carpetbaggers played a disproportionately large role in southern politics. They won a large share of Reconstruction offices, particularly in Florida, South Carolina, and Louisiana and in areas with large African American constituencies.

The third major group of southern Republicans were the native whites pejoratively termed "scalawags." They had even more diverse backgrounds and motives than the northern-born Republicans. Some were prominent prewar Whigs who saw the Republican Party as their best chance to regain political influence. Others viewed the party as an agent of modernization and economic expansion. "Yankees and Yankee notions are just what we want in this country," argued Thomas Settle of North Carolina. "We want their capital to build factories and workshops. We want their intelligence, their energy and enterprise." Their greatest influence lay in the up-country strongholds of southern Unionism, such as eastern Tennessee, western North Carolina, and northern Alabama. Loyalists during the war and traditional enemies of the planter elite (most were small farmers), these white Southerners looked to the Republican Party for help in settling old scores and relief from debt and wartime devastation.

Deep contradictions strained the alliance of these three groups. Southern Republicans touted themselves as the "party of progress and civilization" and promised a new era of material progress for the region. Republican state conventions in 1867 and 1868 voiced support for internal improvements, public schools, debt relief, and railroad building. Yet few white Southerners identified with the political and economic aspirations of African Americans. Nearly every party convention split between "confiscation radicals" (generally African Americans) and moderate elements committed to white control of the party and to economic development that offered more to outside investors than to impoverished African Americans and poor whites.

Reconstructing the States: A Mixed Record

With the old Confederate leaders barred from political participation, and with carpetbaggers and newly enfranchised African Americans representing many of the plantation districts, Republicans managed to dominate the ten southern constitutional conventions of 1867–69. Well-educated carpetbaggers usually chaired the important committees and drafted key provisions of the new constitutions. Most of the delegates were southern white Republicans. African Americans formed a majority of the conventions in Louisiana and South Carolina, but they were generally underrepresented. In all, there were 258 African Americans among the 1,027 convention delegates at the ten conventions.

Most of the conventions produced constitutions that expanded democracy and the public role of the state. The new documents guaranteed the political and civil rights of African Americans, and they abolished property qualifications for officeholding and jury service, as well as imprisonment for debt. They created the first state-funded systems of education in the South, to be administered by state commissioners. The new constitutions also mandated establishment of orphanages, penitentiaries, and homes for the insane. The changes wrought in the South's political landscape seemed quite radical to many. In 1868, only three years after the end of the war, Republicans came to power in most of the southern states. By 1869, new constitutions had been ratified in all the old Confederate states. "These constitutions and governments," one South Carolina Democratic newspaper vowed bitterly, "will last just as long as the bayonets which ushered them into being, shall keep them in existence, and not one day longer."

Republican governments in the South faced a continual crisis of legitimacy that limited their ability to legislate change. They had to balance reform against the need to gain acceptance, especially by white Southerners. Their achievements were thus mixed. In the realm of race relations there was a clear thrust toward equal rights and against discrimination. Republican legislatures followed up the federal Civil Rights Act of 1866 with various antidiscrimination clauses in new constitutions and laws prescribing harsh penalties for civil rights violations. While most African Americans supported autonomous African American churches, fraternal societies, and schools, they insisted that the state be "color-blind." African Americans could now be employed in police forces and fire departments, serve on juries, school boards, and city councils, and they could hold public office at all levels of government.

Segregation, though, became the norm in public school systems. African American leaders often accepted segregation because they feared that insistence on integrated education would jeopardize funding for the new school systems. They generally agreed with Frederick Douglass that separate schools were "infinitely superior" to no schools at all. So while they opposed constitutional language requiring racial segregation in schools, most African Americans were less interested in the abstract ideal of integrated education than in ensuring educational opportunities for their children and employment for African American teachers. Many, in fact, believed all-black schools offered a better chance of securing these goals.

Patterns of discrimination persisted. Demands by African Americans to prohibit segregation in railroad cars, steamboats, theaters, and other public spaces revealed and heightened the divisions within the Republican Party. Moderate white Republicans feared such laws would only further alienate potential white supporters. But by the early 1870s, as black influence and assertiveness grew, laws guaranteeing equal access to transportation and public accommodation were passed in many states. By and large, though, such civil rights laws were difficult to enforce in local communities.

In economic matters, Republican governments failed to fulfill African Americans' hopes of obtaining land. Few former slaves possessed the cash to buy land in the open market, and they looked to the state for help. Republicans tried to weaken the plantation system and promote black ownership by raising taxes on land. Yet even when state governments seized land for nonpayment of taxes, the property was never used to help create black homesteads. In Mississippi, for example, 6 million acres, or about 20 percent of the land, had been forfeited by 1875. Yet virtually all of it found its way back to the original owners after they paid minimal penalties.

Republican leaders emphasized the "gospel of prosperity" as the key to improving the economic fortunes of all Southerners, black and white. Essentially, they envisioned promoting northern-style capitalist development—factories, large towns, and diversified agriculture—through state aid. Much Republican state lawmaking was devoted to encouraging railroad construction. Between 1868 and 1873 state legislatures passed hundreds of bills promoting railroads. Most of the government aid consisted not of direct cash subsidies but of official endorsements of a company's bonds. This government backing gave railroad companies credibility and helped them raise capital. In exchange, states received liens on railroads as security against defaults on payments to bondholders.

Between 1868 and 1872 the southern railroad system was rebuilt and over 3,000 new miles of track added, an increase of almost 40 percent. But in spite of all the new laws, it proved impossible to attract significant amounts of northern and European investment capital. The obsession with railroads withdrew resources from education and other programs. As in the North, it also opened the doors to widespread corruption and bribery of public officials. Finally, the frenzy of railroad promotion soon led to an overextension of credit and to many bankruptcies, saddling Republican governments with enormous debts. Railroad failures eroded public confidence in the Republicans' ability to govern. The "gospel of prosperity" ultimately failed to modernize the economy or solidify the Republican Party in the South.

White Resistance and "Redemption"

The emergence of a Republican Party in the reconstructed South brought two parties but not a two-party system to the region. The opponents of Reconstruction, the Democrats, refused to acknowledge Republicans' right to participate in southern political life. In their view, the Republican Party, supported primarily by the votes of former slaves, was the partisan instrument of the northern Congress. Since Republicans controlled state governments, this denial of legitimacy meant, in effect, a rejection of state authority itself. In each state, Republicans were split between those who urged conciliation in an effort to gain white acceptance and those who emphasized consolidating the party under the protection of the military.

From 1870 to 1872 the Ku Klux Klan fought an ongoing terrorist campaign against Reconstruction governments and local leaders. Although not centrally organized, the Klan was a powerful presence in nearly every southern state. It acted as a kind of guerrilla military force in the service of the Democratic Party, the planter class, and all those who sought the restoration of white supremacy. Klansmen employed violence to intimidate African Americans and white Republicans, murdering innocent people, driving them from their homes, and destroying their property. Planters sometimes employed Klansmen to enforce labor discipline by driving African Americans off plantations to deprive them of their harvest share.

In October 1870, after Republicans carried Laurens County in South Carolina, bands of white people drove 150 African Americans from their homes and murdered 13 black and white Republican activists. In March 1871, three African Americans were arrested in Meridian, Mississippi, for giving "incendiary" speeches. At their court hearing, Klansmen killed two of the defendants and the Republican judge, and thirty more African Americans were murdered in a day of rioting. The single bloodiest episode of Reconstruction era violence took place in Colfax, Louisiana, on Easter Sunday 1873. Nearly 100 African Americans were murdered after they failed to hold a besieged courthouse during a contested election. One former Confederate officer observed that the Klan's goal was "to defy the reconstructed State Governments, to treat them with contempt, and show that they have no real existence."

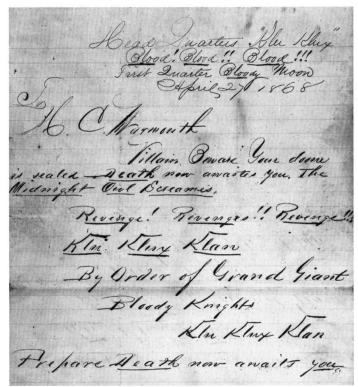

The Ku Klux Klan emerged as a potent political and social force during Reconstruction, terrorizing freed people and their white allies. An 1868 Klan warning threatens Louisiana governor Henry C. Warmoth with death. Warmoth, an Illinois-born "carpetbagger," was the state's first Republican governor. Two Alabama Klansmen, photographed in 1868, wear white hoods to hide their identities.

SOURCE: (a) University of North Carolina Southern Historical Collection; (b) Rutherford B. Hayes Presidential Center.

Southern Republicans looked to Washington for help. In 1870 and 1871 Congress passed three Enforcement Acts designed to counter racial terrorism. These declared that interference with voting was a federal offense. The acts provided for federal supervision of voting, and authorized the president to send the army and to suspend the writ of habeas corpus in districts declared to be in a state of insurrection. The most sweeping measure was the Ku Klux Klan Act of April 1871, which made the violent infringement of civil and political rights a federal crime punishable by the national government. Attorney General Amos T. Akerman prosecuted hundreds of Klansmen in North Carolina and Mississippi. In October 1871 President Grant sent federal troops to occupy nine South Carolina counties and rounded up thousands of Klan members. By the election of 1872, the federal government's intervention had helped break the Klan and restore a semblance of law and order.

The Civil Rights Act of 1875 outlawed racial discrimination in theaters, hotels, railroads, and other public places. But the law proved more an assertion of principle than a direct federal intervention in southern affairs. Enforcement required African Americans to take their cases to the federal courts, a costly and time-consuming procedure.

As wartime idealism faded, northern Republicans became less inclined toward direct intervention in southern affairs. They had enough trouble retaining political control in the North. In 1874 the Democrats gained a majority in the House of Representatives for the first time since 1856. Key northern states also began to fall to the Democrats. Northern Republicans slowly abandoned the freedmen and their white allies in the South. Southern Democrats were also able to exploit a deepening fiscal crisis by blaming Republicans for excessive extension of public credit and the sharp increase in tax rates. Republican governments had indeed spent public money for new state school systems, orphanages, roads, and other internal improvements.

Gradually, conservative Democrats "redeemed" one state after another. Virginia and Tennessee led the way in 1869, North Carolina in 1870, Georgia in 1871, Texas in 1873, and Alabama and Arkansas in 1874. In Mississippi, white conservatives employed violence and intimidation to wrest control in 1875 and "redeemed" the state the following year. Republican infighting in Louisiana in 1873 and 1874 led to a series of contested election results, including bloody clashes between black militia and armed whites, and finally to "redemption" by the Democrats in 1877. Once these states returned to Democratic rule, African Americans faced obstacles to voting, more stringent controls on plantation labor, and deep cuts in social services.

Several Supreme Court rulings involving the Fourteenth and Fifteenth Amendments effectively constrained federal protection of African American civil rights. In the so-called Slaughterhouse cases of 1873, the Court issued its first ruling on the Fourteenth Amendment. The cases involved a Louisiana charter that gave a New Orleans meat-packing company a monopoly over the city's butchering business on the grounds of protecting public health. A rival group of butchers had sued, claiming the law violated the Fourteenth Amendment, which prohibited states from depriving any person of life, liberty, or property without due process of law. The Court held that the Fourteenth Amendment protected only the former slaves, not butchers, and that it protected only national citizenship rights, not the regulatory powers of states. The ruling in effect denied the original intent of the Fourteenth Amendment—to protect against state infringement of national citizenship rights as spelled out in the Bill of Rights.

Three other decisions curtailed federal protection of black civil rights. In *United States* v. *Reese* (1876) and *United States* v. *Cruikshank* (1876), the Court restricted congressional power to enforce the Ku Klux Klan Act. Future prosecution would depend on the states rather than on federal authorities. In these rulings the Court held that the Fourteenth Amendment extended the federal power to protect civil rights only in cases involving discrimination by states; discrimination by individuals or groups was not covered. The Court also ruled that the Fifteenth Amendment did not guarantee a citizen's right to vote; it only barred certain specific grounds for denying suffrage—"race, color, or previous condition of servitude." This interpretation opened the door for southern states to disfranchise African Americans for allegedly nonracial reasons. States back under Democratic control began to limit African American voting by passing laws restricting voter eligibility through poll taxes and property requirements.

Finally, in the 1883 Civil Rights Cases decision, the Court declared the Civil Rights Act of 1875 unconstitutional, holding that the Fourteenth Amendment gave Congress the power to outlaw discrimination by states, but not by private individuals. The majority opinion held that black people must no longer "be the special favorite of the laws." Together, these Supreme Court decisions marked the end of federal attempts to protect African American rights until well into the next century.

White Yeomen, White Merchants, and "King Cotton"

The Republicans' vision of a "New South" remade along the lines of the northern economy failed to materialize. Instead, the South declined into the country's poorest agricultural region. Unlike midwestern and western farm towns burgeoning from trade in wheat, corn, and livestock, southern communities found themselves almost entirely dependent on the price of one commodity. Cotton growing had defined the economic life of large plantations in the coastal regions and black belt communities of the antebellum South. In the post–Civil War years "King Cotton" expanded its realm, as greater numbers of small white farmers found themselves forced to switch from subsistence crops to growing cotton for the market.

The triumph of "King Cotton" reflected the chronic shortage of capital and banking throughout the region. Large planters and town merchants were often the only sources of credit. They advanced loans and supplies to small owners, tenant farmers, and

sharecroppers in exchange for a lien, or claim, on the year's cotton crop. The spread of the "crop lien" system as the South's main form of agricultural credit forced more and more farmers into cotton growing. "Cotton is the thing to get credit on in this country," one small farmer explained to a federal commission investigating commodity prices. "You can always sell cotton. You leave home with a wagon load of cotton and you will go home at night with money in your pocket."

The transition to cotton dependency developed unevenly, at different speeds in different parts of the South. Penetration by railroads, the availability of commercial fertilizers, and the opening up of new lands to

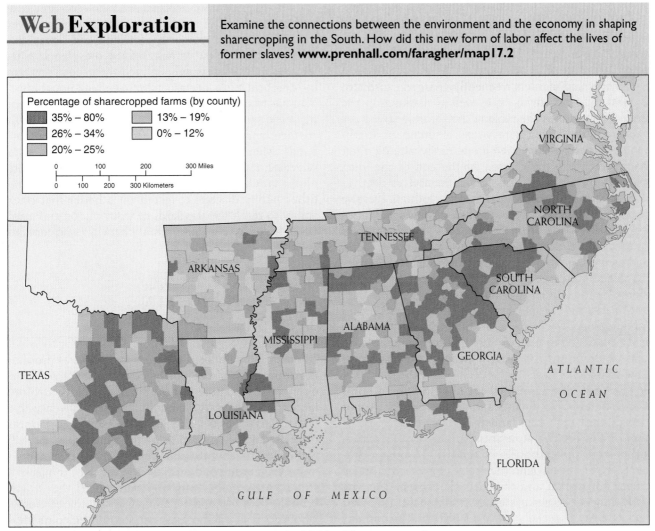

Web Exploration   Examine the connections between the environment and the economy in shaping sharecropping in the South. How did this new form of labor affect the lives of former slaves? **www.prenhall.com/faragher/map17.2**

Southern Sharecropping and the Cotton Belt, 1880   The economic depression of the 1870s forced increasing numbers of southern farmers, both white and black, into sharecropping arrangements. Sharecropping was most pervasive in the cotton belt regions of South Carolina, Georgia, Alabama, Mississippi, and east Texas.

cultivation were key factors in transforming communities from diversified, locally oriented farming to the market-oriented production of cotton. In the South Carolina upcountry, for example, cotton farmers had produced 170,000 bales in 1860; the ravages of war and its aftermath had reduced that figure to 99,000 in 1870. But by 1880 the figure had jumped to 284,000, and by 1890 to 387,000. In the South overall, white farmers had grown only 10 percent of the cotton in 1860; by the mid-1870s they were growing 40 percent of the total, much of it on small farms of 200 acres or less.

The pent-up demand for cotton following the war brought high prices (as much as 43 cents per pound) through the late 1860s. But as the "crop lien" system spread, and as more and more farmers turned to cotton growing as the only way to obtain credit, expanding production depressed prices. Competition from new cotton centers in the world market, such as Egypt and India, accelerated the downward spiral. As cotton prices declined alarmingly, to roughly 11 cents per pound in 1875 to 5 cents by the early 1890s, per capita wealth in the South fell steadily, equaling only one-third that of the East, Midwest, or West by the 1890s. Merchants and planters frequently charged exorbitant interest rates on advances, as well as marking up the prices of the goods they sold in their stores. Taking advantage of the high illiteracy rates among poor Southerners, landlords and merchants easily altered their books to inflate the figures. At the end of the year, sharecroppers and tenants found themselves deep in debt to stores for seed, supplies, and clothing. Despite hard work and even bountiful harvests, few small farmers could escape from heavy debt. Small farmers caught up in a vicious cycle of low cotton prices, debt, and dwindling food crops found their old ideal of independence sacrificed to the cruel logic of the cotton market. When asked how he had fallen into this trap, cotton farmer J. Pope Brown impatiently testified to investigators: "We were poor, had nothing to go on, had no collateral, and we just had to plant the crop that would bring money right away. We did not have time to wait."

By 1880, nearly 40 percent of all Southern farms were operated by tenants and sharecroppers. About one-third of the white farmers and nearly three-quarters of the African American farmers in the cotton states were sharecroppers or tenants. To obtain precious credit, most found themselves forced to produce cotton for market and thus became enmeshed in the debt-ridden crop lien system. In traditional cotton producing areas, especially the black belt, landless farmers growing cotton had replaced slaves growing cotton. In the upcountry and newer areas of cultivation, cotton-dominated commercial agriculture, with landless tenants and sharecroppers as the main workforce, had replaced the more diversified subsistence economy of the antebellum era.

One class of white Southerners benefiting from these arrangements were local merchants. As hundreds of new villages (communities of less than 2,500 people) sprang up in every corner of the South, especially in the new upcountry and Piedmont settlements, local merchants provided both goods and credit for local farmers. In 1866, for example, the mercantile firm of Smith and Melton opened for business in the up-country town of Chester, South Carolina. By 1869 it was advancing some $20,000 per year in credit and supplies to Chester farmers, and could boast over $100,000 in financial backing. By marketing local cotton crops, merchants also served as middlemen between small towns and the larger national economy.

With their power based on control of credit and marketing, merchants emerged as a new economic elite unconnected to the antebellum planters whose power had rested on the ownership of land and slaves. But within both the new towns and the old planter elite, white families increasingly defined their social position by celebrating a certain type of ideal household. Women found meaning in their role as upholders of domestic virtue by creating a comfortable home environment and tending to the needs of children and husbands. Men were to be of strong moral fiber and to provide material support for the family. These elite ideals, articulated in magazines, schools, sermons, and other public discourse, rested on a belief that one's ability to reach the standards of womanhood and manhood rested solely upon moral character and individual choice.

RECONSTRUCTING THE NORTH

Abraham Lincoln liked to cite his own rise as proof of the superiority of the northern system of "free labor" over slavery. "There is no permanent class of hired laborers amongst us," Lincoln asserted. "Twenty-five years ago, I was a hired laborer. The hired laborer of yesterday, labors on his own account today; and will hire others to labor for him tomorrow. Advancement—improvement in condition—is the order of things in a society of equals." But the triumph of the North brought with it fundamental changes in the economy, labor relations, and politics that brought Lincoln's ideal vision into question. The spread of the factory system, the growth of large and powerful corporations, and the rapid expansion of capitalist enterprise all hastened the development of a large unskilled and routinized workforce. Rather than becoming independent producers, more and more workers found themselves consigned permanently to wage labor.

The old Republican ideal of a society bound by a harmony of interests had become overshadowed by a grimmer reality of class conflict. A violent national railroad strike in 1877 was broken only with the direct intervention of federal troops. That conflict struck many Americans as a turning point. Northern society, like the society of the South, appeared more hierarchical than equal. That same year the last federal troops withdrew from their southern posts, marking the end of the Reconstruction era. By then, the North had undergone its own "reconstruction" as well.

The Age of Capital

In the decade following Appomattox, the North's economy continued the industrial boom begun during the Civil War. By 1873, America's industrial production had grown 75 percent over the 1865 level. By that time, too, the number of nonagricultural workers in the North had surpassed the number of farmers. Between 1860 and 1880 the number of wage earners in manufacturing and construction more than doubled, from 2 million to over 4 million. Only Great Britain boasted a larger manufacturing economy than the United States. During the same period, nearly 3 million immigrants arrived in America, almost all of whom settled in the North and West.

The railroad business both symbolized and advanced the new industrial order. Shortly before the Civil War, enthusiasm mounted for a transcontinental line. Private companies took on the huge and expensive job of construction, but the federal government funded the project, providing the largest subsidy in American history. The Pacific Railway Act of 1862 granted the Union Pacific and the Central Pacific rights to a broad swath of land extending from Omaha, Nebraska, to Sacramento, California. An 1864 act bestowed a subsidy of $15,000 per mile of track laid over smooth plains country and varying larger amounts up to $48,000 per mile in the foothills and mountains of the Far West. The Union Pacific employed gangs of Irish American and African American workers to lay track heading west from Omaha, while the Central

Pacific brought in more than 10,000 men from China to handle the difficult work in the Sierra Nevada mountain region.

On May 10, 1869, Leland Stanford, the former governor of California and president of the Central Pacific Railroad, traveled to Promontory Point in Utah Territory to hammer a ceremonial golden spike, marking he finish of the first transcontinental line. Other railroads went up with less fanfare. The Southern Pacific, chartered by the state of California, stretched from San Francisco to Los Angeles, and on through Arizona and New Mexico to connections with New Orleans. The Atchison, Topeka, and Santa Fe reached the Pacific in 1887 by way of a southerly route across the Rocky Mountains. The Great Northern, one of the few lines financed by private capital, extended west from St. Paul, Minnesota, to Washington's Puget Sound.

Railroads paved the way for the rapid settlement of the West, and both rural and urban areas grew dramatically over the next several decades. The combined population of Minnesota, the Dakotas, Nebraska, and Kansas, for example, jumped from 300,000 in 1860 to over 2 million in 1880. In the fifty years after 1870, the nation's railroad system expanded to more than a quarter million miles—more than all the rest of the world's railroad track combined.

Completion of the transcontinental railroad, May 10, 1869, as building crews for the Union Pacific and Central Pacific meet at Promontory Point, Utah. The two locomotive engineers salute each other, while the chief engineers for the two railroads shake hands. Construction had begun simultaneously from Omaha and Sacramento in 1863, with the help of generous subsidies from Congress. Work crews, consisting of thousands of ex-soldiers, Irish immigrants, and imported Chinese laborers, laid nearly 1,800 miles of new track.

SOURCE: The Granger Collection, New York (4E377.23).

Railroad corporations became America's first big businesses. Railroads required huge outlays of investment capital, and their growth increased the economic power of banks and investment houses centered in Wall Street. Bankers often gained seats on the boards of directors of these railroad companies, and their access to capital sometimes gave them the real control of railways. By the early 1870s the Pennsylvania Railroad stood as the nation's largest single company, with more than 20,000 employees. A new breed of aggressive entrepreneur sought to ease cutthroat competition by absorbing smaller companies and forming "pools" that set rates and divided the market. A small group of railroad executives, including Cornelius Vanderbilt, Jay Gould, Collis P. Huntington, and James J. Hill, amassed unheard-of fortunes. When he died in 1877, Vanderbilt left his son $100 million. By comparison, a decent annual wage for working a six-day week was around $350.

A growing number of Republican politicians maintained close connections with railroad interests. Railroad promoters, lawyers, and lobbyists became ubiquitous figures in Washington and state capitals, wielding enormous influence among lawmakers. "The galleries and lobbies of every legislature," one Republican leader noted, "are thronged with men seeking . . . an advantage." Railroads benefited enormously from government subsidies. Between 1862 and 1872, Congress alone awarded more than 100 million acres of public lands to railroad companies and provided them over $64 million in loans and tax incentives.

Some of the nation's most prominent politicians routinely accepted railroad largesse. Republican senator William M. Stewart of Nevada, a member of the Committee on Pacific Railroads, received a gift of 50,000 acres of land from the Central Pacific for his services. Senator Lyman Trumbull of Illinois took an annual retainer from the Illinois Central. The worst scandal of the Grant administration grew out of corruption involving railroad promotion. As a way of diverting funds for the building of the Union Pacific Railroad, an inner circle of Union Pacific stockholders created the dummy Crédit Mobilier construction company. In return for political favors, a group of prominent Republicans received stock in the company. When the scandal broke in 1872, it politically ruined Vice President Schuyler Colfax and led to the censure of two congressmen.

Other industries also boomed in this period, especially those engaged in extracting minerals and processing natural resources. Railroad growth stimulated expansion in the production of coal, iron, stone, and lumber, and these also received significant government aid. For example, under the National Mineral Act of 1866, mining companies received millions of acres of free public land. Oil refining enjoyed a huge expansion in the 1860s and 1870s. As with railroads, an early period of fierce competition soon gave way to concentration. By the late 1870s, John D. Rockefeller's Standard Oil Company controlled almost 90 percent of the nation's oil-refining capacity. The production of pig iron tripled from 1 million tons in 1865 to 3 million tons in 1873. Between 1869 and 1879 both the capital investment and the number of workers in iron nearly doubled. Coal production shot up from 17 million tons in 1861 to 72 million tons in 1880. The size of individual ironworks and coal mines—measured by the number of employees and capital invested—also grew in these years, reflecting the expanding scale of industrial enterprise as a whole.

Liberal Republicans and the Election of 1872

With the rapid growth of large-scale, capital-intensive enterprises, Republicans increasingly identified with the interests of business rather than the rights of freedmen or the antebellum ideology of "free labor." The old Civil War–era Radical Republicans had declined in influence. State Republican parties now organized themselves around the spoils of federal patronage rather than grand causes such as preserving the Union or ending slavery. Despite the Crédit Mobilier affair, Republicans had no monopoly on political scandal. In 1871 New York City newspapers reported the shocking story of how Democratic Party boss William M. Tweed and his friends had systematically stolen tens of millions from the city treasury. The "Tweed Ring" had received enormous bribes and kickbacks from city contractors and businessmen. Grotesquely caricatured by Thomas Nast's cartoons in *Harper's Weekly*, Tweed emerged as the preeminent national symbol of increasingly degraded and dishonest urban politics. But to many, the scandal represented only the most extreme case of the routine corruption that now plagued American political life.

By the end of President Grant's first term, a large number of disaffected Republicans sought an alternative. They were led by a small but influential number of intellectuals, professionals, businessmen, and reformers who articulated an ideology that helped reshape late nineteenth-century politics. The Liberal Republicans, as they called themselves, shared several core values. First, they emphasized the doctrines of classical economics, stressing the law of supply and demand, free trade, defense of property rights, and individualism. They called for a return to limited government, arguing that bribery, scandal, and high taxes all flowed from excessive state interference in the economy.

Liberal Republicans were also suspicious of expanding democracy. "Universal suffrage," Charles Francis Adams Jr. wrote in 1869, "can only mean in plain English the government of ignorance and vice—it means a European, and especially Celtic, proletariat on the Atlantic coast, an African proletariat on the shores of the Gulf, and a Chinese proletariat on the Pacific." Liberal Republicans believed that politics ought to be the province of "the best men"—educated and well-to-do men like themselves, devoted to the "science of government." They proposed civil service reform as the best way to break the hold of party machines on patronage. Competitive examinations, they argued, were the best way to choose employees for government posts. At a time when only a very small fraction of Americans attended college, this requirement would severely restrict the pool of government workers.

Although most Liberal Republicans had enthusiastically supported abolition, the Union cause, and equal rights for freedmen, they now opposed continued federal intervention in the South. The national government had done all it could for the former slaves; they must now take care of themselves. "Root, Hog, or Die" was the harsh advice offered by Horace Greeley, editor of the *New York Tribune*. In the spring of 1872 a diverse collection of Liberal Republicans nominated Greeley to run for president. A longtime foe of the Democratic Party, Greeley nonetheless won that party's presidential nomination as well. He made a new policy for the South the center of his campaign against Grant. The "best men" of both sections, he argued, should support a more generous Reconstruction policy based on "universal amnesty and impartial suffrage." All Americans, Greeley urged, must put the Civil War behind them and "clasp hands across the bloody chasm."

Grant easily defeated Greeley, carrying every state in the North and winning 56 percent of the popular vote. Most Republicans were not willing to abandon the regular party organization, and "waving the bloody shirt" was still a potent vote-getter. But the 1872 election accelerated the trend toward federal abandonment of African American citizenship rights. The Liberal Republicans quickly faded as an organized political force. But their ideas helped define a growing conservative consciousness among the northern public. For the rest of the century, their political and economic views attracted a growing number of middle-class professionals and businessmen. This agenda included retreat from the ideal of racial justice, hostility toward trade unions, suspicion of working-class and immigrant political power,

celebration of competitive individualism, and opposition to government intervention in economic affairs.

The Depression of 1873

In the fall of 1873 the postwar boom came to an abrupt halt as a severe financial panic triggered a deep economic depression. The collapse resulted from commercial overexpansion, especially speculative investing in the nation's railroad system. The investment banking house of Jay Cooke and Company failed in September 1873 when it found itself unable to market millions of dollars in Northern Pacific Railroad bonds. Soon other banks and brokerage houses, especially those dealing in railroad securities, caved in as well, and the New York Stock Exchange suspended operations. By 1876 half the nation's railroads had defaulted on their bonds. Over the next two years more than 100 banks folded and 18,000 businesses shut their doors. The depression that began in 1873 lasted sixty-five months—the longest economic contraction in the nation's history until then.

The human toll of the depression was enormous. As factories began to close across the nation, the unemployment rate soared to about 15 percent. In many cities the jobless rate was much higher; roughly one-quarter of New York City workers were unemployed in 1874. Many thousands of men took to the road in search of work, and the "tramp" emerged as a new and

"The Tramp," *Harper's Weekly*, September 2, 1876. The depression that began in 1873 forced many thousands of unemployed workers to go "on the tramp" in search of jobs. Men wandered from town to town, walking or riding railroad cars, desperate for a chance to work for wages or simply for room and board. The "tramp" became a powerful symbol of the misery caused by industrial depression and, as in this drawing, an image that evoked fear and nervousness among the nation's middle class.

SOURCE: The Picture Bank, Frank & Marie Therese Wood Print Collection.

menacing figure on the social landscape. The Pennsylvania Bureau of Labor Statistics noted that never before had "so many of the working classes, skilled and unskilled . . . been moving from place to place seeking employment that was not to be had." Farmers were also hard hit by the depression. Agricultural output continued to grow, but prices and land values fell sharply. As prices for their crops fell, farmers had a more difficult time repaying their fixed loan obligations; many sank deeper into debt.

During the winter of 1873, New York labor leaders demanded to know what measures would be taken "to relieve the necessities of the 10,000 homeless and hungry men and women of our city whose urgent appeals have apparently been disregarded by our public servants." Mass meetings of workers in New York and other cities issued calls to government officials to create jobs through public works. But these appeals were rejected. Indeed, many business leaders and political figures denounced even meager efforts at charity. E. L. Godkin wrote in the Christmas 1875 issue of *The Nation* that "free soup must be prohibited, and all classes must learn that soup of any kind, beef or turtle, can be had only by being paid for." Men such as Godkin saw the depression as a natural, if painful, part of the business cycle, one that would allow only the strongest enterprises (and workers) to survive. They dismissed any attempts at government interference, in the form of either job creation or relief for the poor.

Increased tensions, sometimes violent, between labor and capital reinforced the feeling of many Americans that the nation was no longer immune from European-style class conflict. The depression of the 1870s prompted workers and farmers to question the old free-labor ideology that celebrated a harmony of interests in northern society. More people voiced anger at and distrust of large corporations that exercised great economic power from outside their communities. Businessmen and merchants, meanwhile, especially in large cities, became more conscious of their own class interests. New political organizations such as Chicago's Citizens' Association united businessmen in campaigns for fiscal conservatism and defense of property rights. In national politics, the persistent depression made the Republican Party, north and south, more vulnerable than ever.

The Electoral Crisis of 1876

With the economy mired in depression, Democrats looked forward to capturing the White House in 1876. New scandals plaguing the Grant administration also weakened the Republican Party. In 1875, a conspiracy surfaced between distillers and U.S. revenue agents to cheat the government out of millions in tax revenues. The government secured indictments against more

than 200 members of this "Whiskey Ring," including Orville E. Babcock, Grant's private secretary. Though acquitted, thanks to Grant's intervention, Babcock resigned in disgrace. In 1876, Secretary of War William W. Belknap was impeached for receiving bribes for the sale of trading posts in Indian Territory, and he resigned to avoid conviction.

Though Grant himself was never implicated in any wrongdoing, Democrats hammered away at his administration's low standard of honesty in government. For president they nominated Governor Samuel J. Tilden of New York, who brought impeccable reform credentials to his candidacy. In 1871 he had helped expose and prosecute the "Tweed Ring" in New York City. As governor he had toppled the "Canal Ring," a graft-ridden scheme involving inflated contracts for repairs on the Erie Canal. In their platform, the Democrats linked the issue of corruption to an attack on Reconstruction policies. They blamed the Republicans for instituting "a corrupt centralism" that subjected southern states to "the rapacity of carpetbag tyrannies," riddled the national government "with incapacity, waste, and fraud," and "locked fast the prosperity of an industrious people in the paralysis of hard times."

Republican nominee Rutherford B. Hayes, governor of Ohio, also sought the high ground. As a lawyer in Cincinnati he had defended runaway slaves. Later he had distinguished himself as a general in the Union

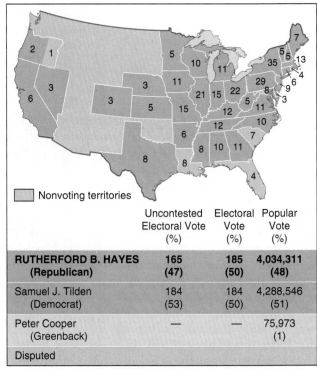

	Uncontested Electoral Vote (%)	Electoral Vote (%)	Popular Vote (%)
RUTHERFORD B. HAYES (Republican)	**165 (47)**	**185 (50)**	**4,034,311 (48)**
Samuel J. Tilden (Democrat)	184 (53)	184 (50)	4,288,546 (51)
Peter Cooper (Greenback)	—	—	75,973 (1)
Disputed			

Nonvoting territories

The Election of 1876 The presidential election of 1876 left the nation without a clear-cut winner.

CHRONOLOGY

1865	Freedmen's Bureau established
	Abraham Lincoln assassinated
	Andrew Johnson begins Presidential Reconstruction
	Black codes begin to be enacted in southern states
	Thirteenth Amendment ratified
1866	Civil Rights Act passed
	Congress approves Fourteenth Amendment
	Ku Klux Klan founded
1867	Reconstruction Acts, passed over President Johnson's veto, begin Congressional Reconstruction
	Tenure of Office Act
	Southern states call constitutional conventions
1868	President Johnson impeached by the House, but acquitted in Senate trial
	Fourteenth Amendment ratified
	Most southern states readmitted to Union
	Ulysses S. Grant elected president
1869	Congress approves Fifteenth Amendment
	Union Pacific and Central Pacific tracks meet at Promontory Point in Utah Territory
	Suffragists split into National Woman Suffrage Association and American Woman Suffrage Association
1870	Fifteenth Amendment ratified
1871	Ku Klux Klan Act passed
	"Tweed Ring" in New York City exposed
1872	Liberal Republicans break with Grant and Radicals, nominate Horace Greeley for president
	Crédit Mobilier scandal
	Grant reelected president
1873	Financial panic and beginning of economic depression
	Slaughterhouse cases
1874	Democrats gain control of House for first time since 1856
1875	Civil Rights Act
1876	Disputed election between Samuel Tilden and Rutherford B. Hayes
1877	Electoral Commission elects Hayes president
	President Hayes dispatches federal troops to break Great Railroad Strike and withdraws last remaining federal troops from the South

army. Republicans charged Tilden with disloyalty during the war, income tax evasion, and close relations with powerful railroad interests. Hayes promised, if elected, to support an efficient civil service system, to vigorously prosecute officials who betrayed the public trust, and to introduce a system of free universal education.

On an election day marred by widespread vote fraud and violent intimidation, Tilden received 250,000 more popular votes than Hayes. But Republicans refused to concede victory, challenging the vote totals in the electoral college. Tilden garnered 184 uncontested electoral votes, one shy of the majority required to win, while Hayes received 165. The problem centered in 20 disputed votes from Florida, Louisiana, South Carolina,

and Oregon. In each of the three southern states two sets of electoral votes were returned. In Oregon, which Hayes had unquestionably carried, the Democratic governor nevertheless replaced a disputed Republican elector with a Democrat.

The crisis was unprecedented. In January 1877 Congress moved to settle the deadlock, establishing an Electoral Commission composed of five senators, five representatives, and five Supreme Court justices; eight were Republicans and seven were Democrats. The commission voted along strict partisan lines to award all the contested electoral votes to Hayes. Outraged by this decision, Democratic congressmen threatened a filibuster to block Hayes's inauguration. Violence and stalemate were avoided when Democrats and Republicans struck a compromise in February. In return for Hayes's ascendance to the presidency, the Republicans promised to appropriate more money for southern internal improvements, to appoint a Southerner to Hayes's cabinet, and to pursue a policy of noninterference ("home rule") in southern affairs.

Shortly after assuming office, Hayes ordered removal of the remaining federal troops in Louisiana and South Carolina. Without this military presence to sustain them, the Republican governors of those two states quickly lost power to Democrats. "Home rule" meant Republican abandonment of freed people, Radicals, carpetbaggers, and scalawags. It also effectively nullified the Fourteenth and Fifteenth Amendments and the Civil Rights Act of 1866. The "Compromise of 1877" completed repudiation of the idea, born during the Civil War and pursued during Congressional Reconstruction, of a powerful federal government protecting the rights of all American citizens. As one black Louisianan lamented, "The whole South—every state in the South—had got into the hands of the very men that held us slaves." Other voices hailed this turning point in policy. "The negro," declared *The Nation*, "will disappear from the field of national politics. Henceforth, the nation, as a nation, will have nothing more to do with him."

CONCLUSION

Reconstruction succeeded in the limited political sense of reuniting a nation torn apart by the Civil War. The Radical Republican vision, emphasizing racial justice, equal civil and political rights guaranteed by the Fourteenth and Fifteenth Amendments, and a new southern economy organized around independent small farmers, never enjoyed the support of the majority of its party or the northern public. By 1877 the political force of these ideals was spent and the national retreat from them nearly complete.

The end of Reconstruction left the way open for the return of white domination in the South. The freed people's political and civil equality proved only temporary. It would take a "Second Reconstruction," the civil rights movement of the next century, to establish full black citizenship rights once and for all. The federal government's failure to pursue land reform left former slaves without the economic independence needed for full emancipation. Yet the newly autonomous black family, along with black-controlled churches, schools, and other social institutions, provided the foundations for the modern African American community. If the federal government was not yet fully committed to protecting equal rights in local communities, the Reconstruction era at least pointed to how that goal might be achieved. Even as the federal government retreated from the defense of equal rights for black people, it took a more aggressive stance as the protector of business interests. The Hayes administration responded decisively to one of the worst outbreaks of class violence in American history by dispatching federal troops to several northern cities to break the Great Railroad Strike of 1877. In the aftermath of Reconstruction, the struggle between capital and labor had clearly replaced "the southern question" as the number one political issue of the day. "The overwhelming labor question has dwarfed all other questions into nothing," wrote an Ohio Republican. "We have home questions enough to occupy attention now."

REVIEW QUESTIONS

1. How did various visions of a "reconstructed" South differ? How did these visions reflect the old political and social divisions that had led to the Civil War?

2. What key changes did emancipation make in the political and economic status of African Americans? Discuss the expansion of citizenship rights in the post–Civil War years. To what extent did women share in the gains made by African Americans?

3. What role did such institutions as the family, the church, the schools, and the political parties play in the African American transition to freedom?

4. How did white Southerners attempt to limit the freedom of former slaves? How did these efforts succeed, and how did they fail?

5. Evaluate the achievements and failures of Reconstruction governments in the southern states.

6. What were the crucial economic changes occurring in the North and South during the Reconstruction era?

RECOMMENDED READING

Paul A. Cimbala and Randall M.Miller, eds., *The Freedmen's Bureau and Reconstruction* (1999). A wide ranging collection of the latest scholarship, with special attention to recapturing the historical voices of freed people.

Jane Dailey, *Before Jim Crow: The Politics of Race in Post Emancipation Virginia* (2000). A fine study that focuses on the tension between the drive to establish white supremacy and the struggle for biracial coalitions in post–Civil War Virginia politics.

Laura F. Edwards, *Gendered Strife & Confusion: The Political Culture of Reconstruction* (1997). An ambitious analysis of how gender ideologies played a key role in shaping the party politics and social relations of the Reconstruction-era South.

Michael W. Fitzgerald, *The Union League Movement in the Deep South* (1989). Uses the Union League as a lens through which to examine race relations and the close connections between politics and economic change in the post–Civil War South.

Eric Foner, *Reconstruction: America's Unfinished Revolution, 1863–1877* (1988). The most comprehensive and thoroughly researched overview of the Reconstruction era.

William Gillette, *Retreat from Reconstruction: A Political History, 1867–1878* (1979). Covers the national political scene, with special attention to the abandonment of the ideal of racial equality.

Jacqueline Jones, *Labor of Love, Labor of Sorrow* (1985). Includes excellent material on the work and family lives of African American women in slavery and freedom.

Leon Litwack, *Been in the Storm So Long: The Aftermath of Slavery* (1979). A richly detailed analysis of the transition from slavery to freedom; excellent use of African American sources.

Scott Reynolds Nelson, *Iron Confederacies: Southern Railways, Klan Violence, and Reconstruction* (1999). Pathbreaking analysis of how conservative southern and northern business interests rebuilt the South's railroad system and also achieved enormous political power within individual states.

Edward Royce, *The Origins of Southern Sharecropping* (1993). A sophisticated, tightly argued work of historical sociology that explains how sharecropping emerged as the dominant form of agricultural labor in the post–Civil War South.

ADDITIONAL BIBLIOGRAPHY

The Politics of Reconstruction

Richard H. Abbott, *The Republican Party and the South, 1855–1877* (1986)

Herman Belz, *Emancipation and Equal Rights* (1978)

Michael Les Benedict, *A Compromise of Principle: Congressional Republicans and Reconstruction* (1974)

———, *The Impeachment and Trial of Andrew Johnson* (1973)

Michael Kent Curtis, *No State Shall Abridge: The Fourteenth Amendment and the Bill of Rights* (1990)

Ellen Carol DuBois, *Feminism and Suffrage* (1978)

Eric Foner, *Politics and Ideology in the Age of the Civil War* (1980)

William C. Harris, *With Charity for All: Lincoln and the Restoration of the Union* (1997)

Robert Kaczorowski, *The Politics of Judicial Interpretation: The Federal Courts, Department of Justice, and Civil Rights, 1866–1876* (1985)

James McPherson, *Ordeal by Fire: The Civil War and Reconstruction* (1982)

Michael Perman, *Emancipation and Reconstruction, 1862–1879* (1987)

Brooks D. Simpson, *The Reconstruction Presidents* (1998)

Kenneth M. Stampp, *The Era of Reconstruction, 1865–1877* (1965)

The Meaning of Freedom

Ira Berlin et al., eds., *Freedom: A Documentary History*, 3 vols. (1985–91)

W. E. B. DuBois, *Black Reconstruction* (1935)

Barbara J. Fields, *Slavery and Freedom on the Middle Ground* (1985)

Eric Foner, *Freedom's Lawmakers: A Directory of Black Officeholders during Reconstruction* (1996)

Noralee Frankel, *Freedom's Women: Black Women and Families in Civil War Era Mississippi* (1999)

Herbert G. Gutman, *The Black Family in Slavery and Freedom* (1976)

Sharon Ann Holt, *Making Freedom Pay: North Carolina Freedpeople Working For Themselves, 1865–1900* (2000)

Thomas Holt, *Black over White: Negro Political Leadership in South Carolina during Reconstruction* (1977)

Lynda J. Morgan, *Emancipation in Virginia's Tobacco Belt* (1992)

Nell Irvin Painter, *Exodusters* (1977)

Howard N. Rabinowitz, *Race Relations in the Urban South, 1865–1890* (1978)

Roger L. Ransom and Richard Sutch, *One Kind of Freedom: The Economic Consequences of Emancipation* (1977)

Leslie A. Schwalm, *A Hard Fight For We: Women's Transition from Slavery to Freedom in South Carolina* (1997)

Southern Politics and Society

Pamela Brandwein, *Reconstructing Reconstruction: The Supreme Court and the Production of Historical Truth* (1999)

Dan T. Carter, *When the War Was Over: The Failure of Self Reconstruction in the South, 1865–1877* (1985)

Richard N. Current, *Those Terrible Carpetbaggers* (1988)

Stephen Hahn, *The Roots of Southern Populism* (1983)

William C. Harris, *The Day of the Carpetbagger: Republican Reconstruction in Mississippi* (1979)

Scott Reynolds Nelson, *Iron Confederacies: Southern Railroads, Klan Violence, and Reconstruction* (1999)

Michael S. Perman, *Reunion without Compromise: The South and Reconstruction, 1865–1868* (1973)

———, *The Road to Redemption: Southern Politics, 1868–1979* (1984)

Howard N. Rabinowitz, *The First New South, 1865–1920* (1991)

Daniel W. Stowell, *Rebuilding Zion: The Religious Reconstruction of the South, 1863–1877* (1998)

Allen W. Trelease, *White Terror: The Ku Klux Klan Conspiracy and Southern Reconstruction* (1971)

Jonathan M. Wiener, *Social Origins of the New South* (1978)

Reconstructing the North

Stephen Buechler, *The Transformation of the Woman Suffrage Movement* (1986)

Morton Keller, *Affairs of State* (1977)

James C. Mohr, ed., *Radical Republicans in the North* (1976)

David Montgomery, *Beyond Equality: Labor and the Radical Republicans, 1862–1872* (1967)

Keith I. Polakoff, *The Politics of Inertia: The Election of 1876 and the End of Reconstruction* (1973)

Amy Dru Stanley, *From Bondage to Contract: Wage Labor, Marriage, and the Market in the Age of Slave Emancipation* (1998)

Mark W. Summers, *Railroads, Reconstruction, and the Gospel of Prosperity* (1984)

———, *The Era of Good Stealings* (1993)

Xi Wang, *The Trial of Democracy: Black Suffrage and Northern Republicans, 1860–1910* (1997)

C. Vann Woodward, *Reunion and Reaction: The Compromise of 1877 and the End of Reconstruction* (1956)

Biography

David Donald, *Charles Sumner and the Rights of Man* (1970)

Russell Duncan, *Freedom's Shore: Tunis Campbell and the Georgia Freedmen* (1986)

William S. McFeely, *Frederick Douglass* (1989)

———, *Grant: A Biography* (1981)

———, *Yankee Stepfather: General O. O. Howard and the Freedmen* (1968)

Hans L. Trefousse, *Andrew Johnson* (1989)

———, *Thaddeus Stevens: Nineteenth Century Egalitarian* (1997)

HISTORY ON THE INTERNET

http://memory.loc.gov/ammem/aaohtml/exhibit/aopart5.html

This American Memory project from the Library of Congress provides primary documents, descriptive narrative, photographs, and drawings of the life of the freedman during Reconstruction.

http://www.lib.auburn.edu/madd/docs/impeach.html

Extensive collection of PDF files on impeachment relating to Andrew Johnson.

http://www.uno.edu/~drcom/Griffith/Birth/

http://www.filmsite.org/birt.html

http://www.library.csi.cuny.edu/dept/history/lavender/birth.html

Each of these sites are related to the 1915 film by D. W. Griffith called *Birth of a Nation* based on the racist book, *The Clansman*. The book and movie portrays the history of Reconstruction from the southern point of view and makes the Ku Klux Klan the heroes of this movie.

Reconstruction Era Primary Documents:

http://www.yale.edu/lawweb/avalon/presiden/inaug/grant1.htm

First Inaugural Address of Ulysses S. Grant, March 4, 1869

http://www.nara.gov/exhall/treasuresofcongress/Images/page_13/44b.html

Wade-Davis Bill

http://odur.let.rug.nl/~usa/P/al16/writings/wdveto.htm

Lincoln's veto of the Wade-Davis Bill

http://www.ncrepublic.org/recon2.html

Reconstruction Act of 1867

http://www.nv.cc.va.us/home/nvsageh/Hist122/Part1/ForceActsEx.htm

The Force Acts of 1870–1871

http://www.yale.edu/lawweb/avalon/presiden/inaug/grant2.htm

Second Inaugural Address of Ulysses S. Grant, March 4, 1873

http://www.yale.edu/lawweb/avalon/presiden/inaug/hayes.htm

Inaugural Address of Rutherford B. Hayes, March 5, 1877

Emigrants to the American West. Colored engraving, 19th century. John Gast, *American Progress*.
SOURCE: The Granger Collection, New York (009675/4E645.28).

AMERICAN COMMUNITIES

The Oklahoma Land Rush

DECADES AFTER THE EVENT, COWBOY EVAN G. BARNARD VIVIDLY recalled the preparations made by settlers when Oklahoma territorial officials announced the opening of No Man's Land to the biggest "land rush" in American history. "Thousands of people gathered along the border. . . . As the day for the race drew near, the settlers practiced running their horses and driving carts." Finally the morning of April 22, 1889, arrived. "At ten o'clock people lined up . . . ready for the great race of their lives." Like many others, Barnard displayed his guns prominently on his hips, determined to discourage competitors from claiming the 160 acres of prime land that he intended to grab for himself.

Evan Barnard's story was one strand in the larger tale of the destruction and creation of communities in the trans-Mississippi West. In the 1830s, the federal government designated what was to become the state of Oklahoma as Indian Territory, reserved for the Five Civilized Tribes (Cherokees, Chickasaws, Choctaws, Creeks, and Seminoles) that had been forcibly removed from their eastern lands. All five tribes had reestablished themselves as sovereign republics in Indian Territory. The Cherokees and Chocktaws became prosperous cotton growers. The Creeks managed large herds of hogs and cattle, and the Chickasaws grazed not only cattle but sheep and goats on their open fields. The Five Tribes also ran sawmills, gristmills, and cotton gins. Indian merchants were soon dealing with other tribespeople as well as licensed white traders and even contracting with the federal government.

The Civil War, however, took a heavy toll on their success. Some tribes, slaveholders themselves, sided with the Confederacy; others with the Union. When the war ended, more than 10,000 people—nearly one-fifth of the population of Indian Territory—had died. To make matters worse, new treaties required the Five Civilized Tribes to cede the entire western half of the territory, including the former northern Indian territory of Nebraska and Kansas, for the resettlement of tribes from other regions.

Western Oklahoma thereby became home to thousands of newly displaced peoples, including the Pawnees, Peorias, Ottawas, Wyandots, and Miamis. Many small tribes readily took to farming and rebuilt their communities. But the nomadic, buffalo-hunting Kiowas, Cheyennes, Comanches, and Arapahoes did not settle so peacefully. They continued to traverse the plains until the U.S. Army finally forced them onto reservations. Eventually, more than 80,000 tribespeople were living on twenty-one separate reservations in western Oklahoma, all governed by agents appointed by the federal government.

The opening of the unassigned far western district of Oklahoma known as No Man's Land to non-Indian homesteading, however, signaled the impending end of Indian sovereignty. Many non-Indians saw this almost 2 million acre strip as a Promised Land, perfect for dividing into thousands of small farms. African Americans, many of whom were former slaves of Indian planters, appealed to the federal government for the right to stake claims there. Another group of would-be homesteaders, known as "Boomers," quickly tired of petitioning and invaded the district in 1880, only to be booted out by the Tenth Cavalry. Meanwhile, the railroads, seeing the potential for lucrative commerce, put constant pressure on the federal government to open No Man's Land for settlement. In 1889 the U.S. Congress finally gave in.

Cowboy Barnard was just one of thousands to pour into No Man's Land on April 22, 1889. Many homesteaders simply crossed the border from Kansas. Southerners, dispossessed by warfare and economic ruin in their own region, were also well represented. Market-minded settlers claimed the land nearest the railroads, and by nightfall of April 22 they had set up tent cities along the tracks. In a little over two months, after 6,000 homestead claims had been filed, the first sod houses appeared, sheltering growing communities of non-Indian farmers, ranchers, and other entrepreneurs.

Dramatic as it was, the land rush of 1889 was only one in a series of events that soon dispossessed Oklahoma's Indians of their remaining lands. First, the federal government broke up the estates held collectively by various tribes in western Oklahoma, assigning to individuals the standard 160-acre allotment and allowing non-Indian homesteaders to claim the rest. Then, in 1898, Congress passed the Curtis Act, formally dissolving Indian Territory and dispossessing the Five Tribes. Members of the former Indian nations were directed to dismantle their governments, abandon their estates, and join the ranks of other homesteaders. They nevertheless retained many of their tribal customs and managed to regain their sovereign status in 1977.

Later generations of Oklahomans often celebrated their his-

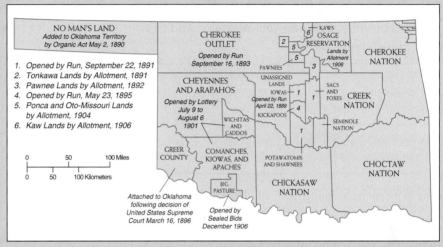

Oklahoma Territory   Land openings to settlers came at different times, making new land available through various means.

toric ties to the Indian nations. At formal ceremonies marking statehood, just before the newly elected governor took the oath of office, a mock wedding ceremony united a tough and virile cowboy with a demure and submissive Indian maiden. By this time, in 1907, tribespeople were outnumbered in Oklahoma by ten to one.

By this time also, nearly one-quarter of the entire population of the United States lived west of the Mississippi River. Hundreds of new communities, supported primarily by cattle ranching, agriculture, mining, or other industries, had not only grown with the emerging national economy but helped to shape it in the process. The newcomers displaced communities that had formed centuries earlier. They also drastically transformed the physical landscape. Through their activities and the support of Easterners, the United States realized an ambition that John L. O'Sullivan had described in 1845 as the nation's "manifest destiny to overspread the continent" and remake it in a new image. ■

KEY TOPICS

- The impact of western expansion on Indian societies

- The West as an "internal empire" and the development of new technologies and new industries

- The creation of new communities and the displacement of old communities

- The West as myth and legend

INDIAN PEOPLES UNDER SIEGE

The tribespeople living west of the Mississippi River keenly felt the pressure of the gradual incorporation of the West into the nation. The Oregon Trail opened the Northwest to large numbers of non-Indian settlers, and by 1845 nearly 5,000 people had braved the six-to-eight-month journey by wagon to reach present-day Oregon and Washington. The following year, the United States reached an agreement with Great Britain for the division of the Oregon Country. Then came the addition of the vast territories taken from Mexico following the Mexican-American War. California quickly became a state in 1850, Oregon in 1859. Congress consolidated the national domain in the next decades by granting territorial status to Utah, New Mexico, Washington, Dakota, Colorado, Nevada, Arizona, Idaho, Montana, and Wyoming. The purchase of Alaska in 1867 added an area twice the size of Texas and extended the nation beyond its contiguous borders so that it reached almost to Russia and the North Pole. The federal government made itself the custodian of all these thinly settled regions, permitting limited self-rule, with appointed governors supervising the transition from territorial status to statehood.

Competition for the land and its resources was central to this encounter. Unlike the settlers wedded to the principles of private property, the tribespeople mainly believed that the land belongs to those who revere it across many generations. Their prospects to preserve their ways of life amid this contest dimmed considerably following the discovery of gold in California in 1848, the opening of western lands to homesteaders in 1862, and the completion of the transcontinental railroad in 1869. White settlers, hoping to build a new life for themselves, rushed into these new territories and repeatedly invaded Indian lands west of the Mississippi. Violent outbreaks between white emigrants and Indian peoples became increasingly commonplace. Since the Jefferson administration, federal officials had promoted the assimilation of Indian peoples; they now became even more determined to break up their tribal councils and to bring them into the American mainstream.

On the Eve of Conquest

Before the European colonists reached the New World, tribespeople of the Great Plains, Southwest, and Far West had occupied the lands for more than 20,000 years. Hundreds of tribes, totaling perhaps a million members, had adapted to such extreme climates as the desert aridity of present-day Utah and Nevada, the bitter cold of the northern Great Plains, and the seasonally heavy rain of the Pacific Northwest. Many cultivated maize (corn), foraged for wild plants, fished, or hunted game. Several tribes built cities with several thousand inhabitants and traded across thousands of miles of western territory.

Invasion by the English, Spanish, and other Europeans brought disease, religious conversion, and new patterns of commerce. But geographic isolation still gave many tribes a margin of survival unknown in the East. At the close of the Civil War, approximately 360,000 Indian people still lived in the trans-Mississippi West, the majority of them in the Great Plains.

The surviving tribes adapted to changing conditions. The Plains Indians learned to ride the horses and shoot the guns introduced by Spanish and British traders. The Pawnees migrated farther westward to evade encroaching non-Indian settlers, while the Sioux and the Comanches fought neighboring tribes to gain control of large stretches of the Great Plains. The southwestern Hopis and Zunis, conquered earlier by the Spanish, continued to trade extensively with the Mexicans who lived near them. Some tribes took dramatic steps toward accommodation with white ways. Even before they were uprooted and moved across the Mississippi River, the Cherokees had learned English, converted to Christianity, established a constitutional republic, and become a nation of farmers.

Web Exploration

Explore the conflicts between Indians and white settlers from 1860 to 1900. Why were the Indians forcibly removed to reservations? www.prenhall.com/faragher/map18.1

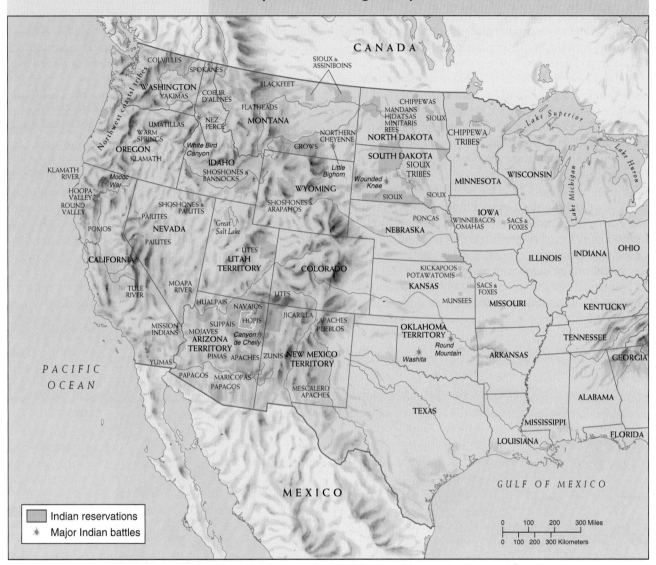

Major Indian Battles and Indian Reservations, 1860–1900 As commercial routes and white populations passed through and occupied Indian lands, warfare inevitably erupted. The displacement of Indians to reservations opened access by farmers, ranchers, and investors to natural resources and to markets.

Legally, the federal government had long regarded Indian tribes as autonomous nations residing within American boundaries and had negotiated numerous treaties with them over land rights and commerce. But pressured by land-hungry whites, several states had violated these federal treaties so often that the U.S. Congress passed the Indian Removal Act of 1830 (see Chapter 10), which provided funds to relocate all eastern tribes by force if necessary. The Cherokees challenged this legislation, and the Supreme Court ruled in their favor in *Cherokee Nation v. Georgia* (1831). Ignoring the Court's decision, President Andrew Jackson, known as a hardened Indian fighter, forced many tribes to cede their land and remove to Indian Territory. There, it was believed, they might live undisturbed by whites and gradually adjust to "civilized" ways. But soon, the onslaught of white settlers, railroad entrepreneurs, and prospectors rushing for gold pressured tribes to cede millions of their acres to the United States. In 1854, to open the Kansas and Nebraska Territories for white settlement, the federal government simply abolished the northern half of Indian Territory.

As demand for resources and land accelerated, the entire plan for a permanent Indian Territory fell apart.

Reservations and the Slaughter of the Buffalo

As early as the 1840s, highly placed officials had outlined a plan to subdue the intensifying rivalry over natural resources and land. Under the terms of their proposal, individual tribes would agree to live within clearly defined zones—reservations—and, in exchange, the Bureau of Indian Affairs would provide guidance while U.S. military forces ensured protection. This reservation policy also reflected the vision of many "Friends of the Indian," educators and Protestant missionaries who aspired to "civilize the savages." By the end of the 1850s eight western reservations had been established where Indian peoples were induced to speak English, take up farming, and convert to Christianity. The U.S. Commissioner of Indian affairs Luke Lea predicted that reservations would speed the "ultimate incorporation" of the Indians "into the great body of our citizen population."

Several tribes did sign treaties, although often under duress. High-handed officials, such as governor Isaac Stevens of Washington Territory, made no attempt at legitimate negotiations, choosing instead to intimidate or deceive Indian peoples into signing away their lands. Most of the tribes in Washington responded by remaining in their old villages. But Stevens finally had his way. State officials moved the Indians onto three reservations after their leaders signed away 45,000 square miles of tribal land. The Suquamish leader Seattle admitted defeat but warned the governor: "Your time of decay may be distant, but it will surely come."

Those tribes that moved to reservations often found federal policies inadequate to their needs. The federal government repeatedly reduced the size of land allotments, forcing tribes to compete with each other for increasingly scarce resources and making subsistence farming on the reservation virtually impossible. The Medicine Lodge Treaty of 1867 assigned reservations in existing Indian Territory to Comanches, Plains (Kiowa) Apaches, Kiowas, Cheyennes, and Arapahoes, bringing these tribes together with Sioux, Shoshones, and Bannocks. All told, more than 100,000 people found themselves competing intensely for survival. Over the next decade, a group of Quakers appointed by President Ulysses S. Grant attempted to mediate differences among the tribes and to supply the starving peoples

Chief Red Cloud in an 1868 photograph. The Oglala Sioux spiritual leader is seen with Red Dog, Little Wound, interpreter John Bridgeman (on his right), American Horse, and Red Shirt (on his left). He ventured to Washington with his delegation to discuss with President Ulysses S. Grant the various provisions of the peace treaty, just signed, to end the violent conflict over the Bozeman Trail.

SOURCE: National Anthropological Archives/Smithsonian Institution (3238/E).

with food and seed. At the same time, white prospectors and miners continued to flood the Dakota Territory. "They crowded in," Iron Teeth recalled bitterly, "so we had to move out." Moreover, corrupt officials of the Bureau of Indian Affairs routinely diverted funds for their own use and reduced food supplies, a policy promoting malnutrition, demoralization, and desperation.

The nomadic tribes that traditionally hunted and gathered over large territories saw their freedom sharply curtailed. The Lakotas, or Western Sioux, a loose confederation of bands scattered across the northern Great Plains, were one of the largest and most adaptive of all Indian nations. Seizing buffalo-hunting territory from their rivals, the Pawnees and the Crows, the Sioux had learned to follow the herds on horseback. Buffalo meat and hides fed and clothed the Sioux and satisfied many of their other needs as well. Images of buffalo appeared in their religious symbols and ceremonial dress. The Sioux were also vision seekers. Young men and women pursued dreams that would provide them guidance for a lifetime; elders themselves followed dreams that might guide the destiny of the entire tribe or nation.

The mass slaughter of the buffalo brought the crisis provoked by the increasing restriction of the nomadic Plains peoples to a peak. In earlier eras, vast herds of buffalo had literally darkened the western horizon. Buffalo grazed over distances of several hundred miles, searching for water and wallowing in mud to fend off insects. The expansion of trade in buffalo robes, involving both tribespeople and Europeans and Americans, proved devastating for the herds and the populations who had come to depend on them. By midcentury, non-Indian traders avidly sought fur for coats, hide for leather, bones for fertilizer, and heads for trophies. As gunpowder and the railroad came to the range, the number of buffalo fell rapidly. New rifles, like the .50 caliber Sharps, could kill at 600 feet; one sharpshooter bragged of killing 3,000 buffalo. Army commanders encouraged the slaughter, accurately predicting that starvation would break tribal resistance to the reservation system. With their food sources practically destroyed, diseases such as smallpox and cholera (brought by fur traders) sweeping through their

villages, and their way of life undermined, many Great Plains tribes, including many Sioux, concluded that they could only fight or die.

The Indian Wars

Under these pressures, a handful of tribes organized themselves and their allies to resist both federal policies and the growing wave of white settlers. The overwhelming majority of tribespeople did not take up arms. But settlers, thousands of them Civil War veterans with weapons close at hand, responded to real or imaginary threats with their own brands of violence.

Large-scale war erupted in 1864. Having decided to terminate all treaties with tribes in eastern Colorado, territorial governor John Evans encouraged a group of white civilians, the Colorado Volunteers, to stage raids through Cheyenne campgrounds. Seeking protection, Chief Black Kettle brought a band of 800 Cheyennes to a U.S. fort and received orders to set up camp at Sand Creek. Feeling secure in this arrangement, Black Kettle sent out most of his men to hunt. Several weeks later, on November 29, 1864, the Colorado Volunteers and soldiers attacked. While Black Kettle held up a U.S. flag and a white truce banner, a disorderly group of 700 men, many of them drunk, slaughtered 105 Cheyenne women and children and 28 men. They

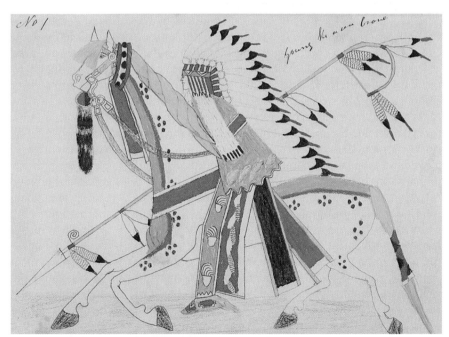

Preparing for a War Expedition, ca. 1887. This sketch on paper was made by an Indian artist, Silverhorn, who had himself taken part in the final revolt of the Kiowas in 1874. He later became a medicine man, and then served as a private in the U.S. Cavalry at Fort Sill, Oklahoma Territory.

SOURCE: Silverhorn, Native American, *Kiowa Preparing for a War Expedition.* From *Sketchbook,* 1887. Graphite ink and crayon. Gift of Mrs. Terrell Bartlett. Collection of the McNay Art Museum.

mutilated the corpses and took scalps back to Denver to exhibit as trophies. Iron Teeth, a Cheyenne woman who survived, remembered seeing a woman "crawling along on the ground, shot, scalped, crazy, but not yet dead." Months after the Sand Creek Massacre, bands of Cheyennes, Sioux, and Arapahoes were still retaliating, burning civilian outposts and sometimes killing whole families.

The Sioux played the most dramatic roles in the Indian Wars. In 1851, believing the U.S. government would recognize their own rights of conquest over other Indian tribes, the Sioux relinquished large tracts of land as a demonstration of good faith. But within a decade, a mass invasion of miners and the construction of military forts along the Bozeman Trail in Wyoming, the Sioux's principal buffalo range, threw the tribe's future into doubt. During the Great Sioux War of 1865–67, the Oglala Sioux warrior Red Cloud fought the U.S. Army to a stalemate and forced the government to abandon its forts, which the Sioux then burned to the ground. The Treaty of Fort Laramie, signed in 1868, created the Great Sioux Reservation, which included the present state of South Dakota west of the Missouri River, but restored only a temporary peace to the region.

The Treaty of Fort Laramie granted the Sioux the right to occupy the Black Hills, or Paha Sapa, their sacred land, "as long as the grass shall grow," but the discovery of gold soon undermined this guarantee. White prospectors hurriedly invaded the territory. Directed to quash rumors of fabulous deposits of the precious metal, Lieutenant Colonel George Armstrong Custer organized a surveying expedition to the Black Hills during the summer of 1874, but, contrary to plan, the Civil War hero described rich veins of ore that could be cheaply extracted. The U.S. Congress then pushed to acquire the territory for Americans. To protect their land, Sioux, Cheyenne, and Arapaho warriors, ranging between 2,000 and 9,000 in number, moved into war camps during the summer of 1876 and prepared for battle.

After several months of skirmishes and battles between the U.S. Army and Sioux warriors, Lieutenant Colonel Custer, the most flamboyant of calvary commanders (and in the eyes of many of his own troops, the most irresponsible) was ordered to move the Seventh Calvary into position to meet another infantry division. Custer abandoned the plan and decided to rush ahead to a site in Montana that was known to white soldiers as Little Bighorn and to Lakotas as Greasy Grass. This foolhardy move offered the allied Cheyenne and Sioux warriors a perfect opportunity to cut off Custer's logistical and military support. On June 25, 1876, Custer and his troops were wiped out by one of the largest Indian contingents ever assembled, an estimated 2,000 to 4,000 warriors.

"Custer's Last Stand" gave Indian-haters the emotional ammunition to whip up public excitement. After Custer's defeat, spiritual leader Sitting Bull reportedly said, "Now they will never let us rest." The U.S. Army tracked down the disbanded Indian contingents one by one and forced them to surrender. In February, 1877, the U.S. government formally took possession of the Black Hills. After the defiant warrior Crazy Horse was fatally stabbed while under arrest at a U.S. Army camp, Sioux leadership in the Indian Wars came to an end.

Among the last to hold out against the reservation system were the Apaches in the Southwest. Most Apache bands had abided by the Medicine Lodge Treaty of 1867, and in 1872 Cochise, one of the ablest Apache chiefs, agreed to live with his people on a reservation on a portion of the tribe's ancestral land. Cochise died two years later, and some of the Apache bands, unable to tolerate the harsh conditions on the reservation, returned to their old ways of seizing territory and stealing cattle. For the next ten years, Cochise's successor Geronimo led intermittent raids against white outposts in the rough Arizona terrain.

Pursued by the U.S. Army, the Apaches earned a reputation as intrepid warriors. Their brilliant strategists and horse-riding braves became legendary for lightning-swift raids followed by quick disappearances. The Kiowas and the Comanches, both powerful tribes, joined the Apaches in one of the bloodiest conflicts, the Red River War of 1874–75. The U.S. Army ultimately prevailed less by military might than by denying Indians access to food. Even after the Red River War, small-scale warfare sputtered on. Not until September 1886, his band reduced to only thirty people, did Geronimo finally surrender, ending the Indian Wars.

The Nez Percé

In crushing the Plains tribes, the U.S. government had conquered those peoples who had most actively resisted the advance of non-Indians into the West. But even tribes that had long tried to cooperate found themselves embattled. The Nez Percé (meaning "pierced nose") had been given their name by French Canadian fur trappers, who thought they had seen members of the tribe wearing shells in their septums. For generations the Nez Percé had regarded themselves as good friends to white traders and settlers. Living in the plateau where Idaho, Washington, and Oregon now meet, they had saved the Lewis and Clark expedition from starvation in 1803. The Nez Percé had occasionally assisted American armies against hostile tribes, and many of them were converts to Christianity.

But the discovery of gold on Nez Percé territory in 1860 changed their relations with whites for the worse. Pressed by prospectors and mining companies, government commissioners, in the treaty of 1863, demanded the Nez Percé cede 6 million acres, nine-tenths of their land, at less than ten cents per acre. Some of the Nez Percé leaders agreed to the terms of the treaty, which had been fraudulently signed on behalf of the entire tribe, but others refused. Old Chief Tuekekas, one of the first to convert to Christianity, threw away his Bible and returned to his old religion. His son and successor, Chief Joseph, swore to protect the peoples of the Wallowa Valley in present-day Oregon. At first, federal officials listened to Nez Percé complaints against the treaty and decided to allow them to remain on their land. But responding to pressure from settlers and politicians, however, they almost immediately reversed their decision, ordering the Nez Percé, including Chief Joseph and his followers, to sell their land and to move onto a reservation.

Intending to comply, Chief Joseph's band set out from the Wallowa Valley with their livestock and all the possessions they could carry. Along the way, some young members of another Indian band traveling with them rode away from camp to avenge the death of one of their own by killing several white settlers. Hoping to explain the situation, a Nez Percé truce team approached U.S. troops. The troops opened fire, and the Indian riders fired back, killing one-third of the soldiers. Chief Joseph and his people then undertook a monumental journey in search of sanctuary in Canada. Brilliantly outmaneuvering vengeful U.S. troops sent to intercept them, the 750 Nez Percé—including women, children, and the elderly—retreated for some 1,400 miles into Montana and Wyoming through mountains and prairies, and across the Bitterroot Range. Along the way, they unintentionally terrified tourists at the newly created Yellowstone National Park. Over the three and a half months of their journey, Nez Percé braves fought 2,000 regular U.S. troops and eighteen Indian auxiliary detachments in eighteen separate engagements and two major battles. U.S. troops finally trapped the Nez Percé in the Bear Paw Mountains of northern Montana, just 30 miles from the Canadian border. Suffering from hunger and cold, they surrendered.

General Sherman remarked admiringly at the Nez Percé's ingenious tactics, courage, and avoidance of cruelty. Newspapers described Chief Joseph as a "Red Napoleon" defying overwhelming odds. (Actually, Joseph did not plan military strategy but mainly attended to the needs of dependent tribal members.)

Promised they would be returned to Oregon, the Nez Percé were sent instead to disease-ridden bottomland near Fort Leavenworth in Kansas, and then to Oklahoma. Arguing for the right of his people to return to their Oregon reservation, Joseph spoke eloquently, through an interpreter, to Congress in 1879. "Treat all men alike. Give them all the same law. Give them all an even chance to live and grow. All men were made by the same Great Spirit Chief," Joseph pleaded. The last remnant of Joseph's band were deported under guard to a non-Nez Percé reservation in Washington, where Chief Joseph died in 1904 "of a broken heart," and where his descendants continue to live in exile to this day.

THE INTERNAL EMPIRE

Since the time of Christopher Columbus, the Americas had inspired in Europeans visions of a land of incredible wealth, free for the taking. In the nineteenth century, the North American continent, stretching across scarcely populated territories toward the Pacific Ocean, revived this fantasy, especially as early reports conjured dreams of mountains of gold and silver. Determined to make their fortunes, be it from copper in Arizona, wheat in Montana, or oranges in California, numerous adventurers traveled west. As a group they carried out the largest migration and greatest commercial expansion in American history.

But the settlers themselves also became the subjects of a huge "internal empire" whose financial, political, and industrial centers of power remained in the East. A vast system of international markets also shaped the development of mines, farms, and new communities, even as Americans romantically imagined the West to be the last frontier of individual freedom and wide open spaces. Only a small number of settlers actually struck it rich in the great extractive industries—mining, lumbering, ranching, and farming—that ruled the western economy. Meanwhile, older populations—Indian peoples, Hispanic peoples, and more recently settled communities like the Mormons—struggled to create places for themselves in this new order.

Mining Towns

The discovery of gold in California in 1848 roused fortune seekers from across the United States, Europe, and as far away as Chile and China. Just ten years later, approximately 35,000 Chinese men were working in mines, some having taken over the camps abandoned by American miners. Meanwhile, prospecting parties overran the western territories, setting a pattern for intermittent rushes for gold, silver, and copper that extended from the Colorado mountains to the Arizona deserts, from California to Oregon and Washington, and from Alaska to the Black Hills of South Dakota. Mining camps and boomtowns soon dotted what had once been thinly settled regions. The population of California alone jumped from 14,000 in 1848 to 223,856 just four years later. More than any other industry or commercial enterprise, mining fostered western expansion.

Web Exploration

Pan across a map of the West during the period 1860–1900. How did the growth of railroads and mining impact the environment and the lives of native peoples?
www.prenhall.com/faragher/map18.2

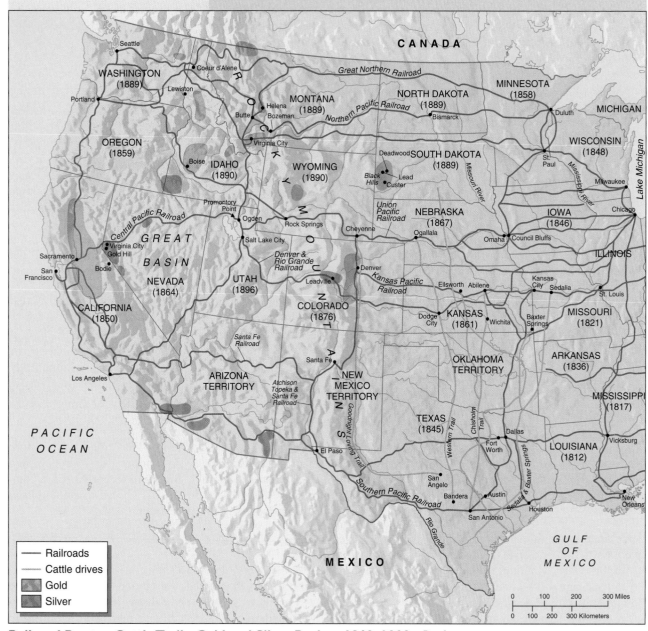

Railroad Routes, Cattle Trails, Gold and Silver Rushes, 1860–1900 By the end of the nineteenth century, the vast region of the West was crosscut by hundreds of lines of transportation and communication. The trade in precious metals and in cattle helped build a population almost constantly on the move, following the rushes for gold or the herds of cattle.

SOURCE: Encyclopedia of American Social History.

The first miners required little preparation to stake their claims. The miner needs nothing, the military governor of California announced, "but his pick and shovel and tin pan with which to dig and wash the gravel." A handful of individual prospectors did strike it rich. Many more found themselves employees of the so-called bonanza kings, the owners or operators of the most lucrative enterprises. Only in 1896–97, with

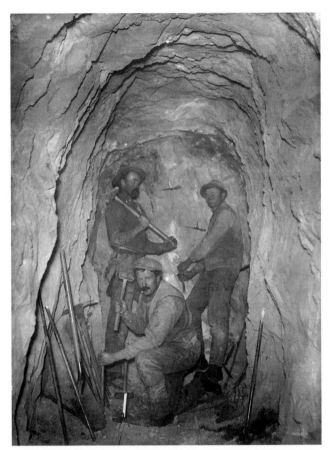

A "hard rock" miner demonstrates the tiring and often dangerous task of hammering a drill into a rock to prepare a blasting hole. New technologies, such as diamond-headed drills, quickly revolutionized the extractive process, but potentially lethal hazards, including cave-ins and poisonous gases, remained great.

SOURCE: Artist unknown, *Miners Underground*, 1897. Glass plate negative. Photograph by Timothy O'Sullivan. Courtesy Colorado Historical Society.

news of "gold on the Klondike" in Alaska, did prospectors again hit on a vein worth millions of dollars.

The mining industry quickly grew from its treasure-hunt origins into a grand corporate enterprise. The Comstock Lode of silver, discovered by Henry Comstock along the Carson River in Nevada in 1859, sent about 10,000 miners across the Sierra Nevada from California, but few individuals came out wealthy. Comstock himself eventually sold his claims for a mere $11,000 and two mules. Those reaping the huge profits were the entrepreneurs who could afford to invest in the heavy—and expensive—equipment necessary to drill more than 3,000 feet deep and to hire engineers with the technical knowledge to manage the operations. Having secured a capital investment of nearly $900,000, the owners of the Gould and Curry mill, built on the Comstock Lode, did very well.

The most successful mineowners bought out the smaller claims and built an entire industry around their stakes. They found investors to finance their expansion and used the borrowed capital to purchase the latest in extractive technology, such as new explosives, compressed-air or diamond-headed rotary drills, and wire cable. They gained access to timber to fortify their underground structures and water to feed the hydraulic pumps that washed down mountains. They built smelters to refine the crude ore into ingots and often financed railroads to transport the product to distant markets. By the end of the century, the Anaconda Copper Mining Company, which had mining interests throughout the West, had expanded into hydroelectricity to become one of the most powerful corporations in the nation.

The mining corporations laid the basis for a new economy as well as an interim government and established many of the region's first white settlements. Before the advent of railroads, ore had to be brought out of, and supplies brought into, mining areas by boats, wagons, and mules traveling hundreds of miles over rough territory. The railroad made transportation of supplies and products easier and faster. The shipping trade meanwhile grew into an important industry of its own, employing thousands of merchants, peddlers, and sailors. Dance halls, saloons, theaters, hospitals, and newspapers followed. Gold Hill and nearby Virginia City, Nevada, began as a cluster of small mining camps and by the early 1860s became a thriving urban community of nearly 6,000 people. A decade later, the population had quadrupled, but it subsequently fell sharply as the mines gave out. Occasionally, ore veins lasted long enough—as in Butte, Montana, center of the copper-mining district—to create permanent cities.

Many short-lived boomtowns were known as "Helldorados." Men outnumbered women by as much as ten to one, and very few lived with families or stayed very long. They often bunked with male kin and worked alongside friends or acquaintances from their hometown or, in the case of Butte, with fellow immigrants from Ireland. Some lived unusually well, feasting on oysters trucked in at great expense. Amateur sporting events, public lectures, and large numbers of magazines and books filled many of their leisure hours. But the town center was usually the saloon, where, as one observer complained, men "without the restraint of law, indifferent to public opinion, and unburdened by families, drink whenever they feel like it, whenever they have the money to pay for it, and whenever there is nothing else to do."

The western labor movement began in these camps, partly as a response to dangerous working conditions. In the hardrock mines of the 1870s, one of every thirty workers was disabled, one of eighty killed. Balladeers back in Ireland sang of Butte as the town "where the streets were paved with Irish bones," and departing emigrants promised their mothers that they would never go underground in Montana. Miners began to organize in the 1860s, demanding good pay for dangerous and life-shortening work. In 1892, miners in the Coeur d'Alene region of Idaho, in the aftermath of a bitter and violent strike, formed the Western Federation of Miners. With organizers traveling to mining towns and camps throughout the West, they established by the end of the century one of the strongest unions in the nation.

Violence on both sides characterized western labor relations. When mineowners' private armies "arrested" strikers or fought their unions with rifle fire, miners burned down the campsites, seized trains loaded with ore, and sabotaged company property. The miners' unions also helped to secure legislation mandating a maximum eight-hour day for certain jobs and workmen's compensation for injuries. Such laws were enacted in Idaho, Arizona, and New Mexico by the 1910s, long before similar laws in most eastern states.

The unions fought hard, but they did so exclusively for the benefit of white workers. The native-born and the Irish and Cornish immigrants (from Cornwall, England) far outnumbered other groups before the turn of the century, when Italians, Slavs, and Greeks began to replace them. Labor unions eventually admitted these new immigrants, but refused Chinese, Mexican, and Indian workers. In 1869 white miners at the Comstock Lode rioted to protest the employment of Chinese miners. In Arizona, Mexican Americans had secured jobs in the copper and silver mines, but they usually received less pay and worked under worse conditions than white workers.

When prices and ore production fell sharply, not even unions could stop the owners from shutting down the mines and leaving ghost towns in their wake. Often they also left behind an environmental disaster. Hydraulic mining, which used water cannons to blast hillsides and expose gold deposits, drove tons of rock and earth into the rivers and canyons. By the late 1860s southern California's rivers were clogged, producing floods that wiped out towns and farms. In 1893, Congress finally passed the Caminetti Act, giving the state the power to regulate the mines. (The act also created the Sacramento River Commission, which began to replace free-flowing rivers with canals and dams.) Underground mining continued unregulated, using up whole forests for timbers and filling the air with dangerous, sulfurous smoke.

Mormon Settlements

While western expansion fostered the growth of new commercial cities such as the numerous if unstable mining towns, it simultaneously placed new restrictions on established communities. The Mormons (members of

the Church of Jesus Christ of Latter-Day Saints) had fled western New York in the 1830s for Illinois and Missouri, only to face greater persecution in the Midwest. When their founder, Joseph Smith, was murdered after proclaiming the doctrine of polygamy (the taking of more than one wife), the community sought refuge in the West. Led by their new prophet, Brigham Young, the Mormons migrated in 1846–47 to the Great Basin in present-day Utah and formed an independent theocratic state called Deseret. However, their dream was cut short in 1850 when Congress set up Utah Territory. In 1857 President James Buchanan declared the Mormons to be in "a state of substantial rebellion" (for being

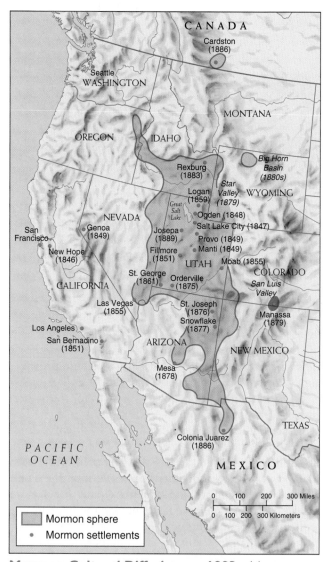

Mormon Cultural Diffusion, ca. 1883 Mormon settlements permeated many sparsely populated sections of Idaho, Nevada, Arizona, Wyoming, Colorado, and New Mexico. Built with church backing and the strong commitment of community members, they survived and even prospered in adverse climates.

an independent state within U.S. territory) and sent the U.S. Army to occupy the territory.

Although federal troops remained until the outbreak of the Civil War in 1861, the Mormon population continued to grow. By 1870, more than 87,000 Mormons lived in Utah Territory, creating relatively stable communities that were unique in the West for their religious and ethnic homogeneity. Contrary to federal law, church officials forbade the selling of land. Mormons instead held property in common. They created sizable settlements complemented by satellite villages joined to communal farmlands and a common pasture. Relying on agricultural techniques learned from local Indian tribes, the Mormons built dams for irrigation and harvested a variety of crops from desert soil. Eventually nearly 500 Mormon communities spread from Oregon to Idaho to northern Mexico.

But as territorial rule tightened, the Mormons saw their unique way of life once again threatened. The newspapers and the courts repeatedly assailed the Mormons for the supposed sexual excesses of their system of "plural marriage," condemning them as heathens and savages. "There is an irrepressible conflict," one journalist wrote, "between the Mormon power and the principles upon which our free institutions are established, and one or the other must succumb." Preceded by prohibitory federal laws enacted in 1862 and 1874, the Supreme Court finally ruled against polygamy in the 1879 case of *United States* v. *Reynolds*, which granted the freedom of belief but not the freedom of practice. In 1882, Congress passed the Edmunds Act, which effectively disfranchised those who believed in or practiced polygamy and threatened them with fines and imprisonment. Equally devastating was the Edmunds-Tucker Act, passed five years later, which destroyed the temporal power of the Mormon Church by confiscating all assets over $50,000 and establishing a federal commission to oversee all elections in the territory. By the early 1890s, Mormon leaders officially renounced the practice of plural marriage.

Polygamy had actually been practiced by no more than 15 to 20 percent of Mormon families, but it had been important to their sense of messianic mission. Forced to abandon the practice, they gave up most other aspects of their distinctive communal life, including the common ownership of land. By the time Utah became a state in 1896, Mormon communities resembled in some ways the society that the original settlers had sought to escape. Nevertheless, they combined their religious cohesion with leadership in the expanding regional economy to become a major political force in the West.

Borderland Communities

American expansionism transformed deserts and grasslands that had been contested for centuries among world powers. In 1845, Texas was annexed as a state, and the following year President James K. Polk whipped up a border dispute with Mexico into a war. The one-sided conflict ended in 1848 with the United States taking fully half of all Mexican territory—the future states of Arizona, California, Nevada, and Utah, most of New Mexico, and parts of Wyoming, and Colorado. The Gadsden Purchase of 1853 rounded off this prize, giving the United States a strip of land from El Paso west to the Colorado River—in short, all the land north of the Rio Grande River.

The Treaty of Guadalupe Hidalgo, which ended the Mexican-American War, allowed the Hispanic people north of the Rio Grande to choose between immigrating to Mexico or staying in what was now the United States. But the new Mexican-American border, one of the longest unguarded boundaries in the world, could not successfully sever communities that had been connected for centuries. Despite the change in sovereignty, elites and common folk alike continued to travel back and forth between the two nations, and the majority of people who became U.S. citizens retained their identity as Mexicans. Even those who migrated farther north, a process that accelerated after the discovery of gold in California and the silver strikes in Nevada, kept their ties with friends and family in Mexico. What gradually emerged was an economically and socially interdependent zone, the Anglo-Hispanic borderlands linking the United States and Mexico.

Equality, however, did not provide the basis for relationships between the two nations and their peoples. Although under the treaty all Hispanics were formally guaranteed citizenship and the "free enjoyment of their liberty and property," local "Anglos" (as the Mexicans called white Americans) often violated these provisions and, through fraud or coercion, took control of the land. The Sante Fe Ring, a group of lawyers, politicians, and land speculators, stole millions of acres from the public domain and grabbed over 80 percent of the Mexicano landholdings in New Mexico alone. More often, Anglos used new federal laws to their own benefit.

For a time, Arizona and New Mexico seemed to hold out hope for a mutually beneficial interaction between Mexicanos and Anglos. A prosperous class of Hispanic landowners, with long-standing ties to Anglos through marriage, had established itself in cities like Albuquerque and Tucson, old Spanish towns that had been founded in the seventeenth and eighteenth centuries. Estevan Ochoa, merchant, philanthropist, and the only Mexican to serve as mayor of Tucson following the Gadsden Purchase, managed to build one of the largest business empires in the West. In Las Cruces, New Mexico, an exceptional family such as the wealthy Amadors could shop by mail from Bloomingdales, travel to the World's Fair in Chicago, and send their children to English-language Catholic schools. Even the small and struggling Mexicano middle class could afford such

Mexican Americans in San Antonio continued to conduct their traditional market bazaar well after the incorporation of this region into the United States. Forced off the land and excluded from the better-paying jobs in the emerging regional economy, many Mexicanos and especially women sought to sell the products of their own handiwork for cash or for bartered food and clothing.

SOURCE: Thomas Allen, *Market Plaza*, 1878–1879. Oil on canvas, 26″ × 39½″. Witte Museum, San Antonio, Texas (36-65/8P).

modern conveniences as kitchen stoves and sewing machines. These Mexican elites, well integrated into the emerging national economy, continued to wield political power as ranchers, landlords, and real estate developers until the end of the century. They secured passage of bills for education in their regions and often served as superintendents of local schools. Several prominent merchants became territorial delegates to Congress.

But the majority of Mexicans who had lived in the mountains and deserts of the Southwest for well over two centuries were less prepared for these changes. Most had worked outside the commercial economy, farming and herding sheep for their own subsistence. Before 1848 they had few contacts with the outside world. With the Anglos came land closures as well as commercial expansion prompted by railroad, mining, and timber industries. Many poor families found themselves crowded onto plots too small for subsistence farming. Many turned to seasonal labor on the new Anglo-owned commercial farms, where they became the first of many generations of poorly paid migratory workers. Other Mexicanos adapted by taking jobs on the railroad or in the mines. Meanwhile their wives and daughters moved to the new towns and cities in such numbers that by the end of the century Mexicanos had become a predominantly urban population, dependent on wages for survival.

Women were quickly drawn into the expanding network of market and wage relations. They tried to make ends meet by selling produce from their backyard gardens; more often they worked as seamstresses or laundresses. Formerly at the center of a communal society, Mexicanas found themselves with fewer options in the cash economy. What wages they could now earn fell below even the low sums paid to their husbands, and women lost status within both the family and community.

Occasionally, Mexicanos organized to reverse these trends or at least to limit the damage done to their communities. In the border town of Brownsville, Texas, in 1859, Juan Nepomuceno Cortina, known as the Red Robber of the Rio Grande, and sixty of his followers pillaged white-owned stores and killed four Anglos who had gone unpunished for murdering several Mexicans. "Cortina's War" marked the first of several sporadic rebellions. As late as the 1880s, Las Gorras Blancas, a band of agrarian rebels in New Mexico, were destroying railroad ties and farm machinery and posting demands for justice on fences of the new Anglo farms and ranches. In 1890 Las Gorras turned from social banditry to political organization, forming *El Partido del Pueblo Unido* (The People's Party). Organized along similar lines, *El Alianzo Hispano-Americano* (The Hispanic-American Alliance) was formed "to protect and fight for the rights of Spanish Americans" through political action. *Mutualistes* (mutual aid societies) provided sickness and death benefits to Mexican families.

Despite many pressures, Mexicanos preserved much of their cultural heritage. Many persisted in older ways simply because they had few choices. In addition, the influx of new immigrants from Mexico helped to reinforce traditional cultural norms. Beginning in the late 1870s, the modernizing policies of Porfirio Diaz, the president of Mexico from 1876 to 1911, brought deteriorating living conditions to the masses of poor people and prompted a migration northward that accelerated through the first decades of the twentieth century. These newcomers revitalized old customs and rituals associated with family and religion. The Roman Catholic Church retained its influence in the community, and most Mexicans continued to turn to the church to baptize infants, to celebrate the feast day of their patron saints, to marry, and to bury the dead. Special saints like the Virgin of Guadalupe and distinctive holy days like the Day of the Dead survived along with fiestas celebrating the change of seasons. Many communities continued to commemorate Mexican national holidays, such as *Cinco de Mayo* (the Fifth of May), marking the Mexican victory over French invaders in the battle of Puebla in 1862. Spanish language and Spanish place names continued to distinguish the Southwest.

But for the encroaching Anglo majority, large regions in the West had been "won" from the populations who had previously settled the region. Americans had brought in commercial capitalism, their political and legal systems, as well as many of their social and cultural institutions. Ironically, though, even after statehood, white settlers would still be only distant representatives of an empire whose financial, political, and industrial centers remained in the Northeast. In return for raw produce or ore drawn out of soil or rock, they received washtubs, clothes, and whiskey; model legal statutes; and doctors, lawyers, and teachers. But they were often frustrated by their continued isolation, and they were enraged at the federal regulations that governed them, and at the eastern investors and lawyers who seemed poised on all sides to rob them of the fruits of their labor. Embittered Westerners, along with Southerners, would form the core of a nationwide discontent that would soon threaten to uproot the American political system.

THE CATTLE INDUSTRY

The slaughter of the buffalo made way for the cattle industry, one of the most profitable businesses in the West. Texas longhorns, introduced by the Spanish, numbered over 5 million at the close of the Civil War and represented a potentially plentiful supply of beef for eastern consumers. In the spring of 1866, entrepreneurs such as Joseph G. McCoy began to build a spectacular cattle market in the eastern part of Kansas, where the Kansas Pacific Railroad provided crucial transportation links to slaughtering and packing houses and commercial distributors in Kansas City, St. Louis, and Chicago.

In 1867 only 35,000 head of cattle reached McCoy's new stockyards in Abilene, but 1868 proved the first of many banner years. Drovers pushed herd after herd north from Texas through Oklahoma on the trail marked out by part-Cherokee trader Jesse Chisholm. Great profits were made on Texas steers bought for $7–$9 a head and sold in Kansas for upward of $30. In 1880 nearly 2 million cattle were slaughtered in Chicago alone. For two decades, cattle represented the West's bonanza industry.

Cowboys

The great cattle drives depended on the cowboy, a seasonal or migrant worker. After the Civil War, cowboys—one for every 300–500 head of cattle on the trail—rounded up herds of Texas cattle and drove them as much as 1,500 miles north to grazing ranches or to the stockyards where they were readied for shipping by rail to eastern markets. The boss supplied the horses, the cowboy his own bedroll, saddle, and spurs. The workday lasted from sunup to sundown, with short night shifts for guarding the cattle. Scurvy, a widespread ailment, could be traced to the basic chuckwagon menu of sowbelly, beans, and coffee, a diet bereft of fruits and vegetables. The cowboy worked without protection from rain or hail, and severe dust storms could cause temporary blindness. As late as 1920, veterans of the range complained that no company would sell life insurance to a cowboy.

In return for his labor, the cowboy received at the best of times about $30 per month. Wages were usually paid in one lump sum at the end of a drive, a policy that encouraged cowboys to spend their money quickly and recklessly in the booming cattle towns of Dodge City, Kansas, or Cheyenne, Wyoming. In the 1880s, when wages began to fall along with the price of beef, cowboys fought back by stealing cattle or by forming unions. In 1883 many Texas cowboys struck for higher wages; nearly all Wyoming cowboys struck in 1886. Aided by the legendary camaraderie fostered in the otherwise desolate conditions of the long drive, cowboys, along with miners, were among the first western workers to organize against employers.

Like other parts of the West, the cattle range was ethnically diverse. Between one-fifth and one-third of all workers were Indian, Mexican, or African American. Indian cowboys worked mainly on the northern plains and in Indian Territory; the *vaqueros*, who had previously worked on the Mexican cattle *haciendas*, or huge estates, predominated in South Texas and California. African American cowboys worked primarily in Texas, where the range cattle industry was founded.

Like the vaqueros, African American cowboys were highly skilled managers of cattle. Some were sons of former slaves who had been captured from the African territory of Gambia, where cattle raising was an age-old art. Unlike Mexicans, they earned wages comparable to those paid to Anglos and especially during the early years worked in integrated drover parties. By the 1880s, as the center of the cattle industry shifted to the more settled regions around the northern ranches, African Americans were forced out, and they turned to other kinds of work. Although the majority of Anglo cowboys also came from the South and shared with former slaves the hope of escaping the postwar economic devastation of their region, they usually remained loyal to the racial hierarchy of the Confederacy.

Cowgirls and Prostitutes

Sally Redus, wife of an early Texas cattleman, once accompanied her husband on the long drive from Texas to Kansas. Carrying her baby on her lap, she most likely rode the enormous distance "sidesaddle," with both legs on one side of the horse. Although few women worked as trail hands, they did find jobs on the ranches, usually in the kitchen or laundry. Occasionally a husband and wife worked as partners, sharing even the labor of wrangling cattle, and following her husband's death, a woman might take over altogether. Elizabeth Collins, for example, turned her husband's large ranch into an extraordinarily prosperous business, earning for herself the title "Cattle Queen of Montana." The majority of women attended to domestic chores, caring for children and maintaining the household. Their daughters, however, enjoyed better prospects. By the end of the century, women, who as girls had accompanied their fathers in outside chores, were riding astride, "clothespin style," roping calves, branding cattle or cutting their ears to mark them, and castrating bulls. But not until 1901 did a woman dare to enter an official rodeo contest.

In cattle towns as well as mining camps, many women worked as prostitutes. During the first cattle drive to Abilene in 1867, a few women were so engaged; but by the following spring, McCoy's assistant recalled, "they came in swarms, & as the weather was warm 4 or 5 girls could huddle together in a tent very comfortably." Although some women worked in trailside "hoghouses," the best-paid prostitutes congregated in "brothel districts" or "tenderloins." Most cattle towns boasted at least one dance hall where prostitutes plied their trade. Dodge city had two: one with white prostitutes for white patrons; another with black prostitutes for both white and black men. Although prostitution was illegal in most towns, the laws were rarely enforced until the end of the century, when reformers led campaigns to shut down the red-light districts.

Perhaps 50,000 women engaged in prostitution west of the Mississippi during the second half of the nineteenth century. Like most cowboys, most prostitutes were unmarried and in their teens or twenties. Often fed up with underpaid jobs in dressmaking or domestic service, they found few alternatives to prostitution in the cattle towns, where the cost of food and lodging was notoriously high. Still, earnings in prostitution were slim, except during the cattle-shipping season when young men outnumbered women by as much as three to one. In the best of times, a fully employed Wichita prostitute might earn $30 per week, nearly two-thirds of which would go for room and board. Injury or even death from violent clients, addiction to narcotics such as cocaine or morphine, and venereal disease were workaday dangers.

Curly Wolves Howled on Saturday Night, a commercial woodcut from the 1870s. The artist, recording this scene at a tavern near Billings, Montana, captured what he called a "Dude and a Waitress" dancing the "Bull Calves' Medley on the Grand Piano." Illustrations depicting a wild and lively West appeared prominently in magazines like *Harper's Weekly,* which circulated mainly among readers east of the Mississippi.

SOURCE: Horace Bradley. Courtesy of the Library of Congress.

Community and Conflict on the Range

The combination of prostitution, gambling, and drinking discouraged the formation of stable communities. According to a Kansas proverb, "There's no Sunday west of Junction City and no god west of Salina." Personal violence was notoriously commonplace on the streets and in the barrooms of cattle towns and mining camps populated mainly by young, single men. Many western towns such as Wichita outlawed the carrying of handguns, but enforcement usually lagged. Local specialty shops and mail-order catalogues continued to sell weapons with little regulation. But contrary to popular belief, gunfights were relatively rare. Local police officers, such as Wyatt Earp and James "Wild Bill" Hickok, worked mainly to keep order among drunken cowboys.

After the Civil War, violent crime, assault, and robbery rose sharply throughout the United States. In the West, the most prevalent crimes were horse theft and cattle rustling, which peaked during the height of the open range period and then fell back by the 1890s. Death by legal hanging or illegal lynching—at "necktie parties" in which the victims were "jerked to Jesus"—was the usual sentence. In the last half of the century, vigilantes acting outside the law mobilized more than 200 times, claiming altogether more than 500 victims.

The "range wars" of the 1870s produced violent conflicts. By this time, both farmers and sheep herders were encroaching on the fields where cattle had once grazed freely. Sheep chew grass down to its roots, making it practically impossible to raise cattle on land they have grazed. Farmers meanwhile set about building fences to protect their domestic livestock and property. Great cattle barons fought back against farmers by ordering cowboys to cut the new barbed-wire fences. Rivalry among the owners of livestock was even more vicious, particularly in the Southwest and Pacific Northwest. In these areas, Mexicano shepherds and Anglo cattlemen often fought each other for land. In Lincoln County, New Mexico, the feuds grew so intense in 1878 that one faction hired gunman Billy the Kid to protect its interests. President Rutherford B. Hayes finally sent troops to halt the bloodshed.

The cattle barons helped to bring about their own demise, but they did not go down quietly. Ranchers eager for greater profits, and often backed by foreign capital, overstocked their herds, and eventually the cattle began to deplete the limited supply of grass. Finally, during 1885–87, a combination of summer drought and winter blizzards killed 90 percent of the cattle in the northern Plains. Prices also declined sharply. Many big ranchers fell into bankruptcy. Along the way, they often took out their grievances against the former cowboys who had gathered small herds for

themselves. They charged these small ranchers with cattle rustling, taking them to court or, in some cases, rounding up lynching parties. As one historian has written, violence was "not a mere sideshow" but "an intrinsic part of western society."

FARMING COMMUNITIES ON THE PLAINS

The vision of a huge fertile garden extending from the Appalachians to the Pacific Ocean had inspired Americans since the early days of the republic. But the first explorers who actually traveled through the Great Plains quashed this dream. "The Great Desert" was the name they gave to the region stretching west from Kansas and Nebraska, north to Montana and the Dakotas, and south again to Oklahoma and Texas. Few trees fended off the blazing sun of summer or promised a supply of lumber for homes and fences. The occasional river or stream flowed with "muddy gruel" rather than pure, sweet water. Economically, the entire region appeared as hopelessly barren as it was vast. It took massive improvements in both transportation and farm technology—as well as unrelenting advertising and promotional campaigns—to open the Great Plains to widescale agriculture.

The Homestead Act

The Homestead Act of 1862 offered the first incentive to prospective white farmers. This act granted a quarter section (160 acres) of the public domain free to any settler who lived on the land for at least five years and improved it; or a settler could buy the land for $1.25 per acre after only six months' residence. Restricting its provisions to unmarried women, the Homestead Act encouraged adventurous and hard-working women to file between 5 and 15 percent of the claims, which allowed approximately 400,000 households to build farms for themselves.

Homesteaders achieved their greatest success in the central and upper Midwest where the soil was rich and weather relatively moderate. But those settlers lured to the Great Plains by descriptions of land "carpeted with soft grass—a sylvan paradise" found themselves locked in a fierce struggle with the harsh climate and arid soil. The average holding could rarely furnish a livelihood, even with hard work. Nearly half of all homesteaders failed to improve the land and therefore lost their claims.

Rather than filing a homestead claim with the federal government, most settlers acquired their land outright. State governments and land companies usually held the most valuable land near transportation and markets, and the majority of farmers were willing to pay a hefty price for these benefits. A few women speculators did very well, particularly in the Dakotas, where they acquired acreage under the generous terms of the Homestead Act, not to farm but to sell when prices for land increased. The big-time land speculators gained even more, plucking choice locations at bargain prices. And the railroads, which received land grants from the federal government, did best, selling off the holding near their routes at top dollar. By the end of the century, farm acreage west of the Mississippi had tripled, but perhaps only 10 percent of all farmers got their start under Homestead Act provisions.

The dream of a homestead nevertheless died hard. Five years after the passage of the Homestead Act, *New York Tribune* editor Horace Greeley still advised his readers to strike off "into the broad, free West" and "make yourself a farm from Uncle Sam's generous domain, you will crowd nobody, starve nobody, and . . . neither you nor your children need evermore beg for Something to Do." He was wrong. Although the Homestead Act did spark the largest migration in American history, it did not lay the foundation for a nation of prosperous family farms.

Populating the Plains

The rapid settlement of the West could not have taken place without the railroad. Although the Homestead Act offered prospective farmers free land, it was the railroad that promoted settlement, brought people to their new homes, and carried crops and cattle to eastern markets. The railroads therefore wielded tremendous economic and political power throughout the West. Their agents—reputed to know every cow in the district—made major decisions regarding territorial welfare. In designing routes and locating depots, railroad companies put whole communities "on the map," or left them behind.

Along with providing transportation links between the East and the West and potential markets as distant as China, the western railroads directly encouraged settlement. Unlike the railroads built before the Civil War, which followed the path of villages and towns, the western lines preceded settlement. Bringing people west became their top priority, and the railroad companies conducted aggressive promotional and marketing campaigns. Agents enticed Easterners and Europeans alike with long-term loans and free transportation by rail to distant points in the West. The railroads also sponsored land companies to sell parcels of their own huge allotments from the federal government. The National Land Company, founded in Chicago in 1869, alone organized sixteen colonies of mainly European

immigrants in parts of Kansas and Colorado. The Santa Fe Railroad sent agent C. B. Schmidt to Germany, where he managed to entice nearly 60,000 Germans to settle along the rail line.

More than 2 million Europeans, many recruited by professional promoters, settled the Great Plains between 1870 and 1900. Some districts in Minnesota seemed to be virtual colonies of Sweden; others housed the largest number of Finns in the New World. In sparsely settled North Dakota, Scandinavians constituted 30 percent of the population, with Norwegians the largest group. Nebraska, whose population as early as 1870 was 25 percent foreign-born, concentrated Germans, Swedes, Danes, and Czechs. Amid this diverse population, Germans outnumbered all other immigrants by far. A smaller portion of European immigrants reached Kansas, still fewer the territories to the south where Indian and Hispanic peoples and African Americans remained the major ethnic populations. By the end of the century, the West was second only to New England in the proportion of foreign-born persons in its regional population.

Many immigrants found life on the Great Plains difficult but endurable. "Living in Nebraska," the locals joked, "is a lot like being hanged; the initial shock is a bit abrupt, but once you hang there for awhile you sort of get used to it." The German-speaking Russians who settled the Dakotas discovered soil similar to that of their homeland but weather that was even more severe. Having earlier fled religious persecution in Germany for Russia, they brought with them heavy coats and the technique of using sun-dried bricks to build houses in areas where lumber was scarce. These immigrants often provided examples for other settlers less familiar with such harsh terrain.

Having traveled the huge distance with kin or members of their Old World villages, immigrants tended to form tight-knit communities on the Great Plains. Often they advised others still at home to join them and thereby gradually enlarged their distinctive settlements. Many married only within their own group. For example, only 3 percent of Norwegian men married women of a different ethnic background. Like many Mexicanos in the Southwest, several immigrant groups retained their languages well into the twentieth century, usually by sponsoring parochial school systems and publishing their own newspapers. A few groups closed their communities to outsiders. The Poles who migrated to central Nebraska in the 1880s, for example, formed an exclusive settlement; and the German Hutterites, who disavowed private property, lived as much as possible in seclusion in the Bon Homme colony of South Dakota, established in 1874.

Among the native-born settlers of the Great Plains, the largest number had migrated from states bordering the Mississippi River. Settling as individual families rather than as whole communities, they faced an exceptionally solitary life on the Great Plains. The usual rectangular homestead of 160 acres placed farm families at least a half-mile and often much farther from each other. To stave off isolation, homesteaders sometimes built their homes on the adjoining corners of their plots. Still, the prospect of doing better, which brought most homesteaders to the Great Plains in the first place, caused many families to keep seeking greener pastures. Mobility was so high that between one-third and one-half of all households pulled up stakes within a decade.

Communities eventually flourished in prosperous towns, like Grand Island, Nebraska; Coffeyville, Kansas; and Fargo, North Dakota, that served the larger agricultural region. Built alongside the railroad, they grew into commercial centers, home to banking, medical, legal, and retail services. Town life fostered a special intimacy; even in the county graveyard, it was said, a town resident remained among neighbors. But closeness did not necessarily promote social equality or even friendship. A social hierarchy based on education (for the handful of doctors and lawyers) and, more important, investment property (held mainly by railroad agents and bankers) governed relationships between individuals and families. Religion also played a large part in defining these differences. Upwards of 70 percent of town residents were church-affiliated, the largest group being Roman Catholics, followed by Methodists, Lutherans, Baptists, and Presbyterians. Reinforced by family ties and ethnic affiliation, religious allegiances just as often provided a basis for conflict as for community.

Work, Dawn to Dusk

By the 1870s the Great Plains, once the home of buffalo and Indian hunters, was becoming a vast farming region populated mainly by immigrants from Europe and white Americans from east of the Mississippi. In place of the first one-room shanties, sod houses, and log cabins stood substantial frame farmhouses, along with a variety of other buildings like barns, smokehouses, and stables. But the built environment took nothing away from the predominating vista—the expansive fields of grain. "You have no idea, Beulah," wrote a Dakota farmer to his wife, "of what [the wheat farms] are like until you see them. For mile after mile there is not a sign of a tree or stone and just as level as the floor of your house. . . . Wheat never looked better and it is nothing but wheat, wheat, wheat."

Most farm families survived, and prospered if they could, through hard work, often from dawn to dusk. Men's activities in the fields tended to be seasonal,

with heavy work during planting and harvest; at other times, their labor centered on construction or repair of buildings and on taking care of livestock. Women's activities were usually far more routine, week in and week out: cooking and canning of seasonal fruit and vegetables, washing, ironing, churning cream for butter, and keeping chickens for their eggs. Women might occasionally take in boarders, usually young men working temporarily in railroad construction, and they tended to the young children. Many women complained about the ceaseless drudgery, especially when they watched their husbands invest in farm equipment rather than in domestic appliances. The majority felt, as one farm woman put it, "quite lonesome & solitary. . . . I have very little female society." Some, however, relished the challenge. An Iowa woman, for example, liked "to have whole control of my house; can say I am monarch of all I survey and none to dispute my right."

Children also joined in the family's labors. Milking the cows, hauling water, and running errands to neighboring farms could be done by the children, once they had reached the age of nine or so. The "one-room school," where all grades learned together, taught the basics of literacy and arithmetic that a future farmer or commercial employee would require. Sons might be expected to work for ten to twenty years on the family farm, generally for their subsistence alone. Older sons and daughters alike might move to the nearest town to find wagework and contribute their earnings to the family coffer.

The harsh climate and unyielding soil nevertheless forced all but the most reclusive families to seek out friends and neighbors. Many hands were needed to clear the land for cultivation or for roadbeds, to raise houses and barns, or to bring in a harvest before a threatening storm. Neighbors might agree to work together haying, harvesting, and threshing grain. They also traded their labor, calculated by the hour, for use of equipment or for special assistance. A well-to-do farmer might "rent" his threshing machine in exchange for a small cash fee and, for instance, three days' labor. His wife might barter her garden produce for her neighbor's bread and milk or for help during childbirth or disability. Women often combined work and leisure in quilting bees and sewing circles, where they made friends while sharing scraps of material and technical information. Whole communities turned out for special events, such as the seasonal husking bees and apple bees, which were organized mainly by women.

Much of this informal barter, however, resulted from lack of cash rather than a lasting desire to cooperate. When annual harvests were bountiful, even the farm woman's practice of bartering goods with neighbors and local merchants—butter and eggs in return for yard

These homesteaders in Nebraska, 1886, confronted the typically harsh conditions of treeless plains by erecting sod huts. They often brought with them an assortment of seeds and seedlings for spring plantings and a small number of livestock. A good fall harvest would provide the cash for building more substantial frame houses and outbuildings and encourage other homesteaders to settle near them. Communities eventually grew from these crude beginnings.

SOURCE: Sylvester Rawding Family sod house, 1884. Nebraska State Historical Society, Solomon D. Butcher Collection (RG2608–1784).

goods or seed—diminished sharply, replaced by cash transactions. Still, wheat production proved unsteady in the last half of the nineteenth century, and few farm families could remain reliant wholly on themselves.

For many farmers, the soil simply would not yield a livelihood, and they often owed more money than they took in. Start-up costs, including the purchase of land and equipment, put many farmers deep in debt to local creditors. Some lost their land altogether. By 1880, when the Bureau of the Census began to compile statistics on tenant-operated farms, nearly 18 percent of the farms in Nebraska were worked by tenants; a decade later the portion had risen to nearly one-quarter. By the turn of the century, more than one-third of all farmers in the United States were tenants on someone else's land.

The Garden of Eden was not to be found on the prairies or on the plains, no matter how hard the average farm family worked. Again and again foreclosures wiped out the small landowner through dips in commodity prices, bad decisions, natural disasters, or illness. In one especially bad year, 1881, a group of farmers in western Iowa chose to burn off rather than harvest their wheat because the yield promised to be so small. Many farmers stood only a step away from financial disaster, wondering if they had chosen the best life for themselves and their families. The swift growth of rural population soon ended. Although writers and orators alike continued to celebrate the family farm as the source of virtue and economic well-being, the hard reality of big money and political power told a far different story.

THE WORLD'S BREADBASKET

During the second half of the nineteenth century commercial farms employed the most intensive and extensive methods of agricultural production in the world. Hard-working farmers brought huge numbers of acres under cultivation, while new technologies allowed them to achieve unprecedented levels of efficiency in the planting and harvesting of crops. As a result, western agriculture became increasingly tied to international trade, and modern capitalism soon ruled western agriculture, as it did the mining and cattle industries.

New Production Technologies

Only after the trees had been cleared and grasslands cut free of roots could the soil be prepared for planting. But as farmers on the Great Plains knew so well, the sod west of the Mississippi did not yield readily to cultivation and often broke the cast-iron plows typically used by eastern farmers. Farther west, some farmers resorted to drills to plant seeds for crops such as wheat and oats. Even in the best locations, where loamy, fertile ground had built up over centuries into eight or more inches of decayed vegetation, the preliminary breaking, or "busting," of the sod required hard labor. One man would guide a team of five or six oxen pulling a plow through the soil, while another regulated the depth of the cut, or furrow. But, as a North Dakota settler wrote to his wife back in Michigan, after the first crop the soil became as "soft as can be, any team [of men and animals] can work it."

This "thirty-three horse team harvester" was photographed at the turn of the century in Walla Walla, Washington. Binding the grain into sheaves before it could hit the ground, the "harvester" cut, threshed, and sacked wheat in one single motion.

SOURCE: ca. 1902. Library of Congress.

Agricultural productivity depended as much on new technology as on the farmers' hard labor. In 1837 John Deere had designed his famous "singing plow" that easily turned prairie grasses under and turned up even highly compacted soils. Around the same time, Cyrus McCormick's reaper began to be used for cutting grain; by the 1850s his factories were turning out reapers in mass quantities. McCormick's design featured ridges of triangular knives, like sharks' teeth, that mechanically sliced through the stalks as the reaper moved forward pulled by horses or, later, by steam- or gasoline-powered engines. The harvester, invented in the 1870s, drew the cut stalks upward to a platform where two men could bind them into sheaves; by the 1880s an automatic knotter tied them together. Drastically reducing the number of people traditionally required for this work, the harvester increased the pace many times over.

Improvements were not limited to the reaper and harvester, although these machines underwent contin-

uous redesign and were enhanced first by steam and eventually gasoline power. From the 1840s on, the U.S. Patent Office recorded an astonishing number of agricultural inventions. The introduction of mechanized corn planters and mowing or raking machines for hay all but completed the technological arsenal.

In the 1890s, the U.S. commissioner of labor measured the impact of technology on farm productivity. Before the introduction of the wire binder in 1875, he reported, a farmer could not plant more than 8 acres of wheat if he were to harvest it successfully without help; by 1890 the same farmer could rely on his new machine to handle 135 acres with relative ease and without risk of spoilage. The improvements in the last half of the century allowed an average farmer to produce up to ten times more than was possible with the old implements.

Scientific study of soil, grain, and climatic conditions was another factor in the record output. Heretofore, farmers relied on tradition or experimented with whatever the grain merchants had to offer. Beginning in the mid-nineteenth century, federal and state governments added inducements to the growing body of expertise, scientific information, and hands-on advice. Through the Morrill Act of 1862, "land-grant" colleges acquired space for campuses in return for promising to institute agricultural programs. The Department of Agriculture, which attained cabinet-level status in 1889, and the Weather Bureau (transferred from the War Department in 1891) also made considerable contributions to farmers' knowledge. The federal Hatch Act of 1887, which created a series of state experimental stations, provided for basic agricultural research, especially in the areas of soil minerals and plant growth. Many states added their own agricultural stations, usually connected with state colleges and universities.

Nature nevertheless often reigned over technological innovation and seemed in places to take revenge against these early successes. West of the 98th meridian—a north-south line extending through western Oklahoma, central Kansas and Nebraska, and eastern Dakota—perennial dryness due to an annual rainfall of less than 20 inches constantly threatened to turn soil into dust and to break plows on the hardened ground. Summer heat burned out crops and ignited grass fires. Mountains of winter snows turned rivers into spring torrents that flooded fields; heavy fall rains washed crops away. Even good weather invited worms and flying insects to infest the crops. During the 1870s grasshoppers in clouds a mile long ate everything organic, including tree bark and clothes. Mormons erected a statue to the

HAND V. MACHINE LABOR ON THE FARM, CA. 1880				
	Time Worked		**Labor Cost**	
Crop	Hand	Machine	Hand	Machine
Wheat	61 hours	3 hours	$3.55	$0.66
Corn	39 hours	15 hours	3.62	1.51
Oats	66 hours	7 hours	3.73	1.07
Loose Hay	21 hours	4 hours	1.75	0.42
Baled Hay	35 hours	12 hours	3.06	1.29

gulls who made a surprise appearance in Utah to eat the "hoppers"; however, most farmers were not as lucky as the Mormons.

Producing for the Market

From the Midwest to the far reaches of the Great Plains, farming changed in important ways during the last third of the nineteenth century. Although the family remained the primary source of labor, farmers tended to put more emphasis on production for exchange rather than for home use. They continued to plant vegetable gardens and often kept fowl or livestock for the family's consumption, but farmers raised crops mainly for the market and measured their own success or failure in terms of cash products.

Most large-scale or "bonanza" farmers specialized in one or two crops, such as corn, rye, or barley, and sent their goods by railroad to eastern distributors and thence to national and international markets. Wheat farmers in particular prospered. With the world population increasing at a rapid rate, the international demand for wheat was enormous, and American farmers made huge profits from the sale of this crop. Wheat production ultimately served as a barometer of the agricultural economy in the West. Farmers in all corners of the region, from Nebraska to California, expanded or contracted their holdings and planned their crops according to the price of wheat.

The new machines and expanding market did not necessarily guarantee success. Land, draft animals, and equipment remained very expensive, and start-up costs could keep a family in debt for decades. A year of good returns often preceded a year of financial disaster. Weather conditions, international markets, and railroad and steamship shipping prices all proved equally unpredictable and heartless.

Farmers who settled on good lands in the 1860s and 1870s were more fortunate than those to follow. These pioneers, who began with only a little capital and worked twenty or thirty years to build up livestock and crops, frequently reached old age knowing that they could leave productive farmland to their sons or daughters. Latecomers found most of the good land already locked up in production or too expensive to acquire.

The new technology and scientific expertise favored the large, well-capitalized farmer over the small one. Such is the story of the large-scale wheat operations in the great Red River Valley of North Dakota. Here a shrewd worker such as Oliver Dalrymple could take advantage of a spectacular bonanza. When Dalrymple started out in 1875, he managed a farm owned by two officials of the Northern Pacific Railroad. He cleared their land, planted wheat, and yielded a sizable harvest the first year. He did much better the second year and

began to invest in his own farm. A decade later his operations included 32,000 acres in wheat and 2,000 in oats. Dalrymple now had the financial resources to use the latest technology to harvest these crops and to employ up to 1,000 seasonal laborers at a time. The majority of farmers with fewer resources expanded at more modest rates. Between 1880 and 1900, average farm size in the seven leading grain-growing states increased from 64.4 acres to more than 100 acres.

California Agribusiness

The trend toward big farms reached an apex in California, where farming as a business surpassed farming as a way of life. The conclusion of the Mexican-American War in 1848 coincided with the beginning of the Gold Rush, and the Anglos flooding the new territory wanted the land that had been held for centuries by the Spanish-speaking peoples, the Californios. The U.S. Congress created the Lands Claims Commission in 1851 to examine the great land-grant system that had been introduced by the Spaniards. Although the Supreme Court ultimately validated many of their holdings, the cost of litigation and steep land taxes forced many Californios into debt. Bankers, railroad magnates, and other Anglos made rich by the Gold Rush took possession of the best farming land in the state. The new owners introduced the latest technologies, built dams and canals, and invested huge amounts of capital, setting the pattern for the state's prosperous agribusiness. Farms of nearly 500 acres dominated the California landscape in 1870; by the turn of the century, two-thirds of the state's arable land was in 1,000-acre farms. As land reformer and social commentator Henry George noted, California was "not a country of farms but a country of plantations and estates."

This scale of production made California the national leader in wheat production by the mid-1880s. But it also succeeded dramatically with fruit and vegetables. Large- and medium-sized growers, shrewdly combined in cooperative marketing associations during the 1870s and 1880s, used the new refrigerator cars to ship their produce in large quantities to the East and even to Europe. By 1890, cherries, apricots, and oranges, packed with mountains of ice, made their way into homes across the United States.

California growers learned quickly that they could satisfy consumer appetites and even create new ones. Orange producers packed their products individually in tissue paper, a technique designed to convince eastern consumers that they were about to eat a luxury fruit. By the turn of the century, advertisers for the California Citrus Growers' Association described oranges as a necessity for good health, inventing the trademark "Sunkist" to be stamped on each orange. Meanwhile

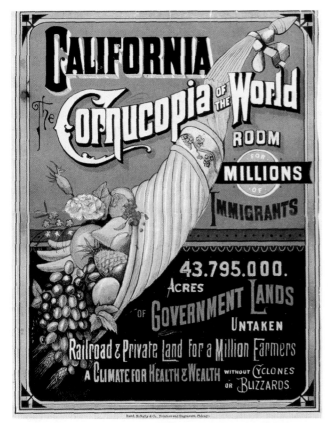

In the decades after the Civil War, agricultural production expanded at a fast pace as farmers migrated farther westward. California farmers, who enjoyed the benefits of a temperate climate, produced a great variety of crops, including wheat, vegetables, fruits, and nuts. Railroad advertisers, hoping to attract prospective farmers to the region, commonly relied on this popular image of California as a region overflowing in fresh produce.

SOURCE: *California, Cornucopia of the World,* ca. 1880. Lithograph poster from the Bella C. Landauer Collection. © Collection of The New York Historical Society. Negative no. 41800.

California's grape growing grew into a big business, led by promoter and winemaker Paul Masson. Long considered inferior to French wines, California wines found a ready market at lower prices. Other grape growers made their fortunes in raisins. By the early twentieth century, one association trademarked its raisins as "Sun Maid" and packaged them for schoolchildren in the famous "nickel" box.

By 1900, California had become the model for American agribusiness, not the home of self-sufficient homesteaders but the showcase of heavily capitalized farm factories. Machines soon displaced animals and even many people. Many Californios tried to hold onto their traditional forms of labor if not their land, only to join the Chinese workers who by 1870 had become the backbone of the state's migrant workforce. Intense

battles in the state legislature over land and irrigation rights underscored the message that powerful forces had gathered in California to promote large-scale agricultural production.

The Toll on the Land

The delicate ecologies of the West perished more quickly under human pressure than those prevailing anywhere else on the continent. Viewing the land as a resource to command, the new inhabitants often looked past the existing flora and fauna toward a landscape remade strictly for commercial purposes. The changes they produced in some areas were nearly as cataclysmic as those that occurred during the Ice Age.

Banishing many existing species, farmers "improved" the land by introducing exotic plants and animals—that is, biological colonies indigenous to other regions and continents. Some of the new plants and animals flourished in alien surroundings; many did not. Farmers also unintentionally introduced new varieties of weeds, insect pests, and rats. Surviving portions of older grasslands and meadows eventually could be found only alongside railroad tracks, in graveyards, or inside national parks.

Numerous species disappeared altogether or suffered drastic reduction. The grizzly bear, for example, an animal exclusive to the West, could once be found in large numbers from the Great Plains to California and throughout much of Alaska; by the early decades of the twentieth century, one nature writer estimated that only 800 survived, mostly in Yellowstone National Park. At the same time the number of wolves declined from perhaps as many as 2 million to just 200,000. "If you count the buffalo for hides and the antelope for backstraps and the passenger pigeons for target practice and the Indian ponies (killed by whites, to keep the Indian poor)," one scholar estimates, "it is conceivable that 500 million creatures died" on the Great Plains alone. By the mid-1880s, no more than 5,000 buffalo survived in the entire United States, and little remained of the once vast herds but great heaps of bones sold for $7.50 per ton.

The slaughter of the buffalo had a dramatic impact, not only on the fate of the species but also on the grasslands of the Great Plains. Overall, the biological diversity of the region had been drastically reduced. Unlike the grizzly and wolf, buffalo had not been exclusively Western animals. Before European colonization they had grazed over an area of 3 million square miles, nearly to the east coast; as the wide-ranging herds moved on, the grasslands were replenished. Having killed off the giant herds, ranchers and farmers quickly shifted to cattle and sheep production. Unlike the roaming buffalo, these livestock did not range widely and soon devoured the native grasses down to their roots. With the ground cover destroyed, the soil eroded and became barren. By the end of the century, huge dust storms formed across the windswept plains.

New forests, many settlers hoped, would improve the weather, restore the soil, and also provide a source for fencing and fuel. In 1873 the U.S. Congress passed the Timber Culture Act, which allotted homesteaders an additional 160 acres of land in return for planting and cultivating forty acres of trees. Because residence was not required, and because tree planting could not be assessed for at least thirteen years, speculators filed for several claims at once, then turned around and sold the land without having planted a single tree. Although some forests were restored, neither the weather nor the soil improved.

Large-scale commercial agriculture also took a heavy toll on inland waters. Before white settlement, rainfall had drained naturally into lakes and underground aquifers, and watering spots were abundant throughout the Great Plains. Farmers mechanically rerouted and dammed water to irrigate their crops, causing many bodies of water to disappear and the water table to drop significantly. Successful farmers pressed for ever greater supplies of water. In 1887 the state of California formed irrigation districts, securing bond issues for the construction of canals, and other western states followed. But by the 1890s, irrigation had seemed to reach its limit without federal support. The Newlands or National Reclamation Act of 1902 added 1 million acres of irrigated land, and state irrigation districts added more than 10 million acres. Expensive to taxpayers, and ultimately benefiting corporate farmers rather than small landowners, these projects further diverted water and totally transformed the landscape.

Although western state politicians and federal officials debated water rights for decades, they rarely considered the impact of water policies on the environment. Lake Tulare in California's Central Valley, for example, had occupied up to 760 square miles. After farmers began to irrigate their land by tapping the rivers that fed

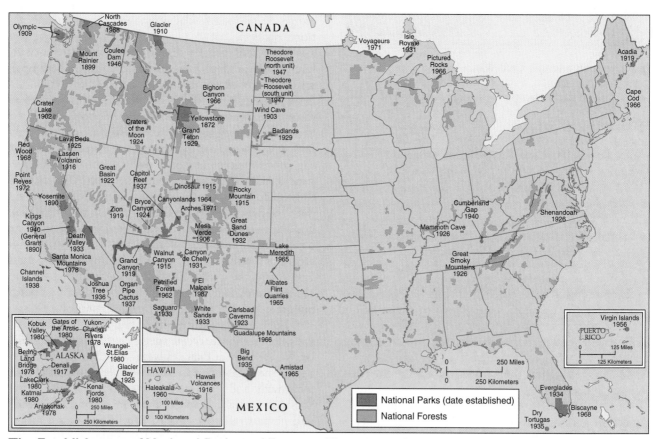

The Establishment of National Parks and Forests The setting aside of land for national parks saved large districts of the West from early commercial development and industrial degradation, setting a precedent for the later establishment of additional parks in economically marginal but scenic territory. The West, home to the vast majority of park space, became a principal site of tourism by the end of the nineteenth century.

Tulare, the lake shrank dramatically, covering a mere 36 square miles by the early twentieth century. Finally the lake, which had supported rich aquatic and avian life for thousands of years, disappeared entirely. The land left behind, now wholly dependent on irrigation, grew so alkaline in spots that it could no longer be used for agricultural purposes.

The need to maintain the water supply indirectly led to the creation of national forests and the Forest Service. Western farmers supported the General Land Revision Act of 1891, which gave the president the power to establish forest reserves to protect watersheds against the threats posed by lumbering, overgrazing, and forest fires. In the years that followed, President Benjamin Harrison established fifteen forest reserves exceeding 16 million acres, and President Grover Cleveland added more than 21 million acres. But only in 1897 did the secretary of the interior finally gain the authority to regulate the use of these reserves.

The Forest Management Act of 1897 and the National Reclamation Act of 1902 set the federal government on the path of large-scale regulatory activities. The Forest Service was established in 1905, and in 1907 forest reserves were transferred from the Department of the Interior to the Department of Agriculture. The federal government would now play an even larger role in economic development of the West, dealing mainly with corporate farmers and ranchers eager for improvements.

THE WESTERN LANDSCAPE

Throughout the nineteenth century, many Americans viewed western expansion as the nation's "manifest destiny," and just as many marveled at the region's natural and cultural wonders. Their fascination grew with the proliferation of printed literature, "Wild West" entertainments, sideshows, and traveling exhibits featuring western themes. The public east of the Mississippi craved stories about the West and visual images of its sweeping vistas. Artists and photographers built their reputations in what they saw and imagined. Scholars, from geologists and botanists to historians and anthropologists, toured the trans-Mississippi West in pursuit of new data. The region and its peoples came to represent what was both unique and magnificent about the American landscape.

Nature's Majesty

Alexis de Tocqueville, the famed commentator on American society, found little beauty in the land west of the Mississippi. Writing in the 1830s, he described the landscape as "more and more uneven and sterile," the soil "punctured in a thousand places by primitive rocks

sticking out here and there like the bones of a skeleton when sinews of flesh have perished." By the end of the century, scores of writers had provided an entirely different image of the American West. They described spectacular, breathtaking natural sites like the Grand Tetons and High Sierras, vast meadows of waving grasses and beautiful flowers, expansive canyons and rushing white rivers, and exquisite deserts covered with sagebrush or dotted with flowering cactus and enticing precisely for their stark qualities. A traveler through Yellowstone country recalled "the varied scenery" of the West and its "stupendous & remarkable manifestations of nature's forces," an impression destined to stay with him "as long as memory lasts."

Landscape painters, particularly the group that became known as the Rocky Mountain School, also piqued the public's interest in western scenery. Exhibited in galleries and museums and reproduced in popular magazines, their sketches and paintings circulated western imagery throughout the country and through much of Europe. In the 1860s, German-born Albert Bierstadt, equipped with a camera, traveled the Oregon Trail. Using his photographs as inspiration, Bierstadt painted mountains so wondrous that they seemed nearly surreal, projecting a divine aura behind the majesty of nature. His "earthscapes"—huge canvases with exacting details of animals and plants—thrilled viewers and sold for tens of thousands of dollars.

Moved by such evidence, the federal government began to set aside huge tracts of land as nature reserves. In 1864 Congress passed the Yosemite Act, which placed the spectacular cliffs and giant sequoias under the management of the state of California. Meanwhile, explorers returned to the East awestruck by the varied terrain of the Rocky Mountains, the largest mountain chain in North America. These early visitors described huge sky-high lakes, boiling mud, and spectacular waterfalls. Finally, in 1871, the federal government funded a major undertaking by a team of researchers from the Geological and Geographical Survey of the Territories, which included the early landscape photographer William H. Jackson and the painter Thomas Moran. These researchers brought back to Congress visual proof of the monumental scenery of the West, including the Grand Canyon. In 1872 Congress named Yellowstone the first national park. Yosemite and Sequoia in California, Crater Lake in Oregon, Mount Ranier in Washington, and Glacier in Montana all became national parks between 1890 and 1910.

Many of the wilderness enthusiasts, however, worked to set aside these territories at the expense of the Indian peoples who occupied them. Aware that tourists fearing Indian presence would avoid national parks, federal officials attempted to fortify the territories. In 1886, the U.S. Army took over the job of protecting

Albert Bierstadt became one of the first artists to capture on enormous canvases the vastness and rugged terrain of mountains and western wilderness. Many other artists joined Bierstadt to form the Rocky Mountain School. In time, the camera largely replaced the paintbrush, and most Americans formed an image of these majestic peaks from postcards and magazine illustrations.

SOURCE: Albert Bierstadt. *Merced River, Yosemite Valley, 1866.* Oil on canvas, 4.36′ × 50″. The Metropolitan Museum of Art. Gift of the Sons of William Paton, 1909 (09.214.1). Photograph © 1982 The Metropolitan Museum of Art.

Yellowstone from the bands of Crow, Shoshone, and Bannock that, by treaty rights, customarily used the park for hunting game. Ten years later, the U. S. Supreme Court ruled that Wyoming, on becoming a state, gained the right to regulate hunting, thus in effect nullifying the preexisting treaties. *Ward* v. *Racehorse*, the deciding court case, significantly diminished the presence of Indian bands in Yellowstone and, as other states followed suit, in all public lands, and it restricted them to reservations except during open hunting seasons.

The Legendary Wild West

Legends of the Wild West grew into a staple of popular culture just as the actual work of cowboys became more routine. By the end of the century, many Americans, rich and poor alike, imagined the West as a land of promise and opportunity and, above all, of excitement and adventure. Future president Theodore Roosevelt helped to promote this view. Soon after his election to the New York State Assembly in 1882, Roosevelt was horrified to see himself lampooned in the newspapers as a dandy and weakling. A year later, after buying a ranch in South Dakota, he began to reconstruct his public image. He wrote three books recounting his adventures in the West, claiming that they had not only instilled in him

personal bravery and "hardihood" but self-reliance. In 1886 he was back in New York, running for mayor as the "Cowboy of the Dakotas." In April 1899, he addressed the members of Chicago's elite Hamilton Club, inviting them to join him in "the strenuous life" as exemplified by their Indian-fighter ancestors. Indeed, by this time many Americans had joined Roosevelt in imagining the West as a source of rejuvenation and virility. Young men at Harvard and Yale universities, for example, had named their hunting clubs after Daniel Boone and Davy Crockett. The West, as Roosevelt insisted, meant "vigorous manhood."

The first "westerns," the "dime novels" that sold in the 1860s in editions of 50,000 or more, reflected these myths. Competing against stories about pirates, wars, crime, and sea adventures, westerns outsold the others. Edward Zane Carroll Judson's *Buffalo Bill, the King of the Border Men,* first published in 1869, spawned hundreds of other novels, thousands of stories, and an entire magazine devoted to Buffalo Bill. Even before farmers had successfully halted the free-grazing of cattle, writers made tough cowboys and high-spirited women into legends of the Wild West. Real-life African American cowboy Nat Love lived on in the imaginations of many generations as Edward L. Wheeler's dime novel hero "Deadwood Dick," who rode the range as a white cowboy in black clothes in over thirty stories. His girlfriend "Calamity Jane"—"the most reckless buchario in ther Hills"—also took on mythic qualities.

Railroad promoters and herd owners actively promoted these romantic and heroic images. Cowman Joseph McCoy staged Wild West shows in St. Louis and Chicago, where Texas cowboys entertained prospective buyers by roping calves and breaking horses. Many cowboys played up this imaginary role, dressing and talking to match the stories told about them. "The drovers of the seventies were a wild and reckless bunch," recalled cowboy Teddy Blue. Typically, they had worn a "wide brimmed beaver hat, black or brown with a low crown, fancy shirts, high heeled boots, and sometimes a vest." In the 1880s cowboys adopted the high-crowned Stetson hat, ornately detailed shirts with pockets, and striped or checked pants. The first professional photographers often made their living touring the West, setting

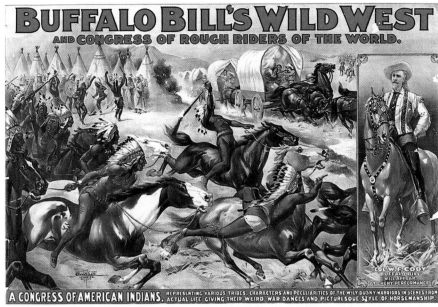

Buffalo Bill's "Wild West Show" poster from 1899. William Cody's theatrical company toured the United States and Europe for decades, reenacting various battles and occasionally switching to football (cowboys versus Indians). Cody's style set the pace for both rodeos and Western silent films.

SOURCE: Library of Congress.

up studios where cowboys and prostitutes posed in elaborate costumes.

For thirty years, Wild West shows toured the United States and Europe. The former Pony Express rider, army scout, and famed buffalo hunter William F. Cody hit upon the idea of an extravaganza that would bring the legendary West to those who could never experience it in person. "Buffalo Bill" Cody made sharpshooter Annie Oakley a star performer. Entrancing crowds with her stunning accuracy with pistol or rifle, Oakley shot dimes in midair and cigarettes from her husband's mouth. Cody also hired Sioux Indians and hundreds of cowboys to perform in mock stagecoach robberies and battles. Shows like Custer's Last Stand thrilled crowds, including Britain's Queen Victoria. Revamped as the rodeo, the Wild West show long outlasted Buffalo Bill, who died in 1917.

With far less fanfare, many veteran cowboys enlisted themselves on "dude ranches" for tourists or performed as rope twirlers or yodeling singers in theaters across the United States. In 1902 Owen Wister's novel *The Virginian* fixed in the popular imagination the scene of the cowboy facing down the villain and saying, "When you call me that, *smile!*"

The "American Primitive"

New technologies of graphic reproduction encouraged painters and photographers to provide new images of the West, authentic as well as fabricated. A young German

American artist, Charles Schreyvogel, saw Buffalo Bill's tent show in Buffalo and decided to make the West his life's work. His canvases depicted Indian warriors and U.S. cavalry fighting furiously but without blood and gore. Charles Russell, a genuine cowboy, painted the life he knew, but also indulged in imaginary scenarios, producing paintings of buffalo hunts and first encounters between Indian peoples and white explorers.

Frederic Remington, the most famous of all the western artists, left Yale Art School to visit Montana in 1881, became a Kansas sheep herder and tavern owner, and then returned to painting. Inspired by newspaper stories of the army's campaign against the Apaches, he made himself into a war correspondent and captured vivid scenes of battle in his sketches. Painstakingly accurate in physical details, especially of horses, his paintings celebrated the "winning of the West" from the Indian peoples. By the turn of the century, Remington was the chief magazine illustrator of western history.

Remington joined hundreds of other painters and engravers in reproducing the most popular historic event: Custer's Last Stand. Totally fictionalized by white artists to show a heroic General Custer personally holding off advancing Indian warriors, these renditions dramatized the romance and tragedy of conquest. Indian artists recorded Custer's defeat in far less noble fashion.

Photographers often produced highly nuanced portraits of Indian peoples. Dozens of early photographers from the Bureau of American Ethnology captured the gaze of noble tribespeople or showed them hard at work digging clams or grinding corn. President Theodore Roosevelt praised Edward Sheriff Curtis for vividly conveying tribal virtue. Generations later, in the 1960s and 1970s, Curtis's photographs again captured the imagination of western enthusiasts, who were unaware or unconcerned that this sympathetic artist had often posed his subjects or retouched his photos to blur out any artifacts of white society.

Painters and photographers led the way for scholarly research on the various Indian societies. The early ethnographer and pioneer of fieldwork in anthropology Lewis Henry Morgan devoted his life to the study of Indian family or kinship patterns, mostly of eastern tribes such as the Iroquois, who adopted him into their Hawk Clan. In 1851 he published *League of the Ho-de-no-sau-nee, or*

Iroquois, considered the first scientific account of an Indian tribe. A decade later Morgan ventured into Cheyenne country to examine the naming patterns of this tribe. In his major work, *Ancient Society,* published in 1877, he posited a universal process of social evolution leading from savagery to barbarism to civilization.

One of the most influential interpreters of the cultures of living tribespeople was the pioneering ethnographer Alice Cunningham Fletcher. In 1879, Fletcher met Suzette (Bright Eyes) La Flesche of the Omaha tribe, who was on a speaking tour to gain support for her people, primarily to prevent their removal from tribal lands. Fletcher, then forty-two years old, accompanied La Flesche to Nebraska, telling the Omahas that she had come "to learn, if you will let me, something about your tribal organization, social customs, tribal rites, traditions and songs. Also to see if I can help you in any way." After transcribing hundreds of songs, Fletcher became well known as an expert on Omaha music. She also supported the Omahas' campaign to gain individual title to tribal lands, eventually drafting legislation that was enacted by Congress as the Omaha Act of 1882. In 1885, Fletcher produced for the U.S. Senate a report titled *Indian Education and Civilization,* one of the first general statements on the status of Indian peoples. As a founder of the American Anthropological Society and president of the American Folk-Lore Society, she encouraged further study of Indian societies.

While white settlers and the federal government continued to threaten the survival of tribal life, Indian lore became a major pursuit of scholars and amateurs alike. Adults and children delighted in turning up arrowheads. Fraternal organizations such as the Elks and Eagles borrowed tribal terminology. The Boy Scouts and Girl Scouts, the nation's premier youth organizations, used tribal lore to instill strength of character. And the U.S. Treasury stamped images of tribal chiefs and buffalo on the nation's most frequently used coins.

THE TRANSFORMATION OF INDIAN SOCIETIES

In 1871, the U.S. government formally ended the treaty system, eclipsing without completely abolishing the sovereignty of Indian nations. Still, the tribes persisted. Using a mixture of survival strategies from farming and trade to the leasing of reservation lands, they both adapted to changing conditions and maintained old traditions.

Reform Policy and Politics

By 1880, many Indian tribes had been forcibly resettled on reservations, but very few had adapted to white ways. For decades, reformers, mainly from the Protestant churches, had lobbied Congress for a program of salvation through assimilation, and they looked to the Board of Indian Commissioners, created in 1869, to carry out this mission. The board often succeeded in

OVERVIEW

MAJOR INDIAN TREATIES AND LEGISLATION OF THE LATE NINETEENTH CENTURY

1863	Nez Percé Treaty	Signed illegally on behalf of the entire tribe in which the Nez Percé abandoned 6 million acres of land in return for a small reservation in northeastern Oregon. Led to Nez Percé wars, which ended in 1877 with the surrender of Chief Joseph.
1867	Medicine Lodge Treaty	Assigned reservations in existing Indian Territory to Comanches, Plains (Kiowa), Appaches, Kiowas, Cheyennes, and Arapahoes, bringing these tribes together with Sioux, Shoshones, Bannocks, and Navajos.
1868	Treaty of Fort Laramie	Successfully ended Red Cloud's war by evacuating federal troops from Sioux Territory along the Bozeman Trail; additionally granted Sioux ownership of the western half of South Dakota and rights to use Powder River county in Wyoming and Montana.
1871		Congress declares end to treaty system.
1887	Dawes Severalty Act	Divided communal tribal land, granting the right to petition for citizenship to those Indians who accepted the individual land allotment of 160 acres. Successfully undermined sovereignty.

mediating conflicts among the various tribes crowded onto reservations but made far less headway in converting them to Christianity or transforming them into prosperous farming communities. The majority of Indian peoples lived in poverty and misery, deprived of their traditional means of survival and more often than not subjected to fraud by corrupt government officials and private suppliers. Reformers who observed these conditions firsthand nevertheless remained unshaken in their belief that tribespeople must be raised out of the darkness of ignorance into the light of civilization. Some conceded, however, that the reservation system might not be the best means to this end.

Unlike most Americans, who saw the conquest of the West as a means to national glory, some reformers were genuinely outraged by the government's continuous violation of treaty obligations and the military enforcement of the reservation policy. One of the most influential was Helen Hunt Jackson, a noted poet and author of children's stories. In 1879 Jackson had attended a lecture in Hartford, Connecticut, by a chief of the Ponca tribe whose destitute people had been forced from their Dakota homeland. Heartstruck, Jackson lobbied former abolitionists such as Wendell Phillips to work for Indians' rights and herself began to write against government policy. Her book-length exposé, *A Century of Dishonor*, published in 1881, detailed the plight of Indian peoples.

Jackson threw herself into the Indian Rights Association, an offshoot of the Women's National Indian Association (WNIA), which had been formed in 1874 to rally public support for a program of assimilation. The two organizations helped to place Protestant missionaries in the West to work to eradicate tribal customs as well as to convert Indian peoples to Christianity. According to the reformers' plans, men would now farm as well as hunt, while women would leave the fields to take care of home and children. Likewise, all communal practices would be abandoned in favor of individually owned homesteads, where families could develop in the "American" manner and even celebrate proper holidays such as the Fourth of July. Children, hair trimmed short, would be placed in boarding schools where, removed from their parents' influence, they

would shed traditional values and cultural practices. By 1882 the WNIA had gathered 100,000 signatures on petitions urging Congress to phase out the reservation system, to establish universal education for Indian children, and to award title to 160 acres to any Indian individual willing to work the land.

The Dawes Severalty Act, passed by Congress in 1887, incorporated many of these measures and established federal Indian policy for decades to come. The act allowed the president to distribute land not to tribes but to individuals legally "severed" from their tribes. The commissioner of Indian affairs rendered the popular interpretation that "tribal relations should be broken up, socialism destroyed and the family and autonomy of the individual substituted. The allotment of land in severalty, the establishment of local courts and police, the development of a personal sense of independence and the universal adoption of the English language are means to this end."

Those individuals who accepted the land allotment of 160 acres and agreed to allow the government to sell unallotted tribal lands (with some funds set aside for education) could petition to become citizens of the United States. A little over a decade after its enactment,

In 1890, the celebrated artist Frederic Remington (1861–1909) produced this color sketch of Oglala Sioux at the Pine Ridge Indian Reservation in South Dakota. By this time, Remington had established himself as a leading illustrator of western themes, including the Indian Wars. He had traveled extensively in the West, gathering information, making sketches, and taking photographs, which he later used at his studio in New Rochelle, New York. Remington sold his illustrations to major magazines, including *Harper's Weekly*.

The ghost dance of 1890, pictured here, provided artists like Remington with vivid imagery. The dancers wore brightly patterned robes and shirts, some decorated with stars symbolizing the coming of a new age for the Indians.

SOURCE: Frederic Remington, *Oglala Sioux performing the Ghost Dance at the Pine Ridge Indian Agency, South Dakota, 1890*/The Granger Collection, New York (4E400.03).

many reformers believed that the Dawes Act had resolved the basis of the "Indian problem." Hollow Horn Bear, a Sioux chief, offered a different opinion, judging the Dawes Act to be "only another trick of the whites."

The Dawes Act successfully undermined tribal sovereignty but offered little compensation. Indian religions and sacred ceremonies were banned, the telling of legends and myths forbidden, and shaman and medicine men imprisoned or exiled for continuing their traditional practices. "Indian schools" forbade Indian languages, clothing styles, and even hair fashions in order to "kill the Indian . . . and save the man," as one schoolmaster put it.

These and other measures did little to integrate Indians into white society. Treated as savages, Indian children fled most white schools. Nor did adults receive much encouragement to become property holders. Government agencies allotted them inferior farmland, inadequate tools, and little training for agricultural self-sufficiency. Seeing scant advantage in assimilating, only a minority of adults dropped their tribal religion for Christianity or their communal ways for the accumulation of private property. Within the next forty years, the Indian peoples lost 60 percent of the reservation land remaining in 1887 and 66 percent of the land allotted to them as homesteaders. The tenets of the Dawes Act were not reversed until 1934. In that year, Congress passed the Indian Reorganization Act, which affirmed the integrity of Indian cultural institutions and returned some land to tribal ownership (see Chapter 24).

The Ghost Dance

After the passage of the Dawes Severalty Act, one more cycle of rebellion remained for the Sioux. In 1888, the Paiute prophet Wovoka, ill with scarlet fever, had a vision during a total eclipse of the sun. In his vision, the Creator told him that if the Indian peoples learned to love each other, they would be granted a special place in the afterlife. The Creator also gave him the Ghost Dance, which the prophet performed for others and soon spread throughout the tribe. The Sioux came to believe that when the day of judgment came, all Indian peoples who had ever lived would return to their lost world and white peoples would vanish from the earth. The chant sounded:

> *The whole world is coming.*
> *A nation is coming, a nation is coming.*
> *The Eagle has brought the message to the tribe.*
> *The father says so, the father says so.*
> *Over the whole earth they are coming.*
> *The buffalo are coming, the buffalo are coming.*
> *The Crow has brought the message to the tribe,*
> *The Father says so, the Father says so.*

Many white settlers and federal officials feared the Ghost Dancers, even though belief in a sudden divine judgment was common among Christians and Jews. Before the Civil War, Protestant groups such as the Millerites, who had renounced personal property and prepared themselves for the millennium, were tolerated by other Americans. But after decades of Indian warfare, white Americans took the Ghost Dance as a warning of tribal retribution rather than a religious ceremony. As thousands of Sioux danced to exhaustion, local whites intolerantly demanded the practice be stopped. The U.S. Seventh Cavalry, led in part by survivors of the Battle of Little Bighorn, rushed to the Pine Ridge Reservation, and a group of the Sioux led by Big Foot, now fearing mass murder, moved into hiding in the Bad Lands of South Dakota. After a skirmish, the great leader Sitting Bull and his young son lay dead.

The Seventh Calvalry pursued the Sioux Ghost Dancers and 300 undernourished Sioux, freezing and without horses, to Wounded Knee Creek on the Pine Ridge Reservation. There, on December 29, 1890, while the peace-seeking Big Foot, who had personally raised a white flag of surrender, lay dying of pneumonia, they were surrounded by soldiers armed with automatic guns. The U.S. troops expected the Sioux to surrender their few remaining weapons, but an accidental gunshot from one deaf brave who misunderstood the command caused panic on both sides.

Within minutes, 200 Sioux had been cut down and dozens of soldiers wounded, mostly by their own cross fire. For two hours soldiers continued to shoot at anything that moved—mostly women and children straggling away. Many of the injured froze to death in the snow; others were transported in open wagons and finally laid out on beds of hay under Christmas decorations at the Pine Ridge Episcopal church. The massacre, which took place almost exactly 400 years after Columbus "discovered" the New World for Christian civilization, seemed to mark the final conquest of the continent's indigenous peoples.

Black Elk later recalled, "I can see that something else died there in the bloody mud, and was buried in the blizzard. A people's dream died there. It was a beautiful dream. . . . The nation's hoop is broken and scattered. There is no center any longer, and the sacred tree is dead."

Endurance and Rejuvenation

The most tenacious tribes were those occupying land rejected by white settlers or those distant from their new communities. Still, not even an insular, peaceful agricultural existence on semiarid, treeless terrain necessarily provided protection. Nor did a total willingness to peacefully accept white offers prevent attack.

The Pimas of Arizona, for instance, had a well-developed agricultural system adapted to a scarce supply of water, and they rarely warred with other tribes. After the arrival of white settlers, they integrated Christian symbolism into their religion, learned to speak English, and even fought with the U.S. cavalry against the Apaches. Still, the Pimas saw their lands stolen, their precious waterways diverted, and their families impoverished.

The similarly peaceful Yana tribes of California, hunters and gatherers rather than farmers, were even less fortunate. Suffering enslavement, prostitution, and multiple new diseases from white settlers, they faced near extinction within a generation. One Yana tribe, the Yahi, chose simply to disappear. For more than a decade, they lived in caves and avoided all contact with white settlers.

Many tribes found it difficult to survive in the proximity of white settlers. The Flatheads, for example, seemed to Indian commissioners in the Bitterroot region of Montana to be destined for quick assimilation. They had refused to join the Ghost Dance and had agreed to sell their rich tribal land and move to a new reservation. But while waiting to be moved, the dispossessed Flatheads nearly starved. When they finally reached the new reservation in October 1891, the remaining 250 Flatheads put on their finest war paint and whooped and galloped their horses, firing guns in the air in celebration. But disappointment and tragedy lay ahead. The federal government drastically reduced the size of the reservation, using a large part of it to provide a national reserve for buffalo. Only handfuls of Flatheads, mostly elderly, continued to live together in pockets of rural poverty.

A majority of tribes, especially smaller ones, sooner or later reached numbers too low to maintain their collective existence. Intermarriage, although widely condemned by the white community, drew many young people outside their Indian communities. Some tribal leaders also deliberately chose a path toward assimilation. The Quapaws, for example, formally disbanded in the aftermath of the Dawes Severalty Act. The minority that managed to prosper in white society as tradespeople or farmers abandoned their language, religious customs, and traditional ways of life. Later generations petitioned the federal government and regained tribal status, established ceremonial grounds and cultural centers (or bingo halls), and built up one of the most durable powwows in the state. Even so, much of the tribal lore that had underpinned distinct identity had simply vanished.

For those tribes who remained on reservations, the aggressively assimilationist policies of the Office of Indian Affairs (OIA) challenged their traditional ways. The Southern Ute, for example, at one time hunted, fished, and gathered throughout a huge region spanning the Rocky Mountains and the Great Basin. In 1848 they began to sign a series of treaties in accord with the reservation policy of the U.S. government. Twenty years later their territory had been reduced to approximately one-quarter of Colorado Territory, and in 1873, they had further relinquished about one-quarter of this land. After the passage of the Dawes Act, the U. S. government, pressured by white settlers, gave the tribe two choices: they could break up their communal land holdings and accept the 160 acres granted to the male heads of families or they could maintain their tribal status and move to a reservation in Utah. The Utes divided over the issue, but a considerable number chose to live on reservations under the administration of the OIA.

Under the terms of the Dawes Act, Southern Ute men and women endured continuous challenges to their egalitarian practices. The OIA assumed, for example, that Ute men would represent the tribe in all official matters, a policy that forced Ute women to petition the U.S. government to recognize their rights and concerns. Similarly, Ute women struggled to hold on to their roles as producers within the subsistence family economy against the efforts of the OIA agents to train them for homemaking alone. In the 1880s, the OIA established a matrons program to teach Ute women to create a "civilizing" home, which included new lessons about sanitation, home furnishings, and health care. But even fifty years later, some Ute preferred to live at least part of the year in a teepee in a multigenerational family rather than in a private residence designed for a single married couple and their children.

A small minority of tribes, grown skillful in adapting to dramatically changing circumstances, managed to persist and even grow. Never numbering more than a few thousand people, during the late eighteenth century the Cheyennes had found themselves caught geographically between aggressive tribes in the Great Lakes region and had migrated into the Missouri area, where they split into small village-sized communities. By the mid-nineteenth century they had become expert horse traders on the Great Plains, well prepared to meet the massive influx of white settlers by shifting their location frequently. They avoided the worst of the pestilence that spread from the diseases white people carried, and likewise survived widespread intermarriage with the Sioux in the 1860s and 1870s. Instructed to settle, many Cheyenne took up elements of the Christian religion and became farmers, also without losing their tribal identity. Punished by revenge-hungry soldiers after the battle of Little Bighorn, their lands repeatedly taken away, they still held on. The Cheyennes were survivors.

The Navajos experienced an extraordinary renewal, largely because they built a life in territory considered worthless by whites. Having migrated to the Southwest from the northwestern part of the continent perhaps 700 years ago, the Diné ("the People") as they called themselves had already survived earlier invasions by the

CHRONOLOGY

1848	Treaty of Guadalupe Hidalgo
1849–60s	California Gold Rush
1853	Gadsden Purchase
1858	Comstock Lode discovered
1859	Cortina's War in South Texas
1862	Homestead Act makes free land available
	Morrill Act authorizes "land-grant" colleges
1865–67	Great Sioux War
1866	Texas cattle drives begin
	Medicine Lodge Treaty established reservation system
	Alaska purchased
1869	Board of Indian Commissioners created
	Buffalo Bill, the King of the Border Men, sets off "Wild West" publishing craze
1870s	Grasshopper attacks on the Great Plains
1872	Yellowstone National Park created
1873	Timber Culture Act
	Red River War
1874–75	Sioux battles in Black Hills of Dakotas
1876	Custer's Last Stand
1877	Defeat of the Nez Percé
1881	Helen Hunt Jackson, *A Century of Dishonor*
1882	Edmunds Act outlaws polygamy
1885–87	Droughts and severe winters cause the collapse of the cattle boom
1887	Dawes Severalty Act
1890	Sioux Ghost Dance movement
	Massacre of Lakota Sioux at Wounded Knee
	Census Bureau announces the end of the frontier line
1887	Forest Management Act gives the federal government authority over forest reserves

Spanish. In 1863 they had been conquered again through the cooperation of hostile tribes led by the famous Colonel Kit Carson. Their crops burned, their fruit trees destroyed, 8,000 Navajo were forced in the 300-mile "Long Walk" to the desolate Bosque Redondo reservation, where they nearly starved. Four years later, the Indian Bureau allowed the severely reduced tribe to return to a fraction of its former lands.

By 1880 the Navajos' population had returned to nearly what it had been before their conquest by white Americans. Quickly depleting the deer and antelope on their hemmed-in reservation, they had to rely on sheep alone as a food reserve during years of bad crops. With their wool rugs and blankets much in demand in the East, the Navajos increasingly turned to crafts, including eventually silver jewelry as well as weaving, to survive. Although living on the economic margin, they persevered to become the largest Indian nation in the United States.

The nearby Hopis, like the Navajos, survived by stubbornly clinging to lands unwanted by white settlers and by adapting to drastically changing conditions. A famous tribe of "desert people," the Hopis had lived for centuries in their cliff cities. Their highly developed theological beliefs, peaceful social system, sand paintings, and kachina dolls interested many educated and influential whites. The resulting publicity helped them gather the public supporters and financial resources needed to fend off further threats to their reservations.

Fortunate northwestern tribes remained relatively isolated from white settlers until the early twentieth century, although they had begun trading with white visitors centuries earlier. Northwestern peoples relied largely on salmon and other resources of the region's rivers and bays. In potlatch ceremonies, leaders redistributed tribal wealth and maintained their personal status and the status of their tribe by giving lavish gifts to invited guests. Northwest peoples also made intricate wood carvings, including commemorative "totem" poles, that recorded their history and identified their regional status. Northwestern peoples maintained their cultural integrity in part through connections with kin in Canada, as did southern tribes with kin in Mexico. In Canada and Mexico, native populations suffered less pressure from new populations and retained more tribal authority than in the United States.

Indian nations approached their nadir as the nineteenth century came to a close. The descendants of the great pre-Columbian civilizations had been conquered by foreigners, their population reduced to fewer than 250,000. Under the pressure of assimilation, the remaining tribespeople became known to non-Indians as "the vanishing Americans." It would take several generations before Indian sovereignty experienced a resurgence.

CONCLUSION

The transformation of the trans-Mississippi West pointed up the larger meaning of expansion. Almost overnight, mines opened, cities grew, and farms and cattle ranches spread out across the vast countryside. New communities formed rapidly and often displaced old ones. In 1890 the director of the U.S. Census announced that the nation's "unsettled area has been so broken into by isolated bodies of settlement that there can hardly be said to be a frontier line."

The development of the West met the nation's demands for mineral resources for its expanding industries and agricultural products for the people of the growing cities. Envisioning the West as a cornucopia whose boundless treasures would offer themselves to the willing pioneer, most of the new residents failed to calculate the odds against their making a prosperous livelihood as miners, farmers, or petty merchants. Nor could they appreciate the long-term consequences of the violence they brought with them from the battlefields of the Civil War to the far reaches of the West.

REVIEW QUESTIONS

1. Discuss the role of federal legislation in accelerating and shaping the course of westward expansion.

2. How did the incorporation of western territories into the United States affect Indian nations such as the Sioux or the Nez Percé? Discuss the causes and consequences of the Indian Wars. Discuss the significance of reservation policy and the Dawes Severalty Act for tribal life.

3. What were some of the major technological advances in mining and in agriculture that promoted the development of the western economy?

4. Describe the unique features of Mexicano communities in the Southwest before and after the mass immigration of Anglos. How did changes in the economy affect the patterns of labor and the status of women in these communities?

5. What role did the Homestead Act play in western expansion? How did farm families on the Great Plains divide chores among their members? What factors determined the likelihood of economic success or failure?

6. Describe the responses of artists, naturalists, and conservationists to the western landscape. How did their photographs, paintings, and stories shape perceptions of the West in the East?

RECOMMENDED READING

William Cronon, George Miles, and Jay Gitlin, eds., *Under an Open Sky: Rethinking America's Western Past* (1992). A useful collection of essays. Reinterpreting older evidence and adding new data, these essays stress the bitter conflicts over territory, the racial and gender barriers against democratic community models, and the tragic elements of western history.

Jon Gjerde, *The Minds of the West: Ethnocultural Evolution in the Rural Middle West, 1830–1914* (1997). A combination cultural and economic history that weighs the importance of ethnicity in the shaping of American identities in the farming regions of the Middle West. Gjerde pays close attention to the religious institutions and systems of belief of European immigrants as the basis of community formation.

Lisbeth Haas, *Conquests and Historical Identities in California, 1769–1936* (1995). A multiethnic history, centered in San Juan Capistrano, that examines the political intersection of geography and community formation. The author studies the processes of Americanization among the Spanish and Indian populations who settled this land.

Robert V. Hine and John Mack Faragher, *The American West: A New Interpretive History* (2000). A sweeping, amply illustrated survey of western history with reference to recent scholarship. The authors emphasize Native Americans and include rich material on ethnicity, the environment, and the role of women.

John C. Hudson, *Making the Corn Belt: A Geographical History of Middle-Western Agriculture* (1994). An ecologically oriented study of corn growing that traces its development from Indians to Southerners moving westward.

Andrew C. Isenberg, *The Destruction of the Bison: An Environmental History, 1750–1920* (2000). A rich study of the forces behind the near-extinction of the bison with special attention to the interplay among Indians, Euroamericans, and the environment of the Great Plains. Isenberg constructs a narrative that is as much cultural as economic in framing the problem.

Karl Jacoby, *Crimes Against Nature: Squatters, Poachers, Thieves, and the Hidden History of American Conservation* (2001). A complex analysis of the origins of national parks in the Adirondacks, Yellowstone, and the Grand Canyon. Rather than focusing on the individuals and groups that led the conservation of vast public lands, Jacoby switches perspective to focus on those who were dispossessed by the process.

Elizabeth Jameson and Susan Armitage, eds., *Writing the Range* (1997). A collection of essays on women in the West that presents an inclusive historical narrative based on the experiences of women of differing backgrounds, races, and ethnic groups.

Katherine M. B. Osburn, *Southern Ute Women: Autonomy and Assimilation on the Reservation, 1887–1934* (1998). Presents a careful analysis of the impact of the Dawes Act on the role and status of women among the Southern Ute. Osburn acknowledges the changes brought by the Office of Indian Affairs programs on the reservations but emphasizes the resistance of the Ute and the retention of old ways.

Glenda Riley, *Building and Breaking Families in the American West* (1996). Essays covering the variety of cultures in the American West and organized topically to highlight courtship, marriage and intermarriage, and separation and divorce.

Thomas E. Sheridan, *Los Tucsonenses: The Mexican Community in Tucson, 1854–1941* (1986). A highly readable account of Mexican-American communities in the Southwest. Sheridan shows how a midcentury accommodation of Anglos and Mexicanos faded with the absorption of the region into the national economy and with the steady displacement of Mexicano community from its agricultural landholdings.

Liping Zhu, *A Chinaman's Chance: The Chinese on the Rocky Mountain Mining Frontier* (1997). Studies the mining communities of Chinese in the Boise Basin of Idaho. Zhu emphasizes the success the Chinese enjoyed not only as miners but as merchants in the face of discriminatory practices and laws.

ADDITIONAL BIBLIOGRAPHY

Indian Peoples and Indian-White Relations

Patricia Albers and Beatrice Medicine Albers, *The Hidden Half: Studies of Plains Indian Women* (1983)

Morris W. Foster, *Being Comanche: A Social History of an American Indian Community* (1991)

Shelley Bowen Hatfield, *Chasing Shadows: Indians Along the United States–Mexico Border, 1876–1911* (1998)

Frederick E. Hoxie, *A Final Promise: The Campaign to Assimilate the Indians, 1880–1920* (1984)

Albert L. Hurtado, *Indian Survival on the California Frontier* (1988)

Patricia Nelson Limerick, *The Legacy of Conquest: The Unbroken Past of the American West* (1987)

John D. McDermott, *A Guide to the Indian Wars of the West* (1998)

Theda Perdue, ed., *Sifters: Native American Women's Lives* (2001)

Catherine Price, *The Oglala People, 1841–1879* (1996)

Glenda Riley, *Women and Indians on the Frontier, 1825–1915* (1984)

Richard White, *The Roots of Dependency: Subsistence, Environment, and Social Change among the Choctaws, Pawnees, and Navajos* (1983)

Elliott West, *The Way to the West: Essays on the Central Plains* (1995)

Internal Empire

Armando C. Alonzo, *Tejano Legacy: Rancheros and Settlers in South Texas, 1734–1900* (1998)

Susan Armitage and Elizabeth Jameson, eds., *The Women's West* (1987)

Susan Armitage, Ruth B. Moynihan, and Christiane Fischer Dichamp, eds., *So Much to Be Done: Women Settlers on the Mining and Ranching Frontier* (1990)

Sarah Deutsch, *No Separate Refuge: Culture, Class and Gender on an Anglo-Hispanic Frontier in the American Southwest, 1880–1940* (1987)

David M. Emmons, *The Butte Irish: Class and Ethnicity in an American Mining Town, 1875–1925* (1989)

Marion S. Goldman, *Gold Diggers and Silver Miners: Prostitution and Social Life on the Comstock* (1981)

B. Carmon Hardy, *Solemn Covenant: The Mormon Polygamous Passage* (1992)

Douglas Monroy, *Thrown among Strangers: The Making of Mexican Culture in Frontier California* (1993)

Lucy E. Salyer, *Laws Harsh as Tigers: Chinese Immigrants and the Shaping of Modern Immigration Law* (1996)

Sally Zanjani, *A Mine of Her Own: Women Prospectors in the American West, 1850–1950*

Ranching and Farming

Allan G. Bogue, *From Prairie to Corn Belt: Farming on the Illinois and Iowa Prairies in the Nineteenth Century* (1963)

Mark Fiege, *The Making of an Agricultural Landscape in the American West* (1999)

Philip Durham and Everett L. Jones, *The Negro Cowboys* (1965)

Dee Garceau, *The Important Things of Life: Women, Work, and Family in Sweetwater County, Wyoming, 1880–1929* (1997)

C. Mark Hamilton, *Nineteenth-Century Mormon Architecture and City Planning* (1995)

Robert C. Haywood, *Victorian West: Class and Culture in Kansas Cattle Towns* (1991)

Stan Hoig, *The Oklahoma Land Rush of 1889* (1984)

Lawrence Jelinek, *Harvest Empire: A History of California Agriculture*, 2d ed. (1982)

Frederick C. Leubke, ed., *European Immigrants in the American West: Community Histories* (1998)

Sonya Salamon, *Prairie Patrimony: Family, Farming, and Community in the Midwest* (1992)

Paul I. Wellman, *The Trampling Herd: The Story of the Cattle Range in America* (1988)

The West, the Land, and the Imagination

Alfred L. Bush and Lee Clark Mitchell, *The Photograph and the American Indian* (1994)

Mick Gidley, *Edward S. Curtis and the North American Indian, Incorporated* (1998)

William H. Goetzmann and William N. Goetzmann, *The West of the Imagination* (1986)

Chris J. Magoc, *Yellowstone: The Creation and Selling of an American Landscape, 1870-1903* (1999)

L. G. Moses, *Wild West Shows and the Images of American Indians, 1883–1933* (1996)

Walter Nugent and Martin Ridge, eds., *The American West: The Readers* (1999)

Paul Reddin, *Wild West Shows* (1999)

Mark David Spence, *Dispossessing the Wilderness: Indian Removal and the Making of the National Parks* (1999)

Richard Slotkin, *Gunfighter Nation: The Myth of the Frontier in 20th-Century America* (1992)

Richard White and Patricia Nelson Limerick, *The Frontier in American Culture* (1994)

Richard White, *"It's Your Misfortune and None of My Own": A History of the American West* (1991)

Donald Worcester, *Rivers of Empire: Water, Aridity, and the Growth of the American West* (1985)

Biography

Matthew Baigell, *Albert Bierstadt* (1981)

Louise Barnett, *Touched by Fire: The Life, Death, and Mythic Afterlife of George Armstrong Custer* (1996)

Robert W. Larson, *Red Cloud: Warrior-Statesman of the Lakota Sioux* (1997)

Joan T. Mark, *A Stranger in Her Native Land: Alice Fletcher and the American Indians* (1988)

Sarah R. Massey, ed., *Black Cowboys of Texas* (2000)

Valerie Mathes, *Helen Hunt Jackson and Her Indian Reform Legacy* (1990)

John G. Neihardt, *Black Elk Speaks: Being the Life Story of a Holy Man of the Oglala Sioux* (1961)

Elinore Pruitt Stewart, *Letters of a Woman Homesteader* (1914; 1989)

Edwin R. Sweeny, *Cochise, Chiricahua Apache Chief* (1991)

Jerry D. Thompson, ed., *Juan Cortina and the Texas-Mexico Frontier, 1859–1877* (1994)

Benson Tong, *Susan La Flesch Picotte, M.D.: Omaha Indian Leader and Reformer* (1999)

Robert M. Utley, *The Lance and the Shield: A Life and Times of Sitting Bull* (1993)

HISTORY ON THE INTERNET

http://www.lib.utah.edu/spc/photo/cent1.html

http://www.lib.utah.edu/spc/photo/cent2.html

http://www.lib.utah.edu/150/

http://www.lib.utah.edu/spc/photo/photo2.html

These sites connect to the University of Utah, Marriott Library photo archive collections and provide visual images, some very good quality, of early Utah history.

http://www.pbs.org/weta/thewest/resources/archives/index.htm

Prepared by the Public Broadcasting Service (PBS) to accompany their video, *The West*, this very large collection contains both photographs and primary documents on westward expansion during the 19th century.

These sites cover Nevada territorial/state history during western expansion:

http://www.vcnevada.com/history.htm

http://www.calliope.org/gold/gold3.html

http://dmla.clan.lib.nv.us/docs/museums/reno/his-soc.htm

These sites detail Arizona history during westward expansion:

http://w3.arizona.edu/~azhist/health.htm

http://dizzy.library.arizona.edu/images/

http://www.rr.gmcs.k12.nm.us/dNMhist.htm

Very large site on New Mexico history including narrative and graphics.

NINETEEN

THE INCORPORATION OF AMERICA

▷ 1865 – 1900

Bessemer steel manufacture at Andrew Carnegie's Pittsburgh steel works in 1886. Contemporary colored engraving.
SOURCE: The Granger Collection, New York (0009141/4E452.14).

AMERICAN COMMUNITIES

Packingtown, Chicago, Illinois

APPROACHING PACKINGTOWN, THE NEIGHBORHOOD ADJOINING the Union Stockyards, the center of Chicago's great meatpacking industry, one noticed first the pungent odor, a mixture of smoke, fertilizer, and putrid flesh, blood, and hair from the slaughtered animals. A little closer, the stench of the uncovered garbage dump blended in. Finally one crossed "Bubbly Creek," a lifeless offshoot of the Chicago River, aptly named for the effect of the carbolic acid gas that formed from the decaying refuse poured in by the meatpacking plants. Railroads crisscrossed the entire area, bringing in thousands of animals each day and carrying out meat for sale in markets across the country.

Packingtown occupied about one square mile of land bounded by stockyards, packing plants, and freight yards. With a population of 30,000 to 40,000 at the end of the nineteenth century, it was a rapidly growing community of old and new immigrants who depended on the meatpacking industry for their livelihood. An average household included six or seven people—parents, two or three children, and two or three boarders. They lived typically in wooden houses divided into four or more flats. Although Irish, Germans, Bohemians, Poles, Lithuanians, and Slovaks were squeezed together in this solidly working-class neighborhood, strong ethnic identities persisted. Few households included residents of more than one nationality, and interethnic marriages were rare. Nearly everyone professed the Roman Catholic faith, yet each ethnic group maintained its own church and often its own parochial school, where children were taught in their parents' language. Political organizations, fraternal societies, and even gymnastic clubs and drama groups reflected these ethnic divisions.

The one local institution that bridged the different groups was the saloon. Located on virtually every street corner, saloons offered important services to the community, hosting weddings and dances, providing meeting places for trade unions and fraternal societies, and cashing paychecks. During the frequent seasons of unemployment, Packingtown workers spent a lot of time in saloons. Here they often made friends across ethnic divisions, an extension of their common work experience in the nearby stockyard and packinghouses.

Most of the meatpacking industry's first "knife men"—the skilled workers in the "killing gangs" that managed the actual slaughtering and cutting operations—were German and Irish. Many had learned their butcher's craft in the Old Country. Below them were the common laborers, mainly recent immigrants from eastern Europe. Having no previous experience in meatpacking, these workers found themselves in the lowest paid jobs, such as the by-product manufacturing of glue and oleo. A sizable portion had never before earned wages. They soon discovered, as one Lithuanian laborer put it, that "money was everything and a man without money must die." But the money available—a daily wage of $2 (or less)—was often not enough. The death rate from tuberculosis in Packingtown was thought to be the highest in Chicago and among the highest in the nation.

The Packingtown community, small and insular as it seemed to the residents, was bound into an elaborate economic network that reached distant parts of the United States, transforming the way farmers raised livestock and grains, railroads operated, and consumers ate their meals. These workers helped make Chicago a gateway city, a destination point for raw materials coming in from the West as well as a point of export for products of all kinds.

Chicago meatpackers, led by the "big five" of Armour, Cudahy, Morris, Schwarzschild and Sulzberger, and Swift, expanded more than 900 percent between 1870 and 1890, dominating the national market for meat and establishing a standard for monopoly capitalism in the late nineteenth century. In the process, they also became the city's largest manufacturing employer. They built huge, specialized factories during the 1860s and 1870s that speeded the killing process and—thanks to mountains of ice brought by rail from ponds and lakes—operated year round. The introduction of an efficiently refrigerated railroad car in the 1880s made it possible to ship meat nationwide. Consumers had long believed that only meat butchered locally was safe to eat, but now cheap Chicago-packed beef and pork began to appear on every meateater's table. Local packinghouses throughout the Midwest succumbed to the ruthless competition from Chicago.

Chicago's control of the mass market for meat affected all aspects of the industry. Midwestern farmers practically abandoned raising calves on open pastures. Instead, they bought two-year-old steers from the West and fattened them on homegrown corn in feedlots, making sure that bulk went into edible parts rather than muscle and bone. The feedlot—a kind of rural factory—replaced pasture just as pasture had earlier supplanted prairie grasslands.

Few of the workers in Chicago's stockyards had seen a farm since they left their homelands. But as the working hands of what poet Carl Sandburg would later call the "Hog butcher for the world, . . . City of the big shoulders," they played their part, along with the farmer, the grain dealer, the ironworker, the teamster, and many others in bringing together the neighboring countryside, distant regions, and the city in a common endeavor. ■

Chicago

KEY TOPICS

- The rise of big business and the formation of the national labor movement
- The transformation of southern society
- The growth of cities

- The Gilded Age
- Changes in education
- Commercial amusements and organized sports

THE RISE OF INDUSTRY, THE TRIUMPH OF BUSINESS

At the time of the Civil War, the typical American business firm was a small enterprise, owned and managed by a single family, and producing goods for a local or regional market. By the turn of the century, businesses depending on large-scale investments had organized as corporations and grown to unforeseen size. These mammoth firms could afford to mass-produce goods for national and even international markets. At the helm stood unimaginably wealthy men such as Andrew Carnegie, Philip Danforth Armour, Jay Gould, and John D. Rockefeller, all powerful leaders of a new national business community.

A Revolution in Technology

In the decades after the Civil War, American industry transformed itself into a new wonder of the world. The Centennial Exposition of 1876, held in Philadelphia, celebrated not so much the American Revolution 100 years earlier as the industrial and technological promise of the century to come. Its central theme was power. In the main building—at the time the largest on earth—the visiting emperor of Brazil marked the opening day by throwing a switch on a giant steam engine. Examining the telephone, which he had never before seen in operation, he gasped, "My God, it talks!" Patented that year by Alexander Graham Bell, the telephone signaled the rise of the United States to world leadership in industrial technology.

The year 1876 also marked the opening of Thomas Alva Edison's laboratory in Menlo Park, New Jersey, one of the first devoted to industrial research. Not yet thirty years old, Edison could already claim credit for the mimeograph, the multiplex telegraph, and the stock ticker. In October 1879 his research team hit upon its most marketable invention, an incandescent lamp that burned for more than thirteen hours. On December 31 Edison brought 3,000 people by a special train to witness the sight of hundreds of electric lights illuminating his shop and neighborhood streets. By 1882 the Edison Electric Light Company had launched its service in New York City's financial district. A wondrous source of light and power, electricity revolutionized both industry and urban life.

A whimsical rendition of Thomas Edison's laboratories in Menlo Park, New Jersey, ca. 1880. The commercial artist imagined a giant electric light illuminating the entire region. Six weeks after Edison announced the invention of the electric light in 1879, the stock market turned jittery and gas company shares fell sharply: investors feared his "magic."

SOURCE: Hebert Orth, *Edison's Menlo Park Laboratories*, a fanciful painting. U.S. Department of the Interior, National Park Service, Edison National Historic Site.

By this time American inventors, who had filed nearly half a million patents since the close of the Civil War, were previewing the marvels of the next century. Henry Ford, working as an electrical engineer for the Detroit Edison Company, was already experimenting with the gasoline-burning internal combustion engine and designing his own automobile. By 1900 American companies had produced more than 4,000 automobiles. The prospect of commercial aviation emerged in 1903 when Wilbur and Orville Wright staged the first airplane flight near Kitty Hawk, North Carolina.

A major force behind economic growth was the vast transcontinental railroad, completed in 1869. The addition of three more major rail lines (the Southern Pacific; the Northern Pacific; and the Atchison, Topeka, and Santa Fe) in the early 1880s, and the Great Northern a decade later, completed the most extensive transportation network in the world. As the nation's first big busi-

ness, railroads linked cities in every state and served a nationwide market for goods. Freight trains carried the bountiful natural resources, such as iron, coal, and minerals that supplied the raw materials for industry, as well as food for the growing urban populations.

The monumental advances in transportation and communication facilitated the progressively westward relocation of industry. The geographic center of manufacturing (as computed by the gross value of products) was near the middle of Pennsylvania in 1850, in western Pennsylvania by 1880, and near Mansfield, Ohio, in 1900. The geographic center of flour milling moved from the East Coast to Rochester, New York, then to Ohio, and finally to Minneapolis and Kansas City. Similarly, the centers for the manufacture of agricultural equipment moved from central New York to Illinois and Wisconsin, while the production of wire moved from Massachusetts to Illinois.

Web Exploration

Explore patterns of industry in each region of the United States in 1900. Why did industrial patterns differ from region to region?
www.prenhall.com/faragher/map19.1

Patterns of Industry, 1900 Industrial manufacturing concentrated in the Northeast and Midwest, while the raw materials for production came mostly from other parts of the nation.

Industry grew at a pace that was not only unprecedented but previously unimaginable. In 1865 the annual production of goods was estimated at $2 billion; by 1900 it stood at $13 billion, transforming the United States from fourth to first in the world in terms of productivity. By the early twentieth century, American industry manufactured one-third of the world's goods.

Mechanization Takes Command

This second industrial revolution depended on many factors, but none was more important than the application of new technologies to increase the productivity of labor and the volume of goods. Machines, factory managers, and workers together created a system of continuous production by which more could be made, and faster, than anywhere else on earth. Higher productivity depended not only on machinery and technology but on economies of scale and speed, reorganization of factory labor and business management, and the unparalleled growth of a market for goods of all kinds.

All these changes depended in turn on anthracite coal, a new source of fuel, which was widely used after 1850. Reliable and inexpensive sources of energy made possible dramatic changes in the industrial uses of light, heat, and motion. Equally important, coal fueled the great open-hearth furnaces and mills of the iron and steel industry. By the end of the century, the U.S. steel industry was the world's largest, churning out rails to carry trains and parts to make more machines to produce yet more goods.

New systems of mass production replaced wasteful and often chaotic practices and speeded up the delivery of finished goods. In the 1860s meatpackers set up one of the earliest production lines. The process of converting livestock into meat began with a live animal. A chain around the hind leg whirled the body to an overhead rail, which carried it to slaughter—all in barely half a minute's time. Then hair and bristles were removed by a scraping machine, the carcass shifted to a conveyer belt where the chest was split and the organs removed, and the body placed in a cooler. This "disassembly line" displaced patterns of hand labor that were centuries old. The production line became standard in most areas of manufacturing.

Sometimes the invention of a single machine could instantly transform production, mechanizing every stage from processing the raw material to packaging the product. The cigarette-making machine, patented in 1881, shaped the tobacco, encased it in an endless paper tube, and snipped off the tube at cigarette-length intervals. This machine could produce more than 7,000 cigarettes per hour, replacing the worker who at best made 3,000 per day. After a few more improvements, fifteen machines could meet the total demand for American cigarettes. Within a generation, continuous production also revolutionized the making of furniture, cloth, grain products, soap, and canned goods; the refining, distilling, and processing of animal and vegetable fats; and eventually the manufacture of automobiles.

The Expanding Market for Goods

To distribute the growing volume of goods, businesses demanded new techniques of marketing and merchandising. For generations, legions of sellers, or "drummers," had worked their routes, pushing goods, especially hardware and patent medicines, to individual buyers and retail stores. The appearance of mail-order houses after the Civil War accompanied the consolidation of the railroad lines and the expansion of the postal system. Rates were lowered for freight and postage alike, and railroad stations opened post offices and sold money orders. By 1896 rural free delivery had reached distant communities.

Growing directly out of these services, the successful Chicago-based mail-order houses drew rural and urban consumers into a common marketplace. Sears, Roebuck and Company and Montgomery Ward offered an enormous variety of goods, from shoes to buggies to gasoline stoves and cream separators. The Montgomery Ward catalogue provided "a real link between us and civilization," a Nebraska farmwoman wrote. The mail-order catalogue also returned to rural folks the fruits of their own labor, now processed and packaged for easy use. The Sears catalogue offered Armour's summer sausage as well as Aunt Jemima's Pancake Flour and Queen Mary Scotch Oatmeal, both made of grains that came from the agricultural heartland. In turn, the purchases made by farm families through the Sears catalogue sent cash flowing into Chicago.

The chain store achieved similar economies of scale. By 1900, a half-dozen grocery chains had sprung up. The largest was A&P, originally named the Great Atlantic and Pacific Tea Company to celebrate the completion of the transcontinental railroad. Frank and Charles Woolworth offered inexpensive variety goods in five-and-ten-cent stores, of which more than 1,000 were established in the United States and Great Britain by 1919. Other chains selling drugs, costume jewelry, shoes, cigars, and furniture soon appeared, offering a greater selection of goods and lower prices than the small, independent stores. Hurt financially by this competition, community-based retailers headed the lobby for antichain legislation.

The department stores reigned over the urban market. These palaces of merchandise, with their attractive displays and convenient arrangements of goods, enticed

John D. Rockefeller, who formed the Standard Oil Company in 1870, sought to control all aspects of the industry, from the transportation of crude oil to the marketing and distribution of the final products. By the end of the decade, after making shrewd deals with the railroads and underselling his rivals, he managed to control 90 percent of the oil-refining industry. To further consolidate his interests, in 1882 Rockefeller created the Standard Oil Trust, which, by integrating both vertically and horizontally, became a model for other corporations and an inspiration for critical commentary and antitrust legislation.

This cartoon, published in *Puck* in 1904, shows the stranglehold Standard Oil had on government and industry alike. In 1911, in response to an antitrust suit, the Supreme Court ordered the company to break up.

SOURCE: Courtesy of the Library of Congress (LCUS264-435).

buyers and browsers alike. Opening shortly after the Civil War, department stores began to take up much of the business formerly enjoyed by specialty shops, offering a spectrum of services that included restaurants, rest rooms, ticket agencies, nurseries, reading rooms, and post offices. Elegantly appointed with imported carpets, sweeping marble staircases, and crystal chandeliers, the department store raised retailing to new heights. By the close of the century, the names of Marshall Field of Chicago, Filene's of Boston, The Emporium of San Francisco, Wanamaker's of Philadelphia, and Macy's of New York had come to represent the splendors of those great cities as well as the apex of mass retailing.

Advertising lured customers to the department stores, the chains, and the independent neighborhood shops. The advertising revolution began in 1869, when Francis Wayland Ayer founded the earliest advertising agency, but the firm did not hire its first full-time copy writers until 1891. Ayer's handled the accounts of such companies as Montgomery Ward, Procter & Gamble,

and the National Biscuit Company. With the help of this new sales tool, gross revenues of retailers raced upward from $8 million in 1860 to $102 million in 1900.

Integration, Combination, and Merger

The business community aspired to exercise greater control of the economy and to enlarge the commercial empire. From the source of raw materials to the organization of production, from the conditions of labor to the climate of public opinion, business leaders acted shrewdly. Economic cycles alternating between rapid growth and sharp decline also promoted the rise of big business. Major economic setbacks in 1873 and 1893 wiped out weaker competitors, allowing the strongest firms to rebound swiftly and to expand their sales and scale of operation during the recovery period.

Businesses grew in two distinct, if overlapping, ways. Through *vertical integration* a firm gained control of production at every step of the way—from raw materials through processing to transport and merchandising of the finished items. In 1899 the United Fruit Company began to build a network of wholesale houses, and within two years it had opened distribution centers in twenty-one major cities. Eventually it controlled an elaborate system of Central American plantations and temperature-controlled shipping and storage facilities for its highly perishable bananas. The firm became one of the nation's largest corporations, its "empire in bananas" dominating the economic and political life of whole nations in Central America.

The second means of growth, *horizontal combination*, entailed gaining control of the market for a single product. The most famous case was the Standard Oil Company, founded by John D. Rockefeller in 1870. Operating out of Cleveland in a highly competitive but lucrative field, Rockefeller first secured preferential rates from railroads eager to ensure a steady supply of oil. He then convinced or coerced other local oil operators to sell their stock to him. The Standard Oil Trust, established in 1882, controlled over 90 percent of the nation's oil-refining industry. Rockefeller understood the larger implications of his success, writing that he had "revolutionized the way of doing business all over the world. . . . The day of combination is here to stay."

In 1890 Congress passed the Sherman Antitrust Act to restore competition by encouraging small business and outlawing "every . . . combination . . . in restraint of trade." Ironically, the courts interpreted the law in ways that inhibited the organization of trade unions (on the ground that they restricted the free flow of labor) and actually helped the consolidation of business. More than 2,600 firms vanished between 1898 and 1902 alone. By 1910 the industrial giants that would dominate the American economy until the last half of the twentieth century—U.S. Rubber, Goodyear, American Smelting and Refining, Anaconda Copper, General Electric, Westinghouse, Nabisco, Swift and Company, Armour, International Harvester, Eastman Kodak, and American Can—had already formed.

The Gospel of Wealth

The preeminent financiers and corporation magnates not only took pride in the collective triumph of the business community but felt spiritually fulfilled by the accumulation of wealth. Ninety percent of the nation's business leaders were Protestant, and the majority attended church services regularly. They attributed their personal achievement to hard work and perseverance and made these the principal tenets of a new faith that imbued the pursuit of wealth with old-time religious zeal. "God gave me my money," declared John D. Rockefeller. Baptist minister Russell Conwell's pamphlet *Acres of Diamonds*, which sold more than 1 million copies,

argued that to build a fortune was a profound Christian duty. "To make money honestly," he preached, "is to preach the gospel."

One version of this "gospel of wealth" justified the ruthless behavior of entrepreneurs who accumulated unprecedented wealth and power through shady deals and conspiracies. Speculator Jay Gould, known in the popular press as the "Worst Man in the World," wrung his fortune, it was widely believed, from the labor of others. Through a series of financial maneuvers (one of which allegedly drove a partner to suicide) and such high-handed measures as sending armed employees to seize a factory, he rose quickly from his modest origins in western New York state. After abandoning his tanning business, he turned to stock trading and became a major player on Wall Street.

Speculation in railroads proved to be Gould's forte. He took over the Erie Railroad, paying off New York legislators to get the state to finance its expansion, and he acquired the U.S. Express Company by pressuring and tricking its stockholders. When threatened with arrest, Gould sold off his shares for $9 million and moved on to the Union Pacific, where he cut wages, precipitated strikes, and manipulated elections in the western and Plains states. Tired of being caricatured in the press as a great swindler, he bought the leading newspapers. At his death, one obituary described Jay Gould as "an incarnation of cupidity and sordidness" whose life symbolized "idolatrous homage [to] the golden calf."

Andrew Carnegie—the "Richest Man in the World"—offered a strikingly different model. He represented the "captain of industry" who had risen from the ranks through diligence and who refused to worship wealth for its own sake. Late in his life, he outlined his personal philosophy in a popular essay, *The Gospel of Wealth* (1889), explaining that "there is no genuine, praiseworthy success in life if you are not honest, truthful, and fair-dealing."

A poor immigrant from Scotland, Carnegie spent his boyhood studying bookkeeping at night while working days in a textile mill. At age thirteen he had become a messenger for Western Union, and by age seventeen he was the fastest telegraph key operator in Pittsburgh. In 1852 he became the personal secretary of the superintendent of the Pennsylvania Railroad's western division. Well placed to learn the principles of the business, Carnegie stepped into the superintendent's job seven years later. While improving passenger train service, he invested brilliantly to build funds for his next venture.

Carnegie built an empire in steel. A genius at vertical integration, he undercut his competitors by using the latest technology and designing his own system of cost analysis. By 1900 Carnegie managed the most efficient steel mills in the world, which accounted for one-third of the nation's output. When he sold out to J. P. Morgan's

The Two Philanthropists by Joseph Keppler, from *Puck Magazine,* February 23, 1888. This famous artist of the late nineteenth century drew caricatures of magnates Jay Gould and Cornelius Vanderbilt, stressing not their "good works" but their less than beneficent control of the nation's railroads and telegraph systems. Illustrated magazines, such as *Puck,* reproduced such drawings in quantity, due in part to technological advances in the lithographic process.

SOURCE: Color engraving by J. Keppler (1838–94) from *Puck,* February 23, 1881, Collection of the New-York Historical Society, New York City (#48872).

new United States Steel Corporation in 1901, his personal share of the proceeds came to $225 million.

Carnegie was well known as a civic leader. From one point of view, he was a factory despot who underpaid his employees and ruthlessly managed their working conditions. But to the patrons of the public libraries, art museums, concert halls, colleges, and universities that he funded, Carnegie appeared to be the single greatest philanthropist of the age. By the time he died, he had given away his massive personal fortune.

Whether following the rough road of Gould or the smooth path of Carnegie, the business community worked together to fashion the new conservative ideology of social Darwinism, which purportedly explained, and justified, why some Americans grew rich while others remained poor. Derived from the famed British naturalist Charles Darwin's scientific theories of evolution presented in *On the Origin of Species* (1859), social Darwinism superimposed the brutal struggle for existence that supposedly dominated nature onto modern society and underscored the principle of "survival of the fittest." The Yale professor William Graham Sumner gave this idea an economic spin. In an essay published in 1883 entitled *What Social Classes Owe to Each Other,* he argued that only a few individuals were capable of putting aside selfish pleasures to produce the capital needed to drive the emerging industrial economy and, moreover, they were fully deserving of their great fortunes. In contrast, the vast majority, too lazy or profligate to rise above poverty, deserved their own miserable fates. To tamper with this "natural" order by establishing welfare programs to help the poor or redistributing wealth in any way would be hazardous to society. Meanwhile, the popular writer Horatio Alger produced a more temperate version of this credo. Publishing more than 100 rags-to-riches novels, he created heroes who manage to rise out of poverty by both hard work and luck and ultimately acquire, if not vast wealth, middle-class respectability and comfort.

LABOR IN THE AGE OF BIG BUSINESS

It was a common item of faith among most working people that, as labor reformer George E. McNeill put it in 1877, "labor produces all the wealth of the world. . . . [The laborer] makes civilization possible." Like the gospel of wealth, the "gospel of work" affirmed the dignity of hard work, the virtue of thrift, and the importance of individual initiative. Both doctrines elaborated the simple phrase adorning many needlework samplers, "Work Is Prayer." But unlike business leaders, the philosophers of American working people did not believe in riches as the proof of work well done, or in the lust for power as the driving force of progress. On the contrary, they contended that honesty and competence should become the cornerstones of a society "so improved that labor shall become a blessing instead of a curse," recognized by all as the badge of the morally responsible citizen.

This faith inspired a slender minority, less than 3 percent of the workforce, to form unions in various trades and industries. Despite its small size, the labor movement represented the most significant and lasting response of workers to the rise of big business and the consolidation of corporate power.

The Wage System

The accelerating growth of industry, especially the steady mechanization of production, dramatically changed employer-employee relations and created new categories of workers. Self-employment became less common. The 1870 census revealed that the number of people working for wages already totaled almost 5 million (3.5 million in industry) of the nearly 13 million people who were gainfully employed. Farmers still accounted for 3 million or so, agricultural laborers for nearly 4 million. But by the end of the century, two-thirds of all Americans were working not for themselves but for wages. Many of these workers were also employed by large firms. For example, just sixty-six companies of Chicago's 3,000 largest firms employed nearly one-fifth of the city's entire wage-earning population in 1890.

For most craft workers, the new system destroyed long-standing practices, chipped away at their customary autonomy, and placed them in competition with other, mainly unskilled workers. Frederick Winslow Taylor, the pioneer of scientific management, explained that managers must "take all the important decisions . . . out of the hands of workmen." Teams of ironworkers, for example, had previously set the rules of production as well as their wages while the company supplied equipment and raw materials. Once steel replaced iron, most companies gradually introduced a new system. Managers now constantly supervised workers, set the pace of production and rate of payment, and introduced new, faster machinery that made many skills obsolete. In the woodworking trades, highly skilled cabinetmakers, who for generations had brought their own tools to the factory, were largely replaced with "green hands"—immigrants, including many women—who with only minimal training and close supervision could operate new woodworking machines at cheaper rates of pay.

Not all trades conformed to this pattern. The garment industry, for example, grew at a very fast pace in New York, Boston, Chicago, Philadelphia, Cleveland, and St. Louis but retained older systems of labor along with the new. The highly mechanized factories that employed hundreds of thousands of young immigrant women, while the outwork system, established well before the Civil War, contracted ever-larger numbers of families to work in their homes on sewing machines or by hand. However, companies fostered extreme competition between these two groups of workers by continually increasing daily production quotas. Paid by the piece—a seam stitched, a collar turned, a button attached—workers labored faster and longer at home

or in the factory to forestall a dip in wages. Meanwhile, in some older trades such as machine tooling and textiles, the surviving craft jobs continued to pass from fathers to sons, nephews, or family friends.

The new system of production required a vast number of people. Lured by the promise of a paying job in industry, many young men and women fled the family farm for the factory. A smaller number escaped the peonage system of agricultural labor in the South. By far the largest proportion came from Europe or Asia. Between 1860 and 1890, 10 million people immigrated to the United States. A 1910 report on twenty-one industries estimated that nearly 53 percent of all wage workers were foreign-born, with two-thirds coming from southern and eastern Europe. In many occupations—meat processing, clothing and textile manufacturing, cigar making, and mining, for example—immigrants predominated.

Industrial expansion also offered new opportunities for women to work outside the home. African American and immigrant women found employment in trades least affected by technological advances, such as domestic service. In contrast, English-speaking white women moved into the better-paying clerical and sales positions in the rapidly expanding business sector. After the typewriter and telephone came into widespread use in the 1890s, the number of women employed in office work rose even faster. At the turn of the century, 8.6 million women worked outside their homes—nearly triple the number in 1870.

By contrast, African American men found themselves excluded from many fields. In Cleveland, for example, the number of black carpenters declined after 1870, just as the volume of construction was rapidly increasing. African American men were also systematically driven from restaurant service and barred from newer trades such as boilermaking, plumbing, electrical work, and paperhanging, which European immigrants secured for themselves.

Discriminatory or exclusionary practices fell hardest on workers recruited earlier from China. Driven by severe famine and political turmoil in their homeland and drawn by news of jobs in the California Gold Rush and railroad construction, young men mostly between the ages of sixteen and twenty-four immigrated to the United States. They worked in the mines, in the construction of the railroads, and in market gardening. From the 1860s on, many Chinese established laundries and restaurants in west coast cities where they were viewed as potential competitors by white workers and proprietors of small businesses. A potent and racist anti-Chinese movement organized to protest "cheap Chinese labor" and to demand a halt to Chinese immigration. By the late 1870s white rioters were insistently calling for deportation measures and razing Chinese neighborhoods. In 1882 Congress passed the Chinese

Between 1852 and the Chinese Exclusion Act of 1882, approximately 322,000 Chinese immigrated to the United States. Many helped to build the Central Pacific Railroad and, after fulfilling their labor contracts, moved on to work as cooks or laundry workers in mining and timber camps. Nearly 90 percent of all American Chinese settled in the West. This family, celebrating a wedding, posed for a photographer in Idaho City, Idaho, their new hometown.

SOURCE: The Denver Public Library—Western History Collection.

Exclusion Act, which suspended Chinese immigration, limited the civil rights of resident Chinese, and forbade their naturalization.

For even the best-placed wage earners, the new workplace could be unhealthy, even dangerous. Meatpacking produced its own hazards—the dampness of the pickling room, the sharp blade of the slaughtering knife, and the noxious odors of the fertilizer department. Factory owners often failed to mark high-voltage wires, locked fire doors, and allowed the emission of toxic fumes. Extractive workers, such as coal and copper miners, labored in mineshafts where the air could suddenly turn poisonous and where cave-ins were possible and deadly. Moreover, machines ran faster in American factories than anywhere else in the world, and workers who could not keep up or suffered serious injury found themselves without a job.

Even under less hazardous conditions, workers complained about the tedium of performing repetitive tasks for many hours each day. Although federal employees had been granted the eight-hour day in 1868, most workers still toiled upward of ten or twelve hours. "Life in a factory," one textile operative grumbled, "is perhaps, with the exception of prison life, the most monotonous life a human being can live." Nor could glamour be found in the work of saleswomen in the elegant department stores. Clerks could not sit down, despite workdays as long as sixteen hours in the busy season, or hold "unnecessary conversations" with customers or other clerks. Despite these disadvantages, most women preferred sales and manufacturing jobs to domestic service, which required live-in servants to be on call seven days a week, enjoying at best an occasional afternoon off.

Moreover, steady employment was rare. Between 1866 and 1897, fourteen years of prosperity stood against seventeen of hard times. The major depressions of 1873–79 and 1893–97 were the worst in the nation's history up to that time. Three "minor" recessions (1866–67, 1883–85, and 1890–91) did not seem insignificant to the millions who lost their jobs during those periods. "At one time they drive us like slaves," a labor official complained in 1883, "and at other times we have to beg for work." During that year, 40 percent of all industrial workers lived below the poverty line ($500 per year). Whereas a highly skilled worker who earned between $800 and $1,000 per year might be able to save for a "rainy day," a common laborer who received only $1.50 for a day's work could not.

The Knights of Labor

The Noble and Holy Order of the Knights of Labor, founded by a group of Philadelphia garment cutters in 1869, grew to become the largest labor organization in the nineteenth century. Led by Grand Master Workman Terence V. Powderly, the order sought to bring together all wage earners regardless of skill. Only by organizing widely, one member insisted, would workers be able to achieve their "emancipation" from wage slavery.

The Knights endorsed a variety of reform measures—child labor reform, a graduated income tax, more land set aside for homesteading, the abolition of contract labor, and monetary reform—to offset the power of the industrialists. They believed that the "producing classes," once freed from the grip of corporate monopoly and the curses of ignorance and alcohol, would transform the United States into a genuinely democratic society.

The Knights promoted economic cooperation as the alternative to the wage system and advocated a system of producers' cooperatives. In these factories workers collectively made all decisions on prices and wages and shared all the profits. Local assemblies launched thousands of these small co-ops, such as the Our Girls Co-operative Manufacturing Company, which was established by Chicago seamstresses in the 1880s. The Knights also ran small cooperative cigar shops and grocery stores, often housed in their own assembly buildings. Successful for a time, most cooperatives could not complete against the heavily capitalized enterprises and ultimately failed.

The Knights reached their peak during the great campaign for a shorter workday. The Eight-Hour League, led by Ira Steward, advocated a "natural" rhythm of eight hours for work, eight hours for sleep, and eight hours for leisure. After staging petition campaigns, marches, and a massive strike in New York City, the movement collapsed during the economic recession of the 1870s. The Knights helped revive it in the next decade, and their newspapers ran advertisements promoting "eight-hour" shoes, "eight-hour" romance novels, and "eight-hour" picnics and concerts sponsored by groups eager for the reform. This time the campaign aroused widespread support from consumers, who boycotted brands of beer, bread, and other products made in longer-hour shops.

During the first weeks of May 1886, more than a third of a million workers walked off their jobs. Approximately 200,000 of them won shorter hours, including Packingtown's workers, who joined the Knights of Labor en masse. To celebrate, the community staged a huge parade of twelve marching bands and twenty-eight decorated wagons.

The eight-hour campaign swelled the ranks of the Knights of Labor. The organization grew from a few thousand in 1880 to nearly three-quarters of a million six years later. Nearly 3,000 women formed their own "ladies assemblies" or joined mixed locals. The organization was already committed to securing "for both sexes equal pay for equal work," but Leonora Barry, who was now appointed to organize women, helped to increase their share of membership to 10 percent. African Americans also joined the Knights—20,000 to 30,000 nationally—mainly in separate assemblies within the organization.

In Chicago, the shorter-hours campaign ended in tragedy. On May 4, 1886, following a series of confrontations between strikers and authorities, a protest against police violence at Haymarket Square seemed to be ending quietly until someone threw a bomb that killed one policeman and left seven others fatally wounded. Police responded by firing wildly into the crowd, killing an equal number. After Chicago authorities arrested anarchist leaders, a sensational trial ended in death sentences, although no evidence linked

THE GOSPEL OF THE KNIGHTS OF LABOR.
"We work not selfishly for ourselves alone, but extend the hand of fellowship to all mankind."—*Mr. Powderly, at Richmond.*

This anti-labor cartoon was published in the satirical magazine *Puck,* October 13, 1886, shortly after the national convention of the Knights of Labor in Richmond, Virginia, which attracted attention for the prominent role played by African American delegates. At this meeting, Grand Master Terence Powderly had declared, "We work not selfishly for ourselves alone but extend the hand of fellowship to all mankind." Joseph Keppler, *Puck* editor and artist, parodies Powderly's pronouncement by depicting him as belligerent in his defense of unionized workers.

SOURCE: The Granger Collection, New York (0008409).

the accused to the bombing. Four of the convicted were hanged, one committed suicide, and three other "Haymarket Martyrs," as they were called, remained jailed until pardoned in 1893 by Illinois governor John Peter Altgeld.

The Knights of Labor had suffered an irreparable setback. Employers' associations successfully pooled funds to rid their factories of troublesome organizers and announced that companies would no longer bargain with unions. In Packingtown, the Big Five firms drew up a blacklist to get rid of labor organizers and quickly reinstituted the ten-hour day. The Knights' membership dropped precipitously. The wage system had triumphed.

The American Federation of Labor

The events of 1886 also signaled the rise of a very different kind of organization, the American Federation of Labor (AFL). Unlike the Knights, the AFL accepted the wage system. Following a strategy of "pure and simple unionism," the AFL sought to gain recognition of its union status to bargain with employers for better working conditions, higher wages, and shorter hours. In return, it offered compliant firms the benefit of amenable day-to-day relations with the most highly skilled wage earners. Only if companies refused to bargain in good faith would union members strike.

The new federation, with twelve national unions and 140,000 affiliated members, declared war on the Knights of Labor. In the wake of the Haymarket tragedy and the collapse of the eight-hour movement, the AFL pushed ahead of its rival by organizing craft workers. AFL president Samuel Gompers refused to include unskilled workers, racial minorities, women, and immigrants, believing they were impossible to organize and even unworthy of equal status. Under his leadership, the AFL member became the "aristocrat of labor," the best-paid worker in the world.

Far from the national leadership of Gompers, who served as president until 1924, local AFL members recuperated some of the best qualities of the Knights of Labor and establish a firm basis for the survival of the labor movement. Across the country, Central Federations of Labor formed in cities and small industrial towns. Often they published their own weekly newspaper. Always they sought to coordinate the activities of affiliated locals, from providing support to strikers, to gathering votes for prolabor political candidates, to conducting mass social gatherings in the warm summer months.

Chicago's Central Labor Federation embodied the new spirit of the AFL. After the Haymarket tragedy, labor activists worked more closely with urban reformers. Finding allies among women's clubs and church groups, within the state legislature and even among some socially minded members of the business community, unionists cultivated an atmosphere of civic responsibility. The Illinois Factory Investigation Act of 1893 offered evidence of their hard work and patience, securing funds from the state legislature to monitor working conditions and particularly to improve the woeful situation of the many women and children who worked in sweatshops. Although craft unionism represented only a small minority of working Americans—about 10 percent at the end of the century—local federations of skilled workers often played important roles in their communities. They may not have been able to slow the steady advance of mechanization, which diminished the craft worker's autonomy and eliminated some of the most desirable jobs, but AFL members managed to make their presence felt. Local politicians courted their votes, and Labor Day, first celebrated in the 1880s, became a national holiday in 1894.

THE NEW SOUTH

"Fifteen years have gone over" since the Civil War, journalist Whitelaw Reid complained, yet the South "still sits crushed, wretched, busy displaying and bemoaning her wounds." Physically and financially devastated by the war, the South had little investment capital and relatively few banks to manage it. The area was economically stagnant, its per capita wealth only 27 percent of that of the northeastern states. The South's remote countryside receded into greater isolation, while its few urban regions moved very slowly into the era of modern industry and technology. As late as 1880 mining and manufacturing employed only 5 percent of Alabama's workforce. At the turn of the century southern industries lagged far behind enterprises in other regions of the country. Their progress was held back by dependence on northern finance capital, continued reliance on cotton production, and the legacy of slavery.

An Internal Colony

In the 1870s a vocal and powerful new group of Southerners headed by Henry Woodfin Grady, editor of the *Atlanta Constitution*, insisted that the region enjoyed a great potential in its abundant natural resources of coal, iron, turpentine, tobacco, and lumber. Grady and his peers envisioned a "New South" where modern textile mills operated efficiently and profitably, close to the sources of raw goods, the expansive fields of cotton, and a plentiful and cheap supply of labor, unrestricted by unions or by legal limitations on the employment of children. Arguing against those planters who aspired to rejuvenate the agricultural economy based on the cultivation of a few staple crops, this group forcefully promoted industrial development and welcomed northern investors.

Northern investors secured huge concessions from southern state legislatures, including land, forest, and mineral rights and large tax exemptions. Exploiting the incentives, railroad companies laid over 22,000 miles of new track, connecting the region to national markets and creating new cities. By 1890 a score of large railroad companies, centered mainly in New York, held more than half of all the track in the South. Northern-owned lumber companies meanwhile stripped southern forests.

Northerners also employed various means to protect their investments from southern competition. By the late 1870s, southern merchants, with help from foreign investors, had begun to run iron factories around Birmingham, Alabama. Southern iron production was soon encroaching on the northeastern market. Andrew Carnegie toured the city's iron mills and then declared, "The South is Pennsylvania's most formidable industrial enemy." To stave off this competition, Carnegie ordered the railroads to charge higher freight fees to Birmingham's iron producers. New York bankers later succeeded in expatriating Birmingham's profits through stock ownership in southern firms. After the turn of the century, U.S. Steel simply bought out the local merchants and took over much of Birmingham's production.

The production of cotton textiles followed a similar course. Powerful merchants and large landowners, realizing that they could make high profits by controlling the cotton crop from field to factory, promoted the vertical integration of the cotton industry. The Mississippi Valley Cotton Planters' Association, for example, advised planters to "set up spindles in the cotton fields"—that is, to build mills on their land. Meanwhile, New South promoters in Atlanta hosted the International Cotton Exposition of 1881 in a bold public relations campaign to attract investors. The number of mills in the South grew from 161 in 1880 to 400 in 1900. Southern investors supplied large amounts of the capital for the industrial expansion and technological improvements. The latest machines ran the new mills, and the South boasted the first factory fully equipped with electricity. Production in the four leading cotton-manufacturing states—North Carolina, South Carolina, Georgia, and Alabama—skyrocketed, far outpacing the New England mills.

Recognizing the potential for great profit in these new factories with their cheap labor, northern manufacturers, including many New England mill owners, shifted their investments to the South. By the 1920s, northern investors held much of the South's wealth, including the major textile mills, but returned through employment or social services only a small share of the profits to the region's people.

Beyond iron or steel and textiles, southern industry remained largely extractive and, like the South itself, rural. Turpentine and lumbering businesses pushed ever farther into diminishing pine forests, the sawmills and distilleries moving with them. Toward the end of the century, fruit canning and sugar refining flourished. For the most part, southern enterprises mainly produced raw materials for consumption or use in the North, thereby perpetuating the economic imbalance between the sections.

The governing role of capital investments from outside the region reinforced long-standing relationships. Even rapid industrialization—in iron, railroads, and textiles—did not carry the same consequences achieved in the North. The rise of the New South reinforced, rather than diminished, the region's status as the nation's internal colony.

Southern Labor

The advance of southern industry did little to improve the working lives of most African Americans. The majority of African Americans lived in the southern states,

making up 35 percent of the region's population as late as 1910. In several states, such as Mississippi and South Carolina, they represented the majority. Although black workers continued to prevail in the agricultural economy, large numbers were moving to the new manufacturing centers and growing cities in search of better-paying jobs. African American men did find work with the railroads; in booming cities like Atlanta they even gained skilled positions in the construction trades and worked as bricklayers, carpenters, and painters. For the most part, however, African Americans were limited to unskilled, low-paying jobs. In the textile mills and cigarette factories, which employed both black and white workers, the workforce was rigidly segregated. African Americans were assigned mainly to janitorial jobs and rarely worked alongside the white workers who tended the machines. Nearly all African American women who earned wages did so as household workers. By 1880 Atlanta's washerwomen outnumbered the African American men who worked as common laborers. While the vast majority of adult women did laundry, girls as young as ten years worked as domestics or as nurses for white children.

In general, white workers fiercely protected their relatively privileged positions. Locals of the all-white carpenters' union maintained a segregation policy so absolute that if too few members were available for a job, the union would send for out-of-town white workers rather than employ local members of the black carpenters' union. In an Atlanta mill in 1897, 1,400 white women operatives went on strike when the company proposed to hire two black spinners.

Only at rare moments did southern workers unite across racial lines. In the 1880s, the Knights of Labor briefly organized both black and white workers. At its high point, the Knights' local union, District Assembly 92, enrolled two-thirds of Richmond's 5,000 tobacco operatives and made significant inroads among quarry workers, coopers, typographers, iron molders, and builders. But when white politicians and local newspapers began to raise the specter of black domination, the Knights were forced to retreat. Across the region their assemblies collapsed. Other unions remained the exclusive preserve of white skilled workers.

With few of the new immigrant groups that had found work in northern industries, the South depended on its own regional labor market and therefore maintained low wages for both black and white workers. In 1890, white skilled workers in Richmond's iron trades, including plumbers, carpenters, and gas fitters, made 10 to 30 percent less in 1890 than comparable workers elsewhere in the United States. Southern textile workers' wages were barely half those of New Englanders. In the 1880s, when investors enjoyed profits ranging from 30 percent to 75 percent, southern mill workers earned as little as 12 cents per hour. Black men earned at or below the poverty line of $300 per year, while black women rarely earned more than $120, and white women about $220, annually. The poorest paid workers were children, the mainstay of southern mill labor.

As industry expanded throughout the nation, so too did the number of children earning wages. This was especially so in the South. In 1896 only one in twenty Massachusetts mill workers was younger than sixteen, but one in four North Carolina cotton mill operatives was that age or younger. Traditions rooted in the agricultural economy reinforced the practice of using the labor of all family members, even the very young. In oyster-canning factories, for example, even five-year-olds joined their parents in work. Seasonal labor, such as picking crops or grinding sugarcane, put families on the move, making formal education all but impossible. Not until well into the twentieth century did compulsory school attendance laws effectively restrict child labor in the South.

The processing of raw tobacco employed thousands of African American women, who sorted, stripped, stemmed, and hung tobacco leaves as part of the redrying process. After mechanization was introduced, white women took jobs as cigarette rollers, but black women kept the worst, most monotonous jobs in the tobacco factories. The women shown in this photograph are stemming tobacco in a Virginia factory while their white male supervisor oversees their labor.

SOURCE: Cook Collection, Valentine Museum/Richmond History Center.

A system of convict labor also thrived in the South. Bituminous coal mines and public work projects of all kinds, especially in remote areas, employed disciplinary methods and created living and working conditions reminiscent of slavery. With African Americans constituting up to 90 percent of the convict workforce, public officials felt little need to justify the occasional practice of capturing unsuspecting black strangers and placing them alongside criminals in labor gangs. Transported and housed like animals—chained together by day and confined in portable cages at night—these workers suffered high mortality rates. Southern leaders took pride in what they called the "good roads movement"—the chief use of convict labor—as proof of regional progress.

The Transformation of Piedmont Communities

The impact of the New South was nowhere greater than in the Piedmont, the region extending from southern Virginia and the central Carolinas into northern Alabama and Georgia. After 1870, long-established farms and plantations gave way to railroad tracks, textile factories, numerous mill villages, and a few sizable cities. By the turn of the century, five Piedmont towns had populations over 10,000. Even more dramatic was the swelling number of small towns with populations between 1,000 and 5,000—from fourteen in 1870 to fifty-two in 1900. Once the South's backcountry, the Piedmont now surpassed New England in the production of yarn and cloth to stand first in the world.

Rural poverty and the appeal of a new life encouraged many farm families to strike out for a mill town. As prices of cotton or tobacco fell and farmers' debts to the merchants rose, many families turned to tenant farming and its life of hopeless indebtedness. Those with the least access to land and credit—mainly widows and their children and single women—were the first to go into the mills. Then families sent their children. Some families worked in the mills on a seasonal basis, between planting and harvesting. But as the agricultural crisis deepened, more and more people abandoned the countryside entirely for what they called "public work." Hoping to do better, the majority of these families soon found themselves residents of a company town, owned "lock, stock and barrel" by the manufacturers who employed them.

A mill community typically comprised rows of single-family houses, a small school, several churches, a company-owned store, and the home of the superintendent who governed everyone's affairs. The manager of the King Cotton Mill in Burlington, North Carolina, not only kept the company's accounts in order, purchased raw material, and sold the finished yarn, but even bought Christmas presents for the workers' children. It was not unknown for a superintendent to prowl the neighborhood to see which families burned their lanterns past nine o'clock at night and, finding a violator, to knock on the door and tell the offenders to go to bed. Millworkers frequently complained that they had no private life at all. A federal report published shortly after the turn of the century concluded that "all the affairs of the village and the conditions of living of all the people are regulated entirely by the mill company. Practically speaking, the company owns everything and controls everything, and to a large extent controls everybody in the mill village."

Mill superintendents also relied on schoolteachers and clergy to set the tone of community life. They hired and paid the salaries of Baptist and Methodist ministers to preach a faith encouraging workers to be thrifty, orderly, temperate, and hardworking. Ministers conducted evening prayer services, brought men and women into the choir, and sponsored Bible classes and missionary societies. The schools, similarly subsidized by the company, reinforced the lesson of moral and social discipline required of industrial life and encouraged students to follow their parents into the mill. But it was mainly young children between six and eight years old who attended school. When more hands were needed in the mill, superintendents plucked out these youngsters and sent them to join their older brothers and sisters who were already at work.

Piedmont mill villages like Greenville, South Carolina, and Burlington, Charlotte, and Franklinville, North Carolina, nevertheless developed a cohesive character typical of isolated rural communities. The new residents maintained many aspects of their agricultural pasts, tilling small gardens and keeping chickens, pigs, and cows in their yards. Factory owners rarely paved roads or sidewalks or provided adequate sanitation. Mud, flies, and diseases such as typhoid fever flourished. Millworkers endured poverty and health hazards by strengthening community ties through intermarriage. Within a few generations, most of the village residents had, according to one study, "some connection to each other, however distant, by marriage," blood, or both. Even the men and women without families boarded in households where privacy was scarce and collective meals created a familylike atmosphere. Historians have called this complex of intimate economic, family, and community ties the customs of incorporation.

THE INDUSTRIAL CITY

Before the Civil War, manufacturing had centered in the countryside, in burgeoning factory towns such as Lowell, Massachusetts, and Troy, New York. The expanding rail system of the postwar decades promoted new growth in the older commercial cities of Boston, Philadelphia, and New York and created urban outposts like Minneapolis, Kansas City, and Denver. By the end of the nineteenth century, 90 percent of all manufacturing took place in cities. The metropolis stood at the center of the growing industrial economy, a magnet drawing raw material, capital, and labor, and a key distribution point for manufactured goods.

The industrial city inspired both great hope and great trepidation. Civic leaders often bragged about its size and rate of growth; immigrants wrote to their countryfolk of its pace, both exciting and exhausting. Philosopher Josiah Strong described the city as the nation's "storm center." "Here luxuries are gathered—everything that dazzles the eye, or tempts the appetite" as well as, he pointedly added, "the desperation of starvation." Whatever the assessment, the city dominated the nation's economic, social, and cultural life.

Populating the City

The United States was on its way to becoming an urban nation. The population of cities grew at double the rate of the nation's population as a whole. In 1860 only sixteen cities had more than 50,000 residents. By 1890 one-third of all Americans were city dwellers. Eleven cities claimed more than 250,000 people. Both Chicago and Philadelphia had 1 million inhabitants. But although New York City in 1900 was home to almost 3.5 million people, the West had become the nation's most urbanized region in terms of both the proportion of people living in cities and the concentration of wealth in urban areas. In California, for example, 40 percent of the state's population lived in the two urban areas of San Francisco–Oakland and Los Angeles.

The growth of cities in the western and southern states reflected the expansion of the nation's railroads in those regions and the efficient transportation of goods and people that expansion made possible. The growth of Atlanta, for example, was tied to the expansion of the southern rail system. Like Chicago in the Midwest and Los Angeles in the West, Atlanta became a hub and distribution center for regionally produced goods.

The nation's largest cities—New York, Chicago, Philadelphia, St. Louis, Boston, and Baltimore—achieved international fame for the size and diversity of their populations. Many of their new residents had migrated from rural communities within the United States. Between 1870 and 1910, an average of nearly 7,000 African Americans moved north each year, hoping to escape the poverty and oppression prevailing in the South and to find better-paying jobs. By the end of the century, nearly 80 percent of African Americans in the North lived in urban areas. Among those aged sixteen to thirty-five in all native-born groups, urban women outnumbered men. Whereas young white men in particular aspired to inherit the family farm or seek a fortune in the West, their sisters sought jobs in urban manufacturing, commercial trades, and housekeeping.

Immigrants and their children were the major source of urban population growth in the late nineteenth century. Most of those in the first wave of immigration, before the Civil War, had settled in the countryside. In contrast, after the war it was the industrial city that drew the so-called new immigrants, who came primarily from eastern and southern Europe. In 1880 San Francisco claimed the highest proportion of foreign born (45 percent), although not the largest number. By the turn of the century Chicago had more Germans than all but a few German cities and more Poles than most Polish cities; New York had more Italians than a handful of the largest Italian cities, and Boston had nearly as many Irish as Dublin. In almost every group except the Irish, men outnumbered women.

Like rural migrants, immigrants came to the American city to take advantage of the expanding opportunities for employment. While many hoped to build a new home in the land of plenty, many others intended to work hard, save money, and return to their families in the Old Country. In the 1880s, for example, nearly half of all Italian, Greek, and Serbian men returned to their native lands. Others could not return to their homelands or did not wish to. Jews, for instance, had emigrated to escape persecution in Russia and Russian-dominated Polish and Romanian lands. A Yiddish writer later called this generation the "Jews without Jewish memories. . . . They shook them off in the boat when they came across the seas. They emptied out their memories." Those Chinese immigrants who could not return home during their lifetime often requested that their bodies or ashes be sent back to China.

Of all groups, Jews had the most experience with urban life. Forbidden to own land in most parts of Europe and boxed into *shtetls* (villages), Jews had also formed thriving urban communities in Vilna, Berlin, London, and Vienna. Many had worked in garment manufacturing, in London's East End, for example, and followed a path to American cities like New York, Rochester, Philadelphia, or Chicago where the needle trades flourished.

Other groups, the majority coming from rural parts of Europe, sought out their kinfolk in American cities, where they could most easily find housing and employment. Bohemians settled largely in Chicago, Pittsburgh, and Cleveland. They often lived and worked near German immigrants, although in poorer housing and in less-skilled jobs as lumberyard workers, cigar rollers, and garment workers. French Canadians, a relatively small group of a few hundred thousand, emigrated from Quebec and settled almost exclusively in New England and upper New York State. Finding work mainly in textile mills, they transformed smaller industrial cities like Woonsocket, Rhode Island, into French-speaking communities. Cubans, themselves often first- or second-generation immigrants from Spain, moved to Ybor City, a section of Tampa, Florida, to work in cigar factories. Still other groups tended toward cities dominated by fishing, shoemaking, or even glassblowing, a craft carried directly from the Old Country. Italians, the most numerous among the new immigrants, settled mainly in northeastern cities. With few skills and little education, they often became laborers, laying railroad track, excavating subways, and erecting buildings.

Resettlement in an American city did not necessarily mark the end of the immigrants' travels. Newcomers, both native-born and immigrant, moved frequently from one neighborhood to another and from one city to another. As manufacturing advanced outward from the city center, working populations followed. American cities experienced a total population turnover three or four times during each decade of the last half of the century.

The American city was transformed under the pressure of these various groups. In 1882, when 1.2 million people immigrated to the United States, the novelist Henry James described what he called a "sharp sense of dispossession." To the immigrants, the scene was also disquieting. Before he left his village, Allesandro DeLuca remembered hearing that New York was not only bigger but better than any city in Italy. After he arrived, he felt disillusioned and doubted that he would ever "find here my idea."

The Urban Landscape

Faced with a population explosion and an unprecedented building boom, the cities encouraged the creation of many beautiful and useful structures, including commercial offices, sumptuous homes, and efficient public services—but at a cost. Builders and city planners often disregarded the natural beauty and the architectural landmarks of earlier generations. Laid out in a simple geometric gridiron pattern, streets and housing ran over the sites of hills that had been leveled, ponds that had been filled, farmlands and farm houses that had been eradicated. Factories often occupied the best sites, near waterways where goods could be easily transported and wastes dumped.

In New York City, the majority of the population who worked in dingy factories lived in crowded tenements designed to maximize the use of space by impoverished families. Built by the thousands after the Civil War, the typical "dumbbell" model sat on a lot 25 by 100 feet and rose to five stories. Each floor was subdivided

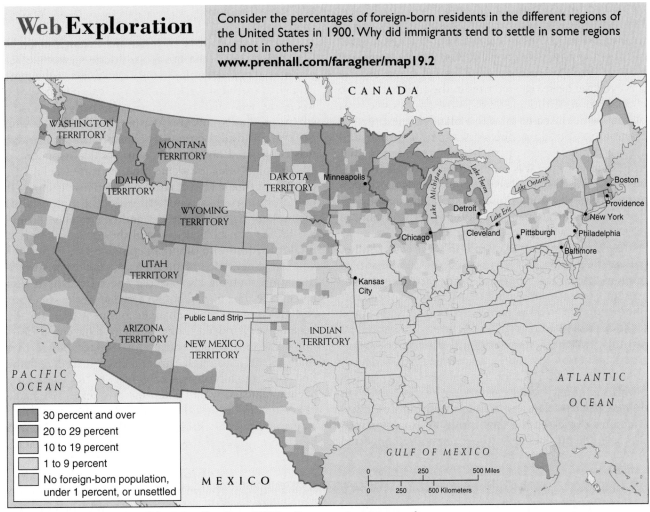

Web Exploration

Consider the percentages of foreign-born residents in the different regions of the United States in 1900. Why did immigrants tend to settle in some regions and not in others?
www.prenhall.com/faragher/map19.2

Population of Foreign Birth by Region, 1880   European immigrants after the Civil War settled primarily in the industrial districts of the northern Midwest and parts of the Northeast. French Canadians continued to settle in Maine, Cubans in Florida, and Mexicans in the Southwest, where earlier immigrants had established thriving communities.

SOURCE: Clifford L. Lord and Elizabeth H. Lord, *Lord & Lord Historical Atlas of the United States* (New York: Holt, 1953).

into four family units of no more than three rooms each. One room served as a combined cooking and living room, the remaining two as bedrooms. By 1890 New York's Lower East Side packed more than 700 people per acre into back-to-back buildings, producing one of the highest population densities in the world.

At the other end of the urban social scale, New York's Fifth Avenue, St. Paul's Summit Avenue, Chicago's Michigan Avenue, and San Francisco's Nob Hill fairly gleamed with new mansions and town houses. Commonwealth Avenue marked Boston's fashionable Back Bay district, built on a filled-in 450-acre tidal flat. State engineers planned this community, with its magnificent boulevard, uniform five-story brownstones, and back

alleys designed for deliveries. Like wealthy neighborhoods in other cities, Back Bay also provided space for the city's magnificent public architecture, its stately public library, fine arts and science museums, and orchestra hall. Back Bay opened onto the Fenway Park system designed by the nation's premier landscape architect, Frederick Law Olmsted.

Cities such as Boston, Chicago, Baltimore, and San Francisco managed to rebuild after major fires, employing the latest technological and architectural innovations. The Chicago Fire broke out in October 1871—though not, as legend had it, because "Mrs. O'Leary's cow" had kicked over a lantern—and swept through the ramshackle wooden houses that had been thrown up for workers. By the time it was doused, the fire had destroyed more than 60,000 buildings within four square miles, including much of the commercial district, and had left nearly 100,000 people homeless. Louis H. Sullivan, recently schooled in Europe, eagerly surveyed the newly cleared sites in the aftermath of the conflagration. Although he did little to improve residential living, he came up with a plan for a new type of commercial building, the skyscraper, a "proud and soaring thing, rising in [such] sheer exultation that from bottom to top it is a unit without a single dissenting line." Emphasizing vertical grandeur rising as high as twenty stories, and using iron, steel, and masonry to deter fires, Sullivan made the skyscraper the symbol of the modern city.

Architects played a key role in what is sometimes called the American Renaissance or City Beautiful movement. Grand concrete boulevards were constructed at enormous public cost. New sports amphitheaters dazzled the public and evoked pride in the city's accomplishments. New schools, courthouses, capitols, hospitals, museums, and department stores arose. Influenced by the Parisian Beaux-Arts style, architects regularly replaced the simple Greek Revival buildings constructed earlier in the century with domed palaces. These massive, often highly ornate structures expressed the city's pride in its commercial success. The city center also became more congested and noisy, making it a more desirable place to visit than to live.

The city also inspired other architectural marvels. Opened in 1883, the Brooklyn Bridge won wide acclaim from engineers, journalists, and poets as the most original American construction. Designed by John Roebling, who died from an accident early in its construction, and by his son Washington Roebling, who became an invalid during its construction, the bridge was considered an aesthetic and practical wonder. Its soaring piers, elegant arches, and intricate steel cables convey an image of strength and elasticity, inspiring a belief among artists and writers in the potential of technology to unite function and beauty. The Brooklyn Bridge also helped to speed the transformation of rural townships into suburban communities.

The emergence of inexpensive, rapid mass transportation systems also altered the spatial design of cities. Like the railroad but on a smaller scale, streetcars and elevated railroads changed business dramatically because they moved traffic of many different kinds—information, people, and goods—faster and farther than before. Although San Francisco introduced the first mechanically driven cable car in 1873, within a decade Chicago would claim the most extensive cable car system in the world. The first electrified street railway was tested in Richmond, Virginia in 1888, and by 1895 more than 800 communities operated systems of electrically powered cars or trolleys on track totaling 10,000 miles. Two years later Boston rerouted a mile and a half of track underground, establishing the nation's first subway trolley. In 1902 New York opened its subway system, which would grow to become the largest in the nation.

Mass transit, by bringing so many people into the heart of the city, played a large part in boosting the value of real estate and promoting the development of central business districts. The value of property in Chicago's "Loop" district, for example, increased by 700 percent between 1877 and 1991. Soon financial, commercial, and cultural institutions replaced small factories and private residences, which moved to neighborhoods where property and rent were less expensive. In turn, the new structures made fuller use of the land, rising high to maximize the space available to tenants.

In his watercolor *The Bowery at Night,* painted in 1885, W. Louis Sonntag, Jr. shows a New York City scene transformed by electric light. Electricity transformed the city in other ways as well, as seen in the electric streetcars and elevated railroad.

SOURCE: *The Bowery at Night,* 1885. Watercolor. Museum of the City of New York.

At the same time, by making it possible for a great number of workers to live in communities distant from their place of employment, mass transportation also allowed the metropolitan region to grow dramatically. By the end of the nineteenth century, suburban trains were bringing nearly 100,000 riders daily into the city of Chicago. Outside Boston, suburbs like Dorchester and Brookline sprang up, offering many professional workers quiet residential retreats from the city's busy downtown. New retail and service businesses followed as the dynamism of the great city radiated outward while the bulk of industry and pollution remained behind.

The City and the Environment

Electric trolleys eliminated the tons of waste from horse-cars that had for decades fouled city streets. But the new rail systems also increased congestion and created new safety hazards for pedestrians. During the 1890s, 600 people were killed each year by Chicago's trains. To relieve congestion, Chicago as well as New York and Boston elevated portions of their rapid transit systems and in the process placed entire communities under the shadow of noisy and rickety wooden platforms. Despite many technological advances, the quality of life in the nation's cities did not necessarily improve.

In the half-century after the Civil War, efforts to improve sanitary conditions absorbed many urban tax dollars. Although cast iron pipes and steam pumps had delivered water into cities since the early part of the century, the filtration systems introduced in the 1890s greatly improved water quality and, by providing cleaner water, played an important role in reducing the incidence of typhoid. By the 1880s, bathrooms with showers and flush toilets had become standard features in hospitals and in many middle-class homes. In turn, the greater quantity of water as well as waste required larger and better drainage and sewer systems. Modern water and sewer systems now constituted a hidden city of pipes and wires mirroring the growth of the visible city above ground.

These advances did not in themselves eradicate serious environmental or health problems. Most cities continued to dump sewage into nearby bodies of water. Moreover, rather than outlawing upriver dumping by factories, municipal governments usually moved to establish separate clean-water systems through the use of reservoirs. Meanwhile the filthy rivers, such as the Providence and Woonasquatucket Rivers in Providence, Rhode Island, were paved over as they passed through downtown. The Chicago River was reversed through an engineering feat so as to transport sewage away from Lake Michigan, the city's source of drinking water. Chicago's residents enjoyed cleaner tap water, but downriver communities began to complain about the unendurable stench from the diverted flow.

The unrestricted burning of coal to fuel the railroads and to heat factories and homes after 1880 greatly intensified urban air pollution. Noise levels continued to rise in the most compacted living and industrial areas. Overcrowded conditions and inadequate sanitary facilities bred tuberculosis, smallpox, and scarlet fever, among other contagious diseases. Children's diseases like whooping cough and measles spread rapidly through poor neighborhoods such as Packingtown. A major yellow fever epidemic in 1878 prompted the creation of the National Board of Health, which in turn began to advise state and city officials and provide emergency assistance. However, in several states, local health officials refused to cooperate with the new national board and directed their representatives in Congress to reduce its appropriations and, finally, to abolish the national board in 1893. Meanwhile, scientific advances in the field of bacteriology prompted local hospital administrators and physicians to supplement public health measures, such as inproved sanitation, with efforts to control disease. By the 1890s many urban school systems employed doctors and nurses to screen children for common contagious diseases. But only after the turn of the century, amid an intensive campaign against municipal corruption, did laws and administrative practices address the serious problems of public health (see Chapter 21).

Meanwhile the distance between the city and the countryside narrowed. Naturalists had hoped for large open spaces—a buffer zone—to preserve farmland and wild areas, protect future water supplies, and diminish regional air pollution. But soon the industrial landscape invaded the countryside. Nearby rural lands not destined for private housing or commercial development became sites for water treatment and sewage plants, garbage dumps, and graveyards—services essential to the city's growing population.

CULTURE AND SOCIETY IN THE GILDED AGE

The growth of industry and spread of cities had a profound impact on all regions of the United States. During the final third of the nineteenth century the standard of living climbed, although unevenly and erratically. Real wages (pay in relation to the cost of living) rose, fostering improvements in nutrition, clothing, and housing. More and cheaper products were within the reach of all but the very poor. Food from the farms became more abundant and varied—grains for bread or beer; poultry, pork, and beef; fresh fruits and vegetables from California. Although many

Americans continued to acknowledge the moral value of hard work, thrift, and self-sacrifice, the explosion of consumer goods and services promoted sweeping changes in behavior and beliefs. Leisure, play, and consumption became part of a new ideal and measure of success. Nearly everyone felt the impact of the transformation from an economy grounded in production toward one based on consumption, although in vastly and increasingly different ways.

"Conspicuous Consumption"

Labeled the "Gilded Age" by humorist and social critic Mark Twain, the era following the Civil War favored the growth of a new class united in its pursuit of money and leisure. The well-to-do enjoyed great status throughout the nineteenth century, but only after the war did upper-class Americans form national networks to consolidate their power. Business leaders built diverse stock portfolios and often served simultaneously on the boards of several corporations. Similarly, they intertwined their interests by joining the same religious, charitable, athletic, and professional societies. They sent their sons to private boarding schools such as St. Paul's, then on to Harvard, Yale, or Princeton. During the summer months, their wives and children vacationed together in the sumptuous new seashore and mountain resorts, while they themselves made deals at their leisure in new downtown social clubs and on the golf links of suburban country clubs. During the winter, high society regrouped in Palm Beach, Florida, linked by rail to points north and lined with fine, warm-weather resorts. Just as Dun and Bradstreet ranked the leading corporations, the Social Register identified the 500 families that controlled most of the nation's wealth.

According to economist and social critic Thorstein Veblen, the rich had created a new style of "conspicuous consumption." The Chicago mansion of real estate tycoon Potter Palmer, for example, was constructed in 1885 without exterior doorknobs. Not only could no one enter uninvited, but a visitor's calling card supposedly passed through the hands of twenty-seven servants before admittance was allowed. At the nearby McCormick mansion, dinner guests chose from a menu printed in French. A vice president of the Chicago & Northwestern Railroad, Perry H. Smith, built his marble palace in the style of the Greek Renaissance. Its ebony staircase was trimmed in gold, its butler's pantry equipped with faucets not only for hot and cold water but for iced champagne. The women who oversaw these elaborate households themselves served as measures of their husbands' status, according to Veblen, by adorning themselves in jewels, furs, and dresses of the latest Paris design.

Conspicuous consumption reached toward new heights of extravagance. In New York, wealthy families hosted dinner parties for their dogs or pet monkeys, dressing the animals in fancy outfits for the occasion. Railroad magnate "Diamond Jim" Brady commonly enjoyed after-theater snacks at the city's "lobster palaces," where he consumed vast quantities of food—oysters for an appetizer, two soups, fish, a main dinner of beef and vegetables, punches and sherbet on the side, dessert, coffee, and quarts of orange juice.

Perhaps no display of wealth matched the ostentation of the "cottages" of Newport, Rhode Island, where the rich created a summer community centering on consumption. Architect H. H. Richardson and his protégés built manor houses more magnificent than the English homes they mimicked. Here wealthy young men and women engaged in new amateur sports such as polo, rowing, and lawn tennis. Young and old alike joined in yachting and golf tournaments.

Toward the end of the century, the wealthy added a dramatic public dimension to the "high life." New York's Waldorf-Astoria hotel, which opened in 1897, incorporated the grandeur of European royalty but with an important difference. Because rich Americans wanted to be watched, the elegantly appointed corridors and restaurants were visible to the public through huge windows, and floor-to-ceiling mirrors allowed diners to observe one another. The New York rich also established a unique custom to welcome the New Year: they opened wide the curtains of their Fifth Avenue mansions so that passersby could marvel at the elegant decor.

The wealthy also became the leading patrons of the arts as well as the chief importers of art treasures from Europe and Asia. They provided the bulk of funds for the new symphonies, operas, and ballet companies, which soon rivaled those of Continental Europe. Nearly all major museums and art galleries, including the Boston Museum of Fine Arts, the Philadelphia Museum of Art, the Art Institute of Chicago, and the Metropolitan Museum of Art in New York, were founded during the last decades of the nineteenth century. Many were the gifts of individual donors, such as the libraries, museums, and galleries in Pittsburgh that all bore the name "Carnegie."

Gentility and the Middle Class

A new middle class, very different from its predecessor, formed during the last half of the century. The older middle class comprised the owners or superintendents of small businesses, doctors, lawyers, teachers, and ministers and their families. The new middle class included these professionals but also the growing number of salaried employees—the managers, technicians, clerks, and engineers who worked in the complex web of corporations and government. Long hours of labor earned their families a modest status and sufficient income to live securely in style and comfort and, equally important, to separate work and home.

Most middle-class American families valued their home not simply as a sign of their social station but as a haven from the tumultuous society outside. For as little as $10 a month, a family could finance the construction of a suburban retreat from the noise, filth, and dangers of the city. This peaceful domestic setting, with its manicured lawns and well-placed shrubs, afforded family members both privacy and rejuvenation. But to accomplish this goal, middle-class families had to separate business activities from leisure, and the breadwinner from his family for most of the day. Assisted by modern transportation systems, men often traveled one to two hours each day, five or six days a week, to their city offices and back again. Women and children stayed behind.

The interior design of middle-class homes reflected a desire for refinement. A rush of new magazines and volumes on homemaking, like Harriet Spofford's *Art Decoration* (1879), set the standards, including elaborate front entryways, wallpapers stenciled by housewives themselves, stained-glass windows, and solid furniture. Reserved for visitors, the parlor featured upholstered furniture, inexpensive prints of famous paintings, and framed photographs of family members. Outside, the fenced-in yard served as a safe playground for small children and their pets.

Middle-class women found themselves devoting a large part of their day to housework. They frequently employed one or two servants but relied increasingly on the many new household appliances to get their work done. Improvements in the kitchen stove, such as the conversion from wood fuel to gas, saved a lot of time. Yet, simultaneously, with the widespread circulation of cookbooks and recipes in newspapers and magazines, as well as the availability of new foods, the preparation of meals became more complex and time-consuming. New devices such as the eggbeater speeded some familiar tasks, but the era's fancy culinary practices offset any gains in saving time. Similarly, the new carpet sweepers surpassed the broom in efficiency, but the fashionable high-napped carpeting demanded more care. The foot-powered treadle sewing machine, a staple of the middle-class home, encouraged the fashion-conscious housewife to produce fancier clothing for herself and her family. Thus, rather than diminishing with technological innovation, household work expanded to fill the time available.

Almost exclusively white, Anglo-Saxon, and Protestant, the new middle class embraced "culture" not for purposes of conspicuous consumption but as a means of self-improvement and moral uplift. Whole families visited the new museums and art galleries. One of the most cherished institutions, the annual season of lectures at the Chautauqua campgrounds in upstate New York, brought thousands of families together in pursuit of knowledge of literature and the fine arts. The middle class also provided the bulk of patrons for the new public libraries.

Middle-class families applied the same standards to their leisure activities. What one sporting-goods entrepreneur rightly called the "gospel of EXERCISE" involved men and women in calisthenics and outdoor activities, not so much for pleasure as for physical and mental discipline. Hiking was a favorite among both men and women and required entirely new outfits: for women, loose upper garments and skirts short enough to prevent dragging; for men, rugged outer wear and jaunty hats. Soon men and women began camping out, with almost enough amenities to re-create a middle-class home in the woods. Roller skating and ice skating, which became crazes shortly after the Civil War, took place in specially designed rinks in almost every major town. By the 1890s, the "safety" bicycle had also been marketed. It replaced the large-wheel variety, which was difficult to keep upright. A good-quality "bike" cost $100 and, like the piano, was a symbol of middle-class status. In 1995 Chicago hosted thirty-three cycle clubs comprising nearly 10,000 members.

Leisure became the special province of middle-class childhood. Removed from factories and shops and freed from many domestic chores, children enjoyed creative play and physical activity. Summer camps, offering several weeks of sports and handicrafts, attracted many children to New England during this period. The toy market boomed, and lower printing prices helped children's literature flourish. The *Brownie Book* (1898), about imaginary elflike beings, was tremendously popular. Children's magazines such as *St. Nicholas* and *Youth's Companion* were filled with stories, poems, and pictures. Slightly older children read westerns, sports novels of many kinds, and such perennial and uplifting classics as *Little Women* and *Black Beauty.*

Life in the Streets

Immigrants often weighed the material abundance they found in the United States against their memories of the Old Country. One could "live better" here, but only by working much harder. In letters home, immigrants described the riches of the new country but warned friends and relatives not to send weaklings, who would surely die of stress and strain. Even if their bodies thrived, their spirits might sink amid the alien and intense commercialism of American society. In many immigrant communities, alcoholism and suicide rates did soar above contemporary European standards. Germans in

Chicago, it was said half jokingly, drank more beer and whiskey than all the Germans in Germany. Each group had its own phrase to express its feelings of disenchantment. Embittered German immigrants called their new land *Malhuerica*, "misfortune"; Jews called it *Ama Reka*, Hebrew for "without soul"; and Slavs referred to it as *Dollerica*.

To alleviate the stress of adjustment to life in an unfamiliar city, newcomers often established close-knit ethnic communities. European immigrants usually preferred to live together with people from their own country of origin, if possible from their home district. The poorest of new immigrants, like the Italians of Providence, Rhode Island, or the Slavs of Homestead, Pennsylvania, made special sacrifices to resettle with people who would be familiar to them. Aunts and uncles became almost as dear as parents, cousins as close as brothers and sisters. Young adults married within their communities, often setting up households within a few blocks of their parents and not infrequently within the same "triple-decker" or tenement.

Many newcomers, having little choice about their place of residence, concentrated in districts marked off by racial or ethnic lines. In San Francisco, city ordi-

nances prevented Chinese from operating laundries in most of the city's neighborhoods, and the city's schools excluded their children. In the 1880s, Chinese San Franciscans, representing 10 percent of the city's population, were crowded into a dozen blocks of restaurants, shops, and small factories known as Chinatown. In Los Angeles and San Antonio, Mexicans lived in distinctive barrios. In most cities, African American families were similarly compelled to remain in the dingiest, most crime-ridden, and dangerous sections of town.

Young people who had left their families behind, whether in Europe or in the American countryside, usually took rooms in small residential hotels or boardinghouses. The Young Men's Christian Association (YMCA), established in the 1850s, and the Young Women's Christian Association (YWCA), organized a decade later, provided temporary residences mainly to native-born, white, self-supporting men and women. The most successful "women adrift," such as clerical workers and retail clerks, lived in the new furnished-room districts bordering the city's business center. The least prosperous landed on "skid row," where homeless people spent time in the rough taverns, eating free lunches in return for purchased beer, waiting for casual labor, and sometimes trading sexual favors for money.

The working-class home did not necessarily ensure privacy or offer protection from the dangers of the outside world. In the tenements, families often shared their rooms with other families or paying boarders. During the summer heat, adults, children, and boarders alike competed for a sleeping place on the fire escape or roof, and all year round noise resounded through paper-thin walls. But so complex and varied were income levels and social customs that no single pattern emerged. Packingtown's Slovaks, Lithuanians, and Poles, for example, frequently took in boarders, yet Bohemians rarely did. Neither did the skilled iron rollers who worked at the Carnegie Steel Company in Homestead, Pennsylvania. These well-paid craft workers often owned their own homes, boasting parlors and even imported Belgian carpets. At the other extreme, Italian immigrants, who considered themselves fortunate to get work with a shovel, usually lived in overcrowded rented apartments, just a paycheck away from eviction.

Whether it was a small cottage or a tenement flat, the working-class home involved women and children in routines of household labor without the aid of the new mechanical devices. In addition to cooking and cleaning, women used their cramped domestic space for work that provided a small income. They gathered their children—and their husbands after a hard day's labor—to sew garments, wrap cigars, string beads, or paint vases for a contractor who paid them by the piece. And they cooked and cleaned for the boarders whose rent supple-

The intersection of Orchard and Hester Streets on New York's Lower East Side, photographed ca. 1905. Unlike the middle classes, who worked and played hidden away in offices and private homes, the Jewish lower-class immigrants who lived and worked in this neighborhood spent the greater parts of their lives on the streets.

SOURCE: Oil over a photograph. The Granger Collection (4E534.23).

mented the family income. In short, the home was a second work place, usually involving the entire family.

Despite working people's slim resources, their combined buying power created new and important markets for consumer goods. Often they bought shoddy replicas of products sold to the middle class: cheaper canned goods, inferior cuts of meat, and partially spoiled fruit. Several leading clothing manufacturers specialized in inexpensive ready-to-wear items, usually copied from patterns designed for wealthier consumers but constructed hastily from flimsy materials. Patent medicines for ailments caused by working long periods in cramped conditions sold well in working-class communities, where money for doctors was scarce. These nostrums failed to restore health, except perhaps through the power of suggestion. On the other hand, their high alcohol content might lift a person's spirits, if only temporarily.

The close quarters of the urban neighborhood allowed immigrants to preserve many Old World customs. In immigrant communities such as Chicago's Packingtown, Pittsburgh's Poletown, New York's Lower East Side, or San Francisco's Chinatown, people usually spoke their native language while visiting their friends and relatives. The men might play cards while women and children gathered in the stairwell or on the front stoop to trade stories. In good weather they walked and talked, an inexpensive pastime common in European cities. No organization was as important as the fraternal society, which sponsored social clubs and provided insurance benefits. Social organizations, known as *huiguan*, were especially important in preserving clan and dialect among the largely male unmarried population of Chinese San Francisco. Immigrants also re-created Old World religious institutions such as the temple, church, or synagogue, or secular institutions such as German family-style taverns or Russian Jewish tearooms. Chinese theaters, in inexpensive daily and nightly performances, presented dramas depicting historical events or explicating moral teachings and thereby preserved much of Chinese native culture. Immigrants also replicated their native cuisine (as much as available foods allowed) and sang their own songs, accompanied by the polka, mazurka, or tamburitza, according to tradition. They married, baptized children, and buried their dead according to Old World customs.

In the cosmopolitan cities, immigrants, by being innovative entrepreneurs as well as the best customers, helped to shape the emerging popular culture. German immigrants, for example, created Tin Pan Alley, the center of the popular music industry, and wrote such well-liked ballads as "Down by the Old Mill Stream." They also became the first promoters of ragtime, which found its way north from Storyville, the red-light district of New Orleans. Created by African American and creole bands, ragtime captivated those teenage off-spring of immigrants who rushed to the new dance halls. Disdaining their parents' sentimental favorites, such as "Beautiful Dreamer," the youngsters seemed to associate the new syncopated sounds with the pulse of urban life. They also gave ragtime musicians paying work and budding musical entrepreneurs the idea that music with African American roots could become the biggest commercial entertainment of all.

In the same years, the first great amusement parks began to enthrall masses of immigrants and other city dwellers. The most spectacular was Coney Island, at the southern edge of Brooklyn, New York, which grew out of a series of fancy hotels and gambling (and prostitution) parlors. When developers realized that "wholesome fun" for the masses could pay better than upper-class leisure or lower-class vice, they decided to transform Coney Island into a magnificent seaside park filled with ingenious amusements such as water slides, mechanized horse races, carousels, roller coasters, and fun houses. Three amusement parks opened between 1895 and 1903. On the rides or at the nearby beach, young men and women could easily meet apart from their parents, cast off their inhibitions, and enjoy a hug or kiss. Or they could simply stroll through the grounds, looking at exotic performers, enjoying make-believe trips to the Far East or even the moon, entranced by fantastic towers, columns, minarets, and lagoons lit up at night to resemble dreams rather than reality. At Coney Island or at Riverview, Chicago's oldest amusement park located on the city's North Side, millions of working-class people enjoyed cheap thrills that offset the hardships of their working lives.

CULTURES IN CONFLICT, CULTURE IN COMMON

The new commercial entertainments gave Americans from various backgrounds more in common than they would otherwise have had. On New York's Lower East Side, for instance, theater blossomed with dramas that Broadway would adopt years later, while children dreamed of going "uptown" where the popular songs they heard on the streets were transcribed onto sheet music and sold in stores throughout the city. Even so, nothing could smooth the tensions caused by conflicting claims to the same resources, such as public schools and urban parks.

Education

As industries grew and cities expanded, so did the nation's public school system. Business and civic leaders realized that the welfare of society now depended on an educated population, one possessing the skills and knowledge required to keep both industry and government running. In the last three decades of the nineteenth century, the idea of universal free schooling, at least for white children, took hold. Kindergartens in particular flourished. St. Louis, Missouri, opened the first public school kindergarten in 1873, and by the turn of the century more than 4,000 similar programs throughout the country enrolled children between the ages of three and seven.

The number of public high schools, which were rare before the Civil War, also increased, from 160 in 1870 to 6,000 by the end of the century. In Chicago alone, average daily attendance increased sixfold. Despite this spectacular growth, which was concentrated in urban industrial areas, as late as 1890 only 4 percent of children between the ages of fourteen and seventeen were enrolled in school, the majority of them girls planning to become teachers or office workers. Most high schools continued to serve mainly the middle class. In 1893 the National Education Association reaffirmed the major purpose of the nation's high schools as preparation for college, rather than for work in trades or industry, and endorsed a curriculum of rigorous training in the classics, such as Latin, Greek, and ancient history. The expected benefits of this kind of education rarely outweighed the immediate needs of families who depended on their children's wages. At the end of the century, 50 percent of the children in Chicago between the ages of ten and twelve were working for wages.

Higher education also expanded along several lines. Agricultural colleges formed earlier in the century developed into institutes of technology and took their places alongside the prestigious liberal arts colleges. To extend learning to the "industrial classes," Representative Justin Morrill of Vermont sponsored the Morrill Federal Land Grant Act of 1862, which funded a system of state colleges and universities for teaching agriculture and mechanics "without excluding other scientific and classic studies." Meanwhile, established private institutions like Harvard, Yale, Princeton, and Columbia grew, with the help of huge endowments from business leaders such as Rockefeller and Carnegie. By 1900, sixty-three Catholic colleges were serving mainly the children of immigrants from Ireland and eastern and southern Europe. Still, as the overall number of colleges and universities grew from 563 in 1870 to nearly 1,000 by 1910, only 3 percent of the college-age population took advantage of these new opportunities.

One of the most important developments occurred in the area of professional training. Although medical and law schools dated from the mid-eighteenth century, their numbers grew rapidly after the Civil War. Younger professions, such as engineering, pharmacy, and journalism, also established specialized training institutions. In 1876 the Johns Hopkins University pioneered a program of research and graduate studies, and by the end of the century several American universities, including Stanford University and the University of Chicago, offered advanced degrees in the arts and sciences.

This expansion benefited women, who previously had had little access to higher education. After the Civil War, a number of women's colleges were founded, beginning in 1865 with Vassar, which set the academic standard for the remainder of the century. Smith and Wellesley followed in 1875, Bryn Mawr in 1885. By the end of the century, 125 women's colleges offered a first-rate education comparable to that given to men at Harvard, Yale, or Princeton. Meanwhile, coeducation grew at an even faster rate; by 1890, 47 percent of the nation's colleges and universities admitted women. The proportion of women college students changed dramatically. Women constituted 21 percent of undergraduate enrollments in 1870, 32 percent in 1880, and 40 percent in 1910. Despite these gains, many professions remained closed to women.

An even greater number of women enrolled in vocational courses. Normal schools, which offered one- or two-year programs for women who planned to become elementary school teachers, developed a collegiate character after the Civil War and had become accredited state teachers' colleges by the end of the century. Normal schools enrolled many women from rural areas, particularly from poor families. Upon graduation, these women filled the personnel ranks of the rapidly expanding system of public education. Other institutions, many founded by middle-class philanthropists, also prepared women for vocations. For example, the first training school for nurses opened in Boston in 1873, followed in 1879 by a diet kitchen that taught women to become cooks in the city's hospitals. Founded in 1877, the Women's Educational and Industrial Union offered a multitude of classes to Boston's wage-earning women, ranging from elementary French and German, to drawing, watercoloring, and oil and china painting, to dressmaking and millinery, stenography and typing, as well as crafts less familiar to women, such as upholstering, cabinetmaking, and carpentry. In the early 1890s, when the entering class at a large women's college like Vassar still averaged under 100, the Boston Women's Educational and Industrial Union reported that its staff of 83 served an estimated 1,500 clients per day. By that time, one of its most well-funded programs was a training school for domestic servants.

The leaders of the business community had also begun to promote manual training for working-class and immigrant boys. One leading San Francisco merchant described the philosophy behind this movement as a desire to train boys "to earn a living with little study and plenty of work." Craft unionists in several cities actively opposed this development, preferring their own methods of apprenticeship to training programs they could not control. But local associations of merchants and manufacturers lobbied hard for "industrial education" and raised funds to supplement the public school budget. In 1884 the Chicago Manual Training School opened, teaching "shop work" along with a few academic subjects, and by 1895 all elementary and high schools in the city offered courses that trained working-class boys for future jobs in industry and business.

The expansion of education did not benefit all Americans or benefit them all in the same way. Because African Americans were prohibited from enrolling in colleges attended by white students, special colleges were founded in the southern states shortly after the Civil War. All-black Atlanta and Fisk universities both soon offered a rigorous curriculum in the liberal arts. Other institutions, such as Hampton, founded in 1868, specialized in vocational training, mainly in manual trades. Educator Booker T. Washington encouraged African Americans to resist "the craze for Greek and Latin learning" and to strive for practical instruction. In 1881 he founded the Tuskegee Institute in Alabama to provide industrial education and moral uplift. By the turn of the century, Tuskegee enrolled 1,400 men and women in more than thirty different vocational courses, including special cooking classes for homemakers and domestic servants. Black colleges, including Tuskegee, trained so many teachers that by the century's end the majority of black schools were staffed by African Americans.

The nation's educational system was becoming more inclusive and yet more differentiated. The majority of children attended school for several years or more. At the same time, students were tracked—by race, gender, and class—to fill particular roles in an industrial society.

Leisure and Public Space

Most large cities set aside open land for leisure-time use by residents. New York's Central Park opened for ice skating in 1858, providing a model for urban park systems across the United States. In 1869, planners in Chicago secured funds to create a citywide system comprising six interconnected large parks, and within a few years, Lincoln Park, on the city's north side, was attracting crowds of nearly 30,000 on Sundays. These parks were rolling expanses, cut across by streams and pathways and footbridges and set off by groves of trees, ornamental shrubs, and neat flower gardens. According to the designers' vision, the urban middle class might find here a respite from the stresses of modern life. To ensure this possibility, posted regulations forbade many activities, ranging from walking on the grass to gambling, picnicking, or ball playing without permission, to speeding in carriages.

The working classes had their own ideas about the use of parks and open land. Trapped in overcrowded tenements or congested neighborhoods, they wanted space for sports, picnics, and lovers' trysts. Young people openly defied ordinances that prohibited play on the grassy knolls, while their elders routinely voted against municipal bonds that did not include funds for more recreational space in their communities. Immigrant ward representatives on the Pittsburgh city council, for instance, argued that band shells for classical music meant little to their constituents, while spaces suitable for sports meant much.

Eventually, most park administrators set aside some sections for playgrounds and athletic fields and others for public gardens and band shells. Yet intermittent conflicts erupted. The Worcester, Massachusetts, park system, for example, allowed sports leagues to schedule events but prohibited pickup games. This policy gave city officials more control over the use of the park for outdoor recreation but at the same time forced many

George Washington Carver (1864–1943), who had been born in slavery, had been invited by Booker T. Washington to direct agricultural research at the Tuskegee Institute in Alabama. A leader in development of agriculture in the New South, Carver promoted crop diversification to rejuvenate soil that was depleted by the continuous planting of cotton and encouraged the cultivation of alternative, high-protein crops such as peanuts and soybeans. He designed his programs in sustainable agriculture mainly for African American farmers and sharecroppers rather than for commercial purposes.

SOURCE: ca. 1900. The Granger Collection, New York (0002916).

ball-playing boys into the streets. When working-class parents protested, city officials responded by instituting programs of supervised play, to the further dismay of the children.

Public drinking of alcoholic beverages, especially on Sunday, provoked similar disputes. Pittsburgh's "blue laws," forbidding businesses to open on Sunday, were rigidly enforced when it came to neighborhood taverns, while large firms like the railroads enjoyed exemptions. Although the Carnegie Institute hoped to discourage Sunday drinking by sponsoring alternative events, such as free organ recitals and other concerts, many working people, especially beer-loving German immigrants, continued to treat Sunday as their one day of relaxation. In Chicago, when not riding the streetcars to the many beer gardens and taverns that thrived on the outskirts, Germans gathered in large numbers for picnics in the city's parks.

Toward the end of the century, many park administrators relaxed the rules and expanded the range of permitted activities. By this time, large numbers of the middle class had become sports enthusiasts and pressured municipal governments to turn meadowlands into tennis courts and golfing greens. In the 1890s bicycling brought many women into the parks. Still, not all city residents enjoyed these facilities. Officials in St. Louis, for example, barred African Americans from the city's grand Forest Park and set aside the smaller Tandy Park for their use. After challenging this policy in court, African Americans won a few concessions, such as the

right to picnic at any time in Forest Park and to use the golf course on Monday mornings.

National Pastimes

Toward the end of the century, the younger members of the urban middle class had begun to find common ground in lower-class pastimes, especially ragtime music. Introduced to many Northerners by the African American composer Scott Joplin at the Chicago World's Fair of 1893, "rag" quickly became the staple of entertainment in the new cabarets and nightclubs. Middle-class urban dwellers began to seek out ragtime bands and congregated in nightclubs and even on the rooftops of posh hotels to listen and dance and even to drink.

Vaudeville, the most popular form of commercial entertainment since the 1880s, also bridged middle- and working-class tastes. Drawing on a variety-show tradition of singers, dancers, comedians, jugglers, and acrobats, who had entertained Americans since colonial days, "vaude" became a big business that made ethnic and racial stereotypes and the daily frustrations of city life into major topics of amusement. Vaudeville palaces—ten in New York, six in Philadelphia, five in Chicago, and at least one in every other large city—attracted huge, "respectable" crowds that sampled between twenty and thirty dramatic, musical, and comedy acts averaging fifteen minutes each. One study estimated that before vaudeville gave way to movie theaters in the 1920s, between 14 and 16 percent of all city dwellers attended shows at least once a week. Sunday matinees were especially popular with women and children.

Sports, however, outdistanced all other commercial entertainments in appealing to all kinds of fans and managing to create a sense of national identity. No doubt the most popular parks in the United States were the expanses of green surrounded by grandstands and marked by their unique diamond shape—the baseball field. During the last quarter of the nineteenth century the amateur sport of gentlemen and Union soldiers suddenly became the "national pastime." Both American and English children had for years been playing a form of baseball, known mainly as "rounders," when a group of young men in Manhattan formed the Knickerbocker Base Ball Club in 1845 and proceeded to set down the game's rules in

One of the finest American painters of the period, known for realistic depictions of physical exertion in amateur athletics, Thomas Eakins here turned his attention to the commercial baseball park. The batter and catcher appear as well-poised athletes, dignified in their dress and manner—everything that the baseball player of the late nineteenth century was not very likely to be.

SOURCE: Thomas Eakins, *Baseball Players*, 1875. Watercolor. The Rhode Island School of Design Museum of Art (36.172).

CHRONOLOGY

1862	Morrill Act authorizes "land-grant" colleges
1869	Knights of Labor founded
1870	Standard Oil founded
1871	Chicago Fire
1873	Financial panic brings severe depression
1876	Baseball's National League founded
	Alexander Graham Bell patents the telephone
1879	Thomas Edison invents the incandescent bulb
	Depression ends
1881	Tuskegee Institute founded
1882	Peak of immigration to the United States (1.2 million) in the nineteenth century
	Chinese Exclusion Act passed
	Standard Oil Trust founded
1883	William Graham Sumner published the social Darwinist classic *What Social Classes Owe to Each Other*
1886	Campaigns for eight-hour workday peak
	Haymarket riot and massacre discredit the Knights of Labor
	American Federation of Labor founded
1890	Sherman Antitrust Act passed
1893	Stock market panic precipitates severe depression
1895	Coney Island opens
1896	Rural free delivery begins
1900	Andrew Carnegie's *Gospel of Wealth* recommends honesty and fair dealing
1901	U.S. Steel Corporation formed

writing. Baseball clubs soon formed in many cities, and shortly after the Civil War traveling teams with regular schedules made baseball a professional sport. The formation of the National League in 1876 encouraged other spectator sports, but for generations baseball remained the most popular.

Rowdy behavior gave the game a working-class ambience. Well-loved players known for their saloon brawls occasionally disappeared for a few days on "benders." Team owners, themselves often proprietors of local breweries, counted heavily on beer sales in the parks. Having to contend with hundreds of drunken fans, officials maintained order only with great difficulty. Outfielders occasionally leaped into the grandstand to punch spectators who had heckled them. To attract more subdued middle-class fans, the National League raised admission prices, banned the sale of alcohol, and observed Sunday blue laws. Catering to a working-class audience, the American Association kept the price of admission low, sold liquor, and played ball on Sunday.

Baseball, like many other sports, soon became tied to the larger business economy. In Chicago, for example, the first baseball clubs organized in the 1850s. After the Civil War local merchants, such as Marshall Field, began to support teams and by the end of the decade there were more than fifty company-sponsored teams playing the local leagues. By 1870, a Chicago Board of Trade team emerged as the city's first professional club, the White Stockings. Capitalized as a joint stock company, the White Stockings soon succeeded in recruiting a star pitcher from the Boston Red Stockings, Albert Spalding, who eventually became manager and then president of the team. Spalding also came to see baseball as a source of multiple profits. He procured the exclusive rights to manufacture the official ball and the rule book, while producing large varieties of other sporting equipment. Meanwhile, he built impressive baseball parks in Chicago with seating for 10,000 and special private boxes above the grandstands for the wealthy. He easily became the foremost figure in the National League.

Spalding also succeeded in tightening the rules of participation in the sport. In 1879 he dictated the "reserve clause," which prevented players from negotiating a better deal and leaving the team that originally signed them. He encouraged his player-manager "Cap" Anson to forbid the White Stockings from playing against any team with an African American member. The firing of Moses "Fleet" Walker, an African-American, from the Cincinnati team in 1884 marked the first time the color line had been drawn in a major professional sport.

Effectively excluded, African Americans organized their own traveling teams. In the 1920s they formed the Negro Leagues, which produced some of the nation's finest ballplayers.

Players occasionally organized to regain control over their sport. They frequently complained about low wages and arbitrary rules, and like factory workers in the 1880s they formed their own league, the Brotherhood of Professional Base Ball Players, with profits divided between participants and investors. This effort failed, partly because fans would not desert the established leagues, but mostly because successful baseball franchises demanded large quantities of capital. American sports had become big business.

As attendance continued to grow, the enthusiasm for baseball straddled major social divisions, bringing together Americans of many backgrounds, if only on a limited basis. By the end of the century, no section of the daily newspaper drew more readers than the sports pages. Although it interested relatively few women, sports news riveted the attention of men from all social classes. Loyalty to the "home team" helped to create an urban identity, while individual players became national heroes.

CONCLUSION

By the end of the nineteenth century, industry and the growing cities had opened a new world for Americans. Fresh from Europe or from the native countryside, ordinary urban dwellers struggled to form communities of fellow newcomers through work and leisure, in the factory, the neighborhood, the ballpark, and the public school. Meanwhile, their "betters," the wealthy and the new middle class, made and executed the decisions of industry and marketing, established the era's grand civic institutions, and set the tone for high fashion and art.

Rich and poor alike shared many aspects of the new order. Yet inequality persisted and increased, as much a part of the new order as the Brooklyn Bridge or advertising. During the mostly prosperous 1880s, optimists believed that unfair treatment based on region, on class, and perhaps even on race and gender might ease in time. By the depressed 1890s, however, these hopes had worn thin, and the lure of overseas empire appeared as one of the few goals that held together a suffering and divided nation.

REVIEW QUESTIONS

1. Discuss the sources of economic growth in the decades after the Civil War. Historians often refer to this period as the era of the "second industrial revolution." Do you agree with this description?

2. Describe the impact of new technologies and new forms of production on the routines of industrial workers. How did these changes affect African American and women workers in particular? What role did trade unions play in this process?

3. Choose one major city, such as Boston, New York, Chicago, Birmingham, or San Francisco, and discuss changes in its economy, population, and urban space in the decades after the Civil War.

4. Discuss the role of northern capital in the development of the New South. How did the rise of industry affect the lives of rural Southerners? Analyze these changes from the point of view of African Americans.

5. How did urban life change during the Gilded Age? How did economic development affect residential patterns? How did the middle class aspire to live during the Gilded Age? How did their lifestyles compare with those of working-class urbanites?

6. How did the American educational system change to prepare children for their adult roles in the new industrial economy?

7. How did the rise of organized sports and commercial amusements reflect and shape social divisions at the end of the century? Which groups were affected most (or least) by new leisure activities?

RECOMMENDED READING

Cindy S. Aron, *Working at Play: A History of Vacations in the United States* (1999). Covers the expansion of vacations from wealthy families to the middle class in the nineteenth century. Aron examines several types of settings, ranging from the grand summer hotels and posh resorts to camping vacations in the new national parks.

James R. Barrett, *Work and Community in the Jungle* (1987). A very close study of the Packingtown district of Chicago, Illinois, at the turn of the century. Barrett describes the transformation of animals to meat in great stockyards and processing plants. He also provides rich documentation of neighborhood life.

Alfred D. Chandler Jr., *The Visible Hand: The Managerial Revolution in American Business* (1977). A highly acclaimed study of corporate management. Chandler shows how the rapid growth in the scale of business, as well as its influence in public life, brought about a new type of executive with skills for national decision making and close links with others of his kind.

William Cronon, *Nature's Metropolis* (1991). Analyzes the changing economic and political relationship between the city of Chicago and the surrounding countryside. Cronon demonstrates through a variety of evidence the tight interdependence of urban and rural regions.

Herbert G. Gutman, *Work, Culture and Society in Industrializing America: Essays in American Working-Class and Social History* (1977). Influential essays on the formation of working-class communities in the nineteenth century. Gutman focuses on the role of immigrants in transforming the values and belief systems of working-class Americans in the throes of industrialization.

Alice Kessler-Harris, *Out to Work: A History of Wage-Earning Women in the United States* (1982). A comprehensive survey of women's increasing participation in the labor force. Kessler-Harris documents women's role in trade unions and the impact on family patterns and ideas about women's roles in American society.

Kenneth L. Kusmer, *A Ghetto Takes Shape, Black Cleveland, 1870–1930* (1976). A keen analysis of a long-standing African American community. Kusmer shows how blacks suffered downward mobility and increased segregation as their skilled jobs and small-business opportunities were given to European immigrants.

Lawrence H. Larsen, *The Rise of the Urban South* (1985). Studies of the changing South. In Larson's view, the true New South was the city, for relatively few had lived there before the late nineteenth century, but rural values remained vital, especially in religious life and voting patterns.

David F. Noble, *America by Design: Science, Technology and the Rise of Corporate Capitalism* (1977). A view of scientific advancement and its connections with the expanding economy. Noble shows how scientific breakthroughs were often created for, but especially adapted to, corporate purposes.

Dave Roediger and Franklin Rosemont, eds., *Haymarket Scrapbook* (1986). A large, beautifully illustrated book about the events and consequences of the Haymarket tragedy.

Roy Rosenzweig, *Eight Hours for What We Will: Workers and Leisure in an Industrial City, 1870–1920* (1983). Analyzes class and cultural conflicts over recreational space. This valuable book treats the city park as the arena for conflict over whether public community life should be uplifting (devoted to nature walks and concerts) or entertaining (for drinking, courting, and amusement).

Alan Trachtenberg, *The Incorporation of America: Culture and Society in the Gilded Age* (1982). One of the best and most readable overviews of the post–Civil War era. Trachtenberg devotes great care to describing the rise of the corporation to the defining institution of national life, and the reorientation of culture to reflect the new middle classes employed by the corporation.

ADDITIONAL BIBLIOGRAPHY

Science, Technology, and Industry

David A. Hounshell, *From the American System to Mass Production, 1800–1932* (1984)

Walter Licht, *Industrializing America: The Nineteenth Century* (1995)

A. J. Millard, *Edison and the Business of Innovation* (1990)

Leonard S. Reich, *The Making of American Industrial Research: Science and Business at G. E. and Bell, 1876–1926* (1985)

Business and the Economy

Wendy Gambler, *The Female Economy: The Millinery and Dressmaking Trades, 1860–1930* (1997)

Naomi R. Lamoreaux, *The Great Merger Movement in American Business, 1895–1904* (1985)

Pamela Walker Laird, *Advertising Progress: American Business and the Rise of Consumer Marketing* (1998)

Daniel Nelson, *Managers and Workers: Origins of the Factory System in the United States, 1880–1920* (1975)

Sarah Lyons Watts, *Order against Chaos: Business Culture and Labor Ideology in America, 1800–1915* (1991)

William G. Roy, *Socializing Capital: The Rise of the Large Industrial Corporation in America* (1997)

Olivier Zunz, *Making America Corporate, 1870–1920* (1990)

Working Class and Labor

Eric Arnesen, *Waterfront Workers of New Orleans: Race, Class, and Politics, 1863–1923* (1991)

John Bodnar, *Immigration and Industrialization: Ethnicity in an American Mill Town* (1977)

Lisa M. Fine, *The Souls of the Skyscraper: Female Clerical Workers in Chicago, 1870–1930* (1990)

David M. Katzman, *Seven Days a Week: Women and Domestic Service in Industrializing America* (1978)

David Montgomery, *The Fall of the House of Labor: The Workplace, the State, and American Labor Activism, 1865–1925* (1987)

Daniel T. Rodgers, *The Work Ethic in Industrial America, 1850–1920* (1978)

Robert E. Weir, *Beyond Labor's Veil: The Culture of the Knights of Labor* (1996)

The Industrial City

John S. Garner, ed., *The Midwest in American Architecture* (1991)

Dolores Hayden, *The Grand Domestic Revolution: A History of Feminist Designs for American Homes, Neighborhoods, and Cities* (1981)

Scott Molloy, *Trolley Wars: Streetcar Workers on the Line* (1996)

Mark H. Rose, *Cities of Light and Heat: Domesticating Gas and Electricity in Urban America* (1995)

Roy Rosenzweig and Elizabeth Blackmar, *The Park and the People: A History of Central Park* (1993)

John R. Stilgoe, *Borderland: Origins of the American Suburb, 1820–1939* (1988)

The New South

Edward L. Ayers, *The Promise of the New South* (1992)

Don Doyle, *New Men, New Cities, New South* (1990)

Jacquelyn D. Hall, et al., *Like a Family: The Making of a Southern Cotton Mill World* (1987)

Tara W. Hunter, *To 'Joy My Freedom: Southern Black Women's Lives and Labors after the Civil War* (1997)

Gerald D. Jaynes, *Branches without Roots: Genesis of the Black Working Class in the American South, 1862–1882* (1986)

Cathy McHugh, *Mill Family: The Labor System in the Southern Textile Industry, 1880–1915* (1988)

Karin A. Shapiro, *A New South Rebellion: The Battle Against Convict Labor in the Tennessee Coalfields, 1871–1896* (1998)

Society and Culture

Elaine S. Abelson, *When Ladies Go A-Thieving* (1989)

Stuart Blumin, *The Emergence of the Middle Class* (1989)

Sarah Burns, *Inventing the Modern Artists: Art and Culture in Gilded Age America* (1999)

Yong Chen, *Chinese San Francisco, 1850–1943* (2000)

Priscilla Ferguson Clement, *Growing Pains: Children in the Industrial Age, 1850–1890* (1997)

Steven Conn, *Museums and American Intellectual Life, 1876–1926* (1998)

Perry Duis, *Challenging Chicago: Coping with Everyday Life, 1837–1920* (1998)

Katherine C. Grier, *Culture and Comfort: Parlor Making and Middle-Class Identity, 1850–1930* (1988, 1997)

Judy Hilkey, *Character Is Capital: Success Manuals and Manhood in Gilded Age America* (1997)

John F. Kasson, *Amusing the Millions: Coney Island at the Turn of the Century* (1978)

Lawrence W. Levine, *Highbrow/Lowbrow: The Emergence of Cultural Hierarchy in America* (1988)

Patricia Marks, *Bicycles, Bangs, and Bloomers: The New Woman in the Popular Press* (1990)

Steven A. Riess, *City Games: The Evolution of American Urban Society and the Rise of Sports* (1989)

Barbara M. Solomon, *In the Company of Educated Women: A History of Women and Higher Education in America* (1985)

Biography

Robert V. Bruce, *Alexander Graham Bell and the Conquest of Solitude* (1973)

Helen Lefkowitz Horowitz, *The Power and Passion of M. Carey Thomas* (1994)

Stuart B. Kaufman, *Samuel Gompers and the Rise of the American Federation of Labor, 1884–1896* (1973)

Murray Klein, *The Life and Legend of Jay Gould* (1986)

Robert C. Twombly, *Louis Sullivan* (1986)

Michael Zuckerman, *Almost Chosen People: Oblique Biographies in the American Grain* (1993)

HISTORY ON THE INTERNET

http://trainweb.org/wnyrhs/historyFrame1Source1.htm

An interesting article appears at this site on the history of railroading in Western New York State in conjunction with the 1901 Pan-American Exposition and is sponsored by the Western New York Railway Historical Society.

http://www.fordham.edu/halsall/mod/1889carnegie.html

Andrew Carnegie's article containing the concepts of the Gospel of Wealth.

http://www.history.rochester.edu/fuels/tarbell/MAIN.HTM

The University of Rochester has posted this electronic version of Ida Tarbell's famous history of John D. Rockefeller's Standard Oil Company as it was printed in 1904 in *McClure's*.

http://www.financialhistory.org/photo-history.htm

A flattering family history of those immediately around John D. Rockefeller, Sr. including his parents, wife, and himself, this site was posted by the Museum of American Financial History located in New York City.

http://douglass.speech.nwu.edu/grad_a12.htm

This site contains Henry W. Grady's "The New South" speech given December 22, 1886 before the New England Society of New York.

Representing Chicago's History

Packingtown occupies a unique niche in Chicago's historical memory in that it came to represent the very essence of the city. As the poet Carl Sandburg wrote, Chicago was "the city of big shoulders," "hog butcher to the world." There was a certain grittiness and muscularity about the Midwestern metropolis that for generations delighted residents and intrigued visitors.

This image of Chicago began to circulate widely after the publication of Upton Sinclair's muckraking novel, *The Jungle.* Commissioned by a socialist newspaper to write a novel about immigrant workers in the meat packing houses, Sinclair collected a $500 advance and spent nearly two months researching the working and living conditions of Packingtown. In *The Jungle*, which was published in 1905, he described in vivid detail the blood and guts of the killing floors and the squalid neighborhood that adjoined the stock yards. His story revolved around a family of recent immigrants from Lithuania, and he provided close descriptions of their everyday life, down to the clothes they wore. Sinclair, a socialist himself, hoped to mobilize his readers to overthrow the system that created the grave social injustices that put so much strain on the immigrant community, but he succeeded mainly in buttressing a campaign for the regulation of the food industry. "I aimed at the public's heart," he lamented, "and by accident hit it in the stomach." Partly in a response to his best-selling novel, Congress passed the Pure Food and Drug Act and the Meat Inspection Act in 1906. But *The Jungle*, which within a few years sold more than 150,000 copies and was published in 17 languages, also enhanced Packingtown's reputation as symbol of the industrial city at its prime.

Despite Sinclair's intention, *The Jungle* helped to make Packingtown the focal point of Chicago history. By the time of its publication, the Union Stock Yards were already attracting tourists from all over the world. In 1893, more people went to see the killing floors than the famed world's fair, the Columbian Exposition. Ironically, Sinclair's vivid descriptions of the gore further piqued their curiosity about work and life in Packingtown. Well into the 1940s, the big packinghouses like Armour and Swift's maintained a special visitors entrance for tourists who continued to come by the trainload to see the way meat was mass produced.

Established in 1865, Chicago's Union Stockyards was processing more than 9 million livestock by the turn of the century. "The Yards" covered more than a square mile of land on the city's South Side. The livestock, brought in by trainloads, were held in pens until moved to the "killing floors" for slaughter. It wasn't a "pretty sight," as one Chicagoan remarked, but the meatpacking industry "put Chicago into contention as a world-class city." SOURCE: © CORBIS.

Chicagoans themselves nurtured this aspect of their history. They took pride in being the center of the meat packing industry, which, after steel, reigned for nearly a century as the city's largest industry. They described the Union Stock Yards as one of the wonders of the world. They even bragged about the notorious stench of the neighborhood. As one long-time member of the community noted, "the first memory" of anybody from Packingtown was "the overpowering smell from the packing houses and the fertilizer plants." Scratch any Chicagoan, a popular saying went, and some stockyard smell would come out. Contrary to Sinclair's intention to expose the degradation of Packingtown's residents, Chicagoans took pride in themselves as survivors of harsh conditions. However, by end of the twentieth century, few Chicagoans could nurture this memory.

Since its origin as a primarily German and Irish neighborhood in the 1860s and transformation into a community of Eastern European immigrants when the stockyards were at their peak, slaughtering 15 million livestock a year and employing 44,000 people, Packingtown underwent a series of dramatic changes. After

The Chicago Department of Cultural Affairs promoted the *Cows on Parade* exhibit by presenting the 320 cows on display as "works of art to be treasured" as well as "'worthy trophies of Chicago history." Chicago multimedia artist Joyce Martin Perz fashioned the cow shown here, "Jazz Chicago! Merci Henri!" as a tribute to the French modernist artist Henri Matisse. It was one of several cows featured in the "Mooseum Campus," which was located near the downtown. SOURCE: Photograph by AFP. © AFP/CORBIS.

World War II, as a consequence of the decentralization of the meat packing industry, the stock yards began a period of sharp decline. By the late 1950s, when some of the biggest firms closed their doors, new populations moved in. Meanwhile, postwar prosperity had encouraged the majority of Poles and Lithuanians to find cleaner jobs in other industries and to flee to the suburbs. Mexicans and African Americans took their place and stayed. At one time there were a dozen Polish-American Catholic parishes; after 1971, when the Union Stock Yards finally shut down, the parishes that remained were Mexican. In the 1980s, the City of Chicago, partnering with the Back of the Yards Council, a community organization founded in the late 1930s, launched a redevelopment plan that laid the foundation for the Stockyards Industrial Park. The new complex of small businesses and retail stores employed about one-third the number of workers as the packing houses and retained a link to the past in name only. All that remained of the scenes made famous by Upton Sinclair and celebrated by Chicagoans themselves was the limestone arch that marks the entryway to the old stockyards complex. By the time Chicago designated the old stone gate as an official landmark in 1972, only the memories of old-timers kept this chapter of Chicago's history alive.

By the end of the twentieth century, a new generation of Chicagoans were poised to celebrate not the city's gritty past but its future in finance, service, and tourist industries. In 1999, the city sponsored "Cows on Parade," a public art project that brought to downtown sidewalks more than 200 "cows" made of a fiberglass-polyester mixture and painted in a rainbow of colors and a variety of styles. One cow perched atop a skateboard, for example, another was on skis. The cows had cute names, such as Rhinestone Cowgirl, Cowbelle de Fruits, and Wow Cow. Local businesses and art patrons vied to purchase a cow of their own for a standard fee of $3,500, and at the end of the summer they could either take home their trophy or donate it to a public auction for charity. "Cows on Parade" enchanted children, tourists, and the thousands of office workers who filled the downtown skyscrapers—including the Sears Tower, which, since 1974, stood as the city's new source of pride as the tallest building in the nation.

A few Chicagoans, however, complained that "Cows on Parade" had supplanted the stockyards as the city's chief symbol and, in the process, obliterated much of its history. "Chicago seems to be erasing its gritty, less-glitzy past," one local critic observed. "The hog (and cattle) butcher to the world," he added, "has become a Technicolor, DisneyQuest, chrome-and-glass kinda town." Another detractor refused to relinquish the time-tested symbol, insisting that the "true monument to Chicago's past" was not the whimsical cows currently on display but "a bull named Sherman." Named after one of the founders of the Union Stock yard, John B. Sherman, this rugged bust of the prize-winning steer still tops the old stone gate.

But what remains of the historical memory of Chicago as the nation's premier industrial city and community of hard-working Eastern European immigrants?

During the summer of 1999, while upscale Chicago basked in the publicity garnered from "Cows on Parade," the new residents of what had once been Packingtown displayed their own cows, a trio of colorfully painted figures contributed not by the big-name artists who crafted the downtown versions but by local schoolchildren and community groups. Few Chicagoans from other parts of the city bothered to visit them. "And there they sit," as one nostalgic observer recorded at the time: "No tourists or cameras. Just three forgotten cows marking Chicago's forgotten past." ■

TWENTY

COMMONWEALTH AND EMPIRE

1870–1900

Fred Pansing, *Simpson and Schley Leading the Fleet into New York Harbor, August 20, 1898.*
SOURCE: © Museum of the City of New York/CORBIS (NY001109).

The Cooperative Commonwealth

EDWARD BELLAMY'S *LOOKING BACKWARD* (1888), THE CENTURY'S best-selling novel after Harriet Beecher Stowe's *Uncle Tom's Cabin*, tells the story of a young man who awakens in the year 2000 after a sleep lasting more than 100 years. He is surprised to learn that Americans had solved their major problems. Poverty, crime, war, taxes, air pollution—even housework—no longer exist. Nor are there politicians, capitalists, bankers, or lawyers. Most amazing, gone is the great social division between the powerful rich and the suffering poor. In the year 2000 everyone lives in material comfort, happily and harmoniously. No wonder Bellamy's hero shudders at the thought of returning to the late nineteenth century, a time of "worldwide bloodshed, greed and tyranny."

Community and cooperation are the key concepts in Bellamy's utopian tale. The nation's businesses, including farms and factories, have been given over to the collective ownership of the people. Elected officials now plan the production and distribution of goods for the common well-being. With great efficiency, they even manage huge department stores and warehouses full of marvelous manufactured goods and oversee majestic apartment complexes with modern facilities for cooking, dining, and laundering. To get the necessary work done, an industrial army enlists all adult men and women, but automated machinery has eliminated most menial tasks. The workday is only four hours; vacations extend to six months of each year. At forty-five everyone retires to pursue hobbies, sports, and culture.

Bellamy envisioned his technological utopia as promoting the "highest possible physical, as well as mental, development for everyone." There was nothing fantastic in this plan, the author insisted. It simply required Americans to share equally the abundant resources of their land. If the nation's citizens actually lived up to their democratic ideals, Bellamy declared, the United States would become a "cooperative commonwealth," that is, a nation governed by the people for their common welfare.

Bellamy, a journalist and writer of historical fiction from Chicopee Falls, Massachusetts, moved thousands of his readers to action. His most ardent fans endorsed his program for a "new nation" and formed the Nationalist movement, which by the early 1890s reached an apex of 165 clubs. Terence V. Powderly of the Knights of Labor declared himself a Nationalist. Many leaders of the woman suffrage movement also threw in their support. They endorsed *Looking Backward*'s depiction of marriage as a union of "perfect equals" and admired Bellamy's sequel, *Equality* (1897), which showed how women might become "absolutely free agents" by ending their financial dependence on men.

During the 1890s Bellamy's disciples actually attempted to create new communities along the lines set forth in *Looking Backward*. The best known and longest lasting of these settlements was established in Point Loma, California, in 1897. Situated on 330 acres, with avenues winding through gardens and orchards newly planted with groves of eucalyptus trees, Point Loma was known for its physical beauty. Many young married couples chose to live in small bungalows, which were scattered throughout the colony's grounds; others opted for private rooms in a large communal building. Either way, they all met twice daily to share meals and usually spent their leisure hours together. On the ocean's edge the residents constructed an outdoor amphitheater and staged plays and concerts.

The colony's founder, Katherine Tingley, described Point Loma as "a practical illustration of the possibility of developing a higher type of humanity." No one earned wages, but all 500 residents lived comfortably. They dressed simply in clothes manufactured by the community's women. The majority of the men worked in agriculture. They conducted horticultural experiments that yielded new types of avocados and tropical fruits and eventually produced over half of the community's food supply. Children, who slept in a special dormitory from the time they reached school age, enjoyed an outstanding education. They excelled in the fine arts, including music and drama, and often demonstrated their talents to audiences in nearby San Diego.

The Point Loma community never met all its expenses, but with the help of donations from admirers across the country it remained solvent for decades. Baseball entrepreneur Albert Spalding, who lived there during his retirement,

Point Loma

helped make up the financial deficit. As late as the 1950s the community still had some seventy-five members living on about 100 acres of land.

Even relatively successful cooperative communities such as Point Loma, however, could not bring about the changes that Bellamy hoped to see, and he knew it. Only a mobilization of citizens nationwide could overturn the existing hierarchies and usher in the egalitarian order depicted in *Looking Backward*. Without such a rigorous challenge, the economic and political leadership that had been emerging since the Civil War would continue to consolidate its power and become even further removed from popular control.

The last quarter of the nineteenth century saw just such a challenge, producing what one historian calls "a moment of democratic promise." Ordinary citizens sought to renew the older values of community through farm and labor organizations as well as philanthropic and charitable societies. They could not clearly see, however, that the fate of the nation depended increasingly on events beyond its territorial boundaries. Business leaders and politicians had proposed their own vision of the future: an American empire extending to far distant lands.

KEY TOPICS

- The growth of federal and state governments and the consolidation of the modern two-party system

- The development of mass protest movements

- Economic and political crisis in the 1890s

- The United States as a world power

- The Spanish-American War

TOWARD A NATIONAL GOVERNING CLASS

The basic structure of government changed dramatically in the last quarter of the nineteenth century. Mirroring the fast-growing economy, public administration expanded at all levels—municipal, county, state, and federal—and took on greater responsibility for regulating society, especially market and property relations. Whereas most political theorists continued to advise that the best government is the one that governs least, governments began to do much more than simply maintain order.

This expansion offered ample opportunities for politicians who were eager to compete against one another for control of the new mechanisms of power. Political campaigns, especially those staged for the presidential elections, became mass spectacles, and votes became precious commodities. The most farsighted politicians attempted to rein in the growing corruption and to promote both efficiency and professionalism in the expanding structures of government.

The Growth of Government

Before the Civil War, local governments attended mainly to the promotion and regulation of trade and relied on private enterprise to supply vital services such as fire protection and water supply. As cities became more responsible for their residents' well-being, they introduced professional police and firefighting forces and began to finance school systems, public libraries, and parks. Municipal ownership and administration of basic services became so common that by the end of the century only nine of the nation's fifty largest cities still depended on private corporations for their water supplies.

This expansion demanded huge increases in local taxation. Boston, for example, spent five times more per resident in 1875 than it had just thirty years earlier, and its municipal debt rose from $784,000 to more than $27 million. The city now paid the salaries of many civil servants, including a growing class of sanitary engineers. By 1880 one of every eight New York voters appeared on a government payroll.

At the national level, mobilization for the Civil War and Reconstruction had demanded an unprecedented degree of coordination, and the federal government continued to expand under the weight of new tasks and responsibilities. Federal revenues also skyrocketed, from $257 million in 1878 to $567 million in 1900. The administrative bureaucracy also grew dramatically, from 50,000 employees in 1871 to 100,000 only a decade later.

The modern apparatus of departments, bureaus, and cabinets took shape amid this upswing. The Department of Agriculture was established in 1862 to provide information to farmers and to consumers of farm products. The Department of the Interior, which had been created in 1849, grew into the largest and most important federal department after the Post Office. It came to comprise more than twenty agencies, including the Bureau of Indian Affairs, the U.S. Geological Survey, and the Bureau of Territorial and International Affairs. The Department of the Treasury, responsible for collecting federal taxes and customs as well as printing money and stamps, grew from 4,000 employees in 1873 to nearly 25,000 in 1900. The Pension Act of 1890 made virtually every Union army veteran and his dependents eligible for benefits; within a decade the Veterans Bureau became known as "the largest executive bureau in the world," employing nearly 60,000 men and women.

The nation's first independent regulatory agency took charge of the nation's most important industry. The Interstate Commerce Commission (ICC) was created in 1887 to bring order to the growing patchwork of state laws concerning railroads. The five-member commission appointed by the president approved freight and passenger rates set by the railroads. The ICC could take public testimony on possible violations, examine company records, and generally oversee enforcement of the law.

This first regulatory agency set a precedent for future regulation of trade as well as for positive government—that is, for the intervention of the government into the affairs of private enterprise. It also marked a shift in the balance of power from the states to the federal government.

The Machinery of Politics

Only gradually did Republicans and Democrats adapt to the demands of governmental expansion. The Republican Party continued to run on its Civil War record, pointing to its achievements in reuniting the nation and in passing new reform legislation. Democrats, by contrast, sought to reduce the influence of the federal government, slash expenditures, repeal legislation, and protect states' rights. While Republicans held on to their long-time constituencies, Democrats gathered support from southern white voters and immigrants newly naturalized in the North. But neither party commanded a clear majority of votes until the century drew to a close.

Presidents in the last quarter of the century— Rutherford B. Hayes (1877–81), James A. Garfield (1881), Chester A. Arthur (1881–85), Grover Cleveland (1885–89), Benjamin Harrison (1889–93), and Cleveland again (1893–97)—did not espouse a clear philosophy of government. They willingly yielded power to Congress and the state legislatures. Only 1 percent of the popular vote separated the presidential candidates in three of five elections between 1876 and 1892. Congressional races were equally tight, less than 2 percentage points separating total votes for Democratic and Republican candidates in all but one election in the decade before 1888. Democrats usually held a majority in the House and Republicans a majority in the Senate, but neither party had sufficient strength to govern effectively. One result was that Congress passed little legislation before 1890.

One major political issue of the late nineteenth century was the tariff. First instituted in 1789 to raise revenue for the young republic, the tariff imposed a fee on imported goods, especially manufactured commodities. Soon its major purpose became the protection of the nation's "infant industries" from foreign competition. Manufacturing regions, especially the Northeast, favored a protective policy, while agricultural regions like the South opposed high tariffs as unfair to farmers who had to pay the steep fees on imported necessities. Democrats, with a stronghold among southern voters, argued for sharp reductions in the tariff as a way to save the rural economy and to give a boost to workers. Republicans, who represented mainly business interests, raised tariffs to new levels on a wide array of goods during the Civil War and retained high tariffs as long as they held power.

Although their platforms encompassed broad national issues, none more important than the tariff, both political parties operated essentially as state or local organizations. Successful politicians responded primarily to the particular concerns of their constituents. To please local voters, Democrats and Republicans repeatedly crosscut each other by taking identical positions on controversial issues.

Political campaigns were great spectacles in the late nineteenth century. Candidates of both parties pursued swing voters furiously. "We work through one campaign," quipped one candidate, "take a bath and start in on the next." Election paraphernalia—leaflets or pamphlets, banners, hats, flags, buttons, inscribed playing cards, or clay pipes featuring a likeness of a candidate's face or the party symbol—became a major expense for both parties. Partisans embraced the Democratic donkey or the Republican elephant as symbols of party fidelity. And voters did turn out. During the last quarter of the century, participation in presidential elections peaked at nearly 80 percent of those eligible to vote. Thousands, in fact, voted several times on any given election day; voters who had died, or had never lived, also miraculously cast ballots.

The rising costs of maintaining local organizations and orchestrating mammoth campaigns drove party leaders to seek ever-larger sources of revenue. Winners often seized and added to the "spoils" of office through an elaborate system of payoffs. Legislators who supported government subsidies for railroad corporations, for instance, commonly received stock in return and sometimes cash bribes. At the time, few politicians or business leaders regarded these practices as unethical.

At the local level, powerful bosses and political machines dominated both parties. Democrats William Marcy Tweed of New York's powerful political organization, Tammany Hall, and Michael "Hinky Dink" Kenna of Chicago specialized in giving municipal jobs to loyal voters and holiday food baskets to their families. Tweed's machine wooed working-class voters by expanding city services in their neighborhoods and even by staging major sporting events or entertainments for the Irish Americans and German Americans who made up over half of New York City's population. Hundreds of smaller political machines ruled cities and rural courthouses through a combination of "boodle" (bribe money) and personal favors.

A large number of federal jobs, meanwhile, changed hands each time the presidency passed from one party to another. More than 50 percent of all federal jobs were

This wooden noisemaker was designed for Grover Cleveland's presidential campaign in 1892. Pursuing the voters, political campaigners devised ingenious signs, buttons, and other miscellaneous novelties for supporters to display, especially at public demonstrations. When shaken vigorously, noisemakers literally demanded the attention of bystanders.

SOURCE: Cleveland campaign noisemaker, 1892. Museum of American Political Life, University of Hartford. Photo by Sally Andersen-Bruce.

patronage positions—nearly 56,000 in 1881—jobs that could be awarded to loyal supporters as part of the "spoils" of the winner. Observers estimated that decisions about congressional patronage filled one-third of all legislators' time. No wonder Bellamy's utopian community operated without politicians and political parties.

One Politician's Story

A typical politician of the age was James Garfield, the nation's twentieth president. Born in a frontier Ohio log cabin in 1831, Garfield briefly worked as a canal boat driver, an experience he later exploited as proof of his humble origins. A Civil War hero—he fought at Shiloh, was honored for gallantry at Chickamauga, and was a major general when he took a seat in Congress in 1863— the Ohio legislator carefully prepared his move into the national political arena.

While serving in Congress, Garfield seemed at first committed to social reform. He introduced a bill to cre-

ate a Department of Education, arguing that public education would prove the best stepping-stone to equality. He denounced his own Republican Party for allowing corruption to flourish during Ulysses S. Grant's administration. The nation's "next great fight," he insisted, would pit the people against the corporations.

With the failure of Reconstruction, Garfield shifted his stance and began to espouse more conservative views. Nearly defeated in a Democratic congressional landslide in 1874, he concluded that "the intelligence of the average American citizen" fell short of the demands of the democratic system. As a result, he came out against universal suffrage. Garfield now looked to the probusiness faction of the Republican Party as a vehicle for realizing his personal ambition. After six years of shrewd maneuvering, trading votes and favors to build his reputation, Garfield became the party's candidate for the 1880 presidential election. In a mediocre race with no outstanding issues, Garfield won by less than 40,000 popular votes out of 9 million cast.

Garfield the idealist had grown into Garfield the machine politician and lackluster president. He had already shown himself indecisive and even indifferent to governing when a frustrated patronage seeker shot him just 200 days after his inauguration. Like other presidents of his era, Garfield assumed that the nation's chief executive served as his party's titular leader and played mainly a ceremonial role in office.

The Spoils System and Civil Service Reform

As early as 1865, Republican representative Thomas A. Jenckes of Rhode Island proposed a bill for civil service reform. Congress feared that such a measure would hamper candidates in their relentless pursuit of votes. President Hayes took up the cause, introducing a few reforms in the New York Customhouse and federal post offices, but Congress again refused to join in a major reform effort. Finally, a group consisting of mainly professors, newspaper editors, lawyers, and ministers organized the Civil Service Reform Association and enlisted Democratic senator George H. Pendleton to sponsor reform legislation.

In January 1883, a bipartisan congressional majority passed the Pendleton Civil Service Reform Act. This measure allowed the president to create, with Senate approval, a three-person commission to draw up a set of guidelines for executive and legislative appointments. The commission established a system of standards for various federal jobs and instituted "open, competitive examinations for testing the fitness of applicants for public service." The Pendleton Act also barred political candidates from soliciting campaign contributions from government workers. Patronage did not disappear, but public service did improve.

Many departments of the federal government took on a professional character similar to that which doctors, lawyers, and scholars were imposing on their fields through regulatory societies such as the American Medical Association and the American Historical Association. At the same time, the federal judiciary began to act more aggressively to establish the parameters of government. With the Circuit Courts of Appeals Act of 1891, Congress granted the U.S. Supreme Court the right to review all cases at will.

Despite these reforms, many observers still viewed government as a reign of outsiders, people pulling the levers of the party matchinery or spending money to influence important decisions. Edward Bellamy agreed. He advised Americans to organize their communities for the specific purpose of wresting control of government from the hands of politicians.

FARMERS AND WORKERS ORGANIZE THEIR COMMUNITIES

Farmers and workers began to organize in the late 1860s and succeeded in building powerful national organizations to oppose, as a Nebraska newspaper put it, "the wealthy and powerful classes who want the control of government to plunder the people." It was clear by that time that the nation's political agenda was shifting from the issues raised by the Civil War and Reconstruction to the increasingly tense relationship between capital and labor as well as between work and wages. This relationship became increasingly strained as industrial employers, responding to a series of business downturns, not only increased their scale of production and formed cartels but moved aggressively to cut labor costs. In the process, many of the agreements made with the craft unions fell by the wayside. Meanwhile, farmers in the West and South saw prices for their crops drop while rates for credit and transportation rose.

The railroad, as the most important industry in the nineteenth century and at the peak of its own "system building" into a national network, played a large part in generating protest from workers and farmers. By the end of the century the communities whose livelihoods depended directly or indirectly on the railroads presented the most significant challenge to the political system since the Civil War—the Populist movement.

The Grange

In 1867 farmers on the Great Plains formed the Patrons of Husbandry for their own "social, intellectual, and moral improvement." Led by Oliver H. Kelley, an em-

ployee of the Department of Agriculture, this fraternal society resembled the secretive Masonic order. Whole families staffed a complex array of offices engaged in mysterious rituals involving passwords, flags, songs, and costumes. In many farming communities, the headquarters of the local chapter, known as the Grange (a word for "farm"), became the center of social activity, the site of summer dinners and winter dances.

The Grange movement spread rapidly, especially in areas where farmers were experiencing their greatest hardships. Great Plains farmers barely survived the blizzards, grasshopper infestations, and droughts of the early 1870s. Meanwhile, farmers throughout the trans-Mississippi West and the South watched the prices for grains and cotton fall year by year in the face of growing competition from producers in Canada, Australia, Argentina, Russia, and India. In the hope of improving their condition through collective action, many farmers joined their local Grange. The Patrons of Husbandry soon swelled to more than 1.5 million members.

Grangers blamed hard times on a band of "thieves in the night"—especially railroads and banks—that

The symbols chosen by Grange artists represented their faith that all social value could be traced to honest labor and most of all to the work of the entire farm family. The hardworking American required only the enlightenment offered by the Grange to build a better community.

SOURCE: *Kingfisher Reformer*, May 3, 1894, Library of Congress.

charged exorbitant fees for service. They fumed at American farm equipment manufacturers, such as Cyrus McCormick, who sold farm equipment more cheaply in Europe than in the United States. To purchase equipment and raw materials, farmers borrowed money and accrued debts averaging twice that of Americans not engaged in business.

Grangers mounted their greatest assault on the railroad corporations. By bribing state legislators, railroads enjoyed a highly discriminatory rate policy, commonly charging farmers more to ship their crops short distances than over long hauls. In 1874 several midwestern states responded to pressure and passed a series of so-called Granger laws establishing maximum shipping rates. Grangers also complained to their lawmakers about the price-fixing policies of grain wholesalers, warehousers, and operators of grain elevators. In 1873 the Illinois legislature passed a Warehouse Act establishing maximum rates for storing grains. Chicago firms challenged the legality of this measure, but in *Munn* v. *Illinois* (1877) the Supreme Court upheld the law, ruling that states had the power to regulate private property in the public interest.

Determined to buy less and produce more, Grangers created a vast array of cooperative enterprises for both the purchase of supplies and the marketing of crops. They established local grain elevators, set up retail stores, and even manufactured some of their own farm machinery. As early as 1872, the Iowa Grange claimed to control one-third of the grain elevators and warehouses in the state. In other states Grangers ran banks as well as fraternal life and fire insurance companies.

The deepening depression of the late 1870s wiped out most of these cooperative programs. By 1880 Grange membership had fallen to 100,000. Meanwhile, the Supreme Court overturned most of the key legislation regulating railroads. Despite these setbacks, the Patrons of Husbandry had nonetheless promoted a model of cooperation that would remain at the heart of agrarian protest movements until the end of the century.

The Farmers' Alliance

Agrarian unrest did not end with the downward turn of the Grange but instead moved south. In the 1880s farmers organized in communities where both poverty and the crop-lien system prevailed (see Chapter 17). New South newspaper writers and politicians advised farmers to trim expenditures and to diversify out of cotton into other crops. But with household budgets falling from $50 to as low as $10 a year, southern farmers had no leeway to cut expenses. And the cost of shipping perishable crops made diversification untenable despite the low price of cotton. In response to these conditions, Texas farmers—proclaiming "Equal Rights to All, Special Privileges to None"—began to organize.

In 1889, several regional organizations joined forces to create the National Farmers' Alliance and Industrial Union. Within a year the combined movement claimed 3 million white members. Separately, the Colored Farmers' Alliance and Cooperative Union grew from its beginnings in Texas and Arkansas in 1888 and quickly spread across the South to claim more than a million members of its own. These parallel organizations reflected both increasing racial segregation and the racism of white farmers.

In the South, the falling price of cotton underscored the need for action, and farmers readily translated their anger into intense loyalty to the one organization pledged to improve their lot. With more than 500 chapters in Texas alone, and cooperative stores complemented by the cooperative merchandising of crops, the Southern Farmers' Alliance became a viable alternative to the capitalist marketplace—if only temporarily.

The Northern Farmers' Alliance took shape in the Great Plains states, drawing upon larger organizations in Minnesota, Nebraska, Iowa, Kansas, and the Dakota Territory. During 1886 and 1887, summer drought followed winter blizzards and ice storms, reducing wheat harvests by one-third on the Plains. Locusts and cinch bugs ate much of the rest. As if this were not enough, prices on the world market fell sharply for what little remained. Many farmers left the land; western Kansas lost nearly half its population by the early 1890s. Skilled agitators played upon these hardships—especially the overpowering influence of railroads over the farmers' lives—boosting the alliance movement. By 1890 the Kansas Alliance alone claimed 130,000 members.

Grangers had pushed legislation that would limit the salaries of public officials, provide public school students with books at little or no cost, establish a program of teacher certification, and widen the admissions policies of the new state colleges. But only rarely did they put up candidates for office. In comparison, the Farmers' Alliance had few reservations about taking political stands or entering electoral races. At the end of the 1880s, regional alliances drafted campaign platforms demanding state ownership of the railroads, a graduated income tax, lower tariffs, restriction of land ownership to citizens, and easier access to money through "the free and unlimited coinage of silver." In several states, alliance candidates for local and state office won elections. By 1890 the alliances had gained control of the Nebraska legislature and held the balance of power in Minnesota and South Dakota.

Workers Search for Power

The depression following the Panic of 1873, which produced 25 percent unemployment in many cities, served as a catalyst for workers to organize their communities. In New York City, a group marched to City Hall to present a petition on behalf of 10,000 workers who were without jobs or homes. Turned back repeatedly by the police, the organizers decided to stage a rally to advertise their demand for a steady job at a living wage. City officials refused to grant a permit. When 7,000 working-class men and women showed up on January 13, 1874, a battalion of 1,600 police—nearly two-thirds of the city's force—rushed into the crowd and began striking out indiscriminately with their clubs. This incident, known as the Tompkins Square Riot, inaugurated an era of unprecedented labor conflict and violence.

The railroad, which played a key role in the industrial and urban transformations following the Civil War, became the focus of protests by workers and farmers alike. Within the few months after the Panic of 1873, workers struck so many times that the *New York Railroad Gazette* complained, "Strikes are . . . as much a disease of the body politic as the measles or indigestion are of our physical organization." Although most of these strikes ended in failure, they revealed the readiness of workers to spell out their grievances in a direct and dramatic manner. They also suggested how strongly many townspeople, including merchants who depended on workers' wages, would support local strikes and turn them into community uprisings.

Despite these warnings, the railroad corporations were unprepared for the Great Uprising of 1877, the first nationwide strike. The strike began in Martinsburg, West Virginia, where workers protesting a 10 percent wage cut uncoupled all engines. No trains would run, they promised, until wages were restored. Within a few days, the strike had spread along the railroad routes to New York, Buffalo, Pittsburgh, Chicago, Kansas City, and San Francisco. In all these cities, workers in various industries and masses of the unemployed formed angry crowds, defying armed militia ordered to disperse them by any means. Young men and boys gathered at railroad crossings to throw stones at the trains that ran right through the heart of their neighborhoods. Angry at these ironhorse intruders, the crowds halted train traffic, sometimes pulling up entire rails and seizing carloads of food for hungry families. Energized by the activity, workers in St. Louis even took over the city's administration.

The rioting persisted for nearly a week, spurring business leaders to call for the deportation, arrest, or execution of strike leaders. Law and Order Leagues swept through working-class neighborhoods and broke up union meetings. Fearing a "national insurrection," President Hayes set a precedent by calling in the U.S. Army to suppress the strike. In Pittsburgh, federal troops equipped with semiautomatic machine guns fired into a crowd and killed more than twenty people. By the time the strike finally ended, more than 100 people were dead.

Memories of the Uprising of 1877 haunted business and government officials for decades, prompting the creation of the National Guard and the construction of armories in working-class neighborhoods. Workers also drew lessons from the events. Before the end of the century, more than 6 million workers would strike in industries ranging from New England textiles to southern tobacco factories to western mines. The labor movement also expanded its sphere of influence to the halls of city government. While the Farmers' Alliance put up candidates in the South and Plains states, workers

The Great Uprising of 1877, which began as a strike of railroad workers, spread rapidly to communities along the railroad routes. Angry crowds defied the armed militia and the vigilantes hired to disperse them. In Philadelphia, for example, strikers set fire to the downtown, destroying many buildings before federal troops were brought in to stop them. More than a hundred people died before the strike ended, and the railroad corporations suffered about $10 million loss in property.

SOURCE: Contemporary engraving. The Granger Collection, New York (0008654).

launched labor parties in dozens of industrial towns and cities.

In New York City, popular economist and land reformer Henry George, with the ardent support of the city's Central Labor Council and the Knights of Labor, put himself forward in 1886 as candidate for mayor on the United Labor Party ticket. His best-selling book *Progress and Poverty* (1879), advocated a sweeping tax on all property to generate enough revenue to allow all Americans to live in comfort. Especially popular among Irish Americans, who had seen their homeland swallowed up by British landlords, George's ideas also appealed to German Americans, who, with the Irish, made up the heart of the city's labor movement. George called upon "all honest citizens" to join in independent political action as "the only hope of exposing and breaking up the extortion and speculation by which a standing army of professional politicians corrupt the people whom they plunder."

Tammany Hall delivered many thousands of the ballots cast for George straight into the Hudson River. Nevertheless, George managed to finish a respectable second with 31 percent of the vote, running ahead of young patrician Theodore Roosevelt. Although his campaign ended in defeat, George had issued a stern warning to the entrenched politicians. Equally important, his impressive showing encouraged labor groups in other cities to form parties calling for the defeat of the "power of aggregated wealth." The results, in local elections around the country, stunned Republicans and Democrats alike.

In the late 1880s labor parties won seats on many city councils and state legislatures. The Milwaukee People's Party elected the mayor, a state senator, six assemblymen, and one member of Congress. In smaller industrial towns where workers outnumbered the middle classes, labor parties did especially well. In Rochester, New Hampshire, with a population of only 7,000, workers, mainly shoemakers, elected a majority slate, from city council to mayor.

Women Build Alliances

Women helped build both the labor and agrarian protest movements while campaigning for their own rights as citizens. Like woman suffrage leader Elizabeth Cady Stanton, many women believed that "government based on caste and class privilege cannot stand." In its place, as Bellamy predicted in *Equality*, would arise a new cooperative order in which women would be "absolutely free agents in the disposition of themselves."

Women in the Knights of Labor endorsed the order's political planks while putting forth their own set of demands. In 1886 sixteen women attending the national convention lobbied for the creation of a special department "to investigate the abuses of which our sex is subjected by unscrupulous employers, to agitate the principles which our Order teaches of equal pay for equal work and the abolition of child labor." The delegates accepted the plan with little dissent and appointed knit-goods worker Leonora M. Barry general investigator. With perhaps 65,000 women members at its peak, the Knights ran day-care centers for the children of wage-earning mothers and occasionally even set up bakery cooperatives to reduce the drudgery of cooking.

Women made a similar mark on farmers' organizations. The Patrons of Husbandry issued a charter to a local chapter only when women were well represented on its rolls, and in the 1870s delegates to its conventions routinely gave speeches endorsing woman suffrage and even dress reform. The Farmers' Alliance continued this policy, enjoining women to assist their fathers, husbands, or sons in agitation efforts. Whole families shared in social programs, such as songfests on Sunday afternoons, lecture series, and contests featuring antimonopoly games. In both the Northern and Southern Alliances, women made up perhaps one-quarter of the membership, and several advanced through the ranks to become leading speakers and organizers. Mary E. Lease, who achieved lasting fame for advising farmers to raise less corn and more hell, vividly expressed their sense of purpose. "Ours is a grand, a holy mission," she proclaimed, "to drive from our land and forever abolish the triune monopoly of land, money, and transportation."

Women in both the Knights of Labor and the Farmers' Alliance found their greatest leader in Frances E. Willard, the most famous woman of the nineteenth century. Willard assumed that women, who guarded their families' physical and spiritual welfare, would, if granted the right to vote, extend their influence throughout the

Strikes by State, 1880 Most strikes after the Uprising of 1877 could be traced to organized trades, concentrated in the manufacturing districts of the Northeast and Midwest.

SOURCE: Carville Earle, *Geographical Inquiry and American Historical Problems* (Stanford, CA: Stanford University Press, 1992).

Susan B. Anthony and Elizabeth Cady Stanton, on the platform, founded the National Woman Suffrage Association in 1869. They found many supporters for their cause among the Knights of Labor, the Farmers' Alliance, and the Woman's Christian Temperance Union.

SOURCE: Contemporary colored engraving. The Granger Collection, New York (4E26.32).

whole society. From 1878 until her death in 1897, Willard presided over the Woman's Christian Temperance Union (WCTU), at the time the largest organization of women in the world, and encouraged her numerous followers to "do everything." She mobilized nearly 1 million women to, in her words, "make the whole world HOMELIKE." WCTU members preached total abstinence from the consumption of alcohol, but they also worked to reform the prison system, eradicate prostitution, and eliminate the wage system. Willard went so far as to draw up plans for a new system of government whereby all offices, right up to the presidency, would be shared jointly by men and women. She also became a member of the Knights of Labor and endorsed the platform of the Farmers' Alliance.

Under Willard's leadership, the WCTU grew into the major force behind the campaign for woman suffrage, far surpassing the American Woman Suffrage Association and the National Woman Suffrage Association. By 1890, when the two rival suffrage associations merged to form the National American Woman Suffrage Association, the WCTU had already pushed the heart of the suffrage campaign into the Great Plains states and the West. In Iowa, Nebraska, Colorado, and especially Kansas, agitation for the right to vote provided a political bridge among women organized in the WCTU, Farmers' Alliance, Knights of Labor, and various local suffrage societies.

In 1891 representatives from various women's organizations formed the National Women's Alliance. The founding convention called for "full equality of the sexes," "harmony and unity of action among the Sisterhood" of the nation, "prevention of war," and the rejection of alcohol, tobacco, and narcotics as injurious to health. The organization's newspaper, the *Farmer's Wife,* spelled out basic principles in epigrams like "Give our women encouragement and victory is yours" and "Put 1,000 women lecturers in the field and the revolution is here."

Although women lecturers such as Kansas's Annie Diggs were outstanding crowd pleasers, women in the Knights of Labor and the Farmers' Alliance failed to gain equality within the protest movements. Most political parties endorsed by these organizations included planks calling for equal wages for equal work but refused to endorse woman suffrage. Only in Colorado did local third-party candidates support the 1893 campaign that secured women's right to vote in that state. In the Southern Alliance, women themselves opposed women's enfranchisement. It was, however, an increasing emphasis on electoral politics that effectively placed voteless women on the sidelines.

Farmer-Labor Unity

In December 1890 the Farmers' Alliance called a meeting at Ocala, Florida, to press for a national third-party movement. This was a risky proposition because the Southern Alliance hoped to capture control of the Democratic Party, whereas many farmers in the Plains states voted Republican. In some areas, however, the Farmers' Alliance established its own parties, put up full slates of candidates for local elections, won majorities in state legislatures, and even sent a representative to Congress. Reviewing these successes, delegates at Ocala decided to push ahead and form a national party, and they appealed to other farm, labor, and reform organizations to join them. Edward Bellamy advised his followers to take advantage of "the largest opportunity yet presented in the history of our movement" and support the third-party effort.

The time had come, the Alliance announced, "to establish the moral solidarity of the farmer and toiler societies." In February 1892, representatives from the Farmers' Alliance, the Knights of Labor, and the National Colored Farmers' Alliance, among others, met in St. Louis under a broad banner that read: "We do not ask for sympathy or pity. We ask for justice." The 1,300 delegates adopted a platform for the new People's Party. It called for government ownership of railroads, banks, and telegraph lines, prohibition of large land-holding companies, a graduated income tax, an eight-hour workday, and restriction of immigration. The People's Party convened again in Omaha in July 1892 and nominated James Baird Weaver of Iowa for president and, to please the South, the Confederate veteran James Field from Virginia for vice president.

The Populists, as supporters of the People's Party styled themselves, quickly became a major factor in American politics. In some southern states, Populists cooperated with local Republicans in sponsoring "pepper and salt" state and local tickets that put black and white candidates on a single slate. To hold their voters, some Democrats adopted the Populist platform wholesale; others resorted to massive voter fraud and intimidation. In the West, Democrats threw their weight behind the Populist ticket mainly to defeat the ruling Republicans.

Although Democrat Grover Cleveland regained the presidency in 1892 (he had previously served from 1885 to 1889), Populists scored a string of local victories. In Idaho, Nevada, Colorado, Kansas, and North Dakota, they won 50 percent or more of the vote. Nationwide, they elected three governors, ten representatives to Congress, and five senators. The national ticket received more than 1 million votes (8.5 percent of the total) and 22 electoral college votes—the only time since the Civil War that a third party had received any electoral votes. Despite poor showings among urban workers east of the Mississippi, Populists looked forward to the next round of state elections in 1894. But the great test would come with the presidential election in 1896.

THE CRISIS OF THE 1890s

Populist Ignatius Donnelly wrote in the preface to his pessimistic novel *Caesar's Column* (1891) that industrial society appears to be a "wretched failure" to "the great mass of mankind." On the road to disaster rather than to the egalitarian community that Bellamy had envisioned, "the rich, as a rule, hate the poor; and the poor are coming to hate the rich . . . society divides itself into two hostile camps. . . . They wait only for the drum beat and the trumpet to summon them to armed conflict."

A series of events in the 1890s shook the confidence of many citizens in the reigning political system. But nothing was more unsettling than the severe economic depression that consumed the nation and lasted for five years. Many feared—while others hoped—that the entire political system would topple.

Financial Collapse and Depression

Railroads were at the center of the economic growth of the late nineteenth century. By the early 1890s they represented capital totaling $2.5 billion. As a result,

when the nation's major rail lines went bankrupt in 1893, the business boom of nearly two decades ended and the entire economy ground to a halt. The depression that followed made the hard times of the 1870s appear a mere rehearsal for worse misery to come.

Although the economic downturn began in agriculture and mining, the crisis came when the railroads registered the impact of the loss of income from these principal shippers. In March 1883, the collapse of the Philadelphia and Reading Railroad, followed by the downfall of the National Cordage Company, precipitated a crash in the stock market and sent waves of panic splashing over banks across the country. In a few months, more than 150 banks went into receivership and hundreds more closed; nearly 200 railroads and more than 15,000 businesses also slipped into bankruptcy. In the steel industry alone thirty companies collapsed within six months of the panic. Agricultural prices meanwhile continued to plummet until they reached new lows. The economy slowly began to pick up again in 1897, but new century arrived before prosperity returned.

In many cities, unemployment rates reached 25 percent; Samuel Gompers, head of the American Federation of Labor (AFL), estimated nationwide unemployment at 3 million. "I have seen more misery in this last week than I ever saw in my life before," wrote a young reporter from Chicago. Few people starved, but millions suffered. Inadequate diets prompted a rise in communicable diseases, such as tuberculosis and pellagra. Unable to buy food, clothes, or household items, families learned to survive with the barest minimum.

Tens of thousands "rode the rails" or went "on the tramp" to look for work, hoping that their luck might change in a new city or town. Some panhandled for the nickel that could buy a mug of beer and a free lunch at a saloon. By night they slept in parks or, in the colder months, flocked to the "bum tanks" of the city jail or to fleabag hotels. Vagrancy laws (enacted during the 1870s) forced many into prison. In New York City alone, with more than 20,000 homeless people, thousands ended up in jail. Newspapers warned against this "menace" and blamed the growing crime rates on the "dangerous classes."

Another Populist, Jacob Sechler Coxey, decided to gather the masses of unemployed into a huge army and then to march to Washington, D.C., to demand from Congress a public works program. On Easter Sunday, 1894, Coxey left Massillon, Ohio, with several hundred followers. Meanwhile, brigades from Boston, Los Angeles, San Francisco, Tacoma, Denver, Salt Lake City, Reno, Butte, and Omaha joined his "petition in boots." Communities across the country welcomed the marchers, but U.S. attorney general Richard C. Olney, a former lawyer for the railroad companies, conspired with state and local officials to halt them. Only 600 men and women reached the nation's capital,

Jacob Coxey's "Commonwealth of Christ Army," April 1894. Attracting the sympathetic attention of working people and the hostility of most of the wealthier classes, "Industrial Armies" marched through U.S. cities en route to the nation's capital.

SOURCE: Library of Congress.

where the police first clubbed and then arrested the leaders for trespassing on the grass. "Coxey's Army" quickly disbanded, but not before voicing the public's growing impatience with government apathy toward the unemployed.

Strikes and Labor Solidarity

Meanwhile, in several locations the conflict between labor and capital had escalated to the brink of civil war. Wage cuts in the silver and lead mines of northern Idaho led to one of the bitterest conflicts of the decade. To put a brake on organized labor, mineowners had formed a "protective association," and in March 1892 they announced a lower wage scale throughout the Coeur d'Alene district. After the miners' union refused to accept the cut, the owners locked out all union members and brought in strikebreakers by the train-load. Unionists tried peaceful methods of protest. But after three months of stalemate, they loaded a railcar with explosives and blew up a mine. Strikebreakers fled while mineowners appealed to the Idaho governor for assistance. A force of 1,500 state and federal troops occupied the district, and more than 300 union members were herded into bullpens, where they were kept under unsanitary conditions for several weeks before their

trial. Ore production meanwhile resumed with "scab" labor, and by November, when the troops were withdrawn, the mineowners declared a victory. But the miners' union survived, and most members eventually regained their jobs. "We have made a fight that we are proud of and propose to continue it to the end," one striker declared. The following spring, Coeur d'Alene miners sent delegates to Butte, Montana, where they helped form the Western Federation of Miners, which soon became one of the strongest labor organizations in the nation.

Coeur d'Alene strikers had been buoyed by the news that steelworkers at Homestead, Pennsylvania, had likewise taken guns in hand to defend their union. Members of the Amalgamated Iron, Steel and Tin Workers, the most powerful union of the AFL, had carved out an admirable position for themselves in the Carnegie Steel Company. Well paid, proud of their skills, the unionists customarily directed their unskilled helpers without undue influence of company supervisors. But, determined to gain control over every stage of production, Carnegie and his chairman, Henry C. Frick, decided not only to lower wages but to break the union.

In 1892, when the Amalgamated's contract expired, Frick announced a drastic wage cut. He also ordered a wooden stockade built around the factory, with grooves for rifles and barbed wire on top. When Homestead's city government refused to assign police to disperse the strikers, Frick dispatched a barge carrying a private army armed to the teeth. Gunfire broke out and continued throughout the day. After the governor sent the Pennsylvania National Guard to restore order, Carnegie's factory reopened, with strikebreakers doing the work.

After four months, the union was forced to concede a crushing defeat, not only for itself but, in effect, for all steelworkers. The Carnegie company reduced its workforce by 25 percent, lengthened the workday, and cut wages 25 percent for those who remained on the job. If the Amalgamated Iron, Steel and Tin Workers, known throughout the industry as the "aristocrats of labor," could be brought down, less-skilled workers could expect little from the corporate giants. Within a decade, every major steel company operated without union interference.

But the spirit of labor solidarity did not die. Just two years after the strikes at Coeur d'Alene and Homestead, the greatest railway strike since 1877 again dramatized the importance of the railroad as well as the extent of collusion between the government and corporations to crush the labor movement.

Unlike Packingtown, Pullman, Illinois, just south of Chicago, had been constructed as a model industrial community. Its creator and proprietor, George M. Pullman, had manufactured luxurious "sleeping cars" for railroads since 1881. He built his company as a self-contained community, with the factory at the center, surrounded by modern cottages, a library, churches, parks, an independent water supply, even its own cemetery, but no saloons. The Pullman Palace Car Company deducted rent, library fees, and grocery bills from each worker's weekly wages. In good times workers enjoyed a decent livelihood, although many resented Pullman's autocratic control of their daily affairs.

When times grew hard, the company cut wages by as much as one-half, in some cases down to less than $1 a day. Charges for food and rent remained unchanged. Furthermore, factory supervisors sought to make up for declining profits by driving workers to produce more. In May 1894, after Pullman fired members of a committee that had drawn up a list of grievances, workers voted to strike.

Pullman workers found their champion in Eugene V. Debs, who had recently formed the American Railway Union (ARU) in order to bring railroad workers across the vast continent into one organization. Debs, the architect of the ARU's victory over the Great Northern rail line just one month earlier, advised caution, but delegates to an ARU convention voted to support a nationwide boycott of all Pullman cars. This action soon turned into a sympathy strike by railroad workers across the country. Support for the strike was especially strong in the western states.

Compared to the Uprising of 1877, the orderly Pullman strike at first produced little violence. ARU officials urged strikers to ignore all police provocations and hold their ground peacefully. But Attorney General Richard C. Olney, claiming that the ARU was disrupting mail shipments (actually Debs had banned such interference), issued a blanket injunction against the strike. On July 4, President Cleveland sent federal troops to Chicago, over Illinois governor John Peter Altgeld's objections. After a bitter confrontation that left thirteen people dead and more than fifty wounded, the army dispersed the strikers. For the next week, railroad workers in twenty-six other states resisted federal troops, and a dozen more people were killed. On July 17, the strike finally ended when federal marshals arrested Debs and other leaders.

"The Debs of fable," wrote the editor of a Unitarian weekly, "lighted a fire in the car yards of Chicago. The Debs of fact lighted an idea in the dangerous shadows of the Republic." Assailing the arrogance of class privilege that encouraged the government to use brute force against its citizens, Debs concluded that the labor movement could not regain its dignity under the present system. An avid fan of Bellamy's *Looking Backward*, he came out of jail committed to the ideals of socialism and in 1898 helped to form a political party dedicated to its principles.

Across the industrial belt and in the West and Southwest, in railroad towns, factory villages, and farms, tens of thousands of people supported Debs. Declining nomination on the Populist ticket in 1896, he ran for president as a socialist in 1900 and in four subsequent elections. The odds against him grew with the scale of the

In 1894, to protest a cut in wages, the workers of the Pullman Palace Car Company struck. Eugene V. Debs, president of the American Railway Union, ordered a nationwide boycott against the Pullman Company. The United States Cavalry was brought in to escort the trains run by "scab" laborers.

SOURCE: Library of Congress (49255/3526).

booming economy, but Debs made his point on moral grounds. His friend James Whitcomb Riley, the nation's most admired sentimental poet, wrote in rural dialect that Debs had "the kindest heart that ever beat/betwixt here and the jedgment [judgment] seat."

The Social Gospel

Like Edward Bellamy, a growing number of Protestant and Catholic clergy and lay theologians noted a discrepancy between the ideals of Christianity and prevailing attitudes toward the poor. Like Bellamy, they could no longer sanction an economic system that allowed so many to toil long hours under unhealthy conditions and for subsistence wages. They demanded that the church lead the way to a new cooperative order. In 1889 Episcopalian clergyman W. D. P. Bliss, a charter member of Boston's Bellamy Nationalist club, began to publish a monthly magazine, *The Dawn*, whose motto was "He works for God who works for man."

Coinciding with an upswing in religious revivals in the nation's cities, some liberal congregations broke away from established churches to side with the working class and the immigrant poor. Ministers called for civil service reform and the end of child labor. Supporting labor's right to organize and, if necessary, to strike, they petitioned government officials to regulate corporations and place a limit on profits. Washington Gladden, a Congregationalist minister, warned that if churches continued to ignore pressing social problems they would devolve into institutions whose sole purpose was to preserve obscure rituals and superstitions. In the wake of the Great Uprising of 1877, he had called upon his congregation in Columbus, Ohio, to take an active part in the fight against social injustice. Gladden's *Applied Christianity* (1886) appealed to the nation's business leaders to return to Christ's teachings.

Less famous but more numerous, local Protestant ministers and community leaders likewise sought to restore what they considered the true spirit of Christianity. As labor reformer George McNeill wrote in 1890, some ministers might be the servants of wealth, but in the long run "the influence of the teachings of the Carpenter's Son" will "counteract the influence of Mammon," the biblical embodiment of greed. McNeill looked forward to the day when "every man shall have according to his needs." Although the social gospel spread most rapidly through the northern industrial cities, southern African Americans espoused their own version. They reinterpreted the Gospel as Jesus' promise to emancipate their race from satanic white power brokers. The biblical republic of "Beulahland" became their model of redemption.

The depression of the 1890s produced an outpouring of social gospel treatises. The very popular *If Christ Came to Chicago* (1894), by British journalist W. T. Stead, forced readers to confront the "ugly sight" of a city with 200 millionaires and 200,000 unemployed men. It inspired Edward Everett Hale's *If Jesus Came to Boston* (1894), which similarly questioned social inequalities. The most famous tract, *In His Steps* (1896), by Methodist minister Charles M. Sheldon of Topeka, Kansas, urged readers to rethink their actions in the light of the simple question "What would Jesus do?" By 1933 Sheldon's book had sold more than 23 million copies.

Catholics, doctrinally more inclined than Protestants to accept poverty as a natural condition, joined the social gospel movement in smaller numbers. In the early 1880s Polish Americans broke away from the Roman Catholic Church to form the Polish National Church, which was committed to the concerns of working people. Irish Americans, especially prominent in the Knights of Labor, encouraged priests to ally themselves with the labor movement. Pope Leo XIII's encyclical *Rerum Novarum* (1891) endorsed the right of workers to form trade unions.

Women guided the social gospel movement in their communities. In nearly every city, groups of women affiliated with various evangelical Protestant sects raised money to establish small, inexpensive residential hotels for working women, whose low wages rarely covered the price of safe, comfortable shelter. Many of these groups joined to form the Young Women's Christian Association (YWCA), which by 1900 had more than 600 local chapters. The "Y" sponsored a range of services for needy Christian women, ranging from homes for the elderly and for unmarried mothers to elaborate programs of vocational instruction and physical fitness. The Girls Friendly Societies, an organization of young women affiliated with Episcopal churches, sponsored similar programs. Meanwhile Catholic lay women and nuns served the poor women of their faith, operating numerous schools, hospitals, and orphanages.

Although centered in the cities, the social gospel rallied many small-town and rural women, especially ardent admirers of Frances Willard. "The time will come," Willard insisted, "when the human heart will be so much alive that no one could sleep in any given community; if any of that group of human beings were cold, hungry, or miserable."

POLITICS OF REFORM, POLITICS OF ORDER

The severe hardships of the 1890s, following a quarter of a century of popular unrest and economic uncertainty, led to a crisis in the two-party system, making the presidential election of 1896 a turning point in

American politics. Republicans and Democrats continued to enjoy long-standing voter loyalties among specific groups or regions. Particularly in the South, the Democrats could generally depend on the masses of white voters to unite against any movement threatening to compromise the "color line." But Populists were tenacious contenders.

The election of 1896, however, indicated not merely the regrouping of American voters. It also revealed the power of the conservative ascendancy. By the 1890s, the reform movements were losing ground while nativist and racist sentiments were consolidating, even within the reform movements themselves.

The Free Silver Issue

Grover Cleveland owed his victory in 1892 over Republican incumbent Benjamin Harrison to the predictable votes of the Democratic "solid South" and to the unanticipated support of such northern states as Illinois and Wisconsin, whose German-born voters turned against the increasingly nativist Republicans. But when the economy collapsed the following year, Cleveland and the Democrats who controlled Congress faced a public eager for action. Convinced that the economic crisis was "largely the result of financial policy . . . embodied in unwise laws," the president called a special session of Congress to reform the nation's currency.

For generations, reformers had advocated "soft" currency—that is, an increase in the money supply that would loosen credit. During the Civil War the federal government took decisive action, replacing state bank notes with a national paper currency popularly called "greenbacks" (from the color of the bills). Then, in 1873 the Coinage Act tightened the money supply by eliminating silver from circulation, prompting farmers who depended on credit to call it "the Crime of '73." This measure actually had little real impact on the economy but opened the door to yet more tinkering and, especially during hard times, the currency question simmered. For the most part, the business community consistently advocated the gold-standard. A compromise was reached with the passage of the Sherman Silver Purchase Act of 1890. The act directed the Treasury to increase the amount of currency coined from silver mined in the West and also permitted the U.S. government to print paper currency backed by the silver. In turn, Westerners who stood to benefit most from this reform, agreed to support the McKinley Tariff of 1890 that, in establishing the highest import duties yet on foreign goods, pleased the business community.

Following the crash of 1893, as the economy fell into ruins, a desperate President Cleveland demanded the repeal of the Sherman Act, insisting that only the gold standard could pull the nation out of depression. By exerting intense pressure on congressional Democrats, Cleveland succeeded in October 1893, but not without ruining his chances for renomination. The midterm elections in 1894 brought the largest shift in congressional power in American history: the Republicans gained 117 seats, while the Democrats lost 113. The "Silver Democrats" of Cleveland's own party vowed revenge and began to look to the Populists, mainly Westerners and farmers who favored "free silver"—that is, the unlimited coinage of silver. Republicans confidently began to prepare for the presidential election of 1896, known as the "battle of the standards."

Populism's Last Campaigns

Populists had been buoyed by the 1894 election, which delivered to their candidates nearly 1.5 million votes, a gain of 42 percent over their 1892 totals. They made impressive inroads into several southern states. West of the Mississippi, political excitement steadily increased. David Waite, the Populist governor of Colorado, talked of a coming revolution and declared, "It is better, infinitely better, that blood should flow [up] to the horses' bridles rather than our national liberties should be destroyed." Still, even in the Midwest where Populists doubled their vote, they managed to win less than 7 percent of the total.

As Populists prepared for the 1896 election, they found themselves at a crossroad: What were they to do with the growing popularity of Democrat William Jennings Bryan? Son of an Illinois judge who had run unsuccessfully for Congress, Bryan had relocated to Nebraska, where he practiced law. A spellbinding orator, he won a congressional seat in 1890. After seizing the Populist slogan "Equal Rights to All, Special Privilege to None," Bryan became a major contender for president of the United States.

Noting the surging interest in free silver, Bryan became its champion. "I don't know anything about free silver," he once admitted, but "the people of Nebraska are for free silver and I am for free silver. I will look up the arguments later." For two years before the 1896 election, Bryan wooed potential voters in a speaking tour that took him to every state in the nation. Pouring new life into his divided party, Bryan pushed Silver Democrats to the forefront.

At the 1896 party convention, the thirty-six-year-old orator thrilled delegates with his evocation of agrarian ideals. "Burn down your cities and leave our farms," Bryan preached, "and your cities will spring up again as if by magic; but destroy our farms and the grass will grow in the streets of every city in the country." What became one of the most famous speeches in American political history closed on a yet more dramatic note. Spreading his arms to suggest the crucified Christ figure,

Bryan pledged to answer all demands for a gold standard by saying, "You shall not press down upon the brow of labor this crown of thorns, you shall not crucify mankind upon a cross of gold." The next day, Bryan won the Democratic presidential nomination.

The Populists knew that the Democrats, in nominating Bryan, had stolen their thunder. Although many feared that the growing emphasis on currency would overshadow their more important planks calling for government ownership of the nation's railroads and communications systems, few Populists had expected either major party to come out for free silver. As the date of their own convention approached, delegates divided over strategy: they could endorse Bryan and give up their independent status; or they could run an independent campaign and risk splitting the silver vote. Neither

This Republican campaign poster of 1896 depicts William McKinley standing on sound money and promising a revival of prosperity. The depression of the 1890s shifted the electorate into the Republican column.

choice was good. "If we fuse," one Populist explained, "we are sunk; if we don't fuse, all the silver men we have will leave us for the more powerful Democrats."

In the end, the Populists nominated Bryan for president and chose one of their own ranks, the popular Georgian Tom Watson, for the vice presidential candidate. Most of the state Democratic Party organizations, however, refused to put the "fusion" ticket on the ballot, and Bryan and his Democratic running mate Arthur Sewall simply ignored the Populist campaign.

The Republican Triumph

After Cleveland's blunders, Republicans anticipated an easy victory in 1896, but Bryan's nomination, as party stalwart Mark Hanna warned, "changed everything." Luckily, they had their own handsome, knowledgeable, courteous, and ruthless candidate, Civil War veteran William McKinley.

The Republican campaign in terms of sheer expense and skill of coordination outdid all previous campaigns and established a precedent for future presidential elections. Hanna guided a strategy that raised up to $7 million and outspent Bryan more than ten to one. Using innumerable pamphlets, placards, hats, and parades, Republicans advertised their promise to "rebuild out of the ruins of the last four years the stately mansions of national happiness, prosperity and self-respect." MCKinley even invited voters to his home, managing to attract as many as 750,000 people to his famous "Front Porch." In the campaign's final two weeks, organizers dispatched 1,400 speakers to spread the word. Fearful that the silver issue could divide their own ranks, Republicans stepped around it while emphasizing the tariff. Delivering a hard-hitting negative camapign, they consistently cast adversary Bryan as a dangerous naysayer willing to risk the nation's well-being and cost voters their jobs or worse.

McKinley triumphed in the most important presidential election since Reconstruction. Bryan managed to win 46 percent of the popular vote but failed to carry the Midwest, West Coast, or Upper South. Moreover, the free silver campaign rebuffed traditionally Democratic urban voters who feared that soft money would bring higher prices. Many Catholics uncomfortable with Bryan's Protestant moral piety also deserted the Democrats. Finally, neither the reform-minded middle classes nor impoverished blue-collar workers were convinced that Bryan's grand reform vision really included them. The Populist following, disappointed and disillusioned, dwindled away, and for the next sixteen years, Democrats dominated no region but the South. Voter apathy set in, and participation began to spiral downward from its 1896 peak, when upwards of 80 percent of the electorate turned out.

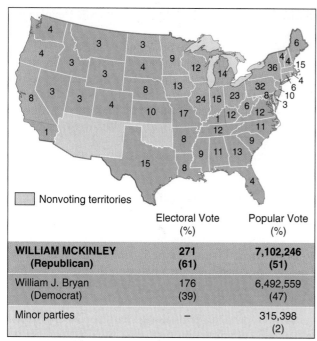

	Electoral Vote (%)	Popular Vote (%)
WILLIAM MCKINLEY (Republican)	**271 (61)**	**7,102,246 (51)**
William J. Bryan (Democrat)	176 (39)	6,492,559 (47)
Minor parties	–	315,398 (2)

Election of 1896 Democratic candidate William Jennings Bryan carried most of rural America but could not overcome Republican William McKinley's stronghold in the populous industrial states.

Once in office, McKinley promoted a mixture of probusiness and expansionist measures. He supported the Dingley Tariff of 1897, which raised import duties to an all-time high. In 1897 McKinley also encouraged Congress to create the United States Industrial Commission, which would plan business regulation; in 1898 he promoted a bankruptcy act that eased the financial situation of small businesses; and he proposed the Erdman Act of the same year, which established a system of arbitration to avoid rail strikes. The Supreme Court ruled in concert with the president, finding eighteen railways in violation of antitrust laws and granting states the right to regulate hours of labor under certain circumstances. In 1900 he oversaw the passage of the Gold Standard Act.

McKinley's triumph ended the popular challenge to the nation's governing system. With prosperity returning by 1898 and nationalism rising swiftly, McKinley encouraged Americans to go for "a full dinner pail," the winning Republican slogan of the 1900 presidential election. With news of his second triumph, stock prices on Wall Street skyrocketed.

Nativism and Jim Crow

Campaign rhetoric aside, McKinley and Bryan differed only slightly on the major problems facing the nation in 1896. Neither Bryan the reformer nor McKinley the prophet of prosperity addressed the escalation of racism and nativism (antiimmigrant feeling) throughout the nation. After the election, McKinley made white supremacy a major tenet of his foreign policy; Bryan, twice more a presidential contender, championed the white race and deemed "social equality" impossible.

Toward the end of the century, many political observers noted, the nation's patriotic fervor took on a strongly nationalistic and antiforeign tone. Striking workers and their employers alike tended to blame "foreigners" for the hard times. AFL leader Samuel Gompers, himself a Jewish immigrant from Europe, lobbied Congress to restrict immigration from eastern and southern Europe, and even the sons and daughters of earlier immigrants attacked the newcomers as unfit for democracy. Imagining a Catholic conspiracy directed by the pope, semisecret organizations such as the American Protective Association sprang up to defend American institutions. Fourth of July orators continued to celebrate freedom and liberty but more often boasted about the might and power of their nation.

In the South, white racism tightened its grip on the region. Local and state governments codified racist ideology by passing discriminatory and segregationist legislation, which became known as Jim Crow laws. The phrase, dating from the early decades of the nineteenth century, was made popular by a white minstrel in black face who used the name "Jim Crow" to characterize all African Americans. Before the Civil War, abolitionists described segregated railroad cars as "Jim Crow." By the end of the century, "Jim Crow" referred to the customs of segregation that were becoming codified by law and practice throughout the South. With nine of every ten black Americans living in this region, the significance of this development was sweeping.

"The supremacy of the white race of the South," New South promoter Henry W. Grady declared in 1887, "must be maintained forever . . . because the white race is the superior race." To secure their privileges, Grady and other white Southerners acted directly to impose firm standards of segregation and domination and to forestall any appearance of social equality. State after state in the South enacted new legislation to cover facilities such as restaurants, public transportation, and even drinking fountains. Signs "White Only" and "Colored" appeared over theaters, parks, rooming houses, and toilets. In banks, post offices, and stores, blacks were required to wait until all whites had been served, and special rules prohibited such common practices as trying on shoes or hats before purchasing them.

The United States Supreme Court upheld the new discriminatory legislation. Its decisions in the *Civil Rights Cases* (1883) overturned the Civil Rights Act of

1875, and in *Plessy* v. *Ferguson* (1896) the Court upheld a Louisiana state law formally segregating railroad cars on the basis of the "separate but equal" doctrine. In *Cumming* v. *Richmond County Board of Education* (1899), the Court allowed separate schools for blacks and whites, even where facilities for African American children did not exist.

The new restrictions struck especially hard at the voting rights of African Americans. Southern states enacted new literacy tests and property qualifications for voting, demanding proof of $300 to $500 in property and the ability to read and write. Loopholes permitted poor whites to vote even under these conditions, except where they threatened the Democratic Party's rule. "Grandfather clauses," invented in Louisiana, exempted from all restrictions those who had been entitled to vote on January 1, 1867, together with their sons and grandsons, a measure that effectively enfranchised whites while barring African Americans. In 1898, the Supreme Court ruled that poll taxes and literacy requirements enacted in order to prevent blacks (and some poor whites) from voting were a proper means of restricting the ballot to "qualified" voters. By this time, only 5 percent of the southern black electorate voted, and African Americans were barred from public office and jury service. Supreme Court Justice John Marshall Harlan, the lone dissenter in *Plessy* v. *Ferguson*, lamented that the Court's majority rulings gave power to the states "to place in a condition of legal inferiority a large body of American citizens." Depriving African Americans of equal rights and protection under the law, Jim Crow legislation encouraged states outside the South to pass similar measures.

THE SPREAD OF DISFRANCHISEMENT

Year	State	Restrictions
1889	Florida	Poll tax
	Tennessee	Poll tax
1890	Mississippi	Poll tax, literacy test, understanding clause
1891	Arkansas	Poll tax
1893, 1901	Alabama	Poll tax, literacy test, grandfather clause
1894, 1895	South Carolina	Poll tax, literacy test, understanding clause
1894, 1902	Virginia	Poll tax, literacy test, understanding clause
1897, 1898	Louisana	Poll tax, literacy test, grandfather clause
1899, 1900	North Carolina	Poll tax, literacy test, grandfather clause
1902	Texas	Poll tax
1908	Georgia	Poll tax, literacy test, understanding clause, grandfather clause

Racial violence in turn escalated. Not only race riots but thousands of lynchings took place. Between 1882 and the turn of the century, the number of lynchings usually exceeded 100 each year; 1892 produced a record 230 deaths (161 black, 69 white). Mobs often burned or dismembered victims in order to drag out their agony and entertain the crowd of onlookers. Announced in local newspapers, lynchings became public spectacles for entire white families, and railroads sometimes offered special excursion rates for travel to these events.

Antilynching became the one-woman crusade of Ida B. Wells, young editor of a black newspaper in Memphis. After three local black businessmen were lynched in 1892, Wells vigorously denounced the outrage, blaming the white business competitors of the victims. Her stand fanned the tempers of local whites, who destroyed her press and forced the outspoken editor to leave the city.

Wells set out to investigate lynching in a systematic fashion. She paid special attention to the common defense of lynching—that it was a necessary response to attempts by black men to rape white women. Her 1895 pamphlet *A Red Record* showed that the vast majority of black lynching victims had not even been accused of rape. In fact, Wells showed, lynching was primarily a brutal device to eliminate African Americans who

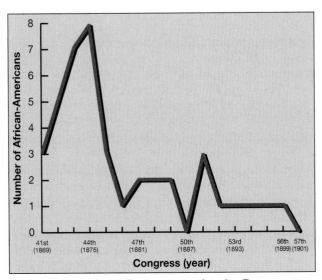

African-American Representation in Congress, 1867–1900   Black men served in the U.S. Congress from 1870 until 1900. All were Republicans.

had become too prosperous or competed with white businesses.

Wells launched an international movement against lynching, lecturing across the country and in Europe, demanding an end to the silence about this barbaric crime. Her work also inspired the growth of a black women's club movement. The National Association of Colored Women, founded in 1896, provided a home for black women activists who had been excluded from white women's clubs. United by a growing sense of racial pride, black women's clubs took up the antilynching cause and also fought to protect black women from exploitation by white men and from charges of sexual depravity.

Tom Watson

Few white reformers rallied to defend African Americans. At its 1899 convention, the National American Woman Suffrage Association appeased new southern white members by voting down a resolution condemning racial segregation in public facilities. A far greater tragedy was a racist turn in the Populist movement, whose leaders even in the South had at times challenged white supremacy. The story of Thomas E. Watson, briefly a champion of interracial unity, illustrates the rise and fall of hopes for an egalitarian South.

Son of a prosperous cotton farmer who had been driven into bankruptcy during the depression of the 1870s, Tom Watson had once campaigned to restore the civil rights of southern African Americans. "Why is not the colored tenant [farmer] open to the conviction that he is in the same boat as the white tenant; the colored laborer with the white laborer?" he asked. Watson planned to overturn Democratic rule by capturing and building up the black vote for the People's Party.

Watson's followers in Georgia were jailed, shot at, denied the protection of the courts, and driven from their churches. Yet tens of thousands regarded him as a savior. Flowers decorated the bridges along his speaking routes, crowds standing in pouring rain begged him to continue speaking, and wagons of loyalists carried Winchester rifles to defend him from armed attack. Preaching government ownership of railroads and banks and political equality for both races, Watson stirred the only truly grass-roots interracial movement the South had yet seen.

By early 1896, however, Watson perceived that the increasing ardor for free silver and the move toward cooperation with Democrats would doom the Populist movement. He nevertheless accepted the nomination for vice president on the "fusion" ticket and campaigned in several states. After McKinley's triumph, Watson withdrew from politics, returning to his Georgia farm to write popular histories of the United States and to plot his future.

Watson returned to public life after the turn of the century but with a totally different approach to race relations. He still bitterly attacked the wealthy classes but now blamed black citizens for conspiring against poor whites. Political salvation now hinged, he concluded, on accommodation to white supremacy. Watson expressed a southern variation of the new national creed that prepared Americans to view the luckless inhabitants of distant lands as ripe for colonization by the United States.

"IMPERIALISM OF RIGHTEOUSNESS"

Many Americans attributed the crisis of 1893–97 not simply to the collapse of the railroads and the stock market but to basic structural problems: an overbuilt economy and an insufficient market for goods. Profits from total sales of manufactured and agricultural products had grown substantially over the level achieved in the 1880s, but output increased even more rapidly. While the number of millionaires shot up from 500 in 1860 to more than 4,000 in 1892, the majority of working people lacked enough income to buy back a significant portion of what they produced. As Republican Senator Albert J. Beveridge of Indiana put it, "We are raising more than we can consume . . . making more than we can use. Therefore, we must find new markets for our produce, new occupation for our capital, new work for our labor."

In 1893 Frederick Jackson Turner reminded Americans that the continent had now been settled. Having passed "from the task of filling up the vacant spaces of the continent," the nation is now "thrown back upon itself," the young historian concluded. Obviously, Americans required a new "frontier" if democracy were to survive.

The White Man's Burden

Turner read his famous essay, "The Significance of the Frontier in American History," at the meeting of the American Historical Association, which was held in Chicago at the time of the World's Fair, less than two months after the nation's economy had collapsed. On May Day 1893, crowds flocked to the fair—"a little ideal world, a realization of Utopia . . . [foreshadowing] some far away time when the earth should be as pure, as beautiful, and as joyous as the White City itself." A complex of more than 400 buildings, newly constructed in beaux arts design, commemorated the four hundredth anniversary of Columbus's landing. Such expositions, President McKinley explained, served as "timekeepers of progress."

The captains of Chicago's industry—Armour, Swift, McCormick, Field, and Pullman—had campaigned hard to bring the fair to Chicago and delighted in its triumphant display of American business ingenuity. Agriculture Hall showcased the production of corn, wheat, and other crops and featured a gigantic globe encircled by samples of American-manufactured farm machinery. The symbolism was evident: all eyes were on worldwide markets for American products. Another building housed a model of a canal cut across Nicaragua, suggesting the ease with which American traders might reach Asian markets if transport ships could travel directly from the Caribbean to the Pacific. One of the most popular exhibits, attracting 20,000 people a day, featured a mock ocean liner built to scale by the International Navigation Company, where fairgoers could imagine themselves as "tourists," sailing in luxury to distant parts of the world.

The World's Fair also "displayed" representatives of the people who populated foreign lands. The Midway Plaisance, a strip nearly a mile long and more than 600 feet wide, was an enormous sideshow of re-created Turkish bazaars and South Sea island huts. There were Javanese carpenters, Dahomean drummers, Egyptian swordsmen, and Hungarian Gypsies as well as Eskimos, Syrians, Samoans, and Chinese. Very popular was the World Congress of Beauty, parading "40 Ladies from 40 Nations" dressed in native costume. Another favorite attraction was "Little Egypt," who performed at the Persian Palace of Eros; her *danse du ventre* became better known as the hootchy-kootchy. According to the guidebook, all these peoples had come "from the night-some North and the splendid South, from the wasty West and the effete East, bringing their manners, customs, dress, religions, legends, amusements, that we might know them better." One of the exposition's directors, Frederick Ward Putnam, head of Harvard's Peabody Museum of American Archeology and Ethnology, explained more fully that the gathering gave fairgoers "a grand opportunity to see . . . the material advantages which civilization brings to mankind."

By celebrating the brilliance of American industry and simultaneously presenting the rest of the world's people as a source of exotic entertainment, the planners of the fair delivered a powerful message. Former abolitionist Frederick Douglass, who attended the fair on "Colored People's Day," recognized it immediately. He noted that the physical layout of the fair, by carefully grouping exhibits, sharply divided the United States and Europe from the rest of the world, namely from the nations of Africa, Asia, and the Middle East. Douglass objected to the stark contrast setting off Anglo-Saxons from people of color, an opposition between "civiliza-

tion" and "savagery." Douglass and Ida B. Wells jointly wrote a pamphlet that referred to the famed exposition as "a whited sepulcher." Wells advised African Americans to boycott the fair, but Douglass chose to attend. He used the occasion to deliver a speech upbraiding those white Americans who labeled the African American "a moral monster."

The Chicago World's Fair gave material shape to prevalent ideas about the superiority of American civilization and its racial order. At the same time, by showcasing American industries, it made a strong case for commercial expansion abroad. Social gospeler Josiah Strong, a Congregational minister who had begun his career trying to convert Indians to Christianity, provided a timely synthesis. He argued that the United States, as the most economically advanced and most Christian nation in the world, commanded a providential role. Thus linking economic and spiritual expansion, Strong advocated an "imperialism of righteousness." The rest of the world "is to be Christianized and civilized," Strong insisted, by the white Americans, who were best suited to this greatest task of all time. "Pure spiritual Christianity" and a "genius for colonizing" compelled Americans to move beyond their own national interests to consider the needs of the people of Africa and the Pacific and beyond. It was the white American, Strong argued, who had been "divinely commissioned to be, in a peculiar sense, his brother's keeper."

Senator Beveridge faithfully carried this message to Congress, insisting that God "has made us [white, English-speaking people] adept in government that we may administer governments among savages and senile peoples. . . . He has marked the American people as His chosen nation to finally lead in the regeneration of the world." According to many newspaper reporters and editorialists, it would be morally wrong for Americans to shirk what the British poet Rudyard Kipling called the "White Man's Burden."

Foreign Missions

The push for overseas expansion coincided with a major wave of religious evangelism and foreign missions. Early in the nineteenth century, Protestant missionaries, hoping to fulfill what they believed to be a divine command to carry God's message to all peoples and to win converts for their church, had focused on North America. Many disciples, like Josiah Strong himself, headed west and stationed themselves on Indian reservations. Others worked among the immigrant populations of the nation's growing cities. As early as the 1820s, however, a few missionaries had traveled to the Sandwich Islands (Hawai'i) in an effort to supplant the indigenous religion with Christianity. After the Civil War, following the formation of the Women's Union Missionary Society of

American Protestant missionaries opened refuge homes for Chinese women, many brought to the United States as prostitutes or under contracts resembling indentured servitude, and offered shelter, vocational training, and religious instruction. The Chinese women pictured here, all with bound feet, are studying with the matron.

SOURCE: Harvard University.

Americans for Heathen Lands, the major evangelical Protestant denominations all sponsored missions directed at foreign lands.

Funded by wealthy men and the vigorous campaigns of female church members, these societies soon attracted a large membership. By the 1890s, college campuses blazed with missionary excitement, and the intercollegiate Student Volunteers for Foreign Missions spread rapidly under the slogan "The Evangelicization of the World in This Generation." Magazines bristled with essays such as "The Anglo-Saxon and the World's Redemption." Young Protestant women rushed to join foreign missionary societies. In 1863 there had been only 94 Methodist women missionaries in China; by 1902 the number had jumped to 783. In all, some twenty-three American Protestant churches had established missions in China by the turn of the century, the majority staffed by women. By 1915, more than 3 million women had enrolled in forty denominational missionary societies, surpassing in size all other women's organizations in the United States. Their foreign missions ranged from India and Africa to Syria, the Pacific Islands, and nearby Latin America.

With so many agents in the field, missionaries scored numerous successes. They recruited many "natives," including the "rice-Christians" who feigned conversion in order to be fed by the missions. By 1898 Protestants claimed to have made Christians of more than 80,000

Chinese, a tiny portion of the population but a significant stronghold for American interests in their nation. The missionaries did more than spread the gospel. They taught school, provided rudimentary medical care, offered vocational training programs, and sometimes encouraged young men and women to pursue a college education in preparation for careers in their homelands. Such work depended on, and in turn inspired, enthusiastic church members in the United States.

Outside the churches proper, the YMCA and YWCA, which had set up nondenominational missions for the working poor in many American cities, also embarked on a worldwide crusade to reach non-Christians. By the turn of the century, the YWCA had foreign branches in Ceylon (present-day Sri Lanka) and China. After foreign branches multiplied in the next decade, a close observer ironically suggested that the United States had three great occupying forces: the army, the navy, and the "Y." He was not far wrong.

Missionaries played an important role both in generating public interest in foreign lands and in preparing the way for American economic expansion. As Josiah Strong aptly put it, "Commerce follows the missionary."

An Overseas Empire

Not only missionaries but business and political leaders had set their sights on distant lands, which, in turn, meant new markets. In the 1860s, Secretary of State William Henry Seward, under Abraham Lincoln and then under Andrew Johnson, encouraged Americans to defer to "a political law—and when I say political law, I mean higher law, a law of Providence—that empire has [had], for the last three thousand years." Seward correctly predicted that foreign trade would play an increasingly important part in the American economy. Between 1870 and 1900 exports more than tripled, from about $400 million to over $1.5 billion, with textiles and agricultural products leading the way. But as European markets for American goods began to contract, business and political leaders of necessity looked more eagerly to Asia as well as to lands closer by.

Since the American Revolution, many Americans had regarded all nearby nations as falling naturally within their own territorial realm, destined to be acquired when opportunity allowed. Seward advanced these imperialist principles in 1867 by negotiating the purchase of Alaska (known at the time as Seward's Icebox) from Russia for $7.2 million, and he hoped someday to see the American flag flying over Canada and Mexico. Meanwhile, with European nations launched on their own imperialist missions in Asia and Africa, the United States increasingly viewed the Caribbean as an "American lake" and all of Latin America as a vast potential market for U.S. goods. The crisis of the 1890s transformed this long-standing desire into a perceived economic necessity. Large-scale conquest, however, appeared to American leaders more expensive and less appealing than economic domination and selective colonization. Unlike European imperialists, powerful Americans dreamed of empire without large-scale permanent military occupation and costly colonial administration.

Americans focused their expansionist plans on the Western Hemisphere, determined to dislodge the dominant power, Great Britain. In 1867, when Canada became a self-governing dominion, American diplomats hoped to annex their northern neighbor, believing that

Great Britain would gladly accede in order to concentrate its imperial interests in Asia. But Great Britain refused to give up Canada, and the United States backed away. Central and South America proved more accommodating to American designs.

Republican stalwart James G. Blaine, secretary of state under presidents Garfield and Harrison, determined to work out a Good Neighbor policy (a phrase coined by Henry Clay in 1820). "What we want," he explained, "are the markets of these neighbors of ours that lie to the south of us. We want the $400,000,000 annually which to-day go to England, France, Germany and other countries. With these markets secured new life would be given to our manufactures, the product of the Western farmer would be in demand, the reasons for and inducements to strikers, with all their attendant evils,

Web Exploration   Consider the global reach of America in 1900. What fueled this expansion overseas?
www.prenhall.com/faragher/map20.1

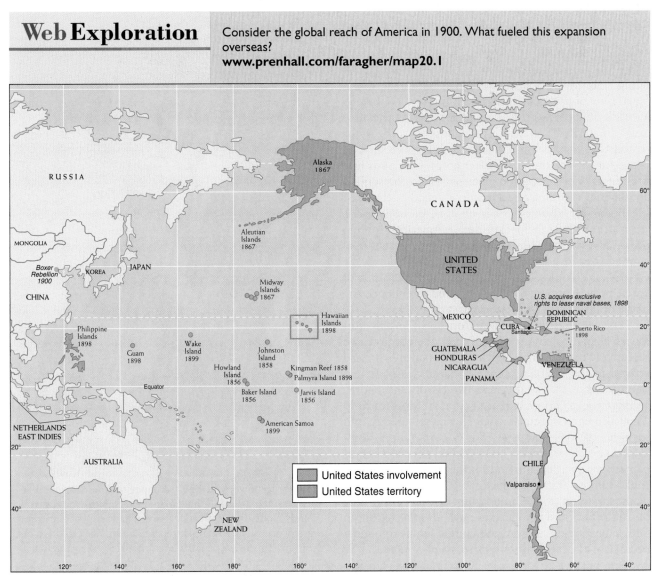

The American Domain, ca. 1900   The United States claimed numerous islands in the South Pacific and intervened repeatedly in Latin America to secure its economic interests.

would cease." Bilateral treaties with Mexico, Colombia, the British West Indies, El Salvador, and the Dominican Republic allowed American business to dominate local economies, importing their raw materials at low prices and flooding their local markets with goods manufactured in the United States. Often American investors simply took over the principal industries of these small nations, undercutting national business classes. The first Pan-American Conference, held in 1889–90, marked a turning point in hemispheric relations.

The Good Neighbor policy depended, Blaine knew, on peace and order in the Latin American states. As early as 1875, when revolt shook Venezuela, the Department of State warned European powers not to meddle. If popular uprisings proved too much for local officials, the U.S. Navy would intervene and return American allies to power.

In 1883, wishing to enforce treaties and protect overseas investments, Congress appropriated funds to build up American seapower. Beginning with ninety small ships, over one-third of them wooden, the navy grew quickly to include modern steel fighting ships. The hulls of these ships were painted a gleaming white, and the armada was known as the Great White Fleet. One of the most popular exhibits at the Chicago World's Fair featured full-sized models of the new armor-plated steel battleships. Congress also established the Naval War College in Newport, Rhode Island, in 1884 to train the officer corps. One of its first presidents, Captain Alfred Thayer Mahan, prescribed an imperialist strategy based on command of the seas. His book, *The Influence of Sea Power upon American History, 1660–1873* (1890), helped to define American foreign policy at the time. Mahan insisted that international strength rested not only on open markets but on the control of colonies. He advocated the annexation of bases in the Caribbean and the Pacific to enhance the navy's ability to threaten or wage warfare.

The annexation of Hawai'i on July 7, 1898, followed nearly a century of economic penetration and diplomatic maneuver. American missionaries, who had arrived in the 1820s to convert Hawai'ians to Christianity, began to buy up huge parcels of land and to subvert the existing feudal system of landholding. They also encouraged American businesses to buy into sugar plantations, and by 1875 U.S. corporations dominated the sugar trade. They tripled the number of plantations by 1880 and sent Hawai'ian sugar duty-free to the United States. By this time Hawai'i appeared, in Blaine's opinion, to be "an outlying district of the state of California," and he began to push for annexation. In 1887 a new treaty allowed the United States to build a naval base at Pearl Harbor on the island of Oahu.

The next year, American planters took a step further, arranging the overthrow of the weak king Kalakaua

and securing a new government allied to their economic interests. In 1891, the new ruler, Queen Liliuokalani, struck back by issuing a constitution granting her more discretionary power. The U.S. minister, prompted by the pineapple magnate Sanford B. Dole, responded by calling for military assistance. On January 16, 1893, U.S. sailors landed on Hawai'i to protect American property. Liliuokalani was deposed, a new provisional government was installed, and Hawai'i was proclaimed an American protectorate (a territory protected and partly controlled by the United States). The American diplomat John L. Stevens, stationed in Hawai'i, eagerly wired Washington that the "Hawai'ian pear is now fully ripe, and this is the golden hour for the United States to pluck it." President Cleveland refused to consider annexation, but five years later McKinley affirmed a joint congressional resolution under which Hawai'i would

Brought to power with the assistance of American businessmen, Queen Liliuokalani nevertheless sought to limit the outsiders' influence. American marines, Christian missionaries, and sugar planters joined in 1893 to drive her from her throne. A century later, the U.S. government apologized to native Hawai'ians for this illegal act.

SOURCE: Library of Congress.

become an American territory in 1900. The residents of Hawai'i were not consulted about this momentous change in their national identity.

Hawai'i was often viewed as a steppingstone to the vast Asian markets. A U.S. admiral envisioned the happy future: "The Pacific is the ocean bride of America—China, Japan and Korea—and their innumerable islands, hanging like necklaces about them, are the bridesmaids. . . . Let us as Americans . . . determine while yet in our power, that no commercial rival or hostile flag can float with impunity over the long swell of the Pacific sea."

To accelerate railroad investment and trade, a consortium of New York bankers created the American China Development Company in 1896. They feared, however, that the tottering Manchu dynasty would fall to European, Russian, and Japanese colonial powers, which would then prohibit trade with the United States. Secretary of State John Hay responded in 1899 by proclaiming the Open Door policy. According to this doctrine, outlined in notes to six major powers, the United States enjoyed the right to advance its commercial interests anywhere in the world, at least on terms equal to those of the other imperialist nations. The Chinese marketplace was too important to lose.

Chinese nationalist rebellion, however, threatened to overwhelm all the outsiders' plans for China. An antiforeign secret society known as the Harmonious Righteous Fists (dubbed "Boxers" by the Western press) rioted repeatedly in 1898 and 1899, actually occupying the capital city of Beijing and surrounding the foreign embassies. Shocked by the deaths of thousands, including many Chinese converts to Christianity, and determined to maintain American economic interests, President McKinley, not bothering to request congressional approval, contributed 5,000 U.S. troops to an international army that put down the Boxer uprising. The Boxer Rebellion dramatized the Manchu regime's inability to control its own subjects and strengthened John Hay's determination to preserve the economic status quo. A second series of Open Door notes by the secretary of state restated the intention of the United States to trade in China and laid the basis for twentieth-century foreign policy.

THE SPANISH–AMERICAN WAR

During his 1896 campaign, William McKinley firmly committed himself to the principle of economic expansion. It was for him the proper alternative to Edward Bellamy's program for a cooperative commonwealth. Indeed, he once described his "greatest ambition" as achieving American supremacy in world markets. As president, McKinley not only reached out for markets but took his nation into war while proclaiming its humanitarian and democratic goals.

The Spanish-American War was the most popular war since the American war for independence from Great Britain. It was short, lasting only sixteen weeks. It claimed relatively few lives—about 2,500 men died from diseases, mainly yellow fever, typhoid, or malaria—ten times the number killed in combat. And the war cost the government only $250 million. When it ended, the United States waged another war and annexed the Philippines. By the end of the century, the nation had joined Europe and Japan in the quest for empire and had become a formidable world power with territories spread out across the Carribean Sea and Pacific Ocean.

A "Splendid Little War" in Cuba

"I have ever looked on Cuba," Thomas Jefferson wrote, "as the most interesting addition which could ever be made to our system of States." Before the Civil War, Southerners hoped to acquire Cuba, still owned by Spain, for the expansion of slavery in its sugar mills, tobacco plantations, and mines. After attempting several times to buy the island outright, the United States settled for the continuation of the status quo, reaffirming Jefferson's conclusion that preserving Cuba's "independence against all the world, *except* Spain . . . would be nearly as valuable to us as if it were our own." Throughout the nineteenth century, the United States resolved to protect Spain's sovereignty over Cuba against the encroachment of other powers, including Cuba itself.

In Cuba, a movement for independence began in the mid-1860s when Spain, its empire in ruins, began to impose stiff taxes on the island. After defeat during the Ten Years War of 1868–78 and yet another series of setbacks, the insurgents rallied under the nationalist leadership of José Martí. In May 1895 Spanish troops ambushed and killed Martí, turning him into a martyr and fanning the flames of rebellion. By July, the rebels declared Cuba a republic and established a rudimentary government. Meanwhile, the war for independence moved closer to Havana, the island's seat of power.

Many Americans, invoking the legacy of their own war for independence, supported the movement for *Cuba Libre*. Grisly stories of Spain's treatment of captured insurrectionists circulated in American newspapers and aroused popular sympathy for the Cuban cause. In 1896 both the Democratic and Republican parties adopted planks supporting Cuba's freedom. President Cleveland refused to back the Cuban revolutionaries and instead urged Spain to grant the island a limited autonomy. Even when Congress passed a resolution in 1896 welcoming the future independence of Cuba, Cleveland and his advisers demurred.

Web Exploration

Look at both theaters of action in the Spanish-American War. What did the United States gain from victories in each of these conflicts?
www.prenhall.com/faragher/map20.2

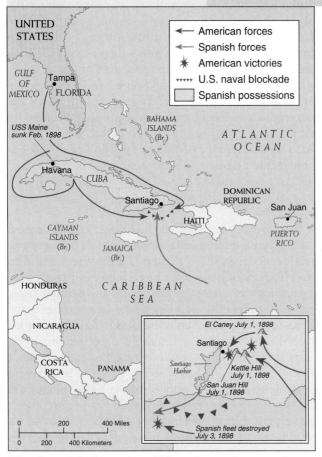

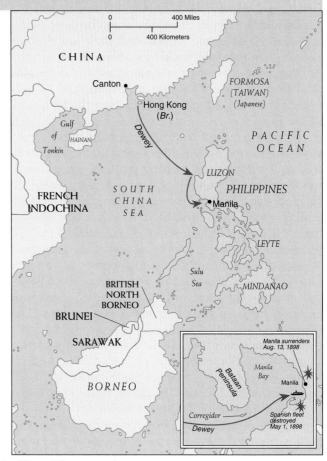

The Spanish-American War In two theaters of action, the United States used its naval power adeptly against a weak foe.

After he took over the office, President McKinley also drew back. In his Inaugural Address he declared, "We want no wars of conquest; we must avoid the temptation of territorial aggression." The tide turned, however, when Spain appeared unable to maintain order. In early 1898 public indignation, whipped up by tabloid press headlines and sensational stories, turned into frenzy on February 15, when an explosion ripped through the battleship USS *Maine,* stationed in Havana harbor ostensibly to rescue American citizens.

McKinley, suspecting war was close, had already begun to prepare for intervention. Newspapers ran banner headlines charging a Spanish conspiracy, although there was no proof. The impatient public meanwhile demanded revenge for the death of 266 American sailors. Within days a new slogan appeared: "Remember the Maine! To Hell with Spain!"

Finally, on April 11, McKinley asked Congress for a declaration of war against Spain. Yet Congress barely passed the war resolution on April 25, and only with the inclusion of an amendment by Senator Henry Teller of Colorado that disclaimed "any disposition or intention to exercise sovereignty, jurisdiction or control over said island, except for the pacification thereof." McKinley called for 125,000 volunteers, and men seeking to enlist nearly overwhelmed the administration. For the first time, former Confederates served in the higher ranks of the U.S. Army, symbolically uniting North and South in this patriotic endeavor. African Americans volunteered in great numbers, in a display of patriotism and also in sympathy with Cubans who were, like themselves, a generation or less away from slavery. By the end of April, the fighting had begun.

Charles Post, *Spanish Civil War.* Badly supplied Cuban insurrectos had practiced guerrilla warfare against the Spanish colonizers since the mid-1890s, but after the explosion on the USS *Maine*, American forces took over the war and abandoned the cause of Cuban self-determination. This picture, by the young U.S. volunteer, was one of a series of sketches later transformed into watercolor and oil paintings.

SOURCE: Library of Congress. Courtesy of Mrs. Charles Johnson Post and Miss Phyllis B. Post.

An outpouring of patriotic joy inspired massive parades, topical songs, and an overpowering enthusiasm. "Populists, Democrats, and Republicans are we," went one jingle, "But we are all Americans to make Cuba free." Just as the Civil War inspired masses of women to form relief societies so, too, did the Spanish–American war. The Women's Relief Corps and women's clubs across the country raised money and sent food and medical supplies to U.S. military camps.

Ten weeks later the war was all but over. On land, Lieutenant Colonel Theodore Roosevelt—who boasted of killing Spaniards "like jackrabbits"—led his Rough Riders to victory. On July 3, the main Spanish fleet near Santiago Bay was destroyed; two weeks later Santiago itself surrendered, and the war drew to a close. Although fewer than 400 Americans died in battle, disease and the inept treatment of the wounded created a medical disaster, spreading sickness and disease to more than 20,000 in the regiments. Roosevelt nevertheless felt invigorated by the conflict, agreeing with John Hay that it had been a "splendid little war."

On August 12, at a small ceremony in McKinley's office marking Spain's surrender, the United States

secured Cuba's independence from Spain but not its own sovereignty. One member of Congress thus announced the unanticipated outcome of the war from Cuba's point of view: "What greater liberty, freedom, and independence can be obtained than that enjoyed under the protection of our flag?" On January 1, 1899, at ceremonies in Havana marked the end of four hundred years of Spanish rule and the passage of sovereignty over the island to the United States. The Cubans who waged the struggle for independence for nearly forty years sat on the sidelines, the words of José Martí—"Cuba must be free from Spain and the United States"—receding into the distant past.

American businesses proceeded to tighten their hold on Cuban sugar plantations, while U.S. military forces oversaw the formation of a constitutional convention that made Cuba a protectorate of the United States. Under the Platt Amendment, sponsored by Republican senator Orville H. Platt of Connecticut in 1901, Cuba was required to provide land for American bases; to devote national revenues to pay back debts to the United States; to sign no treaty that would be detrimental to American interests; and to acknowledge the right of the United States to intervene at any time to protect its interests in Cuba. During the occupation, which lasted until 1902, there were more U.S. troops in Cuba than during the war. After the U.S. withdrawal, the terms of the Platt amendment were incorporated into the Cuban-American Treaty of 1903. This treaty, which remained in place until 1934, paved the way for American domination of the island's sugar industry and contributed to anti–American sentiment among Cuban nationalists.

War in the Philippines

The Philippines, another of Spain's colonies, seemed an especially attractive prospect, its 7,000 islands a natural way station to the markets of mainland Asia. In 1897 Assistant Secretary of the Navy Theodore Roosevelt and President McKinley had discussed the merits of taking the Pacific colony in the event of war with Spain. At the first opportunity, McKinley acted to bring these islands into the U.S. strategic orbit. Shortly after Congress declared war on Spain, on May 4, the president dispatched 5,000 troops to occupy the Philippines. George Dewey, a Civil War veteran who commanded the American Asiatic Squadron, was ordered to "start offensive action." During the first week of the conflict, he demolished the Spanish fleet in Manila Bay through seven hours of unimpeded target practice. Once the war ended, McKinley refused to sign the armistice unless Spain relinquished all claims to its Pacific islands. When Spain conceded, McKinley quickly drew up plans for colonial administration. He pledged "to educate the Filipinos, and to uplift and civilize and Christianize them." But after centuries of Spanish rule, the majority of islanders—already Christians—were eager to create their own nation.

The Filipino rebels, like the Cubans, at first welcomed American troops and fought with them against Spain. But when the Spanish-American War ended and they perceived that American troops were not preparing to leave, the rebels, led by Emilio Aguinaldo, turned against their former allies and attacked the American base of operations in Manila in February 1899. Predicting a brief skirmish, American commanders seriously underestimated the population's capacity to endure great suffering for the sake of independence.

U.S. troops had provoked this conflict in various ways. Military leaders, the majority veterans of the Indian Wars, commonly described the natives as "gugus," and reported themselves, as one said, as "just itching to get at the niggers." While awaiting action, American soldiers repeatedly insulted or physically abused civilians, raped Filipino women, and otherwise whipped up resentment.

The resulting conflict took the form of modern guerrilla warfare, with brutalities on both sides. By the time the fighting slowed down in 1902, 4,300 American lives had been lost, and one of every five Filipinos had died in battle or from starvation or disease. On some of the Philippine islands, intermittent fighting lasted until 1935.

The United States nevertheless refused to pull out. In 1901 William Howard Taft headed a commission that established a government controlled by Americans; after 1905, the president appointed a Filipino governor general to maintain the provincial government. Meanwhile, Americans bought up the best land and invested heavily in the island's sugar economy.

The conquest of the Philippines, which remained a U.S. territory until 1946, evoked for its defenders the vision of empire. At the very least, the Philippines joined Hawai'i as yet another steppingstone for U.S. merchants en route to China. At the end of the Spanish-American War, the United States advanced its interests in the Caribbean to include Puerto Rico, ceded by Spain, and eventually the Virgin Islands of St. Thomas, St. John, and St. Croix, purchased from Denmark in 1917. The acquisition of Pacific territories, including Guam, marked the emergence of the United States as a global colonial power.

Once again, Josiah Strong proclaimed judgment over an era. His famous treatise *Expansion* (1900) roundly defended American overseas involvements by carefully distinguishing between freedom and independence. People could achieve freedom, he argued, only under the rule of law. And because white Americans had proven themselves superior in the realm of

government, they could best bring "freedom" to nonwhite peoples by setting aside the ideal of national independence for a period of enforced guidance. Many began to wonder, however, whether the United States could become an empire without sacrificing its democratic spirit, and to ask whether the subjugated people were really so fortunate under the rule of the United States.

Critics of Empire

No mass movement formed to forestall U.S. expansion, but distinguished figures like Mark Twain, Andrew Carnegie, William Jennings Bryan, and Harvard philosopher William James voiced their opposition strongly. Dissent followed two broad lines of argument. In 1870, when President Grant urged the annexation of Santo Domingo, the nation-state occupying half of the island of Hispaniola (Haiti occupying the other half), opponents countered by insisting that the

"Uncle Sam Teaches the Art of Self-Government," editorial cartoon, 1898. Expressing a popular sentiment of the time, a newspaper cartoonist shows the rebels as raucous children who constantly fight among themselves and need to be brought into line by Uncle Sam. The Filipino leader, Emilio Aguinaldo, appears as a dunce for failing to learn properly from the teacher. The two major islands where no uprising took place, Puerto Rico and Hawai'i, appear as passive but exotically dressed women, ready to learn their lessons.

SOURCE: Library of Congress.

CHRONOLOGY

1867	Grange founded
	Secretary of State Seward negotiates the purchase of Alaska
1874	Tompkins Square Riot
	Granger laws begin to regulate railroad shipping rates
1877	Rutherford B. Hayes elected president
	Great Uprising of 1877
1879	Henry George publishes *Progress and Poverty*
1881	President James A. Garfield assassinated; Chester A. Arthur becomes president
1883	Pendleton Act passed
1884	Grover Cleveland elected president
1887	Interstate Commerce Act creates the Interstate Commerce Commission
1888	Edward Bellamy publishes *Looking Backward*
	National Colored Farmers' Alliance and Cooperative Union formed
	Benjamin Harrison elected president
1889	National Farmers' Alliance and Industrial Union formed
1890	Sherman Silver Purchase Act
	McKinley tariff enacted
	National American Woman Suffrage Association formed
1891	National Women's Alliance formed
	Populist (People's) Party formed
1892	Coeur d'Alene miners' strike
	Homestead strike
	Ida B. Wells begins crusade against lynching
1893	Western Federation of Miners formed
	Financial panic and depression
	World's Columbian Exhibition opens in Chicago
1894	"Coxey's Army" marches on Washington, D.C.
	Pullman strike and boycott
1896	*Plessy* v. *Ferguson* upholds segregation
	William McKinley defeats William Jennings Bryan for president
1897	Dingley tariff again raises import duties to an all-time high
1898	Eugene V. Debs helps found Social Democratic Party
	Hawai'i is annexed
	Spanish-American War begins
	Anti-Imperialist League formed
1899	*Cumming* v. *Richmond County Board of Education* sanctions segregated education
	Secretary of State John Hay announces Open Door policy
	Guerrilla war begins in the Philippines
1900	Gold Standard Act
	Josiah Strong publishes *Expansion*

United States stood unequivocally for the right of national self-determination and the consent of the governed. Others opposed annexation on the ground that dark-skinned and "ignorant" Santo Domingans were unworthy of American citizenship. These two contrary arguments, democratic and racist, were sounded repeatedly as the United States joined other nations in the armed struggle for empire.

Organized protest to military action, especially against the widely reported atrocities in the Philippines, owed much to the Anti-Imperialist League, which was founded by a small group of prominent Bostonians. In historic Faneuil Hall, which had witnessed the birth of both the American Revolution and the antislavery movement, a mass meeting was convened in June 1898 to protest the "insane and wicked ambition which is driving the nation to ruin." Within a few months, the league reported 25,000 members. Most supported American economic expansion but advocated free trade rather than political domination as the means to reach this goal. All strongly opposed the annexation of new territories. The league drew followers from every walk of life, including such famous writers as Charles Francis Adams and Mark Twain, *Nation* editor E. L. Godkin, African American scholar W. E. B. Du Bois, and Civil War veteran Thomas Wentworth Higginson.

The Anti-Imperialist League brought together like-minded societies from across the country, encouraged mass meetings, and published pamphlets, poems, and broadsides. The *National Labor Standard* expressed the common hope that all those "who believe in the Republic against Empire should join." By 1899, the league claimed a half-million members. A few outspoken anti-imperialists, such as former Illinois governor John Peter Altgeld, openly toasted Filipino rebels as heroes. Morrison Swift, leader of the Coxey's Army contingent from Massachusetts, formed a Filipino Liberation Society and sent antiwar materials to American troops. Others, such as Samuel Gompers, a league vice president, felt no sympathy for conquered peoples, describing Filipinos as "perhaps nearer the condition of savages and barbarians than any island possessed by any other civilized nation on earth." Gompers simply wanted to prevent colonized nonwhites from immigrating into the United States and "inundating" American labor.

Military leaders and staunch imperialists did not distinguish between racist and nonracist antiimperialists. They called all dissenters "unhung traitors" and demanded their arrest. Newspaper editors accused universities of harboring antiwar professors, although college students as a group were enthusiastic supporters of the war.

Within the press, which overwhelmingly supported the Spanish-American War, the voices of opposition appeared primarily in African American and labor papers. The *Indianapolis Recorder* asked rhetorically in 1899, "Are the tender-hearted expansionists in the United States Congress really actuated by the desire to save the Filipinos from self-destruction or is it the worldly greed for gain?" The *Railroad Telegrapher* similarly commented, "The wonder of it all is that the working people are willing to lose blood and treasure in fighting another man's battle."

Most Americans put aside their doubts and welcomed the new era of imperialism. Untouched by the private tragedies of dead or wounded American soldiers and the mass destruction of civilian society in the Philippines, the vast majority could approve Theodore Roosevelt's defense of armed conflict: "No triumph of peace is quite so great as the supreme triumphs of war."

CONCLUSION

The conflicts marking the last quarter of the nineteenth century that pitted farmers, workers, and the proprietors of small businesses against powerful outside interests had offered Americans an important moment of democratic promise. By the end of the century, however, the rural and working-class campaigns to retain a large degree of self-government in their communities had been defeated, their organizations destroyed, their autonomy eroded. The rise of a national governing class and its counterpart, the large bureaucratic state, established new rules of behavior, new sources of prestige, and new rewards for the most successful citizens.

But the nation would pay a steep price, in the next era, for the failure of democratic reform. Regional antagonisms, nativist movements against the foreign-born, and above all deepening racial tensions blighted American society. As the new century opened, progressive reformers moved to correct flaws in government while accepting the framework of a corporate society and its overseas empire. But they found the widening divisions in American society difficult—if not impossible—to overcome.

REVIEW QUESTIONS

1. Discuss some of the problems accompanying the expansion of government during the late nineteenth century. What role did political parties play in this process? Explain how a prominent reformer such as James Garfield might become a leading "machine" politician?

2. What were the major causes and consequences of the Populist movement of the 1880s and 1890s? Why did the election of 1896 prove so important to the future of American politics?

3. Discuss the role of women in both the Grange and the People's Party. What were their specific goals?

4. Discuss the causes and consequences of the financial crisis of the 1890s. How did various reformers and politicians respond to the event? What kinds of programs did they offer to restore the economy or reduce poverty?

5. How did the exclusion of African Americans affect the outcome of populism? Explain the rise of Jim Crow legislation in the South, and discuss its impact on the status of African Americans.

6. Describe American foreign policy during the 1890s. Why did the United States intervene in Cuba and the Philippines? What were some of the leading arguments for and against overseas expansion?

RECOMMENDED READING

Ruth Bordin, *Woman and Temperance: The Quest for Power and Liberty, 1873–1900* (1981). Relates the history of the WCTU to other campaigns for women's emancipation in the late nineteenth century and highlights the leadership of Frances E. Willard. Bordin demonstrates the central position temperance occupied in the political struggles of the era.

Matthew Freye Jacobson, *Barbarian Virtues: The United Sates Encounters Foreign Peoples at Home and Abroad, 1876–1917* (2000). Links the histories of immigration and empire-building to examine public discussions about foreign people, especially their "fitness" for self-government. Jacobson casts the search for markets as backdrop for cultural history.

Michael Kazin, *The Populist Persuasion: An American History* (1995, rev. ed., 1998). A fresh interpretation of Populist-style movements through the nineteenth and twentieth century that suggests such movements can be either "right" or "left" depending upon circumstances.

Walter LaFeber, *The New Empire: An Interpretation of American Expansion, 1860–1898* (1963, 1998). The best overview of U.S. imperial involvement in the late nineteenth century. LaFeber shows how overseas commitments grew out of the economic expansionist assumptions of American leaders and expanded continuously, if often chaotically, with the opportunities presented by the crises experienced by the older imperial powers.

Leon F. Litwack, *Trouble in Mind: Black Southerners in the Age of Jim Crow* (1998). An expansive social history of the first generation of African Americans born in freedom and surviving a period of extraordinary violent and repressive race relations in the South. Litwack examines the retrenchment of their political and civil rights but emphasizes their resourcefulness and resistance.

Nell Irvin Painter, *Standing at Armageddon: The United States, 1877–1919* (1987). Presents a broad overview of racial and industrial conflicts and the political movements that formed in their wake. Painter attempts to show how this period proved decisive to the future history of the United States.

Emily S. Rosenberg, *Spreading the American Dream: American Economic and Cultural Expansion, 1890–1945* (1982). Insightfully examines the significance of expansionist ideology. Rosenberg studies the cultural and social roots of American foreign policy.

Elizabeth Sanders, *Roots of Reform: Farmers, Workers, and the American State, 1877–1917* (1999). A painstaking reconstruction of the legislative history of congressional bills with emphasis on the lobbying of dirt farmers as well as their search for allies. Sanders, a political scientist, shines new light on familiar conflicts between debtors and creditors and the political processes of the Gilded Age.

David O. Stowell, *Streets, Railroads, and the Great Strike of 1877* (1999). Examines in close detail the uprising of 1877 in Buffalo, Albany, and Syracuse, New York, casting the strike simultaneously as a struggle between workers and the railroad corporations and an attempt by the community to protest against usurpation of streets by the trains. Stowell emphasizes the importance of the urban setting of this strike and provides ample data on the physical injuries inflicted by trains on local residents.

William Appleman Williams, *Empire as a Way of Life: An Essay on the Causes and Character of America's Present Predicament* (1982). A lucid general exploration of American views of empire. Williams shows that Americans allowed the idea of empire and, more generally, economic expansion, to dominate their concept of democracy, especially in the last half of the nineteenth century.

ADDITIONAL BIBLIOGRAPHY

The Nation and Politics

Paula C. Baker, *The Moral Frameworks of Public Life: Gender, Politics and the State in Rural New York, 1870–1930* (1991)

Rebecca Edwards, *Angels in the Machinery: Gender in American Party Politics from the Civil War to the Progressive Era* (1997)

Michael Lewis Goldberg, *An Army of Women: Gender and Politics in Gilded Age Kansas* (1997)

J. William Harris, *Deep Souths: Delta, Piedmont, and Sea Island Society in the Age of Segregation* (2001)

Gwendolyn Mink, *Old Labor and New Immigrants in American Political Development* (1986)

Douglas Steeples and David O. Whitten, *Democracy in Desperation: The Depression of 1893* (1998)

Brook Thomas, Plessy v. Ferguson: *A Brief History with Documents* (1997)

David Traxel, *1898: The Birth of the American Century* (1998)

C. Vann Woodward, *The Strange Career of Jim Crow*, 3rd rev. ed. (1974)

Populism

Lawrence Goodwyn, *Democratic Promise: The Populist Moment in America* (1976)

Steven Hahn, *The Roots of Southern Populism* (1983)

Robert C. McMath, *American Populism: A Social History* (1993)

Scott G. McNall, *The Road to Rebellion: Class Formation and Kansas Populism 1865–1900* (1988)

Norman Pollack, *The Human Economy: Populism, Capitalism and Democracy* (1990)

Protest and Reform Movements

Susan Curtis, *A Consuming Faith: The Social Gospel and Modern American Culture* (1991)

Barbara Leslie Epstein, *The Politics of Domesticity: Women, Evangelism, and Temperance in Nineteenth-Century America* (1981)

Paul Krause, *The Battle for Homestead, 1880–1892* (1992)

Ralph E. Luker, *The Social Gospel in Black and White* (1991)

Alison M. Parker, *Purifying America: Women, Cultural Reform, and Pro-Censorship Activism* (1997)

Gretchen Ritter, *Goldbugs and Greenbacks: The Antimonopoloy Tradition and the Politics of Finance in America, 1865–1896* (1997)

Richard Schneirov, Shelton Stromquist, and Nick Salvatore, eds., *The Pullman Strike and the Crisis of the 1890s: Essays on Labor and Politics* (1999)

Carlos A. Schwantes, *Coxey's Army* (1985)

Imperialism and Empire

Tunde Adeleke, *Unafrican Americans: Nineteenth-Century Black Nationalists and the Civilizing Mission* (1998)

Nupur Chauduri and Margaret Strobel, eds., *Western Women and Imperialism* (1992)

Willard B. Gatewood, Jr., *Black Americans and the White Man's Burden* (1975)

Patricia Hill, *The World Their Household: The American Women's Foreign Mission Movement and Cultural Transformation, 1870–1920* (1985)

Amy Kaplan and Donald E. Pease, eds., *Cultures of United States Imperialism* (1993)

Robert W. Rydell, *All the World's a Fair: Vision of Empire at the American International Expositions, 1876–1916* (1984)

Anders Stephanson, *Manifest Destiny: American Expansion and the Empire of Right* (1995)

Spanish-American War and the Philippines

H. W. Brands, *Bound to Empire: The United States and the Philippines* (1992)

Kristin L. Hoganson, *Fighting for American Manhood: How Gendeer Politics Provoked the Spanish–American and Philippine–American Wars* (1998)

Stuart Creighton Miller, *"Benevolent Assimilation": The American Conquest of the Philippines, 1899–1903* (1982)

Ivan Musicant, *Empire By Default: The Spanish-American War and the Dawn of the American Century* (1998)

Louis A. Perez, Jr., *The War of 1898: The United States and Cuba in History and Historiography* (1998)

Harvey Rosenfeld, *Diary of a Dirty Little War: The Spanish–American War of 1898* (2000)

Angel Smith and Emma Davila-Cox, ed., *The Crisis of 1898: Colonial Redistribution and Nationalist Mobilization* (1999)

Biography

Ruth Bordin, *Frances Willard: A Biography* (1986)

Mari Jo Buhle, Paul Buhle, and Harvey J. Kaye, eds., *The American Radical* (1995)

Edward P. Crapol, *James G. Blaine: Architect of Empire* (2000)

Jane Taylor Nelson, *A Prairie Populist: The Memoirs of Luna Kellie* (1992)

Allan Peskin, *Garfield: A Biography* (1978)

Ben Procter, *William Randolph Hearst: The Early Years, 1863–1910* (1998)

Nick Salvatore, *Eugene V. Debs* (1982)

Peggy Samuels and Harold Samuels, *Teddy Roosevelt at San Juan: The Making of a President* (1997)

Mildred Thompson, *Ida B. Wells-Barnett: An Exploratory Study of an American Black Woman* (1990)

C. Van Woodward, *Tom Watson* (1963)

HISTORY ON THE INTERNET

http://www.history.navy.mil/photos/events/spanam/eve-pge.htm

This is a U.S. Navy historical site containing photographs with informative captions from the Spanish American War era.

http://oyez.nwu.edu/

The Oyez Project of Northwestern University provides information on Supreme Court decisions, especially the written Court opinions. For this chapter search for *Plessy* v. *Ferguson* (1896).

http://memory.loc.gov/ammem/aaohtml/exhibit/aopart6.html

This American Memory exhibition from the Library of Congress describes the America of African Americans from the 1870s to World War I as Booker T. Washington gained prominence as a black leader.

http://www.boondocksnet.com/gallery/us_intro.html

http://www.boondocksnet.com/gallery/ads_index.html

Boondocksnet presents political cartoons and commercial advertisements of America's age of Imperialism and the Spanish American War on this site.

URBAN AMERICA AND THE PROGRESSIVE ERA

1900–1917

John Sloan (1871–1951), *Italian Procession, New York*, 1913–1925. Oil on canvas, 24″ × 28″. SOURCE: San Diego Museum of Art, gift of Mr. and Mrs. Appleton S. Bridges.

The Henry Street Settlement House: Women Settlement House Workers Create a Community of Reform

A SHY AND FRIGHTENED YOUNG GIRL APPEARED IN THE DOORWAY OF A weekly home-nursing class for women on Manhattan's Lower East Side. The teacher beckoned her to come forward. Tugging on the teacher's skirt, the girl pleaded in broken English for the teacher to come home with her. "Mother," "baby," "blood," she kept repeating. The teacher gathered up the sheets that were part of the interrupted lesson in bed making. The two hurried through narrow, garbage-strewn, foul-smelling streets, then groped their way up a pitch-dark, rickety staircase. They reached a cramped, two-room apartment, home to an immigrant family of seven and several boarders. There, in a vermin-infested bed, en-crusted with dried blood, lay a mother and her newborn baby. The mother had been abandoned by a doctor because she could not afford his fee.

The teacher, Lillian Wald, was a twenty-five-year-old nurse at New York Hospital. Years later she recalled this scene as her baptism by fire and the turning point in her life. Born in 1867, Wald had enjoyed a com-fortable upbringing in a middle-class German Jewish family in Rochester. Despite her parents' objections, she had moved to New York City to become a professional nurse. Resentful of the disdainful treatment nurses received from doctors and horrified by the inhumane conditions at a juvenile asylum she worked in, Wald determined to find a way of caring for the sick in their neighborhoods and homes. With nursing school classmate Mary Brewster, Wald rented a fifth-floor walk-up apartment on the Lower East Side and established a visiting nurse service. The two pro-vided professional care in the home to hundreds of families for a nominal fee of 10 to 25 cents. They also offered each family they visited informa-tion on basic health care, sanitation, and disease prevention. In 1895, philanthropist Jacob Schiff generously donated a red brick Georgian house on Henry Street as a new base of operation.

The Henry Street Settlement stood in the center of perhaps the most overcrowded neighborhood in the world, New York's Lower East Side. Roughly 500,000 people were packed into an area only as large as a midsized Kansas farm. Population density was about 500 per acre, roughly four times the figure for the rest of New York City and far more concentrated than even the worst slums of London or Calcutta. A single city block might have as many as 3,000 residents. Home for most Lower East Siders was a small tenement apartment that might include paying boarders squeezed in alongside the immediate family. Residents were mostly recent immigrants from southern and eastern Europe: Jews, Ital-ians, Germans, Greeks, Hungarians, Slavs. Men, women, and children toiled in the garment shops, small factories, retail stores, breweries, and warehouses to be found on nearly every street. An Irish-dominated ma-chine controlled local political affairs.

The Henry Street Settlement became a model for a new kind of re-form community composed essentially of college-educated women who encouraged and supported one another in a wide variety of humanitarian, civic, political, and cultural activities. Settlement house living arrangements closely resembled those in the dormitories of such new women's colleges as Smith, Wellesley, and Vassar. Like these colleges, the settlement house was an "experiment," but one designed, in settlement house pioneer Jane Addams's words, "to aid in the solution of the social and industrial problems which are engendered by the modern conditions of urban life." Unlike earlier moral reformers who tried to impose their ideas from outside, settlement house residents lived in poor communities and worked for immediate improvements in the health and welfare of those communities. Yet, as Addams and others repeatedly stressed, the college-educated women were beneficiaries as well. The settlement house allowed them to preserve a collegial spirit, satisfy the desire for service, and apply their academic training.

With its combined moral and social appeal, the settlement house movement attracted many educated young women and grew rapidly. There were six settlement houses in the United States in 1891, some 74 in 1897, more than 200 by 1900, and more than 400 by 1910. Few women made settlement work a career. The average stay was less than five years. Roughly half of those who worked in the movement eventually married. Those who did make a career of settlement house work, however, typically chose not to marry, and most lived together with female companions. As the movement flourished, settlement house residents called attention to the plight of the poor and fostered respect for different cultural heritages in countless articles and lectures. Leaders of the movement, including Jane Addams, Lillian Wald, and Florence Kelley, emerged as influential political figures during the progressive era.

Wald attracted a dedicated group of nurses, educators, and reformers to live at the Henry Street Settlement. By 1909 Henry Street had more than forty residents, supported by the donations of well-to-do New Yorkers. Wald and her allies convinced the New York Board of Health to assign a nurse to every public school in the city. They lobbied the Board of Education to create the first school lunch programs. They persuaded the city to set up municipal milk stations to ensure the purity of milk. Henry Street also pioneered tuberculosis treatment and prevention. Its leaders became powerful advocates for playground construction, improved street cleaning, and tougher housing inspection. The settlement's Neighborhood Playhouse became an internationally acclaimed center for innovative theater, music, and dance.

As settlement house workers expanded their influence from local neighborhoods to larger political and social circles, they became, in the phrase of one historian, "spearheads for reform." Lillian Wald became a national figure—an outspoken advocate of child labor legislation and woman suffrage and a vigorous opponent of American involvement in World War I. She offered Henry Street as a meeting place to the National Negro Conference in 1909, out of which emerged the National Association for the Advancement of Colored People. It was no cliché for Wald to say, as she did on many occasions, "The whole world is my neighborhood." ■

New York City

KEY TOPICS

- The political, social, and intellectual roots of progressive reform

- Tensions between social justice and social control

- The urban scene and the impact of new immigration

- Political activism by the working class, women, and African Americans

- Progressivism in national politics

THE CURRENTS OF PROGRESSIVISM

Between the 1890s and World War I, a large and diverse number of Americans claimed the political label "progressive." Progressives could be found in all classes, regions, and races. They shared a fundamental ethos, or belief, that America needed a new social consciousness to cope with the problems brought on by the enormous rush of economic and social change in the post–Civil War decades. Yet progressivism was no unified movement with a single set of principles. It is best understood as a varied collection of reform communities, often fleeting, uniting citizens in a host of political, professional, and religious organizations, some of which were national in scope.

Progressivism drew from deep roots in hundreds of local American communities. At the state level it flowered in the soil of several key issues: ending political corruption, bringing more businesslike methods to governing, and offering a more compassionate legislative response to the excesses of industrialism. As a national movement, progressivism reached its peak in 1912, when the four major presidential candidates all ran on some version of a progressive platform. This last development was an important measure of the extent to which local reform movements, like the Henry Street Settlement, and new intellectual currents had captured the political imagination of the nation.

The many contradictions and disagreements surrounding the meaning of progressivism have led some historians to dismiss the term as hopelessly vague. Some progressives focused on expanding state and federal regulation of private interests for the public welfare. Others viewed the rapid influx of new immigrants and the explosive growth of large cities as requiring more stringent social controls. Another variant emphasized eliminating corruption in the political system as

the key to righting society's wrongs. In the South, progressivism was for white people only. Progressives could be forward looking in their vision or nostalgic for a nineteenth-century world rapidly disappearing. Self-styled progressives often found themselves facing each other from opposite sides of an issue.

Yet at the local, state, and finally national levels, reform rhetoric and energy shaped most of the political and cultural debates of the era. Understanding progressivism in all its complexity thus requires examining what key reform groups, thinkers, and political figures actually did and said under its ambiguous banner.

Unifying Themes

Three basic attitudes underlay the various crusades and movements that emerged in response to the fears gnawing at large segments of the population. The first was anger over the excesses of industrial capitalism and urban growth. At the same time, progressives shared an essential optimism about the ability of citizens to improve social and economic conditions. They were reformers, not revolutionaries. Second, progressives emphasized social cohesion and common bonds as a way of understanding how modern society and economics actually worked. They largely rejected the ideal of individualism that had informed nineteenth-century economic and political theory. For progressives, poverty and success hinged on more than simply individual character; the economy was more than merely a sum of individual calculations. Progressives thus opposed social Darwinism, with its claim that any effort to improve social conditions would prove fruitless because society is like a jungle in which only the "fittest" survive. Third, progressives believed in the need for citizens to intervene actively, both politically and morally, to improve social conditions. They pushed for a stronger government role in regulating the economy and solving the nation's social problems.

OVERVIEW

CURRENTS OF PROGRESSIVISM

	Key Figures	Issues	Institutions/Achievements
Local Communities	Jane Addams, Lillian Wald, Florence Kelley, Frederic C. Howe, Samuel Jones	■ Improving health, education, welfare in urban immigrant neighborhoods ■ Child labor, eight-hour day ■ Celebrating immigrant cultures ■ Reforming urban politics ■ Municipal ownership/regulation of utilities	■ Hull House Settlement ■ Henry Street Settlement ■ National Consumers League ■ New York Child Labor Committee ■ Bureau of Municipal Research
State	Robert M. LaFollette, Hiram Johnson, Al Smith	■ Limiting power of railroads, other corporations ■ Improving civil service ■ Direct democracy ■ Applying academic scholarship to human needs	■ "Wisconsin Idea" ■ State Workmen's Compensation ■ Unemployment Insurance ■ Public utility regulation
	James K. Vardaman, Hoke Smith	■ Disfranchisement of African Americans	■ Legalized segregation
National	Theodore Roosevelt	■ Trustbusting ■ Conservation and Western development ■ National regulation of corporate and financial excesses	■ Reclamation Bureau (1902) ■ U.S. Forest Service (1905) ■ Food and Drug Administration (1906) ■ Meat Inspection Act (1906) ■ Hepburn Act–ICC (1906)
	Woodrow Wilson	■ National regulation of corporate and financial excesses ■ Reform of national banking	■ Graduated Income Tax (1913) ■ Federal Reserve Act (1913) ■ Clayton Antitrust Act (1914) ■ Federal Trade Commission (1914)
Intellectual/ Cultural	Jacob Riis	■ Muckraking	■ *How the Other Half Lives* (1890)
	Lincoln Steffens, Ida Tarbell, Upton Sinclair, S. S. McClure		■ *Shame of the Cities* (1902) ■ *History of Standard Oil* (1904) ■ *The Jungle* (1906) ■ *McClure's Magazine*
	John Dewey	■ Education reform	■ *Democracy and Education* (1916)
	Louis Brandeis	■ Sociological jurisprudence	■ *Muller v. Oregon* (1908)
	Edwin A. Ross	■ Empowering "ethical elite"	■ *Social Control* (1901)

Progressive rhetoric and methods drew on two distinct sources of inspiration. One was evangelical Protestantism, particularly the late nineteenth-century social gospel movement. Social gospelers rejected the idea of original sin as the cause of human suffering. They emphasized both the capacity and the duty of Christians to purge the world of poverty, inequality, and economic greed. A second strain of progressive thought looked to natural and social scientists to develop rational measures for improving the human condition, believing that experts trained in statistical analysis and engineering could make government and industry more efficient. Progressivism thus offered an uneasy combination of social justice and social control, a tension that would characterize American reform for the rest of the twentieth century.

Women Spearhead Reform

In the 1890s the settlement house movement had begun to provide an alternative to traditional concepts of private charity and humanitarian reform. Settlement workers found they could not transform their neighborhoods without confronting a host of broad social questions: chronic poverty, overcrowded tenement houses, child labor, industrial accidents, public health. As on Henry Street, college-educated, middle-class women constituted a key vanguard in the crusade for social justice. As reform communities, settlement houses soon discovered the need to engage the political and cultural life of the larger communities that surrounded them.

Photographer Lewis Hine, one of the pioneers of social documentary photography, made this evocative 1908 portrait of "Mamie," a typical young spinner working at a cotton mill in Lancaster, South Carolina. The National Child Labor Committee hired Hine to help document, publicize, and curb the widespread employment of children in industrial occupations. "These pictures," Hine wrote, "speak for themselves and prove that the law is being violated."

SOURCE: Lewis Hine (American, 1874–1940), *A Carolina Spinner*, 1908. Gelatin silver print, 4 3/4 × 7 in. Milwaukee Art Museum, Gift of the Sheldon M. Barnett Family. (M1973.83).

Jane Addams founded one of the first settlement houses, Hull House, in Chicago in 1889 after years of struggling to find work and a social identity equal to her talents. A member of one of the first generation of American women to attend college, Addams was a graduate of Rockford College. Many educated women were dissatisfied with the life choices conventionally available to them: early marriage or the traditional female professions of teaching, nursing, and library work. Settlement work provided these women with an attractive alternative. Hull House was located in a run-down slum area of Chicago. It had a day nursery, a dispensary for medicines and medical advice, a boardinghouse, an art gallery, and a music school. Addams often spoke of the "subjective necessity" of settlement houses. By this she meant that they gave young, educated women a way to satisfy their powerful desire to connect with the real world. "There is nothing after disease, indigence and guilt," she wrote, "so fatal to life itself as the want of a proper outlet for active faculties."

Social reformer Florence Kelley helped direct the support of the settlement house movement behind groundbreaking state and federal labor legislation. Arriving at Hull House in 1891, Kelley found what she described as a "colony of efficient and intelligent women." In 1893, she wrote a report detailing the dismal conditions in sweatshops and the effects of long hours on the women and children who worked in them. This report became the basis for landmark legislation in Illinois that limited women to an eight-hour workday, barred children under fourteen from working, and abolished tenement labor. Illinois governor John Peter Altgeld appointed Kelley as chief inspector for the new law. In 1895 Kelley published *Hull House Maps and Papers*, the first scientific study of urban poverty in America. Moving to Henry Street Settlement in 1898, Kelley served as general secretary of the new National Consumers' League. With Lillian Wald she established the New York Child Labor Committee and pushed for the creation of the U.S. Children's Bureau, established in 1912.

Kelley, Addams, Wald, and their circle consciously used their power as women to reshape politics in the progressive era. Electoral politics and the state were historically male preserves, but female social progressives turned their gender into an advantage. They built upon the tradition of female moral reform, where women had long operated outside male-dominated political institutions to agitate and organize. Activists like Kelley used their influence in civil society to create new state powers in the service of social justice. They left a legacy that simultaneously expanded the social welfare function of the state and increased women's public authority and influence.

The young Jane Addams, founder of the Hull House settlement in south Chicago, and a leading voice for a variety Progressive era reform campaigns. Addams inspired thousands of educated, middle class American women to put their intelligence, energy, and moral passion into serving the needs of the urban poor.

SOURCE: Jane Addams Memorial Collection (JAMC neg.21), The University Library, University of Illinois at Chicago.

The Urban Machine

Women had to work outside existing political institutions not just because they could not vote, but also because city politics had become a closed and often corrupt system. By the turn of the century Democratic Party machines, usually dominated by first- and second-generation Irish, controlled the political life of most large American cities. The keys to machine strength were disciplined organization and the delivery of essential services to both immigrant communities and business elites. The successful machine politician viewed his work as a business, and he accumulated his capital by serving people who needed assistance. For most urban dwellers, the city was a place of economic and social insecurity. Recent immigrants in particular faced frequent unemployment, sickness, and discrimination. In exchange for votes, machine politicians offered their constituents a variety of services. These included municipal jobs in the police and

fire departments, work at city construction sites, intervention with legal problems, and food and coal during hard times.

For those who did business with the city—construction companies, road builders, realtors—staying on the machine's good side was simply another business expense. In exchange for valuable franchises and city contracts, businessmen routinely bribed machine politicians and contributed liberally to their campaign funds. George Washington Plunkitt, a stalwart of New York's Tammany Hall machine, good-naturedly defended what he called "honest graft": making money from inside information on public improvements. "It's just like lookin' ahead in Wall Street or in the coffee or cotton market. . . . I seen my opportunities and I took 'em."

The machines usually had close ties to a city's vice economy and commercial entertainments. Organized prostitution and gambling, patronized largely by visitors to the city, could flourish only when "protected" by politicians who shared in the profits. Many machine figures began as saloonkeepers, and liquor dealers and beer brewers provided important financial support for "the organization." Vaudeville and burlesque theater, boxing, horse racing, and professional baseball were other urban enterprises with economic and political links to machines. Entertainment and spectacle made up a central element in the machine political style as well. Constituents looked forward to the colorful torch-light parades, free summer picnics, and riverboat excursions regularly sponsored by the machines.

On New York City's Lower East Side, where the Henry Street Settlement was located, Timothy D. "Big Tim" Sullivan embodied the popular machine style. Big Tim, who had risen from desperate poverty, remained enormously popular with his constituents until his death in 1913. "I believe in liberality," he declared. "I am a thorough New Yorker and have no narrow prejudices. I never ask a hungry man about his past; I feed him, not because he is good, but because he needs food. Help your neighbor but keep your nose out of his affairs." Critics charged that Sullivan controlled the city's gambling and made money from prostitution. But his real fortune came through his investments in vaudeville and the early movie business. Sullivan, whose district included the largest number of immigrants and transients in the city, provided shoe giveaways and free Christmas dinners to thousands every winter. To help pay for these and other charitable activities, he informally taxed the saloons, theaters, and restaurants in the district.

Progressive critics of machine politics routinely exaggerated the machine's power and influence. State legislatures, controlled by Republican rural and small-town elements, proved a formidable check on what city-based machines could accomplish. Reform campaigns that publicized excessive graft and corruption sometimes led voters to throw machine-backed mayors and aldermen out of office. And there were never enough patronage jobs for all the people clamoring for appointments. In the early twentieth century, to expand their base of support, political machines in the Northeast began concentrating more on passing welfare legislation beneficial to working-class and immigrant constituencies. In this way machine politicians often allied themselves with progressive reformers in state legislatures. In New York, for example, Tammany Hall figures such as Robert Wagner, Al Smith, and Big Tim Sullivan worked with middle-class progressive groups to pass child labor laws, factory safety regulations, worker compensation plans, and other efforts to make government more responsive to social needs. As Jewish and Catholic immigrants expanded in number and proportion in the city population, urban machines also began to champion cultural pluralism, opposing prohibition and immigration restrictions and defending the contributions made by new ethnic groups in the cities.

Political Progressives and Urban Reform

Political progressivism originated in the cities. It was both a challenge to the power of machine politics and a response to deteriorating urban conditions. City governments, especially in the Northeast and industrial Midwest, seemed hardly capable of providing the basic services needed to sustain large populations. For example, an impure water supply left Pittsburgh with one of the world's highest rates of death from typhoid, dysentery, and cholera. Most New York City neighborhoods rarely enjoyed street cleaning, and playgrounds were nonexistent. "The challenge of the city," Cleveland progressive Frederic C. Howe said in 1906, "has become one of decent human existence."

Reformers placed much of the blame for urban ills on the machines and looked for ways to restructure city government. The "good government" movement, led by the National Municipal League, fought to make city management a nonpartisan, even nonpolitical, process by bringing the administrative techniques of large corporations to cities. Reformers revised city charters in favor of stronger mayoral power and expanded use of appointed administrators and career civil servants. The New York Bureau of Municipal Research, founded in 1906, became a prototype for similar bureaus around the country. It drew up blueprints for model charters, ordinances, and zoning plans designed by experts trained in public administration.

Business and professional elites became the biggest boosters of structural reforms in urban government. In the summer of 1900 a hurricane in the Gulf of Mexico unleashed a tidal wave on Galveston, Texas. To cope with this disaster, leading businessmen convinced the state legislature to replace the mayor-council government with a small board of commissioners. Each commissioner was elected at large, and each was responsible for a different city department. Under this plan voters could more easily identify and hold accountable those responsible for city services. The city commission, enjoying both policy-making and administrative powers, proved very effective in rebuilding Galveston. By 1917 nearly 500 cities, including Houston, Oakland, Kansas City, Denver, and Buffalo, had adopted the commission form of government. Another approach, the city manager plan, gained popularity in small and midsized cities. In this system, a city council appointed a professional, nonpartisan city manager to handle the day-to-day operations of the community.

Progressive politicians who focused on the human problems of the industrial city championed a different kind of reform, one based on changing policies rather than the political structure. In Toledo, Samuel "Golden Rule" Jones served as mayor from 1897 to 1904. A capitalist who had made a fortune manufacturing oil well machinery, Jones created a strong base of working-class and ethnic voters around his reform program. He advocated municipal ownership of utilities, built new parks and schools, and established an eight-hour day and a minimum wage for city employees. In Cleveland, wealthy businessman Thomas L. Johnson served as mayor from 1901 to 1909. He emphasized both efficiency and social welfare. His popular program included lower streetcar fares, public baths, milk and meat inspection, and an expanded park and playground system.

Progressivism in the Statehouse: West and South

Their motives and achievements were mixed, but progressive politicians became a powerful force in many state capitals. In Wisconsin, Republican dissident Robert M. La Follette forged a coalition of angry farmers, small businessmen, and workers with his fiery attacks on railroads and other large corporations. Leader of the progressive faction of the state Republicans, "Fighting Bob" won three terms as governor (1900–06), then served as a U.S. senator until his death in 1925. As governor he pushed through tougher corporate tax rates, a direct primary, an improved civil service code, and a railroad commission designed to regulate freight charges. La Follette used faculty experts at the University of Wisconsin to help research and write his bills. Other states began copying the "Wisconsin Idea"—the application of academic scholarship and theory to the needs of the people.

La Follette railed against "the interests" and invoked the power of the ordinary citizen. In practice, however, his railroad commission accomplished far less than progressive rhetoric claimed. It essentially represented special interests—commercial farmers and businessmen seeking reduced shipping rates. Ordinary consumers did not see lower passenger fares or reduced food prices. And as commissioners began to realize, the national reach of the railroads limited the effectiveness of state regulation. Although La Follette championed a more open political system, he also enrolled state employees in a tight political machine of his own. The La Follette family would dominate Wisconsin politics for forty years.

Western progressives displayed the greatest enthusiasm for institutional political reform. In the early 1900s, Oregon voters approved a series of constitutional amendments designed to strengthen direct democracy. The two most important were the *initiative*, which allowed a direct vote on specific measures put on the state ballot by petition, and the *referendum*, which allowed voters to decide on bills referred to them by the legislature. Other reforms included the direct *primary*, which allowed voters to cross party lines, and the *recall*, which gave voters the right to remove elected officials by popular vote. Widely copied throughout the West, all these measures intentionally weakened political parties.

Western progressives also targeted railroads, mining and timber companies, and public utilities for reform. Large corporations such as Pacific Gas and Electric and the Southern Pacific Railroad had amassed enormous wealth and political influence. They were able to corrupt state legislatures and charge consumers exorbitant rates. An alliance between middle-class progressives and working-class voters reflected growing disillusionment with the ideology of individualism that had helped pave the way for the rise of the big corporation. In California, attorney Hiram Johnson won a 1910 progressive campaign for governor on the slogan "Kick the Southern Pacific Railroad Out of Politics." In addition to winning political reforms, Johnson also put through laws regulating utilities and child labor, mandating an eight-hour day for working women, and providing a state-worker compensation plan.

In the South, the populist tradition of the 1880s and 1890s had been based in part on a biracial politics of protest. But southern progressivism was for white people only. Indeed, southern progressives believed that the disfranchisement of black voters and the creation of a legally segregated public sphere were necessary preconditions for political and social reform. Reform governors, such as James Vardaman of Mississippi and Hoke Smith of Georgia, made strident racism a key element in their campaigns against entrenched conservative Democratic machines. With African Americans removed from political life, white southern progressives argued, the direct primary system of nominating candidates would give white voters more influence. Between 1890 and

1910 southern states passed a welter of statutes specifying poll taxes, literacy tests, and property qualifications with the explicit goal of preventing voting by blacks. This systematic disfranchisement of African American voters stripped black communities of any political power. To prevent the disfranchisement of poor white voters under these laws, states established so-called understanding and grandfather clauses. Election officials had discretionary power to decide whether an illiterate person could understand and reasonably interpret the Constitution when read to him. Unqualified white men were also registered if they could show that their grandfathers had voted.

Southern progressives also supported the push toward a fully segregated public sphere. Between 1900 and 1910 southern states strengthened "Jim Crow" laws requiring separation of races in restaurants, streetcars, beaches, and theaters. Schools were separate but hardly equal. A 1916 Bureau of Education study found that per capita expenditures for education in southern states averaged $10.32 a year for white children and $2.89 for black children. And African American teachers received far lower salaries than their white counterparts. Black taxpayers, in effect, subsidized improved schools for whites, even as they saw their own children's educational opportunities deteriorate. The legacy of southern progressivism was thus closely linked to the strengthening of the legal and institutional guarantees of white supremacy.

Based mostly in New South towns and cities, and with growing strength among educated professionals, small businessmen, and women's benevolent societies, southern progressives organized to control both greedy corporations and "unruly" citizens. Citizens groups, city boards of trade, and newspapers pressed reluctant legislators to use state power to regulate big business. Between 1905 and 1909 nearly every southern state moved to regulate railroads by mandating lower passenger and freight rates. Prohibition enjoyed wide appeal in the South, as progressives active in the Anti-Saloon League argued that banning the alcohol trade would protect the family structure and victimized women, as well as reducing crime among African Americans. Employing aggressive lobbying, petitions, and massive parades, prohibition forces succeeded in pushing six southern states to ban the manufacture and sale of alcoholic beverages by 1909. Southern progressives also directed their energies at the related problems of child labor and educational reform. In 1900, at least one-quarter of all southern cotton mill workers were between the ages of ten and sixteen, many of whom worked over sixty hours per week. Led by reform minded ministers Edgar Gardner Murphy and Alexander McKelway, and drawing upon the activism of white club women, reformers attacked child labor by focusing on the welfare of children and their mothers and emphasizing the degradation of "Anglo Saxons." In 1903 Alabama and North Carolina enacted the first state child labor laws, setting twelve as a minimum age for employment. But the laws were weakened by many exemptions and no provisions for enforcement, as lawmakers also heard the loud complaints from parents and mill owners who resented the efforts of reformers to limit their choices. Progressives also mounted related state campaigns for compulsory education, as the South lagged behind the rest of the nation in literacy rates, school attendance, and overall spending. In 1906 the General Education Board, funded by John D. Rockefeller, Jr., began working with southern state boards of education and local officials to build high schools, lengthen the school year, and improve teachers' salaries. By 1920 only half as many southern children were illiterate as in 1900, and thousands of new school buildings had been constructed throughout the region.

New Journalism: Muckraking

Changes in journalism helped fuel a new reform consciousness by drawing the attention of millions to urban poverty, political corruption, the plight of industrial workers, and immoral business practices. As early as 1890, journalist Jacob Riis had shocked the nation with his landmark book *How the Other Half Lives,* a portrait of New York City's poor. A Danish immigrant who arrived in New York City in 1871, Riis became a newspaper reporter, covering the police beat and learning about the city's desperate underside. Riis's book included a remarkable series of photographs he had taken in tenements, lodging houses, sweatshops, and saloons. These striking pictures, combined with Riis's analysis of slum housing patterns, had a powerful impact on a whole generation of urban reformers.

Within a few years, magazine journalists had turned to uncovering the seamier side of American life. The key innovator was S. S. McClure, a young Midwestern editor who in 1893 started America's first large-circulation magazine, *McClure's.* Charging only a dime for his monthly, McClure effectively combined popular fiction with articles on science, technology, travel, and recent history. He attracted a new readership among the urban middle class through aggressive subscription and promotional campaigns, as well as newsstand sales. By the turn of the century *McClure's* and several imitators—*Munsey's, Cosmopolitan, Collier's, Everybody's,* and the *Saturday Evening Post*—had circulations in the hundreds of thousands. Making extensive use of photographs and illustrations, these cheap upstarts soon far surpassed older, more staid and expensive magazines such as the *Atlantic Monthly* and *Harper's* in circulation.

In 1902 McClure began hiring talented reporters to write detailed accounts of the nation's social problems. Lincoln Steffens's series *The Shame of the Cities* (1902) revealed the widespread graft at the center of American urban politics. He showed how big-city bosses routinely worked hand in glove with businessmen seeking lucrative municipal contracts for gas, water, electricity, and mass transit. Ida Tarbell, in her *History of the Standard Oil Company* (1904), thoroughly documented how John D. Rockefeller ruthlessly squeezed out competitors with unfair business practices. Ray Stannard Baker wrote detailed portraits of life and labor in Pennsylvania coal towns.

McClure's and other magazines discovered that "exposure journalism" paid off handsomely in terms of increased circulation. The middle-class public responded to this new combination of factual reporting and moral exhortation. A series such as Steffens's fueled reform campaigns that swept individual communities. Between 1902 and 1908, magazines were full of articles exposing insurance scandals, patent medicine frauds, and stock market swindles. Upton

This picture of Bohemian immigrant cigar makers at work in a New York City tenement first appeared in Jacob Riis's How the Other Half Lives (1890), a pathbreaking work of "exposure journalism." Apartments like these, owned and rented out by cigar manufacturers, served as both living quarters and workshops, leading to filthy and unhealthy conditions. Note how the entire family works together to roll as many cigars as possible.

SOURCE: Bohemian Cigar Makers at Work in Their Tenement, ca. 1890. Museum of the City of New York, The Jacob A. Riis Collection, (#147.90.13.1.150).

Sinclair's 1906 novel *The Jungle,* a socialist tract set among Chicago packinghouse workers, exposed the filthy sanitation and abysmal working conditions in the stockyards and the meatpacking industry. In an effort to boost sales, Sinclair's publisher devoted an entire issue of a monthly magazine it owned, *World's Work,* to articles and photographs that substantiated Sinclair's devastating portrait.

In 1906, David Graham Phillips, in a series for *Cosmopolitan* called "The Treason of the Senate," argued that many conservative U.S. senators were no more than mouthpieces for big business. President Theodore Roosevelt, upset by Phillips's attack on several of his friends and supporters, coined a new term when he angrily denounced Phillips and his colleagues as "muckrakers" who "raked the mud of society and never looked up." Partly due to Roosevelt's outburst, the muckraking vogue began to wane. By 1907, S. S. McClure's original team of reporters had broken up. But muckraking had demonstrated the powerful potential for mobilizing public opinion on a national scale. Reform campaigns need not be limited to the local community. Ultimately, they could engage a national community of informed citizens.

Intellectual Trends Promoting Reform

On a deeper level than muckraking, a host of early twentieth-century thinkers challenged several of the core ideas in American intellectual life. Their new theories of education, law, economics, and society provided effective tools for reformers. The emergent fields of the social sciences—sociology, psychology, anthropology, and economics—emphasized empirical observation of how people actually lived and behaved in their communities. Progressive reformers linked the systematic analysis of society and the individual characteristic of these new fields of inquiry to the project of improving the material conditions of American society. In doing so, they called on the academy for something it had never before been asked to provide—practical help in facing the unprecedented challenges of rapid industrialization and urbanization.

Sociologist Lester Frank Ward, in his pioneering work *Dynamic Sociology* (1883), offered an important critique of social Darwinism, the then orthodox theory that attributed social inequality to natural selection and the "survival of the fittest." Ward argued that the conservative social theorists responsible for social Darwinism, such as Herbert Spencer and William Graham Sumner, had wrongly applied evolutionary theory to human affairs. They had confused organic evolution with social evolution. Nature's method was genetic: unplanned, involuntary, automatic, and me-

chanical. An octopus had to lay 50,000 eggs to maintain itself; a codfish hatched a million young fish a year in order that two might survive. By contrast, civilization had been built on successful human intervention in the natural processes of organic evolution. The human method was telic: planned, voluntary, rational, dynamic. "Every implement or utensil," Ward argued, "every mechanical device, every object of design, skill, and labor, every artificial thing that serves a human purpose, is a triumph of mind over the physical forces of nature in ceaseless and aimless competition."

Philosopher John Dewey criticized the excessively rigid and formal approach to education found in most American schools. In books such as *The School and Society* (1899) and *Democracy and Education* (1916), Dewey advocated developing what he called "creative intelligence" in students, which could then be put to use in improving society. Schools ought to be "embryonic communities," miniatures of society, where children were encouraged to participate actively in different types of experiences. By cultivating imagination and openness to new experiences, schools could develop creativity and the habits required for systematic inquiry. Dewey placed excessive faith in the power of schools to promote community spirit and democratic values. But his belief that education was the "fundamental method of social progress and reform" inspired generations of progressive educators.

At the University of Wisconsin, John R. Commons founded the new field of industrial relations and organized a state industrial commission that became a model for other states. Working closely with Governor Robert M. La Follette, Commons and his students helped draft pioneering laws in worker compensation and public utility regulation. Another Wisconsin faculty member, economist Richard Ely, argued that the state was "an educational and ethical agency whose positive aim is an indispensable condition of human progress." Ely believed the state must directly intervene to help solve public problems. He rejected the doctrine of laissez faire as merely "a tool in the hands of the greedy." Like Commons, Ely worked with Wisconsin lawmakers, applying his expertise in economics to reforming the state's labor laws.

Progressive legal theorists began challenging the conservative view of constitutional law that had dominated American courts. Since the 1870s, the Supreme Court had interpreted the Fourteenth Amendment (1868) as a guarantee of broad rights for corporations. That amendment, which prevented states from depriving "any person of life, liberty, or property, without due process of law," had been designed to protect the civil rights of African Americans against violations by the states. But the Court, led by Justice Stephen J. Field, used the due process clause to strike down state laws regulating business and labor conditions. The Supreme Court and state courts had thus made the Fourteenth Amendment a bulwark for big business and a foe of social welfare measures.

The most important dissenter from this view was Oliver Wendell Holmes Jr. A scholar and Massachusetts judge, Holmes believed the law had to take into account changing social conditions. And courts should take care not to invalidate social legislation enacted democratically. After his appointment to the Supreme Court in 1902, Holmes authored a number of notable dissents to conservative court decisions overturning progressive legislation. Criticizing the majority opinion in *Lochner* v. *New York* (1905), in which the Court struck down a state law setting a ten-hour day for bakers, Holmes insisted that the Constitution "is not intended to embody a particular theory."

Holmes's pragmatic views of the law seldom convinced a majority of the Supreme Court before the late 1930s. But his views influenced a generation of lawyers who began practicing what came to be called sociological jurisprudence. In *Muller* v. *Oregon* (1908), the Court upheld an Oregon law limiting the maximum hours for working women, finding that the liberty of contract "is not absolute." Noting that "woman's physical structure and the performance of maternal functions place her at a disadvantage," the Court found that "the physical well-being of woman becomes an object of public interest and care." Louis Brandeis, the state's attorney, amassed statistical, sociological, and economic data, rather than traditional legal arguments, to support his arguments. The "Brandeis Brief" became a common strategy for lawyers defending the constitutionality of progressive legislation.

The new field of American sociology concentrated on the rapidly changing nature of community. German social theorist Ferdinand Tönnies developed an extremely influential model for describing the recent evolution of Western society from *Gemeinschaft* to *Gesellschaft*: from a static, close-knit, morally unified community to a dynamic, impersonal, morally fragmented society. If the new urban-industrial order had weakened traditional sources of morality and values—the family, the church, the small community—then where would the mass of people now learn these values?

This question provided the focus for Edward A. Ross's landmark work *Social Control* (1901), a book whose title became a key phrase in progressive thought. Ross argued that society needed an "ethical elite" of citizens "who have at heart the general welfare and know what kinds of conduct will promote this welfare." The "surplus moral energy" of this elite—ministers, educators, professionals—would have to guide the new mechanisms of social control needed in America's *Gesellschaft* communities.

SOCIAL CONTROL AND ITS LIMITS

Many middle- and upper-class Protestant progressives feared that immigrants and large cities threatened the stability of American democracy. They worried that alien cultural practices were disrupting what they viewed as traditional American morality. Viewing themselves as part of what sociologist Edward Ross called the "ethical elite," progressives often believed they had a mission to frame laws and regulations for the social control of immigrants, industrial workers, and African Americans. This was the moralistic and frequently xenophobic side of progressivism, and it provided a powerful source of support for the regulation of drinking, prostitution, leisure activities, and schooling. Organizations devoted to social control constituted other versions of reform communities. But these attempts at moral reform met with mixed success amid the extraordinary cultural and ethnic diversity of America's cities.

The more extreme proponents of these views also embraced the new pseudoscience of eugenics, based on the biological theories of the English scientist Francis Galton. Eugenicists stressed the primacy of inherited traits over environmental conditions for understanding human abilities and deficiencies. They argued that human society could be bettered only by breeding from the best stock and limiting the offspring of the worst. By the 1920s, these theories had gained enough influence to contribute to the drastic curtailing of immigration to America (see Chapter 23).

The Prohibition Movement

During the last two decades of the nineteenth century, the Woman's Christian Temperance Union had grown into a powerful mass organization. The WCTU appealed especially to women angered by men who used alcohol and then abused their wives and children. It directed most of its work toward ending the production, sale, and consumption of alcohol. But local WCTU chapters put their energy into nontemperance activities as well, including homeless shelters, Sunday schools, prison reform, child nurseries, and woman suffrage. The WCTU thus provided women with a political forum in which they could fuse their traditional moral posture as guardians of the home with broader public concerns. By 1911 the WCTU, with a quarter million members, was the largest women's organization in American history.

Other temperance groups had a narrower focus. The Anti-Saloon League, founded in 1893, began by organizing local-option campaigns in which rural counties and small towns banned liquor within their geographical limits. It drew much of its financial support from local businessmen, who saw a link between closing a community's saloons and increasing the productivity of workers. The league was a one-issue pressure group that played effectively on antiurban and antiimmigrant prejudice. League lobbyists targeted state legislatures, where big cities were usually underrepresented. They hammered away at the close connections among saloon culture, liquor dealers, brewers, and big-city political machines.

The prohibition movement found its core strength among Protestant, native-born, small-town, and rural Americans. But prohibition found support as well in the cities, where the battle to ban alcohol revealed deep ethnic and cultural divides within America's urban communities. Opponents of alcohol were generally "pietists," who viewed the world from a position of moral absolutism. These included native-born, middle-class Protestants associated with evangelical churches along with some old-stock Protestant immigrant denominations. Opponents of prohibition were generally "ritualists" with less arbitrary notions of personal morality. These were largely new-stock, working-class Catholic and Jewish immigrants, along with some Protestants, such as German Lutherans.

The Social Evil

Many of the same reformers who battled the saloon and drinking also engaged in efforts to eradicate prostitution. Crusades against "the social evil" had appeared at intervals throughout the nineteenth century. But they reached a new level of intensity between 1895 and 1920. In part, this new sense of urgency stemmed from the sheer growth of cities and the greater visibility of prostitution in red-light districts and neighborhoods. Antiprostitution campaigns epitomized the diverse makeup and mixed motives of so much progressive reform. Male business and civic leaders joined forces with feminists, social workers, and clergy to eradicate "commercialized vice."

Between 1908 and 1914 exposés of the "white slave traffic" became a national sensation. Dozens of books, articles, and motion pictures alleged an international conspiracy to seduce and sell girls into prostitution. Most of these materials exaggerated the practices they attacked. They also made foreigners, especially Jews and southern Europeans, scapegoats for the sexual anxieties of native-born whites. In 1910 Congress passed legislation that permitted the deportation of foreign-born prostitutes or any foreigner convicted of procuring or employing them. That same year, the Mann Act made it a federal offense to transport women across state lines for "immoral purposes."

But most antiprostitution activity took place at the local level. Between 1910 and 1915, thirty-five cities and states conducted thorough investigations of prostitution. The progressive bent for defining social problems through statistics was nowhere more evident than in these reports. Vice commission investigators combed red-light districts, tenement houses, hotels, and dance halls, drawing up detailed lists of places where prostitution took place. They interviewed prostitutes, pimps, and customers. These reports agreed that commercialized sex was a business run by and for the profit and pleasure of men. They also documented the dangers of venereal disease to the larger community. The highly publicized vice reports were effective in forcing police crackdowns in urban red-light districts.

Reformers had trouble believing that any woman would freely choose to be a prostitute; such a choice was antithetical to conventional notions of female purity and sexuality. But for wage-earning women, prostitution was a rational choice in a world of limited opportunities. Maimie Pinzer, a prostitute, summed up her feelings in a letter to a wealthy female reformer: "I don't propose to get up at 6:30 to be at work at 8 and work in a close, stuffy room with people I despise, until dark, for $6 or $7 a week! When I could, just by phoning, spend an afternoon with some congenial person and in the end have more than a week's work could pay me." The antivice crusades succeeded in closing down many urban red-light districts and larger brothels, but these were replaced by the streetwalker and call girl, who were more vulnerable to harassment and control by policemen and pimps. Rather than eliminating prostitution, reform efforts transformed the organization of the sex trade.

The Redemption of Leisure

Progressives faced a thorny issue in the growing popularity of commercial entertainment. For large numbers of working-class adults and children, leisure meant time and money spent at vaudeville and burlesque theaters, amusement parks, dance halls, and motion picture houses. These competed with municipal parks, libraries, museums, YMCAs, and school recreation centers. For many cultural traditionalists, the flood of new urban commercial amusements posed a grave threat. As with prostitution, urban progressives sponsored a host of recreation and amusement surveys detailing the situation in their individual cities. "Commercialized leisure," warned Frederic C. Howe in 1914, "must be controlled by the community, if it is to become an agency of civilization rather than the reverse."

By 1908 movies had become the most popular form of cheap entertainment in America. One survey estimated that 11,500 movie theaters attracted 5 million patrons each day. For 5 or 10 cents "nickelodeon" theaters offered programs that might include a slapstick

Movies, by John Sloan, 1913, the most talented artist among the so-called Ashcan realist school of painting. Active in socialist and bohemian circles, Sloan served as art editor for *The Masses* magazine for several years. His work celebrated the vitality and diversity of urban working-class life and leisure, including the new commercial culture represented by the motion picture.

SOURCE: John Sloan, *Movies*, 1913. Oil painting. The Toledo Museum of Art.

comedy, a Western, a travelogue, and a melodrama. Early movies were most popular in the tenement and immigrant districts of big cities, and with children. As the films themselves became more sophisticated and as "movie palaces" began to replace cheap storefront theaters, the new medium attracted a large middle-class clientele as well.

Progressive reformers seized the chance to help regulate the new medium as a way of improving the commercial recreation of the urban poor. Movies held out the promise of an alternative to the older entertain-

ment traditions, such as concert saloons and burlesque theater, that had been closely allied with machine politics and the vice economy. In 1909, New York City movie producers and exhibitors joined with the reform-minded People's Institute to establish the voluntary National Board of Censorship (NBC). Movie entrepreneurs, most of whom were themselves immigrants, sought to shed the stigma of the slums, attract more middle-class patronage, and increase profits. A revolving group of civic activists reviewed new movies, passing them, suggesting changes, or condemning them. Local censoring committees all over the nation subscribed to the board's weekly bulletin. They aimed at achieving what John Collier of the NBC called "the redemption of leisure." By 1914 the NBC was reviewing 95 percent of the nation's film output.

Standardizing Education

Along with reading, writing, and mathematics, schools inculcated patriotism, piety, and respect for authority. Progressive educators looked to the public school primarily as an agent of "Americanization." Elwood Cubberley, a leading educational reformer, expressed the view that schools could be the vehicle by which immigrant children could break free of the parochial ethnic neighborhood. "Our task," he argued in *Changing Conceptions of Education* (1909), "is to break up these groups or settlements, to assimilate and amalgamate these people as a part of our American race, and to implant in their children, so far as can be done, the Anglo-Saxon conception of righteousness, law and order, and popular government."

The most important educational trends in these years were the expansion and bureaucratization of the nation's public school systems. In most cities, centralization served to consolidate the power of older urban elites who felt threatened by the large influx of immigrants. Children began school earlier and stayed there longer. Kindergartens spread rapidly in large cities. They presented, as one writer put it in 1903, "the earliest opportunity to catch the little Russian, the little Italian, the little German, Pole, Syrian, and the rest and begin to make good American citizens of them." By 1918 every state had some form of compulsory school attendance. High schools also multiplied, extending the school's influence beyond the traditional grammar school curriculum. In 1890 only 4 percent of the nation's youth between fourteen and seventeen were enrolled in school; by 1930 the figure was 47 percent.

High schools reflected a growing belief that schools be comprehensive, multifunctional institutions. In 1918 the National Education Association offered a report defining Cardinal Principles of Secondary Education. These included instruction in health, family life, citizenship, and ethical character. Academic programs prepared a small number of students for college. Vocational programs trained boys and girls for a niche in the new industrial order. Boys took shop courses in metal trades, carpentry, and machine tools. Girls learned typing, bookkeeping, sewing, cooking, and home economics. The Smith-Hughes Act of 1917 provided federal grants to support these programs and set up a Federal Board for Vocational Education.

Educational reformers also established national testing organizations such as the College Entrance Exami-

nation Board (founded in 1900) and helped standardize agencies for curriculum development and teacher training. In 1903, E. L. Thorndike published *Educational Psychology*, which laid the groundwork for education research based on experimental and statistical investigations. Progressives led in the development of specialized fields such as educational psychology, guidance counseling, and educational administration.

WORKING-CLASS COMMUNITIES AND PROTEST

The Industrial Revolution, which had begun transforming American life and labor in the nineteenth century, reached maturity in the early twentieth. In 1900, out of a total labor force of 28.5 million, 16 million people worked at industrial occupations and 11 million on farms. By 1920, in a labor force of nearly 42 million, almost 29 million were in industry, but farm labor had declined to 10.4 million. The world of the industrial worker included large manufacturing towns in New England; barren mining settlements in the West; primitive lumber and turpentine camps in the South; steelmaking and coal-mining cities in Pennsylvania and Ohio; and densely packed immigrant ghettos from New York to San Francisco, where workers toiled in garment trade sweatshops.

All these industrial workers shared the need to sell their labor for wages in order to survive. At the same time, differences in skill, ethnicity, and race proved powerful barriers to efforts at organizing trade unions that could bargain for improved wages and working conditions. So, too, did the economic and political power of the large corporations that dominated much of American industry. Yet there were also small, closely knit groups of skilled workers, such as printers and brewers, who exercised real control over their lives and labors. And these years saw many labor struggles that created effective trade unions or laid the groundwork for others. Industrial workers also became a force in local and national politics, adding a chorus of insistent voices to the calls for social justice.

New Immigrants from Two Hemispheres

On the eve of World War I, close to 60 percent of the industrial labor force was foreign-born. Most of these workers were among the roughly 9 million new immigrants from southern and eastern Europe who arrived in the United States between 1900 and 1914. In the nineteenth century, much of the overseas migration had come from the industrial districts of northern and western Europe. English, Welsh, and German artisans had brought with them skills critical for emerging

IMMIGRATION TO THE UNITED STATES (1901–1920)		
Total: 14,532,000		% of Total
Italy	3,157,000	22%
Austria-Hungary	3,047,000	21
Russia and Poland	2,524,000	17
Canada	922,000	6
Great Britain	867,000	6
Scandinavia	709,000	5
Ireland	487,000	3
Germany	486,000	3
France and Low Countries (Belgium, Netherlands, Switz.)	361,000	2
Mexico	268,000	2
West Indies	231,000	2
Japan	213,000	2
China	41,000	*
Australia and New Zealand	23,000	*

*Less than 1% of total

SOURCE: U.S. Bureau of the Census, *Historical Statistics of the United States from Colonial Times to 1970,* Washington, DC, 1975.

industries such as steelmaking and coal mining. Unlike their predecessors, nearly all the new Italian, Polish, Hungarian, Jewish, and Greek immigrants lacked industrial skills. They thus entered the bottom ranks of factories, mines, mills, and sweatshops.

These new immigrants had been driven from their European farms and towns by several forces, including the undermining of subsistence farming by commercial agriculture; a falling death rate that brought a shortage of land; and religious and political persecution. American corporations also sent agents to recruit cheap labor. Except for Jewish immigrants, a majority of whom fled virulent anti-Semitism in Russia and Russian Poland, most newcomers planned on earning a stake and then returning home. Hard times in America forced many back to Europe. In the depression year of 1908, for example, more Austro-Hungarians and Italians left than entered the United States.

The decision to migrate usually occurred through social networks—people linked by kinship, personal acquaintance, and work experience. These "chains," extending from places of origin to specific destinations in the United States, helped migrants cope with the considerable risks entailed by the long and difficult journey. A study conducted by the U.S. Immigration Commission in 1909 found that about 60 percent of the new immigrants had their passage arranged by

In 1892 the federal government opened the immigration station on Ellis Island, located in New York City's harbor, where about 80 percent of the immigrants to the United States landed. As many as 5,000 passengers per day reported to federal immigration officers for questions about their background and for physical examinations, such as this eye exam. Only about 1 percent were quarantined or turned away for health problems.

SOURCE: Brown Brothers.

immigrants already in America. An Italian who joined his grandfather and cousins in Buffalo in 1906 recalled, "In western New York most of the first immigrants from Sicily went to Buffalo, so that, from 1900 on, the thousands who followed them to this part of the state also landed in Buffalo."

Immigrant communities used ethnicity as a collective resource for gaining employment in factories, mills, and mines. One Polish steelworker recalled how the process operated in the Pittsburgh mills: "Now if a Russian got his job in a shear department, he's looking for a buddy, a Russian buddy. He's not going to look for a Croatian buddy. And if he sees the boss looking for a man he says, 'Look, I have a good man,' and he's picking out his friends. A Ukrainian department, a Russian department, a Polish department. And it was a beautiful thing in a way." Such specialization of work by ethnic origin was quite common throughout America's industrial communities.

The low-paid, backbreaking work in basic industry became nearly the exclusive preserve of the new immigrants. In 1907, of the 14,359 common laborers employed at Pittsburgh's U.S. Steel mills, 11,694 were eastern Europeans. For twelve-hour days and seven-day weeks, two-thirds of these workers made less than $12.50 a week, one-third less than $10.00. This was far less than the $15.00 that the Pittsburgh Associated Charities had estimated as the minimum for providing necessities for a family of five. Small wonder that the new immigration was disproportionately male. One-third of the immigrant steelworkers were single, and among married men who had been in the country less than five years, about two-thirds reported that their wives were still in Europe. Workers with families generally supplemented their incomes by taking in single men as boarders.

Not all the new immigrants came from Europe, as hemispheric migration increased sharply as well. Over 300,000 French Canadians arrived in the U.S. between 1900 and 1930, settling mostly in New England. But the maturing continental railroad system had widened the choice of destinations to communities in upstate New York and Detroit, which had the largest number of French Canadian migrants outside New England. The pull of jobs in New England's textile industry, along with its physical proximity, attracted male farmers and laborers unable to make a living in the rural districts of Quebec. Roughly one-third of female migrants were domestic servants looking for the higher pay and greater independence associated with factory labor. The significant French Canadian presence in communities such as Lowell, Holyoke, Manchester, Nashua, and Waterville often made them the largest single ethnic group. By 1918, for example, one quarter of the Fall River, Massa-

chusetts, population of 28,000 was French Canadian. French language churches, newspapers, private schools, and mutual benefit societies reinforced the distinctive cultural milieu, and the presence of kin or fellow villagers facilitated the arrival of largely rural migrants into these new, highly industrialized, and urbanized settings. As Bruno Noury, a single eighteen-year-old farm laborer who emigrated from Quebec to Mainville, Rhode Island, recalled: "When I left, I wasn't sure whether it was temporary or to stay. I had two of my older brothers there, so I said, 'I'll do like them.' I wanted to try what they had done."

Mexican immigration also grew in these years, providing a critical source of labor for the West's farms, railroads, and mines. Between 1900 and 1914, the number of people of Mexican descent living and working in the United States tripled, from roughly 100,000 to 300,000. Economic and political crises spurred tens of thousands of Mexico's rural and urban poor to emigrate north. Large numbers of seasonal agricultural workers regularly came up from Mexico to work in the expanding sugar beet industry, and then returned. But a number of substantial resident Mexican communities also emerged in the early twentieth century.

Throughout Texas, California, New Mexico, Arizona, and Colorado, western cities developed *barrios*, distinct communities of Mexicans. Mexican immigrants attracted by jobs in the smelting industry made El Paso the most thoroughly Mexican city in the United States. In San Antonio, Mexicans worked at shelling pecans, becoming perhaps the most underpaid and exploited group of workers in the country. By 1910, San Antonio contained the largest number of Mexican immigrants of any city. In southern California, labor agents for railroads recruited Mexicans to work on building new interurban lines around Los Angeles. Overcrowding, poor sanitation, and deficient public services made many of these enclaves unhealthy places to live. Mexican barrios suffered much higher rates of disease and infant mortality than surrounding Anglo communities.

Between 1898 and 1907 more than 80,000 Japanese entered the United States. The vast majority were young men working as contract laborers in the West, mainly in California. American law prevented Japanese immigrants (the *Issei*) from obtaining American citizenship, because they were not white. This legal discrimination, along with informal exclusion from many occupations, forced the Japanese to create niches for themselves within local economies. Most Japanese settled near Los Angeles, where they established small communities centered around fishing, truck farming, and the flower and nursery business. In 1920 Japanese farmers produced 10 percent of the dollar volume of

California agriculture on 1 percent of the farm acreage. By 1930 over 35,000 Issei and their children (the *Nisei*) lived in Los Angeles.

Urban Ghettos

In large cities, new immigrant communities took the form of densely packed ghettos. By 1920, immigrants and their children constituted almost 60 percent of the population of cities over 100,000. They were an even larger percentage in major industrial centers such as Chicago, Pittsburgh, Philadelphia, and New York. The sheer size and dynamism of these cities made the immigrant experience more complex than in smaller cities and more isolated communities. Workers in the urban garment trades toiled for low wages and suffered layoffs, unemployment, and poor health. But conditions in the small, labor-intensive shops of the clothing industry differed significantly from those in the large-scale, capital-intensive industries like steel.

New York City had become the center of both Jewish immigration and America's huge ready-to-wear clothing industry. The city's Jewish population was 1.4 million in 1915, almost 30 percent of its inhabitants. New York produced 70 percent of all women's clothing and 40 percent of all men's clothing made in the country. In small factories, lofts, and tenement apartments some 200,000 people, most of them Jews, some of them Italians, worked in the clothing trades. Most of the industry operated on the grueling piece-rate, or task, system, in which manufacturers and subcontractors paid individuals or teams of workers to complete a certain quota of labor within a specific time.

The garment industry was highly seasonal. A typical work week was sixty hours, with seventy common during busy season. But there were long stretches of unemployment in slack times. Even skilled cutters, all men, earned an average of only $16 per week. Unskilled workers, nearly all of them young single women, made only $6 or $7 a week. Perhaps a quarter of the workforce, classified as "learners," earned only $3 to $6 a week. Often forced to work in cramped, dirty, and badly lit rooms, garment workers strained under a system in which time equaled money. Morris Rosenfeld, a presser of men's clothing who wrote Yiddish poetry, captured the feeling:

The tick of the clock is the boss in his anger
The face of the clock has the eye of a foe
The clock—I shudder—Dost hear how it draws me?
It calls me "Machine" and it cries to me "Sew!"

In November 1909 two New York garment manufacturers responded to strikes by unskilled women workers by hiring thugs and prostitutes to beat up pickets. The strikers won the support of the Women's Trade Union League, a group of sympathetic female reformers

that included Lillian Wald, Mary Dreier, and prominent society figures. At a dramatic mass meeting in Cooper Union Hall, Clara Lemlich, a teenage working girl speaking in Yiddish, made an emotional plea for a general strike. She called for everyone in the crowd to take an old Jewish oath: "If I turn traitor to the cause I now pledge, may this hand wither from the arm I now raise." The Uprising of the 20,000, as it became known, swept through the city's garment district.

The strikers demanded union recognition, better wages, and safer and more sanitary conditions. They drew support from thousands of suffragists, trade unionists, and sympathetic middle-class women as well. Hundreds of strikers were arrested, and many were beaten by police. After three cold months on the picket line, the strikers returned to work without union recognition. But the International Ladies Garment Workers Union (ILGWU), founded in 1900, did gain strength and negotiated contracts with some of the city's shirtwaist makers. The strike was an important breakthrough in the drive to organize unskilled workers into industrial unions. It opened the doors to women's involvement in the labor movement and created new leaders, such as Clara Lemlich, Pauline Newman, and Rose Schneiderman.

On March 25, 1911, the issues raised by the strike took on new urgency when a fire raced through three

New York City Police set up this makeshift morgue to help identify victims of the disastrous Triangle Shirtwaist Company fire, March 25, 1911. Unable to open the locked doors of the sweatshop and desperate to escape from smoke and flames, many of the 146 who died had leaped eight stories to their death.

SOURCE: UPI/CORBIS.

floors of the Triangle Shirtwaist Company. As the flames spread, workers found themselves trapped by exit doors that had been locked from the outside. Fire escapes were nonexistent. Within half an hour, 146 people, mostly young Jewish women, had been killed by smoke or had leaped to their death. In the bitter aftermath, women progressives led by Florence Kelley and Frances Perkins of the National Consumers' League joined with Tammany Hall leaders Al Smith, Robert Wagner, and Big Tim Sullivan to create a New York State Factory Investigation Commission. Under Perkins's vigorous leadership, the commission conducted an unprecedented round of public hearings and on-site inspections, leading to a series of state laws that dramatically improved safety conditions and limited the hours for working women and children.

Company Towns

Immigrant industrial workers and their families often established their communities in a company town, where a single large corporation was dominant. Cities such as Lawrence, Massachusetts; Gary, Indiana; and Butte, Montana, revolved around the industrial enterprises of Pacific Woolen, U.S. Steel, and Anaconda Copper. Workers had little or no influence over the economic and political institutions of these cities. In the more isolated company towns, residents often had no alternative but to buy their food, clothing, and supplies at company stores, usually for exorbitantly high prices. But they did maintain some community control in other ways. Family and kin networks, ethnic lodges, saloons, benefit societies, churches and synagogues, and musical groups affirmed traditional forms of community in a setting governed by individualism and private capital.

On the job, modern machinery and industrial discipline meant high rates of injury and death. In Gary, non–English speaking immigrant steelworkers suffered twice the accident rate of English-speaking employees, who could better understand safety instructions and warnings. A 1910 study of work accidents revealed that nearly a fourth of all new steelworkers were killed or injured each year. As one Polish worker described the immigrant's lot to his wife: "If he comes home sick then it is trouble, because everybody is looking only for money to get some of it, and during the sickness most will be spent." Mutual aid associations, organized around ethnic groups, offered some protection through cheap insurance and death benefits.

In steel and coal towns, women not only maintained the household and raised the children, they also boosted the family income by taking in boarders, sewing, and laundry. Many women also tended gardens and raised chickens, rabbits, and goats. Their produce and income helped reduce dependence on the company store.

Working-class women felt the burdens of housework more heavily than their middle-class sisters. Pump water, indoor plumbing, and sewage disposal were often available only on a pay-as-you-go basis. The daily drudgery endured by working-class women far outlasted the "man-killing" shift worked by the husband. Many women struggled with the effects of their husbands' excessive drinking and faced early widowhood.

The adjustment for immigrant workers was not so much a process of assimilation as adaptation and resistance. Efficiency experts, such as Frederick Taylor (see Chapter 19), carefully observed and analyzed the time and energy needed for each job, then set standard methods for each worker. In theory, these standards would increase efficiency and give managers more control over their workers. But work habits and Old World cultural traditions did not always mesh with factory discipline or Taylor's "scientific management." A Polish wedding celebration might last three or four days. A drinking bout following a Sunday funeral might cause workers to celebrate "St. Monday" and not show up for work. Employers made much of the few Slavs allowed to work their way up into the ranks of skilled workers and foremen. But most immigrants were far more concerned with job security than with upward mobility. The newcomers learned from more skilled and experienced British and American workers that "slowing down" or "soldiering" spread out the work. As new immigrants became less transient and more permanently settled in company towns, they increased their involvement in local politics and union activity.

The power of large corporations in the life of company towns was most evident among the mining communities of the West, as was violent labor conflict. The Colorado Fuel and Iron Company (CFI) employed roughly half of the 8,000 coal miners who labored in that state's mines. In mining towns such as Ludlow and Trinidad, the CFI thoroughly dominated the lives of miners and their families. "The miner," one union official observed, "is in this land owned by the corporation that owns the homes, that owns the boarding houses, that owns every single thing there is there . . . not only the mines, but all the grounds, all the buildings, all the places of recreation, as well as the school and church buildings." By the early twentieth century, new immigrants, such as Italians, Greeks, Slavs, and Mexicans, composed a majority of the population in these western mining communities. About one-fifth of CFI miners spoke no English.

In September 1913, the United Mine Workers led a strike in the Colorado coalfields, calling for improved safety, higher wages, and recognition of the union. Thousands of miners' families moved out of company housing and into makeshift tent colonies provided by the union. In October, Governor Elias Ammons ordered the Colorado National Guard into the tense strike region to keep order. The troops, supposedly neutral, proceeded to ally themselves with the mine operators. By spring the strike had bankrupt the state, forcing the governor to remove most of the troops. The coal companies then brought in large numbers of private mine guards who were extremely hostile toward the strikers. On April 20, 1914, a combination of guardsmen and private guards surrounded the largest of the tent colonies at Ludlow, where more than a thousand mine families lived. A shot rang out (each side accused the other of firing), and a pitched battle ensued that lasted until the poorly armed miners ran out of ammunition. At dusk, the troops burned the tent village to the ground, routing the families and killing fourteen, eleven of them children. Enraged strikers attacked mines throughout southern Colorado in an armed rebellion that lasted ten days, until President Woodrow Wilson ordered the U.S. Army into the region. News of the Ludlow Massacre shocked millions and aroused widespread protests and demonstrations against the policies of Colorado Fuel and Iron and its owner, John D. Rockefeller Jr.

The AFL: "Unions, Pure and Simple"

Following the depression of the 1890s, the American Federation of Labor (AFL) emerged as the strongest and most stable organization of workers. Samuel Gompers's strategy of recruiting skilled labor into unions organized by craft had paid off. Union membership climbed from under 500,000 in 1897 to 1.7 million by 1904. Most of this growth took place in AFL affiliates in coal mining, the building trades, transportation, and machine shops. The national unions—the United Mine Workers of America, the Brotherhood of Carpenters and Joiners, the International Association of Machinists—represented workers of specific occupations in collective bargaining. Trade autonomy and exclusive jurisdiction were the ruling principles within the AFL.

But the strength of craft organization also gave rise to weakness. In 1905 Gompers told a union gathering in Minneapolis that "caucasians" would not "let their standard of living be destroyed by negroes, Chinamen, Japs, or any others." Those "others" included the new immigrants from eastern and southern Europe, men and women, who labored in the steel mills and garment trades. Each trade looked mainly to the welfare of its own. Many explicitly barred women and African Americans from membership. There were some important exceptions. The United Mine Workers of America (UMWA) followed a more inclusive policy, recruiting both skilled underground pitmen and the unskilled aboveground workers. The UMWA even tried to recruit strikebreakers brought in by coal operators. With

260,000 members in 1904, the UMWA became the largest AFL affiliate.

AFL unions had a difficult time holding on to their gains. Economic slumps, technological changes, and aggressive counterattacks by employer organizations could be devastating. Trade associations using management-controlled efficiency drives fought union efforts to regulate output and shop practices. The National Association of Manufacturers (NAM), a group of smaller industrialists founded in 1903, launched an "open shop" campaign to eradicate unions altogether. "Open shop" was simply a new name for a workplace where unions were not allowed. The NAM supplied strikebreakers, private guards, and labor spies to employers. It also formed antiboycott associations to prevent unions in one trade from supporting walkouts in another.

Unfriendly judicial decisions also hurt organizing efforts. In 1906 a federal judge issued a permanent injunction against an iron molders strike at the Allis Chalmers Company of Milwaukee. In the so-called Danbury Hatters' Case (*Loewe* v. *Lawler*, 1908), a federal court ruled that secondary boycotts, aimed by strikers at other companies doing business with their employer, such as suppliers of materials, were illegal under the Sherman Antitrust Act. Long an effective labor tactic, secondary boycotts were now declared a conspiracy in restraint of trade. Not until the 1930s would unions be able to count on legal support for collective bargaining and the right to strike.

The IWW: "One Big Union"

Some workers developed more radical visions of labor organizing. In the harsh and isolated company towns of Idaho, Montana, and Colorado, miners suffered from low wages, poor food, and primitive sanitation, as well as injuries and death from frequent cave-ins and explosions. The Western Federation of Miners (WFM) had gained strength in the metal mining regions of the West by leading several strikes marred by violence. In 1899, during a strike in the silver mining district of Coeur d'Alene, Idaho, the Bunker Hill and Sullivan Mining Company had enraged the miners by hiring armed detectives and firing all union members. Desperate miners retaliated by destroying a company mill with dynamite. Idaho's governor declared martial law and obtained federal troops to enforce it. In a pattern that would become familiar in western labor relations, the soldiers served as strikebreakers, rounding up hundreds of miners and imprisoning them for months in makeshift bullpens.

In response to the brutal realities of labor organizing in the West, most WFM leaders embraced socialism and industrial unionism. In 1905, leaders of the WFM, the Socialist Party, and various radical groups gathered in Chicago to found the Industrial Workers of the World (IWW). The IWW charter proclaimed bluntly, "The working class and the employing class have nothing in common. . . . Between these two classes a struggle must go on until the workers of the world unite as a class, take possession of the earth and the machinery of production, and abolish the wage system."

William D. "Big Bill" Haywood, an imposing, one-eyed, hard-rock miner, emerged as the most influential and flamboyant spokesman for the IWW, or Wobblies, as they were called. Haywood, a charismatic speaker and effective organizer, regularly denounced the AFL for its conservative emphasis on organizing skilled workers by trade. He insisted that the IWW would exclude no one from its ranks. The Wobblies concentrated their efforts on miners, lumberjacks, sailors, "harvest stiffs," and other casual laborers. They glorified transient and unskilled workers in speeches and songs, aiming to counter their hopelessness and degradation. Openly contemptuous of bourgeois respectability, the IWW stressed the power of collective direct action on the job—strikes and, occasionally, sabotage.

The IWW briefly became a force among eastern industrial workers, tapping the rage and growing militance of the immigrants and unskilled. In 1909, an IWW–led steel strike at McKees Rocks, Pennsylvania, challenged the power of U.S. Steel. In the 1912 "Bread and Roses" strike in Lawrence, Massachusetts, IWW organizers turned a spontaneous walkout of textile workers into a successful struggle for union recognition. Wobbly leaders such as Haywood, Elizabeth Gurley Flynn, and Joseph Ettor used class-conscious rhetoric and multilingual appeals to forge unity among the ethnically diverse Lawrence workforce of 25,000.

These battles gained the IWW a great deal of sympathy from radical intellectuals, along with public scorn from the AFL and employers' groups. The IWW failed to establish permanent organizations in the eastern cities, but it remained a force in the lumber camps, mines, and wheat fields of the West. In spite of its militant rhetoric, the IWW concerned itself with practical gains. "The final aim is revolution," said one Wobbly organizer, "but for the present let's see if we can get a bed to sleep in, water enough to take a bath in and decent food to eat."

The occasional use of violence by union organizers sometimes backfired against the labor movement. On October 1, 1910, two explosions destroyed the printing plant of the *Los Angeles Times*, killing twenty-one workmen. When John and James McNamara, two brothers active in the ironworkers' union, were charged with the bombing and indicted for murder, unionists of all political persuasions rallied to their defense. Leaders of the AFL, IWW, and Socialist Party joined in a massive campaign that stressed the labor-

versus-capital aspects of the case. The *Los Angeles Times* and its influential owner Harrison Gray Otis, they noted, were strongly antiunion and had helped keep Los Angeles a largely nonunion city. Some even suggested that Otis himself, looking to give labor a black eye, was responsible for the bombs. On Labor Day 1911, as the trial approached, huge crowds in America's largest cities gathered to proclaim the McNamara brothers innocent. But they were guilty. In the middle of the trial, the McNamaras confessed to the dynamiting, shocking their many supporters. A Socialist candidate for mayor of Los Angeles, favored to win the election, was decisively defeated, and the city remained a nonunion stronghold.

Rebels in Bohemia

During the 1910s, a small but influential community of painters, journalists, poets, social workers, lawyers, and political activists coalesced in the New York City neighborhood of Greenwich Village. These cultural radicals, nearly all of middle-class background and hailing from provincial American towns, shared a deep sympathy toward the struggles of labor, a passion for modern art, and an openness to socialism and anarchism. "Village bohemians," especially the women among them, challenged the double standard of Victorian sexual morality, rejected traditional marriage and sex roles, advocated birth control, and experimented with homosexual relations. They became a powerful national symbol for rebellion and the merger of political and cultural radicalism.

The term "bohemian" referred to anyone who had artistic or intellectual aspirations and who lived with disregard for conventional rules of behavior. Other American cities, notably Chicago at the turn of the century, had supported bohemian communities. But the Village scene was unique, if fleeting. The neighborhood offered cheap rents, studio space, and good ethnic restaurants, and it was close to the exciting political and labor activism of Manhattan's Lower East Side. The worldview of the Village's bohemian community found expression in *The Masses*, a monthly magazine founded in 1911 by socialist critic Max Eastman, who was also its editor. "The broad purpose of *The Masses*," wrote John Reed, one of its leading writers, "is a social one—to everlastingly attack old systems, old morals, old prejudices—the whole weight of outworn thought that dead men have saddled upon us." Regular contributors included radical labor journalist Mary Heaton Vorse, artists John Sloan and George Bellows, and writers Floyd Dell and Sherwood Anderson.

At private parties and public events, the Village brought together a wide variety of men and women looking to combine politics, art, and support for the labor movement. Birth control activist Margaret Sanger found a sympathetic audience, as did IWW leader Big Bill Haywood. Journalist Walter Lippmann lectured on the new psychological theory of Sigmund Freud. Anarchist and feminist Emma Goldman wooed financial supporters for her magazine *Mother Earth*. Photographer Alfred Stieglitz welcomed artists to his gallery-studio "291."

For some, Greenwich Village offered a chance to experiment with sexual relationships or work arrangements. For others, it was an escape from small-town conformity or a haven for like-minded artists and activists. Yet the Village bohemians were united in their search for a new sense of community. Mary Heaton Vorse expressed their deeply pessimistic conviction that modern American society could no longer satisfy the elemental needs of community. "This is our weakness," she wrote. "Our strength does not multiply in our daily lives. There is a creative force in people doing things together." Intellectuals and artists, as well as workers, feeling alienated from the rest of society, sought shelter in the collective life and close-knit social relations of the Village community.

The Paterson, New Jersey, silk workers' strike of 1913 provided the most memorable fusion of bohemian sensibility and radical activism. After hearing Haywood speak about the strike at Mabel Dodge's apartment, John Reed offered to organize a pageant on the strikers' behalf at Madison Square Garden. The idea was to publicize the strike to the world and also raise money. The Villagers helped write a script, designed sets and scenery, and took care of publicity. A huge crowd watched more than a thousand workers reenact the silk workers' strike, complete with picket line songs, a funeral, and speeches by IWW organizers.

The spectacular production was an artistic triumph. One critic described the pageant as "a new art form, a form in which the workers would present their own story without artifice or theatricality, and therefore with a new kind of dramatic power." But the pageant was also a financial disaster. The Village bohemia lasted only a few years, a flame snuffed out by the chill political winds accompanying America's entry into World War I. Yet for decades Greenwich Village remained a mecca for young men and women searching for alternatives to conventional ways of living.

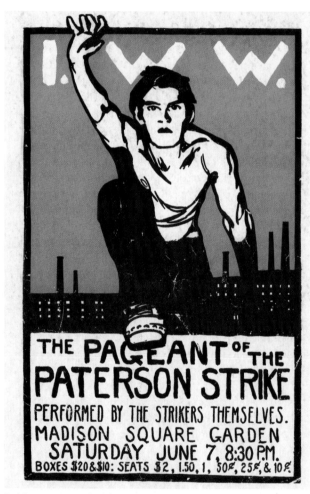

Publicity poster for the 1913 pageant, organized by John Reed and other Greenwich Village radicals, supporting the cause of striking silk workers in Paterson, New Jersey. This poster drew on aesthetic styles associated with the Industrial Workers of the World, typically including a heroic, larger than life image of a factory laborer.

SOURCE: The original Paterson Pageant Program, on which this drawing appeared, is part of the collection of the American Labor Museum/Botto House National Landmark. The poster is a copy of the program cover.

WOMEN'S MOVEMENTS AND BLACK AWAKENING

Progressive era women were at the forefront of several reform campaigns, such as the settlement house movement, prohibition, suffrage, and birth control. Millions of others took an active role in new women's associations that combined self-help and social mission. These organizations gave women a place in public life, increased their influence in civic affairs, and nurtured a new generation of female leaders.

In fighting racial discrimination, African Americans had a more difficult task. As racism gained ground in the political and cultural spheres, black progressives fought defensively to prevent the rights they had secured during Reconstruction from being further undermined. Still, they managed to produce leaders, ideas, and organizations that would have a long-range impact on American race relations.

The New Woman

The settlement house movement discussed in the opening of this chapter was just one of the new avenues of opportunity that opened to progressive era women. A steady proliferation of women's organizations attracted growing numbers of educated, middle-class women in the early twentieth century. With more men working in offices, more children attending school, and family size declining, the middle-class home was emptier. At the same time, more middle-class women were graduating from high school and college. In 1900, only 7 percent of Americans went to high school, but 60 percent of those who graduated were women. Moreover, in 1870, only 1 percent of college-age Americans had attended college, about 20 percent of them women; by 1910 about 5 percent of college-age Americans attended college, but the proportion of women among them had doubled to 40 percent.

Single-sex clubs brought middle-class women into the public sphere by celebrating the distinctive strengths associated with women's culture: cooperation, uplift, service. The formation of the General Federation of Women's Clubs in 1890 brought together 200 local clubs representing 20,000 women. By 1900 the federation boasted 150,000 members, and by World War I it claimed to represent over a million women. The women's club movement combined an earlier focus on self-improvement and intellectual pursuits with newer benevolent efforts on behalf of working women and children. The Buffalo Union, for example, sponsored art lectures for housewives and classes in typing, stenography, and bookkeeping for young working women. It also maintained a library, set up a "noon rest" downtown where women could eat lunch, and ran a school for training domestics. In Chicago the Women's Club became a powerful ally for reformers, and club member Louise Bowen, a Hull House trustee, gave the settlement three-quarters of a million dollars.

For many middle-class women the club movement provided a new kind of female-centered community. As one member put it: "What college life is to the young woman, club life is to the woman of riper years, who amidst the responsibilities and cares of home life still wishes to keep abreast of the time, still longs for the companionship of those who, like herself, do not wish to cease to be students because they have left school." Club activity often led members to participate in other civic ventures, particularly "child-saving" reforms, such as child labor laws and mothers' pensions. Some took up the cause of working-class women, fighting for protective legislation and offering aid to trade unions. As wives and daughters of influential and well-off men in their communities, clubwomen had access to funds and could generate support for projects they undertook.

Other women's associations made even more explicit efforts to bridge class lines between middle-class homemakers and working-class women. The National Consumers' League (NCL), started in 1898 by Maud Nathan and Josephine Lowell, sponsored a "white label" campaign in which manufacturers who met safety and sanitary standards could put NCL labels on their food and clothing. Under the dynamic leadership of Florence Kelley, the NCL took an even more aggressive stance by publicizing labor abuses in department stores and lobbying for maximum-hour and minimum-wage laws in state legislatures. In its efforts to protect home and housewife, worker and consumer, the NCL embodied the ideal of "social housekeeping." "The home does not stop at the street door," said Marion Talbot, dean of women at the University of Chicago in 1911. "It is as wide as the world into which the individual steps forth."

Birth Control

The phrase "birth control," coined by Margaret Sanger around 1913, described her campaign to provide contraceptive information and devices for women. Sanger had seen her own mother die at age forty-nine after bearing eleven children. In 1910, Sanger was a thirty-year-old nurse and housewife living with her husband and three children in a New York City suburb. Excited by a socialist lecture she had attended, she convinced her husband to move to the city, where she threw herself into the bohemian milieu. She became an organizer for the IWW, and in 1912 she wrote a series of articles on female sexuality for a socialist newspaper.

When postal officials confiscated the paper for violating obscenity laws, Sanger left for Europe to learn more about contraception. She returned to New York determined to challenge the obscenity statutes with her own magazine, the *Woman Rebel*. Sanger's journal celebrated female autonomy, including the right to sexual expression and control over one's body. When she distributed her pamphlet *Family Limitation*, postal inspectors confiscated copies and she found herself facing forty-five years in prison. In October 1914 she fled to Europe again. In her absence, anarchist agitator Emma Goldman and many women in the Socialist Party took up the cause.

An older generation of feminists had advocated "voluntary motherhood," or the right to say no to a husband's sexual demands. The new birth control advocates embraced contraception as a way of advancing sexual freedom for middle-class women as well as responding to the misery of those working-class women who bore numerous children while living in poverty. Sanger returned to the United States in October 1915. After the government dropped the obscenity charges, she embarked on a national speaking tour. In 1916 she again defied the law by opening a birth control clinic in a working-class neighborhood in Brooklyn and offering birth control information without a physician present. Arrested and jailed, she gained more publicity for her crusade. Within a few years, birth control leagues and clinics could be found in every major city and most large towns in the country.

Racism and Accommodation

At the turn of the century, four-fifths of the nation's 10 million African Americans still lived in the South, where most eked out a living working in agriculture. In the cities, most blacks were relegated to menial jobs, but a small African American middle class of entrepreneurs and professionals gained a foothold by selling services and products to the black community. They all confronted a racism that was growing in both intensity and influence in American politics and culture. White racism came in many variants and had evolved significantly since slavery days. The more virulent strains, influenced by Darwin's evolutionary theory, held that blacks were a "degenerate" race, genetically predisposed to vice, crime, and disease and destined to lose the struggle for existence with whites. By portraying blacks as incapable of improvement, racial Darwinism justified a policy of repression and neglect toward African Americans.

Southern progressives articulated a more moderate racial philosophy. They also assumed the innate inferiority of blacks, but they believed that black progress was necessary to achieve the economic and political progress associated with a vision of the New South. Their solution to the "race problem" stressed paternalist uplift. Edgar Gardner Murphy, an Episcopal clergyman and leading Alabama progressive, held that African Americans need not be terrorized. The black man, Murphy asserted, "will accept in the white man's country the place assigned him by the white man, will do his work, not by stress of rivalry, but by genial cooperation with the white man's interests."

African Americans also endured a deeply racist popular culture that made hateful stereotypes of black people a normal feature of political debate and everyday life. Benjamin Tillman, a U.S. senator from South Carolina, denounced the African American as "a fiend, a wild beast, seeking whom he may devour." Thomas Dixon's popular novel *The Clansman* (1905) described the typical African American as "half child, half animal, the sport of impulse, whim, and conceit . . . a being who, left to his will, roams at night and sleeps in the day, whose speech knows no word of love, whose passions, once aroused, are as the fury of a tiger." In northern cities "coon songs," based on gross caricatures

of black life, were extremely popular in theaters and as sheet music. As in the antebellum minstrel shows, these songs reduced African Americans to creatures of pure appetite—for food, sex, alcohol, and violence. The minstrel tradition of white entertainers "blacking up"—using burnt cork makeup to pretend they were black—was still a widely accepted convention in American show business.

Amid this political and cultural climate, Booker T. Washington won recognition as the most influential black leader of the day. Born a slave in 1856, Washington was educated at Hampton Institute in Virginia, one of the first freedmen's schools devoted to industrial education. In 1881 he founded Tuskegee Institute, a black school in Alabama devoted to industrial and moral education. He became the leading spokesman for racial accommodation, urging blacks to focus on economic improvement and self-reliance, as opposed to political and civil rights. In an 1895 speech delivered at the Cotton States Exposition in Atlanta, Washington outlined the key themes of accommodationist philosophy. "Cast down your buckets where you are," Washington told black people, meaning they should focus on improving their vocational skills as industrial workers and farmers. "In all things that are purely social," he told attentive whites, "we can be as separate as the fingers, yet one as the hand in all things essential to mutual progress."

Washington's message won him the financial backing of leading white philanthropists and the respect of progressive whites. His widely read autobiography, *Up from Slavery* (1901), stands as a classic narrative of an American self-made man. Written with a shrewd eye toward cementing his support among white Americans, it stressed the importance of learning values such as frugality, cleanliness, and personal morality. But Washington also gained a large following among African Americans, especially those who aspired to business success. With the help of Andrew Carnegie he founded the National Negro Business League to preach the virtue of black business development in black communities.

Presidents Theodore Roosevelt and William Howard Taft consulted Washington on the few political patronage appointments given to African Americans. Washington also had a decisive influence on the flow of private funds to black schools in the South. Publicly he insisted that "agitation of questions of social equality is the extremest folly." But privately Washington also spent money and worked behind the scenes trying to halt disfranchisement and segregation. He offered secret financial support, for example, for court cases that challenged Louisiana's grandfather clause, the exclusion of blacks from Alabama juries, and railroad segregation in Tennessee and Georgia.

Racial Justice, the NAACP, Black Women's Activism

Washington's focus on economic self-help remained deeply influential in African American communities long after his death in 1915. But alternative black voices challenged his racial philosophy while he lived. In the early 1900s, scholar and activist W. E. B. Du Bois created a significant alternative to Washington's leadership. A product of the black middle class, Du Bois had been educated at Fisk University and Harvard, where in 1895 he became the first African American to receive a Ph.D. His book *The Philadelphia Negro* (1899) was a pioneering work of social science that refuted racist stereotypes by, for example, discussing black contributions to that city's political life and describing the wide range of black business activity. In *The Souls of Black Folk* (1903), Du Bois declared prophetically that "the problem of the twenti-

eth century is the problem of the color line." Through essays on black history, culture, education, and politics, Du Bois explored the concept of "double consciousness." Black people, he argued, would always feel the tension between an African heritage and their desire to assimilate as Americans.

Unlike Booker T. Washington, Du Bois did not fully accept the values of the dominant white society. He worried that "our material wants had developed much faster than our social and moral standards." *Souls* represented the first effort to embrace African American culture as a source of collective black strength and something worth preserving. Spiritual striving, rooted in black folklore, religion, music, and history, were just as important as industrial education.

Du Bois criticized Booker T. Washington's philosophy for its acceptance of "the alleged inferiority of the Negro." The black community, he argued, must fight for the right to vote, for civic equality, and for higher education for the "talented tenth" of their youth. In 1905 Du Bois and editor William Monroe Trotter brought together a group of educated black men to oppose Washington's conciliatory views. Discrimination they encountered in Buffalo, New York, prompted the men to move their meeting to Niagara Falls, Ontario. "Any discrimination based simply on race or color is barbarous," they declared. "Persistent manly agitation is the way to liberty." The Niagara movement protested legal segregation, the exclusion of blacks from labor unions, and the curtailment of voting and other civil rights.

The Niagara movement failed to generate much change. But in 1909 many of its members, led by Du Bois, attended a National Negro Conference held at the Henry Street Settlement in New York. The group included a number of white progressives sympathetic to the idea of challenging Washington's philosophy. A new, interracial organization emerged from this conference, the National Association for the Advancement of Colored People. Du Bois, the only black officer of the original NAACP, founded and edited the *Crisis*, the influential NAACP monthly journal. For the next several decades the NAACP would lead struggles to overturn legal and economic barriers to equal opportunity.

The disfranchisement of black voters in the South severely curtailed African American political influence. In response, African American women created new strategies to challenge white supremacy and improve life in their communities. As Sallie Mial, a North Carolina Baptist home missionary told her male brethren, "We have a peculiar work to do. We can go where you cannot afford to go." Founded in 1900, the Women's Convention of the National Baptist Convention, the largest black denomination in the United States, offered African American women a new public space to pursue reform work and "racial uplift." They organized

In July 1905, a group of African American leaders met in Niagara Falls, Ontario, to protest legal segregation and the denial of civil rights to the nation's black population. This portrait was taken against a studio backdrop of the falls. In 1909, the leader of the Niagara movement, W. E. B. Du Bois (second from right, middle row) founded and edited *The Crisis*, the influential monthly journal of the National Association for the Advancement of Colored People.

SOURCE: Photographs and Print Division, Schomburg Center for Research in Black Culture, The New York Public Library, Astor, Lenox and Tilden Foundations.

settlement houses and built playgrounds; they created day-care facilities and kindergartens; they campaigned for women's suffrage, temperance, and advances in public health. In effect, they transformed church missionary societies into quasi social service agencies. In close alliance with the Women's Convention, the National Association of Black Women's Clubs provided a secular umbrella for African American women's activism. Using the motto "Lifting as We Climb," the NACW by 1914 boasted 50,000 members in 1,000 clubs nationwide.

NATIONAL PROGRESSIVISM

The progressive impulse had begun at local levels and percolated up. Progressive forces in both major political parties pushed older, entrenched elements to take a more aggressive stance on the reform issues of the day. Both Republican Theodore Roosevelt and Democrat Woodrow Wilson laid claim to the progressive mantle during their presidencies—a good example of how on the national level progressivism animated many perspectives. In their pursuit of reform agendas, both significantly reshaped the office of the president. As progressivism moved to Washington, nationally organized interest groups and public opinion began to rival the influence of the old political parties in shaping the political landscape.

Theodore Roosevelt and Presidential Activism

The assassination of William McKinley in 1901 made forty-two-year-old Theodore Roosevelt the youngest man to ever hold the office of president. Born to a wealthy New York family in 1858, Roosevelt overcame a sickly childhood through strenuous physical exercise and rugged outdoor living. After graduating from Harvard he immediately threw himself into a career in the rough and tumble of New York politics. He won election to the state assembly, ran an unsuccessful campaign for mayor of New York, served as president of the New York City Board of Police Commissioners, and went to Washington as assistant secretary of the navy. During the Spanish-American War, he won national fame as leader of the Rough Rider regiment in Cuba. Upon his return, he was elected governor of New York and then in 1900 vice president. Roosevelt viewed the presidency as a "bully pulpit"—a platform from which he could exhort Americans to reform their society—and he aimed to make the most of it.

Roosevelt was a uniquely colorful figure, a shrewd publicist, and a creative politician. His three-year stint as a rancher in the Dakota Territory; his fondness for hunting and nature study; his passion for scholarship, which resulted in ten books before he became president—all these set "T. R." apart from most of his upper-class peers. Roosevelt preached the virtues of "the strenuous life," and he believed that educated and wealthy Americans had a special responsibility to serve, guide, and inspire those less fortunate.

In style, Roosevelt made key contributions to national progressivism. He knew how to inspire and guide public opinion. He stimulated discussion and aroused curiosity like no one before him. In 1902 Roosevelt demonstrated his unique style of activism when he personally intervened in a bitter strike by anthracite coal miners. Using public calls for conciliation, a series of White House bargaining sessions, and private pressure on the mine owners, Roosevelt secured a settlement that won better pay and working conditions for the miners, but without recognition of their union. Roosevelt also pushed for efficient government as the solution to social problems. Unlike most nineteenth-century Republicans, who had largely ignored economic and social inequalities, Roosevelt frankly acknowledged them. Administrative agencies run by experts, he believed, could find rational solutions that could satisfy everyone.

Trustbusting and Regulation

One of the first issues Roosevelt faced was growing public concern with the rapid business consolidations taking place in the American economy. In 1902 he directed the Justice Department to begin a series of prosecutions under the Sherman Antitrust Act. The first target was the Northern Securities Company, a huge merger of transcontinental railroads brought about by financier J. P. Morgan. The deal would have created a giant holding company controlling nearly all the long-distance rail lines from Chicago to California. The Justice Department fought the case all the way through a hearing before the Supreme Court. In *Northern Securities* v. *United States* (1904), the Court held that the stock transactions constituted an illegal combination in restraint of interstate commerce.

This case established Roosevelt's reputation as a "trustbuster." During his two terms, the Justice Department filed forty-three cases under the Sherman Antitrust Act to restrain or dissolve business monopolies. These included actions against the so-called tobacco and beef trusts and the Standard Oil Company. Roosevelt viewed these suits as necessary to publicize the issue and assert the federal government's ultimate authority over big business. But he did not really believe in the need to break up large corporations. Unlike many progressives, who were nostalgic for smaller companies and freer competition, Roosevelt accepted centralization as a fact of modern economic life.

Roosevelt considered government regulation the best way to deal with big business. After easily defeating Democrat Alton B. Parker in the 1904 election, Roosevelt felt more secure in pushing for regulatory legislation. In 1906 Roosevelt responded to public pressure for greater government intervention and, overcoming objections from a conservative Congress, signed three important measures into law. The Hepburn Act strengthened the Interstate Commerce Commission (ICC), established in 1887 as the first independent regulatory agency, by authorizing it to set maximum railroad rates and inspect financial records.

Two other laws passed in 1906 also expanded the regulatory power of the federal government. The battles surrounding these reforms demonstrate how progressive measures often attracted supporters with competing motives. The Pure Food and Drug Act established the Food and Drug Administration (FDA), which tested and approved drugs before they went on the market. The Meat Inspection Act empowered the Department of Agriculture to inspect and label meat products. In both cases, supporters hailed the new laws as providing consumer protection against adulterated or fraudulently labeled food and drugs. Sensational exposés by muckrakers, documenting the greed, corruption, and unhealthy practices in the meatpacking and patent medicine industries, contributed to public support for the measures. Upton Sinclair's best-selling novel *The Jungle*, depicting the horrible conditions in Chicago's packinghouses, was the most sensational and influential of these.

But regulatory legislation found advocates among American big business as well. Large meatpackers such as Swift and Armour strongly supported stricter federal regulation as a way to drive out smaller companies that could not meet tougher standards. The new laws also helped American packers compete more profitably in the European export market by giving their meat the official seal of federal inspectors. Large pharmaceutical manufacturers similarly supported new regulations that would eliminate competitors and patent medicine suppliers. Thus these reforms won support from large corporate interests that viewed stronger federal regulation as a strategy for consolidating their economic power. Progressive era expansion of the nation-state had its champions among—and benefits for—big business as well as American consumers.

Conservation, Preservation, and the Environment

As a naturalist and outdoorsman, Theodore Roosevelt also believed in the need for government regulation of the natural environment. He worried about the destruction of forests, prairies, streams, and the wilderness. The conservation of forest and water resources, he argued, was a national problem of vital import. In 1905 he created the U.S. Forest Service and named conservationist Gifford Pinchot to head it. Pinchot recruited a force of forest rangers to manage the reserves. By 1909 total timber and forest reserves had increased from 45 to 195 million acres, and more than 80 million acres of mineral lands had been withdrawn from public sale. Roosevelt also sponsored a National Conservation Commission, which produced the first comprehensive study of the nation's mineral, water, forest, and soil resources.

On the broad issue of managing America's natural resources, the Roosevelt administration took the middle ground between preservation and unrestricted commercial development. Pinchot established the basic pattern of federal regulation based on a philosophy of what he called the "wise use" of forest reserves. "Wilderness is waste," Pinchot was fond of saying, reflecting an essentially utilitarian vision that balanced the demands of business with wilderness conservation. But other voices championed a more radical vision of conservation, emphasizing the preservation of wilderness lands against the encroachment of commercial exploitation.

The most influential and committed of these was John Muir, an essayist and founder of the modern environmentalist movement. Muir made a passionate and spiritual defense of the inherent value of the American wilderness. Wild country, he argued, had a mystical power to inspire and refresh. "Climb the mountains and get their good tidings," he advised. "Nature's peace will flow into you as the sunshine into the trees. The winds will blow their freshness into you, and the storms their energy, while cares will drop off like autumn leaves."

Muir had been a driving force behind the Yosemite Act of 1890. Yosemite Park, located in a valley amid California's majestic Sierra Nevada range, became the nation's first preserve consciously designed to protect wilderness. Muir served as first president of the Sierra Club, founded in 1892 to preserve and protect the mountain regions of the west coast as well as Yellowstone National Park in Wyoming, Montana, and Idaho. Muir was a tireless publicist, and his writings won wide popularity among Americans, who were increasingly drawn to explore and enjoy the outdoors. By the turn of the century, misgivings about the effects of "overcivilization" and the association of untamed lands with the nation's frontier and pioneer past had attracted many to his thinking.

A bitter, drawn-out struggle over new water sources for San Francisco revealed the deep conflicts between conservationists, represented by Pinchot, and preservationists, represented by Muir. After a devastating earthquake in 1906, San Francisco sought federal approval to

William Hahn, *Yosemite Valley from Glacier Point* (1874). Congress established Yosemite as a national park in 1890. Paintings like this one, along with contemporary photographs, helped convince Congress of the uniqueness of Yosemite's natural beauty.

SOURCE: William Hahn (1829–1887), *Yosemite Valley from Glacier Point*, 1874, 271/4″ × 461/4″. California Historical Society, gift of Albert M. Bender.

dam and flood the spectacular Hetch Hetchy Valley, located 150 miles from the city in Yosemite National Park. The project promised to ease the city's chronic freshwater shortage and to generate hydroelectric power. Conservationists and their urban progressive allies argued that developing Hetch Hetchy would be a victory for the public good over greedy private developers, since the plan called for municipal control of the water supply. To John Muir and the Sierra Club, Hetch Hetchy was a "temple" threatened with destruction by the "devotees of ravaging commercialism."

Both sides lobbied furiously in Congress and wrote scores of articles in newspapers and magazines. Congress finally approved the reservoir plan in 1913; utility and public development triumphed over the preservation of nature. Although they lost the battle for Hetch Hetchy, the preservationists gained much ground in the larger campaign of alerting the nation to the dangers of a vanishing wilderness. A disappointed John Muir took some consolation from the fact that "the conscience of the whole country has been aroused from sleep." Defenders of national parks now realized that they could not make their case simply on scenic merit alone. They began to use their own utilitarian rationales, arguing that national parks would encourage economic growth through tourism and provide Americans with a healthy escape from urban and industrial areas. In 1916 the preservationists obtained their own bureaucracy in Washington with the creation of the National Park Service.

The Newlands Reclamation Act of 1902 represented another important victory for the conservation strategy of Roosevelt and Pinchot. With the goal of turning arid land into productive family farms through irrigation, the act established the Reclamation Bureau within the Department of the Interior and provided federal funding for dam and canal projects. But in practice, the bureau did more to encourage the growth of large-scale agribusiness and western cities than small farming. The Roosevelt Dam on Arizona's Salt River, along with the forty-mile Arizona Canal, helped develop the Phoenix area. The Imperial Dam on the Colorado River diverted water to California's Imperial and Coachella Valleys. The bureau soon became a key player in western life and politics, with large federally funded water projects providing flood control and the generation of electricity, as well as water for irrigation. The Newlands Act thus established a growing federal presence in managing water resources, the critical issue in twentieth-century western development.

Republican Split

When he won reelection in 1904, Roosevelt proclaimed his support for a "Square Deal" for all people. He was still essentially a conservative who supported progressive reform as the best way to head off the potential of class war. By the end of his second term, Roosevelt had moved beyond the idea of regulation to push for the most far-reaching federal economic and social programs ever proposed. He saw the central problem as "how to exercise . . . responsible control over the business use of vast wealth." To that end, he proposed restrictions on the use of court injunctions against labor strikes, as well as an eight-hour day for federal employees, a worker compensation law, and federal income and inheritance taxes.

In 1908, Roosevelt kept his promise to retire after a second term. He chose Secretary of War William Howard Taft as his successor. Taft easily defeated Democrat William Jennings Bryan in the 1908 election. During Taft's presidency, the gulf between "insurgent" progressives and the "stand pat" wing split the Republican Party wide open. To some degree, the battles were as much over style as substance. Compared with Roosevelt, the reflective and judicious Taft brought a much more restrained concept of the presidency to the White House. He supported some progressive measures, including the constitutional amendment legalizing a graduated income tax (ratified in 1913), safety codes for mines and railroads, and the creation of a federal Children's Bureau (1912). But in a series of bitter political fights involving tariff, antitrust, and conservation policies, Taft alienated Roosevelt and many other progressives.

After returning from an African safari and a triumphant European tour in 1910, Roosevelt threw himself back into national politics. He directly challenged Taft for the Republican Party leadership. In a dozen bitter state presidential primaries (the first ever held), Taft and Roosevelt fought for the nomination. Although Roosevelt won most of these contests, the old guard still controlled the national convention and renominated Taft in June 1912. Roosevelt's supporters stormed out, and in August the new Progressive Party nominated Roosevelt and Hiram Johnson of California as its presidential ticket. Roosevelt's "New Nationalism" presented a vision of a strong federal government, led by an activist president, regulating and protecting the various interests in American society. The platform called for woman suffrage, the eight-hour day, prohibition of child labor, minimum-wage standards for working women, and stricter regulation of large corporations.

The Election of 1912: A Four-Way Race

With the Republicans so badly divided, the Democrats sensed a chance for their first presidential victory in twenty years. They chose Governor Woodrow Wilson

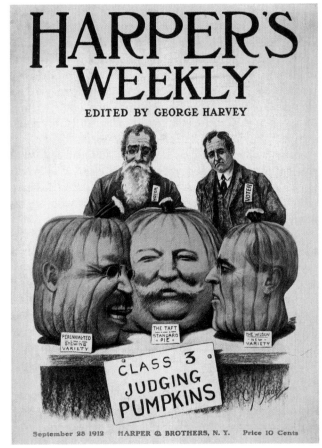

This political cartoon, drawn by Charles Jay Budd, appeared on the cover of *Harper's Weekly*, September 28, 1912. It employed the imagery of autumn county fairs to depict voters as unhappy with their three choices for president. Note that the artist did not include the fourth candidate, Socialist Eugene V. Debs, who was often ignored by more conservative publications such as *Harper's*.

SOURCE: Theodore Roosevelt Collection, Harvard College Library.

of New Jersey as their candidate. Although not nearly as well known nationally as Taft and Roosevelt, Wilson had built a strong reputation as a reformer. The son of a Virginia Presbyterian minister, Wilson spent most of his early career in academia. He studied law at the University of Virginia and then earned a Ph.D. in political science from Johns Hopkins. After teaching history and political science at several schools, he became president of Princeton University in 1902. In 1910, he won election as New Jersey's governor, running against the state Democratic machine. He won the Democratic nomination for president with the support of many of the party's progressives, including William Jennings Bryan.

Wilson declared himself and the Democratic Party to be the true progressives. Viewing Roosevelt rather than Taft as his main rival, Wilson contrasted his New Freedom campaign with Roosevelt's New Nationalism.

Crafted largely by progressive lawyer Louis Brandeis, Wilson's platform was far more ambiguous than Roosevelt's. The New Freedom emphasized restoring conditions of free competition and equality of economic opportunity. Wilson did favor a variety of progressive reforms for workers, farmers, and consumers. But in sounding older, nineteenth-century Democratic themes of states' rights and small government, Wilson argued against allowing the federal government to become as large and paternalistic as Roosevelt advocated. "What this country needs above everything else," Wilson argued, "is a body of laws which will look after the men who are on the make rather than the men who are already made."

Socialist party nominee Eugene V. Debs offered the fourth and most radical choice to voters. The Socialists had more than doubled their membership since 1908, to more than 100,000. On election days Socialist strength was far greater than that, as the party's candidates attracted increasing numbers of voters. By 1912 more than a thousand Socialists held elective office in thirty-three states and 160 cities. Geographically, Socialist strength had shifted to the trans-Mississippi South and West.

Debs had been a national figure in American politics since the 1890s, and he had already run for president three times. An inspiring orator who drew large and sympathetic crowds wherever he spoke, Debs proved especially popular in areas with strong labor movements and populist traditions. He wrapped his socialist message in an apocalyptic vision. Socialists would "abolish this monstrous system and the misery and crime which flow from it." His movement would "tear up all privilege by the roots, and consecrate the earth and all its fullness to the joy and service of all humanity." Debs and the Socialists also took credit for pushing both Roosevelt and Wilson further toward the left. Both the Democratic and Progressive Party platforms contained proposals that had been considered extremely radical only ten years earlier.

In the end, the divisions in the Republican Party gave the election to Wilson. He won easily, polling 6.3 million votes to Roosevelt's 4.1 million. Taft came in third with 3.5 million. Eugene Debs won 900,000 votes, 6 percent of the total, for the strongest Socialist showing in American history. Even though he won with only 42 percent of the popular vote, Wilson swept the electoral college with 435 votes to Roosevelt's 88 and Taft's 8, giving him the largest electoral majority up to that time. In several respects, the election of 1912 was the first "modern" presidential race. It featured the first direct primaries, challenges to traditional party loyalties, an issue-oriented campaign, and a high degree of interest group activity.

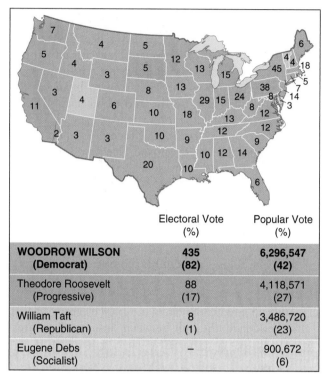

	Electoral Vote (%)	Popular Vote (%)
WOODROW WILSON (Democrat)	**435 (82)**	**6,296,547 (42)**
Theodore Roosevelt (Progressive)	88 (17)	4,118,571 (27)
William Taft (Republican)	8 (1)	3,486,720 (23)
Eugene Debs (Socialist)	–	900,672 (6)

The Election of 1912   The split within the Republican Party allowed Woodrow Wilson to become only the second Democrat since the Civil War to be elected president. Eugene Debs's vote was the highest ever polled by a Socialist candidate.

Woodrow Wilson's First Term

As president, Wilson followed Roosevelt's lead in expanding the activist dimensions of the office. He became more responsive to pressure for a greater federal role in regulating business and the economy. This increase in direct lobbying—from hundreds of local and national reform groups, Washington-based organizations, and the new Progressive Party—was itself a new and defining feature of the era's political life. With the help of a Democratic-controlled Congress, Wilson pushed through a significant battery of reform proposals. By 1916 his reform program looked more like the New Nationalism that Theodore Roosevelt had run on in 1912 than Wilson's own New Freedom platform. Four legislative achievements in Wilson's first term stand out.

The Underwood-Simmons Act of 1913 substantially reduced tariff duties on a variety of raw materials and manufactured goods, including wool, sugar, agricultural machinery, shoes, iron, and steel. Taking advantage of the newly ratified Sixteenth Amendment, which gave Congress the power to levy taxes on income, it also imposed the first graduated tax (up to 6 percent) on personal incomes. The Federal Reserve Act that same year restructured the nation's banking and currency system. It created twelve Federal Reserve Banks, regulated by a central board in Washington. Member banks were required to keep a portion of their cash reserves in the Federal Reserve Bank of their district. By raising or lowering the percentage of reserves required, "the Fed" could either discourage or encourage credit expansion by member banks. Varying the interest rate charged on loans and advances by federal reserve banks to member banks also helped regulate both the quantity and cost of money circulating in the national economy. By giving central direction to banking and monetary policy, the Federal Reserve Board diminished the power of large private banks.

Wilson also supported the Clayton Antitrust Act of 1914, which replaced the old Sherman Act of 1890 as the nation's basic antitrust law. The Clayton Act reflected the growing political clout of the American Federation of Labor. It exempted unions from being construed as illegal combinations in restraint of trade, and it forbade federal courts from issuing injunctions against strikers. But Wilson adopted the view that permanent federal regulation was necessary for checking the abuses of big business. The Federal Trade Commission (FTC), established in 1914, sought to give the federal government the same sort of regulatory control over corporations that the ICC had over railroads. Wilson believed a permanent federal body like the FTC would provide a method for corporate oversight superior to the erratic and time-consuming process of legal trustbusting. Wilson's hope that the FTC would usher in an era of harmony between government and business recalled the aims of Roosevelt and his big business backers in 1912.

On social issues, Wilson proved more cautious in his first two years. His initial failure to support federal child labor legislation and rural credits to farmers angered many progressives. A Southerner, Wilson also sanctioned the spread of racial segregation in federal offices. "I would say," he explained in 1913, "that I do approve of the segregation that is being attempted in several of the departments." As the reelection campaign of 1916 approached, Wilson worried about defections from the labor and social justice wings of his party. He proceeded to support a rural credits act providing government capital to federal farm banks, as well as federal aid to agricultural extension programs in schools. He also came out in favor of a worker compensation bill for federal employees, and he signed the landmark Keating-Owen Act, which banned children under fourteen from working in enterprises engaged in interstate commerce. Although it covered less than 10 percent of the nation's 2 million working children, the new law established a minimum standard of protection and put the power of federal authority behind the prin-ciple of regulating child labor. But by 1916 the dark cloud of war in Europe had already begun to cast its long shadow over progressive reform.

CONCLUSION

The American political and social landscape was significantly altered by progressivism, but these shifts reflected the tensions and ambiguities of progressivism itself. A review of changes in election laws offers a good perspective on the inconsistencies that characterized progressivism. Nearly every new election law had the effect of excluding some people from voting while including others. For African Americans, progressivism largely meant disfranchisement from voting altogether. Direct primary laws eliminated some of the most blatant abuses of big-city machines, but in cities and states dominated by one party, the majority party's primary effectively decided the general election. Stricter election laws made it more difficult for third parties to get on the ballot, another instance in which progressive reform had the effect of reducing political options available to voters. Voting itself steadily declined in these years.

Overall, party voting became a less important form of political participation. Interest group activity, congressional and statehouse lobbying, and direct appeals to public opinion gained currency as ways of influencing government. Business groups such as the National Association of Manufacturers and individual trade associations were among the most active groups pressing their demands on government. Political action often shifted from legislatures to the new administrative agencies and commissions created to deal with social and economic problems. Popular magazines and journals grew significantly in both number and circulation, becoming more influential in shaping and appealing to national public opinion.

Social progressives and their allies could point to significant improvements in the everyday lives of ordinary Americans. On the state level, real advances had been made through a range of social legislation covering working conditions, child labor, minimum wages, and worker compensation. Social progressives, too, had discovered the power of organizing into extraparty lobbying groups such as the National Consumers' League and the National American Woman Suffrage Association. Yet the tensions between fighting for social justice and the urge toward social control remained unresolved. The emphasis on efficiency, uplift, and rational administration often collided with humane impulses to aid the poor, the immigrant, the slum dweller. The

CHRONOLOGY

1889	Jane Addams founds Hull House in Chicago
1890	Jacob Riis publishes *How the Other Half Lives*
1895	Booker T. Washington addresses Cotton States Exposition in Atlanta, emphasizing an accommodationist philosophy
	Lillian Wald establishes Henry Street Settlement in New York
1898	Florence Kelley becomes general secretary of the new National Consumers' League
1900	Robert M. La Follette elected governor of Wisconsin
1901	Theodore Roosevelt succeeds the assassinated William McKinley as president
1904	Lincoln Steffens publishes *The Shame of the Cities*
1905	President Roosevelt creates U.S. Forest Service and names Gifford Pinchot head
	Industrial Workers of the World is founded in Chicago
1906	Upton Sinclair's *The Jungle* exposes conditions in the meatpacking industry
	Congress passes Pure Food and Drug Act and Meat Inspection Act and establishes Food and Drug Administration
1908	In *Muller v. Oregon* the Supreme Court upholds a state law limiting maximum hours for working women

1909	Uprising of 20,000 garment workers in New York City's garment industries helps organize unskilled workers into unions
	National Association for the Advancement of Colored People (NAACP) is founded
1911	Triangle Shirtwaist Company fire kills 146 garment workers in New York City
	Socialist critic Max Eastman begins publishing *The Masses*
1912	Democrat Woodrow Wilson wins presidency, defeating Republican William H. Taft, Progressive Theodore Roosevelt, and Socialist Eugene V. Debs
	Bread and Roses strike involves 25,000 textile workers in Lawrence, Massachusetts
	Margaret Sanger begins writing and speaking in support of birth control for women
1913	Sixteenth Amendment, legalizing a graduated income tax, is ratified
1914	Clayton Antitrust Act exempts unions from being construed as illegal combinations in restraint of trade
	Federal Trade Commission is established
	Ludlow Massacre occurs
1916	National Park Service is established

large majority of African Americans, blue-collar workers, and urban poor remained untouched by federal assistance programs.

Progressives had tried to confront the new realities of urban and industrial society. What had begun as a discrete collection of local and state struggles had by 1912 come to reshape state and national politics. Politics itself had been transformed by the calls for social justice. Federal and state power would now play a more decisive role than ever in shaping work, play, and social life in local communities. That there was so much contention over the "true meaning" of progressivism is but one measure of its defining role in shaping early twentieth-century America.

REVIEW QUESTIONS

1. Discuss the tensions within progressivism between the ideals of social justice and the urge for social control. What concrete achievements are associated with each wing of the movement? What were the driving forces behind them?
2. Describe the different manifestations of progressivism at the local, state, and national levels. To what extent did progressives redefine the role of the state in American politics?
3. What gains were made by working-class communities in the progressive era? What barriers did they face?
4. How did the era's new immigration reshape America's cities and workplaces? What connections can you draw between the new immigrant experience and progressive era politics?
5. Analyze the progressive era from the perspective of African Americans. What political and social developments were most crucial, and what legacies did they leave?
6. Evaluate the lasting impact of progressive reform. How do the goals, methods, and language of progressives still find voice in contemporary America?

RECOMMENDED READING

Robert M. Crunden, *Ministers of Reform: The Progressives' Achievement in American Civilization, 1889–1920* (1982). Emphasizes the moral and religious traditions of middle-class Protestants as the core of the progressive ethos.

Alan Dawley, *Struggles for Justice: Social Responsibility and the Liberal State* (1991). Offers an important interpretation of progressivism that focuses on how the working class and women pushed the state toward a more activist role in confronting social problems.

Susan A. Glenn, *Daughters of the Shtetl: Life and Labor in the Immigrant Generation* (1990). A sensitive analysis of the experiences of immigrant Jewish women in the garment trades.

Dewey Grantham, *Southern Progressivism: The Reconciliation of Progress and Tradition* (1982). Examines the contradictions within the southern progressive tradition.

Morton Keller, *Regulating A New Society: Public Policy and Social Change in America, 1900–1930* (1994). A comprehensive study of public policymaking on local and national levels in early twentieth-century America.

Arthur Link and Richard L. McCormick, *Progressivism* (1983). The best overview of progressivism and electoral politics.

Daniel T. Rodgers, *Atlantic Crossings: Social Politics in A Progressive Age* (1998). A magisterial work of comparative history focusing on the transnational conversations that deeply influenced American progressive thinkers and reformers.

Elizabeth Sanders, *Roots of Reform: Farmers, Workers, and the American State, 1877–1917* (1999). Arguing for the centrality of agrarian movements in shaping progressive era reform, Sanders explores the irony of how these efforts led to an increasingly bureaucratic state.

Kathryn Kish Sklar, *Florence Kelley and the Nation's Work* (1995). The first installment in a two-volume biography, this book brilliantly brings Florence Kelley alive within the rich context of late nineteenth-century women's political culture.

Christine Stansell, *American Moderns: Bohemian New York and the Creation of A New Century* (2000). Vividly written account that places radical politics and "New Women" at the center of the shaping of modernism.

ADDITIONAL BIBLIOGRAPHY

The Currents of Progressivism

Walter M. Brasch, *Forerunners of Revolution: Muckrakers and the American Social Conscience* (1990)

John D. Buenker, *Urban Liberalism and Progressive Reform* (1973)

Mina Carson, *Settlement Folk: Social Thought and the American Settlement Movement, 1885–1930* (1990)

Leon Fink, *Progressive Intellectuals and the Dilemmas of Democratic Commitment* (1997)

Richard Hofstadter, *The Age of Reform: From Bryan to FDR* (1955)

James T. Kloppenberg, *Uncertain Victory: Social Democracy and Progressivism in European and American Thought, 1870–1920* (1986)

William A. Link, *The Paradox of Southern Progressivism, 1880–1930* (1992)

Richard McCormick, *The Party Period and Public Policy* (1986)

Robert Wiebe, *The Search for Order, 1877–1920* (1967)

Social Control and Its Limits

Paul M. Boyer, *Urban Masses and Moral Order in America, 1820–1920* (1978)

Eldon J. Eisenach, *The Lost Promise of Progressivism* (1994)

Ruth Rosen, *The Lost Sisterhood: Prostitutes in America, 1900–1918* (1982)

Andrea Tone, *The Business of Benevolence: Industrial Paternalism in Progressive America* (1997)

Working-Class Communities and Protest

John Bodnar, *The Transplanted* (1985)

James R. Green, *The World of the Worker: Labor in Twentieth Century America* (1980)

Alice Kessler-Harris, *Out to Work: A History of Wage Earning Women in the United States* (1982)

David Montgomery, *The Fall of the House of Labor* (1987)

Kathy Peiss, *Cheap Amusements: Working Women and Leisure in Turn of the Century New York* (1986)

Roy Rosenzweig, *Eight Hours for What We Will* (1983)

Ronald Takaki, *Strangers from a Different Shore: A History of Asian Americans* (1989)

Women's Movements and Black Awakening

Paula Baker, *The Moral Frameworks of Public Life* (1991)

Mari Jo Buhle, *Women and American Socialism* (1983)

Rebecca Edwards, *Angels in the Machinery: Gender in American Party Politics from the Civil War to the Progressive Era* (1997)

Linda Gordon, *Woman's Body, Woman's Right: A Social History of Birth Control* (1976)

Molly Ladd-Taylor, *Mother Work: Women, Child Welfare, and the State, 1890–1930* (1994)

National Progressivism

Kendrick A. Clements, *The Presidency of Woodrow Wilson* (1992)

John M. Cooper Jr., *The Warrior and the Priest: Theodore Roosevelt and Woodrow Wilson* (1983)

Lewis L. Gould, *The Presidency of Theodore Roosevelt* (1991)

Michael McGerr, *The Decline of Popular Politics* (1986)

Biography

Ellen Chesler, *Woman of Valor: Margaret Sanger and the Birth Control Movement in America* (1992)

Allen F. Davis, *American Heroine: The Life and Legend of Jane Addams* (1973)

Louis R. Harlan, *Booker T. Washington: Wizard of Tuskegee, 1901–1915* (1983)

J. Joseph Huthmacher, *Senator Robert F. Wagner and the Rise of Urban Liberalism* (1971)

David Levering Lewis, *W.E.B. Du Bois: Biography of a Race, 1868–1919* (1993)

Nick Salvatore, *Eugene V. Debs: Citizen and Socialist* (1982)

Patricia A. Schechter, *Ida B. Wells-Barnett and American Reform, 1880–1930* (2001)

Bernard A. Weisberger, *The LaFollettes of Wisconsin* (1994)

Robert Westbrook, *John Dewey and American Democracy* (1991)

HISTORY ON THE INTERNET

http://www.nara.gov/exhall/picturing_the_century/ portfolios/port_hine.html

This small collection of child labor and industrial photos features the work of Lewis Hind and the National Child Labor Committee. More Hine photos are available on the following Library of Congress site: **http://lcweb.loc.gov/rr/ print/coll/207-b.html**

http://oyez.nwu.edu/cases/cases.cgi

The Oyez Project of Northwestern University provides information on Supreme Court decisions, especially the written Court opinions. Use the search program of this site to find Muller v. Oregon, 208 U.S. 412 (1908).

http://www.yale.edu/amstud/inforev/riis/title.html

Yale University maintains this hypertext version of Jacob Riis' *How the Other Half Lives*, a classic 1890 study of tenement live in New York City.

http://lcweb.loc.gov/rr/print/070_immi.html

This Library of Congress exhibit is entitled: "Selected Images of Ellis Island and Immigration, ca. 1880–1920" from the Prints and Photographs Division.

http://www.ilr.cornell.edu/trianglefire/

Cornell University has posted a comprehensive online history of the Triangle Shirtwaist Company Fire (1911).

Battle for the Lower East Side

When Lillian Wald opened the doors of the Henry Street Settlement House in 1893, the surrounding Lower East Side of New York was the poorest and most polyglot neighborhood in the city, as well as the most overcrowded quarter in the world. Settlement house workers dedicated themselves to helping recent immigrants and the working poor cope with lives scarred by poverty, disease, poor food, and dank tenements. Henry Street Settlement offered a variety of programs, including a free visiting nurse service, advice on cooking and child rearing, art classes, a theater, and a music school. Wald and other settlement house leaders soon saw that, in order to improve the miserable conditions they observed in their communities, they needed to get involved in larger political struggles to improve sanitation, health care, housing, and education. Henry Street Settlement often made common cause in these battles with some of the other political activists who flourished in the Lower East Side community, including socialists, anarchists, trade unionists, woman suffragists, socially conscious artists, and public health reformers.

Over most of the twentieth century the character of the Lower East Side remained fairly stable, though its dominant ethnic groups changed. By the 1950s the Italian, German, and Eastern European Jewish immigrants had largely moved away, while Puerto Ricans, Ukranians, and Asians poured in. But regardless of ethnicity, the neighborhood was still one of the city's poorest, and decent affordable housing remained difficult to get. Tens of thousands of poor working class people still lived in old, dilapidated nineteenth century tenements. The neighborhood's historic reputation as a center for political and cultural radicalism also attracted newcomers. Many Beat poets and jazz musicians settled there in the 1950s, and during the 1960s and 70s the area became a magnet for hippies, rock bands, and young runaways. Local concert halls like the Fillmore East and C.B.G.B.'s, cheap ethnic restaurants, funky clothing shops, and a flourishing drug culture also made the area something of a tourist attraction for young people from around the country and the world. Tompkins Square, a ten-acre park that provided the only swatch of green in the neighborhood, became a popular rallying point for anti-Vietnam War protest, the Black Panther Party, and other political causes.

But by the late 1980s two new groups appeared on the scene and their presence sparked tense debate over

Uniformed young women, part of the Visiting Nurse Service founded by Lillian Wald, leave the Henry Street Settlement for their rounds among tenement families of New York's Lower East Side. By the early 1900s the service was sending scores of trained nurses on tens of thousands of visits every year to provide health care for the poor. SOURCE: ©Bettman/CORBIS.

the historical legacy of the Lower East Side. Hundreds of homeless people began living in Tompkins Square Park, and hundreds of "squatters" occupied abandoned buildings in the surrounding blocks. The area's homeless represent only a small fraction of New York's total, estimated to be in the tens of thousands. At the same time, a wave of young urban professionals arrived, attracted by the downtown Manhattan location and old apartments newly renovated by real estate developers. Young couples expecting to enjoy the grassy park were afraid to walk near the grungy shantytown that had sprung up. "We've had an ongoing battle," said the Rev. George Kuhn of nearby St. Brigid's Church, "between the people who believe they are going to be displaced here and the people who are moving into the area." A loose coalition

New York City police try to control an angry crowd of 400 protesters in Tompkins Square Park in August, 1988. These demonstrators opposed the forcible removal of homeless people from the park, as well as the continuing "gentrification" of the surrounding Lower East Side neighborhood.
SOURCE: AP/Wide World Photos.

of neighborhood squatters, young radicals, artists, and punk rockers took up the cause of the homeless, defending their right to live in the park and attacking the influx of "yuppies." These protesters invoked the Lower East Side's historic traditions of tolerance and sympathy for the down and out. In the summer of 1988 the city announced it would enforce a 1 a.m. curfew in Tompkins Square Park, setting the stage for a violent confrontation. On August 7 over 400 riot equipped police swept through the park, forcibly removing the homeless colony, and clashing with hundreds of demonstrators. Throughout the night, angry protesters hurled bottles, fireworks, and insults as squads of policemen on horseback charged into crowds on nearby streets.

In the bitter aftermath of the riot, deep disagreements over the meaning of the neighborhood's history emerged. "We've always had a fairly diverse, progressive tradition," said Barbara Ingram who ran Children's Liberation daycare center and expressed support for the homeless. "It's something that everyone has tried to protect, because this community *is* different. In this neighborhood, people try to show concern for one another." Tom Calley, a 24 year-old artist and self-described anarchist, thought "this trouble in the park has been great. It's been a rallying point for people who once fought, like blacks and whites." "We can't ignore this problem any longer," argued another young political organizer. "The homeless shouldn't have been carted off, and a lot of activists are going to be demonstrating here this summer." But Maryann Williams, who with her husband and young daughter had just moved to the neighborhood, spoke for many newcomers: "I sympathize with the homeless. I consider myself pro-homeless. But people don't have a right to live in the park. Isn't it supposed to be for everyone? Or am I crazy?" Some, like the neighborhood's City Councilman Antonio Pagan, denounced the protesters for "living out their revolutionary fantasies. They are white, middle class young people from the suburbs hiding behind the banner of helping the homeless." He noted that "poor and working people have not had access to that park," and he asked, "why should a poor, working class neighborhood serve as the burning torch of homelessness for the city of New York?" Edgy conflict continued for years. The city closed the park for renovations in 1991, once again removing hundreds of homeless. Mass evictions of squatters also continued, as did raucous, sometimes violent protests against these police actions.

Henry Street Settlement celebrated its centennial anniversary in 1993 with a giant street festival and parade. Its current community service programs include a battered women's shelter, a day-care facility, art education, and feeding the homeless. Like Lillian Wald and other settlement house pioneers, today's advocates for the poor insist on connecting their plight to policies made far away from the neighborhood. "The community is overwhelmed by the terrible problems of homelessness and drug abuse," declared the Lower East Side Planning Council, a coalition of churches and synagogues. "The lack of affordable housing is the major reason for this situation." Gentrification has meant skyrocketing rents for apartment dwellers and small businesses. A recent survey showed more than half the area's families pay over 30% of their income for housing, and two-thirds reported their apartments had some vital malfunction—no heat, hot water, or electricity. Grinding poverty remains a grim fact of life for much of the Lower East Side, where the median family income is only one-third the city average. The 1997 Broadway musical "Rent" became a smash hit by glamorizing the Lower East Side's roiling world of poverty, struggling artists, yuppie ambition, and escalating housing costs. But as one late 90s protester and longtime resident ironically noted, "Now, for the first time in the Lower East Side's history, the poor can't afford to live here." ▪

Dodge Macknight (American, 1860–1950), *Flags, Mills Street,* 1918. Watercolor, 60.32 × 42.71 cm (23³/₄ × 16¹³/₁₆″).
Bequest of Mrs. Stephen S. Fitzgerald. SOURCE: Museum of Fine Arts, Boston. Reproduced with permission. © 2000
Museum of Fine Arts, Boston. All Rights Reserved (64.1907).

AMERICAN COMMUNITIES

Vigilante Justice in Bisbee, Arizona

ARLY IN THE MORNING OF JULY 12, 1917, 2,000 ARMED VIGILANTES swept through Bisbee, Arizona, acting on behalf of the Phelps-Dodge mining company and Bisbee's leading businessmen to break a bitter strike that had crippled Bisbee's booming copper industry. The vigilantes seized miners in their homes, on the street, and in restaurants and stores. Any miner who wasn't working or willing to work was herded into Bisbee's downtown plaza, where two machine guns commanded the scene. From the Plaza more than 2,000 were marched to the local baseball park. There, mine managers gave them a last chance to return to work. Hundreds accepted and were released. The remaining 1,400 were forced at gunpoint onto a freight train, which took them 173 miles east to Columbus, New Mexico, where they were dumped in the desert.

The Bisbee deportation occurred against a complex backdrop. America had just entered World War I, corporations were seeking higher profits, and labor militancy was on the rise. Bisbee was only one of many American communities to suffer vigilantism during the war. Any number of offenses—not displaying a flag, failing to buy war bonds, criticizing the draft, alleged spying, any apparently "disloyal" behavior—could trigger vigilante action. In western communities like Bisbee, vigilantes used the superpatriotic mood to settle scores with labor organizers and radicals.

Arizona was the leading producer of copper in the United States. With a population of 8,000, Bisbee lay in the heart of the state's richest mining district. The giant Phelps-Dodge Company dominated Bisbee's political and social life. It owned the town's hospital, department store, newspaper, library, and largest hotel. With the introduction of new technology and open pit mining after 1900, unskilled laborers—most of them Slavic, Italian, Czech, and Mexican immigrants—had increasingly replaced skilled American and English-born miners in Bisbee's workforce.

America's entry into the war pushed the price of copper to an all-time high, prompting Phelps-Dodge to increase production. Miners viewed the increased demand for labor as an opportunity to flex their own muscle and improve wages and working conditions. Two rival union locals, one affiliated with the American Federation of Labor (AFL), the other with the more radical Industrial Workers of the World (IWW), or "Wobblies," sought to organize Bisbee's workers. On June 26, 1917, Bisbee's Wobblies went on strike. They demanded better mine safety, an end to discrimination against union workers, and a substantial pay increase. The IWW, making special efforts to attract lower-paid, foreign-born workers to their cause, even hired two Mexican organizers. Although the IWW had only 300 or 400 members in Bisbee, more than half the town's 4,700 miners supported the strike.

The walkout was peaceful, but Walter Douglas, district manager for Phelps-Dodge, was unmoved. "There will be no compromise," he declared, "because you cannot compromise with a rattlesnake." Douglas, Cochise County Sheriff Harry Wheeler, and Bisbee's leading businessmen met secretly to plan the July 12 deportation. The approximately 2,000 men they deputized to carry it out were members of Bisbee's Citizens' Protective League and the Workers Loyalty League. These vigilantes included company officials, small businessmen, professionals, and antiunion workers. Local telephone and telegraph offices agreed to isolate Bisbee by censoring outgoing messages. The El Paso and Southwestern Railroad, a subsidiary of Phelps-Dodge, provided the waiting boxcars.

The participants in this illegal conspiracy defended themselves by exaggerating the threat of organized labor. They also appealed to patriotism and played on racial fears. The IWW opposed American involvement in the war, making it vulnerable to charges of disloyalty. A proclamation, posted in Bisbee the day of the deportation, claimed, "There is no labor trouble—we are sure of that—but a direct attempt to embarrass and injure the government of the United States." Sheriff Wheeler told a visiting journalist he worried that Mexicans "would take advantage of the disturbed conditions of the strike and start an uprising, destroying the mines and murdering American women and children."

An army census of the deportees, who had found temporary refuge at an army camp in Columbus, New Mexico, offered quite a different picture. Of the 1,400 men, 520 owned property in Bisbee. Nearly 500 had already registered for the draft, and more than 200 had purchased Liberty Bonds. More than 400 were married with children; only 400 were members of the IWW. Eighty percent were immigrants, including nearly 400 Mexicans. A presidential mediation committee concluded that "conditions in Bisbee were in fact peaceful and free from manifestations of disorder or violence." The deported miners nonetheless found it difficult to shake the accusations that their strike was anti-American and foreign inspired.

At their camp, the miners organized their own police force and elected an executive committee to seek relief. In a letter to President Wilson, they claimed "Common American citizens here are now convinced that they have no constitutional rights." They promised to return to digging copper if the federal government operated the

nation's mines and smelters. IWW leader William D. "Big Bill" Haywood threatened a general strike of metal miners and harvest workers if the government did not return the deportees to their homes. The presidential mediation committee criticized the mine companies and declared the deportation illegal. But it also denied that the federal government had any jurisdiction in the matter. Arizona's attorney general refused to offer protection for a return to Bisbee.

In September, the men began gradually to drift away from Columbus. Only a few ever returned to Bisbee. The events convinced President Wilson that the IWW was a subversive organization and a threat to national security. The Justice Department began planning an all-out legal assault that would soon cripple the Wobblies. But Wilson could not ignore protests against the Bisbee outrage from such prominent and patriotic Americans as Samuel Gompers, head of the American Federation of Labor. To demonstrate his administration's commitment to harmonious industrial relations, the president appointed a special commission to investigate and mediate wartime labor conflicts. But Arizona's mines would remain union free until the New Deal era of the 1930s.

America's entry into the war created a national sense of purpose and an unprecedented mobilization of resources. Unifying the country and winning the war now took precedence over progressive reforms. The war also aroused powerful political emotions and provided an excuse for some citizens to try to cleanse their communities of anyone who did not conform. In a 1918 speech, Arizona State Senator Fred Sutter hailed the benefits of vigilante justice. "And what are the results in Bisbee since the deportation?" he asked. "They are, sir, a practically 100 percent American camp; a foreigner to get a job there today had to give a pretty good account of himself. The mines are today producing more copper than ever before and we are a quiet, peaceful, law-abiding community and will continue so, so long as the IWWs or other enemies of the government let us alone." ■

Bisbee

KEY TOPICS

- America's expanding international role

- From neutrality to participation in the Great War

- Mobilizing the society and the economy for war

- Dissent and its repression

- Woodrow Wilson's failure to win the peace

BECOMING A WORLD POWER

In the first years of the new century the United States pursued a more vigorous and aggressive foreign policy than it had in the past. Presidents Theodore Roosevelt, William Howard Taft, and Woodrow Wilson all contributed to "progressive diplomacy," in which commercial expansion was backed by a growing military presence in the Caribbean, Asia, and Mexico. This policy reflected a view of world affairs that stressed moralism, order, and a special, even God-given, role for the United States. By 1917, when the United States entered the Great War, this policy had already secured the country a place as a new world power.

Roosevelt: The Big Stick

Theodore Roosevelt left a strong imprint on the nation's foreign policy. Like many of his class and background, "T.R." took for granted the superiority of Protestant Anglo-American culture and the goal of spreading its values and influence. He believed that to maintain and increase its economic and political stature, America must be militarily strong. In 1900 Roosevelt summarized his activist views, declaring, "I have always been fond of the West African proverb, 'Speak softly and carry a big stick, you will go far.'"

Roosevelt brought the "big stick" approach to several disputes in the Caribbean region. Since the 1880s, several British, French, and American companies had pursued various plans for building a canal across the Isthmus of Panama, thereby connecting the Atlantic and Pacific Oceans. The canal was a top priority for Roosevelt, and he tried to negotiate a leasing agreement with Colombia, of which Panama was a province. But when the Colombian Senate rejected a final American offer in the fall of 1903, Roosevelt invented a new strategy. A combination of native forces and foreign promoters associated with the canal project plotted a revolt against Colombia. Roosevelt kept in touch with at least one leader of the revolt, Philippe Bunau-Varilla, an engineer and agent for the New Panama Canal Company, and the president let him know that U.S. warships were steaming toward Panama.

On November 3, 1903, just as the USS *Nashville* arrived in Colón harbor, the province of Panama declared itself independent of Colombia. The United States immediately recognized the new Republic of Panama. Less than two weeks later, Bunau-Varilla, serving as a minister from Panama, signed a treaty granting the United States full sovereignty in perpetuity over a ten-mile-wide canal zone. America guaranteed Panama's independence and agreed to pay it $10 million initially and an additional $250,000 a year for the canal zone. Years after the canal was completed, the U.S. Senate voted another $25 million to Colombia as compensation.

The Panama Canal was a triumph of modern engineering and gave the United States a tremendous strategic and commercial advantage in the Western Hemisphere. It took eight years to build and cost hundreds of poorly paid manual workers their lives. Several earlier attempts to build a canal in the region had failed. But with better equipment and a vigorous campaign against disease, the United States succeeded. In 1914, after $720 million in construction costs, the first merchant ships sailed through the canal.

"The inevitable effect of our building the Canal," wrote Secretary of State Elihu Root in 1905, "must be to require us to police the surrounding premises." Roosevelt agreed. He was especially concerned that European powers might step in if America did not. In 1903 Great Britain, Germany, and Italy had imposed a blockade on Venezuela in a dispute over debt payments owed to private investors. To prevent armed intervention by the Europeans, Roosevelt in 1904 proclaimed what became known as the Roosevelt Corollary to the Monroe Doctrine. "Chronic wrongdoing, or an impotence which results in a general loosening of the ties of civilized society," the statement read, justified "the exercise

THE WORLD'S CONSTABLE.

This 1905 cartoon portraying President Theodore Roosevelt, "The World's Constable," appeared in *Judge* magazine. In depicting the president as a strong but benevolent policeman bringing order in a contentious world, the artist Louis Dalrymple drew on familiar imagery from Roosevelt's earlier days as a New York City police commissioner.

SOURCE: The Granger Collection (4E218.07).

of an international police power" anywhere in the hemisphere. Roosevelt invoked the corollary to justify U.S. intervention in the region, beginning with the Dominican Republic in 1905. To counter the protests of European creditors (and the implied threat of armed intervention), Washington assumed management of the Dominican debt and customs services. Roosevelt and later presidents cited the corollary to justify armed intervention in the internal affairs of Cuba, Haiti, Nicaragua, and Mexico.

American diplomacy in Asia reflected the Open Door policy formulated by Secretary of State John Hay in 1899. Japan and the western European powers had carved key areas of China into spheres of influence, in which individual nations enjoyed economic dominance. The United States was a relative latecomer to the potentially lucrative China market, and Hay sought guarantees of equal opportunity for its commercial interests there. In a series of diplomatic notes, Hay won approval for the so-called Open Door approach, giving all nations equal access to trading and development rights in China. The outbreak of war between Japan and Russia in 1905 threatened this policy. Roosevelt worried that a total victory by Russia or Japan could upset the balance of power in East Asia and threaten American business enterprises there. He became especially concerned after the Japanese scored a series of military victories over Russia and began to loom as a dominant power in East Asia.

Roosevelt mediated a settlement of the Russo-Japanese War at Portsmouth, New Hampshire, in 1905 (for which he was awarded the 1906 Nobel Peace Prize). In this settlement, Japan won recognition of its dominant position in Korea and consolidated its economic control over Manchuria. Yet repeated incidents of anti-Japanese racism in California kept American-Japanese relations strained. In 1906, for example, the San Francisco school board, responding to nativist fears of a "yellow peril," ordered the segregation of Japanese, Chinese, and Korean students. Japan angrily protested. In 1907, in the so-called gentlemen's agreement, Japan agreed not to issue passports to Japanese male laborers looking to emigrate to the United States and Roosevelt promised to fight anti-Japanese discrimination. He then persuaded the San Francisco school board to exempt Japanese students from the segregation ordinance.

But Roosevelt did not want these conciliatory moves to be interpreted as weakness. He thus built up American naval strength in the Pacific, and in 1908 he sent battleships to visit Japan in a muscle-flexing display of sea power. In that same year, the two burgeoning Pacific powers reached a reconciliation. The Root-Takahira Agreement affirmed the "existing status quo" in Asia, mutual respect for territorial possessions in the Pacific, and the Open Door trade policy in China. From the Japanese perspective, the agreement recognized Japan's colonial dominance in Korea and southern Manchuria.

Taft: Dollar Diplomacy

Roosevelt's successor, William Howard Taft, believed he could replace the militarism of the big stick with the more subtle and effective weapon of business investment. Taft and his secretary of state, corporate lawyer Philander C. Knox, followed a strategy (called "dollar diplomacy" by critics) in which they assumed that political influence would follow increased U.S. trade and investment. As Taft explained in 1910, he advocated "active intervention to secure for our merchandise and our capitalists opportunity for profitable investment." He hoped to substitute "dollars for bullets," but he was to discover limits to this approach in both the Caribbean and Asia.

Web Exploration

Examine "dollar diplomacy" in the Caribbean. Why was the United States so heavily involved in this region?
www.prenhall.com/faragher/map22.1

NEBRASKA IOWA
NEW YORK
COLORADO
ILLINOIS INDIANA OHIO PENNSYLVANIA
KANSAS MISSOURI UNITED STATES WEST VIRGINIA DELAWARE MARYLAND
KENTUCKY VIRGINIA
NEW MEXICO OKLAHOMA TENNESSEE NORTH CAROLINA
ARKANSAS SOUTH CAROLINA
Columbus TEXAS MISSISSIPPI ALABAMA GEORGIA
ATLANTIC OCEAN

U.S. Expeditionary Force, 1916-17
Santa Ysabel
Houston New Orleans LOUISIANA FLORIDA

Parral CHIHUAHUA
GULF OF MEXICO
Miami

U.S. troops, 1915-34
Financial supervision, 1916-41

Sinking of Maine, 1898

BAHAMA ISLANDS (Br.)

Revolutions, 1868-78, 1895-98
U.S. troops, 1898-02, 1906-09,
1912, 1917-22
Platt Amendment, 1903-34
U.S. exports to, 1865-1917, equaled $1.6 billion

MEXICO
Tampico

U.S. attempted to buy, 1869
U.S. takes control of customs houses, 1905
U.S. troops, 1916-24
Financial supervision, 1905-41

Havana
CUBA

U.S. seizure, 1914

Mexico City

Guantanamo
U.S. possession after 1898

Veracruz
U. S. Naval Base, 1903
DOMINICAN REPUBLIC
VIRGIN ISLANDS (purchased from Denmark, 1917)

JAMAICA (Br.) HAITI
PUERTO RICO

BRITISH HONDURAS
U. S. troops, 1907, 1924-25
GUADELOUPE (Fr.)

Americans controlled 43% of Mexican property, 1910
U.S. exports to, 1865-1917, equaled $1.3 billion

GUATEMALA
HONDURAS

U.S. troops 1909-10, 1912-25, 1926-33
Financial supervision, 1911-24
MARTINIQUE (Fr.)

EL SALVADOR
NICARAGUA
CARIBBEAN SEA

United Fruit Co. organized for banana trade, 1899
U.S. leased Corn Islands, 1914
BARBADOS (Br.)

COSTA RICA
Caracas
TRINIDAD (Br.)

Canal option, 1916
PANAMA
Venezuelan debt crisis, 1903-04
VENEZUELA

PACIFIC OCEAN
U.S. acquired Canal Zone, 1903
Canal completed, 1914
Bogota
COLOMBIA
BRAZIL

The United States in the Caribbean, 1865–1933 An overview of U.S. economic and military involvement in the Caribbean during the late nineteenth and early twentieth centuries. Victory in the Spanish-American War, the Panama Canal project, and rapid economic investment in Mexico and Cuba all contributed to a permanent and growing U.S. military presence in the region.

Overall American investment in Central America grew rapidly, from $41 million in 1908 to $93 million by 1914. Most of this money went into railroad construction, mining, and plantations. The United Fruit Company alone owned about 160,000 acres of land in the Caribbean by 1913. But dollar diplomacy ended up requiring military support. The Taft administration sent the navy and the marines to intervene in political disputes in Honduras and Nicaragua, propping up factions pledged to protect American business interests. A contingent of U.S. Marines remained in Nicaragua until 1933. The economic and political structures of Honduras and Nicaragua were controlled by both the dollar and the bullet.

In China, Taft and Knox pressed for a greater share of the pie for U.S. investors. They gained a place for

U.S. bankers in the European consortium building the massive new Hu-kuang Railway in southern and central China. But Knox blundered by attempting to "neutralize" the existing railroads in China. He tried to secure a huge international loan for the Chinese government that would allow it to buy up all the foreign railways and develop new ones. Both Russia and Japan, which had fought wars over their railroad interests in Manchuria, resisted this plan as a threat to the arrangements hammered out at Portsmouth with the help of Theodore Roosevelt. Knox's "neutralization" scheme, combined with U.S. support for the Chinese Nationalists in their 1911 revolt against the ruling Manchu dynasty, prompted Japan to sign a new friendship treaty with Russia. The Open Door to China was now effectively closed, and American relations with Japan began a slow deterioration that ended in war thirty years later.

Wilson: Moralism and Realism in Mexico

Right after he took office in 1913, President Woodrow Wilson observed that "it would be the irony of fate if my administration had to deal chiefly with foreign affairs." His political life up to then had centered on achieving progressive reforms in the domestic arena. As it turned out, Wilson had to face international crises from his first day in office. These were of a scope and complexity unprecedented in U.S. history. Wilson had no experience in diplomacy, but he brought to foreign affairs a set of fundamental principles that combined a moralist's faith in American democracy with a realist's understanding of the power of international commerce. He believed that American economic expansion, accompanied by democratic principles and Christianity, was a civilizing force in the world. "Our industries," he told the Democratic National Convention in 1912, "have expanded to such a point that they will burst their jackets if they cannot find a free outlet to the markets of the world. . . . Our domestic markets no longer suffice. We need foreign markets."

Wilson, like most corporate and political leaders of the day, emphasized foreign investments and industrial exports as the keys to the nation's prosperity. He believed that the United States, with its superior industrial efficiency, could achieve supremacy in world commerce if artificial barriers to free trade were removed. He championed and extended the Open Door principles of John Hay, advocating strong diplomatic and military measures "for making ourselves supreme in the world from an economic point of view." Wilson often couched his vision of a dynamic, expansive American capitalism in terms of a moral crusade. As he put it in a speech to a congress of salesmen, "[Since] you are Americans and are meant to carry liberty and justice and the principles of humanity wherever you go, go out and sell goods that will make the world more comfortable and more happy,

and convert them to the principles of America." Yet he quickly found that the complex realities of power politics could interfere with moral vision.

Wilson's policies toward Mexico, which foreshadowed the problems he would encounter in World War I, best illustrate his difficulties. The 1911 Mexican Revolution had overthrown the brutally corrupt dictatorship of Porfirio Díaz, and popular leader Francisco Madero had won wide support by promising democracy and economic reform for millions of landless peasants. U.S. businessmen, however, were nervous about the future of their investments, which totaled over $1 billion, an amount greater than Mexico's own investment and more than all other foreign investment in that country combined. Wilson at first gave his blessing to the revolutionary movement, expressed regret over the Mexican-American War of 1846–48, and disavowed any interest in another war. "I have constantly to remind myself," he told a friend, "that I am not the servant of those who wish to enhance the value of their Mexican investments."

But right before he took office, Wilson was stunned by the ousting and murder of Madero by his chief lieutenant, General Victoriano Huerta. Other nations, including Great Britain and Japan, recognized the Huerta regime, but Wilson refused. He announced that the United States would support only governments that rested on the rule of law. An armed faction opposed to Huerta, known as the Constitutionalists and led by Venustiano Carranza, emerged in northern Mexico. Both sides rejected an effort by Wilson to broker a compromise between them. Carranza, an ardent nationalist, pressed for the right to buy U.S. arms, which he won in 1914. Wilson also isolated Huerta diplomatically by persuading the British to withdraw their support in exchange for American guarantees of English property interests in Mexico.

But Huerta stubbornly remained in power. In April 1914 Wilson used a minor insult to U.S. sailors in Tampico as an excuse to invade. American naval forces bombarded and then occupied Veracruz, the main port through which Huerta received arms shipments. Nineteen Americans and 126 Mexicans died in the battle, which brought the United States and Mexico close to war and provoked anti-American demonstrations in Mexico and throughout Latin America. Wilson accepted the offer of the ABC Powers—Argentina, Brazil, and Chile—to mediate the dispute. Huerta rejected a plan for him to step aside in favor of a provisional government. But then in August, Carranza managed to overthrow Huerta. Playing to nationalist sentiment, Carranza too denounced Wilson for his intervention.

As war loomed in Europe, Mexico's revolutionary politics continued to frustrate Wilson. For a brief period Wilson threw his support behind Francisco "Pancho" Villa, Carranza's former ally who now led a rebel army of his own in northern Mexico. But Carranza's

Mexican revolutionary leaders and sometime allies Francisco "Pancho" Villa (center) and Emiliano Zapata (right) are shown at the National Palace in Mexico City, ca. 1916. Zapata's army operated out of a base in the southern agricultural state of Morelos, while Villa's army controlled large portions of Mexico's north. In 1914 Villa captured the imagination of American reformers, journalists, and moviemakers with his military exploits against the oppressive Huerta regime. But in 1916, after several border clashes between his forces and U.S. military units, President Wilson dispatched a punitive expedition in pursuit of Villa.

SOURCE: Culver Pictures, Inc. (PE0151CP007023)

forces dealt Villa a major setback in April 1915. In October, its attention focused on the war in Europe, the Wilson administration recognized Carranza as Mexico's de facto president. Meanwhile Pancho Villa, feeling betrayed, turned on the United States and tried to provoke a crisis that might draw Washington into war with Mexico. In 1916, Villa led several raids in Mexico and across the border into the United States that killed a few dozen Americans. The man once viewed by Wilson as a fighter for democracy was now dismissed as a dangerous bandit.

In March 1916, enraged by Villa's defiance, Wilson dispatched General John J. Pershing and an army that eventually numbered 15,000 to capture him. For a year, Pershing's troops chased Villa in vain, penetrating 300 miles into Mexico. The invasion made Villa a symbol of national resistance in Mexico, and his army grew from 500 men to 10,000 by the end of 1916. Villa's effective hit-and-run guerrilla tactics kept the U.S. forces at bay. A frustrated General Pershing complained that he felt "just a little bit like a man looking for a needle in a haystack." He urged the U.S. government to occupy the northern Mexican state of Chihuahua and later called for the occupation of the entire country.

Pershing's invasion angered the Carranza government and the Mexican public. Skirmishes between American forces and Carranza's army brought the two nations to the brink of war again in June 1916. Wilson prepared a message to Congress asking permission for American troops to occupy all of northern Mexico. But he never delivered it. There was fierce opposition to war with Mexico throughout the country. Perhaps more important, mounting tensions with Germany caused Wilson to hesitate. He told an aide that "Germany is anxious to have us at war with Mexico, so that our minds and our energies will be taken off the great war across the sea." Wilson thus accepted negotiations by a face-saving international commission. In early 1917, with America moving toward direct involvement in the European war, Wilson began withdrawing American troops. Just a month before the United States entered World War I, Wilson officially recognized the Carranza regime.

Wilson's attempt to guide the course of Mexico's revolution and protect U.S. interests left a bitter legacy of suspicion and distrust in Mexico. It also suggested the limits of a foreign policy tied to a moral vision rooted in the idea of American exceptionalism. Militarism and imperialism, Wilson had believed, were hallmarks of the old European way. American liberal values—rooted in capitalist development, democracy, and free trade—were the wave of the future. Wilson believed the United States could lead the world in establishing a new international system based on peaceful commerce and political stability. In both the 1914 invasion and the 1916 punitive expedition, Wilson declared that he had no desire to interfere with Mexican sovereignty. But in both cases that is exactly what he did. The United States, he argued, must actively use its enormous moral and material power to create the new order. That principle would soon engage America in Europe's bloodiest war and its most momentous revolution.

THE GREAT WAR

World War I, or the Great War, as it was originally called, took an enormous human toll on an entire generation of Europeans. The unprecedented slaughter on the battlefields of Verdun, Ypres, Gallipoli, and scores of other places appalled the combatant nations. At the war's start in August 1914, both sides had confidently predicted a quick victory. Instead, the killing dragged on for more than four years and in the end transformed the old power relations and political map of Europe. The United States entered the war reluctantly, and American forces played a supportive rather than a central role in the military outcome. Yet the wartime experience left a sharp imprint on the nation's economy, politics, and cultural life—one that would last into the next decades.

The Guns of August

In August 1914 a relatively minor incident plunged the European continent into the most destructive war in its history until then. The last decades of the nineteenth century had seen the major European nations, especially Germany, enjoy a great rush of industrial development. During the same period, these nations acquired extensive colonial empires in Africa, Asia, and the Middle East. Only a complex and fragile system of alliances had kept the European powers at peace with each other since 1871. Two great competing camps had evolved by 1907: the Triple Alliance (also known as the Central Powers), which included Germany, Austria-Hungary, and Italy; and the Triple Entente (also known as the Allies), which included Great Britain, France, and Russia. At the heart of this division was the competition between Great Britain, long the world's dominant colonial and commercial power, and Germany, which had powerful aspirations for an empire of its own.

The alliance system managed to keep small conflicts from escalating into larger ones for most of the late nineteenth and early twentieth centuries. But its inclusiveness was also its weakness: the alliance system threatened to entangle many nations in any war that did erupt. On June 28, 1914, Archduke Franz Ferdinand, heir to the throne of the unstable Austro-Hungarian Empire, was assassinated in Sarajevo, Bosnia. The archduke's killer was a Serbian nationalist who believed the Austro-Hungarian province of Bosnia ought to be annexed to neighboring Serbia. Germany pushed Austria-Hungary to retaliate against Serbia, and the Serbians in turn asked Russia for help.

By early August both sides had exchanged declarations of war and begun mobilizing their forces. Germany invaded Belgium and prepared to move across the French border. But after the German armies were stopped at the River Marne in September, the war settled into a long, bloody stalemate. New and grimly efficient weapons, such as the machine gun and the tank, and the horrors of trench warfare meant unprecedented casualties for all involved. Centered in northern France, the fighting killed 5 million people over the next two and a half years.

American Neutrality

The outbreak of war in Europe shocked Americans. President Wilson issued a formal proclamation of neutrality and urged citizens to be "impartial in thought as well as in action." Most of the country shared the editorial view expressed that August in the *New York Sun:* "There is nothing reasonable in such a war, and it would be folly for the country to sacrifice itself to the frenzy of dynastic policies and the clash of ancient hatreds which is urging the Old World to destruction."

In practice, powerful cultural, political, and economic factors made the impartiality advocated by Wilson impossible. The U.S. population included many ethnic groups with close emotional ties to the Old World. Out of a total population of 92 million in 1914, about one-third were "hyphenated" Americans, either foreign-born or having one or both parents who were immigrants. Strong support for the Central Powers could be found among the 8 million German Americans, as well as the 4 million Irish Americans, who shared their ancestral homeland's historical hatred of English rule. On the other side, many Americans were at least mildly pro-Allies due to cultural and language bonds with Great Britain and the tradition of Franco-American friendship.

Both sides bombarded the United States with vigorous propaganda campaigns. The British effectively exploited their bonds of language and heritage with Americans. Reports of looting, raping, and the killing of innocent civilians by German troops circulated widely in the press. Many of these atrocity stories were exaggerated, but verified German actions—the invasion of neutral Belgium, submarine attacks on merchant ships, and the razing of towns—lent them credibility. German propagandists blamed the war on Russian expansionism and France's desire to avenge its defeat by Germany in 1870–71. It is difficult to measure the impact of war propaganda on American public opinion. As a whole, though, it highlighted the terrible human costs of the war and thus strengthened the conviction that America should stay out of it.

Economic ties between the United States and the Allies were perhaps the greatest barrier to true neutrality. Early in the war Britain imposed a blockade on all shipping to Germany. The United States, as a neutral country, might have insisted on the right of nonbelligerents to trade with both sides, as required by international law. But in practice, although Wilson protested the blockade, he wanted to avoid antagonizing Britain and disrupting trade between the United States and the Allies. Trade with Germany all but ended while trade with the Allies increased dramatically. As war orders poured in from Britain and France, the value of American trade with the Allies shot up from $824 million in 1914 to $3.2 billion in 1916. By 1917 loans to the Allies exceeded $2.5 billion compared to loans to the Central Powers of only $27 million. Through exclusive contracts with the British government, J. P. Morgan and Company emerged as the world's single largest purchaser of goods. It brokered more than than 4,000 contracts between the Allies and U.S. companies that sold munitions, chemicals, cotton, machine tools, and foodstuffs. As America's annual export trade jumped from $2 billion in 1913 to nearly $6 billion in 1916, the nation enjoyed a great economic boom—transforming the economy in places like Bisbee, Arizona—and the United States became neutral in name only.

The *New York Times* printed a special Extra edition announcing that a German submarine had torpedoed the British passenger liner Lusitania on May 7, 1915, off the Irish coast. The ship's manifest later revealed that the *Lusitania* carried a shipment of arms along with its passengers. The 1,198 lives lost included 128 Americans, and the incident helped push the United States toward "preparedness" for war.

SOURCE: ©Bettmann/CORBIS (PG3064A).

Preparedness and Peace

In February 1915, Germany declared the waters around the British Isles to be a war zone, a policy that it would enforce with unrestricted submarine warfare. All enemy shipping, despite the requirements of international law to the contrary, would be subject to surprise submarine attack. Neutral powers were warned that the problems of identification at sea put their ships at risk. The United States issued a sharp protest to this policy, calling it "an indefensible violation of neutral rights," and threatened to hold Germany accountable.

On May 7, 1915, a German U-boat sank the British liner *Lusitania* off the coast of Ireland. Among the 1,198 people who died were 128 American citizens. The *Lusitania* was in fact secretly carrying war materials, and passengers had been warned about a possible attack. Wilson nevertheless denounced the sinking as illegal and inhuman, and the American press loudly condemned the act as barbaric. An angry exchange of diplomatic notes led Secretary of State William Jennings Bryan to resign in protest against a policy he thought too warlike.

Tensions heated up again in March 1916 when a German U-boat torpedoed the *Sussex*, an unarmed French passenger ship, injuring four Americans. President Wilson threatened to break off diplomatic relations with Germany unless it abandoned its methods of submarine warfare. He won a temporary diplomatic victory when Germany promised that all vessels would be visited prior to attack. But the crisis also prompted

Wilson to begin preparing for war. The National Security League, active in large eastern cities and bankrolled by conservative banking and commercial interests, helped push for a bigger army and navy and, most important, a system of universal military training. In June 1916, Congress passed the National Defense Act, which more than doubled the size of the regular army to 220,000 and integrated the state National Guards under federal control. In August, Congress passed a bill that dramatically increased spending for new battleships, cruisers, and destroyers.

Not all Americans supported these preparations for battle, and opposition to military buildup found expression in scores of American communities. As early as August 29, 1914, 1,500 women clad in black had marched down New York's Fifth Avenue in the Woman's Peace Parade. Out of this gathering evolved the American Union against Militarism, which lobbied against the preparedness campaign and against intervention in Mexico. Antiwar feeling was especially strong in the South and Midwest. Except for its vitally important cotton exports, the South generally had weaker economic ties to the Allies than other parts of the nation, as well as a historical suspicion of military power concentrated in Washington. The Midwest included communities with large German and socialist influences, both of which opposed U.S. aid to the Allies.

A group of thirty to fifty House Democrats, led by majority leader Claude Kitchin of North Carolina, stubbornly opposed Wilson's military buildup. Jane Addams, Lillian D. Wald, and many other prominent progressive reformers spoke out for peace. A large reservoir of popular antiwar sentiment flowed through the culture in various ways. Movie director Thomas Ince won a huge audience for his 1916 film *Civilization*, which depicted Christ returning to reveal the horrors of war to world leaders. Two of the most popular songs of 1915 were "Don't Take My Darling Boy Away" and "I Didn't Raise My Boy to Be a Soldier."

To win reelection in 1916, Wilson had to acknowledge the active opposition to involvement in the war. In the presidential campaign, Democrats adopted the winning slogan "He Kept Us Out of War." Wilson made a strong showing in the West, where antiwar sentiment was vigorous, and he managed to draw hundreds of thousands of votes away from the anti-war Socialist Party as well. Wilson made a point of appealing to progressives of all kinds, stressing his support for the eight-hour day and his administration's efforts on behalf of farmers. The war-induced prosperity no doubt helped him to defeat conservative Republican Charles Evans Hughes in a very close election. But Wilson knew that the peace was as fragile as his victory.

Safe for Democracy

By the end of January 1917, Germany's leaders had decided against a negotiated peace settlement, placing their hopes instead in a final decisive offensive against the Allies. On February 1, 1917, with the aim of breaking the British blockade, Germany declared unlimited submarine warfare, with no warnings, against all neutral and belligerent shipping. This strategy went far beyond the earlier, more limited use of the U-boat. The decision was made with full knowledge that it might bring America into the conflict. In effect, German leaders were gambling that they could destroy the ability of the Allies to fight before the United States would be able to effectively mobilize manpower and resources.

Wilson was indignant and disappointed. He still hoped for peace, but Germany had made it impossible for him to preserve his twin goals of U.S. neutrality and freedom of the seas. Reluctantly, Wilson broke off diplomatic relations with Germany and called on Congress to approve the arming of U.S. merchant ships. On March 1, the White House shocked the country when it made public a recently intercepted coded message, sent by German foreign secretary Arthur Zimmermann to the German ambassador in Mexico. The Zimmer-

mann note proposed that an alliance be made between Germany and Mexico if the United States entered the war. Zimmermann suggested that Mexico take up arms against the United States and receive in return the "lost territory in New Mexico, Texas, and Arizona." The note caused a sensation and became a very effective propaganda tool for those who favored U.S. entry into the war. "As soon as I saw it," wrote Republican senator Henry Cabot Lodge of Massachusetts, an interventionist, "I knew it would arouse the country more than any other event." The specter of a German-Mexican alliance helped turn the tide of public opinion in the Southwest, where opposition to U.S. involvement in the war had been strong.

Revelation of the Zimmermann note stiffened Wilson's resolve. He issued an executive order in mid-March authorizing the arming of all merchant ships and allowing them to shoot at submarines. In that month, German U-boats sank seven U.S. merchant ships, leaving a heavy death toll. Anti-German feeling increased, and thousands took part in prowar demonstrations in New York, Boston, Philadelphia, and other cities. Wilson finally called a special session of Congress to ask for a declaration of war.

On April 2, on a rainy night before a packed and very quiet assembly, Wilson made his case. He reviewed the escalation of submarine warfare, which he called "warfare against mankind," and said that neutrality was no longer feasible or desirable. But the conflict was not merely about U.S. shipping rights, Wilson argued. He employed highly idealistic language to make the case for war, reflecting his deeply held belief that America had a special mission as mankind's most enlightened and advanced nation:

> It is a fearful thing to lead this great peaceful people into war, into the most terrible and disastrous of all wars, civilization itself seeming to be in the balance. But the right is more precious than peace, and we shall fight for the things which we have always carried nearest to our hearts—for democracy, for the right of those who submit to authority to have a voice in their own governments, for the rights and liberties of small nations, for a universal dominion of right by such a concert of free peoples as shall bring peace and safety to all nations and make the world itself at last free.

This was a bold bid to give the United States a new role in international affairs. It asserted not just the right to protect U.S. interests but called also for change in basic international structures. Wilson's eloquent speech won over the Congress, most of the press, and even his bitterest political critics, such as Theodore Roosevelt. The Senate adopted the war resolution 82 to 6, the House 373 to 50. On April 6, President Wilson signed

Halt the Hun. This 1918 Liberty Loan poster used anti-German sentiment to encourage the purchase of war bonds. Its depiction of an American soldier as the protector of an innocent mother and child implied that the Germans were guilty of unspeakable war crimes.

SOURCE: Howard Chandler Christy, *Hold the Hun! Fight or Buy Bonds,* poster, 1917. Museum of the City of New York, gift of John Campbell. The Granger Collection (4E695.09).

the declaration of war. All that remained was to win over the American public.

AMERICAN MOBILIZATION

The overall public response to Wilson's war message was enthusiastic. Most newspapers, religious leaders, state legislatures, and prominent public figures endorsed the call to arms. But the Wilson administration was less certain about the feelings of ordinary Americans and their willingness to fight in Europe. It therefore took immediate steps to win over public support for the war effort, to place a legal muzzle on antiwar dissenters, and to establish a universal military draft. War mobilization was above all a campaign to unify the country.

Selling the War

Just a week after signing the war declaration, Wilson created the Committee on Public Information (CPI) to organize public opinion. It was dominated by its civilian chairman, the journalist and reformer George Creel. He had become a personal friend of Wilson's while handling publicity for the 1916 Democratic campaign. Creel quickly transformed the CPI from its original function as coordinator of government news into a sophisticated and aggressive agency for promoting the war. Creel remarked that his aim was to mold Americans into "one white-hot mass . . . with fraternity, devotion, courage, and deathless determination."

To sell the war, Creel raised the art of public relations to new heights. He enlisted more than 150,000 people to work on a score of CPI committees. They produced more than 100 million pieces of literature—pamphlets, articles, books—that explained the causes and meaning of the war. The CPI also created posters, slides, newspaper advertising, and films to promote the war. It called upon movie stars such as Charlie Chaplin, Mary Pickford, and Douglas Fairbanks to help sell war bonds at huge rallies. Famous journalists like the muckraker Ida Tarbell and well-known artists like Charles Dana Gibson were recruited. Across the nation, a volunteer army of 75,000 "Four Minute Men" gave brief patriotic speeches before stage and movie shows.

Three major themes dominated the materials disseminated by the CPI: America as a unified moral community; the war as an idealistic crusade for peace and freedom; and the enemy as a despicable foe. The last of these featured an aggressively negative campaign against all things German. Posters and advertisements depicted the Germans as Huns, bestial monsters outside the civilized world. The CPI supported films such as *The Kaiser: The Beast of Berlin* and *The Prussian Cur.* German music and literature, indeed the German language itself, were suspect, and were banished from the concert halls, schools, and libraries of many communities. The CPI also urged ethnic Americans to abandon their Old World ties, to become "unhyphenated Americans." The CPI's push for conformity would soon encourage thousands of local, sometimes violent, campaigns of harassment against German Americans, radicals, and peace activists.

Fading Opposition to War

By defining the call to war as a great moral crusade, President Wilson was able to win over many Americans who had been reluctant to go to war. In particular, many liberals and progressives were attracted to the possibilities of war as a positive force for social change. Many progressives identified with President Wilson's definition of the war as an idealistic crusade to defend democracy, spread liberal principles, and redeem European decadence and militarism. John Dewey, the influ-

"I Summon you to Comradeship in the Red Cross"
Woodrow Wilson

Founded by Clara Barton after the Civil War, the American Red Cross grew in both size and importance during World War I. Female volunteers, responding to humanitarian and patriotic appeals combined in posters like this one, provided most of the health and sanitary services to military and civilian casualties of the war.

SOURCE: Library of Congress.

ential philosopher, believed the war offered great "social possibilities" for developing the public good through science and greater efficiency.

Social welfare advocates, suffragists, tax reformers, even many socialists, now viewed war as a unique opportunity. War would require greater direct and coordinated involvement by the government in nearly every phase of American life. A group of prominent progressives quickly issued a statement of support for Wilson's war policy. They argued that "out of the sacrifice of war we may achieve broader democracy in Government, more equitable distribution of wealth, and greater national efficiency in raising the level of the general welfare."

The writer and cultural critic Randolph Bourne was an important, if lonely, voice of dissent among intellectuals. A former student of Dewey's at Columbia University, Bourne wrote a series of antiwar essays warning of the disastrous consequences for reform movements of all kinds. He was particularly critical of "war intellectuals" such as Dewey who were so eager to shift their energies to serving the war effort. "War is essentially

the health of the State," Bourne wrote, and he accurately predicted sharp infringements on political and intellectual freedoms.

The Woman's Peace Party, founded in 1915 by feminists opposed to the preparedness campaign, dissolved. Most of its leading lights—Florence Kelley, Lillian D. Wald, and Carrie Chapman Catt—threw themselves into volunteer war work. Catt, leader of the huge National American Woman Suffrage Association (NAWSA), believed that supporting the war might help women win the right to vote. She joined the Women's Committee of the Council of National Defense and encouraged suffragists to mobilize women for war service of various kinds. A few lonely feminist voices, such as Jane Addams, continued steadfastly to oppose the war effort. But war work proved very popular among activist middle-class women. It gave them a leading role in their communities—selling bonds, coordinating food conservation drives, and working for hospitals and the Red Cross.

"You're in the Army Now"

The central military issue facing the administration was how to raise and deploy U.S. armed forces. When war was declared, there were only about 200,000 men in the army. Traditionally, the United States had relied on volunteer forces organized at the state level. But volunteer rates after April 6 were less than they had been for the Civil War or the Spanish-American War, reflecting the softness of prowar sentiment. The administration thus introduced the Selective Service Act, which provided for the registration and classification for military service of all men between ages twenty-one and thirty-five. Secretary of War Newton D. Baker was anxious to prevent the widespread, even violent, opposition to the draft that had occurred during the Civil War. Much of the anger over the Civil War draft stemmed from the unpopular provision that allowed draftees to buy their way out by paying $300 for a substitute. The new draft made no such allowances. Baker stressed the democratic procedures for registration and the active role of local draft boards in administering the process.

On June 5, 1917, nearly 10 million men registered for the draft. There was scattered organized resistance, but overall, registration records offered evidence of national support. A supplemental registration in August 1918 extended the age limits to eighteen and forty-five. By the end of the war some 24 million men had registered. Of the 2.8 million men eventually called up for service, about 340,000, or 12 percent, failed to show up. Another 2 million Americans volunteered for the various armed services.

The vast, polyglot army posed unprecedented challenges of organization and control. But progressive elements within the administration also saw opportunities for pressing reform measures involving education, alcohol, and sex. Army psychologists gave the new Stanford-Binet intelligence test to all recruits and were shocked to find illiteracy rates as high as 25 percent. The low test scores among recent immigrants and rural African Americans undoubtedly reflected the cultural biases embedded in the tests and a lack of proficiency in English for many test takers. Most psychologists at the time, however, interpreted low scores in terms of racial theories of innate differences in intelligence. After the war, intelligence testing became a standard feature of America's educational system.

Ideally, the army provided a field for social reform and education, especially for the one-fifth of U.S. soldiers born in another country. "The military tent where they all sleep side by side," Theodore Roosevelt predicted, "will rank next to the public schools among the great agents of democratization." The recruits themselves took a more lighthearted view, while singing the army's praises:

> *Oh, the army, the army, the democratic army,*
> *They clothe you and feed you because the army needs you*
> *Hash for breakfast, beans for dinner, stew for suppertime,*
> *Thirty dollars every month, deducting twenty-nine.*
> *Oh, the army, the army, the democratic army,*
> *The Jews, the Wops, and the Dutch and Irish Cops,*
> *They're all in the army now!*

U.S. soldiers leaving training camp, on their way to the European front, 1918. In just over a year national mobilization expanded the armed forces twentyfold, to nearly 5 million men and women. By November 1918, when the fighting ended, more than 2 million American troops were in Europe.

SOURCE: 69th New York City Infantry going off to WWI. National Archives and Records Administration.

Racism in the Military

But African Americans who served found severe limitations in the U.S. military. They were organized into totally segregated units, barred entirely from the marines and the Coast Guard, and largely relegated to working as cooks, laundrymen, stevedores, and the like in the army and navy. Thousands of black soldiers endured humiliating, sometimes violent treatment, particularly from southern white officers. African American servicemen faced hostility from white civilians as well, North and South, often being denied service in restaurants and admission to theaters near training camps. The ugliest incident occurred in Houston, Texas, in August 1917. Black infantrymen, incensed over continual insults and harassment by local whites, seized weapons from an armory and killed seventeen civilians. The army executed thirty black soldiers and imprisoned forty-one others for life, denying any of them a chance for appeal.

More than 200,000 African Americans eventually served in France, but only about one in five saw combat, as opposed to two out of three white soldiers. Black combat units served with distinction in various divisions of the French army. The all-black 369th U.S. Infantry, for example, saw the first and longest service of any American regiment deployed in a foreign army, serving in the trenches for 191 days. The French government awarded the Croix de Guerre to the entire regiment, and 171 officers and enlisted men were cited individually for exceptional bravery in action. African American soldiers by and large enjoyed a friendly reception from French civilians as well. The contrast with their treatment at home would remain a sore point with these troops upon their return to the United States.

Americans in Battle

Naively, many Americans had assumed that the nation's participation in the war could be limited to supplying economic aid and military hardware. At first, the main contribution came on the sea. German U-boats were sinking Allied ships at a rate of 900,000 tons each month; one of four British ships never returned to port. The United States began sending warships and destroyers to protect large convoys of merchant ships and to aid the British navy in assaulting U-boats. Within a year,

African American troops advance toward the sound of gunfire in northern France, 1918. Nearly 400,000 black men served in World War I, but due to the racist beliefs held by most military and political leaders, only 42,000 went into combat. "Many of the white field officers," wrote black Lieutenant Howard H. Long, "seemed far more concerned with reminding their Negro subordinates that they were Negroes than they were in having an effective unit that would perform well in combat."

SOURCE: Brown Brothers (F149).

shipping tonnage lost each month to submarine warfare had been reduced to 200,000; the flow of weapons, supplies, and troops continued. No American soldiers were lost on the way to Europe.

President Wilson appointed General John J. Pershing, recently returned from pursuing Pancho Villa in Mexico, as commander of the American Expeditionary Force (AEF). Pershing insisted that the AEF maintain its own identity, distinct from that of the French and British armies. He was also reluctant to send American troops into battle before they had received at least six months' training. The AEF's combat role would be brief but intense: not until early 1918 did AEF units reach the front in large numbers; eight months later the war was over.

Like Ulysses S. Grant, Pershing believed the object of war to be total destruction of the enemy's military power. He expressed contempt for the essentially defensive tactics of trench warfare pursued by both sides. But the brutal power of modern military technology had made trench warfare inevitable from 1914 to 1917. The awesome firepower of the machine gun and long-range artillery made the massed frontal confrontations of the Civil War era obsolete. The grim reality of life in the trenches—cold, wet, lice-ridden, with long periods of boredom and sleeplessness—also made a mockery of older notions about the glory of combat.

In the early spring of 1918 the Germans launched a major offensive that brought them within fifty miles of Paris. In early June about 70,000 AEF soldiers helped the French stop the Germans in the battles of Château-Thierry and Belleau Wood. In July, Allied forces led by Marshal Ferdinand Foch of France, began a counteroffensive designed to defeat Germany once and for all. American reinforcements began flooding the ports of Liverpool in England and Brest and Saint-Nazaire in France. The "doughboys" (a nickname for soldiers dating back to Civil War–era recruits who joined the army for the money) streamed in at a rate of over 250,000 a month. By September, General Pershing had more than a million Americans in his army.

In late September 1918, the AEF took over the southern part of a 200-mile front in the Meuse-Argonne offensive. In seven weeks of fighting, most through terrible mud and rain, U.S. soldiers used more ammunition than the entire Union army had in the four years of the Civil War. The Germans, exhausted and badly outnumbered, began to fall back and look for a cease-fire. On November 11, 1918, the war ended with the signing of an armistice.

The massive influx of American troops and supplies no doubt hastened the end of the war. About two-thirds of the U.S. soldiers saw at least some fighting, but even they managed to avoid the horrors of the sustained trench warfare that had marked the earlier years of the war. For most Americans at the front, the war experience was a mixture of fear, exhaustion, and fatigue. Their time in France would remain a decisive moment in their lives. In all, more than 52,000 Americans died in battle. Another 60,000 died from influenza and pneumonia, half of these while still in training camp. More than 200,000 Americans were wounded in the war. These figures, awful as they were, paled against the estimated casualties (killed and wounded) suffered by the European nations: 9 million for Russia, more than 6 million for Germany, nearly 5 million for France, and over 2 million each for Great Britain and Italy.

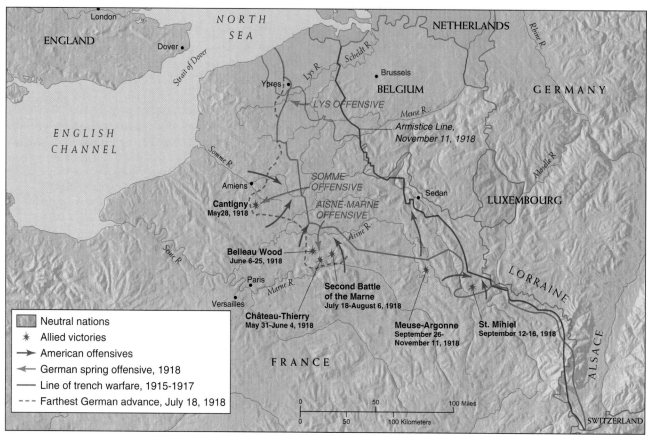

The Western Front, 1918 American units saw their first substantial action in late May, helping to stop the German offensive at the Battle of Cantigny. By September, more than 1 million American troops were fighting in a counteroffensive campaign at St. Mihiel, the largest single American engagement of the war.

OVER HERE

In one sense, World War I can be understood as the ultimate progressive crusade, a reform movement of its own. Nearly all the reform energy of the previous two decades was turned toward the central goal of winning the war. The federal government would play a larger role than ever in managing and regulating the wartime economy. Planning, efficiency, scientific analysis, and cooperation were key principles for government agencies and large volunteer organizations. Although much of the regulatory spirit was temporary, the war experience started some important and lasting organizational trends in American life.

Organizing the Economy

In the summer of 1917 President Wilson established the War Industries Board (WIB) as a clearinghouse for industrial mobilization to support the war effort. Led by the successful Wall Street speculator Bernard M. Baruch, the WIB proved a major innovation in expanding the regulatory power of the federal government. It was given broad authority over the conversion of industrial plants to wartime needs, the manufacture of war materials, and the purchase of supplies for the United States and the Allies. The WIB had to balance price controls against war profits. Only by ensuring a fair rate of return on investment could it encourage stepped-up production.

The WIB eventually handled 3,000 contracts worth $14.5 billion with various businesses. Standardization of goods brought large savings and streamlined production. Baruch continually negotiated with business leaders, describing the system as "voluntary cooperation with the big stick in the cupboard." At first Elbert Gary of U.S. Steel refused to accept the government's price for steel and Henry Ford balked at limiting private car production. But when Baruch warned that he would instruct the military to take over their plants, both industrialists backed down.

In August 1917, Congress passed the Food and Fuel Act, authorizing the president to regulate the production and distribution of the food and fuel necessary for the war effort. To lead the Food Administration (FA), Wilson appointed Herbert Hoover, a millionaire engineer who had already won fame for directing a program of war relief for Belgium. He became one of the best-known figures of the war administration. Hoover imposed price controls on certain agricultural commodities, such as sugar, pork, and wheat. These were purchased by the government and then sold to the public through licensed dealers. The FA also raised the purchase price of grain so that farmers would increase production. But Hoover stopped short of imposing mandatory food rationing, preferring to rely on persuasion, high prices, and voluntary controls.

Hoover's success, like George Creel's at the CPI, depended on motivating hundreds of thousands of volunteers in thousands of American communities. The FA coordinated the work of local committees that distributed posters and leaflets urging people to save food, recycle scraps, and substitute for scarce produce. The FA directed patriotic appeals for "Wheatless Mondays, Meatless Tuesdays, and Porkless Thursdays." Hoover exhorted Americans to "go back to simple food, simple clothes, simple pleasures." He urged them to grow their own vegetables. These efforts resulted in a sharp cutback in the consumption of sugar and wheat as well as a boost in the supply of livestock. The resultant increase in food exports helped sustain the Allied war effort.

The enormous cost of fighting the war, about $33 billion, required unprecedentedly large expenditures for the federal government. The tax structure shifted dramatically as a result. Taxes on incomes and profits replaced excise and customs levies as the major source of revenue. The minimum income subject to the graduated federal income tax, in effect only since 1913, was lowered to $1,000 from $3,000, increasing the number of Americans who paid income tax from 437,000 in 1916 to 4,425,000 in 1918. Tax rates were as steep as 70 percent in the highest brackets.

The bulk of war financing came from government borrowing, especially in the form of the popular Liberty Bonds sold to the American public. Bond drives became highly organized patriotic campaigns that ultimately raised a total of $23 billion for the war effort. The administration also used the new Federal Reserve Banks to expand the money supply, making borrowing easier. The federal debt jumped from $1 billion in 1915 to $20 billion in 1920.

The Business of War

Overall, the war meant expansion and high profits for American business. Between 1916 and 1918, Ford Motor Company increased its workforce from 32,000 to 48,000, General Motors from 10,000 to 50,000. Total capital expenditure in U.S. manufacturing jumped from $600 million in 1915 to $2.5 billion in 1918. Corporate profits as a whole nearly tripled between 1914 and 1919, and many large businesses did much better than that.

Annual prewar profits for United States Steel had averaged $76 million; in 1917 they were $478 million. The Bethlehem Shipbuilding Company increased its annual profits from $6 million in peacetime to $49 million in wartime. Du Pont quadrupled its assets. The demand for foodstuffs led to a boom in agriculture as well. The total value of farm produce rose from $9.8 billion in 1914 to $21.3 billion by 1918. Expanded farm acreage and increased investment in farm machinery led to a jump of 20–30 percent in overall farm production.

The most important and long-lasting economic legacy of the war was the organizational shift toward corporatism in American business. The wartime need for efficient management, manufacturing, and distribution could be met only by a greater reliance on the productive and marketing power of large corporations. Never before had business and the federal government cooperated so closely. Under war administrators like Baruch and Hoover, entire industries (such as radio manufacturing) and economic sectors (such as agriculture and energy) were organized, regulated, and subsidized. War agencies used both public and private power—legal authority and voluntarism—to hammer out and enforce agreements. Here was the genesis of the modern bureaucratic state.

Some Americans worried about the wartime trend toward a greater federal presence in their lives. As *The Saturday Evening Post* noted, "All this government activity will be called to account and re-examined in due time." Although many aspects of the government–business partnership proved temporary, some institutions and practices grew stronger in the postwar years. Among these were the Federal Reserve Board, the income tax system, the Chamber of Commerce, the Farm Bureau, and the growing horde of lobbying groups that pressed Washington for special interest legislation.

One key example of the long-range impact of the government–business partnership was the infant radio industry. Wireless communication technology found many uses among naval and ground forces in wartime. As in most industries, the Justice Department guaranteed radio manufacturers protection against patent infringement and antitrust suits. These guarantees helped stimulate research and the mass production of radios for airplanes, ships, and infantry. In 1919 the government helped create the Radio Corporation of America (RCA), which bought out a British company that had dominated America's wireless system. As part of the deal, the U.S. military was allowed a permanent representative on the RCA board of directors. The creation of RCA, jointly owned by General Electric, American Telephone and Telegraph, and Westinghouse, assured the United States a powerful position in the new age of global communications. It also set the stage for the new radio broadcasting industry of the 1920s.

Labor and the War

Organized labor's power and prestige, though by no means equal to those of business or government, clearly grew during the war. The expansion of the economy, combined with army mobilization and a decline in immigration from Europe, caused a growing wartime labor shortage. As the demand for workers intensified, the federal government was forced to recognize that labor, like any other resource or commodity, would have to be more carefully tended to than in peacetime. For the war's duration, working people generally enjoyed higher wages and a better standard of living. Trade unions, especially those affiliated with the American Federation of Labor (AFL), experienced a sharp rise in membership. In effect, the government took in labor as a junior partner in the mobilization of the economy.

Samuel Gompers, president of the AFL, emerged as the leading spokesman for the nation's trade union movement. An English immigrant and cigar maker by trade, Gompers had rejected the socialism of his youth for a philosophy of "business unionism." By stressing the concrete gains that workers could win through collective bargaining with employers, the AFL had reached a total membership of about 2 million in 1914. Virtually all its members were skilled white males, organized in highly selective crafts in the building trades, railroads, and coal mines.

Gompers pledged the AFL's patriotic support for the war effort, and in April 1918 President Wilson appointed him to the National War Labor Board (NWLB). During 1917 the nation had seen thousands of strikes involving more than a million workers. Wages were usually at issue, reflecting workers' concerns with spiraling inflation and higher prices. The NWLB, co-chaired by labor attorney Frank Walsh and former president William H. Taft, acted as a kind of supreme court for labor, arbitrating disputes and working to prevent disruptions in production. The great majority of these interventions resulted in improved wages and reduced hours of work.

Most important, the NWLB supported the right of workers to organize unions and furthered the acceptance of the eight-hour day for war workers—central aims of the labor movement. It also backed time-and-a-half pay for overtime, as well as the principle of equal pay for women workers. AFL unions gained more than a million new members during the war, and overall union membership rose from 2.7 million in 1914 to more than 5 million by 1920. The NWLB established important precedents for government intervention on behalf of labor.

Wartime conditions often meant severe disruptions and discomfort for America's workers. Overcrowding, rapid workforce turnover, and high inflation rates were typical in war-boom communities. In Bridgeport, Connecticut, a center for small-arms manufacturing, the pop-

ulation grew by 50,000 in less than a year. In 1917 the number of families grew by 12,000, but available housing stock increased by only 6,000 units. Chronic congestion became common in many cities; Philadelphia reported the worst housing shortage in its history.

In the Southwest, the demand for wartime labor temporarily eased restrictions against the movement of Mexicans into the United States. The Immigration Act of 1917, requiring a literacy test and an $8 head tax, had cut Mexican immigration nearly in half, down to about 25,000 per year. But employers complained of severe shortages of workers. Farmers in Arizona's Salt River Valley and southern California needed hands to harvest grain, alfalfa, cotton, and fruit. El Paso's mining and smelting industries, Texas's border ranches, and southern Arizona's railroads and copper mines insisted they depended on unskilled Mexican labor as well.

Responding to these protests, in June 1917, the Department of Labor suspended the immigration law for the duration of the war and negotiated an agreement with the Mexican government permitting some 35,000 Mexican contract laborers to enter the United States. Mexicans let in through this program had to demonstrate they had a job waiting before they could cross the border. They received identification cards and transportation to their place of work from American labor contractors. Pressure from southwestern employers kept the exemptions in force until 1921, well after the end of the war, demonstrating the growing importance of cheap Mexican labor to the region's economy.

If the war boosted the fortunes of the AFL, it also spelled the end for more radical elements of the U.S. labor movement. The Industrial Workers of the World (IWW) had followed a different path from the "pure and simple" trade unionism of Gompers. Unlike the AFL, the IWW concentrated on organizing unskilled workers into all-inclusive industrial unions. The Wobblies denounced capitalism as an unreformable system based on exploitation, and they opposed U.S. entry into the war. IWW leaders advised their members to refuse induction for "the capitalists' war."

With vigorous organizing, especially in the West, the IWW had grown in 1916 and 1917. It gained strength among workers in several areas crucial to the war effort: copper mining, lumbering, and wheat harvesting. In September 1917, just after the vigilante attack in Bisbee and the IWW's efforts to expose it, the Wilson administration responded to appeals from western business leaders for a crackdown on the Wobblies. Justice Department agents, acting under the broad authority of the recently passed Espionage Act, swooped down on IWW offices in more than sixty towns and cities, arresting more than 300 people and confiscating files. The mass trials and convictions that followed broke the back of America's radical labor movement and marked the beginning of a powerful wave of political repression.

Women at Work

World War I marked the first time that women were mobilized directly into the armed forces. Over 16,000 women served overseas with the AEF in France, where most worked as nurses, clerical workers, telephone operators, and canteen operators. Another 12,000 women served stateside in the navy and U.S. Marine Corps, and tens of thousands of civilian women were employed in army offices and hospitals. But the war's impact on women was greatest in the broader civilian economy. For many of the 8 million women already in the labor force, the war meant a chance to switch from low-paying jobs, such as domestic service, to higher-paying industrial employment. About a million women workers joined the labor force for the first time. Of the estimated 9.4 million workers directly engaged in war work, some 2.25 million were women. Of these, 1.25 million worked in manufacturing. Female munitions plant workers, train engineers, drill press operators, streetcar conductors, and mail carriers became a common sight around the country.

Women workers at the Midvale Steel and Ordinance Company in Pennsylvania, 1918. Wartime labor shortages created new opportunities for over one million women to take high wage manufacturing jobs like these. The opening proved temporary, however, and with the war's end nearly all of these women lost their jobs. By 1920 the number of women employed in manufacturing was lower than it had been in 1910.

SOURCE: National Archives and Records Administration (1-SC-31731).

In response to the widened range of female employment, the Labor Department created the Women in Industry Service (WIS). Directed by Mary Van Kleeck, the service advised employers on using female labor and formulated general standards for the treatment of women workers. The WIS represented the first attempt by the federal government to take a practical stand on improving working conditions for women. Its standards included the eight-hour day, equal pay for equal work, a minimum wage, the prohibition of night work, and the provision of rest periods, meal breaks, and restroom facilities. These standards had no legal force, however, and WIS inspectors found that employers often flouted them. They were accepted nonetheless as goals by nearly every group concerned with improving the conditions of working women.

Many women resented the restrictiveness of the WIS guidelines. Myrtle Altenburg, a Wisconsin widow, complained of being prevented from working on a local railroad. "It is my belief," she wrote the state railway commission, "that a woman can do everything that a man can do that is within her strength. Hundreds and hundreds of women might work and release men for war or war work, could they, the women, be employed on the railroads." Even when hired, women suffered discrimination over pay. Government surveys found that women's average earnings were roughly half of men's in the same industries.

At war's end, women lost nearly all their defense-related jobs. Wartime women railroad workers, for example, were replaced by returning servicemen through the application of laws meant to protect women from hazardous conditions. But the war accelerated female employment in fields already dominated by women. By 1920, more women who worked outside the home did so in white-collar occupations—as telephone operators, secretaries, and clerks, for example—than in manufacturing or domestic service. The new awareness of women's work led Congress to create the Women's Bureau in the Labor Department, which continued the WIS wartime program of education and investigation through the postwar years.

Woman Suffrage

The presence of so many new women wageworkers, combined with the highly visible volunteer work of millions of middle-class women, helped finally to secure the vote for women. Volunteer war work—selling bonds, saving food, organizing benefits—was very popular among housewives and clubwomen. These women played a key role in the success of the Food Administration, and the Women's Committee of the Council of National Defense included a variety of women's organizations.

Until World War I, the fight for woman suffrage had been waged largely within individual states. Western states and territories had led the way. Various forms of woman suffrage had become law in Wyoming in 1869, followed by Utah (1870), Colorado (1893), Idaho (1896), Washington (1910), California (1911), Arizona and Oregon (1912), and Montana and Nevada (1914). The reasons for this regional pattern had less to do with dramatically different notions of gender roles in the West than with the distinctiveness of western politics and society. Rocky Mountain and Pacific coast states did not have the sharp ethnocultural divisions between Catholics and Protestants that hindered suffrage efforts in the East. The close identification in the East between the suffrage and prohibition movements led many Catholic immigrants and German Lutherans to oppose the vote for women because they feared it would lead to prohibition. Mormons in Utah supported woman suffrage as a way to preserve polygamy and defend their distinctive social order from attack.

The U.S. entry into the war provided a unique opportunity for suffrage groups to shift their strategy to a national campaign for a constitutional amendment granting the vote to women. The most important of these groups was the National American Woman Suffrage Association. Before 1917, most American suffragists had opposed the war. Under the leadership of Carrie Chapman Catt, the NAWSA threw its support behind the war effort and doubled its membership to 2 million. Catt gambled that a strong show of patriotism would help clinch the century-old fight to win the vote for women. The NAWSA pursued a moderate policy of lobbying Congress for a constitutional amendment and calling for state referendums on woman suffrage.

At the same time, more militant suffragists led by the young Quaker activist Alice Paul, injected new energy and more radical tactics into the movement. Paul had spent several years in England working with militant suffragists there, and in 1913 she returned to the United States to form the Congressional Union within the NAWSA to lobby for a federal amendment. Dissatisfied with the NAWSA's conservative strategy of quiet lobbying and orderly demonstrations, Paul left the organization in 1916. She joined forces with western women voters to form the National Woman's Party. Borrowing from English suffragists, this party pursued a more aggressive and dramatic strategy of agitation. Paul and her supporters picketed the White House, publicly burned President Wilson's speeches, and condemned the presi-

Members of the National Woman's Party picketed President Wilson at the White House in 1917. Their militant action in the midst of the war crisis aroused both anger and sympathy. The NWP campaign helped push the president and the Congress to accept woman suffrage as a "war measure."

SOURCE: Library of Congress.

dent and the Democrats for failing to produce an amendment. In one demonstration they chained themselves to the White House fence and after their arrest went on a hunger strike in jail. The militants generated a great deal of publicity and sympathy.

Although some in the NAWSA objected to these tactics, Paul's radical approach helped make the NAWSA position more acceptable to Wilson. Carrie Chapman Catt used the president's war rhetoric as an argument for granting the vote to women. The fight for democracy, she argued, must begin at home, and she urged passage of the woman suffrage amendment as a "war measure." She won Wilson's support, and in 1917 the president urged Congress to pass a woman suffrage amendment as "vital to the winning of the war." The House did so in January 1918 and a more reluctant Senate approved it in June 1919. Another year of hard work was spent convincing the state legislatures. In August 1920, Tennessee gave the final vote needed to ratify the Nineteenth Amendment to the Constitution, finally making woman suffrage legal nationwide.

Prohibition

Significantly, another reform effort closely associated with women's groups triumphed at the same time. The movement to eliminate alcohol from American life

Web Exploration

Chart the progress of the women's suffrage movement. What were the reasons behind the regional differences in support of women's suffrage?
www.prenhall.com/faragher/map22.2

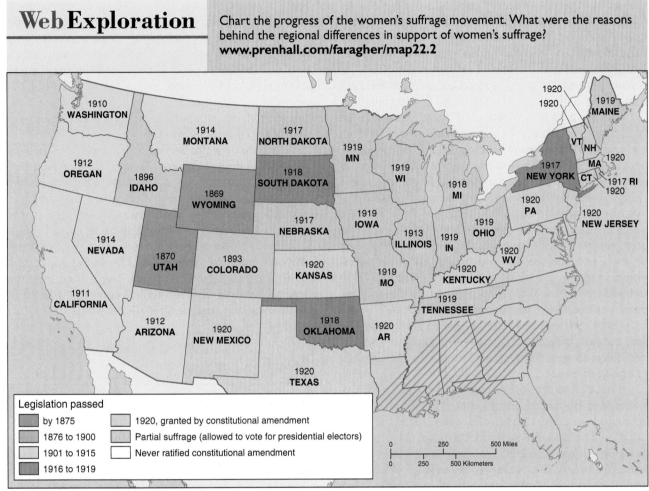

Woman Suffrage by State, 1869–1919 Dates for the enactment of woman suffrage in the individual states. Years before ratification of the Nineteenth Amendment in 1920, a number of western states had legislated full or partial voting rights for women. In 1917 Montana suffragist Jeannette Rankin became the first woman elected to Congress.

SOURCE: Barbara G. Shortridge, *Atlas of American Women* (New York: Macmillan, 1987).

had attracted many Americans, especially women, since before the Civil War. Temperance advocates saw drinking as the source of many of the worst problems faced by the working class, including family violence, unemployment, and poverty. By the early twentieth century the Woman's Christian Temperance Union, with a quarter-million members, had become the single largest women's organization in American history.

The moral fervor that accompanied America's entry into the war provided a crucial boost to the cause. With so many breweries bearing German names, the movement benefited as well from the strong anti-German feeling of the war years. Outlawing beer and whiskey would also help to conserve precious grain, prohibitionists argued.

In 1917, a coalition of progressives and rural fundamentalists in Congress pushed through a constitutional amendment providing for a national ban on alcoholic

drinks. The Eighteenth Amendment was ratified by the states in January 1919 and became the law of the land one year later. Although Prohibition would create a host of problems in the postwar years, especially as a stimulus for the growth of organized crime, many Americans, particularly native Protestants, considered it a worthy moral reform.

Public Health

Wartime mobilization brought deeper government involvement with public health issues, especially in the realm of sex hygiene, child welfare, and disease prevention. The rate of venereal disease among draftees was as high as 6 percent in some states, presenting a potential manpower problem for the army. In April 1917, the War Department mounted a vigorous campaign against venereal disease, which attracted the energies of progressive era sex reformers—social hygienists and antivice crusaders. Under the direction of Raymond Fosdick and the Commission on Training Camp Activities, the military educated troops on the dangers of contracting syphilis and gonorrhea and distributed condoms to soldiers. "A Soldier who gets a dose," warned a typical poster, "is a Traitor." More than a hundred red-light districts near military bases were closed down, and the army established five-mile "pure zones" to keep prostitutes away from the camps. Yet the sexual double standard still operated. Female activists angrily protested when military authorities, while refusing to arrest soldiers for patronizing prostitutes, arrested the women en masse and held them in detention centers.

The scientific discussions of sex to which recruits were subjected in lectures, pamphlets, and films were surely a first for the vast majority of them. Venereal disease rates for soldiers declined by more than 300 percent during the war. The Division of Venereal Diseases, created in the summer of 1918 as a branch of the U.S. Public Health Service, established clinics offering free medical treatment to infected persons. It also coordinated an aggressive educational campaign through state departments of health.

The wartime boost to government health work continued into the postwar years. The Children's Bureau, created in 1912 as a part of the Labor Department, undertook a series of reports on special problems growing out of the war: the increase in employment of married women, the finding of day care for children of working mothers, and the growth of both child labor and delinquency. In 1918 Julia C. Lathrop, chief of the bureau, organized a "Children's Year" campaign designed to promote public protection of expectant mothers and infants and to enforce child labor laws. Millions of health education pamphlets were distributed nationwide, and mothers were encouraged to have their infants and children weighed and measured. Thousands of community-based committees enrolled some 11 million women in the drive.

In 1917, Lathrop, who had come to the Children's Bureau from the settlement house movement, proposed a plan to institutionalize federal aid to the states for protection of mothers and children. Congress finally passed the Maternity and Infancy Act in 1921, appropriating over $1 million a year to be administered to the states by the Children's Bureau. In the postwar years, clinics for prenatal and obstetrical care grew out of these efforts and greatly reduced the rate of infant and maternal mortality and disease.

The disastrous influenza epidemic of 1918–19 offered the most serious challenge to national public health during the war years. Part of a worldwide pandemic that claimed as many as 20 million lives, few Americans paid attention to the disease until it swept through military camps and eastern cities in September 1918. A lethal combination of the "flu" and respiratory complications (mainly pneumonia) killed roughly 550,000 Americans in ten months. Most victims were young adults between the ages of twenty and forty. Professional groups such as the American Medical Association called for massive government appropriations to search for a cure. Congress did appropriate a million dollars to the Public Health Service to combat and suppress the epidemic, but it offered no money for research.

The Public Health Service found itself overwhelmed by calls for doctors, nurses, and treatment facilities. Much of the care for the sick and dying came from Red Cross nurses and volunteers working in local communities across the nation. With a war on, and the nation focused on reports from the battlefront, even a public health crisis of this magnitude went relatively unnoticed. Although funding for the Public Health Service continued to grow in the 1920s, public and private expenditures on medical research were barely one-fiftieth of what they would become after World War II.

REPRESSION AND REACTION

World War I exposed and intensified many of the deepest social tensions in American life. On the local level, as exemplified by the Bisbee deportations, vigilantes increasingly took the law into their own hands to punish those suspected of disloyalty. The push for national unity led the federal government to crack down on a wide spectrum of dissenters from its war policies. The war inflamed racial hatred, and the worst race riots in the nation's history exploded in several cities. At war's end, a newly militant labor movement briefly asserted itself in mass strikes around the nation. Over all these developments loomed the 1917 Bolshevik Revolution in Russia. Radicals around the world had drawn inspiration from what looked like the first successful revolution against a capitalist state. Many conservatives worried that similar revolutions were imminent. From 1918 through 1920 the federal government directed a repressive antiradical campaign that had crucial implications for the nation's future.

Muzzling Dissent: The Espionage and Sedition Acts

The Espionage Act of June 1917 became the government's key tool for the suppression of antiwar sentiment. It set severe penalties (up to twenty years' imprisonment and a $10,000 fine) for anyone found guilty of aiding the enemy, obstructing recruitment, or causing insubordination in the armed forces. The act also empowered the postmaster general to exclude from the mails any newspapers or magazines he thought treasonous. Within a year the mailing rights of forty-five newpapers had been revoked. These included several anti-British and pro-Irish publications, as well as such leading journals of American socialism as the Kansas- based *Appeal to Reason,* which had enjoyed a prewar circulation of half a million, and *The Masses.*

To enforce the Espionage Act, the government had to increase its overall police and surveillance machinery. Civilian intelligence was coordinated by the newly created Bureau of Investigation in the Justice Department. This agency was reorganized after the war as the Federal Bureau of Investigation (FBI). In May 1918 the Sedition Act, an amendment to the Espionage Act, outlawed "any disloyal, profane, scurrilous, or abusive language intended to cause contempt, scorn, contumely, or disrepute" to the government, Constitution, or flag.

In all, more than 2,100 cases were brought to trial under these acts. They became a convenient vehicle for striking out at socialists, pacifists, radical labor activists, and others who resisted the patriotic tide. The most celebrated prosecution came in June 1918 when federal agents arrested Eugene V. Debs in Canton, Ohio, after he gave a speech defending antiwar protesters. Sentenced to ten years in prison, Debs defiantly told the court: "I have been accused of having obstructed the war. I admit it. Gentlemen, I abhor war. I would oppose the war if I stood alone." Debs served thirty-two months in federal prison before being pardoned by President Warren G. Harding on Christmas Day 1921.

The Supreme Court upheld the constitutionality of the acts in several 1919 decisions. In *Schenck* v. *United States* the Court unanimously agreed with Justice Oliver Wendell Holmes's claim that Congress could restrict speech if the words "are used in such circumstances and are of such a nature as to create a clear and present danger." The decision upheld the conviction of

Charles Schenck for having mailed pamphlets urging potential army inductees to resist conscription. In *Debs* v. *United States,* the Court affirmed the guilt of Eugene V. Debs for his antiwar speech in Canton, even though he had not explicitly urged violation of the draft laws. Finally, in *Abrams* v. *United States,* the Court upheld Sedition Act convictions of four Russian immigrants who had printed pamphlets denouncing American military intervention in the Russian Revolution. The nation's highest court thus endorsed the severe wartime restrictions on free speech.

The deportation of striking miners in Bisbee offered an extreme case of vigilante activity. Thousands of other instances took place as government repression and local vigilantes reinforced each other. The American Protective League, founded with the blessing of the Justice Department, mobilized 250,000 self-appointed "operatives" in more than 600 towns and cities. Members of the league, mostly businessmen, bankers, and former policemen, spied on their neighbors and staged a series of well-publicized "slacker" raids on antiwar protesters and draft evaders. Many communities, inspired by Committee on Public Information campaigns, sought to ban the teaching of the German language in their schools or the performance of German music in concert halls.

The Great Migration and Racial Tensions

Economic opportunity brought on by war prosperity triggered a massive migration of rural black Southerners to northern cities. From 1914 to 1920, somewhere between 300,000 and 500,000 African Americans left the rural South for the North. Chicago's black population increased by 65,000, or 150 percent; Detroit's by 35,000, or 600 percent. Acute labor shortages led northern factory managers to recruit black migrants to the expanding industrial centers. The Pennsylvania Railroad alone drew 10,000 black workers from Florida and

THE GREAT MIGRATION: BLACK POPULATION GROWTH IN SELECTED NORTHERN CITIES, 1910–1920					
City	1910		1920		Percent Increase
	No.	Percent	No.	Percent	
New York	91,709	1.9%	152,467	2.7%	66.3%
Chicago	44,103	2.0	109,458	4.1	148.2
Philadelphia	84,459	5.5	134,229	7.4	58.9
Detroit	5,741	1.2	40,838	4.1	611.3
St. Louis	43,960	6.4	69,854	9.0	58.9
Cleveland	8,448	1.5	34,451	4.3	307.8
Pittsburgh	25,623	4.8	37,725	6.4	47.2
Cincinnati	19,739	5.4	30,079	7.5	53.2

SOURCE: U.S. Department of Commerce.

south Georgia. Black workers eagerly left low-paying jobs as field hands and domestic servants for the chance at relatively high-paying work in meatpacking plants, shipyards, and steel mills.

Kinship and community networks were crucial in shaping what came to be called the Great Migration. They spread news about job openings, urban residential districts, and boardinghouses in northern cities. Black clubs, churches, and fraternal lodges in southern communities frequently sponsored the migration of their members, as well as return trips to the South. Single African American women often made the trip first because they could more easily obtain steady work as maids, cooks, and laundresses. One recalled that "if [white employers] liked the way the women would work in their homes or did ironing, they might throw some work to your husband or son." Relatively few African American men actually secured high-paying skilled jobs in industry or manufacturing. Most had to settle for work as construction laborers, teamsters, janitors, porters, or other low-paying jobs.

The persistence of lynching and other racial violence in the South no doubt contributed to the Great Migration. But racial violence was not limited to the South. Two of the worst race riots in American history occurred as a result of tensions brought on by wartime migration. On July 2, 1917, in East St. Louis, Illinois, a

This southern African American family is shown arriving in Chicago around 1910. Black migrants to northern cities often faced overcrowding, inferior housing, and a high death rate from disease. But the chance to earn daily wages of $6 to $8 (the equivalent of a week's wages in much of the South), as well as the desire to escape persistent racial violence, kept the migrants coming.

SOURCE: Stock Montage, Inc./Historical Pictures Collection.

ferocious mob of whites attacked African Americans, killing at least 200. Before this riot, some of the city's manufacturers had been steadily recruiting black labor as a way to keep local union demands down. Unions had refused to allow black workers as members, and politicians had cynically exploited white racism in appealing for votes. In Chicago, on July 27, 1919, antiblack rioting broke out on a Lake Michigan beach. For two weeks white gangs hunted African Americans in the streets and burned hundreds out of their homes. Twenty-three African Americans and fifteen whites died, and more than 500 were injured.

In both East St. Louis and Chicago, local authorities held African Americans responsible for the violence. President Wilson refused requests for federal intervention or investigation. A young black veteran who had been chased by a mob in the Chicago riot asked: "Had the ten months I spent in France been all in vain? Were all those white crosses over dead bodies of those dark skinned boys lying in Flanders field for naught? Was democracy a hollow sentiment?"

In terms of service in the armed forces, compliance with the draft, and involvement in volunteer work, African Americans had supported the war effort as faithfully as any group. In 1917, despite a segregated army and discrimination in defense industries, most African Americans thought the war might improve their lot. "If we again demonstrate our loyalty and devotion to our country," advised the *Chicago Defender*, "those injustices will disappear and the grounds for complaint will no longer exist." By the fall of 1919, writing in *The Crisis*, the journal of the National Association for the Advancement of Colored People (NAACP), black author James Weldon Johnson gloomily concluded that "an increased hatred of race was an integral part of wartime intolerance."

Black disillusionment about the war grew quickly. So did a newly militant spirit. A heightened sense of race consciousness and activism was evident among black veterans and the growing black communities of northern cities. Taking the lead in the fight against bigotry and injustice, the NAACP held a national conference in 1919 on lynching. It pledged to defend persecuted African Americans, publicize the horrors of lynch law, and seek federal legislation against "Judge Lynch." By 1919 membership in the NAACP had reached 60,000 and the circulation of its journal exceeded half a million.

Labor Strife

The relative labor peace of 1917 and 1918 dissolved after the armistice. More than 4 million American workers were involved in some 3,600 strikes in 1919 alone. This unprecedented strike wave had several causes. Most of the modest wartime wage gains were wiped out by spiraling inflation and high prices for food, fuel, and housing. With the end of government controls on industry, many employers withdrew their recognition of unions. Difficult working conditions, such as the twelve-hour day in steel mills, were still routine in some industries.

Several of the postwar strikes received widespread national attention. They seemed to be more than simple economic conflicts, and they provoked deep fears about the larger social order. In February 1919, a strike in the shipyards of Seattle, Washington, over wages escalated into a general citywide strike involving 60,000 workers. The local press and Mayor Ole Hanson denounced the strikers as revolutionaries. Hanson effectively ended the strike by requesting federal troops to occupy the city.

In September, Boston policemen went out on strike when the police commissioner rejected a citizens' commission study that recommended a pay raise. Massachusetts governor Calvin Coolidge called in the National Guard to restore order and won a national reputation by crushing the strike. The entire police force was fired. Coolidge declared, "There is no right to strike against the public safety by anybody, anywhere, any time."

The biggest strike took place in the steel industry, involving some 350,000 steelworkers. Centered in several midwestern cities, this epic struggle lasted from September 1919 to January 1920. The AFL had hoped to build on wartime gains in an industry that had successfully resisted unionization before the war. The major demands were union recognition, the eight-hour day, and wage increases. The steel companies used black strikebreakers and armed guards to keep the mills running. Elbert Gary, president of U.S. Steel, directed a sophisticated propaganda campaign that branded the strikers as revolutionaries. Public opinion turned against the strike and condoned the use of state and federal troops to break it. The failed steel strike proved to be the era's most bitter and devastating defeat for organized labor.

AN UNEASY PEACE

The armistice of November 1918 ended the fighting on the battlefield, but the war continued at the peace conference. In the old royal palace of Versailles near Paris, delegates from twenty-seven countries spent five months hammering out a settlement. Yet neither Germany nor Russia was represented. The proceedings were dominated by leaders of the "Big Four": David Lloyd George (Great Britain), Georges Clemenceau (France), Vittorio Orlando (Italy), and Woodrow Wilson (United States). President Wilson saw the peace conference as a historic opportunity to project his domestic liberalism onto the world stage. But the stubborn realities of power politics would frustrate Wilson at Versailles and lead to his most crushing defeat at home.

The Fourteen Points

Wilson arrived in Paris with the United States delegation in January 1919. He believed the Great War revealed the bankruptcy of diplomacy based on alliances and the "balance of power." Peacemaking, he thought, meant an opportunity for America to lead the rest of the world toward a new vision of international relations. He brought with him a plan for peace that he had outlined a year earlier in a speech to Congress on U.S. war aims. The Fourteen Points, as they were called, had originally served wartime purposes: to appeal to antiwar factions in Austria-Hungary and Germany, to convince Russia to stay in the war, and to help sustain Allied morale. As a blueprint for peace, they contained three main elements. First, Wilson offered a series of specific proposals for setting postwar boundaries in Europe and creating new countries out of the collapsed Austro-Hungarian and Ottoman empires. The key idea here was the right of all peoples to "national self-determination." Second, Wilson listed general principles for governing international conduct, including freedom of the seas, free trade, open covenants instead of secret treaties, reduced armaments, and mediation for competing colonial claims. Third, and most important, Wilson called for a League of Nations to help implement these principles and resolve future disputes.

The Fourteen Points offered a plan for world order deeply rooted in the liberal progressivism long associated with Wilson. The plan reflected a faith in efficient government and the rule of law as means for solving international problems. It advocated a dynamic democratic capitalism as a middle ground between Old World autocracy and revolutionary socialism. Wilson's vision was a profoundly moral one, and he was certain it was the only road to a lasting and humane peace.

The most controversial element, both at home and abroad, would prove to be the League of Nations. The heart of the League covenant, Article X, called for collective security as the ultimate method of keeping the peace: "The members of the League undertake to respect and preserve as against external aggression the territorial integrity and existing political independence of all Members." In the United States, Wilson's critics would focus on this provision as an unacceptable surrender of the nation's sovereignty and independence in foreign affairs. They also raised constitutional objections, arguing that the American system vested the power to declare war with the Congress. Would membership in the League violate this basic principle of the Constitution?

Wilson in Paris

The president was pleased when the conference at first accepted his plan as the basis for discussions. He also enjoyed wildly enthusiastic receptions from the public in Paris and several other European capitals he visited.

Woodrow Wilson, Georges Clemenceau, and David Lloyd George are among the central figures depicted in John Christen Johansen's *Signing of the Treaty of Versailles*. But all the gathered statesmen appear dwarfed by their surroundings.

SOURCE: John Christen Johansen, *Signing of the Treaty of Versailles*, 1919. National Portrait Gallery, Smithsonian Institution, Washington, D.C./Art Resource, New York (S0022240).

France's Clemenceau was less enamored. He sarcastically observed, "God gave us the Ten Commandments, and we broke them. Wilson gave us the Fourteen Points. We shall see." Wilson's plan could not survive the hostile atmosphere at Versailles.

Much of the negotiating at Versailles was in fact done in secret among the Big Four. The ideal of self-determination found limited expression. The independent states of Austria, Hungary, Poland, Yugoslavia, and Czechoslovakia were carved out of the homelands of the beaten Central Powers. But the Allies resisted Wilson's call for independence for the colonies of the defeated nations. A compromise mandate system of protectorates gave the French and British control of parts of the old German and Turkish empires in Africa and West Asia. Japan won control of former German colonies in China. Among those trying, but failing, to influence the treaty negotiations were the sixty-odd delegates to the first Pan African Congress, held in Paris at the same time as the peace talks. The group included Americans W. E. B. Du Bois and William Monroe Trotter as well as representatives from Africa and the West Indies. All were disappointed with the failure of the peace conference to grant self-determination to thousands of Africans living in former German colonies.

Another disappointment for Wilson came with the issue of war guilt. He had strongly opposed the extraction of harsh economic reparations from the Central Powers. But the French and British, with their awful war losses fresh in mind, insisted on making Germany pay. The final treaty contained a clause attributing the war to "the aggression of Germany," and a commission later set German war reparations at $33 billion. Bitter resentment in Germany over the punitive treaty helped sow the seeds for the Nazi rise to power in the 1930s.

The final treaty was signed on June 28, 1919, in the Hall of Mirrors at the Versailles palace. The Germans had no choice but to accept its harsh terms. President Wilson had been disappointed by the secret deals and the endless compromising of his ideals, no doubt underestimating the stubborn reality of power politics in the wake of Europe's most devastating war. He had nonetheless won a commitment to the League of Nations, the centerpiece of his plan, and he was confident that the American people would accept the treaty. The tougher fight would be with the Senate, where a two-thirds vote was needed for ratification.

The Treaty Fight

Preoccupied with peace conference politics in Paris, Wilson had neglected politics at home. His troubles had actually started earlier. Republicans had captured both the House and the Senate in the 1918 elections. Wilson had then made a tactical error by including no prominent Republicans in the U.S. peace delegation. He therefore faced a variety of tough opponents to the treaty he brought home.

Wilson's most extreme enemies in the Senate were a group of about sixteen "irreconcilables," opposed to a treaty in any form. Some were isolationist progressives, such as Republicans Robert M. La Follette of Wisconsin and William Borah of Idaho, who opposed the League of Nations as steadfastly as they opposed American entry into the war. Others were racist xenophobes like Democrat James Reed of Missouri. He objected, he said, to submitting questions to a tribunal "on which a nigger from Liberia, a nigger from Honduras, a nigger from India, and an unlettered gentleman from Siam, each have votes equal to the great United States of America."

The less dogmatic but more influential opponents were led by Republican Henry Cabot Lodge of Massachusetts, powerful majority leader of the Senate. They had strong reservations about the League of Nations, especially the provisions for collective security in the event of a member nation's being attacked. Lodge argued that this provision impinged on congressional authority to declare war and placed unacceptable restraints on the nation's ability to pursue an independent foreign policy. Lodge proposed a series of amendments that would have weakened the League. But Wilson refused to compromise, motivated in part by the long-standing hatred he and Lodge felt toward each other.

In September, Wilson set out on a speaking tour across the country to drum up support for the League and the treaty. His train traveled 8,000 miles—through the Midwest, to the Pacific, and then back East. The crowds were large and responsive, but they did not change any votes in the Senate. The strain took its toll. On September 25, after speaking in Pueblo, Colorado, the sixty-three-year-old Wilson collapsed from exhaustion. His doctor canceled the rest of the trip. A week later, back in Washington, the president suffered a stroke that left him partially paralyzed. In November, Lodge brought the treaty out of committee for a vote, having appended to it fourteen reservations—that is, recommended changes. A bedridden Wilson stubbornly refused to compromise and instructed Democrats to vote against the Lodge version of the treaty. On November 19, Democrats joined with the "irreconcilables" to defeat the amended treaty, 39 to 55.

Wilson refused to budge. In January, he urged Democrats to either stand by the original treaty or vote it down. The 1920 election, he warned, would be "a great and solemn referendum" on the whole issue. In the final vote, on March 19, 1920, twenty-one Democrats broke with the president and voted for the Lodge version, giving it a majority of 49 to 35. But this was seven votes short of the two-thirds needed for ratification. As a result, the United States never signed the Versailles Treaty, nor did it join the League of Nations. The absence of the United States weakened the League and made it more difficult for the organization to realize Wilson's dream of a peaceful community of nations.

The Russian Revolution and America's Response

Since early 1917, the turmoil of the Russian Revolution had changed the climate of both foreign affairs and domestic politics. The repressive and corrupt regime of Czar Nicholas II had been overthrown in March 1917 by a coalition of forces demanding change. The new provisional government, headed by Alexander Kerensky, vowed to keep Russia in the fight against Germany. But the war had taken a terrible toll on Russian soldiers and civilians, and had become very unpopular. The radical Bolsheviks, led by V. I. Lenin, gained a large following by promising "peace, land, and bread," and they began plotting to seize power. The Bolsheviks followed the teachings of German revolutionary Karl Marx, emphasizing the inevitability of class struggle and the replacement of capitalism by communism.

In November 1917 the Bolsheviks took control of the Russian government. In March 1918, to the dismay of the Allies, the new Bolshevik government negotiated a separate peace with Germany, the Treaty of Brest-Litovsk. Russia was now lost as a military ally, and her

defection made possible a massive shift of German troops to the Western Front. As civil war raged within Russia, British and French leaders wanted to help counterrevolutionary forces overthrow the new Bolshevik regime, as well as reclaim military supplies originally sent for use against the Germans.

Although sympathetic to the March revolution overthrowing the czar, President Wilson refused to recognize the authority of the Bolshevik regime. Bolshevism represented a threat to the liberal-capitalist values that Wilson believed to be the foundation of America's moral and material power and that provided the basis for the Fourteen Points. At the same time, however, Wilson at first resisted British and French pressure to intervene in Russia, citing his commitment to national self-determination and noninterference in other countries' internal affairs. "I believe in letting them work out their own salvation, even though they wallow in anarchy for a while," he wrote to one Allied diplomat.

By August 1918, as the Russian political and military situation became increasingly chaotic, Wilson agreed to British and French plans for sending troops to Siberia and northern Russia. Meanwhile, Japan poured troops into Siberia and northern Manchuria in a bid to control the commercially important Chinese Eastern and Trans-Siberian railways. After the Wilson administration negotiated an agreement that placed these strategic railways under international control, the restoration and protection of the railways became the primary concern of American military forces in Russia. Wilson justified the intervention on trade and commercial grounds, telling Congress, "It is essential that we maintain the policy of the Open Door." But, however reluctantly, the United States had in fact become an active, anti-Bolshevik participant in the Russian civil war.

Wilson's idealistic support for self-determination had succumbed to the demands of international power politics. Eventually, some 15,000 American troops served in northern and eastern Russia, with some remaining until 1920. They stayed for two reasons: to counter Japanese influence, and because Wilson did not want to risk alienating the British and French, who opposed withdrawal. The Allied armed intervention widened the gulf between Russia and the West. In March 1919, Russian Communists established the Third International, or Comintern. Their call for a worldwide revolution deepened Allied mistrust, and the Paris Peace Conference essentially ignored the new political reality posed by the Russian Revolution.

The Red Scare

In the United States, strikes, antiwar agitation, even racial disturbances were increasingly blamed on foreign radicals and alien ideologies. Pro-German sentiment, socialism, the IWW, and trade unionism in general—all were conveniently lumped together. The accusation of Bolshevism became a powerful weapon for turning public opinion against strikers and political dissenters of all kinds. In the 1919 Seattle general strike, for example, Mayor Ole Hanson claimed, contrary to all evidence, that the strikers "want to take possession of our American Government and try to duplicate the anarchy of Russia." In truth, by 1919 the American radicals were already weakened and badly split. The Socialist Party had around 40,000 members. Two small Communist Parties, made up largely of immigrants, had a total of perhaps 70,000. In the spring of 1919, a few extremists mailed bombs to prominent business and political leaders. That June, simultaneous bombings in eight cities killed two people and damaged the residence of Attorney General A. Mitchell Palmer. With public alarm growing, state and federal officials began a coordinated campaign to root out subversives and their alleged Russian connections.

Palmer used the broad authority of the 1918 Alien Act, which enabled the government to deport any immigrant found to be a member of a revolutionary organization prior to or after coming to the United States. In a series of raids in late 1919, Justice Department agents in eleven cities arrested and roughed up several hundred members of the IWW and the Union of Russian Workers. Little evidence of revolutionary intent was found, but 249 people were deported, including prominent anarchists Emma Goldman and Alexander Berkman. In early 1920, some 6,000 people in thirty-three cities, including many U.S. citizens and noncommunists, were arrested and herded into prisons and bullpens. Again, no evidence of a grand plot was found, but another 600 aliens were deported. The Palmer raids had a ripple effect around the nation, encouraging other repressive measures against radicals. In New York, the state assembly refused to seat five duly elected Socialist Party members.

A report prepared by a group of distinguished lawyers questioned the legality of the attorney general's tactics. Palmer's popularity had waned by the spring of 1920, when it became clear that his predictions of revolutionary uprisings were wildly exaggerated. But the Red Scare left an ugly legacy: wholesale violations of constitutional rights, deportations of hundreds of innocent people, fuel for the fires of nativism and intolerance. Business groups, such as the National Association of Manufacturers, found "Red-baiting" to be an effective tool in postwar efforts to keep unions out of their factories. Indeed, the government-sanctioned Red Scare reemerged later in the century as a powerful political force.

The Red Scare took its toll on the women's movement as well. Before the war, many suffragists and feminists had maintained ties and shared platforms with socialist and labor groups. The suffrage movement in particular had brought together women from very different class backgrounds and political perspectives. But the calls for "100 percent Americanism" during and after the war destroyed the fragile alliances that had made a group such as the National American Woman Suffrage Association so powerful. After the war, many women's organizations that had been divided over American involvement in the war reunited under the umbrella of the National Council for Prevention of War. But when military spokesmen in the early 1920s attacked the group for advocating communism, two of its largest affiliates—the General Federation of Women's Clubs and the Parent-Teacher Association—withdrew in fear. Hostility to radicalism marked the political climate of the 1920s, and this atmosphere narrowed the political spectrum for women activists.

The Election of 1920

The presidential contest of 1920 suggested that Americans wanted to retreat from the internationalism, reform fervor, and social tensions associated with the war. Woodrow Wilson had wanted the 1920 election to be a "solemn referendum" on the League of Nations and his conduct of the war. Ill and exhausted, Wilson did not run for reelection. A badly divided Democratic Party compromised on Governor James M. Cox of Ohio as its candidate. A proven vote-getter, Cox distanced himself from Wilson's policies, which had come under withering attack from many quarters.

The Republicans nominated Senator Warren G. Harding of Ohio. A political hack, the handsome and genial Harding had virtually no qualifications to be president, except that he looked like one. Harding's campaign was vague and ambiguous about the Versailles Treaty and almost everything else. He struck a chord with the electorate in calling for a retreat from Wilsonian idealism. "America's present need," he said, "is not heroics but healing; not nostrums but normalcy; not revolution but restoration."

The notion of a "return to normalcy" proved very attractive to voters exhausted by the war, inflation, big government, and social dislocation. Harding won the greatest landslide in history to that date, carrying every state outside the South and taking the popular vote by 16 million to 9 million. Republicans retained their majorities in the House and Senate as well. Socialist Eugene V. Debs, still a powerful symbol of the dream of radical social change, managed to poll 900,000 votes from jail. But the overall vote repudiated Wilson and the progressive movement. Americans seemed eager to pull back from moralism in public and international controversies. Yet many of the economic,

CHRONOLOGY

1903	U.S. obtains Panama canal rights
1905	President Theodore Roosevelt mediates peace treaty between Japan and Russia at Portsmouth Conference
1908	Root-Takahira Agreement with Japan affirms status quo in Asia and Open Door policy in China
1911	Mexican Revolution begins
1914	U.S. forces invade Mexico
	Panama Canal opens
	World War I begins in Europe
	President Woodrow Wilson issues proclamation of neutrality
1915	Germany declares war zone around Great Britain
	German U-boat sinks *Lusitania*
1916	Pancho Villa raids New Mexico, is pursued by General Pershing
	Wilson is reelected
	National Defense Act establishes preparedness program
1917	February: Germany resumes unrestricted submarine warfare
	March: Zimmermann Note, suggesting a German-Mexican alliance, shocks Americans

	April: U.S. declares war on the Central Powers
	May: Selective Service Act is passed
	June: Espionage Act is passed
	November: Bolshevik Revolution begins in Russia
1918	January: Wilson unveils Fourteen Points
	May: Sedition Act is passed
	June: U.S. troops begin to see action in France
	November: Armistice ends war
1919	January: Eighteenth Amendment (Prohibition) is ratified
	Wilson serves as Chief U.S. negotiator at Paris Peace Conference
	June: Versailles Treaty is signed in Paris
	July: Race riot breaks out in Chicago
	Steel strike begins in several midwestern cities
	November: Palmer raids begin
1920	March: Senate finally votes down Versailles Treaty and League of Nations
	August: Nineteenth Amendment (woman suffrage) is ratified
	November: Warren G. Harding is elected president

social, and cultural changes wrought by the war would accelerate during the 1920s. In truth, there could never be a "return to normalcy."

CONCLUSION

Compared to the casualties and social upheavals endured by the European powers, the Great War's impact on American life might appear slight. Yet the war created economic, social, and political dislocations that helped reshape American life long after Armistice Day. Republican administrations invoked the wartime partnership between government and industry to justify an aggressive peacetime policy fostering cooperation between the state and business. Wartime production needs contributed to what economists later called "the second industrial revolution." Patriotic fervor and the exaggerated specter of Bolshevism were used to repress radicalism, organized labor, feminism, and the entire legacy of progressive reform.

The wartime measure of national prohibition evolved into perhaps the most contentious social issue of peacetime. Sophisticated use of sales techniques, psychology, and propaganda during the war helped define the newly powerful advertising and public relations industries of the 1920s. The growing visibility of immigrants and African Americans, especially in the nation's cities, provoked a xenophobic and racist backlash in the politics of the 1920s. More than anything else, the desire for "normalcy" reflected the deep anxieties evoked by America's wartime experience.

REVIEW QUESTIONS

1. What central issues drew the United States deeper into international politics in the early years of the century? How did American presidents justify a more expansive role? What diplomatic and military policies did they exploit for these ends?

2. Compare the arguments for and against American participation in the Great War. Which Americans were most likely to support entry? Which were more likely to oppose it?

3. How did mobilizing for war change the economy and its relationship to government? Which of these changes, if any, spilled over to the postwar years?

4. How did the war affect political life in the United States? What techniques were used to stifle dissent? What was the war's political legacy?

5. To what extent was the war an extension of progressivism?

6. Analyze the impact of the war on American workers. How did the conflict affect the lives of African Americans and women?

7. What principles guided Woodrow Wilson's Fourteen Points? How would you explain the United States' failure to ratify the Treaty of Versailles?

RECOMMENDED READING

Marc Allen Eisner, *From Warfare State to Welfare State: World War I, Compensatory State Building, and the Limits of the Modern Order* (2000). Demonstrates how, to compensate for the limited capacities of the state to wage total war, policymakers incorporated business organizations and structures into the network of committees coordinating the war effort.

Kathleen Kennedy, *Disloyal Mothers and Scurrilous Citizens: Women and Subversion During World War I* (1999). Analyzes the Federal government's campaign against antiwar women activists and their refusal to adhere to accepted notions of "patriotic motherhood."

Thomas J. Knock, *To End All Wars: Woodrow Wilson and the Quest for a New World Order* (1992). A persuasive analysis of Wilson's internationalism, its links to his domestic policies, and his design for the League of Nations.

Walter LaFeber, *The American Age* (1989). A fine survey of the history of U.S. foreign policy that includes an analysis of the pre–World War I era.

Paul L. Murphy, *World War I and the Origin of Civil Liberties* (1979). A good overview of the various civil liberties issues raised by the war and government efforts to suppress dissent.

Ronald Schaffer, *America in the Great War: The Rise of the War Welfare State* (1991). Excellent material on how the war transformed the relationship between business and government and spurred improved conditions for industrial workers.

Joe William Trotter Jr., ed., *The Great Migration in Historical Perspective* (1991). An excellent collection of essays examining the Great Migration, with special attention to issues of class and gender within the African American community.

Neil A. Wynn, *From Progressivism to Prosperity: World War I and American Society* (1986). An illuminating account of the social impact of the war on American life. Effectively connects the war experience with both progressive era trends and postwar developments in the 1920s.

Robert H. Zieger, *America's Great War: World War I and the American Experience* (2000). The best new one volume synthesis on how the war transformed the United States and its role in the world.

Susan Zeiger, *In Uncle Sam's Service: Women Workers With the American Expeditionary Force, 1917–1919* (1999). The first in depth study of American women's experiences with the armed forces overseas.

ADDITIONAL BIBLIOGRAPHY

Becoming a World Power

Richard H. Collin, *Theodore Roosevelt's Caribbean* (1990)

Friedrich Katz, *The Secret War in Mexico* (1981)

Walter LaFeber, *The Panama Canal* (1978)

Lester E. Langley, *The Banana Wars: An Inner History of American Empire, 1900–1934* (1983)

Mary A. Renda, *Taking Haiti: Military Occupation and the Culture of U.S. Imperialism, 1915–1940* (2001)

The Great War

Lloyd E. Ambrosius, *Woodrow Wilson and the American Diplomatic Tradition* (1987)

Paul Fussell, *The Great War and Modern Memory* (1973)

Martin Gilbert, *The First World War: A Complete History* (1994)

James Joll, *The Origins of the First World War* (1984)

American Mobilization

A. E. Barbeau and Florette Henri, *The Unknown Soldiers: Black American Troops in World War I* (1974)

John W. Chambers, *To Raise an Army: The Draft in Modern America* (1987)

Edward M. Coffman, *The War to End All Wars* (1968)

Stephen Vaughn, *Holding Fast the Inner Lines: Democracy, Nationalism, and the Committee on Public Information* (1980)

Over Here

Allen J. Brandt, *No Magic Bullet: A Social History of Venereal Disease in the United States since 1880* (1985)

Leslie M. DeBauche, *Reel Patriotism: The Movies and World War I* (1997)

Frances R. Early, *A World Without War: How U.S. Feminists and Pacifists Resisted World War I* (1997)

Robert H. Ferrell, *Woodrow Wilson and World War I* (1985)

Margaret Mary Finnegan, *Selling Suffrage: Consumer Culture and Votes for Women* (1999)

Maureen Greenwald, *Women, War, and Work* (1980)

Ellis W. Hawley, *The Great War and the Search for Modern Order*, 2d ed. (1992)

Jeffrey Haydu, *Making American Industries Safe for Democracy* (1997)

David M. Kennedy, *Over Here* (1980)

David Montgomery, *The Fall of the House of Labor* (1987)

Barbara Steinson, *American Women's Activism in World War I* (1982)

Repression and Reaction

James P. Grossman, *Land of Hope: Chicago, Black Southerners, and the Great Migration* (1989)

Frederick C. Luebke, *Bonds of Loyalty: German Americans and World War I* (1974)

William Preston, Jr., *Aliens and Dissenters: Federal Suppression of Radicals, 1903–1933* (1966)

William M. Tuttle, Jr., *Race Riot: Chicago in the Red Summer of 1919* (1970)

An Uneasy Peace

Dana Frank, *Purchasing Power: Consumer Organizing, Gender, and the Seattle Labor Movement, 1919–1929* (1994)

Lloyd Gardner, *Safe for Democracy: The Anglo-American Response to Revolution, 1913–1923* (1984)

Robert D. Johnson, *The Peace Progressives and American Foreign Relations* (1995)

Richard Polenberg, *Fighting Faiths: The Abrams Case, the Supreme Court, and Free Speech* (1987)

Stuart Rochester, *American Liberal Disillusionment in the Wake of World War I* (1977)

Daniel D. Stid, *The President As Statesman: Woodrow Wilson and the Constitution* (1998)

Biography

Kendrick Clements, *Woodrow Wilson: World Statesman* (1987)

Ellen Carol Dubois, *Harriot Stanton Blatch and the Winning of Woman Suffrage* (1997)

Jordan Schwarz, *The Speculator: Bernard M. Baruch in Washington, 1917–1965* (1981)

Frank E. Vandiver, *Black Jack: The Life and Times of John J. Pershing* (1977)

Jacqueline van Voris, *Carrie Chapman Catt* (1987)

HISTORY ON THE INTERNET

http://www.tamu.edu/scom/pres/speeches/wilson.html

On this Texas A&M site, examine Woodrow Wilson's War Message (1918) and his appeal to the nation to force the Senate to approve the Covenant of the League of Nations (1919).

http://www.history.navy.mil/photos/prs-tpic/females/yeoman-f.htm

This is a U.S. Navy historical site that records the contributions of women in the Navy during World War I.

http://lcweb.loc.gov/rr/print/076_vfw.html

This Library of Congress site presents a selected collection of photographs and some prints from the suffrage movement beginning in the late 1890s, focusing upon the War years, and ending with the 1920s.

http://raven.cc.ukans.edu/~kansite/ww_one/photos/greatwar.htm

This University of Kansas site contains an extensive collection of World War I photographs.

http://gulib.lausun.georgetown.edu/dept/speccoll/amposter.htm

This Georgetown University site contains twenty-five World War I posters.

SOURCE: Thomas Hart Benton, *City Activities with Dance Hall* from America Today, 1930. Distemper and egg tempera with oil glaze on gessoed linen, 92″ × 134 1/2″. Collection, The Equitable Life Assurance Society of the U.S. © T. H. Benton and R. P. Benton Testamentary Trusts/Licensed by VAGA, New York, N.Y.

AMERICAN COMMUNITIES

The Movie Audience and Hollywood: Mass Culture Creates a New National Community

INSIDE MIDTOWN MANHATTAN'S MAGNIFICENT NEW ROXY THEATER, A sellout crowd eagerly settled in for opening night. Outside, thousands of fans cheered wildly at the arrival of movie stars such as Charlie Chaplin, Gloria Swanson, and Harold Lloyd. A squadron of smartly uniformed ushers guided patrons under a five-story-tall rotunda to some 6,200 velvet-covered seats. The audience marveled at the huge gold and rose-colored murals, classical statuary, plush carpeting, and Gothic-style windows. It was easy to believe newspaper reports that the theater had cost $10 million to build. Suddenly, light flooded the orchestra pit and 110 musicians began playing "The Star Spangled Banner." A troupe of 100 performers took the stage, dancing ballet numbers and singing old southern melodies such as "My Old Kentucky Home" and "Swanee River." Congratulatory telegrams from President Calvin Coolidge and other dignitaries flashed on the screen. Finally, the evening's feature presentation, *The Love of Sunya*, starring Gloria Swanson, began. Samuel L. "Roxy" Rothapfel, the theater's designer, had realized his grand dream—to build "the cathedral of the motion picture."

When Roxy's opened in March 1927, nearly 60 million Americans "worshiped" each week at movie theaters across the nation. The "movie palaces" of the 1920s were designed to transport patrons to exotic places and different times. As film pioneer Marcus Loew put it, "We sell tickets to theaters, not movies." Every large community boasted at least one opulent movie theater. Houston's Majestic was built to represent an ancient Italian garden; it had a ceiling made to look like an open sky, complete with stars and cloud formations. The Tivoli in Chicago featured opulent French Renaissance decor; Grauman's Egyptian in Los Angeles re-created the look of a pharaoh's tomb; and Albuquerque's Kimo drew inspiration from Navajo art and religion.

The remarkable popularity of motion pictures, and later radio, forged a new kind of community. A huge national audience regularly went to the movies, and the same entertainment could be enjoyed virtually anywhere in the country by just about everyone. Movies emerged as the most popular form in the new mass culture, with an appeal that extended far beyond the films themselves, or even the theaters. Americans embraced the cult of celebrity, voraciously consuming fan magazines, gossip columns, and news of the stars. By the 1920s, the production center for this dream world was Hollywood, California, a suburb of Los Angeles that had barely existed in 1890.

Motion picture companies found Hollywood an alluring alternative to the east coast cities where they had been born. Its reliably sunny and dry climate was ideal for year-round filming. Its unique surroundings offered a perfect variety of scenic locations—mountains, desert, ocean—and downtown Los Angeles was only an hour away. Land was cheap and plentiful. And because Los Angeles was the leading nonunion, open-shop city in the country, so was labor. By the early 1920s Hollywood produced more than 80 percent of the nation's motion pictures and was assuming mythical status. The isolation of the town, its great distance from the eastern cities, its lack of traditional sources of culture and learning—all contributed to movie folk looking at life in a self-consciously "Hollywood" way.

With its feel of a modern frontier boomtown, Hollywood was a new kind of American community. It lured the young and cosmopolitan with the promise of upward mobility and a new way of life. Most of the top studio executives were Jewish immigrants from eastern and central Europe. In contrast to most Americans, who hailed from rural areas or small towns, more than half of Hollywood's writers, directors, editors, and actors were born in cities of over 100,000. Two-thirds of its performers were under thirty-five, and three-fourths of its actresses were under twenty-five. More than 90 percent of its writers (women made up one-third to one-half of this key group) had attended college or worked in journalism. The movies this untypical community created evoked the pleasures of leisure, consumption, and personal freedom, redefining the nation's cultural values in the 1920s.

Movie stars dominated Hollywood. Charlie Chaplin, Mary Pickford, Rudolph Valentino, Gloria Swanson, and Douglas Fairbanks became popular idols as much for their highly publicized private lives as for their roles on screen. Many accumulated great wealth, becoming the nation's experts on how to live well. Movie folk built luxurious mansions in a variety of architectural styles and outfitted them with swimming pools, tennis courts, golf courses, and lavish gardens.

Visitors often noted that Hollywood had no museums, art galleries, live theater, or other traditional institutions of high culture. How would the town's wealthy movie elite spend their time and money? By 1916 Charlie Chaplin, a working-class immigrant from the London slums, was earning $10,000 a week for the comedies that made his the most famous face in the world. He recalled trying to figure out what to do with his new wealth. "The money I earned was legendary, a symbol in figures, for I had never actually seen it. I therefore had to do something to prove I had it. So I procured a secretary, a valet, a car, a chauffeur."

Ordinary Americans found it easy to identify with movie stars despite their wealth and status. Unlike industrialists or politicians, stars had no social authority over large groups of employees or voters. They, too, had to answer to a boss, and most had risen from humble beginnings. But above all, Hollywood, like the movies it churned out, represented for millions of Americans new possibilities: freedom, material success, upward mobility, and the chance to remake one's very identity. By the end of the decade the Hollywood "dream factory" had helped forge a national community whose collective aspirations and desires were increasingly defined by those possibilities, even if relatively few Americans realized them during the 1920s. ■

Hollywood

KEY TOPICS

- A second industrial revolution that transforms the economy

- The promise and limits of prosperity in the 1920s

- New mass media and the culture of consumption

- Republican Party dominance

- Political and cultural opposition to modern trends

POSTWAR PROSPERITY AND ITS PRICE

Republican Warren G. Harding won the presidency in 1920, largely thanks to his nostalgic call for a "return to normalcy." But in the decade following the end of World War I, the American economy underwent profound structural changes that guaranteed life would never be "normal" again. The 1920s saw an enormous increase in the efficiency of production, a steady climb in real wages, a decline in the length of the average employee's work week, and a boom in consumer goods industries. Americans shared unevenly in the postwar prosperity, and by the end of the decade certain basic weaknesses in the economy helped to bring on the worst depression in American history. Yet overall, the nation experienced crucial transformations in how it organized its business, earned its living, and enjoyed its leisure time.

The Second Industrial Revolution

The prosperity of the 1920s rested on what historians have called the "second industrial revolution" in American manufacturing, in which technological innovations made it possible to increase industrial output without expanding the labor force. Electricity replaced steam as the main power source for industry in these years, making possible the replacement of older machinery with more efficient and flexible electric machinery. In 1914 only 30 percent of the nation's factories were electrified; by 1929, 70 percent relied on the electric motor rather than the steam engine.

Much of the newer, automatic machinery could be operated by unskilled and semiskilled workers, and it boosted the overall efficiency of American industry. Thus in 1929 the average worker in manufacturing produced roughly three-quarters more per hour than he or she had in 1919. The machine industry itself, particularly the manufacture of electrical machinery, led in productivity gains, enjoying one of the fastest rates of expansion. It employed more workers than any other manufacturing sector—some 1.1 million in 1929—supplying not only a growing home market but 35 percent of the world market as well.

During the late nineteenth century, heavy industries such as machine tools, railroads, iron, and steel had pioneered mass-production techniques. These industries manufactured what economists call producer-durable goods. In the 1920s, modern mass-production techniques were increasingly applied as well to newer consumer-durable goods—automobiles, radios, washing machines, and telephones—permitting firms to make large profits while keeping prices affordable. Other consumer-based industries, such as canning, chemicals, synthetics, and plastics, began to change the everyday lives of millions of Americans. With more efficient management, greater mechanization, intensive product research, and ingenious sales and advertising methods, the consumer-based industries helped to nearly double industrial production in the 1920s.

America experienced a building boom during the 1920s, and its construction industry played a large role in the new prosperity. Expenditures for residential housing, nonresidential building, and public construction projects all showed steady growth after 1921. The demand for new housing was unprecedented, particularly with the backlog created during World War I, when little new construction took place. The growth in automobile ownership, as well as improvements in public mass transit, made suburban living more attractive to families and suburban construction more profitable for developers. Commercial banks, savings and loan associations, and insurance companies provided greatly expanded credit for home buying. America's residential mortgage debt jumped from about $8 billion in 1919 to $27 billion in 1929.

The Modern Corporation

The organization and techniques of American business underwent crucial changes during the postwar decade. In the late nineteenth century, individual entrepreneurs such as John D. Rockefeller in oil and Andrew Carnegie in steel had provided a model for success. They maintained both corporate control (ownership) and business leadership (management) in their enterprises. In the 1920s, a managerial revolution increasingly divorced ownership of corporate stock from the everyday control of businesses. The new corporate ideal was to be found in men such as Alfred P. Sloan of General Motors and Owen D. Young of the Radio Corporation of America. A growing class of salaried executives, plant managers, and engineers formed a new elite who made corporate policy without themselves having a controlling interest in the companies they worked for. They stressed scientific management and the latest theories of behavioral psychology in their effort to make their workplaces more productive, stable, and profitable.

During the 1920s, the most successful corporations were those that led in three key areas: the integration of production and distribution, product diversification, and the expansion of industrial research. Until the end of World War I, for example, the chemical manufacturer Du Pont had specialized in explosives such as gunpowder. After the war, Du Pont moved aggressively into the consumer market with a diverse array of products. The company created separate but integrated divisions that produced and distributed new fabrics (such as rayon),

paints, dyes, and celluloid products (such as artificial sponges). The great electrical manufacturers—General Electric and Westinghouse—similarly transformed themselves after the war. Previously concentrating on lighting and power equipment, they now diversified into household appliances like radios, washing machines, and refrigerators. The chemical and electrical industries also led the way in industrial research, hiring personnel to develop new products and test their commercial viability.

By 1929 the 200 largest corporations owned nearly half the nation's corporate wealth—that is, physical plant, stock, and property. Half the total industrial income—revenue from sales of goods—was concentrated in 100 corporations. Oligopoly—the control of a market by a few large producers—became the norm. Four companies packed almost three-quarters of all American meat. Another four rolled nine out of every ten cigarettes. National chain grocery stores, clothing shops, and pharmacies began squeezing out local neighborhood businesses. One grocery chain alone, the Great Atlantic and Pacific Tea Company (A&P), accounted for 10 percent of all retail food sales in America. Its 15,000 stores sold a greater volume of goods than Ford Motor Company at its peak. These changes meant that Americans were increasingly members of national consumer communities, buying the same brands all over the country, as opposed to locally produced goods.

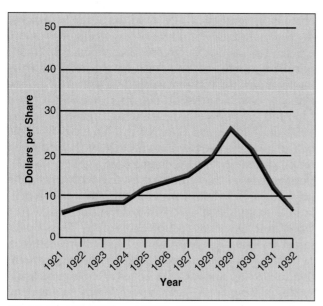

Stock Market Prices, 1921–1932 Common stock prices rose steeply during the 1920s. Although only about 4 million Americans owned stocks during the period, "stock watching" became something of a national sport.

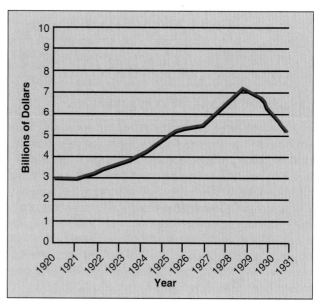

Consumer Debt, 1920–1931 The expansion of consumer borrowing was a key component of the era's prosperity. These figures do not include mortgages or money borrowed to purchase stocks. They reveal the great increase in "installment buying" for such consumer durable goods as automobiles and household appliances.

The A&P grocery chain expanded from 400 stores in 1912 to more than 15,000 by the end of the 1920s, making it a familiar sight in communities across America. A&P advertisements, like this one from 1927, emphasized cleanliness, order, and the availability of name brand goods at discount prices.

SOURCE: From Ladies Home Journal. A&P Food Stores LTD.

Welfare Capitalism

The wartime gains made by organized labor and the active sympathy shown to trade unions by government agencies such as the National War Labor Board troubled most corporate leaders. To challenge the power and appeal of trade unions and collective bargaining, large employers aggressively promoted a variety of new programs designed to improve worker well-being and morale. These schemes, collectively known as welfare capitalism, became a key part of corporate strategy in the 1920s.

One approach was to encourage workers to acquire property through stock-purchase plans or, less frequently, home ownership plans. By 1927, 800,000 employees had more than $1 billion invested in more than 300 companies. Other programs offered workers insurance policies covering accidents, illness, old age, and death. By 1928 some 6 million workers had group insurance coverage valued at $7.5 billion. Many plant managers and personnel departments consciously worked to improve safety conditions, provide medical

services, and establish sports and recreation programs for workers. Employers hoped such measures would encourage workers to identify personally with the company and discourage complaints on the job. To some extent they succeeded. But welfare capitalism could not solve the most chronic problems faced by industrial workers: seasonal unemployment, low wages, long hours, and unhealthy factory conditions.

Large corporations also mounted an effective antiunion campaign in the early 1920s called "the American plan," a name meant to associate unionism with foreign and un-American ideas. Backed by powerful business lobbies such as the National Association of Manufacturers and the Chamber of Commerce, campaign leaders called for the open shop, in which no employee would be compelled to join a union. If a union existed, nonmembers would still get whatever wages and rights the union had won—a policy that put organizers at a disadvantage in signing up new members.

The open shop undercut the gains won in a union shop, where new employees had to join an existing union, or a closed shop, where employers agreed to hire only union members. As alternatives, large employers such as U.S. Steel and International Harvester began setting up company unions. Their intent was to substitute largely symbolic employee representation in management conferences for the more confrontational process of collective bargaining. Company unions were often established simultaneously with antiunion campaigns in specific industries or communities.

These management strategies contributed to a sharp decline in the ranks of organized labor. Total union membership dropped from about 5 million in 1920 to 3.5 million in 1926. A large proportion of the remaining union members were concentrated in the skilled crafts of the building and printing trades. A conservative and timid union leadership was also responsible for the trend. William Green, who became president of the American Federation of Labor after the death of Samuel Gompers in 1924, showed no real interest in getting unorganized workers, such as those in the growing mass-production industries of automobiles, steel, and electrical goods, into unions. The federal government, which had provided limited wartime support for unions, now reverted to a more probusiness posture. The Supreme Court in particular was unsympathetic toward unions, consistently upholding the use of injunctions to prevent strikes, picketing, and other union activities.

The Auto Age

In their classic community study *Middletown* (1929), sociologists Robert and Helen Lynd noted the dramatic impact of the car on the social life of Muncie, Indiana. "Why on earth do you need to study what's changing this country?" asked one lifelong Muncie resident in 1924. "I can tell you what's happening in just four letters: A-U-T-O!" This remark hardly seems much of an exaggeration today. No other single development could match the impact of the postwar automobile explosion on the way Americans worked, lived, and played. The auto industry offered the clearest example of the rise to prominence of consumer durables. During the 1920s, America made approximately 85 percent of all the world's passenger cars. By 1929 the motor vehicle industry was the most productive in the United States in terms of value. In that year the industry added 4.8 million new cars to the more than 26 million—roughly one for every five people—already on American roads.

This extraordinary new industry had mushroomed in less than a generation. Its great pioneer, Henry Ford, had shown how the use of a continuous assembly line could drastically reduce the number of worker hours required to produce a single vehicle. Ford revolutionized the factory shop floor with new, custom-built machinery, such as the engine-boring drill press and the pneumatic wrench, and a more efficient layout. "Every piece of work in the shop moves," Ford boasted. "It may move on hooks or overhead chains, going to assembly in the exact order in which the parts are required; it may travel on a moving platform, or it may go by gravity, but the point is that there is no lifting or trucking of anything other than materials." In 1913 it took thirteen hours to produce one automobile. In 1914, at his sprawling new Highland Park assembly plant just outside Detroit, Ford's system finished one car every ninety minutes. By 1925, cars were rolling off his assembly line at the rate of one every ten seconds.

In 1914 Ford startled American industry by inaugurating a new wage scale: $5 for an eight-hour day. This was roughly double the going pay rate for industrial labor, along with a shorter workday as well. But in defying the conventional economic wisdom of the day, Ford acted less out of benevolence than out of shrewdness. He understood that workers were consumers as well as producers, and the new wage scale helped boost sales of Ford cars. It also reduced the high turnover rate in his

Finished automobiles roll off the moving assembly line at the Ford Motor Company, Highland Park, Michigan, ca. 1920. During the 1920s Henry Ford achieved the status of folk hero, as his name became synonymous with the techniques of mass production. Ford cultivated a public image of himself as the heroic genius of the auto industry, greatly exaggerating his personal achievements.

SOURCE: Brown Brothers.

labor force and increased worker efficiency. Roughly two-thirds of the labor force at Ford consisted of immigrants from southern and eastern Europe. By the early 1920s Ford also employed about 5,000 African Americans, more than any other large American corporation. Ford's mass-production system and economies of scale permitted him to progressively reduce the price of his cars, bringing them within the reach of millions of Americans. The famous Model T, thoroughly standardized and available only in black, cost just under $300 in 1924—about three months' wages for the best-paid factory workers.

By 1927 Ford had produced 15 million Model Ts. But by then the company faced stiff competition from General Motors, which had developed an effective new marketing strategy. Under the guidance of Alfred P. Sloan, GM organized into separate divisions, each of which appealed to a different market segment. Cadillac, for example, produced GM's most expensive car, which was targeted at the wealthy buyer; Chevrolet produced its least expensive model, which was targeted at working-class and lower middle-class buyers. The GM business structure, along with its attempts to match production with demand through sophisticated market research and sales forecasting, became a widely copied model for other large American corporations.

The auto industry provided a large market for makers of steel, rubber, glass, and petroleum products. It stimulated public spending for good roads and extended the housing boom to new suburbs. Showrooms, repair shops, and gas stations appeared in thousands of communities. New small enterprises, from motels to billboard advertising to roadside diners, sprang up as motorists took to the highway. The rapid development of Florida and California, in particular, was partly a response to the growing influence of the automobile and the new possibilities it presented for seeing far-off places.

Automobiles widened the experience of millions of Americans. They made the exploration of the world outside the local community easier and more attractive. For some the car merely reinforced old social patterns, making it easier for them to get to church on Sunday, for example, or visit neighbors. Others used their cars to go to new places, shop in nearby cities, or take vacations. The automobile made leisure, in the sense of getting away from the routines of work and school, a more regular part of everyday life. It undoubtedly also changed the courtship practices of America's youth. Young people took advantage of the car to gain privacy and distance from their parents. "What on earth do you want me to do?" complained one "Middletown" high school girl to her anxious father. "Just sit around home all evening?" Many had their first sexual experiences in a car.

Cities and Suburbs

Cars also promoted urban and suburban growth. The federal census for 1920 was the first in American history in which the proportion of the population that lived in urban places (those with 2,500 or more people) exceeded the proportion of the population living in rural areas. More revealing of urban growth was the steady increase in the number of big cities. In 1910 there were sixty cities with more than 100,000 inhabitants; in 1920 there were sixty-eight; and by 1930 there were ninety-two. During the 1920s New York grew by 20 percent to nearly 7 million, whereas Detroit, home of the auto industry, doubled its population, to nearly 2 million.

Cities promised business opportunity, good jobs, cultural richness, and personal freedom. They attracted millions of Americans, white and black, from small towns and farms, as well as immigrants from abroad. Im-

migrants were drawn to cities by the presence there of family and people of like background in already established ethnic communities. In a continuation of the Great Migration that began during World War I, roughly 1.5 million African Americans from the rural South migrated to cities in search of economic opportunities during the 1920s, doubling the black populations of New York, Chicago, Detroit, and Houston.

Cities grew both vertically and horizontally in these years. Skylines around the country were remade as architects took advantage of steel-skeleton construction technology to build skyscrapers. By 1930, American cities boasted nearly 400 buildings more than twenty stories tall. New York's Empire State Building, completed in 1931, was the tallest building in the world, rising 1,250 feet into the sky. It had room for 25,000 commercial and residential tenants in its 102 stories.

Houston offers a good example of how the automobile shaped an urban community. In 1910 it was a sleepy railroad town with a population of about 75,000 that served the Texas Gulf coast and interior. The enormous demand for gasoline and other petroleum products

Until 1924 Henry Ford had disdained national advertising for his cars. But as General Motors gained a competitive edge by making yearly changes in style and technology, Ford was forced to pay more attention to advertising. This ad was directed at "Mrs. Consumer," combining appeals to both female independence and motherly duties.

helped transform the city into a busy center for oil refining. Its population soared to 300,000 by the end of the 1920s. Abundant cheap land and the absence of zoning ordinances, combined with the availability of the automobile, pushed Houston to expand horizontally rather than vertically. It became the archetypal decentralized, low-density city, sprawling miles in each direction from downtown, and thoroughly dependent upon automobiles and roads for its sense of community. Other Sunbelt cities, such as Los Angeles, Miami, and San Diego, experienced similar land-use patterns and sharp population growth during the decade.

Suburban communities grew at twice the rate of their core cities, also thanks largely to the automobile boom. Undeveloped land on the fringes of cities became valuable real estate. Grosse Pointe, near Detroit, and Elmwood Park, near Chicago, grew more than 700 percent in ten years. Long Island's Nassau County, just east of New York City, tripled in population. All the new "automobile suburbs" differed in important ways from earlier suburbs built along mass transit lines. The car allowed for a larger average lot size, and in turn lower residential density. It also became essential for commuting to work and encouraged the movement of workplaces out of the central city. The suburbs would increasingly become not only places to live but centers for working and shopping as well.

Exceptions: Agriculture, Ailing Industries

Amid prosperity and progress, there were large pockets of the country that lagged behind. Advances in real income and improvements in the standard of living for workers and farmers were uneven at best. During the 1920s, one-quarter of all American workers were employed in agriculture, yet the farm sector failed to share in the general prosperity. The years 1914–19 had been a kind of golden age for the nation's farmers. Increased wartime demand, along with the devastation of much of European agriculture, had led to record-high prices for many crops. In addition, the wartime Food Administration had encouraged a great increase in agricultural production. But with the war's end, American farmers began to suffer from a chronic worldwide surplus of such farm staples as cotton, hogs, and corn.

Prices began to drop sharply in 1920. Cotton, which sold at 37 cents a pound in mid-1920, fell to 14 cents by year's end. Hog and cattle prices declined nearly 50 percent. By 1921 net farm income was down more than half from the year before. Land values also dropped, wiping out billions in capital investment. Behind these aggregate statistics were hundreds of thousands of individual human tragedies on the nation's 6 million farms. A 1928 song, "Eleven Cent Cotton," expressed the farmer's lament:

'Leven cent cotton, forty cent meat,
How in the world can a poor man eat?
Pray for the sunshine, 'cause it will rain,
Things gettin' worse, drivin' us insane.

During the war many farmers had gone heavily into debt to buy land and expand operations with new machinery. Farm mortgages doubled between 1910 and 1920, from $3.3 billion to $6.7 billion, and another $2.7 billion was added to the total by 1925. These debts saddled farmers with fixed expenses that grew crushingly burdensome as commodity prices spiraled downward. American farm products, moreover, faced stiffer competition abroad from reviving European agriculture and the expanding output from Canada, Argentina, and Australia. Efforts to ease the farmer's plight through governmental reform were largely unsuccessful. Individual farmers, traditionally independent, could not influence the price of commodities they sold or bought. It was extremely difficult for farmers to act collectively.

In the South, farmers dependency on "King Cotton" deepened, as the region lagged farther behind the rest of the nation in both agricultural diversity and standard of living. Cotton acreage expanded as large and heavily mechanized farms opened up new land in Oklahoma, west Texas, and the Mississippi-Yazoo delta. But in most of the South, from North Carolina to east Texas, small one- and two-mule cotton farms, most under 50 acres, still dominated the countryside. While editors, state officials, and reformers preached the need for greater variety of crops, southern farmers actually raised less corn and livestock by the end of the decade. With few large urban centers and inadequate transportation, even those southern farmers who had access to capital found it extremely difficult to find reliable markets for vegetables, fruit, poultry, or dairy products. The average southern farm had land and buildings worth $3,525; for northern farms, the figure was $11,029. The number of white tenant farmers increased by 200,000 during the 1920s, while black tenantry declined slightly as a result of the Great Migration. Some 700,000 southern farmers, roughly half white and half black, still labored as sharecroppers. Modern conveniences such as electricity, indoor plumbing, automobiles, and phonographs remained far beyond the reach of the great majority of southern farmers. Widespread rural poverty, poor diet, little access to capital—the world of southern agriculture had changed very little since the days of Populist revolt in the 1890s.

To be sure, some farmers thrived. Wheat production jumped more than 300 percent during the 1920s. Across the plains of Kansas, Nebraska, Colorado, Oklahoma, and Texas, wheat farmers brought the methods of industrial capitalism to the land. They hitched disc plows and combined harvester-threshers to gasoline-powered tractors, tearing up millions of acres of grassland to create a vast wheat factory. With prices averaging above $1 per bushel over the decade, mechanized farming created a new class of large-scale wheat entrepreneurs on the plains. Ida Watkins, "the Wheat Queen" of Haskell County, Kansas, made a profit of $75,000 from her 2,000 acres in 1926. Hickman Price needed twenty-five combines to harvest the wheat on his Plainview, Texas, farm—34,500 acres stretching over fifty-four square miles. When the disastrous dust storms of the 1930s rolled across the grassless plains, the long-range ecological impact of destroying so much native vegetation became evident.

Improved transportation and chain supermarkets allowed for a wider and more regular distribution of such foods as oranges, lemons, and fresh green vegetables. Citrus, dairy, and truck farmers in particular profited from the growing importance of national markets. But per capita farm income remained well below what it had been in 1919, and the gap between farm and nonfarm income widened. By 1929 the average income per person on farms was $223, compared with $870 for nonfarm workers. By the end of the decade, hundreds of thousands had quit farming altogether for jobs in mills and factories. And fewer farmers owned their land. In 1930, 42 percent of all farmers were tenants, compared with 37 percent in 1919.

The most important initiatives for federal farm relief were the McNary-Haugen bills, a series of complicated measures designed to prop up and stabilize farm prices. The basic idea, borrowed from the old Populist proposals of the 1890s, was for the government to purchase farm surpluses and either store them until prices rose or sell them on the world market. The result was supposed to be higher domestic prices for farm products. But President Calvin Coolidge viewed these measures as unwarranted federal interference in the economy and vetoed the McNary-Haugen Farm Relief bill of 1927 when it finally passed Congress. Hard-pressed farmers would not benefit from government relief until the New Deal programs implemented in response to the Great Depression in the 1930s.

Other large sectors of American industry also failed to share in the decade's general prosperity. As oil and natural gas gained in importance, America's coal mines became a less important source of energy. A combination of shrinking demand, new mining technology, and a series of losing strikes reduced the coal labor force by one-quarter. The United Mine Workers, perhaps the strongest AFL union in 1920 with 500,000 members, had shrunk to 75,000 by 1928. Economic hardship was widespread in many mining communities dependent on coal, particularly in Appalachia and the southern Midwest. And those miners who did work earned lower hourly wages.

The number of miles of railroad track actually decreased after 1920 as automobiles and trucks began to displace trains. In textiles, shrinking demand and overcapacity (too many factories) were chronic problems. The women's fashions of the 1920s generally required less material than had earlier fashions, and competition from synthetic fibers such as rayon depressed demand for cotton textiles. To improve profit margins, textile manufacturers in New England and other parts of the Northeast began a long-range shift of operations to the South, where nonunion shops and substandard wages became the rule. Between 1923 and 1933, 40 percent of New England's textile factories closed and nearly 100,000 of the 190,000 workers employed there lost their jobs. Older New England manufacturing centers such as Lawrence, Lowell, Nashua, Manchester, and Fall River were hard hit by this shift.

The center of the American textile industry shifted permanently to the Piedmont region of North and South Carolina. Southern mills increased their work force from 220,000 to 257,000 between 1923 and 1933. By 1933 they employed nearly 70 percent of the workers in the industry. One of the biggest new textile communities was Gastonia, North Carolina, which proudly called itself the "South's City of Spindles." As the dominant employers and overall economic powers in southern textile communities, manufacturers aggressively tried to improve productivity and cut costs. Southern mills generally operated night and day, used the newest labor-saving machinery, and cut back on the wage gains of the World War I years. Southern mill hands paid the price for what they called "stretch-out"—a catchall term describing the changes that had them tending more and more machines, receiving lower wages, working nights, and losing nearly all control over the pace and method of production.

THE NEW MASS CULTURE

New communications media reshaped American culture in the 1920s. The phrase "Roaring Twenties" captures the explosion of image- and sound-making machinery that came to dominate so much of American life. Movies, radio, new kinds of journalism, the recording industry, and a more sophisticated advertising industry were deeply connected with the new culture of consumption. They also encouraged the parallel emergence of celebrity as a defining element in modern life. As technologies of mass impression, the media established national standards and norms for much of our culture—habit, dress, language, sounds, social behavior. For millions of Americans, the new media radically altered the rhythms of everyday life and redefined what it meant to be "normal." To be sure, most working-class families had only limited access to the world of mass consumption—and many had only limited interest in it. But the new mass culture helped redefine the ideal of "the good life" and made the images, if not the substance, of it available to a national community.

Movie-Made America

The early movie industry, centered in New York and a few other big cities, had made moviegoing a regular habit for millions of Americans, especially immigrants and the working class. They flocked to cheap, storefront theaters, called nickelodeons, to watch short Westerns, slapstick comedies, melodramas, and travelogues. By 1914 there were about 18,000 "movie houses" showing motion pictures, with more than 7 million daily admissions and $300 million in annual receipts. With the shift of the industry westward to Hollywood, movies entered a new phase of business expansion.

Large studios such as Paramount, Fox, Metro-Goldwyn-Mayer (M-G-M), Universal, and Warner Brothers dominated the business with longer and more expensively produced movies—feature films. These companies were founded and controlled by immigrants from Europe, all of whom had a talent for discovering and exploiting changes in popular tastes. Adolph Zukor, the Hungarian-born head of Paramount, had been a furrier in New York City. Warsaw-born Samuel Goldwyn, a founder of M-G-M, had been a glove salesman. William Fox, of Fox Pictures, began as a garment cutter in Brooklyn. Most of the immigrant moguls had started in the business by buying or managing small movie theaters before beginning to produce films.

The studio system, which came to dominate moviemaking, was based on industrial principles. Each studio combined the three functions of production, distribution, and exhibition, and each controlled hundreds of movie theaters around the country. The era of silent films ended when Warner Brothers scored a huge hit in 1927 with *The Jazz Singer*, starring Al Jolson, which successfully introduced sound. New genres—musicals, gangster films, and screwball comedies—soon became popular. The higher costs associated with "talkies" also increased the studios' reliance on Wall Street investors and banks for working capital.

At the heart of Hollywood's success was the star system and the accompanying cult of celebrity. Stars became vital to the fantasy lives of millions of fans. For many in the audience, there was only a vague line separating the on-screen and off-screen adventures of the stars. Studio publicity, fan magazines, and gossip columns reinforced this ambiguity. Film idols, with their mansions, cars, parties, and private escapades, became the national experts on leisure and consumption. Their movies generally emphasized sexual themes and celebrated youth, athleticism, and the liberating power of consumer goods. Young Americans in particular looked to movies to learn how to dress, wear their hair, talk, or kiss. One researcher looking into the impact of moviegoing on young people asked several to keep "motion picture diaries." "Upon going to my first dance I asked the hairdresser to fix my hair like Greta Garbo's," wrote one eighteen-year-old college student. "In speaking on graduation day I did my best to finish with the swaying-like curtsy which Pola Negri taught me from the screen."

Moviemakers attracted new fans by producing more spectacular movies and by building elegant "movie palaces," like the Roxy Theater described in the opening of this chapter, in which to watch them. But many Americans, particularly in rural areas and small towns, worried about Hollywood's impact on traditional sexual morality. They attacked the permissiveness associated with Hollywood life, and many states created censorship boards to screen movies before allowing them to be shown in theaters. In 1921, the popular comedian Roscoe "Fatty" Arbuckle became embroiled in a

Mary Pickford, one of the most popular movie stars of the 1910s and 1920s, shown here reading a feminist newspaper in a publicity photo ca. 1917. Pickford frequently portrayed young women struggling for economic freedom from men. She wrote weekly columns for women in which she backed suffrage and urged her female readers to be more self-sufficient. Pickford embodied the new, mass media-based "celebrity" of the 1920s.

SOURCE: Culver Pictures, Inc.

highly publicized sex scandal when he was accused of raping and murdering actress Virginia Rappe. Although Arbuckle was acquitted, the sensational atmosphere surrounding the case badly frightened studio heads. They resolved to improve their public image.

To counter growing calls for government censorship, Hollywood's studios came up with a plan to censor themselves. In 1922 they hired Will Hays to head the Motion Picture Producers and Distributors of America. Hays was just what the immigrant moguls needed. An Indiana Republican, elder in the Presbyterian Church, and former postmaster general under President Harding, he personified midwestern Protestant respectability. As the movie industry's czar, Hays lobbied against censorship laws, wrote pamphlets defending the movie business, and began setting guidelines for what could and could not be depicted on the screen. He insisted that movies be treated like any other industrial enterprise, for he understood the relationship between Hollywood's success and the growth of the nation's consumer culture. "More and more," Hays argued in 1926, "is the motion picture being recognized as a stimulant to trade. No longer does the girl in Sullivan, Indiana, guess what the styles are going to be in three months. She knows because she sees them on the screen."

Radio Broadcasting

In the fall of 1920, Westinghouse executive Harry P. Davis noticed that amateur broadcasts from the garage of an employee had attracted attention in the local Pittsburgh press. A department store advertised radio sets capable of picking up these "wireless concerts." Davis converted this amateur station to a stronger one at the Westinghouse main plant. Beginning with the presidential election returns that November, station KDKA offered regular nightly broadcasts that were probably heard by only a few hundred people. Radio broadcasting, begun as a service for selling cheap radio sets left over from World War I, would soon sweep the nation.

Before KDKA, wireless technology had been of interest only to the military, the telephone industry, and a few thousand "ham" (amateur) operators who enjoyed communicating with each other. The "radio mania" of the early 1920s was a response to the new possibilities offered by broadcasting. By 1923 nearly 600 stations had been licensed by the Department of Commerce, and about 600,000 Americans had bought radios. Early programs included live popular music, the playing of phonograph records, talks by college professors, church services, and news and weather reports. For millions of Americans, especially in rural areas and small towns, radio provided a new and exciting link to the larger national community of consumption.

Who would pay for radio programs? In the early 1920s, owners and operators of radio stations included radio equipment manufacturers, newspapers, department stores, state universities, cities, ethnic societies, labor unions, and churches. But by the end of the decade commercial (or "toll") broadcasting emerged as the answer. The dominant corporations in the industry—General Electric, Westinghouse, Radio Corporation of America (RCA), and American Telephone and Telegraph (AT&T)—settled on the idea that advertisers would foot the bill for radio. Millions of listeners might be the consumers of radio shows, but sponsors were to be the customers. Only the sponsors and their advertising agencies enjoyed a direct relationship with broadcasters. Sponsors advertised directly or indirectly to the mass audience through such shows as the *Eveready Hour,* the *Ipana Troubadors,* and the *Taystee Loafers.* AT&T leased its nationwide system of telephone wires to allow the linking of many stations into powerful radio networks, such as the National Broadcasting Company (1926) and the Columbia Broadcasting System (1928).

Radio broadcasting created a national community of listeners, just as motion pictures created one of viewers. NBC and CBS led the way in creating popular radio programs that relied heavily on older cultural forms. The variety show, hosted by vaudeville comedians, became network radio's first important format. Radio's first truly national hit, The *Amos 'n' Andy Show* (1928), was a direct descendant of nineteenth-century "blackface" minstrel entertainment. Radio did more than any previous medium to publicize and commercialize previously isolated forms of American music such as country-and-western, blues, and jazz. Broadcasts of baseball and college football games proved especially popular. In 1930, some 600 stations were broadcasting to more than 12 million homes with radios, or roughly 40 percent of American families. By that time all the elements that characterize the present American system of broadcasting—regular daily programming paid for and produced by commercial advertisers, national networks carrying shows across the nation, and mass ownership of receiver sets in American homes—were in place.

Since it transcended national boundaries, broadcasting had a powerful hemispheric impact as well. In Canada, American manufacturers supplied most of the radio receivers and the larger U.S. stations in cities such as Detroit and Buffalo could easily be heard in Toronto and Montreal. American signals thus interfered with Canadian ones. In response, the 1929 Royal Commission on Radio Broadcasting created a national Canadian broadcasting system, establishing a public network (run by the Canadian Broadcasting Corporation), but also allowing private stations to operate. In a bid to counter American influence, both the public and private elements of the system were charged with providing Canadian programing for their audiences. Yet despite these efforts to "Canadianize" broadcasting, American shows—and advertising—continued to dominate Canadian airwaves. Similarly, U.S. broadcasting interests helped shape early Mexican radio. The 1926 Law of Electric Communications declared the radio spectrum a national resource and created a system combining government-owned stations with private commercial broadcasters licensed by the state. Large private Mexican radio stations were often started in partnership with American corporations such as RCA, as a way to create demand for receiving sets. Language barriers limited the direct impact of U.S. broadcasts, but American advertisers became the backbone of commercial radio in Mexico. They encouraged Mexican broadcasters to adapt successful U.S.-radio formulas, as when Colgate Palmolive pioneered the *radionovela* format similar to the North American soap opera. In both Canada and Mexico, then, governments established national broadcasting systems to bolster cultural and political nationalism. But radio broadcasting significantly amplified the influence of American commercialism throughout the hemisphere.

New Forms of Journalism

A new kind of newspaper, the tabloid, became popular in the postwar years. The *New York Daily News*, founded in 1919 by Joseph M. Patterson, was the first to develop the tabloid style. Its folded-in-half page size made it convenient to read on buses or subways. The *Daily News* devoted much of its space to photographs and other illustrations. With a terse, lively reporting style that emphasized sex, scandal, and sports, *Daily News* circulation reached 400,000 in 1922 and 1.3 million by 1929.

This success spawned a host of imitators in New York and elsewhere. New papers like the *Chicago Times* and the *Los Angeles Daily News* brought the tabloid style to cities across America, while some older papers, such as the *Denver Rocky Mountain News*, adopted the new format. The circulation of existing dailies was little affected. Tabloids had instead discovered an audience of millions who had never read newspapers before. Most of these new readers were poorly educated working-class city dwellers, many of whom were immigrants or children of immigrants.

The tabloid's most popular new feature was the gossip column, invented by Walter Winchell, an obscure former vaudevillian who began writing his column "Your Broadway and Mine" for the *New York Daily Graphic* in 1924. Winchell described the secret lives of public figures with a distinctive, rapid-fire, slangy style that made the reader feel like an insider. He chronicled the connections among high society, show business

stars, powerful politicians, and the underworld. By the end of the decade, scores of newspapers "syndicated" Winchell's column, making him the most widely read—and imitated—journalist in America.

Many critics dismissed the tabloids for being, as one put it, "synonomous with bad taste, vulgarity, and a degenerate sensationalism." But the popularity of the tabloids forced advertising agencies to expand their definition of the consumer market to include working-class and immigrant readers. And advertisers borrowed freely from tabloid techniques—"true confession" stories, racy headlines, shocking photos, sexually charged images—to reach that market.

Journalism followed the larger economic trend toward consolidation and merger. Newspaper chains like Hearst, Gannett, and Scripps-Howard flourished during the 1920s. There was a sizable increase in the number of these chains and in the percentage of total daily circulation that was chain-owned. By the early 1930s, the Hearst organization alone controlled twenty-six dailies in eighteen cities, accounting for 14 percent of the nation's newspaper circulation. One of every four Sunday papers sold in America was owned by the Hearst group. One journalist lamented this standardization in 1930: "When one travels through the country on a Sunday on a fast train and buys Sunday papers, one finds the same 'comics,' the same Sunday magazines, the same special 'features' in almost all of them and, of course, in most of them precisely the same Associated Press news." New forms of journalism, like radio and the movies, contributed to the growth of a national consumer community.

Advertising Modernity

A thriving advertising industry both reflected and encouraged the growing importance of consumer goods in American life. Previously, advertising had been confined mostly to staid newspapers and magazines and offered little more than basic product information. The most creative advertising was usually for dubious products, such as patent medicines. The successful efforts of the government's Committee on Public Information, set up to "sell" World War I to Americans, suggested that new techniques using modern communication media could convince people to buy a wide range of goods and services. As a profession, advertising reached a higher level of respectability, sophistication, and economic power in American life during the 1920s. Total advertising volume in all media—newspapers, magazines, radio, billboards—jumped from $1.4 billion in 1919 to $3 billion in 1929.

The larger ad agencies moved toward a more scientific approach by sponsoring market research and welcoming the language of psychology to their profession.

Cigarette smoking increased enormously in the 1920s among both men and women, and tobacco companies were among the largest national advertisers. This ad linked smoking to male sexual prowess.

SOURCE: 1918 Murad ad showing men and women at the beach. Gaslight Advertising Archives, Commack, N.Y.

Advertisers began focusing on the needs, desires, and anxieties of the consumer rather than on the qualities of the product. "There are certain things that most people believe," noted one ad agency executive in 1927. "The moment your copy is linked to one of those beliefs, more than half your battle is won." Ad agencies and their clients invested extraordinary amounts of time, energy, and money trying to discover and, to some extent, shape those beliefs. Leading agencies such as Lord and Thomas in Chicago and J. Walter Thompson in New York combined knowledge gained from market research and consumer surveys with carefully prepared ad copy and graphics to sell their clients' wares.

High-powered ad campaigns made new products like Fleischmann's Yeast and Kleenex household words across the country. One of the more spectacular examples of advertising effectiveness involved an old product, Listerine, which had been marketed as a general antiseptic for years by Lambert Pharmaceutical Com-

pany. A new ad campaign touting Listerine as a cure for halitosis—a scientific-sounding term for bad breath—boosted Lambert's profits from $100,000 in 1922 to more than $4 million in 1927.

Above all, advertising celebrated consumption itself as a positive good. In this sense the new advertising ethic was a therapeutic one, promising that products would contribute to the buyer's physical, psychic, or emotional well-being. Certain strategies, such as appeals to nature, medical authority, or personal freedom, were used with great success. Many of these themes and techniques are still familiar today. Well-financed ad campaigns were especially crucial for marketing newer consumer goods such as cars, electrical appliances, and personal hygiene products.

The Phonograph and the Recording Industry

Like radio and movies, the phonograph came into its own in the 1920s as a popular entertainment medium. Originally marketed in the 1890s, early phonographs used wax cylinders that could both record and replay. But the sound quality was poor, and the cylinders were difficult to handle. The convenient permanently grooved disc recordings introduced around World War I were eagerly snapped up by the public, even though the discs could not be used to make recordings at home. The success of records transformed the popular music business, displacing both cylinders and sheet music as the major source of music in the home.

Dance crazes such as the fox trot, tango, and grizzly bear, done to complex ragtime and Latin rhythms, boosted the record business tremendously. Dixieland jazz, which recorded well, also captured the public's fancy in the early 1920s, and records provided the music for new popular dances like the Charleston and the black bottom. In 1921 more than 200 companies produced some 2 million records and annual record sales exceeded 100 million.

Record sales declined toward the end of the decade due to competition from radio. But in a broader cultural sense, records continued to transform American popular culture. Record companies discovered lucrative regional and ethnic markets for country music, which appealed primarily to white Southerners, and blues and jazz, which appealed primarily to African Americans. Country musicians like the Carter Family and Jimmie Rodgers, and blues singers like Blind Lemon Jefferson and Ma Rainey, had their performances put on records for the first time. Their records sold mainly in specialized "hillbilly" and "race" markets. Yet they were also played over the radio, and millions of Americans began to hear musical styles and performers who had previously been isolated from the general population. Blues great Bessie Smith sold hundreds of thousands of records and single-handedly kept the fledgling Columbia Record Company profitable. The combination of records and radio started an extraordinary cross-fertilization of American musical styles that continues to this day.

Sports and Celebrity

During the 1920s, spectator sports enjoyed an unprecedented growth in popularity and profitability. As radio, newspapers, magazines, and newsreels exhaustively documented their exploits, athletes took their place alongside movie stars in defining a new culture of celebrity. Big-time sports, like the movies, entered a new corporate phase. Yet it was the athletes themselves, performing extraordinary feats on the field and transcending their often humble origins, who attracted millions of new fans. The image of the modern athlete—rich, famous, glamorous, and often a rebel against social convention—came into its own during the decade.

Major league baseball had more fans than any other sport, and its greatest star, George Herman "Babe" Ruth, embodied the new celebrity athlete. In 1920 the game had suffered a serious public relations disaster with the unfolding of the "Black Sox" scandal. The previous year, eight members of the poorly paid Chicago White Sox had become involved in a scheme to "throw" the World Series in exchange for large sums of money from gamblers. Although they were acquitted in the courts, baseball commissioner Judge Kenesaw Mountain Landis, looking to remove any taint of gambling from the sport, banned the accused players for life. Landis's actions won universal acclaim, but doubts about the integrity of the "national pastime" lingered.

Ruth did more than anyone to repair the damage and make baseball more popular than ever. Born in 1895, he was a product of Baltimore's rough waterfront district. After spending most of his youth in an orphanage for delinquent boys, he broke into baseball as a pitcher for the Boston Red Sox. Traded to the New York Yankees in 1920, he switched to the outfield and began attracting enormous attention with the length and frequency of his home runs. He hit fifty-four in his first year in New York, eclipsing the old record by twenty-nine. The next year he hit fifty-nine. "The Sultan

of Swat," as one sportswriter dubbed him, transformed the game. Before Ruth, the "homer" was an infrequent event in a game built around pitching, defense, and speed. Fans now flocked to games in record numbers to see the new, more offensive-oriented baseball.

Ruth was a larger-than-life character off the field as well as on. In New York, media capital of the nation, newspapers and magazines chronicled his enormous appetites—for food, whiskey, expensive cars, and big-city nightlife. He hobnobbed with politicians, movie stars, and gangsters, and he regularly visited sick children in hospitals. Ruth became the first athlete avidly sought after by manufacturers for celebrity endorsement of their products. As one of the most photographed individuals of the era, Ruth's round, beaming face became a familiar image around the world. In 1930, at the onset of the Great Depression, when a reporter told him that his $80,000 salary was more than President Herbert Hoover's, the Babe replied good naturedly, "Well, I had a better year than he did."

Baseball attendance exploded during the 1920s, reaching a one-year total of 10 million in 1929. The attendance boom prompted urban newspapers to increase their baseball coverage, and the larger dailies featured separate sports sections. The best sportswriters, such as Grantland Rice, Heywood Broun, and Ring

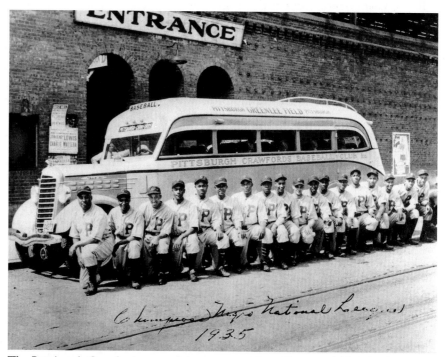

The Pittsburgh Crawfords, one of the most popular and successful baseball teams in the Negro National League, organized in 1920. Excluded from major league baseball by a "whites only" policy, black ballplayers played to enthusiastic crowds of African Americans from the 1920s through the 1940s. The "Negro leagues" declined after major league baseball finally integrated in 1947. SOURCE: 1935 Pittsburgh Crawfords, champion Negro National League. National Baseball Hall of Fame Library, Cooperstown, N.Y.

Lardner, brought a poetic sensibility to descriptions of the games and their stars. William K. Wrigley, owner of the Chicago Cubs, discovered that by letting local radio stations broadcast his team's games, the club could win new fans, especially among housewives.

Baseball owners solidified their monopolistic control of the game in 1922 when the Supreme Court, ruling in an antitrust suit, declared that baseball, while obviously a business, was not "trade or commerce in the commonly accepted use of those words." By exempting baseball from antitrust prosecution, the Court gave the game a uniquely favored legal status and also ensured the absolute control of owners over their players. Among those excluded from major league baseball were African Americans, who had been banned from the game by an 1890s' "gentleman's agreement" among owners.

During the 1920s black baseball players and entrepreneurs developed a world of their own, with several professional and semiprofessional leagues catering to expanding African American communities in cities. The largest of these was the Negro National League, organized in 1920 by Andrew "Rube" Foster. Black ballclubs also played exhibitions against, and frequently defeated, teams of white major leaguers. African Americans had their own baseball heroes, such as Josh Gibson and Satchel Paige, who no doubt would have been stars in the major leagues if not for racial exclusion.

The new media configuration of the 1920s created heroes in other sports as well. Radio broadcasts and increased journalistic coverage made college football a big-time sport, as millions followed the exploits of star players such as Illinois's Harold E. "Red" Grange and Stanford's Ernie Nevers. Teams like Notre Dame, located in sleepy South Bend, Indiana, but coached by the colorful Knute Rockne, could gain a wide national following. Sportswriter Grantland Rice contributed to the school's mystique when he dubbed its backfield the "Four Horsemen of Notre Dame." The earnings potential of big-time athletics was not lost on college administrators, and it blurred the old lines separating amateur and professional sports. The center of college football shifted from the old elite schools of the Ivy League to the big universities of the Midwest and Pacific coast, where most of the players were now second-generation Irish, Italians, and Slavs. Athletes like boxers Jack Dempsey and Gene Tunney, tennis players Bill Tilden and Helen Wills, and swimmers Gertrude Ederle and Johnny Weissmuller became household names who brought legions of new fans to their sports.

A New Morality?

Movie stars, radio personalities, sports heroes, and popular musicians became the elite figures in a new culture of celebrity defined by the mass media. They were the model for achievement in the new age. Great events and abstract issues were made real through movie close-ups, radio interviews, and tabloid photos. The new media relentlessly created and disseminated images that are still familiar today: Babe Ruth trotting around the bases after hitting a home run; the wild celebrations that greeted Charles Lindbergh after he completed the first solo transatlantic airplane flight in 1927; the smiling gangster Al Capone, bantering with reporters who transformed his criminal exploits into important news events.

But images do not tell the whole story. Consider one of the most enduring images of the "Roaring Twenties," the flapper. She was usually portrayed on screen, in novels, and in the press as a young, sexually aggressive woman with bobbed hair, rouged cheeks, and short skirt. She loved to dance to jazz music, enjoyed smoking cigarettes, and drank bootleg liquor in cabarets and dance halls. She could also be competitive, assertive, and a good pal. As writer Zelda Fitzgerald put it in 1924: "I think a woman gets more happiness out of being gay, light-hearted, unconventional, mistress of her own fate. . . . I want [my daughter] to be a flapper, because flappers are brave and gay and beautiful."

This 1925 *Judge* cartoon, "Sheik with Sheba," drawn by John Held, Jr., offered one view of contemporary culture. The flashy new automobile, the hip flask with illegal liquor, the cigarettes, and the stylish "new woman" were all part of the "Roaring Twenties" image.

SOURCE: The Granger Collection (4E746.21).

Was the flapper a genuine representative of the 1920s? Did she embody the "new morality" that was so widely discussed and chronicled in the media of the day? The flapper certainly did exist, but she was neither as new nor as widespread a phenomenon as the image would suggest. The delight in sensuality, personal pleasure, and rhythmically complex dance and music had long been key elements of subcultures on the fringes of middle-class society: bohemian enclaves, communities of political radicals, African American ghettos, working-class dance halls. In the 1920s, these activities became normative for a growing number of white middle-class Americans, including women. Jazz, sexual experimentation, heavy makeup, and cigarette smoking spread to college campuses.

Several sources, most of them rooted in earlier years, can be found for the increased sexual openness of the 1920s. Troops in the armed forces during World War I had been exposed to government-sponsored sex education. New psychological and social theories like those of Havelock Ellis, Ellen Key, and Sigmund Freud stressed the central role of sexuality in human experience, maintaining that sex is a positive, healthy impulse that, if repressed, could damage mental and emotional health. The pioneering efforts of Margaret Sanger in educating women about birth control had begun before World War I (see Chapter 21). In the 1920s, Sanger campaigned vigorously—through her journal *Birth Control Review*, in books, on speaking tours—to make contraception freely available to all women.

Advertisers routinely used sex appeal to sell products. Tabloid newspapers exploited sex with "cheesecake" photos, but they also provided features giving advice on sex hygiene and venereal disease. And movies, of course, featured powerful sex symbols such as Rudolph Valentino, Gloria Swanson, John Gilbert, and Clara Bow. Movies also taught young people an etiquette of sex. One typical eighteen-year-old college student wrote in the motion picture diary she kept for a sociological study: "These passionate pictures stir such longings, desires, and urges as I never expected any person to possess. Just the way the passionate lover held his sweetheart suggests so many beautiful and intimate relations, which even my reenacting a scene does not satisfy any more."

Sociological surveys also suggested that genuine changes in sexual behavior began in the prewar years among both married and single women. Katherine Bement Davis's pioneering study of 2,200 middle-class women, carried out in 1918 and published in 1929, revealed that most used contraceptives and described sexual relations in positive terms. A 1938 survey of 777 middle-class females found that among those born between 1890 and 1900, 74 percent were virgins before marriage; for those born after 1910 the figure dropped

to 32 percent. Women born after the turn of the century were twice as likely to have had premarital sex as those born before 1900. The critical change took place in the generation that came of age in the late teens and early twenties. By the 1920s, male and female "morals" were becoming more alike.

THE STATE, THE ECONOMY, AND BUSINESS

Throughout the 1920s, a confident Republican Party dominated national politics, certain that it had ushered in a "new era" in American life. A new and closer relationship between the federal government and American business became the hallmark of Republican policy in both domestic and foreign affairs during the administrations of three successive Republican presidents: Warren Harding (1921–23), Calvin Coolidge (1923–29), and Herbert Hoover (1929–33). And Republicans never tired of claiming that the business-government partnership their policies promoted was responsible for the nation's economic prosperity.

Harding and Coolidge

Handsome, genial, and well-spoken, Warren Harding may have looked the part of a president—but acting like one was another matter. Harding was a product of small-town Marion, Ohio, and the machine politics in his native state. Republican Party officials had made a point of keeping Senator Harding, a compromise choice, as removed from the public eye as possible in the 1920 election. They correctly saw that active campaigning could only hurt their candidate by exposing his shallowness and intellectual weakness. Harding understood his own limitations. He sadly told one visitor to the White House shortly after taking office, "I knew that this job would be too much for me."

Harding surrounded himself with a close circle of friends, the "Ohio gang," delegating to them a great deal of administrative power. The president often conducted business as if he were in the relaxed, convivial, and masculine confines of a small-town saloon. Alice Roosevelt Longworth, Theodore Roosevelt's daughter, described the scene she encountered in Harding's crony-filled study when she tagged along with her husband, Congressman Nicholas Longworth, to a card game: "The air heavy with tobacco smoke, trays with bottles containing every imaginable brand of whiskey [standing] about, cards and poker chips ready at hand—a general atmosphere of waistcoat unbuttoned, feet on the desk, and spitoons alongside." In the summer of 1923 Harding began to get wind of the scandals for which his administration is best remembered. He wearily told his friend Kansas journalist William Allen White: "This is a hell of a job! I have no trouble with my enemies. . . . But my damned friends,. . . White, they're the ones that keep me walking the floor nights."

A series of congressional investigations soon revealed a deep pattern of corruption. Attorney General Harry M. Daugherty had received bribes from violators of the Prohibition statutes. He had also failed to investigate graft in the Veterans Bureau, where Charles R. Forbes had pocketed a large chunk of the $250 million spent on hospitals and supplies. The worst affair was the Teapot Dome scandal involving Interior Secretary Albert Fall. Fall received hundreds of thousands of dollars in payoffs when he secretly leased navy oil reserves in Teapot Dome, Wyoming, and Elk Hills, California, to two private oil developers. He eventually became the first cabinet officer ever to go to jail.

But the Harding administration's legacy was not all scandal. Andrew Mellon, an influential Pittsburgh banker, served as secretary of the treasury under all three Republican presidents of the 1920s. One of the richest men in America, and a leading investor in the Aluminum Corporation of America and Gulf Oil, Mellon believed government ought to be run on the same conservative principles as a corporation. He was a leading voice for trimming the federal budget and cutting taxes on incomes, corporate profits, and inheritances. These cuts, he argued, would free up capital for new investment and thus promote general economic growth. Mellon's program sharply cut taxes for both higher-income brackets and for businesses. By 1926, a person with an income of a million a year paid less than a third of the income tax he or she had paid in 1921. Overall, Mellon's policies succeeded in rolling back much of the progressive taxation associated with Woodrow Wilson.

When Harding died in office of a heart attack in August 1923, Calvin Coolidge succeeded to the presidency. Coolidge seemed to most people the temperamental opposite of Harding. Born and raised in rural Vermont, elected governor of Massachusetts, and coming to national prominence only through the 1919 Boston police strike (see Chapter 22), "Silent Cal" was the quintessential New England Yankee. Taciturn, genteel, and completely honest, Coolidge believed in the least amount of government possible. He spent only four hours a day at the office. His famous aphorism, "The business of America is business," perfectly captured the core philosophy of the Republican new era. He was in awe of wealthy men such as Andrew Mellon, and he thought them best suited to make society's key decisions.

Coolidge easily won election on his own in 1924. He benefited from the general prosperity and the contrast he provided with the disgraced Harding. Coolidge

Calvin Coolidge combined a spare, laconic political style with a flair for publicity. He frequently posed in the dress of a cowboy, farmer, or Indian chief.

SOURCE: Calvin Coolidge in headdress and robes after joining Sioux Indians as Chief Leading Eagle, c. 1928. CORBIS.

defeated little-known Democrat John W. Davis, the compromise choice of a party badly divided between its rural and urban wings. Also running was Progressive Party candidate Robert M. La Follette of Wisconsin, who mounted a reform campaign that attacked economic monopolies and called for government ownership of utilities.

In his full term, Coolidge showed most interest in reducing federal spending, lowering taxes, and blocking congressional initiatives. He saw his primary function as clearing the way for American businessmen. They, after all, were the agents of the era's unprecedented prosperity.

Herbert Hoover and the "Associative State"

The most influential figure of the Republican new era was Herbert Hoover, who as secretary of commerce dominated the cabinets of Harding and Coolidge before becoming president himself in 1929. A successful engineer, administrator, and politician, Hoover effectively embodied the belief that enlightened business, encouraged and informed by the government, would act in the public interest. In the modern industrial age, Hoover believed, the government needed only to advise private citizens' groups about what national or international polices to pursue. "Reactionaries and radicals," he wrote in *American Individualism* (1922), "would assume that all reform and human advance must come through government. They have forgotten that progress must come from the steady lift of the individual and that the measure of national idealism and progress is the quality of idealism in the individual."

Hoover thus fused a faith in old-fashioned individualism with a strong commitment to the progressive possibilities offered by efficiency and rationality. Unlike an earlier generation of Republicans, Hoover wanted not just to create a favorable climate for business but to actively assist the business community. He spoke of creating an "associative state," in which the government would encourage voluntary cooperation among corporations, consumers, workers, farmers, and small businessmen. This became the central occupation of the Department of Commerce under Hoover's leadership. Under Hoover, the Bureau of Standards became one of the nation's leading research centers, setting engineering standards for key American industries such as machine tools and automobiles. The bureau also helped standardize the styles, sizes, and designs of many consumer products such as canned goods and refrigerators.

Hoover actively encouraged the creation and expansion of national trade associations. By 1929 there were about 2,000 of them. At industrial conferences called by the Commerce Department, government officials explained the advantages of mutual cooperation in figuring prices and costs and then publishing the information. The idea was to improve efficiency by reducing competition. To some this practice violated the spirit of antitrust laws, but in the 1920s the Justice Department's Antitrust Division took a very lax view of its responsibility. In addition, the Supreme Court consistently upheld the legality of trade associations. Hoover also had a strong influence on presidential appointments to regulatory commissions; most of these went to men who had worked for the very firms the commissions had been designed to supervise. Regulatory commissions thus benefited from the technical expertise brought by industry leaders, but they in turn tended to remain uncritical of the industries they oversaw.

The government thus provided an ideal climate for the concentration of corporate wealth and power. The trend toward large corporate trusts and holding companies had been well under way since the late nineteenth century, but it accelerated in the 1920s. By 1929, the 200 largest American corporations owned almost half the total corporate wealth and about a fifth of the total national wealth. Concentration was particularly strong

in manufacturing, retailing, mining, banking, and utilities. The number of vertical combinations—large, integrated firms that controlled the raw materials, manufacturing processes, and distribution networks for their products—also increased. Vertical inegration became common not only in older industries but also in the automobile, electrical, radio, motion picture, and other new industries as well.

War Debts, Reparations, Keeping the Peace

The United States emerged from World War I the strongest economic power in the world. The war transformed it from the world's leading debtor nation to its most important creditor. European governments owed the U.S. government about $10 billion in 1919. In the private sector, the war ushered in an era of expanding American investment abroad. As late as 1914 foreign investments in the United States were about $3 billion more than the total of American capital invested abroad. By 1919 that situation was reversed: America had $3 billion more invested abroad than foreigners had invested in the United States. By 1929 the surplus was $8 billion. New York replaced London as the center of international finance and capital markets.

During the 1920s, war debts and reparations were the single most divisive issue in international economics. In France and Great Britain, which both owed the United States large amounts in war loans, many concluded that the Uncle Sam who had offered assistance during wartime was really a loan shark in disguise. In turn, many Americans viewed Europeans as ungrateful debtors. As President Coolidge acidly remarked, "They hired the money, didn't they?" In 1922 the U.S. Foreign Debt Commission negotiated an agreement with the debtor nations that called for them to repay $11.5 billion over a sixty-two-year period. But by the late 1920s, the European financial situation had become so desperate that the United States agreed to cancel a large part of these debts. Continued insistence by the United States that the Europeans pay at least a portion of the debt fed anti-American feeling in Europe and isolationism at home.

The Germans believed that war reparations, set at $33 billion by the Treaty of Versailles, not only unfairly punished the losers of the conflict but, by saddling their civilian economies with such massive debt, also deprived them of the very means to repay. In 1924 Herbert Hoover and Chicago banker Charles Dawes worked out a plan to aid the recovery of the German economy. The Dawes Plan reduced Germany's debt, stretched out the repayment period, and arranged for American bankers to lend funds to Germany. These measures helped stabilize Germany's currency and allowed it to make reparations payments to France and

Great Britain. The Allies, in turn, were better able to pay their war debts to the United States.

The horrors of the Great War led millions of citizens, as well as government officials, to advocate curbs on the world's armed forces. In 1921 Secretary of State Charles Evans Hughes took the initiative on arms limitations by inviting representatives from Great Britain, Japan, Italy, France, and China to meet in Washington to discuss reductions in military budgets. Hughes offered to scrap thirty major American ships and asked for comparable actions by the British and Japanese. He asked for a ten-year moratorium on the construction of new battleships and cruisers and proposed limiting naval tonnage. The following year the Five-Power Treaty agreed to this scaling down of navies and also pledged to respect the territorial integrity of China. But the Italians and Japanese soon complained about the treaty's restraints, and ultimately the limits placed on navy construction were abandoned.

The United States never joined the League of Nations, but it maintained an active, if selective, involvement in world affairs. In addition to the Dawes Plan and the American role in naval disarmament, the United States joined the league-sponsored World Court in 1926 and was represented at numerous league conferences. In 1928, with great fanfare, the United States and sixty-two other nations signed the Pact of Paris (better known as the Kellogg-Briand Pact for the U.S. Secretary of State Frank B. Kellogg and French Foreign Minister Aristide Briand who initiated it), which grandly and naively renounced war in principle. Peace groups, such as the Woman's Peace Party and the Quaker-based Fellowship of Reconciliation, hailed the pact for formally outlawing war. But critics charged that the Kellogg-Briand Pact was essentially meaningless since it lacked powers of enforcement and relied solely on the moral force of world opinion. Within weeks of its ratification, the U.S. Congress had appropriated $250 million for new battleships.

Commerce and Foreign Policy

Secretary of State Charles Evans Hughes, a former governor of New York and the Republican candidate for president in 1916, played a leading role in shaping America's postwar foreign policy. Hughes argued that the United States must seek "to establish a Pax Americana maintained not by arms but by mutual respect and good will and the tranquilizing processes of reason." Hughes's push for the arms reduction agreements of 1921 went hand in hand with his deep belief that America's economic wealth—not military or political power—could help create a new and prosperous international system free of the rivalries that had led to the disastrous Great War.

Throughout the 1920s, Hughes and other Republican leaders pursued policies designed to expand American economic activity abroad. They understood that capitalist economies must be dynamic; they must expand their markets if they were to thrive. The focus must be on friendly nations and investments that would help foreign citizens to buy American goods. Toward this end, Republican leaders urged close cooperation between bankers and the government as a strategy for expanding American investment and economic influence abroad. They insisted that investment capital not be spent on U.S. enemies, such as the new Soviet Union, or on nonproductive enterprises such as munitions and weapons. Throughout the 1920s, investment bankers routinely submitted loan projects to Hughes and Secretary of Commerce Hoover for informal approval, thus reinforcing the close ties between business investment and foreign policy.

Foreign policymakers were not shy about brandishing America's postwar economic power to gain advantage. In 1926, the British tried to drive up the world price of rubber, a crucial product for the burgeoning automobile industry. Hoover retaliated by threatening a less friendly U.S. attitude toward British loans and war debts and by encouraging American investors to enlarge their rubber plantations in Southeast Asia and Liberia. Within three months, Hoover had succeeded in driving down the price of rubber from $1.21 a pound to 40 cents. For Hoover and other policymakers, American business abroad was simply rugged individualism at work around the globe.

American oil, autos, farm machinery, and electrical equipment supplied a growing world market. Much of this expansion took place through the establishment of branch plants overseas by American companies. America's overall direct investment abroad increased from $3.8 billion in 1919 to $7.5 billion in 1929. Leading the American domination of the world market were General Electric, Ford, and Monsanto Chemical. American oil companies, with the support of the State Department, also challenged Great Britain's dominance in the oil fields of the Middle East and Latin America, forming powerful cartels with English firms.

The strategy of maximum freedom for private enterprise, backed by limited government advice and assistance, significantly boosted the power and profits of American overseas investors. But in Central and Latin America, in particular, aggressive U.S. investment also fostered chronically underdeveloped economies, dependent on a few staple crops (sugar, coffee, cocoa, bananas) grown for export. American investments in Latin America more than doubled between 1924 and 1929, from $1.5 billion to over $3.5 billion. A large part of this money went to taking over vital mineral resources, such as Chile's copper and Venezuela's oil. The growing wealth and power of U.S. companies made it more difficult for these nations to grow their own food or diversify their economies. U.S. economic dominance in the hemisphere also hampered the growth of democratic politics by favoring autocratic, military regimes that could be counted on to protect U.S. investments.

During the 1920s, U.S. negotiators peacefully resolved long-simmering disputes with Mexico over oil and mineral holdings of American companies. The United States withdrew its marines from the Dominican Republic in 1924, after many years of direct military intervention. But in Nicaragua, American troops continued to prop up the conservative government of Adolfo Díaz, who had worked closely with the State Department since the first U.S. intervention in 1911. When a popular revolt led by General Augustino Sandino broke out in 1927, American marines landed and wound up supervising Nicaraguan elections over the next five years. They were not finally withdrawn until 1933, leaving a bitter legacy that would lead to crisis once again in the 1980s.

RESISTANCE TO MODERNITY

One measure of the profound cultural changes of the 1920s was the hostility and opposition expressed toward them by large sectors of the American public. Deep and persistent tensions, with ethnic, racial, and geographical overtones, characterized much of the decade's politics. The postwar Red Scare had given strength to the forces of antiradicalism in politics and traditionalism in culture. Resentments over the growing power of urban culture were very strong in rural and small-town America. The big city, in this view, stood for all that was alien, corrupt, and immoral in the country's life. Several trends and mass movements reflected this anger and the longing for a less complicated past.

Prohibition

The Eighteenth Amendment, banning the manufacture, sale, and transportation of alcoholic beverages, took effect in January 1920. Prohibition was the culmination of a long campaign that associated drinking with the degradation of working-class family life and the worst evils of urban politics. Supporters, a coalition of women's temperance groups, middle-class progressives, and rural Protestants, hailed the new law as "a noble experiment." But it became clear rather quickly that enforcing the new law would be extremely difficult. The Volstead Act of 1919 established a federal Prohibition Bureau to enforce the Eighteenth Amendment. Yet the bureau was severely understaffed, with only about 1,500 agents to police the entire country.

The public demand for alcohol, especially in the big cities, led to widespread lawbreaking. Drinking was such a routine part of life for so many Americans that bootlegging quickly became a big business. Illegal stills and breweries, as well as liquor smuggled in from Canada, supplied the needs of those Americans who continued to drink. Nearly every town and city had at least one "speakeasy," where people could drink and enjoy music and other entertainment. Local law enforcement personnel, especially in the cities, were easily bribed to overlook these illegal establishments. By the early 1920s many eastern states no longer made even a token effort at enforcing the law.

But because liquor continued to be illegal, Prohibition gave an enormous boost to violent organized crime. The profits to be made in the illegal liquor trade dwarfed the traditional sources of criminal income—gambling, prostitution, and robbery. The pattern of organized crime in the 1920s closely resembled the larger trends in American business: smaller operations gave way to larger and more complex combinations. Successful organized crime figures, like Chicago's Al "Scarface" Capone, became celebrities in their own right and received heavy coverage in the mass media. Capone himself shrewdly used the rhetoric of the Republican new era to defend himself: "Everybody calls me a racketeer. I call myself a businessman. When I sell liquor it's bootlegging. When my patrons serve it on a silver tray on Lake Shore Drive, it's hospitality."

Organized crime, based on its huge profits from liquor, also made significant inroads into legitimate businesses, labor unions, and city government. By the time Congress and the states ratified the Twenty-first Amendment in 1933, repealing Prohibition, organized crime was a permanent feature of American life. Politically, Prohibition continued to be a controversial issue in national politics, as "wets" and "drys" debated the merits of the law. Prohibition did, in fact, significantly reduce per capita consumption of alcohol. In 1910, annual per capita consumption stood at 2.6 gallons; in 1934 the figure was less than a gallon. Many drinkers—especially wage earners—probably consumed less because of the higher price of bootleg beer and spirits. Yet among young people, especially college students, the excitement associated with speakeasies and lawbreaking contributed to increased drinking during Prohibition.

Immigration Restriction

Sentiment for restricting immigration, growing since the late nineteenth century, reached its peak immediately after World War I. Antiimmigrant feeling reflected the growing preponderance after 1890 of "new immigrants"—those from southern and eastern

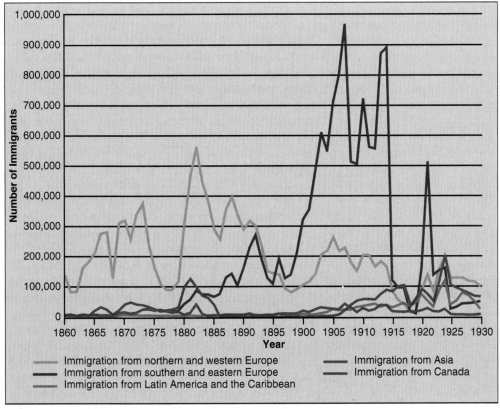

Annual Immigration to the United States, 1860–1930

Europe—over the immigrants from northern and western Europe who had predominated before 1890. Between 1891 and 1920, roughly 10.5 million immigrants arrived from southern and eastern Europe. This was nearly twice as many as arrived during the same years from northern and western Europe.

The "new immigrants" were mostly Catholic and Jewish, and they were darker-skinned than the "old immigrants." To many Americans they seemed more exotic, more foreign, and less willing and able to assimilate the nation's political and cultural values. They were also relatively poorer, more physically isolated in the nation's cities, and less politically strong than earlier immigrants. In the 1890s, the anti-Catholic American Protective Association called for a curb on immigration, and by exploiting the economic depression of that decade it reached a membership of 2.5 million. In 1894 a group of prominent Harvard graduates, including Henry Cabot Lodge and John Fiske, founded the Immigration Restriction League, providing an influential forum for the fears of the nation's elite. The league used newer scientific arguments, based on a flawed application of Darwinian evolutionary theory and genetics, to support its call for immigration restriction.

Theories of scientific racism, which had become more popular in the early 1900s, reinforced antiimmi-grant bias. The most influential statement of racial hierarchy was Madison Grant's *The Passing of the Great Race* (1916), which distorted genetic theory to argue that America was committing "race suicide." According to Grant, inferior Alpine, Mediterranean, and Jewish stock threatened to extinguish the superior Nordic race that had made America great. Eugenicists, who enjoyed considerable vogue in these years, held that heredity determined almost all of a person's capacities and that genetic inferiority predisposed people to crime and poverty. Such pseudoscientific thinking sought to explain historical and social development solely as a function of "racial" differences.

Against this background, the war and its aftermath provided the final push for immigration restriction. The "100 percent American" fervor of the war years fueled nativist passions. So did the Red Scare of 1919–20, which linked foreigners with Bolshevism and radicalism of all kinds in the popular mind. The postwar depression coincided with the resumption of massive immigration, bringing much hostile comment on the relationship between rising unemployment and the new influx of foreigners. The American Federation of Labor proposed stopping all immigration for two years. Sensational press coverage of organized crime figures, many of them Italian or Jewish, also played a part.

In 1921 Congress passed the Immigration Act, setting a maximum of 357,000 new immigrants each year. Quotas limited annual immigration from any European country to 3 percent of the number of its natives counted in the 1910 U.S. census. But restrictionists complained that the new law still allowed too many southern and eastern Europeans in, especially since the northern and western Europeans did not fill their quotas. The Johnson-Reed Immigration Act of 1924 revised the quotas to 2 percent of the number of foreign-born counted for each nationality in the census for 1890, when far fewer southern or eastern Europeans were present in the United States. The maximum total allowed each year was also cut, to 164,000. The quota laws did not apply to Canada, Mexico, or any other nation in the western hemisphere.

The immigration restriction laws reversed earlier practices and became a permanent feature of national policy. Republican congressman Albert Johnson of Washington, coauthor of the 1924 act, defended it by claiming that "our capacity to maintain our cherished institutions stands diluted by a stream of alien blood, with all its inherited misconceptions respecting the relationships of the governing power to the governed. . . . The day of unalloyed welcome to all peoples, the day of indiscriminate acceptance of all races, has definitely ended." In effect, Congress had accepted the racial assumptions of such popular, pseudoscientific writers as Madison Grant, basing immigration restriction on a presumed hierarchy of superior and inferior "races."

The Ku Klux Klan

If immigration restriction was resurgent nativism's most significant legislative expression, a revived Ku Klux Klan was its most effective mass movement. The original Klan had been formed in the Reconstruction South as an instrument of white racial terror against newly freed slaves (see Chapter 17). It had died out in the 1870s. The new Klan, born in Stone Mountain, Georgia, in 1915, was inspired by D. W. Griffith's racist spectacle *The Birth of a Nation*, a film released in that year depicting the original KKK as a heroic organization. The new Klan patterned itself on the secret rituals and antiblack hostility of its predecessor, and until 1920 it was limited to a few local chapters in Georgia and Alabama.

When Hiram W. Evans, a dentist from Dallas, became imperial wizard of the Klan in 1922, he transformed the organization. Evans hired professional fundraisers and publicists and directed an effective recruiting scheme that paid a commission to sponsors of new members. The Klan advocated "100 percent Americanism" and "the faithful maintenance of White Supremacy." The Klan also staunchly supported the enforcement of Prohibition, and it attacked birth control and Darwinism. The new Klan made a special target of the Roman Catholic Church, labeling it a hostile and dangerous alien power. In a 1926 magazine piece titled "The Klan's Fight for Americanism," Evans alleged that the Church's "theocratic autocracy and its claim to full authority in temporal as well as spiritual matters, all make it impossible for it as a church, or for its members if they obey it, to cooperate in a free democracy in which Church and State have been separated."

The new Klan presented itself as the righteous defender of the embattled traditional values of small-town Protestant America. But ironically, to build its membership rolls, it relied heavily on the publicity, public relations, and business techniques associated with modern urban culture. By 1924 the new Klan counted more than 3 million members across the country. President Harding had joined in a special White House ceremony. Its slogan, "Native, White, Protestant Supremacy," proved especially attractive in the Midwest and South, including many cities. Klansmen boycotted businesses, threatened families, and sometimes resorted to violence—public whippings, arson, and lynching—against their chosen enemies. The Klan's targets sometimes included white Protestants accused of sexual promiscuity, blasphemy, or drunkenness, but most victims were African Americans, Catholics, and Jews. Support for Prohibition enforcement probably united Klansmen more than any single issue.

On another level, the Klan was a popular social movement. Many members were more attracted by the Klan's spectacular social events and its efforts to reinvigorate community life than by its attacks on those considered outsiders. Perhaps a half million women joined the Women of the Ku Klux Klan, and women constituted nearly half of the Klan membership in some states. Klanswomen drew on family and community traditions, such as church suppers, kin reunions, and gossip campaigns, to defend themselves and their families against what they saw as corruption and immorality. One northern Indiana Klanswoman recalled, "Store owners, teachers, farmers . . . the good people, all belonged to the Klan. They were going to clean up the government, and they were going to improve the school books that were loaded with Catholicism." The Klan's power was strong in many communities precisely because it fit so comfortably into the everyday life of white Protestants.

Studies of Klan units suggest that the appeal and activities of the organization varied greatly from community to community. Local conditions and circumstances often attracted followers more than the extremist and nativist appeals of the national office. In

Women members of the Ku Klux Klan in New Castle, Indiana, August 1, 1923. The revived Klan was a powerful presence in scores of American communities during the early 1920s, especially among native-born white Protestants who feared cultural and political change. In addition to preaching "100 percent Americanism," local Klan chapters also served as a social function for members and their families.

SOURCE: Ball State University Libraries, Archives & Special Collections, W.A. Swift Photo Collection.

Anaheim, California, for example, most Klansmen were migrants from midwestern states who attended mainstream Protestant churches. They focused their anger on the local economic elite, whom they held responsible for a failure to enforce Prohibition, a rising crime rate, and runaway economic growth. In Colorado, Prohibition and vice law violations appeared to be the main concern. Vigilante attacks on Catholic priests and Jewish synagogues were more prevalent in cities like Denver and Pueblo, which had small but visible nonwhite Protestant communities.

At its height, the Klan also became a powerful force in Democratic Party politics in Texas, Oklahoma, Indiana, Colorado, Oregon, and other states. It had a strong presence among delegates to the 1924 Democratic National Convention. The Klan began to fade in 1925 when its Indiana leader, Grand Dragon David C. Stephenson, became involved in a sordid personal affair. Stephenson had picked up a young secretary at a party, got her drunk on bootleg liquor, and then assaulted her on a train. After the woman took poison and died, Stephenson was convicted of manslaughter. With one of its most famous leaders disgraced and in

jail, the new Klan began to lose members and influence. The success of immigration restriction, the receding concern over Bolshevism, wrangling among Klan leaders, and the general economic prosperity also contributed to the movement's rapid decline by the late 1920s.

Religious Fundamentalism

Paralleling political nativism in the 1920s was the growth of religious fundamentalism. In many Protestant churches, congregations focused less on religious practice and worship than on social and reform activities in the larger community. By the early 1920s, a fundamentalist revival had developed in reaction to these tendencies. The fundamentalists emphasized a literal reading of the Bible, and they rejected the tenets of modern science as inconsistent with the revealed word of God. Fundamentalist publications and Bible colleges flourished, particularly among Southern Baptists.

One special target of the fundamentalists was the theory of evolution, first set forth by Charles Darwin in his landmark work *The Origin of Species* (1859). Using

Clarence Darrow (left) and William Jennings Bryan at the Scopes Trial in Dayton, Tennessee, in 1925. Their courtroom battle embodied the larger cultural conflict between religious fundamentalism and secular values. In the trial's most dramatic moment, Darrow called Bryan to the witness stand to testify as an expert on the Bible.

SOURCE: AP/Wide World Photos.

The Scopes "monkey trial"— so called because fundamentalists trivialized Darwin's theory into a claim that humans were descended from monkeys—became one of the most publicized and definitive moments of the decade. The real drama was the confrontation between Darrow and Bryan. Darrow, denied by the judge the right to call scientists to testify for the defense, put the "Great Commoner," Bryan, himself on the stand as an expert witness on the Bible. Bryan delighted his supporters with a staunch defense of biblical literalism. But he also drew scorn from many of the assembled journalists, including cosmopolitan types such as H. L. Mencken of the *Baltimore Sun*, who ridiculed Bryan's simplistic faith. Scopes's guilt was never in question. The jury convicted him quickly, although the verdict was later thrown out on a technicality. Bryan died a week after the trial; his epitaph read simply, "He kept the Faith." The struggle over the teaching of evolution continued in an uneasy stalemate; state statutes were not repealed, but prosecutions for teaching evolution ceased. Fundamentalism, a religious creed and a cultural defense against the uncertainties of modern life, continued to have a strong appeal for millions of Americans.

fossil evidence, evolutionary theory suggested that over time many species had become extinct and that new ones had emerged through the process of natural selection. These ideas directly contradicted the account of one, fixed creation in the Book of Genesis. Although most Protestant clergymen had long since found ways of blending the scientific theory with their theology, fundamentalists launched an attack on the teaching of Darwinism in schools and universities. By 1925 five southern state legislatures had passed laws restricting the teaching of evolution.

A young biology teacher, John T. Scopes, deliberately broke the Tennessee law prohibiting the teaching of Darwinism in 1925 in order to challenge it in court. The resulting trial that summer in Dayton, a small town near Chattanooga, drew international attention to the controversy. Scopes's defense team included attorneys from the American Civil Liberties Union and Clarence Darrow, the most famous trial lawyer in America. The prosecution was led by William Jennings Bryan, the old Democratic standard-bearer who had thrown himself into the fundamentalist and antievolutionist cause. Held in a circus atmosphere in sweltering heat, the trial attracted thousands of reporters and partisans to Dayton and was broadcast across the nation by the radio.

PROMISES POSTPONED

The prosperity of the 1920s was unevenly distributed and enjoyed across America. Older, progressive reform movements that had pointed out inequities faltered in the conservative political climate. But the Republican new era did inspire a range of critics deeply troubled by unfulfilled promises in American life. Feminists sought to redefine their movement in the wake of the suffrage victory. Mexican immigration to the United States shot up, and in the burgeoning Mexican American communities of the Southwest and Midwest, economic and social conditions were very difficult. African Americans, bitterly disappointed by their treatment during and after the Great War, turned to new political and cultural strategies. Many American intellectuals found themselves deeply alienated from the temper and direction of modern American society.

Feminism in Transition

The achievement of the suffrage removed the central issue that had given cohesion to the disparate forces of female reform activism. In addition, female activists of all persuasions found themselves swimming against a national tide of hostility to political idealism. During the 1920s, the women's movement split into two main wings over a fundamental disagreement about female identity. Should activists stress women's differences from men—their vulnerability and the double burden of work and family—and continue to press for protective legislation, such as laws that limited the length of the work week for women? Or should they emphasize the ways that women were like men—sharing similar aspirations—and push for full legal and civil equality?

In 1920, the National American Woman Suffrage Association reorganized itself as the League of Women Voters. The league represented the historical mainstream of the suffrage movement, those who believed that the vote for women would bring a nurturing sensibility and a reform vision to American politics. This view was rooted in politicized domesticity, the notion that women had a special role to play in bettering society: improving conditions for working women, abolishing child labor, humanizing prisons and mental hospitals, and serving the urban poor. Most league members continued working in a variety of reform organizations, and the league itself concentrated on educating the new female electorate, encouraging women to run for office, and supporting laws for the protection of women and children.

A newer, smaller, and more militant group was the National Woman's Party (NWP), founded in 1916 by militant suffragist Alice Paul. The NWP downplayed the significance of suffrage and argued that women were still subordinate to men in every facet of life. The NWP opposed protective legislation for women, claiming that such laws reinforced sex stereotyping and prevented women from competing with men in many fields. Largely representing the interests of professional and business women, the NWP focused on passage of a brief Equal Rights Amendment (ERA) to the Constitution, introduced in Congress in 1923: "Men and women shall have equal rights throughout the United States and every place subject to its jurisdiction."

Since the ERA would wipe out sex as a legal category, its opponents worried about the loss of hard-won protective legislation that benefited poor and working-class women. Many of the older generation of women reformers opposed the ERA as elitist, arguing that far more women benefited from protective laws than were injured by them. "So long as men cannot be mothers," Florence Kelley declared, "so long legislation adequate for them can never be adequate for wage-earning

women; and the cry Equality, Equality, where nature has created inequality, is as stupid and as deadly as the cry of Peace, Peace, where there is no Peace." Mary Anderson, director of the Women's Bureau in the Department of Labor, argued that "women who are wage earners, with one job in the factory and another in the home, have little time and energy left to carry on the fight to better their economic status. They need the help of other women and they need labor laws."

ERA supporters countered that maximum hours laws or laws prohibiting women from night work prevented women from getting many lucrative jobs. According to Harriot Stanton Blatch, daughter of feminist pioneer Elizabeth Cady Stanton, "In many highly paid trades women have been pushed into the lower grades of work, limited in earning capacity, if not shut out of the trade entirely by these so-called protective laws." M. Carey Thomas, president of Bryn Mawr College, defended the ERA with language reminiscent of laissez faire: "How much better by one blow to do away with discriminating against women in work, salaries, promotion and opportunities to compete with men in a fair field with no favour on either side!"

But most women's groups did not think there was a "fair field." Positions solidified. The League of Women Voters, the National Consumers' League, and the Women's Trade Union League opposed the ERA. ERA supporters generally stressed individualism, competition, and the abstract language of "equality" and "rights." ERA opponents emphasized the grim reality of industrial exploitation and the concentration of women workers in low-paying jobs in which they did not compete directly with men. ERA advocates dreamed of a labor market that might be, one in which women might have the widest opportunity. Anti-ERA forces looked at the labor market as it was, insisting it was more important to protect women from existing exploitation. The NWP campaign failed to get the ERA passed by Congress, but the debates it sparked would be echoed during the feminist movement of the 1970s, when the ERA became a central political goal of a resurgent feminism.

A small number of professional women made real gains in the fields of real estate, banking, and journalism. The press regularly announced new "firsts" for women, such as Amelia Earhart's 1928 airplane flight across the Atlantic. Anne O'Hare McCormick won recognition as the "first lady of American journalism" for her reporting and editorial columns in the *New York Times*. As business expanded, a greater percentage of working women were employed in white-collar positions, as opposed to manufacturing and domestic service. In 1900 less than 18 percent of employed women worked in clerical, managerial, sales, and professional areas. By 1930 the number was 44 percent. But studies showed that most of these women were clustered in the low-paying areas of typing, stenography, bookkeeping, cashiering, and sales clerking. Men still dominated in the higher-paid and managerial white-collar occupations.

The most significant, if limited, victory for feminist reformers was the 1921 Sheppard-Towner Act, which established the first federally funded health-care program, providing matching funds for states to set up prenatal and child health care centers. These centers also provided public health nurses for house calls. Although hailed as a genuine reform breakthrough, especially for women in rural and isolated communities, the act aroused much opposition. The NWP disliked it for its assumption that all women were mothers. Birth control advocates such as Margaret Sanger complained that contraception was not part of the program. The American Medical Association (AMA) objected to government-sponsored health care and to nurses who functioned outside the supervision of physicians. By 1929, largely as a result of intense AMA lobbying, Congress cut off funds for the program.

Mexican Immigration

While immigration restriction sharply cut the flow of new arrivals from Europe, the 1920s also brought a dramatic influx of Mexicans to the United States. Mexican immigration, which was not included in the immigration laws of 1921 and 1924, had picked up substantially after the outbreak of the Mexican Revolution in 1911, when political instability and economic hardships provided incentives to cross the border to *El Norte.* According to the U.S. Immigration Service, an estimated 459,000 Mexicans entered the United States between 1921 and 1930, more than double the number for the previous decade. The official count no doubt underrepresented the true numbers of immigrants from Mexico. Many Mexicans shunned the main border crossings at El Paso, Texas; Nogales, Arizona; and Calexico, California, and thus avoided paying the $8 head tax and $10 visa fee.

The primary pull was the tremendous agricultural expansion occurring in the American Southwest. Irrigation and large-scale agribusiness had begun transforming California's Imperial and San Joaquin Valleys from arid desert into lucrative fruit and vegetable fields. Cotton pickers were needed in the vast plantations of Lower Rio Grande Valley in Texas and the Salt River Valley in Arizona. The sugar beet fields of Michigan, Minnesota, and Colorado also attracted many Mexican farm workers. American industry had also begun recruiting Mexican workers, first to fill wartime needs and later to fill the gap left by the decline in European immigration.

The new Mexican immigration appeared more permanent than previous waves—that is, more and more

newcomers stayed—and, like other immigrants, settled in cities. This was partly the unintended consequence of new policies designed to make immigration more difficult. As the Border Patrol (established in 1924) made border crossing more difficult (through head taxes, visa fees, literacy tests, and document checks), what had once been a two-way process for many Mexicans became a one-way migration. Permanent communities of Mexicans in the U.S. grew rapidly. By 1930, San Antonio's Mexican community accounted for roughly 80,000 people out of a total population of a quarter million. Around 100,000 Mexicans lived in central and east Los Angeles, including 55,000 who attended city schools. Substantial Mexican communities also flourished in midwestern cities such as Chicago, Detroit, Kansas City, and Gary. Many of the immigrants alternated between agricultural and factory jobs, depending on the seasonal availability of work. Mexican women often worked in the fields alongside their husbands. They also had jobs as domestics and seamstresses or took in laundry and boarders.

Racism and local patterns of residential segregation confined most Mexicans to barrios. Housing conditions were generally poor, particularly for recent arrivals, who were forced to live in rude shacks without running water or electricity. Disease and infant mortality rates were much higher than average, and most Mexicans

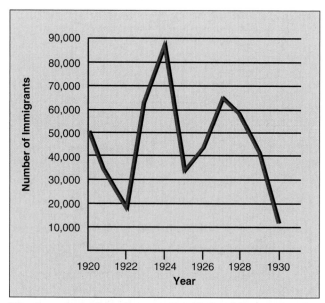

Mexican Immigration to the United States in the 1920s Many Mexican migrants avoided official border crossing stations so they would not have to pay visa fees. Thus these official figures probably underestimated the true size of the decade's Mexican migration. As the economy contracted with the onset of the Great Depression, immigration from Mexico dropped off sharply.

Mexican workers gathered outside a San Antonio labor bureau in 1924. These employment agencies contracted Mexicans to work for Texas farmers, railroads, and construction companies. Note the three Anglo men in front (wearing suits and ties), who probably owned and operated this agency. During the 1920s, San Antonio's Mexican population doubled from roughly 40,000 to over 80,000, making it the second largest *colonia* in *El Norte* after Los Angeles.

SOURCE: Goldbeck Collection, Harry Ransom Humanities Research Center, University of Texas at Austin. Photo by Summerville (46ND).

worked at low-paying, unskilled jobs and received inadequate health care. Legal restrictions passed by states and cities made it difficult for Mexicans to enter teaching, legal, and other professions. Mexicans were routinely banned from local public works projects as well. Many felt a deep ambivalence about applying for American citizenship. Loyalty to the Old Country was strong, and many cherished dreams of returning to live out their days in Mexico.

Ugly racist campaigns against Mexicans were common in the 1920s, especially when "cheap Mexican labor" was blamed for local unemployment or hard times. Stereotypes of Mexicans as "greasers" or "wetbacks" were prevalent in newspapers and movies of the day. Nativist efforts to limit Mexican immigration were thwarted by the lobbying of powerful agribusiness interests. The Los Angeles Chamber of Commerce typically employed racist stereotyping in arguing to keep the borders open. Mexicans, it claimed, were naturally suited for agriculture, "due to their crouching and bending habits. . . , while the white is physically unable to adapt himself to them."

Mutual aid societies—*mutualistas*—became key social and political institutions in the Mexican communities of the Southwest and Midwest. They provided death benefits and widows' pensions for members and also served as centers of resistance to civil rights violations and discrimination. In 1928, the Federation of Mexican Workers Unions formed in response to a large farm labor strike in the Imperial Valley of California. A group of middle-class Mexican professionals in Texas organized the League of United Latin American Citizens (LULAC) in 1929. The founding of these organizations marked only the beginnings of a long struggle to bring economic, social, and racial equality to Mexican Americans.

The "New Negro"

The Great Migration spurred by World War I showed no signs of letting up during the 1920s, and African American communities in northern cities grew rapidly. By far the largest and most influential of these communities was New York City's Harlem. Previously a

Web Exploration   Examine the Great Migration in more detail. Why were African Americans drawn to northern cities?
www.prenhall.com/faragher/map23.1

Black Population, 1920   Although the Great Migration had drawn hundreds of thousands of African Americans to the urban north, the southern states of the former Confederacy still remained the center of the African American population in 1920.

residential suburb, Harlem began attracting middle-class African Americans in the prewar years. After the war, heavy black migration from the South and the Caribbean encouraged real estate speculators and landlords to remake Harlem as an exclusively black neighborhood. Between 1920 and 1930 some 120,000 new black arrivals settled in Harlem, giving it a black population of roughly 200,000.

Harlem emerged as the demographic and cultural capital of black America, but it's appeal transcended national borders as mass migration from the Caribbean helped reshape the community. Between 1900 and 1930 some 300,000 West Indians emigrated to the United States, roughly half of whom settled in New York City. By the late 1920s about one-quarter of Harlem's population had been born in Jamaica, Barbados, Trinidad, the Bahamas, and other parts of the Caribbean. Some of the leading cultural, business, and political figures of the

era—poet Claude McKay, newspaper publisher P. M. H. Savory, labor organizer Hubert Harrison, black nationalist Marcus Garvey—had roots in the West Indies. Most black Caribbean migrants came from societies where class differences mattered more than racial ones, and many refused to accept racial bigotry without protest. A large number also carried with them entrepreneurial experience that contributed to their success in running small businesses. Intraracial tensions and resentment between American-born blacks and an increasingly visible West Indian population was one reflection of Harlem's transformation into a hemispheric center for black people.

The demand for housing in this restricted geographical area led to skyrocketing rents, but most Harlemites held low-wage jobs. This combination produced extremely overcrowded apartments, unsanitary conditions, and the rapid deterioration of housing stock. Disease

A 1925 pensive portrait of Langston Hughes, one of the leading literary voices of the Harlem Renaissance. Winold Reiss's work suggested Hughes's determination to create poetry out of the everyday life experiences of Harlem's burgeoning African American population.

SOURCE: Winold Reiss, Portrait of Langston Hughes (1902–1967 Poet) © 1925. National Portrait Gallery, Washington, DC, USA. Art Resource, N.Y. (S0041021)

and death rates were abnormally high. Harlem was well on its way to becoming a slum. Yet Harlem also boasted a large middle-class population and supported a wide array of churches, theaters, newspapers and journals, and black-owned businesses. It became a magnet for African American intellectuals, artists, musicians, and writers from all over the world. Poet Langston Hughes expressed the excitement of arriving in the community in 1921: "I can never put on paper the thrill of the underground ride to Harlem. I went up the steps and out into the bright September sunlight. Harlem! I stood there, dropped my bags, took a deep breath and felt happy again."

Harlem became the political and intellectual center for what writer Alain Locke called the "New Negro." Locke was referring to a new spirit in the work of black writers and intellectuals, an optimistic faith that encour-

aged African Americans to develop and celebrate their distinctive culture, firmly rooted in the history, folk culture, and experiences of African American people. This faith was the common denominator uniting the disparate figures associated with the Harlem Renaissance. The assertion of cultural independence resonated in the poetry of Langston Hughes and Claude McKay, the novels of Zora Neale Hurston and Jessie Fauset, the essays of Countee Cullen and James Weldon Johnson, the acting of Paul Robeson, and the blues singing of Bessie Smith. Most would agree with Johnson when he wrote in 1927 that "nothing can go farther to destroy race prejudice than the recognition of the Negro as a creator and contributor to American civilization."

There was a political side to the "New Negro" as well. The newly militant spirit that black veterans had brought home from World War I matured and found a variety of expressions in the Harlem of the 1920s. New leaders and movements began to appear alongside established organizations like the National Association for the Advancement of Colored People. A. Philip Randolph began a long career as a labor leader, socialist, and civil rights activist in these years, editing the *Messenger* and organizing the Brotherhood of Sleeping Car Porters. Harlem was also headquarters to Marcus Garvey's Universal Negro Improvement Association. An ambitious Jamaican immigrant who had moved to Harlem in 1916, Garvey created a mass movement that stressed black economic self-determination and unity among the black communities of the United States, the Caribbean, and Africa. His newspaper, *Negro World*, spoke to black communities around the world, urging black businesses to trade among themselves. With colorful parades and rallies and a central message affirming pride in black identity, Garvey attracted as many as a million members worldwide.

Garvey's best-publicized project was the Black Star Line, a black-owned and -operated fleet of ships that would link people of African descent around the world. But insufficient capital and serious financial mismanagement resulted in the spectacular failure of the enterprise. In 1923, Garvey was found guilty of mail fraud in his fundraising efforts; he later went to jail and was subsequently deported to England. Despite the disgrace, Harlem's largest newspaper, the *Amsterdam News*, explained Garvey's continuing appeal to African Americans: "In a world where black is despised, he taught them that black is beautiful. He taught them to admire and praise black things and black people."

Harlem in the 1920s also became a popular tourist attraction for "slumming" whites. Nightclubs like the Cotton Club were often controlled by white organized crime figures. They featured bootleg liquor, floor shows, and the best jazz bands of the day, led by Duke Ellington, Fletcher Henderson, Cab Calloway, and

Louis Armstrong. Yet these clubs were rigidly segregated. Black dancers, singers, and musicians provided the entertainment, but no African Americans were allowed in the audience. Chronicled in novels and newspapers, Harlem became a potent symbol to white America of the ultimate good time. Yet the average Harlemite never saw the inside of a nightclub. For the vast majority of Harlem residents, working menial jobs for low wages and forced to pay high rents, the day-to-day reality was depressingly different.

Intellectuals and Alienation

War, Prohibition, growing corporate power, and the deep currents of cultural intolerance troubled many intellectuals in the 1920s. Some felt so alienated from the United States that they left to live abroad. In the early 1920s Gertrude Stein, an American expatriate writer living in Paris, told the young novelist Ernest Hemingway: "All of you young people who served in the war, you are a lost generation." The phrase "a lost generation" was widely adopted as a label for American writers, artists, and intellectuals of the postwar era. Yet it is difficult to generalize about so diverse a community. For one thing, living abroad attracted only a handful of American writers. Alienation and disillusion with American life were prominent subjects in the literature and thought of the 1920s, but artists and thinkers developed these themes in very different ways.

The mass slaughter of World War I provoked revulsion and a deep cynicism about the heroic and moralistic portrayal of war so popular in the nineteenth century. Novelists Hemingway and John Dos Passos, who both served at the front as ambulance drivers, depicted the war and its aftermath in world-weary and unsentimental tones. The search for personal moral codes that would allow one to endure life with dignity and authenticity was at the center of Hemingway's fiction. In the taut, spare language of *The Sun Also Rises* (1926) and *A Farewell to Arms* (1929), he questioned idealism, abstractions, and large meanings. As Jake Barnes, the wounded war hero of *The Sun Also Rises* explained, "I did not care what it was all about. All I wanted to know was how to live it."

Hemingway and F. Scott Fitzgerald were the most influential novelists of the era. Fitzgerald joined the army during World War I but did not serve overseas. His work celebrated the youthful vitality of the "Jazz Age" (a phrase he coined) but was also deeply distrustful of the promises of American prosperity and politics. His first novel, *This Side of Paradise* (1920), won a wide readership around the country with its exuberant portrait of a "new generation," "dedicated more than the last to the fear of poverty and the worship of success;

grown up to find all Gods dead, all wars fought, all faiths in man shaken." Fitzgerald's finest work, *The Great Gatsby* (1925), written in the south of France, depicted the glamorous parties of the wealthy while evoking the tragic limits of material success.

At home, many American writers engaged in sharp attacks on small-town America and what they viewed as its provincial values. Essayist H. L. Mencken, caustic editor of the *American Mercury*, heaped scorn on fundamentalists, Prohibition, and nativists, while ridiculing what he called the "American booboisie." Mencken understood the power of the small town and despaired of reforming politics. "Our laws," he wrote, "are invented, in the main, by frauds and fanatics, and put upon the statute books by poltroons and scoundrels." Fiction writers also skewered small-town America, achieving commercial and critical success in the process. Sherwood Anderson's *Winesburg, Ohio* (1919) offered a spare, laconic, pessimistic yet compassionate view of middle America. He had a lasting influence on younger novelists of the 1920s.

The most popular and acclaimed writer of the time was novelist Sinclair Lewis. In a series of novels satirizing small-town life, such as *Main Street* (1920) and especially *Babbitt* (1922), Lewis affectionately mocked his characters. His treatment of the central character in *Babbitt*—George Babbitt of Zenith—also had a strong element of self-mockery, for Lewis could offer no alternative set of values to Babbitt's crass self-promotion, hunger for success, and craving for social acceptance. In 1930 Lewis became the first American author to win the Nobel Prize for literature.

The playwright Eugene O'Neill revolutionized the American stage with his naturalistic and brooding dramas. O'Neill's depictions of the darker side of family life and his exploration of race relations helped push American theater past the melodramatic conventions of the late nineteenth century. Among his influential early plays were *Beyond the Horizon* (1920), *The Emperor Jones* (1921), and *The Great God Brown* (1926). Two expatriate poets, T. S. Eliot and Ezra Pound, were breaking Victorian conventions by pushing American verse in revolutionary new directions. Eliot's *The Waste Land* (1922), perhaps the most influential poem of the century, used the metaphor of impotence to comment on the postwar world.

In the aftermath of the postwar Red Scare, American radicalism found itself on the defensive throughout the 1920s. But one *cause celebre* did attract a great deal of support from intellectuals. In 1921 two Italian American immigrants, Nicola Sacco and Bartolomeo Vanzetti, were tried and convicted for murder in the course of robbing a shoe factory in South Braintree, Massachusetts. Neither Sacco, a shoemaker, nor Vanzetti, a fish peddler, had criminal records, but both had long been active in militant anarchist circles, labor organizing, and antiwar agitation. Their trial took place amidst an intense atmosphere of nativist and antiradical feeling, and both the judge and prosecuting attorney engaged in clearly prejudicial conduct toward the defendants. A six year struggle to save Sacco and Vanzetti following the trial failed, despite attracting support from a broad range of liberal intellectuals including Harvard law professor and future Supreme Court justice Felix Frankfurter. The two men were finally executed in 1927, and for many years their case would remain a powerful symbol of how the criminal justice system could be tainted by political bias and antiimmigrant fervor. Many intellectuals agreed with literary critic Edmund Wilson who wrote that the Sacco and Vanzetti case "revealed the whole anatomy of American life with all its classes, professions, and points of view and all their relations, and it raised almost every fundamental question of our political and social system."

Another side of intellectual alienation was expressed by writers critical of industrial progress and the new mass culture. The most important of these were a group of poets and scholars centered in Vanderbilt University in Nashville, Tennessee, collectively known as the Fugitives. They included Allen Tate, John Crowe Ransom, Donald Davidson, and Robert Penn Warren, all of whom invoked traditional authority, respect for the past, and older agrarian ways as ideals to live by. The Fugitives attacked industrialism and materialism as modern-day ills. Self-conscious Southerners, they looked to the antebellum plantation-based society as a model for a community based on benevolence toward dependents (such as black people and women) and respect for the land. Their book of essays, *I'll Take My Stand* (1930), was a collective manifesto of their ideas.

Not all intellectuals, of course, were critics of modern trends. Some, like the philosopher John Dewey, retained much of the prewar optimism and belief in progress. But many others, such as Walter Lippmann and Joseph Wood Krutch, articulated a profound uneasiness with the limits of material growth. In his 1929 book *A Preface to Morals*, the urbane and sophisticated Lippmann expressed doubts about the moral health of the nation. Modern science and technological advances could not address more cosmic questions of belief. The erosion of old religious faiths and moral standards, along with the triumph of the new mass culture, had left many people with nothing to believe in. Lippmann called for a new "religion of the spirit" to offer a guide for living an ethical life. He was unclear as to just what the "religion of the spirit" might be. But he was certain that the moralist would have to persuade rather than command people to live the good life. His job would be "not to exhort men to be good but to elucidate what the good is."

The Election of 1928

The presidential election of 1928 served as a kind of national referendum on the Republican new era. It also revealed just how important ethnic and cultural differences had become in defining American politics. The contest reflected many of the deepest tensions and conflicts in American society in the 1920s: native-born versus immigrant; Protestant versus Catholic;

Clifford K. Berryman's 1928 political cartoon interpreted that year's presidential contest along sectional lines. It depicted the two major presidential contenders as each setting off to campaign in the regions where their support was weakest. For Democrat Al Smith, that meant the West, and for Republican Herbert Hoover, the East.

SOURCE: *Copyright, 1928, Lost Angeles Times.* Reprinted by permission.

Prohibition versus legal drinking; small-town life versus the cosmopolitan city; fundamentalism versus modernism; traditional sources of culture versus the new mass media.

The 1928 campaign featured two politicians who represented profoundly different sides of American life. Al Smith, the Democratic nominee for president, was a pure product of New York City's Lower East Side. Smith came from a background that included Irish, German, and Italian ancestry, and he was raised as a Roman Catholic. After attending parochial school and working in the Fulton Fish Market, he rose through the political ranks of New York's Tammany Hall machine. A personable man with a deep sympathy for poor and working-class people, Smith won a reputation as an effective state legislator in Albany. He served four terms as governor of New York, pushing through an array of laws reforming factory conditions, housing, and welfare programs. Two of his closest advisers were the progressives Frances Perkins and Belle Moskowitz. Smith thus fused older-style machine politics with the newer reform emphasis on state intervention to solve social problems.

Herbert Hoover easily won the Republican nomination after Calvin Coolidge announced he would not run for reelection. Hoover epitomized the successful and forward-looking American. An engineer and self-made millionaire, he offered a unique combination of experience in humanitarian war relief, administrative efficiency, and probusiness policies. Above all, Hoover stood for a commitment to voluntarism and individualism as the best method for advancing the public welfare. He was one of the best-known men in America and promised to continue the Republican control of national politics.

Smith himself quickly became the central issue of the campaign. His sharp New York accent, jarring to many Americans who heard it over the radio, marked him clearly as a man of the city. So did his brown derby and fashionable suits, as well as his promise to work for the repeal of Prohibition. As the first Roman Catholic nominee of a major party, Smith also drew a torrent of anti-Catholic bigotry, especially in the South and Midwest. Nativists and Ku Klux Klanners shamelessly exploited old anti-Catholic prejudices and intimidated participants in Democratic election rallies. But Smith was also attacked from more respectable quarters. Bishop James Cannon, head of the Southern Methodist Episcopal Church, insisted that "no subject of the Pope" should be permitted to occupy the White House. William Allen White, the old and influential progressive editor from Kansas, denounced Smith as the candidate of gambling, prostitution, and liquor interests.

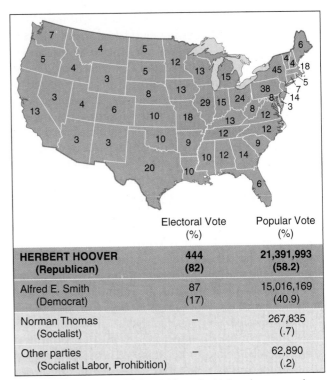

	Electoral Vote (%)	Popular Vote (%)
HERBERT HOOVER **(Republican)**	**444** **(82)**	**21,391,993** **(58.2)**
Alfred E. Smith (Democrat)	87 (17)	15,016,169 (40.9)
Norman Thomas (Socialist)	–	267,835 (.7)
Other parties (Socialist Labor, Prohibition)	–	62,890 (.2)

The Election of 1928   Although Al Smith managed to carry the nation's twelve largest cities, Herbert Hoover's victory in 1928 was one of the largest popular and electoral landslides in the nation's history.

For his part, Smith ran a largely conservative race. He appointed John Raskob, a Republican vice president of General Motors, to manage his campaign, and tried to outdo Hoover in his praise for business. He avoided economic issues such as the unevenness of the prosperity, the plight of farmers, or the growing unemployment. Democrats remained regionally divided over Prohibition, Smith's religion, and the widening split between rural and urban values. Hoover did not have to do much, other than take credit for the continued prosperity.

In retrospect, probably no Democrat could have won in 1928. The incumbent majority party would not lose during prosperous times. Hoover polled 21 million votes to Smith's 15 million, and swept the electoral college 444 to 87, including New York State. Even the Solid South, reliably Democratic since the Civil War, gave five states to Hoover—a clear reflection of the ethnocultural split in the party. Yet the election offered important clues to the future of the Democrats. Smith ran better in the big cities of the North and East than any Democrat in modern times. He outpolled Hoover in the aggregate vote of the nation's twelve largest cities

CHRONOLOGY

1920	Prohibition takes effect			Johnson-Reed Immigration Act tightens quotas established in 1921
	Warren G. Harding is elected president		1925	Scopes trial pits religious fundamentalism against modernity
	Station KDKA in Pittsburgh goes on the air			F. Scott Fitzgerald publishes *The Great Gatsby*
	Census reports that urban population is greater than rural population for the first time		1926	National Broadcasting Company establishes first national radio network
1921	First immigration quotas are established by Congress		1927	McNary-Haugen Farm Relief bill finally passed by Congress but is vetoed by President Coolidge as unwarranted federal interference in the economy
	Sheppard-Towner Act establishes first federally funded health-care program			Warner Brothers produces *The Jazz Singer*, the first feature-length motion picture with sound
1922	Washington conference produces Five-Power Treaty, scaling down navies			Charles Lindbergh makes first solo flight across the Atlantic Ocean
1923	Equal Rights Amendment is first introduced in Congress		1928	Kellogg-Briand Pact renounces war
	Harding dies in office; Calvin Coolidge becomes president			Herbert Hoover defeats Al Smith for the presidency
1924	Ku Klux Klan is at height of its influence		1929	Robert and Helen Lynd publish their classic community study *Middletown*
	Dawes Plan for war reparations stabilizes European economies			

and carried six of them, thus pointing the way to the Democrats' future dominance with urban, Northeastern, and ethnic voters.

CONCLUSION

America's big cities, if not dominant politically, now defined the nation's cultural and economic life as never before. The mass media of motion pictures, broadcasting, and chain newspapers brought cosmopolitan entertainments and values to the remotest small communities. The culture of celebrity knew no geographic boundaries. New consumer durable goods associated with mass-production techniques—automobiles, radios, telephones, household appliances—were manufactured largely in cities. The advertising and public relations companies that sang their praises were also distinctly urban enterprises. Even with the curtailing of European immigration, big cities attracted a kaleido-

scopic variety of migrants: white people from small towns and farms, African Americans from the rural South, Mexicans from across the border, intellectuals and professionals looking to make their mark.

Many Americans, of course, remained deeply suspicious of postwar cultural and economic trends. Yet the partisans of Prohibition, members of the Ku Klux Klan, and religious fundamentalists usually found themselves on the defensive against what they viewed as alien cultural and economic forces centered in the metropolis. Large sectors of the population did not share in the era's prosperity. But the large numbers who did—or at least had a taste of good times—ensured Republican political dominance throughout the decade. Thus America in the 1920s balanced dizzying change in the cultural and economic realms with conservative politics. The reform crusades that attracted millions during the progressive era were a distant memory. Political activism was no match for the new pleasures promised by technology and prosperity.

REVIEW QUESTIONS

1. Describe the impact of the "second industrial revolution" on American business, workers, and consumers. Which technological and economic changes had the biggest impact on American society?

2. Analyze the uneven distribution of the 1920's economic prosperity. Which Americans gained the most, and which were largely left out?

3. How did an expanding mass culture change the contours of everyday life in the decade following World War I? What role did new technologies of mass communication play in shaping these changes? What connections can you draw between the "culture of consumption," then and today?

4. What were the key policies and goals articulated by Republican political leaders of the 1920s? How did they apply these to both domestic and foreign affairs?

5. How did some Americans resist the rapid changes taking place in the post–World War I world? What cultural and political strategies did they employ?

6. Discuss the 1928 election as a mirror of the divisions in American society.

RECOMMENDED READING

Nancy F. Cott, *The Grounding of American Feminism* (1987). Includes a sophisticated analysis of the debates among feminists during the 1920s.

Lynn Dumenil, *The Modern Temper: America in the 1920s* (1995). An excellent synthesis of recent scholarship, which emphasizes the ambivalence that many Americans felt toward the emergence of modern society.

James J. Flink, *The Car Culture* (1975). The best single volume on the history of the automobile and how it changed American life.

David J. Goldberg, *Discontented America: The United States in the 1920s* (1999). Focuses on Americans' continuing discomfort with racial, ethnic, religious, and class difference during the decade.

Ellis W. Hawley, *The Great War and the Search for Modern Order* (1979). An influential study of the relations between the state and business and the growth of mass consumer society.

Desmond King, *Making Americans: Immigration, Race, and the Origins of Diverse Democracy* (2000). Fine analysis of the shift of U.S. immigration policies in the 1920s, with special attention to the influence of eugenics, and the long-term consequences of the new restrictive legislation.

Nancy Maclean, *Behind the Mask of Chivalry: The Making of the Second Ku Klux Klan* (1994). An excellent case study of the KKK in Athens, Georgia, with important insights on the Klan's relationship to issues involving gender and class difference.

Roland Marchand, *Advertising the American Dream: Making Way for Modernity, 1920–1940* (1985). A superb, beautifully illustrated account of the rise of the modern advertising industry.

Emily S. Rosenberg, *Spreading the American Dream* (1982). A fine study of American economic and cultural expansion around the world from 1890 to 1945.

Susan Smulyan, *Selling Radio: The Commercialization of American Broadcasting, 1920–1934* (1994). The best analysis of the rise of commercial radio broadcasting in the 1920s.

ADDITIONAL BIBLIOGRAPHY

Postwar Prosperity and Its Price

David Brody, *Workers in Industrial America* (1980)

Gilbert C. Fite, *Cotton Fields No More: Southern Agriculture, 1865–1980* (1984)

Kenneth T. Jackson, *Crabgrass Frontier* (1985)

William Leuchtenberg, *The Perils of Prosperity, 1914–1932* (1958)

Clay McShane, *Down the Asphalt Path* (1994)

Gwendolyn Wright, *Building the American Dream* (1981)

Gerald Zahavi, *Workers, Managers, and Welfare Capitalism* (1988)

The New Mass Culture

Beth A. Bailey, *From Front Porch to Back Seat: Courtship in Twentieth Century America* (1988)

Daniel J. Czitrom, *Media and the American Mind* (1982)

John D'Emilio and Estelle B. Freedman, *Intimate Matters: A History of Sexuality in America* (1988)

Susan J. Douglas, *Listening In: Radio and the American Imagination* (1999)

Michele Hilmes, *Radio Voices: American Broadcasting, 1922–1952* (1997)

Pamela Walker Laird, *Advertising Progress: American Business and the Rise of Consumer Marketing* (1998)

Jackson Lears, *Fables of Abundance: A Cultural History of Advertising in America* (1994)

Steven J. Ross, *Working Class Hollywood: Silent Film and the Shaping of Class in America* (1998)

Robert Sklar, *Movie Made America,* rev. ed. (1995)

The State, the Economy, and Business

Kendrick A. Clements, *Hoover, Conservation, and Consumerism: Engineering the Good Life* (2000)

Warren I. Cohen, *Empire without Tears* (1987)

Louis Galambos and Joseph Pratt, *The Rise of the Corporate Commonwealth* (1988)

John Earl Haynes, ed., *Calvin Coolidge and the Coolidge Era* (1998)

Roland Marchand, *Creating the Corporate Soul: The Rise of Public Relations and Corporate Imagery in American Big Business* (1998)

Charles L. Mee, *The Ohio Gang: The World of Warren G. Harding* (1981)

Resistance to Modernity

Katherine M. Blee, *Women and the Klan: Racism and Gender in the 1920s* (1991)

John Higham, *Strangers in the Land: Patterns of American Nativism, 1860–1925* (1955)

Thomas R. Pegram, *Battling Demon Rum: The Struggle for a Dry America, 1800–1933* (1998)

Promises Postponed

Ruth Schwartz Cowan, *More Work for Mother* (1982)

Ann Douglas, *Terrible Honesty: Mongrel Manhattan in the 1920s* (1995)

Nathan I. Huggins, *Harlem Renaissance* (1971)

Cary D. Mintz, *Black Culture and the Harlem Renaissance* (1988)

Kathy H. Ogren, *The Jazz Revolution: Twenties America and the Meaning of Jazz* (1989)

George J. Sanchez, *Becoming Mexican American* (1993)

Judith Stein, *The World of Marcus Garvey* (1985)

Biography

Edith L. Blumhofer, *Aimee Semple McPherson* (1993)

David Burner, *Herbert Hoover: The Public Life* (1979)

Robert Creamer, *Babe: The Legend Comes to Life* (1975)

Neal Gabler, *Winchell: Gossip, Power, and the Culture of Celebrity* (1994)

David Levering Lewis, *W. E. B. DuBois: The Fight for Equality and the American Century, 1919–1963* (2000)

Fred Hobson, *Mencken: A Life* (1994)

David Nasaw, *The Chief: The Life of William Randolph Hearst* (2000)

Arnold Rampersad, *The Life of Langston Hughes,* 2 vols. (1986–88)

David Robinson, *Chaplin* (1985)

Robert A. Slayton, *Empire Statesman: The Rise and Redemption of Al Smith* (2001)

HISTORY ON THE INTERNET

http://jurist.law.pitt.edu/trials17.htm

This University of Missouri–Kansas City Law School site contains a legal analysis of the Sacco-Vanzetti trial.

The Inaugural Addresses of the three Republican presidents of the 1920s:

http://www.bartleby.com/124/pres46.html

Warren G. Harding

http://www.bartleby.com/124/pres47.html

Calvin Coolidge

http://www.bartleby.com/124/pres48.html

Herbert Hoover

http://www.nara.gov/education/cc/prohib.html

Several original photographs, primary documents, and the laws relating to Prohibition are posted on this National Archives site.

http://www.law.umkc.edu/faculty/projects/ftrials/ scopes/scopes.htm

This University of Missouri–Kansas City Law School site has a very thorough site on the Scopes Monkey Trial (1925).

THE GREAT DEPRESSION AND THE NEW DEAL

▷ 1929–1940

Reginald Marsh (1898–1954), *The Park Bench*, 1933. Tempera on masonite on panel, 24 × 36 in. Sheldon Memorial Art Gallery, University of Nebraska–Lincoln, Nebraska Art Association Collection 1938.N–43.

AMERICAN COMMUNITIES

Sit-Down Strike at Flint: Automobile Workers Organize a New Union

IN THE GLOOMY EVENING OF FEBRUARY 11, 1937, 400 TIRED, UNSHAVEN, but very happy strikers marched out of the sprawling automobile factory known as Fisher Body Number 1. Most carried American flags and small bundles of clothing. A makeshift banner on top of the plant announced "Victory Is Ours." A wildly cheering parade line of a thousand supporters greeted the strikers at the gates. Shouting with joy, honking horns, and singing songs, the celebrants marched to two other factories to greet other emerging strikers. After forty-four days, the great Flint sit-down strike was over.

Flint, Michigan, was the heart of production for General Motors, the largest corporation in the world. In 1936 GM's net profits had reached $285 million, and its total assets were $1.5 billion. Originally a center for lumbering and then carriage making, Flint had boomed with the auto industry during the 1920s. Thousands of migrants streamed into the city, attracted by assembly-line jobs averaging about $30 a week. By 1930 Flint's population had grown to about 150,000 people, 80 percent of whom depended on work at General Motors. A severe housing shortage made living conditions difficult. Tar-paper shacks, tents, even railroad cars were the only shelter available for many. Parts of the city resembled a mining camp.

The Great Depression hit Flint very hard. Employment at GM fell from a 1929 high of 56,000 to fewer than 17,000 in 1932. As late as 1938 close to half the city's families were receiving some kind of emergency relief. By that time, as in thousands of other American communities, Flint's private and county relief agencies had been overwhelmed by the needs of the unemployed and their families. Two new national agencies based in Washington, D.C., the Federal Emergency Relief Administration and the Works Progress Administration, had replaced local sources of aid during the economic crisis.

The United Automobile Workers (UAW) came to Flint in 1936 seeking to organize GM workers into one industrial union. The previous year, Congress had passed the National Labor Relations Act (also known as the Wagner Act), which made union organizing easier by guaranteeing the right of workers to join unions and to bargain collectively. The act established the National Labor Relations Board to oversee union elections and prohibit illegal antiunion activities by employers. But the obstacles to labor organizing were still enormous. Unemployment was high, and GM had maintained a vigorous antiunion policy for years. By the fall of 1936, the UAW had signed up only a thousand members. The key moment came with the seizure of two Flint GM plants by a few hundred auto workers on December 30, 1936. The idea was to stay in the factories until strikers could achieve a collective bargaining agreement with General Motors. "We don't aim to keep the plants or try to run them," explained one sit-downer to a reporter, "but we want to see that nobody takes our jobs. We don't think we're breaking the law, or at least we don't think we're doing anything really bad."

The sit-down strike was a new and daring tactic that gained popularity among American industrial workers during the 1930s. In 1936 there were forty-eight sit-downs involving nearly 90,000 workers, and in 1937 some 400,000 workers participated in 477 sit-down strikes. Sit-downs expressed the militant exuberance of the rank and file. As one union song of the day put it:

When they tie the can to a union man,
Sit down! Sit down!
When they give him the sack they'll take him back,
Sit down! Sit down!
When the speed up comes, just twiddle your thumbs,
Sit down! Sit down!
When the boss won't talk don't take a walk,
Sit down! Sit down!

The Flint strikers carefully organized themselves into what one historian called "the sit-down community." Each plant elected a strike committee and appointed its own police chief and sanitary engineer. Strikers were divided into "families" of fifteen, each with a captain. No alcohol was allowed, and strikers were careful not to destroy company property. Committees were organized for every conceivable purpose: food, recreation, sanitation, education, and contact with the outside. Sit-downers formed glee clubs and small orchestras to entertain themselves. Using loud-speakers, they broadcast concerts and speeches to their supporters outside the gates. A Women's Emergency Brigade—the strikers' wives, mothers, and daughters—provided crucial support preparing food and maintaining militant picket lines.

As the sit-down strike continued through January 1937, support in Flint and around the nation grew. Overall production in the GM empire dropped from 53,000 vehicles per week to 1,500. Reporters and union supporters flocked to the plants. On January 11, in the so-called Battle of Running Bulls, strikers and their supporters clashed violently with Flint police and private GM guards. Michigan governor Frank Murphy, sympathetic to the strikers, brought in the National Guard to protect them. He refused to enforce an injunction obtained by GM to evict the strikers.

In the face of determined unity by the sit-downers, GM gave in and recognized the UAW as the exclusive bargaining agent in all sixty of its factories. The strike was perhaps the most important in American labor history, sparking a huge growth in union membership in the automobile and other mass-production industries. Rose Pesotta, a textile union organizer, described the wild victory celebration in Flint's overflowing Pengelly Building: "People sang and joked and laughed and cried, deliriously joyful. Victory meant a freedom they had never known before. No longer would they be afraid to join unions."

Out of the tight-knit, temporary community of the sit-down strike emerged a looser yet more permanent kind of community: a powerful, nationwide trade union of automobile workers. The UAW struggled successfully to win recognition and collective bargaining rights from other carmakers, such as Chrysler and Ford. The national UAW, like other new unions in the mass-production industries, was composed of locals around the country. The permanent community of unionized auto workers won significant improvements in wages, working conditions, and benefits. Locals also became influential in the political and social lives of their larger communities—industrial cities such as Flint, Detroit, and Toledo. Nationally, organized labor became a crucial component of the New Deal political coalition and a key power broker in the Democratic Party. The new reality of a national community of organized labor would alter the national political and economic landscape for decades to come. ■

Flint

KEY TOPICS

- Causes and consequences of the Great Depression

- The politics of hard times

- Franklin D. Roosevelt and the two New Deals

- The expanding federal sphere in the West

- American cultural life during the 1930s

- Legacies and limits of New Deal reform

HARD TIMES

No event of the twentieth century had a more profound impact on American life than the Great Depression of the 1930s. Statistics can document a slumping economy, mass unemployment, and swelling relief rolls—but these numbers tell only part of the story. The emotional and psychological toll of these years, what one writer called "the invisible scar," must also be considered in understanding the worst economic crisis in American history. Even today, Depression-era experiences retain a central, even mythical, place in the lives and memories of millions of American families.

The Bull Market

Stock trading in the late 1920s captured the imagination of the broad American public. The stock market resembled a sporting arena, millions following stock prices as they did the exploits of Babe Ruth or Jack Dempsey. Many business leaders and economists as much as told Americans that it was their duty to buy stocks. John J. Raskob, chairman of the board of General Motors, wrote an article for the *Ladies' Home Journal* titled "Everybody Ought to Be Rich." A person who saved $15 each month and invested it in good common stocks would, he claimed, have $80,000 within twenty years. *The Saturday Evening Post* printed a poem that captured the fever:

> *Oh, hush thee, my babe, granny's bought some more shares*
> *Daddy's gone out to play with the bulls and the bears,*
> *Mother's buying on tips and she simply can't lose,*
> *And baby shall have some expensive new shoes!*

During the bull market of the 1920s, stock prices increased at roughly twice the rate of industrial production. Paper value far outran real value. By the end of the decade, stocks that had been bought mainly on the basis of their earning power, which was passed on to stockholders in the form of dividends, now came to be purchased only for the resale value after their prices rose. Anyone reading the financial pages of a newspaper would be amazed at the upward climb. In 1928 alone, for example, the price of Radio Corporation of America stock shot up from $85 to $420; Chrysler stock more than doubled, from $63 to $132.

Yet only about 4 million Americans owned any stocks at all, out of a total population of 120 million. Many of these stock buyers had been lured into the market through easy-credit, margin accounts. Margin accounts allowed investors to purchase stocks by making a small down payment (as low as 10 percent), borrowing the rest from a broker, and using the shares as collateral, or security, on the loan. Just as installment plans had stimulated the automobile and other industries, "buying on the margin" brought new customers to the stock market. Investment trusts, similar to today's mutual funds, attracted many new investors with promises of high returns based on their managers' expert knowledge of the market. Corporations with excess capital found that lending money to stockbrokers was more profitable than plowing it back into their own plants to develop new technologies. All these new approaches to buying stock contributed to an expansive and optimistic atmosphere on Wall Street.

The Crash

Although often portrayed as a one- or two-day catastrophe, the Wall Street crash of 1929 was in reality a steep downward slide. The bull market peaked in early September, and prices drifted downward. On October 23 the Dow Jones industrials lost 21 points in one hour, and many large investors concluded the boom was over. The boom itself rested on expectations of continually rising prices; once those expectations began to melt, the market had to decline. On Monday, October 28, the Dow lost 38 points, or 13 percent of its value. On October 29, "Black Tuesday," the bottom

Stockbrokers, their customers, and employees of the New York Stock Exchange gather nervously on Wall Street during the stock market crash of 1929. October 29 was the worst single day in the 112-year history of the exchange, as panic selling caused many stocks to lose half their value.

SOURCE: Brown Brothers (010634-1).

seemed to fall out. Over 16 million shares, more than double the previous record, were traded as panic selling took hold. For many stocks no buyers were available at any price.

The situation worsened. The market's fragile foundation of credit, based on the margin debt, quickly crumbled. Many investors with margin accounts had no choice but to sell when stock values fell. Since the shares themselves represented the security for their loans, more money had to be put up to cover the loans when prices declined. By mid-November about $30 billion in the market price of stocks had been wiped out. Half the value of the stocks listed in the *New York Times* index was lost in ten weeks.

The nation's political and economic leaders downplayed the impact of Wall Street's woes. "The fundamental business of the country," President Herbert Hoover told Americans in late October, "is on a sound and prosperous basis." Secretary of the Treasury Andrew Mellon spoke for many in the financial world when he described the benefits of the slump: "It will purge the rottenness out of the system. High costs of living and high living will come down. People will work harder, live a more moral life. Values will be adjusted, and enterprising people will pick up the wrecks from less competent people." At the end of 1929 hardly anyone was predicting that a depression would follow the stock market crash.

	DISTRIBUTION OF TOTAL FAMILY INCOME AMONG VARIOUS SEGMENTS OF THE POPULATION, 1929–1944 (IN PERCENTAGES)					
Year	Poorest Fifth	Second Poorest Fifth	Middle Fifth	Second Wealthiest Fifth	Wealthiest Fifth	Wealthiest 5 Percent
1929	12.5		13.8	19.3	54.4	30.0
1935–1936	4.1	9.2	14.1	20.9	51.7	26.5
1941	4.1	9.5	15.3	22.3	48.8	24.0
1944	4.9	10.9	16.2	22.2	45.8	20.7

SOURCE: Adapted from U.S. Bureau of the Census, *Historical Statistics of the United States, Colonial Times to 1970,* Bicentennial ed. (Washington, D.C.: U.S. Government Printing Office, 1975), p. 301.

Underlying Weaknesses

It would be oversimple to say that the stock market crash "caused" the Great Depression. But like a person who catches a chill, the economy after the crash became less resistant to existing sources of infection. The resulting sickness revealed underlying economic weaknesses left over from the previous decade. First, workers and consumers by and large received too small a share of the enormous increases in labor productivity. Better machinery and more efficient industrial organization had increased labor productivity enormously. But wages and salaries had not risen nearly as much.

In effect, the automobile of American capitalism had one foot pressed to the accelerator of production and another on the brake of consumption. Between 1923 and 1929 manufacturing output per worker-hour increased by 32 percent. But wages during the same period rose only 8 percent, or one-quarter the rise in productivity. Moreover, the rise in productivity itself had encouraged overproduction in many industries. The farm sector had never been able to regain its prosperity of the World War I years. Farmers suffered under a triple burden of declining prices for their crops, a drop in exports, and large debts incurred by wartime expansion (see Chapter 23).

The most important weakness in the economy was the extremely unequal distribution of income and wealth. In 1929, the top 0.1 percent of American families (24,000 families) had an aggregate income equal to that of the bottom 42 percent (11.5 million families). The top 5 percent of American families received 30 percent of the nation's income; the bottom 60 percent got only 26 percent. About 71 percent of American families had annual incomes below $2,500. Nearly 80 percent of the nation's families (21.5 million households) had no savings; the top 0.1 percent held 34 percent of all savings. The top 0.5 percent of Americans owned 32.4 percent of the net wealth of the entire population—the greatest such concentration of wealth in the nation's history.

The stock market crash undermined the confidence, investment, and spending of businesses and the well-to-do. Manufacturers decreased their production and began laying off workers, and layoffs brought further declines in consumer spending and another round of production cutbacks. A spurt of consumer spending might have checked this downward spiral, but consumers had less to spend as industries laid off workers and reduced work hours. With a shrinking market for products, businesses were hesitant to expand. A large proportion of the nation's banking funds were tied to the speculative bubble of Wall Street stock buying. Many banks began to fail as anxious depositors withdrew their funds, which were uninsured. Thousands of families lost their savings to these failures. An 86 percent plunge in agricultural prices between 1929 and 1933, compared to a decline in agricultural production of only 6 percent, brought suffering to America's farmers.

Mass Unemployment

At a time when unemployment insurance did not exist and public relief was completely inadequate, the loss of a job could mean economic catastrophe for workers and their families. Massive unemployment across America became the most powerful sign of a deepening depression. In 1930 the Department of Labor estimated that 4.2 million workers, or roughly 9 percent of the labor force, were out of work. These figures nearly doubled in 1931, and by 1933, 12.6 million workers—over one-quarter of the labor force—were without jobs. Other sources put the figure that year above 16 million, or nearly one out of every three workers. None of these statistics tells us how long people were unemployed or how many Americans found only part-time work.

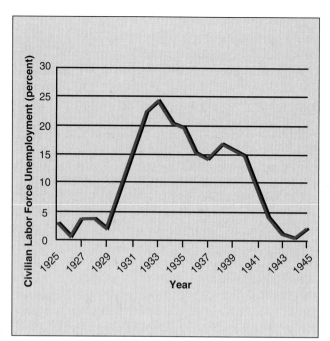

Unemployment, 1929–1945 In 1939, despite six years of New Deal programs, unemployment still hovered around 18 percent of the workforce. Only the onset of World War II ended the unemployment crisis.

SOURCE: U.S. Bureau of the Census, *Historical Statistics of the United States, Colonial Times to 1970*, Bicentennial ed. (Washington, D.C.: U.S. Government Printing Office, 1975), p. 135.

Dorothea Lange captured the lonely despair of unemployment in *White Angel Bread Line*, San Francisco, 1933. During the 1920s Lange had specialized in taking portraits of wealthy families, but by 1932 she could no longer stand the contradiction between her portrait business and "what was going on in the street." She said of this photograph: "There are moments such as these when time stands still and all you can do is hold your breath and hope it will wait for you."

SOURCE: Dorothea Lange, *White Angel Bread Line, San Francisco, 1933*. Copyright, the Dorothea Lange Collection, The Oakland Museum of California, City of Oakland. Gift of Paul S. Taylor.

What did it mean to be unemployed and without hope in the early 1930s? Figures give us only an outline of the grim reality. Many Americans, raised believing that they were responsible for their own fate, blamed themselves for their failure to find work. Contemporary journalists and social workers noted the common feelings of shame and guilt expressed by the unemployed. Even those who did not blame themselves struggled with feelings of inadequacy, uselessness, and despair. One unemployed Houston woman told a relief caseworker, "I'm just no good, I guess. I've given up ever amounting to anything. It's no use." "Drives a man crazy, or drives him to drink, hangin' around," said an out-of-work Connecticut knife maker. For many, nighttime was the worst. "What is going to become of us?" wondered an Arizona man. "I've lost twelve and a half pounds this month, just thinking. You can't sleep, you know. You wake up about 2 A.M., and you lie and think." A West Virginia man wrote his senator to complain, "My children have not got no shoes and clothing to go to school with, and we haven't got enough bed clothes to keep us warm." For the most desperate, contemplating suicide was not unusual. "Can you be so kind as to advise me as to which would

be the most humane way to dispose of my self and family, as this is about the only thing that I see left to do," one despondent Pennsylvania man inquired of a state relief agency.

Joblessness proved especially difficult for men between the ages of thirty-five and fifty-five, the period in their lives when family responsibilities were heaviest. Nathan Ackerman, a psychiatrist who went to Pennsylvania to observe the impact of prolonged unemployment on coal miners, found an enormous sense of "internal distress":

They hung around street corners and in groups. They gave each other solace. They were loath to go home because they were indicted, as if it were their fault for being unemployed. A jobless man was a lazy good-for-nothing. The women punished the men for not bringing home the bacon, by withholding themselves sexually. . . . These men suffered from depression. They felt despised, they were ashamed of themselves. They cringed, they comforted one another. They avoided home.

Unemployment upset the psychological balance in many families by undermining the traditional authority of the male breadwinner. Women, because their labor was cheaper than men's, found it easier to hold onto jobs. Female clerks, secretaries, maids, and waitresses earned much less than male factory workers, but their jobs were more likely to survive hard times. Men responded in a variety of ways to unemployment. Some withdrew emotionally; others became angry or took to drinking. A few committed suicide. One Chicago social worker, writing about unemployment in 1934, summed up the strains she found in families: "Fathers feel they have lost their prestige in the home; there is much nagging, mothers nag at the fathers, parents nag at the children. Children of working age who earn meager salaries find it hard to turn over all their earnings and deny themselves even the greatest necessities and as a result leave home."

Pressures on those lucky enough to have a job increased as well. Anna Novak, a Chicago meat packer, recalled the degrading harassment at the hands of foremen: "You could get along swell if you let the boss slap you on the behind and feel you up. God, I hate that stuff, you don't know!" Fear of unemployment and a deep desire for security marked the Depression generation. "I mean there's a conditioning here by the Depression," a sanitation worker told an interviewer many years later. "I'm what I call a security cat. I don't dare switch [jobs]. 'Cause I got too much whiskers on it, seniority."

Hoover's Failure

The enormity of the Great Depression overwhelmed traditional—and meager—sources of relief. In most communities across America these sources were a patchwork of private agencies and local government units, such as towns, cities, or counties. They simply lacked the money, resources, and staff to deal with the worsening situation. In large urban centers like Detroit and Chicago, unemployment approached 50 percent by 1932. Smaller communities could not cope either. One West Virginia coal-mining county with 1,500 unemployed miners had only $9,000 to meet relief needs for that year. Unemployed transients, attracted by warm weather, posed a special problem for communities in California and Florida. By the end of 1931, Los Angeles had 70,000 nonresident jobless and homeless men; new arrivals numbered about 1,200 a day.

There was great irony, even tragedy, in President Hoover's failure to respond to human suffering. He had administered large-scale humanitarian efforts during World War I with great efficiency. Yet he seemed to most people a man with little personal warmth. Hoover made his reputation as an engineer and as one who believed in the importance of objective studies of social and economic problems, yet he failed to face the facts of the Depression. He ignored all the mounting evidence to the contrary when he claimed in his 1931 State of the Union Address, "Our people are providing against distress from unemployment in true American

Isaac Soyer's *Employment Agency*, a 1937 oil painting, offered one of the decade's most sensitive efforts at depicting the anxiety and sense of isolation felt by millions of Depression-era job hunters.

SOURCE: Isaac Soyer, *Employment Agency*, 1937. Oil on canvas, 34½″ × 45″, (87 × 114.3 cm). Whitney Museum of American Art, New York.

fashion by magnificent response to public appeal and by action of the local governments."

Hoover resisted the growing calls from Congress and local communities for a greater federal role in relief efforts or public works projects. He worried, as he told Congress after vetoing one measure, about injuring "the initiative and enterprise of the American people." The President's Emergency Committee for Unemployment, established in 1930, and its successor, the President's Organization for Unemployment Relief (POUR), created in 1931, did little more than encourage local groups to raise money to help the unemployed. Walter S. Gifford, chairman of POUR and president of AT&T, insisted that local relief groups could handle the needs of Americans in distress. "My sober and considered judgement," he told Congress in early 1932, "is that at this stage Federal aid would be a disservice to the unemployed."

Hoover's plan for recovery centered on restoring business confidence. His administration's most important institutional response to the depression was the Reconstruction Finance Corporation (RFC), established in early 1932 and based on the War Finance Corporation of the World War I years. The RFC was designed to make government credit available to ailing banks, railroads, insurance companies, and other businesses, thereby stimulating economic activity. The key assumption here was that the credit problem was one of supply (for businesses) rather than demand (from consumers). But given the public's low purchasing power, most businesses were not interested in obtaining loans for expansion.

The RFC managed to save numerous banks and other businesses from going under, but its approach did not hasten recovery. And Hoover was loath to use the RFC to make direct grants to states, cities, or individuals. In July 1932, congressional Democrats pushed through the Emergency Relief Act, which authorized the RFC to lend $300 million to states that had exhausted their own relief funds. Hoover grudgingly signed the bill, but less than $30 million had actually been given out by the end of 1933. Although Congress authorized the RFC to spend money on public works, only a small fraction of its $2 billion budget went to such programs.

Protest and the Election of 1932

By 1932, the desperate mood of many Americans was finding expression in direct, sometimes violent protests that were widely covered in the press. On March 7, Communist organizers led a march of several thousand Detroit auto workers and unemployed to the Ford River Rouge factory in nearby Dearborn. When the demonstrators refused orders to turn back, Ford-controlled police fired tear gas and bullets, killing four and seriously wounding fifty others. Some 40,000 people attended a tense funeral service a few days later. Desperate farmers in Iowa organized the Farmers' Holiday Association, aimed at raising prices by refusing to sell produce. In August, some 1,500 farmers turned back cargo trucks outside Sioux City, Iowa, and made a point by dumping milk and other perishables into ditches.

The spring of 1932 also saw the "Bonus Army" begin descending on Washington, D.C. This protest took its name from a 1924 act of Congress that had promised a $1,000 bonus—in the form of a bond that would not mature until 1945—to every veteran of World War I. The veterans who were gathering in Washington demanded immediate payment of the bonus in cash. By summer they and their families numbered around 20,000 and were camped out all over the capital city. Their lobbying convinced the House to pass a bill for immediate payment, but the Senate rejected the bill and most of the veterans left. At the end of July, U.S. Army troops led by Chief of Staff General Douglas MacArthur forcibly evicted the remaining 2,000 veterans from their encampment. MacArthur exaggerated the menace of the peaceful demonstrators, insisting they were driven by "the essence of revolution." The spectacle of these unarmed and unemployed men, the heroes of 1918, being driven off by bayonets and bullets provided the most disturbing evidence yet of the failure of Hoover's administration.

The congressional elections of 1930 had already revealed a growing dissatisfaction with Hoover's approach. Democrats had won control of the House of Representatives for the first time since 1916 and gained eight seats in the Senate. In 1932, Democrats nominated Franklin D. Roosevelt, governor of New York, as their candidate. Roosevelt's acceptance speech stressed the need for reconstructing the nation's economy. "I pledge you, I pledge myself," he said, "to a new deal for the American people."

Roosevelt's plans for recovery were vague at best. He frequently attacked Hoover for reckless and extravagant spending and accused him of trying to center too much power in Washington. He also spoke of the need for government to meet "the problem of underconsumption" and to help in "distributing wealth and products more equitably." Hoover bitterly condemned Roosevelt's ideas as a "radical departure" from the American way of life. But with the Depression growing worse every day, probably any Democrat would have defeated Hoover. The Democratic victory was overwhelming. Roosevelt carried forty-two states, taking the electoral college 472 to 59 and the popular vote by about 23 million to 16 million. Democrats won big majorities in both the House and the Senate. The stage was set for FDR's "new deal."

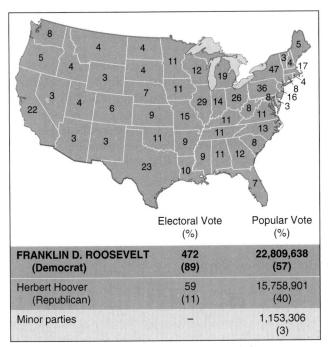

	Electoral Vote (%)	Popular Vote (%)
FRANKLIN D. ROOSEVELT (Democrat)	**472 (89)**	**22,809,638 (57)**
Herbert Hoover (Republican)	59 (11)	15,758,901 (40)
Minor parties	–	1,153,306 (3)

The Election of 1932 Democrats owed their overwhelming victory in 1932 to the popular identification of the Depression with the Hoover administration. Roosevelt's popular vote was about the same as Hoover's in 1928, and FDR's electoral college margin was even greater.

FDR AND THE FIRST NEW DEAL

No president of this century had a greater impact on American life and politics than Franklin Delano Roosevelt. To a large degree, the New Deal was a product of his astute political skills and the sheer force of his personality. The only president ever elected to four terms, FDR would loom as the dominant personality in American political life through depression and war. Roosevelt's leadership also inaugurated a forty-year-long period during which the Democrats would be the nation's majority party.

FDR the Man

Franklin Delano Roosevelt was born in 1882 in Dutchess County, New York, where he grew up an only child, secure and confident, on his family's vast estate. Franklin's father, James, had made a fortune through railroad investments, but he was already in his fifties when Franklin was born, and it was his mother, Sara Delano, who was the dominant figure in his childhood. Roosevelt's education at Groton, Harvard, and Columbia Law School reinforced the aristocratic values of his family: a strong sense of civic duty, the importance of competitive athletics, and a commitment to public service.

In 1905, Franklin married his distant cousin, Anna Eleanor Roosevelt, niece of President Theodore Roosevelt. Eleanor would later emerge as an influential adviser and political force on her own. Franklin turned to politics as a career early on. He was elected as a Democrat to the New York State Senate in 1910, served as assistant navy secretary from 1913 to 1920, and was nominated for vice president by the Democrats in the losing 1920 campaign.

In the summer of 1921 Roosevelt was stricken with polio at his summer home. He was never to walk again without support. The disease strengthened his relationship with Eleanor, who encouraged him not only to fight his handicap but to continue his political career. The disease and FDR's response to it proved a turning point. His patience and determination in fighting the illness transformed him. The wealthy aristocrat, for whom everything had come relatively easy, now personally understood the meaning of struggle and hardship. "Once I spent two years lying in bed trying to move my big toe," he recalled. "After that anything else seems easy."

Elected governor of New York in 1928, Roosevelt served two terms and won a national reputation for reform. As governor, his achievements included instituting unemployment insurance, strengthening child labor laws, providing tax relief for farmers, and providing pensions for the old. As the Depression hit the state, he slowly increased public works and set up a Temporary Emergency Relief Administration. With his eye on the White House, he began assembling a group of key advisers, the "brains trust," who would follow him to Washington. The central figures were Columbia Law School professor and progressive Raymond Moley; two economists, Rexford G. Tugwell and Adolf A. Berle; and attorneys Samuel Rosenman, Basil O'Connor, and Felix Frankfurter. The "brain trusters" shared a faith in the power of experts to set the economy right and a basic belief in government–business cooperation. They rejected the old progressive dream of re-creating an ideal society of small producers. Structural economic reform, they argued, must accept the modern reality of large corporate enterprise based on mass production and distribution.

Restoring Confidence

In the first days of his administration Roosevelt conveyed a sense of optimism and activism that helped restore the badly shaken confidence of the nation. "First of all," he told Americans in his Inaugural Address on March 4, 1933, "let me assert my firm belief that the only thing we have to fear is fear itself." The very next day he issued an executive order calling for a four-day "bank holiday" to shore up the country's ailing financial system. More than 1,300 banks failed in 1930, more than 2,000 in 1931. Contemporary investigations had revealed a disquieting pattern of stock manipulation, illegal loans to bank officials, and tax evasion that helped erode public confidence in the banking system. Between election day and the inauguration, the banking system had come alarmingly close to shutting down altogether due to widespread bank failures and the hoarding of currency.

Roosevelt therefore called for a special session of Congress to deal with the banking crisis as well as with unemployment aid and farm relief. On March 12 he broadcast his first "fireside chat" to explain the steps he had taken to meet the financial emergency. These radio broadcasts became a standard part of Roosevelt's political technique, and they proved enormously suc-

This *New Yorker* magazine cover depicted an ebullient Franklin D. Roosevelt riding to his 1933 inauguration in the company of a glum Herbert Hoover. This drawing typified many mass media images of the day contrasting the different moods and temperaments of the new President and the defeated incumbent. SOURCE: By Peter Arno, March 4, 1933. Franklin D. Roosevelt Library (CT65-521).

cessful. They gave courage to ordinary Americans and communicated a genuine sense of compassion from the White House.

Congress immediately passed the Emergency Banking Act, which gave the president broad discretionary powers over all banking transactions and foreign exchange. It authorized healthy banks to reopen only under licenses from the Treasury Department and provided for greater federal authority in managing the affairs of failed banks. By the middle of March about half the country's banks, holding about 90 percent of the nation's deposits, were open for business again. Banks began to attract new deposits from people who had been holding back their money. The bank crisis had passed.

The Hundred Days

From March to June of 1933—the "Hundred Days"—FDR pushed through Congress an extraordinary number of acts designed to combat various aspects of the Depression. What came to be called the New Deal was no unified program to end the Depression but rather an improvised series of reform and relief measures, some of which seemed to contradict each other. Roosevelt responded to pressures from Congress, from business, and from organized labor, but he also used his own considerable influence over public opinion to get his way. His program focused on reviving both the industrial and agricultural sectors of the economy along with providing emergency relief for the unemployed.

Five measures were particularly important and innovative. The Civilian Conservation Corps (CCC), established in March 1933 as an unemployment relief effort, provided work for jobless young men in protecting and conserving the nation's natural resources. Road construction, reforestation, flood control, and national park improvements were some of the major projects performed in work camps across the country. CCC workers received room and board and $30 each month, up to $25 of which had to be sent home to dependents. By the time the program was phased out in 1942, more than 2.5 million youths had worked in some 1,500 CCC camps.

In May, Congress authorized $500 million for the Federal Emergency Relief Administration (FERA). Half the money went as direct relief to the states; the rest was distributed on the basis of a dollar of federal aid for every three dollars of state and local funds spent for relief. This system of outright federal grants differed significantly from Hoover's approach, which provided only for loans. Establishment of work relief projects, however, was left to state and local governments.

The Agricultural Adjustment Administration (AAA) was set up to provide immediate relief to the nation's farmers. The AAA established a new federal role in agri-

OVERVIEW

KEY LEGISLATION OF THE FIRST NEW DEAL ("HUNDRED DAYS," MARCH 9–JUNE 16, 1933)

Legislation	Purpose
Emergency Banking Relief Act	Enlarged federal authority over private banks Government loans to private banks
Civilian Conservation Corps	Unemployment relief Conservation of natural resources
Federal Emergency Relief Administration	Direct federal money for relief, funneled through state and local governments
Agricultural Adjustment Administration	Federal farm-aid based on parity pricing and subsidy
Tennessee Valley Authority	Economic development and cheap electricity for Tennessee Valley
National Industrial Recovery Act	Self-regulating industrial codes to revive economic activity
Public Works Administration	Federal public works projects to increase employment and consumer spending

cultural planning and price setting. It established parity prices for basic farm commodities, including corn, wheat, hogs, cotton, rice, and dairy products. The concept of parity pricing was based on the purchasing power that farmers had enjoyed during the prosperous years of 1909 to 1914. That period now became the benchmark for setting the prices of farm commodities. The AAA also incorporated the principle of subsidy, whereby farmers received benefit payments in return for reducing acreage or otherwise cutting production where surpluses existed. The funds for these payments were to be raised from new taxes on food processing.

The AAA raised total farm income and was especially successful in pushing up the prices of wheat, cotton, and corn. But it had some troubling side effects as well. Landlords often failed to share their AAA payments with tenant farmers, and they frequently used benefits to buy tractors and other equipment that displaced sharecroppers. Many Americans were disturbed, too, by the sight of surplus crops, livestock, and milk being destroyed while millions went hungry. The Southern Tenant Farmers Union (STFU), founded in 1934, emerged as an important voice of protest against AAA policies. Active in six states and composed of about 30,000 tenant farmers (over half of whom were black), the STFU protested evictions, called strikes to raise farm labor wages, and challenged landlords to give tenants their fair share of subsidy payments. The STFU succeeded in drawing national attention to the plight of sharecroppers and tenant farmers, but it failed

to influence national farm policy. The 1937 Bankhead-Jones Tenancy Act offered a very limited program of loans to tenant farmers, and the AAA remained a boon to large landlords.

The Tennessee Valley Authority (TVA) proved to be one of the most unique and controversial projects of the New Deal era. It had its origins in the federal government's effort during World War I to build a large hydroelectric power complex and munitions plant on the Tennessee River at Muscle Shoals, Alabama. During the 1920s, Republican senator George W. Norris of Nebraska had led an unsuccessful fight to provide for permanent government operation of the Muscle Shoals facilities on behalf of the area's population. The TVA, an independent public corporation, built dams and power plants, produced cheap fertilizer for farmers, and, most significantly, brought cheap electricity for the first time to thousands of people in six southern states. Denounced by some as a dangerous step toward socialism, the TVA stood for decades as a model of how careful government planning could dramatically improve the social and economic welfare of an underdeveloped region.

On the very last of the Hundred Days, Congress passed the National Industrial Recovery Act, the closest attempt yet at a systematic plan for economic recovery. It had two main parts. The National Recovery Administration (NRA) sought to stimulate production and competition in business by means of industrial codes regulating prices, output, and trade practices. In theory,

A recruitment poster represents the Civilian Conservation Corps as much more than simply an emergency relief measure, stressing character building and the opportunity for self-improvement. By the time the CCC expired in 1942 it had become one of the most popular of all the New Deal programs.

SOURCE: Albert M. Bender, *CCC—A Young Man's Opportunity for Work, Play, Study and Health,* 1941. © CORBIS (IH151596).

each industry would be self-governed by a code hammered out by representatives of business, labor, and the consuming public. Once approved by the NRA in Washington, led by General Hugh Johnson and symbolized by the distinctive Blue Eagle stamp, the codes would have the force of law. In practice, almost all the NRA codes were written by the largest firms in any given industry; labor and consumers got short shrift. The sheer administrative complexities involved with code writing and compliance made a great many people unhappy with the NRA's operation. Overall, the NRA looked to business and industry leaders to find a way to recovery.

The second component, the Public Works Administration (PWA), led by Secretary of the Interior Harold Ickes, authorized $3.3 billion for the construction of roads, public buildings, and other projects. The idea was to provide jobs and thus stimulate the economy through increased consumer spending. A favorite image for this kind of spending was "priming the pump." Just as a farmer had to prime a pump with water before it could draw more water from the well, the government had to prime the economy with jobs for the unemployed. Eventually the PWA spent over $4.2 billion building roads, schools, post offices, bridges, courthouses, and other public buildings around the country. In thousands of communities today, these structures remain the most tangible reminders of the New Deal era.

LEFT TURN AND THE SECOND NEW DEAL

The Hundred Days legislative package tried to offer something for everybody. Certainly the active, can-do spirit in Washington brought reassurance that the nation was back on track. Yet the Depression remained a stark reality for many millions. From the beginning, the New Deal had loud and powerful critics who complained bitterly that FDR had overstepped the traditional boundaries of government action. Others were angry that Roosevelt had not done nearly enough. These varied voices of protest helped shape the political debates of FDR's first term. Ultimately, they would push the New Deal in more radical directions.

Roosevelt's Critics

Criticism of the New Deal came from the right and the left. On the right, pro-Republican newspapers and the American Liberty League, a group of conservative businessmen organized in 1934, denounced Roosevelt and his advisers. They held the administration responsible for what they considered an attack on property rights, for the growing welfare state, and for the decline of personal liberty. Dominated by wealthy executives of Du Pont and General Motors, the league attracted support from a group of conservative Democrats, including Al Smith, the former presidential candidate, who declared the New Deal's laws "socialistic." The league supported anti-New Dealers for Congress, but in the 1934 election Democrats built up their majorities from 310 to 319 in the House and from 60 to 69 in the Senate—an unusually strong showing for the incumbent party in a midterm election.

Some of Roosevelt's staunchest early supporters turned critical. Father Charles E. Coughlin, a Catholic priest in suburban Detroit, attracted a huge national radio audience of 40 million listeners with passionate sermons attacking Wall Street, international bankers, and "plutocratic capitalism." Coughlin at first supported Roosevelt and the New Deal, and he tried to build a close personal relationship with the president. But by 1934 the ambitious Coughlin, frustrated by his limited influence on the administration, began attacking FDR. Roosevelt was a tool of special interests, he charged, who wanted dictatorial powers. New Deal policies were part of a Communist conspiracy, threatening community autonomy with centralized federal power. Coughlin finally broke with FDR and founded the National Union for Social Justice. In 1936 the Coughlin-dominated Union Party nominated William Lemke, an obscure North Dakota congressman, to run for president. Lemke polled only 900,000 votes, but Coughlin continued his biting attacks on Roosevelt through 1940.

More troublesome for Roosevelt and his allies were the vocal and popular movements on the left. These found the New Deal too timid in its measures. In California, well-known novelist and socialist Upton Sinclair entered the 1934 Democratic primary for governor by running on a program he called EPIC, for End Poverty in California. He proposed a $50 a month pension for all poor people over age sixty. His campaign also emphasized a government-run system of "production for use" (rather than profit) workshops for the unemployed. Sinclair shocked local and national Democrats by winning the primary easily. He lost a close general election only because the Republican candidate received heavy financial and tactical support from wealthy Hollywood studio executives and frightened regular Democrats.

Another Californian, Francis E. Townsend, a retired doctor, created a large following among senior citizens with his Old Age Revolving Pension plan. He called for payments of $200 per month to all people over sixty, provided the money was spent within thirty days. The pensions would be financed by a national 2 percent tax on all commercial transactions. This plan managed to attract a nationwide following of more than 3 million by 1936. But Townsend's plan was essentially regressive, since it proposed to tax all Americans equally, regardless of their income.

Huey Long, Louisiana's flamboyant backcountry orator, posed the greatest potential threat to Roosevelt's leadership. Long had captured Louisiana's governorship in 1928 by attacking the state's entrenched oil industry and calling for a radical redistribution of wealth. In office, he significantly improved public education, roads, medical care, and other public services, winning the loyalty of the state's poor farmers and industrial workers. Elected to the U.S. Senate in 1930, Long came to Washington with national ambitions. He at first supported Roosevelt, but in 1934 his own presidential

ambitions and his impatience with the pace of New Deal measures led to a break with Roosevelt.

Long organized the Share Our Wealth Society. Its purpose, he thundered, "was to break up the swollen fortunes of America and to spread the wealth among all our people." Limiting the size of large fortunes, Long promised, would mean a homestead worth $5,000 and a $2,500 annual income for everyone. Although Long's economics were fuzzy at best, he undoubtedly touched a deep nerve with his "Every Man a King" slogan. The Democratic National Committee was shocked when a secret poll in the summer of 1935 revealed that Long might attract 3 or 4 million votes. Only his assassination that September by a disgruntled political enemy prevented Long's third-party candidacy, which might have proved disastrous for FDR.

In the nation's work places and streets, a rejuvenated and newly militant labor movement also loomed as a force to be reckoned with. In many industrial cities Unemployed Councils, organized largely by the Communist Party, held marches and rallies demanding public works projects and relief payments. Section 7a of the National Industrial Recovery Act required that workers be allowed to bargain collectively with employers, through representatives of their own choosing. Though this provision of the NIRA was not enforced, it did help raise expectations and spark union organizing. Almost 1.5 million workers took part in some 1,800 strikes in 1934. But employers resisted unionization nearly everywhere, often with violence and the help of local and state police.

In Minneapolis, a local of the International Brotherhood of Teamsters won a bloody strike against the combined opposition of the union's own national officials, vehemently antiunion employers, and a brutal city police force. Violence against strikers helped unite the city's working classes. The Minneapolis Central Labor Union was prepared to support a general strike, and the funeral of a striker shot by police drew 100,000 people. In San Francisco in 1934, a general strike in support of striking members of the International Longshoremen's Association (ILA) effectively shut down the city. Employer use of strikebreakers and violent intimidation prompted an outpouring of support for the ILA from the city's working class, as well as from many shopkeepers and middle-class professionals. When the ILA accepted government arbitration, it won on its main issue—control over the hiring halls on the waterfront. In both Minneapolis and San Francisco, workers had demonstrated the power of labor solidarity and mass protest.

The Second Hundred Days

The popularity of leaders like Sinclair, Townsend, and Long suggested Roosevelt might be losing electoral support among workers, farmers, the aged, and the

OVERVIEW

KEY LEGISLATION OF THE SECOND NEW DEAL (1935–1938)

Legislation	Purpose
Emergency Relief Appropriations Act (1935) (includes Works Progress Administration)	Large-scale public works program for the jobless
Social Security Act (1935)	Federal old-age pensions and unemployment insurance
National Labor Relations Act (1935)	Federal guarantee of right to organize trade unions and collective bargaining
Resettlement Administration (1935)	Relocation of poor rural families Reforestation and soil erosion projects
National Housing Act (1937)	Federal funding for public housing and slum clearance
Fair Labor Standards Act (1938)	Federal minimum wage and maximum hours

unemployed. In early 1935, Roosevelt and his closest advisers responded by turning left and concentrating on a new program of social reform. They had three major goals: strengthening the national commitment to creating jobs; providing security against old age, unemployment, and illness; and improving housing conditions and cleaning slums. What came to be called the "Second Hundred Days" marked the high point of progressive lawmaking in the New Deal.

In April the administration pushed through the Emergency Relief Appropriation Act, which allocated $5 billion for large-scale public works programs for the jobless. New Deal economists, following the theories of Britain's John Maynard Keynes, argued that each government dollar spent had a multiplier effect, pumping two or three dollars into the depressed gross national product. The major responsible agency here was the Works Progress Administration (WPA), led by Harry Hopkins. Born and raised in Iowa, Hopkins had pursued a social work career in New York City. Streetwise, driven by a deep moral passion to help the less fortunate, and impatient with bureaucracy, Hopkins emerged as the key figure in New Deal relief programs. People often referred to him as the "assistant president." Over the next seven years Hopkins oversaw the employment of more than 8 million Americans on a vast array of construction projects: roads, bridges, dams, airports, and sewers. Among the most innovative WPA programs were community service projects that employed thousands of jobless artists, musicians, actors, and writers.

The landmark Social Security Act of 1935 provided for old-age pensions and unemployment insurance. A payroll tax on workers and their employers created a fund from which retirees received monthly pensions after age sixty-five. Payment size depended upon how much employees and their employers had contributed over the years. The unemployment compensation plan established a minimum weekly payment and a minimum number of weeks during which those who lost jobs could collect. The Social Security Board administered this complex system of federal-state cooperation. The original law failed to cover domestics and farm workers, many of whom were Latinos and African Americans. It also made no provisions for casual laborers or public employees. The old-age pensions were quite small at first, as little as $10 a month. And to collect unemployment, one had to have first lost a job. But the law, which has since been amended many times, established the crucial principle of federal responsibility for America's most vulnerable citizens.

Roosevelt and congressional New Dealers called for new legislation to strengthen labor's right to organize after the Supreme Court, in May 1935, ruled the National Industrial Recovery Act unconstitutional, including its provisions protecting union organizing. In July 1935, Congress passed the National Labor Relations Act, often called the Wagner Act for its chief sponsor, Democratic senator Robert F. Wagner of New York. The new law had far-reaching implications for American politics and the economy. For the first time, the federal government guaranteed the right of American workers to join or form independent labor unions and bargain collectively for improved wages, benefits, and working conditions. The National Labor Relations Board would conduct secret-ballot elections in shops and factories to determine which union, if any, workers desired as their sole bargaining agent. The law also defined and prohibited unfair labor practices by employers, including firing workers for union activity. The Wagner Act, described as the "Magna Carta for labor," quickly proved a boon to union growth, especially in previously unorganized industries such as automobiles, steel, and textiles. It set the stage for the sit-down strike in Flint and for General Motors' eventual acceptance of union labor in its factories.

Finally, the Resettlement Administration (RA) produced one of the most utopian New Deal programs, one designed to create new kinds of model communities. Established by executive order and led by key brain truster Rexford G. Tugwell, the RA helped destitute farm families relocate to more productive areas. It granted loans for purchasing land and equipment, and it directed reforestation and soil erosion projects, particularly in the hard-hit Southwest. Due to lack of funds and poor administration, however, only about 1 percent of the projected 500,000 families were actually moved.

Tugwell, one of the New Deal's most ardent believers in planning, was more successful in his efforts at creating model greenbelt communities combining the best of urban and rural environments. "My idea," he wrote, "is to go just outside centers of population, pick up cheap land, build a whole community and entice people into it." Though his vision was only partially fulfilled, several of these communities, such as Greenhills, near Cincinnati, and Greendale, near Milwaukee, still thrive.

Labor's Upsurge: Rise of the CIO

In 1932 the American labor movement was nearly dead. Only 2.8 million workers were union members, a half-million fewer than in 1929 and more than 2 million fewer than in 1920. Yet by 1942, unions claimed more than 10.5 million members, nearly a third of the total nonagricultural workforce. This remarkable turnaround was one of the key events of the Depression era. The growth in the size and power of the labor movement permanently changed the work lives and economic status of millions, as well as the national and local political landscapes.

At the core of this growth was a series of dramatic successes in the organization of workers in large-scale, mass-production industries, such as those producing automobiles, steel, rubber, electrical goods, and textiles. Workers in these fields had largely been ignored by the conservative, craft-conscious unions that dominated the American Federation of Labor. At the 1935 AFL convention, a group of more militant union officials led by John L. Lewis (of the United Mine Workers) and Sidney Hillman (of the Amalgamated Clothing Workers) formed the Committee for Industrial Organization

(CIO). Their goal was to organize mass-production workers by industry rather than by craft. They emphasized the need for opening the new unions to all, regardless of a worker's level of skill. And they differed from nearly all old-line AFL unions by calling for the inclusion of black and women workers.

Lewis was the key figure in the CIO. The gruff son of a Welsh miner, Lewis was articulate, ruthless, and very ambitious. He saw the new legal protection given by the Wagner Act as a historic opportunity. But despite the Act—whose constitutionality was unclear until 1937—Lewis knew that establishing permanent unions in the mass-production industries would be a bruising battle. He committed the substantial resources of the United Mine Workers to a series of organizing drives, focusing first on the steel and auto industries. Many CIO organizers were Communists or radicals of other persuasions, and their dedication, commitment, and willingness to work within disciplined organizations proved invaluable in the often dangerous task of creating industrial unions. Of the roughly 200 full-time organizers on the payroll of the Steel Workers Organizing Committee in 1937, almost a third were members of the Communist Party.

Militant rank-and-file unionists were often ahead of Lewis and other CIO leaders. The sit-down strike—refusing to work but staying in the factory to prevent "scab" workers from taking over—emerged as a popular tactic among rubber and auto workers. After the dramatic breakthrough in the Flint sit-down strike at General Motors, membership in CIO unions grew rapidly. In eight months, membership in the United Automobile Workers alone soared from 88,000 to 400,000. CIO victories in the steel, rubber, and electrical industries followed, but often at a very high cost. One bloody example of the perils of union organizing was the 1937 Memorial Day Massacre in Chicago. In a field near the struck Republic Steel Mill in South Chicago, police fired into a crowd of union supporters, killing ten workers and wounding scores more.

Overall, the success of the CIO's organizing drives was remarkable. In 1938 CIO unions, now boasting nearly 4 million members, withdrew from the AFL and reorganized themselves as the Congress of Industrial Organizations. Ahead lay many hard battles organizing workers in such nonunion bastions as the Ford Motor Company and the textile plants of the South. But for the first time ever, the labor movement had gained a permanent place in the nation's mass-production industries. Organized labor took its place as a key power broker in Roosevelt's New Deal and the national Democratic Party. Frances Perkins, FDR's secretary of labor and the nation's first woman cabinet member, captured the close relationship between the new unionism and the New Deal: "Programs long thought of as merely

Philip Evergood, *American Tragedy* (1937). A classic example of the social realism characteristic of much Depression-era art, this painting depicts the police violence against strikers at the Republic Steel Mill. Evergood was one of many artists who found work in the Federal Art Project painting murals in public buildings.

SOURCE: Philip Evergood, *American Tragedy*, 1937. Oil on canvas, 29½″ × 39½″. Private Collection, Terry Dintenfass Gallery. Photo by Philip Evergood.

labor welfare, such as shorter hours, higher wages, and a voice in the terms of conditions of work, are really essential economic factors for recovery."

The New Deal Coalition at High Tide

Did the American public support Roosevelt and his New Deal policies? Both major political parties looked forward to the 1936 elections as a national referendum, and the campaign itself was an exciting and hard-fought contest. Very few political observers predicted its lopsided result.

Republicans nominated Governor Alfred M. Landon of Kansas, who had gained attention by surviving the Democratic landslide of 1934. Landon, an easygoing, colorless man with little personal magnetism, emphasized a nostalgic appeal to traditional American values. His campaign served as a lightning rod for all those, including many conservative Democrats, who were dissatisfied with Roosevelt and the direction he had taken. Al Smith, the Democratic nominee in 1928, categorically denounced the New Deal as "socialistic" and supported Landon. Kansas Republican William Allen White, editor of the *Emporia Gazette*, attacked the New Deal for building up the federal government and creating "a great political machine centered in Washington."

Roosevelt attacked the "economic royalists" who denied that government "could do anything to protect the citizen in his right to work and his right to live." At the same time, FDR was careful to distance himself from radicalism. "It was this administration," he declared, "which saved the system of private profit and free enterprise after it had been dragged to the brink of ruin." As Roosevelt's campaign crossed the country, his advisers were heartened by huge and enthusiastic crowds, especially in large cities like Chicago and Pittsburgh. Still, the vast majority of the nation's newspapers endorsed Landon. And a widely touted "scientific" poll by the *Literary Digest* forecast a Republican victory in November.

Election day erased all doubts. Roosevelt carried every state but Maine and Vermont, polling 61 percent of the popular vote. Democrats increased their substantial majorities in the House and Senate as well. The *Literary Digest*, it turned out, had drawn the sample for its poll from people whose addresses were listed in telephone directories and car registration records, thus omitting the poorer Americans who had no telephones or cars—and who supported Roosevelt. In 1936 the Democrats drew millions of new voters into the political process and at the same time forged a new coalition of voters that would dominate national politics for two generations.

This "New Deal coalition," as it came to be known, included traditional-minded white southern Democrats, big-city political machines, industrial workers of all races, trade unionists, and many Depression-hit farmers. The Democrats' strong showing in the ethnic wards of America's large urban centers amplified a trend that had begun with Al Smith's 1928 campaign. Organized labor put an unprecedented amount of money and people power into Roosevelt's reelection. Black voters in the North and West, long affiliated with the Republicans as the party of Abraham Lincoln, went Democratic in record numbers. The Great Depression was by no means over. But the New Deal's active response to the nation's misery, particularly the bold initiatives taken in 1935, had obviously struck a powerful chord with the American electorate.

Roosevelt was especially popular among first- and second-generation Catholics and Jews, and the New

Deal drew enthusiastic support from millions in the ethnic working class who had never bothered with politics. As one Slovak worker in Chicago's stock yards put it, "Our people did not know anything about the government until the Depression years. In my neighborhood, I don't remember anyone voting." The severity of the Great Depression had overwhelmed the ethnically based support networks—mutual benefit societies, immigrant banks, and religious charities—that had traditionally helped so many to survive hard times. Working-class voters in large cities like New York, Chicago, Detroit, and Philadelphia increasingly took credit for putting and keeping Democrats in power locally and nationally—and their attitudes toward politics changed. The federal government no longer seemed so remote or irrelevant to their lives. Popular federal programs like Social Security, the WPA, and Home Owners Loan Corporation mortgages changed the consciousness of a generation of the ethnic working class. In exchange for their votes, they now looked to the state—especially the federal government—for relief, protection, and help in achieving the American dream.

THE NEW DEAL AND THE WEST

The New Deal had a more profound impact on the West than on any other region in the nation. Western citizens received more from the federal government in per capita payments for welfare, work relief, and loans than the people of any other section. But perhaps more important, New Deal programs, based on a philosophy of rational planning of resource use, transformed western agriculture, water and energy sources, and Indian policy. From Great Plains farming communities in Kansas and Oklahoma to Pacific coast cities such as Los Angeles and Seattle, federal subsidy and management became an integral part of western life. In the process, the New Deal helped propel the West into the modern era. The region's economic development and politics would now be dominated by a combination of Washington-based bureaucracies, large-scale agriculture, and new industrial enterprises.

The Dust Bowl

An ecological and economic disaster of unprecedented proportions struck the southern Great Plains in the mid-1930s. The region had suffered several drought years in the early 1930s. Such dry spells occurred regularly in roughly twenty-year cycles. But this time the parched earth became swept up in violent dust storms the likes of

which had never been seen before. The dust storms were largely the consequence of years of stripping the landscape of its natural vegetation. During World War I, wheat fetched record-high prices on the world market, and for the next twenty years Great Plains farmers had turned the region into a vast wheat factory.

The wide flatlands of the Great Plains were especially suited to mechanized farming, and gasoline-powered tractors, disc plows, and harvester-thresher combines increased productivity enormously. Back in 1830 it had taken some fifty-eight hours of labor to bring an acre of wheat to the granary; in much of the Great Plains a hundred years later it required less than three hours. As wheat prices fell in the 1920s, farmers broke still more land to make up the difference with increased production. Great Plains farmers had

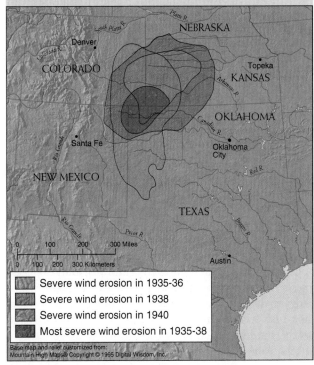

Web Exploration

Through a series of rollover maps, consider the extent of the Dust Bowl from 1935–1940. What were the reasons for this ecological disaster?
www.prenhall.com/faragher/map24.1

The Dust Bowl, 1935–1940   This map shows the extent of the Dust Bowl in the southern Great Plains. Federal programs designed to improve soil conservation, water management, and farming practices could not prevent a mass exodus of hundreds of thousands out of the Great Plains.

created an ecological time bomb that exploded when drought returned in the early 1930s. With native grasses destroyed for the sake of wheat growing, there was nothing left to prevent soil erosion. Dust storms blew away tens of millions of acres of rich topsoil, and thousands of farm families left the region. Those who stayed suffered deep economic and psychological losses from the calamity. The hardest-hit regions were western Kansas, eastern Colorado, western Oklahoma, the Texas Panhandle, and eastern New Mexico. It was the calamity in this southern part of the Great Plains that prompted a Denver journalist to coin the phrase "Dust Bowl."

Black blizzards of dust a mile and a half high rolled across the landscape, darkening the sky and whipping the earth into great drifts of dust that settled over hundreds of miles. Dust storms made it difficult for humans and livestock to breathe and destroyed crops and trees over vast areas. Dust storms turned day into night, terrifying those caught in them. "Dust pneumonia" and other respiratory infections afflicted thousands, and many travelers found themselves stranded in automobiles and trains unable to move. The worst storms occurred in the early spring of 1935. A Garden City, Kansas, woman gave an account of her experience for the *Kansas City Times*:

> All we could do about it was just sit in our dusty chairs, gaze at each other through the fog that filled the room and watch that fog settle slowly and silently, covering everything—including ourselves—in a thick, brownish gray blanket. When we opened the door swirling whirlwinds of soil beat against us unmercifully. The door and windows were all shut tightly, yet those tiny particles seemed to seep through the very walls. It got into cupboards and clothes closets; our faces were as dirty as if we had rolled in the dirt; our hair was gray and stiff and we ground dirt between our teeth.

Several federal agencies intervened directly to relieve the distress. Many thousands of Great Plains farm families were given direct emergency relief by the Resettlement Administration. Other federal assistance included crop and seed loans, moratoriums on loan payments, and temporary jobs with the Works Progress Administration. In most Great Plains counties, from one-fifth to one-third of the families applied for relief; in the hardest-hit communities, as many as 90 percent of the families received direct government aid. The Agricultural Adjustment Administration paid wheat farmers millions of dollars not to grow what they could not sell and encouraged the diversion of acreage from soil-depleting crops like wheat to soil-enriching crops such as sorghum.

Years of Dust. This 1936 poster by the artist and photographer Ben Shahn served to publicize the work of the Resettlement Administration, which offered aid to destitute farm families hit hard by the Dust Bowl. Shahn's stark imagery here was typical of the documentary aesthetic associated with Depression-era art and photography.

SOURCE: The Granger Collection (4EBU96).

To reduce the pressure from grazing cattle on the remaining grasslands, the Drought Relief Service of the Department of Agriculture purchased more than 8 million head of cattle in 1934 and 1935. For a brief time, the federal government was the largest cattle owner in the world. This agency also lent ranchers money to feed their remaining cattle. The Taylor Grazing Act of 1934 brought stock grazing on 8 million acres of public domain lands under federal management.

The federal government also pursued longer-range policies designed to alter land-use patterns, reverse soil erosion, and nourish the return of grasslands. The Department of Agriculture, under Secretary Henry A. Wallace, sought to change farming practices. The spearhead for this effort was the Soil Conservation Service (SCS), which conducted research into controlling wind and water erosion, set up demonstration projects, and offered technical assistance, supplies, and equipment to farmers engaged in conservation work on farms and ranches. The SCS pumped additional federal funds into the Great Plains and created a new rural organization, the soil conservation district, which administered conservation regulations locally.

By 1940 the acreage subject to blowing in the Dust Bowl area of the southern Plains had been reduced from roughly 50 million acres to less than 4 million acres. In the face of the Dust Bowl disaster, New Deal farm policies had restricted market forces in agriculture. But the return of regular rainfall and the outbreak of World War II led many farmers to abandon the techniques that the SCS had taught them to accept. Wheat farming expanded and farms grew as farmers once again pursued commercial agriculture with little concern for its long-term effects on the land.

While large landowners and ranchers reaped sizable benefits from AAA subsidies and other New Deal programs in the southern Plains, tenant farmers and sharecroppers received very little. In the cotton lands of Texas, Oklahoma, Missouri, and Arkansas, thousands of tenant and sharecropper families were forced off the land. They became part of a stream of roughly 300,000 people, disparagingly called "Okies," who migrated to California in the 1930s. California migrants included victims of the Dust Bowl, but the majority were blue-collar workers and small businessmen looking to improve their economic lot. California suffered from the Depression along with the rest of the nation, but it still offered more jobs, higher wages, and higher relief payments than the states of the southern Plains. Most Okies could find work only as poorly paid agricultural laborers in the fertile San Joaquin and Imperial Valley districts. There they faced discrimination and scorn as "poor white trash" while they struggled to create communities amid the squalor of migrant labor camps. Only with the outbreak of World War II and the pressing demand for labor were migrants able to significantly improve their situation.

Mexican farm laborers faced stiff competition from Dust Bowl refugees. By the mid-1930s they no longer dominated California's agricultural workforce. In 1936 an estimated 85 to 90 percent of the state's migratory workers were white Americans, as compared to less than 20 percent before the Depression. Mexican farm worker families who managed to stay employed in California, Texas, and Colorado saw their wages plummet. Southwestern communities, responding to racial hostility from unemployed whites and looking for ways to reduce their welfare burden, campaigned to deport Mexicans and Mexican Americans. Employers, private charities,

and the Immigration and Naturalization Service joined in this effort. Authorities made little effort to distinguish citizens from aliens; most of the children they deported had been born in the United States and were citizens. Los Angeles County had the most aggressive campaign, using boxcars to ship out more than 13,000 Mexicans between 1931 and 1934. The hostile climate convinced thousands more to leave voluntarily. Overall, over 400,000 left the United States during the decade. Some Mexican deportees crossed the border with a melancholy song on their lips:

> And so I take my leave,
> may you be happy.
> Here the song ends,
> but the Depression goes on forever.

Water Policy

The New Deal ushered in an era of large-scale water projects designed to provide irrigation and cheap power and to prevent floods. The long-range impact of these undertakings on western life was enormous. The key government agency in this realm was the Bureau of Reclamation of the Department of the Interior, established under the National Reclamation Act of 1902. The bureau's original responsibility had been to construct dams and irrigation works and thereby encourage the growth of small farms throughout the arid regions of the West. Until the late 1920s the bureau's efforts had been of little consequence, providing irrigation for only a very small portion of land. But its fortunes changed when its focus shifted to building huge multipurpose dams designed to control entire river systems.

The first of these projects was the Boulder Dam (later renamed the Hoover Dam). The dam, actually begun during the Hoover administration, was designed to harness the Colorado River, wildest and most isolated of the major western rivers. Its planned benefits included flood prevention, the irrigation of California's Imperial Valley, the supplying of domestic water for southern California, and the generation of cheap electricity for Los Angeles and southern Arizona. Hoover, however, had opposed the public power aspect of the project, arguing that the government ought not to compete with private utility companies. This position was contrary to that of most Westerners, who believed cheap public power was critical for development. Roosevelt's support for government-sponsored power projects was a significant factor in his winning the political backing of the West in 1932 and subsequent election years.

Boulder Dam was completed in 1935 with the help of funds from the Public Works Administration. Its total cost was $114 million, which was to be offset by the sale of the hydroelectric power it generated.

Web Exploration   Consider the many water projects sponsored by federal agencies during the New Deal. Why were many of these projects located in the West?
www.prenhall.com/faragher/map24.2

The New Deal and Water   This map illustrates U.S. drainage areas and the major large-scale water projects begun or completed by federal agencies during the New Deal. By providing irrigation, cheap power, flood control, and recreation areas, these public works had a historically unprecedented impact on America's western communities.

Los Angeles and neighboring cities built a 259-mile aqueduct, costing $220 million, to channel water to their growing populations. Lake Mead, created by construction of the dam, became the world's largest artificial lake, extending 115 miles up the canyon and providing a popular new recreation area. The dam's irrigation water helped make the Imperial Valley, covering over 500,000 acres, one of the most productive agricultural districts in the world.

The success of Boulder Dam transformed the Bureau of Reclamation into a major federal agency with huge resources at its disposal. In 1938 it completed the All-American Canal—an 80-mile channel connecting the Colorado River to the Imperial Valley, with a 130-mile branch to the Coachella Valley. The canal

cost $24 million to build and carried a flow of water equal to that of the Potomac River. More than a million acres of desert land were opened up to the cultivation of citrus fruits, melons, vegetables, and cotton. Irrigation districts receiving water promised to repay, without interest, the cost of the canal over a forty-year period. This interest-free loan was in effect a huge government subsidy to the private growers who benefited from the canal.

In 1935 the bureau began the giant Central Valley Project (CVP). The Central Valley, stretching through the California interior, is a 500-mile oblong watershed with an average width of 125 miles. The idea was to bring water from the Sacramento River in the north down to the arid lands of the larger San Joaquin Valley in the south. Completed in 1947, the project eventually cost $2.3 billion. The CVP stored water and transferred it to the drier southern regions of the state. It also provided electricity, flood control, and municipal water. The federal government, local municipalities, and buyers of electric power paid most of the cost, and the project proved a boon to large-scale farmers in the Sacramento and San Joaquin river valleys.

The largest power and irrigation project of all was the Grand Coulee Dam, northwest of Spokane, Washington. Completed in 1941, it was designed to convert the power of the Columbia River into cheap electricity and to irrigate previously uncultivated land, thereby stimulating the economic development of the Pacific Northwest. The construction of Grand Coulee employed tens of thousands of workers and pumped millions of dollars into the region's badly depressed economy. Between 1933 and 1940 Washington State ranked first in per capita federal expenditures. In the longer run, Grand Coulee provided the cheapest electricity in the United States and helped attract new manufacturing to a region previously dependent on the export of raw materials, such as lumber and metals.

These technological marvels and the new economic development they stimulated were not without an environmental and human cost. The Grand Coulee and smaller dams nearby reduced the Columbia River, long a potent symbol of the western wilderness, to a string of lakes. Spawning salmon could no longer run the river above the dam. In California, the federal guarantee of river water made a relative handful of large farmers fabulously wealthy. But tens of thousands of farm workers, mostly of Mexican descent, labored in the newly fertile fields for very low wages, and their health suffered from contact with pesticides. The Colorado River, no longer emptying into the Pacific, began to build up salt deposits, making its water increasingly unfit for drinking or irrigation. Water pollution in the form of high salinity continues to plague the 2,000-mile river to this day.

A New Deal for Indians

The New Deal brought important changes and some limited improvements to the lives of Indians. In 1933 some 320,000 Indian people, belonging to about 200 tribes, lived on reservations. Most were in Oklahoma, Arizona, New Mexico, and South Dakota. Indian people suffered from the worst poverty of any group in the nation and an infant mortality rate twice that of the white population. The incidence of alcoholism and other diseases, such as tuberculosis and measles, was much higher on the reservations than off. Half of all those on reservations were landless, forced to rent or live with relatives. The Bureau of Indian Affairs

(BIA), oldest of the federal bureaucracies in the West, had a long history of corruption and mismanagement. The BIA had for years tried to assimilate Indians through education and had routinely interfered with Indian religious affairs and tribal customs. In 1928 the Merriam Report, prepared by the Institute for Government Research, had offered a scathing and widely publicized critique of BIA mismanagement. But the Hoover administration made no effort to reform the agency.

In 1933 President Roosevelt appointed John Collier to bring change to the BIA. Collier had deep roots in progressive-era social work and community organizing in eastern big-city slums. During the 1920s he had become passionately interested in Indian affairs after spending time in Taos, New Mexico. He became involved with the struggle of the Pueblo Indians to hold onto their tribal lands, and he had served as executive secretary of the American Indian Defense Association. As the new BIA head, Collier pledged to "stop wronging the Indians and to rewrite the cruel and stupid laws that rob them and crush their family lives." Collier brought a reformer's zeal to his new job, and he quickly demonstrated his bureaucratic skills. He halted the sale of Indian lands, obtained emergency conservation work for 77,000 Indians under the CCC program, and secured millions of dollars in PWA funds to finance Indian day schools on the reservations. He also fired incompetent and corrupt BIA officials and insisted that those who remained respect tribal customs.

Most important, Collier became the driving force behind the Indian Reorganization Act (IRA) of 1934. The IRA reversed the allotment provisions of the Dawes Severalty Act of 1887, which had weakened tribal sovereignty by shifting the distribution of land from tribes to individuals (see Chapter 18). The new legislation permitted the restoration of surplus reservation lands to tribal ownership and allocated funds for the purchase of additional lands and for economic development. At its heart, the IRA sought to restore tribal structures by making the tribes instruments of the federal government. Any tribe that ratified the IRA could then elect a tribal council that would enjoy federal recognition as the legal tribal government. In this way, Collier argued, tribes would be "surrounded by the protective guardianship of the federal government and clothed with the authority of the federal government." He fought first to get the legislation through a reluctant Congress, which, uneasy with reversing the long-standing policy of Indian assimilation, insisted on many changes to Collier's original plan.

The more difficult battle involved winning approval by Indian peoples. Collier's efforts to win acceptance of the IRA met with mixed results on the reservations. Linguistic barriers made it nearly impossible for some tribes to fully assess the plan. The Papagos of southern Arizona, for example, had no words for "budget" and "representative." Their language made no distinction among the terms "law," "rule," "charter," and "constitution," and they used the same word for "president," "reservation agent," "king," and "Indian commissioner." In all, 181 tribes organized governments under the IRA, while seventy-seven tribes rejected it.

The Navajos, the nation's largest tribe with over 40,000 members, rejected the IRA, illustrating some of the contradictions embedded in federal policy. The Navajo refusal came as a protest against the BIA's forced reduction of their livestock, part of a soil conservation program. The government blamed Navajo sheep for the gullying and erosion that threatened to fill in Lake Mead and make Boulder Dam inoperable. But the hundreds of thousands of sheep in the Navajos' herds were central to their economy and society. They used sheep for barter, to pay religious leaders, and as their primary source of meat.

The Navajos believed the erosion stemmed not from overgrazing but from lack of sufficient water and inadequate acreage on the reservation. Howard Gorman, a Navajo political leader, angrily responded to Collier's last-minute personal appearance before the tribal council: "This thing, the thing you said that will make us strong, what do you mean by it? We have been told that not once but many times this same thing, and all it is is a bunch of lies. . . . You're wasting your time coming here and talking to us." Facing loss of half their sheep, Navajos took their anger out on Collier, rejecting the reorganization plan.

Under Collier's tenure, the BIA became much more sensitive to Indian cultural and religious freedom. The number of Indian people employed by the BIA itself increased from a few hundred in 1933 to more than 4,600 in 1940. Collier trumpeted the principle of Indian political autonomy, a radical idea for the day. But in practice, both the BIA and Congress regularly interfered with reservation governments, especially in money matters. Collier often dictated economic programs for tribes, which Congress usually underfunded. For the long run, Collier's most important legacy was the reassertion of the status of Indian tribes as semisovereign nations. In 1934 a Department of the Interior lawyer, Nathan Margold, wrote a legal opinion that tribal governments retained all their original powers—their "internal sovereignty"—except when these were specifically limited by acts of Congress. In later years U.S. courts would uphold the Margold Opinion, leading to a significant restoration of tribal rights and land to Indian peoples of the West.

DEPRESSION-ERA CULTURE

American culture in the 1930s, like all other aspects of national life, was profoundly shaped by the Great Depression. The themes and images in various cultural forms frequently reflected Depression-related problems. Yet contradictory messages coexisted, sometimes within the same novel or movie. With American capitalism facing its worst crisis, radical expressions of protest and revolution were more common than ever. But there were also strong celebrations of individualism, nostalgia for a simpler, rural past, and searches for core American virtues. The 1930s also saw important shifts in the organization and production of culture. For a brief but significant moment, the federal government offered substantial and unprecedented support to artists and writers. In the realm of popular culture, Hollywood movies, network radio broadcasting, and big-band jazz achieved a central place in the everyday lives of Americans.

A New Deal for the Arts

The Depression hit America's writers, artists, and teachers just as hard as blue-collar workers. In 1935, the WPA allocated $300 million for the unemployed in these fields. Over the next four years, Federal Project No. 1, an umbrella agency covering writing, theater, music, and the visual arts, proved to be one of the most innovative and successful New Deal programs. "Federal One," as it was called, offered work to desperate artists and intellectuals, enriched the cultural lives of millions, and left a substantial legacy of artistic and cultural production. Nearly all these works were informed by the spirit of the documentary impulse, a deep desire to record and communicate the experiences of ordinary Americans. Photographer Lewis Hine defined the documentary attitude simply and clearly: "I wanted to show the things that had to be corrected. I wanted to show the things that had to be appreciated."

At its height, the Federal Writers Project (FWP) employed 5,000 writers on a variety of programs. Most notably, it produced a popular series of state and city guidebooks, each combining history, folklore, and tourism. The 150-volume "Life in America" series included valuable oral histories of former slaves, studies of ethnic and Indian cultures, and pioneering collections of American songs and folk tales. Work on the Writers Project helped many American writers to survive, hone their craft, and go on to great achievement and prominence. These included Ralph Ellison, Richard Wright, Margaret Walker, John Cheever, Saul Bellow, and Zora Neale Hurston. Novelist Anzia Yezierska recalled a strong spirit of camaraderie among

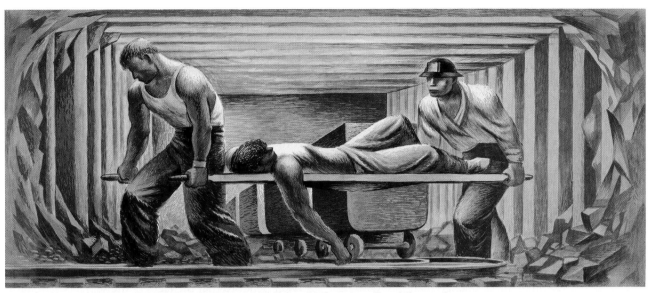

Fletcher Martin painted *Mine Rescue* (1939) in the Kellogg, Idaho post office. The work was part of a Treasury Department program that employed unemployed artists to beautify government buildings. The mural was eventually removed under pressure from local citizens who worried that it might upset those who had lost loved ones in mine accidents.

SOURCE: Fletcher Martin (1904–1979), *Mine Rescue*, 1939. Copyright Smithsonian American Art Museum, Washington, DC/Art Resource, NY (SO137776).

the writers: "Each morning I walked to the Project as lighthearted as if I were going to a party." For poet Muriel Rukeyser, the FWP embodied an essential part of the era: "The key to the 30s was the joy to awake and see life entire and tell the stories of real people."

The Federal Theater Project (FTP), under the direction of the dynamic Hallie Flanagan of Vassar College, reached as many as 30 million Americans with its productions. The FTP sought to expand the audience for theater beyond the regular patrons of the commercial stage. Tickets for its productions were cheap, and it made variety of dramatic forms available. Among its most successful productions were the "Living Newspaper" plays based on contemporary controversies and current events. *Power* concerned the public ownership of utilities; *Triple A Plowed Under* dealt with farm problems; *Injunction Granted* documented unionizing struggles. Other FTP productions brought classics as well as new plays to communities. Among the most successful productions were T. S. Eliot's *Murder in the Cathedral*, Maxwell Anderson's *Valley Forge*, and Orson Welles's version of *Macbeth*, set in Haiti with an all-black cast.

The FTP often came under attack from congressional critics who found it too radical. But Flanagan defended her vision of a theater that confronted political issues. If the plays were mixed with politics, she wrote, "it was because life in our country was mixed with politics. These Arts projects were coming up,

through, and out of the people." The FTP supported scores of community-based theatrical units around the country, giving work and experience to actors, playwrights, directors, and set designers. It brought vital and exciting theater to millions who had never attended before.

Two smaller but similar programs were the Federal Music Project (FMP) and the Federal Art Project (FAP). The FMP, under Nikolai Sokoloff of the Cleveland Symphony Orchestra, employed 15,000 musicians and financed hundreds of thousands of low-priced public concerts by touring orchestras. The Composers' Forum Laboratory supported new works by American composers such as Aaron Copland and William Schuman.

Among the painters who received government assistance through the FAP were Willem de Kooning, Jackson Pollock, and Louise Nevelson. The FAP also employed painters and sculptors to teach studio skills and art history in schools, churches, and settlement houses. The Index of American Design was a comprehensive compilation of American folk art from colonial times. The FAP also commissioned artists to paint hundreds of murals on the walls of post offices, meeting halls, courthouses, and other government buildings. Many of these, done in the style of the revolutionary Mexican muralists Diego Rivera and José Clemente Orozco, emphasized political and social themes. All these projects, declared Holger Cahill, director of the FAP, were aimed at "raising a generation sensitive to their visual environment and capable of helping to improve it."

The Documentary Impulse

"You can right a lot of wrongs with 'pitiless publicity,'" Franklin Roosevelt once declared. Social change, he argued, "is a difficult thing in our civilization unless you have sentiment." During the 1930s an enormous number of artists, novelists, journalists, photographers, and filmmakers tried to document the devastation wrought by the Depression in American communities. They also depicted people's struggles to cope with and reverse hard times. Some of these efforts were consciously linked to promoting political action, often as part of a radical commitment to overthrowing capitalism. Others were interested less in fomenting social change than in recording vanishing ways of life. Mainstream mass media, such as the photo essays found in *Life* magazine or "March of Time" newsreels, also adapted this stance.

Regardless of political agendas or the medium employed, what one historian calls the "documentary impulse" became a prominent style in 1930s cultural expression. At its core, the documentary impulse directly influenced its audience's intellect and feelings through documentary "evidence" of social problems and human suffering. The most direct and influential expression of the documentary style was the photograph. In 1935 Roy Stryker, chief of the Historical Section of the Resettlement Administration (later part of the Farm Security Administration), gathered a remarkable group of photographers to help document the work of the agency. Stryker encouraged them to photograph whatever caught their interest, even if the pictures had no direct connection with RA projects. These photographers, including Dorothea Lange, Walker Evans, Arthur Rothstein, Russell Lee, Ben Shahn, and Marion Post Wolcott, left us the single most significant visual record of the Great Depression.

The photographers traveled through rural areas, small towns, and migrant labor camps, often not stopping even long enough to learn the names of their subjects. They produced powerful images of despair and resignation as well as hope and resilience. These photographs were reproduced in newspapers and magazines across America. Individual images could be interpreted in different ways, depending on context and captions. Stryker believed that the faces of the subjects were most memorable. "You could look at the people," he wrote, "and see fear and sadness and desperation. But you saw something else, too. A determination that not even the Depression could kill. The photographers saw it—documented it."

That double vision, combining a frank portrayal of pain and suffering with a faith in the possibility of overcoming disaster, could be found in many other cultural works of the period. John Steinbeck's *Grapes of Wrath* (1939) sympathetically portrayed the hardships of Oklahoma Dust Bowl migrants on their way to California. "We ain't gonna die out," Ma Joad asserts near the end of the book. "People is goin' on—changin' a

The Joad family prepares to leave the Dust Bowl in Oklahoma for a new life in California in this still-photo from the movie "The Grapes of Wrath" (1940). Director John Ford's adaptation of John Steinbeck's novel reflected the influence of the "documentary impulse" in Hollywood films and other forms of Depression-era popular culture.

SOURCE: The Museum of Modern Art/Film Stills Archive.

little, maybe, but goin' right on." A similar, if more personal, ending could be found in Margaret Mitchell's 1936 bestseller *Gone with the Wind*. Although this romantic novel was set in the Civil War–era South, many Americans identified with Scarlett O'Hara's determination to overcome the disaster of war and the loss of Rhett Butler. "With the spirit of her people who would not know defeat, even when it stared them in the face, she raised her chin. She could get Rhett back. She knew she could."

Many writers interrupted their work to travel around the country and discover the thoughts and feelings of ordinary people. "With real events looming larger than any imagined happenings," novelist Elizabeth Noble wrote, "documentary films and still photographs, reportage and the like have taken the place once held by the grand invention." Writers increasingly used documentary techniques to communicate the sense of upheaval around the nation. In *Puzzled America* (1935), Sherwood Anderson wrote of the psychological toll taken by unemployment. American men, especially, he wrote, were losing "that sense of being some part of the moving world of activity, so essential to an American man's sense of his manhood—the loss of this essential something in the joblessness can never be measured in dollars." Yet writers also found a remarkable absence of bitterness and a great deal of faith. James Rorty, in *Where Life Is Better* (1936), was actually encouraged by his cross-country trip. "I had rediscovered for myself a most beautiful land, and a most vital, creative, and spiritually unsubdued people."

Waiting for Lefty

For some, the capitalist system itself, with its enormous disparities of private wealth amid desperate poverty, was the culprit responsible for the Great Depression. Relatively few Americans became Communists or socialists in the 1930s (at its height, the Communist Party of the United States had perhaps 100,000 members), and many of these remained active for only a brief time. Yet Marxist analysis, with its emphasis on class conflict and the failures of capitalism, had a wide influence on the era's thought and writing.

Some writers joined the Communist Party believing it to be the best hope for political revolution. They saw in the Soviet Union an alternative to an American system that appeared mired in exploitation, racial inequality, and human misery. Communist writers, like the novelist Michael Gold and the poet Meridel LeSueur, sought to radicalize art and literature, and they celebrated collective struggle over individual achievement. Gold's *Jews without Money* (1930) was one of the more successful attempts at a proletarian novel. It dramatized the sense of being locked into a system

that could deliver only despair rather than prosperity. Granville Hicks, an editor of the Communist magazine the *New Masses*, flatly declared: "If there is any other working interpretation of the apparent chaos than that which presents itself in terms of the class struggle, it has not been revealed."

A more common pattern for intellectuals, especially when they were young, was brief flirtation with communism. Many African American writers, attracted by the Communist Party's militant opposition to lynching, job discrimination, and segregation, briefly joined the party or found their first supportive audiences there. These included Richard Wright, Ralph Ellison, and Langston Hughes. Many playwrights and actors associated with New York's influential Group Theater were part of the Communist Party orbit in those years. One production of the group, Clifford Odets's *Waiting for Lefty* (1935), depicted a union organizing drive among taxi drivers. At the play's climax, the audience was invited to join the actors in shouting "Strike!" A commercial and political success, it offered perhaps the most celebrated example of radical, politically engaged art.

Left-wing influence reached its height after 1935 during the "Popular Front" period. Alarmed by the rise of fascism in Europe, communists around the world followed the Soviet line of uniting with liberals and all other antifascists. The American Communist Party adopted the slogan "Communism is Twentieth-Century Americanism." Communists became strong supporters of Roosevelt's New Deal, and their influence was especially strong within the various WPA arts projects. Some 3,200 Americans volunteered for the Communist Party–organized Abraham Lincoln Brigade, which fought in the Spanish civil war on the republican side against the fascists led by Francisco Franco. The Lincoln Brigade's sense of commitment and sacrifice appealed to millions of Americans sympathetic to the republican cause. Communists and other radicals, known for their dedication and effectiveness, also played a leading role in the difficult CIO unionizing drives in the auto, steel, and electrical industries. The successful sit-down strike at General Motors in Flint benefited from the organizing efforts of Communist Party activists who lent their expertise and helped keep the strikers and their families focused and supplied with food.

Hollywood in the 1930s

Commercial popular culture also boomed in the Depression years. The coming of "talking pictures" toward the end of the 1920s helped make movies the most popular entertainment form of the day. More than 60 percent of Americans attended one of the nation's 20,000 movie

Reginald Marsh, *Twenty Cent Movie*, 1936. Marsh documented the urban landscape of the 1930s with great empathy, capturing the city's contradictory mix of commercialism, optimism, energy, and degradation. The popularity of Hollywood films and their stars reached new heights during the Great Depression.

SOURCE: Reginald Marsh, *Twenty Cent Movie*, 1936. Egg tempera on composition board, 40″ × 40″. Whitney Museum of American Art, New York.

houses each week. Through fan magazines and gossip columns they followed the lives and careers of movie stars more avidly than ever. With so many movies being churned out by Hollywood studios for so many fans, it is difficult to generalize about the cultural impact of individual films. Moviegoing itself, usually enjoyed with friends, family, or a date, was perhaps the most significant development of all.

It is too easy to dismiss movies as mere escapism. The more interesting question is, What were people escaping to? Several film genres proved enormously popular during the 1930s. Gangster films did very well in the early Depression years. *Little Caesar* (1930), starring Edward G. Robinson, and *Public Enemy* (1931), with James Cagney, set the standard. They all depicted violent criminals brought to justice by society—but along

the way they gave audiences a vicarious exposure to the pleasures of wealth, power, and lawbreaking. Social disorder could also be treated comically, as in such Marx Brothers films as *Duck Soup* (1933) and *A Night at the Opera* (1935). Mae West's popular comedies, such as *She Done Him Wrong* (1933) and *I'm No Angel* (1933), made people laugh by subverting expectations about sex roles. West was an independent woman, not afraid of pleasure. When Cary Grant asked her, "Haven't you ever met a man who could make you happy?" she replied, "Sure, lots of times."

Movie musicals offered audiences extravagant song-and-dance spectacles, as in Busby Berkeley's *Gold Diggers of 1933* and *42nd Street* (1933). "Screwball comedies" featured sophisticated, fast-paced humor and usually paired popular male and female stars: Clark

Gable and Claudette Colbert in *It Happened One Night* (1934), Katharine Hepburn and Cary Grant in *Bringing Up Baby* (1938). A few movies, notably from the Warner Brothers studio, tried to offer a more "socially conscious" view of Depression-era life. These included *I Am a Fugitive from a Chain Gang* (1932), *Wild Boys of the Road* (1933), and *Black Legion* (1936). By and large, however, Hollywood avoided confronting controversial social or political issues.

Some 1930s filmmakers expressed highly personal visions of core American values. Two who succeeded in capturing both popular and critical acclaim were Walt Disney and Frank Capra. By the mid-1930s, Disney's animated cartoons had become moral tales that stressed keeping order and following the rules. The Mickey Mouse cartoons and the full-length features, such as *Snow White and the Seven Dwarfs* (1937), pulled back from the fantastic stretching of time and space in earlier cartoons. Capra's comedies, such as *Mr. Deeds Goes to Town* (1936) and *You Can't Take It with You* (1938), idealized a small-town America with close families and comfortable homes. Although Capra's films dealt with contemporary problems more than most—unemployment, government corruption, economic monopoly—he made no critique of the social and economic system. Rather, he seemed to suggest that most of the country's ills could be solved if only its leaders learned the old-fashioned values of "common people"—kindness, loyalty, charity.

The Golden Age of Radio

Radio broadcasting emerged as the most powerful medium of communication in the home, profoundly changing the rhythms and routines of everyday life. In 1930 roughly 12 million American homes, 40 percent of the total, had a radio set. By the end of the decade radios could be found in 90 percent of the nation's homes. Advertisers dominated the structure and content of American radio, forming a powerful alliance with the two large networks, the National Broadcasting Company (NBC) and the Columbia Broadcasting System (CBS). The Federal Communications Commission (FCC), established in 1934, continued long-standing policies that favored commercial broadcasting over other arrangements, such as municipal or university programming. By 1937 NBC and CBS controlled about 90 percent of the wattage in the American broadcasting industry. Nearly all network shows were produced by advertising agencies.

The Depression actually helped radio expand. An influx of talent arrived from the weakened worlds of vaudeville, ethnic theater, and the recording industry. The well-financed networks offered an attractive outlet to advertisers seeking a national audience. Radio pro-

gramming achieved a regularity and professionalism absent in the 1920s, making it much easier for a listener to identify a show with its sponsor. Companies with national distribution paid thousands of dollars an hour to networks; by 1939 annual radio advertising revenues totaled $171 million.

Much of network radio was based on older cultural forms. The variety show, hosted by comedians and singers and based on the old vaudeville format, was the first important style. It featured stars like Eddie Cantor, Ed Wynn, Kate Smith, and Al Jolson, who constantly plugged the sponsor's product. The use of a studio audience re-created the human interaction so necessary in vaudeville. The popular comedy show *Amos 'n' Andy* adapted the minstrel "blackface" tradition to the new medium. White comedians Freeman Gosden and Charles Correll used only their two voices to invent a world of stereotyped African Americans for their millions of listeners.

The spectacular growth of the daytime serial, or soap opera, dominated radio drama. Aimed mainly at women working in the home, these serials alone constituted 60 percent of all daytime shows by 1940. Soaps such as *Ma Perkins*, *Helen Trent*, and *Clara Lou and Em* revolved around strong, warm female characters who provided advice and strength to weak, indecisive friends and relatives. Action counted very little; the development of character and relationships was all-important. Contemporary studies found that the average soap opera fan regularly tuned in to six or more different series. Evening radio dramas included thrillers such as *Inner Sanctum* and *The Shadow*, which emphasized crime and suspense. These shows made great use of music and sound effects to sharpen their impact.

In the late 1930s serious drama bloomed briefly, independent of commercial sponsorship, over CBS's Columbia Workshop. Archibald MacLeish's *Fall of the City*, a parable about fascism, and Orson Welles's *War of the Worlds*, a superrealistic adaptation of the H. G. Wells classic, proved the persuasive power of radio. Welles's show convinced many who tuned in that a Martian invasion was actually underway. Radio became a key factor in politics as well, as President Roosevelt showed early on with his popular "fireside" chats.

Finally, radio news arrived in the 1930s, showing the medium's potential for direct and immediate coverage of events. Network news and commentary shows multiplied rapidly over the decade. Complex political and economic issues and the impending European crisis fueled a news hunger among Americans. A 1939 survey found that 70 percent of Americans relied on the radio as their prime source of news. Yet commercial broadcasting, dominated by big sponsors and large radio manufacturers, failed to cover politically controversial events, such as labor struggles. The most powerful station in the country, WLW in Cincinnati, refused to even mention strikes on the air. NBC routinely canceled programs it feared might undermine "public confidence and faith."

The Swing Era

One measure of radio's cultural impact was its role in popularizing jazz. Before the 1930s, jazz was heard largely among African Americans and a small coterie of white fans and musicians. Regular broadcasts of live performances began to expose a broader public to the music. So did radio disc jockeys who played jazz records on their shows. Bands led by black artists such as Duke Ellington, Count Basie, and Benny Moten began to enjoy reputations outside of traditional jazz centers like Chicago, Kansas City, and New York.

Benny Goodman became the key figure in the "swing era," largely through radio exposure. Goodman, a white, classically trained clarinetist, had been inspired by African American band-

The Benny Goodman band at the Meadowbrook Lounge, Cedar Grove, New Jersey, September 1941. After his breakthrough into national prominence in 1935, Goodman became one of the first white bandleaders to hire and feature African American musicians. Although most in the audience were undoubtedly dancing to the "King of Swing," note the crowd of serious listeners gathered around the bandstand.

SOURCE: Frank Driggs Collection.

leaders Fletcher Henderson and Don Redman. These men created arrangements for big bands that combined harmonic call-and-response patterns with breaks for improvised solos. Goodman purchased a series of arrangements from Henderson, smoothing out the sound but keeping the strong dance beat. His band's late-Saturday-night broadcasts began to attract attention.

In 1935, at the Palomar Ballroom in Los Angeles, Goodman made the breakthrough that established his enormous popularity. When the band started playing the Henderson arrangements, the young crowd, primed by the radio broadcasts, roared its approval and began to dance wildly. Goodman's music was perfect for doing the jitterbug or lindy hop, dances borrowed from African American culture. As the "King of Swing," Goodman helped make big-band jazz a hit with millions of teenagers and young adults from all backgrounds. In the late 1930s, big-band music by the likes of Goodman, Basie, Jimmie Lunceford, and Artie Shaw accounted for the majority of million-selling records.

Despite the Depression, the mass culture industry expanded enormously during the 1930s. Millions of

Americans no doubt used mass culture as a temporary escape from their problems, but the various meanings they drew from movies, radio, and popular music were by no means monolithic. In most communities, Americans, especially young people, identified more closely than ever with the national communities forged by modern media. If mass culture offered little in the way of direct responses to the economic and social problems of the day, it nonetheless played a more integral role than ever in shaping the rhythms and desires of the nation's everyday life.

THE LIMITS OF REFORM

In his second Inaugural Address Roosevelt emphasized that much remained to be done to remedy the effects of the Depression. Tens of millions of Americans were still denied the necessities for a decent life. "I see one-third of a nation ill-housed, ill-clad, ill-nourished," the president said. With his stunning electoral victory, the future for further social reform seemed bright. Yet by 1937 the New Deal was in retreat. A rapid political turnaround over the next two years put continuing social reform efforts on the defensive.

Court Packing

FDR and his advisers were frustrated by several Supreme Court rulings declaring important New Deal legislation unconstitutional. In May 1935, in *Schecter* v. *United States*, the Court found the National Recovery Administration unconstitutional in its entirety. The grounds included excessive delegation of legislative power to the executive and the regulation of business that was intrastate, as opposed to interstate or national, in character. In early 1936, ruling in *Butler* v. *United States*, the Court invalidated the Agricultural Adjustment Administration, declaring it an unconstitutional attempt at regulating agriculture. The Court was composed mostly of Republican appointees, six of whom were over seventy. Roosevelt looked for a way to get more friendly judges on the high court.

In February 1937, FDR asked Congress for legislation that would expand the Supreme Court from nine to a maximum of fifteen justices. The president would be empowered to make a new appointment whenever an incumbent judge failed to retire upon reaching age seventy. Roosevelt argued that age prevented justices from keeping up with their workload, but few people believed this logic. Newspapers almost unanimously denounced FDR's "court-packing bill."

Even more damaging was the determined opposition from a coalition of conservatives and outraged New Dealers in the Congress, such as Democratic senator Burton K. Wheeler of Montana. The president gamely fought on, maintaining that his purpose was simply to restore the balance of power among the three branches of the federal government. As the battle dragged on through the spring and summer, FDR's claims weakened. Conservative justice Willis Van Devanter announced plans to retire, giving Roosevelt the chance to make his first Court appointment.

More important, the Court upheld the constitutionality of some key laws from the second New Deal, including the Social Security Act and the National Labor Relations Act. At the end of August, FDR backed off from his plan and accepted a compromise bill that reformed lower court procedures but left the Supreme Court untouched. FDR lost the battle for his judiciary proposal, but he may have won the war for a more responsive Court. Still, the political price was very high. The Court fight badly weakened Roosevelt's relations with Congress. Many more conservative Democrats now felt free to oppose further New Deal measures.

The Women's Network

The Great Depression and the New Deal brought some significant changes for women in American economics and politics. Most women continued to perform unpaid domestic labor within their homes, work that was not covered by the Social Security Act. A growing minority, however, also worked for wages and salaries outside the home. Women represented 24.3 percent of all workers in 1930; by 1940, 25.1 percent of the workforce was female. There was also an increase in married working women as a result of hard times. Between 1930 and 1940 the proportion of married women among the female workforce jumped from 28.8 percent to 35 percent. Jobs in which men predominated, such as construction and heavy industry, were hardest hit by the Depression. In contrast, secretarial, sales, and other areas long associated with women's labor were less affected. But sexual stereotyping still routinely forced women into low-paying and low-status jobs.

The New Deal brought a measurable, if temporary, increase in women's political influence. For those women associated with social reform, the New Deal opened up possibilities to effect change. A "women's network," linked by personal friendships and professional connections, made its presence felt in national politics and government. Most of the women in this network had long been active in movements promoting suffrage, labor law reform, and welfare programs.

Eleanor Roosevelt became a powerful political figure in her own right, actively using her prominence as First Lady to fight for the liberal causes she believed in. She revolutionized the role of the political wife by taking a position involving no institutional duties and turning it into a base for independent action. Privately, she enjoyed great influence with her husband, and her support for a cause could give it instant credibility. She worked behind the scenes with a wide network of women professionals and reformers whom she had come to know in the 1920s. She was a strong supporter of protective labor legislation for women, and her overall outlook owed much to the social reform tradition of the women's movement. "When all is said and done," she wrote in *It's Up to the Women* (1933), "women are different from men. They are equal in many ways, but they cannot refuse to acknowledge their differences. . . . Their physical functions in life are different and perhaps in the same way the contributions which they are to bring to the spiritual side of life are different."

One of Eleanor Roosevelt's first public acts as First Lady was to convene a White House Conference on the Emergency Needs of Women in November 1933. She helped Ellen Woodward, head of women's projects in the Federal Emergency Relief Administration, find

Eleanor Roosevelt on a campaign tour with her husband in Nebraska, 1935. Long active in women's organizations and Democratic Party circles, she used political activity both to maintain her independence and make herself a valuable ally to FDR. "The attitude of women toward change in society," she argued, "is going to determine to a great extent our future in this country."

SOURCE: UPI/CORBIS (UP11).

jobs for 100,000 women, ranging from nursery school teaching to sewing. Roosevelt worked vigorously for antilynching legislation, compulsory health insurance, and child labor reform, and she fought racial discrimination in New Deal relief programs. She saw herself as the guardian of "human values" within the administration, a buffer between Depression victims and government bureaucracy. She frequently testified before legislative committees, lobbied her husband privately and the Congress publicly, and wrote a widely syndicated newspaper column.

Eleanor Roosevelt's closest political ally was Molly Dewson. A long-time social worker and suffragist, Dewson wielded a good deal of political clout as director of the Women's Division of the national Democratic Party. Under her leadership, women for the first time played a central role in shaping the party platform and running election campaigns. Dewson proved a tireless organizer, traveling to cities and towns around the country and educating women about Democratic

policies and candidates. Her success impressed the president, and he relied on her judgment in recommending political appointments. Dewson placed more than a hundred women in New Deal positions.

Perhaps Dewson's most important success came in persuading FDR to appoint Frances Perkins secretary of labor—the first woman cabinet member in U.S. history. A graduate of Mount Holyoke College and a veteran activist for social welfare and reform, Perkins had served as FDR's industrial commissioner in New York before coming to Washington. As labor secretary, Perkins embodied the gains made by women in appointive offices. Her department was responsible for creating the Social Security Act and the Fair Labor Standards Act of 1938, both of which incorporated protective measures long advocated by women reformers. Perkins defined feminism as "the movement of women to participate in service to society." Yet despite the best efforts of the "women's network," women never constituted more than 19 percent of those employed by work relief programs, even though they made up 37 percent of the unemployed.

New Deal agencies opened up spaces for scores of women in the federal bureaucracy. These women were concentrated in Perkins's Labor Department, the FERA and WPA, and the Social Security Board. In addition, the social work profession, which remained roughly two-thirds female in the 1930s, grew enormously in response to the massive relief and welfare programs. In sum, although the 1930s saw no radical challenges to existing male and female roles, working-class women and professional women held their own and managed to make some gains.

A New Deal for Minorities?

"The Negro was born in Depression," recalled Clifford Burke. "It only became official when it hit the white man." Long near the bottom of the American economic ladder, African Americans suffered disproportionately through the difficult days of the 1930s. The old saying among black workers that they were "last hired, first fired" was never more true than during times of high unemployment. With jobs made scarce by the Depression, even traditional "Negro occupations"—domestic service, cooking, janitorial work, elevator operating— were coveted. One white clerk in Florida expressed a widely held view among white Southerners when he defended a lynch mob attack on a store with black employees: "A nigger hasn't got no right to have a job when there are white men who can do the work and are out of work."

Overall, the Roosevelt administration made little overt effort to combat the racism and segregation entrenched in American life. FDR was especially worried about offending the powerful southern Democratic congressmen who were a key element in his political coalition. And local administration of many federal programs meant that most early New Deal programs routinely accepted discrimination. The CCC established separate camps for African Americans. The NRA labor codes tolerated lower wages for black workers doing the same jobs as white workers. African Americans could not get jobs with the TVA. In Atlanta, relief payments for black clients averaged $19.29 per month, compared with $32.66 for white clients. When local AAA committees in the South reduced acreage and production to boost prices, thousands of black sharecroppers and farm laborers were forced off the land. Racism was also embedded in the entitlement provisions of the Social Security Act. The act excluded domestics and casual laborers—workers whose ranks were disproportionately African Americans—from old-age insurance.

Yet some limited gains were made. President Roosevelt issued an executive order in 1935 banning discrimination in WPA projects. In the cities, the WPA, paying minimum wages of $12 a week, enabled thousands of African Americans to survive. Between 15 and 20 percent of all WPA employees were black people, although African Americans made up less than 10 percent of the nation's population. The Public Works Administration, under Harold Ickes, constructed a number of integrated housing complexes and employed more than its fair share of black workers in construction.

FDR appointed several African Americans to second-level positions in his administration. This group became known as "the Black Cabinet." Mary McLeod Bethune, an educator who rose from a sharecropping background to found Bethune-Cookman College, proved a superb leader of the Office of Minority Affairs in the National Youth Administration. Her most successful programs substantially reduced black illiteracy.

Harvard-trained Robert Weaver advised the president on economic affairs and in 1966 became the first black cabinet member when he was appointed secretary of housing and urban development. Yet Roosevelt himself was diffident about advancing civil rights. Typically, he spoke out against lynching in the South, but unlike his wife, he refused to support legislation making it a federal crime. Nor would he risk alienating white Southerners by working for long-denied voting rights for African Americans in the South.

Hard times were especially trying for Mexican Americans as well. As the Great Depression drastically reduced the demand for their labor, they faced massive layoffs, deepening poverty, and deportation. During the 1930s over 400,000 Mexican nationals and their children returned to Mexico, often coerced by local officials unwilling to provide them with relief but happy to offer train fare to border towns. Many native-born Americans argued that deporting Mexicans could reduce unemployment for U.S. citizens. But these claims reflected deep racial prejudice inflamed by the economic crisis. In Detroit, deportations reduced the size of that city's thriving Mexican *colonia* from 15,000 to 3,000 by 1933. In Los Angeles, where 100,000 Mexicans constituted the largest *colonia* in the Unites States, fully one third became *repatriados*. For those who stayed, the New Deal programs did little to help. The AAA benefited large growers, not stoop laborers. Neither the National Labor Relations Act nor the Social Security Act made any provisions for farm laborers. The Federal Emergency Relief Administration and the Works Progress Administration did, at first, provide relief and jobs to the needy irrespective of citizenship status. But after 1937, the WPA eliminated aliens from eligibility, causing great hardship for thousands of Mexican families. Yet both mass repatriation and New Deal public works programs would have profound long-range implications for Mexican American communities. By World War II, colonias would be increasingly dominated by the American-born second generation, rather than those born in Mexico. And since only citizens or aliens who had begun the process of naturalization were eligible for public works jobs, these programs motivated more Mexican immigrants to become U.S. citizens.

The New Deal record for minorities was mixed at best. African Americans, especially in the cities, benefited from New Deal relief and work programs, though this assistance was not colorblind. Black industrial workers made inroads into labor unions affiliated with the CIO. The New Deal made no explicit attempt to attack the deeply rooted patterns of racism and discrimination in American life. The deteriorating economic and political conditions faced by Mexicans and Mexican Americans resulted in a mass reverse exodus.

Yet by 1936, for the first time ever, a majority of black voters had switched their political allegiance to the Democrats—concrete evidence that they supported the directions taken by FDR's New Deal.

The Roosevelt Recession

The nation's economy had improved significantly by 1937. Unemployment had declined to "only" 14 percent (9 million people), farm prices had improved to 1930 levels, and industrial production was slightly higher than the 1929 mark. Economic traditionalists, led by Secretary of the Treasury Henry Morgenthau, called for reducing the federal deficit, which had grown to more than $4 billion in fiscal year 1936. Roosevelt, always uneasy about the growing national debt, called for large reductions in federal spending, particularly in WPA and farm programs. Federal Reserve System officials, worried about inflation, tightened credit policies.

Rather than stimulating business, the retrenchment brought about a steep recession. The stock market collapsed in August 1937, and industrial output and farm prices plummeted. Most alarming was the big increase in unemployment. By March 1938, the jobless rate hovered around 20 percent, with more than 13 million people looking for work. As conditions worsened, Roosevelt began to blame the "new depression" on a "strike of capital," claiming businessmen had refused to invest because they wanted to hurt his prestige. In truth, the administration's own severe spending cutbacks were more responsible for the decline.

The blunt reality was that even after five years the New Deal had not brought about economic recovery. Throughout 1937 and 1938 the administration drifted. Roosevelt received conflicting advice on the economy. Some advisers, suspicious of the reluctance of business to make new investments, urged a massive antitrust campaign against monopolies. Others urged a return to the strategy of "priming the economic pump" with more federal spending. Emergency spending bills in the spring of 1938 pumped new life into the WPA and the PWA. But Republican gains in the 1938 congressional elections (eighty seats in the House, seven in the Senate) made it harder than ever to get new reform measures through.

There were a couple of important exceptions. The 1938 Fair Labor Standards Act established the first federal minimum wage (25 cents an hour) and set a maximum work week of forty-four hours for all employees engaged in interstate commerce. The National Housing Act of 1937, also known as the Wagner-Steagall Act, funded public housing construction and slum clearance and provided rent subsidies for low-income families. But by and large, by 1938 the reform whirlwind of the New Deal was over.

CONCLUSION

Although American capitalism and democracy survived the cataclysm of the Great Depression, the New Deal failed in its central mission. It was never able to bring full economic recovery or end the scourge of mass unemployment. Only the economic boom that accompanied World War II would do that. Far from being the radical program its conservative critics charged, the New Deal did little to alter fundamental property relations or the distribution of wealth. Indeed, most of its programs largely failed to help the most powerless groups in America—migrant workers, tenant farmers and sharecroppers, African Americans, and other minorities.

But the New Deal profoundly changed many areas of American life. Overall, it radically increased the role of the federal government in American lives and communities. Western and southern communities in particular were transformed through federal intervention in water, power, and agricultural policies. Relief programs and the Social Security system established at least the framework for a welfare state. For the first time in American history, the national government took responsibility for assisting its needy citizens. And also for the first time, the federal government guaranteed the right of workers to join trade unions, and it set standards for minimum wages and maximum hours. In politics, the New Deal established the Democrats as the majority party. Some version of the Roosevelt New Deal coalition would dominate the nation's political life for another three decades.

Compared to other hemispheric responses to the Great Depression, the New Deal looks even more sweeping in its innovations. In Canada, where the Great Depression brought massive industrial unemployment and extremely hard times for western farmers, the country's economic and political structure in 1939 remained essentially unchanged. Both the Conservative government led by Richard B. Bennett and the Liberal government of Mackenzie King largely avoided taking on new federal responsibility for unemployment, insisting that this was a provincial or local responsibility. They did little to promote farm relief, old-age insurance, or public works projects. The few new federal initiatives, such as the Bank of Canada and the Canadian Wheat Board, focused on regulating business, avoiding deficit spending, and maintaining high tariffs. In Mexico, fiscal and monetary responses also dominated. Hard times in the United States had triggered a steep decline in the demand for Mexican goods and services, producing widespread unemployment and sharp contraction in the money supply. The Bank of Mexico abandoned the gold standard in response, printing paper money that

CHRONOLOGY

1929	Stock market crash		Committee for Industrial Organization (CIO) established
1930	Democrats regain control of the House of Representatives		Dust storms turn the southern Great Plains into the Dust Bowl
1932	Reconstruction Finance Corporation established to make government credit available		Boulder Dam completed
	Bonus Army marches on Washington	**1936**	Roosevelt defeats Alfred M. Landon in reelection landslide
	Franklin D. Roosevelt elected president		Sit-down strike begins at General Motors plants in Flint, Michigan
1933	Roughly 13 million workers unemployed	**1937**	General Motors recognizes United Automobile Workers
	The "hundred days" legislation of the First New Deal		Roosevelt's "Court-packing" plan causes controversy
	Twenty-first Amendment repeals Prohibition (Eighteenth Amendment)		Memorial Day Massacre in Chicago demonstrates the perils of union organizing
1934	Indian Reorganization Act repeals Dawes Severalty Act and reasserts the status of Indian tribes as semisovereign nations		"Roosevelt recession" begins
	Growing popularity of Father Charles E. Coughlin and Huey Long, critics of Roosevelt	**1938**	CIO unions withdraw from the American Federation of Labor to form the Congress of Industrial Organizations
1935	Second New Deal		Fair Labor Standards Act establishes the first federal minimum wage

helped ease the crisis and permitted the government to engage in more public spending. The devaluation of the peso helped revive the export sector as well. Populist President Lazaro Cardenas (1934–40) widened the power of the federal government by aggressively pushing land reform and nationalizing the oil business. He reorganized his party and named it the *Partido Revolucionario Institucional* (Institutional Revolutionary Party), which would dominate Mexican political life for the rest of the century.

The New Deal's efforts to end racial and gender discrimination were modest at best. Some of the more ambitious programs, such as subsidizing the arts or building model communities, enjoyed only brief success. Other reform proposals, such as national health insurance, never got off the ground. Conservative counterpressures, especially after 1937, limited what could be changed.

Still, the New Deal did more than strengthen the presence of the national government in people's lives. It also fed expectations that the federal presence would intensify. Washington became a much greater center of economic regulation and political power, and the federal bureaucracy grew in size and influence. With the coming of World War II, the direct role of national government in shaping American communities would expand beyond the dreams of even the most ardent New Dealer.

REVIEW QUESTIONS

1. What were the underlying causes of the Great Depression? What consequences did it have for ordinary Americans, and how did the Hoover administration attempt to deal with the crisis?

2. Analyze the key elements of Franklin D. Roosevelt's first New Deal program. To what degree did these succeed in getting the economy back on track and in providing relief to suffering Americans?

3. How did the so-called Second New Deal differ from the first? What political pressures did Roosevelt face that contributed to the new policies?

4. How did the New Deal reshape western communities and politics? What specific programs had the greatest impact in the region? How are these changes still visible today?

5. Evaluate the impact of the labor movement and radicalism on the 1930s. How did they influence American political and cultural life?

6. To what extent were the grim realities of Depression reflected in popular culture? To what degree were they absent?

7. Discuss the long- and short-range effects of the New Deal on American political and economic life. What were its key successes and failures? What legacies of New Deal–era policies and political struggles can you find in contemporary America?

RECOMMENDED READING

Anthony J. Badger, *The New Deal: The Depression Years, 1933–1940* (1989). Very useful overview that emphasizes the limited nature of New Deal reforms.

Alan Brinkley, *The End of Reform: New Deal Liberalism in Recession and War* (1995). A sophisticated analysis of the political and economic limits faced by New Deal reformers from 1937 through World War II.

Lizabeth Cohen, *Making a New Deal: Industrial Workers in Chicago, 1919–1939* (1990). A brilliant study that demonstrates the transformation of immigrant and African American workers into key actors in the creation of the CIO and in New Deal politics and illuminates the complex relationship between ethnic cultures and mass culture.

Michael Denning, *The Cultural Front: The Laboring of American Culture in the Twentieth Century* (1997). A provocative reinterpretation of 1930s culture, emphasizing the impact of the Popular Front and its lasting influence on American modernism and mass culture.

Ronald Edsforth, *The New Deal: America's Response to the Great Depression* (2000). A concise political history of the 1930s, offering an excellent synthesis of the massive secondary literature.

David M. Kennedy, *Freedom From Fear: The American People in Depression and War* (1999). An absorbing, magisterial narrative account of the U.S. experience in depression and war.

Richard Lowitt, *The New Deal and the West* (1984). A comprehensive study of the New Deal's impact in the West, with special attention to water policy and agriculture.

Robert S. McElvaine, *The Great Depression: America, 1929–1941* (1984). The best one-volume overview of the Great Depression. It is especially strong on the origins and early years of the worst economic calamity in American history.

Lois Scharf, *To Work and to Wed* (1980). Examines female employment and feminism during the Great Depression.

Harvard Sitkoff, *A New Deal for Blacks* (1978). Focuses on the narrow gains made by African Americans from New Deal measures, as well as the racism that pervaded most government programs.

ADDITIONAL BIBLIOGRAPHY

Hard Times

Michael A. Bernstein, *The Great Depression* (1987)

Michael D. Bordo, et.al., eds., *The Defining Moment: The Great Depression and the American Economy in the Twentieth Century* (1998)

Maury Klein, *Rainbow's End: The Crash of 1929* (2001)

Robert S. McElvaine, ed., *Down and Out in the Great Depression* (1983)

Jeff Singleton, *The American Dole: Unemployment Relief and the Welfare State in the Great Depression* (2000)

Studs Terkel, *Hard Times* (1970)

T. H. Watkins, *The Hungry Years: A Narrative History of the Great Depression in America* (1999)

FDR and the First New Deal

Steve Fraser and Gary Gerstle, eds., *The Rise and Fall of the New Deal Order* (1988)

William Leuchtenberg, *The FDR Years* (1995)

George McJimsey, *The Presidency of Franklin Delano Roosevelt* (2000)

James S. Olson, *Saving Capitalism* (1988)

Theodore M. Saloutos, *The American Farmer and the New Deal* (1982)

Left Turn and the Second New Deal

Irving Bernstein, *The Turbulent Years: A History of the American Worker, 1933–1941* (1970)

Alan Brinkley, *Voices of Protest: Huey Long, Father Coughlin, and the New Deal* (1982)

Gary Gerstle, *Working Class Americanism* (1989)

Kenneth J. Heineman, *A Catholic New Deal: Religion and Reform in Depression Pittsburgh* (1999)

Robin D. G. Kelley, *Hammer and Hoe: Alabama Communists during the Great Depression* (1990)

Robert H. Zieger, *The CIO, 1935–1955* (1995)

The New Deal and the West

James M. Gregory, *American Exodus: The Dust Bowl Migration and Okie Culture in California* (1989)

Laurence Kelly, *The Assault on Assimilation: John Collier and the Origins of Indian Policy Reform, 1920–1954* (1983)

Vicki Ruiz, *Cannery Women/Cannery Lives: Mexican Women, Unionization, and the California Food Processing Industry, 1930–1950* (1987)

Charles J. Shindo, *Dust Bowl Migrants in the American Imagination* (1997)

Kevin Starr, *Endangered Dreams: The Great Depression in California* (1996)

Donald Worster, *Dust Bowl* (1979)

Depression-Era Culture

Thomas P. Doherty, *Pre-Code Hollywood: Sex, Immorality, and Insurrection in American Cinema, 1930-1934* (1999)

Lewis A. Erenberg, *Swingin' the Dream: Big Band Jazz and the Rebirth of American Culture* (1998)

Vivian Gornick, *The Romance of American Communism* (1976)

Harvey Klehr, *The Heyday of American Communism* (1984)

Anthony W. Lee, *Painting on the Left* (1999)

Richard McKinzie, *The New Deal for Artists* (1973)

Barbara Melosh, *Engendering Culture: Manhood and Womanhood in New Deal Public Art and Theater* (1991)

Thomas Schatz, *The Genius of the System: Hollywood Filmmaking in the Studio Era* (1988)

William Stott, *Documentary Expression and Thirties America* (1973)

The Limits of Reform

Francisco E. Balderrama, *Decade of Betrayal: Mexican Repatriation in the 1930's* (1995)

Suzanne Mettler, *Dividing Citizens: Gender and Federalism in New Deal Public Works* (1998)

Mark Naison, *Communists in Harlem during the Depression* (1983)

Landon R. Y. Storrs, *Civilizing Capitalism: The National Consumers' League, Women's Activism, and Labor Standards in the New Deal Era* (2000)

Patricia Sullivan, *Days of Hope: Race and Democracy in the New Deal Era* (1996)

Susan Ware, *Beyond Suffrage: Women in the New Deal* (1981)

G. Edward White, *The Constitution and the New Deal* (2000)

Biography

Blanche W. Cook, *Eleanor Roosevelt: A Life* (1992)

Kenneth S. Davis, *FDR*, 4 vols. (1972, 1975, 1986, 1992)

Steven Fraser, *Labor Will Rule: Sidney Hillman and the Rise of American Labor* (1991)

June Hopkins, *Harry Hopkins: Sudden Hero, Brash Reformer* (1999)

J. Joseph Huthmacher, *Robert F. Wagner and the Rise of Urban Liberalism* (1968)

Nelson Lichtenstein, *The Most Dangerous Man in Detroit: Walter Reuther and the Fate of American Labor* (1995)

Naomi E. Pasachoff, *Frances Perkins: Champion of the New Deal* (1999)

Lois Scharf, *Eleanor Roosevelt* (1987)

Robert Zieger, *John L. Lewis* (1988)

HISTORY ON THE INTERNET

http://newdeal.feri.org/library/index.htm#4

The New Deal Network is sponsored by the Franklin and Eleanor Roosevelt Instituted and based at Columbia University.

http://lcweb.loc.gov/rr/print/085_disc.html

This site is a Library of Congress exhibit entitled: "Photographs of Signs Enforcing Racial Discrimination: Documentation by Farm Security Administration-Office of War Information Photographers" from the Prints and Photographs Division.

http://lcweb.loc.gov/rr/print/128_migm.html

Dorothea Lange's "Migrant Mother" photograph became one of the classic photos illustrating the deprivation and hunger of the Great Depression. This Library of Congress site provides background information on that photo as well as others taken about the same time by Lange.

http://www.mhric.org/fdr/fdr.html

This site provides electronic texts of Roosevelt's thirty "Fireside Chats" with the American people during the Great Depression and World War II.

TWENTY-FIVE

WORLD WAR II

> 1941–1945

SOURCE: Thomas Hart Benton, *Back Him Up*. Courtesy Christie's Images, Inc. (NYAMP 310585284)

Los Alamos, New Mexico

ON MONDAY, JULY 16, 1945, AT 5:29:45 A.M., MOUNTAIN WAR Time, the first atomic bomb exploded in a brilliant flash visible in three states. Within just seven minutes, a huge, multicolored, bell-shaped cloud soared 38,000 feet into the atmosphere and threw back a blanket of smoke and soot to the earth below. The heat generated by the blast was four times the temperature at the center of the sun, and the light produced rivaled that of nearly twenty suns. Even ten miles away people felt a strong surge of heat. The giant fireball ripped a crater a half-mile wide in the ground, fusing the desert sand into glass. The shock wave blew out windows in houses more than 200 miles away. The blast killed every living creature—squirrels, rabbits, snakes, plants, and insects—within a mile and the smells of death lingered for nearly a month.

Very early that morning, Ruby Wilkening had driven to a nearby mountain ridge, where she joined several other women waiting for the blast. Wilkening worried about her husband, a physicist, who was already at the test site. No one knew exactly what to expect, not even the scientists who developed the bomb.

The Wilkenings were part of a unique community of scientists who had been marshaled for war. President Franklin D. Roosevelt, convinced by Albert Einstein and other physicists that the Nazis might successfully develop an atomic bomb, had inaugurated a small nuclear research program in 1939. Soon after the United States entered World War II, the president released resources to create the Manhattan Project and placed it under the direction of the Army Corps of Engineers. By December 1942 a team headed by Italian-born Nobel Prize–winner Enrico Fermi had produced the first chain reaction in uranium under the University of Chicago's football stadium. Now the mission was to build a new, formidable weapon of war, the atomic bomb.

The government moved the key researchers and their families to Los Alamos, New Mexico, a remote and sparsely populated region of soaring peaks, ancient Indian ruins, modern Pueblos, and villages occupied by the descendents of the earliest Spanish settlers. The scientists and their families arrived in March 1943. They occupied a former boys' preparatory school until new houses could be built. Some families doubled up in rugged log cabins or nearby ranches. Telephone service to the outside world was poor, and the mountain roads were so rough that changing flat tires became a tiresome but familiar routine. Construction of new quarters proceeded slowly, causing nasty disputes between the "longhairs" (scientists) and the "plumbers" (army engineers) in charge of the grounds. Despite the chaos, outstanding American and European scientists eagerly signed up. Most were young, with an average age of twenty-seven, and quite a few were recently married. Many couples began their families at Los Alamos, producing a total of nearly a thousand babies between 1943 and 1949.

The scientists and their families formed an exceptionally close-knit community, united by the need for secrecy and their shared antagonism toward their army guardians. The military atmosphere was oppressive.

Homes and laboratories were cordoned off by barbed wire and guarded by military police. Everything, from linens to food packages, was stamped "Government Issue." The scientists were followed by security personnel whenever they left Los Alamos. Several scientists were reprimanded for discussing their work at home, although many of their wives worked forty-eight hours a week in the Technical Area. All outgoing mail was censored. Well-known scientists commonly worked under aliases—Fermi became "Eugene Farmer"—and code names were used for such terms as atom, bomb, and uranium fission. The birth certificates of babies born at Los Alamos listed their place of birth simply as rural Sandoval County, and children registered without surnames at nearby public schools. Even automobile accidents went unreported, and newspapers carried no wedding announcements or obituaries. Only a group thoroughly committed to the war effort could accept such restrictions on personal liberty.

A profound urgency motivated the research team, which included refugees from Nazi Germany and Fascist Italy and a large proportion of Jews. The director of the project, California physicist J. Robert Oppenheimer, promoted a scientific élan that offset the military style of commanding general Leslie Groves. Just thirty-eight, slightly built, and deeply emotional, "Oppie" personified the idealism that helped the community of scientists overcome whatever moral reservations they held about placing such a potentially ominous weapon in the hands of the government.

In the Technical Area of Los Alamos, Oppenheimer directed research from an office with a desk, long tables, and blackboard along the walls in a typical two-story army building. At seven o'clock each workday morning, the siren dubbed "Oppie's Whistle" called the other scientists to their laboratories to wrestle with the theoretical and practical problems of building an atomic device. Once a week Oppenheimer called together the heads of the various technical divisions to discuss their work in round-table conferences. From May to November 1944, after the bomb had been designed, the key issue was testing it. Many scientists feared a test might fail, scattering the precious plutonium at the bomb's core and discrediting the entire project. Finally, with plutonium production increasing, the Los Alamos team agreed to test "the gadget" at a site 160 miles away.

The unprecedented scientific mobilization at Los Alamos mirrored changes occurring throughout American society as the nation rallied behind the war effort. Sixteen million men and women left home for military service and nearly as many moved to take advantage of wartime jobs. Several states in the South and Southwest experienced huge surges in population. California alone grew by 2 million people, a large proportion from Mexico. Many broad social changes with roots in earlier times—the economic expansion of the West, the erosion of farm tenancy among black people in the South and white people in Appalachia, and the increasing employment of married women—accelerated during the war. The United States, initially reluctant to enter the war, emerged from it the world's leading superpower and free from the weight of the Great Depression. The events of the war eroded old communities, created new ones like Los Alamos, and transformed nearly all aspects of American society. ■

Los Alamos

KEY TOPICS

- The events leading to Pearl Harbor and the declaration of war

- The marshaling of national resources for war

- American society during wartime

- The mobilization of Americans into the armed forces

- The war in Europe and Asia

- Diplomacy and the atomic bomb

THE COMING OF WORLD WAR II

The Great Depression was not confined to the United States. It was a worldwide economic decline that further undermined a political order that had been shaky since World War I. Production declined by nearly 40 percent, international trade dropped by as much as two-thirds, and unemployment rose. While rivalries for markets and access to raw materials intensified, political unrest spread across Europe and Asia. Demagogues played upon nationalist hatreds, fueled by old resentments and current despair, and offered solutions in the form of territorial expansion by military conquest.

Preoccupied with restoring the domestic economy, President Franklin D. Roosevelt had no specific plan to deal with growing conflict elsewhere in the world. Moreover, the majority of Americans strongly opposed foreign entanglements. But as debate over diplomatic policy heated up, terrifying events overseas pulled the nation steadily toward war.

The Shadows of War

War spread first across Asia. Militarist-imperialist leaders in Japan, which suffered economically from loss of trade during the 1930s, determined to make their nation the richest in the world. The Japanese army seized control of Manchuria in 1931 and in 1932 installed a puppet government there. When reprimanded by the League of Nations, Japan simply withdrew from the organization. In 1937 Japan provoked full-scale war with an invasion of northern China. When it seized control of the capital city of Nanking, Japan's army murdered as many as 300,000 Chinese men, women, and children and destroyed much of the city. Within the year Japan controlled all but China's western interior and threatened all Asia and the Pacific.

Meanwhile, the rise of authoritarian nationalism in Italy and Germany cast a dark shadow over Europe. The economic hardships brought on by the Great Depression—and, in Germany, resentment over the harsh terms of the Treaty of Versailles, which ended World War I—fueled the rise of demagogic mass movements. Glorifying war as a test of national virility, the Italian Fascist dictator Benito Mussolini, who had seized power in 1922, declared, "We have buried the putrid corpse of liberty." In Germany, the National Socialists (Nazis), led by Adolf Hitler, combined militaristic rhetoric with a racist doctrine of Aryan (Nordic) supremacy that claimed biological superiority for the blond-haired and blue-eyed peoples of northern Europe and classified nonwhites, including Jews, as "degenerate races."

Hitler, who became chancellor of Germany in January 1933 with the backing of major industrialists and about a third of the electorate, prepared for war. With his brown-shirted storm troopers ruling the streets, he quickly destroyed opposition parties and effectively made himself dictator of the strongest nation in central Europe. Renouncing the disarmament provisions of the Versailles treaty, he began, with no effective protest from France and Britain, to rebuild Germany's armed forces. Intending to make Germany the center of a greater Reich that would last a millennium, the Nazi leader built up a vast industrial infrastructure for an army of a half-million men poised to conquer Europe.

The prospect of war grew as both Mussolini and Hitler began to act on their imperial visions. In 1935 Italy invaded Ethiopia and formally claimed the impoverished African kingdom as a colony. In 1936 Hitler sent 35,000 troops to occupy the Rhineland, a region demilitarized by the Versailles treaty. When the Spanish Civil War broke out later that year, Italy and Germany both supported the fascist insurrection of General Francisco Franco and then, in November, drew up a formal alliance to become the Rome-Berlin Axis. Hitler was now nearly ready to put into operation his plan to secure *Lebensraum*—living space for Germany's growing population—through further territorial expansion.

After annexing his native Austria, Hitler turned his attention to Czechoslovakia, a country which both Britain and France were pledged by treaty to assist. War seemed imminent. But Britain and France surprised

Hitler by agreeing, at a conference in Munich the last week of September 1938, to allow Germany to annex the Sudetenland, a part of Czechoslovakia bordering Germany. In return, Hitler pledged to stop his territorial advance. Less than six months later, in March 1939, Hitler seized the rest of Czechoslovakia.

By this time, much of the world was aware of the horror of Hitler's regime, especially its virulent racist doctrines. After 1935, when Hitler published the notorious Nuremberg Laws denying civil rights to Jews, the campaign against them became steadily more vicious. On the night of November 9, 1938, Nazi storm troopers rounded up Jews, beating them mercilessly and murdering an untold number. They smashed windows in Jewish shops, hospitals, and orphanages and burned synagogues to the ground. This attack came to be known as *Kristallnacht*, "the Night of Broken Glass." The Nazi government soon expropriated Jewish property and excluded Jews from all but the most menial forms of employment. Pressured by Hitler, Hungary and Italy also enacted laws against Jews.

Isolationism

World War I had left a legacy of strong isolationist sentiment in the United States. Senseless slaughter might be a centuries-old way of life in Europe, many Americans reasoned, but not for the United States, which, as Thomas Jefferson had advised, should stay clear of "entangling alliances." While Hollywood movies such as *All Quiet on the Western Front* (1930) graphically depicted the horrors of war, historians published scores of popular books criticizing the abandonment of America's isolationist policy during the Great War. As late as 1937, nearly 70 percent of Americans responding to a Gallup poll stated that U.S. involvement in World War I had been a mistake.

This sentiment won strong support in Congress. In 1934, a special committee headed by Republican senator Gerald P. Nye of North Dakota had charged weapons manufacturers with driving the United States into World War I in the hopes of windfall profits, which, in fact, many realized. In 1935, Congress passed the first of five Neutrality Acts to deter future entanglements, requiring the president to declare an embargo on the sale and shipment of munitions to all belligerent nations.

College students, seeing themselves as future cannon fodder, strongly opposed foreign entanglements. In 1933, 39 percent of those polled stated that they would refuse to fight in any war; 33 percent would fight only if the United States were attacked. Three years later, 500,000 boycotted classes in a nationwide "student strike" to demonstrate their opposition to any preparation for war.

Isolationism spanned the political spectrum. In 1938 socialist Norman Thomas gathered leading liberals and trade unionists into the Keep America Out of War Congress; the communist-influenced American League against War and Fascism claimed more than 1 million members. Meanwhile, Republican senator Robert A. Taft of Ohio, son of former president William Howard Taft, argued that a new war would harm American democracy by enlarging the federal government and tightening its grip on the citizenry.

In 1940 the arch-conservative America First Committee was formed to oppose U.S. intervention. The group was particularly strong in the Midwest. Some America Firsters championed the Nazis while others simply advocated American neutrality. Chaired by top Sears executive Robert E. Wood, the America First Committee quickly gained attention because its members included such well-known personalities as movie stars Robert Young and Lillian Gish, automobile manufacturer Henry Ford, and Charles A. Lindbergh, famous for his 1927 solo flight across the Atlantic. Within a year, America First had launched more than 450 chapters.

Roosevelt Readies for War

While Americans looked on anxiously, the twists and turns of world events prompted President Franklin D. Roosevelt to ready the nation for war. In October 1937 he had called for international cooperation to "quarantine the aggressors." "Let no one imagine that America will escape, that America may expect mercy, that this Western Hemisphere will not be attacked." But a poll of Congress revealed that a two-thirds majority opposed economic sanctions, calling any such plan a "back door to war." Forced to draw back, Roosevelt nevertheless won from Congress $1 billion in appropriations to enlarge the navy. But as late as January 1939, in his annual address to Congress, Roosevelt insisted that the United States must use all means "short of war" to deter aggression.

Everything changed on September 1, 1939, when Hitler invaded Poland. Committed by treaty to defend Poland against unprovoked attack, Great Britain and France issued a joint declaration of war against Germany two days later. After the fall of Warsaw at the end of the month, the fighting slowed to a near halt. Even along their border, French and German troops did not exchange fire. From the east, however, the invasion continued. Just two weeks before Hitler overran Poland, the Soviet Union had stunned the world by signing a nonaggression pact with its former enemy. The Red Army now entered Poland, and the two great powers proceeded to split the hapless nation between them. Soviet forces then headed north, invading Finland on November 30. The European war had begun.

Calculating that the United States would stay out of the war, Hitler began a crushing offensive against western Europe in April 1940. Using the technique of

Blitzkrieg (lightning war)—massed, fast-moving columns of tanks supported by air power—that had overwhelmed Poland, Nazi troops moved first against Germany's northern neighbors. After taking Denmark and Norway, the Nazi armored divisions swept over Holland, Belgium, and Luxembourg and sent more than 338,000 British troops into retreat across the English Channel from Dunkerque. Hitler's army, joined by the Italians, easily conquered France in June 1940. Hitler now turned toward England. In the Battle of Britain, Nazi bombers pounded population and industrial centers while U-boats cut off incoming supplies.

Even with Great Britain under attack, opinion polls indicated Americans' determination to stay out of the war. But most Americans, like Roosevelt himself, believed that the security of the United States depended on both a strong defense and the defeat of Germany. Invoking the Neutrality Act of 1939, which permitted the sale of arms to Britain, France, and China, the president clarified his position: "all aid to the Allies short of war." In May 1940 he began to transfer surplus U.S. planes and equipment to the Allies. In September the president secured the first peacetime military draft in American history, the Selective Service Act of 1940, which sent 1.4 million men to army training camps by July 1941. Yet even when he secured huge congressional appropriations for the production of airplanes and battleships, Roosevelt did so in the name of "hemispheric defense," not intervention. President Roosevelt could not yet admit the inevitability of U.S. involvement—especially during an election year. His popularity had dropped with the "Roosevelt recession" that began in 1937, raising doubts that he could win what would be an unprecedented third term. Waiting until July 1940, the eve of the Democratic Party convention, Roosevelt announced that world events compelled him to accept a party "draft" for renomination. In his campaign he promised voters not to "send your boys to any foreign wars." Roosevelt and his vice presidential candidate Henry Wallace won by a margin of 5 million popular votes over the Republican darkhorse candidate, Wendell L. Willkie of Indiana.

Roosevelt now moved more aggressively to aid the Allies in their struggle with the Axis powers. In his annual

Gallup Polls: European War and World War I, 1938–1940   These three polls conducted by the American Institute of Public Opinion indicate the persistence of isolationist sentiment and popular criticism of U.S. involvement in World War I. Many respondents believed the United States, despite its commitments to European allies, should stay out of war. After 1940, in the aftermath of Nazi military victories in Europe, many Americans reconsidered their opposition, fearing a threat to democracy in their own nation.

OCTOBER 2, 1938
EUROPEAN WAR

If England and France go to war against Germany do you think the United States can stay out?

Yes	57%
No	43

By Region

	Yes	No
New England	46%	54%
Middle Atlantic	61	39
East Central	60	40
West Central	57	43
South	60	40
West	51	49

Interviewing Date 9/15–20/1938, Survey #132, Question #4

FEBRUARY 21, 1940
EUROPEAN WAR

If it appears that Germany is defeating England and France, should the United States declare war on Germany and send our army and navy to Europe to fight?

Yes	23%
No	77

7 percent expressed no opinion.

Interviewing Date 2/2–7/1940, Survey #183-K, Question #6

DECEMBER 16, 1940
EUROPEAN WAR

Do you think it was a mistake for the United States to enter the last World War?

Yes	39%
No	42
No opinion	19

By Political Affiliation
Democrats

Yes	33%
No	46
No opinion	21

Republicans

Yes	46%
No	38
No opinion	16

Interviewing Date 11/21–30/1940, Survey #244-K, Question #6

message to Congress, he proposed a bill that would allow the president to sell, exchange, or lease arms to any country whose defense appeared vital to U.S. security. Passed by Congress in March, 1941, the Lend-Lease Act made Great Britain the first beneficiary of massive aid. Roosevelt also extended the U.S. "security zone" nearly halfway across the Atlantic Ocean and ordered the Coast Guard to seize any German-controlled or German ships that entered an American port. He directed Germany and Italy to close their U.S. consulates and ordered U.S. ships to shoot any Nazi vessel in U.S. "defensive waters" on sight. After Congress authorized the merchant marine

to sail fully armed while conveying lend-lease supplies directly to Britain, a formal declaration of war was only a matter of time.

In August 1941 Roosevelt met secretly at sea off Newfoundland with British prime minister Winston Churchill to map military strategy and declare common goals for the postwar world. Known as the Atlantic Charter, their proclamation specified the right of all peoples to live in freedom from fear, want, and tyranny. The Atlantic Charter also called for free trade among all nations, an end to territorial seizures, and disarmament. Eventually endorsed by the Soviet Union and

Japanese attack planes devastated the U.S. fleet stationed on the Hawaiian island of Oahu. Before December 7, 1941, few Americans had heard of Pearl Harbor, but the "sneak" attack became a symbol of Japanese treachery and the necessity for U.S. revenge.

SOURCE: National Archives and Records Administration.

fourteen other nations, the Atlantic Charter pledged to all nations—vanquished as well as victors—the right to self-determination.

By this time the European war had moved to a new stage. Hitler had conquered the Balkans and then set aside the expedient Nazi-Soviet Pact to resume his quest for the entire European continent. In June 1941 Hitler launched an invasion of the Soviet Union, promising its rich agricultural land to German farmers. Observing this dramatic escalation, the United States moved closer to intervention.

Pearl Harbor

Throughout 1940 and much of 1941 the United States focused on events in Europe, but the war in Asia went on. Roosevelt, anticipating danger to American interests in the Pacific, had directed the transfer of the Pacific Fleet from bases in California to Pearl Harbor, on the island of Oahu, Hawai'i, in May 1940. On September 27 Japan formally joined Germany and Italy as the Asian partner of the Axis alliance. Under the terms of the expanded alliance, Germany would support Japan's seizure of Dutch, British, and French colonial possessions as part of Japan's attempt to create a regional bloc under its rule.

The United States and Japan each played for time. Roosevelt wanted to save his resources to fight against Germany, while Japan's leaders gambled that America's preoccupation with Europe might allow them to conquer all of Southeast Asia, including the French colonies in Indochina (Vietnam, Cambodia, and Laos) and the British possessions of Burma and India. When Japan occupied Indochina in July 1941, however, Roosevelt responded by freezing Japanese assets in the United States and cutting off its oil supplies. Confrontation with Japan now looked likely. U.S. intelligence had broken the Japanese diplomatic code, and the president knew that Japan was preparing for war against the Western powers. Roosevelt's advisers expected an attack somewhere in the Pacific and by the end of November placed all American forces there on high alert.

Japan, however, intended to knock the United States out of the Pacific in a single blow. Early Sun-day morning, December 7, 1941, Japanese carriers launched an attack on Pearl Harbor that caught American forces completely off guard. Sailors on the decks of American ships looked up to see Japanese dive-bombers in the sky above them. Loudspeakers warned: "Japs are coming! Japs attacking us! Go to your battle stations!" Within two hours, Japanese pilots had destroyed nearly 200 American planes and badly damaged the fleet; more than 2,400 Americans were killed and nearly 1,200 wounded. On the same day, Japan struck U.S. bases on the Philippines, Guam, and Wake Island.

On December 8, declaring the attack on Pearl Harbor a day that "will live in infamy," Roosevelt asked Congress for a declaration of war against Japan. With only one dissenting vote—by pacifist Jeannette Rankin of Montana, who had voted against U.S. entry into World War I in 1917—Congress acceded. The United States had not yet declared war on Japan's European allies, but Hitler made that unnecessary when he asked the *Reichstag* on December 11 to support war against the "half Judaized, and the other half Negrified" American nation. Mussolini joined him in the declaration, and the United States on the same day recognized that a state of war existed with Germany and Italy. World War II now began for Americans.

On the day after the attack on Pearl Harbor, President Franklin D. Roosevelt addressed a joint session of Congress and asked for an immediate declaration of war against Japan. The resolution passed with one dissenting vote, and the United States entered World War II.

SOURCE: AP/Wide World Photos.

ARSENAL OF DEMOCRACY

Late in 1940 President Roosevelt called upon all Americans to make the nation a "great arsenal of democracy." During the next three years, the economic machinery that had failed during the 1930s was swiftly retooled for military purposes, with dramatic results. The Great Depression suddenly ended. Never before had the federal government poured so much energy and money into production or assigned such a great army of experts to manage it. This marshaling of resources involved a concentration of power in the federal government that exceeded anything planned by the New Deal.

Mobilizing for War

A few days after the United States declared war on Germany, Congress passed the War Powers Act, which established a precedent for executive authority that would endure long after the war's end. The president gained the power to reorganize the federal government and create new agencies; to establish programs censoring all news and information and abridging civil liberties; to seize property owned by foreigners; and even to award government contracts without competitive bidding.

Roosevelt promptly created special wartime agencies. At the top of his agenda was a massive reorientation and management of the economy, and an alphabet soup of new agencies arose to fill any gaps in production. The Supply Priorities and Allocation Board (SPAB) oversaw the use of scarce materials and resources vital to the war, adjusting domestic consumption (even ending it for some products such as automobiles) to military needs. The Office of Price Administration (OPA) checked the threat of inflation from the government's sudden massive spending by imposing price controls. The National War Labor Board (NWLB) mediated disputes between labor and management, halting strikes and also controlling inflation by limiting wage increases. The War Manpower Commission (WMC) directed the mobilization of military and civilian services. And the Office of War Mobilization (OWM), headed by New Dealer James F. Byrnes, coordinated operations among all these agencies.

Several new agencies focused on domestic propaganda. The attack on Pearl Harbor evoked an outpouring of rage against Japan and effectively quashed much opposition to U.S. intervention. Still, for most Americans, World War II would remain a foreign war, and the government stepped in to fan the fires of patriotism and to shape public opinion. In June 1942 the president created the Office of War Information (OWI) to coordinate information from the multiplying federal agencies and to engage the press, radio, and film industry in an informational campaign—in short, to sell the war to the American people.

The OWI gathered data and controlled the release of news, emphasizing the need to make reports on the war both dramatic and encouraging. Like the Committee on Public Information during World War I, during the first twenty-one months of the war the new agency banned the publication of advertisements, photographs, and newsreels showing American dead, fearing that such images would demoralize the public. In 1943, worrying that Americans had become overconfident, officials changed their policy. A May issue of *Newsweek* featured graphic photographs of Americans wounded in battle, explaining that "to harden home-front morale, the military services have adopted a new policy of letting civilians see photographically what warfare does to men who fight." To spare families unnecessary grief, throughout the war the OWI prohibited the publication of any photograph revealing the identity of the American dead. The OWI also published leaflets and booklets for the armed services and flooded enemy ranks with subversive propaganda.

Propaganda also fueled the selling of war bonds. Secretary of the Treasury Henry Morgenthau, Jr. not only encouraged Americans to buy government bonds to finance the war but planned a campaign "to use bonds to sell the war, rather than vice versa." Bonds, the ads for them claimed, were a good investment that gave everyone an opportunity "to have a financial stake in American democracy." Buying them would "mean bullets in the bellies of Hitler's hordes!" Discovering through research that Americans felt more antagonism to Japan than Germany, Morgenthau directed his staff to use more negative stereotypes of the Japanese in their advertising copy. Polls showed, however, that most Depression-stung Americans bought war bonds— $185.7 billion by war's end—mainly to invest safely, to counter inflation, and to save for postwar purchases.

The federal government also sponsored various measures to prevent subversion of the war effort. Concerned about enemy propaganda, the Office of Facts and Figures hired political scientist Harold Lasswell of Yale University to devise a means to measure the patriotic content of magazines and newspapers. The Federal Bureau of Investigation (FBI) was kept busy, its appropriation rising from $6 million to $16 million in just two years. The attorney general authorized wiretapping in cases of espionage or sabotage, but the FBI used it extensively—and illegally—in domestic surveillance. The Joint Chiefs of Staff created the Office of Strategic Services (OSS) to assess the enemy's military strength, to gather intelligence information, and to oversee espionage activities. Its head, Colonel William Donovan, envisioned the OSS as an "adjunct to military strategy" and engaged leading social scientists to plot psychological warfare against the enemy.

One important outcome of these activities was to increase the size of the government many times over its New Deal level, which conservatives already considered far too large. It cost about $250 million a day to fight the war. As a result, the federal government spent twice as much during the war as it had during the nation's entire history up to then. The federal budget grew to ten times what it had been during the New Deal. Nearly half the revenue required to fight the war was produced by new rates of taxation. The number of Americans filing income tax returns jumped from 4 million before the war to 42.6 million at war's end. At the same time, the number of federal employees nearly quadrupled, from a little over 1 million in 1940 to nearly 4 million by the war's end.

Despite this pattern of expansion, however, the New Deal itself fell victim to the war. As President Roosevelt announced in 1942, "Dr. New Deal" had been replaced by "Dr. Win the War." No longer carrying the heavy responsibility of bringing the nation out of the Great Depression, his administration directed all its resources toward securing the planes, ships, guns, and food required for victory. Moreover, the 1942 elections weakened the New Deal coalition by unseating many liberal Democrats. The Republicans gained forty-six new members in the House of Representatives, nine in the Senate. Republicans now had greater opportunity to quash proposals to extend the social programs instituted during the 1930s. One by one, New Deal agencies vanished. One of the most popular programs, the Civilian Conservation Corps, secured funds from Congress, but only to cover its liquidation. In December 1942, the Works Progress Administration, which handled various forms of work relief, was given, in Roosevelt's words, a "wartime furlough"; a few months later Congress granted the agency an "honorable discharge." Major New Deal agencies, including the National Youth Administration and the Federal Writers Project, were dismantled by 1943.

Economic Conversion

The decisive factor for victory, even more than military prowess and superior strategy, would be, many observers agreed, the ability of the United States to outproduce its enemies. The country enjoyed many advantages to meet this challenge: a large industrial base, abundant natural resources (largely free from interference by the war), and a civilian population large enough to permit it to increase both its labor force and its armed forces. The war would lift the United States out of the Great Depression and create the biggest economic boom in the history of any nation. But first the entire civilian economy had to be both expanded and transformed for the production of arms and other military supplies.

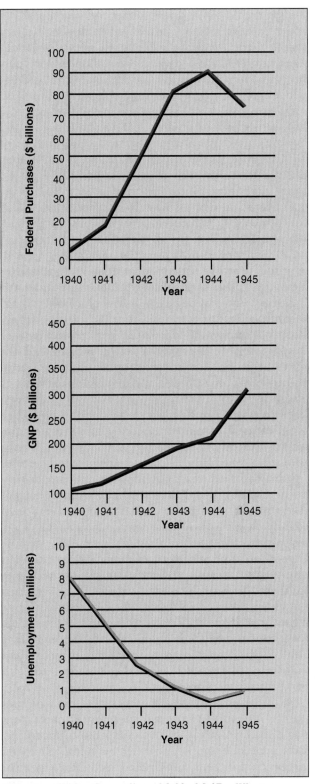

Effects of War Spending, 1940–1945   Wartime spending had a multiplier effect on the U.S. economy. Government contracts with industry rapidly increased the gross national product, and the sharp upswing in production utilized all available workers and sharply reduced unemployment.

SOURCE: Robert L. Heilbroner, *The Economic Transformation of America* (New York: Harcourt, Brace, 1977), p. 205.

Economic conversion resulted from a combination of government spending and foreign orders for military supplies. The American public firmly opposed rearmament until 1938, when expenditures for military purposes amounted to only 1.5 percent of the federal budget. The revision of neutrality legislation in 1939 eased previous restrictions on the sale of war materials to France and Great Britain, creating a huge market and boosting production significantly. By the summer of 1941 the federal government was pouring vast amounts into defense production. Six months after the attack on Pearl Harbor its allocations topped $100 billion for equipment and supplies, which exceeded what American firms had produced in any previous war. Facing war orders too large to fill, American industries were now primed for all-out production. Before the Japanese attack on Pearl Harbor, President Roosevelt counted on American businesses to manage their own war-related industries. After announcing a goal of 60,000 planes, 45,000 tanks, and 8 million tons of ships for 1942, Roosevelt formed the War Production Board in January of that year. He directed the new agency to "exercise general responsibility" for the economy. By June, nearly half of everything produced in the United States was war materiel.

Every economic indicator pointed upward. The gross national product (accounting for inflation) rose from $88.6 billion in 1939 to $198.7 billion in five years. Investment in new plants and equipment, including the manufacture of newly discovered synthetic rubber and fabrics, made possible an increase of 50 percent in the nation's productive capacity and the creation of 17 million jobs. Factories operated around-the-clock, seven days a week. With better equipment and more motivation, American workers proved twice as productive as the Germans, five times as productive as the Japanese. No wonder the actual volume of industrial output expanded at the fastest rate in American history. Military production alone grew from 2 percent of the 1939 total gross national product to 40 percent of the 1943 total. "Something is happening," announced *Time* magazine, "that Adolf Hitler does not understand . . . it is the miracle of production."

Businesses scored huge profits from military contracts. The government provided low-interest loans and even direct subsidies for the expansion of facilities, with generous tax write-offs for retooling. The 100 largest corporations, which manufactured 30 percent of all goods in 1940, garnered 70 percent of all war and civilian contracts and the bulk of the war profits. On the other hand, many small businesses closed, a half-million between 1941 and 1943 alone.

Defense production transformed entire regions. The impact was strongest in the West—the major staging area for the war in the Pacific—where the federal government spent nearly $40 billion for military and industrial expansion. California secured 10 percent of all federal funds, and by 1944 Los Angeles had become the nation's second largest manufacturing center, only slightly behind Detroit. The South also benefited from 60 of the army's 100 new camps. Its textile factories hummed: the army alone required nearly 520 million pairs of socks and 230 million pairs of pants. The southern branch of the Manhattan Project, the Oak Ridge, Tennessee, facility for the production of uranium, employed more than 80,000 workers during 1945, its peak year. The economic boom lifted entire populations out of sharecropping and tenancy into well-paid industrial jobs in the cities and pumped unprecedented profits into southern business. Across the country the rural population decreased by almost 20 percent.

Despite a "Food for Freedom" program, American farmers could not keep up with the rising international demand or even the domestic market for milk, potatoes, fruits, and sugar. The Department of Agriculture reached its goals only in areas such as livestock production, thanks to skyrocketing wholesale prices for meat. The war also speeded the development of large-scale, mechanized production of crops, including the first widespread use of chemical fertilizers and pesticides. By 1945 farm income had doubled, but thousands of small farms had disappeared, never to return.

New Workers

The wartime economy brought an unprecedented number of new workers into the labor force. The *bracero* program, negotiated by United States and Mexico in 1942, brought more than 200,000 Mexicans into the United States for short-term employment as mainly manual laborers and agricultural workers. The program also opened trades previously closed to them, such as shipbuilding on the Pacific coast. In 1944 a survey published by the Bureau of Indian Affairs reported that more than 46,000 Indian peoples were working in either agriculture or industry. The Sioux and Navajos, for example, were hired in large numbers to help build military depots and military training centers. African Americans found new opportunities in industry, in just four years securing a greater variety of jobs than in the seven decades since the outbreak of the Civil War. The number of black workers rose from 2,900,000 to 3,800,000.

The war most dramatically altered the wage-earning patterns of women. The female labor force grew by over 50 percent, reaching 19.5 million in 1945. The rate of growth proved especially high for white women over the age of thirty-five, and for the first time married women became the majority of female wage earners. The employment rate changed comparatively little for African

Facing a shortage of workers and increased production demands, the War Manpower Commission and the Office of War Information conducted a campaign to recruit women into the labor force. Women were encouraged to "take a job for your husband/son/brother" and to "keep the world safe for your children." Higher wages also enticed many women to take jobs in factories producing aircraft, ships, and ordnance. This photograph shows women working on the assembly line at Douglas Aircraft's plant in Long Beach, California, in 1944.

SOURCE: The Granger Collection (4E887.35).

Their skill with a vacuum cleaner easily translated into riveting on huge ships. "Instead of cutting a cake," one newsreel explained, "this woman [factory worker] cuts the pattern of aircraft parts. Instead of baking a cake, this woman is cooking gears to reduce the tension in the gears after use."

In practice, however, many stereotypes broke down. Women mined coal, repaired aircraft engines, cut and welded sheet metal, and operated forklifts and drill presses. On the Pacific coast, more than one-third of all workers in aircraft and shipbuilding were women. One female African American ship welder recalled: "There is nothing in the training to prepare you for the excruciating noise you get down in the ship. Any who were not heart-and-soul determined to stick it out would fade out right away. . . . And it isn't only your muscles that must harden. It's your nerve, too."

Compared to the Great Depression, when married women were barred from many jobs, World War II opened up new fields. The number of women automobile workers, for example, jumped from 29,000 to 200,000, that of women electrical workers from 100,000 to 374,000. Polled near the end of the war, the overwhelming majority—75 percent—of women workers expressed a desire to keep working, preferably at the same jobs. One woman spoke for many in describing her wartime work as "thrilling" and "exciting," adding that it was also "something women have never been allowed to do before." Many also candidly admitted that they most of all liked earning good money. One woman reported that her assembly-line job in the aircraft industry paid $1.15 per hour, a huge increase over the hourly wage she formerly earned as a waitress: 20 cents, with no tips allowed.

Although wartime employment changed the lives and raised the expectations of many new workers, the major advances proved short-lived. As early as 1943 some industries began planning to lay off women as war production wound down. With jobs reserved for returning veterans, women in industry saw their numbers diminish rapidly; as many as 4 million lost their jobs between 1944 and 1946. Although skyrocketing inflation propelled many married women back into the

American women; fully 90 percent had been in the labor force in 1940. However, many black women left domestic service for higher-paying jobs in manufacturing.

Despite this jump in employment rates, neither government nor industry rushed to recruit women. Well into the summer of 1942 the Department of War advised businesses to hold back from hiring women "until all available male labor in the area had first been employed." Likewise, neither government nor industry expected women to stay in their jobs when the war ended. Recruitment campaigns targeted "Mrs. Stay-at-Home" yet underscored the temporary aspect of her wartime service. "Rosie the Riveter" appeared in posters and advertisements as the model female citizen, but only "for the duration." In Washington, D.C., women bus drivers were given badges to wear on their uniforms that read: "I am taking the place of a man who went to war."

For the most part, advertisers used conventional gender stereotypes to make wartime jobs appealing to women. Recruitment posters and informational films depicted women's new industrial jobs as simple variations of domestic tasks. Where once housewives sewed curtains for their kitchens, they now produced silk parachutes.

labor force by the end of the decade, they did not pick up lucrative jobs in heavy industry.

Wartime Strikes

Although the wartime economy drained just about all pools of unemployed labor remaining from the Great Depression, the gains from the 17 million new jobs were not evenly distributed. Wages during wartime increased by as much as 50 percent but never as fast as profits or prices. This widely reported disparity produced one of the most turbulent periods in American labor history.

Labor strife began even before U.S. involvement in World War II. Only two weeks after the 1940 election, workers struck at the Vultee aircraft plant in Los Angeles. After the attorney general denounced the strikers as unpatriotic and the FBI began to harass participants, workers throughout the city walked off their jobs in sympathy with the aircraft workers. In April 1941 the president himself intervened in a large strike at Allis-Chalmers near Milwaukee, threatening seizure of the plant and forcing a settlement after seventy-five days of work stoppage. Later that year Roosevelt ordered troops to break the North American Aviation strike at Inglewood, California.

More workers went on strike in 1941, before the United States entered the war, than in any previous year except 1919. Rising production orders and tightening labor markets made strikes feasible: jobs were plentiful, and business leaders, anticipating hefty profits, had reason to settle quickly. This climate prompted a militant union drive at Ford Motor Company's enormous River Rouge plant, and the United Auto Workers (UAW) emerged as one of the most powerful labor organizations in the world.

Once the United States entered the war, the major unions dutifully agreed to no-strike pledges for its duration. The National War Labor Board, with representatives from business and labor, encouraged employers to allow unions in their plants, and unions secured contracts that included automatic dues checkoff, high wages, and new fringe benefits such as pension plans. Total union membership increased from 10.5 million to 14.7 million, with the women's share alone rising from 11 to 23 percent.

Unions also enrolled 1,250,000 African Americans, twice the prewar number. But many white workers resisted this change. "Hate strikes" broke out in plants across the country when African Americans were hired or promoted to jobs customarily held by white workers. For example, at a U.S. Rubber Company factory in Detroit, more than half the workers walked out in 1943 when African American women began to operate the machinery. Such strikes usually ended quickly because black workers refused to back down.

Rank-and-file union members staged other illegal "wildcat" strikes. The most dramatic, a walkout of more than a half-million coal miners in 1943 led by the rambunctious John L. Lewis, withstood the attacks of the government and the press. Roosevelt repeatedly ordered the mines seized, only to find, as Lewis retorted, that coal could not be mined with bayonets. The Democratic majority in Congress passed the first federal antistrike bill, giving the president power to penalize strikers, even to draft them. And yet the strikes grew in size and number, reaching a level greater than in any other four-year period in American history. Most, however, were of short duration and did not interrupt the war effort.

		STRIKES AND LOCKOUTS IN THE UNITED STATES, 1940–1945		
Year	Number of Strikes	Number of Workers Involved	Number of Man-Days Idle	Percent of Total Employed
1940	2,508	576,988	6,700,872	2.3
1941	4,288	2,362,620	23,047,556	8.4
1942	2,968	839,961	4,182,557	2.8
1943	3,752	1,981,279	13,500,529	6.9
1944	4,956	2,115,637	8,721,079	7.0
1945	4,750	3,467,000	38,025,000	12.2

Despite "no-strike" pledges, workers staged wildcat strikes in the war years. Union leaders negotiated shorter hours, higher wages, and seniority rules and helped to build union membership to a new height. When the war ended, nearly 30 percent of all nonagricultural workers were union members.
SOURCE: "Work Stoppages Caused by Labor-Management Disputes in 1945," *Monthly Labor Review,* May 1946, p. 720; and Martin Glaberman, *War Time Strikes* (Detroit: Bewick, 1980), p. 36.

THE HOME FRONT

Most Americans thoroughly appreciated the burst of prosperity brought on by wartime production. But they also experienced dramatic and unanticipated changes in the ways they worked and lived. Food rationing, long workdays, and separation from loved ones were just a few of the new conditions of daily life. Americans in communities across the country endured four intense years of adjustment.

Most Americans were happy and proud to make whatever sacrifices they could to help bring about the Allied victory. But alongside national unity ran deep conflicts on the home front. Racial and ethnic hostilities flared repeatedly and on several occasions erupted in violence.

Families in Wartime

Despite the uncertainties of wartime, or perhaps because of them, men and women rushed into marriage. The surge in personal income caused by the wartime economic boom meant that many young couples could afford to set up their own households—something their counterparts in the 1930s had not been able to do. As one social scientist remarked at the time, "Economic conditions were ripe for a rush to the altar." For other couples, the prospect of separation provided the incentive. The U.S. Census Bureau estimated that between 1940 and 1943 at least a million more people married than would have been expected had there been no war. The marriage rate skyrocketed, peaking in 1946. The median age for first marriage for women dropped to an unprecedented low of 20.3 years. But by 1946 the number of divorces also set records.

Housing shortages were acute, and rents were high. So scarce were apartments that taxi drivers became, for an extra fee, up-to-the-minute guides to vacancies. Able to set their own terms, landlords frequently discriminated against families with children and even more so against racial minorities. To ease these pressures, the National Housing Agency kicked off the "Share Your Home" campaign, which ultimately encouraged 1.5 million families to open their homes to friends, relatives, or

Students at Officers' Training School at Northwestern University, who were not allowed to marry until they were commissioned as ensigns, apply for marriage licenses in Chicago, August 20, 1943, shortly before graduation. These young couples helped the marriage rate skyrocket during World War II.

SOURCE: CORBIS (CS/695089).

strangers. The federal government also financed the construction of low-cost housing projects, which furnished approximately 2 million new residential units.

Supplying a household was scarcely less difficult. Although retailers extended their store hours into the evenings and weekends, shopping had to be squeezed in between long hours on the job. Extra planning was necessary for purchasing government-rationed staples such as meat, cheese, sugar, milk, coffee, gasoline, and even shoes. To free up commercially grown produce for the troops overseas, many families grew their own fruits and vegetables. In 1943, the peak year of Victory Gardens, three-fifths of the population were "growing their own," which amounted to a staggering 8 million tons of food that year.

Although the Office of Price Administration tried to prevent inflation and ensure an equitable distributions of foodstuffs, many women found it nearly impossible to manage both a demanding job and a household. This dual responsibility contributed to high turnover and absentee rates in factories. A 1943 survey reported that 40 percent of all women who left war plants did so for marital or household reasons rather than because of unsatisfactory wages or working conditions.

The care of small children became a major problem. Wartime employment or military service often separated husbands and wives, leaving children in the hands of only one parent. But even when families stayed together, both adults often worked long hours, sometimes on different shifts. Although the War Manpower Commission estimated that as many as 2 million children needed some form of child care, federally funded day-care centers served less than 10 percent of defense workers' children. Polls indicated that the majority of mothers would in any case refuse to send their youngsters to a public child-care center. In some communities, industries and municipal governments established limited facilities that could not keep up with the rapid increase in the number of "latchkey" children.

Juvenile delinquency rose during the war. With employers often relaxing minimum age requirements for employment, many teenagers quit school for the high wages of factory jobs. Between 1941 and 1944 high school enrollments decreased by 1.2 million. Runaways drifted from city to city, finding temporary work at wartime plants or at military installations. Gangs formed in major urban areas, leading to brawling, prostitution, or automobile thefts for joy rides. Overall, however, with so many young men either employed or serving in the armed forces, crime by juvenile as well as adult males declined. In contrast, complaints against girls, mainly for sexual offenses or for running away from home, increased significantly. In response, local officials created various youth agencies and charged them with developing more recreational and welfare programs.

In 1944 the U.S. Office of Education and the Children's Bureau inaugurated a back-to-school campaign. Local school boards appealed to employers to hire only older workers, and toward the end of the war the student dropout rate began to decline. The public schools, meanwhile, expanded their curriculums to include nutrition, hygiene, first aid, and the political context of the war itself. Although many teachers had quit to take better-paying jobs in industry, those who remained often organized scrap and salvage missions, war bond drives, Victory Gardens, and letter-writing campaigns. In many localities, the school stood at the center of community war efforts.

Public health improved greatly during the war. Forced to cut back on expenditures for medical care during the Great Depression, many Americans now spent large portions of their wartime paychecks on doctors, dentists, and prescription drugs. But even more important were the benefits provided to the more than 16 million men inducted into the armed forces and their dependents. The majority of young, well-trained physicians and dentists worked in uniform, providing their services at government expense. The number of doctors and dentists also increased dramatically: the graduating classes of 1944 were twice as large as those of any pre-war year. Nationally, incidences of such communicable diseases as typhoid fever, tuberculosis, and diphtheria dropped considerably, the infant death rate fell by more than a third, and life expectancy increased by three years. The death rate in 1942, excluding battle deaths, was the lowest in the nation's history. In the South and Southwest, however, racism and widespread poverty combined to halt or even reverse these trends. These regions continued to have the highest infant and maternal mortality rates in the nation.

The Internment of Japanese Americans

After the attack on Pearl Harbor, many Americans feared an invasion of the mainland and suspected Japanese Americans of secret loyalty to an enemy government. On December 8, 1941, the federal government froze the financial assets of those born in Japan, known as Issei, who had been barred from U.S. citizenship. Politicians, patriotic organizations, and military officials, meanwhile, called for the removal of all Americans of Japanese descent from Pacific coastal areas. Although a State Department intelligence report certified their loyalty, Japanese Americans—two-thirds of whom were American-born citizens—became the only ethnic group singled out for legal sanctions.

Charges of sedition masked long-standing racial prejudices. The press began to use the word "Jap" in headlines, while political cartoonists employed blatant racial stereotypes. Popular songs appeared with titles like

"You're a Sap, Mister Jap, to Make a Yankee Cranky." The head of the army's Western Defense Command, General John L. DeWitt, called the Japanese "an enemy race," bound by "racial affinities" to their homeland no matter how many generations removed. "The very fact that no sabotage has taken place to date," an army report suggested, with twisted logic, "is a disturbing and confirming indication that action will be taken."

On February 19, 1942, President Roosevelt signed Executive Order 9066, suspending the civil rights of Japanese Americans and authorizing the exclusion of more than 112,000 men, women, and children from designated military areas, mainly in California, but also in Oregon, Washington, and southern Arizona. At first, sectors of the small, insular communities voluntarily moved away from the Pacific coast, planning to resettle in the Midwest or East. When several governors objected to Japanese migration to their states, General DeWitt issued a "freeze order." The army prepared for forced evacuation, rounding up and removing Japanese Americans from the communities where they had lived and worked, sometimes for generations.

During the spring of 1942, Japanese American families received one week's notice to close up their businesses and homes before being transported to one of the ten internment camps managed by the War Relocation Authority. The guarded camps were located as far away as Arkansas, although the majority had been set up in isolated and arid districts of Utah, Colorado, Idaho, Arizona, Wyoming, and California. Karl G. Yoneda described his quarters at Manzanar in northern California:

> There were no lights, stoves, or window panes. My two cousins and I, together with seven others, were crowded into a 25 × 30 foot room. We slept on army cots with our clothes on. The next morning we discovered that there were no toilets or washrooms. . . . We saw GIs manning machine guns in the watchtowers. The barbed wire fence which surrounded the camp was visible against the background of the snow-covered Sierra mountain range. "So this is the American-style concentration camp," someone remarked.

Byron Takashi Tsuzuki, *Forced Removal, Act II*, 1944. This Japanese American artist illustrates the forced relocation of Japanese Americans from their homes to one of ten inland camps in 1942. About 110,000 Japanese Americans were interned during World War II, some for up to four years. Beginning in January 1945, they were allowed to return to the Pacific coast.

SOURCE: Byron Takashi Tsuzuki, *Forced Removal, Act II*, 1944. Japanese American National Museum, Collection of August and MASKO (Kitty) Nakagawa.

By August, virtually every West Coast resident who had at least one Japanese grandparent had been interned. The majority in the camps were young, 75 percent under the age of twenty-five, and approximately 6,000 more were born there.

The Japanese American Citizens League charged that "racial animosity" rather than military necessity had dictated the internment policy. Despite the protest of the American Civil Liberties Union and several church groups against the abridgment of the civil rights of Japanese Americans, the Supreme Court in *Korematsu* v. *United States* (1944) upheld the constitutionality of relocation on grounds of national security. By this time a program of gradual release was in place, although the last center, at Tule Lake, California, did not close until March 1946. In protest, nearly 6,000 Japanese Americans renounced their U.S. citizenship. Japanese Americans had lost homes and businesses valued at $500 million in what many historians judge as being the worst violation of American civil liberties during the war. Not until 1988 did the U.S. Congress vote reparations of $20,000 and a public apology to each of the 60,000 surviving victims.

Civil Rights and Race Riots

Throughout the war, African American activists conducted a "Double V" campaign, mobilizing not only for Allied victory but for their own rights as citizens. "The army is about to take me to fight for democracy," one Detroit resident said, "but I would as leave fight for democracy right here." Black militants demanded, at a minimum, fair housing and equal employment opportunities. President Roosevelt responded in a lukewarm fashion, supporting advances in civil rights that would not, in his opinion, disrupt the war effort.

Before the United States entered the war, A. Philip Randolph, president of both the Brotherhood of Sleeping Car Porters and the National Negro Congress, had organized the March on Washington Movement. At a planning meeting in Chicago a black woman had proposed sending African Americans to Washington, D.C., "from all over the country, in jalopies, in trains, and any way they can get there until we get some action from the White House." Local rallies were held across the country in preparation for the "great rally" of no less than 100,000 people at the Lincoln Memorial on the Fourth of July.

Eager to stop the movement, President Roosevelt met with Randolph, who proposed an executive order "making it mandatory that Negroes be permitted to work." Randolph reviewed several drafts before approving the text that became, on June 25, 1941, Executive Order 8802, banning discrimination in defense industries and government. The president later appointed a Fair Employment Practices Committee to hear complaints and to take "appropriate steps to redress grievances." Randolph called off the march but did not disband his all-black March on Washington organization. He remained determined to "shake up white America."

Other civil rights organizations formed during wartime to fight both discrimination and Jim Crow practices, including segregation in the U.S. armed forces. The interracial Congress of Racial Equality (CORE), formed by pacifists in 1942, staged sit-ins at Chicago, Detroit, and Denver restaurants that refused to serve African Americans. In several cities, CORE used nonviolent means to challenge racial segregation in public facilities. Meanwhile, membership in the National Association for the Advancement of Colored People (NAACP), which took a strong stand against discrimination in the military, grew from 50,000 in 1940 to 450,000 in 1946.

The struggle for equality took shape within local communities. Approximately 1.2 million African Americans left the rural South to take jobs in wartime industries. They faced not only serious housing shortages but whites who were determined to keep them out of the best jobs and neighborhoods. In February 1942, when twenty black families attempted to move into new federally funded apartments adjacent to a Polish American community in Detroit, a mob of 700 white protesters halted the moving vans and burned a cross on the project's grounds. The police overlooked the white rioters but arrested black youths. Finally, two months later, 1,000 state troopers supervised the move of these families into the Sojourner Truth Homes, named after the famous abolitionist and former slave.

Racial violence reached its wartime peak during the summer of 1943, when 274 conflicts broke out in nearly fifty cities. In Detroit, where the black population had grown by more than a third since the beginning of the war, twenty-five blacks and nine whites were killed and more than 700 were injured. After the riot, one writer reported: "I thought that I had witnessed an experience

This painting is by Horace Pippin, a self-taught African American artist who began painting as therapy for an injury suffered while serving with the U.S. Army's 369th Colored Infantry Regiment during World War I. It is one of a series drawn during World War II illustrating the contradiction between the principles of liberty and justice, for which Americans were fighting abroad, and the reality of race prejudice at home.

SOURCE: Horace Pippin (1888–1946), *Mr. Prejudice*, 1943. Oil on canvas, 18″ × 14″. Philadelphia Museum of Art, Gift of Dr. and Mrs. Matthew T. Moore. Photo by Graydon Wood (1984–108–1).

peculiar to the Deep South. On the streets of Detroit I saw again the same horrible exhibition of uninhibited hate as they fought and killed one another—white against black—in a frenzy of homicidal mania, without rhyme or reason." The poet Langston Hughes, who supported U.S. involvement in the war, wrote:

> *Looky here, America*
> *What you done done—*
> *Let things drift*
> *Until the riots come*
>
> *Yet you say we're fighting*
> *For democracy.*
> *Then why don't democracy*
> *Include me?*
>
> *I ask you this question*
> *Cause I want to know*
> *How long I got to fight*
> *BOTH HITLER—AND JIM CROW.*

The poet and educator Pauli Murray summed up the situation in a letter sent to President Roosevelt: "It is my conviction . . . that the problem of race, intensified by economic conflict and war nerves . . . will eventually . . . occupy a dominant position as a national domestic problem." Her words proved prescient.

Zoot-suit Riots

On the night of June 4, 1943, sailors poured into nearly 200 cars and taxis to drive through the streets of East Los Angeles in search of Mexican Americans dressed in zoot suits. The sailors assaulted their victims at random, even chasing one youth into a movie theater and stripping him of his clothes while the audience cheered. Riots broke out and continued for five days.

Two communities had collided, with tragic results. The sailors had only recently been uprooted from their hometowns and regrouped under the strict discipline of boot camp. Now stationed in southern California while awaiting departure overseas, they came face-to-face with Mexican American teenagers wearing long-draped coats, pegged pants, pocket watches with oversized chains, and big floppy hats. To the sailors, the zoot suit was not just a flamboyant fashion. Unlike the uniform the young sailors wore, the zoot suit signaled a lack of patriotism.

The zoot-suiters, however, represented less than 10 percent of their community's youth. More than 300,000 Mexican Americans were serving in the armed forces (a number representing a greater proportion of their draft-age population than other Americans), and they served in the most hazardous branches, the paratrooper and marine corps. Many others were employed in war

industries in Los Angeles, which had become home to the largest community of Mexican Americans in the nation. For the first time Mexican Americans were finding well-paying jobs, and, like African Americans, they expected their government to protect them from discrimination.

There were several advances during the war. The Fair Employment Practices Committee fostered a limited expansion of civil rights. The Spanish-Speaking People's Division in the Office of Inter-American Affairs established centers in Denver, Salt Lake City, and Los Angeles to bring together community, business, and educational leaders in programs on Latin American culture. The office also developed programs to instill cultural pride and self-esteem among Mexican American children. School districts in California and throughout the Southwest introduced lessons on the Mexican heritage and encouraged bilingual education. Many schools also added vocational training classes to channel graduates into wartime industry.

But these new programs did little to ease the bitter racial and cultural conflict that on occasion became vicious. In Los Angeles, military and civilian authorities eventually contained the zoot-suit riots by ruling several sections of the city off limits to military personnel. The Los Angeles City Council passed legislation making the wearing of a zoot suit in public a criminal offense. Later, the Joint Finding Committee on Un-American Activities in California conducted hearings to determine whether foreign enemy agents had plotted the unrest. Nevertheless, many Mexican Americans expressed concern about their personal safety; some feared that, after the government rounded up the Japanese, they would be the next group sent to internment camps.

Popular Culture and "The Good War"

Global events shaped the lives of American civilians but appeared to touch them only indirectly in their everyday activities. Food shortages, long hours in the factories, and even fears for loved ones abroad did not take away all the pleasures of full employment and prosperity. With money in their pockets, Americans spent freely at vacation resorts, country clubs, race-tracks, nightclubs, dance halls, and movie theaters. Sales of books skyrocketed, and spectator sports attracted huge audiences.

Popular culture, especially music, seemed to bridge the growing racial divisions of the neighborhood and the work place. Transplanted southern musicians, black and white, brought their regional styles to northern cities and adapted them quickly to the electric amplification of nightclubs and recording studios. "They'd made them steel guitars cry and whine," Ray Charles later remembered. Played on jukeboxes in bars, bus stations, and cafes, "country" and "rhythm & blues" not only won over new audiences but also inspired musicians themselves to crisscross old boundaries. The International Sweethearts of Rhythm, a group of black and white women singers, started in the Mississippi Delta but soon pleased audiences throughout the United States.

Many songs featured war themes. Personal sentiment meshed with government directive to depict a "good war," justifying massive sacrifice. The war was to be seen as a worthy and even noble cause. The plaintive "A Rainbow at Midnight" by country singer Ernest Tubb expressed the hope of a common "dogface" soldier looking beyond the misery and horror to the promise of a brighter tomorrow. "Till Then," recorded by the Mills Brothers, a harmonious black quartet, offered the prospect of a romantic reunion when "the world will be free." The era's best-known tune, Irving Berlin's "White Christmas," evoked a lyrical nostalgia of past celebrations with family and friends close by. On the lighter side, novelty artist Spike Jones made his name with the "razz" or "Bronx cheer," in "We're Going to Ffft in the Fuehrer's Face."

Hollywood artists meanwhile threw themselves into a perpetual round of fundraising and morale-boosting public events. Movie stars called on fans to buy war bonds and to support the troops. Combat films such as *Action in the North Atlantic* made heroes of ordinary Americans under fire, depicting GIs of different races and ethnicities discovering their common humanity. Movies with antifascist themes, such as *Tender Comrade*, promoted friendship among Russians and Americans, while films like *Since You Went Away* portrayed the loyalty and resilience of families with servicemen stationed overseas.

The wartime spirit also infected the juvenile world of comics. The climbing sales of nickel "books" spawned a proliferation of patriotic superheroes such as Flash, Hawkman, the Green Lantern, Captain Marvel, and the more comical Plastic Man. Captain America, created by the famed comic artist Jack Kirby, was a frail soldier who, when injected with a wonder drug, began delivering punches at Adolf Hitler even before the United States entered the war. Kirby went on to create "boy Commandos," intensifying juvenile identification with battlefield action. Even Bugs Bunny put on a uniform and fought sinister-looking enemies.

Fashion designers did their part. Padded shoulders and straight lines became popular for both men and women; BVD, a leading manufacturer of underwear, designed civilian clothing to resemble military attire. Patriotic Americans, such as civil defense volunteers and Red Cross workers, fancied uniforms, and women employed in defense plants wore pants, often for the first time. Restrictions on materials also influenced

fashion. Production of nylon stockings was halted because the material was needed for parachutes. To save material, women's skirts were shortened, while the War Production Board encouraged cuffless "Victory Suits" for men. Executive Order M-217 restricted the colors of shoes manufactured during the war to "black, white, navy blue, and three shades of brown."

Never to see a single battle, safeguarded by two oceans, many Americans nevertheless experienced the war years as the most intense of their entire lives. Popular music, Hollywood movies, radio programs, and advertisements—all screened by the Office of War Information—encouraged a sense of personal involvement in a collective effort to preserve democracy at home and to save the world from fascism. No one was excluded, no action considered insignificant. Even casual conversation came under the purview of the government, which warned that "Loose Lips Sink Ships."

MEN AND WOMEN IN UNIFORM

During World War I, American soldiers served for a relatively brief period and in small numbers. A quarter-century later, World War II mobilized 16.4 million Americans into the armed forces. Although only 34 percent of men who served in the army saw combat—the majority during the final year of the war—the experience had a powerful impact on nearly everyone. Whether working in the steno pool at Great Lakes Naval Training Center in northern Illinois or slogging through mud with rifle in hand in the Philippines, many men and women saw their lives reshaped in unpredictable ways. Uprooted from their communities, they suddenly found themselves among strangers, in an unfamiliar geographical setting, and under a severe military regimen. For those who survived, World War II often proved to be the defining experience of their lives.

Creating the Armed Forces

Before the European war broke out in 1939, the majority of the 200,000 men in the U.S. armed forces were employed as military police, engaging in such tasks as patrolling the Mexican border or occupying colonial possessions, such as the Philippines. Neither the army nor the navy was prepared for the scale of combat World War II entailed. Only the U.S. Marine Corps, which had been planning since the 1920s to wrest control of the western Pacific from Japan, was poised to fight. Once mobilized for war, however, the United States became a first-rank military power.

On October 16, 1940, National Registration Day, all men between the ages of twenty-one and thirty-six were legally obligated to register for military service.

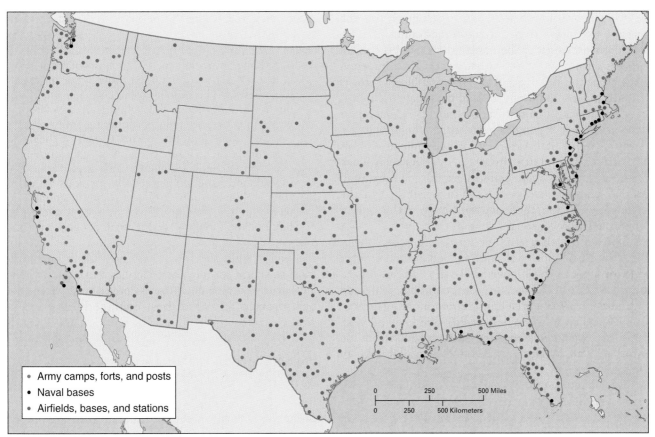

Wartime Army Camps, Naval Bases, and Airfields Their locations chosen for political as well as defense reasons, military facilities were rapidly constructed in every state. The many facilities located in the South and West helped open these areas to economic development and an influx of new migrants.

SOURCE: Clifford L. Lord and Elizabeth H. Lord, *Lord & Lord Historical Atlas of the United States*, rev. ed. (New York: Holt, 1953), p. 309.

Just two weeks later more than 5,000 local draft boards began to draw the first numbers to send men off to camps for one year of training. After the United States entered the war, the draft age was lowered to eighteen, and local boards were instructed to choose first from the youngest.

One-third of the men examined by the Selective Service were rejected. Surprising numbers were refused induction because they were physically unfit for military service. For the first time, men were screened for "neuropsychiatric disorders or emotional problems," and approximately 1.6 million were rejected on this reason. At a time when only one American in four graduated from high school, induction centers turned away many conscripts because they were functionally illiterate.

But those who passed the screening tests joined the best-educated army in history: nearly half of white draftees had graduated from high school and 10 percent had attended college. Once inducted, a soldier went off to one of 242 training centers. At Fort Benning, near Columbus, Georgia, up to 100,000 inductees at a time learned basic military skills such as shooting a rifle, pitching a tent, digging a foxhole, and saluting an officer before advancing to specialized training.

The officer corps, whose top-ranking members were from the Command and General Staff School at Fort Leavenworth, tended to be highly professional, politically conservative, and personally autocratic. General Douglas MacArthur, supreme commander in the Pacific theater, was said to admire the discipline of the German army and to disparage political democracy. General Dwight D. Eisenhower, however, supreme commander of the Allied forces in Europe, projected a new and contrasting spirit. Distrusted by MacArthur and many of the older brass, Eisenhower appeared to his troops a model of leadership. "The idea is to get people working together," he wrote, "because they instinctively want to do it for you. . . . [E]ssentially, you must be devoted to duty, sincere, fair and cheerful."

The democratic rhetoric of the war and the sudden massive expansion of the armed forces contributed to this transformation of the officer corps. A shortage of officers during World War I had prompted a huge expansion of the Reserve Officer Training Corps, but its drilling and discipline alone could not create good officers, and it was still insufficient to meet the demand for trained officers. Racing to make up for the deficiency, Army Chief of Staff George Marshall opened schools for officer candidates. In 1942, in seventeen-week training periods, these schools produced more than 54,000 platoon leaders. Closer in sensibility to the civilian population, these new officers were the kind of leaders Eisenhower sought.

Most GIs (short for "government issue"), who were the vast majority of draftees, had limited contact with officers at the higher levels and instead forged bonds with their company commanders and men within their own combat units. "Everyone wants someone to look up to when he's scared," one GI explained. Most of all, soldiers depended on the solidarity of the group and the loyalty of their buddies to pull through the war.

The majority of these citizen-soldiers endured military discipline "to get the task done," as revealed in numerous polls. They longed foremost for peace. "In the magazines," wrote the popular war correspondent Ernie Pyle,

> war seemed romantic and exciting, full of heroics and vitality. . . . Certainly there were great tragedies, unbelievable heroism, even a constant undertone of comedy. But when I sat down to write, I saw instead men . . . suffering and wishing they were somewhere else . . . all of them desperately hungry for somebody to talk to besides themselves, no women to be heroes in front of, damned little wine to drink, precious little song, cold and fairly dirty, just toiling from day to day in a world full of insecurity, discomfort, homesickness and a dulled sense of danger.

Pledged to fight for democracy, most GIs hoped foremost to return soon to their families and communities. The majority were nevertheless proud to serve in "the best-dressed, best-fed, best-equipped army in the world."

Women Enter the Military

With the approach of World War II, Massachusetts Republican congresswoman Edith Nourse Rogers proposed legislation for the formation of a women's corps. The army instead drafted its own bill, which both Rogers and Eleanor Roosevelt supported, creating in May 1942 the Women's Army Auxiliary Corps (WAAC), later changed to Women's Army Corps (WAC). In 1942–43 other bills established a women's division of the navy (WAVES), the Women's Airforce Service Pilots, and the Marine Corps Women's Reserve. Overall, more than 350,000 women served in World War II, two-thirds of them in the WACS and WAVES. As a group, they were better educated and more skilled—although paid less—than the average soldier.

Although barred from combat, women were not necessarily protected from danger. Nurses accompanied the troops into combat in Africa, Italy, and France, treated men under fire, and dug and lived in their own foxholes. More than 1,000 women flew planes, although not in combat missions. Others worked as photographers and cryptoanalysts.

New recruits to the Women's Army Corps (WAC) pick up their clothing "issue" (allotment). These volunteers served in many capacities, from nursing men in combat to performing clerical and communications duties "state-side" (within the United States). Approximately 140,000 women served in the WACS during World War II.

SOURCE: National Archives and Records Administration.

The vast majority remained far from battlefronts, however, stationed mainly within the United States, where they served in administration, communications, clerical, or health-care facilities.

The WACS and WAVES were both subject to hostile commentary and bad publicity. The overwhelming majority of soliders believed that most WACS were prostitutes, and the War Department itself, fearing "immorality" among women in the armed forces, closely monitored their conduct and established much stricter rules for women than for men. The U.S. Marine Corps even used intelligence officers to ferret out suspected lesbians or women who showed "homosexual tendencies" (as opposed to homosexual acts), both causes for dishonorable discharge.

Eventually some of these discriminatory practices eased, but only after women demanded fair treatment. High-ranking female officers, for example, argued for a repeal of a military policy prohibiting women from supervising male workers, even in offices. The armed forces did not, however, lift its ban on women with children.

Like the armed forces in general, the women's services were marked by racial segregation, despite government declarations of egalitarianism. Black women and white women ate in separate mess halls and slept in separate barracks. At the beginning of the war, black nurses were admitted to serve only black soldiers, and the WAVES refused all black women on the ground that the navy had no black airmen to attend. Only in 1944 did Roosevelt order the navy to incorporate black WAVES, and fewer than 100 served.

Old Practices and New Horizons

The Selective Service Act, in response to the demands of African American leaders, specified that "there shall be no discrimination against any person on account of race or color." The draft brought hundreds of thousands of young black men into the army, and African Americans enlisted at a rate 60 percent above their proportion of the general population. By 1944 black soliders represented 10 percent of the army's troops, and overall approximately 1 million African Americans served in the armed forces during World War II. The army, however, channeled black recruits into segregated, poorly equipped units, which were commanded by white officers. Secretary of War Henry Stimson refused to challenge this policy, saying that the army could not operate effectively as "a sociological laboratory." The majority served in the Signal, Engineer, and Quartermaster Corps, mainly in construction or stevedore work. Only toward the end of the war, when the shortage of infantry neared a crisis, were African Americans permitted to rise to combat status. The all-black 761st Tank Battalion,

the first African American unit in combat, won a Medal of Honor after 183 days in action. And despite the very small number of African Americans admitted to the Air Force, the 99th Pursuit Squadron earned high marks in action against the feared German air force, the Luftwaffe. Even the Marine Corps and the Coast Guard agreed to end their historic exclusion of African Americans, although they recruited and promoted only a small number.

The ordinary black soldier, sailor, or marine experienced few benefits from the late-in-the-war gains of a few. They encountered discrimination everywhere, from the army canteen to the religious chapels. Even the blood banks kept blood segregated by race (although a black physician, Dr. Charles Drew, had invented the process for storing plasma). The year 1943 marked the peak of unrest, with violent confrontations between blacks and whites breaking out at military installations, especially in the South where the majority of African American soliders were stationed. Toward the end of the war, to improve morale among black servicemen, the army relaxed its policy of segregation, mainly in recreational facilities. Although enforcement was uneven and haphazard, the new policy paved the way for integration within a decade of the war's end.

The army also grouped Japanese Americans into segregated units, sending most to fight far from the Pacific theater. Better educated than the average soldier, many Nisei soldiers who knew Japanese served state-side as interpreters and translators. When the army decided to create a Nisei regiment, more than 10,000 volunteers stepped forward, only one in five of whom was accepted. The Nisei 442nd fought heroically in Italy and France and became the most decorated regiment in the war.

Despite segregation, the armed forces ultimately pulled Americans of all varieties out of their communities. Many Jews and other second-generation European immigrants, for example, described their stint in the military as an "Americanizing" experience. Many Indian peoples left reservations for the first time, approximately 25,000 serving in the armed forces. Many Navajo "code talkers," for example, who used a special code based on their native language to transmit information among military units, learned English in special classes established by the marines. For many African Americans, military service provided a bridge to postwar civil rights agitation. Amzie Moore, who later helped to organize the Mississippi Freedom Democratic Party, traced his understanding that "people are just people" to his experiences in the armed forces during World War II.

Many homosexuals also discovered a wider world. Despite a policy barring them from military service, most slipped through mass screening at induction centers.

Moreover, the emotional pressures of wartime, especially the fear of death, encouraged close friendships, and homosexuals in the military often found more room than in civilian life to express their sexual orientation openly. In army canteens, for example, men often danced with one another, whereas in civilian settings they would have been subject to ridicule or even arrest for such activity. "The war is a tragedy to my mind and soul," one gay soldier confided, "but to my physical being, it's a memorable experience." Lesbian WACS and WAVES had similar tales.

Most soldiers looked back at the war, with all its dangers and discomforts, as the greatest experience they would ever know. As the *New Republic* predicted in 1943, they met fellow Americans from every part of the country and recognized for the first time in their lives "the bigness and wholeness of the United States." "Hughie was a Georgia cracker, so he knew something about moonshine," remembered one soldier. Another fondly recalled "this fellow from Wisconsin we called 'Moose.'" The army itself promoted these expectations of new experience. *Twenty-Seven Soldiers* (1944), a government-produced film for the troops, showed Allied soldiers of several nationalities all working together in harmony.

The Medical Corps

The chance of being killed in combat was surprisingly small, estimated at less than 1 in 50, but the risk of injury was much higher. By the time the war ended, the army reported 949,000 casualties, including 175,000 who had been killed in action. Although the European Theater produced the greatest number of casualties, the Pacific held grave dangers in addition to artillery fire. For the soliders fighting in hot, humid jungles, malaria, typhus, diarrhea, or dengue fever posed the most common threat to their lives. For the 25th Infantry Division, which landed in Guadalcanal in 1943, the malaria-carrying mosquito proved a more formidable enemy than Japanese forces.

The prolonged stress of combat also took a toll in the form of "battle fatigue." Despite the rigorous screening of recruits, more than 1 million soldiers suffered at one time or another from debilitating psychiatric symptoms, and the number of men discharged for neuropsychiatric reasons was 2.5 times greater than in previous wars. The cause, psychiatrists concluded, was not individual weakness but long stints in the front lines. In France, for example, where soldiers spent up to 200 days in the field without a break from fighting, thousands cracked, occasionally inflicting wounds on themselves in order to be sent home. One who simply fled the battlefront, Private Eddie Slovik, was tried and executed for desertion—the first such execution since the Civil War. In 1944 the army concluded that eight months in combat was the maximum and instituted,

when replacements were available, a rotation system to relieve exhausted soldiers.

To care for sick and wounded soldiers, the army depended on a variety of medical personnel. Soldiers received first aid training as part of basic training, and they went into battle equipped with bandages to treat minor wounds. For the most part, however, they relied on the talents of trained physicians and medics. The Army Medical Corps sent doctors to the front lines. Working in make-shift tent hospitals, these physicians advanced surgical techniques and, with the use of new "wonder" drugs such as penicillin, saved the lives of many wounded soldiers. Of the soldiers who underwent emergency surgery on the field, more than 85 percent survived. Over all, less than 4 percent of all soldiers who received medical care died as a result of their injuries. Much of the success in treatment came from the use of blood plasma, which reduced the often lethal effect of shock from severe bleeding. By 1945, the American Red Cross Blood Bank, which was formed four years earlier, had collected more than 13 million units of blood from volunteers, converted most of it into dried plasma, and made it readily available throughout the European Theater.

Grateful for the care of skilled surgeons, many soldiers nevertheless named medics the true heroes of the battlefront. Between thirty to forty medics were attached to each infantry battalion, and they were responsible for emergency first-aid and for transporting the wounded to the aid station and if necessary on to the field hospital. Many medics were recruited from the approximately 35,000 conscientious objectors, who were defined by the Selective Service as a person "who, by reason of religious training and belief, is conscientiously opposed to participation in war in any form."

In the military hospitals, American nurses supplied the bulk of care to recovering soldiers. Before World War II, the Army Nurse Corps, created in 1901, was scarcely a military organization, with recruits earning neither military pay nor rank. To overcome the short supply of nurses, Congress extended military rank to nurses in 1944, although only for the duration and for six months after the war ended. In 1945 Congress came close to passing a bill to draft nurses. Like medics, army nurses went first to training centers in the United States, learning how to dig foxholes and dodge bullets before being sent overseas. By 1945, approximately 56,000 women, including 500 African American women, were on active duty in the Army Nurse Corps, staffing medical facilities in every theater of the war.

Prisoners of War

Approximately 120,000 Americans became prisoners of war (POWs). Those captured by the Germans were taken back to camps—*Oflags* for officers or *Stalags* for enlisted men—where they sat out the remainder of the

A painting by Sidney Simon of American POWs freed from Japanese captors at Bilibid prison, in Manila, 1945, after the U.S. reconquest of the Philippines. The battle of the Philippine Sea and the battle of Leyte Gulf during the previous year had nearly broken Japanese resistance in the area, but the clean-up process revealed the awful price that Americans and their Filipino allies had paid. As prisoners of war, they had suffered terribly from malnutrition and improperly attended wounds and from an unsparing and inhumane Japanese military code of behavior.

SOURCE: Sidney Simon, *P.O.W.s at Bilibid Prison*, 1945. Oil on canvas, 25″ × 30″. Center of Military History, U.S. Army (CC/103010).

war, mainly fighting boredom. Registered by the Swiss Red Cross, they could receive packages of supplies and occasionally join work brigades. By contrast, Russian POWs were starved and occasionally murdered in German camps.

Conditions for POWs in the Pacific were, however, worse than abysmal. Of the 20,000 Americans captured in the Philippines early in the war, only 40 percent survived to return home in 1945. At least 6,000 American and Filipino prisoners, beaten and denied food and water, died on the notorious eighty-mile "Death March" through the jungles on the Bataan Peninsula in 1942.

After the survivors reached the former U.S. airbase Camp O'Donnell, hundreds died weekly in a cesspool of disease and squalor.

The Japanese army felt only contempt for POWs; its own soldiers evaded capture by killing themselves. The Imperial Army assigned its most brutal troops to guard prisoners and imposed strict and brutal discipline in the camps. In a postwar survey, 90 percent of former POWs from the Pacific reported that they had been beaten. A desire for retribution, as well as racist attitudes, prompted GIs to treat Japanese prisoners far more brutally than enemy soldiers captured in Europe or Africa.

THE WORLD AT WAR

During the first year of declared war, the Allies remained on the defensive. Hitler's forces held the European Continent and pounded England with aerial bombardments while driving deep into Russia and across northern Africa to take the Suez Canal. The situation in the Pacific was scarcely better. Just two hours after the attack on Pearl Harbor, Japanese planes struck the main U.S. base in the Philippines and demolished half the air force commanded by General Douglas MacArthur. Within a short time, MacArthur was forced to withdraw his troops to the Bataan Peninsula, admitting that Japan had practically seized the Pacific. Roosevelt called the news "all bad," and his military advisers predicted a long fight to victory.

But the Allies enjoyed several important advantages: vast natural resources and a skilled workforce with sufficient reserves to accelerate the production of weapons and ammunitions; the determination of millions of antifascists throughout Europe and Asia; and the capacity of the Soviet Union to endure immense losses. Slowly at first, but then with quickening speed, these advantages made themselves felt.

Soviets Halt Nazi Drive

The weapons and tactics of World War II were radically different from those of World War I. Unlike World War I, which was fought by immobile armies kept in trenches by bursts of machine-gun fire, World War II was a war of offensive maneuvers punctuated by surprise attacks. Its chief weapons were tanks and airplanes, combining mobility and concentrated firepower. Also of major importance were artillery and explosives, which according to some estimates accounted for over 30 percent of the casualties. Major improvements in communication systems, mainly two-way radio transmission and radio-telephony that permitted commanders to stay in contact with division leaders, also played a decisive role from the beginning of the war.

Early on, Hitler had used these methods to seize the advantage, purposefully creating terror among the stricken populations of western Europe as he routed their armies. The Royal Air Force, however, fought the Luftwaffe to a standstill in the Battle of Britain, frustrating Hitler's hopes of invading England. In the summer of 1941, he turned his attention to the east, hoping to invade and conquer the Soviet Union before the United States entered the war. But he had to delay the invasion in order to support Mussolini, whose weak army had been pushed back in North Africa and Greece. The attack on Russia did not come until June 22, six weeks later than planned and too late to achieve its goals before the brutal Russian winter began.

The burden of the war now fell on the Soviet Union. From June to September, Hitler's forces overran the Red Army, killing or capturing nearly 3 million soldiers and leaving thousands to die from exposure or starvation. But Nazi commanders did not count on civilian resistance. The Soviets rallied, cutting German supply lines and sending every available resource to Soviet troops concentrated just outside Moscow. After furious fighting and the onset of severe winter weather, the Red Army launched a massive counterattack, catching the freezing German troops off guard. For the first time, the Nazi war machine suffered a major setback.

Turning strategically away from Moscow, during the summer of 1942 German troops headed toward Crimea and the rich oil fields of the Caucasus. Still set on conquering the Soviet Union and turning its vast resources to his own use, Hitler decided to attack Stalingrad, a major industrial city on the Volga River. The Soviets suffered more casualties during the following battles than Americans did during the entire war. But intense house-to-house and street fighting and a massive Soviet counteroffensive took an even greater toll on the Nazi fighting machine. By February 1943, the German Sixth Army had met defeat, overpowered by Soviet troops and weapons. More than 100,000 German soldiers surrendered.

Already in retreat but plotting one last desperate attempt to halt the Red Army, the Germans threw most of their remaining armored vehicles into action at Kursk, in the Ukraine, in July 1943. The clash quickly developed into the greatest land battle in history. More than 2 million troops and 6,000 tanks went into action. After another stunning defeat, the Germans had decisively lost the initiative. Their only option was to delay the advance of the Red Army against their homeland.

Meanwhile, the Soviet Union had begun to recover from its early losses, even as tens of millions of its own people remained homeless and near starvation. Assisted by the U.S. Lend-Lease program, by 1942 the Soviets were outproducing Germany in many types of weapons and other supplies. Nazi officers and German civilians alike began to doubt that Hitler could win the war. The Soviet victories had turned the tide of the war.

The Allied Offensive

In the spring of 1942, Germany, Italy, and Japan commanded a territory extending from France to the Pacific Ocean. They controlled central Europe and a large section of the Soviet Union as well as considerable parts of China and the southwestern Pacific. But their momentum was flagging. American shipbuilding outpaced the punishment Nazi submarines inflicted on Allied shipping, and sub-sinking destroyers greatly reduced the submarines' threat. The United States

Web Exploration

Examine the strategies of the Axis and the Allies. What were the key turning points of the war in Europe?
www.prenhall.com/faragher/map25.1

Legend:
- Axis Powers before World War II
- Extent of Axis control early Nov. 1942
- Allies
- Neutral nations
- Allied troop movements
- Major battles/Allied victories

ICELAND

ATLANTIC OCEAN

NORWAY

SWEDEN

FINLAND

Petsamo

Finnish territory annexed by Soviet Union

SOVIET UNION

NORTH SEA

NORTHERN IRELAND

GREAT BRITAIN

REPUBLIC OF IRELAND

Leningrad besieged Sept. 1941–Jan. 19, 1943

ESTONIA

LATVIA

Moscow

Sept. 1944

LITHUANIA

DENMARK

Danzig Free State

EAST PRUSSIA (Germany)

Battle of the Bulge Dec. 16, 1944–Jan. 31, 1945

July 1944

Stalingrad besieged Aug. 1942–Jan. 31, 1943

London

NETHERLANDS

Berlin surrendered May 2, 1945

Warsaw

BELGIUM

GERMANY

POLAND

D-Day June 6, 1944

NORMANDY

Paris liberated Aug. 1945

Dresden

Aug. 1944

UKRAINE

CASPIAN SEA

SWITZ.

ALPS

AUSTRIA

SLOVAKIA

HUNGARY

Territory annexed by Hungary

RUTHENIA

ROMANIA

VICHY FRANCE occupied Nov. 1942

Yalta

CAUCASUS MOUNTAINS

PORTUGAL

SPAIN

YUGOSLAVIA

ITALY

BLACK SEA

BULGARIA

CORSICA

SARDINIA

Rome liberated June 4, 1944

ALBANIA (Italy)

TURKEY

MEDITERRANEAN SEA

SICILY

GREECE

RHODES (Italy)

CYPRUS (British)

SYRIA

IRAQ

SPANISH MOROCCO

July 1943

CRETE (Greece)

LEBANON

PALESTINE (British)

MOROCCO

ALGERIA

Kasserine Pass Feb. 14–22, 1943

TRANSJORDAN

FRENCH NORTH AFRICA (Vichy France)
Joined Allies Nov. 1942

TUNISIA

Suez Canal

SAUDI ARABIA

0   500   1000 Miles
0   500   1000 Kilometers

LIBYA (Italy)

El Alamein Oct. 23–Nov. 5, 1942

EGYPT

RED SEA

Base map and relief customized from
Mountain High Maps® Copyright © 1995 Digital Wisdom, Inc.

The War in Europe   The Allies remained on the defensive during the first years of the war, but by 1943 the British and Americans, with an almost endless supply of resources, had turned the tide.

far outstripped Germany in the production of landing craft and amphibious vehicles, two of the most important innovations of the war. Also outnumbered by the Allies, the German air force was limited to defensive action. On land, the United States and Great Britain had the trucks and jeeps to field fully mobile armies, while German troops marched in and out of Russia with packhorses.

Still, German forces represented a mighty opponent on the European Continent. Fighting the Nazis almost alone, the Soviets repeatedly appealed for the creation of a Second Front, an Allied offensive against Germany from the west. The Allies focused instead on securing North Africa and then on an invasion of Italy, hoping to move from there into central Europe.

On the night of October 23–24, 1942, near El Alamein in the desert of western Egypt, the British Eighth Army halted a major offensive by the German Afrika Korps, headed by General Erwin Rommel, the famed "Desert Fox." Although suffering heavy losses—approximately 13,000 men and more than 500 tanks—British forces destroyed the Italian North African Army and much of Germany's Afrika Korps. Americans entered the war in Europe as part of Operation Torch, the landing of British and American troops on the coast of Morocco and Algeria in November 1942, the largest amphibious military landing to that date. The Allies then fought their way along the coast, entering Tunis in triumph six months later. With the surrender of a quarter-million Germans and Italians in Tunisia in May 1943, the Allies controlled North Africa and had a secure position in the Mediterranean. During the North African campaign, the Allies announced that they would accept nothing less than the unconditional surrender of their enemies. In January

1943, Roosevelt and Churchill had met in Casablanca in Morocco and ruled out any possibility of negotiation with the Axis powers. Roosevelt's supporters hailed the policy as a clear statement of goals, a promise to the world that the scourge of fascism would be completely banished. Stalin, who did not attend the meeting, criticized the policy, fearing that it would only increase the enemy's determination to fight to the end. Other critics similarly charged that the demand for total capitulation would serve to prolong the war and lengthen the casualty list.

Allied aerial bombing further increased pressure on Germany. Many U.S. leaders believed that in the B-17 Flying Fortress, the air force possessed the ultimate weapon, "the mightiest bomber ever built." The U.S. Army Air Corps described this bomber as a "humane" weapon, capable of hitting specific military targets and sparing the lives of civilians. But when weather or darkness required pilots to depend on radar for sightings, they couldn't distinguish clearly between factories and schools or between military barracks and private homes, and bombs might fall within a range of nearly two miles from the intended target. American pilots preferred to bomb during daylight hours, while the British bombed during the night. Bombing missions over the Rhineland and the Ruhr successfully took out many German factories. But the Germans responded by relocating their plants, often dispersing light industry to the countryside.

Determined to break German resistance, the Royal Air Force redirected its main attack away from military sites to cities, including fuel dumps and public transportation. Hamburg was practically leveled. Between 60,000 and 100,000 people were killed, and 300,000 buildings were destroyed. Sixty other cities were hit hard, leaving 20 percent of Germany's total residential area in ruins. The very worst air raid of the war—650,000 incendiary bombs dropped on the city of Dresden, destroying 8 square miles and killing 135,000 civilians—had no military value.

The Allied strategic air offensive weakened the German economy and undermined civilian morale. Moreover, in trying to defend German cities and factories, the Luftwaffe sacrificed many of its fighter planes. When the Allies

As part of the air war on Germany, Allied bombers launched a devastating attack on Dresden, a major economic center, in February 1945. Of the civilians who died, most from burns or smoke inhalation during the firestorm, a large number were women and children, refugees from the Eastern Front. The city was left in ruins.

SOURCE: Commuters boarding a tram. Getty Images, Inc. Photo by Fred Ramage (97K/HATY/7781/08).

finally invaded western Europe in the summer and fall of 1944, they would enjoy superiority in the air.

The Allied Invasion of Europe

During the summer of 1943, the Allies began to advance on southern Italy. On July 10, British and American troops stormed Sicily from two directions and conquered the island in mid-August. King Vittorio Emmanuel dismissed Mussolini, calling him "the most despised man in Italy," and Italians, by now disgusted with the Fascist government, celebrated in the streets. Italy surrendered to the Allies on September 8, and Allied troops landed on the southern Italian peninsula. But Hitler sent new divisions into Italy, occupied the northern peninsula, and effectively stalled the Allied campaign. When the European war ended, the German and Allied armies were still battling on Italy's rugged terrain.

Elsewhere in occupied Europe, armed uprisings against the Nazis spread. The brutalized inhabitants of Warsaw's Jewish ghetto repeatedly rose up against their tormentors during the winter and spring of 1943. Realizing that they could not hope to defeat superior forces, they finally sealed off their quarter, executed collaborators, and fought invaders, street by street and house by house. Scattered revolts followed in the Nazi labor camps, where military prisoners of war and civilians were being worked to death on starvation rations.

Partisans were active in many sections of Europe, from Norway to Greece and from Poland to France. Untrained and unarmed by any military standard, organized groups of men, women, and children risked their lives to distribute antifascist propaganda, taking action against rich and powerful Nazi collaborators. They smuggled food and weapons to clandestine resistance groups and prepared the way for Allied offensives. As Axis forces grew weaker and partially withdrew, the partisans worked more and more openly, arming citizens to fight for their own freedom.

Meanwhile, Stalin continued to push for a second front. Stalled in Italy, the Allies prepared in early 1944 for Operation Overlord, a campaign to retake the Continent with a decisive counterattack through France. American and British forces began by filling the southern half of England with military camps. All leaves were canceled. New weapons, such as amphibious armored vehicles, were carefully camouflaged. Fortunately, Hitler had few planes or ships left, so the Germans could defend the coast only with fixed bunkers whose location the Allies ascertained. Operation Overlord began with a preinvasion air assault that dropped 76,000 tons of bombs on Nazi targets.

The Allied invasion finally began on "D-Day," June 6, 1944. Under steady German fire the Allied fleet brought to the shores of Normandy more than 175,000 troops and more than 20,000 vehicles—an accomplishment unimaginable in any previous war. Although the Germans had responded slowly, anticipating an Allied strike at Calais instead of Normandy, at Omaha Beach they had prepared their defense almost perfectly. Wave after wave of Allied landings met machine-gun and mortar fire, and the tides filled with corpses and those pretending to be dead. Some 2,500 troops died, many before they could fire a shot. Nevertheless, in the next six weeks, nearly 1 million more Allied soldiers came ashore, broke out of Normandy, and prepared to march inland.

As the fighting continued, all eyes turned to Paris, the premier city of Europe. Allied bombers pounded factories producing German munitions on the outskirts of the French capital. As dispirited German soldiers

D-Day landing, June 6, 1944, marked the greatest amphibious maneuver in military history. Troop ships ferried Allied soldiers from England to Normandy beaches. Within a month, nearly 1 million men had assembled in France, ready to retake western and central Europe from German forces.

SOURCE: Photo by Robert Capa. CORBIS.

retreated, many now hoping only to survive, the French Resistance unfurled the French flag at impromptu demonstrations on Bastille Day, July 14. On August 10, railway workers staged one of the first successful strikes against Nazi occupiers, and three days later the Paris police defected to the Resistance, which proclaimed in leaflets that "the hour of liberation has come." General Charles de Gaulle, accompanied by Allied troops, arrived in Paris on August 25 to become president of the reestablished French Republic.

One occupied European nation after another now swiftly fell to the Allied armies. But the Allied troops had only reached a resting place between bloody battles.

The High Cost of European Victory

In September 1944 Allied commanders searched for a strategy to end the war quickly. Missing a spectacular chance to move through largely undefended territory and on to Berlin, they turned north instead, intending to open the Netherlands for Allied armies on their way to Germany's industrial heartland. Faulty intelligence reports overlooked a well-armed German division at Arnhem, Holland, waiting to cut Allied paratroopers to pieces. By the end of the battle, the Germans had captured 6,000 Americans.

In a final, desperate effort to reverse the Allied momentum, Hitler directed his last reserves, a quarter-million men, at Allied lines in the Belgian forest of the Ardennes. In what is known as the Battle of the Bulge, the Germans took the Allies by surprise, driving them back 50 miles before they were stopped. This last effort—the bloodiest single campaign Americans had been involved in since the battle of Gettysburg—exhausted the German capacity for counterattack. After Christmas day 1944, the Germans fell back, retreating into their own territory.

The end was now in sight. In March 1945 the Allies rolled across the Rhine and took the Ruhr Valley with its precious industrial resources. The defense of Germany, now hopeless, had fallen into the hands of young teenagers and elderly men. By the time of the German surrender, May 8, Hitler had committed suicide in a Berlin bunker and high Nazi officials were planning their escape routes. The casualties of the Allied European campaign had been enormous, if still small compared to those of the Eastern Front: more than 200,000 killed and almost 800,000 wounded, missing, or dead in nonbattle accidents and unrelated illness.

The War in Asia and the Pacific

The war that had begun with Pearl Harbor rapidly escalated into scattered fighting across a region of the world far larger than all of Europe, stretching from Southeast Asia to the Aleutian Islands. Japan followed up its early advantage by cutting the supply routes between Burma and China, crushing the British navy, and seizing the Philippines, Hong Kong, Wake Island, British Malaya, and Thailand. Although China offically joined the Allies on December 9, 1941, and General Stillwell arrived in March as commander of the China-Burma-India theater, the military mission there remained on the defensive. Meanwhile, after tenacious fighting on the Bataan Peninsula and on the island of Corregidor, the U.S. troops not captured or killed retreated to Australia.

At first, nationalist and anticolonial sentiment played into Japanese hands. Japan succeeded with only 200,000 men because so few inhabitants of the imperial colonies of Britain and France would fight to defend them. Japan installed puppet "independent" governments in Burma and the Philippines. But the new Japanese empire proved terrifyingly cruel. A panicky exodus of refugees precipitated a famine in Bengal, India, which took nearly 3,500,000 lives in 1943. Nationalists from Indochina to the Philippines turned against the Japanese, establishing guerrilla armies that cut Japanese supply lines and prepared the way for Allied victory.

Six months after the disaster at Pearl Harbor, the United States began to regain naval superiority in the central Pacific and halt Japanese expansion. In an aircraft carrier duel with spectacular aerial battles during the Battle of the Coral Sea on May 7 and 8, the United States blocked a Japanese threat to Australia. A month later, the Japanese fleet converged on Midway Island, which was strategically vital to American communications and the defense of Hawai'i. American strategists, however, thanks to specialists who had broken Japanese codes, knew when and where the Japanese planned to attack. The two carrier fleets, separated by hundreds of miles, clashed at the Battle of Midway on June 4. American planes sank four of Japan's vital aircraft carriers and destroyed hundreds of planes, ending Japan's offensive threat to Hawai'i and the west coast of the United States.

But the war for the Pacific was far from over. By pulling back their offensive perimeter, the Japanese concentrated their remaining forces. Their commanders calculated that bitter fighting, with high casualties on both sides, would wear down the American troops. The U.S. command, divided between General Douglas MacArthur in the southwest Pacific and Admiral Chester Nimitz in the central Pacific, needed to develop a counterstrategy to strangle the Japanese import-based economy and to retake strategic islands closer to the homeland.

The Allies launched their counteroffensive campaign on the Solomon Islands and Papua, near New Guinea. American and Australian ground forces fought together through the jungles of Papua, while the marines prepared to attack the Japanese stronghold of

Web Exploration

Consider the war in the Pacific in more detail. How did strategies in this theater differ from those in Europe?
www.prenhall.com/faragher/map25.2

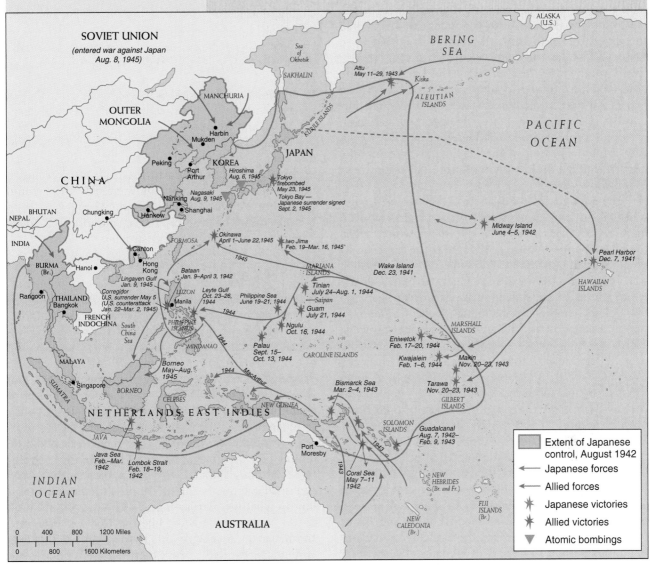

War in the Pacific   Across an ocean battlefield utterly unlike the European theater, Allies battled Japanese troops near their homeland.

Guadalcanal. American forces ran low on food and ammunition during the fierce six-month struggle on Guadalcanal, while the Japanese were reduced to eating roots and berries. American logistics were not always well planned: a week before Christmas in the subtropical climate, a shipment of winter coats arrived! But with strong supply lines secured in a series of costly naval battles, the Americans were finally victorious in February 1943, proving that they could defeat Japanese forces in brutal jungle combat.

For the next two years, the U.S. Navy and Marine Corps, in a strategy known as "island hopping," pushed to capture a series of important atolls from their well-armed Japanese defenders and open a path to Japan. The first of these assaults, which cost more than 1,000 marines their lives, was on Tarawa, in November 1943, in the Gilbert Islands. In subsequent battles in 1944, American forces occupied Guam, Saipan, and Tinian in the Marianas Islands, within air range of the Japanese home islands. In another decisive naval engagement, the Battle of the Philippine Sea, fought in June 1944, the Japanese fleet suffered a crippling loss.

In October 1944, General MacArthur led a force of 250,000 to retake the Philippines. In a bid to defend the islands, practically all that remained of the Japanese navy threw itself at the American invaders in the Battle of Leyte Gulf, the largest naval battle in history. The Japanese lost eighteen ships, leaving the United States in control of the Pacific. While MacArthur continued to advance toward Luzon, the marines waged a successful battle on the small but important island of Iwo Jima. The death toll, however, was high, with casualties estimated at nearly 27,000. The ground fighting in the Philippines, meanwhile, cost 100,000 Filipino civilians their lives and left Manila devastated.

The struggle for the island of Okinawa, 350 miles southwest of the home islands of Japan, proved even more bloody. The invasion of the island, which began on Easter Sunday, April 1, 1945, was the largest amphibious operation mounted by Americans in the Pacific war. It was met by waves of Japanese *kamikaze* ("divine wind") pilots flying suicide missions in planes with a 500-pound bomb and only enough fuel for a one-way flight. On the ground, U.S. troops used flame-throwers, each with three hundred gallons of napalm, against the dug-in Japanese. More Americans died or were wounded here than at Normandy. By the end of June, the fighting had killed more than 200,000 people, with the civilian death toll ranging between 80,000 and 160,000 or more.

With the war over in Europe, the Allies concentrated on Japan, and their air and sea attacks on mainland Japan began to take their toll. U.S. submarines drastically reduced the ability of ships to reach Japan with supplies. Since the taking of Guam, American bombers had been able to reach Tokyo and other Japanese cities, with devastating results. Massive fire bombings burned thousands of civilians alive in their mostly wood or bamboo homes and apartments and left hundreds of thousands homeless.

Japan could not hold out forever. Without a navy or air force, the government could not transport the oil, tin, rubber, and grain needed to maintain its soldiers. Great Britain and particularly the United States, however, pressed for quick unconditional surrender. They had special reasons to hurry. Earlier they had sought a commitment from the Soviet Union to invade Japan, but now they looked beyond the war, determined to prevent the Red Army from taking any territories held by the Japanese. These calculations and the anticipation that an invasion would be extremely bloody set the stage for the use of a secret weapon that American scientists had been preparing: the atomic bomb.

THE LAST STAGES OF WAR

From the attack on Pearl Harbor until mid-1943, President Roosevelt and his advisers had focused on military strategy rather than on plans for peace. But once the defeat of Nazi Germany appeared in sight, high government officials began to reconsider their diplomatic objectives. Roosevelt wanted both to crush the Axis powers and to establish a system of collective security to prevent another world war. He knew he could not succeed without the cooperation of the other key leaders, Stalin and Churchill.

During 1944 and 1945, the "Big Three" met to hammer out the shape of the postwar world. Although none of these nations expected to reach a final agreement, neither did they anticipate how quickly they would be confronted with momentous global events. It soon became clear that the only thing holding the Allies together was the mission of destroying the Axis.

The Holocaust

Not until the last stages of the war did Americans learn the extent of Hitler's atrocities. As part of his "final solution to the Jewish question," Hitler had ordered the systematic extermination of not only Jews, but Gypsies, other "inferior races," homosexuals, and anyone deemed an enemy of the Reich. Beginning in 1933, and accelerating after 1941, the Nazis murdered millions of people from Germany and the European nations they conquered.

During the war the U.S. government released little information on what came to be known as the Holocaust. Although liberal magazines such as the *Nation* and small committees of intellectuals tried to call attention to what was happening in German concentration camps, major news media like the *New York Times* and *Time* magazine treated reports of the camps and killings as minor news items. The experience of World War I, during which the press had published stories of German atrocities that proved in most cases to have been fabricated by the British, had bred a skeptical attitude in the American public. As late as 1943, only 43 percent of Americans polled believed that Hitler was systematically murdering European Jews.

Roosevelt and his advisers maintained that the liberation of European Jews depended primarily on a speedy and total Allied victory. When American Jews pleaded for a military strike against the rail lines leading to the notorious extermination camp in Auschwitz, Poland, the War Department replied that Allied armed forces would not be employed "for the purpose of rescuing victims of enemy oppression unless such rescues are the direct result of military operations conducted with the objective

Belsen Camp: The Compound for Women, painted by American artist Leslie Cole, depicts Belsen as the Allied troops found it when they invaded Germany in 1945.

SOURCE: Leslie Cole, *Belsen Camp. The Compound for Women*. Imperial War Museum, London.

of defeating the armed forces of the enemy." In short, the government viewed civilian rescue as a diversion of precious resources.

Allied troops discovered the death camps when they invaded Germany and liberated Poland. When Eisenhower and General George S. Patton visited the Ohrdruf concentration camp in April 1945, they found barracks crowded with corpses and crematories still reeking of burned flesh. "I want every American unit not actually in the front lines to see this place," Eisenhower declared. "We are told that the American soldier does not know what he is fighting for. Now, at least, he will know what he is fighting against." At Buchenwald in the first three months of 1944, more than 14,000 prisoners were murdered. In all, the Holocaust claimed the lives of as many as 6 million Jews, 250,000 Gypsies, and 60,000 homosexuals, among others.

The Yalta Conference

In preparing for the end of the war, Allied leaders began to reassess their goals. The Atlantic Charter, drawn up before the United States had entered the war, stated noble objectives for the world after the defeat of fascism: national self-determination, no territorial aggrandizement, equal access of all peoples to raw materials and collaboration for the improvement of economic opportunities, freedom of the seas, disarmament, and "freedom from fear and want." Now, four years later, Roosevelt—ill and exhausted—realized that neither Great Britain nor the Soviet Union intended to abide by any code of conduct that compromised its national security or conflicted with its economic interests in other nations or in colonial territories. Stalin and Churchill soon reached a new agreement, one that projected their respective "spheres of influence" over the future of central Europe.

In early February 1945, Roosevelt held his last meeting with Churchill and Stalin at Yalta, a Crimean resort on the Black Sea. Seeking their cooperation, the president recognized that prospects for postwar peace also depended on compromise. Although diplomats avoided the touchy phrase "spheres of influence"—the principle according to which the great powers of the nineteenth century had described their claims to dominance over other nations—it was clear that this principle guided all negotiations. Neither the United States nor Great Britain did more than object to the Soviet Union's plan to retain the Baltic states and part of Poland as a buffer zone to protect it against any future German aggression. In return, Britain planned to reclaim its empire in Asia, and the United States hoped to hold several Pacific islands in order to monitor any military resurgence in Japan. The delegates also negotiated the terms of membership in the United Nations, which had been outlined at a meeting several months earlier.

The biggest and most controversial item on the agenda at Yalta was the Soviet entry into the Pacific war, which Roosevelt believed necessary for a timely Allied victory. After driving a hard bargain involving rights to territory in China, Stalin agreed to declare war against Japan within two or three months of Germany's surrender.

Roosevelt announced to Congress that the Yalta meeting had been a "great success," proof that the wartime alliance remained intact. Privately, however, the president concluded that the outcome of the conference revealed that the Atlantic Charter had been nothing more than "a beautiful idea."

The death of Franklin Roosevelt of a stroke on April 12, 1945, cast a dark shadow over all hopes for long-term, peaceful solutions to global problems. Stung by a Republican congressional comeback in 1942, Roosevelt had rebounded in 1944 to win an unprecedented fourth term as president. In an overwhelming electoral college victory (432 to 99), he had defeated Republican New York governor Thomas E. Dewey. Loyal Democrats continued to link their hopes for peace to Roosevelt's leadership, but the president did not live to witness the surrender of Germany on May 8, 1945. And now, as new and still greater challenges were appearing, the nation's great pragmatic idealist was gone.

The Atomic Bomb

Roosevelt's death made cooperation among the Allied nations much more difficult. His successor, Harry Truman, who had been a Kansas City machine politician, a Missouri judge, and a U.S. senator, lacked diplomatic experience as well as Roosevelt's personal finesse. As a result, negotiations at the Potsdam Conference, held just outside Berlin from July 17 to August 2, 1945, lacked the spirited cooperation characteristic of the wartime meetings of Allied leaders that Roosevelt had attended. The American, British, and Soviet delegations had a huge agenda, including reparations, the future of Germany, and the status of other Axis powers such as Italy. Although they divided sharply over most issues, they held fast to the demand of Japan's unconditional surrender.

It was during the Potsdam meetings that Truman first learned about the successful testing of an atomic bomb in New Mexico. Until this time, the United States had been pushing the Soviet Union to enter the Pacific war as a means to avoid a costly U.S. land invasion, and at Potsdam Truman secured Stalin's promise to be in the war against Japan by August 15. But after Secretary of War Stimson received a cable reading "Babies satisfactorily born," U.S. diplomats concluded that Soviet assistance was no longer needed to bring the war to an end.

On August 3, 1945, Japan wired its refusal to surrender. Three days later, the Army Air Force B-29 bomber *Enola Gay* dropped the bomb that destroyed the Japanese city of Hiroshima. As estimated 40,000 people died instantly; in the following weeks 100,000 more died from radiation poisoning or burns; by 1950 the death toll reached 200,000.

An editorialist wrote in the Japanese *Nippon Times*, "This is not war, this is not even murder; this is pure nihilism . . . a crime against God which strikes at the very basis of moral existence." In the United States, several leading religious publications echoed this view. The *Christian Century* interpreted the use of the bomb as a "moral earthquake" that made the long-denounced use of poison gas by Germany in World War I utterly insignificant by comparison. Albert Einstein, whose theories about the atom provided the foundation for Manhattan Project, observed, that the atomic bomb had changed everything except the nature of man.

Most Americans learned about the atomic bomb for the first time on August 7, when the news media reported the destruction and death it had wrought in Hiroshima. But concerns about the implications of this new weapon were soon overwhelmed by an outpouring of relief when Japan surrendered on August 14 after a second bomb destroyed Nagasaki, killing another 70,000 people.

The Allied insistence on unconditional surrender and the decision to use the atomic bomb against Japan remain two of the most controversial aspects of the war. Although Truman stated in his memoirs, written much later, that he gave the order with the expectation of saving "a half a million American lives" in ground combat, no such official estimate exists. An intelligence document of April 30, 1946, states, "The dropping of the bomb was the pretext seized upon by all leaders as the reason for ending the war, but . . . [even if the bomb had not been used] the Japanese would have capitulated upon the entry of Russia into the war." There is no question, however, that the use of nuclear force did strengthen the U.S. diplomatic mission. It certainly intimidated the Soviet Union, which would soon regain its status as a major enemy of the United States. Truman and his advisers in the State Department knew that their atomic monopoly could not last, but they hoped that in the meantime the United States could play the leading role in building the postwar world.

CONCLUSION

The new tactics and weapons of the Second World War, such as massive air raids and the atomic bomb, made warfare incomparably more deadly than before to both military and civilian populations. Between 40 and 50 million people died in World War II—four times the number in World War I—and half the casualties were women and children. More than 405,000 Americans died, and more than 670,000 were wounded. Although slight compared to the casualties suffered by other Allied nations—more than 20 million Soviets died during the war—the human cost of World War II for Americans was second only to that of the Civil War.

CHRONOLOGY

1931	September: Japan occupies Manchuria
1933	March: Adolf Hitler seizes power
	May: Japan quits League of Nations
1935	October: Italy invades Ethiopia
1935–1937	Neutrality Acts authorize the president to block the sale of munitions to belligerent nations
1937	August: Japan invades China
	October: Franklin D. Roosevelt calls for international cooperation against aggression
1938	March: Germany annexes Austria
	September: Munich Agreement lets Germany annex Sudetenland of Czechoslovakia
	November: *Kristallnacht,* Nazis attack Jews and destroy Jewish property
1939	March: Germany annexes remainder of Czechoslovakia
	August: Germany and the Soviet Union sign nonaggression pact
	September: Germany invades Poland; World War II begins
	November: Soviet Union invades Finland
1940	April–June: Germany's *Bliztkrieg* sweeps over Western Europe
	September: Germany, Italy, and Japan—the Axis powers—conclude a military alliance
	First peacetime military draft in American history
	November: Roosevelt is elected to an unprecedented third term
1941	March: Lend-Lease Act extends aid to Great Britain
	May: German troops secure the Balkans
	A. Philip Randolph plans March on Washington movement for July
	June: Germany invades Soviet Union

	Fair Employment Practices Committee formed
	August: The United States and Great Britain agree to the Atlantic Charter
	December: Japanese attack Pearl Harbor; United States enters the war
1942	January: War mobilization begins
	February: Executive order mandates internment of Japanese Americans
	May–June: Battles of Coral Sea and Midway give the United States naval superiority in the Pacific
	August: Manhattan Project begins
	November: United States stages amphibious landing in North Africa; Operation Torch begins
1943	January: Casablanca Conference announces unconditional surrender policy
	February: Soviet victory over Germans at Stalingrad
	April–May: Coal miners strike
	May: German Afrika Korps troops surrender in Tunis
	July: Allied invasion of Italy
	Summer: Race riots break out in nearly fifty cities
1944	June–August: Operation Overlord and liberation of Paris
	November: Roosevelt elected to fourth term
1945	February: Yalta Conference renews American-Soviet alliance
	February–June: United States captures Iwo Jima and Okinawa in Pacific
	April: Roosevelt dies in office; Harry Truman becomes president
	May: Germany surrenders
	July–August: Potsdam Conference
	August: United States drops atomic bombs on Hiroshima and Nagasaki; Japan surrenders

Coming at the end of two decades of resolutions to avoid military entanglements, the war pushed the nation's leaders to the center of global politics and into risky military and political alliances that would not outlive the war. The United States emerged the strongest nation in the world, but in a world where the prospects for lasting peace appeared increasingly remote. If World War II raised the nation's international commitments to a new height, its impact on ordinary Americans was not so easy to gauge. Many new communities formed as Americans migrated in mass numbers to new regions that were booming as a result of the wartime economy. Enjoying a rare moment of full employment, many workers new to well-paying industrial jobs anticipated further advances against discrimination. Exuberant at the Allies' victory over fascism and the return of the troops, the majority were optimistic as they looked ahead.

REVIEW QUESTIONS

1. Describe the response of Americans to the rise of nationalism in Japan, Italy, and Germany during the 1930s. How did President Franklin D. Roosevelt ready the nation for war?
2. What role did the federal government play in gearing up the economy for wartime production?
3. How did the war affect the lives of American women?
4. Discuss the causes and consequences of the Japanese American internment program.
5. Describe the role of popular culture in promoting the war effort at home.
6. How did military service affect the lives of those who served in World War II?
7. What were the main points of Allied military strategy in both Europe and Asia?
8. How successful were diplomatic efforts in ending the war and in establishing the terms of peace?

RECOMMENDED READING

Stephen E. Ambrose, *D-Day, June 6, 1944: The Climactic Battle of World War II* (1994). A vivid and extremely readable, moment-by-moment reconstruction of the preparation and battle, relying heavily upon the oral histories of American veterans.

Philip D. Beidler, *The Good War's Greatest Hits: World War II and American Remembering* (1998). Examines the popular culture produced about World War II, such as movies, photographs, cartoons, and books, to show how these sources created a lasting image of World War II as the "good war."

Amy Bentley, *Eating for Victory: Food Rationing and the Politics of Domesticity* (1998). Brings together several areas of scholarship, including the social history of food and women's history, and provides a fascinating overview of rationing programs and Victory Gardens during World War II.

Allan Berube, *Coming Out under Fire: The History of Gay Men and Women in World War Two* (1991). A study of government policy toward homosexuals during the war and the formation of a gay community. Berube offers many insights into the new opportunities offered homosexuals through travel and varied companionship and of the effects of sanctions against them.

Paul Boyer, *By the Bomb's Early Light: American Thought and Culture at the Dawn of the Atomic Age* (1985). An analysis of the intellectual and cultural assumptions in relation to atomic weaponry. Boyer examines the development of a political logic, on the part of President Harry Truman and others, that made use of atomic weapons against the Japanese inevitable.

Wayne S. Cole, *Roosevelt and the Isolationists, 1932–45* (1983). Shows the president and his critics sparring over foreign policy issues. Cole analyzes the complexities of liberal-conservative divisions over war and offers insights into the logic of conservatives who feared the growth of a permanent bureaucratic, militarized state.

Richard M. Dalfiume, *Desegregation of the U.S. Armed Forces: Fighting on Two Fronts, 1939–1953* (1969). Analyzes wartime race relations in the military. By examining the official mechanisms to end discrimination and the remaining patterns of racism in the armed forces, Dalfiume reveals how changing attitudes from the top ran up against old assumptions among enlisted men and women.

Roger Daniels, *Concentration Camps USA: Japanese Americans and World War II* (1981). Perhaps the best account of Japanese American internment. Daniels details the government programs, the experiences of detention and camp life, and the many long-term consequences of lost liberty.

Sherna Berger Gluck, *Rosie the Riveter Revisited: Women, the War, and Social Change* (1987). An oral history-based study of women workers during World War II. Gluck's interviewees reveal the diversity of experiences and attitudes of women workers as well as their common feelings of accomplishment.

Laura Hein and Mark Selden, eds., *Living With the Bomb: American and Japanese Cultural Conflict in the Nuclear Age* (1997). Essays dealing with the ambiguous legacy of the atomic bomb in both the United States and Japan. Reviews the "official story" of the bomb as the symbol of U.S. triumph in the "Good War" in light of the growing number of dissenting voices and the impact of both views on memorials and museum exhibits.

John W. Jeffries, *Wartime America: The World War II Homefront* (1996). Provides a useful synthesis of scholarship and assesses the major differences in the interpretations of leading historians.

Gerald F. Linderman, *The World within War: America's Combat Experience in World War II* (1997). Emphasizes the less glamorous aspects of war, mainly the strains placed on the combat soldiers on the front lines. Linderman examines in especially close detail the grim experiences of army infantrymen and the marine riflemen who fought in the Pacific campaign and provides a nuanced analysis of their complex responses to the horror of war.

Katrina R. Mason, *Children of Los Alamos: An Oral History of the Town Where the Atomic Age Began* (1995). Recollections of those who spent their childhood in Los Alamos. They describe their affection for the geographical setting as well as sense of safety growing up in a community so well protected. They also comment on the ethnic diversity of those who populated the town and on the pride they took in their parents' contribution to building the bomb and ending the war.

Neil R. McMillan, ed., *Remaking Dixie: The Impact of World War II on the American South* (1997). A collection of essays on the impact of World War II on the South that pay special attention to the experiences of African Americans and women. Several authors question the degree to which southern society was transformed by wartime mobilization.

Robert J. Moskin, *Mr. Truman's War: The Final Victories of World War II and the Birth of the Postwar World* (1996). A lively history of the final stages of World War II, including the surrender of Germany and the emergence of postwar foreign policy. Moskin provides an assessment of the impact of the war on social and economic conditions in the United States.

William M. Tuttle, Jr., *"Daddy's Gone to War": The Second World War in the Lives of America's Children* (1993). Draws from 2,500 letters that the author solicited from men and women in their fifties and sixties about their wartime childhood memories.

David S. Wyman, *The Abandonment of the Jews: America and the Holocaust, 1941–1945* (1984). A detailed examination of U.S. immigration policy and response to Hitler's program of genocide. Wyman shows both the indifference of the Roosevelt administration to appeals for Allied protection of Jews and the inclinations of leading American Jewish organizations to stress the formation of a future Jewish state instead of the protection of European Jewry.

ADDITIONAL BIBLIOGRAPHY

Coming of World War II

Akira Iriye, *The Origins of the Second World War in Asia and the Pacific* (1988)

Deborah Lipstadt, *Beyond Belief: The American Press and the Coming of the Holocaust, 1933–1945* (1992)

Ernest Mandel, *The Meaning of the Second World War* (1986)

Frank P. Mintz, *Revisionism and the Origins of Pearl Harbor* (1985)

Geoffrey S. Smith, *To Save a Nation* (1992)

Arsenal of Democracy and the Home Front

Karen Anderson, *Wartime Women* (1981)

Alison R. Bernstein, *American Indians and World War II* (1991)

Dominic J. Capeci and Martha Wilkerson, *Layered Violence: The Detroit Rioters of 1943* (1991)

Paul D. Casdorph, *Let the Good Times Roll: Life at Home in America during World War II* (1989)

Thomas Doherty, *Hollywood, American Culture and World War II* (1993)

Lewis A. Erenberg and Susan E. Hirsch, eds., *The War in American Culture: Society and Consciousness during World War II* (1996)

Rachel Waltner Goosen, *Women Against the Good War: Conscientious Objection and Gender on the American Home Front, 1941–1947* (1997)

John W. Jeffries, *Wartime America* (1996)

Gary Y. Okihiro, *Whispered Silences: Japanese Americans and World War II* (1996)

George H. Roeder, *The Censored War: American Visual Experience during World War II* (1993)

Lawrence R. Samuel, *Pledging Allegiance: American Identity and the Bond Drive of World War II* (1997)

Bartholomew H. Sparrow, *From the Outside In: World War II and the American State* (1996)

World at War

Alison Bernstein, *American Indians and World War II* (1991)

Conrad C. Crane, *Bombs, Cities, and Civilians* (1993)

John W. Dower, *War without Mercy* (1986)

Akira Iriye, *Power and Culture: The Japanese-American War, 1941–1945* (1981)

Lee Kennett, *G.I.: The American Soldier in World War II* (1987)

Eric Markusen and David Kopf, *The Holocaust and Strategic Bombing: Genocide and Total War in the Twentieth Century* (1995)

Peter Maslowski, *Armed with Cameras: The American Military Photographers of World War II* (1996)

Murray Williamson and Allan R. Millett, *A War to be Won: Fighting the Second World War* (2000)

Brenda L. Moore, *To Serve My Country: The Story of the Only African American WACS Stationed Overseas During World War II* (1996)

Barbara Brooks Tomblin, *G.I. Nightingales: The Army Nurse Corps in World War II* (1996)

Last Stages of War

John D. Chappell, *Before the Bomb: How America Approached the End of the Pacific War* (1997)

Lloyd C. Gardner, *Spheres of Influence: The Great Powers Partition Europe, from Munich to Yalta* (1993)

Peter Schrijvers, *The Crash of Ruin: American Combat Soldiers in Europe during World War II* (1998)

Michael S. Sherry, *The Rise of American Air Power* (1987)

Atomic Bomb

Gar Alperovitz, *The Decision to Use the Atomic Bomb and the Architecture of an American Myth* (1995)

Paul Boyer, *By the Bomb's Early Light: American Thought and Culture at the Dawn of the Atomic Age* (1985)

Peter Bacon Hales, *Atomic Spaces: Living on the Manhattan Project* (1997)

Ruth H. Howes, *Their Day in the Sun: Women of the Manhattan Project* (1999)

Samuel J. Walker, *Prompt and Utter Destruction: Truman and the Use of Atomic Bombs against Japan* (1997)

Eileen Welsome, *The Plutonium Files: America's Secret Medical Experiments in the Cold War* (1999)

Biography/Memoir

Stephen E. Ambrose, *Supreme Commander: War Years of General Dwight D. Eisenhower* (1970)

Mark M. Anderson, ed., *Hitler's Exiles: Personal Stories of the Flight from Nazi Germany to America* (1998)

Carlo D'Este, *Patton: A Genius for War* (1995)

Paula F. Pfeffer, *A. Philip Randolph* (1990)

John Hubbard Preston, *Apocalypse Undone: My Survival of Japanese Imprisonment during World War II* (1990)

Robert Underhill, *FDR and Harry: Unparalleled Lives* (1996)

HISTORY ON THE INTERNET

http://www.loc.gov/exhibits/british/brit-3.html

With political posters, graphic drawings, and cartoons, this Library of Congress site documents the evolution of British-American foreign policy relations from the War of 1812 to the end of World War II.

http://www.nara.gov/exhall/powers/powers.html

This National Archives site documents posters of World War II.

http://www.fdrlibrary.marist.edu/wwphotos.html

Available through the Franklin D. Roosevelt Presidential Library are literally hundreds of photographs of the American home front and battlefield action in every theater of the war.

http://www.history.navy.mil/photos/sh-fornv/japan/japsh-s/shokaku.htm

http://www.history.navy.mil/photos/sh-fornv/germany/ger-name.htm

These two sites, official U.S. Navy historical records, provide photographs of the major vessels of the Japanese and German fleets during World War II.

http://lcweb.loc.gov/rr/print/coll/109_anse.html

http://lcweb.loc.gov/rr/print/coll/109-b.html

These two sites connect to the Ansel Adams' photos of the Manzanar Japanese Internment camp of World War II.

http://lcweb.loc.gov/rr/print/126_rosi.html

Extensive collection of Library of Congress photos, wartime posters, and cartoons concerning women war industry workers during the Second World War.

Exhibiting the *Enola Gay*

When news of the successful detonation of the atomic bomb over Hiroshima reached Los Alamos, New Mexico, horns and sirens blared in exultation. The community took pride in its achievement and, like other Americans, welcomed the prospect of Japan's surrender and the end of the devastating conflict. Chief scientist J. Robert Oppenheimer nevertheless expressed a sentiment equally common at the time, reporting that he was a "little scared of what I have made." Nearly a half-century later, Americans are no more certain about the meaning of this event.

In 1994, a major controversy erupted as the curatorial staff of the Smithsonian Institution's National Air and Space Museum (NASM) circulated their plans for an exhibition on the *Enola Gay*, the B-29 aircraft that carried "Little Boy," the weapon used on the Hiroshima mission. After reading drafts of a script that was to accompany the display, critics charged that the museum staff had crafted a message that was lop-sided at best, anti-American at worst. A writer in *Time* magazine accused the NASM curators of portraying the Japanese as "more or less innocent victims of American beastliness and lust for revenge." A columnist in the *Washington Post* expressed his opinion more bluntly, calling them a bunch of "politically correct pinheads." These judgments came as a surprise to those at the museum who had prepared the script. They had already received a positive report from a group of scholars who had reviewed the draft and judged it, in the words of a distinguished military historian, "comprehensive and dramatic" and needing only a "bit of 'tweaking.'" However, many Air Force veterans strongly disagreed, and they launched a campaign to block the proposed exhibit.

At the center of the controversy were two nagging questions. Both had been addressed by political and military leaders in August 1945 but never answered—and perhaps can never be answered—satisfactorily: was the atomic bomb necessary to end the war quickly and to save the lives of hundreds of thousands of Americans? Was the decision to deploy the bomb morally unambiguous, given the death toll of Japanese civilians?

The NASM curators had wrestled with these hard questions in preparing the original script. They decided, for example, not to use the conventional estimate of a half-million American lives saved as too high. This figure, they noted, had been projected only after the war had ended and often to rebut critics of the Hiroshima

On his official website, Brigadier General Paul W. Tibbets (USAF Retired) offered for sale replicas of the *Enola Gay*, with signed certificates of authenticity, as well as commemorative coins and stamps, books, and videos about the dropping of the first atomic bomb. SOURCE: © Reuters NewMedia Inc./CORBIS (UT 0012163).

bombing. Instead, the curators relied on the actual wartime estimates by military leaders that projected perhaps tens of thousands of American casualties if a land invasion of Japan were to ensue. They also cited the U.S. Strategic Bombing Survey, which was completed soon after Japan's surrender, that concluded that even without the bomb the war would "certainly" have ended by November or December of 1945.

Many veterans who had served in the Pacific Theater objected strongly even to raising such questions. They continued to have no doubt that Truman had made the decision to drop the atomic bomb to save American lives and to shorten the war. They accused the museum staff of intentionally distorting history. Their collective memory of the battles of Guadacanal, Iwo Jima, and Okinawa, the risks posed by the ground invasion of Japan, and the torture inflicted on prisoners of war in the Japanese death camps ran directly counter to the script that read, "It is possible that there was a last opportunity to end the war without either atomic bombings or an invasion of Japan." The nation's largest veteran organization, the American Legion, issued a public letter to President Clinton calling for the cancellation of the exhibit as planned.

In 1937, Paul W. Tibbets, Jr., enlisted as a flying cadet in the Army Aircorps, and during World war II he became a test pilot for the B-29, the airplane that he helped to redesign to deliver the atomic bomb.

The controversy eventually pulled in General Paul W. Tibbets, the pilot of the *Enola Gay* (he had painted his mother's maiden name on the nose of the plane). He, too, objected to the museum staff's "second-guessing the decision to use the atomic weapons." He wanted a simple, straightforward label for the fifty-six feet of fuselage inside the museum hall: "'This airplane was the first one to drop an atomic bomb.'"

Eventually, the U.S. Congress stepped into the fray. The Senate passed a nonbinding resolution reminding the NASM staff of its "obligation to portray history in the proper context of the time." The museum, at the time averaging about 8.2 million visitors a year, more than any other museum in the world, depended mainly on government funding and therefore relied on those who controlled the federal budget, the Congress.

The NASM staff did have support for their plans, particularly among other professional historians. The Organization of American Historians condemned the intervention by members of Congress. An independent group of "historians and scholars" protested this "transparent attempt at historical cleansing."

On June 28, 1995, the exhibit finally opened, although in greatly reduced form. The original plans for photographs of "ground zero" in Hiroshima, for example, were scrapped, and what remained were several restored components of the B-29 aircraft, such as its fuselage, propellers, and cockpit. As to the *Enola Gay's* mission, one photograph featured the crew before take-off, another of the mushroom cloud as seen from the tail gunner's position. The wall text read simply:

> Tibbets piloted the aircraft on its mission to drop an atomic bomb on Hiroshima on Aug. 6, 1945. That bomb and the one dropped on Nagasaki three days later destroyed much of the two cities and caused tens of thousands of deaths. However, the use of the bombs led to the immediate surrender of Japan and made unnecessary the planned invasion of the Japanese home islands. Such an invasion, especially if undertaken for both main islands, would have led to very heavy casualties among American and Allied troops and Japanese civilians and military. It was thought highly unlikely that Japan, while in a very weakened military condition, would have surrendered unconditionally without such an invasion."

"The aircraft speaks for itself in this exhibit," Smithsonian director I. Michael Heyman said, "and, 50 years after its mission, it continues to evoke strong emotions, in those who look at it."

The legacy of the atomic bomb, including the scientific research done at Los Alamos during the 1940s, remains so uncertain and contentious that an attempted explanation of the mission of the *Enola Gay* was abandoned for a celebration of the aircraft's design as an engineering marvel. Historians and military veterans seemed to speak different languages. Meanwhile, a Gallup Poll conducted at the time of the controversy surrounding the *Enola Gay* exhibit indicated that a quarter of Americans did not even know that World War II ended with the explosion of an atomic bomb over Japan. ▪

TWENTY-SIX

THE COLD WAR

▷ 1945 – 1952

Poster from 1947: *Is This Tomorrow—America under Communism!* Michael Barson (ID #002).

University of Washington, Seattle: Students and Faculty Face the Cold War

I N MAY 1948, A PHILOSOPHY PROFESSOR AT THE UNIVERSITY OF WASH-
ington in Seattle answered a knock on his office door. Two state legislators, members of the state's Committee on Un-American
Activities, entered. "Our information," they charged, "puts you in the
center of a Communist conspiracy."

The accused professor, Melvin Rader, had never been a Communist.
A self-described liberal, Rader drew fire because he had joined several
organizations supported by Communists. During the 1930s, in response
to the rise of Nazism and fascism, Rader had become a prominent political activist in his community. At one point he served as president of the
University of Washington Teacher's Union, which had formed during
the upsurge of labor organizing during the New Deal. When invited to
join the Communist Party, Rader bluntly refused. "The experience of
teaching social philosophy had clarified my concepts of freedom and
democracy," he later explained. "I was an American in search of a way—
but it was not the Communist way."

Despite this disavowal, Rader was caught up in a Red Scare that curtailed free speech and political activity on campuses throughout the
United States. At some universities, such as Yale, the Federal Bureau of
Investigation (FBI) set up camp with the consent of the college administration, spying on students and faculty, screening the credentials of job
or scholarship applicants, and seeking to entice students to report on
their friends or roommates. The University of Washington administration turned down the recommendation of the Physics Department to
hire J. Robert Oppenheimer because the famed atomic scientist had become a vocal opponent of the arms race and the proliferation of nuclear
weapons.

Although one state legislator claimed that "not less than 150 members" of the University of Washington faculty were subversives, the
state's Committee on Un-American Activities turned up just six members
of the Communist Party. These six were brought up before the university's Faculty Committee on Tenure and Academic Freedom, charged
with violations ranging from neglect of duty to failing to inform the university administration of their party membership. Three were ultimately
dismissed, while the other three were placed on probation.

What had provoked this paranoia? Instead of peace in the wake of
World War II, a pattern of cold war—icy relations—prevailed between
the United States and the Soviet Union. Uneasy allies during World
War II, the two superpowers now viewed each other as arch-enemies,
and nearly all other nations lined up with one or the other of them.
Within the United States, the cold war demanded pledges of absolute
loyalty from citizens in every institution, from the university to trade
unions and from the mass media to government itself.

If not for the outbreak of the cold war, this era would have marked
one of the most fruitful in the history of higher education. The Servicemen's Readjustment Act, popularly known as the G.I. Bill of Rights,

passed by Congress in 1944, offered stipends covering tuition and living expenses to veterans attending vocational schools or college. By the 1947–48 academic year, the federal government was subsidizing nearly half of all male college students. Between 1945 and 1950, 2.3 million students benefited from the G.I. Bill, at a cost of more than $10 billion.

At the University of Washington the student population in 1946 had grown by 50 percent over its prewar peak of 10,000, and veterans represented fully two-thirds of the student body. A quickly expanded faculty taught into the evening to use classroom space efficiently. Meanwhile, the state legislature pumped in funds for the construction of new buildings, including dormitories and prefabricated units for married students.

According to many observers, a feeling of community flourished among these war-weary undergraduates. Often the first in their families to attend college, they joined fellow students in campaigns to improve the campus. Married, often fathers of young children, they expected university administrators to treat them as adults. They wanted less supervision of undergraduate social life, more affordable housing, and better cultural opportunities than had previously been the case. On some campuses, film societies and student-run cooperatives vied with fraternities and sororities as centers of undergraduate social activity.

The cold war put a damper on these community-building efforts. FBI director J. Edgar Hoover testified that the college campuses were centers of "red propaganda," full of teachers "tearing down respect for agencies of government, belittling tradition and moral custom and . . . creating doubts in the validity of the American way of life." Due to Communistic teachers and "Communist-line textbooks," a senator lamented, thousands of parents sent "their sons and daughters to college as good Americans," only to see them return home "four years later as wild-eyed radicals."

Although these extravagant charges were never substantiated, several states, including Washington, enacted or revived loyalty-security programs, obligating all state employees to swear in writing their loyalty to the United States and to disclaim membership in any subversive organization. Nationwide, approximately 200 faculty members were dismissed outright and many others were denied tenure. Thousands of students simply left school, dropped out of organizations, or changed friends after "visits" from FBI agents or interviews with administrators. The main effect on campus was the restraint of free speech generally and fear of criticizing U.S. racial, military, or diplomatic policies in particular.

This gloomy mood reversed the wave of optimism that had swept through America only a few years earlier. V-J Day, marking victory over Japan, had erupted into a two-day national holiday of wild celebrations, complete with ticker-tape parades, spontaneous dancing, and kisses for returned G.I. Americans, living in the richest and most powerful nation in the world, finally seemed to have gained the peace they had fought and sacrificed to win. But peace proved fragile and elusive. ■

Seattle

KEY TOPICS

- Prospects for world peace at end of World War II

- Diplomatic policy during the cold war

- The Truman presidency

- Anticommunism and McCarthyism

- Cold war culture and society

- The Korean War

GLOBAL INSECURITIES AT WAR'S END

The war that had engulfed the world from 1939 to 1945 created an international interdependence that no country could ignore. The legendary African American folk singer Leadbelly (Huddie Ledbetter) added a fresh lyric to an old spiritual melody: "We're in the same boat, brother. . . . And if you shake one end you're going to rock the other." Never before, not even at the end of World War I, had hopes been so strong for a genuine "community of nations." With Japan and Germany defeated and occupied and the European empires disintegrating, most Americans recognized, a 1945 opinion poll revealed, that prospects for a durable peace rested to a large degree on harmony between the Soviet Union and the United States.

Rivalry between these two competitors for world leadership had been placed on hold while the United States and the Soviet Union joined in the Grand Alliance to defeat fascism. This coalition, always uneasy, began to crumble during the last stages of the war. Within a year after V-J Day, the world's two most powerful nations had emerged as arch-adversaries in conceiving the shape of the postwar order. The United States viewed the Soviet Union as a ruthless, totalitarian power intent, through an aggressive policy of expansion, to bring about a global Communist revolution. In turn, the USSR considered the United States an imperialist power bent on destroying communism and committed to a capitalist world order compatible with its own economic interests. It was within a context that allowed little possibiity for accommodation or negotiation that the United States defined its national purpose with new energy as nothing less than "to lead the free world."

Financing the Future

In 1941 Henry Luce, publisher of *Time, Life,* and *Fortune* magazines, had forecast the dawn of "the American Century." Americans must, he wrote, "accept whole-heartedly our duty and our opportunity as the most powerful and vital nation in the world and in consequence to assert upon the world the full impact of our influence, for such means as we see fit." Indeed, immediately after the bombing of Hiroshima, President Truman pronounced the United States "the most powerful nation in the world—the most powerful nation, perhaps, in all history." The president and his advisors declared a definitive end to the era of isolation and pledged themselves to bring to fruition Luce's prophecy. The United States would serve not only as the model of democracy—the "City on the Hill" that John Winthrop had imagined in 1630—but the carrier of the torch of freedom throughout the world.

Americans had good reason to be confident about their prospects for setting the terms of reconstruction. Compared with Great Britain and France, reduced to second-rate powers too weak to hold their once vast empires, the United States had not only escaped the ravages of the war but had actually prospered. By June 1945, the capital assets of manufacturing had increased 65 percent over prewar levels and were equal in value to approximately half the entire world's goods and services.

Yet many Americans recognized that it was the massive government spending associated with wartime industry, rather than New Deal programs, that had ended the nightmare of the 1930s. A great question loomed: What would happen when wartime production slowed and millions of troops returned home?

"We need markets—big markets—in which to buy and sell," answered Assistant Secretary of State for Economic Affairs Will Clayton. Just to maintain the current level of growth, the United States needed an estimated $14 billion in exports—an unprecedented amount. Many business leaders even looked to the Soviet Union as a potential trading partner. With this prospect vanishing, Eastern European markets threatened, and large chunks of former colonial territories closed off, U.S. business and government leaders became determined to integrate Western Europe and Asia into a liberal international economy open to American trade and investment.

During the final stages of the war, President Roosevelt's advisers laid plans to establish U.S. primacy in the postwar global economy. In July 1944 representatives from forty-four Allied nations met at Bretton Woods, New Hampshire, and established the International Bank for Reconstruction and Development (World Bank) and the International Monetary Fund (IMF) to help rebuild war-torn Europe and to assist the nations of Asia, Latin America, and Africa. By stabilizing exchange rates to permit the expansion of international trade, the IMF would deter currency conflicts and trade wars—two maladies of the 1930s that were largely responsible for the political instability and national rivalries leading to World War II. As the principal supplier of funds for the IMF and the World Bank—more than $7 billion to each—the United States, in essence, could unilaterally shape the world economy by determining the allocation of loans. "The main prize of the victory" over the Axis powers is, a State Department document noted in 1945, a "limited and temporary power to establish the kind of world we want to live in."

The Soviet Union participated in the Bretton Woods conference but refused to ratify the agreements that, in essence, allowed the United States to rebuild the world economy along capitalist lines. By spurning both the World Bank and the IMF, Soviet Union cut off the possibility of aid to its own people as well as to its Eastern European client states and, equally important, isolated itself economically.

The Division of Europe

The Atlantic Charter of 1941 committed the Allies to recognize the right of all nations to self-determination and to renounce all claims to new territories as the spoils of war. The Allied leaders themselves, however, violated the charter's main points before the war had ended by dividing occupied Europe into spheres of influence (see Chapter 25).

So long as Franklin Roosevelt remained alive, this strategy had seemed reconcilable with world peace. The president had balanced his own international idealism with his belief that the United States was entitled to extraordinary influence in Latin America and the Philippines and that other great powers might have similar privileges or responsibilities elsewhere. Roosevelt also recognized the diplomatic consequences of the brutal ground war that had been fought largely on Soviet territory: the Soviet Union's unnegotiable demand for territorial security along its European border.

From the early days of the war, the USSR was intent on reestablishing its 1941 borders, and by the time of the Potsdam Conference in July 1945 the Soviets had not only regained but extended their territory. Much of eastern Europe, including a large portion of Poland and the little Baltic nations, was now under its control as client states. Only the Yugoslavians and Albanians, who had turned back fascist forces without the Red Army's assistance, could claim nominal independence. But the question remained: Did Stalin aim to bring all of Europe into the Communist domain?

When the Allies turned to plan the future of Germany, this question loomed over all deliberations. France, Great Britain, the Soviet Union, and the United States agreed to dismember Germany and eventually decided to divide the conquered nation into four occupation zones, each governed by one of the Allied nations. But the Allies could not agree on long-term plans. Having borne the brunt of German aggression, France and the USSR both opposed reunification. The latter, in addition, demanded heavy reparations along with a limit on postwar reindustrialization. Roosevelt appeared to agree with the Soviets. But American business leaders, envisioning a new center for U.S. commerce, shared Winston Churchill's hope of rebuilding Germany into a powerful counterforce against the Soviet Union and a strong market for U.S. and British goods.

After the war, continuing disagreements about the future Germany darkened hopes for cooperation between the Soviet Union and the United States. By July 1946, Americans had begun to withhold reparations from their zone and to institute a program of amnesty for former Nazis. Then, in December, the American and British merged their zones and extended an invitation to France and the USSR to join. Although France accepted the offer, the Soviets, fearing a resurgence of united Germany, held out.

The United States and the Soviet Union were now at loggerheads. Twice in the twentieth century, Germany had invaded Russia, and the USSR now interpreted these U.S. moves toward consolidation of Germany an act of supreme hostility. For its part, the United States envisioned a united Germany as a bulwark against Soviet expansion.

The United Nations and Hopes for Collective Security

A thin hope remained amid the gloom of disunity between the two superpowers. A month after the conference at Bretton Woods, Allied leaders met to lay plans for a system of collective security, the United Nations (UN). The dream of postwar international cooperation had been seeded earlier by President Roosevelt. In late summer and fall 1944 at the Dumbarton Oaks Conference in Washington, D.C., and again in April 1945 in

Appointed to the UN delegation by President Harry Truman in 1946, Eleanor Roosevelt (1884–1962) pressured the organization to adopt the Declaration of Human Rights in 1948. In this photograph, taken in 1946, the former First Lady is exchanging ideas with Warren Austin, also a delegate to the United Nations.

SOURCE: UPI/CORBIS–Bettmann.

San Francisco, the Allies worked to shape the United Nations as an international agency that would arbitrate disputes among members as well as impede aggressors, by military force if necessary.

The terms of membership, however, limited the UN's ability to mediate disputes. Although all member nations enjoyed representation in the General Assembly, only five members (the United States, Great Britain, the Soviet Union, France, and Nationalist China) served permanently on on the Security Council, which had the "primary responsibility for the maintenance of international peace and security," and each enjoyed absolute veto power over the decisions of the other members. By this arrangement, the Security Council could censure an act of aggression by any of its members only if that nation made the unlikely decision of abstaining from the vote.

The UN achieved its greatest success with its humanitarian programs. Its relief agency provided the war-torn countries of Europe and Asia with billions of dollars for medical supplies, food, and clothing. The UN also dedicated itself to protecting human rights, and its high standards of human dignity owed much to the lobbying of Eleanor Roosevelt, one of the first delegates from the United States.

On other issues, however, the UN operated strictly along lines dictated by the cold war. The Western nations allied with the United States held the balance of power and maintained their position by controlling the admission of new member nations. They successfully excluded Communist China, for example. Moreover,

the polarization between East and West made negotiated settlements virtually impossible.

THE POLICY OF CONTAINMENT

With the world seemingly dividing into two hostile camps, the dream of a community of nations dissolved. But perhaps it had never been more than a fantasy contrived to maintain a fragile alliance amid the urgency of World War II. In March 1946, in a speech delivered in Fulton, Missouri, Winston Churchill spoke to the new reality. With President Harry Truman at his side, the former British prime minister declared that "an iron curtain has descended across the [European] continent." He called directly upon the United States, standing "at this time at the pinnacle of world power," to recognize its "awe-inspiring accountability to the future" and to act assertively to turn back Soviet expansion.

Although Truman responded cautiously to Churchill's pronouncement, he and his administration ultimately decided to meet the challenge. Within a short time, they were wholeheartedly committed to securing U.S. leadership in the world and, equally important, preventing communism from spreading further. As a doctrine uniting military, economic, and diplomatic strategies, the "containment" of communism also fostered an ideological opposition, an "us"-versus-"them" theme that divided the world into "freedom" and "slavery," "democracy" and "autocracy," and "tolerance" and "coercive force." The Truman Doctrine laid down the first plank in a global campaign against communism.

The Truman Doctrine

Many Americans believed that Franklin D. Roosevelt, had he lived, would have been able to stem the tide of tensions between the Soviet Union and the United States. His successor sorely lacked FDR's talent for diplomacy. More comfortable with machine politicians than with polished New Dealers, the new president liked to talk tough and act defiantly. Just ten days after he took office, Truman complained that U.S.–Soviet negotiations had been a "one-way street." He vowed to "baby" them no longer.

A perceived crisis in the Mediterranean prompted President Truman to show his colors. On February 21, 1947, amid a civil war in Greece, Great Britain informed the U.S. State Department that it could no longer afford to prop up the anti-Communist government there and announced its intention to withdraw all aid. Without U.S. intervention, Truman concluded, Greece, Turkey, and perhaps the entire oil-rich Middle East would fall under Soviet control.

OVERVIEW

MAJOR COLD WAR POLICIES

Policy	Date	Provisions
Truman Doctrine	1947	Pledged the United States to the containment of communism in Europe and elsewhere. The doctrine was the foundation of Truman's foreign policy. It impelled the United States to support any nation whose stability was threatened by communism or the Soviet Union.
Federal Employees Loyalty program and Security Program	1947	Established by Executive Order 9835, this barred Communists and fascists from federal employment and outlined procedures for investigating current and prospective federal employees.
Marshall Plan	1947	U.S. program to aid war-torn Europe, also known as the European Recovery Program. The Marshall Plan was a cornerstone in the U.S. use of economic policy to contain communism.
National Security Act	1947	Established Department of Defense (to coordinate the three armed services), the National Security Council (to advise the president on security issues), and the Central Intelligence Agency (to gather and evaluate intelligence data).
Smith-Mundt Act	1948	Launches an overseas campaign of anti-Communist propaganda.
North Atlantic Treaty Organization (NATO)	1948	A military alliance of twelve nations formed to deter possible aggression of the Soviet Union against Western Europe.
NSC-68	1950	National Security Council Paper calling for an expanded and aggressive U.S. defense policy, including greater military spending and higher taxes.
Internal Security Act (also known as the McCarran Act and the Subversive Activities Control Act)	1950	Legislation providing for the registration of all Communist and totalitarian groups and authorizing the arrest of suspect persons during a national emergency.
Psychological Strategy Board created	1951	Created to coordinate anti–Communist propaganda campaigns
Immigration and Nationality Act (also known as McCarran-Walter Immigration Act)	1952	Reaffirmed the national origins quota system but tightened immigration controls, barring homosexuals and people considered subversive from entering the United States.

On March 12, 1947, the president made his argument before Congress in bold terms: "At the present moment in world history, nearly every nation must choose between alternative ways of life. . . . One way of life is based upon the will of the majority, and is distinguished by free institutions . . . and freedom from political oppression. The second way of life is based upon the will of a minority forcibly imposed on the majority . . . and the suppression of personal freedoms." Never mentioning the Soviet Union by name, he appealed for all-out resistance to a "certain ideology" wherever it appeared in the world. The preservation of peace and

the freedom of all Americans depended, the president insisted, on containing communism.

Congress approved a $400 million appropriation in aid for Greece and Turkey, which helped the monarchy and right-wing military crush the rebel movement. Truman's victory buoyed his popularity for the upcoming 1948 election. It also helped to generate popular support for a campaign against communism, both at home and abroad.

The significance of what became known as the Truman Doctrine far outlasted the events in the Mediterranean: the United States had declared its right to intervene to save other nations from communism. As early as February 1946, foreign-policy adviser George F. Kennan had sent an 8,000-word "long telegram" to the State Department insisting that Soviet fanaticism made cooperation impossible. The USSR intended to extend its realm not by military means alone, he explained, but by "subversion" within "free" nations. In addition, the Truman Doctrine described the differences between the United States and the Soviet Union as absolute and irreconcilable, as an ideological breach that resonated far beyond foreign policy. It was now the responsibility of the United States, Truman insisted, to safeguard the "Free World" by diplomatic, economic, and, if necessary, military means. He had, in sum, fused anticommunism and internationalism into an aggressive foreign policy.

The Marshall Plan

The Truman Doctrine complemented the European Recovery Program, commonly known as the Marshall Plan. Introduced in a commencement speech at Harvard University on June 5, 1947, by secretary of state and former army chief of staff George C. Marshall, the plan sought to reduce "hunger, poverty, desperation, and chaos" and to restore "the confidence of the European people in the economic future of their own countries and of Europe as a whole." Although Marshall added that "our policy is directed not against any country or doctrine," the plan that bore his name additionally aimed to turn back both socialist and Communist electoral bids for power in northern and western Europe while promoting democracy through economic renewal.

Considered by many historians the most successful postwar U.S. diplomatic venture, the Marshall Plan supplemented the Bretton Woods agreements by further improving the climate for a viable capitalist economy in western Europe and, in effect, bringing recipients of aid into a bilateral agreement with the United States. In addition, the western European nations, seventeen in all, ratified the General Agreement on Tariffs and Trade (GATT), which reduced commercial barriers among member nations and opened all to U.S. trade and investment. The plan was costly to Americans, in its initial year taking 12 percent of the federal budget, but effective. Industrial production in the European nations covered by the plan rose by 200 percent between 1947 and 1952. Although deflationary programs cut wages and increased unemployment, profits soared and the standard of living improved. Supplemented by a multimedia propaganda campaign, the Marshall Plan introduced many Europeans to American consumer goods and lifestyle.

The Marshall Plan drove a deeper wedge between the United States and the Soviet Union. Although invited to participate, Stalin denounced the plan for what it was, an American scheme to rebuild Germany and to incorporate it into an anti-Soviet bloc that encompassed all western Europe. The president readily acknowledged that the Marshall Plan and the Truman Doctrine were "two halves of the same walnut."

The Berlin Crisis and the Formation of NATO

As Stalin recognized, the Marshall Plan also sought to rebuild and integrate the western zones of Germany into unified region compatible with U.S. political and economic interests. Within a year of its introduction, the United States and Britain moved closer to this goal by introducing a common currency in the western zones. Stalin reacted to this challenge on June 24, 1948, by halting all traffic to West Berlin, formally controlled by the Western allies but situated deep within the Soviet-occupied zone.

The Berlin blockade created both a crisis and an opportunity for the Truman administration to test its mettle. In a show of strength, the president dispatched to Britain sixty B-29s, "atomic bombers" that could be carrying nuclear weapons but were not. Then, with help from the Royal Air Force, the United States began an around-the-clock airlift of historic proportions—Operation Vittles—that delivered nearly 2 million tons of supplies to West Berliners. The Soviet Union finally lifted the blockade in May 1949, clearing the way for the Western powers to merge their occupation zones into a single nation, the Federal Republic of West Germany. The USSR countered by establishing the German Democratic Republic in their sector.

The Berlin Crisis made a U.S.–led military alliance against the USSR attractive to western European nations. In April 1949 ten European nations, Canada, and the United States formed the North Atlantic Treaty Organization (NATO), a mutual defense pact in which "an armed attack against one or more of them . . . shall be considered an attack against them all." NATO complemented the Marshall Plan, strengthening economic ties among the member nations by, according to one analyst, keeping "the Russians out, the Americans in, and the Germans down." It also deepened divisions between eastern and western Europe, making a permanent military mobilization on both sides almost inevitable.

By mid-1949, Truman and his advisers were basking in the glow of these victories for containment. The U.S. Senate had ratified the first formal military treaty with a European nation since the Revolutionary War era—a giant step away from isolationism. Congress also approved $1.3 billion in military aid, which involved the creation of U.S. Army bases and the deployment of American troops abroad. Critics, such as isolationist senator Robert A. Taft, warned that the United States could not afford to police all Europe without sidetracking domestic policies and undercutting the UN.

But opinion polls revealed strong support for Truman's tough line against the Soviets.

Between 1947 and 1949, the Truman administration had defined the policies that would shape the cold war for decades to come. The Truman Doctrine explained the ideological basis of containment; the Marshall Plan put into place its economic underpinnings in western Europe; and NATO created the mechanisms for military enforcement. When NATO extended membership to a rearmed West Germany in May 1955, the Soviet Union responded by creating a counterpart, the Warsaw Pact, including East Germany. The division of East and West was complete.

Atomic Diplomacy

The policy of containment depended on the ability of the United States to back up its commitments through military means, and Truman invested his faith in the U.S. monopoly of atomic weapons. The United States began to build atomic stockpiles and to conduct tests on the Bikini Islands in the Pacific. By 1950, as a scientific adviser subsequently observed, the United States "had a stockpile capable of somewhat more than reproducing World War II in a single day."

Despite warnings to the contrary by leading scientists, U.S. military analysts estimated it would take the

Web **Exploration**

Examine Europe during the Cold War. Which countries were aligned with the United States, and which with the Soviet Union?
www.prenhall.com/faragher/map26.1

Divided Europe   During the cold war, Europe was divided into opposing military alliances, the North American Treaty Organization (NATO) and the Warsaw Pact (Communist bloc).

Soviet Union three to ten years to produce an atomic bomb. In August 1949, the Soviet Union proved them wrong by testing its own atomic bomb. "There is only one thing worse than one nation having the atomic bomb," Nobel prize-winning scientist Harold C. Urey said, "that's two nations having it."

Within a few years, both the United States and the Soviet Union had tested hydrogen bombs a thousand times more powerful than the weapons dropped on Hiroshima and Nagasaki in 1945. Both proceeded to stockpile bombs attached to missiles, inaugurating the fateful nuclear arms race that scientists had feared since 1945.

The United States and the Soviet Union were now firmly locked into the cold war. The nuclear arms race imperiled their futures, diverted their economies, and fostered fears of impending doom. Prospects for global peace had dissipated, and despite the Allied victory in World War II, the world had again divided into hostile camps.

COLD WAR LIBERALISM

Truman's aggressive, gutsy personality suited the confrontational mood of the cold war. He linked the Soviet threat in Europe to the need for a strong presidency. Pressed to establish his own political identity, "Give 'em Hell" Harry successfully portrayed himself as a fierce fighter against all challengers, yet loyal to Roosevelt's legacy.

Truman set out to enlarge the New Deal but managed mainly to consolidate FDR's bequest of a strong federal government. Social and economic justice at home went the way of peace and cooperation abroad. The compromise that Truman ultimately struck was a modest domestic agenda to promote social welfare and an antiisolationist, fiercely anti-Communist foreign policy. Fatefully, during the course of his administration, domestic and foreign policy became increasingly entangled to lay the basis of a distinctive brand of liberalism—cold war liberalism.

"To Err Is Truman"

Within a year of assuming office, Harry Truman rated lower in public approval than any twentieth-century president except Roosevelt's own predecessor, Herbert Hoover, who had been blamed for the Great Depression. The responsibilities of reestablishing peacetime conditions seemed to overwhelm the new president's administration. "To err is Truman," critics jeered.

In handling the enormous task of reconverting the economy to peacetime production, Truman appeared both inept and mean-spirited. The president faced mil-lions of restless would-be consumers tired of rationing and eager to spend their wartime savings on shiny cars, new furniture, choice cuts of meat, and colorful clothing. The demand for consumer items rapidly outran supply, fueling inflation and creating a huge black market. When Congress proposed to extend wartime price controls, Truman vetoed the bill and prices skyrocketed.

In 1945 and 1946, the country appeared ready to explode. While homemakers protested rising prices by boycotting neighborhood stores, industrial workers struck in unprecedented numbers. Employers, fearing a rapid decline to Depression-level profits, determined to slash wages or at least hold them steady; workers wanted a bigger cut of the huge war profits they had heard about. The spectacle of nearly 4.6 million workers on picket lines alarmed the new president. In May 1946, Truman proposed to draft strikers into the army who refused to return to work under a presidential order. The usually conservative Senate killed this plan.

Congress defeated most of Truman's proposals to revive the New Deal. One week after Japan's surrender, the president introduced a twenty-one-point program that included greater unemployment compensation, higher minimum wages, and housing assistance. Later he added proposals for national health insurance and atomic energy legislation. Congress turned back the bulk of these bills, passing the Employment Act of 1946 only after substantial modification. The act created a new executive body, the Council of Economic Advisers, which would confer with the president and formulate policies for maintaining employment, production, and purchasing power. But the measure did not include funding mechanisms to guarantee full employment, thus falling far short of the bill's intent.

By 1946 Truman's popularity had dipped to 32 percent. One joke began with a reflection on what Roosevelt would do if still alive, only to end by asking "What would Truman do if he were alive?" Republicans, sensing victory in the upcoming off-year elections, asked the voters, "Had enough?" Apparently the voters had. They gave Republicans majorities in both houses of Congress and in the state capitols. And in a symbolic repudiation of Roosevelt, they passed an amendment to the Constitution establishing a two-term limit for the presidency.

The Republicans, dominant in Congress for the first time since 1931, prepared a counteroffensive against the New Deal, beginning with an attack on organized labor. Unions had by this time reached a peak in size and prestige, with membership topping 15 million and encompassing nearly 40 percent of all wage earners. Concluding that labor had gone too far, the Republican-dominated Eightieth Congress aimed to outlaw many practices approved by the Wagner Act of 1935 (see Chapter 24).

Police and strikers confront each other in Los Angeles during one of many postwar strikes in 1946. Employers wanted to cut wages, and workers refused to give up the higher living standard achieved during the war.

SOURCE: AP/Wide World Photos.

The Labor-Management Relations Act of 1947, better known as Taft-Hartley Act, brought to an end the closed shop, the secondary boycott, and the use of union dues for political activities. It also mandated an eighty-day cooling-off period in the case of strikes affecting national safety or health. Taft-Hartley furthermore required all union officials to swear under oath that they were not Communists—a cold war mandate that abridged freedoms ordinarily guaranteed by the First Amendment. Unions that refused to cooperate were denied the services of the National Labor Relations Board, which arbitrated strikes and issued credentials to unions.

Truman regained some support from organized labor when he vetoed the Taft-Hartley Act, saying it would "conflict with important principles of our democratic society." Congress, however, overrode his veto, and Truman himself went on to invoke the act against strikers.

The 1948 Election

Although lacking a strong candidate, Democrats gingerly approached the 1948 election—the first presidential contest since the inauguration of the cold war—as

an opportunity to campaign for their own post–New Deal agenda. In preparation, a group headed by Eleanor Roosevelt, labor leaders Philip Murray and Walter Reuther, and theologian Reinhold Niebuhr, among others, met in January 1947 to form Americans for Democratic Action (ADA). The most important liberal lobby of the postwar era, the ADA forged a new coalition of Democrats who wished to preserve the legacy of the New Deal and at the same time take a strong stand against communism.

The ADA identified its chief adversary in Truman's contender for the office of president, Henry A. Wallace. Truman had personally fired Wallace as secretary of commerce in 1946 for advocating a more conciliatory policy toward the Soviet Union. Wallace, however, would not retreat and made plans to run for president as candidate of the newly formed Progressive Party. Having served as Roosevelt's vice president and secretary of agriculture, he was well known as a long-time champion of the New Deal. Wallace now vowed to expand Roosevelt's programs, to move swiftly and boldly toward full employment, racial equality, and stronger trade unions, and to work in harmony with the Soviet Union. As the election neared, he remarked after a speech before 32,000 enthusiastic supporters, "We're on the march. We're really rolling now." However, the deepening cold war soon quashed Wallace's chances.

The ADA rallied around Truman and denounced Wallace and the Progressive Party for lining up "with the force of Soviet totalitarianism." Truman himself, as well as many conservatives, accused Wallace of being a tool of Communists. These timely Red-baiting attacks took a toll on the poorly organized and underfunded Wallace campaign, driving many liberals from its ranks. Moreover, Wallace, who never subscribed to communism, refused to fend off these charges, considering them a dangerous by-product of anti-Communist hysteria.

Meanwhile, Truman repositioned himself to discredit congressional Republicans. He proposed programs calling for federal funds for education and new housing and a national program of medical insurance that he knew the Republicans would oppose, and he called Congress back for a fruitless special session in 1948. He then hammered away at the Republican controlled "do-nothing Congress" to good effect in his re-election campaign.

A second tactic seemed to backfire. Pressed by ADA leaders to cut Wallace's lead on civil rights, Truman issued executive orders in July 1948 desegregating the armed forces and banning discrimination in the federal civil service. In response, some 300 southern delegates bolted from the Democratic National Convention and formed a States' Rights ("Dixiecrat") ticket, headed by Governor J. Strom Thurmond of South Carolina, known for his segregationist views. With the South as good as lost, and popular New York governor Thomas E. Dewey heading the Republican ticket, Truman appeared hopelessly far from victory.

Yet as the election neared, Truman campaigned vigorously and managed to revive the New Deal coalition. Fear of the Republicans won back the bulk of organized labor, while the recognition of the new State of Israel in May 1948 helped prevent the defection of many liberal Jewish voters from Democratic ranks. The success of the Berlin airlift also buoyed the president's popularity. By election time, Truman had deprived Henry Wallace of nearly all his liberal support. Meanwhile, Dewey, who had run a hard-hitting campaign against Roosevelt in 1944, expected to coast to victory.

"Harry Truman won the election," concluded the *New Republic*, "because Franklin Roosevelt had worked so well." Although he lost four states to Thurmond, foreshadowing the decline of Democratic strength in the South, Truman won the popular vote by a margin of 5 percent and trounced Dewey 303 to 189 in the electoral college. Moreover, Democrats again had majorities in both houses of Congress. But, as it turned out, Truman had hit the highest point of his popularity and was about to begin a steady slide downhill.

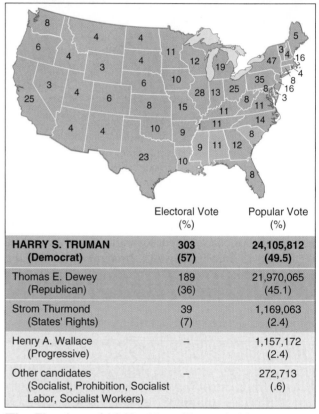

	Electoral Vote (%)	Popular Vote (%)
HARRY S. TRUMAN (Democrat)	**303 (57)**	**24,105,812 (49.5)**
Thomas E. Dewey (Republican)	189 (36)	21,970,065 (45.1)
Strom Thurmond (States' Rights)	39 (7)	1,169,063 (2.4)
Henry A. Wallace (Progressive)	–	1,157,172 (2.4)
Other candidates (Socialist, Prohibition, Socialist Labor, Socialist Workers)	–	272,713 (.6)

The Election of 1948 Harry Truman holds up a copy of the Chicago Tribune with headlines confidently and mistakenly predicting the victory of his opponent, Thomas E. Dewey. An initially unpopular candidate, Truman made a whistle-stop tour of the country by train to win 49.5 percent of the popular vote to Dewey's 45.1 percent.

SOURCE: UPI/CORBIS (U885941B).

The Fair Deal

"Every segment of our population and every individual has a right," Truman announced in January 1949, "to expect from our Government a fair deal." The return of

Democratic congressional majorities, he hoped, would enable him to translate campaign promises into concrete legislative achievements and expand the New Deal. But a powerful bloc of conservative southern Democrats and midwestern Republicans turned back his domestic agenda.

Truman broke no new ground. Congress passed a National Housing Act in 1949, promoting federally funded construction of low-income housing. It also raised the minimum wage from 40 to 75 cents per hour and expanded the Social Security program to cover an additional 10 million people. Otherwise, Truman made little headway. He and congressional liberals introduced a variety of bills to weaken southern segregationism: a federal antilynching law; outlawing the poll tax; prohibiting discrimination in interstate transportation. These measures were all defeated by southern-led filibusters. Proposals to create a national health insurance plan, provide federal aid for education, and repeal or modify Taft-Hartley remained bottled up in committees. Truman himself appeared to lose interest in the liberal agenda as his cold war foreign policy increasingly took priority over domestic issues.

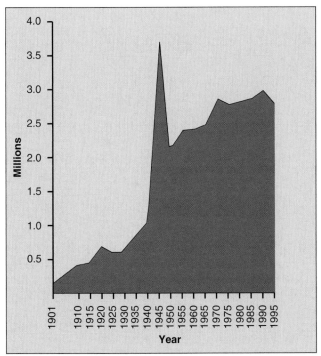

Number of Employees in the Executive Branch, 1901–1995   The federal bureaucracy, which reached a peak of nearly 4 million people during World War II, remained at unprecedentedly high levels during the cold war.

SOURCE: U.S. Bureau of the Census, *Historical Statistics of the United States, Colonial Times through 1970; Statistical Abstract of the United States, 1997.*

Truman managed best to lay out the basic principles of cold war liberalism. Toning down the rhetoric of economic equality espoused by the visionary wing of the Roosevelt coalition, his Fair Deal exalted economic growth—not the reapportionment of wealth or political power—as the proper mechanism for ensuring social harmony and national welfare. His administration insisted, therefore, on an ambitious program of expanded foreign trade, while relying on the federal government to encourage high levels of productivity at home. Equally important, Truman further tempered liberalism by making anticommunism a key element in both foreign policy and the domestic agenda.

THE COLD WAR AT HOME

"Communists . . . are everywhere—in factories, offices, butcher shops, on street corners, in private businesses," Attorney General J. Howard McGrath warned in 1949: "At this very moment [they are] busy at work—undermining your government, plotting to destroy the liberties of every citizen, and feverishly trying in whatever way they can, to aid the Soviet Union." Republican senator Joseph R. McCarthy even claimed to have in his personal possession a list of communists serving secretly in government agencies. By this time, the Communist Party, U.S.A., which had formed in 1919, was steadily losing ground since its peak of only 40,000 to 50,000 members in 1945 when the United States and the Soviet Union were wartime allies.

Nevertheless, during the earliest days of the cold war, anticommunism already occupied center stage in domestic politics. Thus FBI director J. Egar Hoover characteristically warned Americans not to be complacent in the face of low numbers of Communists because "for every party member there are ten others ready, willing, and able to do the Party's work" in infiltrating and corrupting "various spheres of American life." Hoover also helped to set the tone, using hyperbolic rhetoric to describe "the diabolic machinations of sinister figures engaged in un-American activities."

The federal government, with the help of the media, would lead the campaign, finding in the threat of communism a rationale for the massive reordering of its operation and the quieting of the voices of dissent. In this far-reaching quest for security, Americans moved toward a greater concentration of power in government, and, while promising to lead the "free world," allowed many of their own rights to be circumscribed. The United States was readying for permanent military preparedness and perpetual confrontation with its Soviet enemy.

The National Security Act of 1947

The imperative of national security destroyed old-fashioned isolation, forcing the United States into international alliances such as NATO and into the role of world leader. "If we falter in our leadership," Truman warned, "we may endanger the peace of the world–and we shall surely endanger the welfare of this nation." Such a responsibiity required a massive amount of resources. Truman went on, therefore, to argue successfully that national security demanded a substantial increase in the size of the federal government, including both military forces and surveillance agencies. Security measures were required to keep the nation in a steady state of preparedness, readily justified during wartime, now extended into the very uneasy peacetime. As a result, federal expenditures, which had dropped briefly at the end of World War II, grew to be at least seven times greater than during their New Deal peak in the 1930s.

The National Security Act of 1947, passed by Congress in July, laid the foundation for this expansion. The act established the Department of Defense and the National Security Council (NSC) to administer and coordinate defense policies and to advise the president. The Department of Defense replaced the War Department and united the armed forces—the army, navy, and air force—under the jurisdiction of a single secretary with cabinet-level status. As result, with the distinction between citizen and soldier blurred, the ties between the armed forces and the State Department grew closer, as former military officers routinely began to fill positions in the State Department and diplomatic corps. The act also created the National Security Resources Board (NSRB) to coordinate plans throughout the government "in the event of war" and, for the first time in American history, to maintain a program of military preparedness in peacetime.

The Department of Defense, together with the NSRB, became the principal sponsor of scientific research during the first ten years of the cold war. It was commonly recognized at the time that World War II had been "a physicists' war," leading to the creation of the ultimate weapon, the atom bomb, but also to major advances in military technology in areas of systems of navigation and detection, strategic targeting, and communication. Many scientists anticipated that, at the end of the war the special relationship between science and government would continue under the auspices of a new federal agency that would channel funds mainly to universities for basic research under civilian control. Indeed, in 1950, the National Science Foundation (NSF) was created for education and research. However, the NSF sponsored research with little military relevance, and its miniscule budget compared unfavorably to the $85 million per year that the Office of Naval Research directed toward basic research and development. Federal agencies tied to military projects meanwhile supplied well over 90 percent of funding for research in the physical sciences, a large part of the research being located in major universities.

The National Security Act added to this system of defense in 1947 by establishing the Central Intelligence Agency (CIA). With roots in the wartime Office of Strategic Services, the CIA now became a permanent operation devoted to collecting political, military, and economic information for security purposes throughout the world. Although information about the CIA was classified—that is, secret from both Congress and the public—historians have estimated that the agency soon dwarfed the State Department in number of employees and size of budget.

The national security state required a huge workforce. Before World War II, approximately 900,000 civilians worked for the federal government, with about 10 percent engaged in security work; by the beginning of the cold war, nearly 4 million people were on the government's payroll, with 75 percent working in national security agencies. The Pentagon, which had opened in 1943 as the largest office building in the world, how housed the Joint Chiefs of Staff and 35,000 military personnel. Similarly, when the State Department consolidated its various divisions in 1961, it moved into an eight-story structure covering an area the size of four city blocks.

National security took up increasingly large portions of the nation's resources and required an enormous increase in the size of the defense budget. By the end of Truman's second term, defense allocations accounted for 10 percent of the gross national product, directly or indirectly employed hundreds of thousands of well-paid workers, and subsidized some of the nation's most profitable corporations. This vast financial outlay created the rationale for permanent, large-scale military spending as a basic stimulus to economic growth. As early as 1947, Harrison Baldwin of the *New York Times* noted this ominous trend toward "militarization of [the] government and of the American state of mind."

The Loyalty-Security Program

National security also required required increased surveillance at home. Within two weeks of proclamating the Truman Doctrine, the president signed Executive Order 9835 on March 21, 1947, and thereby established a loyalty program for all federal employees. The new Federal Employees Loyalty and Security Program, directed at members of the Communist Party—as well as fascists and anyone guilty of "sympathetic association" with either—in effect established a political test for federal employment. It also outlined procedures for investigating current and prospective federal employees. The loyalty review boards often asked employees about their opinions on the Soviet Union, the Marshall Plan, or NATO, or if they would report fellow workers if they found out they were Communists. Any employee could be dismissed merely on "reasonable grounds" rather than on proof of disloyalty. Later amendments added "homosexuals" as potential security risks on the grounds that they might succumb to blackmail by enemy agents. By early 1952, the FBI, which administered the program, had screened approximately 2 million federal employees.

Many state and municipal governments enacted loyalty programs and required public employees, including teachers at all levels, to sign loyalty oaths. In Detroit, the loyalty review board included city officials, FBI agents, and executives from the auto industry. Positions involving security clearances were closed off to many scientists and engineers, including several who had worked on the Manhattan Project. Only his prominence kept J. Robert Oppenheimer, who spoke critically about the atom bomb, from losing his security clearance until 1953.

Attorney General Clark aided this effort by publishing a list of hundreds of potentially subversive organizations selected by criteria so vague that any views "hostile or inimical to the American form of government" (as Clark's assistants noted in a memo) could make an organization liable for investigation and prosecution. There was, moreover, no right of appeal. Although designed primarily to screen federal employees, the attorney general's list effectively outlawed many political and social organizations, indirectly stigmatizing hundreds of thousands of individuals who had done nothing illegal. Church associations, civil rights organizations, musical groups, and even summer camps appeared on the list. Some, like the Civil Rights Congress, played important roles in defending imprisoned African Americans. Others, like the Jewish Music Alliance and Camp Kinderland, mainly served the cultural interests of Jewish Americans. The FBI compiled separate lists, and by 1960 had created files and collected information on more than 430,000 allegedly subversive individuals and groups.

Membership in a listed group provided the rationale for dismissal at nearly every level of government. Fraternal and social institutions, especially popular among aging European immigrants of various nationalities, were among the largest organizations destroyed. The state of New York, for example, legally dismantled the International Workers' Order, which had provided insurance to nearly 200,000 immigrants and their families. Only a handful of organizations had the funds to challenge the listing legally; most simply closed their doors. Even past membership in a listed group—during the desperate 1930s many liberals had been briefly active in Communist or Communist-related movements—quickly became grounds for suspicion and likely dismissal. Many private employers also used the attorney general's list to institute similar loyalty programs.

Leaders of the labor movement, after initially resisting federal interference, carried out their own sweeping purge of Communists from their affiliated unions. Rather than cooperating with the loyalty program, several major unions withdrew from the Congress of Industrial Organizations, and nine more were expelled at the CIO's 1950 convention. The CIO, now lacking progressive leadership, narrowed its agenda by putting aside the goal of organizing women and racial minorities and foreclosed upon unionism as a social movement. At the same time, the new leaders prepared for merger with the less visionary American Federation of Labor, with George Meany as "business union" president, in 1956.

In all, some 6.6 million people underwent loyalty and security checks. An estimated 500 government workers were fired and perhaps as many as 6,000 more chose to resign. No spies or saboteurs turned up.

In 1950 Congress overrode the president's veto to pass a bill that Truman called "the greatest danger to freedom of press, speech, and assembly since the Sedition Act of 1798." The Internal Security (McCarran) Act required Communist organizations to register with the Subversive Activities Control Board and authorized the arrest of suspect persons during a national emergency. The Immigration and Nationality Act, also sponsored by Republican senator Pat McCarran of Nevada and adopted in 1952, again over Truman's veto, barred people deemed "subversive" or "homosexual" from becoming citizens or even from visiting the United States. It also empowered the attorney general to deport immigrants who were members of Communist organizations, even if they had become citizens. Challenged repeatedly on constitutional grounds, the Subversive Activities Control Board remained in place until 1973, when it was terminated.

The Red Scare in Hollywood

Anti-Communist Democratic representative Martin Dies of Texas, who had chaired a congressional committee on "un-American activities" since 1938, told reporters at a press conference in Hollywood in 1944:

> Hollywood is the greatest source of revenue in this nation for the Communists and other subversive groups. . . . Two elements stand out in . . . the making of pictures which extoll foreign ideology—propaganda for a cause which seeks

to spread its ideas to our people[,] and the "leftist" or radical screenwriters. . . . In my opinion, [motion picture executives] will do well to halt the propaganda pictures and eliminate every writer who has un-American ideas.

A few years later, Dies's successor, J. Parnell Thomas of New Jersey (later convicted and imprisoned for bribery), directed the committee to investigate supposed Communist infiltration of the movie industry.

Renamed and made a permanent standing committee in 1945, the House Un-American Activities Committee (HUAC) had the power to subpoena witnesses and to compel them to answer all questions or face contempt of Congress charges. The results were sometimes absurd. In well-publicized hearings held in Hollywood in October 1947, the mother of actress Ginger Rogers defended her daughter by saying that she had been duped into appearing in the pro-Soviet wartime film *Tender Comrade* (1943) and "had been forced" to read the subversive line "Share and share alike, that's democracy." Conservative novelist Ayn Rand added that *The Song of Russia* (1944) had intentionally deceived the American public by showing Russians smiling! HUAC encouraged such testimony by "friendly witnesses," including Ronald Reagan and Gary Cooper. The committee intimated many others who feared the loss of their careers into naming former friends and co-workers in order to be cleared for future work in Hollywood.

A small but prominent minority refused to cooperate with HUAC. By claiming the freedoms of speech and association guaranteed by the First and Sixth Amendments to the Constitution, they became known as "unfriendly witnesses." Many had worked in Hollywood films celebrating America's working people, a popular Depression-era theme but now considered indicative of subversive intentions. During World War II, many of these same screenwriters and actors had teamed up on films attacking fascism. Among the most prominent "unfriendly witnesses" were actors Orson Welles, Zero Mostel, and Charlie Chaplin, and Oscar-winning screenwriter Ring Lardner, Jr. Humphrey Bogart led a stars' delegation to "Defend the First Amendment" before Congress, but generated only headlines. A handful served prison sentences for contempt of Congress.

Hollywood studios refused to employ any writer, director, or actor who refused to cooperate with HUAC. The resulting blacklist remained in effect until the 1960s and limited the production of films dealing directly with social or political issues. Meanwhile, the privately published *Red Channels: The Report of Communist Influence in Radio and Television* (1950) persuaded advertisers to cancel their accounts with many programs considered friendly to the Soviet Union, the United Nations, or liberal causes.

Spy Cases

In August 1948, Whittaker Chambers, a *Time* magazine editor, appeared before HUAC to name Alger Hiss as a fellow Communist in the Washington underground during the 1930s. Hiss, then president of the prestigious Carnegie Endowment for International Peace and former member of FDR's State Department, denied the charges and sued his accuser for slander. Chambers then revealed his trump card, a cache of films of secret documents—hidden in and then retrieved from a hallowed-out pumpkin on his farm in Maryland—that he claimed Hiss had passed to him for transmission to the USSR. Republican representative Richard Nixon of California described the so-called "Pumpkin Papers" as proof of "the most serious series of treasonable activities . . . in the history of America." The statute of limitations for espionage having run out, a federal grand jury in January 1950 convicted Hiss of perjury (for denying he knew Chambers), and he received a five-year prison term. Hiss was released two years later, still proclaiming his innocence.

Many Democrats, including Truman himself, at first dismissed the allegations against Hiss—conveniently publicized at the start of the 1948 election campaign—as a red herring, a Republican maneuver to gain votes. Indeed, Nixon himself circulated a pamphlet entitled *The Hiss Case* to promote his own candidacy for vice president. Nevertheless, the highly publicized allegations against Hiss proved detrimental to Democrats, suggesting that both FDR and Truman had allowed Communists to infiltrate the federal government.

The most dramatic spy case of the era involved Julius Rosenberg, former government engineer, and his wife, Ethel, who were accused of stealing and plotting to convey atomic secrets to Soviet agents during World War II. The government had only a weak case against Ethel Rosenberg, hoping that her conviction would force her husband to "break." The case against Julius Rosenberg depended on documents too highly classified to present as evidence at a public trial and therefore rested on the testimony of his supposed accomplices, some of them secretly coached by the FBI. Although the Rosenbergs maintained their innocence to the end, in March 1951 a jury found them guilty of conspiring to commit espionage. The American press showed them no sympathy, but around the world the Rosenbergs were defended by citizens' committees and their convictions protested in large-scale demonstrations. Scientist Albert Einstein, the pope, and the president of France, among many prominent figures, all pleaded for clemency. Julius and Ethel Rosenberg died in the electric chair on June 19, 1953.

The tables turned on Senator Joseph McCarthy (1908–57) after he instigated an investigation of the U.S. Army for harboring Communists. A congressional committee then investigated McCarthy for attempting to make the army grant special privileges to his staff aide, Private David Schine. During the televised hearings, Senator McCarthy—shown here with his staff assistant Roy Cohn—discredited himself. In December 1954, the Senate voted to censure him.

SOURCE: Photo by Hank Walker. TimePix (3701).

McCarthyism

In a sensational Lincoln Day speech to the Republican Women's Club of Wheeling, West Virginia, on February 9, 1950, Republican senator Joseph R. McCarthy of Wisconsin announced that the United States had been sold out by the "traitorous actions of those who have been treated so well by the nation." These "bright young men who have been born with silver spoons in their mouths"—such as Secretary of State Dean Acheson, whom McCarthy called a "pompous diplomat in striped pants, with a phony English accent"—were part of a conspiracy, he charged, of more than 200 Communists working in the State Department.

McCarthy refused to reveal names, however, and a few days later, after a drinking bout, he told persistent reporters: "I'm not going to tell you anything. I just want you to know I've got a pailful [of dirt] . . . and I'm going to use it where it does the most good." Although investigations uncovered not a single Communist in the

State Department, McCarthy launched a flamboyant offensive against New Deal Democrats and the Truman administration for failing to defend the nation's security. His name provided the label for the entire campaign to silence critics of the cold war: McCarthyism.

Behind the blitz of publicity, the previously obscure junior senator from Wisconsin had struck a chord. Communism seemed to many Americans to be much more than a military threat—indeed, nothing less than a demonic force capable of undermining basic values. It compelled patriots to proclaim themselves ready for atomic warfare: "Better Dead Than Red." McCarthy also had help from organizations such as the American Legion and the Chamber of Commerce, and prominent religious leaders and union leaders.

Civil rights organizations faced the severest persecution since the 1920s. The Civil Rights Congress and the Negro Youth Council, for instance, were destroyed after frequent charges of Communist influence. W. E. B. Du Bois, the renowned African American historian, and famed concert singer (and former All-American football hero) Paul Robeson had public appearances canceled and their right to travel abroad abridged.

In attacks on women's organizations and homosexual groups, meanwhile, anti-Communist rhetoric cloaked deep fears about changing sexual mores. HUAC published a pamphlet quoting a Columbia professor as saying that "girls' schools and women's colleges contain some of the most loyal disciples of Russia . . . often frustrated females." Republican Party chair Guy Gabrielson warned that "sexual perverts" who were possibly "as dangerous as actual Communists" had infiltrated the government. Aided by FBI reports, the federal government fired up to sixty homosexuals per month in the early 1950s. Dishonorable discharges from the U.S. armed forces for homosexuality, an administrative procedure without appeal, also increased dramatically, to 2,000 per year. Noted historian Arthur Schlesinger, Jr. suggested that critics of cold war policies were not "real" men or, perhaps, "real" women either.

Much of McCarthy's rhetoric was merely opportunistic, his campaign a ruthless attempt to gain power and fame by exploiting cold war fears. He succeeded partly because he brilliantly used the media to his own advantage. McCarthy also perfected the inquisitorial technique, asking directly, "Are you now, or have you ever been, a member of the Communist Party?"

Joseph McCarthy and his fellow Red-hunters eventually burned themselves out. During televised congressional hearings in 1954, not only did McCarthy fail to prove wild charges of Communist infiltration of the army, but in the glare of the television cameras he appeared deranged. Cowed for years, the Senate finally condemned him for "conduct unbecoming a member."

COLD WAR CULTURE

The anti-Communist campaigns and loyalty programs represented only the most palpable elements in the domestic cold war. As the Truman Doctrine clearly specified, the cold war did not necessarily depend on military confrontation; nor was it defined exclusively by a quest for economic supremacy. The cold war embodied the struggle of one "way of life" against another. It was, in short, a contest of values. The president therefore pledged the United States to "contain" communism from spreading beyond the parameters of the Soviet Union and its client states and simultaneously called for fortifications at home. If Americans were to rebuild the world based on their own values, they must rededicate themselves to the defense of their birthright: freedom and democracy. To do so required a total mobilization covering all aspects of American life, not just its formal political institutions. And to prepare Americans for this challenge, it might be necessary first—as Republican senator Arthur Vandenberg advised Truman—to "scare hell out of the country."

An Anxious Mood

At the end of World War II, while much of the world lay in rubble, the United States began the longest, steadiest period of economic growth and prosperity in its history. "We have about 50 percent of the world's wealth," George Kennan noted in 1948, "but only 3.6 percent of its population." Very large pockets of poverty remained, and not all Americans benefited from the postwar abundance. Nonetheless, millions of Americans achieved middle-class status, often through new programs subsidized by the federal government.

Prosperity did not dispel an anxious mood, fueled in part by the reality and the rhetoric of the cold war. Many Americans also feared an economic backslide. If war production had ended the hardships of the Great Depression, how would the economy fare in peacetime? No one could say. Above all, peace itself seemed precarious. President Truman himself suggested that World War III appeared inevitable, and his secretary of state, Dean Acheson, warned the nation to keep "on permanent alert." McCarthyism raised the spectre of internal as well as distant enemies.

Anxieties intensified by the cold war surfaced as major themes in popular culture. One of the most acclaimed Hollywood films of the era, the winner of nine Academy Awards, *The Best Years of Our Lives* (1946), followed the stories of three returning veterans as they tried to readjust to civilian life. The former soldiers found that the dreams of reunion with family and loved ones that had sustained them through years of fighting now seemed hollow. In some cases, their wives and children had become so self-reliant that the men had no clear function to perform in the household; in other cases, the prospect for employment appeared dim. The feeling of community shared with wartime buddies dissipated, leaving only a profound sense of loneliness.

The genre of *film noir* (French for "black") deepened this mood into an aesthetic. Movies like *Out of the Past, Detour,* and *They Live by Night* featured stories of ruthless fate and betrayal. Their protagonists were usually strangers or loners falsely accused of crimes or trapped into committing them. The high-contrast lighting of these black and white films accentuated the difficulty of distinguishing friend from foe. Feelings of frustration and loss of control came alive in tough, cynical characters played by actors such as Robert Mitchum and Robert Ryan.

Plays and novels also described alienation and anxiety in vivid terms. Playwright Arthur Miller in *Death of a Salesman* (1949) sketched an exacting portrait of self-destructive individualism. Willy Loman, the play's hero, is obsessively devoted to his career in sales but is nevertheless a miserable failure. Worse, he has trained his sons to excel in personal presentation and style— the very methods prescribed by standard American success manuals—making them both shallow and materialistic. J. D. Salinger's widely praised novel *Catcher in the Rye* (1951) explored the mental anguish of a teenage boy estranged from the crass materialism of his parents.

Cold war anxiety manifested itself in a flurry of unidentified flying object (UFO) sightings. Thousands of Americans imagined that a Communist-like invasion from outer space was already under way, or they hoped that superior creatures might arrive to show the way to world peace. The U.S. Air Force discounted the sightings of flying saucers, but dozens of private researchers and faddists claimed to have been contacted by aliens. Hollywood films fed these beliefs. The popular movie *The Day the Earth Stood Still* (1951) delivered a message of world peace in which a godlike being implores earthlings to abandon their weaponry before they destroy the planet. Other popular science fiction films carried a different message. In *The Invasion of the Body Snatchers* (1956), for example, a small town is captured by aliens who take over the minds of its inhabitants when they fall asleep, a subtle warning against apathy toward the threat of communist "subversion."

Hollywood studios played directly into the mounting fears, releasing by 1954 more than forty films with titles such as *I Married a Communist* (1950) and *The Red Menace* (1949) that sensationalized the Communist threat. The television industry sponsored the dramatic series *The Hunter*, featuring the adventures of an American businessman fighting Communist agents throughout the Free World. Few of these films or programs were popular, however.

The Family as Bulwark

Postwar prosperity helped to strengthen the ideal of domesticity, although many Americans interpreted their rush toward marriage and parenthood, as one writer put it, as a "defense—an impregnable bulwark" against the anxieties of the era. Even the ultimate symbol of postwar prosperity, the new home in the suburbs, reflected more than simple self-confidence. In 1950 the *New York Times* ran advertisements that captured a chilling quality of the boom in real estate: country properties for the Atomic Age located at least fifty miles outside major cities—the most likely targets, it was believed, of a Soviet nuclear attack. Not a few suburbanites built new additions to their homes, underground bomb shelters made of steel-reinforced concrete and outfitted with provisions to maintain a family for several weeks after an atomic explosion. Financial well-being could not in itself offset the insecurities provoked by the cold war.

Many young couples nevertheless sought security by marrying younger and producing more children than at any time in the past century. The national fertility rate had reached an all-time low during the Great Depression, bottoming out in 1933 at 75 per 1,000 women. A decade later, after wartime production had revived the economy, the birthrate climbed to nearly 109 per 1,000 women. The U.S. Census Bureau predicted that this "baby boom" would be temporary. To everyone's surprise, the birthrate continued to grow at a record pace, peaking at over 118 per 1,000 women in 1957.

The new families who enjoyed postwar prosperity inaugurated a spending spree of trailblazing proportions. "The year 1946," *Life* magazine proclaimed, "finds the U.S. on the threshold of marvels, ranging from run-less stockings and shineless serge suits to jet-propelled airplanes that will flash across the country in just a little less than the speed of sound." The conversion from wartime to peacetime production took longer than many eager shoppers had hoped, but by 1950 the majority of Americans could own consumer durables, such as automatic washers, and small appliances, from do-it-yourself power tools to cameras. By the time Harry Truman left office two-thirds of all American households claimed at least one television set.

These two trends—the baby boom and high rates of consumer spending—encouraged a major change in the middle-class family. Having worked during World War II, often in occupations traditionally closed to them, many women wished to continue in full-time employment. Reconversion to peacetime production forced the majority from their factory positions, but most women quickly returned, taking jobs at a faster rate than men and providing half the total growth of the labor force. By 1952, 2 million more wives worked than during the war. Gone, however, were the high-paying unionized jobs in manufacturing. Instead, most women found minimum-wage jobs in the expanding service sector: clerical work, health care and education, and restaurant, hotel, and retail services. Older women whose children were grown might work because they had come to value a job for its own sake. Younger women often worked for reasons of "economic necessity"—that is, to maintain a middle-class standard of living that now required more than one income. Indeed, mothers of young children were the most likely to be employed.

DISTRIBUTION OF TOTAL PERSONAL INCOME AMONG VARIOUS SEGMENTS OF THE POPULATION, 1947–1970 (IN PERCENTAGES)*

Year	Poorest Fifth	Second Poorest Fifth	Middle Fifth	Second Wealthiest Fifth	Wealthiest Fifth	Wealthiest 5 Percent
1947	3.5	10.6	16.7	23.6	45.6	18.7
1950	3.1	10.5	17.3	24.1	45.0	18.2
1960	3.2	10.6	17.6	24.7	44.0	17.0
1970	3.6	10.3	17.2	24.7	44.1	16.9

Despite the general prosperity of the postwar era, the distribution of income remained essentially unchanged.

*Monetary income only.

SOURCE: Adapted from U.S. Bureau of the Census, *Historical Statistics of the United States, Colonial Times to 1970*, Bicentennial ed. (Washington, D.C.: U.S. Government Printing Office, 1975), p. 292.

This model is displaying the ideal kitchen of the 1950s. The "American way of life," defined as a high standard of living, was one of the tangible fruits of U.S. victory in World War II.

SOURCE: CORBIS (GNGN10375).

for their families. In the first edition of *Baby and Child Care* (1946), the child-rearing advice manual that soon outsold the Bible, Benjamin Spock similarly advised women to devote themselves full time, if financially possible, to their maternal responsibilities.

Patterns of women's higher education reflected this conservative trend. Having made slight gains during World War II when college-age men were serving in the armed forces or working in war industries, women lost ground after the G.I. Bill created a huge upsurge in male enrollment. Women represented 40 percent of all college graduates in 1940 but only 25 percent a decade later.

With a growing number of middle-class women working to help support their families, these cold war policies and prescriptions worked at cross-purposes. As early as 1947, *Life* magazine registered concern in a thirteen-page feature, "American Woman's Dilemma." How could women comfortably take part in a world beyond the home and at the same time heed the advice of FBI director J. Edgar Hoover, who exhorted the nation's women to fight

Even though most women sought employment primarily to support their families, they ran up against popular opinion and expert advice urging them to return to their homes. Public opinion registered resounding disapproval—by 86 percent of those surveyed—of a married woman's working if jobs were scarce and her husband could support her. Noting that most Soviet women worked in industry, commentators appealed to women to return home and make the family a bulwark against communism. Just as the Truman Doctrine and the Marshall Plan responded to pitfalls abroad, the American family could "contain" dangers at home—if "restored" to an imaginary "traditional" form where men alone were breadwinners and women stayed happily at home.

This campaign began on a shrill note. Ferdinand Lundberg and Marynia Farnham, in their best-selling *Modern Woman: The Lost Sex* (1947), attributed the "super-jittery age in which we live" to women's abandonment of the home to pursue careers. To counter this trend, they proposed federally funded psychotherapy to readjust women to their housewifely roles and cash subsidies to encourage them to bear more children.

Articles in popular magazines, television shows, and high-profile experts chimed in with similar messages. Talcott Parsons, the distinguished Harvard sociologist, delineated the parameters of the "democratic" family: husbands served as breadwinners while wives— "the emotional hub of the family"—stayed home to care

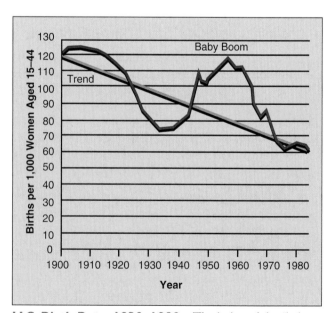

U.S. Birth Rate, 1930–1980 The bulge of the "baby boom," a leading demographic factor in the postwar economy, stands out for this fifty-year period.

"the twin enemies of freedom—crime and communism" by fulfilling their singular role as "homemakers and mothers"?

Military-Industrial Communities in the West

All regions of the United States felt the impact of the cold war but perhaps none so directly as the Trans-Mississippi West. Defense spending during World War II had stimulated the western economy and encouraged a mass migration of people eager to find employment in wartime industry. Following the war, many cities successfully converted to peacetime production; Los Angeles, for example, attracted one-eighth of all new business in the nation during the late 1940s. However, the cold war, by reviving defense funding, provided the most important boost to the western economy. The Department of Defense and private corporations and subcontractors generated billions of dollars for research and development of military equipment of various kinds.

The federal government poured so much defense money—nearly 10 percent of the entire military budget—into California that the state's rate of economic growth between 1949 and 1952 outpaced that of the nation as a whole, with nearly 40 percent coming from the manufacture of aircraft alone. Ten years later, it was estimated that one-third of all workers in Los Angeles were employed by defense industries, particularly aerospace, and that their absolute number was far greater than during the peak of production in World War II. The concentration of defense workers was even greater in the suburbs of Los Angeles. Orange County, for example, grew quickly during the cold war to become a major producer of communication equipment. The San Francisco Bay Area also benefited economically from defense spending, and cities such as Sunnyvale, Mountain View, and San Jose began their ascendance as home to the nation's budding high-technology industry.

The cold war also pumped new life into communities that had grown up during World War II. Hanford, Washington, and Los Alamos, New Mexico, both centers of the Manhattan Project, employed a greater number of people in the construction of the cold war nuclear arsenal than in the development of the atom bomb that brought an end to World War II. Los Alamos grew from its rural origins at such a fast pace that thirty years later its population density was one of the highest in the state, second only to the metropolitan region of Albuquerque. The community lost little of its secretive quality, with entry restricted to mainly well-paid workers and residents who could neither own land or homes within its boundary. Meanwhile, the federal government continued to place its distinctive stamp on the ar-

chitecture, with institutional and purely functional aesthetics governing the design of concrete structures with hospital-green interiors.

Other parts of New Mexico were virtually transformed by cold war exigencies. Three hundred miles southeast of Los Alamos, Espanola Valley, home to a population nearly 90 percent Hispanic and Native American, saw its economy grow as it became the location of Waste Isolation Pilot Project, the dump site of the laboratory's waste projects. Alamogordo, New Mexico, experienced more than a 200 percent increase in population during the first decade of the cold war because of its location next to White Sands Missile Range and Holloman Air Force Base.

New communities accompanied the growth of the U.S. military bases and training camps in the western states. Many of these installations, as well as hospitals and supply depots, not only survived but expanded during the transition from the actual warfare of World War II to the virtual warfare of the cold war. Between 1950 and 1953 approximately twenty western bases were reopened. California became at least a temporary home to more military personnel than any other state, but Texas was not far behind. The availability of public lands with areas of sparse population made western states especially attractive to military planners commissioned to design dangerous and secretive installations such as the White Sands Missile Range in the New Mexican desert.

Many older communities also benefited from such expansion. San Antonio, Texas, for example, came to depend economically on the military personnel stationed near the city in four air force bases, an army fort and hospital, the headquarters of the Fifth Army, and several Marine Corps and navy units. Fort Riley, Kansas developed an even greater degree of interdependency with Junction City, which grew through the cold war era from a tiny town to a small city. Many Mormon communities switched from farming to manufacturing when Utah came to lead all other states in the proportion of federal military dollars making up the state's total income. Nearly equidistant from the major cold war producers of San Diego, Los Angeles, San Francisco, and Seattle, Utah emerged as a prime distribution center for military goods as well as a major storage site.

Local politicians, real estate agents, and merchants usually welcomed these projects as sources of revenue and employment for the residents of their communities. There were, however, heavy costs for speedy and unplanned federally induced growth. To accommodate the new populations, the government poured money into new highway systems and did little to bolster or build public transportation. Uncontrolled spawl, traffic congestion, air pollution, and strains on limited water and energy resources all grew with the military-industrial communities in the West. For those populations living near nuclear weapons testing grounds, environmental degradation complemented the ultimate threat to their own physical well-being, as cancer rates soared over the next forty years.

Zeal for Democracy

World War II revitalized patriotism by rallying Americans to define themselves and their institutions against Nazi and fascist forces abroad. Pledging allegiance to the flag, for example, gained new symbolic meaning as school children were directed to avoid saluting, a gesture now perceived as disturbingly similar to the militaristic Nazi hand-raising, and were instead told to hold their right hand steadily over their heart. By 1941, the celebration of Flag Day moved even President Roosevelt, who previously showed no interest in the event, to implore Americans to show their colors "when the principles of unity and freedom symbolized by Old Glory are under attack."

Following the massive V-J Day celebrations that marked the end of World War II, Americans began to retreat from public displays of patriotism but were soon chastized for their "national apathy" by organizations like the Freedoms Foundation of Valley Forge, which aimed to mobilize a "vast articulate, creative army of ministers, teachers, professional people, students, men and women from the farm and factory" to defend "the American Way." Soon, other new groups, such as the American Heritage Foundation, founded in 1947, joined such stalwarts as the American Legion, the Chamber of Commerce, and local business and veterans groups in this endeavor.

During the tense election year of 1948, for example, the Junior Chamber of Commerce of Kansas City, Missouri, sponsored "Democracy Beats Communism" Week and prepared a small army of speakers to explain the virtues of American democracy over Soviet slavery, focusing to a large extent on superiority of free enterprise over a state-controlled economy. Students in the city's high schools thus learned that whereas one in every five Americans had a phone, only one in 188 Russians did. The week climaxed in a "Torch of Freedom" parade, a caravan of automobiles, trucks, and marching bands carrying the message to all parts of the city.

The American Legion of Mosinee, Wisconsin, utilized political theatre to inculcate the virtues of the American way, orchestrating an imaginary Communist coup of the small community. In 1950 on May Day, the traditional Communist holiday, "Communist agents," followed by more than sixty reporters, forced the mayor from his home and announced that the Council of People's Commissars had taken over the local government. The chief of police met with a similar fate,

and roadblocks were put up to prevent any of the residents from escaping to "free" territory. The restaurants served only Soviet fare: black bread, potato soup, and coffee. The local newspaper, the *Mosinee Times*, printed a special edition on pink stock under its new masthead, "Red Star." The citizens of Mosinee discovered that all private property had been confiscated by the state and that all rights guaranteed by the Constitution had been anulled. Moreover, every adult was required "to contribute to the State four extra hours of labor without compensation." That evening, after a full day of Communist indoctrination, the local residents rallied in "Red Square" where they declared an end to the Communist rule of their community. Mosinee's defenders of freedom raised the American flag and headed home to the refrain of "God Bless America." The national media, including *Life* magazine and all the radio networks, covered Mosinee's "Day Under Communism."

Meanwhile, Attorney General Tom Clark, with the support of President Truman, funding from private donors, and planning by the American Heritage Foundation, had been putting on track the "Freedom Train." Carrying documents illustrating basic American rights and liberties, such as the Bill of Rights and the Constitution, the Freedom Train traveled to various cities across the United States where local citizens got aboard to view various patriotic displays at the average rate of 8,500 people per day. The popular songwriter Irving Berlin memorialized the Freedom Train, lyrically assuring the expectant viewers who endured long lines that inside "you'll find a precious freight."

Patriotic messages also permeated public education. According to guidelines set down by the Truman administration, teachers were to "strengthen national security through education," specifically designing their lesson plans to illustrate the superiority of the American democratic system over Soviet communism. In 1947 the federal Office of Education launched the "Zeal for Democracy" program for implementation by school boards nationwide. The program veered toward propaganda, announcing its intention to "promote and strengthen democratic thinking and practice, just as the schools of totalitarian states have so effectively promoted the ideals of their respective cultures." Meanwhile, as part of a separate program in civil defense, schoolchildren were taught to "duck" under their desks and "cover" their heads to protect themselves in the event of a surprise nuclear attack by the Soviets.

Lessons in the American way also found their way into the books of the nation's leading historians, such as Samuel Eliot Morison, who shaped his interpretation of past events to highlight American values, particularly the sanctity of private property. Richard Hofstadter in his prize-winning *American Political Tradition* (1948), similarly described the uniquely American faith in "the economic virtues of capitalist culture as necessary qualities of man."

There were voices of protest to these cold war programs. The black poet Langston Hughes, for example, expressed his skepticism in verse, writing that he hoped the Freedom Train would carry no Jim Crow car. A fearless minority of scholars protested infringements on their academic freedom by refusing to sign loyalty oaths and by writing books pointing out the potential dangers of aggressively nationalistic foreign and domestic policies. But the chilling atmosphere, such as the political climate pervading the campus of the University of Washington, made many individuals reluctant to express contrary opinions or ideas.

END OF THE DEMOCRATIC ERA

Cold war tensions festered first in Europe. Following the announcement of the Marshall Plan, the Soviet Union tightened relationships among Communist parties in Eastern Europe as well as in France and Italy by establishing the Cominform. Then, in February 1948, Communists seized power in Czechoslovakia, a move that speeded up plans by the British, French, and Americans to consolidate their occupation zones in Germany. By spring of that year, the Berlin Crisis had pushed the United States and Soviet Union to the brink of armed conflict. With so much happening in Europe, neither superpower would have predicted that events in Asia would soon transform their political and ideological competition into a war threatening to destroy the world. Yet, in 1949, Communists in China seized power in the most heavily populated nation in the world. Then, a few months later, in June 1950, Communists threatened to take over all of Korea. The precarious balance of power was seemingly shifting.

Trapped by his own tough cold war rhetoric, Truman asked Americans to sanction a limited war in Korea, and within a few years more than 1.8 millions Americans had been sent to fight a war with no victory in sight. For Truman, the "loss" of China to communism and the stalemate in Korea proved political suicide. The raging controversy that ensued ended the twenty-year Democratic lock on the presidency and the greatest era of reform in U.S. history.

The "Loss" of China

At the close of World War II, the United States acted deliberately to secure Japan firmly in its realm. General Douglas MacArthur directed an interim government in a modest reconstruction program that included land

reform, the creation of independent trade unions, the abolition of contract marriages, the granting of woman suffrage, sweeping demilitarization, and, eventually, a constitutional democracy that barred Communists from all posts. American leaders worked to rebuild the nation's economy along capitalist lines and integrate Japan, like West Germany, into an anti-Soviet bloc. Japan also housed huge U.S. military bases, thus placing U.S. troops and weapons strategically close to the Soviet Union's Asian rim. The "Strategic Importance of Japan," according to a CIA report, derived from its potential to become a stabilizing force in Asia, particularly in relation to China.

The situation in China could not be handled so easily. After years of civil war, the pro-Western Nationalist government of Jiang Jeishi (Chiang Kai-shek) collapsed. Since World War II, the United States had been sending aid to the unpopular government while warning Jiang that without major reforms the Nationalists were heading for defeat. Moreover, they tried to convince him to accept a coalition government. After refusing to intervene on their behalf, the United States watched as Jiang's troops were finally forced to surrender to the Communists, led by Mao Zedong, who enjoyed the support of the Chinese countryside, where 85 percent of the population lived. Surrendering to Mao the entire China mainland, the defeated Nationalist government withdrew to the island of Formosa (Taiwan). On October 1, 1949, the People's Republic of China (PRC) was formally established.

The news of China's "fall" to communism created an uproar in the United States. The Asia First wing of the Republican Party, which envisioned the Far East rather than Europe as the prime site of U.S. trade and investment, blamed the Truman administration for the "loss" of China. In February 1950, when the USSR and the PRC joined in a formal alliance, Truman's adversaries capitalized on the growing threat of "international" communism and referred to the Democrats as a "party of treason."

The Korean War

At the end of World War II, the Allies had divided the small peninsula of Korea, ceded by Japan, at the 38th parallel. Although all parties hoped to reunite the nation under its own government, the line between North and South instead hardened. The United States backed the unpopular government of Syngman Rhee (the Republic of Korea), and the Soviet Union sponsored a rival government in North Korea under Kim Il Sung.

On June 25, 1950, the U.S. State Department received a cablegram reporting a military attack on South Korea by the Communist-controlled North. "If we are tough enough now," President Truman pledged, "if we

American soldiers fought in Korea under the command of General Douglas MacArthur until President Truman named General Matthew Ridgway as his replacement in April 1951. Nearly 1.8 million Americans served in Korea.

SOURCE: National Archives and Records Administration.

paign that halted the Communist drive. By October, UN troops had retaken South Korea.

Basking in victory, the Truman administration could not resist the temptation to expand its war aims. Hoping to prove that Democrats were not "soft" on communism, the president and his advisers decided to roll back the Communists beyond the 38th parallel and ultimately to reunite Korea as a showcase for democracy. Until this point, China had not been actively involved in the war. But it now warned that any attempt to cross the dividing line would be interpreted as a threat to its own national security. Truman flew to Wake Island in the Pacific on October 15 for a conference with MacArthur, who assured the president of a speedy victory.

MacArthur had sorely miscalculated. Chinese troops massed just above the UN offensive line, at the Yalu River. Suddenly, and without any air support, the Chinese attacked in human waves. MacArthur's force was all but crushed. The Chinese drove the UN troops back into South Korea, where they regrouped along the 38th parallel. By summer 1951 a stalemate had been reached very near the old border. Negotiations for a settlement went on for the next eighteen months amid heavy fighting.

"There is no substitute for victory," MacArthur insisted as he tried without success to convince Truman to prepare for a new invasion of Communist territory. Encouraged by strong support at home, he continued to provoke the president by speaking out against official policy, calling for bombing of supply lines in China and a naval blockade of the Chinese coast—actions certain to lead to a Chinese-American war. Finally, on April 10, 1951, Truman dismissed MacArthur for insubordination and other unauthorized activities.

The Price of National Security

The Korean War had profound implications for the use of executive power. By instituting a peacetime draft in 1948 and then ordering American troops into Korea, Truman had bypassed congressional authority. Repub-

stand up to them like we did in Greece three years ago, they won't take any next steps." The Soviet Union, on the other hand, regarded the invasion as Kim Il Sung's affair. Despite Soviet disclaimers, Truman sought approval from the UN Security Council to send in troops to South Korea. Because of the absence of the Soviet delegate, who could have vetoed the decision, the Security Council agreed. Two-thirds of Americans polled approved the president's decision to send troops under the command of General Douglas MacArthur.

Military events seemed at first to justify the president's decision. Seoul, the capital of South Korea, had fallen to North Korean troops within weeks of the invasion, and Communist forces continued to push south until they had taken most of the peninsula. The situation appeared grim until Truman authorized MacArthur to carry out an amphibious landing at Inchon, which he did on September 15, 1950. With tactical brilliance and good fortune, the general orchestrated a military cam-

Web Exploration

Examine the United States military campaign in Korea. How did this reflect Truman's doctrine of containment?
www.prenhall.com/faragher/map26.2

The Korean War The intensity of battles underscored the strategic importance of Korea in the cold war.

lican Senator Robert Taft called the president's actions "a complete usurpation" of democratic checks and balances and charged Truman with transforming his office into an "imperial presidency." For awhile, Truman sidestepped such criticisms and their constitutional implications by declaring a national emergency and by carefully referring to the military deployment not as a U.S. war but as a UN-sanctioned "police action."

The president derived his authority from NSC-68, a paper released to him by the National Security Council in April 1950 that reinterpreted both the basic policy of containment and decision making at the highest levels of government. Demonizing communism as "a new fanatic faith" that "seeks to impose its absolute authority over the rest of the world," NSC-68 pledged the United States not only to "contain" communism but to take a further step to drive back Communist influence wherever it appeared and to "foster the seeds of destruction within the Soviet Union." Moreover, the document designated the struggle between the United States and Soviet Union as "permanent," the era one of "total war." It specified that American citizens must be willing to make sacrifices—"to give up some of the benefits which they have come to associate with their freedom"—to defend their way of life. NSC-68 articulated the intellectual and psychological rationale behind U.S. national security policies for the next forty years.

Initially reluctant, Truman fulfilled the prescriptions of NSC-68 after the outbreak of the Korean War and agreed to its mandate for a rapid and permanent military buildup. By the time the conflict subsided, the defense budget had quadrupled, from $13.5 billion to more than $52 billion in 1953. The U.S. Army had grown to 3.6 million, or six times its size at the beginning of the conflict. At the same time, the federal government accelerated the development of both conventional and nonconventional weapons. In the first instance, it began to stockpile nuclear bombs and weapons, including the first hydrogen, or H-bomb, which was tested in November 1952. NCS-68 also proposed expensive "large-scale covert operations" for the "liberation" of Communist countries, particularly in Eastern Europe.

The Korean War also provided the rationale for the expansion of anti-Communist propaganda. At the end of World War II President Truman had taken steps to transform the Office of War Information into a peacetime program that operated on a much smaller budget. But by 1948 Congress was ready to pass with bipartisan support the Smith-Mundt Act, designed "to promote the better understanding of the United States among the peoples of the world and to strengthen cooperative international relations." Within a year, Congress doubled the budget for such programming, granting $3 million to revive the Voice of America, the short-wave international radio program that had been established in 1942. The new legislation also funded the development of film, print media, cultural exchange programs, and exhibitions, and it created a foundation to promote anti-Communist propaganda throughout the world. By mid-1950, the immediate goal was the "reorientation" of North Korea toward the Free World.

The government's vast "information programs" were designed less to "contain" communism that to "liberate" those countries already under Communist rule by causing disaffection among the people. By 1951 a massive "Campaign of Truth" was reaching 93 nations, and the Voice of America was broadcasting anti-Communist programming in 45 languages. Project Troy, which was initially designed by professors from Harvard and the Massachusetts Institute of Technology, aimed to penetrate the Iron Curtain, for example, by using air balloons to distribute leaflets and cheap American goods, such as playing cards and plastic chess sets. Army pilots joined the effort, dropping leaflets on North Korean troops reading "ENJOY LIFE and plenty of cigarettes away from the war by coming over to the UN side. Escape. Save your life." On April 4, 1951, President Truman signed the order that created the Psychological Strategy Board to coordinate various operations aimed to rollback Soviet power. In his annual message to Congress that year, he had requested $115 million to fund these programs but, as the Korean War bogged down, he managed to get only $85 million.

By the time it ended, the Korean War had cost the United States approximately $100 billion and inaugurated an era of huge deficits in the federal budget and massive national debt but did nothing to improve the case for rolling back communism. Negotiations and fighting proceeded in tandem until the summer of 1953, when a settlement was reached in which both North Korea and South Korea occupied almost the same territory as when the war began. Approximately 54,000 Americans died in Korea; the North Koreans and Chinese lost well over 2 million people. The UN troops had employed both "carpet bombing" (an intense, destructive attack on a given area) and napalm (jellied gasoline bombs), destroying most of the housing and food supplies in both Koreas. True to the pattern of modern warfare, which emerged during World War II, the majority of civilians killed were women and children. Nearly 1 million Koreans were left homeless.

For the United States, the Korean War enlarged the geographical range of the cold war to include East Asia. The war also lined up the People's Republic of China and the United States as unwavering enemies for the next twenty years and heightened the U.S. commitment to Southeast Asia. Now, as one historian commented, the "frontiers on every continent were going to remain frontiers in the traditional American meaning of a frontier—a region to penetrate and control and police and civilize."

The Korean War, moreover, did much to establish an ominous tradition of "unwinnable" conflicts that left many Americans skeptical of official policy. Truman had initially rallied popular support for U.S. intervention by contrasting the Communist North with the "democratic" South, thus casting the conflict in the ideological terms of the cold war. MacArthur's early victories had promised the liberation of North Korea and even the eventual disintegration of the Soviet and Chinese regimes. But with the tactical stalemate came mass disillusionment.

In retrospect many Americans recognized that Truman, in fighting communism in Korea, had pledged the United States to defend a corrupt government and a brutal dictator. Decades later the Korean War inspired the dark comedy *M*A*S*H*, adapted for television from the film written by Hollywood screenwriter Ring Lardner, Jr., an "unfriendly witness" before HUAC, who was jailed during the Korean War for contempt of Congress. As late as 1990, members of Congress were still debating the terms of a Korean War memorial. "It ended on a sad note for Americans," one historian has concluded, "and the war and its memories drifted off into a void."

The Election of 1952

There was only one burning issue during the election campaign of 1952: the Korean War. Truman's popularity had wavered continually since he took office in 1945, but it sank to an all-time low in the early 1950s shortly after he dismissed MacArthur as commander of the UN troops in Korea. Congress received thousands of letters and telegrams calling for Truman's impeachment. "Oust President Truman" bumper stickers could be seen. MacArthur, meanwhile, returned home a hero, welcomed by more than 7 million fans in New York City alone.

Popular dissatisfaction with Truman increased. The Asia First lobby argued that if the president had acted more aggressively to turn back communism in China, the "limited war" in Korea would not have been necessary. Following these charges were accusations of large-scale corruption in his administration. Newspapers reported that several agencies had been dealing in 5 percent kickbacks for government contracts. Business and organized labor complained about the price and wage freezes imposed during the Korean War. A late-1951 Gallup poll showed the president's approval rating at 23 percent. In March 1952, Truman announced he would not run for reelection, a decision rare for a president eligible for another term.

In accepting political defeat and disgrace, Truman turned to the popular but uncharismatic governor of Illinois, Adlai E. Stevenson, Jr. Admired for his honesty and intelligence, Stevenson offered no solutions to the conflict in Korea, the accelerating arms race, or the cold war generally. Accepting the Democratic nomination, he candidly admitted that "the ordeal of the twentieth century is far from over," a prospect displeasing to voters aching for peace.

The Republicans made the most of the Democrats' dilemma. Without proposing any sweeping answers of their own, they pointed to all the obvious shortcomings of their opponents. Their campaign strategy, known as "K_1C_2"—Korea, Communism, and Corruption—took steady aim at the Truman administration, and when opinion polls showed that Dwight Eisenhower possessed an "unprecedented" 64 percent approval rating, they found in "Ike" the perfect candidate to head the ticket.

Eisenhower styled himself the representative of "modern Republicanism." He wisely avoided the nega-

Richard Nixon used the new medium of television to convince American voters that he had not established an illegal slush fund in his campaign for the vice presidency in 1952. Viewers responded enthusiastically to his melodramatic delivery and swamped the Republican campaign headquarters with telegrams endorsing his candidacy.

SOURCE: *Checkers* speech, September 24, 1952. AP/Wide World Photos.

tive impressions made by the unsuccessful 1948 Republican candidate, Thomas Dewey, who had seemed as aggressive as Truman on foreign policy and simultaneously eager to overturn the New Deal domestic legislation. Eisenhower knew better: voters wanted peace and a limited welfare state. He referred to New Deal reforms as "a solid floor that keeps all of us from falling into the pit of disaster." And athough he did not go into specifics, he promised to end the Korean War with "an early and honorable" peace. Whenever he was tempted to address questions of finance or the economy, his advisers warned him: "The chief reason that people want to vote for you is because they think you have more ability to keep us out of another war."

Meanwhile, Eisenhower's vice presidential candidate, Richard Nixon, waged a relentless and defamatory attack on Stevenson, calling him "Adlai the Appeaser." Senator Joseph McCarthy chimed in, proclaiming that with club in hand he might be able to make "a good American" of Stevenson. A month before the election, McCarthy went on network television with his requisite "exhibits" and "documents," this time purportedly showing that the Democratic presidential candidate had promoted communism at home and

CHRONOLOGY

1941 Henry Luce forecasts the dawn of "the American Century"

1944 G.I. Bill of Rights benefits World War II veterans

International Monetary Fund and World Bank founded

1945 Franklin D. Roosevelt dies in office; Harry S. Truman becomes president

United Nations charter signed

World War II ends

Strike wave begins

Truman proposes program of economic reforms

1946 Employment Act creates Council of Economic Advisers

Churchill's Iron Curtain speech

Atomic Energy Act establishes Atomic Energy Commission

Republicans win control of Congress

Benjamin Spock publishes *Baby and Child Care*

1947 Americans for Democratic Action founded

Truman Doctrine announced; Congress appropriates $400 million in aid for Greece and Turkey

Federal Employees Loyalty and Security Program established and attorney general's list of subversive organizations authorized

Marshall Plan announced

Taft-Hartley Act restricts union activities

National Security Act establishes Department of Defense, the National Security Council, and the Central Intelligence Agency

House Un-American Activities Committee hearings in Hollywood

1948 Smith-Mundt Act passed by Congress

Ferdinand Lundberg and Marynia Farnham publish *Modern Woman: The Lost Sex*

State of Israel founded

Berlin blockade begins

Henry Wallace nominated for president on Progressive Party ticket

Truman announces peacetime draft and desegregates U.S. armed forces and civil service

Truman wins election; Democrats sweep both houses of Congress

1949 Truman announces Fair Deal

North Atlantic Treaty Organization (NATO) created

Communists, led by Mao Zedong, take power in China

Berlin blockade ends

Soviet Union explodes atomic bomb

1950 Alger Hiss convicted of perjury

Senator Joseph McCarthy begins anti-Communist crusade

Soviet Union and the People's Republic of China sign an alliance

Adoption of NSC-68 consolidates presidential war powers

Korean War begins

Internal Security (McCarran) Act requires registration of Communist organizations and arrest of Communists during national emergencies

1951 Truman dismisses General Douglas MacArthur

Psychological Strategy Board created

Armistice talks begin in Korea

1952 Immigration and Nationality Act retains quota system, lifts ban on immigration of Asian and Pacific peoples, but bans "subversives" and homosexuals

United States explodes first hydrogen bomb

Dwight D. Eisenhower wins presidency; Richard Nixon becomes vice president

1953 Julius and Ethel Rosenberg executed for atomic espionage

Armistice ends fighting in Korea

1954 Army-McCarthy hearings end

1955 Warsaw Pact created

abroad. These outrageous charges kept the Stevenson campaign off balance.

The Republican campaign was itself not entirely free of scandal: Nixon had been caught accepting personal gifts from wealthy benefactors. Pleading his case on national television, he described his wife Pat's "good Republican cloth coat" and their modest style of living. He then contritely admitted that he had indeed accepted one gift, a puppy named Checkers that his daughters loved and that he refused to give back. "The Poor Richard Show," as critics called the event, defused the scandal without answering the most important charges.

Unaffected by the scandal, Eisenhower continued to enchant the voters as a peace candidate. Ten days before the election he dramatically announced, "I shall go to Korea" to settle the war. Eisenhower received 55 percent of the vote and carried thirty-nine states, in part because he brought out an unusually large number of voters in normally Democratic areas. He won the popular vote in much of the South and in the northern cities of New York, Chicago, Boston, and Cleveland. Riding his coattails, the Republicans regained narrow control of Congress. The New Deal coalition of ethnic and black voters, labor, northern liberals, and southern conservatives no longer commanded a majority.

CONCLUSION

In his farewell address, in January 1953, Harry Truman reflected: "I suppose that history will remember my term in office as the years when the 'cold war' began to overshadow our lives. I have hardly had a day in office that has not been dominated by this all-embracing struggle."

The election of Dwight Eisenhower helped to diminish the intensity of this dour mood without actually bringing a halt to the conflict. The new president pledged himself to liberate the world from communism by peaceful means rather than force. "Our aim is more subtle," he announced during his campaign, "more pervasive, more complete. We are trying to get the world, by peaceful means, to believe the truth. . . ." Increasing the budget of the CIA, Eisenhower took the cold war out of the public eye by relying to a far greater extent than Truman on psychological warfare and covert operations.

"The Eisenhower Movement," wrote journalist Walter Lippmann, was a "mission in American politics" to restore a sense of community among the American people. In a larger sense, many of the issues of the immediate post–World War II years seemed to have been settled, or put off for a distant future. The international boundaries of communism were frozen with the Chinese Revolution, the Berlin Crisis, and now the Korean War. Meanwhile, at home cold war defense spending had become a permanent part of the national budget, an undeniable drain on tax revenues but an important element in the government contribution to economic prosperity. If the nuclear arms race remained a cause for anxiety, joined by more personal worries about the changing patterns of family life, a sense of relative security nevertheless spread. Prospects for world peace had dimmed, but the worst nightmares of the 1940s had eased as well.

REVIEW QUESTIONS

1. Discuss the origins of the cold war and the sources of growing tensions between the United States and the Soviet Union at the close of World War II.
2. Describe the basic elements of President Harry Truman's policy of containment. How did the threat of atomic warfare affect this policy?
3. Compare the presidencies of Franklin D. Roosevelt and Harry S. Truman, both Democrats.
4. Describe the impact of McCarthyism on American political life. How did the anti-Communist campaigns affect the media? What were the sources of Senator Joseph McCarthy's popularity? What brought about his downfall?
5. How did the cold war affect American culture?
6. Discuss the role of the United States in Korea in the decade after World War II. How did the Korean War affect the 1952 presidential election?
7. Why did Dwight D. Eisenhower win the 1952 presidential election?

RECOMMENDED READING

Mark S. Byrnes, *The Truman Years, 1945–1953* (2000). A concise history of the Truman administration and its role at the moment when the United States became the dominant economic power in the world. Byrnes covers this transformation with particular attention to the way the president helped to shape a view of the world that presented the United States and the Soviet Union as permanent enemies in a struggle for domination. Includes a set of twenty-one key documents and a detailed chronology of events.

Warren I. Cohen, *America in the Age of Soviet Power, 1945–1991* (1993). A highly readable volume in the "Cambridge History of American Foreign Relations" series, this study examines the origins of the cold war in policies ending World War II, including the breakup of the colonial empires, and concludes with the collapse of communism in the Soviet Union in 1991.

Kevin J. Fernlund, ed., *The Cold War American West, 1945–1989* (1998). Ten essays illustrating the impact of the cold war on the region of the United States that housed the bulk of military bases, airfields, nucelar testing grounds, and toxic waste dumps. Presenting a variety of interpretations, the contributors ask a common question: Was the West transformed or deformed by the policies of the growing national security state?

John Fousek, *To Lead the Free World: American Nationalism and the Cultural Roots of the Cold War* (2000). Examines the "public culture" of the cold war through an innovative study of various responses to the official doctrines and declarations of the Truman administration. Fousek pays special attention to the publications of major civil rights organizations and the two largest labor unions of the period and argues that "a broad public consensus" supported Truman's nationalistic foreign policy.

Richard M. Fried, *The Russians Are Coming! The Russians Are Coming!: Pageantry and Patriotism in Cold-War America* (1998). Examines, through vivid example, the creation of the fear of communism and its translation into patriotic zeal. Fried takes as his thesis that rallying the public to "fight" the cold war required as much organization and energy as mobilizing Americans to defend the home front during World War II.

Margot A. Henriksen, *Dr. Strangelove's America: Society and Culture in the Atomic Age* (1997). Argues in a lively fashion that the atomic bomb played the "central, defining role" in American culture and society from 1945 into the early 1980s. Henriksen's culls evidence from a wide range of sources, including novels, movies, TV programs, and rock 'n' roll songs.

George Lipsitz, *A Rainbow at Midnight: Labor and Culture in the 1940s* (1994). A vivid account of economic and cultural hopes, uneasiness, and disappointments after World War II. Lipsitz shows how struggles for economic democracy were defeated and how popular culture—for example, country-and-western music and rock 'n' roll, as well as stock car racing and roller derby—arose in blue-collar communities.

Elaine Tyler May, *Homeward Bound: American Families in the Cold War Era* (1988). A lively account of the effects on family life and women's roles of the national mood of "containment." May argues that government policy became part of a popular culture that solidified the cold war era's "feminine mystique."

David G. McCullough, *Truman* (1992). A heroic rendition of Truman's personal life and political career. Through personal correspondence and other documents, McCullough details Truman's view of himself and the generally favorable view of him held by supporters of cold war liberalism.

Patrick McGilligan and Paul Buhle, *Tender Comrades: A Backstory of the Hollywood Blacklist* (1997). A collection of interviews with thirty-five victims of the Hollywood Blacklist, including some of the most important writers, directors, and film stars. The collection is especially valuable for its detailing of film production during the years of World War II and afterward, including the creation of *film noir.*

Joanne Meyerowitz, ed., *Not June Cleaver: Women and Gender in Postwar America, 1945–1960* (1994). A collection of essays that refute the common stereotype of women as homebound during the postwar era.

Stanley Weintraub, *MacArthur's War: Korea and the Undoing of an American Hero* (2000). Tells the story of the downfall of the commander of U.S. forces in the Far East, who was "senior to everyone but God" in the military services. The author additionally offers a detailed description of the horror and ruin accompanying the brutal ground war in Korea.

ADDITIONAL BIBLIOGRAPHY

Global Insecurities and the Policy of Containment

Christian G. Appy, ed., *Cold War Constructions: The Political Culture of United States Imperialism, 1945–1966* (2000)

H. W. Brands, Jr., *The Devil We Knew: Americans and the Cold War* (1993)

Robert Frazier, *Anglo-American Relations with Greece: The Coming of the Cold War, 1942–47* (1991)

John Gaddis, *We Now Know: Rethinking Cold War History* (1997)

John L. Harper, *American Visions of Europe: Franklin D. Roosevelt, George F. Kennan, and Dean G. Acheson* (1995)

Walter Hixson, *Parting the Curtain: Propaganda, Culture, and the Cold War, 1945–1961* (1997)

Townsend Hoopes and Douglas Brinkley, *FDR and the Creation of the U.N.* (1997)

Walter LeFeber, *America, Russia, and the Cold War, 1945–1992,* 7th ed. (1993)

Richard Rhodes, *Dark Sun: The Making of the Hydrogen Bomb* (1995)

Michael Schaller, *American Occupation of Japan: The Origins of the Cold War in Asia* (1985)

The Truman Presidency

Gary A. Donaldson, *Truman Defeats Dewey* (1999)

Harold I. Gullan, *The Upset That Wasn't: Harry S. Truman and the Crucial Election of 1948* (1998)

Melvyn P. Leffler, *A Preponderance of Power: National Security, the Truman Administration, and the Cold War* (1992)

Sean J. Savage, *Truman and the Democratic Party* (1997)

The Cold War at Home

Noam Chomsky, ed., *The Cold War and the University: Toward an Intellectual History of the Postwar Years* (1997)

Larry Ceplair and Steven Englund, *The Inquisition in Hollywood: Politics in the Film Community, 1930–1960* (1980)

Sigmund Diamond, *Compromised Campus: The Collaboration of Universities with the Intelligence Communities, 1945–1995* (1992)

Michael J. Hogan, *A Cross of Iron: Harry S. Truman and the Origins of the National Security States, 1945–1954* (1998)

Scott Lucas, *Freedom's War: The U.S. Crusade Against the Soviet Union, 1945–56* (1999)

Elaine McClarnand and Steve Goodson, eds., *The Impact of the Cold War on American Popular Culture* (1999)

Lisle A. Rose, *The Cold War Comes to Main Street: America in 1950* (1999)

Ellen W. Schrecker, *No Ivory Tower: McCarthyism in the Universities* (1988)

Ellen Schrecker, *Many Are the Crimes: McCarthyism in America* (1998)

Age of Anxiety

Michael Barson, *"Better Dead Than Red!" A Nostalgic Look at the Golden Years of Russiaphobia, Red-Baiting, and Other Commie Madness* (1992)

Stuart W. Leslie, *The Cold War and American Science* (1993)

J. Fred MacDonald, *Television and the Red Menace* (1985)

Lary May, ed., *Recasting America: Culture and Politics in the Age of the Cold War* (1989)

Nora Sayre, *Running Time: Films of the Cold War* (1982)

Jessica Wang, *American Science in an Age of Anxiety: Scientists, Anticommunism, and the Cold War* (1999)

Korean War

William T. Bowers, *William M. Hammond, George L. MacGarrigle, Black Solider, White Army: The 24th Infantry Regiment in Korea* (1996)

Albert E. Cowdrey, *The Medics' War* (1987)

Stephen Endicott and Edward Hagerman, *The United States and Biological Warfare: Secrets from the Early Cold War and Korea* (1998)

Paul G. Pierpaoli, Jr., *Truman and Korea: The Political Culture of the Early Cold War* (1999)

Stanley Sandler, *The Korean War: No Victors, No Vanquished* (1999)

Biography

Allida M. Black, *Casting Her Own Shadow: Eleanor Roosevelt and the Shaping of Postwar Liberalism* (1996)

Martin Bauml Duberman, *Paul Robeson* (1988)

Curt Gentry, *J. Edgar Hoover: The Man and the Secrets* (1991)

Alonzo L. Hamby, *Man of the People: A Life of Harry Truman* (1995)

Arthur Herman, *Joseph McCarthy: Reexamining the Life and Legacy of America's Most Hated Senator* (1999)

Wilson D. Miscamble, *George F. Kennan and the Making of American Foreign Policy, 1947–1950* (1992)

Geoffrey Perret, *Old Soldiers Never Die: The Life of Douglas MacArthur* (1996)

Graham White and John Maze, *Henry A. Wallace: His Search for New World Order* (1995)

HISTORY ON THE INTERNET

http://www.nara.gov/exhall/picturing_the_century/galleries/postwar.html

This site is from the American Memory by the National Archives and includes a small, but interesting collection of photos, one of the most interesting being a snapshot of American troops on November 1, 1951 at Yucca Flats, Nevada.

http://www.history.navy.mil/photos/events/wwii-dpl/hd-state/potsdam.htm

Official U.S. Navy photos of President Truman traveling to the Potsdam Conference aboard the *USS Augusta*, some photos at the conference site, and photos of the president on the return voyage.

http://www.historyplace.com/speeches/ironcurtain.htm

Winston Churchill's "Iron Curtain Speech" delivered March 5, 1946 at Westminster College, in Fulton, Missouri.

http://www.whistlestop.org/study_collections/korea/large/

Truman Presidential Library site on the Korean War with links to many other sites and to Korean War photographs.

TWENTY-SEVEN
AMERICA AT MIDCENTURY

▷ 1 9 5 2 – 1 9 6 3

SOURCE: Photo by Willinger. Getty Images, Inc. (cat #3632)

AMERICAN COMMUNITIES

Popular Music in Memphis

THE NINETEEN-YEAR-OLD SINGER WAS PEERING NERVOUSLY OUT OVER the large crowd. He knew that people had come to Overton Park's outdoor amphitheater that hot, sticky July day in 1954 to hear the headliner, country music star Slim Whitman. Sun Records, a local Memphis label, had just released the teenager's first record, and it had begun to receive some airplay on local radio. But the singer and his two bandmates had never played in a setting even remotely as large as this one. And their music defied categories: it wasn't black and it wasn't white; it wasn't pop and it wasn't country. But when the singer launched into his version of a black blues song called "That's All Right," the crowd went wild. "I came offstage," the singer later recalled, "and my manager told me that they was hollering because I was wiggling my legs. I went back out for an encore, and I did a little more, and the more I did, the wilder they went." Elvis Presley had arrived.

Elvis combined a hard-driving, rhythmic approach to blues and country music with a riveting performance style, inventing the new music known as rock 'n' roll. An unprecedented cultural phenomenon, rock 'n' roll was a music made largely for and by teenagers. In communities all over America, rock 'n' roll brought teens together around jukeboxes, at sock hops, in cars, and at private parties. It demonstrated the enormous consumer power of American teens. Rock 'n' roll also embodied a postwar trend accelerating the integration of white and black music. This cultural integration prefigured the social and political integration won by the civil rights movement.

Located halfway between St. Louis and New Orleans on the Mississippi River, Memphis had become a thriving commercial city by the 1850s, with an economy centered on the lucrative cotton trade of the surrounding delta region. It grew rapidly in the post–Civil War years, attracting a polyglot population of white businessmen and planters, poor rural whites and blacks, and German and Irish immigrants. By the early twentieth century Memphis also boasted a remarkable diversity of popular theater and music, including a large opera house, numerous brass bands, vaudeville and burlesque, minstrel shows, jug bands, and blues clubs.

Like most American cities, Memphis enjoyed healthy growth during World War II, with lumber mills, furniture factories, and chemical manufacturing supplementing the cotton market as sources of jobs and prosperity. And like the rest of the South, Memphis was a legally segregated city; whites and blacks lived, went to school, and worked apart. Class differences among whites were important as well. Like thousands of other poor rural whites in these years, Elvis Presley had moved from Mississippi to Memphis in 1949, where his father found work in a munitions plant. The Presleys were poor enough to qualify for an apartment in Lauderdale Courts, a Memphis public housing project. To James Conaway, who grew up in an all-white, middle-class East Memphis neighborhood, people like the Presleys were "white trash." Negroes, he recalled, were "not necessarily below the rank of a country boy like Elvis, but of another universe, and yet there was more affection for them than for some whites."

839

Gloria Wade-Gayles, who lived in the all-black Foote Homes housing project, vividly remembered that her family and neighbors "had no illusion about their lack of power, but they believed in their strength." For them, strength grew from total immersion in a black community that included ministers, teachers, insurance men, morticians, barbers, and entertainers. "Surviving meant being black, and being black meant believing in our humanity, and retaining it, in a world that denied we had it in the first place."

Yet in the cultural realm, class and racial barriers could be challenged. Elvis Presley grew up a dreamy, shy boy, who turned to music for emotional release and spiritual expression. He soaked up the wide range of music styles available in Memphis. The Assembly of God Church his family attended featured a renowned hundred-voice choir. Elvis and his friends went to marathon all-night "gospel singings" at Ellis Auditorium, where they enjoyed the tight harmonies and emotional style of white gospel quartets.

Elvis also drew from the sounds he heard on Beale Street, the main black thoroughfare of Memphis and one of the nation's most influential centers of African American music. In the postwar years, local black rhythm and blues artists like B. B. King, Junior Parker, and Muddy Waters attracted legions of black and white fans with their emotional power and exciting showmanship. At the Handy Theater on Beale Street, the teenaged Elvis Presley, like thousands of other white young people, heard black performers at the "Midnight Rambles"—late shows for white people only. Elvis himself performed along with black contestants in amateur shows at Beale Street's Palace Theater. Nat D. Williams, a prominent black Memphis disc jockey and music promoter, recalled how black audiences responded to Elvis's unique style. "He had a way of singing the blues that was distinctive. He could sing 'em not necessarily like a Negro, but he didn't sing 'em altogether like a typical white musician. . . . Always he had that certain humanness about him that Negroes like to put in their songs."

The expansion of the broadcasting and recording indus-tries in the postwar years also contributed to the weakening of racial barriers in the musical realm. Two Memphis radio stations featured the hard-driving rhythm and blues music that was beginning to attract a strong following among young white listeners. These Memphis stations also featured spirituals by African American artists such as Mahalia Jackson and Clara Ward.

Elvis himself understood his debt to black music and black performers. "The colored folks," he told an interviewer in 1956, "been singing and playing it just like I'm doing now, man, for more years than I know. They played it like that in the shanties and in their juke joints and nobody paid it no mind until I goosed it up. I got it from them."

Dissatisfied with the cloying pop music of the day, white teenagers across the nation were increasingly turning to the rhythmic drive and emotional intensity of black rhythm and blues. They quickly adopted rock 'n' roll (the term had long been an African American slang expression for dancing and sexual intercourse) as their music. But it was more than just music: it was also an attitude, a celebration of being young, and a sense of having something that adult authority could not understand or control.

When Sun Records sold Presley's contract to RCA Records in 1956, Elvis became an international star. Records like "Heartbreak Hotel," "Don't Be Cruel," and "Jailhouse Rock" shot to the top of the charts and blurred the old boundaries between pop, country, and rhythm and blues. By helping to accustom white teenagers to the style and sound of black artists, Elvis helped establish rock 'n' roll as an interracial phenomenon. Institutional racism would continue to plague the music business—many black artists were routinely cheated out of royalties and severely underpaid—but the music of postwar Memphis at least pointed the way toward the exciting cultural possibilities that could emerge from breaking down the barriers of race. It also gave postwar American teenagers a new-found sense of community. ■

Memphis

AMERICAN SOCIETY AT MIDCENTURY

With the title of his influential work, *The Affluent Society* (1958), economist John Kenneth Galbraith gave a label to postwar America. Galbraith observed that American capitalism had worked "quite brilliantly" in the years since World War II. But Americans, he argued, needed to spend less on personal consumption and devote more public funds to schools, medical care, cultural activities, and social services. For most Americans, however, strong economic growth was the defining fact of the postwar period. A fierce desire for consumer goods and the "good life" imbued American culture, and the deeply held popular belief in a continuously expanding economy and a steadily increasing standard of living—together with the tensions of the cold war—shaped American social and political life.

The Eisenhower Presidency

Dwight D. Eisenhower's landslide election victory in 1952 set the stage for the first full two-term Republican presidency since that of Ulysses S. Grant. At the core of Eisenhower's political philosophy lay a conservative vision of community. He saw America as a corporate commonwealth, similar to the "associative state" envisioned by Herbert Hoover a generation earlier (see Chapter 23). Eisenhower believed the industrial strife, high inflation, and fierce partisan politics of the Truman years could be corrected only through cooperation,

Presidential contender Dwight D. Eisenhower hosts a group of Republican National Committee women at his campaign headquarters in 1952. Ike's status as America's biggest war hero, along with his genial public persona, made him an extremely popular candidate with voters across party lines.

SOURCE: © Bettmann/CORBIS (BEO36973).

self-restraint, and disinterested public service. As president, Eisenhower emphasized limiting the New Deal trends that had expanded federal power, and he encouraged a voluntary, as opposed to regulatory, relationship between government and business. Social harmony and "the good life" at home were closely linked, in his view, to maintaining a stable and American-led international order abroad.

Eisenhower viewed his leadership style as crucial for achieving the goal of a harmonious, corporate-led society. That style owed something to his roots in turn-of-the-century Kansas and his socialization in the military. In the army he had risen through the command structure by playing it safe, keeping his own counsel, and allowing his subordinates to apprise him of his options. He once described his views on leadership to a critic: "It's persuasion—and conciliation—and patience. It's long, slow, tough work. That's the only kind of leadership I know or believe in—or will practice."

Consciously, Eisenhower adopted an evasive style in public, and he was fond of the phrase "middle of the road." He told a news conference, "I feel pretty good when I'm attacked from both sides. It makes me more certain I'm on the right track." Intellectuals and liberals found it easy to satirize Eisenhower for his blandness, his frequent verbal gaffes, his vagueness, and his often contradictory pronouncements. The majority of the American public, however, evidently agreed with Eisenhower's easygoing approach to his office. He kept the conservative and liberal wings of his party united and appealed to many Democrats and independents.

Eisenhower wanted to run government in a businesslike manner while letting the states and corporate interests guide domestic policy and the economy. He appointed nine businessmen to his first cabinet, including three with ties to General Motors. Former GM chief Charles Wilson served as secretary of defense and epitomized the administration's economic views with his famous aphorism "What was good for our country was good for General Motors, and vice versa." In his appointments to the Federal Trade Commission, the Federal Communications Commission, and the Federal Power Commission, Eisenhower favored men congenial to the corporate interests they were charged with regulating. Eisenhower also secured passage of the Submerged Lands Act in 1953, which transferred $40 billion worth of disputed offshore oil lands from the federal government to the Gulf states. This transfer ensured a greater role for the states and private companies in the oil business—and cost the Treasury billions in lost revenues.

In the long run, the Eisenhower administration's lax approach to government regulation accelerated a trend toward the destruction of the natural environment. Oil exploration in Louisiana's bayous, for example, began the massive degradation of America's largest wetlands. Water diversion policies in Florida seriously damaged the biggest tropical forest in the United States. The increased use of toxic chemicals, begun during World War II and largely unregulated by law, placed warehouses of poisons in hundreds of sites, many abutting military installations. Virtually unregulated use and disposal of the pesticide DDT poisoned birds and other animals and left permanent toxic scars in the environment.

At the same time, Eisenhower accepted the New Deal legacy of greater federal responsibility for social welfare. He rejected calls from conservative Republicans, for example, to dismantle the Social Security system. His administration agreed to a modest expansion of Social Security and unemployment insurance and small increases in the minimum wage. Ike also created the Department of Health, Education and Welfare, appointing Oveta Culp Hobby as its secretary, making her the second woman to hold a cabinet post. In agriculture, Eisenhower continued the policy of parity payments designed to sustain farm prices. Between 1952 and 1960, federal spending on agriculture jumped from about $1 billion to $7 billion.

Eisenhower proved hesitant to use fiscal policy to pump up the economy, which went into recession after the Korean War ended in 1953 and again in 1958, when the unemployment rate reached 7.5 percent. The administration refused to cut taxes or increase spending to stimulate growth. Eisenhower feared starting an inflationary spiral more than he worried about unemployment or poverty. By the time he left office, he could proudly point out that real wages for an average family had risen 20 percent during his term. With low inflation and steady, if modest, growth, the Eisenhower years brought greater prosperity to most Americans. Long after he retired from public life, Ike liked to remember his major achievement as having created "an atmosphere of greater serenity and mutual confidence."

Subsidizing Prosperity

During the Eisenhower years the federal government played a crucial role in subsidizing programs that helped millions of Americans achieve middle-class status. Federal aid helped people to buy homes, attend college and technical schools, and live in newly built suburbs. Much of this assistance expanded on programs begun during the New Deal and World War II. The Federal Housing Administration (FHA), established in 1934, extended the government's role in subsidizing the housing industry. The FHA insured long-term mortgage loans made by private lenders for home building. By putting the full faith and credit of the federal government behind residential mortgages, the FHA attracted new private capital into home building and revolutionized the industry. A typical FHA mortgage required less than 10 percent for a down payment and spread low-interest monthly payments over thirty years.

Yet FHA policies also had long-range drawbacks. FHA insurance went overwhelmingly to new residential developments, usually on the fringes of urban areas, hastening the decline of older, inner-city neighborhoods. A bias toward suburban, middle-class communities manifested itself in several ways: it was FHA policy to favor the construction of single-family projects while discouraging multi-unit housing, to refuse loans for the repair of older structures and rental units, and to require for any loan guarantee an "unbiased professional estimate" rating the property, the prospective borrower, and the neighborhood. In practice, these estimates resulted in blatant discrimination against communities that were racially mixed. The FHA's Underwriting Manual bluntly warned: "If a neighborhood is to retain stability, it is necessary that properties shall continue to be occupied by the same social and racial classes." FHA policies in effect inscribed the racial and income segregation of suburbia in public policy.

The majority of suburbs were built as planned communities. One of the first was Levittown, which opened in Hempstead, Long Island, in 1947, on 1,500 acres of former potato fields. Developer William Levitt, who described his firm as "the General Motors of the hous-

ing industry," was the first entrepreneur to bring mass-production techniques to home building. All building materials were precut and prefabricated at a central factory, then assembled on-site into houses by largely unskilled, nonunion labor. In this way Levitt put up hundreds of identical houses each week. Eventually, Levittown encompassed more than 17,000 houses and 82,000 people. Yet in 1960 not one of Levittown's residents was African American, and owners who rented out their homes were told to specify that their houses would not be "used or occupied by any person other than members of the Caucasian race." Levitt himself angrily rejected any criticism of his racial policies: "As a company our position is simply this: we can solve a housing problem, or we can try to solve a racial problem, but we cannot combine the two."

The revolution in American life wrought by the 1944 Servicemen's Readjustment Act, known as the GI Bill of Rights, extended beyond its impact on higher education (see Chapter 26). In addition to educational grants, the act provided returning veterans with low-interest mortgages and business loans, thus subsidizing the growth of the suburbs as well as the postwar expansion of higher education. Through 1956, nearly 10 million veterans received tuition and training benefits under the act. Veteran's Administration–insured loans totaled more than $50 billion by 1962, providing assistance to millions of former GIs who started businesses.

The Federal Highway Act of 1956 gave another key boost to postwar growth, especially in the suburbs. It originally authorized $32 billion for the construction of a national interstate highway system. Financing was to come from new taxes on gasoline, as well as on oil, tires, buses, and trucks. Key to this ambitious program's success was that these revenues were held separately from general taxes in a Highway Trust Fund. By 1972 the program had become the single largest public works program in American history; 41,000 miles of highway were built at a cost of $76 billion. Federal subsidy of the interstate highway system stimulated both the automobile industry and suburb building. But it also accelerated the decline of American mass transit and older cities. By 1970, the nation possessed the world's best roads and one of its worst public transportation systems.

The shadow of the cold war prompted the federal government

This photo, which appeared in a 1950 issue of *Life* magazine, posed a family of pioneer suburbanites in front of their Levittown, New York, home. The prefabricated house was built in 1948.

SOURCE: Bernard Hoffman/Life Magazine/© 1950 TimePix (Set #31949).

to take new initiatives in aid for education. After the Soviet Union launched its first Sputnik satellite in the fall of 1957, American officials worried that the country might be lagging behind the Soviets in training scientists and engineers. The Eisenhower administration, with the bipartisan support of Congress, pledged to strengthen support for educating American students in mathematics, science, and technology. The National Defense Education Act (NDEA) of 1958 allocated $280 million in grants—tied to matching grants from the states—for state universities to upgrade their science facilities. The NDEA also created $300 million in low-interest loans for college students, who had to repay only half the amount if they went on to teach in elementary or secondary school after graduation. In addition, the NDEA provided fellowship support for graduate students planning to go into college and university teaching. The NDEA represented a new consensus on the importance of high-quality education to the national interest.

Suburban Life

The suburban boom strengthened the domestic ideal of the nuclear family as the model for American life. In particular, the picture of the perfect suburban wife—efficient, patient, always charming—became a dominant image in television, movies, and magazines. Suburban domesticity was usually presented as women's only path to happiness and fulfillment. This cultural image often masked a stifling existence defined by housework, child care, and boredom. In the late 1950s, Betty Friedan, a wife, mother, and journalist, began a systematic survey of her Smith College classmates. She found "a strange discrepancy between the reality of our lives as women and the image to which we were trying to conform." Friedan expanded her research and in 1963 published *The Feminine Mystique*, a landmark book that articulated the frustrations of suburban women and helped to launch a revived feminist movement.

The postwar rebirth of religious life was strongly associated with suburban living. In 1940 less than half the American population belonged to institutionalized churches; by the mid-1950s nearly three-quarters identified themselves as church members. A church-building boom was centered in the expanding suburbs. Best-selling religious authors such as Norman Vincent Peale and Bishop Fulton J. Sheen offered a shallow blend of reassurance and "the power of positive thinking." They stressed individual solutions to problems, opposing social or political activism. Their emphasis on the importance of belonging, of fitting in, meshed well with suburban social life and the ideal of family-centered domesticity.

California came to embody postwar suburban life. At the center of this lifestyle was the automobile. Cars were a necessity for commuting to work. California also led the nation in the development of drive-in facilities: motels, movies, shopping malls, fast-food restaurants, and banks. More than 500 miles of highways would be constructed around Los Angeles alone. In Orange County, southeast of Los Angeles, the "centerless city" emerged as the dominant form of community. The experience of one woman resident was typical: "I live in Garden Grove, work in Irvine, shop in Santa Ana, go to the dentist in Anaheim, my husband works in Long Beach, and I used to be the president of the League of Women Voters in Fullerton."

Contemporary journalists, novelists, and social scientists contributed to the popular image of suburban life as essentially dull, conformist, and peopled exclusively by the educated middle class. John Cheever, for example, won the National Book Award for *The Wapshot Chronicle* (1957), a novel set in fictional Remsen Park, "a community of four thousand identical homes." Psychiatrist

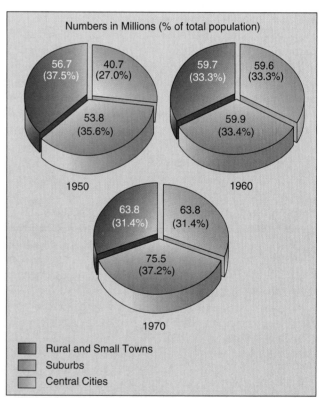

The Growth of the Suburbs, 1950–1970 Suburban growth, at the expense of older inner cities, was one of the key social trends in the twenty-five years following World War II. By 1970, more Americans lived in suburbs than in either inner cities or rural areas.

SOURCE: Adapted from U.S. Bureau of the Census, *Current Censuses, 1930–1970* (Washington, D.C.: U.S. Government Printing Office, 1975).

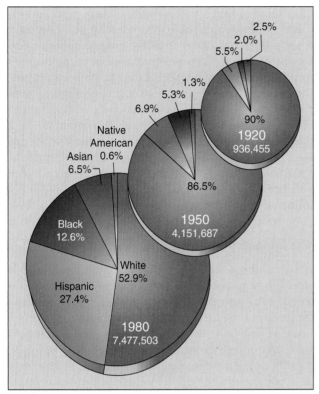

2.5%
2.0%
5.5%

1.3%
5.3%
6.9%

Native
American
Asian   **0.6%**
6.5%

90%
1920
936,455

86.5%
1950
4,151,687

Black
12.6%

White
52.9%

Hispanic
27.4%

1980
7,477,503

L.A. County Population

Richard Gordon's *Split Level Trap* (1960) focused on the emotional problems he observed among the suburban families of Bergen County, New Jersey. Yet these writers tended to obscure the real class and ethnic differences found among and between suburban communities. Many new suburbs had a distinctively blue-collar cast. Milpitas, California, for example, grew up around a Ford auto plant about fifty miles outside San Jose. Its residents were blue-collar assembly-line workers and their families, rather than salaried, college-educated, white-collar employees. Self-segregation and zoning ordinances gave some new suburbs distinctively Italian, Jewish, or Irish ethnic identities, similar to older urban neighborhoods. For millions of new suburbanites, architectural and psychological conformity was an acceptable price to pay for the comforts of home ownership, a small plot of land, and a sense of security and status.

Organized Labor and the AFL-CIO

By the mid-1950s American trade unions reached an historic high-point in their penetration of the labor market, reflecting the enormous gains made during the organizing drives in core mass-production industries during the New Deal and World War II. Whereas only one in eight nonagricultural workers were union members on the eve of the Great Depression, twenty-five years later the fig-

ure stood at one in three. Union influence in political life, especially within the Democratic Party, had also increased. Yet the Republican sweep to power in 1952 meant that for the first time in a generation organized labor was without an ally in the White House. New leaders in the nation's two major labor organizations, the American Federation of Labor (dominated by old line construction and craft unions) and the Congress of Industrial Organizations (centered around unions in mass-production industry), now pushed for a merger of the two rival groups as way to protect and build on the movement's recent gains.

George Meany, the gruff, cigar-chomping head of the AFL, seemed the epitome of the modern labor boss. Originally a plumber, he had worked his way through the AFL bureaucracy and had played a leading role on National War Labor Board during World War II. An outspoken anti-Communist, Meany had pushed the AFL closer to the Democratic Party, and he took pride in never having been on a strike or a picket line. Unions, he believed, must focus on improving the economic well-being of their members. Meany's counterpart in the CIO was Walter Reuther, originally a tool-and-die maker in the auto shops of Detroit. Reuther had come to prominence as a leader of the United Automobile Workers during the tumultuous organizing drives of the 1930s and 1940s. Although he had moved away from his early socialist leanings, Reuther believed strongly that American unions ought to stand for something beyond the bread and butter needs of their members. His support of a broader social vision, including racial equality, aggressive union organizing, and expansion of the welfare state, reflected the more militant tradition of CIO unions. Despite their differences, both Meany and Reuther believed a merger of their two organizations offered the best strategy for the labor movement. In 1955 the newly combined AFL-CIO brought some 12.5 million union members under one banner, with Meany as president and Reuther as director of the Industrial Union Department.

The merger marked the apex of trade union membership, and after 1955 its share of the labor market began a slow and steady decline. To be sure, union membership helped bring the trappings of middle-class prosperity to millions of workers and their families: home ownership, higher education for children, travel, and comfortable retirement. But the AFL-CIO showed little commitment to bringing unorganized workers into the fold. Scandals involving union corruption and racketeering hurt the labor movement's public image. In 1957 the AFL-CIO expelled its largest single affiliate, the International Brotherhood of Teamsters, because of its close ties to organized crime. In 1959, after highly publicized hearings into union corruption, Congress passed the Landrum-Griffin Act, which widened government control over union affairs and further restricted union use of picketing and secondary boycotts during strikes. While union membership as a percentage of the total workforce declined, important growth did take place in new areas, reflecting a broader shift in the American work place from manufacturing to service jobs. During the 1950s and 1960s union membership among public sector employees, especially at the state and local level, increased dramatically. Only 400,000 government workers belonged to unions in 1955. By the early 1970s the figure reached 4 million, as civil servants, postal employees, teachers, police, and firefighters joined unions for the first time. Unions such as the American Federation of State, County, and Municipal Employees (AFSCME) and the American Federation of Teachers (AFT) would emerge as powerful players within the evolving AFL-CIO.

Lonely Crowds and Organization Men

Perhaps the most ambitious and controversial critique of postwar suburban America was sociologist David Riesman's *The Lonely Crowd* (1950). Riesman argued that modern America had given birth to a new kind of character type, the "other-directed" man. Previously the nation had cultivated "inner-directed" people— self-reliant individualists who early on in life had internalized self-discipline and moral standards. By contrast, the "other-directed" person typical of the modern era was peer-oriented. Morality and ideals came from the overarching desire to conform. Americans, Riesman thought, were now less likely to take risks or act independently. Their thinking and habits had come to be determined by cues they received from the mass media.

Similarly, William H. Whyte's *Organization Man* (1956), a study of the Chicago suburb of Park Forest, offered a picture of people obsessed with fitting into their communities and jobs. In place of the old Protestant ethic of hard work, thrift, and competitive struggle, Whyte believed, middle-class suburbanites now strove mainly for a comfortable, secure niche in the system. They held to a new social ethic, he argued: "a belief in the group as the source of creativity; a belief in 'belongingness' as the ultimate need of the individual." Sloan Wilson's *Man in the Grey Flannel Suit*, a 1955 best-seller, featured a hero who rejects the top position at his firm. His boss sympathizes with this reluctance to sacrifice, telling him, "There are plenty of good positions where it's not necessary for a man to put in an unusual amount of work."

The most radical critic of postwar society, and the one with the most enduring influence, was Texas-reared sociologist C. Wright Mills. In *White Collar* (1951), Mills analyzed the job culture that typified life for middle-class salaried employees, office workers, and bureaucrats. "When white collar people get jobs," he wrote, "they sell not only their time and energy, but their personalities as well. They sell by the week or month their smiles and their kindly gestures, and they must practice the prompt repression of resentment and aggression." In *The Power Elite* (1956), Mills argued that a small, interconnected group of corporate executives, military men, and political leaders had come to dominate American society. The arms race in particular, carried out in the name of cold war policies, had given an unprecedented degree of power to what President Eisenhower later termed the military-industrial complex.

The Expansion of Higher Education

American higher education experienced rapid growth after the war. This expansion both reflected and reinforced other trends in postwar society. The number of students enrolled in colleges and universities climbed from 2.6 million in 1950 to 3.2 million in 1960. It then more than doubled—to 7.5 million—by 1970, as the baby boom generation came of age. Most of these new students attended greatly enlarged state university systems. Main campuses at state universities in Michigan, Wisconsin, California, and other states grew bigger than ever, enrolling as many as 40,000 students. Technical colleges and "normal schools" (designed originally for the training of teachers) were upgraded and expanded into full-fledged universities, as in the branches of the State University of New York, founded in 1948.

Several factors contributed to this explosion. A variety of new federal programs, including the GI Bill and the National Defense Education Act, helped subsidize college education for millions of new students. Government spending on research and development in universities, especially for defense-related projects, pumped further resources into higher education. Much of this money supported programs in graduate work, reflecting an important postwar shift in the priorities of American universities. Graduate education and faculty research now challenged traditional undergraduate teaching as the main locus of university activity and power.

Colleges and universities by and large accepted the values of postwar corporate culture. By the mid-1950s, 20 percent of all college graduates majored in business or other commercial fields. The college degree was a gateway to the middle class. It became a requirement for a whole range of expanding white-collar occupations in banking, insurance, real estate, advertising and marketing, and other corporate enterprises. As much as educating young people, colleges trained them for careers in technical, professional, and management positions. Most administrators accommodated large business interests, which were well represented on university boards of trustees. Universities themselves were increasingly run like businesses, with administrators adopting the language of input-output, cost effectiveness, and quality control.

Researchers found college students in the 1950s generally absorbed the conventions and attitudes associated with working in a corporate environment. A typical Iowa State student told one writer, "You have to be very careful not to associate with the wrong clan of people, an introvert that isn't socially acceptable, guys who dress in the fashion of ten years ago. These people are just not accepted—and, if you associate with them, you're not accepted either."

Health and Medicine

Dramatic improvements in medical care allowed many Americans to enjoy longer and healthier lives. During the war the federal government had poured unprecedented amounts of money into medical research and the diffusion of new techniques. The armed forces had immunized and treated millions of servicemen and women for diseases ranging from syphilis to tuberculosis. New antibiotics such as penicillin were manufactured and distributed on a mass basis, and after the war they became widely available to the general population. Federal support for research continued after the war with the reorganization of the National Institutes of Health in 1948. Federal agencies, led by the National Institute of Mental Health, founded in 1949, also expanded research on and treatment of mental illness.

By 1960 many dreaded epidemic diseases, such as tuberculosis, diphtheria, whooping cough, and measles, had virtually disappeared from American life. Perhaps the most celebrated achievement of postwar medicine was the victory over poliomyelitis. Between 1947 and 1951 this disease, which usually crippled those it did not kill, struck an annual average of 39,000 Americans. In 1952, 58,000 cases, most of them children, were reported. Frightened parents warned children to stay away from crowded swimming pools and other gathering places. In 1955 Jonas Salk pioneered the first effective vaccine against the disease, using a preparation of killed virus. A nationwide program of polio vaccination, later supplemented by the oral Sabin vaccine, virtually eliminated polio by the 1960s.

Yet the benefits of "wonder drugs" and advanced medical techniques were not shared equally by all Americans. More sophisticated treatments and expensive new hospital facilities sharply increased the costs of health care. The very poor and many elderly Americans found themselves unable to afford modern medi-

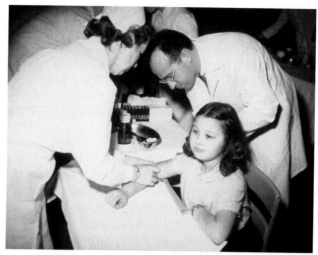

Dr. Jonas E. Salk and nurse administered polio vaccine to Pauline Antloger, a student at Sunnyside School in Pittsburgh, 1955. Dr. Salk's scientific breakthrough of a killed-virus polio vaccine led to an array of viral vaccines to cure other diseases, such as hepatitis.

SOURCE: © Bettmann/CORBIS (U.1122024).

cine. Thousands of communities, especially in rural areas and small towns, lacked doctors or decent hospital facilities. Critics of the medical establishment charged that the proliferation of medical specialists and large hospital complexes had increased the number of unnecessary surgical operations, especially for women and children. The decline of the general practitioner—the family doctor—meant fewer physicians made house calls; more and more people went to hospital emergency rooms or outpatient clinics for treatment. Unreasonable faith in sophisticated medical technologies also contributed to the proliferation of iatrogenic ailments—sickness brought on by treatment for some other illness.

The American Medical Association (AMA), which certified medical schools, did nothing to increase the flow of new doctors. The number of physicians per 100,000 people actually declined between 1950 and 1960; the shortage was made up by doctors trained in other countries. The AMA also lobbied hard against efforts to expand government responsibility for the public's health. President Harry Truman had advanced a plan for national health insurance, to be run along the lines of Social Security. President Dwight Eisenhower had proposed a program that would offer government assistance to private health insurance companies. The AMA denounced both proposals as "socialized medicine." It helped block direct federal involvement in health care until the creation of Medicare (for the elderly) and Medicaid (for the poor) in 1965.

YOUTH CULTURE

The term "teenager," describing someone between thirteen and nineteen, entered standard usage only at the end of World War II. According to the *Dictionary of American Slang*, the United States is the only country with a word for this age group and the only country to consider it "a separate entity whose influence, fads, and fashions are worthy of discussion apart from the adult world." The fifteen years following World War II saw unprecedented attention to America's adolescents. Deep fears were expressed about everything from teenage sexuality and juvenile delinquency to young people's driving habits, hairstyles, and choice of clothing. At the same time, advertisers and businesses pursued the disposable income of America's affluent youth with a vengeance. Teenagers often found themselves caught between their desire to carve out their own separate sphere and the pressure to become an adult as quickly as possible.

The Youth Market

Birthrates had accelerated gradually during the late 1930s and more rapidly during the war years. The children born in those years had by the late 1950s grown into the original teenagers, the older siblings of the celebrated baby boomers of 1946–64. They came of age in a society that, compared with that of their parents and the rest of the world, was uniquely affluent. Together, the demographic growth of teens and the postwar economic expansion created a burgeoning youth market. Manufacturers and advertisers rushed to cash in on the special needs and desires of young consumers: cosmetics, clothing, radios and phonographs, and cars.

Before Elvis Presley became the ultimate teen idol, his life in Memphis mirrored the experiences of millions of American teenagers. In high school he was an average student at best, and he took part-time jobs to help out the family; after graduation he worked as a truck driver and as an electrician's helper. He enjoyed making the rounds of movies, roller rinks, and burger joints with his friends, and he dreamed of owning his own Cadillac. Like many teens, Elvis obsessed over the latest stylish clothing—which he could not afford. He could often be found haunting the shop windows at the Lansky Brothers clothing store on Beale Street in Memphis.

In 1959, *Life* summarized the new power of the youth market. "Counting only what is spent to satisfy their special teenage demands," the magazine reported, "the youngsters and their parents will shell out about $10 billion this year, a billion more than the total sales of GM." In addition, advertisers and market researchers found that teenagers often played a critical, if hard-to-measure, role as "secret persuaders" in a family's large purchase decisions. Specialized market research organizations, such as Eugene Gilbert & Company and Teen-Age Survey Incorporated, sprang up to serve business clients eager to attract teen consumers and instill brand loyalty. Through the 1950s and into the 1960s, teenagers had a major, sometimes dominant, voice in determining America's cultural fads.

To many parents, the emerging youth culture was a dangerous threat to their authority. One mother summarized this fear in a revealing, if slightly hysterical, letter to *Modern Teen*:

> Don't you realize what you are doing? You are encouraging teenagers to write to each other, which keeps them from doing their school work and other chores. You are encouraging them to kiss and have physical contact before they're even engaged, which is morally wrong and you know it. You are encouraging them to have faith in the depraved individuals who make rock and roll records when it's common knowledge that ninety per cent of these rock and roll singers are people with no morals or sense of values.

The increasing uniformity of public school education also contributed to the public recognition of the special status of teenagers. In 1900, about one of every eight teenagers was in school; by the 1950s, the figure was six out of eight. Psychologists wrote guidebooks for parents, two prominent examples being Dorothy Baruch's *How to Live with Your Teenager* (1953) and Paul Landis's *Understanding Teenagers* (1955). Social scientists stressed the importance of peer pressure for understanding teen behavior. "The teenage group," Landis observed in *Understanding Teenagers*, "is self-sufficient now as in no previous generation." The larger point here is that traditional sources of adult authority and socialization—the marketplace, schools, child-rearing manuals, the mass media—all reinforced the notion of teenagers as a special community, united by age, rank, and status.

"Hail! Hail! Rock 'n' Roll!"

The demands of the new teen market, combined with structural changes in the postwar American mass media, reshaped the nation's popular music. As television broadcasting rapidly replaced radio as the center of family entertainment, people began using radios in new ways. The production of portable transistor radios and car radios grew rapidly in the 1950s as listeners increasingly tuned them in for diversion from or an accompaniment to other activities. Locally produced radio shows, featuring music, news, and disc jockeys,

This photo of Elvis Presley singing at a 1956 state fair in Memphis captured his dramatic stage presence. Performing with only a trio, his sound was spare but hard driving. Both the music and Presley's stage moves owed a great deal to African American rhythm and blues artists.

SOURCE: Getty Images, Inc. (C422)

replaced the old star-studded network programs. By 1956, some 2,700 AM radio stations were on the air across the United States, with about 70 percent of their broadcast time given to record shows. Most of these concentrated on popular music for the traditional white adult market: pop ballads, novelty songs, and show tunes.

In the recording industry, meanwhile, a change was in the air. Small independent record labels led the way in aggressively recording African American rhythm and blues artists. Atlantic Records, in New York, developed the most influential galaxy of artists, including Ray Charles, Ruth Brown, the Drifters, Joe Turner, LaVerne Baker, and the Clovers. Chess, in Chicago, had the blues-based, singer-songwriter-guitarists Chuck Berry and Bo Diddley, and the "doo-wop" group the Moonglows. In New Orleans, Imperial had the veteran pianist-singer Fats Domino, while Specialty unleashed the outrageous Little Richard on the world. On radio, over jukeboxes, and in record stores, all of these African American artists "crossed over," adding millions of white teenagers to their solid base of black fans.

The older, more established record companies, such as RCA, Decca, M-G-M, and Capitol, had largely ignored black music. Their response to the new trend was to offer slick, toned-down "cover" versions by white pop singers of rhythm and blues originals. Cover versions were invariably pallid imitations, artistically inferior to the originals. One has only to compare,

say, Pat Boone's covers of Fats Domino's "Ain't That a Shame" or Little Richard's "Tutti Frutti" with the originals to hear how much was lost. While African American artists began to enjoy newfound mass acceptance, there were limits to how closely white kids could identify with black performers. Racism, especially in so sexually charged an arena as musical performance, was still a powerful force in American life. Because of the superior promotional power of the major companies and the institutional racism in the music business, white cover versions almost always outsold the black originals.

Alan Freed, a popular white Cleveland disc jockey, refused to play cover versions on his "Moondog Matinee" program. He played only original rhythm and blues music, and he popularized the term "rock 'n' roll" to describe it. Freed promoted concerts around the Midwest featuring black rhythm and blues artists, and these attracted enthusiastic audiences of both black and white young people. In 1954 the music trade magazine *Billboard* noted this trend among white teenagers: "The present generation has not known the rhythmically exciting dance bands of the swing era. It therefore satisfies its hunger for 'music with a beat' in modern r&b (rhythm and blues) groups." The stage was thus set for the arrival of white rock 'n' roll artists who could exploit the new sounds and styles.

As a rock 'n' roll performer and recording artist, Elvis Presley reinvented American popular music. His success challenged the old lines separating black music from white, and pop from rhythm and blues or country. As a symbol of rebellious youth and as the embodiment of youthful sexuality, Elvis revitalized American popular culture. In his wake came a host of white rock 'n' rollers, many of them white Southerners like Elvis: Jerry Lee Lewis, Buddy Holly, the Everly Brothers, Roy Orbison. But the greatest songwriter and the most influential guitarist to emerge from this first "golden age of rock 'n' roll" was Chuck Berry, an African American from St. Louis who worked part-time as a beautician and house painter. Berry proved especially adept at capturing the teen spirit with humor, irony, and passion. He composed hits around the trials and tribulations of school ("School Days"), young love ("Memphis"), cars ("Maybellene"), and making it as a rock 'n' roller ("Johnny B. Goode"). As much as anyone, Berry created music that defined what it meant to be young in postwar America.

Almost Grown

At least some of the sense of difference, of uniqueness, associated with adolescence came from teens themselves. Teenage consumers remade the landscape of popular music into their own turf. The dollar value of annual record sales nearly tripled between 1954 and 1959, from $213 million to $603 million. New magazines aimed exclusively at teens flourished in the postwar years. *Modern Teen, Teen Digest,* and *Dig* were just a few. Most teen magazines, like rock 'n' roll music, focused on the rituals, pleasures, and sorrows surrounding teenage courtship. Paradoxically, behavior patterns among white middle-class teenagers in the 1950s and early 1960s exhibited a new kind of youth orientation and at the same time a more pronounced identification with adults.

While many parents worried about the separate world inhabited by their teenage children, many teens seemed determined to become adults as quickly as possible. Postwar affluence multiplied the number of two-car families, making it easier for sixteen-year-olds to win driving privileges formerly reserved for eighteen-year-olds. Girls began dating, wearing brassieres and nylon stockings, and using cosmetics at an earlier age than before—twelve or thirteen rather than fifteen or sixteen. Several factors contributed to this trend, including a continuing decline in the age of menarche (first menstruation), the sharp drop in the age of marriage after World War II, and the precocious social climate of junior high schools (institutions that became widespread only after 1945). The practice of going steady, derived from the college custom of fraternity and sorority pinning, became commonplace among high schoolers. By the late 1950s, eighteen had become the most common age at which American females married.

Teenagers often felt torn between their identification with youth culture and pressures to assume adult responsibilities. Many young people juggled part-time jobs with school and very active social lives. Teen-oriented magazines, music, and movies routinely dispensed advice and sympathy regarding this dilemma. Rock 'n' roll songs offered the most sympathetic treatments of the conflicts teens experienced over work ("Summertime Blues"), parental authority ("Yakety Yak"), and the desire to look adult ("Sweet Little Sixteen"). By 1960, sociologist James S. Coleman reflected a growing consensus when he noted that postwar society had given adolescents "many of the instruments which can make them a functioning community: cars, freedom in dating, continual contact with the opposite sex, money, and entertainment, like popular music and movies, designed especially for them."

Deviance and Delinquency

Many adults held rock 'n' roll responsible for the apparent decline in parental control over teens. A psychiatrist writing in the *New York Times* described rock 'n' roll as "a cannibalistic and tribalistic kind of music" and "a communicable disease." Many clergymen and church leaders declared it "the devil's music." Much of the opposition to rock 'n' roll, particularly in the South, played on long-standing racist fears that white females might be attracted to black music and black performers. The undercurrent beneath all this opposition was a deep anxiety over the more open expression of sexual feelings by both performers and audiences.

Paralleling the rise of rock 'n' roll was a growing concern with an alleged increase in juvenile delinquency. An endless stream of magazine articles, books, and newspaper stories asserted that criminal behavior among the nation's young was chronic. Gang fights, drug and alcohol abuse, car theft, and sexual offenses received the most attention. The U.S. Senate established a special subcommittee on juvenile delinquency. Highly publicized hearings in 1955 and 1956 convinced much of the public that youthful criminals were terrorizing the country. Although crime statistics do suggest an increase in juvenile crime during the 1950s, particularly in the suburbs, the public perception of the severity of the problem was surely exaggerated.

In retrospect, the juvenile delinquency controversy tells us more about anxieties over family life and the erosion of adult authority than about crime patterns. Teenagers seemed more defined by and loyal to their peer culture than to their parents. A great deal of their music, speech, dress, and style was alien and threatening. The growing importance of the mass media in defining youth culture brought efforts to regulate or censor media forms believed to cause juvenile delinquency. In 1954, for example, psychiatrist Fredric Wertham published *Seduction of the Innocent,* arguing that crime comic books incited youngsters to criminal acts. Mass culture, he believed, could overwhelm the traditional influences of family, school, and religion. He led a highly publicized crusade that forced the comic book industry to adopt a code strictly limiting the portrayal of violence and crime.

As reactions to two of the most influential "problem youth" movies of the postwar era indicate, teens and their parents frequently interpreted depictions of youthful deviance in the mass media in very different ways. In *The Wild One* (1954), Marlon Brando played the crude, moody leader of a vicious motorcycle gang. Most adults thought of the film as a critique of mindless gang violence, but many teenagers identified with the Brando character, who, when asked, "What are you rebelling against?" coolly replied, "Whattaya got?" In *Rebel without a Cause* (1955), James Dean, Natalie Wood, and Sal Mineo played emotionally troubled youths in an affluent California suburb. The movie suggests that parents can cause delinquency when they fail to conform to conventional roles—Dean's father wears an apron and his mother is domineering. But on another level, the film suggests that young people can form their own families, without parents.

Brando and Dean, along with Elvis, were probably the most popular and widely imitated teen idols of the era. For most parents, they were vaguely threatening figures whose sexual energy and lack of discipline placed them outside the bounds of middle-class respectability. For teens, however, they offered an irresistible combination of rough exterior and sensitive core. They embodied, as well, the contradiction of individual rebellion versus the attractions of a community defined by youth.

MASS CULTURE AND ITS DISCONTENTS

No mass medium ever achieved such power and popularity as rapidly as television. The basic technology for broadcasting visual images with sound had been developed by the late 1930s, and television demonstrations were among the most popular exhibits at the 1939 New York World's Fair. But World War II and corporate competition postponed television's introduction to the public until 1946. By 1960, nearly nine in ten American families owned at least one set, which was turned on an average of more than five hours a day. Television reshaped leisure time and political life. It also helped create a new kind of national community defined by the buying and selling of consumer goods.

Important voices challenged the economic trends and cultural conformity of the postwar years. Academics, journalists, novelists, and poets offered a variety of works criticizing the overall direction of American life. These critics of what was dubbed "mass society" were troubled by the premium American culture put on conformity, status, and material consumption. Although a distinct minority, these critics were persistent. Many of their ideas and prescriptions would reverberate through the political and cultural upheavals of the 1960s and 1970s.

Television: Tube of Plenty

Television constituted a radical change from radio, and its development as a mass medium was quicker and less chaotic. The three main television networks—NBC, CBS, ABC—grew directly from radio organizations. A short-lived fourth network, Dumont, grew from a tele-

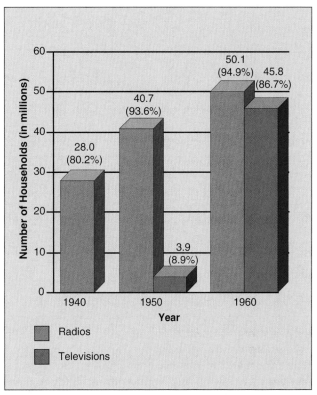

Radio and Television Ownership, 1940–1960
By 1960 nearly 90 percent of American households owned at least one television set, as TV replaced radio as the nation's dominant mass medium of entertainment. Radio ownership rose as well, but Americans increasingly listened to radio as an accompaniment to other activities, such as driving.

vision manufacturing business. The Federal Communications Commission oversaw the licensing of stations and set technical standards. The networks led the industry from the start, rather than following individual stations, as radio had done. Nearly all TV stations were affiliated with one or more of the networks; only a handful of independent stations could be found around the country.

Television not only depended on advertising, it also transformed the advertising industry. The television business, like radio, was based on the selling of time to advertisers who wanted to reach the mass audiences tuning into shows. Radio had offered entire shows produced by and for single sponsors, usually advertisers who wanted a close identification between their product and a star. But the higher costs of television production forced key changes. Sponsors left the production of programs to the networks, independent producers, and Hollywood studios.

Sponsors now bought scattered time slots for spot advertisements rather than bankrolling an entire show. Ad agencies switched their creative energy to producing slick thirty-second commercials rather than entertainment programs. A shift from broadcasting live shows to filming them opened up lucrative opportunities for reruns and foreign export. The total net revenue of the TV networks and their affiliated stations in 1947 was about $2 million; by 1957 it was nearly $1 billion. Advertisers spent $58 million on TV shows in 1949; ten years later the figure was almost $1.5 billion.

The staple of network radio, the comedy-variety show, was now produced with pictures. The first great national TV hit, *The Milton Berle Show*, followed this format when it premiered in 1948. Radio stars such as Jack Benny, Edgar Bergen, George Burns and Gracie Allen, and Eddie Cantor switched successfully to television. Boxing, wrestling, the roller derby, and other sporting events were also quite popular. For a brief time, original live drama flourished on writer-oriented shows such as *Goodyear Television Playhouse* and *Studio One*. In addition, early television featured an array of situation comedies with deep roots in radio and vaudeville.

Set largely among urban ethnic families, early shows like *I Remember Mama*, *The Goldbergs*, *The Life of Riley*, *Life with Luigi*, and *The Honeymooners* often featured working-class families struggling with the dilemmas posed by consumer society. Most plots turned around comic tensions created and resolved by consumption: contemplating home ownership, going out on the town, moving to the suburbs, buying on credit, purchasing a new car. Generational discord and the loss of ethnic identity were also common themes. To some degree, these early shows mirrored and spoke to the real dilemmas facing families that had survived the Great Depression and the Second World War and were now finding their place in a prosperous consumer culture.

By the late 1950s all the urban ethnic comedy shows were off the air. A new breed of situation comedies presented nonethnic white, affluent, and insular suburban middle-class families. Shows like *Father Knows Best*, *Leave It to Beaver*, *The Adventures of Ozzie and Harriet*, and *The Donna Reed Show* epitomized the ideal suburban American family of the day. Their plots focused on genial crises, usually brought on by children's mischief and resolved by kindly fathers. In retrospect, what is most striking about these shows is what is absent—politics, social issues, cities, white ethnic groups, African Americans, and Latinos were virtually unrepresented.

Television cut deeply into the filmgoing habits of Americans. The audience for movies began a steep decline from the high point of 1948. Hollywood tried desperately to compete with its new rival by pushing spectacular new techniques such as Cinerama, CinemaScope, and 3-D. By the mid-1950s, studios had begun to sell off their valuable backlog of films to the networks; old movies thus became a staple of television programming. Many TV shows were produced on the same Hollywood back lots that had churned out "B" pictures in the 1930s and 1940s. Two of the most popular genres of television in these years were old movie standbys: westerns (*Gunsmoke*, *Cheyenne*,

Ricky and Ozzie Nelson play piano together as David and Harriet Nelson watch, in a scene from the long-running 1950s television sit-com "Ozzie and Harriet." The show epitomized the white, suburban, middle class family ideal that dominated TV through the mid-1960s.

SOURCE: © Springer/Bettmann/CORBIS (JS-296).

The Rifleman) and crime dramas (*Dragnet*, *Highway Patrol*, *The Untouchables*).

Television also demonstrated a unique ability to create overnight fads and crazes across the nation. Elvis Presley's 1956 appearances on several network television variety shows, including those hosted by Milton Berle and Ed Sullivan, catapulted him from regional success to international stardom. Successful television advertising campaigns made household names out of previously obscure products. A memorable example of TV's influence came in 1955 when Walt Disney produced a series of three one-hour shows on the life of frontier legend Davy Crockett. The tremendous success of the series instantly created a $300 million industry of Davy Crockett shirts, dolls, toys, and coonskin caps.

Television and Politics

Prime-time entertainment shows carefully avoided any references to the political issues of the day. Network executives bowed to the conformist climate created by the domestic cold war. Any hint of political controversy could scare off sponsors, who were extremely sensitive to public protest. Anti-Communist crusaders set themselves up as private watchdogs, warning of alleged subversive influence in the broadcasting industry. In 1950 one such group published *Red Channels* (see Chapter 26), a book branding 151 of the most well-known writers, directors, and actors in radio and television as Communists or Communist dupes. Television executives responded by effectively blacklisting many talented individuals.

As in Hollywood, the cold war chill severely restricted the range of political discussion on television. Any honest treatment of the conflicts in American society threatened the consensus mentality at the heart of the television business. Even public affairs and documentary programs were largely devoid of substantial political debate. An important exception was Edward R. Murrow's *See It Now* on CBS—but that show was off the air by 1955. Television news did not come into its own until 1963, with the beginning of half-hour nightly network newscasts. Only then did television's extraordinary power to rivet the nation's attention during a crisis become clear.

Still, some of the ways that TV would alter the nation's political life emerged in the 1950s. Television made Democratic senator Estes Kefauver of Tennessee a national political figure through live coverage of his 1951 Senate investigation into organized crime. It also contributed to the political downfall of Senator Joseph McCarthy in 1954 by showing his cruel bullying tactics during Senate hearings into alleged subversive Communist influence in the army. In 1952, Republican vice presidential candidate Richard M. Nixon effectively used an emotional, direct television appeal to voters— the "Checkers" speech—to counter charges of corruption (see Chapter 26).

The 1952 election also brought the first use of TV political advertising for presidential candidates. The Republican Party hired a high-powered ad agency, Batten, Barton, Durstine & Osborn (BBD&O), to create a series of short, sophisticated advertisements touting Dwight D. Eisenhower. The Democrats were content to buy a few half-hour blocks of TV time for long speeches by their nominee, Adlai Stevenson. The BBD&O campaign saturated TV with twenty-second Eisenhower spots for two weeks before election day. Ever since then, television image-making has been the single most important element in American electoral politics.

Culture Critics

From both the left and the right, an assortment of writers expressed anger, fear, and plain disgust with the power of American mass culture. It would, they feared, overwhelm traditional standards of beauty, truth, and

quality. Indeed, the urge to denounce the mass media for degrading the quality of American life tended to unite radical and conservative critics. Thus Marxist writer Dwight Macdonald sounded an old conservative warning when he described mass culture as "a parasite, a cancerous growth on High Culture." Society's most urgent problem, Macdonald claimed, was a "a tepid, flaccid Middlebrow Culture that threatens to engulf everything in its spreading ooze."

Critics of mass culture argued that the audiences for the mass media were atomized, anonymous, and detached. The media themselves had become omnipotent, capable of manipulating the attitudes and behavior of the isolated individuals in the mass. These critics undoubtedly overestimated the power of the media. They ignored the preponderance of research suggesting that most people watched and responded to mass media in family, peer group, and other social settings. The critics also missed the genuine vitality and creative brilliance to be found within mass culture: African American music; the films of Nicholas Ray, Elia Kazan, and Howard Hawks; the experimental television of Ernie Kovacs; the satire of *Mad* magazine.

Many of these critics achieved great popularity themselves, suggesting that the public was deeply ambivalent about mass culture. One of the best-selling authors of the day was Vance Packard, whose 1957 exposé *The Hidden Persuaders* showed how advertisers exploited motivational research into the irrational side of human behavior. Paul Goodman won a wide audience for his *Growing Up Absurd* (1960), which charged that America made it very difficult for young people to find meaningful work, sexual fulfillment, or a true sense of community. Goodman was only one of the thinkers at the end of the decade whose work pointed toward the coming youth rebellion in culture and politics.

Some of the sharpest dissents from the cultural conformity of the day came from a group of writers known collectively as the Beats. Led by the novelist Jack Kerouac and the poet Allen Ginsberg, the Beats shared a distrust of the American virtues of progress, power, and material gain. The Beat sensibility celebrated spontaneity, friendship, jazz, open sexuality, drug use, and the outcasts of American society. Kerouac, born and raised in a working-class French Canadian family in Lowell, Massachusetts, coined the term "beat" in 1948. It meant for him a "weariness with all the forms of the modern industrial state"—conformity, militarism, blind faith in technological progress. Kerouac's 1957 novel *On the Road*, chronicling the tumultuous adventures of Kerouac's circle of friends as they traveled by car back and forth across America, became the Beat manifesto. Allen Ginsberg had grown up in New Jersey in an immigrant Jewish family. His father was a poet and teacher, and his mother had a history of mental problems. After being expelled from Columbia University,

Jack Kerouac, founding voice of the Beat literary movement, in front of a neon lit bar, ca. 1950. Kerouac's public readings, often to the accompaniment of live jazz music, created a performance atmosphere underlining the connections between his writing style and the rhythms and sensibility of contemporary jazz musicians.

SOURCE: Globe Photos, Inc. (YULSMAN).

Ginsberg grew close to Kerouac and another writer, William Burroughs. At a 1955 poetry reading in San Francisco, Ginsberg introduced his epic poem *Howl* to a wildly enthusiastic audience:

> I saw the best minds of my generation destroyed
> by madness, starving hysterical naked,
> dragging themselves through the negro streets at dawn
> looking for an angry fix,
> angelheaded hipsters burning for the ancient heavenly
> connection
> to the starry dynamo in the machinery of night.

Howl became one of the best-selling poetry books in the history of publishing, and it established Ginsberg as an important new voice in American literature.

Beat writers received a largely antagonistic, even virulent reception from the literary establishment. But millions of young Americans read their work and became intrigued by their alternative visions. The mass media soon managed to trivialize the Beats. A San Francisco journalist coined the term "beatnik," and by the late 1950s it had become associated with affected men and women dressed in black, wearing sunglasses and berets, and acting rebellious and alienated. But Beat writers like Kerouac, Ginsberg, Burroughs, Diane DiPrima, Gary Snyder, LeRoi Jones, and others continued to produce serious work that challenged America's official culture. They foreshadowed the mass youth rebellion and counterculture to come in the 1960s.

THE COLD WAR CONTINUED

Eisenhower's experience in foreign affairs had been one of his most attractive assets as a presidential candidate. His success as supreme commander of the Allied forces in World War II owed as much to diplomatic skill as to military prowess. As president, Eisenhower sustained the anti-Communist rhetoric of cold war diplomacy, and his administration persuaded Americans to accept the cold war stalemate as a more or less permanent fact. Eisenhower developed new strategies for containment and for the support of United States power abroad, including a greater reliance on nuclear weapons and the aggressive use of the Central Intelligence Agency (CIA) for covert action. Yet Eisenhower also resolved to do everything he could to forestall an all-out nuclear conflict. He recognized the limits of raw military power. He accepted a less than victorious end to the Korean War, and he avoided a full military involvement in Indochina. Ironically, Eisenhower's promotion of high-tech strategic weaponry fostered development of a military-industrial complex. By the time he left office in 1961, he felt compelled to warn the nation of the growing dangers posed by burgeoning military spending.

The "New Look" in Foreign Affairs

Although Eisenhower recognized that the United States was engaged in a long-term struggle with the Soviet Union, he feared that permanent mobilization for the cold war might overburden the American economy and result in a "garrison state." He therefore pursued a high-tech, capital intensive defense policy that emphasized America's qualitative advantage in strategic weaponry. The "new look" in foreign affairs promised to reduce the military budget by exploiting America's atomic and air superiority.

The emphasis on massive retaliation, the administration claimed, would also make possible cuts in the military budget. As Secretary of Defense Charles Wilson said, the goal was to "get more bang for the buck." Eisenhower largely succeeded in stabilizing the defense budget. Between 1954 and 1961 absolute spending rose only $800 million, from $46.6 billion to $47.4 billion. Military spending as an overall percentage of the federal budget fell from 66 percent to 49 percent during his two terms. Much of this saving was gained through the increased reliance on nuclear weapons and long-range delivery systems, which were relatively less expensive than conventional forces.

Secretary of State John Foster Dulles emerged as a key architect of American policy, giving shape to Eisenhower's views. Raised a devout Presbyterian and trained as a lawyer, Dulles had been involved in diplomatic affairs since World War I. He brought a strong sense of righteousness to his job, an almost missionary belief in America's responsibility to preserve the "free world" from godless, immoral communism. Dulles articulated a more assertive policy toward the Communist threat by calling not simply for containment but for a "roll-

Soviet Premier Nikita Khrushchev enjoys a bite to eat during his tour of an Iowa farm in 1959. A colorful, earthy, and erratic man, Khrushchev loomed as the most visible human symbol of the USSR for Americans. On this trip he called for Soviet-American friendship, yet also boasted "We will bury you."

SOURCE: © Bettmann/CORBIS (BE031798).

back." The key would be greater reliance on America's nuclear superiority. This policy appealed to Republicans, who had been frustrated by the restriction of United Nations forces to conventional arms during the Korean War.

The "new look" conflicted, however, with Eisenhower's own sense of caution, especially during moments of crisis in Eastern Europe and potential military confrontation with the Soviet Union. The limits of a policy based on nuclear strategy became painfully clear when American leaders faced tense situations that offered no clear way to intervene without provoking full-scale war.

When East Berliners rebelled against the Soviets in 1953, cold war hard-liners thought they saw the long awaited opportunity for rollback. But precisely how could the United States respond? Public bitterness over the Korean conflict merged with Eisenhower's sense of restraint and in the end, apart from angry denunciations, the United States did nothing to prevent the Soviets from crushing the rebellion. U.S. leaders faced the same dilemma on a grander scale when Hungarians revolted against their Soviet-dominated Communist rulers in 1956, staging a general strike and taking over the streets and factories in Budapest and other cities. The United States opened its gates to thousands of Hungarian refugees, but despite urgent requests, it refused to intervene when Soviet tanks and troops crushed the revolt. Eisenhower recognized that the Soviets would defend their own borders, and all of Eastern Europe as well, by all-out military force if necessary.

The death of Josef Stalin in 1953 and the worldwide condemnation of his crimes, revealed by his successor, Nikita Khrushchev, in 1956, gave Eisenhower fresh hope for a new spirit of peaceful coexistence between the two superpowers. Khrushchev, in a gesture of goodwill, withdrew Soviet troops from Austria. The first real rollback had been achieved by negotiations and a spirit of common hope, not threats or force. In 1958 Khrushchev, probing American intentions and hoping to redirect the Soviet economy toward the production of more consumer goods, unilaterally suspended nuclear testing. Tensions rose again that year when the Soviet leader, threatened by a revived West Germany, demanded that the Western Allies leave Berlin within six months. But after Khrushchev made a twelve-day trip to America in 1959, he suspended the deadline and relations warmed. Khrushchev visited an Iowa farm, went sightseeing in Hollywood, and spent time with Eisenhower at Camp David, the presidential retreat in Maryland.

The two leaders achieved nothing concrete, but with summit diplomacy seeming to offer at least a psychological thaw in the cold war, the press began referring to the "spirit of Camp David." In early 1960

Khrushchev called for another summit in Paris, to discuss German reunification and nuclear disarmament. Eisenhower, meanwhile, planned his own friendship tour of the Soviet Union. But in May 1960 the Soviets shot down an American U-2 spy plane gathering intelligence on Soviet military installations. A deeply embarrassed Eisenhower at first denied the existence of U-2 flights, but the Soviets produced the pilot, Francis Gary Powers, who readily confessed. The summit collapsed when Eisenhower refused Khrushchev's demands for an apology and an end to the spy flights. The U-2 incident demonstrated the limits of personal diplomacy in resolving the deep structural rivalry between the superpowers.

Eisenhower often provided a moderate voice on issues of defense spending and missile development. The Soviet Union's dramatic launch of Sputnik, the first space-orbiting satellite, in October 1957 upset many Americans' precarious sense of security. In particular, this demonstration of Soviet technological prowess raised fears about Russian ability to deploy intercontinental ballistic missiles (ICBMs) against American cities. Critics attacked the Eisenhower administration for failure to keep up with the enemy. Senator Stuart Symington (D-MO) bluntly warned that, "Unless our defense policies are promptly changed, the Soviets will move from superiority to supremacy." In addition to huge increases in defense spending, some urged a massive program to build "fallout shelters" for the entire population in case of nuclear attack. But Eisenhower rejected these more radical responses. He knew from evidence provided by U-2 spy planes that the Soviet Union in fact trailed far behind the U.S. in ICBM development, but he kept this knowledge secret. Instead of panicking before Sputnik, he held to a doctrine of "sufficiency": maintaining enough military strength to survive any foreign attack and enough nuclear capability to deliver a massive counterattack. In 1958 Eisenhower did support creation of the National Aeronautics and Space Agency (NASA), to coordinate space exploration and missile development. And he also backed the National Defense Education Act that year, which funneled more federal aid into science and foreign language education. Yet, in Congress a bipartisan majority voted to increase the military budget by another $8 billion in 1958, thereby accelerating the arms race and expanding the defense sector of the economy.

Covert Action

Eisenhower combined the overt threat of massive retaliation in his "new look" approach to foreign affairs with a heavy reliance on covert interventions by the Central Intelligence Agency (CIA). He had been an enthusiastic supporter of covert operations during World War II, and during his presidency CIA-sponsored covert para-

military operations became a key facet of American foreign policy. With the American public wary of direct U.S. military interventions, the CIA promised a cheap, quick, and quiet way to depose hostile or unstable regimes. Eisenhower increasingly relied on the CIA to destabilize emerging third world governments deemed too radical or too friendly with the Soviets. Covert actions also proved vital for propping up more conservative regimes under siege by indigenous revolutionaries. These actions were particularly effective in the former colonial areas of Asia, Africa, and the Caribbean.

For CIA director, Eisenhower named Allen Dulles, brother of the secretary of state and a former leader in the CIA's World War II precursor, the Office of Strategic Services. The CIA's mandate was to collect and analyze information, but it did much more under Dulles's command. Thousands of covert agents stationed all over the world carried out a wide range of political activities. Some agents arranged large, secret financial payments to friendly political parties, such as the conservative Christian Democrats in Italy and in Latin America, or foreign trade unions opposed to socialist policies. Other agents secretly funded and guided intellectuals in, for instance, the Congress of Cultural Freedom, a prestigious group of liberal writers in Europe and the United States.

While the United States moderated its stance toward the Soviet Union and its Eastern European satellites, it hardened its policies in the third world. The need for anti-Communist tactics short of all-out military conflict pushed the Eisenhower administration to develop new means of fighting the cold war. The premise rested on encouraging confusion or rivalry within the Communist sphere and on destabilizing or destroying anticapitalist movements around the world.

The Soviet Union tried to win influence in Africa, Asia, and Latin America by appealing to a shared "anti-imperialism" and by offering modest amounts of foreign aid. In most cases, Communists played only small roles in third world independence movements. But the issue of race and the popular desire to recover national resources from foreign investors inflamed already widespread anti-European and anti-American feelings. When new nations or familiar allies threatened to interfere with U.S. regional security arrangements, or to expropriate the property of American businesses, the Eisenhower administration turned to covert action and military intervention.

Intervening around the World

The Central Intelligence Agency produced a swift, major victory in Iran in 1953. The country's popular prime minister, Mohammed Mossadegh, had nationalized Britain's Anglo-Iranian Oil Company, and the State Department

Web Exploration

Compare American intervention in the Caribbean from 1948–1966 with intervention in this region earlier in the twentieth century (chapter 22). What are the similarities? What are the differences?
www.prenhall.com/faragher/map27.1

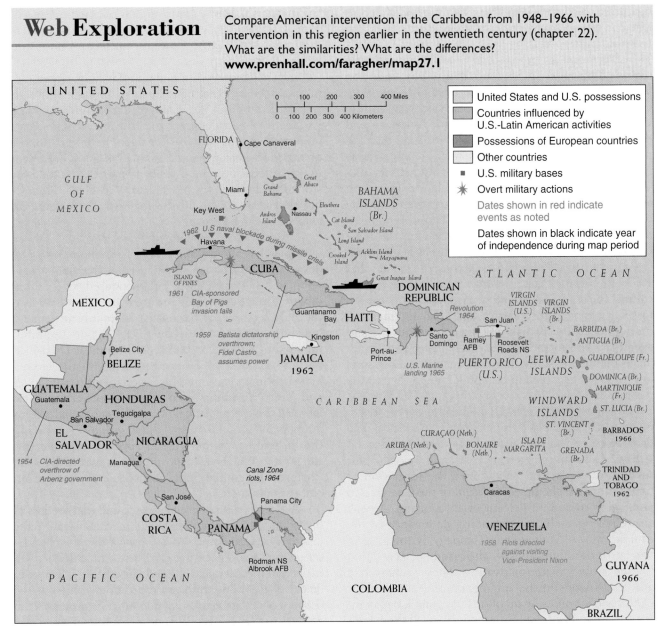

The U.S. in the Caribbean, 1948–1966 U.S. military intervention and economic presence grew steadily in the Caribbean following World War II. After 1960, opposition to the Cuban Revolution dominated U.S. Caribbean policies.

worried that this might set a precedent throughout the oil-rich Middle East. Kermit Roosevelt, CIA chief in Iran, organized and financed an opposition to Mossadegh within the Iranian army and on the streets of Teheran. This CIA-led movement forced Mossadegh out of office and replaced him with Riza Shah Pahlavi. The shah proved his loyalty to his American sponsors by renegotiating oil contracts so as to assure American companies 40 percent of Iran's oil concessions.

The rivalry between Israel and its Arab neighbors complicated U.S. policy in the rest of the Middle East. The Arab countries launched an all-out attack on Israel in 1948 immediately after the United States and the Soviet Union had recognized its independence. Israel repulsed the attack, drove thousands of Palestinians from their homes, occupied territory that hundreds of thousands of others had fearfully fled, and seized lands far in excess of the terms of a United Nations–sponsored armistice of 1949. The Arab states refused to recognize Israel's right to exist and subjected it to a damaging economic boycott. Meanwhile, hundreds of thousands of Palestinians languished in refugee camps. Eisenhower believed that Truman had perhaps been too hasty in encouraging the Israelis. Yet most Americans supported the new Jewish state as a refuge for a people who had suffered so much persecution, especially during the Holocaust.

Israel stood as a reliable U.S. ally in an unstable region. Arab nationalism continued to vex American policymakers, culminating in the Suez crisis of 1956. Egyptian president Gamal Abdel Nasser, a leading voice of Arab nationalism, looked for American and British economic aid. He had long dreamed of building the Aswan High Dam on the Nile to create more arable land and provide cheap electric power. When negotiations broke down, Nasser announced he would nationalize the strategically sensitive Suez Canal, and he turned to the Soviet Union for aid. Eisenhower refused European appeals for U.S. help in seizing the Suez Canal and returning it to the British. When British, French, and Israeli forces attacked Egypt in October 1956, the United States sponsored a UN resolution calling for a cease-fire and a withdrawal of foreign forces. Yielding to this pressure and to Soviet threats of intervention, the British and French withdrew, and eventually so did the Israelis. Eisenhower had won a major diplomatic battle through patience and pressure, but he did not succeed in bringing lasting peace to the troubled region.

The most publicized CIA intervention of the Eisenhower years took place in Guatemala, where a fragile democracy had taken root in 1944. President Jácobo Arbenz Guzmán, elected in 1950, aggressively pursued land reform and encouraged the formation of trade unions. At the time, 2 percent of the Guatemalan population owned 72 percent of all farmland. Arbenz also challenged the long-standing dominance of the American-based United Fruit Company by threatening to expropriate hundreds of thousands of acres that United Fruit was not cultivating. The company had powerful friends in the administration (CIA director Dulles had sat on its board of trustees), and it began intensive lobbying for U.S. intervention. United Fruit linked the land-reform program to the evils of international communism, and the CIA spent $7 million training antigovernment dissidents based in Honduras.

The American navy stopped ships bound for Guatemala and seized their cargoes, and on June 14, 1954, a U.S.–sponsored military invasion began. Guatemalan citizens resisted by seizing United Fruit buildings, but U.S. Air Force bombing saved the invasion effort. Guatemalans appealed in vain to the United Nations for help. Meanwhile, President Eisenhower publicly denied any knowledge of CIA activities. The newly appointed military leader, Carlos Castillo Armas, flew to the Guatemalan capital in a U.S. embassy plane. Widespread terror followed, unions were outlawed, and thousands arrested. United Fruit circulated photos of Guatemalans murdered by

the invaders, labeling them "victims of communism." In 1957 Castillo Armas was assassinated, and a decades-long civil war ensued between military factions and peasant guerrillas.

American intervention in Guatemala increased suspicion of and resentment against American foreign policy throughout Central and Latin America. Vice President Nixon declared that the new Guatemalan government had earned "the overwhelming support of the Guatemalan people." But in 1958, while making a "goodwill" tour of Latin America, Nixon was stoned by angry mobs in Caracas, Venezuela, suggesting that U.S. actions in the region had triggered an anti-American backlash.

In Indochina, the United States provided France with massive military aid and CIA cooperation in its desperate struggle to maintain its colonial empire. From 1950 to 1954 the United States poured $2.6 billion (about three-quarters of the total French costs) into the fight against the nationalist Vietminh movement, led by Communist Ho Chi Minh. When Vietminh forces surrounded 25,000 French troops at Dien Bien Phu in March 1954, France pleaded with the United States to intervene directly. Secretary of State Dulles and Vice President Nixon, among others, recommended the use of tactical nuclear weapons and a commitment of ground troops. But Eisenhower, recalling the difficulties of the Korean conflict, rejected this call. "I can conceive of no greater tragedy," he said, "than for the United States to become engaged in all-out war in Indochina."

At the same time, Eisenhower feared that the loss of one country to communism would inevitably lead to the loss of others. As he put it, "You have a row of dominoes set up, and you knock over the first one and what will happen to the last one is the certainty that it will go over quickly." According to this so-called domino theory, the "loss" of Vietnam would threaten other Southeast Asian nations, such as Laos, Thailand, the Philippines, and perhaps even India and Australia. After the French surrender at Dien Ben Phu, a conference in Geneva established a cease-fire and a temporary division of Vietnam along the 17th parallel into northern and southern sectors. The Geneva accord called for reunification and national elections in 1956. But the United States, although it had attended the conference along with the Soviet Union and China, refused to sign the accord. In response to the Vietnam situation the Eisenhower administration created the Southeast Asia Treaty Organization (SEATO) in 1954. This NATO-like security pact included the United States, Great Britain, France, Australia, New Zealand, Thailand, the Philippines, and Pakistan, and was dominated by the United States.

South Vietnamese leader Ngo Dinh Diem, a former Japanese collaborator and a Catholic in a country that

Venezuelan soldiers (right) tried to disperse rioters who attacked Vice President Richard M. Nixon's car in Caracas during his 1958 "goodwill tour." Demonstrations such as these revealed a reservoir of resentment in Latin America against the interventionist policies of the United States in the region.

was 90 percent Buddhist, quickly alienated many peasants with his corruption and repressive policies. American economic and military aid, along with continuing covert CIA activity, was crucial in keeping the increasingly isolated Diem in power. Both Diem and Eisenhower refused to permit the 1956 elections stipulated in Geneva because they knew popular hero Ho Chi Minh would easily win. By 1959 Diem's harsh and unpopular government in Saigon faced a civil war; thousands of peasants had joined guerrilla forces determined to drive him out. Eisenhower's commitment of military advisers and economic aid to South Vietnam, based on cold war assumptions, laid the foundation for the Vietnam War of the 1960s.

Ike's Warning: The Military-Industrial Complex

Throughout the 1950s small numbers of peace advocates in the United States had pointed to the ultimate illogic of the "new look" in foreign policy. The increasing reliance on nuclear weapons, they argued, did not

strengthen national security but rather threatened the entire planet with extinction. They demonstrated at military camps, atomic-test sites, and missile-launching ranges, often getting arrested to make their point. Reports of radioactive fallout around the world rallied a larger group of scientists and prominent intellectuals against further nuclear testing. In Europe, a Ban the Bomb movement gained a wide following; an American counterpart, the National Committee for a Sane Nuclear Policy (SANE), claimed 25,000 members by 1958. The Women's International League for Peace and Freedom collected petitions calling for a test ban. The Student Peace Union, founded in 1959, established units on many campuses. Small but well-publicized actions against civil defense drills took place in several big cities: protesters marched on the streets rather than entering bomb shelters.

As he neared retirement, President Eisenhower came to share some of the protesters' anxiety and doubts about the arms race. Ironically, Eisenhower found it difficult to restrain the system he helped create. He chose to devote his Farewell Address, delivered in January 1961, to warning the nation about the dangers of what he termed the "military-industrial complex." Its total influence, he cautioned, "economic, political, even spiritual—is felt in every city, every statehouse, every office of the federal government." The conjunction of a large military establishment and a large arms industry, Eisenhower noted, was new in American history. "The potential for the disastrous rise of misplaced power exists and will persist. We must never let the weight of this combination endanger our liberties or democratic processes."

The old soldier understood perhaps better than most the dangers of raw military force. Eisenhower's public posture of restraint and caution in foreign affairs accompanied an enormous expansion of American economic, diplomatic, and military strength. Yet the Eisenhower years also demonstrated the limits of power and intervention in a world that did not always conform to the simple dualistic assumptions of cold war ideology.

JOHN F. KENNEDY AND THE NEW FRONTIER

No one could have resembled Dwight Eisenhower less in personality, temperament, and public image than John Fitzgerald Kennedy. The handsome son of a prominent, wealthy Irish American diplomat, husband of a fashionable, trend-setting heiress, forty-two-year-old JFK embodied youth, excitement, and sophistication. As only the second Catholic candidate for president—the first was Al Smith in 1928—Kennedy ran under the banner of the New Frontier. His liberalism inspired idealism and hope in millions of young people at home and abroad. In foreign affairs, Kennedy generally followed, and in some respects deepened, the cold war precepts that dominated postwar policymaking. But by the time of his assassination in 1963, he may have been veering away from the hard-line anti-Communist ideology he had earlier embraced. What a second term might have brought remains debatable, but his death ended a unique moment in American public life.

The Election of 1960

John F. Kennedy's political career began in Massachusetts, which elected him to the House in 1946 and then the Senate in 1952. Kennedy won the Democratic nomination after a bruising series of primaries in which he defeated party stalwarts Hubert Humphrey of Minnesota and Lyndon B. Johnson of Texas. Unlike Humphrey and Johnson, Kennedy had not been part of the powerful group of insiders who dominated the Senate. But he drew strength and financial support from a loyal coterie of friends and family, including his father, Joseph P. Kennedy, and his younger brother Robert. Vice President Richard M. Nixon, the Republican nominee, had faithfully served the Eisenhower administration for eight years, and was far better known than his younger opponent. The Kennedy campaign stressed its candidate's youth and his image as a war hero. During his World War II tour of duty in the Pacific, Kennedy had bravely rescued one of his crew after their PT boat had been sunk. Kennedy's supporters also pointed to his intellectual ability. JFK had won the Pulitzer Prize in 1957 for his book *Profiles in Courage,* which in fact had been written largely by his aides.

The election featured the first televised presidential debates. Political analysts have long argued over the impact of these four encounters, but agree that they moved television to the center of presidential politics, making image and appearance more critical than ever. Nixon appeared nervous and the camera made him look unshaven. Kennedy, in contrast, benefited from a confident manner and telegenic good looks. Both candidates emphasized foreign policy. Nixon defended the Republican record and stressed his own maturity and experience. Kennedy hammered away at the alleged "missile gap" with the Soviet Union and promised more vigorous executive leadership. He also countered the anti-Catholic prejudice of evangelical Protestants with a promise to keep church and state separate.

Kennedy squeaked to victory in the closest election since 1884. He won by a little more than 100,000 votes

Presidential candidate John F. Kennedy smiles while listening to his opponent Richard M. Nixon during one of their televised debates in the 1960 election. Eighty-five million viewers watched at least one of the debates, which both reflected and increased the power of television in the electoral process.

SOURCE: AP/Wide World Photos.

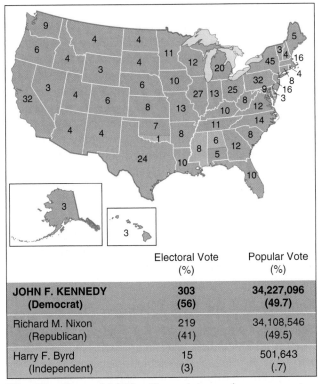

	Electoral Vote (%)	Popular Vote (%)
JOHN F. KENNEDY (Democrat)	**303** **(56)**	**34,227,096** **(49.7)**
Richard M. Nixon (Republican)	219 (41)	34,108,546 (49.5)
Harry F. Byrd (Independent)	15 (3)	501,643 (.7)

The Election of 1960 Kennedy's popular vote margin over Nixon was only a little over 100,000, making this one of the closest elections in American history.

out of nearly 69 million cast. He ran poorly in the South, but won the Catholic vote so overwhelmingly that he carried most of the Northeast and Midwest. Though the margin of victory was tiny, Kennedy was a glorious winner. Surrounding himself with prestigious Ivy League academics, Hollywood movie stars, and talented artists and writers, he imbued the presidency with an aura of celebrity. The inauguration brought out a bevy of poets, musicians, and fashionably dressed politicians from around the world. The new administration promised to be exciting and stylish, a modern-day Camelot peopled by heroic young men and beautiful women. The new president's ringing inaugural address ("Ask not what your country can do for you—ask what you can do for your country") had special resonance for a whole generation of young Americans.

New Frontier Liberalism

Kennedy promised to revive the long-stalled liberal domestic agenda. His New Frontier advocated such liberal programs as a higher minimum wage, greater federal aid for education, increased Social Security benefits, medical care for the elderly, support for public housing, and various antipoverty measures. Yet the thin margin of his victory and the stubborn opposition

of conservative southern Democrats in Congress made it difficult to achieve these goals. Congress refused, for example, to enact the administration's attempt to extend Social Security and unemployment benefits to millions of uncovered workers. Congress also failed to enact administration proposals for aid to public schools, mass-transit subsidies, and medical insurance for retired workers over sixty-five.

There were a few New Frontier victories. Congress did approve a modest increase in the minimum wage (to $1.25 per hour), agreed to a less ambitious improvement in Social Security, and appropriated $5 billion for public housing. It also passed the Manpower Retraining Act, appropriating $435 million to train the unemployed. The Area Redevelopment Act provided federal funds for rural, depressed Appalachia. The Higher Education Act of 1963 offered aid to colleges for constructing buildings and upgrading libraries. One of the best-publicized New Frontier programs was the Peace Corps, in which thousands of mostly young men and women traveled overseas for two-year stints in underdeveloped countries. There they provided technical and educational assistance in setting up health-care programs and improving agricultural efficiency. As a force for change, the Peace Corps produced modest results, but it epitomized Kennedy's promise to provide opportunities for service for a new generation of idealistic young people.

Kennedy helped revive the issue of women's rights with his Presidential Commission on the Status of Women, led by Eleanor Roosevelt. The commission's 1963 report was the most comprehensive study of women's lives ever produced by the federal government. It documented the ongoing discrimination faced by American women in the work place and in the legal system, as well as the inadequacy of social services such as day care. It called for federally supported day-care programs, continuing education programs for women, and an end to sex bias in Social Security and unemployment benefits. The commission also insisted that more women be appointed to policy-making positions in government. One concrete legislative result, the Equal Pay Act of 1963, made it illegal for employers to pay men and women different wages for the same job. The law did not do much to improve women's economic status, since most working women were employed in job categories, such as secretary or clerk, that included no men. But the issue of economic inequality had at least been put on the public agenda. President Kennedy also directed executive agencies to prohibit sex discrimination in hiring and promotion. The work of the commission contributed to a new generation of women's rights activism.

Taking a more aggressive stance on stimulating economic growth and creating new jobs than had Eisenhower, Kennedy relied heavily on Walter Heller, chair of the Council of Economic Advisers (CEA). Heller emphasized the goal of full employment, which he believed could be attained through deficit spending, encouragement of economic growth, and targeted tax cuts. The administration thus pushed lower business taxes through Congress, even at the cost of a higher federal deficit. The Revenue Act of 1962 encouraged new investment and plant renovation by easing tax depreciation schedules for business. Kennedy also gained approval for lower U.S. tariffs as a way to increase foreign trade. To help keep inflation down, he intervened in the steel industry in 1961 and 1962, pressuring labor to keep its wage demands low and management to curb price increases.

Kennedy also increased the federal commitment to a wholly new realm of government spending: the space program. The National Aeronautics and Space Administration (NASA) had been established under Eisenhower in response to the Soviet success with Sputnik. In 1961, driven by the cold war motivation of beating the Soviets to the moon and avoiding "another Sputnik," Kennedy won approval for a greatly expanded space program. He announced the goal of landing an American on the moon by the end of the decade. NASA eventually spent $33 billion before reaching this objective in 1969. This program of manned space flight—the Apollo missions—appealed to the public, acquiring a science fiction aura. In space, if not on earth, the New Frontier might actually be reached.

Overall, Kennedy's most long-lasting achievement as president may have been his strengthening of the

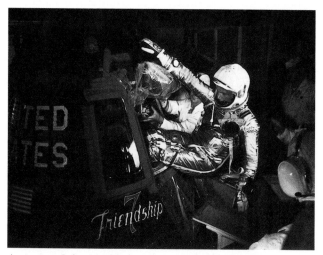

Astronaut John H. Glenn as he prepared for the first American manned space orbit of the earth. The space program of the early 1960s emphasized the technical training and courage of astronauts, consciously creating a set of public heroes as a way to ensure popular support and congressional funding.

SOURCE: NASA Headquarters.

executive branch itself. He insisted on direct presidential control of details that Eisenhower had left to advisers and appointees. Moreover, under Kennedy the White House staff assumed many of the decision-making and advisory functions previously held by cabinet members. This arrangement increased Kennedy's authority, since these appointees, unlike cabinet secretaries, escaped congressional oversight and confirmation proceedings. White House aides also lacked an independent constituency; their power and authority derived solely from their ties to the president. Kennedy's aides, "the best and the brightest," as he called them, dominated policymaking. With men such as McGeorge Bundy directing foreign affairs and Theodore Sorensen coordinating domestic issues, Kennedy began a pattern whereby American presidents increasingly operated through small groups of fiercely loyal aides, often acting in secret.

Kennedy and the Cold War

During Kennedy's three years in office his approach to foreign policy shifted from aggressive containment to efforts at easing U.S.–Soviet tensions. Certainly when he first entered office, Kennedy and his chief aides considered it their main task to confront the Communist threat. In his first State of the Union Address, in January 1961, Kennedy told Congress that America must seize the initiative in the cold war. The nation must "move outside the home fortress, and . . . challenge the enemy in fields of our own choosing." To head the State Department Kennedy chose Dean Rusk, a conservative former assistant to Truman's secretary of state, Dean Acheson. Secretary of Defense Robert McNamara, a Republican and Ford Motor Company executive, was determined to streamline military procedures and weapons buying. McNamara typified the technical, cost-efficient, superrational approach to policymaking. Allen Dulles, Eisenhower's CIA director, remained at his post. These and other officials believed with Kennedy that Eisenhower had timidly accepted stalemate when the cold war could have been won.

Kennedy built up American nuclear and conventional weapons systems. Between 1960 and 1962 defense appropriations increased by nearly a third, from $43 billion to $56 billion. JFK expanded Eisenhower's policy of covert operations, deploying the army's elite Special Forces as a supplement to CIA covert operations in counterinsurgency battles against third world guerrillas. These soldiers, fighting under the direct orders of the president, could provide "rapid response" to "brush-fire" conflicts where Soviet influence threatened American interests. The Special Forces, authorized by Kennedy to wear the green berets that gave them their unofficial name, reflected the president's desire as president to acquire greater flexibility, secrecy, and independence in the conduct of foreign policy.

The limits on the ability of covert action and the Green Berets to further American interests became apparent in Southeast Asia. In Laos, where the United States had ignored the 1954 Geneva agreement and installed a friendly military regime, the CIA-backed government could not defeat Soviet-backed Pathet Lao guerrillas. The president had to arrange with the Soviets to neutralize Laos. In neighboring Vietnam, the situation proved more difficult. When Communist Vietcong guerrillas launched a civil war in South Vietnam against the U.S.–supported government in Saigon, Kennedy began sending hundreds of Green Berets and other military advisers to support the rule of Ngo Dinh Diem. In May 1961, in response to North Vietnamese aid to the Vietcong, Kennedy ordered a covert action against Ho Chi Minh's government that included sabotage and intelligence gathering.

Kennedy's approach to Vietnam reflected an analysis of the situation in that country by two aides, General Maxwell Taylor and Walt Rostow, who saw it through purely cold war eyes. "The Communists are pursuing a clear and systematic strategy in Southeast Asia," Taylor and Rostow concluded, ignoring the inefficiency, corruption, and unpopularity of the Diem government. By 1963, with Diem's army unable to contain the Vietcong rebellion, Kennedy had sent nearly 16,000 support and combat troops to South Vietnam. By then, a wide spectrum of South Vietnamese society had joined the revolt against the hated Diem, including highly respected Buddhist monks and their students. Americans watched in horror as television news reports showed footage of Buddhists burning themselves to death on the streets of Saigon—the ultimate protest against Diem's repressive rule. American press and television also reported the mounting casualty lists of U.S. forces in Vietnam. The South Vietnamese army, bloated by U.S. aid and weakened by corruption, continued to disintegrate. In the fall of 1963, American military officers and CIA operatives stood aside with approval as a group of Vietnamese generals removed President Diem, killing him and his top advisers. It was the first of many coups that racked the South Vietnamese government over the next few years.

In Latin America, Kennedy looked for ways to forestall various revolutionary movements that were gaining ground. The erosion of peasant landholdings had accelerated rapidly after 1950. Huge expanses of fertile land long devoted to subsistence farming were converted to business-dominated agriculture that grew staple crops for export (bananas, coffee, sugar). Millions of impoverished peasants were forced to relocate to already overcrowded cities. In 1961 Kennedy unveiled the Alliance for Progress, a ten-year, $100 billion plan to spur economic development in Latin America. The United States committed $20 billion to the project, with the Latin nations responsible for the rest. The main goals included greater industrial growth and agricultural productivity, more equitable distribution of income, and improved health and housing.

Kennedy intended the Alliance for Progress as a kind of Marshall Plan that would benefit the poor and middle classes of the continent. The alliance did help raise growth rates in Latin American economies. But the expansion in export crops and in consumption by the tiny upper class did little to aid the poor or encourage democracy. The United States hesitated to challenge the power of dictators and extreme conservatives who were staunch anti-Communist allies. Thus the alliance soon degenerated into just another foreign aid program, incapable of generating genuine social change.

The Cuban Revolution and the Bay of Pigs

The direct impetus for the Alliance for Progress was the Cuban Revolution of 1959, which loomed over Latin America. The U.S. economic domination of Cuba that began with the Spanish American War (see Chapter 20) had continued through the 1950s. American-owned businesses controlled all of Cuba's oil production, 90 percent of its mines, and roughly half of its railroads and sugar and cattle industries. Havana, the island's capital, was an attractive tourist center for Americans, and U.S. crime syndicates shared control of the island's lucrative gambling, prostitution, and drug trade with dictator Fulgencio Batista.

As a response to this, in the early 1950s, a peasant-based revolutionary movement, led by Fidel Castro, began gaining strength in the rural districts and mountains outside Havana. On New Year's Day 1959, after years of guerrilla war, the rebels entered Havana and seized power amid great public rejoicing. For a brief time, Castro seemed a hero to many North Americans as well. The *New York Times* had conducted sympathetic interviews with Castro in 1958, while he was still fighting in Cuba's mountains. Many young people visited the island and returned with enthusiastic reports. Famous writers such as James Baldwin and Ernest Hemingway embraced Castro. The CIA and President Eisenhower, however, shared none of this exuberance. Castro's land-reform program, involving the seizure of acreage from the tiny minority that controlled much of the fertile land, threatened to set an example for other Latin American countries. Although Castro had not joined the Cuban Communist Party, he turned to the Soviet Union after the United States withdrew economic aid. He began to sell sugar to the Soviets and soon nationalized American-owned oil companies and other enterprises. Eisenhower established an economic boycott of Cuba in 1960, then severed diplomatic relations.

Kennedy inherited from Eisenhower plans for a U.S. invasion of Cuba, including the secret arming and training of Cuban exiles. The CIA drafted the invasion plan, which was based on the assumption that a U.S.–led invasion would trigger a popular uprising of the Cuban people and bring down Castro. Kennedy went along with the plan, but at the last moment decided not to supply an Air Force cover for the operation. On April 17, 1961, a ragtag army of 1,400 counterrevolutionaries led by CIA operatives landed at the Bay of Pigs, on Cuba's south coast. Castro's efficient and loyal army easily subdued them. At the United Nations, Ambassador Adlai Stevenson, deceived by presidential aides, flatly denied any U.S. involvement, only to learn the truth later.

The debacle revealed that the CIA, blinded by cold war assumptions, had failed to understand the Cuban Revolution. There was no popular uprising against Castro. Instead, the invasion strengthened Castro's standing among the urban poor and peasants, already attracted by his programs of universal literacy and medical care. As Castro stifled internal opposition, many Cuban intellectuals and professionals fled to the United States. An embarrassed Kennedy reluctantly took the blame for the abortive invasion, and his administration was censured time and again by third world delegates to the United Nations. American liberals criticized Kennedy for plotting Castro's overthrow, while conservatives blamed him for not supporting the invasion. Despite the failure, Kennedy remained committed to getting rid of Castro and keeping up the economic boycott. The CIA continued to support anti-Castro operations and launched at least eight attempts to assassinate the Cuban leader.

The Missile Crisis

The aftermath of the Bay of Pigs led to the most serious confrontation of the cold war: the Cuban missile crisis of October 1962. Frightened by U.S. belligerency, Castro asked Soviet premier Khrushchev for military help. Khrushchev responded in the summer of 1962 by shipping to Cuba a large amount of sophisticated weaponry, including intermediate-range nuclear missiles. In early October, U.S. reconnaissance planes found camouflaged missile silos dotting the island. Several Kennedy aides demanded an immediate bombing of Cuban bases, arguing that the missiles had decisively eroded the strategic global advantage the United States had previously enjoyed. Other aides rejected this analysis, pointing out that American cities had been vulnerable to Soviet intercontinental ballistic missiles (ICBMs) since 1957.

The president and his advisers pondered their options in a series of tense meetings. Secretary of Defense McNamara was probably closest to the truth when he asserted, "I don't believe it's primarily a military prob-

lem. It's primarily a domestic political problem." Kennedy's aggressive attempts to exploit Cuba in the 1960 election now came back to haunt him, as he worried that his critics would accuse him of weakness in failing to stand up to the Soviets. The disastrous Bay of Pigs affair still rankled. Even some prominent Democrats, including Senator J. William Fulbright, chair of the Senate Foreign Relations Committee, called for an invasion of Cuba.

Kennedy went on national television on October 22. He announced the discovery of the missile sites, demanded the removal of all missiles, and ordered a strict naval blockade of all offensive military equipment shipped to Cuba. He also requested an emergency meeting of the UN Security Council and promised that any missiles launched from Cuba would bring "a full retaliatory response upon the Soviet Union." For a tense week, the American public wondered if nuclear Armageddon was imminent. Eyeball to eyeball, the two superpowers waited for each other to blink. On October 26 and 27 Khrushchev yielded, ordering twenty-five Soviet ships off their course to Cuba, thus avoiding a challenge to the American blockade.

Khrushchev offered to remove all the missiles in return for a pledge from the United States not to invade Cuba. Khrushchev later added a demand for removal of American weapons from Turkey, as close to the Soviet Union as Cuba is to the United States. Kennedy secretly assured Khrushchev that the United States would dismantle the obsolete Jupiter missiles in Turkey. On November 20, after weeks of delicate negotiations, Kennedy publicly announced the withdrawal of Soviet missiles and bombers from Cuba. He also pledged to respect Cuban sovereignty, and promised that U.S. forces would not invade the island.

The crisis had passed. The Soviets, determined not to be intimidated again, began the largest weapons buildup in their history. For his part Kennedy, perhaps chastened by this flirtation with nuclear disaster, made important gestures toward peaceful coexistence with the Soviets. In a June 1963 address at American University, Kennedy called for a rethinking of cold war diplomacy. Both sides, he said, had been "caught up in a vicious and dangerous cycle in which suspicion on one side breeds suspicion on the other, and new weapons beget counterweapons." It was important "not to see only a distorted and desperate view of the other side. . . . No government or social system is so evil that its people must be considered as lacking in virtue."

Shortly after, Washington and Moscow set up a "hot line"—a direct phone connection to permit instant communication during times of crisis. More substantial was the Limited Nuclear Test-Ban Treaty, signed in August 1963 by the United States, the Soviet Union, and Great Britain. The treaty prohibited above-ground, outer space, and underwater nuclear weapons tests. It eased international anxieties over radioactive fallout. But underground testing continued to accelerate for years. The limited test ban was perhaps more symbolic than substantive, a psychological breakthrough in East-West relations after a particularly tense three years.

The Assassination of President Kennedy

The assassination of John F. Kennedy in Dallas on November 22, 1963, sent the entire nation into shock and mourning. Just forty-six years old and president for only three years, Kennedy quickly ascended to martyrdom in the nation's consciousness. Millions had identified his strengths—intelligence, optimism, wit, charm, coolness under fire—as those of American society. In life, Kennedy had helped place television at the center of American political life. Now in the aftermath of his death, television riveted a badly shocked nation. One day after the assassination, the president's accused killer, an obscure political misfit named Lee Harvey Oswald, was himself gunned down before television cameras covering his arraignment in Dallas. Two days later tens of millions watched the televised spectacle of Kennedy's funeral, trying to make sense of the brutal murder. Although a special commission headed by Chief Justice Earl Warren found the killing to be the work of Oswald acting alone, many Americans doubted this conclusion. Kennedy's death gave rise to a host of conspiracy theories, none of which seems provable. In 1979 a House committee concluded that more than one gunman had fired on the presidential motorcade; but FBI scientists disputed this finding.

As Adlai Stevenson, one of Kennedy's longtime political rivals in the Democratic Party, noted in his eulogy to the president, "No one will ever know what this blazing political talent might have accomplished had he been permitted to live and labor long in the cause of freedom." We will never know, of course, what Kennedy might have achieved in a second term. But in his 1,000 days as president, he demonstrated a capacity to change and grow in office. Having gone to the brink during the mis-

sile crisis, he managed to launch new initiatives toward peaceful coexistence. At the time of his death, relations between the United States and the Soviet Union were more amicable than at any time since the end of World War II. Much of the domestic liberal agenda of the New Frontier would be finally implemented by Kennedy's successor, Lyndon B. Johnson, who dreamed of creating a Great Society.

CONCLUSION

America in 1963 still enjoyed the full flush of its postwar economic boom. To be sure, millions of Americans, particularly African Americans and Latinos, did not share in the good times. But millions of others had managed to achieve middle-class status since the early 1950s. An expanding economy, cheap energy, government subsidies, and a dominant position in the world marketplace had made the hallmarks of "the good life" available to more Americans than ever. The postwar "American dream" promised home ownership, college education, secure employment at decent wages, affordable appliances, and the ability to travel—for one's children if not for one's self. The nation's public culture—its schools,

Vice President Lyndon B. Johnson took the oath of office as president aboard *Air Force One* after the assassination of John F. Kennedy, November 22, 1963. Onlookers included the grief-stricken Jacqueline Kennedy (right) and Lady Bird Johnson (left). This haunting photo captured both the shock of Kennedy's assassination and the orderly succession of power that followed.

SOURCE: AP/Wide World Photos.

CHRONOLOGY

1950	David Riesman publishes *The Lonely Crowd*
1952	Dwight D. Eisenhower is elected president
1953	CIA installs Riza Shah Pahlavi as leader of Iran
1954	Vietminh force French surrender at Dien Bien Phu
	CIA overthrows government of Jácobo Arbenz Guzmán in Guatemala
	United States explodes first hydrogen bomb
1955	Jonas Salk pioneers vaccine for polio
	James Dean stars in the movie *Rebel without a Cause*
1956	Federal Highway Act authorizes Interstate Highway System
	Elvis Presley signs with RCA
	Eisenhower is reelected
	Allen Ginsberg publishes *Howl*
1957	Soviet Union launches Sputnik, first space-orbiting satellite
	Jack Kerouac publishes *On the Road*
1958	National Defense Education Act authorizes grants and loans to college students
1959	Nikita Khrushchev visits the United States
1960	Soviets shoot down U-2 spy plane
	John F. Kennedy is elected president
	Almost 90 percent of American homes have television
1961	President Kennedy creates "Green Berets"
	Bay of Pigs invasion of Cuba fails
1962	Cuban missile crisis brings the world to the brink of a superpower confrontation
1963	Report by the Presidential Commission on the Status of Women documents ongoing discrimination
	Betty Friedan publishes *The Feminine Mystique*
	Limited Nuclear Test-Ban Treaty is signed
	President Kennedy is assassinated

mass media, politics, advertising—presented a powerful consensus based on the idea that the American dream was available to all who would work for it.

The presidential transition from the grandfatherly Dwight Eisenhower to the charismatic John F. Kennedy symbolized for many a generational shift as well. By 1963 young people had more influence than ever before in shaping the nation's political life, its media images, and its burgeoning consumer culture. Kennedy himself inspired millions of young Americans to pursue public service and to express their political idealism. But even by the time of Kennedy's death, the postwar consensus and the conditions that nurtured it were beginning to unravel.

REVIEW QUESTIONS

1. How did postwar economic prosperity change the lives of ordinary Americans? Which groups benefited most and which were largely excluded from "the affluent society"?

2. What role did federal programs play in expanding economic opportunities?

3. Analyze the origins of postwar youth culture. How was teenage life different in these years from previous eras? How did popular culture both reflect and distort the lives of American youth?

4. How did mass culture become even more central to American everyday life in the two decades following World War II? What problems did various cultural critics identify with this trend?

5. How did cold war politics and assumptions shape American foreign policy in these years? What were

the key interventions the United States made in Europe and the third world?

6. Evaluate the domestic and international policies associated with John F. Kennedy and the New Frontier. What continuities with Eisenhower-era politics do you find in the Kennedy administration? How did JFK break with past practices?

RECOMMENDED READING

Roslayn Fraad Baxandall and Elizabeth Ewen, *Picture Windows: How the Suburbs Happened* (2000). The best new account of postwar suburbs, emphasizing the demand for affordable housing and making fine use of the voices of suburbanites.

Lawrence Freedman, *Kennedy's Wars: Berlin, Cuba, Laos, and Vietnam* (2000). A comprehensive new analysis of JFK's foreign policy, emphasizing the context of cold war liberalism.

James B. Gilbert, *A Cycle of Outrage* (1986). An insightful examination of juvenile delinquency and its treatment by social scientists and the mass media during the 1950s.

Kenneth T. Jackson, *Crabgrass Frontier* (1985). The most comprehensive overview of the history of American suburbs. Jackson provides a broad historical context for understanding postwar suburbanization, and offers an excellent analysis of the impact of government agencies such as the Federal Housing Administration.

David E. Kaiser, *American Tragedy: Kennedy, Johnson, and the Origins of the Vietnam War* (2000). The most detailed account yet of how the contradictions of cold war thinking pushed policymakers in three administrations toward an unnecessary and unwinnable war.

Zachary Karabell, *Architects of Intervention: The United States, the Third World, and the Cold War, 1946–1962* (1999). A wide-ranging analysis of U.S. involvement in various Third World countries, with special emphasis on the active role played by indigenous, non-American participants.

George Lipsitz, *Time Passages* (1990). An illuminating set of essays charting developments in American popular culture, especially strong analysis of music and early television.

Elaine Tyler May, *Homeward Bound: American Families in the Cold War* (1988). A thoughtful social history linking family life of the 1950s with the political shadow of the cold war.

Grace Palladino, *Teenagers: An American History* (1996). A lively and witty narrative account of the emergence of teenagers as a new social class.

James T. Patterson, *Grand Expectations: Postwar America, 1945–1974* (1996). A comprehensive overview of postwar life that centers on the "grand expectations" evoked by unprecedented prosperity.

Mark J. White, ed., *Kennedy: The New Frontier Revisited* (1998). Wide ranging collection of recent essays that together offer a balanced view of Kennedy's presidency.

ADDITIONAL BIBLIOGRAPHY

American Society at Mid-Century

Stephanie Coontz, *The Way We Never Were* (1992)
John P. Diggins, *The Proud Decades: America in War and Peace, 1941–1960* (1988)
Benita Eisler, *Private Lives: Men and Women of the Fifties* (1986)
Delores Hayden, *Redesigning the American Dream* (1984)
Kenneth W. Olson, *The GI Bill, the Veterans, and the Colleges* (1974)

Youth Culture

Wini Breines, *Young, White, and Miserable: Growing Up Female in the Fifties* (1992)
Thomas Doherty, *Teen Pics* (1994)
Nelson George, *The Death of Rhythm and Blues* (1988)
William Graebner, *Coming of Age in Buffalo* (1990)

Douglas T. Miller and Marion Novak, *The Fifties: The Way We Really Were* (1977)
Jim Miller, *Flowers in the Dustbin: The Rise of Rock and Roll, 1947–1977* (1999)

Mass Culture and Its Discontents

Erik Barnouw, *Tube of Plenty* (1982)
Nancy E. Bernhard, *U.S. Television News and Cold War Propaganda, 1947–1960* (1999)
Joel Foreman, ed., *The Other Fifties: Interrogating Midcentury American Icons* (1997)
George Lipsitz, *Class and Culture in Cold War America* (1981)
J. Fred MacDonald, *Television and the Red Menace* (1985)
David Marc, *Demographic Vistas: Television and American Culture* (1984)

Lynn Spigel, *Make Room for TV* (1992)

Stephen J. Whitfield, *The Culture of the Cold War* (1991)

The Cold War Continued

James G. Blight and Peter Kornbluh, eds., *Politics of Illusion: The of Bay Pigs Invasion Reexamined* (1999)

Robert R. Bowie, *Waging Peace: How Eisenhower Shaped An Enduring Cold War Strategy* (1998)

Nick Cullather, *Secret History: The CIA's Classified Account of its Operations in Guatemala, 1952–1954* (1999)

Paul Dickson, *Sputnik: The Shock of the Century* (2001)

Piero Gleijeses, *Shattered Hope: The Guatemalan Revolution and the United States, 1944–1954* (1991)

Richard A. Melanson and David A. Mayers, eds., *Reevaluating Eisenhower* (1986)

John F. Kennedy and the New Frontier

Michael Beschloss, *The Crisis Years* (1991)

Thomas Brown, *JFK: The History of an Image* (1988)

Trumbull Higgins, *The Perfect Failure: Kennedy, Eisenhower and the CIA at the Bay of Pigs* (1988)

Walter LaFeber, *Inevitable Revolutions* (1983)

Thomas G. Paterson, ed., *Kennedy's Quest for Victory* (1989)

Gerald L. Posner, *Case Closed: Lee Harvey Oswald and the Assassination of JFK* (1993)

Richard E. Welch, Jr., *Response to Revolution: The United States and Cuba, 1959–1961* (1985)

Garry Wills, *The Kennedy Imprisonment* (1983)

Biography

Stephen Ambrose, *Eisenhower*, 2 vols. (1983, 1984)

Chuck Berry, *The Autobiography* (1987)

David Burner, *John F. Kennedy and a New Generation* (1988)

Carol George, *God's Salesman: Norman Vincent Peale and the Power of Positive Thinking* (1993)

Peter Guralnick, *Last Train to Memphis: The Rise of Elvis Presley* (1994)

Daniel Horowitz, *Betty Friedan and the Making of the Feminine Mystique* (1998)

Barry Miles, *Allen Ginsberg* (1989)

Gerald Nicosia, *Memory Babe: A Critical Biography of Jack Kerouac* (1983)

Geoffrey Perret, *Eisenhower* (1999)

HISTORY ON THE INTERNET

http://www.tamu.edu/scom/pres/archive.html

The Center for Presidential Studies at Texas A&M University has a collection of presidential speeches from Washington through George Bush. Examine Kennedy's foreign policy problems through his Inaugural Address (1961), Berlin Crisis Address (1961), Cuban Missile Crisis Speech (1962), American University Speech (1963), and his speech on the Nuclear Test Ban Treaty (1963).

http://www.bartleby.com/124/pres54.html

First Inaugural Address of Dwight D. Eisenhower, January 20, 1953

http://www.bartleby.com/124/pres55.html

Second Inaugural Address of Dwight D. Eisenhower, January 21, 1957

http://www.ukans.edu/carrie/docs/texts/ddefarew.html

Eisenhower's "Farewell Address," January 17, 1961 (Excerpts)

http://www.bartleby.com/124/pres56.html

Inaugural Address of John F. Kennedy, January 20, 1961

http://www.fordham.edu/halsall/mod/1962kennedy-cuba.html

Kennedy's Address on the Cuban Crisis October 22, 1962

http://tigger.uic.edu/~pbhales/Levittown.html

http://www.lihistory.com/specsec/levmain.htm

Two large sites with a rich history of Levittown, among the first of the post war suburbs.

TWENTY-EIGHT

THE CIVIL RIGHTS MOVEMENT

▶ 1945 – 1966

Jacob Lawrence, *Four Students*, 1961. Photograph by Geoffrey Clements. SOURCE: CORBIS. © Geoffrey Clements/CORBIS (IE001007).

AMERICAN COMMUNITIES

The Montgomery Bus Boycott: An African American Community Challenges Segregation

A STEADY STREAM OF CARS AND PEDESTRIANS JAMMED THE STREETS around the Holt Street Baptist Church in Montgomery, Alabama. By early evening a patient, orderly, and determined crowd of more than 5,000 African Americans had packed the church and spilled over onto the sidewalks. Loudspeakers had to be set up for the thousands who could not squeeze inside. After a brief prayer and a reading from Scripture, all attention focused on the twenty-six-year-old minister who was to address the gathering. "We are here this evening," he began slowly, "for serious business. We are here in a general sense because first and foremost we are American citizens, and we are determined to apply our citizenship to the fullness of its means."

Sensing the expectant mood of the crowd, the minister got down to specifics. Rosa Parks, a seamstress and well-known activist in Montgomery's African American community, had been taken from a bus, arrested, and put in jail for refusing to give up her seat to a white passenger on December 1, 1955. Composing roughly half the city's 100,000 people, Montgomery's black community had long endured the humiliation of a strictly segregated bus system. Drivers could order a whole row of black passengers to vacate their seats for one white person. And black people had to pay their fares at the front of the bus and then step back outside and reenter through the rear door. The day of the mass meeting, more than 30,000 African Americans had answered a hastily organized call to boycott the city's buses in protest of Mrs. Parks's arrest. As the minister quickened his cadence and drew shouts of encouragement, he seemed to gather strength and confidence from the crowd. "You know, my friends, there comes a time when people get tired of being trampled over by the iron feet of oppression. There comes a time, my friends, when people get tired of being flung across the abyss of humiliation, when they experience the bleakness of nagging despair."

Even before he concluded his speech, it was clear to all present that the bus boycott would continue for more than just a day. The minister laid out the key principles that would guide the boycott—nonviolence, Christian love, unity. In his brief but stirring address the minister created a powerful sense of communion. "If we are wrong, justice is a lie," he told the clapping and shouting throng. "And we are determined here in Montgomery to work and fight until justice runs down like water and righteousness like a mighty stream." Historians would look back at Montgomery, he noted, and have to say: " 'There lived a race of people, black people, fleecy locks and black complexion, of people who had the moral courage to stand up for their rights.' And thereby they injected a new meaning into the veins of history and of civilization."

The Reverend Dr. Martin Luther King, Jr. made his way out of the church amid waves of applause and rows of hands reaching out to touch him. His prophetic speech catapulted him into leadership of the Montgomery bus boycott—but he had not started the movement. When Rosa Parks was arrested, local activists with deep roots in the black protest tradition galvanized the community with the idea of a boycott. Mrs. Parks herself had served for twelve years as secretary of the local NAACP chapter. She was a committed opponent of segregation and was thoroughly respected in the city's African American community. E. D. Nixon, president of the Alabama NAACP and head of the local Brotherhood of Sleeping Car Porters union, saw Mrs. Parks's arrest as the right case on which to make a stand. It was Nixon who brought Montgomery's black ministers together on December 5 to coordinate an extended boycott of city buses. They formed the Montgomery Improvement Association (MIA) and chose Dr. King as their leader. Significantly, Mrs. Parks' lawyer was Clifford Durr, a white liberal with a history of representing black clients. His politically active wife Virginia, for whom Mrs. Parks worked as a seamstress, had been a longtime crusader against the poll tax which prevented many blacks from voting. And two white ministers, Rev. Robert Graetz and Rev. Glenn Smiley, would offer important support to the MIA.

While Nixon organized black ministers, Jo Ann Robinson, an English teacher at Alabama State College, spread the word to the larger black community. Robinson led the Women's Political Council (WPC), an organization of black professional women founded in 1949. With her WPC allies, Robinson wrote, mimeographed, and distributed 50,000 copies of a leaflet telling the story of Mrs. Parks's arrest and urging all African Americans to stay off city buses on December 5. They did. Now the MIA faced the more difficult task of keeping the boycott going. Success depended on providing alternate transportation for the 30,000 to 40,000 maids, cooks, janitors, and other black working people who needed to get to work.

The MIA coordinated an elaborate system of car pools, using hundreds of private cars and volunteer drivers to provide as many as 20,000 rides each day. Many people walked. Local authorities, although shocked by the discipline and sense of purpose shown by Montgomery's African American community, refused to engage in serious negotiations. With the aid of the NAACP, the MIA brought suit in federal court against bus segrega-tion in Montgomery. Police harassed boycotters with traffic tickets and arrests. White racists exploded bombs in the homes of Dr. King and E. D. Nixon. The days turned into weeks, then months, but still the boycott continued. All along, mass meetings in Montgomery's African American churches helped boost morale with singing, praying, and stories of individual sacrifice. One elderly woman, refusing all suggestions that she drop out of the boycott on account of her age, made a spontaneous remark that became a classic refrain of the movement: "My feets is tired, but my soul is rested."

The boycott reduced the bus company's revenues by two-thirds. In February 1956, city officials obtained indictments against King, Nixon, and 113 other boycotters under an old law forbidding hindrance to business without "just cause or legal excuse." A month later King went on trial. A growing contingent of newspaper reporters and TV crews from around the country watched as the judge found King guilty, fined him $1,000, and released him on bond pending appeal. But on June 4, a panel of three federal judges struck down Montgomery's bus segregation ordinances as unconstitutional. On November 13 the Supreme Court affirmed the district court ruling. After eleven hard months and against all odds, the boycotters had won.

The struggle to end legal segregation took root in scores of southern cities and towns. African American communities led these fights, developing a variety of tactics, leaders, and ideologies. With white allies, they engaged in direct-action protests such as boycotts, sit-ins, and mass civil disobedience as well as strategic legal battles in state and federal courts. The movement was not without its inner conflicts. Tensions between local movements and national civil rights organizations flared up regularly. Within African American communities, long-simmering distrust between the working classes and rural folk on the one hand and middle-class ministers, teachers, and business people on the other sometimes threatened to destroy political unity. There were generational conflicts between African American student activists and their elders. But overall, the civil rights movement created new social identities for African Americans and profoundly changed American society. ■

Montgomery

KEY TOPICS

- Legal and political origins of the African American civil rights struggle

- Martin Luther King's rise to leadership

- Student protesters and direct action in the South

- Civil rights and national politics

- Civil Rights Act of 1964 and Voting Rights Act of 1965

- America's other minorities

ORIGINS OF THE MOVEMENT

The experiences of African Americans during World War II and immediately after laid the foundation for the civil rights struggle of the 1950s and 1960s. Nearly 1 million black men and women had served in the armed forces. The discrepancy between fighting totalitarianism abroad while enduring segregation and other racist practices in the military embittered many combat veterans and their families. Between 1939 and 1945 nearly 2 million African Americans found work in defense plants, and another 200,000 entered the federal civil service. Black union membership doubled, reaching more than 1.2 million. But the wartime stress on national unity and consensus largely muted political protests. With the war's end, African Americans and their white allies determined to push ahead for full political and social equality.

Civil Rights after World War II

The boom in wartime production spurred a mass migration of nearly a million black Southerners to northern cities. Forty-three northern and western cities saw their black population double during the 1940s. Although racial discrimination in housing and employment was by no means absent in northern cities, greater economic opportunities and political freedom continued to attract rural African Americans after the war. With the growth of African American communities in northern cities, black people gained significant influence in local political machines in such cities as New York, Chicago, and Detroit. Within industrial unions such as the United Automobile Workers and the United Steel Workers, white and black workers learned the power of biracial unity in fighting for better wages and working conditions. Harlem congressman Adam Clayton Powell, Jr. captured the new mood of 1945 when he wrote that black people were eager "to make the dream of America become flesh and blood, bread and butter, freedom and equality."

After the war, civil rights issues returned to the national political stage for the first time since Reconstruction. Black voters had already begun to switch their allegiance from the Republicans to the Democrats during the New Deal. A series of symbolic and substantial acts by the Truman administration solidified that shift. In 1946 Truman created a President's Committee on Civil Rights. Its report, *To Secure These Rights* (1947), set out an ambitious program to end racial inequality. Recommendations included a permanent civil rights division in the Justice Department, voting rights protection, antilynching legislation, and a legal attack on segregated housing. Yet, although he publicly endorsed nearly all the proposals of the new committee, Truman introduced no legislation to make them law.

Truman and his advisers walked a political tightrope on civil rights. They understood that black voters in several key northern states would be pivotal in the 1948 election. At the same time, they worried about the loyalty of white southern Democrats adamantly opposed to changing the racial status quo. In July 1948, the president made his boldest move on behalf of civil rights, issuing an executive order barring segregation in the armed forces. When liberals forced the Democratic National Convention to adopt a strong civil rights plank that summer, a group of outraged Southerners walked out and nominated Governor Strom Thurmond of South Carolina for president on a States' Rights ticket. Thurmond carried four southern states in the election. But with the help of over 70 percent of the northern black vote, Truman barely managed to defeat Republican Thomas E. Dewey in November. The deep split over race issues would continue to rack the national Democratic Party for a generation.

Electoral politics was not the only arena for civil rights work. During the war, membership in the National Association for the Advancement of Colored People had mushroomed from 50,000 to 500,000. Working- and middle-class urban black people provided the backbone of this new membership. The NAACP conducted voter registration drives and lobbied against discrimination in housing and employment. Its Legal Defense and Education Fund, vigorously led by special counsel Thurgood Marshall, mounted several significant legal challenges to segregation laws. In *Morgan* v. *Virginia* (1946), the Supreme Court declared that segregation on interstate buses was an undue burden on interstate commerce. Other Supreme Court decisions struck down all-white election primaries, racially restrictive housing covenants, and the exclusion of blacks from law and graduate schools.

The NAACP's legal work demonstrated the potential for using federal courts in attacking segregation. Courts were one place where black people, using the constitutional language of rights, could make forceful arguments that could not be voiced in Congress or at political conventions. But federal enforcement of court decisions was often lacking. In 1947 a group of black and white activists tested compliance with the *Morgan* decision by traveling on a bus through the Upper South. This "Freedom Ride" was cosponsored by the Christian pacifist Fellowship of Reconciliation (FOR) and its recent offshoot, the Congress of Racial Equality (CORE), which was devoted to interracial, nonviolent direct action. In North Carolina, several riders were arrested and sentenced to thirty days on a chain gang for refusing to leave the bus.

Two symbolic "firsts" raised black expectations and inspired pride. In 1947 Jackie Robinson broke the color barrier in major league baseball, winning rookie-of-the-year honors with the Brooklyn Dodgers. Robinson's courage in the face of racial epithets from fans and players paved the way for the black ballplayers who soon followed him to the big leagues. In 1950 United Nations diplomat Ralph Bunche won the Nobel Peace Prize for arranging the 1948 Arab-Israeli truce. Bunche, however, later declined an appointment as undersecretary of state because he did not want to subject his family to the humiliating segregation laws of Washington, D.C.

Cultural change could have political implications as well. In the 1940s, African American musicians created a new form of jazz that revolutionized American music and asserted a militant black consciousness. Although black musicians had pioneered the development of swing and, earlier, jazz, white bandleaders and musicians had reaped most of the recognition and money from the public. Artists such as Charlie Parker, Dizzy Gillespie, Thelonius Monk, Bud Powell, and Miles Davis revolted against the standard big-band format of swing, preferring small groups and competitive jam sessions to express their musical visions. The new music, dubbed "bebop" by critics and fans, demanded a much more sophisticated knowledge of harmony and melody and featured more complex rhythms and extended improvisation than previous jazz styles.

Charlie Parker (alto sax) and Miles Davis (trumpet) with their group in 1947, at the Three Deuces Club in New York City. Parker and Davis were two creative leaders of the "bebop" movement of the 1940s. Working in northern cities, boppers reshaped jazz music and created a distinct language and style that was widely imitated by young people. They challenged older stereotypes of African American musicians by insisting that they be treated as serious artists.

SOURCE: Frank Driggs Collection.

In urban black communities the "boppers" consciously created a music that, unlike swing, white popularizers found difficult to copy or sweeten. These black artists insisted on independence from the white-defined norms of show business. Serious about both their music and the way it was presented, they refused to cater to white expectations of grinning, easygoing black performers. Although most boppers had roots in the South, they preferred the relative freedom they found in northern urban black communities. Many northern black (and white) youths identified with the distinctive music, language, and dress of the boppers. In both their music and their public image, these musicians presented a rebellious alternative to the traditional image of the African American entertainer.

The Segregated South

In the postwar South, still home to over half the nation's 15 million African Americans, the racial situation had changed little since the Supreme Court had sanctioned "separate but equal" segregation in *Plessy* v. *Ferguson* (discussed in Chapter 20). In practice, segregation meant separate but unequal. A tight web of state and local ordinances enforced strict separation of the races in schools, restaurants, hotels, movie theaters, libraries, restrooms, hospitals, even cemeteries, and the facilities for black people were consistently inferior to those for whites. There were no black policemen in the Deep South and only a handful of black lawyers. "A white man," one scholar observed, "can steal from or maltreat a Negro in almost any way without fear of reprisal, because the Negro cannot claim the protection of the police or courts."

In the late 1940s only about 10 percent of eligible southern black people voted, most of these in urban areas. A combination of legal and extralegal measures kept all but the most determined black people disfranchised. Poll taxes, all-white primaries, and discriminatory registration procedures reinforced the belief that voting was "the white man's business." African Americans who insisted on exercising their right to vote, especially in remote rural areas, faced physical violence—beatings, shootings, lynchings. A former president of the Alabama Bar Association expressed a commonly held view when he declared, "No Negro is good enough and no Negro will ever be good enough to participate in making the law under which the white people of Alabama have to live."

Outsiders often noted that despite Jim Crow laws (see Chapter 20) contact between blacks and whites was ironically close. The mass of black Southerners worked on white-owned plantations and in white households. One black preacher neatly summarized the nation's regional differences this way: "In the South, they don't care how close you get as long as you don't get too big; in the North, they don't care how big you get as long as you don't get too close." The South's racial code forced African Americans to accept, at least outwardly, social conventions that reinforced their low standing with whites. A black person did not shake hands with a white person, or enter a white home through the front door, or address a white person except formally.

In these circumstances, survival and self-respect depended to a great degree on patience and stoicism. Black people learned to endure humiliation by keeping their thoughts and feelings hidden from white people.

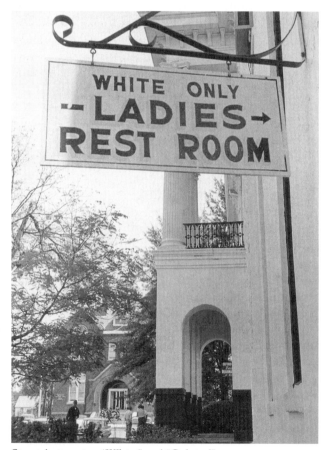 

Signs designating "White" and "Colored" rest rooms, waiting rooms, entrances, benches, and even water fountains were a common sight in the segregated South. They were a constant reminder that legal separation of the races in public spaces was the law of the land.

SOURCE: (a) Photo by Dan McCoy. Black Star; (b) Segregation trailways. CORBIS.

Paul Laurence Dunbar, an African American poet, captured this bitter truth in his turn-of-the-century poem "We Wear the Mask."

We wear the mask that grins and lies,
It hides our cheeks and shades our eyes,
This debt we pay to human guile;
With torn and bleeding hearts we smile,
And mouth with myriad subtleties.
Why should the world be over-wise,
In counting all our tears and sighs?
Nay, let them only see us, while
We wear the mask.

Brown v. Board of Education

Since the late 1930s, the NAACP had chipped away at the legal foundations of segregation. Rather than making a frontal assault on the *Plessy* separate-but-equal rule, civil rights attorneys launched a series of suits seeking complete equality in segregated facilities. The aim of this strategy was to make segregation so prohibitively expensive that the South would be forced to dismantle it. In the 1939 case *Missouri v. ex.rel. Gaines*, the Supreme Court ruled that the University of Missouri law school must either admit African Americans or build another, fully equal law school for them. NAACP lawyers pushed their arguments further, asserting that equality could not be measured simply by money or physical plant. In *McLaurin v. Oklahoma State Regents* (1950), the Court agreed with Thurgood Marshall's argument that regulations forcing a black law student to sit, eat, and study in areas apart from white students inevitably created a "badge of inferiority."

By 1951, Marshall had begun coordinating the NAACP's legal resources for a direct attack on the separate-but-equal doctrine. The goal was to overturn *Plessy* and the constitutionality of segregation itself. For a test case, Marshall combined five lawsuits challenging segregation in public schools. One of these suits argued the case of Oliver Brown of Topeka, Kansas, who sought to overturn a state law permitting cities to maintain segregated schools. The law forced Brown's eight-year-old daughter Linda to travel by bus to a black school even though she lived only three blocks from an all-white elementary school. The Supreme Court heard initial arguments on the cases, grouped together as *Brown v. Board of Education*, in December 1952.

In his argument before the Court, Thurgood Marshall tried to establish that separate facilities, by definition, denied black people their full rights as American citizens. Marshall used sociological and psychological evidence that went beyond standard legal arguments. For example, he cited the research of African American psychologist Kenneth B. Clark, who had studied the self-esteem of black children in New York City and in segregated schools in the South. Using black and white dolls and asking the children which they preferred, Clark illustrated how black children educated in segregated schools developed a negative self-image. When Chief Justice Fred Vinson died suddenly in 1953, President Dwight Eisenhower appointed California Governor Earl Warren to fill the post. After hearing further arguments, the Court remained divided on the issue of overturning *Plessy*. Warren, eager for a unanimous decision, patiently worked at convincing two holdouts. Using his political skills to persuade and achieve compromise, Warren urged his colleagues to affirm a simple principle as the basis for the decision.

On May 17, 1954, Warren read the Court's unanimous decision aloud. "Does segregation of children in public schools solely on the basis of race . . . deprive the children of the minority group of equal educational opportunities?" The chief justice paused. "We believe that it does." Warren made a point of citing several of the psychological studies of segregation's effects. He ended by directly addressing the constitutional issue. Segregation deprived the plaintiffs of the equal protection of the laws guaranteed by the Fourteenth Amendment. "We conclude that in the field of public education the doctrine of 'separate but equal' has no place. Separate educational facilities are inherently unequal." "Any language in *Plessy v. Ferguson* contrary to this finding is rejected."

African Americans and their liberal allies around the country hailed the decision and the legal genius of Thurgood Marshall. Marshall himself predicted that all segregated schools would be abolished within five years. Black newspapers were full of stories on the imminent dismantling of segregation. The *Chicago Defender* called the decision "a second emancipation proclamation." But the issue of enforcement soon dampened this enthusiasm. To gain a unanimous decision, Warren had had to agree to let the Court delay for one year its ruling on how to implement desegregation. This second *Brown* ruling, handed down in May 1955, assigned responsibility for desegregation plans to local school boards. The Court left it to federal district judges to monitor compliance, requiring only that desegregation proceed "with all deliberate speed." Thus, although the Court had made a momentous and clear constitutional ruling, the need for compromise dictated gradual enforcement by unspecified means.

Crisis in Little Rock

Resistance to *Brown* took many forms. Most affected states passed laws transferring authority for pupil assignment to local school boards. This prevented the NAACP from bringing statewide suits against segregated school

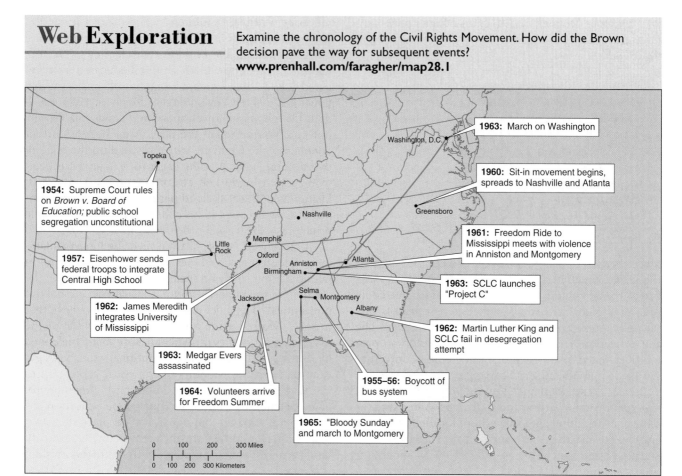

Web Exploration

Examine the chronology of the Civil Rights Movement. How did the Brown decision pave the way for subsequent events?
www.prenhall.com/faragher/map28.1

1954: Supreme Court rules on *Brown v. Board of Education;* public school segregation unconstitutional

1957: Eisenhower sends federal troops to integrate Central High School

1962: James Meredith integrates University of Mississippi

1963: Medgar Evers assassinated

1964: Volunteers arrive for Freedom Summer

1965: "Bloody Sunday" and march to Montgomery

1955–56: Boycott of bus system

1962: Martin Luther King and SCLC fail in desegregation attempt

1963: SCLC launches "Project C"

1961: Freedom Ride to Mississippi meets with violence in Anniston and Montgomery

1960: Sit-in movement begins, spreads to Nashville and Atlanta

1963: March on Washington

Map of the Civil Rights Movement Key battlegrounds in the struggle for racial justice in communities across the South.

systems. Counties and towns created layers of administrative delays designed to stop implementation of *Brown.* Some school boards transferred public school property to new, all-white private "academies." State legislatures in Virginia, Alabama, Mississippi, and Georgia, resurrecting pre–Civil War doctrines, passed resolutions declaring their right to "interpose" themselves between the people and the federal government and to "nullify" federal laws. In 1956, 101 congressmen from the former Confederate states signed the Southern Manifesto, urging their states to refuse compliance with desegregation. President Dwight Eisenhower declined to publicly endorse *Brown,* contributing to the spirit of southern resistance. "I don't believe you can change the hearts of men with laws or decisions," he said. Privately, the president opposed the *Brown* decision, and he later called his appointment of Earl Warren as chief justice "the biggest damn fool mistake I ever made."

In Little Rock, Arkansas, the tense controversy over school integration became a test case of state versus federal power. A federal court ordered public schools to begin desegregation in September 1957, and the local school board made plans to comply. But Governor Orval Faubus, facing a tough reelection fight, decided to make a campaign issue out of defying the court order. He dispatched Arkansas National Guard troops to Central High School to prevent nine black students from entering. For three weeks, armed troops stood guard at the school. Screaming crowds, encouraged by Faubus, menaced the black students, beat up two black reporters, and chanted "Two, four, six, eight, we ain't going to integrate." Moderate whites, such as *Arkansas Gazette* editor Harry Ashmore, opposed Faubus, fearing that his controversial tactics would make it harder to attract new businesses and investment capital to the city.

At first, President Eisenhower tried to intervene quietly, gaining Faubus's assurance that he would protect the nine black children. But when Faubus suddenly withdrew his troops, leaving the black students at the mercy of the white mob, Eisenhower had to move. On September 24 he placed the Arkansas National Guard under federal control and ordered a thousand paratroopers of the 101st Airborne Division to Little Rock. The nine black students arrived in a U.S. Army car.

With fixed bayonets, the soldiers protected the students as they finally integrated Central High School in Little Rock. Eisenhower, the veteran military commander, justified his actions on the basis of upholding federal authority and enforcing the law. He also defended his intervention as crucial to national prestige abroad, noting the propaganda victory Faubus had handed to the Soviet bloc. "Our enemies," the President argued, "are gloating over this incident and using it everywhere to misrepresent our whole nation." But he made no endorsement of desegregation. But as the first president since Reconstruction to use armed federal troops in support of black rights, Eisenhower demonstrated that the federal government could, indeed, protect civil rights. Unfazed, Governor Faubus kept Little Rock high schools closed during the 1958–59 academic year to prevent what he called "violence and disorder."

NO EASY ROAD TO FREEDOM, 1957–62

The legal breakthrough represented by the *Brown* decision heartened opponents of segregation everywhere. Most important, *Brown* demonstrated the potential for using the federal court system as a weapon against discrimination and as a means of protecting the full rights of citizenship. Yet the widespread opposition to *Brown* and its implications showed the limits of a strictly legal strategy. In Little Rock, the ugly face of white racism received wide coverage in the mass media and quickly sobered the more optimistic champions of integration. However welcome Eisenhower's intervention, his reluctance to endorse desegregation suggested that civil rights activists could still not rely on federal help. As the Montgomery bus boycott had proved, black communities would have to help themselves first.

Martin Luther King and the SCLC

When it ended with the Supreme Court decision in November 1956, the 381-day Montgomery bus boycott had made Martin Luther King a prominent national figure. In January 1957 *Time* magazine put King on its cover. The *New York Times Magazine* published a detailed history of the bus boycott, focusing on King's role. NBC's *Meet the Press* invited him to become only the second African American ever to appear on that program. Speaking invitations poured in from universities and organizations around the country. King himself was an extraordinary and complex man. Born in 1929 in Atlanta, he enjoyed a middle-class upbringing as the son of a prominent Baptist minister. After graduating from prestigious Morehouse College, an all-black school, King earned a divinity degree at Crozer Theological

Seminary in Pennsylvania and a Ph.D. in theology from Boston University.

In graduate school King explored a very diverse range of philosophers and political thinkers—the ancient Greeks, French Enlightenment thinkers, the German idealists, and Karl Marx. He was drawn to the social Christianity of American theologian Walter Rauschenbusch, who insisted on connecting religious faith with struggles for social justice. Above all, King admired Mohandas Gandhi, a lawyer turned ascetic who had led a successful nonviolent resistance movement against British colonial rule in India. Gandhi taught his followers to confront authorities with a readiness to suffer, in order to expose injustice and force those in power to end it. This tactic of nonviolent civil disobedience required discipline and sacrifice from its followers, who were sometimes called upon to lay their lives on the line against armed police and military forces. Crucially, King believed Gandhian nonviolence to be not merely a moral imperative but a potent political strategy that had "muzzled the guns of the British empire in India and freed more than three hundred and fifty million people from colonialism."

Like Gandhi and many of the Christian saints he had studied, King grappled with inner doubts about his faith and true mission. Since childhood he had suffered from extreme mood swings. He was charming and popular, but also self-restrained and dignified. Even after becoming pastor of Montgomery's Dexter Avenue Baptist Church in 1954, King often agonized over his inner emotions, including his religious faith. The rigorous discipline required by the philosophy of nonviolence helped King to master his inner turmoil. A unique blend of traditional African American folk preacher and erudite intellectual, King used his passion and intelligence to help transform a community's pain into a powerful moral force for change.

In a December 1956 address celebrating the Montgomery bus boycott victory, King laid out six key lessons from the year-long struggle: "(1) We have discovered that we can stick together for a common cause; (2) our leaders do not have to sell out; (3) threats and violence do not necessarily intimidate those who are sufficiently aroused and nonviolent; (4) our church is becoming militant, stressing a social gospel as well as a gospel of personal salvation; (5) we have gained a new sense of dignity and destiny; (6) we have discovered a new and powerful weapon—nonviolent resistance." The influence of two visiting northern pacifists, Bayard Rustin of the War Resisters' League and Glenn Smiley of the Fellowship of Reconciliation, had helped deepen King's own commitment to the Gandhian philosophy.

King recognized the need to exploit the momentum of the Montgomery movement. In early 1957, with the help of Rustin and other aides, he brought together nearly 100 black ministers to found the Southern Christian Leadership Conference (SCLC). The clergymen elected King president and his close friend, the Reverend Ralph Abernathy, treasurer. The SCLC called upon black people "to understand that nonviolence is not a symbol of weakness or cowardice, but as Jesus demonstrated, nonviolent resistance transforms weakness into strength and breeds courage in the face of danger."

But King and other black leaders also understood that the white South was no monolith. They believed white Southerners could be divided roughly into three groups: a tiny minority—often with legal training, social connections, and money—that might be counted on to help overthrow segregation; extreme segregationists who were willing and able to use violence and terror in defense of white supremacy; and a broad middle group who favored and benefited from segregation, but who were unwilling to take personal risks to prevent its destruction. In the battles to come, civil rights leaders made this nuanced view of the white South a central part of their larger political strategy. Extreme segregationists could be counted on to overreact, often violently, to civil rights campaigns, and thereby help to win sympathy and support for the cause. White moderates, especially in the business community, might be reluctant to initiate change, but they would try to distance themselves from the desperate violence of extremists and present themselves as pragmatic supporters of order and peace.

Previously, the struggle for racial equality had been dominated by a northern elite focusing on legal action. The SCLC now envisioned the southern black church, preaching massive nonviolent protest, as leading the fight. The SCLC gained support among black ministers, and King vigorously spread his message in speeches and writings. But the organization failed to generate the kind of mass, direct-action movement that had made history in Montgomery. Instead, the next great spark to light the fire of protest came from what seemed at the time a most unlikely source: black college students.

Sit-Ins: Greensboro, Nashville, Atlanta

On Monday, February 1, 1960, four black freshmen from North Carolina Agricultural and Technical College in Greensboro sat down at the whites-only lunch counter in Woolworth's. They politely ordered coffee and doughnuts. As the students had anticipated while planning the action in their dorm rooms, they were refused service. Although they could buy pencils or toothpaste, black people were not allowed to eat in Woolworth's. But the four students stayed at the counter until closing time. Word of their actions spread quickly, and the next day they returned with over two dozen supporters. On the third day, students occupied sixty-three of the sixty-six lunch counter seats. By Thursday they had been joined by three white students from the Women's College of the University of North Carolina in Greensboro. Scores of sympathizers overflowed Woolworth's and started a sit-in down the street in S. H. Kress. On Friday hundreds of black students and a few whites jammed the lunch counters.

The week's events made Greensboro national news. City officials, looking to end the protest, offered to negotiate in exchange for an end to demonstrations. But white business leaders and politicians proved unwilling to change the racial status quo, and the sit-ins resumed on April 1. In response to the April 21 arrest of forty-five students for trespassing, an outraged African American community organized an economic boycott of targeted stores. With the boycott cutting deeply into merchants' profits, Greensboro's leaders reluctantly gave in. On July 25, 1960, the first African American ate a meal at Woolworth's.

The Greensboro sit-in sent a shock wave throughout the South. During the next eighteen months 70,000 people—most of them black students, a few of them white allies—participated in sit-ins against segregation in dozens of communities. More than 3,000 were arrested. African Americans had discovered a new form of direct-action protest, dignified and powerful, which white people could not ignore. The sit-in movement also transformed participants' self-image, empowering them psychologically and emotionally. Franklin McCain, one of the original four Greensboro students, later recalled a great feeling of soul cleansing: "I probably felt better on that day than I've ever felt in my life. Seems like a lot of feelings of guilt or what-have-you suddenly left me, and I felt as though I had gained my manhood, so to speak, and not only gained it, but had developed quite a lot of respect for it."

In Nashville, Reverend James Lawson, a northern-born black minister, had led workshops in nonviolent resistance since 1958. Lawson had served a jail term as a conscientious objector during the Korean War and had become active in the Fellowship of Reconciliation. He had also spent three years as a missionary in India, where he had learned close-up the Gandhian methods of promoting social change. Lawson gathered around him a group of deeply committed black students from Fisk, Vanderbilt, and other Nashville colleges. Young activists there talked not only of ending segregation but also of creating a "Beloved Community" based on Christian idealism and Gandhian principles.

In the spring of 1960 more than 150 Nashville students were arrested in disciplined sit-ins aimed at desegregating downtown lunch counters. Lawson, who preached the need for sacrifice in the cause of justice, found himself expelled from the divinity school

The second day of the sit-in at the Greensboro, North Carolina, Woolworth lunch counter, February 2, 1960. From left: Joseph McNeil, Franklin McCain, Billy Smith, and Clarence Henderson. The Greensboro protest sparked a wave of sit-ins across the South, mostly by college students, demanding an end to segregation in restaurants and other public places.

SOURCE: Photo by John G. Moebes. Greensboro News & Record.

at Vanderbilt. Lawson and other veterans of the Nashville sit-ins, such as John Lewis, Diane Nash, and Marion Barry, would go on to play influential roles in the national civil rights movement. The Nashville group developed rules of conduct that became a model for protesters elsewhere: "Don't strike back or curse if abused. . . . Show yourself courteous and friendly at all times. . . . Report all serious incidents to your leader in a polite manner. Remember love and nonviolence."

The most ambitious sit-in campaign developed in Atlanta, the South's largest and richest city, home to the region's most powerful and prestigious black community. Students from Morehouse, Spelman, and the other all-black schools that made up Atlanta University took the lead. On March 15, 1960, 200 young black people staged a well-coordinated sit-in at restaurants in City Hall, the State Capitol, and other government offices. Police arrested and jailed seventy-six demonstrators that day, but the experience only strengthened the activists' resolve. Led by Julian Bond and Lonnie King,

two Morehouse undergraduates, the students formed the Committee on an Appeal for Human Rights. In full-page advertisements in Atlanta newspapers, the students demanded an end to segregation and also demanded jobs, equal housing and education, and better health services for the city's black people. We will "use every legal and nonviolent means at our disposal to secure full citizenship rights as members of this great democracy of ours," the students promised. Over the summer they planned a fall campaign of large-scale sit-ins at major Atlanta department stores and a boycott of downtown merchants. Their slogan became "Close out your charge account with segregation, open up your account with freedom." In October 1960 Martin Luther King and thirty-six students were arrested when they sat down in the all-white Magnolia Room restaurant in Rich's Department Store. As in Greensboro and Montgomery, the larger African American community in Atlanta supported the continuing sit-ins, picketing, and boycotts. The campaign stretched on for months, and hundreds of protesters went to jail. The city's business leaders finally relented in September 1961, and desegregation came to Atlanta.

SNCC and the "Beloved Community"

The sit-in movement pumped new energy into the civil rights cause, creating a new generation of activists and leaders. Mass arrests, beatings, and vilification in the southern white press only strengthened the resolve of those in the movement. Students also had to deal with the fears of their families, many of whom had made great sacrifices to send them off to college. John Lewis, a seminary student in Nashville, remembered his mother in rural Alabama pleading with him to "get out of that mess, before you get hurt." Lewis wrote to his parents that he acted out of his Christian conscience: "My soul will not be satisfied until freedom, justice, and fair play become a reality for all people."

The new student militancy also caused discord within black communities. The authority of local African American elites had traditionally depended on their influence and cooperation with the white establishment. Black lawyers, schoolteachers, principals, and businessmen had to maintain regular and cordial relations with white judges, school boards, and politicians. Student calls for freedom disturbed many community leaders worried about upsetting traditional patronage networks. Some black college presidents, pressured by trustees and state legislators, sought to moderate or stop the movement altogether. The president of Southern University in Baton Rouge, the largest black college in the nation, suspended eighteen sit-in leaders in 1960 and forced the entire student body of 5,000 to reapply to the college so that agitators could be screened out.

An April 1960 conference of 120 black student activists in Raleigh, North Carolina, underlined the generational and radical aspects of the new movement. The meeting had been called by Ella Baker, executive director of the SCLC, to help the students assess their experiences and plan future actions. Fifty-five at the time, Baker had for years played an important behind-the-scenes role in the civil rights cause, serving as a community organizer and field secretary for the NAACP before heading the staff of the SCLC. She understood the psychological importance of the students' remaining independent of adult control. She counseled them to resist affiliating with any of the national civil rights organizations. Baker also encouraged the trend toward group-centered leadership among the students. She later commented that social movements needed "the development of people who are interested not in being leaders as much as in developing leadership among other people."

With Baker's encouragement, the conference voted to establish a new group, the Student Nonviolent Coordinating Committee (SNCC). The strong influence of the Nashville students, led by James Lawson, could be found in the SNCC statement of purpose:

> We affirm the philosophical or religious ideal of nonviolence as the foundation of our purpose, the presupposition of our faith, and the manner of our action. Nonviolence as it grows from Judaic-Christian tradition seeks a social order of justice permeated by love. Integration of human endeavor represents the crucial first step towards such a society.
>
> By appealing to conscience and standing on the moral nature of human existence, nonviolence nurtures the atmosphere in which reconciliation and justice become actual possibilities.

In the fall of 1960 SNCC established an organizational structure, a set of principles, and a new style of civil rights protest. The emphasis was on fighting segregation through direct confrontation, mass action, and civil disobedience. SNCC fieldworkers initiated and supported local, community-based activity. Three-quarters of the first fieldworkers were less than twenty-two years old. Leadership was vested in a nonhierarchical Coordinating Committee, but local groups were free to determine their own direction. SNCC people distrusted bureaucracy and structure; they stressed spontaneity and improvisation. Bob Moses, a former Harvard graduate student and New York City schoolteacher, best expressed the freewheeling SNCC attitude: "Go where the spirit say go and do what the spirit say do." A small but dedicated group of young white southerners, inspired by SNCC's idealism and activism, joined the cause. Groups such as the Southern Student Organizing Committee, led by Sam Shirah and Sue Thrasher, as well as SNCC activists like Bob Zellner, looked for ways to extend SNCC's radicalism to white communities. Over the next few years SNCC was at the forefront of nearly every major civil rights battle.

The Election of 1960 and Civil Rights

The issue of race relations was kept from center stage during the very close presidential campaign of 1960. As vice president, Richard Nixon had been a leading Republican voice for stronger civil rights legislation. In contrast, Democratic nominee Senator John F. Kennedy had played virtually no role in the congressional battles over civil rights during the 1950s. But during the campaign, their roles reversed. Kennedy praised the sit-in movement as part of a revival of national reform spirit. He declared, "It is in the American tradition to stand up

A Freedom Riders' bus burns after being firebombed in Anniston, Alabama, May 14, 1961. After setting the bus afire, whites attacked the passengers fleeing the smoke and flames. Violent scenes like this one received extensive publicity in the mass media and helped compel the Justice Department to enforce court rulings banning segregation on interstate bus lines.

SOURCE: UPI/CORBIS (U12 79611 < 25).

worry about alienating conservative southern Democrats who chaired key congressional committees. Passage of major civil rights legislation would be virtually impossible. The new president told leaders such as Roy Wilkins of the NAACP that a strategy of "minimum legislation, maximum executive action" offered the best road to change. The president did appoint some forty African Americans to high federal positions, including Thurgood Marshall to the federal appellate court. He established a Committee on Equal Employment Opportunity, chaired by Vice President Lyndon B. Johnson, to fight discrimination in the federal civil service and in corporations that received government contracts.

Most significantly, the Kennedy administration sought to invigorate the Civil Rights Division of the Justice Department. That division had been created by the Civil Rights Act of 1957, which authorized the attorney general to seek court injunctions to protect people denied their right to vote. But the Eisenhower administration had made little use of this new power. Robert Kennedy, the new attorney general, began assembling a staff of brilliant and committed attorneys, headed by Washington lawyer Burke Marshall. Kennedy encouraged them to get out of Washington and get into the field wherever racial troubles arose. In early 1961, when Louisiana school officials balked at a school desegregation order, Robert Kennedy warned them that he would ask the federal court to hold them in contempt. When Burke Marshall started court proceedings, the state officials gave in. But the new, more aggressive mood at Justice could not solve the central political dilemma: how to move forward on civil rights without alienating southern Democrats. Pressure from the newly energized southern civil rights movement soon revealed the true difficulty of that problem. The movement would also provoke murderous outrage from white extremists determined to maintain the racial status quo.

for one's rights—even if the new way is to sit down." While the Republican platform contained a strong civil rights plank, Nixon, eager to court white southern voters, minimized his own identification with the movement. In October, when Martin Luther King, Jr. was jailed after leading a demonstration in Atlanta, Kennedy telephoned King's wife, Coretta Scott King, to reassure her and express his personal support. Kennedy's brother Robert telephoned the judge in the case and angrily warned him that he had violated King's civil rights and endangered the national Democratic ticket. The judge released King soon afterward.

News of this intervention did not gain wide attention in the white South, much to the relief of the Kennedys. The race was tight, and they knew they could not afford to alienate traditional white southern Democrats. But the campaign effectively played up the story among black voters all over the country. Kennedy won 70 percent of the black vote, which helped put him over the top in such critical states as Illinois, Texas, Michigan, and Pennsylvania and secure his narrow victory over Nixon. Many civil rights activists optimistically looked forward to a new president who would have to acknowledge his political debt to the black vote.

But the very closeness of his victory constrained Kennedy on the race question. Democrats had lost ground in the House and Senate, and Kennedy had to

Freedom Rides

In the spring of 1961 James Farmer, national director of CORE, announced plans for an interracial Freedom Ride through the South. The goal was to test compliance with court orders banning segregation in interstate travel and terminal accommodations. CORE had just recently made Farmer its leader in an effort to revitalize the organization. One of the founders of CORE in 1942, Farmer had worked for various pacifist and socialist groups and served as program director for the NAACP. He designed the Freedom Ride to induce a crisis, in the spirit of the sit-ins. "Our intention," Farmer declared, "was to provoke the southern authorities into arresting us and thereby prod the Justice Department into enforcing the law of the land." CORE received financial and tactical support from the SCLC and several NAACP branches. It also informed the Justice Department and the Federal Bureau of Investigation of its plans, but received no reply.

On May 4 seven blacks and six whites split into two interracial groups and left Washington on public buses bound for Alabama and Mississippi. At first the two buses encountered only isolated harassment and violence as they headed south. But when one bus entered Anniston, Alabama, on May 14, an angry mob surrounded it, smashing windows and slashing tires. Six miles out of town, the tires went flat. A firebomb tossed through a window forced the passengers out. The mob then beat the Freedom Riders with blackjacks, iron bars, and clubs, and the bus burst into flames. A caravan of cars organized by the Birmingham office of the SCLC rescued the wounded. Another mob attacked the second bus in Anniston, leaving one Freedom Rider close to death and permanently brain-damaged.

The violence escalated. In Birmingham, a mob of forty whites waited on the loading platform and attacked the bus that managed to get out of Anniston. Although police had been warned to expect trouble, they did nothing to stop the mob from beating the Freedom Riders with pipes and fists, nor did they make any arrests. FBI agents observed and took notes but did nothing. The remaining Freedom Riders decided to travel as a single group on the next lap, from Birmingham to Montgomery, but no bus would take them. Stranded and frightened, they reluctantly boarded a special flight to New Orleans arranged by the Justice Department. On May 17 the CORE-sponsored Freedom Ride disbanded.

But that was not the end of the Freedom Rides. SNCC leaders in Atlanta and Nashville assembled a fresh group of volunteers to continue the trip. On May 20, twenty-one Freedom Riders left Birmingham for Montgomery. The bus station in the Alabama capital was eerily quiet and deserted as they pulled in. But when the passengers left the bus a mob of several hundred whites rushed them, yelling "Get those niggers!" and clubbing people to the ground. James Zwerg, a white Freedom Rider from the University of Wisconsin, had his spinal cord severed. John Lewis, veteran of the

Nashville sit-in movement, suffered a brain concussion. As he lay in a pool of blood, a policeman handed him a state court injunction forbidding interracial travel in Alabama. The mob indiscriminately beat journalists and clubbed John Siegenthaler, a Justice Department attorney sent to observe the scene. It took police more than an hour to halt the rioting. Montgomery's police commissioner later said, "We have no intention of standing guard for a bunch of troublemakers coming into our city."

The mob violence and the indifference of Alabama officials made the Freedom Ride page-one news around the country and throughout the world. Newspapers in Europe, Africa, and Asia denounced the hypocrisy of the federal government. The Kennedy administration, preparing for the president's first summit meeting with Soviet premier Nikita Khrushchev, saw the situation as a threat to its international prestige. On May 21, an angry mob threatened to invade a support rally at Montgomery's First Baptist Church. A hastily assembled group of 400 U.S. marshals, sent by Robert Kennedy, barely managed to keep the peace. The attorney general called for a cooling-off period, but Martin Luther King, Jr., James Farmer, and the SNCC leaders announced that the Freedom Ride would continue. When Robert Kennedy warned that the racial turmoil would embarrass the president in his meeting with Khrushchev, Ralph Abernathy of the SCLC replied, "Doesn't the attorney general know that we've been embarrassed all our lives?"

A bandaged but spirited group of twenty-seven Freedom Riders prepared to leave Montgomery for Jackson, Mississippi, on May 24. To avoid further violence Robert Kennedy arranged a compromise through Mississippi senator James Eastland. In exchange for a guarantee of safe passage through Mississippi, the federal government promised not to interfere with the arrest of the Freedom Riders in Jackson. This Freedom Ride and several that followed thus escaped violence. But more than 300 people were arrested that summer in Jackson on charges of traveling "for the avowed purpose of inflaming public opinion." Sticking to a policy of "jail, no bail," Freedom Riders clogged the prison, where they endured beatings and intimidation by prison guards that went largely unreported in the press. Their jail experiences turned most of them into committed core leaders of the student movement.

The Justice Department eventually petitioned the Interstate Commerce Commission to issue clear rules prohibiting segregation on interstate carriers. At the end of 1962, CORE proclaimed victory in the battle against Jim Crow interstate travel. By creating a crisis, the Freedom Rides had forced the Kennedy administration to act. But they also revealed the unwillingness of the federal government to fully enforce the law of the land. The Freedom Rides exposed the ugly face of southern racism to the world. At the same time, they reinforced white resistance to desegregation. The jailings and brutality experienced by Freedom Riders made clear to the civil rights community the limits of moral suasion alone for effecting change.

The Albany Movement: The Limits of Protest

Where the federal government chose not to enforce the constitutional rights of black people, segregationist forces tenaciously held their ground, especially in the more remote areas of the Deep South. In Albany, a small city in southwest Georgia, activists from SNCC, the NAACP, and other local groups formed a coalition known as the Albany movement. Starting in October 1961 and continuing for more than a year, thousands of Albany's black citizens marched, sat in, and boycotted as part of a citywide campaign to integrate public facilities and win voting rights. More than a thousand people spent time in jail. In December, the arrival of Martin Luther King, Jr. and the SCLC transformed Albany into a national symbol of the struggle.

But the gains at Albany proved minimal. Infighting among the various civil rights organizations hurt the cause. Local SNCC workers opposed the more cautious approach of NAACP officials, even though the more established organization paid many of the campaign's expenses. The arrival of King guaranteed national news coverage, but local activists worried that his presence might undermine the community focus and their own influence. Most important, Albany police chief Laurie Pritchett shrewdly deprived the movement of the kind of national sympathy won by the Freedom Riders. Pritchett filled the jails with black demonstrators, kept their mistreatment to a minimum, and prevented white mobs from running wild. "We met 'nonviolence' with 'nonviolence,'" he boasted.

King himself was twice arrested in the summer of 1962, but Albany officials quickly freed him to avoid negative publicity. The Kennedy administration kept clear of the developments in Albany, hoping to help the gubernatorial campaign of "moderate" Democrat Carl Sanders. By late 1962 the Albany movement had collapsed, and Pritchett proudly declared the city "as segregated as ever." One activist summed up the losing campaign: "We were naive enough to think we could fill up the jails. Pritchett was hep to the fact that we couldn't. We ran out of people before he ran out of jails." Albany showed that mass protest without violent white reaction and direct federal intervention could not end Jim Crow.

The successful battle to integrate the University of Mississippi in 1962 contrasted with the failure at Albany and reinforced the importance of federal intervention

for guaranteeing civil rights to African Americans. In the fall of 1962 James Meredith, an air force veteran and a student at all-black Jackson State College, tried "to register as the first black student at the university. Governor Ross Barnett defied a federal court order and personally blocked Meredith's path at the admissions office. When Barnett refused to assure Robert Kennedy that Meredith would be protected, the attorney general dispatched 500 federal marshals to the campus. Over the radio, Barnett encouraged resistance to the "oppressive power of the United States," and an angry mob of several thousand whites, many of them armed, laid siege to the campus on September 30. A night of violence left 2 people dead and 160 marshals wounded, 28 from gunfire. President Kennedy ordered 5,000 army troops onto the campus to stop the riot. A federal guard remained to protect Meredith, who graduated the following summer.

THE MOVEMENT AT HIGH TIDE, 1963–65

The tumultuous events of 1960–62 convinced civil rights strategists that segregation could not be dismantled merely through orderly protest and moral persuasion. Only comprehensive civil rights legislation, backed by the power of the federal government, could guarantee full citizenship rights for African Americans. To build the national consensus needed for new laws, civil rights activists looked for ways to gain broader support for their cause. By 1963, their sense of urgency had led them to plan dramatic confrontations that would expose the violence and terror routinely faced by southern blacks. With the whole country—indeed, the whole world—watching, the movement reached the peak of its political and moral power.

Birmingham

At the end of 1962, Martin Luther King, Jr. and his SCLC allies decided to launch a new campaign against segregation in Birmingham, Alabama. After the failure in Albany, King and his aides looked for a way to shore up his leadership and inject new momentum into the freedom struggle. They needed a major victory. Birmingham was the most segregated big city in America, and it had a deep history of racial violence. African Americans endured total segregation in schools, restaurants, city parks, and department store dressing rooms. Although black people constituted more than 40 percent of the city's population, fewer than 10,000 of Birmingham's 80,000 registered voters were black. The city's prosperous steel industry relegated black workers to menial jobs.

Police dogs attacked a seventeen-year-old civil rights demonstrator for defying an antiparade ordinance in Birmingham, Alabama, May 3, 1963. He was part of the "children's crusade" organized by SCLC in its campaign to fill the city jails with protesters. More than 900 Birmingham schoolchildren went to jail that day.

SOURCE: Photo by Bill Hudson. AP/Wide World Photos.

Working closely with local civil rights groups led by the longtime Birmingham activist Reverend Fred Shuttlesworth, the SCLC carefully planned its campaign. The strategy was to fill the city jails with protesters, boycott downtown department stores, and enrage Public Safety Commissioner Eugene "Bull" Connor. In April, King arrived with a manifesto demanding an end to racist hiring practices and segregated public accommodations and the creation of a biracial committee to oversee desegregation. "Here in Birmingham," King told reporters, "we have reached the point of no return." Connor's police began jailing hundreds of demonstrators, including King himself, who defied a state court injunction against further protests.

Held in solitary confinement for several days, King managed to write a response to a group of Birmingham clergy who had deplored the protests. King's *Letter from Birmingham Jail* was soon widely reprinted and circulated as a pamphlet. It set out the key moral issues at stake, and scoffed at those who claimed the campaign was illegal and ill timed. King wrote:

> We know through painful experience that freedom is never voluntarily given by the oppressor; it must be demanded by the oppressed. Frankly, I have never yet engaged in a direct-action campaign that was "well timed" in the view of those who have not suffered unduly from the disease of segregation. For years now I have heard the word "Wait!" It rings in the ear of every Negro with a piercing familiarity. This "Wait" has almost always meant "Never." We must come to see, with one of our distinguished jurists, that "justice too long delayed is justice denied."

After King's release on bail, the campaign intensified. The SCLC kept up the pressure by recruiting thousands of Birmingham's young students for a "children's crusade." In early May, Bull Connor's forces began using high-powered water cannons, billy clubs, and snarling police dogs to break up demonstrations. Millions of Americans reacted with horror to the violent scenes from Birmingham shown on national television. Many younger black people, especially from the city's poor and working-class districts, began to fight back, hurling bottles and bricks at police. On May 10, mediators from the Justice Department negotiated an uneasy truce. The SCLC agreed to an immediate end to the protests. In exchange, businesses would desegregate and begin hiring African Americans over the next three months, and a biracial city committee would oversee desegregation of public facilities.

King claimed the events in Birmingham represented "the most magnificent victory for justice we've ever seen in the Deep South." But whites such as Bull Connor and Governor George Wallace denounced the agreement. A few days after the announcement, more than a thousand robed Ku Klux Klansmen burned a cross in a park on the outskirts of Birmingham. When bombs rocked SCLC headquarters and the home of King's brother, a Birmingham minister, enraged blacks took to the streets and pelted police and firefighters with stones and bottles. President Kennedy ordered 3,000 army troops into the city and prepared to nationalize the Alabama National Guard. The violence receded, and white business people and politicians began to carry out the agreed-upon pact. But in September a bomb killed four black girls in a Birmingham Baptist church, reminding the city and the world that racial harmony was still a long way off.

The Birmingham campaign and the other protests it sparked over the next seven months engaged more than 100,000 people and led to nearly 15,000 arrests. The civil rights community now drew support from millions of Americans, black and white, who were inspired by the protesters and repelled by the face of southern bigotry. At the same time, Birmingham changed the nature of black protest. The black unemployed and working poor who joined in the struggle brought a different perspective from that of the students, professionals, and members of the religious middle class who had dominated the movement before Birmingham. They cared less about the philosophy of nonviolence and more about immediate gains in employment and housing and an end to police brutality. The urgent cries for "Freedom now!" were more than simply a demand to end legal segregation, and they were a measure as well of how far the movement had traveled in the seven years since the end of the Montgomery bus boycott.

JFK and the March on Washington

The growth of black activism and white support convinced President Kennedy the moment had come to press for sweeping civil rights legislation. Continuing white resistance in the South also made clearer than ever the need for federal action. In June 1963, Alabama governor George Wallace threatened to personally block the admission of two black students to the state university. Only the deployment of National Guard troops, placed under federal control by the president, ensured the students' safety and their peaceful admission into the University of Alabama.

It was a defining moment for Kennedy. Even more than for Eisenhower at Little Rock, the realities of international cold war politics pushed Kennedy toward support for civil rights. On June 11 the president went on national television and offered his personal endorsement of the civil rights activism: "Today we are committed to a worldwide struggle to promote and protect the rights of all who wish to be free. And when Americans are sent to Vietnam or West Berlin, we do not ask for whites only . . . Are we to say to the rest of the world, and much more importantly, to each other, that this is a land of the free except for Negroes?" Reviewing the racial situation, Kennedy told his audience that "We face . . . a moral crisis as a country and a people. It cannot be met by repressive police action. It cannot be left to increased demonstrations in the streets. It cannot be quieted by token moves or talk. It is a time to act in the Congress, in your state and local legislative body, and, above all, in all our daily lives." The next week Kennedy asked Congress for a broad law that would ensure voting rights, outlaw segregation in public facilities, and bolster federal authority to deny funds for discriminatory programs. Knowing they would face a stiff fight from

As the Civil Rights movement received greater coverage in the international press, editorial cartoonists in America expressed fears that white resistance to integration provided an effective propaganda weapon to the Soviet Union and its allies. This *Oakland Tribune* cartoon appeared on September 11, 1957, in the midst of the crisis in Little Rock.

SOURCE: *Right into Their Hands.* The Oakland Tribune.

congressional conservatives, administration officials began an intense lobbying effort in support of the law. After three years of fence sitting, Kennedy finally committed his office and his political future to the civil rights cause.

Movement leaders lauded the president's initiative. Yet they understood that racial hatred still haunted the nation. Only a few hours after Kennedy's television speech, a gunman murdered Medgar Evers, leader of the Mississippi NAACP, outside his home in Jackson, Mississippi. To pressure Congress and demonstrate the urgency of their cause, a broad coalition of civil rights groups planned a massive, nonviolent March on Washington. The idea had deep roots in black protest. A. Philip Randolph, head of the Brotherhood of Sleeping Car Porters, had originally proposed such a march in 1941 to protest discrimination against blacks in the wartime defense industries. Now, more than twenty years later, Randolph, along with his aide Bayard Rustin, revived the concept and convinced leaders of the major civil rights groups to support it.

The Kennedy administration originally opposed the march, fearing it would jeopardize support for the president's civil rights bill in Congress. But as plans for the rally solidified, Kennedy reluctantly gave his approval. Leaders from the SCLC, the NAACP, SNCC, the Urban League, and CORE—the leading organizations in the civil rights community—put aside their tactical differences to forge a broad consensus for the event. John Lewis, the young head of SNCC, who had endured numerous brutal assaults, planned a speech that denounced the Kennedys as hypocrites. Lewis's speech enraged Walter Reuther, the white liberal leader of the United Auto Workers union, which had helped finance the march. Reuther threatened to turn off the loudspeakers he was paying for, believing Lewis's speech would embarrass the Kennedys. Randolph, the acknowledged elder statesman of the movement, convinced Lewis at the last moment to tone down his remarks. "We've come this far," he implored. "For the sake of unity, change it."

Reverend Dr. Martin Luther King, Jr., acknowledging the huge throng at the historic March on Washington for "jobs and freedom," August 28, 1963. The size of the crowd, the stirring oratory and song, and the live network television coverage produced one of the most memorable political events in the nation's history.

SOURCE: George Ballis/Take Stock.

On August 28, 1963, more than a quarter of a million people, including 50,000 whites, gathered at the Lincoln Memorial to rally for "jobs and freedom." Union members, students, teachers, clergy, professionals, musicians, actors—Americans from all walks of life joined the largest political assembly in the nation's history until then. The sight of all those people holding hands and singing "We Shall Overcome," led by the white folk singer Joan Baez, would not be easily forgotten. At the end of a long, exhilarating day of speeches and freedom songs, Martin Luther King, Jr. provided an emotional climax. Combining the democratic promise of the Declaration of Independence with the religious fervor of his Baptist heritage, King stirred the crowd with his dream for America:

> I have a dream today that one day this nation will rise up and live out the true meaning of its creed: "We hold these truths to be self-evident—that all men are created equal." . . . When we allow freedom to ring, when we let it ring from every village and every hamlet, from every state and every city, we will be able to speed up that day when all of God's children—black men and white men, Jews and Gentiles, Protestants and Catholics—will be able to join hands and sing in the words of the old Negro spiritual, "Free at last! Free at last! Thank God Almighty, we are free at last!"

LBJ and the Civil Rights Act of 1964

An extraordinary demonstration of interracial unity, the March on Washington stood as the high-water mark in the struggle for civil rights. It buoyed the spirits of movement leaders as well as the liberals pushing the new civil rights bill through Congress. But the assassination of John F. Kennedy on November 22, 1963, in Dallas threw an ominous cloud over the whole nation and the civil rights movement in particular. In the Deep South, many ardent segregationists welcomed the president's death because of his support for civil rights. Most African Americans probably shared the feelings of Coretta Scott King, who recalled her family's vigil: "We felt that President Kennedy had been a friend of the Cause and that with him as President we could continue to move forward. We watched and prayed for him."

Lyndon Baines Johnson, Kennedy's successor, had never been much of a friend to civil rights. As a senator from Texas (1948–60, including six years as majority leader), Johnson had been one of the shrewdest and most powerful Democrats in Congress. Throughout the 1950s he had worked to obstruct the passage and enforcement of civil rights laws—though as vice president he had ably chaired Kennedy's working group on equal employment. Johnson reassured a grieving nation that "the ideas and the ideals which [Kennedy] so nobly represented must and will be translated into effective action." Even so, civil rights activists looked upon Johnson warily as he took over the Oval Office.

As president, Johnson realized that he faced a new political reality, one created by the civil rights movement. Eager to unite the Democratic Party and prove himself as a national leader, he seized on civil rights as a golden political opportunity. "I knew that if I didn't get out in front on this issue," he later recalled, "they [the liberals] would get me. They'd throw up my background against me, they'd use it to prove that I was incapable of bringing unity to the land I loved so much. . . . I had to produce a civil rights bill that was even stronger than

the one they'd have gotten if Kennedy had lived." Throughout the early months of 1964, the new president let it be known publicly and privately that he would brook no compromise on civil rights.

Johnson exploited all his skills as a political insider. He cajoled, flattered, and threatened key members of the House and Senate. Working with the president, the fifteen-year-old Leadership Conference on Civil Rights coordinated a sophisticated lobbying effort in Congress. Groups such as the NAACP, the AFL-CIO, the National Council of Churches, and the American Jewish Congress made the case for a strong civil rights bill. The

OVERVIEW

LANDMARK CIVIL RIGHTS LEGISLATION, SUPREME COURT DECISIONS, AND EXECUTIVE ORDERS

Year	Decision, law, or executive order	Significance
1939	*Missouri v. ex. rel. Gaines*	Required University of Missouri Law School either to admit African Americans or build another fully equal law school
1941	Executive Order 8802 (by President Roosevelt)	Banned racial discrimination in defense industry and government offices; established Fair Employment Practices Committee to investigate violations
1946	*Morgan v. Virginia*	Ruled that segregation on interstate buses violated federal law and created an "undue burden" on interstate commerce
1948	Executive Order 9981 (by President Truman)	Desegregated the U.S. armed forces
1950	*McLaurin v. Oklahoma State Regents*	Ruled that forcing an African American student to sit, eat, and study in segregated facilities was unconstitutional because it inevitably created a "badge of inferiority"
1950	*Sweatt v. Painter*	Ruled that an inferior law school created by the University of Texas to serve African Americans violated their right to equal protection and ordered Herman Sweatt to be admitted to University of Texas Law School
1954	*Brown v. Board of Education of Topeka I*	Declared "separate educational facilities are inherently unequal," thus overturning *Plessy v. Ferguson* (1896) and the "separate but equal" doctrine as it applied to public schools
1955	*Brown v. Board of Education of Topeka II*	Ordered school desegregation to begin with "all deliberate speed," but offered no timetable
1957	Civil Rights Act	Created Civil Rights Division within the Justice Department
1964	Civil Rights Act	Prohibited discrimination in employment and most places of public accommodation on basis of race, color, religion, sex, or national origin; outlawed bias in federally assisted programs; created Equal Employment Opportunity Commission
1965	Voting Rights Act	Authorized federal supervision of voter registration in states and counties where fewer than half of voting age residents were registered; outlawed literacy and other discriminatory tests in voter registration

House passed the bill in February by a 290–130 vote. The more difficult fight would be in the Senate, where a southern filibuster promised to block the bill or weaken it. But by June, Johnson's persistence had paid off and the southern filibuster had collapsed.

On July 2, 1964, Johnson signed the Civil Rights Act of 1964. Every major provision had survived intact. This landmark law represented the most significant civil rights legislation since Reconstruction. It prohibited discrimination in most places of public accommodation; outlawed discrimination in employment on the basis of race, color, religion, sex, or national origin; outlawed bias in federally assisted programs; authorized the Justice Department to institute suits to desegregate public schools and other facilities; created the Equal Employment Opportunity Commission; and provided technical and financial aid to communities desegregating their schools.

Mississippi Freedom Summer

While President Johnson and his liberal allies won the congressional battle for the new civil rights bill, activists in Mississippi mounted a far more radical and dangerous campaign than any yet attempted in the South. In the spring of 1964, a coalition of workers led by SNCC launched the Freedom Summer project, an ambitious effort to register black voters and directly challenge the iron rule of segregation. Mississippi stood as the toughest test for the civil rights movement, racially and economically. It was the poorest, most backward state in the nation, and had remained largely untouched by the freedom struggle. African Americans constituted 42 percent of the state's population, but fewer than 5 percent could register to vote. Median black family income was under $1,500 a year, roughly one-third that of white families. A small white planter elite controlled most of the state's wealth, and a long tradition of terror against black people had maintained the racial caste system.

Bob Moses of SNCC and Dave Dennis of CORE planned Freedom Summer as a way of opening up this closed society to the glare of national publicity. The project recruited over 900 volunteers, mostly white college students, to aid in voter registration, teach in "freedom schools," and help build a "freedom party" as an alternative to Mississippi's all-white Democratic Party. Organizers expected violence, which was precisely why they wanted white volunteers. Dave Dennis later explained their reasoning: "The death of a white college student would bring on more attention to what was going on than for a black college student getting it. That's cold, but that was also in another sense speaking the language of this country." Mississippi authorities prepared for the civil rights workers as if expecting a foreign army, beefing up state highway patrols and local police forces.

Bob Moses of the Student Nonviolent Coordinating Committee was one of the driving forces behind the 1964 Freedom Summer Project. Here he instructs student volunteers gathered in Oxford, Ohio before they leave for voter registration and other community organizing work in Mississippi. Moses, who had been working for voting rights in Mississippi since 1961, played a key role in persuading SNCC to accept white volunteers from the North.

SOURCE: Photo by Steve Shapiro. Black Star (PER 13SC HA000102).

On June 21, while most project volunteers were still undergoing training in Ohio, three activists disappeared in Neshoba County, Mississippi, when they went to investigate the burning of a black church that was supposed to serve as a freedom school. Six weeks later, after a massive search belatedly ordered by President Johnson, FBI agents discovered the bodies of the three—white activists Michael Schwerner and Andrew Goodman, and a local black activist, James Chaney—buried in an earthen dam. Goodman and Schwerner had been shot once; Chaney had been severely beaten before being shot three times. Over the summer, at least three other civil rights workers died violently. Project workers suffered 1,000 arrests, 80 beatings, 35 shooting incidents, and 30 bombings in homes, churches, and schools.

Within the project, simmering problems tested the ideal of the Beloved Community. Black veterans of SNCC resented the affluent white volunteers, many of whom had not come to terms with their own racial prejudices. White volunteers, staying only a short time in the state, often found it difficult to communicate in the southern communities with local African Americans, who were wary of breaking old codes of deference. Sexual tensions between black male and white female volunteers also strained relations. A number of both black and white women, led by Ruby Doris Robinson, Mary King, and Casey Hayden, began to raise the issue of women's equality as a companion goal to racial equality. The day-to-day reality of violent reprisals, police harassment, and constant fear took a hard toll on everyone.

The project did manage to rivet national attention on Mississippi racism, and it won enormous sympathy from northern liberals. Among their concrete accomplishments, the volunteers could point with pride to more than forty freedom schools that brought classes in reading, arithmetic, politics, and African American history to thousands of black children. Some 60,000 black voters signed up to join the Mississippi Freedom Democratic Party (MFDP). In August 1964 the MFDP sent a slate of delegates to the Democratic National Convention looking to challenge the credentials of the all-white regular state delegation.

In Atlantic City, the idealism of Freedom Summer ran into the more cynical needs of the national Democratic Party. Lyndon Johnson opposed the seating of the MFDP because he wanted to avoid a divisive floor fight. He was already concerned that Republicans might carry a number of southern states in November. But MFDP leaders and sympathizers gave dramatic tes-

timony before the convention, detailing the racism and brutality in Mississippi politics. "Is this America," asked Fannie Lou Hamer, "the land of the free and the home of the brave, where we are threatened daily because we want to live as decent human beings?" Led by vice presidential nominee Senator Hubert Humphrey, Johnson's forces offered a compromise that would have given the MFDP a token two seats on the floor. Bitter over what they saw as a betrayal, the MFDP delegates turned the offer down. Within SNCC, the defeat of the MFDP intensified African American disillusionment with the Democratic Party and the liberal establishment.

Malcolm X and Black Consciousness

Frustrated with the limits of nonviolent protest and electoral politics, younger activists within SNCC found themselves increasingly drawn to the militant rhetoric and vision of Malcolm X, who since 1950 had been the preeminent spokesman for the black nationalist religious sect, the Nation of Islam (NOI). Founded in Depression-era Detroit by Elijah Muhammad, the NOI, like the followers of black nationalist leader Marcus Garvey in the 1920s (see Chapter 23) aspired to create a self-reliant, highly disciplined, and proud community—a separate "nation" for black people. Elijah Muhammad preached a message of racial solidarity and self-help, criticized crime and drug use, and castigated whites as "blue-eyed devils" responsible for the world's evil. During the 1950s the NOI (also called Black Muslims) successfully organized in northern black communities, appealing especially to criminals, drug addicts, and others living on the margins of urban life. It operated restaurants, retail stores, and schools as models for black economic self-sufficiency.

The man known as Malcolm X had been born Malcolm Little in 1925 and raised in Lansing, Michigan. His father, a preacher and a follower of Marcus Garvey, was killed in a racist attack by local whites. In his youth, Malcolm led a life of petty crime, eventually serving a seven-year prison term for burglary. While in jail he educated himself and converted to the Nation of Islam. He took the surname "X" to symbolize his original African family name, lost through slavery. Emerging from jail in 1952, he became a dynamic organizer, editor, and speaker for

After they were barred from the floor of the August 1964 Democratic National Convention, members of the Mississippi Freedom Democratic Party were led by Fanny Lou Hamer in a song-filled protest outside the hotel. SOURCE: Women from right: Fannie Lou Hamer, Eleanor Holmes Norton, and Ella Baker. Photo by George Ballis. Take Stock-Images of Change (0812023).

Born Malcolm Little, Malcolm X (1925–65) took the name "X" as a symbol of the stolen identity of African slaves. He emerged in the early 1960s as the foremost advocate of racial unity and black nationalism. The Black Power movement, initiated in 1966 by SNCC members, was strongly influenced by Malcolm X.

SOURCE: Malcolm X in Egypt, 1964. Photo by John Launois. Black Star.

the Nation of Islam. He spoke frequently on college campuses as well on the street corners of black neighborhoods like New York's Harlem. He encouraged his audiences to take pride in their African heritage and to consider armed self-defense rather than relying solely on nonviolence—in short, to break free of white domination "by any means necessary."

Malcolm ridiculed the integrationist goals of the civil rights movement. Black Muslims, he told audiences, do not want "to integrate into this corrupt society, but to separate from it, to a land of our own, where we can reform ourselves, lift up our moral standards, and try to be godly." In his best-selling *Autobiography of Malcolm X* (1965), he admitted that his position was extremist. "The black race here in North America is in extremely bad condition. You show me a black man who isn't an extremist," he argued, "and I'll show you one who needs psychiatric attention."

In 1964, troubled by Elijah Muhammad's personal scandals (he faced paternity suits brought by two young female employees) and eager to find a more politically effective approach to improving conditions for blacks, Malcolm X broke with the Nation of Islam. He made a pilgrimage to Mecca, the Muslim holy city, where he met Islamic peoples of all colors and underwent a "radical alteration in my whole outlook about 'white' men." He returned to the United States as El-Hajj Malik El-Shabazz, abandoned his black separatist views, and founded the Organization of Afro-American Unity. Malcolm now looked for common ground with the civil rights movement, addressing a Mississippi Freedom Democrats rally in Harlem and meeting with SNCC activists. He stressed the international links between the civil rights struggle in America and the problems facing emerging African nations. On February 21, 1965, Malcolm X was assassinated during a speech at Harlem's Audubon Ballroom. His assailants were members of a New Jersey branch of the NOI, possibly infiltrated by the FBI.

"More than any other person," remarked black author Julius Lester, "Malcolm X was responsible for the new militancy that entered The Movement in 1965." SNCC leader John Lewis thought Malcolm had been the most effective voice "to articulate the aspirations, bitterness, and frustrations of the Negro people," forming "a living link between Africa and the civil rights movement in this country." In his death he became a martyr for the idea that soon became known as Black Power. As much as anyone, Malcolm X pointed the way to a new black consciousness that celebrated black history, black culture, the African heritage, and black self-sufficiency.

Selma and the Voting Rights Act of 1965

Lyndon Johnson won reelection in 1964 by a landslide, capturing 61 percent of the popular vote. Of the 6 million black people who voted in the election, 2 million more than in 1960, an overwhelming 94 percent cast their ballots for Johnson. Republican candidate Senator Barry Goldwater managed to carry only his home state of Arizona and five Deep South states, where fewer than 45 percent of eligible black people could vote. With Democrats in firm control of both the Senate and the House, civil rights leaders believed the time was ripe for further legislative gains. Johnson and his staff began drafting a tough voting rights bill in late 1964, partly with an eye toward countering Republican gains in the Deep South with newly registered black and Democratic voters. Martin Luther King and the SCLC shared this goal of passing a strong voting rights law that would provide southern black people with direct federal protection of their right to vote.

Once again, movement leaders plotted to create a crisis that would arouse national indignation, pressure

Voting rights demonstrators rallied in front of the state capitol in Montgomery, Alabama, March 25, 1965, after a four day, fifty-four mile trek from Selma. The original 3,000 marchers were joined by over 30,000 supporters by the end of their journey. SOURCE: Photo by Matt Herron. Media Image Resource Alliance (0001A030).

Congress, and force federal action. King and his aides chose Selma, Alabama, as the target of their campaign. Selma, a city of 27,000 some fifty miles west of Montgomery, had a notorious record of preventing black voting. Of the 15,000 eligible black voters in Selma's Dallas County, registered voters numbered only in the hundreds. In 1963, local activists Amelia Boynton and Reverend Fred Reese had invited SNCC workers to aid voter registration efforts in the community. But they had met a violent reception from county sheriff Jim Clark. Sensing that Clark might be another Bull Connor, King arrived in Selma in January 1965, just after accepting the Nobel Peace Prize in Oslo. "We are not asking, we are demanding the ballot," he declared. King, the SCLC staff, and SNCC workers led daily marches on the Dallas County Courthouse, where hundreds of black citizens tried to get their names added to voter lists.

By early February, Clark had imprisoned more than 3,000 protesters.

Despite the brutal beating of Reverend James Bevel, a key SCLC strategist, and the killing of Jimmy Lee Jackson, a young black demonstrator in nearby Marion, the SCLC failed to arouse the level of national indignation it sought. Consequently, in early March SCLC staffers called on black activists to march from Selma to Montgomery, where they planned to deliver a list of grievances to Governor Wallace. On Sunday, March 7, while King preached to his church in Atlanta, a group of 600 marchers crossed the Pettus Bridge on the Alabama River, on their way to Montgomery. A group of mounted, heavily armed county and state lawmen blocked their path and ordered them to turn back. When the marchers did not move, the lawmen attacked with billy clubs and tear gas, driving the protesters back over the bridge in a bloody rout. More than fifty marchers had to be treated in local hospitals.

The dramatic "Bloody Sunday" attack received extensive coverage on network television, prompting a national uproar. Demands for federal intervention poured into the White House from all over the country. King issued a public call for civil rights supporters to come to Selma for a second march on Montgomery. But a federal court temporarily enjoined the SCLC from proceeding with the march. King found himself trapped. He reluctantly accepted a face-saving compromise: in return for a promise from Alabama authorities not to harm marchers, King would lead his followers across the Pettus Bridge, stop, pray briefly, and then turn back. This plan outraged the more militant SNCC activists and sharpened their distrust of King and the SCLC.

But just when it seemed the Selma movement might die, white racist violence revived it. A gang of white toughs attacked four white Unitarian ministers who had come to Selma to participate in the march. One of them, Reverend James J. Reeb of Boston, died of multiple skull fractures. His death brought new calls for federal action. On March 15, President Johnson delivered a televised address to a joint session of Congress to request passage of a voting rights bill. In a stirring speech, the president fused the political power of his office with the moral power of the movement. "Their cause must be our cause, too. Because it is not just Negroes, but really all of us who must overcome the crippling legacy of bigotry and injustice. And," he concluded firmly, invoking the movement's slogan, "we shall overcome." Johnson also prevailed upon federal judge Frank Johnson to issue a ruling allowing the march to proceed, and he warned Governor Wallace not to interfere.

On March 21 Martin Luther King led a group of more than 3,000 black and white marchers out of Selma on the road to Montgomery, where the bus boycott that marked the beginning of his involvement had occurred nine years before. Four days later they arrived at the

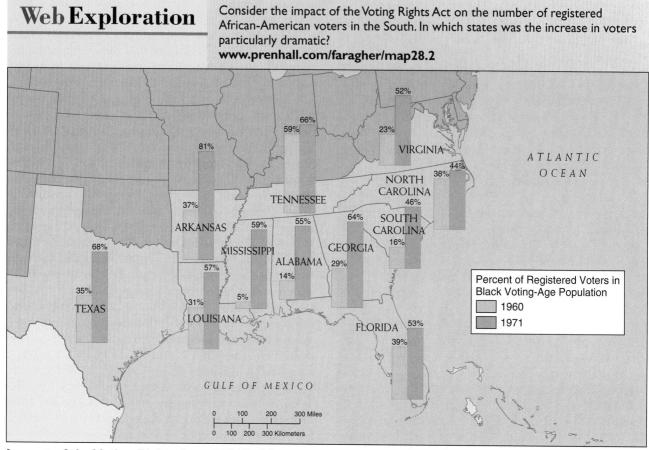

Web Exploration

Consider the impact of the Voting Rights Act on the number of registered African-American voters in the South. In which states was the increase in voters particularly dramatic?
www.prenhall.com/faragher/map28.2

Impact of the Voting Rights Act of 1965 Voter registration among African Americans in the South increased significantly between 1960 and 1971.

Alabama statehouse. Their ranks had been swelled by more than 30,000 supporters, including hundreds of prominent politicians, entertainers, and black leaders. "I know some of you are asking today," King told the crowd, "'How long will it take?'" He went on in a rousing, rhythmic cadence:

> I come to say to you this afternoon, however difficult the moment, however frustrating the hour, it will not be long because truth pressed to earth will rise again. How long? Not long, because no lie can live forever. How long? Not long, because you will reap what you sow. How long? Not long, because the arc of the moral universe is long but it bends toward justice. How long? Not long, because mine eyes have seen the glory of the coming of the Lord!

In August 1965 President Johnson signed the Voting Rights Act into law. It authorized federal supervision of registration in states and counties where fewer than half of voting-age residents were registered. It also outlawed literacy and other discriminatory tests that had been

used to prevent blacks from registering to vote. Between 1964 and 1968, black registrants in Mississippi leaped from 7 percent to 59 percent of the statewide black population; in Alabama, from 24 percent to 57 percent. In those years the number of southern black voters grew from 1 million to 3.1 million. For the first time in their lives, black Southerners in hundreds of small towns and rural communities could enjoy full participation in American politics. Ten years after the Montgomery bus boycott, the civil rights movement had reached a peak of national influence and interracial unity.

FORGOTTEN MINORITIES, 1945–65

The civil rights movement revolved around the aspirations and community strength of African Americans. The historic injustices of slavery, racism, and segregation gave a moral and political urgency to the black struggle for full citizenship rights. Yet other minorities as well had long been denied their civil rights. After World War II, Latinos, Indian peoples, and Asian Americans began making their own halting efforts to improve their political, legal, and economic status. They faced strong opposition from institutional racism and various economic interests that benefited from keeping these groups in a subordinate position. By the late 1960s, the success of the black civil rights movement had inspired these minority groups to adopt more militant strategies of their own.

Mexican Americans

The Mexican American community in the West and Southwest included both longtime U.S. citizens—who found white authorities nonetheless unwilling to recognize their rights—and noncitizen immigrants from Mexico. After World War II, several Mexican American political organizations sought to secure equal rights and equal opportunity for their community by stressing its American identity. The most important of these groups were the League of United Latin American Citizens (LULAC), founded in Texas in 1928, and the G.I. Forum, founded in Texas in 1948 by Mexican American veterans of World War II. Both emphasized the learning of English, assimilation into American society, improved education, and the promotion of

political power through voting. LULAC successfully pursued two important legal cases that anticipated *Brown v. Board of Education.* In *Mendez v. Westminster,* a 1947 California case, and in the 1948 *Delgado* case in Texas, the Supreme Court upheld lower-court rulings that declared segregation of Mexican Americans unconstitutional. Like *Brown,* these two decisions did not immediately end segregation, but they offered path-breaking legal and psychological victories to Mexican American activists. LULAC won another significant legal battle in the 1954 *Hernandez* decision, in which the Supreme Court ended the exclusion of Mexican Americans from Texas jury lists.

Mexican migration to the United States increased dramatically during and after World War II. The *bracero* program, a cooperative effort between the U.S. and Mexican governments, brought some 300,000 Mexicans to the United States during the war as temporary agricultural and railroad workers. American agribusiness came to depend on Mexicans as a key source of cheap farm labor, and the program continued after the war. Most braceros endured harsh work, poor food, and substandard housing in the camps in which they lived. Some migrated into the newly emerging barrio neighborhoods in cities such as San Antonio, Los Angeles, El Paso, and Denver. Many braceros and their children became American citizens, but most returned to

Delegates to the 1948 National Convention of the League of United Latin American Citizens met in Kingsville, Texas. After World War II, LULAC grew to about 15,000 members active in 200 local councils, mostly in Texas and California.

SOURCE: Benson Latin American Collection.

Mexico. Another group of postwar Mexican immigrants were the *mojados*, or "wetbacks," so called because many swam across the Rio Grande River to enter the United States illegally.

In 1954, in an effort to curb the flow of undocumented immigrants from Mexico, the Eisenhower administration launched the massive "Operation Wetback." Over the next three years Immigration Service agents rounded up some 3.7 million allegedly illegal migrants and sent them back over the border. Immigration agents made little effort to distinguish the so-called illegals from braceros and Mexican American citizens. Many families were broken up, and thousands who had lived in the United States for a decade or more found themselves deported. Many deportees were denied basic civil liberties, such as due process, and suffered physical abuse and intimidation. Most Mexican Americans had ambivalent feelings about mojados and Operation Wetback. The deportations tended to improve job opportunities and wages for those who remained. Yet the so-called illegals were considered members of *la raza*, the larger Mexican American community, and family ties between these groups were common. LULAC and the *Asociación Nacional Mexico-Americana*, founded in 1950, tried in vain to curb abuses against aliens and Mexican Americans. Among Mexican Americans, Operation Wetback left a bitter legacy of deep mistrust and estrangement from Anglo culture and politics.

Puerto Ricans

The United States took possession of the island of Puerto Rico in 1898, during the final stages of the Spanish-American War. The Jones Act of 1917 made the island an unincorporated territory of the United States and granted U.S. citizenship to all Puerto Ricans. Over the next several decades, Puerto Rico's economic base shifted from a diversified, subsistence-oriented agriculture to a single export crop—sugar. U.S. absentee owners dominated the sugar industry, claiming most of the island's arable land, previously tilled by small farmers growing crops for local consumption. Puerto Rico's sugar industry grew enormously profitable, but few island residents benefited from this expansion. By the 1930s, unemployment and poverty were widespread and the island was forced to import its foodstuffs.

Small communities of Puerto Rican migrants had begun to form in New York City during the 1920s. The largest was on the Upper East Side of Manhattan—*el barrio* in East Harlem. During World War II, labor shortages led the federal government to sponsor the recruitment of Puerto Rican workers for industrial jobs in New Jersey, Philadelphia, and Chicago. But the "great migration" took place from 1945 to 1964. During these two

decades the number of Puerto Ricans living on the mainland jumped from less than 100,000 to roughly 1 million. Economic opportunity was the chief impetus for this migration, for the island suffered from high unemployment rates and low wages.

The advent of direct air service between Puerto Rico and New York in 1945 made the city easily accessible. The Puerto Rican community in East (or Spanish) Harlem mushroomed, and new communities in the South Bronx and Brooklyn began to emerge. By 1970 there were about 800,000 Puerto Ricans in New York—more than 10 percent of the city's population. New Puerto Rican communities also took root in Connecticut, Massachusetts, New Jersey, and the Midwest. Puerto Ricans frequently circulated between the island and the mainland, often returning home when economic conditions on the mainland were less favorable.

The experience of Puerto Rican migrants both resembled and differed from that of other immigrant groups in significant ways. Like Mexican immigrants, Puerto Ricans were foreign in language, culture, and experience, yet unlike them they entered the United States as citizens. Many Puerto Ricans were also African Americans. Racial and ethnic discrimination came as a double shock, since Puerto Ricans, as citizens, entered the United States with a sense of entitlement. In New York, Puerto Ricans found themselves barred from most craft unions, excluded from certain neighborhoods, and forced to take jobs largely in the low-paying garment industry and service trades. Puerto Rican children were not well served by a public school system insensitive to language differences and too willing to track Spanish-speaking students into obsolete vocational programs.

By the early 1970s, Puerto Rican families were substantially poorer on average than the total population of the country, and they had the lowest median income of any Latino groups. The steep decline in manufacturing jobs and in the garment industry in New York during the 1960s and 1970s hit the Puerto Rican community especially hard. So did the city's fiscal crisis, which brought sharp cuts in funding for schools, health care, libraries, government jobs, and other public services traditionally available to immigrant groups. The structural shift in the U.S. economy away from manufacturing and toward service and high-technology jobs reinforced the Puerto Rican community's goal of improving educational opportunities for its members. The struggle to establish and improve bilingual education in schools became an important part of this effort. Most Puerto Ricans, especially those who had succeeded in school and achieved middle-class status, continued to identify strongly with their Puerto Rican heritage and the Spanish language.

George Gillette (left foreground), chairman of the Fort Berthold Indian Council, wept as Secretary of Interior J. A. Krug signed a contract buying 155,000 acres of the tribe's best land in North Dakota for a reservoir project, May 20, 1948. "The members of the tribal council sign this contract with heavy hearts," Gillette said.

SOURCE: CORBIS.

Indian Peoples

The postwar years also brought significant changes in the status and lives of Indian peoples. Congress reversed the policies pursued under the New Deal, which had stressed Indian sovereignty and cultural independence. Responding to a variety of pressure groups, including mining and other economic interests wishing to exploit the resources on Indian reservations, Congress adopted a policy known as "termination," designed to cancel Indian treaties and terminate sovereignty rights. In 1953, Congress passed House Concurrent Resolution 108, which allowed Congress to terminate a tribe as a political entity by passing legislation specific to that tribe. The leader of the termination forces, Senator Arthur Watkins of Utah, declared the new law meant that "the concept that the Indian people exist within the United States as independent nations has been rejected." Supporters of termination had varied motives, but the policy added up to the return of enforced assimilation for solving the "Indian problem."

Between 1954 and 1962, Congress passed twelve termination bills covering more than sixty tribes, nearly all in the West. Even when tribes consented to their own termination, they discovered that dissolution brought unforeseen problems. For example, members of the Klamaths of Oregon and the Paiutes of Utah received large cash payments from the division of tribal assets.

But after these one-time payments were spent, members had to take poorly paid, unskilled jobs to survive. Many Indian peoples became dependent on state social services and slipped into poverty and alcoholism.

Along with termination, the federal government gave greater emphasis to a relocation program aimed at speeding up assimilation. The Bureau of Indian Affairs encouraged reservation Indians to relocate to cities, where they were provided housing and jobs. For some, relocation meant assimilation, intermarriage with whites, and the loss of tribal identity. Others, homesick and unable to adjust to an alien culture and place, either returned to reservations or wound up on the margins of city life. Still others regularly traveled back and forth. In some respects, this urban migration paralleled the larger postwar shift of rural peoples to cities and suburbs.

Indians increasingly came to see termination as a policy geared mainly to exploiting resources on Indian lands. By the early 1960s, a new movement was emerging to defend Indian sovereignty. The National Congress of American Indians (NCAI) condemned termination, calling for a review of federal policies and a return to self-determination. The NCAI led a political and educational campaign that challenged the goal of assimilation and created a new awareness among white people that Indians had the right to remain Indians. When the termination policy ended in the early 1960s, it had affected only about 3 percent of federally recognized Indian peoples.

Taking their cue from the civil rights movement, Indian activists used the court system to reassert sovereign rights. Indian and white liberal lawyers, many with experience in civil rights cases, worked through the Native American Rights Fund, which became a powerful force in western politics. A series of Supreme Court decisions, culminating in *United States v. Wheeler* (1978), reasserted the principle of "unique and limited" sovereignty. The Court recognized tribal independence except where limited by treaty or Congress.

The Indian population had been growing since the early years of the century, but most reservations had trouble making room for a new generation. Indians suffered increased rates of poverty, chronic unemployment, alcoholism, and poor health. The average Indian family in the early 1960s earned only one-third of the average family income in the United States. Those who remained in the cities usually became "ethnic Indians," identifying themselves more as Indians than as members of specific tribes. By the late 1960s, ethnic Indians had begun emphasizing civil rights over tribal rights, making common cause with African Americans and other minorities. The National Indian Youth Council (NIYC), founded in 1960, tried to unite the two causes of equality for individual Indians and special status for tribes.

But the organization faced difficult contradictions between a common Indian identity, emphasizing Indians as a single ethnic group, and tribal identity, stressing the citizenship of Indians in separate nations.

Asian Americans

The harsh relocation program of World War II devastated the Japanese American community on the west coast (see Chapter 25). But the war against Nazism also helped weaken older notions of white superiority and racism. During the war the state of California had aggressively enforced an alien land law by confiscating property declared illegally held by Japanese. In November 1946 a proposition supporting the law appeared on the state ballot. But, thanks in part to a campaign by the Japanese American Citizens League (JACL) reminding voters of the wartime contributions of Nisei (second-generation Japanese Americans) soldiers, voters overwhelmingly rejected the referendum. One JACL leader hailed the vote as proof that "the people of California will not approve discriminatory and prejudiced treatment of persons of Japanese ancestry." Two years later the Supreme Court declared the law unconstitutional, calling it "nothing more than outright racial discrimination."

The 1952 Immigration and Nationality Act (see Chapter 26) removed the old ban against Japanese immigration, and also made Issei (first-generation Japanese Americans) eligible for naturalized citizenship. Japanese Americans, who lobbied hard for the new law, greeted it with elation. "It gave the Japanese equality with all other immigrants," said JACL leader Harry Takagi, "and that was the principle we had been struggling for from the very beginning." By 1965 some 46,000 immigrant Japanese, most of them elderly Issei, had taken their citizenship oaths. One of these wrote a poem to celebrate the achievement:

> Going steadily to study English,
> Even through the rain at night,
> I thus attain,
> Late in life,
> American citizenship.

The Immigration and Nationality Act allowed immigration from the "Asian-Pacific Triangle." It was nonetheless racially discriminatory, in that each country in Asia was permitted only 100 immigrants a year. In addition, the act continued the national-origins quotas of 1924 for European countries. The civil rights struggle helped spur a movement to reform immigration policies. "Everywhere else in our national life, we have eliminated discrimination based on national origins," Attorney General Robert Kennedy told Congress in 1964. "Yet, this system is still the foundation of our immigration law."

In 1965 Congress passed a new Immigration and Nationality Act, abolishing the national-origins quotas and providing for the admission each year of 170,000 immigrants from the Eastern Hemisphere and 120,000 from the Western Hemisphere. The new law set a limit of 20,000 per country from the Eastern Hemisphere—these immigrants to be admitted on a first-come, first-served basis—and established preference categories for professional and highly skilled immigrants.

The 1965 act would have a profound effect on Asian American communities, opening the way for a new wave of immigration. In the twenty years following the act, the number of Asian Americans soared from 1 million to 5 million. Four times as many Asians settled in the United States in this period as in the entire previous history of the nation. This new wave also brought a strikingly different group of Asian immigrants to America. In 1960 the Asian American population was 52 percent Japanese, 27 percent Chinese, and 20 percent Filipino. In 1985, the composition was 21 percent Chinese, 21 percent Filipino, 15 percent Japanese, 12 percent Vietnamese, 11 percent Korean, 10 percent Asian Indian, 4 percent Laotian, and 3 percent Cambodian. These newcomers included significant numbers of highly educated professionals and city dwellers, a sharp contrast with the farmers and rural peoples of the past.

CONCLUSION

The mass movement for civil rights was arguably the most important domestic event of the twentieth century. The struggle that began in Montgomery, Alabama, in December 1955 ultimately transformed race relations in thousands of American communities. By the early 1960s this community-based movement had placed civil rights at the very center of national political life. It achieved its greatest successes by invoking the law of the land to destroy legal segregation and win individual freedom for African Americans. The Civil Rights Act of 1964 and the Voting Rights Act of 1965 testified to the power of an African American and white liberal coalition. Yet the persistence of racism, poverty, and ghetto slums challenged a central assumption of liberalism: that equal protection of constitutional rights would give all Americans equal opportunities in life. By the mid-1960s, many black people had begun to question the core values of liberalism, the benefits of alliance with whites, and the philosophy of nonviolence. At the same time, a conservative white backlash against the gains made by African Americans further weakened the liberal political consensus.

In challenging the persistence of widespread poverty and institutional racism, the civil rights movement called

CHRONOLOGY

1941	Executive Order 8802 forbids racial discrimination in defense industries and government
1946	In *Morgan v. Virginia*, U.S. Supreme Court rules that segregation on interstate buses is unconstitutional
	President Harry Truman creates the Committee on Civil Rights
1947	Jackie Robinson becomes the first African American on a major league baseball team
1948	President Truman issues executive order desegregating the armed forces
1954	In *Brown v. Board of Education*, Supreme Court rules segregated schools inherently unequal
1955	Supreme Court rules that school desegregation must proceed "with all deliberate speed"
	Montgomery bus boycott begins
1956	Montgomery bus boycott ends in victory as the Supreme Court affirms a district court ruling that segregation on buses is unconstitutional
1957	Southern Christian Leadership Conference (SCLC) is founded
	President Dwight Eisenhower sends in federal troops to protect African American students integrating Little Rock, Arkansas, high school
1960	Sit-in movement begins as four college students sit at a lunch counter in Greensboro, North Carolina, and ask to be served
	Student Nonviolent Coordinating Committee (SNCC) founded

1960	Board of Indian Commissioners is created
	Buffalo Bill, the King of the Border Men, sets off "Wild West" publishing craze
1961	Freedom Rides begin
1962	James Meredith integrates the University of Mississippi
	The Albany movement fails to end segregation in Albany, Georgia
1963	SCLC initiates campaign to desegregate Birmingham, Alabama
	Medgar Evers, leader of the Mississippi NAACP, is assassinated
	March on Washington; Martin Luther King, Jr. delivers his historic "I Have a Dream" speech
1964	Mississippi Freedom Summer project brings students to Mississippi to teach and register voters
	President Johnson signs the Civil Rights Act of 1964
	Civil rights workers Michael Schwerner, James Chaney, and Andrew Goodman are found buried in Philadelphia, Mississippi
	Mississippi Freedom Democratic Party (MFDP) is denied seats at the 1964 Democratic Presidential Convention
1965	SCLC and SNCC begin voter registration campaign in Selma, Alabama
	Malcolm X is assassinated
	Civil rights marchers walk from Selma to Montgomery
	Voting Rights Act of 1965 is signed into law

for deep structural changes in American life. By 1967, Martin Luther King, Jr. was articulating a broad and radical vision linking the struggle against racial injustice to other defects in American society. "The black revolution," he argued, "is much more than a struggle for the rights of Negroes. It is forcing America to face all its interrelated flaws—racism, poverty, militarism, and materialism. It is exposing evils that are deeply rooted in the whole structure of our society." Curing these ills would prove far more difficult than ending legal segregation.

REVIEW QUESTIONS

1. What were the key legal and political antecedents to the civil rights struggle in the 1940s and early 1950s? What organizations played the most central role? Which tactics continued to be used, and which were abandoned?

2. How did African American communities challenge legal segregation in the South? Compare the strategies of key organizations, such as the NAACP, SNCC, SCLC, and CORE.

3. Discuss the varieties of white resistance to the civil rights movement. Which were most effective in slowing the drive for equality?

4. Analyze the civil rights movement's complex relationship with the national Democratic Party between 1948 and 1964. How was the party transformed by its association with the movement? What political gains and losses did that association entail?

5. What legal and institutional impact did the movement have on American life? How did it change American culture and politics? Where did it fail?

6. What relationship did the African Americans who struggled for civil rights have with other American minorities? How—if at all—did these minorities benefit? Did they build their own versions of the movement?

RECOMMENDED READING

Taylor Branch, *Parting the Waters: America in the King Years, 1954–1963* (1988); *Pillar of Fire: America in the King Years, 1963–1965* (1998). A deeply researched and monumental narrative history of the southern civil rights movement organized around the life and influence of Reverend Martin Luther King, Jr.

Clayborne Carson, *In Struggle: SNCC and the Black Awakening of the 1960s* (1981). The most comprehensive history of the Student Nonviolent Coordinating Committee, arguably the most important civil rights organization. Carson stresses the evolution of SNCC's radicalism during the course of the decade.

William Chafe, *Civilities and Civil Rights: Greensboro, North Carolina, and the Black Struggle for Equality* (1980). Examines the community of Greensboro from 1945 to 1975. Chafe focuses on the "etiquette of civility" and its complex relationship with the promise of racial justice, along with black protest movements and relations between the city's blacks and whites.

David Chappell, *Inside Agitators: White Southerners in the Civil Rights Movement* (1994). A thoughtful and sophisticated analysis of the varying roles played by whites in the movement.

Mary L. Dudziak, *Cold War Civil Rights: Race and the Image of American Democracy* (2000). Excellent analysis of the connections between the struggle for racial equality in America and the nation's contest with communism abroad.

Sara Evans, *Personal Politics: The Roots of Women's Liberation in the Civil Rights Movement and the New Left* (1979). A pathbreaking study showing the important connections between the struggle for black rights and the rebirth of feminism.

Aldon D. Morris, *The Origins of the Civil Rights Movement: Black Communities Organizing for Change* (1984). An important study combining history and social theory. Morris emphasizes the key role of ordinary black people, acting through their churches and other community organizations before 1960.

Howell Raines, *My Soul Is Rested: Movement Days in the Deep South Remembered* (1977). The best oral history of the civil rights movement, drawing from a wide range of participants and points of view. It is brilliantly edited by Raines, who covered the events as a journalist.

Jo Ann Gibson Robinson, *The Montgomery Bus Boycott and the Women Who Started It.* ed. David J. Garrow (1987). An important memoir by one of the key behind-the-scenes players in the Montgomery bus boycott. Robinson stresses the role of middle- and working-class black women in the struggle.

Robert Weisbrot, *Freedom Bound: A History of America's Civil Rights Movement* (1990). One of the best single-volume syntheses of the movement. Weisbrot is especially strong on the often turbulent relations between black activists and white liberals and the relationship between civil rights and broader currents of American reform.

ADDITIONAL BIBLIOGRAPHY

Origins of the Movements
Michael R. Belknap, *Federal Law and Southern Order* (1987)
Scott DeVeaux, *The Birth of BeBop* (1998)
Grace Elizabeth Hale, *Making Whiteness: The Culture of Segregation in the South, 1890–1940* (1998)
Charles P. Henry, *Ralph Bunche: Model Negro or American Other* (1999)
Grace Williams O'Brien, *The Color of the Law: Race, Violence, and Justice in the Post–World War II South* (1999)
Bernard Schwartz, *The NAACP's Legal Strategy against Segregated Education* (1987)
Mark Tushnet, *Making Civil Rights Law: Thurgood Marshall and the Supreme Court, 1936–1961* (1994)
Jules Tygiel, *Baseball's Great Experiment: Jackie Robinson and His Legacy* (1983)

No Easy Road to Freedom, 1957–62
Constance Curry, et.al., *Deep In Our Hearts: Nine White Women in the Freedom Movement* (2000)
John Dittmer, *Local People: The Struggle for Civil Rights in Mississippi* (1994)
James Farmer, *Lay Bare the Heart* (1985)
James Forman, *The Making of Black Revolutionaries* (1985)
David J. Garrow, *The FBI and Martin Luther King, Jr.* (1983)
Cheryl L. Greenberg, ed., *A Circle of Trust: Remembering SNCC* (1998)
Charles M. Payne, *I've Got the Light of Freedom: The Organizing Tradition and the Mississippi Freedom Struggle* (1995)
Miles Wolff, *Lunch at the 5&10* (1990)
Howard Zinn, *SNCC: The New Abolitionists* (1965)

The Movement at High Tide, 1963–65
Seth Cagin and Philip Dray, *We Are Not Afraid* (1988)
Henry Hampton and Steve Fayer, *Voices of Freedom: An Oral History of the Civil Rights Movement* (1990)
Doug McAdam, *Freedom Summer* (1988)
Belinda Robnett, *How Long? How Long? African American Women in the Struggle for Civil Rights* (1997)
Debra L. Schultz, *Going South: Jewish Women in the Civil Rights Movement* (2001)

Clive Webb, *Fight Against Fear: Southern Jews and Black Civil Rights* (2001)

Forgotten Minorities, 1945–65
Rodolfo Acuna, *Occupied America*, 3d ed. (1981)
Larry Burt, *Tribalism in Crisis: Federal Indian Policy, 1953–1961* (1982)
Thomas W. Conger, *The National Congress of American Indians* (1999)
Donald Fixico, *Termination and Relocation: Federal Indian Policy, 1945–1960* (1986)
Manuel G. Gonzalez, *Mexicanos: A History of Mexicans in the United States* (1999)
Gary Y. Okihiro, *The Columbia Guide to Asian American History* (2001)
David Palumbo-Liu, *Asian Americans: Historical Crossings of a Racial Frontier* (1999)
Maria E. Perez y Gonzalez, *Puerto Ricans in the United States* (2000)
Kenneth R. Philip, *Termination Revisited: American Indians on the Trail to Self Determination, 1933–1953* (1999)
Cora T. Whalen, *From Puerto Rico to Philadelphia: Puerto Rican Workers and Postwar Economies* (2001)

Biography
Robert Dallek, *Flawed Giant: Lyndon B. Johnson and His Times, 1961–1973* (1998)
Michael Eric Dyson, *I May Not Get There With You: The True Martin Luther King, Jr.* (2000)
David J. Garrow, *Bearing the Cross: Martin Luther King, Jr., and the Southern Christian Leadership Conference* (1986)
Joann Grant, *Ella Baker: Freedom Bound* (1998)
Chana Kai Lee, *For Freedom's Sake: The Life of Fannie Lou Hamer* (1999)
Daniel Levine, *Bayard Rustin and the Civil Rights Movement* (2000)
John Lewis, *Walking With the Wind: A Memoir of the Movement* (1998)
Malcolm X, with Alex Haley, *The Autobiography of Malcolm X* (1965)

HISTORY ON THE INTERNET

http://supct.law.cornell.edu/supct/cases/historic.htm

The Legal Information Institute of Cornell Law School provides complete transcripts of a few hundred of the most important U.S. Supreme Court decisions. Use this resource to examine the most important decisions of the Warren Court, especially *Brown v. Board of Education of Topeka, Kansas* (1954), *Brown II* (1955), *Gideon v. Wainwright* (1963), *Escobedo v. Illinois* (1964), *Baker v. Carr* (1962), *Miranda v. Arizona* (1966) and others.

http://www.angelfire.com/pa/marchonwashington/

An interesting, detailed description of the 1963 March on Washington.

http://seattletimes.nwsource.com/mlk/movement/PT/phototour.html

A photo history of the Civil Right movement of the 1950s and 1960s sponsored by the *Seattle Times*.

http://www.usbr.gov/laws/civil.html

Links to the full legal text of the Civil Rights Act of 1957, 1960, 1964, and 1968.

http://hcl.chass.ncsu.edu/garson/dye/docs/votrit65.htm

Full legal text of the Voting Rights Act of 1965.

▶ Flying the "Stars and Bars"

In 1956 African-American citizens in Montgomery, Alabama, successfully boycotted the city's segregated bus lines, thus sparking a non-violent mass movement to end legalized segregation in the South. Nearly a century earlier, on the eve of the Civil War, Montgomery had hosted a convention which created the Confederate States of America. As both the "cradle of the Confederacy" and the birthplace of the modern Civil Rights movement, it's not surprising that Montgomery, Alabama has been the site of bitter conflict over the meaning and use of the Confederate flag. Indeed, during the 1990s, widespread controversy in the South over displays of the Confederate flag reflected both the fierce pride many white Southerners maintained for the "Lost Cause" and the enormous changes wrought by the Civil Rights movement of the 1950s and 1960s. The fight over the flag and what it represents provides a perfect example of how communities struggle over the meaning of their history. For as William Faulkner, the South's most distinguished novelist, once put it: "The past is not dead, it isn't even past."

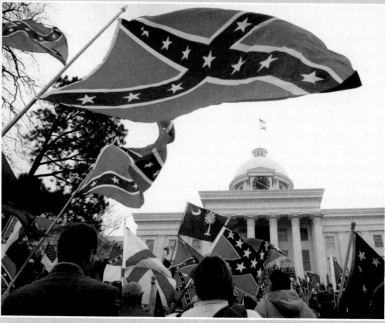

In March, 2000, thousands of demonstrators rallied outside the Capitol in Montgomery, calling on state officials to once again fly the Confederate flag over the building. This rally was organized by the League of the South, an organization dedicated to celebrating white Southern history and culture.

SOURCE: Alabama Department of Archives and History, Montgomery, Alabama (86.3972.1(PN10138, PN10181)).

Throughout the South, the revived use of the Confederate flag began as part of the white backlash against the campaign to end legal segregation. In 1963 Alabama Gov. George C. Wallace ordered the Confederate battle flag to fly on top of the state capitol to protest a visit by Attorney General Robert F. Kennedy, who had come to Montgomery to discuss desegregation of the state's schools. The flag, which had white stars on a blue X-shape against a red background, was the same design as the battle flag carried in the field by Confederate troops during the Civil War. The battle flag flew over the dome, along with the national and state flags, until the spring of 1992, when they were taken down during renovation work. By then, the Confederate flag had become a cultural icon of regional pride and enduring belief in white supremacy in many parts of the South. And around the nation, others adopted it as an all-purpose symbol of rebellion and resistance to authority, displayed on posters, clothing, bumper stickers, and featured in music videos.

But for most African Americans the Confederate flag meant something quite different. In the summer of 1988 fourteen black state legislators were arrested for trespassing on state property when they attempted to scale a chain-link fence and remove the flag. Rep. Alvin Holmes, one of those arrested, said, "When I walk up the Capitol steps, instead of seeing the American flag, the flag that I served under when I was in the United States Army, I see a flag that represents treason, sedition, slavery, and oppression toward my people."

In December 1992 Montgomery prepared to rededicate the 141-year-old state Capitol after a $28 million restoration. When Gov. Guy Hunt insisted that the "Stars and Bars" continue to fly over the building, 24 African-American legislators boycotted the ceremony in protest. Rep. Holmes filed a lawsuit asking for

In the early 1960s three flags flew over the Alabama State Capitol in Montgomery, representing the United States, Alabama, and the Confederacy. Governor George Wallace had insisted on flying the Confederate "Stars and Bars" as a protest against the Civil Rights Movement. It was removed in 1992 after demonstrations and a court challenge led by African American state legislators.

an injunction, claiming an 1896 state law prohibited any flags other than the Alabama and U.S. flags from flying above the Capitol. Alabama citizens expressed a wide range of opinions on the subject. Most whites insisted the old symbol was about regional identity and pride, not race. John Napier, a retired Air Force colonel and leader of the Sons of Confederate veterans argued, "We celebrate our civil rights history. There are those of us who feel the earlier struggle should be commemorated historically, too. While we're running around naming streets for Rosa Parks, which I have no problem with, you're getting into removing all the symbols of the Confederacy." African Americans, for whom the flag symbolized slavery, racism, and segregation, tried to distinguish between private and public displays. "I see nothing wrong with someone flying the Confederate flag even on their front lawn or putting it on their bumper stickers," said Earl Shinhoster, an official of the NAACP. "I do, however, see something wrong when the state promotes something that many people find offensive."

As with the Montgomery bus boycott of 1956, the economic implications of the controversy were not lost on the city's the business community and political leaders. Anna Bishop, spokeswoman for the Montgomery Chamber of Commerce, noted that, "Business people are realizing that the flag contributes to a negative image for Alabama."

The Alabama State Business Council told Gov. Hunt in a letter that "the Confederate flag is detrimental to our image and is dividing our citzenry." Neal Wade of the Economic Development Partnership of Alabama asserted, "Anything that causes division within a state makes it less attractive to a potential employer, particularly from overseas."

In January 1993, just a few weeks after the dedication of the renovated Capitol, Judge William Gordon of Alabama Circuit Court in Montgomery ruled that the 1896 state law did indeed prohibit the state from flying the "Stars and Bars" over the state Capitol. The new governor, Jim Folsom, announced that he would not challenge the decision, and that the Confederate battle flag would fly instead across the street at the First White House of the Confederacy. "This has been a divisive issue in our state," he said, "and I believe it is time we put it behind us and move our state forward." Still, in many parts of the country private and public displays of the Confederate flag have persisted—and so have the continued and deeply felt debates over the historical meanings embedded within it. ■

TWENTY-NINE

WAR ABROAD, WAR AT HOME

▶ 1965 – 1974

Bernard Perlin, *Mayor Richard Daley*, 1968. Collection of Philip J. and Suzanne Schiller, American Social Commentary Art, 1930–70.
SOURCE: Library of Congress.

AMERICAN COMMUNITIES

Uptown, Chicago, Illinois

DURING FREEDOM SUMMER OF 1964, WHILE TEAMS OF NORTHERN college students traveled south to join voter registration campaigns among African Americans, a small group moved to Chicago to help the city's poor people take control of their communities and to demand better city services. They targeted a neighborhood known as Uptown, a one-mile-square section five miles north of the Loop, the city center. The residents, many only recently transplanted from the poverty of the Appalachian South, lived in crowded tenements or in once-elegant mansions now subdivided into tiny, run-down apartments. Four thousand people lived on just one street running four blocks, 20 percent of them on welfare. Chicago civic authorities had also selected this neighborhood for improvement. Designating it a Conservation Area under the terms of the Urban Renewal Act, they applied for federal funds in order to upgrade the housing for middle-income families and, in effect, to clear out the current residents. In contrast, the student organizers intended to mobilize the community "so as to demand an end to poverty and the construction of a decent social order."

With the assistance of the Packinghouse Workers union, the students formed Jobs or Income Now (JOIN), opened a storefront office, and invited local residents to work with them to halt the city's plans. They spent hours and hours listening to people, drawing out their ideas and helping them develop scores of additional programs. Confronting the bureaucracy of the welfare and unemployment compensation offices stood high on their list. They also campaigned against Mayor Richard Daley's policy of "police omnipresence" that had a fleet of squad cars and paddy wagons continually patrolling the neighborhood. To curb police harassment, they demanded the creation of civilian review boards. They also helped establish new social clubs, a food-buying cooperative, a community theater, and a health clinic. Within a few years, Uptown street kids had formed the Young Patriots organization, put out a community newspaper, *Rising Up Angry,* and staffed free breakfast programs.

Chicago JOIN was one of ten similar projects sponsored by Students for a Democratic Society (SDS). Impatient with the nation's chronic poverty and cold war politics, twenty-nine students from nine universities had met in June 1960 to form a new kind of campus-based political organization. SDS soon caught the attention of liberal students, encouraging them, as part of the nation's largest college population to date, to make their voices heard. By its peak in 1968, SDS had 350 chapters and between 60,000 and 100,000 members. Its principle of participatory democracy—with its promise to give people control over the decisions affecting their lives—appealed to a wider following of more than a million students.

In June 1962, in Port Huron, Michigan, the founding members of SDS issued a declaration of principles, drafted mainly by graduate student Tom Hayden. "We are people . . . bred in at least modest comfort, housed now in universities," *The Port Huron Statement* opened, "looking uncomfortably to the world we inherit." The dire effects of poverty and

903

social injustice, it continued, were not the only dismaying things about American society. A deeper ailment plagued American politics. Everyone, including middle-class students with few material wants, suffered from a sense of "loneliness, estrangement, and alienation." *The Port Huron Statement* defined SDS as a new kind of political movement that would bring people "out of isolation and into community." Through participatory democracy, not just the poor but all Americans could overcome their feelings of "powerlessness [and hence] resignation before the enormity of events." As one organizer explained, programs like JOIN were attempts to create a poor people's movement as well as a means for students themselves to live an "authentic life" outside the constraints of middle-class society.

SDS began with a campaign to reform the university, especially to disentangle the financial ties between campus-based research programs and the military-industrial complex. Later it expanded to the nation's cities, sending small groups of students to live and organize in the poor communities of Boston, Louisville, Cleveland, and Newark as well as Chicago. Ultimately, few of these projects succeeded in mobilizing the poor to political action. Protests against local government did little to combat unemployment, and campaigns for better garbage collection or more playgrounds rarely evolved into lasting movements. Nevertheless, organizers did succeed in bringing many neighborhood residents "out of isolation and into community." By late 1967, SDS prepared to leave JOIN in the hands of the people it had organized, which was its goal from the beginning.

Initially, even Lyndon Baines Johnson promoted the ideal of civic participation. The Great Society, as the president called his domestic program, promised more than the abolition of poverty and racial inequality. In May 1964, at the University of Michigan, the president described his goal as a society "where every child can find knowledge to enrich his mind and to enlarge his talents," where "the city of man serves not only the needs of the body and the demands of commerce but the desire for beauty and the hunger for community."

By 1967 the Vietnam War had upset the domestic agendas of both SDS and the Johnson administration. If SDSers had once believed they could work with liberal Democrats to reduce poverty in the United States, they now interpreted social injustice at home as the inevitable consequence of dangerous and destructive foreign policies pursued by liberals and conservatives alike. SDS threw its energies into the movement against the war in Vietnam. President Johnson, meanwhile, pursued a foreign policy that would swallow up the funding for his own plans for a war on poverty and would precipitate a very different war at home, Americans against Americans. As hawks and doves lined up on opposite sides, the Vietnam War created a huge and enduring rift. SDS member Richard Flacks had warned that the nation had to "choose between devoting its resources and energies to maintaining military superiority and international hegemony or rechanneling those resources and energies to meeting the desperate needs of its people." Ultimately, even President Johnson himself understood that the "bitch of a war" in Asia ruined "the woman I really loved—the Great Society." The dream of community did not vanish, but consensus appeared increasingly remote as the United States fought—and eventually lost— the longest war in its history. ■

Chicago

---■ KEY TOPICS ---

■ Widening U.S. involvement in the war in Vietnam

■ The "sixties generation" and the antiwar movement

■ Poverty and urban crisis

■ The election of 1968

■ The rise of "liberation" movements

■ The Nixon presidency and the Watergate conspiracy

VIETNAM: AMERICA'S LONGEST WAR

The Vietnam War had its roots in the Truman Doctrine and its goal of containing communism (see Chapter 26). After the defeat of the French by the Communist forces of Ho Chi Minh in 1954, Vietnam emerged as a major zone of cold war contention. President John Kennedy called it "the cornerstone of the Free World in Southeast Asia, the keystone in the arch, the finger in the dike," a barrier to the spread of communism throughout the region and perhaps the world. President Lyndon Johnson sounded the same note at the beginning of his presidency. He told the public that North Vietnam was intent on conquering South Vietnam, defeating the United States, and extending "the Asiatic dominion of communism." With American security at stake, he concluded, Americans had little choice but to fight for "the principle for which our ancestors fought in the valleys of Pennsylvania."

Vietnam was not Valley Forge, however, and the United States ultimately paid a huge price for its determination to turn back communism in Indochina. More than 50,000 Americans died in an unwinnable overseas war that only deepened divisions at home.

Johnson's War

Although President Kennedy had greatly increased the number of military advisors in South Vietnam (see Chapter 27), it was his successor, Lyndon B. Johnson, who made the decision to engage the United States in a major war there. At first, Johnson simply hoped to stay the course in Vietnam. Facing a presidential election in November 1964, he knew that a major military setback would cripple his election campaign. But he was equally determined to avoid the fate of President Truman, who had bogged down politically after "losing" China to communism and producing a stalemate in Korea. Within days of taking office, the new president said he

intended to do his utmost to help South Vietnam win its "contest against the externally directed and supported Communist conspiracy."

Throughout the winter and spring of 1964, as conditions grew steadily worse in South Vietnam, Johnson and his advisors quietly laid the groundwork for a sustained bombing campaign against North Vietnam. In early August, they found a pretext to set this plan in motion. After two U.S. destroyers in the Gulf of Tonkin, off the coast of North Vietnam, reported attacks by North Vietnamese patrol boats, Johnson retaliated by ordering air strikes against bases in North Vietnam.

Johnson now appealed to Congress to pass a resolution giving him the authority "to take all necessary measures" and "all necessary steps" to defend U.S. armed forces and to protect Southeast Asia "against aggression or subversion." This Tonkin Gulf resolution, secretly drafted six weeks before the incident for which it was named, passed the Senate on August 7 with only two dissenting votes and moved unanimously through the House. It served, in Undersecretary of State Nicholas Katzenbach's words, as the "functional equivalent" of a declaration of war.

Ironically, Johnson had campaigned for the presidency with a call for restraint in Vietnam. He assured voters that "we are not about to send American boys nine or ten thousand miles away from home to do what Asian boys ought to be doing for themselves." This strategy helped him win a landslide victory over conservative Republican Barry Goldwater of Arizona, who had proposed the deployment of nuclear weapons in Vietnam.

With the election behind him, Johnson now faced a hard decision. The limited bombing raids against North Vietnam had failed to slow the movement of the Communist Vietcong forces across the border into the South. Meanwhile, the government in Saigon, the capital city of South Vietnam, appeared near collapse. Faced with the prospect of a Communist victory, the president chose to escalate U.S. involvement in Vietnam massively.

Deeper into the Quagmire

In early February 1965, Johnson found a rationale to justify massive bombing of the North. The Vietcong had fired at the barracks of the U.S. Marine base at Pleiku in the central highlands of Vietnam, killing eight and wounding more than 100 Americans. Waving the list of casualties, the president rushed into an emergency meeting of the National Security Council to announce that the time had passed for keeping "our guns over the mantel and our shells in the cupboard." He ordered immediate reprisal bombing of North Vietnam and one week later, on February 13, authorized Operation Rolling Thunder, a campaign of gradually intensifying air attacks.

Johnson and his advisers hoped that the air strikes against North Vietnam would demonstrate U.S. resolve "both to Hanoi and to the world" and make the deployment of ground forces unnecessary. Intelligence reports, however, suggested that the bombing had little impact and noted, moreover, that North Vietnam was now sending troops into South Vietnam. With retreat his only alternative, Johnson decided to introduce ground troops for offensive operations.

Once Rolling Thunder had begun, President Johnson found it increasingly difficult to speak frankly with the American public about his policies. Initially, he announced that only two battalions of marines were being assigned to Danang to defend the airfields where bombing runs began. But six week later, 50,000 U.S. troops were in Vietnam. By November 1965 the total topped 165,000, and more troops were on the way. But even after Johnson authorized a buildup to 431,000 troops in mid-1966, victory was still nowhere in sight.

The strategy pursued by the Johnson administration and implemented by General William Westmoreland—a war of attrition—was based on the premise that continued bombing would eventually exhaust North Vietnam's resources. Meanwhile, U.S. ground forces would defeat the Vietcong in South Vietnam, forcing its soldiers to defect and supporters to scatter, thereby restoring political stability to South Vietnam's pro-Western government. As Johnson once boasted, the strongest military power in the world surely could crush a Communist rebellion in a "pissant" country of peasants.

In practice, the United States wreaked havoc in South Vietnam, tearing apart its society and bringing ecological devastation to its land. Intending to locate and eradicate the support network of the Vietcong, U.S. ground troops conducted search-and-destroy missions throughout the countryside. They attacked villagers and their homes. Seeking to ferret out Vietcong sympathizers, U.S. troops turned at any one time as many as 4 million people—approximately one-quarter of the population of South Vietnam—into refugees. By late 1968, the United States had dropped more than 3 million tons

Refugees, Binh Dinh Province, 1967. The massive bombing and ground combat broke apart the farming communities of South Vietnam, creating huge numbers of civilian casualties and driving millions into quickly constructed refugee camps or already overcrowded cities. Approximately 25 percent of the South Vietnamese population fled their native villages, many never to return.

SOURCE: Photo by Philip Jones Griffiths. Magnum Photos, Inc.

of bombs on Vietnam, and eventually delivered more than three times the tonnage dropped by the Allies on all fronts during World War II. The United States also conducted the most destructive chemical warfare in history. To deprive the Vietcong of camouflage, American troops used herbicides to defoliate forests. During Operation Ranch Hand, which ran between 1965 and 1971, 17.6 million gallons of Agent Orange were sprayed over approximately 3.6 million acres of South Vietnam.

Several advisers urged the president to inform the American people about his decisions on Vietnam, even to declare a state of national emergency. But Johnson feared he would lose momentum on domestic reform, including his antipoverty programs, if he drew attention to foreign policy. Seeking to avoid "undue excitement in the Congress and in domestic public opinion," he held to a course of intentional deceit.

The Credibility Gap

Johnson's popularity had surged at the time of the Tonkin Gulf resolution, skyrocketing in one day from 42 to 72 percent, according to a Louis Harris poll. But afterward it waned rapidly. The war dragged on. Every night network television news reported the soaring American body count, from 26 per week in 1965 to 180 in 1967. No president had worked so hard to control the news media, but by 1967 Johnson found himself badgered at press conferences by reporters who accused the president of creating a credibility gap.

Scenes of human suffering and devastation recorded by television cameras increasingly undermined the administration's moral justification of the war with claims that it was a necessary defense of freedom and democracy in South Vietnam. During the early 1960s, network news had either ignored Vietnam or had been patriotically supportive of U.S. policy. Beginning with a report on a ground operation against the South Vietnamese village of Cam Ne by Morley Safer for CBS News in August 1965, however, the tenor of news reporting changed. Although government officials described the operation as a strategic destruction of "fortified Vietcong bunkers," the *CBS Evening News* showed pictures of Marines setting fire to the thatched homes of civilians. After CBS aired Safer's report, President Johnson complained bitterly to the news director. But more critical commentary soon followed. By 1967, according to a noted media observer, "every subject tended to become Vietnam." Televised news reports now told of new varieties of American cluster bombs, which released up to 180,000 fiberglass shards, and showed the nightmarish effects of the defoliants used on forests in South Vietnam to uncover enemy strongholds.

Coverage of the war in the print media also became more skeptical of Johnson's policies. By 1967 independent news teams were probing the government's official claims. Harrison Salisbury, Pulitzer Prize–winning *New York Times* reporter, questioned the administration's claims that its bombing of the North precisely targeted military objectives, charging that U.S. planes had bombed the population center of Hanoi, capital of North Vietnam, and intentionally ravaged villages in the South. As American military deaths climbed at the rate of more than 800 per month during the first half of 1967, newspaper coverage of the war focused yet more intently on such disturbing events.

The most vocal congressional critic of Johnson's war policy was Democratic senator J. William Fulbright of Arkansas, who chaired the Senate Foreign Relations Committee and who had personally speeded the passage of the Tonkin Gulf resolution. A strong supporter of the cold war, Fulbright had decided that the war in Vietnam was unwinnable and destructive to domestic reform. In *Arrogance of Power,* a book published in 1966 that became a national bestseller, he proposed a negotiated withdrawal from a neutralized Southeast Asia. At first Fulbright stood nearly alone: in October 1966 only 15 percent of Congress favored a negotiated settlement. But he soon persuaded prominent Democrats in Congress, such as Frank Church, Mike Mansfield, and

George McGovern, to put aside their personal loyalty to Johnson and oppose his conduct of the war. In 1967 the Congress passed a nonbinding resolution appealing to the United Nations to help negotiate an end to hostilities. Meanwhile, some of the nation's most trusted European allies called for restraint in Vietnam.

The impact of the war, which cost Americans $21 billion per year, was also felt at home. Johnson convinced Congress to levy a 10 percent surcharge on individual and corporate taxes. Later adjustments in the national budget tapped the Social Security fund, heretofore safe from interference. Inflation raced upward, fed by spending on the war. Johnson replaced advisers who questioned his policy, but as casualties multiplied, more and more Americans began to question his handling of the war.

A GENERATION IN CONFLICT

As the war in Vietnam escalated, Americans from all walks of life demanded an end to U.S. involvement. Debates raged everywhere, from families to informal community meetings to the halls of Congress. Eventually the antiwar movement won over a majority. But between 1965 and 1971, its years of peak activity, it had a distinctly generational character. At the forefront were the baby boomers who were just coming of age.

This so-called sixties generation, the largest generation in American history, was also the best educated. By the late 1960s, nearly half of all young adults between the ages of 18 and 21 were enrolled in college. In 1965 there were 5 million college students; in 1973 the number had doubled to 10 million. Public universities made the largest gains; by 1970 eight had more than 30,000 students apiece. Although a small minority, groups of students began to combine protest against the war in Vietnam with a broader, penetrating critique of American society. Through music, dress, and even hairstyle, they expressed a deep estrangement from the values and aspirations of their parents' generation. As early as 1967, when opposition to the war had begun to swell, "flower children" were putting daisies in the rifle barrels of troops stationed to quash campus protests, providing a seemingly innocent counterpoint to the grim news of slaughter abroad.

Representing perhaps only one-quarter of the nation's college students, these young people had an impact far beyond their numbers. They promoted a "culture of life" against the "culture of death" symbolized by the war. Campus organizations such as SDS, which had begun in the early 1960s in an attempt to build community, now turned against the government. SDS encouraged many college students to take a militant stand against the war, calling for an immediate and unconditional withdrawal of U.S. troops from Vietnam.

Young women, dressed in hippie garb, flash the peace sign in protest against the war in Vietnam.

SOURCE: Photo by Jeffrey Blankfort. Jeroboam, Inc. (JB24-8183).

"The Times They Are A-Changin'"

The first sign of a new kind of protest was the free speech movement at the University of California at Berkeley in 1964. That fall, civil rights activists returned to the 27,000-student campus from Freedom Summer in Mississippi. They soon began to picket Bay Area stores that practiced discrimination in hiring and to recruit other students to join them. When the university administration moved to prevent them from setting up information booths on campus, eighteen groups protested, including the arch-conservative Students for Goldwater, claiming that their right to free speech had been abridged. The administration responded by sending police to break up the protest rally and arrest participants. University president Clark Kerr met with students, agreed not to press charges, and seemed set to grant them a small space on campus for political activity. Then, under pressure from conservative regents, Kerr reversed himself and announced in November that the university planned to press new charges against the free speech movement's leaders. On December 2 a crowd of 7,000 gathered to protest this decision. Joining folk singer Joan Baez in singing "We Shall Overcome," a group of 1,000 people marched toward the university's administration building, where they planned to stage a sit-in until Kerr rescinded his order. The police arrested nearly 800 protestors in the largest mass arrest in California history.

Mario Savio, a Freedom Summer volunteer and philosophy student, explained that the free speech movement wanted more than just the right to conduct political activity on campus. He spoke for many students when he complained that the university had become a faceless bureaucratic machine rather than a community of learning. Regulating the activities of students while preparing them for colorless lives as corporation clerks, the university made them "so sick at heart" that they had decided to put their "bodies upon the gears" to make it stop.

The free speech movement's social critique resonated among college students. Across the country they began to demand a say in the structuring of their education. Brown University students, for example, demanded a revamp of the curriculum that would eliminate all required courses and make grades optional. Students also protested campus rules that treated students as children instead of as adults. After a string of campus protests, most large universities, including the University of California, relinquished *in loco parentis* (in the place of parents) policies and allowed students to live off-campus and to set their own hours.

Across the bay in San Francisco, other young adults staked out a new form of community—a counterculture. In 1967, the "Summer of Love," the population of the Haight-Ashbury district swelled by 75,000 as youthful adventurers gathered for the most celebrated "be-in" of the era. Although the *San Francisco Chronicle* featured a headline reading "Mayor Warns Hippies to Stay Out of Town," masses of long-haired young men and women dressed in bell-bottoms and tie-dyed T-shirts were undeterred. They congregated in "the Haight" to listen to music, take drugs, and "be" with each other. "If you're going to San Francisco," a popular rock group sang, "be sure to wear some flowers in your hair . . . you're going to meet some gentle people there." In the fall, the majority returned to their own communities, often bringing with them a new lifestyle. *Time* magazine announced the appearance of new "hippie enclaves . . . in every major U.S. city from Boston to Seattle, from Detroit to New Orleans."

The generational rebellion took many forms, including a revolution in sexual behavior that triggered countless quarrels between parents and their maturing sons and daughters. During the 1960s more teenagers experienced premarital sex—by the decade's end three-quarters of all college seniors had engaged in sexual intercourse—and far more talked about it openly than in previous eras. With birth control widely available, including the newly developed "pill," many young women, who were no longer deterred from sex by fear of pregnancy, rejected premarital abstinence. "We've discarded the idea that the loss of virginity is related to degeneracy," one college student explained. "Premarital sex doesn't mean the downfall of society, at least not the kind of society that we're going to build." Many heterosexual couples chose to live together outside marriage, a practice few parents condoned. A much smaller but significant number formed communes—approximately 4,000 by 1970—where members could share housekeeping and child care as well as sexual partners.

Mood-altering drugs played a large part in this counterculture. In the 1950s, doctors had begun to freely prescribe tranquilizers and antidepressants, and alcohol and tobacco were popular stimulants. The drug subculture that emerged in the 1960s, however, was associated primarily with illicit psychoactive substances and hallucinogenic drugs. Harvard professor Timothy Leary urged young people to "turn on, tune in, drop out" and also advocated the mass production and distribution of LSD (lysergic acid diethylamide), which was not criminalized until 1968. Hollywood movies, such as *Easy Rider*, which was released in 1969, cast Peter Fonda and Dennis Hopper as two alienated youth who indulged in both casual sex and drugs. Marijuana, illegal yet readily available, was often paired with rock music in a collective ritual of love and laughter. Singer Bob Dylan taunted adults with the lyrics of his hit single, "Everybody must get stoned."

Music played a large part in defining the counterculture. With the emergence of rock 'n' roll in the 1950s, popular music had begun to express a deliberate generational identity (see Chapter 27), a trend that gained momentum with the emergence of the British rock group The Beatles in 1964. Folk music, which had gained popularity on campuses in the early 1960s with the successful recordings of Peter, Paul, and Mary, Phil Ochs, and Judy Collins, as well as Joan Baez, continued to serve the voice of protest. Shortly after Freedom Summer, folk singer Bob Dylan issued a warning to parents:

> Your sons and your daughters
> are beyond your command
> Your old road is
> rapidly agin'.
> Please get out of the new one
> If you can't lend your hand
> For the times they are a-changin'.

By 1965 Dylan himself had turned to the electric guitar and rock, which triumphed as the musical emblem of a generation.

At a farm near Woodstock, New York, more than 400,000 people gathered in August 1969 for a three-day rock concert and to give witness to the ideals of the counterculture. Richie Havens opened with "Freedom," and performers including Joan Baez, Janis Joplin, Santana, and The Grateful Dead among others entertained the crowd. Thousands took drugs while security officials and local police stood by, some stripped off their clothes to dance or swim, and a few even made love in the grass. "We were exhilarated," one reveler recalled. "We felt as though we were in liberated territory."

The Woodstock Nation, as the counterculture was mythologized, did not actually represent the sentiments of most young Americans. But its attitudes and styles, especially its efforts to create a new community, did speak for the large minority seeking a peaceful alternative to the intensifying climate of war. "We used to think of ourselves as little clumps of weirdos," rock star Janis Joplin explained. "But now we're a whole new minority group." Another interpreter, Charles Reich, whose *The Greening of America* (1970) became a best-seller, defined the counterculture as a generation's attempt to create "a form of community in which love, respect, and a mutual search for wisdom replace the competition and separation of the past." The slogan "Make Love, Not War" linked generational rebellion and opposition to the U.S. invasion of Vietnam.

From Campus Protest to Mass Mobilization

Three weeks after the announcement of Operation Rolling Thunder in 1965, peace activists called for a day-long boycott of classes so that students and faculty might meet to discuss the war. At the University of Michigan in Ann Arbor, more than 3,000 students turned out for sessions held through the night because university administrators had bowed to the pressure of state legislators and had refused to cancel classes. During the following weeks, "teach-ins" spread across the United States and to Europe and Japan as well.

Students also began to protest against war-related research on their campuses. The expansion of higher education in the 1960s had depended largely on federally funded programs, including military research on counterinsurgency tactics and new chemical weapons. Student protesters demanded an end to these programs and, receiving no response from university administrators, turned to civil disobedience. In October 1967, the Dow Chemical Company, manufacturers of napalm, a form of jellied gasoline often used against civilians in Vietnam, sent job recruiters to the University of Wisconsin at Madison despite warnings that a group of students would try to prevent them from conducting interviews. A few hundred students staged a sit-in at the building where the recruitment interviews were scheduled, and 2,000 onlookers gathered outside. Ordered by university administrators to disperse the crowd, the city's police broke glass doors, dragged students through the debris, and clubbed those who refused to move. Suddenly the campus erupted. Students chanted *Sieg Heil* at the police, who attempted to disperse them with tear gas and Mace. Undergraduate students and their teaching assistants boycotted classes for a week. During the first half of 1968 alone, nearly 40,000 students staged more than 200 major demonstrations at more than 100 colleges and universities. During the next three years, the momentum grew, and demonstrations took place on campuses in every region of the country.

Many student strikes and demonstrations merged opposition to the war with other campus and community issues. At Columbia University, students struck in 1968 against the administration's plans to build a new gymnasium in a city park used by residents of neighboring Harlem. In the Southwest, Mexican American students demonstrated against the use of funds for military projects that might otherwise be allocated to antipoverty and educational programs.

By the late 1960s, the peace movement had spread well beyond the campus and commanded a diverse following. While some protesters marched, others held prayer vigils, staged art fairs, distributed leaflets door to door, or simply engaged friends and neighbors in conversation about Vietnam. In April 1967, a day-long antiwar rally at the Sheep Meadow in Manhattan's Central Park drew more than 300,000 people—more than had taken part in the civil rights movement's 1965 March on Washington. Meanwhile, 60,000 protesters turned out in San Francisco. By summer, Vietnam Veterans Against the War had begun to organize returning soldiers and sailors, encouraging them to cast off the medals and ribbons they had won in battle.

The steadily increasing size of antiwar demonstrations provoked conservatives and prowar Democrats to take a stronger stand in support of the war. On the weekend following the huge turnout in Central Park, the Veterans of Foreign Wars staged a "Loyalty Day" parade in New York City under the banner "One

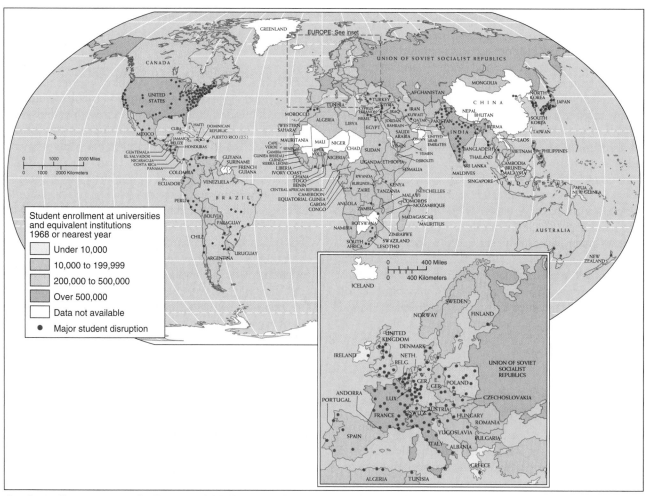

Antiwar Protests on College and University Campuses, 1967–1969
Campus-based protests against the war in Vietnam, at first centered on the East Coast and in California, spread to nearly every region of the country and around the world by the decade's end.

Country, One Flag, Love It or Leave It." Although only 7,500 people participated, the event signaled a hardening of opposition to the peace movement. Several newspaper and magazine editorialists called for the arrest of antiwar leaders on charges of treason. Secretary of State Dean Rusk, appearing on NBC's *Meet the Press*, expressed his concern that "authorities in Hanoi" might conclude, incorrectly, that the majority of Americans did not back their president and that "the net effect of these demonstrations will be to prolong the war, not to shorten it."

Many demonstrators themselves concluded that mass mobilizations alone had little impact on U.S. policy. Some sought to serve as moral witnesses. Despite a congressional act of 1965 providing for a five-year jail term and a $10,000 fine for destroying a draft card, nearly 200 young men destroyed their draft cards at the April Sheep Meadow demonstration and encouraged approximately a half-million more to resist the draft or refuse induction. Two Jesuit priests, Daniel and Philip Berrigan, raided the offices of the draft board in Catonsville, Maryland, in May 1968 and poured homemade napalm over records. A few protesters even doused their clothes with gasoline and set fire to themselves, as Buddhist monks protesting the war had done in Vietnam. Other activists determined to "bring the war home." An estimated 40,000 bombing incidents or bomb threats took place from January 1969 to April 1970; more than $21 million of property was damaged, and forty-three people were killed. Most of the perpetrators were never identified.

Observers at the time noted a similarity between the violence in Vietnam and the violence in the United States. Parallel wars were now being fought, one between two systems of government in Vietnam, another between the American government and masses of its citizens. Those Americans sent to Vietnam were caught in between.

Teenage Soldiers

The Vietnam War era witnessed not only a generation gap but a fissure within the generation of young adults. Whereas the average age of the World War II soldier was twenty-six, the age of those who fought in Vietnam hovered around nineteen. Until late 1969 the Selective Service System—the draft— gave deferments to college students and to workers in selected occupations while recruiting hard in poor communities, advertising the armed forces as a provider of vocational training and social mobility. Working-class young men, disproportionately African American and Latino, signed up in large numbers under these inducements. They also bore the brunt of combat. Whereas college graduates constituted only 12 percent of all soldiers and 9 percent of those who were killed in combat, high school dropouts were the most likely to serve in Vietnam and by far the most likely to die there. The death rate for African Americans was approximately 30 percent higher than the overall death rate for U.S. forces in Southeast Asia. These disparities created a rupture that would last well past the end of the war.

Yet the soldiers were not entirely isolated from the changes affecting their generation. G.I.s in significant numbers smoked marijuana, listed to rock music, and participated in the sexual revolution. In 1968 more than 200 soldiers from Fort Hood, Texas, attended a "be-in." But most condemned antiwar protest as the expressions of their privileged peers who did not have to fight.

As the war dragged on, however, some soldiers began to show their frustration. By 1971 many G.I.s were putting peace symbols on their combat helmets, joining antiwar demonstrations, and staging their own events such as "Armed Farces Day." Sometimes entire companies refused to carry out duty assignments or even to enter battle. A smaller number took revenge by "fragging" reckless commanding officers with grenades meant for the enemy. Meanwhile African American soldiers closed ranks and often flaunted their racial

African American troops in Vietnam, 1970. Serving on the front lines in disproportionate numbers, many black soldiers echoed the growing racial militancy in the United States and increasingly chose to spend their off-duty time apart from white soldiers.

SOURCE: Mark Jury, *The Vietnam Photo Book.*

solidarity by weaving their bootlaces into "slave brace-lets" and carrying Black Power canes, which were ebony-colored and topped with a clenched fist. Some openly complained about being asked to fight "a white man's war" and emblazoned their helmets with slogans like "No Gook Ever Called Me Nigger." By 1971, at least fourteen organizations claimed affiliation with RITA, an acronym for "Resistance in the Army." The largest was the American Servicemen's Union, which claimed more than 10,000 members and published its own newspaper, *The Bond.*

The nature of the war fed feelings of disaffection in the armed forces. U.S. troops entering South Vietnam expected a warm welcome from the people whose home-land they had been sent to defend. Instead, they encoun-tered anti-American demonstrations and placards with slogans like "End Foreign Dominance of Our Country." Hostile Vietnamese civilians viewed the Americans as in-vaders. The enemy avoided open engagements in which the Americans could benefit from their superior arms and air power. Soldiers found themselves instead stumbling into booby traps as they chased an elusive guerrilla foe through deep, leech-infested swamps and dense jungles swarming with fire ants. They could never be sure who was friend and who was foe. Patently false U.S. govern-ment press releases that heralded glorious victories and extolled the gratitude of Vietnamese civilians deepened bitterness on the front lines.

Approximately 8.6 million men and women served in the armed forces, and many returned to civilian life quietly and without fanfare, denied the glory earned by the combat veterans of previous wars. They reen-tered a society divided over the cause for which they had risked their lives. Tens of thousands suffered debil-itating physical injuries. As many as 40 percent of them came back with drug dependencies or symptoms of post-traumatic stress disorder, haunted and de-pressed by troubling memories of atrocities. Moreover, finding and keeping a job proved to be particularly hard in the shrinking economy of the 1970s. The situ-ation was especially bleak for African American veter-ans who returned to communities with unemployment rates at least triple the national average. Many veterans felt betrayed either by members of their own genera-tion who stayed home and protested or by their politi-cal leaders who sent them to fight an unwinnable war.

WARS ON POVERTY

During the early 1960s, the civil rights movement spurred a new awareness of and concern with poverty. As poor African Americans from both the rural South and the urban North got involved in political protests, they added the issues of unemployment, low wages,

and slum housing to the demands for desegregation and voting rights. The civil rights movement also re-vealed the close link between racial discrimination and economic inequalities. What good was winning the right to sit at a lunch counter if one could not afford to buy a hamburger?

One of the most influential books of the times, Michael Harrington's *The Other America* (1962), added fuel to this fire. Harrington argued that one-fifth of the nation—as many as 40 to 50 million people—suffered from bad housing, malnutrition, poor medical care, and other deprivations of poverty. He documented the miseries of what he called the "invisible land of the other Americans," the rejects of society who simply did not exist for affluent suburbanites or the mass media. The other America, Harrington wrote, "is populated by failures, by those driven from the land and bewil-dered by the city, by old people suddenly confronted with the torments of loneliness and poverty, and by minorities facing a wall of prejudice."

These arguments motivated President Johnson to expand the antipoverty program that he had inherited from the Kennedy administration. "That's my kind of program," he told his advisers. "It will help people. I want you to move full speed ahead on it." Ironically, it was another kind of war that ultimately undercut his aspiration to wage "an unconditional war on poverty."

The Great Society

In his State of the Union message in 1964, Johnson announced his plans to build a Great Society. Over the next two years, he used the political momentum of the civil rights movement and the overwhelming Democratic majorities in the House and Senate to push through the most ambitious reform program since the New Deal. In August 1964 the Economic Opportunity Act launched the War on Poverty as a "hand up, not a handout," as the new director, Sargent Shriver, ex-plained. It established an Office of Economic Opportu-nity (OEO), which coordinated a network of federal programs designed to increase opportunities in employ-ment and education.

The programs had mixed results. The Job Corps provided vocational training mostly for urban black youth considered unemployable. Housed in dreary bar-rackslike camps far from home, trainees often found themselves learning factory skills that were already obsolete. The dropout rate was very high. The Neigh-borhood Youth Corps managed to provide work for about 2 million young people aged sixteen to twenty-one. But nearly all of these were low-paying, make-work jobs. Educational programs proved more successful. VISTA (Volunteers in Service to America) was a kind of domestic Peace Corps that brought several thousand

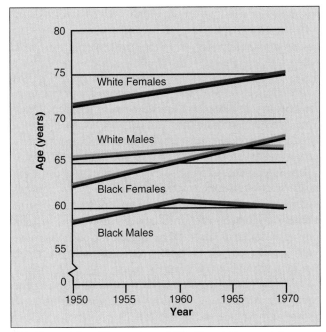

Comparative Figures on Life Expectancy at Birth by Race and Sex, 1950–1970 Shifting mortality statistics suggested that the increased longevity of females increasingly cut across race lines, but did not diminish the difference between white people and black people as a whole.

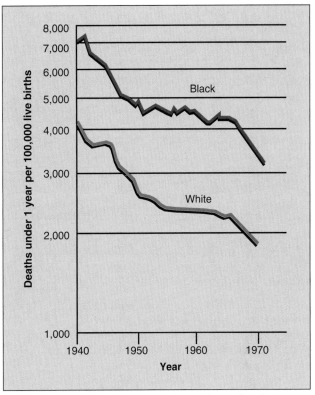

Comparative Figures on Infant Mortality by Race, 1940–1970 The causes of infant mortality such as inadequate maternal diets, prenatal care, and medical services were all rooted in poverty, both rural and urban. Despite generally falling rates of infant mortality, nonwhite people continued to suffer the effects more than white people.

idealistic volunteers into poor communities for social service work.

The most innovative and controversial element of the OEO was the Community Action Program (CAP). The program invited local communities to establish community action agencies (CAAs), to be funded through the OEO. The Economic Opportunity Act included language requiring these agencies to be "developed, conducted, and administered with the maximum feasible participation of residents of the areas and members of the groups served." In theory, as the SDS organizers had also believed, community action would empower the poor by giving them a direct say in mobilizing resources to attack poverty.

By 1966 the OEO was funding more than 1,000 CAAs, mostly in the black neighborhoods of big cities. The traditional powers in cities—mayors, business elites, and political machines—generally resisted institutional change. They looked at CAAs as merely another way to dispense services and patronage, with the federal government picking up the tab. A continual tug-of-war over who should control funding and decision making plagued the CAP in most cities, sparking intense power struggles that helped to cripple the antipoverty effort. Such was the case in Chicago, where Mayor Richard Daley demanded absolute control over the allocation of federal funds. After being challenged by OEO

activists, Daley denounced the program for "fostering class struggle."

The most successful and popular offshoots of the CAAs were the so-called national-emphasis programs, designed in Washington and administered according to federal guidelines. The Legal Services Program, staffed by attorneys, helped millions of poor people in legal battles with housing authorities, welfare departments, police, and slumlords. Head Start and Follow Through reached more than 2 million poor children and significantly improved the long-range educational achievement of participants. Comprehensive Community Health Centers—one-stop clinics—provided basic medical services to poor patients who could not afford to see doctors. Upward Bound helped low-income teenagers develop the skills and confidence needed for college. Birth control programs dispensed contraceptive supplies and information to hundreds of thousands of poor women.

But the root cause of poverty lay in unequal income distribution. The Johnson administration never committed itself to the redistribution of income or wealth.

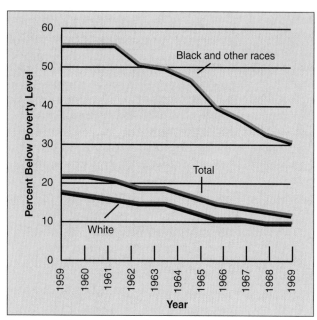

Percent of population below poverty level, by race, 1959–1969
Note: The poverty threshold for a nonfarm family of four was $3,743 in 1969 and $2,973 in 1959.

SOURCE: *Congressional Quarterly, Civil Rights: A Progress Report,* 1971, p. 46.

Spending on social welfare jumped from 7.7 percent of the gross national product in 1960 to 16 percent in 1974. But roughly three-quarters of social welfare payments went to the nonpoor. The largest sums went to Medicare, established by Congress in 1965 to provide basic health care for the aged, and to expanded Social Security payments and unemployment compensation. The major surge in federal spending on poor people resulted from the explosive growth of Aid to Families with Dependent Children (AFDC), a program begun during the New Deal. But the total cost of AFDC in the mid-1970s was only about $5 billion per year, compared with $65 billion annually for the roughly 30 million Americans receiving Social Security payments.

The War on Poverty, like the Great Society itself, became a forgotten dream. "More than five years after the passage of the Economic Opportunity Act," a 1970 study concluded, "the war on poverty has barely scratched the surface. Most poor people have had no contact with it, except perhaps to hear the promises of a better life to come." The OEO finally expired in 1974. Having made the largest commitment to federal spending on social welfare since the New Deal, Johnson could take pride in the gains scored in the War on Poverty. At the same time, he had raised expectations higher than could be reached without a more drastic redistribution of economic and political power. Even in the short run, the president could not sustain the wel-

fare programs and simultaneously fight a lengthy and expensive war abroad.

Crisis in the Cities

As Harrington's *The Other America* pointed out, some of the nation's poorest communities were located in the Appalachian Mountains and in the Deep South. But since World War II, urban areas had suffered disproportionally from a steady process of decay. "White flight"—the exodus of white people to the suburbs—had reduced the tax base for public services of all kinds, especially schools and recreational facilities. Johnson's War on Poverty scarcely addressed the problems plaguing the nation's metropolitan areas (defined by the U.S. Census as those with populations of 250,000 people or more). On the contrary, urban conditions grew worse.

With funds for new construction limited during the Great Depression and World War II, and the postwar boom taking place in the suburbs, the housing stock in the cities diminished and deteriorated. The Federal Housing Administration had encouraged this trend by insuring loans to support the building of new homes in suburban areas (see Chapter 27). The federal government also encouraged "redlining," which left people in poor neighborhoods without access to building loans. In these areas, the supply of adequate housing declined sharply. Slumlords took advantage of this situation, collecting high rents while allowing their properties to deteriorate. City officials meanwhile appealed for federal funds under Title I of the 1949 Housing Act to upgrade housing. Designed as a program of civic revitalization, these urban renewal projects more often than not sliced apart poor neighborhoods with new highways, demolished them in favor of new office complexes, or, as in Chicago's Uptown, favored new developments for the middle class rather than the poor. In 1968 a federal survey showed that 80 percent of those residents who had been displaced under this program were nonwhite, a finding that prompted civil rights leaders to call urban renewal programs "Negro removal." As a result, the inner city became not only increasingly crowded in the 1960s but more segregated.

Urban employment opportunities declined along with the urban housing stock. The industries and corporations that had lured working men and women to the cities a century earlier either automated their plants, thus scaling back their workforces, or relocated to the suburbs or other regions, such as the South and Southwest, that promised lower corporate taxes and nonunion labor. Nationwide, military spending prompted by the escalation of the Vietnam War brought the unemployment rate down from 6 percent, where it was in 1960, to 4 percent in 1966, where it remained until the end of the decade. Black unemployment, however, was nearly twice that of white unemployment. New jobs were concentrated in the defense-related industries in the South and Southwest. In northern cities, the proportion of the workforce employed in the higher-paying manufacturing jobs declined precipitously while the proportion working in minimum-wage service industries rose at a fast rate. In short, African Americans were losing good jobs and steadily falling further behind whites.

Pollution, which had long plagued traffic-congested cities like Los Angeles and industrial cities like steel-producing Pittsburgh, became an increasingly pervasive urban problem. Cities like Phoenix that once had clean air began to issue smog alerts. Pointing to high levels of lead in the blood of urban children, scientists warned of the long-term threat of pollution to public health.

Despite deteriorating conditions, millions of Americans continued to move to the cities, mainly African

Americans from the Deep South, white people from the Appalachian Mountains, and Latinos from Puerto Rico. By the mid-1960s, African Americans had become near majorities in the nation's decaying inner cities. Since World War II nearly 3 million African Americans had left the South for northern cities. In that time, New York's black population had more than doubled, and Detroit's had tripled. The vast majority of these African Americans fled rural poverty only to find themselves earning minimum wages at best and living in miserable, racially segregated neighborhoods.

Urban Uprisings

These deteriorating conditions brought urban pressures to the boiling point in the mid-1960s. In the "long, hot summers" of 1964 to 1968 the nation was rocked by more than 100 urban uprisings. As poet Imamu Amiri

Web Exploration Consider the geographical distribution of urban uprisings from 1965–1968. What were the main factors behind urban unrest? www.prenhall.com/faragher/map29.1

Urban Uprisings, 1965–1968 After World War II urban uprisings precipitated by racial conflict increased in African American communities. In Watts in 1965 and in Detroit and Newark in 1967, rioters struck out at symbols of white control of their communities, such as white-owned businesses and residential properties.

Baraka (formerly LeRoi Jones) noted, these incidents were spontaneous rebellions against authority. Unlike the race riots of the 1920s and 1940s, when angry whites assaulted blacks, masses of African Americans now took revenge for the white domination of their communities and specifically for police abuse.

In 1964, waves of turbulence rippled through the black neighborhoods of Harlem, Rochester, and Philadelphia. The first major uprising erupted in August 1965 in the Watts section of Los Angeles. Here, the male unemployment rate hovered around 30 percent. Watts lacked health-care facilities—the nearest hospital was twelve miles away—and in a city with little public transportation, fewer than one-fifth of its residents owned cars. It took only a minor arrest to set off the uprising, which quickly spread outward for fifty miles. Throwing rocks and bottles through store windows, participants reportedly shouted, "This is for Selma! This is for Birmingham!" and "Burn, baby, burn!" Nearly 50,000 people turned out, and 20,000 National Guard troops were sent in. After six days, 34 people lay dead, 900 were injured, and 4,000 more had been arrested. Los Angeles chief of police William H. Parker blamed civil rights workers, the mayor accused Communists, and both feigned ignorance when the media

reported that white police assigned to "charcoal alley," their name for the Watts district, had for years referred to their nightsticks as "nigger knockers."

The following summer, large-scale uprisings occurred in San Francisco, Milwaukee, Dayton, and Cleveland. On July 12, 1967, in Newark, New Jersey, a city with severe housing shortages and the nation's highest black unemployment rate, the beating and arrest of a black taxi driver by a white police officer provoked a widespread protest. Five days of looting and burning of white-owned buildings ended with twenty-five people dead. One week later the Detroit "Great Rebellion" began. This time a vice squad of the Detroit police had raided a bar and arrested the after-hours patrons. One spectator called out, "Don't let them take our people away. . . . Let's get the bricks and bottles going." *Time* magazine later reported, "Detroit became the scene of the bloodiest uprising in a half century and the costliest in terms of property damage in U.S. history." Army tanks and paratroopers were brought in to quell the massive disturbance, which lasted a week and left 34 people dead and 7,000 under arrest.

The uprisings seemed at first to prompt badly needed reforms. After Watts, President Johnson set up a task force headed by Deputy Attorney General Ramsey Clark and allocated funds for a range of antipoverty programs. Several years later the Kerner Commission, headed by Governor Otto Kerner of Illinois, studied the riots and found that the participants in the uprisings were not the poorest or least-educated members of their communities. They suffered instead from heightened expectations sparked by the civil rights movement and Johnson's promise of a Great Society, expectations that were not to be realized. The Kerner Commission concluded its report by indicting "white racism" for creating an "explosive mixture" of poverty and police brutality and by recommending a yet more extensive program of public housing, integrated schools, 2 million new jobs, and funding for a "national system of income supplementation."

But Congress ignored both the recommendations and the commission's warning that "our nation is moving toward two societies, one black, one white—separate and unequal." Moreover, the costs of

Between 1965 and 1968, racial tensions exploded into violence in more than seventy-five cities. Unlike earlier episodes of racial violence, which often took the form of clashes between black and white residents over contested neighborhoods, the riots of the 1960s were more often attacks by ghetto residents against retail establishments and property owned primarily by whites. Most deaths and injuries resulted from confrontations between police and rioters, not from fighting between black and white residents.

SOURCE: Newark, NJ, 7/14/1967. © Bettmann/CORBIS (BE 020707).

the Vietnam War left little federal money for antipoverty programs. Senator William Fulbright noted, "Each war feeds on the other, and, although the President assures us that we have the resources to win both wars, in fact we are not winning either of them."

1968

The urban uprisings of the summer of 1967 marked the most drawn-out violence in the United States since the Civil War. But, rather than offering a respite, 1968 proved to be even more turbulent. The bloodiest and most destructive fighting of the Vietnam War resulted in a hopeless stalemate that soured most Americans on the conflict and undermined their faith in U.S. invincibility in world affairs. Disillusionment deepened in the spring when two of the most revered political leaders were struck down by assassins' bullets. Once again protesters and police clashed on the nation's campuses and city streets, and millions of Americans asked what was wrong with their country. Why was it so violent? A former graduate student at Columbia University, Mike Wallace, spoke for many when he later recalled, "Nineteen sixty-eight just cracked the universe open for me."

The Tet Offensive

On January 30, 1968, the North Vietnamese and their Vietcong allies launched the Tet Offensive (named for the Vietnamese lunar new year holiday), stunning the U.S. military command in South Vietnam. The Vietcong managed to push into the major cities and provincial capitals of the South, as far as the courtyard of the U.S. embassy in Saigon. U.S. troops ultimately halted the offensive, suffering comparatively modest casualties of 1,600 dead and 8,000 wounded. The North Vietnamese and Vietcong suffered more than 40,000 deaths, about one-fifth of their total forces. Civilian casualties ran to the hundreds of thousands. As many as 1 million South Vietnamese became refugees, their villages totally ruined.

The Tet Offensive, despite the U.S. success in stopping it, shattered the credibility of American officials who had repeatedly

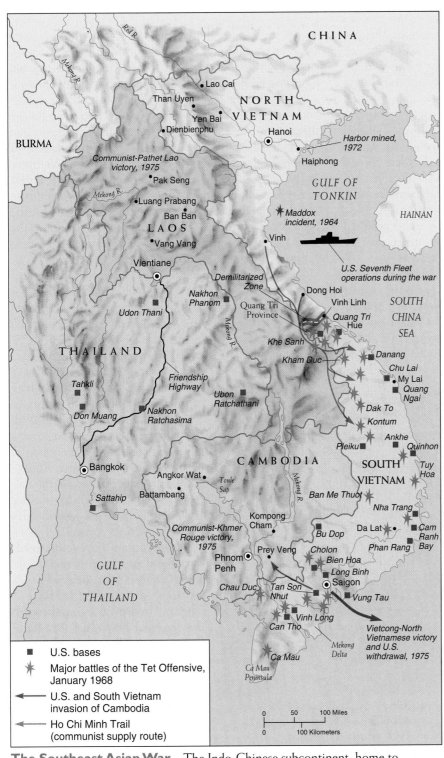

The Southeast Asian War   The Indo-Chinese subcontinent, home to long-standing regional conflict, became the center of a prolonged war with the United States.

claimed the enemy to be virtually beaten. Television and press coverage—including scenes of U.S. personnel shooting from the embassy windows in Saigon—dismayed the public. Americans saw the beautiful, ancient city of Hue devastated almost beyond recognition and heard a U.S. officer casually remark about a village in the Mekong Delta, "We had to destroy it, in order to save it." Television newscasters began to warn parents: "The following scenes might not be suitable viewing for children."

The United States had chalked up a major military victory during the Tet Offensive but lost the war at home. For the first time, polls showed strong opposition to the war, 49 percent concluding that the entire operation in Vietnam was a mistake. The majority believed that the stalemate was hopeless. Meanwhile, in Rome, Berlin, Paris, and London, students and others turned out in huge demonstrations to protest U.S. involvement in Vietnam. At home, sectors of the antiwar movement began to shift from resistance to open rebellion.

The Tet Offensive also opened a year of political drama at home. Congress resoundingly turned down a request for a general increase in troops issued by General Westmoreland. President Johnson, facing the 1968 election campaign, knew the odds were now against him. He watched as opinion polls showed his popularity plummet to an all-time low. After he squeaked to a narrow victory in the New Hampshire primary, Johnson decided to step down. On March 31 he announced

he would not seek the Democratic Party's nomination. He also declared a bombing halt over North Vietnam and called Hanoi to peace talks, which began in Paris in May. Like Truman almost thirty years earlier, and despite his determination not to repeat that bit of history, Johnson had lost his presidency in Asia.

King, the War, and the Assassination

By 1968 the civil rights leadership stood firmly in opposition to the war, and Martin Luther King, Jr. had reached a turning point in his life. The Federal Bureau of Investigation had been harassing King, tapping his telephones and spreading malicious rumors about him. Despite the threat from the FBI (Bureau Chief J. Edgar Hoover had sworn to "destroy the burrhead"), King abandoned his customary caution in criticizing U.S. policy in Vietnam. In the fall of 1965, he began to connect domestic unrest with the war abroad, calling the U.S. government the "greatest purveyor of violence in the world today." As he became more militant in opposing the war, King lost the support of liberal Democrats who remained loyal to Johnson. King refused to compromise.

In the spring of 1968 King chose Memphis, Tennessee, home of striking sanitation workers, as the place to inaugurate a Poor People's Campaign for peace and justice. Noting that the United States was "much, much sicker" than when he had begun working in 1955, he nonetheless delivered, in what was to be his final speech, a message of hope. "I have a dream this afternoon that the brotherhood of man will become a reality," King told the crowd. "With this faith, I will go out and carve a tunnel of hope from a mountain of despair." The next evening, April 4, 1968, as he stepped out on the balcony of his motel, King was shot and killed by a lone assassin, James Earl Ray.

Throughout the world crowds turned out to mourn King's death. The *New York Times* declared King's murder "a national disaster." Cheers, however, rang through the regional FBI office. President Johnson, who had ordered the investigation of King, declined to attend the funeral, sending the vice president in his place. Student Nonviolent Coordinating Committee leader Stokely Carmichael stormed, "When white America killed Dr. King, she declared war on us."

"Martin Luther King," Robert Kennedy said when he heard the news of the assassination of the civil rights leader, "dedicated his life to love and to justice for his fellow human beings, and he died because of that effort." The funeral service for King was held in the Ebenezer Baptist Church in Atlanta on April 7, 1968.

SOURCE: Walk down West Hunter Street, Atlanta. © James L. Amos/CORBIS (JA 004098).

LA	1	2	8,840
	8	20	81,786
MD	1	8	5,304
	4	14	68,640
	1	8	16,640
	2	3	10,816
	5	12	53,300
VA	12	24	101,631
	1	2	8,840
S	7	20	90,987
	4	12	58,731
	1	1	2,080
J	3	3	7,956
	1	2	5,304
	1	1	832
	2	3	9,100
	1	4	3,536
	1	1	5,980
	1	15	55,575
	4	16	63,759
	1	1	1,560

succeed Johnson. But his reputation as a cold war Democrat had become a liability. In the 1950s Humphrey had delivered stirring addresses for civil rights and antipoverty legislation; yet he also sponsored repressive cold war measures and supported huge defense appropriations that diverted needed funds from domestic programs. He fully supported the Vietnam War and had publicly scorned peace activists as cowardly and un-American. Incongruously calling his campaign the "Politics of Joy," Humphrey simultaneously courted Democrats who grimly supported the war and the King-Kennedy wing, which was sickened by it.

Humphrey skillfully cultivated the Democratic power brokers. Without entering a single state primary, he lined up delegates loyal to city bosses, labor leaders, and conservative southern Democrats. As the candidate least likely to rock the boat, he had secured his party's nomination well before delegates met in convention.

"The Whole World Is Watching!"

The events surrounding the Democratic convention in Chicago, August 21–26, demonstrated how deep the divisions within the United States had become. Antiwar activists had called for a massive demonstration at the delegates' hotel and at the convention center. The media focused, however, on the plans announced

Eugene McCarthy. The race for the Democratic nomination positioned McCarthy, the witty philosopher, against Kennedy, the charismatic campaigner. McCarthy garnered support from liberal Democrats and white suburbanites. On college campuses his popularity with idealistic students was so great that his campaign became known as the "children's crusade." Kennedy reached out successfully to African Americans and Latinos and won all but the Oregon primary.

Kennedy appeared to be the Democratic Party's strongest candidate as June 4, the day of the California primary, dawned. But as the final tabulation of his victory came in just past midnight, Robert Kennedy was struck down by the bullet of an assassin, a Jordanian national named Sirhan Sirhan.

Vice President Hubert H. Humphrey, a longtime presidential hopeful, was now the sole Democrat with the credentials to

The "police riot" in Chicago, August 1968, during the Democratic National Convention capped a spring and summer of violence. Mayor Richard Daley had prepared his city for the anticipated protest against the war by assembling more than 20,000 law enforcement officials, including police, National Guard, and U.S. Army troops carrying flame throwers and bazookas. Television cameras and photographers recorded the massive clubbing and teargassing of demonstrators as well as bystanders and news reporters.

SOURCE: Photo by Jeffrey Blankfort. Jeroboam, Inc.

by the "Yippies," or Youth International Party, a largely imaginary organization of politicized hippies led by jokester and counterculture guru Abbie Hoffman. Yippies called for a Festival of Life, including a "nude-in" on Lake Michigan beaches and the release of a greased pig—Pigasus, the Yippie candidate for president. Still reeling from the riots following King's assassination, Chicago's Mayor Richard Daley refused to issue parade permits. According to later accounts, he sent hundreds of undercover police into the crowds to encourage rock throwing and generally to incite violence so that retaliation would appear necessary and reasonable.

Daley's strategy boomeranged when his officers staged what a presidential commission later termed a "police riot," randomly assaulting demonstrators, casual passersby, and television crews filming the events. For one of the few times in American history, the media appeared to join a protest against civil authorities. Angered by the embarrassing publicity, Daley sent his agents to raid McCarthy's campaign headquarters, where Democrats opposed to the war had gathered.

Inside the convention hall, a raging debate over a peace resolution underscored the depth of the division within the party over the war. Representative Wayne Hays of Ohio lashed out at those who substituted "beards for brains . . . [and] pot [for] patriotism." When the resolution failed, McCarthy delegates put on black armbands and followed folk singer Theodore Bikel in singing "We Shall Overcome." Later, as tear gas used against the demonstrators outside turned the amphitheater air acrid, delegates heard the beaming Humphrey praise Mayor Daley and Johnson's conduct of the Vietnam War. When Senator Abraham Ribicoff of Connecticut addressed the convention and protested the "Gestapo tactics" of the police, television cameras focused on Mayor Daley saying, "You Jew son of a bitch . . . , go home!" The crowd outside chanted, "The whole world is watching! The whole world is watching!" Indeed, through satellite transmission, it was.

Protest and social strain spread worldwide. Across the United States the antiwar movement picked up steam. In Paris, students took over campuses and workers occupied factories. Young people scrawled on the walls such humorous and half-serious slogans as "Be Realistic, Demand the Impossible!" Similar protests against authority occurred in eastern Europe. In Prague, Czechoslovakia, students wearing blue jeans and singing Beatles songs threw rocks at Soviet tanks. Meanwhile, demonstrations in Japan, Italy, Ireland, Germany, and England all brought young people into the streets to demand democratic reforms in their own countries and an end to the war in Vietnam.

THE POLITICS OF IDENTITY

The tragic events of 1968 brought whole sectors of the counterculture into political activism. But, remember, hippie Tuli Kupferberg warned them, "the first revolution (but not of course the last) is in your own head." Many young Americans seemed to hear his message, intensifying their protest against the war while at the same time expressing their own political grievances and promoting their own sense of collective identity. United in their opposition to "The Establishment"— that is, the politicians and business leaders who maintained the status quo—these baby boomers sought also to empower themselves and their communities in myriad smaller but vital movements.

With great media fanfare, gay liberation and women's liberation movements emerged in the late 1960s. By the early 1970s, young Latinos, Asian Americans, and Indian peoples had pressed their own claims. In different ways, these groups drew their own lessons from the nationalist movement that formed in the wake of Malcolm X's death—Black Power. Soon, "Brown Power," "Yellow Power," and "Red Power" became the slogans of movements constituted distinctly as new communities of protest.

Black Power

In African American communities, when the Great Society programs failed to lessen poverty and black men began to die in disproportionate numbers in Vietnam, faith in the old ways lapsed. Impatient with the strategies of social change based on voting rights and integration, many younger activists spurned the tactics of civil disobedience of King's generation for direct action and militant self-defense. In 1966, Stokely Carmichael, who had helped turn SNCC into an all-black organization, began to advocate Black Power as a means for African Americans to take control of their own communities.

Derived from a century-long tradition of black nationalism, the key tenets of Black Power were self-determination and self-sufficiency. National conferences of activists, held annually beginning in 1966, adopted separatist resolutions, including a plan to partition the United States into black and white nations. Black Power also promoted self-esteem by affirming the unique history and heritage of African peoples.

The movement's boldest expression was the Black Panther Party for Self-Defense, founded in Oakland, California, in 1966 by Huey P. Newton and Bobby Seale. "We want freedom," Newton demanded. "We want power. . . . We want full employment. . . . We want all black men to be exempt from military service.

OVERVIEW

PROTEST MOVEMENTS OF THE 1960s

Year	Organization/ Movement	Description
1962	Students for a Democratic Society (SDS)	Organization of college students that became the largest national organization of left-wing white students. Calling for "participatory democracy," SDS involved students in community-based campaigns against poverty and for citizens' control of neighborhoods. SDS played a prominent role in the campaign to end the war in Vietnam.
1964	Free Speech Movement	Formed at the University of California at Berkeley to protest the banning of on-campus political fund-raising. Decried the bureaucratic character of the "multiuniversity" and advocated an expansion of student rights.
1965	Anti-Vietnam War Movement	Advocated grass-roots opposition to U.S. involvement in Southeast Asia. By 1970 a national mobilization committee organized a demonstration of a half-million protesters in Washington, D.C.
1965	*La raza*	A movement of Chicano youth to advance the cultural and political self-determination of Mexican Americans. *La raza* included the Brown Berets, which addressed community issues, and regional civil rights groups such as the Crusade for Social Justice, formed in 1965.
1966	Black Power	Militant movement that emerged from the civil rights campaigns to advocate independent institutions for African Americans and pride in black culture and African heritage. The idea of Black Power, a term coined by Stokely Carmichael, inspired the formation of the paramilitary Black Panthers.
1968	American Indian Movement (AIM)	Organization formed to advance the self-determination of Indian peoples and challenge the authority of the Bureau of Indian Affairs. Its most effective tactic was occupation. In February, 1973, AIM insurgents protesting land and treaty violations occupied Wounded Knee, South Dakota, the location of an 1890 massacre, until the FBI and BIA agents drove them out.
1968	Women's Liberation	Movement of mainly young women that took shape following a protest at the Miss America Beauty Pageant. Impatient with the legislative reforms promoted by the National Organization for Women, founded in 1966, activists developed their own agenda shaped by the slogan "The Personal Is Political." Activities included the formation of "consciousness-raising" groups and the establishment of women's studies programs.
1968	Asian American Political Alliance (AAPA)	Formed at the University of California at Berkeley, the AAPA was one of the first pan-Asian political organizations to struggle against racial oppression. The AAPA encouraged Asian Americans to claim their own cultural identity and to protest the war against Asian peoples in Vietnam.
1969	Gay Liberation	Movement to protest discrimination against homosexuals and lesbians that emerged after the Stonewall Riots in New York City. Unlike earlier organizations such as the Mattachine Society, which focused on civil rights, Gay Liberationists sought to radically change American society and government, which they believed were corrupt.

The war in Vietnam contributed to the growing racial militancy in the United States. African Americans served on the front lines in Vietnam in disproportionate numbers, and many came to view the conflict as a "white man's war."
SOURCE: James Meredith march through Mississippi. Photo by Matt Herron. Media Image Resource Alliance (0001A089).

We want . . . an end to POLICE BRUTALITY. . . . We want land, bread, housing, education, clothing, and justice." Armed self-defense was the Panthers' strategy, and they adopted a paramilitary style—black leather jackets, shoes, black berets, and firearms—that infuriated local authorities. Monitoring local police, a practice Panthers termed "patrolling the pigs," was their major activity. In several communities, Panthers also ran free breakfast programs for schoolchildren, established medical clinics, and conducted educational classes. For a time the Panthers became folk heroes. A Harris poll conducted in 1970 found that a quarter of African Americans surveyed admired the Black Panthers "a great deal." Persecuted by local police and the FBI—there were more than thirty raids on Panther offices in eleven states during 1968 and 1969—the Panthers were arrested, prosecuted, and sentenced to long terms in jail that effectively destroyed the organization.

Black Power nevertheless continued to grow during the late 1960s and became a multifaceted movement. The Reverend Jesse Jackson, for example, rallied African

Americans in Chicago to boycott the A&P supermarket chain until the firm hired 700 black workers. A dynamic speaker and skillful organizer, Jackson encouraged African Americans to support their own businesses and services. "We are going to see to it," he explained in 1969, "that the resources of the ghetto are not siphoned off by outside groups. . . . If a building goes up in the black community, we're going to build it." His program, Operation Breadbasket, strengthened community control. By 1970 it had spread beyond Chicago to fifteen other cities.

Cultural nationalism became the most enduring component of Black Power. In their popular book *Black Power* (1967), Stokely Carmichael and Charles V. Hamilton urged African Americans "to assert their own definitions, to reclaim their history, their culture; to create their own sense of community and togetherness." Thousands of college students responded by calling for more scholarships and for more classes on African American history and culture. At San Francisco State University, students formed the Black Student Union and, with help from the Black Panthers, demanded the creation of a black studies department. After a series of failed negotiations with the administration, the black students called for a campuswide strike and in December 1968 shut down the university. In the end, 134 school days later, the administration agreed to fund a black studies department but also fired about twenty-five faculty members and refused to drop charges against 700 arrested campus activists. Strikes for "third world studies" soon broke out on other campuses, including the Newark campus of Rutgers University, the San Diego and Berkeley campuses of the University of California, and the University of Wisconsin at Madison, where the national guard was brought in to quell the protest.

Meanwhile, trend setters put aside Western dress for African-style dashikis and hairdos, and black parents gave their children African names. Many well-known African Americans such as Imamu Amiri Baraka (formerly LeRoi Jones), Muhammad Ali (formerly Cassius Clay), and Kwame Touré (formerly Stokely Carmichael) rejected their "slave names." The African American holiday Kwanzaa began to replace Christmas as a seasonal family celebration. This deepening sense of racial pride and solidarity was summed up in the popular slogan "Black Is Beautiful."

Sisterhood Is Powerful

Betty Friedan's best-selling *Feminine Mystique* (1963) had swelled feelings of discontent among many middle-class white women who had come of age in the 1950s (see Chapter 27) and sparked the formation of the National Organization for Women (NOW) in 1966. NOW pledged itself "to take action to bring women into full participation in the mainstream of American society now." Members spearheaded campaigns for the enforcement of laws banning sex discrimination in work and in education, for maternity leaves for working mothers, and for government funding of day-care centers. NOW also came out for the Equal Rights Amendment, first introduced in Congress in 1923, and demanded the repeal of legislation that prohibited abortion or restricted birth control.

The second half of the decade produced a different kind of movement: women's liberation. Like Black Power, the women's liberation movement especially attracted women who had been active in civil rights, SDS, and campus antiwar movements. These women resented the sexist attitudes and behaviors of their fellow male activists. Women must come to understand, one angry woman wrote, that "they are not inferior—nor chicks, nor bunnies, nor quail, nor cows, nor bitches, nor ass, nor meat," but agents of their own destiny. Like Black Power, the women's liberation movement issued its own separatist plan.

In 1967 small groups of women broke off from male-led protest movements. They formed myriad all-women organizations such as the Radical Women and the Redstockings in New York, the Women's Liberation Union in Chicago, Berkeley, and Dayton, and Bread and Roses and Cell 16 in Boston. Impatient with the legislative reforms promoted by NOW, and angered by the sexism of SNCC and SDS, these women proclaimed "Sisterhood Is Powerful." "Women are an oppressed class. Our oppression is total, affecting every facet of our lives," read the Redstocking Manifesto of 1969. "We are exploited as sex objects, breeders, domestic servants, and cheap labor."

The women's liberation movement developed a scathing critique of patriarchy—that is, the power of men to dominate all institutions, from the family to business to the military to the protest movements themselves. Patriarchy, they argued, was the prime cause of exploitation, racism, and war. Outraged and sometimes outrageous, radical feminists, as they called themselves, conducted "street theater" at the 1968 Miss America Beauty Pageant in Atlantic City, crowning a live sheep as queen and "throwing implements of female torture" (bras, girdles, curlers, and copies of the *Ladies' Home Journal*) into a "freedom trash can." A few months later, the Women's International Terrorist Conspiracy from Hell (WITCH) struck in Lower Manhattan, putting a hex on the male-dominated New York Stock Exchange.

The media focused on the audacious acts and brazen pronouncements of radical feminists, but the majority involved in the women's liberation movement were less flamboyant women who were simply trying to rise above the limitations imposed on them because of their sex. Most of their activism took place outside the limelight in consciousness-raising (CR) groups. CR groups, which multiplied by the thousands in the late 1960s and early 1970s, brought women together to discuss the relationship between public events and private lives, particularly between politics and sexuality. Here women shared their most intimate feelings toward men or other women and established the constituency for the movement's most important belief, expressed in the aphorism "The personal is political." Believing that no aspect of life lacked a political dimension, women in these groups explored the power dynamics of the institutions of family and marriage as well as the workforce and government. "The small group has served as a place where thousands of us have learned to support each other," one participant reported, "where we have gained new feelings of self-respect and learned to speak about what we are thinking and to respect other women."

Participants in the women's liberation movement engaged in a wide range of activities. Some staged sit-ins at *Newsweek* to protest demeaning media depictions of women. Others established health clinics, day-care centers, rape crisis centers, and shelters for women fleeing abusive husbands or lovers. The women's liberation movement also had a significant educational impact. Feminist bookstores and publishing companies, such as the Feminist Press, reached out to eager readers. Scholarly books such as Kate Millett's *Sexual Politics* (1970) found a wide popular audience. By the early 1970s, campus activists were demanding women's studies programs and women's centers. Like black studies, women's studies programs included traditional academic goals, such as the generation of new scholarship, but also encouraged personal change and self-esteem. Between 1970 and 1975, as many as 150 women's studies programs had been established. The movement continued to grow; by 1980 nearly 30,000 women's studies courses were offered at colleges and universities throughout the United States.

The women's liberation movement remained, however, a bastion of white middle-class women. The appeal to sisterhood did not unite women across race or class or even sexual orientation. Lesbians, who charged the early leaders of NOW with homophobia, found large pockets of "heterosexism" in the women's liberation movement and broke off to form their own organizations. Although some African American women were outraged at the posturing of Black Power leaders like Stokely Carmichael, who joked that "the only position for women in SNCC is prone," the majority remained wary of white women's appeals to sisterhood. African American women formed their own "womanist" movement to address their distinct cultural and political concerns. Similarly, by 1970 a Latina feminist movement had begun to address issues uniquely relevant to women of color in an Anglo-dominated society.

Although the women's liberation movement could not dispel ethnic or racial differences, it fostered a sense of community among many women. By August 1970, hundreds of thousands of women responded to NOW's call for a Women's Strike for Equality, a mass demonstration marking the fiftieth anniversary of the woman suffrage amendment and the largest turnout for women's rights in U.S. history.

Gay Liberation

The gay community had been generations in the making but only gained visibility during World War II (see Chapter 25). By the mid-1950s, two pioneering homophile organizations, the Mattachine Society and the Daughters of Bilitis, were campaigning to reduce discrimination against homosexuals in employment, the armed forces, and all areas of social and cultural life. Other groups, such as the Society for Individual Rights, rooted themselves in New York's Greenwich Village, San Francisco's North Beach, and other centers of gay night life. But it was during the tumultuous 1960s that gay and lesbian movements encouraged many men and women to proclaim publicly their sexual identity: "Say It Loud, Gay Is Proud."

The major event prompting gays to organize grew out of repeated police raids of gay bars and the harassment of their patrons. In February 1966 New York City's popular liberal mayor John Lindsay announced a crackdown against "promenading perverts" and assigned police to patrol the bars between Times Square and Washington Square. The American Civil Liberties Union responded by pointing out that the mayor was "confusing deviant social behavior with criminal activity." Lindsay's police commissioner soon announced the end of the entrapment policy by which undercover police had been luring homosexuals into breaking the law, but various forms of individual harassment continued. Finally, on Friday, June 27, 1969, New York police raided the Stonewall Inn, a well-known gay bar in Greenwich Village, and provoked an uprising of angry homosexuals that lasted the entire night. The next day, "Gay Power" graffiti appeared on buildings and sidewalks throughout the neighborhood.

The Stonewall Riot, as it was called, sparked a new sense of collective identity among many gays and lesbians and touched off a new movement for both civil rights and liberation. Gay men and women in New York City formed the Gay Liberation Front (GLF), announcing themselves as "a revolutionary homosexual group of men and women formed with the realization that complete sexual liberation for all people cannot come about unless existing social institutions are abolished. We reject society's attempt to impose sexual roles and definitions of our nature. We are stepping outside these roles and

simplistic myths. We are going to be who we are." The GLF also took a stand against the war in Vietnam and supported the Black Panthers. It quickly adopted the forms of public protest, such as street demonstrations and sit-ins, developed by the civil rights movement and given new direction by antiwar protesters.

Changes in public opinion and policies followed. As early as 1967 a group of Episcopal priests had urged church leaders to avoid taking a moral position against same-sex relationships. The San Francisco–based Council on Religion and Homosexuality established a network for clergy sympathetic to gay and lesbian parishioners. In 1973 the American Psychiatric Association, which since World War II had viewed homosexuality as a treatable mental illness, reclassified it as a normal sexual orientation. Meanwhile, there began a slow process of decriminalization of homosexual acts between consenting adults. In 1975 the U.S. Civil Service Commission ended its ban on the employment of homosexuals.

The founders of gay liberation encouraged not only legal changes and the establishment of supporting institutions but self-pride. "Gay Is Good" (like "Black Is Beautiful" and "Sisterhood Is Powerful") expressed the aspiration of a large hidden minority (estimated at 10 million or more people) to "come out" and demand public acceptance of their sexual identity. The Gay Activist Alliance, founded in 1970, demanded "freedom of expression of our dignity and value as human beings." By the mid-1970s Gay Pride marches held simultaneously in several cities were drawing nearly 500,000 participants.

The Chicano Rebellion

By the mid-1960s young Mexican Americans had created, according to one historian, a moral community founded on collectivist principles and a determination to resist Anglo domination. Mainly high school and college students, they adopted the slang term *Chicano*, in preference to Mexican American, to express a militant ethnic nationalism. Chicano militants demanded not only equality with white people but cultural and political self-determination. Tracing their roots to the heroic Aztecs, they identified *la raza* (the race or people) as the source of a common language, religion, and heritage.

Students played a large role in shaping the Chicano movement. In East Los Angeles, high school students staged "blowouts" or strikes to demand educational reform and a curricular emphasis on the history, literature, art, and language of Mexican Americans. In 1968 President Johnson had signed the Bilingual Education Act, which reversed state laws that prohibited the teaching of classes in any language but English. Nevertheless, as Sal Castro, an East Los Angeles teacher, complained,

"If a kid speaks in Spanish, he is criticized. If a kid has a Mexican accent, he is ridiculed. If a kid talks back, in any language, he is arrested. . . . We have a gunpoint education. The school is a prison." Moreover, Chicanos had one of the highest drop-out rates in the country. Castro encouraged 15,000 students from five Los Angeles schools to strike against poor educational facilities. The police conducted a mass arrest of protesters, and within a short time students in San Antonio and Denver were conducting their own blowouts, holding placards reading "Teachers, Sí, Bigots, No!" By 1969, on September 16, Mexican Independence Day, high school students throughout the Southwest skipped classes in the First National Chicano Boycott. Meanwhile, students organized to demand Mexican American studies on their campuses. In 1969, a group staged a sit-in at the administrative offices of the University of California at Berkeley, which one commentator called "the first important public appearance of something called Brown Power."

In 1967 David Sanchez of East Los Angeles formed the Brown Berets, modeled on the Black Panthers, to address such community issues as housing and employment and generally to encourage teenagers to express *Chicanismo*, or pride in their Mexican American identity and heritage. By 1972, when the organization disbanded, the Brown Berets had organized twenty chapters, published a newspaper, *La Causa*, and run a successful health clinic. From college campuses spread a wider cultural movement that spawned literary journals in "Spanglish" (a mixture of English and Spanish), theatrical companies and music groups, and murals illustrating ethnic themes on buildings in Los Angeles and elsewhere.

Chicano nationalism inspired a variety of regional political movements in the late 1960s. One of these, Rodolfo "Corky" Gonzales's Crusade for Justice, formed in 1965 to protest the failure of the Great Society's antipoverty programs. A former boxer and popular poet, Gonzales was especially well liked by barrio youth and college students. He led important campaigns for greater job opportunities and land reform throughout the Southwest well into the 1970s. In Colorado and New Mexico, the *Alianza Federal de Mercedes*, formed in 1963 by Reies López Tijerina, fought to reclaim land fraudulently appropriated by white settlers. The Texas-based *La Raza Unida Party* (LRUP), meanwhile, increased Mexican American representation in local government and established social and cultural programs. The student-led Mexican American Youth Organization (MAYO) worked closely with the LRUP to help Mexican Americans take political power in Crystal City, Texas. The two organizations registered voters, ran candidates for office, and staged a massive boycott of Anglo-owned businesses.

Mexican American activists, even those who won local office, soon discovered that economic power remained out of community hands. Stifled by poverty, ordinary Mexican Americans had less confidence in the political process, and many fell back into apathy after early hopes of great, sudden change. Despite these setbacks, a sense of collective identity had been forged among many Mexican Americans.

The Chicano movement found vivid expression in the performing and visual arts and in literature. *Teatro*, comprising film and drama, drew creatively on Mexican and Anglo cultural forms to explore the political dimensions of Mexican American society. *La Carpa de los Rasquachis (The Tent of the Underdogs)*, appeared in 1974 as the first full-length Chicano play and was subsequently staged in many communities. One of the most popular and visible media was the mural, often based on the works of Mexican masters such as Diego Rivera. Chicano muralists painted an estimated 1,500 murals on public buildings throughout their communities, from the exteriors of retail shops to freeway overpasses, even to large drainage pipes. Artistic expression found its way into music and dance. The rock group *Los Lobos*, for example, dedicated their first recorded album to the United Farm Workers. One of the most important writers to capture the excitement of the

Labor activist Cesar Chavez spearheaded the organization of Chicano agricultural workers into the United Farm Workers (UFW), the first successful union of migrant workers. In 1965, a strike of grape pickers in the fields around Delano, California, and a nationwide boycott of table grapes brought Chevez and the UFW into the media spotlight. Like Martin Luther King, Jr., he advocated nonviolent methods for achieving justice and equality. SOURCE: EPA Documercia (1927–1933) National Archives and Records Administration.

Chicano movement was Oscar Zeta Acosta, whose *Revolt of the Cockroach*, published in 1973, renders into fiction some of the major events of the era.

Red Power

The phrase "Red Power," attributed to Vine Deloria, Jr., commonly expressed a growing sense of supratribal Indian identity. At the forefront of this movement was the American Indian Movement (AIM), which was founded in 1968. Its members represented mainly urban Indian communities, and its leaders were young and militant. Like the Black Panthers and Brown Berets, AIM was initially organized to monitor law enforcement practices such as police harassment and brutality. It soon played a major role in building a network of urban Indian centers, churches, and philanthropic organizations and in establishing the "powwow circuit" that publicized news of protest activities across the country. Skillful in attracting attention from the news media,

AIM quickly inspired a plethora of new publications and local chapters. Many young Indians turned to their elders to learn tribal ways, including traditional dress and spiritual practices.

The major catalyst of Red Power was the occupation of the deserted federal prison on Alcatraz Island in San Francisco Bay on November 20, 1969. A group of eighty-nine Indians, identifying themselves as "Indians of All Tribes," claimed the island according to the terms of an 1868 Sioux treaty that gave Indians rights to unused federal property on Indian land. The group demanded federal funds for a multifaceted cultural and educational center. For the next year and a half, an occupation force averaging around 100 and a stream of visitors from a large number of tribes celebrated the occupation. Although the protestors ultimately failed to achieve their specific goals, they had an enormous impact on the Indian community. With the occupation at Alcatraz, a participant testified, "we got back our worth, our pride, our dignity, our humanity." At the

Web Exploration

Examine those states with sizeable Indian reservations. How did the Civil Rights Act affect Indian identity?
www.prenhall.com/faragher/map29.2

Major Indian Reservations, 1976   Although sizable areas, designated Indian reservations represented only a small portion of territory occupied in earlier times.

same time, the occupation fostered a new identity, a multitribal ethnicity —the American Indian.

The most dramatic series of events of the Red Power movement began in 1972, when Indian activists left the cities to return to their rural roots. In November, AIM staged an event known as the "Trail of Broken Treaties " that culminated in a week-long occupation of the Bureau of Indian Affairs in Washington, D.C. Emphasizing treaty violation rather than civil rights, AIM insurgents then moved to the Pine Ridge Reservation, the site of the 1890 massacre at Wounded Knee, South Dakota, where in the spring of 1973 they began a seige that lasted ten weeks. AIM activists demanded the removal of the leader of the Oglala Lakota, whom they believed to be a corrupt puppet of the Bureau of Indian Affairs, and the restoration of treaty rights. Dozens of FBI agents then invaded under shoot-to-kill orders, leaving two Indians dead and an unknown number of casualties on both sides. AIM gained widespread support for its actions among young urban Indians but alienated many reservation Indians and their tribal leaders. In the next few years, Indian activists staged a number of occupations on reservations in New York, Wisconsin, New Mexico, South Dakota, and Washington.

The Red Power movement culminated in the "Longest Walk," a five-month protest march that began in San Francisco and ended in Washington, D.C., in July 1978. The event emphasized the history of the forced removal of Indians from their homelands and protested the U.S. government's repeated violation of treaty rights. By this time, several tribes had won in court, by legislation or by administrative fiat, small parts of what had earlier been taken from them. The sacred Blue Lake was returned to Pueblo Indians in Taos, New Mexico, and Alaskan natives were granted legal title to 40 million acres (and compensation of almost $1 billion). The Native American Rights Fund (NARF), established in 1971, gained additional thousands of acres in Atlantic coast states. But despite these victories, a rush of new legislation in Congress threatened to abrogate treaties still in place, and many tribal lands continued to suffer from industrial and government waste dumping and other commercial uses. On reservations and in urban areas with heavy Indian concentrations, alcohol abuse and ill health remained serious problems.

The 1960s also marked the beginning of an "Indian Renaissance" in literature. New books like Vine Deloria, Jr.'s *Custer Died for Your Sins* (1969) and the classic *Black Elk Speaks* (1961), reprinted from the 1930s, reached millions of readers inside and outside Indian communities. A wide variety of Indian novelists, historians, and essayists, such as Pulitzer Prize–winning N. Scott Momaday and Leslie Silko, followed up these successes, and fiction and nonfiction works about Indian life and lore continued to attract a large audience.

The Asian American Movement

Inspired by the Black Power movement, college students of Asian ancestry sought to unite fellow Asian Americans in a struggle against racial oppression "through the power of a consolidated yellow people." In 1968 students at the University of California at Berkeley founded the Asian American Political Alliance (AAPA), one of the first pan-Asian political organizations bringing together Chinese, Japanese, and Filipino American activists. Similar organizations soon appeared on campuses throughout California and spread quickly to the East Coast and Midwest.

These groups took a strong stand against the war in Vietnam, condemning it as a violation of the national sovereignty of the small Asian country. They also protested the racism directed against the peoples of Southeast Asia, particularly the practice common among American soldiers of referring to the enemy as "Gooks." This racist epithet, first used to denigrate Filipinos during the Spanish-American War, implied that Asians were something less than human and therefore proper targets for slaughter. In response, Asian American activists rallied behind the people of Vietnam and proclaimed racial solidarity with their "Asian brothers and sisters."

The antiwar movement brought many young Asian Americans into political organizations such as the AAPA that encouraged them to claim their own cultural identity. In 1968 and 1969 students at San Francisco State College and the University of California at Berkeley, for example, rallied behind the slogan "Shut It Down!" and waged prolonged campus strikes to demand the establishment of ethnic studies programs. These students sought alternatives to the goal of assimilation into mainstream society, promoting instead a unique sense of ethnic identity, a pan-Asian counterculture. Berkeley students, for example, sponsored the "Asian American Experience in America–Yellow Power" conference, inviting their peers to learn about "Asian American history and destiny, and the need to express Asian American solidarity in a predominantly white society."

Between 1968 and 1973, major universities across the country introduced courses on Asian American studies, and a few, such as the City College of New York, set up interdisciplinary departments. Meanwhile, artists, writers, documentary filmmakers, oral historians, and anthropologists worked to recover the Asian American past. Writer Frank Chin, who advocated a language that "coheres the people into a community by organizing and codifying the symbols of the people's common experience," wrote the first Asian American drama, *The Year of the Dragon,* to be produced on national television. It was, however, Maxine Hong Kingston's *Woman Warrior: A Memoir of a Girlhood among Ghosts* (1976) that became the major bestseller.

Looking to the example of the Black Panthers, young Asian Americans also took their struggle into the community. In 1968, activists presented the San Francisco municipal government with a list of grievances about conditions in Chinatown, particularly the poor housing and medical facilities, and organized a protest march down the neighborhood's main street. They led a communitywide struggle to save San Francisco's International Hotel, a low-income residential facility mainly for Filipino and Chinese men, which was ultimately leveled for a new parking lot.

Community activists ranging from college students to neighborhood artists worked in a variety of campaigns to heighten public awareness. The Redress and Reparations Movement, initiated by Sansei (third-generation Japanese Americans), for example, encouraged students to ask their parents about their wartime experiences and prompted older civil rights organizations, such as the Japanese American Citizens League, to bring forward the issue of internment. At the same time, trade union organizers renewed labor organizing among new Asian workers, mainly in service industries, such as hotel and restaurant work, and in clothing manufacturing. Other campaigns reflected the growing diversity of the Asian population. Filipinos, the fastest-growing group, organized to protest the destructive role of U.S.–backed Philippine dictator Ferdinand Marcos. Students from South Korea similarly denounced the repressive government in their homeland. Samoans sought to publicize the damage caused by nuclear testing in the Pacific Islands. Ultimately, however, in blurring intergroup differences, the Asian American movement failed to reach the growing populations of new immigrants, especially the numerous Southeast Asians fleeing their devastated homeland.

Despite its shortcomings, the politics of identity would continue to grow through the next two decades of mainly conservative rule, broadening the content of literature, film, television, popular music, and even the curricula of the nation's schools. Collectively, the various movements for social change pushed issues of race, gender, and sexual orientation to the forefront of American politics and simultaneously spotlighted the nation's cultural diversity as a major resource.

THE NIXON PRESIDENCY

The sharp divisions among Americans in 1968, mainly due to President Johnson's policies in Vietnam, paved the way for the election of Richard Milhous Nixon. The new Republican president inherited not only an increasingly unpopular war but a nation riven by internal discord. Without specifying his plans, he promised a "just and honorable peace" in Southeast Asia and the restoration of law and order at home. Yet, once in office, Nixon puzzled both friends and foes. He ordered unprecedented illegal government action against private citizens while agreeing with Congress to enhance several welfare programs and improve environmental protection. He widened and intensified the war in Vietnam, yet made stunning moves toward détente with the People's Republic of China. An architect of the cold war in the 1950s, Nixon became the first president to foresee its end. Nixon worked hard in the White House, centralizing authority and reigning defiantly as an "Imperial President"—until he brought himself down.

The Southern Strategy

In 1968, Republican presidential contender Richard Nixon deftly built on voter hostility toward youthful protesters and the counterculture. He represented, he said, the "silent majority"—those Americans who worked, paid taxes, and did not demonstrate, picket, or protest loudly, "people who are not haters, people who love their country." Recovering from defeats in elections for the presidency in 1960 and the governorship of California in 1962, Nixon declared himself the one candidate who could restore law and order to the nation.

After signing the landmark Civil Rights Act of 1964, President Johnson said privately, "I think we just delivered the South to the Republicans for a long time to come." Republican strategists moved quickly to make this prediction come true. They also recognized the growing electoral importance of the Sunbelt, where populations grew with the rise of high-tech industries and retirement communities. A powerful conservatism dominated this region, home to many military bases, defense plants, and an increasingly influential Protestant evangelism. Nixon appealed directly to these voters by promising to appoint to federal courts judges who would undercut liberal interpretations of civil rights and be tough on crime. Nixon also promised to roll back the Great Society. "I say it's time," he announced, "to quit pouring billions of dollars into programs that have failed."

Nixon selected as his running mate Maryland governor Spiro T. Agnew, known for his vitriolic oratory. Agnew treated dissent as near treason. He courted the silent majority by attacking all critics of the war as "an effete corps of impudent snobs" and blasted liberal newscasters as "nattering nabobs of negativism." Democratic nominee Hubert Humphrey chose as his running mate Maine senator Edmund Muskie.

The 1968 campaign underscored the antiliberal sentiment of the voting public. The most dramatic example was the relative success of Alabama governor George Wallace's third-party bid for the presidency. Wallace took state office in 1963 promising white

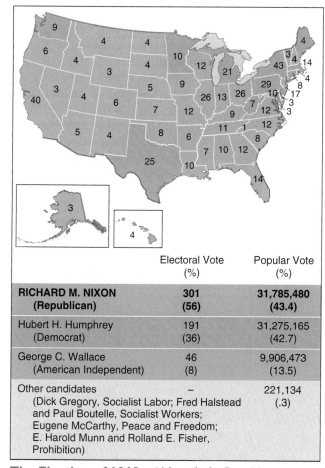

	Electoral Vote (%)	Popular Vote (%)
RICHARD M. NIXON (Republican)	**301 (56)**	**31,785,480 (43.4)**
Hubert H. Humphrey (Democrat)	191 (36)	31,275,165 (42.7)
George C. Wallace (American Independent)	46 (8)	9,906,473 (13.5)
Other candidates (Dick Gregory, Socialist Labor; Fred Halstead and Paul Boutelle, Socialist Workers; Eugene McCarthy, Peace and Freedom; E. Harold Munn and Rolland E. Fisher, Prohibition)	–	221,134 (.3)

The Election of 1968 Although the Republican Nixon-Agnew team won the popular vote by only a small margin, the Democrats lost in most of the northern states that had voted Democratic since the days of FDR. Segregationist Governor George Wallace of Alabama polled more than 9 million votes.

Alabamans "Segregation now! Segregation tomorrow! Segregation forever!" In 1968 he waged a national campaign around a conservative hate list that included school busing, antiwar demonstrations, and urban uprisings. His running mate in the American Independent Party, retired air force general Curtis LeMay, proposed the use of nuclear weapons to "bomb the North Vietnamese back to the Stone Age." Winning only five southern states, Wallace nevertheless captured 13.5 percent of the popular vote.

The Nixon-Agnew team squeaked to victory, capturing the popular vote by the slim margin of 43.4 percent to Humphrey and Muskie's 42.7 percent but taking nearly all the West's electoral votes. Bitterly divided by the campaign, the Democrats would remain out of presidential contention for over two decades, except when the Republicans suffered scandal and disgrace. The Republicans in 1968 had paved the way for the conservative ascendancy.

Nixon's War

Nixon promised to bring "peace with honor." Yet, despite this pledge, the Vietnam War raged for four more years before a peace settlement was reached.

Much of the responsibility for the prolonged conflict rested with Henry A. Kissinger. A dominating personality on the National Security Council, Kissinger insisted that the United States could not retain its global leadership by appearing weak to either allies or enemies. "However we got into Vietnam," he wrote in 1969, the United States "cannot accept a military defeat, or a change in the political structure of South Vietnam brought about by external military forces." Brilliant and ruthless, Kissinger helped Nixon centralize foreign policymaking in the White House. Together, they overpowered those members of the State Department who had concluded that the majority of Americans no longer supported the war.

In public Nixon followed a policy of "Vietnamization." On May 14, 1969, he announced that the time was approaching "when the South Vietnamese . . . will be able to take over some of the fighting." During the next several months, he ordered the withdrawal of 60,000 U.S. troops. Hoping to placate public opinion, Nixon also intended to "demonstrate to Hanoi that we were serious in seeking a diplomatic settlement." In private, with Kissinger's guidance, Nixon mulled over the option of a "knockout blow" to the North Vietnamese.

On April 30, 1970, Nixon made one of the most controversial decisions of his presidency. Without seeking congressional approval, Nixon added Cambodia (through which North Vietnam had been ferrying troops and supplies south) to the war zone. Although Nixon had authorized secret bombing raids of Cambodia in 1969, he now ordered U.S. troops to invade the tiny

---

In view of the developments since we entered the fighting in Vietnam, do you think the United States made a mistake sending troops to fight in Vietnam?

Yes	52%
No	39
No opinion	9

Interviewing Date 1/22–28/1969, Survey #774-K, Question #6/Index #45

Public Opinion on the War in Vietnam By 1969 Americans were sharply divided in their assessments of the progress of the war and peace negotiations. The American Institute of Public Opinion, founded in 1935 by George Gallup, charted a growing dissatisfaction with the war in Vietnam.

SOURCE: *The Gallup Poll: Public Opinion, 1935–1974* (New York: Random House, 1974), p. 2189.

nation. Nixon had hoped in this way to end North Vietnamese infiltration into the South, but he had also decided to live up to what he privately called his "wild man" or "mad bomber" reputation. The enemy would be unable to anticipate the location or severity of the next U.S. strike, Nixon reasoned, and would thus feel compelled to negotiate.

Nixon could not have predicted the outpouring of protest that followed the invasion of Cambodia. The largest series of demonstrations and police-student confrontations in the nation's history took place on campuses and in city streets. At Kent State University in Ohio, twenty-eight National Guardsmen apparently panicked, shooting into an unarmed crowd of about 200 students, killing four and wounding nine. Ten days later, on May 14, at Jackson State University, a black school in Mississippi, state troopers entered a campus dormitory and began shooting wildly, killing two students and wounding twelve others. Demonstrations broke out on fifty campuses.

The nation was shocked. Thirty-seven college and university presidents signed a letter calling on the president to end the war. A few weeks later the Senate adopted a bipartisan resolution outlawing the use of funds for U.S. military operations in Cambodia, starting July 1, 1970. Although the House rejected the resolution, Nixon saw the writing on the wall. He had planned to negotiate a simultaneous withdrawal of North Vietnamese and U.S. troops, but he could no longer afford to hold out for this condition.

The president, still goaded by Kissinger, did not accept defeat easily. In February 1971 Nixon directed the South Vietnamese army to invade Laos and cut supply lines, but the demoralized invading force suffered a quick and humiliating defeat. Faced with enemy occupation of more and more territory during a major offensive in April 1972, Nixon ordered the mining of North Vietnamese harbors and directed B-52s to conduct massively destructive bombing missions in Cambodia and North Vietnam.

Nixon also sent Kissinger to Paris for secret negotiations with delegates from North Vietnam. They agreed to a cease-fire specifying the withdrawal of all U.S. troops and the return of all U.S. prisoners of war. Knowing these terms ensured defeat, South Vietnam's president refused to sign the agreement. On Christmas Day 1972, hoping for a better negotiating position, Nixon ordered one final wave of bomb attacks on North Vietnam's cities. To secure a halt to the bombing, the North Vietnamese offered to resume negotiations. But the terms of the Paris Peace Agreement, signed by North Vietnam and the United States in January 1973, differed little from the settlement Nixon could have procured in 1969, costing hundreds of thousands of deaths that might have been prevented. Beginning in March 1973, the with-

drawal of U.S. troops left the outcome of the war a foregone conclusion. By December of that year only fifty American military personnel remained, and the government of South Vietnam had no future. In April 1975 North Vietnamese troops took over Saigon, and the Communist-led Democratic Republic of Vietnam soon united the small nation. The war was finally over. It had cost the United States 58,000 lives and $150 billion. The country had not only failed to achieve its stated war goal but had lost an important post in Southeast Asia. Equally important, the policy of containment introduced by President Truman had proved impossible to sustain.

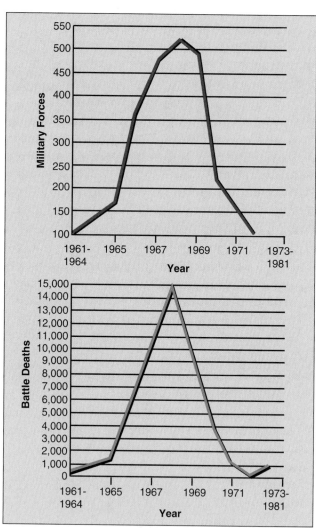

U.S. Military Forces in Vietnam and Casualties, 1961–1981 The United States government estimated battle deaths between 1969 and 1973 for South Vietnamese troops at 107,504 and North Vietnamese and Vietcong at more than a half-million. Although the United States suffered fewer deaths, the cost was enormous.

SOURCE: U.S. Department of Defense, *Selected Manpower Statistics,* annual, and unpublished data; beginning 1981, National Archives and Records Service, "Combat Area Casualty File" (3-330-80-3).

While Nixon was maneuvering to bring about "peace with honor," the chilling crimes of war had already begun to haunt Americans. In 1971 the army court-martialed a young lieutenant, William L. Calley, Jr., for the murder of "at least" twenty-two Vietnamese civilians during a 1968 search-and-destroy mission subsequently known as the My Lai Massacre. Calley's platoon had destroyed a village and slaughtered more than 350 unarmed South Vietnamese, raping and beating many of the women before killing them. "My Lai was not an isolated incident," one veteran attested, but "only a minor step beyond the standard official United States policy in Indochina." Commander of the platoon at My Lai, Calley was first sentenced to life imprisonment before being given a reduced term of ten years. The secretary of the army paroled Calley after he served three years under house arrest in his apartment.

"The China Card"

Apart from Vietnam, Nixon's foreign policy defied the expectations of liberals and conservatives alike. Actually, he followed traditions of previous Republican moderates such as Herbert Hoover and Dwight Eisenhower, who had so effectively "proved" their anticommunism that they could conciliate international foes without undermining their popularity at home. Nixon added a new page, however—a policy of détente that replaced U.S.–Soviet bipolarity with multilateral relations. Nixon could cultivate relations with the People's Republic of China, a rising world power more rigidly Communist than the Soviet Union, to form an alliance against the Soviet Union. And he could easily persuade the Soviet Union to cooperate on trade agreements, thus limiting the two nations' ruthless competition to control governments in Asia, the Middle East, and Africa. Opponents of the Vietnam War accused Nixon of double dealing, while conservatives howled at any compromise with Communist governments. But Nixon persisted in his plans, anticipating an end to the cold war on American terms.

Playing the "China card" was the most dramatic of the president's moves. Early in his political career Nixon had avidly supported the arch-conservative China lobby. But as president he considered the People's Republic of China too important to be isolated by the West and too obviously hostile to the Soviet Union to be discounted as a potential ally. "If there is anything I want to do before I die," he confided to a *Time* magazine reporter, "it is to go to China."

"Ping-pong diplomacy" began in April 1971, when the Chinese hosted a table tennis team from the United States. Henry Kissinger embarked on a secret mission a few months later. Finally, in February 1972, Richard and Pat Nixon flew to Beijing, where they were greeted by foreign minister Zhou Enlai and a band playing "The Star-Spangled Banner." It was a momentous and surprising event, one that marked a new era in East-West diplomacy. Nixon claimed that he had succeeded in bridging "16,000 miles and twenty-two years of hostility." The president's move successfully increased diplomatic pressure on the Soviet Union but simultaneously weakened the Nationalist Chinese government in Taiwan, which now slipped into virtual diplomatic obscurity.

Next the president went to Moscow to negotiate with Soviet leader Leonid Brezhnev, who was anxious about U.S. involvement with China and eager for economic assistance. Declaring, "There must be room in this world for two great nations with different systems to live together and work together," Nixon offered to sell $1 billion of grain to the Soviets. Winning the favor of American wheat farmers, this deal simultaneously relieved U.S. trade deficits and crop surpluses. Afterward, the Soviet leader became visibly more cautious about supporting revolutions in the third world. Nixon also completed negotiations of the Strategic Arms Limitation Treaty (SALT, known later as SALT I). A limited measure, SALT I represented the first success at strategic arms control since the opening of the cold war and a major public relations victory for the leaders of the two superpowers.

Nixon's last major diplomatic foray proved far less effective. The president sent Kissinger on a two-year mission of "shuttle diplomacy" to mediate Israeli-Arab disputes, to ensure the continued flow of oil, and to increase lucrative U.S. arms sales to Arab countries. The Egyptians and Israelis agreed to a cease-fire in their October 1973 Yom Kippur War, but little progress toward peace in the area was achieved.

Domestic Policy

Nixon deeply desired to restore order in American society. "We live in a deeply troubled and profoundly unsettled time," he noted. "Drugs, crime, campus revolts, racial discord, draft resistance—on every hand we find old standards violated, old values discarded." Despite his hostility to liberalism, however, Nixon had some surprises for conservatives. Determined to win reelection in 1972, he supported new Social Security benefits and subsidized housing for the poor and oversaw the creation of the Environmental Protection Agency and the Occupational Safety and Health Administration. Most notable was his support, under the guidance of Democratic adviser Daniel P. Moynihan, for the Family Assistance Plan, which proposed a minimal income for the poor in place of welfare benefits. Conservatives judged the plan too generous while liberals found it inadequate. Moreover, the plan was expensive. Bipartisan opposition ultimately killed the bill.

Nixon also embraced a policy of fiscal liberalism. Early in 1971 he accepted the idea of deficit spending. Later that year he ordered a first: he took the nation off the gold standard. Subsequently, the dollar's value would float on the world market rather than being tied to the value of gold. His ninety-day freeze on wages, rents, and prices, designed to halt the inflation caused by the massive spending on the Vietnam War, also closely resembled Democratic policies. Finally, Nixon's support of "black capitalism"—adjustments or quotas favoring minority contractors in construction projects—created an explosive precedent for "set-aside" programs later blamed on liberals.

Nixon lined up with conservatives, however, on most civil rights issues and thus enlarged southern Republican constituencies. He accepted the principle of school integration but rejected the busing programs required to implement racial balance. His nominees to the Supreme Court were far more conservative than those appointed by Eisenhower. Warren E. Burger, who replaced Chief Justice Earl Warren, steered the Court away from the liberal direction it had taken since the 1950s.

One of the most newsworthy events of Nixon's administration was a distant result of President Kennedy's determination to outshine the Soviets in outer space (see Chapter 27). On July 21, 1969, the lunar module of Apollo 11 descended to the moon's Sea of Tranquility. As millions watched on television, astronauts Neil Armstrong and Buzz Aldrin stepped out to plant an American flag and to bear the message, "We came in peace for all mankind."

WATERGATE

At times Richard Nixon expressed his yearning for approval in strange ways. A few days after the bombing of Cambodia in May 1970, he wandered out of the White House alone at 5:00 in the morning to talk to antiwar demonstrators. He tried to engage them in small talk about football and pleaded, "I know that probably most of you think I'm an SOB, but I want you to know I understand just how you feel." According to H. R. Haldeman, one of Nixon's closest advisers, the student killings at Kent State deeply troubled the president.

Yet only a few months later Nixon ordered illegal wiretaps of news professionals. He also reaffirmed his support of Central Intelligence Agency (CIA) surveillance of U.S. citizens and organizations—a policy specifically forbidden by the CIA charter—and encouraged members of his administration to spy on Democrats planning for the 1972 election campaign. When news of these illegal activities surfaced, one of the most canny politicians in American history found himself the first president since Andrew Johnson to face the likelihood of impeachment proceedings.

Foreign Policy as Conspiracy

Nixon's conduct of foreign policy offered early clues into his political character. Although he had welcomed the publicity surrounding his historic moves toward détente with the Soviet Union and normalized relations with China, Nixon generally handled the nation's foreign affairs in surreptitious fashion. But as opposition to the Vietnam War mounted in Congress, he began to face hard questions about this practice. As early as 1970, Republicans as well as Democrats had condemned covert operations in foreign countries. In response, the president, the Department of State, and the CIA developed plans to tighten security even further. Nixon issued a tough mandate against all leaks of information by government personnel, news specialists, or politicians.

At the time, apart from the highly publicized tour to China, Nixon revealed little about his policy for other parts of the globe. Unknown to most Americans, he accelerated the delivery of arms supplies to foreign dictators, including the shah of Iran, Ferdinand Marcos of the Philippines, and the regime of Pieter William Botha in South Africa. His CIA assistants trained and aided SAVAK, the Iranian secret police force notorious for torturing political dissidents. They also stood behind the South African government in its effort to curtail the activities of the antiapartheid African National Congress. In Latin America, Nixon provided financial assistance and military aid to repressive regimes such as that of Anastasio Somoza of Nicaragua, notorious for its blatant corruption and repeated violations of human rights.

Still more controversial was Nixon's plan to overthrow the legally elected socialist government of Salvador Allende in Chile. With the assistance of nongovernment agencies, such as the AFL-CIO's American Institute for Free Labor Development, the CIA destabilized the regime by funding right-wing parties, launching demonstrations, and preparing the Chilean army for a coup. In September 1973, a military junta killed President Allende and captured, tortured, or murdered thousands of his supporters. Nixon and Kissinger warmly welcomed the new ruler, Augusto Pinochet, granting him financial assistance to restabilize the country.

Toward the end of Nixon's term, members of Congress who had been briefed on these policies began to break silence, and reports of clandestine operations flooded the media. Several former CIA agents issued anguished confessions of their activities in other countries. More troubling to Nixon, in spite of all his efforts the United States continued to lose ground as a superpower.

The Age of Dirty Tricks

As Nixon approached the 1972 reelection campaign, he tightened his inner circle of White House staff who assisted him in withholding information from the public, discrediting critics, and engaging in assorted "dirty tricks." Circle members solicited illegal contributions for the campaign and laundered the money through Mexican bank accounts. They also formed a secret squad, "the plumbers," to halt the troublesome leaks of information. This team, headed by former CIA agent E. Howard Hunt and former FBI agent G. Gordon Liddy, assisted in conspiracy at the highest levels of government.

The first person on the squad's "hit list" was Daniel Ellsberg, a former researcher with the Department of Defense, who in 1971 had turned over to the press secret documents outlining the military history of American involvement in Vietnam. The so-called Pentagon Papers exposed the role of presidents and military leaders in deceiving the public and Congress about the conduct of the United States in Southeast Asia. Nixon sought to bar publication by the *New York Times*, but the Supreme Court ruled in favor of the newspaper on the basis of the First Amendment. Within weeks, a complete version of the Pentagon Papers became a best-selling book, and in 1972 the *New York Times* won a Pulitzer Prize for the series of articles. Frustrated in his attempt to suppress the report, Nixon directed the Department of Justice to prosecute Ellsberg on charges of conspiracy, espionage, and theft. Meanwhile, Hunt and Liddy, seeking to discredit Ellsberg, broke into the office of his former psychiatrist. They found nothing that would make their target less heroic in the eyes of an increasingly skeptical public, and by 1973 the charges against Ellsberg were dropped after the Nixon administration itself stood guilty of misconduct.

At the same time, Nixon ran a skillful negative campaign charging George McGovern, the liberal Democrat who had won his party's nomination on the first ballot, with supporting "abortion, acid [LSD], and amnesty" for those who had resisted the draft or deserted the armed forces. The Republicans also informed the news media that McGovern's running mate, Senator Thomas Eagleton, had once undergone electric shock therapy for depression, thus forcing his resignation from the Democratic team. Voter turnout fell to an all-time low, and McGovern lost every state but Massachusetts. (Later, when Nixon faced disgrace, bumper stickers appeared reading, "Don't Blame Me, I'm from Massachusetts.")

The Committee to Re-Elect the President (CREEP) enjoyed a huge war chest and spent a good portion on dirty tricks designed to divide the Democrats and discredit them in the eyes of the voting public. The most ambitious plan—wiretapping the Democratic National Committee headquarters—backfired.

On June 17, 1972, a security team had tripped up a group of intruders hired by CREEP to install listening devices in the Washington, D.C., Watergate apartment and office complex where the Democrats were headquartered. The police arrested five men, who were later found guilty of conspiracy and burglary. Although

Nixon disclaimed any knowledge of the plan, two *Washington Post* reporters, Bob Woodward and Carl Bernstein, followed a trail of evidence back to the nation's highest office.

Televised Senate hearings opened to public view more than a pattern of presidential wrongdoing: they showed an attempt to impede investigations of the Watergate case. Testifying before the committee, a former Nixon aide revealed the existence of secret tape recordings of conversations held in the Oval Office. After special prosecutor Archibald Cox refused to allow Nixon to claim executive privilege and withhold the tapes, the president ordered Cox fired. This "Saturday Night Massacre," as it came to be called, further tarnished Nixon's reputation and swelled curiosity about the tapes. On June 24, 1974, the Supreme Court voted unanimously that Nixon had to release the tapes to a new special prosecutor, Leon Jaworski.

The Fall of the Executive

The case against the president gained strength. Although incomplete, the Watergate tapes proved damning. They documented Nixon's ravings against his enemies, including anti-Semitic slurs, and his conniving efforts to harass

With impeachment a certainty in the House of Representatives, President Nixon decided to resign his office. On nation-wide television, on August 8, 1974, he said that it had become apparent that "I no longer have a strong enough political base in the Congress to justify continuing" as the President of the United States. He left Washington, D.C. the next day.

SOURCE: AP/Wide World Photos.

CHRONOLOGY

1964 President Lyndon Johnson calls for "an unconditional war on poverty" in his state of the union address

Tonkin Gulf resolution

The Economic Opportunity Act establishes the Office of Economic Opportunity

Free speech movement gets under way at University of California at Berkeley

Johnson defeats conservative Barry Goldwater for president

1965 President Johnson authorizes Operation Rolling Thunder, the bombing of North Vietnam

Teach-ins begin on college campuses

First major march on Washington for peace is organized

Watts uprising begins a wave of rebellions in black communities

1966 J. William Fulbright publishes *The Arrogance of Power*

Black Panther Party is formed

National Organization for Women (NOW) is formed

1967 Antiwar rally in New York City draws 300,000

Vietnam Veterans against the War is formed

Uprisings in Newark, Detroit, and other cities

Hippie "Summer of Love"

1968 U.S. ground troops levels in Vietnam number 500,000

Tet Offensive in Vietnam, followed by international protests against U.S. policies

Martin Luther King, Jr. is assassinated; riots break out in more than 100 cities

Vietnam peace talks begin in Paris

Robert Kennedy is assassinated

Democratic National Convention, held in Chicago, nominates Hubert Humphrey; "police riot" against protesters

Richard Nixon elected president

American Indian Movement (AIM) founded

1969 Woodstock music festival marks the high tide of the counterculture

Stonewall Riot in Greenwich Village sparks the gay liberation movement

Apollo 11 lands on the moon

1970 U.S. incursion into Cambodia sparks campus demonstrations; students killed at Kent State and Jackson State universities

Women's Strike for Equality marks the fiftieth anniversary of the woman suffrage amendment

1971 Lieutenant William Calley, Jr. court-martialed for My Lai Massacre

New York Times starts publishing the Pentagon Papers

1972 Nixon visits China and Soviet Union

SALT I limits offensive intercontinental ballistic missiles

Intruders attempting to "bug" Democratic headquarters in the Watergate complex are arrested

Nixon is reelected in a landslide

Nixon orders Christmas Day bombing of North Vietnam

1973 Paris Peace Agreement ends war in Vietnam

FBI seizes Indian occupants of Wounded Knee, South Dakota

Watergate burglars tried; congressional hearings on Watergate

CIA destabilizes elected Chilean government, which is overthrown

Vice President Spiro T. Agnew resigns

1974 House Judiciary Committee adopts articles of impeachment against Nixon

Nixon resigns the presidency

private citizens through federal agencies. The tapes also proved that Nixon had not only known about plans to cover up the Watergate break-in but had ordered it. The news media enjoyed a field day with the revelations. In July 1974, the House Judiciary Committee adopted three articles of impeachment, charging Nixon with obstructing justice.

Charges of executive criminality had clouded the Nixon administration since his vice president had resigned in disgrace. In 1972 Spiro Agnew had admitted accepting large kickbacks while serving as governor of Maryland. Pleading no contest to this and to charges of federal income tax evasion, Agnew had resigned from office in October 1973. Gerald Ford, a moderate Republican representative from Michigan, had replaced him and now stood in the wings while the president's drama unfolded.

Facing certain impeachment by the House of Representatives, Richard Nixon became, on August 9, 1974, the first U.S. president to resign from office.

CONCLUSION

The resignations of Richard Nixon and Spiro Agnew brought little to relieve the feeling of national exhaustion that attended the Vietnam War. U.S. troops had pulled out of Vietnam in 1973 and the war officially ended in 1975, but bitterness lingered over the unprecedented—and, for many, humiliating—defeat. Morover, confidence in the government's highest office was severely shaken. The passage of the War Powers Act in 1973, written to compel any future president to seek congressional approval for armed intervention abroad, dramatized both the widespread suspicion of presidential intentions and a yearning for peace. But the positive dream of community that had inspired Johnson, King, and a generaton of student activists could not be revived. No other vision took its place.

In 1968 seven prominent antiwar protesters had been brought to trial for allegedly conspiring to disrupt the Democratic National Convention in Chicago. Just a few years later, the majority of Americans had concluded that presidents Johnson and Nixon had conspired to do far worse. They had intentionally deceived the public about the nature and fortunes of the war. This moral failure signaled a collapse at the center of the American political system. Since Dwight Eisenhower left office warning of the potential danger embedded in the "military-industrial complex," no president had survived the presidency with his honor intact. Watergate, then, appeared to cap the politics of the cold war, its revelations only reinforcing futility and cynicism. The United States was left psychologically at war with itself.

REVIEW QUESTIONS

1. Discuss the events that led up to and contributed to U.S. involvement in Vietnam. How did U.S. involvement in the war affect domestic programs?

2. Discuss the reasons the protest movement against the Vietnam War started on college campuses. Describe how these movements were organized and how the opponents of the war differed from the supporters.

3. Discuss the programs sponsored by Johnson's plan for a Great Society. What was their impact on urban poverty in the late 1960s?

4. What was the impact of the assassinations of Martin Luther King, Jr. and Robert Kennedy on the election of 1968? How were various communities affected?

5. How were the "politics of identity" movements different from earlier civil rights organizations? In what ways did the various movements resemble one another?

6. Why did Richard Nixon enjoy such a huge electoral victory in 1972? Discuss his foreign and domestic policies. What led to his sudden downfall?

RECOMMENDED READING

John A. Andrew III, *Lyndon Johnson and the Great Society* (1998). An assessment of the Great Society, with special emphasis on the two major issues of civil rights and poverty. Andrew discusses Johnson's aspirations and the obstacles that kept them out of reach.

Keith Beattie, *The Scar That Binds: American Culture and the Vietnam War* (1998). Examines memoirs, war novels and films, and the Vietnam Veterans Memorial in Washington, D.C., to discuss the cultural legacy of the war.

Alexander Bloom, ed., *Long Time Gone: Sixties America Then and Now* (2001). Ten essays covering various aspects of the social and political movements of the 1960s. The authors draw out the meaning of the "sixties" for today and dispel commonplace myths by providing accurate information and a sound context for interpretation.

Jane F. Gerhard, *Desiring Revolution: Second-Wave Feminism and the Rewriting of American Sexual Thought, 1920–1982* (2001). Discusses the background of the feminist side of the sexual revolution with special attention to popular versions of Freud's theories. Gerhard discusses disagreements among feminists on the meaning and experience of sexual liberation.

Michael H. Hunt, *Lyndon Johnson's War: America's Cold War Crusade in Vietnam, 1945–1968* (1996). Tracks Johnson's decisions to wage all-out war in Vietnam. Hunt interprets Johnson's actions as consistent with the cold war foreign policy that had prevailed since the Truman administration and its pledge to "contain" communism.

Rebecca E. Klatch, *A Generation Divided: The New Left, the New Right, and the 1960s* (1999). Compares and contrasts the respective roles of Students for a Democratic Society and the conservative Young Americans for Freedom on college campuses. Klatch, a sociologist, presents lengthy oral interviews with former student activists in both camps.

Joan Morrison and Robert K. Morrison, eds., *From Camelot to Kent State: the Sixties Experience in the Words of Those Who Lived It* (2001). A collection of 59 oral histories with a range of people who lived through the 1960s. The volume includes stories of better-known activists, such as Eldridge Cleaver and Abbie Hoffman, as well as those who were soldiers in Vietnam or student activists. This edition also contains many photographs.

Joseph Tilden Rhea, *Race Pride and the American Identity* (1997). Examines American Indians, Asian Americans, Latinos, and African Americans in their search for recognition. Rhea emphasizes the importance of political struggles and their impact on historical consciousness, including the establishment of historical sites and museums.

Ruth Rosen, *The World Split Open: How the Modern Women's Movement Changed America* (2000). Discusses the impact of women's liberation on American politics, business, and family life. Through extensive archival research and interviews, Rosen provides compelling evidence for the magnitude of change accompanying second-wave feminism.

Anthony Summers, *The Arrogance of Power: The Secret World of Richard Nixon* (2000). A popular biography of Nixon's life from his early political career in California through his presidency. Summers drew on more than a thousand interviews, including those with Nixon's psychotherapist, to portray the former president's erratic behavior and mental instability during as well as before the disastrous Watergate affair.

Marilyn B. Young, *The Vietnam Wars, 1945–1990* (1991). An excellent overview of the involvement of the French and the American military and diplomatic forces in Vietnam from the 1910s to 1975, and of the various movements against them. Young presents a thematic continuity that highlights the nationalism of the Vietnamese as ultimately more powerful than the troops and weaponry of their opponents.

ADDITIONAL BIBLIOGRAPHY

Vietnam: America's Longest War

Christian G. Appy, *Working–Class War: American Combat Soldiers in Vietnam* (1993)

Larry Berman, *No Peace, No Honor: Nixon, Kissinger, and Betrayal in Vietnam* (2001)

Robert Buzzanco, *Vietnam and the Transformation of American Life* (1999)

Kenton J. Clymer, *The Vietnam War: Its History, Literature and Music* (1998)

Gerald J. DeGroot, *A Noble Cause? America and the Vietnam War* (2000)

Virginia Elwood-Akers, *Women War Correspondents in the Vietnam War, 1961–1975* (1988)

William M Hammond, *Reporting Vietnam: Media and Military at War* (1998)

George C. Herring, *America's Longest War: The United States and Vietnam, 1950–1975*, 3rd ed. (1996)

———, ed., *The Pentagon Papers*, abridged ed. (1993)

Andrew E. Hunt, *The Turning: A History of Vietnam Veterans Against the War* (1999)

Jeffrey Kimball, *Nixon's Vietnam War* (1998)

Fredrik Logevall, *Choosing War: The Lost Chance for Peace and the Escalation of War in Vietnam* (1999)

Robert Mann, *A Grand Illusion: America's Descent into Vietnam* (2001)

James S. Olson and Randy Roberts, *My Lai: A Brief History with Documents* (1998)

Randy Shilts, *Conduct Unbecoming: Lesbians and Gays in the U.S. Military, Vietnam to the Persian Gulf* (1993)

Fred Turner, *Echoes of Combat: The Vietnam War in American Memory* (1996)

James E. Westheider, *Fighting on Two Fronts: African Americans and the Vietnam War* (1997)

A Generation in Conflict

David Allyn, *Make Love, Not War: The Sexual Revolution, Unfettered History* (2000)

Beth Baily, *Sex in the Heartland* (1999)

Alexander Bloom and Wini Breines, eds., *Takin' It to the Streets: A Sixties Reader* (1996)

Aniko Bodroghkozy, *Groove Tube: Sixties Television and the Youth Rebellion* (2001)

Wini Breines, *Community and Organization in the New Left* (1982)

David Farber, *The Age of Great Dreams: America in the 1960s* (1994)

James J. Farrell, *The Spirit of the Sixties: The Making of Postwar Radicalism* (1997)

Maurice Isserman and Michael Kazin, *America Divided: The Civil War of the 1960s* (2000)

Paul Lyons, *New Left, New Right, and the Legacy of the Sixties* (1996)

John C. McWilliams, *The 1960s Cultural Revolution* (2000)

Timothy Miller, *The 60s Communes: Hippies and Beyond* (1999)

George Rising, *Clean for Gene: Eugene McCarthy's 1968 Presidential Campaign* (1997)

William L. Van Deburg, *New Day in Babylon: The Black Power Movement and American Culture, 1965–1975* (1992)

The Politics of Identity

Kathleen C. Berkeley, *The Women's Liberation Movement in America* (1999)

Dudley Clendinen and Adam Nagourney, *Out for Good: The Struggle to Build a Gay Rights Movement in America* (1999)

Susan J. Douglas, *Where the Girls Are: Growing Up Female with the Mass Media* (1994)

Martin Duberman, *Stonewall* (1993)

Gerald Horne, *Fire This Time: The Watts Uprising and the 1960s* (1996)

Blance Linden-Ward, *American Women in the 1960s* (1992)

Marguerite V. Marin, *Social Protest in an Urban Barrio: A Study of the Chicano Movement, 1966–1972* (1991)

Peter Matthiessen, *In the Spirit of Crazy Horse* (1991)

Joane Nagel, *American Indian Ethnic Renewal: Red Power and the Resurgence of Identity and Culture* (1996)

Armando Navarro, *Mexican American Youth Organization: Avant-Garde of the Chicano Movement in Texas* (1995)

Rachel Blau De Plessis and Ann Snitow, *The Feminist Memoir Project: Voices from Women's Liberation* (1998)

The Nixon Presidency and Watergate

Mary C. Brennan, *Turning Right in the Sixties: The Conservative Capture of the GOP* (1995)

Carl Bernstein and Bob Woodward, *All the President's Men* (1974)

Leonard Garment, *In Search of Deep Throat: The Greatest Political Mystery of Our Time* (2000)

Lewis L. Gould, *1968: The Election That Changed America* (1993)

Allen J. Matusow, *Nixon's Economy: Booms, Busts, Dollars and Votes* (1998)

Michael Schudson, *Watergate in American History* (1992)

Biography

David L. Anderson, ed., *The Human Tradition in the Vietnam Era* (2000)

Elaine Brown, *A Taste of Power: A Black Woman's Story* (1992)

Jody Carlson, *George C. Wallace and the Politics of Powerlessness* (1981)

Robert Dallek, *Flawed Giant: Lyndon Johnson and His Times, 1961–1973* (1998)

Robert Alan Goldberg, *Barry Goldwater* (1995)

Elliot Gorn, ed., *Muhammad Ali: The People's Champ* (1996)

Daniel Horowitz, *Betty Friedan and the Making of the Feminine Mystique: The American Left, the Cold War, and Modern Feminism* (1998)

Joan Hoff, *Nixon Reconsidered* (1994)

Jonah Raskin, *For the Hell of It: The Life and Times of Abbie Hoffman* (1996)

Kenneth S. Stern, *Loud Hawk: The United States versus the American Indian Movement* (1994)

Evan Thomas, *Robert Kennedy: His Life* (2000)

Jack Todd, *Desertion: In the Time of Vietnam* (2001)

Irwin Unger and Debi Unger, *LBJ: A Life* (1999)

HISTORY ON THE INTERNET

http://www.yale.edu/lawweb/avalon/tonkin-g.htm

Text of President Johnson's address to Congress on the Gulf of Tonkin incident and the Joint Resolution of Congress H.J. RES 1145 August 7, 1964.

http://seattletimes.nwsource.com/news/nation-world/html98/tett_013098.html

A *Seattle Times* assessment of the impact of the Tet Offensive of 1968.

http://www.gwu.edu/~nsarchiv/NSAEBB/NSAEBB48/supreme.html

Interesting discussion and links on the Pentagon Papers and the court battle to publish that document.

http://www.pbs.org/wgbh/amex/vietnam/trenches/mylai.html

Short but detailed PBS description of the My Lai incident.

http://www.tamu.edu/scom/pres/archive.html

The Center for Presidential Studies at Texas A&M University has a collection of presidential speeches from Washington through George Bush. Trace the development of Johnson's Vietnam policies from the Gulf of Tonkin Speech (1964), to the John Hopkins Speech (1965), to his decision to refuse the 1968 Democratic nomination (1968).

http://www.lib.berkeley.edu/MRC/watergate.html

RealAudio recordings of the Nixon White House tapes. Visit the National Archives link listed here for interesting information concerning the preservation of those tapes.

http://www.washingtonpost.com/wp-srv/national/longterm/watergate/chronology.htm

A very interesting Washington Post timeline of the Watergate events leading to Nixon's resignation with links to Washington Post new stories of the day.

THIRTY

THE CONSERVATIVE ASCENDANCY

▶ 1974–1987

Wayne Thiebaud, *Urban Freeways*, 1979–80. Oil on canvas. 44″ × 36″. Allan Stone Gallery, New York.

Grass Roots Conservatism in Orange County, California

IN 1962 BEE GATHRIGHT, A BROWNIE LEADER AND MOTHER OF THREE young girls, listened to a neighbor's casual request. Would she allow the patio of her suburban Garden Grove home to be used for a meeting bringing together neighbors to hear a talk about liberalism and conservatism by a man from the nearby Knott's Berry Farm Freedom Center? Gathright agreed and found the meeting to be a revelation: "This is when I discovered that I was a conservative," she recalled three decades later. She soon arranged for the speaker to address a larger audience at the local public school. Gathright began to read widely in books and newspapers "because I began to hear that the Communists were going to bury us, were going to take over the world . . . I was afraid." She convinced her skeptical husband Neil, an aerospace engineer, to share her new-found activism. They attended study groups and soon joined the California Republican Assembly, a volunteer organization dedicated to electing conservatives to office. In 1964 the Gathrights' home served as a local headquarters for the presidential campaign of conservative Arizona Senator Barry Goldwater. After winning the Republican nomination Goldwater lost the election to President Lyndon Johnson in one of the biggest landslides in American electoral history. Most political commentators and analysts believed Goldwater's crushing defeat proved that "far Right" conservatism had little future in American politics.

Orange County in the 1960s and 1970 had thousands of "kitchen table" activists like the Gathrights, and they began a transformation of American conservatism and American politics that would culminate in the election of Ronald Reagan as president in 1980. Most of them were middle-class men and women, including large numbers of professionals and people with small businesses. Many were recent migrants to California, attracted by job opportunities in aerospace. Bee Gathright herself had arrived after World War II from Iowa, taking a job as an executive secretary at Douglas Aircraft in Santa Monica. Orange County's 800 square miles lie at the geographic center of the Southern California basin, and large lemon and orange groves dominated the economy until the 1940s. The Second World War and Cold War defense-related spending accelerated Orange County's growth as companies like Hughes Aircraft, Autonetics, and Beckman Instruments created over 30,000 new manufacturing jobs in defense and electronics between 1950 and the early 1960s. The strong demand for housing spurred a highly profitable construction boom and a roaring real estate market. By 1960, over 700,000 people lived in Orange County, an increase of nearly 400 percent since 1940, and the population doubled again to almost 1.5 million by 1970.

While Barry Goldwater's 1964 campaign had ignited great enthusiasm in Orange County, his national defeat forced conservatives to consider how they might shed the "extremism" label and put more emphasis on winning office. In 1966 they succeeeded in electing Ronald Reagan as governor. A former Hollywood actor and New Deal liberal, Reagan had evolved in the 1950s into an effective conservative spokesman and a prominent Republican Party activist. His gubernatorial campaign stressed limiting state support for welfare and other social services, while expanding state power to enforce law and order.

Reagan's electoral success in California, as well as Richard Nixon's election as president in 1968, signaled an important new turn for American conservatives in the 1970s. They still championed anticommunism, but no longer engaged in the kind of loose talk about using nuclear weapons that had hurt Goldwater. They attacked the growth of "big government," but no longer spoke openly about repealing popular New Deal programs like Social Security. Instead, they responded to the concerns over "social issues" that increasingly troubled and mobilized Orange County's grass-roots activists. These issues were largely defined by a "backlash" against the antiwar movement, counterculture, feminist activism, and urban riots, and an emphasis on so-called family issues, in which opposition to sex education, obscenity, abortion rights, and gay liberation were all linked together. On the economic side, conservatives began to tap a deep well of resentment over rising property taxes and high inflation.

Two of the central themes of this new conservatism found powerful expression in Orange County, and resonated with millions of Americans well beyond it. One was the so-called tax revolt led by Howard Jarvis, a flamboyant campaigner long active in Southern California conservative circles. Saying he had been energized and inspired by local taxpayer-protest meetings, Jarvis told his supporters, "Lower taxes and less government became my holy grail. . . . The only way to cut government spending is not to give them the money in the first place." Jarvis relied on local networks to gather 1.3 million signatures to get his Proposition 13 on the ballot—a constitutional amendment that slashed the property tax rate from 3% to 1% of a home's market value, and strictly limited future tax increases. After its passage in 1978, the "tax revolt" soon spread to other states and attracted millions to the conservative message of limiting government and lowering taxes.

Orange County was a center of the second new force reshaping conservatism, the spectacular growth of "born again" evangelical Christianity. Fundamentalist sects had long been associated with the rural poor of the South. But Orange County's religious revival demonstrated how educated professionals and middle class suburbanites were also turning to "born again" Christianity in their search for spirituality and meaning, as a rejection of "permissiveness," and as a way to assert order amidst rapid cultural and social change. One of the most successful fundamentalist ministers was the Reverend Chuck Smith, who pioneered the use of Christian folk music, adopted countercultural symbols and motifs, and conducted mass ocean baptisms in Corona del Mar. By 1978 his mother church in Costa Mesa, Calvary Chapel, had 25,000 members. They found community not only in Sunday services but in a wide range of tightly organized activities: Bible study groups, summer retreats, "singles' fellowships," prayer breakfasts, and "Christian" consumer culture, which allowed people to simultaneously embrace faith, modern business techniques, and worldly goods.

The political implications of the new evangelicalism became clear by the late 1970s. Most fundamentalist preachers tied their sermons and prophesies to conservative political themes, especially fears about the decline of morality and of American power in the world. Reverend Chuck Smith warned that "the decline of the economy and government of the United States will open the doors to the rise of the anti-Christ to world power."

Newly politicized Christian voters worked diligently to elect Ronald Reagan President in 1980. In Orange County they helped Reagan get 68 percent of the vote, the most lopsided victory of any large county in the nation. For Bee Gathright, the former Goldwater supporter who by then had shifted her energies to Christian missionary work, Reagan's victory provided a national vindication of her years of grass-roots activism. For her, as for so many others in Orange County, the "Christian movement" and the conservative movement had become one and the same. ■

Three Mile Island

KEY TOPICS

- Structural shifts in the economy

- The Ford and Carter presidencies

- Crisis in the cities and environment

- Community politics and the rise of the New Right

- Iran hostage crisis

- The Reagan Republican presidential victory

- Reagan's domestic and foreign policies

- The growth of inequality

THE OVEREXTENDED SOCIETY

In the 1970s Americans faced an unfamiliar combination of skyrocketing prices, rising unemployment, and low economic growth. Economists termed this novel condition "stagflation." The annual rate of economic growth slowed by almost one-quarter from its robust 3.2 percent average of the 1950s. By 1975, the unemployment rate had reached nearly 9 percent, its highest level since the Great Depression, and it remained close to 7 percent for most of the rest of the decade. Inflation, meanwhile, reached double-digits.

The United States had come to a turning point in its economic history. Emerging from World War II as the most prosperous nation in the world and retaining this status through the 1960s, the country suddenly found itself falling behind western Europe and Japan. Polls conducted at the end of the 1970s revealed that a majority of Americans believed that conditions would worsen.

The gloomy economy shadowed the nation's political leaders. Republican Gerald Ford and Democrat Jimmy Carter promised little and, as far as many voters were concerned, delivered less. Neither managed to secure a second term in the White House.

A Troubled Economy

In October 1973 gasoline prices nearly doubled, jumping from 40 to nearly 70 cents per gallon. Gas lines grew up to four miles long, and fistfights broke out among frustrated motorists. Several states responded to the shortage by introducing rationing programs.

The oil crisis began suddenly, although it had been decades in the making. The United States, which used about 70 percent of all oil produced in the world, had found the domestic supply sufficient until the late 1950s. But rising demand had outstripped national reserves, and by 1973 the nation was importing one-third of its crude oil, mainly from the Middle East. In that year, following the Arab-Israeli War, oil prices skyrocketed. On October 17, the Organization of Petroleum Exporting Countries (OPEC), a cartel of mainly Arab oil producers, announced an embargo on oil shipments to Israel's allies, including the United States. A few weeks later, President Nixon announced, "We are heading toward the most acute shortage of energy since World War II."

The president responded to the embargo by creating an "energy czar" and paving the way for the creation of the Department of Energy in 1977. He ordered a 10 percent reduction in air travel and appealed to Congress to lower speed limits on interstate highways to 55 miles per hour (incidentally reducing highway deaths in the process), and to extend daylight-saving time into the winter months. Many state governments introduced their own programs, turning down the thermostats in public buildings to a chilly 68 degrees, reducing nonessential lighting, and restricting hours of service.

With the cost of gasoline, oil, and electricity up, many other prices also rose, from apartment rents and telephone bills to restaurant checks. As oil prices continued to rise through the 1970s, many Americans also began to look suspiciously at the pricing practices of U.S. oil companies. Whatever the causes, the oil crisis played a major role in the economic downturn, the worst since the Great Depression.

The economic downturn, according to many experts, had deeper roots in the failure of the United States to keep up with the rising industrial efficiency of Western Europe and Japan. As long as American manufacturers faced scant competition from abroad, they had little incentive to update their machinery or to establish management techniques that took full advantage of the skills of younger, more educated employees.

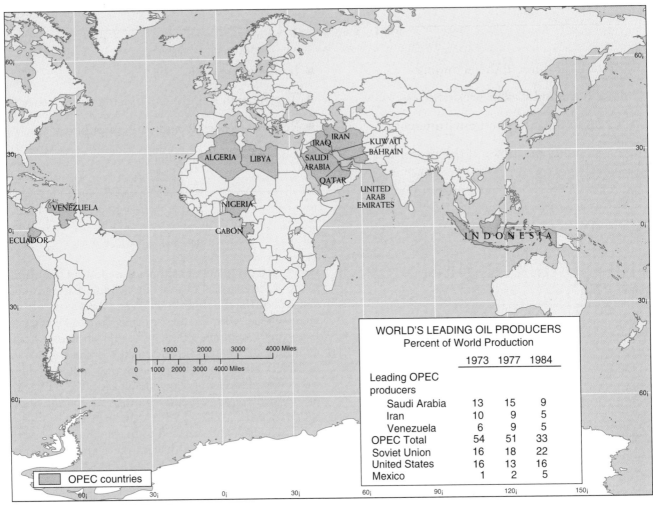

WORLD'S LEADING OIL PRODUCERS Percent of World Production			
	1973	1977	1984
Leading OPEC producers			
Saudi Arabia	13	15	9
Iran	10	9	5
Venezuela	6	9	5
OPEC Total	54	51	33
Soviet Union	16	18	22
United States	16	13	16
Mexico	1	2	5

World's Leading Oil Producers

Manufacturers from Asia, Latin America, and Europe now offered consumers cheaper and better products, including automobiles, long considered the monopoly of Detroit. U.S. automakers, determined to reduce costs, turned to "outsourcing"—that is, making cars and trucks from parts cheaply produced abroad and imported into the United States as semifinished materials (which were subject to a lower tariff than finished goods.) In high-tech electronics, the United States scarcely competed against Japanese-produced televisions, radios, tape players, cameras, and computers. An AFL-CIO leader complained that the United States was becoming "a nation of hamburger stands . . . a country stripped of industrial capacity and meaningful work."

The situation in agriculture was still more grim. The huge increase in oil prices translated into higher gasoline and fertilizer costs, forcing farmers to borrow heavily from banks. Soon the high interest rates on borrowed money threw many family farmers into a state of permanent indebtedness. When overseas sales declined at the end of the 1970s, tens of thousands defaulted on loans and lost their farms to banks and credit companies, ending a way of life generations old. High costs and unstable prices offered a gloomy prospect for all but the leaders in corporate-style agribusiness, the 12 percent of farmers who made 90 percent of all farm income.

Blue-Collar Blues

In past decades labor unions had typically responded to inflation by negotiating new contracts or, if necessary, striking for higher pay. But while factories closed, the National Labor Relations Board increasingly ruled in favor of management, making the organization of new union locals far more difficult. Between 1970 and 1982 the AFL-CIO lost nearly 30 percent of its membership. The only real growth took place among public employees, including teachers, civil service workers, and health professionals—all of them dependent on

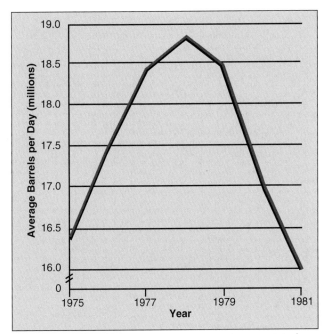

Decline of U.S. Oil Consumption, 1975–1981

SOURCE: Department of Energy, *Monthly Energy Review*, June 1982.

worked as domestics or agricultural laborers in the Southwest. Neither group earned much more than the minimum wage.

Sunbelt/Snowbelt Communities

By the 1970s the Sunbelt offered a rare showplace of American prosperity. It boasted a gross product greater than many nations and more cars, television sets, houses, and even miles of paved roads than the rest of the United States. Large influxes of immigrants from Latin America, the Caribbean, and Asia combined with the shift of Americans from the depressed Northeast to boost the region's population. From 56 million people in 1940, the Sunbelt's population more than doubled to 118 million just four decades later.

This increase had been made possible by a huge outlay of federal funds, including defense spending and the allocation of Social Security funds. The number of residents over the age of sixty-five increased by 30 percent during the 1970s, reaching 26 million by 1980.

sagging public budgets. Union-backed meaures now routinely failed in Congress, despite the Democratic majority.

Typical of hard times, women in increasing numbers sought jobs to support their families. By 1980 more than half of all married women and nearly 60 percent of mothers with children between the ages of six and seventeen were in the labor force. Yet despite these statistical changes, women had lost ground relative to men. In 1955 women earned 64 percent of the average wages paid to men; in 1980 they earned only 59 percent. The reason for this dip was that women were clustered in the clerical and service trades where the lowest wages prevailed.

African American women made some gains. Through Title VII of the Civil Rights Act, which outlawed work place discrimination by sex or race, and the establishment of the Equal Employment Opportunity Commission to enforce it, they managed to climb the lower levels of the job ladder. By 1980, northern black women's median earnings were about 95 percent of white women's earnings. Proportionately, slightly more black women than white were gainfully employed in technical, sales, and administrative jobs.

In contrast, Hispanic women, whose labor force participation leaped by 80 percent during the decade, were restricted to a very few poorly paid occupations. Puerto Ricans found jobs in the garment industry of the Northeast; Mexican Americans more typically

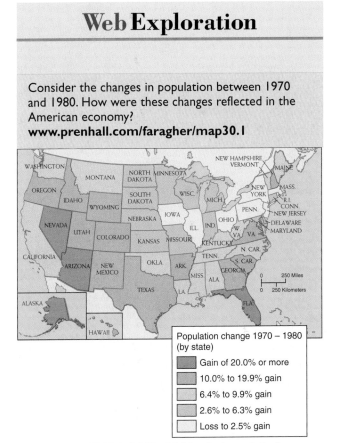

Web Exploration

Consider the changes in population between 1970 and 1980. How were these changes reflected in the American economy?
www.prenhall.com/faragher/map30.1

Population change 1970 – 1980 (by state)

- Gain of 20.0% or more
- 10.0% to 19.9% gain
- 6.4% to 9.9% gain
- 2.6% to 6.3% gain
- Loss to 2.5% gain

Population Shifts, 1970–1980   Industrial decline in the Northeast coincided with an economic boom in the Sunbelt, encouraging millions of Americans to head for warmer climates and better jobs.

Armed with retirement packages won decades earlier, huge "golden age" migrations created new communities in Florida, Arizona, and southern California.

The South witnessed a dramatic turnaround in demographic and economic trends. While manufacturing and highly subsidized agribusiness flourished, southern cities reversed the century-long trend of out-migration among African Americans. The Southwest and West changed yet more dramatically. Aided by air conditioning, water diversions, public improvements, and large-scale development, California became the nation's most populous state; Texas moved to third, behind New York. Former farms and deserts were turned almost overnight into huge metropolitan areas by the automobile and suburbs. Phoenix grew from 664,000 in 1960 to 1,509,000 in 1980, Las Vegas from 127,000 to 463,000.

Much of the Sunbelt wealth tended to be temporary or sharply cyclical, producing a boom-and-bust economy of sudden expansion and disordered sprawl. Corporate office buildings in cities such as Houston emptied almost as fast as they filled. Income was also distributed very unevenly. Older Hispanic populations made only modest gains, while recent Mexican immigrants and Indian peoples suffered from a combination of low wages and poor public services. The Sunbelt states concentrated their tax and federal dollars on strengthening police forces, building roads or sanitation systems for the expanding suburbs, and creating budget surpluses, in contrast to eastern and midwestern states that continued to spend significantly on public housing, education, and mass transit.

The "Snowbelt" (or "Rustbelt") states meanwhile suffered severe population losses accompanying the

These newly built houses in Phoenix, Arizona, a popular retirement community as well as the state capital, helped accommodate a 55 percent rise in the city's population between 1970 and 1980. Like other burgeoning cities of the Mountain West, Phoenix experienced many urban tensions during this decade, including racial conflict, antagonism between affluent suburbs and the decaying downtown, air pollution, traffic congestion, and strained water supplies.

SOURCE: Aerial view. Photo by Guido Alberto Rossi. Getty Images, Inc. (233142A)

sharp decline of industry. Of the nineteen metropolitan areas that lost population during the 1970s, all were old manufacturing centers, topped by New York, Cleveland, Pittsburgh, Boston, Philadelphia, and Buffalo.

A feeling of defeat intensified in the aging industrial cities of the Monogahela River valley in western Pennsylvavnia. Since the late nineeenth century, "Mon Valley" had proudly stood as the steelmaking center of the nation and much of the world. With the decline of steel production, however, major firms such as U.S. Steel increased investments in overseas mining and mineral processing companies, some of which worked closely with foreign steelmakers. This policy of "disinvestment" had a devastating impact on the people and communities who for generations had helped build the nation's basic industries. During the 1980s the Mon Valley lost 30,000 people, or 10 percent of its population.

The community of Clairton epitomized these conditions. Situated on a hill about fifteen miles from Pittsburgh, Clairton was once a bustling small city, with active Slavic, Italian, and Irish communities. At the end of World War II, its coke works were the largest in the world, and its by-products division made components for thousands of different products. By the mid-1980s, however, Clairton was suffering an unemployment rate of about 35 percent and facing bankruptcy. The entire thirteen-member police force had to be laid off, and a state-appointed trustee took over the city's financial affairs.

New York City offered a still more spectacular example. A fiscal crisis in 1975 forced liberal mayor Abraham Beame to choose between wage freezes for public employees and devastating cuts and layoffs. Eventually, with the municipal government teetering on the brink of bankruptcy, he chose both. In response to cutbacks in mass transit and the deterioration of municipal services, a large sector of the middle class fled. At the same time, the proportion of poor people rose from 15 percent in 1969 to nearly 25 percent fourteen years later.

"Lean Years Presidents": Ford and Carter

Gerald R. Ford and Jimmy Carter presided over not only a depressed economy but a nation of disillusioned citizens. The revelations of the Watergate break-in and Nixon's subsequent resignation as president cast a pall over politics. Replacing Nixon in August 1974, Gerald Ford reassured the public that "our long national nightmare is over"—then quickly pardoned Nixon for all the federal crimes he may have committed. The pardon reinforced public cynicism toward government and Ford in particular. Elections later that year added fifty-two Democrats to the House and four to the Senate.

Ford, who issued more vetoes of major bills than any other president in the twentieth century but saw

Congress override most of them, struck most Americans as a pleasant person of modest ability. First Lady Betty Ford was the shining star of the White House. She broke ranks with other Republicans to champion the Equal Rights Amendment. She also won praise for her courage in discussing her mastectomy for breast cancer and her voluntary entry into a substance abuse clinic for a drinking problem. In 1975 *Newsweek* magazine chose her as Woman of the Year.

Ford banked on his incumbency for the 1976 election and welcomed Senator Robert Dole of Kansas as his running mate. Democrats chose Jimmy Carter, a former one-term governor of Georgia, who depicted himself as an antipolitician, an outsider, and someone who was independent of the Washington establishment. When Carter told his mother he was running for president, she reportedly asked, "President of what?"

A "born again" Christian, Carter had been born in Plains, Georgia, in 1924. After a rural childhood and service in the navy, he emerged without a career, so poor that he was the first president to have lived in government-subsidized housing. A successful Southern politician, Carter promoted regional development. In seeking the nomination, he declined to call himself a liberal, offering instead personal integrity as his chief qualification for the nation's highest office.

Carter campaigned as a moderate on domestic policy issues. Counting on support from both conservative and southern voters who would ordinarily vote Republican, he defended existing entitlement programs while opposing Senator Edward Kennedy's call for comprehensive health coverage. He capitalized on Ford's unpopular Nixon pardon and, with his running mate Senator Walter Mondale of Minnesota, won with just over 50 percent of the popular vote and a 297-to-240 margin in the Electoral College. Carter won more than 90 percent of the black vote, which provided his margin of victory in Pennsylvania, Ohio, and seven southern states. But apathy proved the next most important factor. A record 46.7 percent of eligible voters, mainly the nation's poor, did not bother to cast ballots.

In office, Carter seemed to many observers enigmatic, even uninterested in the presidency. His most successful innovation, deregulation of the airlines, brought lower fares for millions of passengers. But by freeing banks from congressional control, he inadvertently encouraged bad investments, outright fraud, and a round of disastrous bank failures. Inflation proved to be his worst enemy. As older Americans could recognize, half of all the inflation since 1940 had occurred in just ten years. Interest rates rose, driving mortgages out of reach for many would-be home buyers. Rents in many locations doubles, sales of automobiles and other consumer products slumped, and many small businesses went under. Tuition costs skyrocketed along

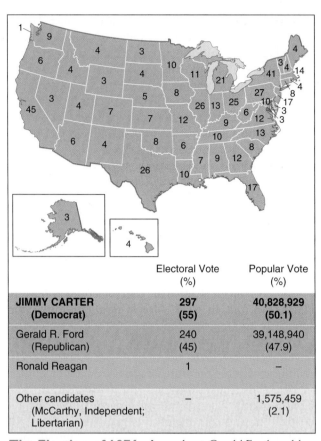

	Electoral Vote (%)	Popular Vote (%)
JIMMY CARTER (Democrat)	**297 (55)**	**40,828,929 (50.1)**
Gerald R. Ford (Republican)	240 (45)	39,148,940 (47.9)
Ronald Reagan	1	–
Other candidates (McCarthy, Independent; Libertarian)	–	1,575,459 (2.1)

The Election of 1976 Incumbent Gerald Ford could not prevail over the disgrace brought to the Republican Party by Richard Nixon. The lingering pall of the Watergate scandal, especially Ford's pardon of Nixon, worked to the advantage of Jimmy Carter, who campaigned as an outsider to national politics. Although Carter and his running mate Walter Mondale won by only a narrow margin, the Democrats gained control of both the White House and Congress.

with unemployment, and many young men and women who could neither afford to go to college nor find a job moved back home. Carter could not deliver on his promise to turn the economy around. By the time he left office in 1980, a majority of those polled agreed that "the people running the country don't really care what happens to you."

COMMUNITIES AND POLITICS

The mass demonstrations of the 1960s gave way in the 1970s to a style of political mobilization centered squarely in communities. Unlike national elections, which after 1968 registered increasing voter apathy, local campaigns brought a great many people to the voting booth and into newly organized voluntary asso-

ciations. "I didn't care so much about my neighborhood until I had children," one city dweller told a sociologist. "I wasn't aware of the various facets of the community. Then came a lot of other things that I began to do as the parent of a child in this neighborhood. We became committed to this area."

The New Urban Politics

In many cities, new groups came into political power. In several college towns, such as Berkeley, California, and Eugene, Oregon, both of which had been centers of political activism during the 1960s, student coalitions were formed to secure seats for their candidates on city councils. In 1973 labor unions, college students, and community groups in Madison, Wisconsin, elected a former student activist to the first of three terms as mayor.

African American candidates scored impressive victories during the 1970s. The newly elected African American mayor of Atlanta, Maynard Johnson, concluded that "politics is the civil rights movement of the 1970s." By 1978, 2,733 African Americans held elected offices in the South, ten times the number a decade earlier. Mississippi, a state where the civil rights movement had encountered violent opposition, had more African American elected officials by 1980 than any other state in the union. Most of these elected officials served on city councils, county commissions, school boards, and law enforcement agencies. But voters elected African American mayors in New Orleans and Atlanta. In other parts of the country, black mayors, such as Coleman Young in Detroit, Richard Hatcher in Gary, and Tom Bradley in Los Angeles, held power along with many minor black officials. Cities with black mayors spent more than other municipalities of similar size on education and social services. They worked hardest to improve community health services and to ensure equity in government employment.

Other racial or ethnic groups advanced more slowly, rarely in proportion to their actual numbers in the population. Mexican Americans had already won offices in Crystal City, Texas, and in 1978 took control of a major city council, in San Antonio, for the first time. They also scored electoral victories in other parts of Texas and in New Mexico and developed strong neighborhood or ward organizations in southern California. Puerto Ricans elected a handful of local officials in New York, mostly in the Bronx. Asian Americans advanced in similar fashion in parts of Hawai'i.

The fiscal crises of the 1970s nevertheless undercut these efforts to reform municipal government. Most new officials found themselves unable to make the sweeping changes they had promised during their campaigns. Community-based job programs could not counteract the effects of factory shutdowns and the disappearance of industrial jobs. Affirmative action programs aroused cries of "reverse discrimination" from angered whites who felt that minorities' progress had been registered at their expense. Conservatives put forward their own candidates, charging that government at all levels favored minorities, the jobless, and criminals over the law-abiding, hard-working, tax-paying majority.

The City and the Neighborhood

The nation's cities inspired a range of responses from residents who chose to resist the pull of the suburbs and from those who simply could not afford to leave. For city dwellers, the city's hospitals, public libraries, symphony orchestras, museums, and art galleries became anchoring institutions requiring public support. Changes in federal policies also encouraged local initiative. The Community Development Act of 1974, signed by President Ford, combined federal grant programs for cities into a single program and put mayors and city managers directly in charge of spending. With grants totaling $8.4 billion over three years, city governments could allocate funds as they saw fit and encourage citizens to take part in local planning. Communities Organized for Public Service (COPS) in San Antonio, Texas, and the Association of Community Organizations for Reform Now (ACORN) in Little Rock, Arkansas, were formed to advise public officials. In other cities, Save the City campaigns engaged residents in defining problems important to the community, such as traffic control, sewerage, and animal control and welfare.

Groups of preservationists organized to save historic buildings and public spaces, to form land trusts for acquiring and refurbishing old houses, and to turn vacant lots into neighborhood parks. In Rhode Island, the Providence Preservation Society worked with city planners and individual donors to restore hundreds of houses. It organized festival tours of neighborhoods to lure prospective buyers, and spurred the formation of similar societies in nearby towns.

Local and national foundations joined federal agencies in funding Community Development Corporations (CDCs) through a series of antipoverty agencies. These community groups promoted "development banks" that would facilitate "sweat equity"—that is, the granting of low-interest mortgage loans to buyers willing to rebuild or refurbish dilapidated housing. They also acted to

Geronimo, 1981, by Victor Orozco Ochoa. During the 1970s public murals appeared in many cities, often giving distinctive expression to a community's racial or ethnic identity. The murals painted in the mid-1970s on the outside of the Centro Cultural de la Raza, in San Diego, were among the most striking. After vandals ruined one section, Ochoa, whose grandmother was Yaqui, replaced it with this enormous representation of Geronimo, surrounded by figures of contemporary Chicano cultural life.

SOURCE: *Untitled,* Geronimo mural. Victor Orozco Ochoa.

prevent local banks from closing when a neighborhood became mainly black. Federal assistance proved vital to maintaining most community-based programs, especially in the late 1970s when cities faced major fiscal crises.

In 1979 President Carter's National Commission on Neighborhoods recommended the strenthening of local institutions "to reorganize our society . . . to a new democratic system of grass-roots involvement." But advocacy groups often learned to their dismay that foundations and federal agencies with money to spend resisted local decision making. While the economy worsened, mortgages moved out of reach for most buyers, and rents in many locations doubled. Local preservationists' dreams sometimes became nightmarish. "Gentrification" often accompanied restoration, with poor residents displaced by the more prosperous Americans who craved the increasingly fashionable old homes.

The Endangered Environment

On March 28, 1979, a series of mechanical problems and judgment errors at the nuclear generating facility at Three Mile Island (TMI), near Harrisburg, Pennsylvania, led to the formation of a dangerously explosive hydrogen bubble and posed the danger of a catastrophic core meltdown. After the news broke, nearly 150,000 residents fled their homes. President and First Lady Rosalynn Carter tried to reassure the stricken community by visiting the site. Ten days later, the Nuclear Regulatory Commission announced that any danger of explosion had passed, but what had seemed an isolated event in one community had already grown into a regional phenomenon with national repercussions. Elevated levels of radioactivity were found in milk supplies several hundred miles away. Massive demonstrations against nuclear power followed the accident, concluding in a rally of more than 200,000 people in New York City. Groups organized in many communites to defeat referendums to fund new nuclear power facilities or rallied around candidates who promised to shut down existing ones. Of the ninety-six under construction and the thirty more planned at the time of the TMI crisis, only a handful were completed.

Earlier in the 1970s, the discovery of high rates of cancer and birth defects in Love Canal, near Buffalo, New York, had offered compelling evidence of a growing danger to many American communities. Here toxic wastes dumped by the Hooker Chemical Laboratory had oozed into basements and backyards, and homemaker Lois Gibbs organized a vigorous publicity campaign to draw attention to the grim situation. Meanwhile, outraged Florida residents realized that the damming of the Everglades for sugar production and housing developments, undertaken by the Army

Corps of Engineers decades earlier, had degraded thousands of acres of wilderness, eliminating natural filtration systems and killing millions of birds and other species.

The roots of the modern environmentalist movement can be traced to the publication of the works of scientist Rachel Carson. In 1962 she published *Silent Spring*, which detailed the devastating effects of DDT and other pesticides. By 1970, opinion polls showed the state of the envronment outranking all other domestic issues. Senator Gaylord Nelson of Wisconsin

Senator Gaylord Nelson of Wisconsin, hoping to direct some of the energy of the anti–Vietnam War protests into environmental activism, organized the first Earth Day, which was celebrated on April 22, 1970. On that day, 20 million Americans demonstrated for a healthy and sustainable environment. Their protest against the deterioration of the environment led to the creation of the Environmental Protection Agency and marks the birth of the modern environmental movement.

SOURCE: Photo by Dennis Brack. Black Star (470/2584).

and Representative Paul "Pete" McCloskey of California invited Americans to devote an entire day— April 22, Earth Day—to discuss the environment. The response was overwhelming; nearly 20 million Americans gathered in local parks, high schools, and colleges, and at the nation's capital. Many wore green peace symbols and sang "All we are saying is give earth a chance," based on a Beatles' tune.

Even before the energy crisis, many Americans had begun to make changes in their own ways of living. Many families began to save glass bottles and newspapers for reuse. Some began to reduce or eliminate their consumption of beef, since beef is far more costly and uses more resources to produce than grain. Backyard vegetable gardens became popular, as did grocers who stocked organic foods. Nutritionist Frances Moore Lappe's popular *Diet for a Small Planet* (1971) sought to counter the logic of excess, while Barry Commoner's *Closing Circle* (1971) helped make the term "ecology" (the name of the branch of biology that deals with the relationship between organisms and their environment) a synonym for environmental balance (*eco* means "home" in Greek).

The environmentalist movement grew stronger in long-standing organizations, such as the Audubon Society and the Wilderness Society. The Sierra Club, formed in 1892 as a small society of western mountain hikers, grew to 100,000 members in 1970 and to 500,000 over the next decade. New groups sprang up in response to the energy crisis, often devoted to developing renewable energy sources such as solar power. Some, like Greenpeace, sponsored direct action campaigns to halt practices that caused harm to the environment.

Cutting across nearly all population groups and regions, environmentalists reached such traditionally conservative areas as the Deep South with warnings of the dangers of toxic wastes, the destruction of wetlands, and the ruin of fishing industries. Sometimes campaigns succeeded in blocking massive construction projects, such as nuclear energy plants; more often they halted small-scale destruction of a natural habitat or historic urban district. These campaigns made the public more aware of the consequences of private and government decisions about the environment.

Responding to organized pressure groups, Congress passed scores of bills designed to protect endangered species, reduce pollution caused by automobile emissions, limit and ban the use of some pesticides, and control strip-mining practices. The Environmental Protection Agency (EPA), established in 1970, grew to become the federal government's largest regulatory agency, employing more than 10,000 people by the end of the decade.

Environmentalists enjoyed only limited success in bringing about large-scale changes in policy. Cities often avoided congressional mandates for reduction in air pollution by requesting lengthy extensions of deadlines for compliance. Despite the introduction of lead-free gasoline, the air in major metropolitan areas grew no better in the long run because automobile traffic increased at a fast pace. Environmentalists lost an important campaign with the approval of the Alaskan Pipeline, 800 miles of pipe connecting oil fields with refining facilities.

Small-Town America

A host of unresolved problems, ranging from air pollution to rising crime rates to higher taxes, encouraged a massive exodus from the nation's cities. Between 1970 and 1975, for every 100 people relocating to metropolitan areas, 138 moved out. Newer residential communities in small towns and in formerly rural areas grew at a fast pace, attracting retirees and others seeking solace or security.

Government programs such as mortgage guarantees and low-interest financing on individual homes promoted these large "low-density" developments of single-family houses. In many regions, the countryside gradually disappeared into "exurbia," a trend that population experts Peter A. Morison and Judith P. Wheeler attributed to the American "wish to love one's neighbor but keep him at arm's length." Opinion poles suggested that many Americans wanted to live in a small town that was not a suburb but was still no more than thirty miles from a major city.

Soon even small towns developed their own suburbs, usually moderate-income tracts of ranch houses squeezed between older wood-frame colonial or Victorian farmhouses. Federal subsidies for the construction of sewerage and water lines, originally intended to aid rural communities, now became springboards for further development. Ironically, shopping malls on former farmland drained commercial activity from the small-town centers, channeling the benefits of development to chain stores rather than to local merchants.

Some communities organized to oppose these trends. Following the publication of E. F. Schumacher's *Small Is Beautiful* (1973), groups of people began to question the advantages of "bigness" and its toll on humanity. They principally sought to rebuild communities on a smaller scale and therefore campaigned to preserve the environment by opposing further development and the construction of new highways, nuclear energy generating plants, and toxic dumps. In Vermont, liberal "hippies" and "back-to-the-landers" joined traditionally conservative landowners to defeat a 1974 gubernatorial plan to attract developers. In other locales, such as the Berkshire Mountains of Massachusetts, community land trusts were organized to encourage common ownership of the land. "From coast to coast," the *New York Times* reported, "environmental, economic and social pressures have impelled hundreds of cities and towns to adopt limitations on the size and character of their populations." To encourage public discussion of land-use issues, President Carter created the Small Community and Rural Development Policy group. Many small towns, especially those in the Plains states, meanwhile collapsed from failing family farms and small businesses. Leaving rundown schools, inadequate medical care, and abandoned movie theaters and grocery stores. Only nursing homes and funeral parlors continued to thrive.

THE NEW CONSERVATISM

Sizable numbers of taxpayers resented the tax hikes required to fund government programs that benefited minorities, provided expanded social services for the poor, or protected the environment at the expense of economic development. In 1978 California voters staged a "taxpayers' revolt," approving Proposition 13, which cut property taxes and government revenues for social programs and education. In other economically hard-pressed urban areas, white voters who resented the gains made by African Americans and Latinos formed a powerful backlash movement. By the end of the decade, the only substantial increase in voter participation was among conservatives.

The New Right

The largest New Right constituency united behind major conservative religious and political leaders to promote what they viewed as traditional values. By the end of the 1970s, more than 50 million Americans had joined the ranks of evangelical Christians. One year after Billy Graham published his fast-selling *How to Be Born Again* (1977), 40 percent of all Americans, including the nation's president, reported that they were indeed "born again." Although not all evangelical Christians were Republicans or conservative, this expanding group became the backbone of key organizations such as the National Conservative Political Action Committee and, most especially, the Moral Majority. The Reverend Jerry Falwell formed the Moral Majority as a political lobbying group to advocate tough laws against homosexuality and pornography, to promote a reduction of government services (especially welfare payments to poor families), and to increase spending for a stronger national defense. Together these groups raised the funds to wage additional well-publicized campaigns against abortion, the ERA, and the busing of schoolchildren.

Conservative political organizations were among the first to employ direct mail campaigns. Greater success came from the work of televangelists. By the late 1960s,

televangelists such as Pat Robertson and Jim Bakker frequently mixed conservative political messages with appeals to prayer. Falwell's *Old-Time Gospel Hour* was broadcast over 200 television stations and 300 radio stations each week. Christian broadcasters generally endorsed Falwell's faith that "the free-enterprise system is clearly outlined in the Book of Proverbs of the Bible." By the end of the 1970s more than 1,400 radio stations and thirty TV stations specialized in religious broadcasts that reached an audience of perhaps 20 million weekly.

Jesse Helms was the first major politician to appeal directly to the New Right and to build his own impressive fundraising empire with its help. A North Carolina

In the aftermath of the *Roe* v. *Wade* decision in 1973, the televangelist Jerry Falwell became increasingly political in his sermons on the *Old-Time Gospel Hour.* He declared a "war against sin" by opposing abortion, homosexual rights, pornography, and crime, and by appealing for financial contributions he generated an annual income of more than $100 million. The Reverend Falwell reached his peak in the early 1980s and was, at that time, the most visible fundamentalist preacher in the United States.

SOURCE: Photo by Eve Arnold. Magnum Photos, Inc. (PER06ARE007001)

journalist who had fought the integration of public schools and defended the Ku Klux Klan, he had often attacked Martin Luther King, Jr. as a Communist-influenced demagogue. Helms entered national politics as a Goldwater supporter in 1964 and ran for the Senate in 1972. Carried to victory with Nixon's success in North Carolina, Helms immediately promoted a host of conservative bills as well as federal support for regional tobacco interests. He introduced legislation to allow automobile owners or dealers to disconnect mandatory antipollution devices. He also defended the Watergate break-ins as necessary to offset the "traitorous conduct" of antiwar activists. By 1978 he had raised $8.1 million, the largest amount ever, for his successful reelection campaign. Helms built a powerful, loyal, and wealthy following.

The political surge rightward gained intellectual respectability from neoconservatives, former liberals who blamed the social movements of the 1960s for the demoralization of the nation. The American Enterprise Institute and the Heritage Foundation, heavily supported by major corporations, established major research centers for conservative scholars. These and other foundations also funded campus publications attacking welfare programs, affirmative action, and environmentalism.

Anti-ERA, Antiabortion

The New Right rallied support for a balanced budget amendment to the Constitution, sought unsuccessfully to return prayer to the public schools, and endorsed the Supreme Court's approval of the death penalty in 1977. Practically all the New Right's campaigns emphasized restoration of the "traditional family values" undermined, they alleged, by the women's liberation movement.

The defeat of the Equal Rights Amendment (ERA) stood at the top of the New Right agenda. Approved by Congress in March 1972, nearly fifty years after its introduction (see Chapter 22), the ERA stated: "Equality of rights under the law shall not be denied or abridged by the United States or by any State on account of sex." Endorsed by both the Democratic and Republican Parties, the amendment appeared likely to be ratified by the individual states. Nearly all mainstream women's organizations, including the Girl Scouts of America, endorsed the ERA. Even the AFL-CIO retracted its long-standing opposition and endorsed the amendment.

Cued by this groundswell of support in favor of the ERA, the New Right swung into action. Phyllis Schlafly, a self-described suburban housewife and popular conservative lecturer, headed the STOP ERA campaign, describing the amendment's supporters as "a bunch of bitter women seeking a constitutional cure for their personal problems." She warned that the ERA would deprive women of their true rights "such as the right of

a wife to be supported by her husband" and that it would lead to unisex public toilets and homosexual marriages. Hostile to "Big Government," antiratificationists believed that the ERA would allow the state to intrude further into the private domain of family by requiring massive changes in laws concerning marriage, divorce, and child custody.

The New Right mounted large, expensive campaigns in each swing state and overwhelmed pro-ERA resources. Although thirty-five states had ratified the ERA by 1979, the amendment remained three votes short of passage. Despite a three-year extension, the ERA died in 1982.

The New Right also waged a steady campaign against abortion, which the women's liberation movement had defined as a woman's right rather than a mere medical issue. In 1973 the Supreme Court had ruled in *Roe* v. *Wade* that state laws decreeing abortion a crime during the first two trimesters of pregnancy constituted a violation of a woman's right to privacy. Opponents of *Roe* rallied for a constitutional amendment defining conception as the beginning of life and arguing that the "rights of the unborn" supersede a woman's right to

---

Asked of those who said they had heard of or read about the Equal Rights Amendment: Do you favor or oppose this amendment?

Favor	58%
Oppose	24%
No opinion	18%

By Sex

Male

Favor	63%
Oppose	22%
No opinion	15%

Female

Favor	54%
Oppose	25%
No opinion	21%

Interviewing Date 3/7–10/1975, Survey #925-K

Gallup Poll on the Equal Rights Amendment, 1975 By 1973 thirty of the thirty-eight states required to ratify the ERA had done so. Although the amendment ultimately failed to achieve ratification and died in June 1982, public support was strong. In the 1976 presidential campaign, the platforms of both Democrats and Republicans included planks favoring its passage.

SOURCE: *The Gallup Poll: Public Opinion, 1935–1974* (New York: Random House, 1974).

Would you favor or oppose a law that would permit a woman to go to a doctor to end pregnancy at any time during the first three months?

Favor	40%
Oppose	50%
No opinion	10%

Interviewing Date 11/12–17/1969, Survey #793-K, Question #4, Index #54

The United States Supreme Court has ruled that a woman may go to a doctor to end pregnancy at any time during the first three months of pregnancy. Do you favor or oppose this ruling?

Favor	47%
Oppose	44%
No opinion	9%

Interviewing Date 3/8–11; 3/15–18/1974, Survey #894-K; 895 -K

Gallup Polls on Abortion: 1969, 1974 During the 1960s, numerous American women began to demand control over their own reproductive processes and the repeal of legislation in place in all fifty states rendering abortion illegal. The American Institute of Public Opinion surveyed Americans in 1969, when abortion was still illegal, and again in 1974, one year after *Roe* v. *Wade*, the Supreme Court ruling that struck down state laws prohibiting abortion during the first three months of pregnancy.

SOURCE: *The Gallup Poll: Public Opinion, 1935–1974* (New York: Random House, 1974).

control her own body. The Roman Catholic Church organized the first antiabortion demonstrations after the Supreme Court's decision and sponsored the formation of the National Right to Life Committee, which claimed 11 million members by 1980.

Antiabortion groups also picketed Planned Parenthood counseling centers, intimidating potential clients. They rallied against government-subsidized day-care centers and against sex education programs in public schools. A small minority turned to more extreme actions and bombed dozens of abortion clinics.

"The Me Decade"

The shift in the political winds of the 1970s registered not only the rise of the New Right but also the disengagement of a sizable number of Americans from politics altogether. In 1976 novelist Tom Wolfe coined the phrase the "Me Decade" to describe an era obsessed with personal well-being and emotional security. Health foods and diet crazes, a mania for physical fit-

ness, and a quest for happiness through therapy involved millions of middle-class Americans. Historian Christopher Lasch provided his own label for this enterprise in the title of his best-selling book *The Culture of Narcissism: American Life in an Age of Diminishing Expectations* (1978). "After the political turmoil of the sixties," he observed, "Americans have returned to purely personal preoccupations."

The rise of the "human potential movement" provided a vivid example of this trend. The most successful was Erhard Seminars Training (EST), a self-help program blending insights from psychology and mysticism. Founded by Werner Erhard (a former door-to-door seller of encyclopedias), the institute taught individuals to form images of themselves as successful and satisfied. Through sixty hours of intensive training involving playacting and humiliation, participants learned one major lesson: "You are the one and only source of your experience. You created it." Priced at $400 for a series of two weekend sessions, EST peaked at 6,000 participants per month, grossing $25 million in revenue in 1980.

Transcendental meditation (TM) promised a shortcut to mental tranquility and found numerous advocates among Wall Street brokers, Pentagon officials, and star athletes. Techniques of TM were taught in more than 200 special teaching centers and practiced by a reputed 350,000 devotees.

Religious cults also formed in large numbers during the 1970s. The Unification Church, founded by the Korean Reverend Sun Myung Moon, extracted intense personal loyalty from its youthful disciples, dubbed by the media as "Moonies." Moon's financial empire, which included hundreds of retail businesses and the conservative *Washington Star*, proved highly lucrative and kept his church solvent despite numerous lawsuits. By contrast, Jim Jones's People's Temple, an interracial movement organized in the California Bay Area, ended in a mass murder and suicide when Jones induced more than 900 of his followers to drink cyanide-laced Kool-Aid in a remote retreat in Guyana in 1978.

Popular music expressed and reinforced many of these trends. The songs of community and hope common in the late 1960s gave way to songs of search for more meaningful personal relationships, and to songs of nostalgia, despair, or nihilism. Bruce Springsteen, whose lyrics lamented the disappearance of the white working class, became the decade's most popular new rock artist. At the same time, heavy metal bands such as Kiss, as well as punk and new wave artists underscored themes of decadence and futility. Meanwhile country and western music hit its peak with crossover hits and numerous new all-C&W radio stations. Charismatic stars like Willie Nelson sang melodic refrains reeking of loneliness and nostalgia and appealing to older, white, working-class Americans.

ADJUSTING TO A NEW WORLD

In April 1975 the North Vietnamese struck Saigon and easily captured the city as the South Vietnamese army, now without U.S. assistance, fell apart. All fighting stopped within a few weeks, and Saigon was renamed Ho Chi Minh City. Vietnam was reunited under a government dominated by Communists. For many Americans, this outcome underscored the futility of U.S. involvement in the Vietnam War.

By the mid-1970s a new realism seemed to prevail in U.S. diplomacy. Presidents Ford and Carter, as well as their chief advisers, acknowledged that the cost of fighting the Vietnam War had been too high, speeding the decline of the United States as the world's reigning superpower. The realists shared with dissatisfied nationalists a single goal: "No More Vietnams."

A Thaw in the Cold War

The military defeat in Vietnam forced the makers of U.S. foreign policy to reassess priorities. The United States must continue to defend its "vital interests," declared Ford's secretary of state Henry Kissinger, but must also recognize that "Soviet-American relations are not designed for tests of manhood." Both nations had experienced a decline of power in world affairs. And both were suffering from the already enormous and relentlessly escalating costs of sustaining a prolonged cold war.

At the close of World War II, the United States could afford to allocate huge portions of its ample economic resources to maintaining and enlarging its global interests. Soon, however, military and defense expenses began to grow at a much faster rate than the economy itself. Whereas the Korean War had cost around $69.5 billion, the Vietnam War cost $172.2 billion. But the expenses of military conflicts accounted for only one portion of the defense budget. Clandestine operations, alliance building, and weapons production accounted for trillions of dollars more.

Military spending at this level eventually took its toll on the American economy, especially as the federal government increasingly relied on deficit spending in an attempt to cover the bill. The federal debt, which stood at $257 billion in 1950, had jumped to $908 billion by 1980, and an increasingly large part of the federal budget went to paying just the interest on this debt. At the same time, military spending diverted funds from programs that could have strengthened the economy. The results were disastrous. While the United States endured falling productivity levels and rates of personal savings, and a disappearing skilled workforce, other nations rushed ahead. When Japan and West Germany emerged in the 1970s as potent economic competitors,

Business Week noted that the American "colossus" was "clearly facing a crisis of the decay of power."

Western European nations acted to nudge U.S. foreign policy away from its cold war premises. In 1975, in Helsinki, Finland, representatives of thirty-five nations approved the national boundaries drawn in eastern and western Europe after World War II, and in return the Soviet Union agreed to enact a more liberal human rights policy, including the loosening of restrictions on the emigration of Soviet Jews. Recognizing that the Soviet Union no longer posed a military threat to their national sovereignty—if indeed it ever had—Western leaders also sought to strengthen economic relations between the two major blocs.

The Soviet Union, whose economy suffered even greater setbacks from defense spending, joined the United States in moving toward détente. The signing of SALT I, the first Strategic Arms Limitation Treaty, during Nixon's administration, followed by the U.S. withdrawal from Vietnam, encouraged new efforts to negotiate on strategic arms control. In November 1974, Ford and Soviet leader Leonid Brezhnev met in Vladivostok to set the terms of SALT II, and President Carter secured the final agreement in 1979. However, the treaty failed to win confirmation from the Senate when the Soviet Union invaded Afghanistan in December 1979.

Although repeated conflicts in the third world continued to slow the pace toward détente, leaders in both the United States and the Soviet Union usually recognized that their economic well-being depended on a reduction in defense spending. However haltingly, steps toward reconciliation had to be taken. "If you think you can run the world and then you find out you can't," the aged journalist Walter Lippmann observed, "you withdraw to what you can run."

Foreign Policy and "Moral Principles"

When he took office, President Carter presented his lack of experience in foreign affairs as an asset. "We've seen a loss of morality," he noted, "and we're ashamed." The "soul" of his policy would be an "absolute" commitment to human rights.

Carter condemned policies that allowed the United States to support "right-wing monarchs and military dictators" in the name of anticommunism. In 1976 a powerful human rights lobby pressured Congress to pass a bill that required the secretary of state to report annually on the status of human rights in all countries receiving aid from the United States and to cut off assistance to any country with a record of "gross violations." Carter's secretary of state, Cyrus R. Vance, and the assistant secretary for human rights and humanitarian affairs, Pat Derrian, worked to punish or at least to censure repressive military regimes in Brazil, Argentina, and Chile. For the first time, leading U.S. diplomats spoke out against the South African apartheid regime rather than commending or quietly supporting that government's avid anticommunism.

In line with this policy, Carter attempted to institute reforms at the Central Intelligence Agency (CIA), particularly to halt the blatant intervention in the affairs of foreign governments. He appointed Admiral Stansfield Turner, a Rhodes scholar, as director and ordered a purge of the "rogue elephants" who had pursued covert operations in Southeast Asia during the Vietnam War. "The CIA must operate within the law," Carter insisted. Under Turner, however, these reforms remained incomplete; they later proved temporary.

Carter nearly triumphed in the Middle East. Early in his administration, Carter met privately with Israeli prime minister Menachem Begin to encourage concilia-

tion with Egypt. When negotiations between the two countries stalled in 1978, Carter brought Begin together with Egyptian president Anwar el-Sadat for a thirteen-day retreat at Camp David, Maryland.

The Camp David Accords, signed in September 1978, set the formal terms for peace in the region. Egypt became the first Arab country to recognize Israel's right to exist, as the two nations established mutual diplomatic relations for the first time since the founding of Israel in 1948. In return, Egypt regained control of the Sinai Peninsula, including important oil fields and airfields. In 1979 Begin and Sadat shared the Nobel Prize for Peace.

But disappointment lay ahead. Carter staked his hopes for regional peace on the final achievement of statehood, or at least political autonomy, for Palestinians in a portion of their former lands now occupied by the Israelis. The accords specified that Israel would eventu-

President Carter signs the Middle East Peace Treaty with Egyptian President Anwar Sadat and Israeli Prime Minister Menachem Begin, in Washington, D.C., March 1979. President Carter had invited both leaders to Camp David, the presidential retreat in Maryland, where for two weeks he mediated between them on territorial rights to the West Bank and Gaza Strip. Considered Carter's greatest achievement in foreign policy, the negotiations, known as the Camp David Peace Accords, resulted in not only the historic peace treaty but the Nobel Peace Prize for Begin and Sadat.

SOURCE: CORBIS.

ally return to its approximate borders of 1967. However, although Begin agreed to dismantle some Israeli settlements in the Sinai, the Israeli government continued to sponsor more and more Jewish settlements, expropriating Palestinian holdings. The final status of the Palestinians remained in limbo, as did that of Jerusalem, which many Christians and Muslims felt should be an autonomous holy city. Meanwhile Sadat grew increasingly isolated within the Arab world. In 1981 he was assassinated by Islamic fundamentalists.

Carter scored his biggest moral victory in foreign affairs by paving the way for Panama to assume the ownership, operation, and defense of the Panama Canal Zone. Negotiations with Panama had begun during Johnson's administration, following riots by Panamanians against U.S. territorial rule in their country. Carter pressured the Senate to ratify new treaties in 1978 (by a vote of 68 to 32) that would turn the Panama Canal over to Panama by the year 2000.

But when it came to nations considered vital to U.S. interests, such as South Korea, the Philippines, and El Salvador, Carter put aside his principles to stabilize repressive regimes and dictatorships. In restoring diplomatic relations with the People's Republic of China in January 1979, Carter likewise overlooked the regular imprisonment of dissidents. "The real problem," a U.S. diplomat observed, was that human rights was "not a policy but an attitude."

(Mis)Handling the Unexpected

Mired in problems inherited from his predecessors, Carter often found himself disoriented by contradictory advice. Washington state senator Henry "Scoop" Jackson, for whom Carter had delivered a nominating speech at the 1972 Democratic National Convention, bitterly opposed Carter's appointment of moderate Paul Warnke as chief negotiator for arms' reduction talks with the Soviet Union, urging a harder line toward the Soviets. Carter's Secretary of state Cyrus Vance recommended well-planned negotiations to soothe Soviet–U.S. relations and resolve disagreements with third world nations. But national security adviser Zbigniew Brzezinski, a bitterly anti-Communist Polish exile, adhered to cold war policies and interpreted events in even remote sections of Africa or South America as plays in a zero-sum game: wherever the United States lost influence, the Soviet Union gained, and vice versa. Despite Carter's commitment to human rights, he allowed U.S. policy to resume cold war postures.

In 1979 the overthrow of the brutal Nicaraguan dictatorship of Anastasio Somoza, long-time ally of the United States, left Carter without a succcessor to support. When the new Sandinista revolutionary govern-

ment pleaded for help, Congress turned down Carter's request for $75 million in aid to Nicaragua. Meanwhile, in El Salvador, the Carter administration continued to back a repressive government even after the assassination of Oscar Romero, a Catholic archbishop and opposition leader. Following the rape and murder of four U.S. Catholic church women, apparently by the ultraright Salvadoran armed forces trained in the United States, peace activists and other Americans pleaded with Carter to withhold further military aid. Conservatives meanwhile demanded yet more funds to bolster the repressive anti-Communist regime.

African nations vacillated between allying with the United States and courting the Soviet Union. In this tricky political territory, UN ambassador (and former civil rights leader) Andrew Young, the first major African American diplomat assigned to Africa, could not persuade Carter to recognize the antiapartheid government of Angola, which had invited 20,000 Cuban troops to help in its fight against South African–backed rebels. Nor did Carter's and Young's verbal criticisms of the South African regime, unaccompanied by economic sanctions, satisfy black Africans. After Carter fired Young for having met secretly with officials of the Palestine Liberation Organization (PLO), the president proved even less effective in negotiating with anti-apartheid leaders.

The Soviet invasion of Afghanistan produced a major stalemate. In December 1979, 30,000 Soviet troops invaded their neighbor to put down a revolt by Islamic fundamentalists against the weakening Soviet-backed government. The invasion succeeded mainly in heating up the civil war, which the American press quickly labeled the "Russian Vietnam." As the war bogged down, Americans heard familiar stories, this time of Soviet soldiers using drugs and expressing disillusionment with their government.

President Carter responded to these events with his own corollary to the Monroe Doctrine. The so-called Carter Doctrine asserted the determination of the United States to protect its interests in yet another area of the world, the Persian Gulf. Carter acted on the advice of Brzezinski, who believed that the Soviet Union would soon try to secure for itself a warm-water port on the gulf, an area rich in oil and now vital to U.S. interests. The president backed up his increasingly hard-line policies by halting exports of grain and high technology to the Soviet Union, supporting Afghani ressistance against the Russians, and by cancelling American participation in the 1980 Moscow Olympics.

By the end of Carter's term, conservatives had swamped liberals within the Democratic Party. With the economy still hurting from the effects of cold war spending, Carter called for ever-larger increases in the military budget. He also signed Presidential Directive 59, guaranteeing the production of weapons alleged necessary to win a prolonged nuclear war. The prospect of peace and détente dried up.

The Iran Hostage Crisis

On November 4, 1979, Iranian fundamentalists seized the U.S. embassy in Tehran and held fifty-two American employees hostage for 444 days. This event made President Carter's previous problems seem small by comparison. "I-R-A-N," Rosalynn Carter later wrote. "Those four letters had become a curse to me."

For decades, U.S. foreign policy in the Middle East had depended on a friendly government in Iran. After the CIA had helped to overthrow the reformist, constitutional government and installed the Pahlavi royal family and the shah of Iran in 1953, millions of U.S. dollars had poured into the Iranian economy and the shah's armed forces. President Carter had toasted the shah for his "great leadership" and overlooked the rampant corruption in government and a well-organized opposition. But, by early 1979, a revolution led by Islamic fundamentalist Ayatollah Ruholla Khomeini had overthrown the shah.

After Carter had allowed Mohammad Reza Pahlavi, the deposed shah, to enter the United States to be treated for cancer in November, a group of Khomeini's followers retaliated, storming the U.S. embassy and taking the American staff as hostages.

Cyrus Vance assured Carter that only negotiations could free the Americans. Caught up in a reelection campaign and lobbied by Brzezinski for decisive action, Carter ordered U.S. military forces to stage a nighttime helicopter rescue mission. But a sandstorm caused some of the aircraft to crash and burn, leaving eight Americans dead, their burned corpses displayed by the enraged Iranians. Short of an all-out attack, which surely would have resulted in the hostages' death, Carter had used up his options.

The political and economic fallout was heavy. Cyrus Vance resigned, the first secretary of state in sixty-five years to leave office over a political difference with the president. The price of oil rose by 60 percent. Carter had failed in the one area he had proclaimed central to the future of the United States: energy. He had also violated his own human rights policy, which was intended to be his distinctive mark on American foreign affairs.

Carter's "Crisis of Confidence"

By 1979 inflation once again soared, and it was clear that Carter's program for economic recovery had failed. In July, with Vice President Walter Mondale increas-

Iranians demonstrate outside the U.S. Embassy in Tehran, raising a poster with a caricature of President Carter. The Iran hostage crisis, which began November 8, 1979, when a mob of Iranians seized the U.S. embassy in Tehran, contributed to Carter's defeat the polls the following year. Fifty-two embassy employees were held hostage for 444 days.

SOURCE: AP/WideWorld Photos.

ingly opposed to his policies and toying with the idea of resigning from office, Carter withdrew with his staff to Camp David to reassess priorities. In his first public speech after the retreat, the president announced that the nation was experiencing a "crisis of confidence," and he called upon the people to change their attitude, to stop wallowing in personal problems, and to show more faith in their leaders.

Carter's "malaise speech," as it was called—although Carter never actually used the term "malaise"—backfired. Many Americans resented the president for heaping blame on the public instead of taking responsibility for his own failures. News analysts now attacked Carter with zeal, breaking stories of minor scandals in his administration and ridiculing the president in various ways. Far from pleasing the public, Carter lost its respect. His prospects for reelection therefore appeared to rest on his conduct of international affairs. If he only could put his human rights policy on a firm ground, move toward lasting peace in the Middle East, or strike a bargain with the Soviets on arms limitation, he might restore voter confidence. If not, his presidency would end after a single term.

Ultimately, Carter's bid for renomination depended more on his incumbency than on his popularity. Until the Iranian incursion, Democrats had been expected to nominate Senator Edward Kennedy, turning aside Carter. But in the face of national humiliation, delegates at the Democratic National Convention unenthusiastically endorsed Carter along with Mondale. On the Republican side, former California governor Ronald Reagan had been building his campaign since his near nomination in 1976. Former CIA director and Texas oil executive George H. W. Bush, more moderate than Reagan, became the Republican candidate for vice president. The Moral Majority placed itself squarely in Reagan's camp, and Senator Jesse Helms's Congressional Club contributed $4.6 million to the campaign.

Reagan repeatedly asked voters, "Are you better off now than you were four years ago?" Although critics questioned Reagan's competence, the attractive, soft-spoken actor shrugged off criticisms while spotlighting the many problems besetting the country.

The Republican ticket cruised to victory. Carter won only 41.2 percent of the popular vote to Reagan's 50.9 percent, 49 votes in the Electoral College to Reagan's 489. The Republicans won control of the Senate for the first time since 1952 and with the largest majority since 1928. Still, barely half of the eligible voters turned out in the 1980 election, bringing Ronald Reagan into office with a mandate of a thin 25 percent.

THE REAGAN REVOLUTION

No other twentieth-century president except Franklin D. Roosevelt has left as deep a personal imprint on American politics as Ronald Reagan. Ironically, Reagan himself began his political life as an ardent New Deal Democrat. Even after his transformation into a conservative Republican, he regularly invoked the words and deeds of FDR and sought to avoid ideological labels. Reagan admired Roosevelt as an inspirational leader who had led the nation through depression and war. But by the time he entered the White House in 1981, Reagan had rejected the activist welfare state legacy of the New Deal era. Following his overwhelming electoral victories in 1980 and 1984, Reagan and his allies tried to reshape the political and social landscape of the nation along conservative lines.

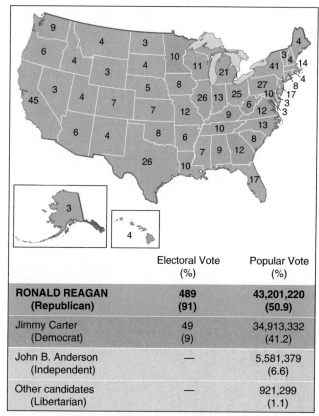

	Electoral Vote (%)	Popular Vote (%)
RONALD REAGAN (Republican)	**489 (91)**	**43,201,220 (50.9)**
Jimmy Carter (Democrat)	49 (9)	34,913,332 (41.2)
John B. Anderson (Independent)	—	5,581,379 (6.6)
Other candidates (Libertarian)	—	921,299 (1.1)

The Election of 1980 Ronald Reagan won a landslide victory over incumbent Jimmy Carter, who managed to carry only six states and the District of Columbia. Reagan attracted millions of traditionally Democratic voters to the Republican camp.

The Great Communicator

Ronald Reagan was born in 1911 and raised in the small town of Dixon, Illinois. His father was a salesman and an alcoholic who had a tough time holding a job. His strong-willed mother was a fundamentalist Christian who kept the family together despite frequent moves. A job with the Works Progress Administration for Reagan's father had helped the family survive the hard times of the Great Depression. As a child, Reagan learned to disconnect himself from the difficult scenes at home, taking refuge in his own world of imaginary stories and plays. Encouraged by his mother, he began acting in church plays and in productions at Eureka College, from which he graduated in 1932.

In 1937 Reagan began a Hollywood acting career that lasted for a quarter-century. Although he was never a big star, on screen he appeared tall, handsome, and affable. In later years, he credited his political success to his acting experience. He told one interviewer: "An actor knows two important things—to be honest in what he's doing and to be in touch with the audience. That's not bad advice for a politician either. My actor's

Ronald and Nancy Reagan at the Inaugural Ball, January 20, 1981. The Reagan's, supported by a circle of wealthy conservative friends from the business world and Hollywood, brought a lavish style to the White House that helped define the culture of the 1980s.

SOURCE: Photo by Dennis Brack. Black Star (1-81-8930).

instincts simply told me to speak the truth as I saw it and felt it."

While serving as president of the Screen Actors Guild from 1947 to 1952, Reagan began to distance himself from New Deal liberalism by becoming a leader of the anti-Communist forces in Hollywood. In 1954 he became the host of a new national television program, General Electric Theater, and began a long stint as a national promoter for GE. In this role he made numerous speeches celebrating the achievements of corporate America and emphasizing the dangers of big government, excessive liberalism, and radical trade unions.

Reagan switched his party affiliation to the Republicans and became a popular fundraiser and speaker for the California GOP. He took a leading role in conservative Republican Barry Goldwater's 1964 presidential campaign. A televised address on Goldwater's behalf thrust Reagan himself to national prominence. At the

core of Reagan's conservative message was an attack on big government. He lashed out at a growing bureaucracy and celebrated the achievements of entrepreneurs unfettered by government regulation or aid.

With the financial backing of a group of wealthy, conservative Californians, Reagan defeated Democratic governor Edmund G. Brown in 1966 and won reelection in 1970. As governor, he cut the state welfare rolls, placed limits on the number of state employees, and funneled a large share of state tax revenues back to local governments. He vigorously attacked student protesters and black militants, thereby tapping into the conservative backlash against the activism of the 1960s.

The conservatism that had been growing since Nixon took office now emerged as the mainstream. When Reagan entered the White House in January 1981, his supporters confidently predicted that the "Reagan revolution" would usher in a new age in American political life.

Reaganomics

During the Reagan presidency, supply-side economic theory, dubbed "Reaganomics," dominated the administration's thinking and helped redirect American economic policy. Supply-side theorists urged a sharp break with the Keynesian policies that had been dominant since the New Deal era (see Chapter 24). Keynesians traditionally favored moderate tax cuts and increases in government spending to stimulate the economy and reduce unemployment during recessions. By putting more money in people's pockets, they argued, greater consumer demand would lead to economic expansion. By contrast, supply-siders called for simultaneous tax cuts and reductions in public spending. This combination, they claimed, would give private entrepreneurs and investors greater incentives to start businesses, take risks, invest capital, and thereby create new wealth and jobs. Whatever revenues were lost in lower tax rates would be offset by revenue from new economic growth. At the same time, spending cuts would keep the federal deficit under control and thereby keep interest rates down.

George Gilder, conservative author of the bestselling *Wealth and Poverty* (1981), summarized the supply-side view: "A successful economy depends on the proliferation of the rich." On the political level, supply-siders looked to reward the most loyal Republican constituencies: the affluent and the business community. At the same time, they hoped to reduce the flow of federal dollars received by two core Democratic constituencies: the recipients and professional providers of health and welfare programs.

Reagan quickly won bipartisan approval for two key pieces of legislation based on these ideas. The Economic Recovery Tax Act of 1981 cut income and corporate taxes by $747 billion over five years. For individuals, the act cut taxes across the board. It also reduced the maximum tax on all income from 70 percent to 50 percent, lowered the maximum capital gains tax—the tax paid on profitable investments—from 28 percent to 20 percent, and eliminated the distinction between earned and unearned income. This last measure proved a boon to the small, richest fraction of the population that derives most of its income from rent, dividends, and interest instead of from wages.

With the help of conservative southern and western Democrats in the House, the administration also pushed through a comprehensive program of spending cuts, awkwardly known as the Omnibus Reconciliation Act of 1981. This bill mandated cuts of $136 billion in federal spending for the period 1982–1984, affecting more than 200 social and cultural programs. The hardest-hit areas included federal appropriations for education, the environment, health, housing, urban aid, food stamps, research on synthetic fuels, and the arts. The conservative coalition in the House allowed only one vote on the entire package of spending cuts, a strategy that allowed conservatives to slash appropriations for a wide variety of domestic programs in one fell swoop. One leading House liberal, Democrat Leon Panetta of California, lamented: "We are dealing with over 250 programs with no committee consideration, no committee hearings, no debate, and no opportunity to offer amendments."

While reducing spending on domestic programs, the Reagan administration greatly increased the defense budget. During the 1980 election campaign, Reagan's calls to "restore America's defenses" helped reinforce the public perception that President Carter had dealt ineffectively with the Iran hostage crisis. Once in office he greatly accelerated a trend already under way during the last two years of the Carter presidency: a sharp increase in defense spending. Overall, the Reagan budgets for military spending totaled $1.6 trillion over five years and indicated a significant shift in federal budget priorities under his administration. In 1980, 28 percent of federal spending went to housing, education, and urban and social services. By 1987, federal outlays for human resources totaled only 22 percent of the total. In the same period, defense spending rose from 23 percent to 28 percent of the federal budget.

Meanwhile, the Reagan administration created a chilly atmosphere for organized labor. In the summer of 1981, some 13,000 federal employees, all members of the Professional Air Traffic Controllers Organization (PATCO), went on strike. The president retaliated against the strikers by firing them, and the Federal Aviation Administration started a crash program to replace them. Conservative appointees to the National Labor Relations Board and the federal courts toughened its antiunion position. The militantly antilabor mood in Washington, combined with the continuing decline of the nation's manufacturing infrastructure, kept trade unions on the defensive. By 1990 fewer than 15 percent of American workers belonged to a labor union, the lowest proportion since before World War II.

Reagan appointed conservatives to head the Environmental Protection Agency, the Occupational Safety and Health Administration, and the Consumer Product Safety Commission. These individuals abolished or weakened hundreds of rules governing environmental protection, work-place safety, and consumer protection, all in the interest of increasing the efficiency and productivity of business. The deregulatory fever dominated cabinet departments as well. Secretary of the Interior James Watt opened up formerly protected wilderness areas and wetlands to private developers. Secretary of Transportation Andrew L. "Drew" Lewis, Jr. eliminated regulations passed in the 1970s aimed at reducing air pollution and improving fuel efficiency in cars and trucks.

Following the tenets of supply-side economics, the Reagan administration weakened the Antitrust Division of the Justice Department, the Securities and Exchange Commission, and the Federal Home Loan Bank Board. Large corporations, Wall Street stock brokerages, investment banking houses, and the savings and loan industry were all allowed to operate with a much freer hand than ever before. The appointment of Alan Greenspan in 1983, to succeed Carter appointee Paul Volker, greatly encouraged trends toward the dominance of speculation in market trading. By the late 1980s, the unfortunate consequences of this freedom would become apparent in a series of unprecedented scandals in the nation's financial and banking industries.

The Election of 1984

As the 1984 election approached, many Americans expressed doubts about the Reagan administration's defense initiatives. Polls showed that more than 70 percent of Americans favored a nuclear freeze with the Soviet Union. In June 1982, three-quarters of a million people—the largest political rally in American history—demonstrated in New York City for a halt to spending on and deployment of nuclear weapons. Many observers noted that Reagan also appeared politically vulnerable for his economic policies and cutbacks in social programs.

Hoping to win back disgruntled voters, Democrats chose Carter's vice president, Walter Mondale, as their nominee. As a former senator from Minnesota, Mondale had close ties with the party's liberal establishment and also the support of its more military-minded wing. At the Democratic National Convention, Mondale named Representative Geraldine Ferraro of New York as his running mate, a first for women in American politics. Charismatic speakers such as the Reverend Jesse Jackson, a dynamic disciple of Martin Luther King, Jr., and Governor Mario Cuomo of New York stirred the delegates and many television viewers with their appeals to compassion, fairness, and brotherhood.

Opinion polls showed Mondale running even with Reagan. But the president's enormous personal popularity, along with the booming economy, overwhelmed the Democratic ticket. While Mondale emphasized the growing deficit and called attention to Americans who were left out of prosperity, Reagan cruised above it all. It was "morning again in America," his campaign ads claimed. In one of the biggest landslides in American history, Reagan won 59 percent of the popular vote and carried every state but Minnesota and the District of Columbia. A majority of blue-collar voters cast their ballots for the president, as did 54 percent of women, despite Ferraro's presence on the Democratic ticket.

Recession, Recovery, Fiscal Crisis

Over the course of his two terms in office, Reagan's economic policies had mixed results. In 1982 a severe recession, the worst since the 1930s, gripped the nation. The official unemployment rate reached nearly 11 percent, or more than 11.5 million people. Another 3 million had been out of work so long they no longer actively looked for jobs and therefore were not counted in official statistics. But by the middle of 1983 the economy had begun to recover, and unemployment dropped to about 8 percent while inflation fell below 5 percent. The stock market boomed, pushing the Dow Jones industrial average from 776 in August 1982 to an all-time high of 2,722 in August 1987. The administration took credit for the turnaround, hailing the supply-side fiscal policies that had drastically cut taxes and domestic spending. But critics pointed to other factors: the Federal Reserve Board's tight-money policies, an energy resource glut and a consequent sharp drop in energy prices, and the billions of dollars pumped into the economy for defense spending.

Few doubted, however, that the supply-side formula intensified an ominous fiscal crisis. Although President Reagan had promised to balance the federal budget, his policies had the opposite effect. The national debt grew from $907 billion in 1980 to over $2 trillion in 1986, more than the federal government had accumulated in its entire previous history. Expenditures for paying just the interest on the national debt reached 14 percent of the annual budget in 1988, double the percentage set aside for that purpose in 1974.

In the Reagan years the fiscal crisis became a structural problem with newly distrubing and perhaps permanent implications for the American economy. Big deficits kept interest rates high, as the government drove up the cost of borrowing the money it needed to pay its own bills. Foreign investors, attracted by high interest rates on government securities, pushed up the value of the dollar in relation to foreign currencies.

The overvalued dollar made it difficult for foreigners to buy American products, while making overseas good cheaper to American consumers. Basic American industries—steel, autos, textiles—thus found it difficult to compete abroad and at home. In 1980, the United States still enjoyed a trade surplus of $166 billion. By 1987 the nation had an indebtedness to foreigners of $340 billion. Since World War I, the United States had been the world's leading creditor; in the mid-1980s it became its biggest debtor.

In late 1986, the Securities and Exchange Commission (SEC) uncovered the biggest stock scandal in history, in the process revealing the inner workings of high finance in the 1980s. Ivan Boesky, one of the nation's leading stock speculators, admitted to using confidential information about upcoming corporate takeovers to trade stocks illegally. Just two years earlier the dapper Boesky had made more than $100 million on just two deals. "Greed is all right," he told a cheering University of California Business School audience in 1985. "Everybody should be a little bit greedy. . . . You shouldn't feel guilty." Now Boesky agreed to cooperate with SEC investigators.

The biggest fish caught in their net was Michael Milken, a Boesky ally. An investment banker for Drexel Burnham Lambert, Milken perfected the art of corporate raiding through creative manipulation of debt. He showed how enormous profits could be earned from weak firms that were tempting targets for takeovers and mergers. Their debt could be used as tax write-offs; less efficient units could be sold off piecemeal; and more profitable units could be retained, merged, or sold again to form new entities. Instead of borrowing from banks, Milken financed his deals by underwriting high-yield, risky "junk bonds" for companies rated below investment grade. Investors in turn reaped huge profits by selling these junk bonds to hostile-takeover dealers.

Milken and other corporate raiders reshaped the financial world, setting off the greatest wave of buying and selling in American business history. Milken himself made a staggering $550 million in one year alone. Just before filing for bankruptcy in 1990, Drexel Burnham Lambert paid its executives $350 million in bonuses—almost as much as it owed its creditors. Milken was eventually convicted of insider trading and stock fraud and sent to prison. Too frequently, profits now depended more on debt manipulation and corporate restructuring rather than investment in research and development or the creation of new products. In 1987, the Hollywood film *Wall Street* dramatized this world of ruthless profiteering.

On Wall Street, the bull market of the 1980s ended abruptly in the fall of 1987. After reaching its new high of 2,722 at the end of August, the Dow Jones average of thirty leading industrial stocks began to slide downward and then crashed. On October 19, the Dow lost almost 23 percent of its value. The panic on

After the Dow-Jones reached an all-time high at the end of August, stocks began to slide and then crashed. On October 19, 1987—"Black Monday"— traders at the New York Stock Exchange panicked, selling off stocks at such a rate that the market lost almost twenty-three percent of its value, marking the end of a five-year "bull" market. The market soon bounced back, and by September 1989 the Dow-Jones had made up all its losses.

SOURCE: AP/Wide World Photos (025473).

the trading floors recalled the pandemonium set off by the stock market crash of 1929. Millions of Americans now feared that the 1987 crash would signal the onset of a great recession or even a depression.

BEST OF TIMES, WORST OF TIMES

The celebration of wealth, moneymaking, and entrepreneurship dominated much of popular culture, politics, and intellectual life in the 1980s. But grimmer realities lay under the surface. A variety of measures strongly

suggested that the nation had moved toward greater inequality, that the middle class was shrinking, and that poverty was on the rise. Analysts disagreed over the causes of these trends. No doubt some reflected structural changes in the American economy and a rapidly changing global marketplace. After eight years of tax cuts, defense buildup, growing budget deficits, and record trade imbalances, the economic future looked uncertain at best. Two of the most cherished basic assumptions about America—that life would improve for most people and their children, and that membership in the comfortable middle-class was available to all who worked for it—looked shaky by the end of the decade.

The Celebration of Wealth

The very wealthy did extremely well during the 1980s. In 1989, the richest 1 percent of American households accounted for 37 percent of the nation's private wealth—up from 31 percent in 1983, a jump of almost 20 percent. This top 1 percent, consisting of 834,000 households with about $5.7 trillion of net worth, owned more than the bottom 90 percent of Americans, the remaining 84 million households, whose total net worth was about $4.8 trillion.

Other affluent Americans also made huge gains. In 1980 the top 5 percent of families earned 15.3 percent of the nation's total income. By 1992 their share had grown to 17.6 percent, an increase of 15 percent; their average income was $156,000 a year. In 1980 the top 20 percent of families earned 41.6 percent of the nation's total. By 1992 their share had grown to 44.6 percent, an increase of about 7 percent, with an average income of $99,000 a year. In contrast, the bottom 40 percent of families had 16.7 percent of aggregate income in 1980. By 1992 their share had declined to 14.9 percent, a drop of nearly 2 percent, with an average income of about $16,500 a year.

PERCENTAGE SHARE OF AGGREGATE FAMILY INCOME, 1980–1992		
	1980	1992
Top 5 Percent	15.3%	17.6%
Highest Fifth	41.6	44.6
Fourth Fifth	24.3	24.0
Third Fifth	17.5	16.5
Second Fifth	11.6	10.5
First Fifth	5.1	4.4

SOURCE: U.S. Bureau of the Census, *Current Population Reports: Consumer Incomes*, Series P-60, Nos. 167 and 184, 1990, 1993. U.S. federal data compiled by Ed Royce, Rollins College.

SHARE OF TOTAL NET WORTH OF AMERICAN FAMILIES		
	1983	1989
Richest 1 percent of families	31%	37%
Next richest 9 percent	35	31
Remaining 90 percent	33	32

SOURCE: *New York Times*, April 21, 1992, from Federal Reserve Survey of Consumer Finances.

MEASURES OF AVERAGE EARNINGS, 1980–1992 (IN 1990 DOLLARS)		
Year	Average Weekly Earnings	Average Hourly Earnings
1980	$373.81	$10.59
1985	363.30	10.41
1992	339.37	9.87

SOURCE: U.S. House of Representatives, Committee on Ways and Means, *Overview of Entitlement Programs* (Washington, D.C.: GPO, 1993), table 35, p. 557. U.S. federal data compiled by Ed Royce, Rollins College.

NUMBER OF POOR, RATE OF POVERTY, AND POVERTY LINE, 1979–1992		
	1979	1992
Millions of poor	26.1	36.9
Rate of poverty	11.7%	14.5%
Poverty line (family of four)	$7,412	$14,335

SOURCE: U.S. Bureau of the Census, *Current Population Reports: Consumer Income*, Series P-60, Nos. 161 and 185, 1988, 1993. U.S. federal data compiled by Ed Royce, Rollins College.

The theme of money, status, and power —the values embraced by the Reagan administration—dominated popular culture. The newly elected president himself set the tone when he responded to a reporter's question asking him what was best about America. "What I want to see above all," Reagan replied, "is that this remains a country where someone can always get rich." Many thousands of Americans made fortunes in the expansive and lucrative sectors of the economy: stock trading, real estate, business services, defense contracting, and high-tech industries. A step below the new rich were the "yuppies," who were defined by their upscale consumer behavior. Yuppies ate gourmet foods, wore designer clothes, drove expensive automobiles, and lived in "gentrified" neighborhoods.

Popular culture reflected and reinforced an obsession with getting rich and living well. Once again, novelist Tom Wolfe gave a name to the cultural phenomenon— "plutography," which represented "graphic depictions of the acts of the rich." Hit TV series like *Dallas* and *Dynasty* (and their imitators) focused on the family wars and business intrigues of oil tycoons and fashion queens. Shows such as *Lifestyles of the Rich and Famous* and *Entertainment Tonight* offered vicarious pleasures by taking viewers into the homes and on the shopping sprees of wealthy celebrities.

Tie-ins proliferated among films, television shows, advertising, newspapers and magazines, popular music, and politicians. A growing concentration of ownership among television networks, movie studios, publishers, and cable companies accelerated this trend. New media forms—the newspaper *USA Today*, the news channel Cable News Network (CNN), the weekly magazine *People*—intensified the national culture of celebrity. Demographic analysis created the most important "communities" in American life—communities of consumers, so that advertisers could define and target them to sell a product or provide a service.

A Two-Tiered Society

During the 1960s, despite the diversion of federal funds to military spending during the Vietnam War, President Johnson's Great Society had brought a higher standard of living to many Americans. By the time Carter took office in 1977, the sinking economy was undercutting these gains. Reagan's supply-side policies enlivened the economy but at the same time widened the gap between rich and poor.

NET NEW JOB CREATION BY WAGE LEVEL, 1979–1987		
	Number of Net New Jobs Created	Percentage of Net New Jobs Created
Low-wage Jobs (less than $11,611)	5,955,000	50.4%
Middle-wage Jobs ($11.612 to $46,444)	4,448,000	31.7%
High-wage Jobs ($46,445 and above)	1,405,000	11.9%

SOURCE: U.S. Senate, Committee on the Budget, *Wages of American Workers in the 1980s* (Washington, D.C.: GPO, 1988). U.S. federal data compiled by Ed Royce, Rollins College.

MEDIAN FAMILY INCOME AND RATIO TO WHITE, BY RACE AND HISPANIC ORIGIN, 1980–1992 (IN 1992 DOLLARS)				
Year	All Races	White	Black	Hispanic
1980	$35,839	$37,341	$21,606 (58%)	$25,087 (67%)
1985	36,164	38,011	21,887 (58%)	25,596 (67%)
1992	36,812	38,909	21,161 (54%)	23,901 (61%)

SOURCE: U.S. Bureau of the Census, *Current Population Reports*, Series P-60, No. 184, 1993. U.S. federal data compiled by Ed Royce, Rollins College.

The number and percentage of Americans in poverty grew at an alarming rate. Since the mid-1970s, most of the new jobs clustered in low-paying service and manufacturing sectors and less than half of them paid more than the $11,611 poverty-level income for a family of four. In 1979 the government classified about 26.1 million people as poor, 11.7 percent of the total population; by 1992 the number of poor had reached 36.9 million, or 14.5 percent of the population, and nearly 22 percent of all American children under eighteen lived in poverty.

The widening gap between rich and poor was sharply defined by race. By 1992, 33 percent of all African Americans lived in poverty, as did 29 percent of Hispanics (the rate was especially high among Puerto Ricans, yet low among Cuban Americans). The gains achieved by the civil rights movement were steadily eroding. In 1954, the year of the *Brown* v. *Board of Education* decision, black families earned about 53 percent of the income of white families. This figure rose to 60 percent in 1969 and peaked at 62 percent in 1975. By 1979, black family income had fallen back to 57 percent and continued to slide during the next decade. Similarly, the number of African Americans attending college peaked in 1976 at 9.3 percent of the black population, a 500 percent increase over the 1960 average.

The majority of African Americans, six out of ten, lived in central cities with high unemployment rates, and the bleak prospects took a toll especially on the young. A black child was twice as likely as a white child to die before reaching the first birthday and four times more likely to be killed between the ages of one and four. Among black teenagers, the unemployment rate topped 40 percent; the few jobs available to them were among the lowest-paid in the economy. Meanwhile, the high school dropout rate skyrocketed, and the number of serious crimes, such as burglary, car theft, and murder, perpetrated by children between the ages of ten and seventeen increased at an alarming rate.

The gap between rich and poor also increased within the African American community. While the poor stayed behind in increasingly segregated urban neighborhod, nearly 45 percent of black families managed to achieve middle-class status by the mid-1970s. This trend dramatically affected the black community. Until the 1970s the majority of African Americans had held to common residential neighborhoods, institutions, and political outlooks. By the end of the decade, growing income and residential disparity, which widened faster among black people than among white people, produced sharp differences among African Americans on social, economic, and political issues.

Moreover, opportunities for advancement into the middle class were dwindling. By 1980 fewer black students attended integrated schools than in 1954, except in the South, where about half the black students did. The turnabout resulted in part from increasing opposition by white parents to court-ordered school busing, which had served since *Brown* v. *Board of Education* as the principal means of achieving racial balance in urban school systems. In 1975 a major clash between local white residents and black parents and their children occurred in Boston when a federally mandated busing plan was put into operation. During the 1980s the busing controversy nearly disappeared because federal judges hesitated to mandate such programs. But more important was the change in the racial composition of American cities. As a consequence of "white flight" to the suburbs, big-city school systems were serving mainly African American and Latino children, making the issue of integration moot. By this time, the dropout rate of black teenagers had reached 50 percent in inner-city schools.

New legal rulings closed off important routes to employment in the professions. A 1978 U.S. Supreme Court decision dealt a sharp blow to affirmative action. To ensure acceptance of a minimum number of minority students, the University of California at Davis Medical School had established a quota system under affirmative action guidelines. In 1973 and 1974 the school denied admission to Allan Bakke, a white student. Bakke sued the university for "reverse discrimination," claiming his academic record was better than that of the sixteen minority students who were admitted. The U.S. Supreme

Court handed down a five-to-four decision on June 18, 1978, stating that the use of an "explicit racial classification" in situations where no earlier discrimination had been demonstrated violated the equal protection clause of the Fourteenth Amendment. The Court ordered the University of California to admit Bakke to its medical school. During the 1980s, therefore, affirmative action programs could operate only when "a legacy of unequal treatment" could be proved.

The Feminization of Poverty

Despite a growing rate of labor force participation, the majority of women gainfully employed earned less than a living wage. Even if employed, women usually lost ground following a divorce, especially as new no-fault divorce laws lowered or eradicated alimony. Moreover, the majority of men defaulted on child-support payments within one year after separation. Whereas divorced men enjoyed a sizable increase in their standard of living, divorced women suffered a formidable decline. During the 1970s alone, the number of poor families headed by women increased nearly 70 percent.

A sharp rise in teenage pregnancy reinforced this pattern. Many of these mothers were too young to have gained either the education or skills to secure jobs that would pay enough to support themselves and their children. Even with Aid to Families with Dependent Children (AFDC) payments and food stamps, it was impossible for these single mothers to keep their families above the poverty line. By 1992, female-headed households, comprising 13.7 million people, accounted for 37 percent of the poor. African American and Latino women and their children had by far the highest poverty rates.

Moreover, political mobilization for protecting the rights of poor women was at a low ebb. Since its founding in 1967, the National Welfare Rights Organization (NWRO), led by African American women, had spearheaded a campaign to enable welfare recipients to have a voice in policy decisions. They demanded adequate day-care facilities and job-training programs and insisted on the legitimacy of female-headed households. NWRO activists occasionally staged sit-ins at welfare agencies to secure benefits for their members. More often, they informed poor women of their existing rights and encouraged them to apply for benefits. In 1975, NWRO, exhausted from fighting cutbacks in the federal welfare system, filed for bankruptcy.

Epidemics: Drugs, AIDS, Homelessness

Drug addiction and drug trafficking took on frightening new dimensions in the early 1980s. The arrival of "crack," a cheap, smokable, and highly addictive form of cocaine, made that drug affordable to the urban poor. As crack addiction spread, the drug trade assumed alarming new proportions both domestically and internationally. Crack ruined hundreds of thousands of lives and led to a dramatic increase in crime rates. Studies showed that over half the men arrested in the nation's largest cities tested positive for cocaine. The crack trade spawned a new generation of young drug dealers who were willing to risk jail and death for enormous profits. In city after city, drug wars over turf took the lives of dealers and innocents, both caught in the escalating violence.

By the end of the 1980s, opinion polls revealed that Americans identified drugs as the nation's number one problem. The Reagan administration declared a highly publicized "war on drugs," a multibillion-dollar campaign to bring the traffic under control. Critics charged that the war on drugs focused on supply from abroad when it needed to look at demand here at home. They urged more federal money for drug education, treatment, and rehabilitation. Drug addiction and drug use, they argued, were primarily health problems, not law enforcement issues.

In 1981 doctors in Los Angeles, San Francisco, and New York began encountering a puzzling new medical phenomenon. Young homosexual men were dying suddenly from rare types of pneumonia and cancer. The underlying cause was found to be a mysterious new viral disease that destroyed the body's natural defenses against illness, making its victims susceptible to a host of opportunistic infections. Researchers at the Centers for Disease Control (CDC) in Atlanta called the new disease acquired immune deficiency syndrome (AIDS). The virus that causes AIDS is transmitted primarily in semen and blood. Full-blown AIDS might not appear for years after initial exposure to the virus. Thus one could infect others without knowing one had the disease. Although tests emerged to determine whether one carried HIV, there was no cure. The majority of early AIDS victims were homosexual men who had been infected through sexual contact. Many Americans thus perceived AIDS as a disease of homosexuals. But other victims became infected through intravenous drug use, blood transfusions, heterosexual transmission, or birth to AIDS-carrying mothers.

AIDS provoked fear, anguish, and anger. It also brought an upsurge of organization and political involvement. In city after city, the gay community responded to the AIDS crisis with energy and determination. Most gay men changed their sexual habits, practicing "safe sex" to lessen the chances of infection. The Reagan administration, playing to antihomosexual prejudices, largely ignored the epidemic. One important exception was Surgeon General C. Everett Koop, who urged a comprehensive sex education program in the nation's schools.

Homelessness emerged as a chronic social problem during the 1980s. Often disoriented, shoeless, and forlorn, growing numbers of street people slept over

In May 1987, members of the Lesbian and Gay Community Services in Downtown Manhattan organized ACT-UP. Protesting what they perceived to be the Reagan administration's mismanagement of the AIDs crisis, they used non-violent direct action, which often took the form of dramatic acts of civil disobedience. ACT-UP grew to more than 70 chapters in the United States and the world.

SOURCE: AP/Wide World Photos.

heating grates, on subways, and in parks. Homeless people wandered city sidewalks panhandling and struggling to find scraps of food. Winters proved especially difficult. In the early 1980s, the Department of Housing and Urban Development placed the number of the nation's homeless at between 250,000 and 350,000. But advocates for the homeless estimated that the number was as high as 3 million.

Who were the homeless? Analysts agreed that at least a third were mental patients who had been discharged from psychiatric hospitals amid the deinstitutionalization trend of the the 1970s. Many more were alcoholics and drug addicts unable to hold jobs. But the ranks of the homeless also included female-headed fami-

lies, battered women, Vietnam veterans, AIDS victims, and elderly people with no place to go. Some critics pointed to the decline in decent housing for poor people and the deterioration of the nation's health-care system as a cause of homelessness. Some communities made strong efforts to place their homeless residents in city-run shelters, but violence and theft in the shelters scared away many people. No matter how large and what its components, the permanent class of American homeless reflected the desperate situation of America's poor.

REAGAN'S FOREIGN POLICY

Throughout his presidency, Reagan campaigned to restore American leadership in world affairs. He revived cold war patriotism and championed American interventionism in the third world, especially in the Caribbean and Central America. His infusion of funds into national security programs would have enormous consequences for the domestic economy as well as for America's international stance. Yet along with its hard-line exhortations against the Soviet Union and international terrorism, the Reagan administraton also pursued a less ideological, more pragmatic approach in key foreign policy decisions. Most important, sweeping and unanticipated internal changes within the Soviet Union made the entire cold war framework of American foreign policy largely irrelevant by the late 1980s.

The Evil Empire

In the early 1980s, the Reagan administration made vigorous anti-Communist rhetoric the centerpiece of its foreign policy. In a sharp turn from President Carter's focus on human rights and President Nixon's pursuit of détente, Reagan described the Soviet Union as "an evil empire . . . the focus of evil in the modern world." The president denounced the growing movement for a nuclear freeze, arguing that "we must find peace through strength."

Administration officials argued that the nation's military strength had fallen dangerously behind that of the Soviet Union during the 1970s. Critics disputed this assertion, pointing out that the Soviet advantage in intercontinental ballistic missiles (ICBMs) was offset by American superiority in submarine-based forces and strategic aircraft. Nonetheless, the administration proceeded with plans to enlarge America's nuclear strike force.

In 1983 President Reagan introduced an unsettling new element into superpower relations when he presented his Strategic Defense Initiative (SDI), the plan for a space-based ballistic-missile defense system that journalists dubbed "Star Wars," after the popular Hollywood film series. This proposal for a five-year $26 billion program promised to give the United States the capacity to shoot down incoming missiles with laser beams and homing rockets. To critics, the plan seemed unworkable, impossibly expensive, and likely to destabilize existing arms treaties. The Reagan administration pressed ahead, spending $17 billion in research before the president left office—without achieving any convincing results. Nevertheless, the Soviets complained that the SDI carried the potential of upsetting the nuclear balance and interpreted the plan as an offensive strategy to ensure a first-strike advantage to the United States.

Attempts at meaningful arms control stalled in this atmosphere, and U.S.–Soviet relations deteriorated. In the fall of 1983, the Soviets shot down a Korean airliner that had strayed over Soviet airspace, killing 269 people. Soviet military officials, believing the plane to be on a spy mission, acted at best in a confused and incompetent manner. President Reagan immediately denounced the act as a deliberate "crime against humanity," and a wave of anti-Soviet sentiment swept the country. The Soviet Union and its Eastern European allies then boycotted the 1984 Olympic Games in Los Angeles, partly in response to the American boycott of the 1980 Moscow games. While Reagan transformed images of enthusiastic Americans chanting "USA! USA!" and "We're number one!" into an effective backdrop for his reelection campaign, the American-Soviet relationship seemed to have fallen to a new low.

The Reagan Doctrine and Central America

Declaring the "Vietnam syndrome" over, the president confidently reasserted America's right to intervene anywhere in the world to fight Communist insurgency. The Reagan Doctrine, as this declaration was later called, assumed that all political instability in the third world resulted not from indigenous factors such as poverty or corruption but from the pernicious influence of the Soviet Union. It found its most important expression in Central America, where the United States hoped to reestablish its historical control over the Caribbean basin.

On the economic front, the Caribbean Basin Initiative (CBI) promised to stimulate the Caribbean economy by encouraging the growth of business corporations and a freer flow of capital through $350 million in U.S. aid. Yet Congress refused to play by the rules of free trade, placing stiff tariffs and quotas on imports of shoes, leather goods, and sugar competing with U.S. products. Many Latin American business leaders opposed key parts of the CBI, such as generous tax breaks for foreign investors. They feared that once large multinational corporations entered their markets, the CBI would strengthen the kind of chronic economic dependency that had shaped so much of the region's past.

Throughout Central America, the Reagan administration believed, as National Security Adviser Richard Allen argued, that all problems stemmed from "Fidel Castro's Soviet directed, armed, and financed marauders" and required a military solution. Between 1980 and 1983 the United States poured more military aid into Central America than it had during the previous thirty years. In October 1983, the administration directed American marines to invade Grenada, claiming that the tiny island had become a base for the Cuban military and therefore posed a dangerous threat to the hemisphere. The easy triumph proved popular with most Grenadans and Americans. In the larger and more complicated nations of El Salvador and Nicaragua, this sort of unilateral military action proved politically and strategically more difficult to carry out.

In El Salvador, the Reagan administration continued to support the repressive regime. Military aid jumped from $6 million in 1980 to $82 million in 1982, and El Salvador received more U.S. economic assistance than any other Latin American country. By 1983 right-wing death squads, encouraged by military elements within the regime, had tortured and assassinated thousands of opposition leaders. The election in 1984 of centrist president José Napoleón Duarte failed to end the bloody civil war. Some 53,000 Salvadorans, more than one out of every hundred, lost their lives in the conflict.

In Nicaragua, the Reagan administration claimed that the revolutionary Sandinista government posed "an unusual and extraordinary threat to the national security." U.S. officials accused the Sandinistas of shipping arms to antigovernment rebels in El Salvador. In December 1981, Reagan approved a $19 million CIA plan arming and organizing Nicaraguan exiles, known as Contras, to fight against the Sandinista government. As Reagan escalated this undeclared war, the aim became not merely the cutting of Nicaraguan aid to Salvadoran rebels but the overthrow of the Sandinista regime itself.

In 1984 the CIA secretly mined Nicaraguan harbors. When Nicaragua won a judgment against the United States in the World Court over this violation of its sovereignty, the Reagan administration refused to recognize the court's jurisdiction in the case and ignored the verdict. Predictably, the U.S. covert war pushed the Sandinistas closer to Cuba and the Soviet bloc. Meanwhile, U.S. grass-roots opposition to Contra aid grew more vocal and widespread. A number of U.S. communities set up sister city projects offering humanitarian and technical assistance to Nicaraguan communities. Scores of U.S. churches offered sanctuary to political refugees from Central America.

In 1984 Congress reined in the covert war by passing the Boland Amendment, introduced by Democratic Representative Edward Boland of Massachusetts. If forbid government agencies from supporting "directly

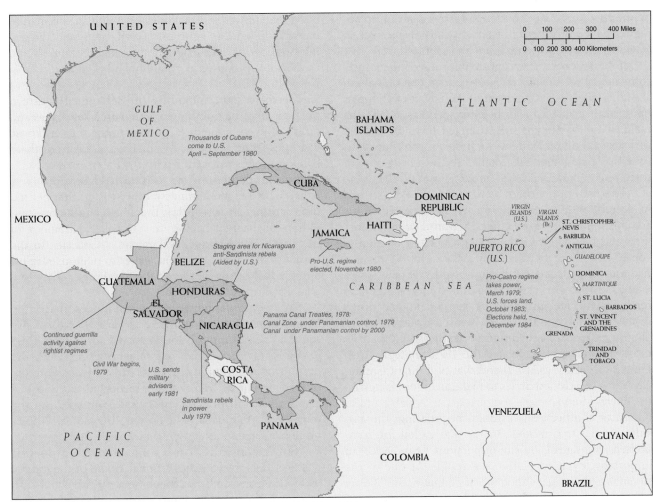

The United States in Central America, 1978–1990   U.S. intervention in Central America reached a new level of intensity with the so-called Reagan Doctrine. The bulk of U.S. aid came in the form of military support for the government of El Salvador and the Contra rebels in Nicaragua.

or indirectly military or paramilitary operations" in Nicaragua. Denied funding by Congress, President Reagan turned to the National Security Council to find a way to keep the Contra war going. Between 1984 and 1986, the NSC staff secretly ran the Contra assistance effort, raising $37 million in aid from foreign countries and private contributors, creating the largest mercenary army in hemispheric history. In 1987 the revelation of this unconstitutional scheme exploded before the public as part of the Iran-Contra affair, the most damaging political scandal of the Reagan years.

Glasnost and Arms Control

Meanwhile, momentous political changes within the Soviet Union led to a reduction in East-West tensions and ultimately the end of the cold war itself. Soviet premier Leonid Brezhnev, in power since 1964, died toward the end of 1982. His successors, Yuri Andropov

and Konstantin Chernenko, both died after brief terms in office. But in 1985 a new, reform-minded leader, Mikhail Gorbachev, won election as general secretary of the Soviet Communist Party. Although a lifelong Communist, Gorbachev represented a new generation of disenchanted party members. He initiated a radical new program of economic and political reform under the rubrics of *glasnost* (openness) and *perestroika* (restructuring).

Gorbachev and his advisers opened up political discussion and encouraged criticism of the Soviet economy and political culture. There was much to criticize. Inefficiency and chronic shortages plagued Soviet production of such staples as meat, grain, clothing, and housing. Even when consumer goods were available, high prices often put them beyond the means of the average Soviet family. The government released longtime dissidents like Andrei Sakharov from prison and took the first halting steps toward profit-based, private initiatives in the economy. This "new thinking" inspired an unprecedented wave of diverse, often critical perspectives in Soviet art, literature, journalism, and scholarship.

In Gorbachev's view, improving the economic performance of the Soviet system depended first on halting the arms race. Over 10 percent of the Soviet GNP (gross national product) went to defense spending, while the majority of its citizens still struggled to find even the most basic consumer items in shops. Gorbachev thus took the lead in negotiating a halt to the arms race with the United States.

The historical ironies were stunning. Reagan had made militant anticommunism the centerpiece of his administration. He staunchly resisted arms control initiatives and presided over the greatest military buildup in American history. But between 1985 and 1988 Reagan had four separate summit meetings with the new Soviet leader. In October 1986, Reagan and Gorbachev met in Reykjavík, Iceland, but this summit bogged down over the issue of SDI. Reagan refused to abandon his plan for a space-based defensive umbrella. Gorbachev insisted that the plan violated the 1972 Strategic Arms Limitation Treaty (SALT I) and that SDI might eventually allow the United States to make an all-out attack on the Soviet Union.

After another year of tough negotiating, the two sides agreed to a modest treaty that called for comprehensive, mutual, on-site inspections. It provided an important psychological breakthrough. At one of the summits a Soviet leader humorously announced, "We are going to do something terrible to you Americans—we are going to deprive you of an enemy."

The Iran-Contra Scandal

The gift of glasnost did not eliminate cold war thinking entirely, especially in the continuing covert war in Central America. Nor could it resolve long-standing and complex international disputes in regions like the Middle East. In 1987 the revelations of the Iran-Contra affair laid bare the continuing contradictions and difficulties attending America's role in world affairs. The affair also demonstrated how overzealous and secretive government officials subverted the Constitution and compromised presidential authority under the guise of patriotism.

The Middle East presented the Reagan administration with its most frustrating foreign policy dilemmas. In Afghanistan, the administration expanded military aid (begun under President Carter) to the forces resisting the Soviet-backed regime. In June 1982 Israel invaded Lebanon in an attempt to destroy the Palestine Liberation Organization (PLO). Hoping to shore up a weak Lebanese government threatened by a brutal civil war, President Reagan dispatched marines to Beirut. In Octo-

ber 1983, however, a terrorist bombing in the marine barracks killed 241 American servicemen, and the administration pulled the marines out of Lebanon, shying away from a long-term commitment of U.S. forces in the Middle East.

Terrorist acts, including the seizing of Western hostages and the bombing of commercial airplanes and cruise ships, redefined the politics of the region. These were desperate attempts by small sects, many of them splinter groups associated with the Palestinian cause or Islamic fundamentalism, to inhibit U.S. support of Israel. The Reagan administration insisted that behind international terrorism lay the sinister influence and money of the Soviet bloc, the Ayatollah Khomeini of Iran, and Libyan leader Muammar el-Qaddafi. In the spring of 1986 the president, eager to demonstrate his antiterrorist resolve, ordered the bombing of Tripoli in a failed effort to kill Qaddafi.

As a fierce war between Iran and Iraq escalated, the administration tilted publicly toward Iraq to please the Arab states around the Persian Gulf. But in 1986 Reagan's advisors began secret negotiations with the revolutionary Iranian government. They eventually offered to supply Iran with sophisticated weapons for use against Iraq in exchange for help in securing the release of Americans held hostage by radical Islamic groups in Lebanon.

Subsequent disclosures elevated the arms-for-hostages deal into a major scandal. Some of the money from the arms deal had been secretly diverted into covert aid for the Nicaraguan Contras. The American public soon learned the sordid details from investigative journalists and through televised congressional hearings held during the summer of 1987. In order to escape congressional oversight of the CIA, Reagan and CIA director William Casey had essentially turned the National Security Council, previously a policy-coordinating body, into an operational agency. Under the direction of National Security Advisers Robert McFarlane and later Admiral John Poindexter, the NSC had sold TOW and Hawk missiles to the Iranians, using Israel as a go-between. Millions of dollars from these sales were then given to the Contras in blatant and illegal disregard of the Boland Amendment.

In the televised congressional hearings, NSC staffer and marine lieutenant colonel Oliver North emerged as the figure running what he euphemistically referred to as "the Enterprise." North defiantly defended his actions in the name of patriotism. Some Americans saw the handsome and dashing North as a hero; most were appalled by his and Poindexter's blithe admissions that they had lied to Congress, shredded evidence, and refused to inform the president of details in order to guarantee his "plausible deniability." A blue-ribbon commission led by former senator John Tower

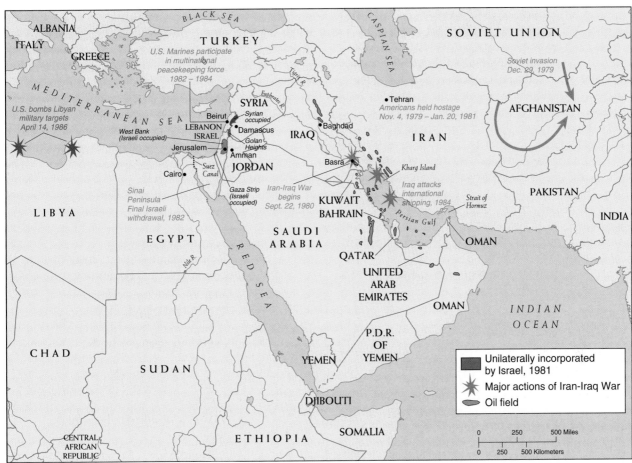

The United States in the Middle East in the 1980s   The volatile combination of ancient religious and ethnic rivalries, oil, and emerging Islamic fundamentalism made peach and stability elusive in the Middle East.

of Texas concluded that Reagan himself "did not seem to be aware" of the policy or its consequences. But the Tower Report offered a stunning portrait of a president who was at best confused and far removed from critical policy-making responsibilities. The joint congressional committee investigating the "profoundly sad" story concluded: "The common ingredients of the Iran and Contra policies were secrecy, deception, and disdain for the law. A small group of senior officials believed that they alone knew what was right."

Ultimately, the Iran-Contra investigation raised more questions than it answered. The full role of CIA director Casey, who died in 1987, particularly his relationships with North and the president, remained murky. The role of Vice President George H. W. Bush remained mysterious as well, and it would return as an issue in the 1992 presidential election. Both North and Poindexter were convicted of felonies, but their convictions were overturned by higher courts on technical grounds, although diplomatic official Elliott Abrams was convicted of lying to Congress and successfully

sentenced to public service. The scandal had mesmerized a national television audience. But Iran-Contra, unlike Watergate, produced no equivalent movement for impeachment. Reagan held fast to his plea of ignorance. When pressed on what had happened, he repeatedly claimed, "I'm still trying to find out."

In December 1992, following his reelection defeat and six years after the scandal broke, President George H. W. Bush granted pardons to six key players in the Iran-Contra affair. The Bush pardons made it unlikely that the full truth about the arms-for-hostages affair would ever be known.

CONCLUSION

The success of conservatives to halt and in some cases actually reverse key trends in American politics, from Franklin Roosevelt's New Deal to Lyndon Johnson's Great Society, was made possible by the legacy of the

CHRONOLOGY

1973	*Roe* v. *Wade* legalizes abortion
	Arab embargo sparks oil crisis in the United States
1974	Richard Nixon resigns presidency; Gerald Ford takes office
	President Ford pardons Nixon and introduces antiinflation program
1975	Unemployment rate reaches nearly 9 percent
	South Vietnamese government falls to communists
	Antibusing protests break out in Boston
1976	Percentage of African Americans attending college peaks at 9.3 percent and begins a decline
	Jimmy Carter is elected president
1977	President Carter announces human rights as major tenet in foreign policy
1978	*Bakke* v. *University of California* decision places new limits on affirmative action programs
	Camp David meeting sets terms for Middle East peace
	California passes Proposition 13, cutting taxes and government social programs

1979	Three Mile Island nuclear accident threatens a meltdown
	Nicaraguan Revolution overthrows Anastasio Somoza
	Iranian fundamentalists seize the U.S. embassy in Tehran and hold U.S. citizens hostage for 444 days
	Soviets invade Afghanistan
1980	Inflation reaches 13.5 percent
	Ronald Reagan is elected president
1981	Reagan adminisration initiates major cuts in taxes and domestic spending.
	Military buildup accelerates
	AIDS is recognized and named
1982	Economic recession grips the nation
1983	Reagan announces the Strategic Defense Initiative, labeled "Star Wars" by critics.
	241 marines killed in Beirut terrorist bombing
1985	Mikhail Gorbachev initates reforms—*glasnost* and *perestroika*—in the Soviet Union
1986	Iran-Contra hearings before Congress reveal arms-for-hostages deal and funds secretly and illegally diverted to Nicaraguan rebels

cold war and the trauma of defeat in Vietnam. But it also owed a great deal to a deepening anxiety of the public about cultural changes and a growing pessimism about the ability of politicians to offer solutions, especially at the national level. Those community activists struggling to extend the protest movements of the 1960s into an updated, comprehensive reformism encompassing such issues as feminism, ecology, and affirmative action readily recognized that the liberal era had ended.

President Ronald Reagan, a charismatic figure who sometimes invented his own past and seemed to believe in it, offered remedies for a weary and nostalgic nation. By insisting that the rebellious 1960s had been a terrible mistake, lowering national self-confidence along with public morals and faith in the power of economic individualism, he successfully wedded the conservatism of

Christian fundamentalists, many suburbanites, and Sunbelt voters with the more traditional conservatism of corporate leaders. In many respects, the Reagan administration actually continued and added ideological fervor to the downscaling of government services and upscaling of military spending already evident under President Jimmy Carter, while offering supporters the hope of a sweeping conservative revolution.

In the end, critics suggested, supporters of Ronald Reagan and Reaganism could not go back to the 1950s—just as the erstwhile rebels of the 1960s could not go back to their favorite era. Economically, conservatives achieved many of their goals, including widespread acceptance of sharper economic divisions within society and fewer restraints on corporations and investments. But socially and culturally, their grasp was much less secure.

REVIEW QUESTIONS

1. Evaluate the significance of the major population shifts in the United States from the 1940s through the 1970s. What was their impact on local and national politics?
2. Discuss the connections between the energy crisis and the rise of the environmental movement.
3. Why was the 1970s dubbed the "Me Decade"? Interpret the decline of liberalism and the rise of conservative political groups. How did these changes affect the outcome of presidential elections?
4. Was the Iran hostage crisis a turning point in American politics or only a thorn in Carter's reelection campaign? How did Iran-Contra affect the Republicans?

5. Describe the central philosophical assumptions behind Reaganomics. What were the key policies by which it was implemented? To what extent were these policies a break with previous economic approaches?
6. Evaluate Reagan's foreign policy. How did it differ from Carter's approach to foreign affairs?
7. Analyze the key structure factors underlying recent changes in American economic and cultural life. Do you see any political solutions for the growth of poverty and inequality?

RECOMMENDED READING

Lee Edwards, *The Conservative Revolution: The Movement That Remade America* (2000). Traces the rise of modern political conservatism from its origins in cold war anticommunism. A longtime conservative activist and writer, Edwards credits much of Reagan's success in office to the presence of a stong, vital, and grass-roots conservative movement.

Frances FitzGerald, *Way Out There in the Blue: Reagan, Star Wars, and the End of the Cold War* (2000). A well-documented study of the conservative mood that made Star Wars both credible and popular among conservatives. FitzGerald provides a sweeping historical context for Star Wars with special attention given to the impact of the cold war on traditional isolationism.

Angela Howard and Sasha Ranae Addams Tarrant, eds., *Reaction to the Modern Women's Movement, 1963 to present* (1997). A collection of essays covering a wide variety of topics concerning the rise of antifeminism. The editors include excerpts from the writings of leading conservatives and analysis by historians.

John Karaagac, *Between Promise and Policy: Ronald Reagan and Conservative Reformism* (2000). Assesses Reagan's major polities, such as increased funding for federal government and regulatory reform, in light of his professed conservative ideals. Karaagac argues that Reagan wielded ideology as a political weapon to gain support for his programs while acting pragmatically and with a good deal of flexibility on particular issues.

Michael B. Katz, *Improving Poor People: The Welfare State, the "Underclass," and Urban Schools as History* (1995). Provides a broad overview of the history of urban poverty, welfare policy, and public education. Katz examines the "underclass" debates of the 1970s as a function of the interaction between politics and economics within the postindustrial inner city.

William M. LeoGrande, *Our Own Backyard: The United States in Central America, 1977–1992* (1998). Assesses the efforts of the Reagan adminstration to gain congressional approval for funding counterrevolutionary operations in El Salvador and Nicaragua. LeoGrande, a former congressional advisor, based his well-documented and detailed study on declassified State Department records, interviews, as well as conventional published sources.

Melani McAlister, *Epic Encounters: Culture, Media, and U.S. Interests in the Middle East, 1945–2000* (2001). A close reading of American popular culture, including films, television news broadcasts, museum exhibits, and fiction, representing relationship between the Middle East and the United States. McAlister considers the importance of the abundance of oil and the Islamic religion of the Middle East as factors shaping U.S. foreign policy.

Lisa McGirr, *Suburban Warriors: The Origins of the New American Right* (2001). Traces the resurgence of American conservatism by analyzing issues that galvanized grass-roots middle-class activism in 1960s and 1970s Southern California.

Bruce J. Schulman, *The Seventies: The Great Shift in American Culture, Society, and Politics* (2001). Examines the move away from the public-spirited universalism that characterized the New Deal and civil rights movement toward the sovereignty of the free market and celebration of private life. With a geopolitical twist that emphasizes the increasing importance of the Sunbelt, Schulman argues that the conservative 1980s actually began a decade earlier.

Judith Stein, *Running Steel, Running America: Race, Economic Policy, and the Decline of Liberalism* (1998). Discusses the impact of the decline of the U.S. steel industry on its large African American labor force. Stein analyzes trade policy, especially under Carter, that benefited foreign steel producers and led to the closing of American plants.

Robert A. Strong, *Working in the World: Jimmy Carter and the Making of American Foreign Policy* (2000). A collection of nine case studies of international affairs covering Carter's presidency. Strong's goal is not to provide new insight into the central crises of the era but to open a window to the range of presidential responsibilities in the diplomatic arena.

Andrew Szasz, *EcoPopulism: Toxic Waste and the Movement for Environmental Justice* (1994). A careful analysis of a turning point in federal regulation of toxic waste. Szasz shows how the prevention of pollution, previously considered a local issue, through strengthened state and federal regulations became a national issue and a springboard for the environmental movement.

Winifred D. Wandersee, *On the Move: American Women in the 1970s* (1988). A highly readable overview of the changes that brought American women into political life but also kept them at the margins of power. This study includes a close description of the National Organization for Women as well as media personalities, such as Jane Fonda, who gave feminism a public face.

ADDITIONAL BIBLIOGRAPHY

Stagflation and the Oil Crisis

Michael A. Bernstein and David E. Adler, eds., *Understanding American Economic Decline* (1994)

Gordon L. Clark, *Unions and Communities under Siege* (1989)

Claudia Goldin, *Understanding the Gender Gap: An Economic History of American Women* (1990)

Burton I. Kaufman, *The Arab Middle East and the United States: Inter-Arab Rivalry and Superpower Diplomacy* (1996)

Paul Krugman, *Peddling Prosperity: Economic Sense and Nonsense in the Age of Diminished Expectations* (1994)

Bruce J. Schulman, *From Cotton Belt to Sun Belt* (1990)

Jon Teaford, *Cities of the Heartland: The Rise and Fall of the Industrial Midwest* (1993)

"Lean Year" Presidents

George C. Edwards III, *At the Margins: Presidential Leadership of Congress* (1989)

Gary M. Fink and Hugh Davis Graham, eds., *The Carter Presidency: Policy Choices in the Post-New Deal Era* (1998)

John Robert Greene, *The Presidency of Gerald R. Ford* (1995)

Alexander P. Lamis, *The Two-Party South*, 2nd ed. (1990)

Gary Sick, *October Surprise: America's Hostages in Iran and the Election of Ronald Reagan* (1991)

Grass-Roots Politics and the New Conservatism

Henry F. Bedford, *Seabrook Station: Citizen Politics and Nuclear Power* (1990)

Nicholas Dagen Bloom, *Suburban Alchemy: 1960s New Towns and the Transformation of the American Dream* (2001)

Elinor Burkett, *The Right Woman: A Journey Through the Heart of Conservative America* (1998)

Dan T. Carter, *From George Wallace to Newt Gingrich: Race in the Conservative Counterrevolution, 1963–1994* (1996)

Craig Cox, *Storefront Revolution: Food Co-ops and the Counterculture* (1994)

Betty A. Dobratz and Stephanie L. Shanks-Meile, *"White Power, White Pride!" The White Separatist Movement in the United States* (1997)

Susan Faludi, *Backlash: The Undeclared War Against American Women* (1991)

David Frum, *How We Got Here: The 70s, The Decade That Brought You Modern Life (For Better or Worse)* (2000)

Lois Gibbs, *Love Canal: The Story Continued* (1998)

Elsebeth Hurup, ed., *The Lost Decade: America in the Seventies* (1996)

William Martin, *With God on Our Side: The Rise of the Religious Right in America* (1996)

Donald G. Mathews and Jane S. De Hart, *Sex, Gender and the Politics of ERA* (1998)

Stephen Paul Miller, *The Seventies Now: Culture as Surveillance* (1999)

Gordana Rabrenovic, *Community Builders: A Tale of Neighborhood Mobilization in Two Cities* (1996)

David Brian Robertson, ed., *Loss of Confidence: Politics and Policy in the 1970s* (1998)

Suzanne Staggenborg, *The Pro-Choice Movement: Organization and Activism in the Abortion Conflict* (1991)

Foreign Policy

William J. Broad, *Teller's War: The Top-Secret Story behind the Star Wars Deception* (1992)

Beth A. Fischer, *The Reagan Reversal: Foreign Policy and the End of the Cold War* (1997)

Christopher Hemmer, *Which Lessons Matter? American Foreign Policy Decision Making in the Middle East, 1979–1987* (2000)

Timothy P. Maga, *The World of Jimmy Carter: U.S. Foreign Policy, 1977–1981* (1994)

Morris Morley, *Washington, Somoza and the Sandinistas: State and Regime in U.S. Policy toward Nicaragua, 1969–1981* (1994)

Bob Woodward, *Veil: The Secret Wars of the CIA* (1987)

The Reagan Revolution

Matthew Dallek, *The Right Moment: Ronald Reagan's First Victory and the Decisive Turning Point in American Politics* (2000)

Rowland Evans and Robert Novak, *The Reagan Revolution* (1991)

Nicholas Laham, *Ronald Reagan and the Politics of Immigration Reform* (2000)

Michael Schaller, *Reckoning with Reagan* (1992)

John W. Sloan, *The Reagon Effect: Economics and Presidential Leadership* (1999)

Best of Times, Worst of Times

James D. Cockcroft, *Outlaws in the Promised Land: Mexican Immigrant Workers and America's Future* (1986)

Barbara Ehrenreich, *Fear of Falling: The Inner Life of the Middle Class* (1989)

Elizabeth Fee and Daniel M. Fox, eds., *AIDS: The Making of a Chronic Disease* (1992)

Jacqueline Jones, *The Dispossessed: America's Underclasses from the Civil War to the Present* (1992)

Michael B. Katz, ed., *The "Underclass" Debate* (1993)

Hilda Scott, *Working Your Way to the Bottom: The Feminization of Poverty* (1985)

Randy Shilts, *And the Band Played On: Politics, People, and the AIDS Epidemic* (1987)

Ruth Sidel, *The Plight of Poor Women in Affluent America* (1986)

Lenore J. Weitzman, *The Divorce Revolution: The Unexpected Social and Economic Consequences for Women and Children in America* (1985)

Richard White, *Rude Awakenings: What the Homeless Crisis Tells Us* (1992)

Biography

Peter G. Bourne, *Jimmy Carter: A Comprehensive Biography From Plains to Postpresidency* (1997)

Jimmy Carter, *Keeping Faith: Memoirs of a President Jimmy Carter* (1982, 1995)

Rosalynn Carter, *First Lady from Plains* (1984)

Adam Clymer, *Edward M. Kennedy: A Biography* (1999)

Jim Cullen, *Born in the U.S.A.: Bruce Springsteen and the American Tradition* (1997)

Betty Ford, with Chris Chase, *Betty, A Glad Awakening* (1987)

Marshall Frady, *Jesse: The Life and Pilgrimage of Jesse Jackson* (1996)

Ernest B. Furgurson, *The Hard Right: The Rise of Jesse Helms* (1986)

Kitty Kelley, *Nancy Reagan* (1991)

Linda J. Lear, *Rachel Carson* (1997)

Peter Meyer, *Defiant Patriot: The Life and Exploits of Lt. Colonel Oliver L. North* (1987)

Edmund Morris, *Dutch: A Memoir of Ronald Reagan* (1999)

Wilbour C. Rich, *Coleman Young and Detroit Politics* (1988)

HISTORY ON THE INTERNET

http://www.ford.utexas.edu/library/speeches/740061.htm

Text of Ford's official pardon of Nixon, September 8, 1974.

http://www.bartleby.com/124/pres60.html

Jimmy Carter's Inaugural Address, January 20, 1977.

http://www.jimmycarterlibrary.org/documents/hostages.phtml

Description of the Iran hostage crisis as described by the Jimmy Carter presidential library.

http://www.yale.edu/lawweb/avalon/mideast/campdav.htm

The Camp David Accords brokered by Jimmy Carter in 1978 between Egypt and Israel.

http://www.loc.gov/exhibits/oliphant/

Pat Oliphant is a Pulitzer Prize-winning cartoonist. This site contains his work for the Nixon, Reagan, and Bush administrations.

http://www.bartleby.com/124/pres61.html

Ronald Reagan's First Inaugural Address, January 20, 1981.

http://www.bartleby.com/124/pres62.html

Ronald Reagan's Second Inaugural Address, January 21, 1985.

Nam June Paik, *Electronic Superhighway*, 1995. Installation view at Holly Solomon Gallery. Courtesy of Nam June Paik and Holly Solomon Gallery.

AMERICAN COMMUNITIES

The World Trade Center, New York, as a Transnational Community

TELMO ALVEAR HAD QUIT HIS JOB AS A BUSBOY IN AUGUST 2001 to become a waiter at Windows on the World, a restaurant on the 106th and 107th floors of the North Tower of the World Trade Center (WTC) that was once described by *New York* magazine as "the most spectacular restaurant in the world." The posh restaurant was huge and elegant. Designed originally as part of a private club for the WTC's business clients, Windows on the World could accommodate as many as 1,000 people. In the decade after it opened in 1976, Windows was one of the most successful restaurants in the world, earning revenues that topped $20 million a year. Much of its success came from its fabulous menu, originally planned with the consultation of James Beard, one of the world's most renowned chefs. In the early 1990s, the reputation of Windows began to slip, and following a terrorist attack on the WTC in February 1993, the restaurant closed. But by the time Alvear found a job there, Windows on the World was once again thriving. Celebrity chef Michael Lomonaco was in charge, earning for the restaurant the Visitors Choice Award of "Grand Prize for Best Restaurant Overall." With views on a clear day extending for forty-five miles, and with a wine cellar and liquor stock that was modestly named "The Greatest Bar on Earth," Windows had become a prime tourist attraction and a popular dining spot for some of the most powerful international traders and merchants in the world. "It's more than a restaurant," one reviewer enthused. "It's a New York experience."

And so it was. Not just Windows on the World but the entire World Trade Center had come to represent both the best and worst of New York City, the commercial capital of the world. The twin skyscrapers, which were designed to be the tallest in the world, were audacious. Completed in 1973 at a cost of $400 million, they rose 110 stories above ground and occupied a thirteen-square-block site in Lower Manhattan, conveniently close to Wall Street and the New York Stock Exchange. When the WTC was first built, many New Yorkers, including distinguished architects, complained that the mammoth, boxy structures destroyed the city's unrivaled skyline. They stood too self-assuredly, critics charged, as tasteless monuments to commerce, wealth, and ambition. But over the years, the WTC became a preeminent symbol of the glory of New York and, by extension, the United States. The image of the twin towers was emblazoned on t-shirts and captured on postcards and sold to tourists from all over the world. The WTC provided office space to hundreds of businesses and government agencies and served as a work place for more than 50,000 people.

The people who worked in the twin towers constituted a remarkable transnational community. Although many were native New Yorkers, a large number were relative newcomers. Alvear himself was one in a huge wave of Hispanic immigration that had been transforming New York City since 1990. Immigrating from Ecuador as a teenager, he represented what census takers term "other Hispanics"—immigrants from the South and Central America, and the Caribbean who had replaced the Puerto Ricans and Cubans as the city's Hispanic majority. Alvear lived with his wife Blanca and their one-year-old son in Queens and spent his hours away from work at soccer games and dance clubs.

At his job, Alvear worked with and served people from a wide array of national backgrounds. Those who worked at Windows on the World proudly described themselves as a "little United Nations" because they represented just about every nation of the world and spoke nearly as many languages. Representing a wide range of cultures, they were well prepared to deal with the restaurant's equally diverse patrons, tourists from around the world and international traders and executives with offices in the WTC.

The Port Authority of New York and New Jersey, which owned the WTC, rented space primarily to tenants engaged in international commerce. Importers, exporters, freight handlers, steamship lines, oil traders, and insurance organizations were among the long-term renters. Many were multinational businesses, the majority with home offices in the United States, but a sizable number represented financial or commercial operations from Latin America, Asia, Africa, and Europe. American-based firms such as Verizon Communications, Morgan Stanley, and the Oppenheimer Funds occupied several floors. But Fuji Bank of Japan, Thai Farmers Bank, Zim-American Israeli Shipping Company, and the Bank of Taiwan also had offices there. To promote transnational exchanges, the World Trade Institute, on the 55th floor of the North Tower,

sponsored training courses in world trade, seminars for international businesspeople, and even language classes. Many of these firms chose to rent space in the WTC not because their businesses benefited directly from physical proximity to other international traders, but because an address at the WTC offered visibility to firms seeking a high profile in the world of commerce. The WTC offered firms the prestige of working in New York's most imposing landmark, a symbol of American wealth and power.

On September 11, 2001, two commercial jetliners hijacked by terrorists crashed into both towers of the World Trade Center and within an hour both towers had collapsed. Telmo Alvear, who usually worked the night shift, had been covering for a friend that morning. At age twenty-five he perished, along with nearly eighty members of the Hotel and Restaurant Workers Union who, like Alvear, were serving a special breakfast meeting. Nearly 3,000 people—citizens of the United States and eighty other nations—died that day. Uncounted were an unknown number of homeless New Yorkers who had sought what they believed to be a safe haven in the cavernous underground spaces of the WTC.

The WTC symbolized, if any building could, the confidence of American leadership in an era when national borders seemed to melt away. It also symbolized the transnationalism that many believed laid the foundation for a new world order based on the democratic liberalism that Americans treasured. Its vulnerability to surprise attack suggested the fragile nature of the swiftly changing society. ■

New York City

KEY TOPICS

- American foreign policy after the cold war
- The impact of the New Economy and the boom of the 1990s
- Revelations of the 2000 Census

- The Clinton presidency and resurgent conservatism
- Globalization
- International Terrorism

A NEW WORLD ORDER

Between 1989 and 1991, Americans watched with amazement as the Soviet empire disintegrated, and the cold war came to an end. But contrary to expectations, this dramatic event did not bring world peace. The end of the cold war let loose a multitude of furies in the form of renewed nationalism, ethnic and religious conflict, and widening divisions between the world's rich and poor. Just as dramatically, as the old geopolitical order disappeared, ideological rivalry shifted to the Middle East and other areas in the world where Islamic militants had forcefully turned against the West.

The presidential administrations of George Herbert Walker Bush (1989–1992) and Bill Clinton (1993–2000) bore the enormous responsibility of reshaping the fundamental premises that had guided the nation's foreign policy since the end of World War II. As the leader of the only surviving superpower, President George H. W. Bush faced a host of problems complicated rather than resolved by the collapse of the Soviet Union, and he brought the nation to war for the first time since Vietnam. Then, in 1992, when the Democrats recaptured the White House after twelve years of Republican control, President Clinton found himself equally entangled in foreign affairs. Threat of economic collapse in Japan and other parts of Asia, the various effects of global economic slowdown on the developing nations of Africa and Latin America, terrorism along with the continuation of localized wars and armed occupations worldwide, nuclear proliferation, and new strains on the world's natural resources—all forced reconsideration of the core principles of the nation's foreign and domestic policies.

The Collapse of Communism

The reforms initiated by Mikhail Gorbachev in the mid–1980s, known as *perestroika,* and, more immediately, the failed Soviet war in Afghanistan led to the

Constructed by the Port Authority of New York and New Jersey in the early 1970s, the World Trade Center provided office space to businesses from around the world. The 110-story twin towers dominated the skyline of Lower Manhattan.

dissolution of the Soviet Union and to the end of Communist rule throughout Eastern Europe. Beginning in June 1989, when Poland held its first free elections since the close of World War II in 1945, prodemocracy demonstrations forced out long-time Communist leaders in Hungary, Czechoslovakia, Bulgaria, and Romania. Most dramatic of all were the events in East Germany. The Berlin Wall, which for thirty years had loomed as the ultimate symbol of cold war division, came down on November 9, 1989. Hundreds of thousands of East Germans immediately rushed into West Berlin. Popular protest intensified, paving the way for German reunification the following year.

Political changes in the Soviet Union came more slowly, accompanied by such drastically reduced living standards that successful transition to a liberal market economy and democratic political system was uncertain. In March 1989 the Soviet Union held its first open elections since 1917, and a new Congress of People's Deputies replaced the old Communist Party–dominated Supreme Soviet. In the next elections the following year, hundreds of party officials went down in defeat in key Russian cities. In August 1991 party hard-liners made a final attempt to hold on to the old order and staged a coup, placing President Gorbachev under house arrest. Although the coup quickly failed, most of the fifteen republics had meanwhile announced their withdrawal from the Soviet Union. Gorbachev found he could no longer control the government. On Christmas Day 1991 the weary and bitter president of the USSR resigned and recognized the new Commonwealth of Independent States.

The Soviet Union had dissolved, marking the end of the great superpower rivalry that had shaped American foreign policy and domestic politics for nearly a half-century. President Bush described the end of the cold war as an event of "biblical proportions." Many scholars have agreed that the changes rivaled the collapse of European empires during World War I and the rise of the cold war after World War II.

President Bush seemed both well positioned and well prepared to deal with this situation. Before serving as vice president under Ronald Reagan, he had held several major appointive offices that had involved him directly in foreign policy—UN ambassador, envoy to China, and director of the CIA. Winning election handily over Massachusetts governor George Dukakis with forty out of fifty states and 56 percent of the popular vote, he believed he could count on popular support. With the end of the cold war, Bush proclaimed, it was "time to move beyond containment to a new policy for the 1990s." But what would be that new policy?

War in the Middle East

The first great post–cold war crisis demonstrated how new kinds of conflicts—economic competition, ethnic hatreds, and regional struggles—were to redefine global politics. Events in the oil-rich Middle East, a region where both the United States and the Soviet Union had vital and often conflicting national interests, brought the two former enemies into diplomatic partnership for the first time since World War II.

On August 2, 1990, 120,000 Iraqi troops backed by 850 tanks swept into neighboring Kuwait and quickly seized control of that tiny monarchy with its rich oil fields. The motives of Saddam Hussein, Iraq's military dictator, were mixed. Like most Iraqis, Hussein believed that oil-rich Kuwait was actually an ancient province of Iraq that had been illegally carved away by British imperial agents in the 1920s as part of the dismemberment of the Ottoman Empire. Control of Kuwait would give Saddam Hussein control of its huge oil reserves, as well as Persian Gulf ports for his landlocked country.

Religion as well as economic rivalry within the Organization of Petroleum Exporting Countries (OPEC) were also major factors. Islamic militants cheered Hussein's action as a brilliant move to counter the growing influence of the United States throughout the Middle East. Just emerging from an exhausting and inconclusive eight-year war with Iran, Iraqis also bitterly resented Kuwait's production of oil beyond OPEC quotas, which had helped send the world price of oil plummeting from the highs of the 1970s and early 1980s.

The United States responded swiftly to news of the invasion. Its first concern was that Saddam Hussein also might attack Saudi Arabia, which the United States had defined as vital to its interests as far back as 1943. On August 15, President George H. W. Bush ordered U.S. forces to Saudi Arabia and the Persian Gulf, calling the action Operation Desert Shield. The president stressed the importance of oil supplies. "Our jobs, our way of life, our own freedom, and the freedom of friendly countries around the world will suffer if control of the world's great oil reserves fall in the hands of that one man, Saddam Hussein." The United States also led a broad coalition in the United Nations, including the Soviet Union, that condemned the Iraqi invasion of Kuwait and declared strict economic sanctions against Iraq if it did not withdraw. By the middle of October, some 230,000 American troops had been sent to the Persian Gulf.

In early November, President Bush announced a change in policy to what he called "an offensive military option," and the U.S. troop deployment quickly doubled and reached 580,000 by January 1991. The president also shifted to the moral high ground in justifying the biggest U.S. troop buildup since the Vietnam

War. "The fight isn't about oil," he insisted. "The fight is about naked aggression that will not stand." Administration officials now demonized Saddam Hussein as another Adolf Hitler. The UN sanctions failed to budge Hussein from Kuwait, and the drift to war now looked inevitable. In January 1991, Congress narrowly passed a joint resolution authorizing the president to use military force.

After a last-minute UN peace mission failed to break the deadlock, President Bush announced, on January 16, 1991, the start of Operation Desert Storm. U.S.–led air strikes began forty-two days of massive bombing of Iraqi positions in Kuwait, as well as Baghdad and other Iraqi cities. U.S. planes dropped 142,000 tons of bombs on Iraq and Kuwait, roughly six times the equivalent of the atomic bomb dropped on Nagasaki in World War II. The ground war, which began on February 24, took only 100 hours to force Saddam Hussein's troops out of Kuwait. Hussein's vaunted military machine—the fourth largest army in the world—turned out to be surprisingly weak. U.S. forces lost only 184 dead, compared to nearly 100,000 Iraqi deaths, mostly from the bombing.

Almost every community in the United States sent men and women to the Gulf, and the vast majority supported Operation Desert Storm. Unlike the media cov-

erage of the Vietnam War, television new reports showed virtually no blood or death. The Pentagon required "military escorts" to accompany all reporters and carefully regulated the release of silent film footage documenting precision bombing runs. Emphasizing the technological feats, television reporters dubbed the conflict the "Nintendo" war. Air strikes looked more like video games than bombing attacks, and military officials insisted that American bombardiers never missed their targets, which were supposedly restricted to Iraqi military sites. But subsequent investigations revealed massive numbers of targeting errors and the devastation of Iraq's infrastructure, from its communications network to its water system.

Politically, the Persian Gulf War marked the high point of Bush's popularity. His approval rating with the public reached nearly 90 percent, higher than President Franklin Roosevelt's during World War II. Basking in his success, Bush proclaimed the responsibility of the United States to lead in the creation of a "new world order" that would be "freer from the threat of terror, stronger in the pursuit of justice, and more secure in the quest for peace, an era in which the nations of the world, East and West, North and South, can prosper and live in harmony."

Victory in the Gulf War rekindled national pride in many people of the United States. But for the 18 million people of Iraq, it produced the worst possible outcome. The ecological damage in the Gulf region was extensive and long-lasting. Oil fires burned out of control. The use of armor-piercing depleted uranium (DN) shells, for the first time in any war, left behind traces of radiation believed to endanger health, especially that of children and the aged. Human rights groups reported an appalling toll among civilians. Congressman Jim McDermott (D-Washington), who visited Iraq during the summer after the war, testified before a House committee on the misery he saw and posed the ethical dilemma created by the continuation of economic sanctions against the Iraqi government: "The Iraqi people did not vote for Saddam Hussein, yet hundreds of thousands of Iraqis, most of them children, are hungry, sick, and dying because of Hussein's intransigence and our commitment to oust Hussein at all cost."

The limits of military power to solve complex political and economic disputes became clear in the aftermath of victory. The Persian Gulf war failed to dislodge Saddam Hussein, who remained in power despite CIA attempts to overthrow him and repeated bombings of Iraqi military positions. Trade sanctions did little to weaken his rule, although the economic boycott, which brought increasing hardship to the civilian population, eventually divided the Western powers, leaving the United States and Great Britain isolated in their sanctions against Iraq.

U.S. Marines swept into Kuwait City, March 1991. After six weeks of intensive bombing and less than five days after the start of a massive ground offensive, U.S. and allied forces overwhelmed the Iraqi army and ended Saddam Hussein's occupation of Kuwait.

SOURCE: Photo by Patrick Downs. © Los Angeles Times. Reprinted by permission.

Moreover, regional tensions worsened in the aftermath of the war. In order to gain support from Egypt, Syria, Jordan, and Saudi Arabia to conduct military operations against Iraq, U.S. diplomats had promised to forge a just peace between the Palestinians and Israelis. President Clinton undertook secret negotiations culminating in a Declaration of Principles in Oslo, Norway, in 1993, which for the first time promised security for the Israelis and self-rule for the Palestinians. For their role in this process, Israeli prime minister Itzakh Rabin and Palestinian leader Yassar Arafat were jointly awarded a Nobel Peace Prize. But the assassination of Rabin by an Israeli religious fundamentalist, the continuing buildup of Israeli "settlements" in the occupied West Bank of the Jordan River, and the resulting violence on both sides deprived Clinton of a major diplomatic triumph.

The repercussions of the Gulf War were longlasting. The leading U.S. ally in the region, the oil-rich kingdom of Saudi Arabia, had served as the launchingpad for the invasion of Iraq, and following the war the Saudis had allowed the continuing presence of U.S. troops and weapons. This occupation of Saudi territory, which included Islamic holy sites, intensified the hatred of Americans among many Muslims and prompted appeals for revenge. Between 1980 and the turn of the twenty-first century, they bitterly observed, the United States had waged seventeen distinct military operations in the Middle East, all against Muslims.

Among those actively opposed to the U.S. role in the region was Saudi millionaire Osama bin Laden, just a few years earlier a close ally of the United States during the Russian invasion of Afghanistan. He now turned squarely against his former arms suppliers and CIA contacts. Using his own funds and a tribal network, bin Laden built his shadowy Al-Qaeda organization, training small groups in terror tactics to be used against Western interests, particularly to force American troops out of the Middle East.

Peacekeeping in the Balkans

The immediate victory in the Persian Gulf and a six-month surge of popularity did little to help President Bush when faced with a formidable candidate, William Jefferson Clinton. Unlike Bush, the last of the World War II veterans to enter the White House, Arkansas governor Clinton belonged to the Vietnam War generation and had opposed U.S. military intervention in Southeast Asia. The electorate awarded him 43 percent of the votes, compared to Bush's 38 percent, and gave the moderate Democrat a solidly Democratic House and Senate.

Despite this strong mandate, Clinton did not enjoy an easy transition. Heightened ethnic nationalism and religious fundamentalism continued to fill the vacuum left by the collapse of communism. Across the globe, from Africa to the Middle East, the Indian subcontinent, and beyond, civil wars created massive civilian casualties and new waves of refugees. Clinton, inexperienced in foreign affairs, created a team of veteran advisers including Secretary of State William Christopher and UN ambassador Madeline Albright. Together, they were compelled to grapple with a major post–cold war crisis that Bush had pushed aside—civil war in the Balkans.

With the collapse of communism, Yugoslavia had quickly fallen to pieces when four of its six states declared independence. Ethnic and religious rivalry among Serbs, Croats, and Muslims living in Bosnia erupted into a violent civil war. Bush and his foreign policy advisers, seeing no threat to American interests, opposed U.S. military intervention. But as reports of "ethnic cleansing"—forced removal and murder of Croats and Muslims by Bosnian Serbs—increased, and as the numbers of refugees grew, Clinton, with congressional support, prepared to act. By late summer 1995, U.S. and NATO fighter pilots were bombing Serbian strongholds in Bosnia. After negotiating with Yugoslavian president Slobodan Milosevic, on November 27 Clinton announced the Dayton Accords, an agreement drawn up in Dayton, Ohio, and signed in Paris that called for a federated, multiethnic state of Bosnia. An International Protection Force, one-third of whom were U.S. troops, was then installed as peacekeepers. One year later, the date Clinton had marked for withdrawal of American troops, Bosnia was still deeply divided, and American troops had settled in for a long haul.

The worst foreign crisis of Clinton's presidency erupted in Kosovo, a Serbian province about 160 miles east of Italy, across the Adriatic Sea. Milosevic, a Serb nationalist, had terminated the autonomy of the province shortly after he took office in 1989, and in response the ethnic Albanians living there organized their own government and declared their independence the following year. While preoccupied by the civil war in Bosnia, Milosevic paid comparatively little attention to Kosovo. However, in 1997, the virtual collapse of the government of neighboring Albania changed the situation dramatically. Armed Albanians poured into Kosovo and joined the rebel forces. Clashes between Serbs and Albanians intensified, and the fighting soon spread to neighboring Macedonia and to Albania itself.

President Clinton once again attempted to negotiate, but he failed to resolve the problems through diplomacy. After NATO authorized air strikes, he addressed Americans on March 24, 1999, stating that U.S. armed forces had that day joined their allies to attack Serbian forces in Kosovo. "All the ingredients for a major war are there," he explained, "ancient grievances, struggling democracies, and in the center of it all a dictator in

Serbia who has done nothing since the cold war ended but start new wars and pour gasoline on the flames of ethnic and religious division." On June 10, after a little more than two months of intensive bombing, he reported that the Serbian army was withdrawing from Kosovo and "for the first time in seventy-nine days, the skies over Yugoslavia are silent." But the bombing had destroyed many beautiful cities, the weapons deployed had left radioactive traces in the soil and water, and resentments among Muslims simmered.

His country in ruins, and voted out of office, Slobodan Milosevic became the first head of state to be brought to trial for war crimes and crimes against humanity by the International War Crimes Tribunal in 2001. Meanwhile, in the Balkans, nationalist and ethnic conflicts continued to flare up, and U.S. peacekeepers remained.

Transnational Human Rights

The nationalist and ethnic conflicts of the post–cold war era pushed human rights to the forefront of foreign policy. This concern dated to 1947, when the UN Commission for Human Rights met for the first time to draft the Universal Declaration of Human Rights (see Chapter 26). The principle of human rights is embedded in Article 3: "Everyone has the right to life, liberty, and security of person." However, it was only in the 1970s that the United States proclaimed its international responsibility to protect and promote democracy, human rights, religious freedom, and workers rights not just as American values but as universal values. In 1976 Congress enacted legislation linking both foreign trade and monetary assistance to human rights and created a bureau within the State Department that would report annually on the status of human rights in individual countries. By the end of the century, the Bureau of Democracy, Human Rights, and Labor was surveying the status of human rights in nearly 200 countries, documenting the rise of transnational human rights networks in the public as well as private sectors, and helping to promote "an international civil society capable of promoting democracy and universal rights."

During the 1990s, with the intensification of nationalist and ethnic conflicts, the UN Commission clarified its intention to focus on the protection of vulnerable groups, including racial minorities, indigenous peoples, women, and children. The commission gave priority to the eradication of violence against women and the attainment of equal rights, and the U.S. Congress followed by creating in 1994 the position of Senior Advisor for Women's Rights.

Meanwhile, in many countries nongovernmental organizations (NGOs) were formed to cooperate with UN agencies and to provide assistance, for example, to

victims of torture or religious persecution. The largest was Human Rights Watch, which had formed in 1978 to assist prodemocracy groups in Moscow, Prague, and Warsaw. In the 1990s, the organization developed into a global network of human rights advocates. It investigated and exposed war-related abuses such indiscriminate shelling of noncombatants as well as the use of rape or starvation as weapons of war. Providing assistance to refugees of civil conflict represented an enormous enterprise. In Kosovo alone, by 1999, approximately 600,000 ethnic Albanians had been driven from their homes and villages by the Serbs, and another 700,000 were living as refugees in nearby countries.

Human rights emerged as a centerpiece of President Clinton's foreign policy. Having held public office as an Arkansas governor, he was relatively inexperienced in foreign policy, and on many issues, differed little from Bush. However, like his Democratic predecessor, Jimmy Carter, he insisted that U.S. foreign policy reflect "the moral principles most American share." Now that the cold war had ended, the United States could replace the strategy of containment with humanitarian goals. Moreover, Clinton insisted, the United States, as the world's strongest nation, had a special responsibility to provide leadership to the new and emerging democracies. In 1993, Secretary of State Warren Christopher directed all American embassies to focus their programming on the advancement of human rights and democracy.

However, human rights was only one aspect of the the liberal internationalism that was the core of Clinton's foreign policy. The president insisted that the campaign for human rights depended on the expansion of democracy, which in turn depended on the simultaneous expansion of the free market throughout the world. In terms of U.S. foreign policy, Clinton therefore proposed to replace the strategy of containment with a "strategy of enlargement—enlargement of the world's free community of market democracies."

This idea drove Clinton's policy toward the People's Republic of China (PRC). The U.S. détente with China, which President Nixon had cultivated, began to fall apart during the Bush administration. During the spring of 1989, Chinese government forces brutally attacked prodemocracy demonstrators in Beijing's Tiananmen Square, resulting in the killing of some 3,000 protestors and the wounding of 10,000 more. Scenes of the massacre were broadcast live on television and provoked outrage around the world. President Bush, who had only recently extended Most Favored Nation (MFN) economic and trading status toward the PRC, hoped to maintain ties but was soon pressured by Congress to impose trade sanctions.

During his election campaign of 1992, Clinton had criticized Bush for continuing "to coddle" China in light of such gross human rights violations. Then, after taking office, he modified his position and, looking for "hopeful seeds of change," recommended restoring MFN status with the PRC. He acknowledged that serious human rights abuses continued, such as China's religious and cultural persecution in Tibet, but he pointed out that China, the world's most populous nation, had the world's fastest growing economy—as well as a nuclear arsenal and veto in the National Security Council of the UN. He defeated congressional opposition to detach human rights from MFN status and instead promoted free enterprise as a principal means to advance democracy in not only the PRC but in other nations, such as Turkey, Saudi Arabia, and Indonesia.

CHANGING AMERICAN COMMUNITIES

The dark side of the post–cold war era seemed to be offset during the 1990s by the unprecedented surge of the U.S. economy and the inclusion of millions of new immigrants, who easily found places for themselves within the rapidly expanding service sector. The patterns of growth indicated a dynamic shift toward a postindustrial economy based upon high technology, wherein today's worker with a high degree of skill and entrepreneurial initiative might be tomorrow's millionaire. After a recession, which had plagued Bush's presidency, bottomed out in 1994, Americans settled in to enjoy record profits, low unemployment rates, and unsurpassed prosperity. The business cycle, many analysts concluded, had simply disappeared, and productivity would just keep growing at a miraculous rate. In cultural as well as in economic life, in the United States and throughout the world, these changes seemed—at least for a time—revolutionary.

The Boom Years

The economy rather than foreign affairs had fueled the 1992 presidential election campaign. Republicans took credit for forcing the fall of communism and reviving America's military strength. But they had also promised to cut government spending and balance the budget. In 1985, the Republican Congress had enacted, amid great fanfare, the Balanced Budget and Emergency Deficit Reduction Act, more popularly known as Gramm-Rudman after its principal authors, senators Phil Gramm and Warren Rudman. The act mandated automatic spending cuts if the government failed to meet fixed deficit reduction goals leading to a balanced budget by 1991. But just as Bush was about to take office in 1989, many of the nation's savings and

loan institutions, which had been deregulated by Reagan, collapsed. Then, on Friday, October 13, 1989, the stock market took its worst nosedive since 1987, signaling the beginning of a major recession. With the national debt reaching an astronomical $4 trillion, the paradoxes of the Reagan-Bush years had become readily apparent.

In the Democrats' campaign headquarters a sign humorously reminded the staff: "It's the economy, stupid." Candidate Bill Clinton promised economic leadership, including deficit reduction and a tax cut for the middle class. He also effectively adopted many of the conservative themes that proved so advantageous to Republicans over the past twelve years. He called for "responsibility" on the part of recipients of social programs, spoke of the importance of stable families, promised to be tough on crime and to reduce the bureaucracy, and stressed the need for encouraging private investment to create new jobs. Economic issues also fueled the independent campaign of Texas billionaire H. Ross Perot, who with his folksy East Texas twang argued that a successful businessman such as himself was better qualified to solve the nation's economic woes than Washington insiders. Clinton interpreted Perot's

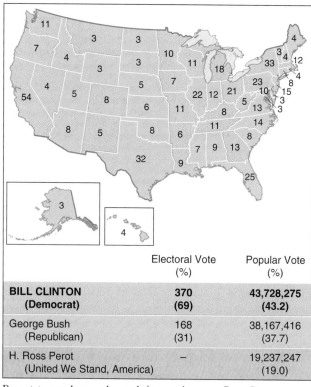

	Electoral Vote (%)	Popular Vote (%)
BILL CLINTON (Democrat)	**370 (69)**	**43,728,275 (43.2)**
George Bush (Republican)	168 (31)	38,167,416 (37.7)
H. Ross Perot (United We Stand, America)	–	19,237,247 (19.0)

Promising to bring about deficit reduction, Ross Perot won the largest percentage of the popular vote of any third-party candidate in U.S. history.

Republican President George Bush, Democrat Bill Clinton, and independent H. Ross Perot debated the issues on television three times during the 1992 presidential campaign. Bush emphasized the "character" issue by hammering away at Clinton's failure to serve during the Vietnam War. Clinton focused on the plight of the "forgotten middle class," many of whom had deserted the Democratic party. Perot appealed to voter frustration with the two major parties.

SOURCE: Corbis/Sygma (280232).

success at the polls to his promise to focus, as he put it, "like a laser beam on the economy."

The Clinton administration succeeded in breaking the political gridlock caused by the traditional Democratic resistance to the "economic discipline" urged by Republicans. He pursued a strategy his advisors called "triangulation," positioning himself above and between the interests of warring Democrats and Republicans. For example, despite his attacks on the Republicans as radicals, Clinton opposed his own party's efforts to block a Republican plan to dismantle the federal welfare system in place since the New Deal. The new legislation—the Welfare Reform Act—abolished the sixty-year-old Aid to Families with Dependent Children program (AFDC). Poor mothers with dependent children would now have access to aid for only a limited period and only if they were preparing for or seeking work. When Congress passed the act in August of 1996, Clinton held a public

signing ceremony and declared "an end to welfare as we know it." At the same time, he pursued this strategy to make investments at home and overseas both easier and more profitable. Clinton thus completed the economic side of the "Reagan Revolution," often with more Republican than Democratic support in Congress. Equally important, he renewed the Reagan appointment of Alan Greenspan, who chaired the Federal Reserve Board and cleverly set interest rates to check inflation and to encourage the economy to keep on growing.

President Clinton pushed two major trade agreements through Congress that built on efforts by the Reagan and Bush administrations to expand markets and encourage "free trade." Approved in November 1993, the North American Free Trade Agreement (NAFTA) eased the international flow of goods, services, and investments among the United States, Mexico, and Canada by eliminating tariffs and other trade barriers. Supplemental agreements called for cooperation on environmental and labor concerns. The stated goal of NAFTA was to improve productivity and living standards through a freer flow of commerce in North America. It created the largest free-trade zone in the world, comprising 360 million people and an annual gross national product of $6 trillion. In 1994 Congress also approved the General Agreement on Tariffs and Trade (GATT), which slashed tariffs on thousands of goods throughout the world and phased out import quotas imposed by the United States and other industrialized nations. It also established the World Trade Organization (WTO) to mediate commercial disputes among 117 nations.

Critics and supporters of NAFTA and GATT argued over whether the agreements would encourage global competition, thereby boosting American export industries and creating new high-wage jobs for American workers, or simply erode the American industrial base and accelerate environmental degradation. Cities on the U.S.–Mexican border, such as Tijuana and San Diego were clear beneficiaries, but the downside was considerable. New *maquiladora* (factories and assembly plants) lacked pollution controls and spewed tons of toxic wastes into the air and groundwater. Despite the boost from NAFTA, the Mexican peso collapsed, and only a $20 billion bailout of the Mexican economy directed by executive order from the White House on January 31, 1995, prevented a serious depression there. From 1994 to 1997 the wages of the average Mexican worker fell from $1.45 per hour to only 78 cents. Trade did boom between the two countries, but a 1997 study conducted by the Department of Labor estimated that some 142,000 U.S. and Canadian jobs had been lost as a direct result of NAFTA.

Perhaps the greatest stimulus to Clinton's economic policy was the soaring stock market of the 1990s, with "tech stocks" leading the way. The record highs of the Bush years, when the Dow Jones index of thirty industrials approached 4,000, paled by comparison to the leap in 1999 when the Dow hit 10,000 in March and then peaked above 11,000 in May. The fastest growing sector of the market was NASDAQ, the acronym for National Association of Securities Dealers Automated Quotations, which was created in 1971 to report on the trading of domestic securities. NASDAQ grew to become the largest securities market in the United States and the prime-trading venue for technology stocks. In 1999, three companies—Intel, Cisco Systems, and Microsoft, which in terms of stock capitalization was the biggest company in the world—made up nearly a quarter of NASDAQ's total value. The market remained volatile during the decade, but profits were extraordinarily high. Annual returns on investments, generally under 6 percent during the 1970s, had risen to more than 18 percent.

Equally remarkable was the involvement "in the market" of ordinary citizens. By the end of the century, Americans had 60 percent of their investments and savings in stocks, more than double the proportion in 1982, when the market had traded at under 800. An estimated 78.7 million people held stocks, often through mutual funds or in retirement fund portfolios managed by their employers or unions. Thousands of white-collar employees working for fast-rising firms like Microsoft also acquired stock options that made them "instant millionaires" at the stocks' peak value.

The down side of the economic boom was nearly invisible. Greenspan enthusiastically announced in 1995 that the boom had solid roots: productivity had risen sharply since the 1970s while labor costs had actually declined, hoisting profits to new levels. But critics observed that while a corporate official had earned around twenty or thirty times the pay of a blue-collar worker at the same company a few decades earlier, corporate executive income was more than two hundred times greater than that of a blue-collar employee. Moreover, "downsizing" became a common strategy for increasing profits levels or defeating negative trends. By the mid-1990s, corporate leaders at IBM had laid off or fired approximately half the company workforce hired since 1980, mainly white-collar workers who usually found other jobs but often at sharply reduced pay. In the blue-collar sector, industrial jobs continued to disappear as factories closed or companies moved production of textiles, auto parts, and even electronics across borders or overseas.

Skyrocketing stock prices, while creating huge profits, inevitably raised worries of a future plunge. Anticipated returns on investments in much of Eastern Europe (especially the Soviet Union) and Latin America often did not materialize. Meanwhile, saving rates of Americans reached an all-time low, warning that a downturn could provoke massive defaults and bankruptcies sending a ripple effect through the economy. In 1998, venture capital investments reached a record $14.3 billion, an extreme example of "risk capital." By the second half of 1999, the "dot-com" internet-related stocks began to tumble, and economic analysts began to wonder if the business cycle had indeed been rendered obsolete.

Silicon Valley

Much of the growth of the 1990s was attributed to the consolidation of the "new economy," a phrased coined by economists in the 1970s to characterize the increasing importance of the service sector, corporate restructuring, and globalization. As illustrated by the successful merger of computer and communication technologies, the most important and dynamic wealth-producing activities were no longer the manufacturing and distribution of material goods but the creation, processing, and sale of information and services.

During the peak years of the new economy, a thirty-by-ten-mile strip of Santa Clara County, California, emerged as both the real and symbolic capital of the most important sector of the new economy—microelectronics. As late as 1960 this region was the major processor of fruits and vegetables in the world; forty years later one-third of the valley's workforce were employed by high-tech companies.

The nucleus for Silicon Valley dated to the early days of the cold war, when the defense industry laid the foundation for information technology. In the 1950s Stanford University began to lease unused land to electronics firms as a way to earn money, and companies such as Schockley Transitor Company, IBM, Hewlett-Packard, and Fairchild Semiconductor, seeking the advantages of proximity to a major research university, expanded to become key players in the new industry. At first, military contracts predominated, but the consumer electronics revolution of the 1970s fueled an explosive new wave of growth. Silicon Valley firms gave birth to pocket calculators, video games, home computers, cordless telephones, digital watches, and almost every other new development in electronics.

Dubbed "Silicon Valley" in 1971 after the semiconductor chip, which is made of silicon, and which became the basic building block of modern microelectronics, the region flourished thanks to its unique combination of research facilities, investment capital, attractive environment, and a large pool of highly educated people. It became home to more than 1,700 high-tech firms that specialized in gathering, processing, or distributing information or in manufacturing information technology. Companies like Atari, Apple, and Intel achieved enormous success and became household names. Silicon Valley boasted the greatest concentration of new wealth in the United States, and it attracted widespread coverage in trade magazines, business periodicals, and the popular press. Stories of millionaires made over night reinforced the powerful popular image of Silicon Valley as a place where technological innovation and great fortunes emerged from a unique culture of youth, inventiveness, and entrepreneurship.

By the end of the century, Silicon Valley had become a continuous sprawl of two dozen cities between San Francisco and San Jose and the home and work place of a diverse population. The white population stood at 44 percent, leaving no ethnic or racial majority. The managers and engineers, nearly all of whom were white males, had settled in affluent communities such as Palo Alto, Mountain View, and Sunnyvale. Manual workers on assembly lines and in low-paying service jobs clustered in San Jose and Gilroy. Most of these were Latino, African American, Vietnamese, Cambo-dian, and Filipino men and women who constituted a cheap, nonunionized labor pool with an extremely high turnover rate. Public services in their communities—schools, welfare, police and fire protection—were poor, the glamorous lifestyle out of their reach.

The prime example of the new economy, Silicon Valley was also part of a global enterprise. Its firms were closely linked to the microelectronic industry of the greater Pacific Rim. The end of the cold war and the accompanying decline in military spending in the United States forced high-tech firms in California into greater competition on the world market and especially against similar companies in Japan, Korea, China, and Malaysia. But many American companies protected themselves against such competition by owning and managing a large share of the plants in these countries. Silicon Valley companies such as Solectron, the largest contract manufacturer of electronics in the world, Seagate Technology, Siebel Systems, and Intel, for example, all had sizable operations in Malaysia.

By the end of the century, the rate of growth showed signs of slowing, as did the infusion of new venture capital into high-tech industries. Young entrepreneurs throughout the Pacific Rim found it more difficult to start successful new companies and to make the leap from a small, start-up company to a large corporation. Then, in 2000, stocks trading on NASDAQ began to spiral downward. Within the first year of the new century, NASDAQ dropped 61 percent, a fall greater than the one caused by the oil crisis in 1973. Led by Cisco Systems, the decline inaugurated a period of retrenchment, with a slowdown in sales matched by rising unemployment throughout Silicon Valley. By this time, scarcity in housing, traffic jams, and an inflated cost of living were already leading many companies and individuals to move out of the area.

An Electronic Culture

The technological developments produced in Silicon Valley helped reconfigure cultural life in the United States and the world. Revolutions in computers and telecommunications merged telephones, televisions, computers, cable, and satellites into a global system of information exchange. The new technologies changed the way people worked and played. They made the nation's cultural life more homogeneous, played a greater role than ever in shaping politics, and ultimately created the "global village" of instant, worldwide communication that the media theorist Marshall McLuhan had predicted in the 1960s.

The twin arrivals of cable and the videocassette recorder (VCR) expanded and redefined the power of television. By the end of the 1980s pay cable services and VCRs had penetrated roughly two-thirds of American homes. Cable and satellite in the 1990s offered television viewers scores of new programming choices, especially sports events and movies. For the first time ever, the mass audience for traditional network programming declined as "narrowcasting"—the targeting of specialized audiences—competed with broadcasting. The VCR revolutionized the way people used their sets, allowing them to organize program watching around their own schedules. Hollywood studios began releasing movies on videotape, and the rental and sale of movies for home viewing quickly outstripped ticket sales at theaters as the main profit source for filmmakers. The VCR thus radically changed the economics of the entertainment business.

The intensification of television's power could be measured in many ways. In 1981, a new cable channel called MTV (for Music Television) began airing videos of popular music stars performing their work. The intent was to boost sales of the stars' audio recordings, but the music video soon became a new art form in itself. MTV redefined popular music by placing as much emphasis on image as on sound, and it revived dance as a popular performance art as well. Artists who best exploited music video, such as Madonna and Michael Jackson, achieved international superstar status. MTV also helped transform smaller, cult musical forms, such as rap and heavy metal, into giant mass-market phenomena. MTV pioneered an imaginative visual style, featuring rapid cutting, animation, and the sophisticated fusion of sound and image. Television producers, filmmakers, advertisers, and political consultants quickly adapted MTV techniques to just about every kind of image making.

More than ever, television drove the key strategies and tactics defining American political life. Politicians and their advisers focused intently on a candidate's television image. Issues, positions, and debate all paled alongside the key question: How did it look on television? In the 1992 campaign Clinton, Bush, and Perot appeared frequently on call-in television and radio talk shows in an effort to circumvent the power of professional journalists and connect more directly with voters. As the first baby-boomer candidate, the forty-six-year-old Clinton made a special effort to reach younger voters by appearing on MTV and youth-oriented programs. Fewer citizens voted or took an active role in campaigns, and most relied on television coverage to make their choices. Thus creating an effective television "character" emerged as perhaps the most crucial form of political discourse.

Perhaps no aspect of the electronics culture was more revolutionary than the creation of cyberspace, the conceptual region occupied by people linked through computers and communications networks. It began with ARPANET, the first computer network,

which was created by the Department of Defense in the early 1970s. Computer enthusiasts known as "hackers" created unexpected grass-roots spinoffs from ARPANET, including electronic mail, computer conferencing, and computer bulletin board systems. In the mid-1980s the boom in cheap personal computers capable of linking to the worldwide telecommunications network began a population explosion in cyberspace. By then, tens of thousands of researchers and scholars at universities and in private industry were linked to the Internet—the U.S. government-sponsored successor to ARPANET—through their institutions' computer centers. The establishment of the World Wide Web and easy-to-use browser software such as Netscape, introduced in 1994, made the "information highway" accessible to millions of Americans with few computer skills and created a popular communications medium with global dimensions.

By the beginning of the new century, the Census Bureau estimated that more than half of all households had at least one computer and more than 40 percent were connected to the Internet. Nearly 85 percent of classrooms in public schools were online. At work, Americans spent an average of 21 hours per week on line. At home, they spent an average of 9.5 hours per week online, gaining access to the Web from independent service providers such as America Online and Earthlink. For a flat monthly fee users could play games, send electronic mail, discuss issues in public forums, and purchase a huge array of goods and services, ranging from books and airline tickets to automobiles and psychotherapy sessions. The Web enticed millions with its advertising and spawned a new system of gambling— "day trading" on the stock market by individuals with relatively little money to spend. By 1998 there were some 320 million websites in the United States, repre-

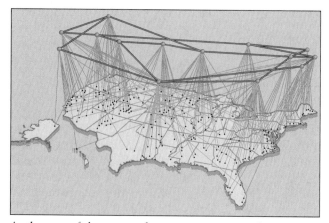

At the turn of the twenty-first century, more and more Americans were finding—and inventing—versions of community on the electronic frontier of cyberspace.

senting everything from large corporations to fringe political groups to personal "home pages."

These new information technologies gave birth to a media community that transcended national boundaries. During the 1980s, exports from Hollywood to the rest of the world doubled in value. The number of hours of television watched throughout the world nearly tripled. MTV was broadcast to an estimated 250 million households throughout the world. By the mid-1990s there were more television sets in China than in the United States. The growth of cable was phenomenal; in the Netherlands, for example, 98 percent of households received programming by cable.

Meanwhile, the ownership of media corporations became increasingly concentrated. Internationally, the News Corporation, established by the Australian Rupert Murdoch, had become a major force by the 1980s, working in nine different media on six continents. Murdoch's empire reached far into the United States. The News Corporation owned many local newspapers and broadcasting networks, such as Fox, and television stations covering more than 40 percent of TV households in the United States. Americans, however, owned a disproportionate share of the largest media corporations in the world, with Microsoft, Disney, and Time Warner in the lead. More than 40 percent of television programs in the world originated in the United States, and in Latin America the percentage of U.S.–produced programs reached 75 percent.

The New Immigrants and Their Communities

The 2000 census showed that the nation's population during the 1990s grew by 32.7 million, a number greater than that of any other decade in U.S. history. Even the 1950s, which witnessed the post–World War II baby boom, could not compete against a decade marked by a huge number of immigrants and a birthrate that surpassed the death rate. At the beginning of the new millennium, Americans numbered 281.4 million. Reflecting the economic boom of the 1990s, the data also indicated a sizable improvement in the standard of living: gains in education, housing, and mobility, and substantial increases in household income.

The 2000 census confirmed what many Americans had observed over the previous decade in their communities and work places. The face of the nation was perceptibly changing and changing on a scale that compared to the first decades of the twentieth century, when immigration from Europe peaked. At the turn of the twenty-first century, more than a third of the nation's population growth came from the influx of new immigrants. Although three-quarters of the newcomers joined many other Americans in flocking to the Sunbelt states, headed by California, Texas, and Florida, they

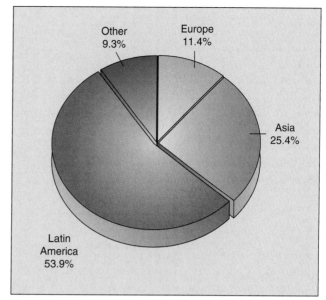

Continent of Birth for Immigrants, 1990–2000
By 2000, the number of foreign-born residents and their children—56 million according to the Census Bureau—had reached the highest level in U.S. history.

not only helped to reverse population loss in such major urban centers as New York and Chicago and slow the decline in Rustbelt cities like Cleveland, Detroit, and Milwaukee, but also for the first time in any census, they played a major role in the population increase in all fifty states. California surpassed all other states in the percent of foreign-born residents. Whereas nationally, the percentage of Americans born outside the United States was 11.2 percent, its highest point since 1930, in California the percentage of foreign born approached 26 percent.

The Immigration Act of 1965, passed almost unnoticed in the context of the egalitarian political climate created by the civil rights movement, had revolutionary consequences, some of them unintended. The act abolished the discriminatory national origins quotas that had been in place since the 1920s. It also limited immigration from the Western Hemisphere for the first time, while giving preferences to people from the nations of the Eastern Hemisphere who had specialized job skills and training. This provision created the conditions for Asian immigrants to become the fasting growing ethnic group in the United States. But in setting limits on Western Hemisphere immigration, the 1965 act tempted many thousands of people from Latin American to enter the United States illegally. By the mid-1980s, growing concern over "illegal aliens" had become a hotly debated political issue, particularly in the Southwest. The Immigration Reform and Control Act of 1986 marked a break with the past attempts to address this problem. Instead of mass deportation programs, the law offered an amnesty to all undocumented workers who had entered the country since 1982. Four years later, additional revisions of this act enlarged the quota of immigrants, once again giving priority to skilled and professional workers. Hispanics and Asians benefited from these changes in immigration law. Within the twenty fastest-growing cities, the number of Hispanics and Asians increased by approximately 70 percent. In contrast, the number of African Americans grew by less than 25 percent and whites by a mere 5 percent. In a dozen large cities, whites became a minority population for the first time.

Demographers predicted that Hispanics, who had grown from 22.4 million in 1990 to 35.3 million in 2000, according to census data, would replace African Americans as the largest minority group in the nation by the middle of the twenty-first century. By 1990 Hispanics had already formed over a third of the population of New Mexico, a quarter of the population of Texas, and over 10 percent of the populations of California, Arizona, and Colorado. Nearly a million Mexican Americans lived in Los Angeles alone.

Hispanic immigration played a large role in shifting the average age of the population. By end of the twentieth century, Americans as a group were gradually aging due to the population bulge caused by baby boomers born between 1945 and 1960. However, the population under the age of eighteen now accounted for nearly 26 percent of the total. Nearly a third of Hispanics were under age eighteen, representing the largest proportion in any major group. In areas of southern and western Texas and large parts of southern California, Hispanics made up nearly half of all the under-eighteen population.

The 2000 census showed that Mexicans were the largest Hispanic group in the United States, at 20.6 million and representing nearly 60 percent of the total Hispanic population. The boom of the U.S. economy in the 1990s, with service, agricultural, and even factory jobs readily available, had provided a significant "pull" for these newcomers. But other factors encouraged many immigrants to make an often difficult and dangerous sojourn. First, a drop in worldwide oil prices followed by the deflation of the Mexican national currency dramatically lowered living standards in Mexico in the mid-1990s. The North American Free Trade Agreement (NAFTA) and the greater integration of the U.S. and Mexican economies brought new jobs but often with increasingly expensive living conditions. Tens and perhaps hundreds of thousands of Mexicans worked in the United States temporarily while planning a permanent move north, with or without legal documentation. By 2001, the government of Mexico estimated that as many as 3 million of its citizens were living illegally in the United States.

According to the 2000 Census, Hispanics were the nation's largest minority group among those 17 and younger. They represented a generation of nearly 12.3 million, the majority living in California and the Southwest.

SOURCE: Photograph by Jose L. Pelaez. Corbis/Stock Market (0-067-0130).

After settling across the border, most new Mexican Americans struggled in low-wage and often dangerous jobs such as meatpacking or construction, and they were more likely to die from work place injuries than other workers. Through education and success in business, a significant number achieved middle-class status and wealth. But almost 20 percent of Mexican Americans lived below the poverty line. They tended to live in segregated neighborhoods and were less likely than non-Hispanic whites to have health insurance or to own their own homes.

Metropolitan New York became a showcase for the new Hispanic immigration. Since the 1920s, Puerto Ricans, as the third largest group of immigrants to the U.S. mainland from the Western Hemisphere, had dominated the Spanish-speaking communities, concentrating especially in "Spanish Harlem" and in sections of the Bronx. Puerto Ricans were a special case because, as U.S. citizens since 1917, they could come and go without restrictions. Between 1945 and 1965, the Puerto

Rican–born population jumped from 100,000 to roughly 1 million. However, during the 1990s, this trend had begun to reverse, their numbers falling by 12 percent. The smaller but highly influential Cuban population declined even more, by 27 percent. Meanwhile, other Latin populations grew at an extraordinary rate of 50 percent. The Mexican-born population more than doubled, and Filipinos, who often speak Spanish as a first language, increased by 27 percent. Immigrants from the Dominican Republic, now second in population size only to Puerto Ricans, dominated sizable sections of Washington Heights and Brooklyn, while immigrants from various countries in Central and South American created new communities throughout the greater metropolitan region.

The cultural implications for all Americans, not just new New Yorkers, were far-reaching. Children born to the new immigrants of the 1980s and 1990s, despite increasing neighborhood segregation by race, played on the streets together, attended the same schools and often married outside their racial group. In the 2000 census, 6.8 million Americans nationwide listed themselves as multiracial. Identities blurred as popular entertainment created new mixes of traditions and styles. "World beat" music (heavily influenced by "Afro-Pop"), *Alternalationo* (alternative Latin music—a mixture of salsa and merenge), Tjano, Reggae, and other music in fusion mixtures became as common to Manhattan or Los Angeles as to Mexico City or Rio. By the 1990s, the West Indian carnival held annually in Brooklyn at the end of summer had become the most popular ethnic festival in Greater New York City.

Although smaller in number than Hispanics, Asians were the fasting-growing racial group in the United States. The number of Asian Americans soared from 7.3 million in 1990 to approximately 10.2 million in 2000. With a steady flow of professionals and workers skilled in technology into their communities, Chinese Americans maintained their status as the largest Asian ethnicity in the United States. However, other groups grew at faster rates, particularly Indo Americans (from the subcontinent of India), whose numbers doubled during the 1990s to 1.68 million to become the third-largest Asian group. Meanwhile Japanese Americans, once the largest and most influential members of the pan-Asian community, declined. Immigration from Japan had virtually ceased during the decade, while many young Japanese Americans married someone of a different race.

Like earlier immigrant groups, new Americans from Korea, Vietnam, and the Philippines tended to cluster in their own communities and maintain a durable group identity. As a whole, Asian Americans made mobility through education a priority, along with pooling family capital and labor to support small businesses. Newcomers selected communities with job

opportunities or where family members and friends had settled previously. This "chain migration" is illustrated by the large numbers of Hmongs, a tribal group from Laos, living in Minneapolis and St. Paul. The stream of Hmongs began with church-sponsored refugee programs, then gained momentum as more and more family members followed. As one of the nation's leading states in the resettlement of refugees, Minnesota saw its total Asian population triple, increasing during the 1980s from 26,000 to 78,000, and then nearly doubling in the next decade. A similar story could be told about Franklin Country, Ohio, where the Asian and Pacific Island population grew by more than 47 percent in the 1990s. Although the community was small, representing less than 3 percent of the overall

Hmong-origin immigrants were among the fastest growing Asian groups in the United States in the 1990s. In Minnesota, they were the leading Asian group coming to the state. The Hmong brought traditional clothing as well as entertainments, food, and sports and established more than 400 businesses in the Minneapolis-St. Paul region.

SOURCE: Photograph by The Merced Sun-Star. AP/Wide World Photos (6090567).

population, Asians were the fasting-growing minority group in the county. Like previous generations of immigrants, they sought opportunities, hoping to secure employment in nearby automobile factories or education at the Ohio State University in Columbus.

A NEW AGE OF ANXIETY

Despite the prosperity of the 1990s, many Americans experienced an uneasiness that resembled the anxiety of mid-twentieth century, when the world seemed on the brink of nuclear destruction. The threat of communism had expired along with the cold war, but doubts and fears about the fate of their own society had multiplied. So many changes had occurred in just the last three decades of the century that a sense of permanence had disappeared. The new economy had transformed the way Americans worked and played. The new wave of immigration had dramatically altered the demographic landscape. Even the way the nation's leaders conducted themselves appeared not only new but potentially hazardous to the moral order. In addition, many Americans had begun to fear for their personal safety, even within their own communities. Perhaps most disturbing was the lack of consensus on the meaning of these changes.

There were indications that Americans were sharply divided. The 2000 census indicated that although the poverty rate had dropped to 11.3 percent of the population, near the lowest level ever recorded, nevertheless approximately 31.1 million people still lived in poverty. Moreover, the new economy had done little to close the gap between the highest and lowest income earners, which remained at a post–World War II high. Women as a group made few gains, earning 73 cents to each dollar earned by men. And with African Americans and Latinos continuing to earn, on average, far less than non-Hispanic whites, race relations benefited little from the economic boom of the 1990s.

The Racial Divide

In the spring of 1992 an upheaval in Los Angeles offered the starkest evidence that racial tensions had not eased. The spark that ignited the worst riot of the century was outrage over police brutality. A year earlier, Rodney King, a black motorist, had been pulled from his vehicle and severely beaten by four white police officers. An amateur videotape of the incident was widely aired on television newshows. When, despite this graphic evidence, a jury acquitted the officers of all but one of eleven counts of assault, several minority communities erupted in anger. Rioters swept through South Central Los Angeles and nearby Koreatown, looting and burning businesses. Fifty-one people were killed, more

than $850 million in damage was reported, and about 500 buildings were destroyed before L.A. police and National Guard troops restored order. Approximately 12,000 people, 45 percent Latino and 41 percent African American, were arrested for looting, arson, and violations of curfew.

More than a quarter-century after the uprising in Watts, the situation in Los Angeles seemed more desperate than ever to most African Americans. The poverty rate in South Los Angeles was 30.3 percent, more than twice the national average. The unemployment rate for adult black males hovered around 40 percent, and a quarter of the population was on welfare. Los Angeles had lost 100,000 manufacturing jobs in the three years before the riot. The passage of a statewide tax cut in 1978 had led to a sharp reduction in public investment in the inner-city educational system. Drug dealing and gang warfare had escalated, reflecting the sense of despair among young people.

The events in Los Angeles exposed the deep animosity among various groups—so much so that the observers referred to the event as a "multicultural riot." Almost 2,000 Korean businesses were destroyed, and Koreans angrily accused the police of making no effort to defend their stores. The division was sharpest, though, between whites and the minority populations. "We are all quite isolated in our own communities," a resident of Westwood, a mostly white middle-class neighborhood, explained. "We don't know and don't care about the problems in the inner cities. Driving to work every day most of us don't even know where South Central is—except many of us saw the fires from that direction when we were stuck in traffic."

The situation in Los Angeles was not unique. The 2000 census showed that segregation was on the rise, and not only in cities but in their surrounding suburbs. For example, in the Atlanta region, which claimed the largest share of black suburbanites in the nation (26 percent), the percent living separately from whites had increased from 52 percent in 1990 to nearly 60 percent by 2000. Similarly, in the nation's schools, the gains from the civil rights era were diminishing and, in some communities, disappearing altogether. A report released in 2001 showed that, despite the increasing racial and ethnic diversity of nation's youth, segregation was becoming more pronounced in grades K–12. Approximately 70 percent of African American children were attending predominantly minority schools, up from 60 percent ten years earlier. The states with the most segregated schools were all in the North, with New York ranking first, followed by Michigan, Illinois, and California.

The widening racial divide also showed itself during the highly publicized trial of celebrity athlete O. J. Simpson, who was accused of brutally murdering Nicole Brown Simpson, his ex-wife, and Ronald Goldman, an acquaintance. Dubbed by the media the "Trial of the Century," the nationally televised proceedings, which lasted 133 days, provided a forum for commentary on race relations in the United States. From the beginning of the trial in January 1995 to the jury's acquittal of the ex-football star and media personality, opinions were polarized. In the end, far more blacks than whites agreed with the verdict.

The publicity generated by the arrests of Rodney King and O. J. Simpson fed several major controversies concerning the U.S. criminal justice system. In 1999 the Bureau of Justice reported that 6.3 million people were on probation, in jail or prison, or on parole, representing 3.1 percent of all adult residents. Incarceration rates, highest in the southern states of Louisiana, Texas, and Mississippi, showed a slight decline in early 2000 but nevertheless had more than tripled since 1980. Racial disparities were pronounced, with ethnic and racial minorities accounting for approximately two-thirds of state prison inmates. Based on these figures, the Bureau of Justice estimated that 28 percent of African American men would enter a state or federal prison during their lifetimes.

Various civil liberties groups reviewed these statistics and concluded that African Americans were not necessarily more prone to criminal activity but were far more likely to be stopped, searched, arrested, convicted, and given harsher penalties than white Americans. They attributed the recent rise in rates to changes in law enforcement policies dating to the Reagan administration's War on Drugs, which led to a tripling of nationwide arrests for drug offenses and accounted for one-third of all federal criminal cases by the end of the century. Critics singled out the practice of "racial profiling" whereby police disportionately stopped African Americans and Latinos as the most likely offenders. Although reports issued by the federal government at the time estimated that 80 percent of cocaine users in the United States were white and typically middle-class, the new law enforcement guidelines resulted in a significant increase in the proportion of African Americans among drug arrestees, from 25 percent in 1980 to 37 percent in 1995. By the end of the decade, in a review of various data nationwide, the National Institute of Drug Abuse estimated that although 12 percent of illegal drug users were black, they now made up 50 percent of all drug possession arrestees. By this time, "driving while black" had become a news item in all the major media, leading to the introduction of a bill into the U.S. Senate in 1999 to collect statistics on traffic stops.

The Forces of Fear

During the 1990s and first years of the new century, anxiety about terrorism and random violence escalated until the catastrophic September 11, 2001, suicide

attack on the World Trade Center and the Pentagon seemed to justify all such fears. According to the CIA, incidents of international terrorism had been declining in number since the 1980s, but the drama and scale of terrorist events since then has suggested otherwise.

On December 21, 1988, Americans responded in horror to the news that a Pam Am plane en route to New York had exploded 31,000 feet over Lockerbie, Scotland, killing all 259 people aboard, including thirty-five college students returning from a Syracuse University overseas study program. This tragedy, later attributed to a bomb planted by two Libyan terrorists, became one in a series that placed Americans at risk in travel abroad.

Within their own borders, Americans were actually far safer from terrorist attacks than the citizens of many other countries. Nevertheless, two events—the attack on the World Trade Center 1993 and the destruction of the federal building in Oklahoma City in 1995—alerted Americans to danger at home.

On February 26, 1993, a small group associated with Osama bin Laden bombed the World Trade Center in New York City. The terrorists used a rented van to deliver explosives that demolished an underground parking lot, killed six people, and injured more than a thousand others. Taken in retaliation for U.S. policies in the Middle East, the attack was the most destructive act of terrorism committed within the United States to that time. It spurred the Antiterrorism and Effective Death Penalty Act of 1996, which greatly expanded the budget and powers of federal authorities to monitor likely terrorists. Despite increased surveillance of terrorist groups, bin Laden's organization struck another lethal blow. On August 7, 1998, car bombings of U.S. embassies in Nairobi, Kenya, and Dar es Salaam, Tanzania, injured more than 5,500 people and killed 225.

The bombing of the Alfred P. Murrah Federal Building in Oklahoma City raised an entirely different specter: terrorism by self-described patriotic Americans. The perpetrators represented the extremist wing of the New Right, the superpatriot movement, which included groups of people who set up "survivalist" encampments in rural areas and organized themselves into armed militias. Inspired by author William Pierce's *Turner Diaries* (1978), which predicted a revolt of "Aryans" against people of color and the federal government, the patriots found their martyrs in the Branch Davidians and their revenge in Oklahoma.

Two years earlier, on February 28, 1993, agents of the FBI and the Federal Bureau of Alcohol, Tobacco, and Firearms (ATF) had conducted a "search and arrest" operation against the Branch Davidians that turned deadly. Their object was David Koresh, the leader of the obscure religious sect who was suspected of stockpiling illegal firearms and ammunition. After a round of shots, which took the lives of four ATF agents and

Rescue workers carried an injured man from the ruble of the U.S. Embassy in Nairobi, Kenya. A terrorist bomb killed more than 100 people and injured more than 1,600 on August 8, 1998.

SOURCE: © AFP/CORBIS (FT0047338).

six Branch Davidians, Koresh's heavily armed followers barricaded themselves in their compound in Waco, Texas. Fifty-one days later, on April 19, government agents brought their siege to a fiery end. Nine Davidians managed to escape the flames engulfing their buildings, while seventy-six others, including twenty-one children, perished.

Many Americans registered their disapproval of the government's actions and their skepticism of the official accounts that assigned blame for the lethal fire to the Davidians themselves. The National Rifle Association, with 3.5 million members, likened AFT and FBI agents to Hitler's storm troopers, who squashed the rights of ordinary citizens. Right-wing paramilitarists vowed revenge. Less than a year later, at a paramilitarist demonstration near the compound, patriot Timothy McVeigh was photographed distributing bumper stickers reading, "Is Your Church AFT-Approved?"

On April 19, 1995, McVeigh and his accomplices took revenge for the tragedy in Waco. Shortly after 9:00 A.M., a bomb went off in the federal office building in Oklahoma City, killing 168 people, including 19 children, and injuring more than 500 others. People living forty miles away felt the impact of the explosion that demolished the nine-story structure in a matter of seconds. Although early news reports pointed to Islamic terrorists, the perpetrators were McVeigh, Terry Nichols, and his brother James Nichols. They had chosen April 19, the anniversary of the federal raid

at Waco, as their "Date of Doom." Arrested within hours of the bombing on a misdemeanor traffic violation, McVeigh was charged in connection with the crime just three days later. After a trial in federal court and demonstrations both for and against the death penalty, he was executed in June 2001.

Immediately after the Oklahoma City bombing, President Clinton declared a national day of mourning for the victims and their families. He addressed the nation, saying "Let us let our own children know that we will stand against the forces of fear. When there is talk of hatred, let us stand up and talk against it. When there is talk of violence, let us stand up and talk against it."

But terrorism continued, with many of the attacks politically or ideologically motivated. For example, medical clinics that provided abortion services to women became a prime target. Although the ratio of abortions to live pregnancies had been declining since 1979, groups opposed to abortion became more belligerent, emphasizing civil disobedience in addition to legal lobbying in order to promote legislation to restrict access to abortion. In 1991, Operation Rescue launched a well-publicized and illegal blockade of three abortion clinics in Wichita, Kansas. Although the "war in Wichita" ended peacefully after forty-six days, antiabortion protests became increasingly violent in its wake. Several medical providers were murdered outside their clinics, including Dr. David Gunn, who was killed by a member of the antiabortion group Rescue America in Pensacola, Florida, in March 1993. In 1994, with the support of President Clinton, Congress enacted the Freedom of Access to Clinic Entrance Act, which provides protection to any abortion clinic requesting it. Although the number of violent incidents declined since the peak of nineteen bombings in 1992 and forty-two murders in 1994, with California leading the nation in the the number of clinics torched and bombed, the attacks did not stop. In 1997, an off-duty police officer died in a bombing of an Atlanta clinic, and by the end of the century arson attacks alone reached nearly 200.

Often, the motivation for acts of domestic terror eluded even experts on the subject. Workers suspended from their jobs, fathers separated from their children, as well as individuals with grudges against the government turned to violence. One of the most highly publicized cases occurred in Littleton, Colorado, a mostly white, middle-class suburb of Denver. On April 20, 1999, two students at Columbine High School, armed with semi-automatic handguns, shotguns, and explosives, opened fire, killing one teacher and twelve of their classmates before killing themselves. Although homicides by young people age seventeen or younger declined by nearly a third in the 1990s, school killings increased. Just one month later, a teenager in Springfield, Oregon, killed his parents and then aimed fire on forty-two of his classmates, killing two.

The Culture Wars

In the 1980s and 1990s, moral and social issues, many observers noted, were replacing long-standing political markers such as religion, ethnicity, and socioeconomic class. Whereas the "New Democrats" of Clinton's administration and conservative Republicans differed little on their perception of the appropriate size and power of the federal government, they were at loggerheads over what constituted American values. Thus what one scholar described as "the struggle to define America" became hotly contested in the 1990s, with politics increasingly centered in discussions about reproductive rights and reproductive technology, homosexuality and gay rights, the curriculum in public schools, codes of speech and standards in the arts, gun control, and scientific developments such as cloning, genetic alteration, and fetal tissue research, and even the validity of Darwin's theory of evolution. With conservative radio talk-show hosts such as Rush Limbaugh and "Doctor" Laura Schlessinger firing debate on public morality, Americans became deeply divided on these and other issues.

The increasing racial and ethnic diversity of American society, as well as the expansion of rights for groups such as women and gays, had become the impetus for a broad and controversial movement known as "multiculturalism." Unlike earlier conceptions of America as a "melting pot," new metaphors such as "salad bowl" or "mosaic" became popular expressions that emphasized the unique attributes and achievements of formerly marginal groups and recent immigrants. This celebration of diversity played a big part in the campaign strategy of Bill Clinton, and he won a large share of votes by tailoring his appeals to specific groups. Like other Democrats, he received upward of 80 percent of black votes, but he won more votes from Latinos and Asian Americans than any other candidate in American history. On college campuses, multiculturalism marked the high point of the curricular reform that had been ongoing since the late 1960s and early 1970s, when specialized programs in women's studies and African American studies were launched (see Chapter 29). At the secondary level, several state legislatures and boards of education mandated instruction that would encourage students to appreciate cultural diversity.

For many conservatives, multiculturalism had replaced communism as the nation's most dangerous enemy, and they rallied to reinstate what they called universal truths and traditional moral values. University of Chicago professor Allan Bloom's best-selling *The Closing of the American Mind* (1987), for example, argued that the new lesson plans failed to prepare Americans for the responsibility of preserving their democratic legacy. In 1992, Florida conservatives contested the new legislative reforms, insisting that lessons on diversity be accompanied by instruction in the "greatness of America," including the notion that American culture is "superior to all other cultures, past and present."

The culture wars were not restricted to the academic world. Americans divided sharply over many issues, including immigration policy. In 1994, a referendum on California's ballot, Proposition 187, called for making all undocumented aliens ineligible for any welfare services, schooling, and nonemergency medical care, and it required teachers and clinic doctors to report illegal immigrants to the police. Proponents such as Republican Governor Pete Wilson argued that illegals created a crushing burden on state and local welfare agencies and school systems. They also hoped the measure would force federal action to stem the flow of illegals. A spokesman for Americans Against Illegal Immigration, a pro-Proposition 187 Southern California group, asserted, "Enough is enough. We're going broke in this state. . . . It's insanity, it doesn't make sense and the average guy in this country is not going to buy into it anymore."

Proposition 187 passed by a three to two margin, but it was immediately challenged in the streets and in the courts. In Los Angeles, more than 70,000 people marched to protest its passage and the city council voted not to enforce it. In 1998, after several years of legal wrangling, a Los Angeles federal district court judge ruled that Proposition 187 unconstitutionally usurped federal authority over immigration policy. In June 2001, the U.S. Supreme Court ruled that immigrants are entitled to same protection by the Constitution as that afforded to citizens.

But the national debate over immigration policy, in which economic issues and racial fears were deeply entangled, continued unabated in California and elsewhere. As one Stanford law professor who had worked to overturn Proposition 187 put it: "Some people genuinely worry about the problem of too many immigrants in a stagnant economy. But for most, economics is a diversion. Underneath it is race." California voters also upheld legislation enacted in 1996 that banned the consideration of race, ethnicity, and gender in college admissions and public employment, and thereby

After the University of California regents voted to end the affirmative action policy governing admissions to the state-wide system, students at the University of California-Irvine protested outside the campus administrations building in October, 1995.

SOURCE: AP/Wide World Photos (000615).

abolished the affirmative-action programs established thirty years earlier.

A similar backlash gathered steam against women and gays. First Lady Hillary Rodham Clinton became the target of sustained attack for redefining and enlarging the role of the president's spouse. She led a failed campaign for reform of health care during her husband's first term, remained a vocal political adviser throughout his presidency, and became the first first lady to run for elective office. Many Americans, especially women, admired her for taking strong stands; others villified her for moving too far beyond the helpmeet role. To conservatives, Hillary Rodham Clinton symbolized the erosion of traditional American values in her support of pay equity, day-care centers, and reproductive rights.

A major controversy erupted around a push for the legal recognition of marriage for same-sex couples. Although the first law suits dated to the early 1970s, in May 1993 the Supreme Court of Hawai`i ruled that the laws barring same-sex couples from getting a marriage license were discriminatory and therefore in violation of the state constitution. This highly controversial decision prompted conservative state legislators to propose an amendment to the state constitution barring same-sex marriages, which the Hawai`ian voters overwhelmingly approved in 1998. Meanwhile, several Republicans in the U.S. Congress, fearing that if any state recognized same-sex marriages all other states would be forced to recognize these marriages as legal, sponsored legislation to deny recognition to these

unions. In 1996, President Clinton signed the Defense of Marriage Act, which specified that gay couples would be ineligible for spousal benefits provided by federal law. By the end of the century, more than thirty states had enacted similar legislation. Vermont, however, stood alone, becoming the first state to recognize civil unions, allowing same-sex couples to receive many, although not all, of the legal benefits of marriage. One year after approving "civil unions" for same-sex couples, Vermont legislators clarified by law by banning "marriage" between members of the same sex.

In other parts of the country, local laws that prohibited bias in employment or housing on the basis of sexual orientation were overturned. In 1992, a conservative group called Colorado for Family Values pushed a referendum to enact an amendment to the state constitution that would annul all gay-rights ordinances. To the surprise of many liberal political observers, the amendment passed easily, winning a majority of votes in fifty-two of sixty-three counties in Colorado. But, in May 1996, the amendment was ruled unconstitutional by the U.S. Supreme Court.

At the end of the century, the antiabortion movement took a new turn by opposing government financing of an area of scientific research that had been growing in importance since the birth of the first test-tube baby in 1981—embryonic stem cell research. Because these microscopic clusters of cells have the potential to grow into any tissue in the body, embryonic stems cells hold promise, scientists believe, for refurbishing or replacing damaged tissues or organs and therefore might prove useful in treating or perhaps even curing diseases such as diabetes, Parkinson's, and Alzheimer's. Conservatives opposed this research because it involves the destruction of human embryos, usually derived from the excess products of *in vitro* fertilization processes and scheduled for disposal by fertility clinics. In 1995, in response to pressure from conservatives groups such as the National Right to Life Committee, Congress enacted legislation banning the use of federal funds for research that involves the destruction of human embryos. However, in his last year in office, Clinton loosened the ban and thereby generated another round of controversy. Most conservative groups remained firm in their opposition, agreeing with the United States Conference of Catholic Bishops, which insisted "that the government must not treat any living human being as research material, as a mere means for benefit to others."

Other areas of science were affected by the culture wars, including one of the most important at the end of the century: research in biological evolution. The Creation Science Movement, which had been founded in 1932 by a small group of Christians, gained widespread support for their idea that the earth was created by a deity less than 10,000 years ago and that life forms had changed little since. Evolutionists, in contrast, contended that the universe came into being 10 to 20 billion years ago, the earth about 4.5 billion year ago, and that all life forms evolved from bacteria by natural rather than divine forces. A 1997 Gallup Poll showed that 44 percent of all adults in the United States sided with the creationists, while only 5 percent of scientists did. Although the National Standards in Education adopted in 1996 specified levels of understanding of evolutionary theory among the nation's school children, many parents resisted this mandate. The Kansas Board of Education, for example, no longer required the teaching evolution in public schools.

High Crimes and Misdemeanors

Questions of private and public morality dogged Bill Clinton's political career. During the 1992 election campaign, while intending to focus on the economy, he found himself offering explanations for past behavior, such as avoiding the draft during the Vietnam War and smoking—but "not inhaling," he claimed—marijuana during his college years. However, once in office, he acted boldly on reproductive rights and put forward a controversial "don't ask, don't tell" policy for gays in the armed forces. Conservatives, including such religious groups as the Christian Coalition, the American Family Association, and the Traditional Values Coalition, as well as many Republicans, struck back.

The culture wars heated up just in time for the 1994 election campaign, making race relations, immigration, and woman's rights "hot buttons" for political candidates. With attacks on welfare, affirmative action, and federal initiatives to aid education and the inner cities, conservatives exploited a continuing white backlash against the limited economic and political gains African Americans had achieved in the previous decades. No major candidates addressed the deepening poverty and economic inequality that put one of every seven Americans, and one of every five children, below the poverty line. However, the Republicans basked in their defeat of one of Clinton's major initiatives, health-care reform, reserving as their trump card an all-out attack on Clinton's character.

During the campaign, the Republicans targeted the key item in Clinton's liberal agenda, reform of the nation's health-care system. Nearly 40 million Americans had no health insurance at all. Many simply could not afford it, and others were denied coverage by private insurers because of preexisting conditions such as AIDS and heart disease. For millions of others, health insurance was tied to the work place; and a loss or change of jobs threatened their coverage. National spending on health care had skyrocketed from roughly $200 billion in 1980 to more than $800 billion in 1992, constituting about one-seventh of the entire domestic economy. Once in office, President Clinton appointed Hillary Rodham Clinton to head a task force charged with preparing a sweeping legislative overhaul of health care. The task force sought a political middle ground between conservative approaches, which stressed fine tuning the system by making private insurance available to all, and more liberal approaches, which would have the federal government guarantee health care as a right. Powerful forces such as the Chamber of Commerce, the National Association of Manufacturers, and most Republicans immediately attacked the proposal. The Health Insurance Association of America spent millions of dollars on negative advertisements. In August, as the 1994 election campaign moved into its final phase, the president conceded that his proposal had died in Congress.

Voter turnout was light in most areas, but the majority who voted turned firmly against Clinton. Republicans gained control of both the House and Senate for the first time in forty years—a disaster of historic proportions for Clinton and the Democratic Party. Congress was now dominated by a new breed of younger, ideologically more conservative Republicans led by the new House Speaker, Newt Gingrich of Georgia.

Gingrich, first elected to Congress in 1978, had quickly won a reputation as a formidable polemicist for the Republican Party's far right. "Sixties values," Gingrich declared, "cripple human beings, weaken cities, make it difficult for us to, in fact, survive as a country." With his scathing denunciations of big government and celebration of entrepreneurship, Gingrich challenged Clinton as the key figure setting the nation's political agenda. His priorities were expressed in a set of proposals labeled the "Contract with America." Invoking the "hundred days" of Franklin D. Roosevelt's New Deal in 1933 (see Chapter 24), Gingrich promised to bring all these proposals to a vote in the House within a hundred days. The House did indeed pass much of the "Contract", including a large tax cut, an increase in military spending, cutbacks in federal regulatory power in the environment and at the work place, a tough anticrime bill, and a sharp reduction in federal welfare programs.

After the 1994 midterm election gave Republicans control of the House of Representatives for the first time in forty years, the new speaker, Newt Gingrich of Georgia, presented a list of legislative initiatives to be completed within the first one hundred days of the new session. On April 7, 1995, he appeared at a rally on Capitol Hill to celebrate the success of the Republican's "Contract with America."

SOURCE: Photograph by John Duricka. AP/Wide World Photos.

Differences with the Senate, however, and the threat of presidential veto ultimately thwarted Gingrich's plans and created conditions that allowed President Clinton to make a political comeback. In December of 1995 the Republican-controlled Congress forced a shutdown of the federal government rather than accede to President Clinton's demand for changes in their proposed budget. The result was a public relations disaster for the Republicans. Gingrich's reputation plummeted, and after little more than a year as Speaker he had become one of the most unpopular figures in American politics.

Meanwhile, Clinton undercut the Republicans by adapting many of their positions to his own. He endorsed the goal of a balanced federal budget and declared, in his January 1996 State of the Union message, that "the era of big government is over." With such deft maneuvers, the president set the theme for his 1996 reelection campaign, portraying himself as a reasonable conservative and the Republicans in Congress as conservative radicals.

While the Republican contender, Robert Dole of Kansas, majority leader of the Senate, waged an inept campaign for president, Clinton and his staff crafted a brilliant and well-funded one. Confounding the predictions of the political pundits who had pronounced his political death, the president won a resounding reelection victory in November of 1996. He won 49 percent of the popular vote compared to Dole's 41 per-

cent, and carried thirty-three states. But it was a victory without coattails: the Republicans retained control of both houses of Congress. In his State of the Union address in 1997, Clinton backed yet further away from liberalism, promising a "new kind of government—not to solve all of our problems for us, but to give all our people the tools to make the most of their own lives." The era of big government may have ended, as the president proclaimed, but the era of divided government would continue.

During his second term as president, Clinton had to answer many questions about his moral conduct. Real estate deals involving both him and Hillary Rodham Clinton blew up into a major scandal known as Whitewater. More predictive of troubles ahead, a former Arkansas state employee, Paula Jones, charged Clinton with sexual assault during his gubernatorial term. Attorney General Janet Reno, under extreme pressure from conservatives, appointed an independent counsel, former judge Kenneth Starr, to investigate allegations. But in the summer of 1998, Starr delivered to the House Judiciary Committee a report focusing on an extramarital affair that the president conducted with a young White House intern, Monica Lewinsky. Starr's report outlined several potential impeachable offenses, including false testimony under oath, witness tampering, and obstruction of justice, all allegedly committed by the president to keep his relationship with Lewinsky secret.

After agreeing to testify before a grand jury empaneled by Starr—a first for an American president—Clinton made an extraordinary television address to the nation. He defended his legal position and attacked the Starr inquiry as politically motivated. The Congress and the American people at large fiercely debated the nature of the charges against the president: Were they truly impeachable—"high crimes and misdemeanors" as the Constitution put it—or merely part of a partisan political effort to overturn the election of 1996? For only the third time in history, in October 1998, the House of Representatives voted to open an inquiry into possible grounds for the impeachment.

Republicans hoping to reap a wholesale victory from the scandal in the fall elections were bitterly disappointed. Contrary to predictions and traditions in off-term elections, the president's party added seats, trimming the Republican majority in the 105th Congress.

Voters evidently had more on their minds than President Clinton's sex life. Democratic candidates benefited from continued strength in the economy, and they made effective appeals on a range of issues, from preserving Social Security and Medicare to protecting a woman's right to choose an abortion. Higher than expected turnout from such core constituencies as union members and African Americans (especially in the South) also contributed to the unexpectedly strong Democratic showing. The election also brought a shakeup in the Republican leadership. Newt Gingrich, under pressure from Republican colleagues angry about a campaign strategy that had narrowly focused on Clinton's impeachment problem, announced his resignation as Speaker of the House and from his seat in Congress. Ironically Gingrich, who had led the Republican resurgence in the 1990s, now appeared to be the first political victim of the Lewinsky scandal.

In the aftermath of the 1998 election, most politicians and analysts, and indeed most Americans, believed the impeachment inquiry to be at a dead end. But the House Judiciary Committee, after raucous televised debate, voted to bring four articles of impeachment—charging President Clinton with perjury, obstruction of justice, witness tampering, and abuse of power—to the full House. But unlike the bipartisan case the Judiciary Committee brought against Richard Nixon in 1974 (see Chapter 29), this time the votes were all along strictly party lines. Neither the 1998 election results, nor polls showing a large majority of Americans opposed to removing the president, curbed the Republican determination to push impeachment through the House and then on to the Senate for trial. On February 12, 1999, the Senate trial concluded with the president's acquittal.

ing as a persistent threat, as witnessed by yet another terrorist attack, the October 12, 2000, bombing of the USS *Cole* in Aden, Yemen, which cost the lives of seventeen American sailors. In this world of growing uncertainties, no one knew how a new Republican administration would respond to the enormous challenges accompanying the new millennium.

The Election of 2000

After a relatively dull campaign season, the 2000 election played out as high drama. Voters went to the polls as usual on election day, watched as late-night television newscasters projected a victory for the Democratic candidate, Clinton's vice president Al Gore, and then woke up the next morning to learn that perhaps the winner was not the vice president but his Republican opponent, Governor George W. Bush of Texas, son of former president George H. W. Bush. It was clear that Gore and his running mate, Connecticut Senator Joseph Lieberman, had won the popular vote, although by the closest margin since John F. Kennedy defeated Richard Nixon in 1961. In doubt was the number of votes in the Electoral College. At 2:15 A.M., the pollsters who had projected Gore as the winner changed their minds. The

THE NEW MILLENNIUM

At the beginning of the twenty-first century, citizens, politicians, and business and religious leaders had to rethink their basic assumptions about the American way of life. American society had become more stratified along lines of race and income. New immigrant groups, especially from Asia and Latin America, had changed the face of the nation's communities, schools, and work places. New media technologies had made cultural life more homogenized and caused the manipulation of image to become more crucial than ever to both politics and entertainment. The New Economy, service-oriented and high-tech, had fundamentally altered the way many Americans did business and earned a livelihood, and it depended not only on American consumers heavily burdened with debt but also on an expanding global market.

The end of the cold war had reconfigured global politics, ending the bilateralism that had dominated international affairs since the end of World War II. The United States alone held fast to its superpower status, but this achievement did not necessarily make Americans more secure or safe. The old enemy, Soviet communism, was succeeded by more fanatic, less predictable foes. It was clear that international terrorism was emerg-

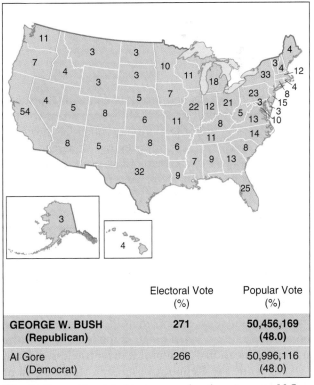

	Electoral Vote (%)	Popular Vote (%)
GEORGE W. BUSH (Republican)	**271**	**50,456,169 (48.0)**
Al Gore (Democrat)	266	50,996,116 (48.0)

The 2000 presidential election was the closest one in U.S. history and the first one to be decided by a decision of the Supreme Court.

An election official examined a disputed punch-card ballot in the Presidential election in Florida in November 2001. He tried to figure out whether the "chad" had been dislodged or merely "dimpled."

SOURCE: © Reuters NewMedia Inc./CORBIS (UT0055362).

cliffhanger in Florida had finally ended with the state's decisive twenty-five electoral votes earmarked for the Republicans. By morning Gore had called Bush to concede. The *New York Times*, however, ran a guarded headline "Bush Appears to Defeat Gore." Only a few hundred votes in Florida gave Bush the edge, and in cases where the margin is so narrow Florida law mandates a machine recount in all sixty-seven counties. Gore soon retracted his concession, putting voters into suspense until the middle of December, when the vice president finally ended his campaign.

Such a spectacular ending to the 2000 campaign could not have been foreseen from the primaries. As the son of a former president, George W. Bush had run a low-key campaign, calling himself a "compassionate conservative" who cared about the underdog and the nation's educational system. He nevertheless did not swerve from the Republican agenda that President Reagan had shaped: tax cuts, strong military defense, and the overhaul of Social Security and Medicare. He also promised relief from environmental regulations,

new judicial appointments that would eventually limit reproductive rights, and the restoration of morality to public life. Albert Gore, Jr., also the son of a prominent politician, carried the burden of association with Bill Clinton and waged an uphill battle. More notable was his running mate, Lieberman, the first Jewish candidate for vice president. Dick Cheney, who had served prominently in the senior Bush's administration, balanced the younger Bush's relative lack of experience in federal government. The emergence of consumer advocate Ralph Nader as Green Party candidate added spice to an often dull campaign.

In November, voters themselves offered few surprises except for a round of congressional defeats for Republicans. Republicans lost ground in both the House of Representatives, where their majority fell to a dozen, and in the Senate, where Democrats and Republicans stood in equal numbers until James Jeffords of Vermont ended the stalemate by quitting the Republican Party early in the new Congress. The one major surprise was the unanticipated victory of Hillary Rodham Clinton, who beat her Republican opponent by a twelve-point margin for a seat in the U.S. Senate from the state of New York.

The 2000 campaign played out as the first disputed presidential election since 1876, when Democrat Samuel J. Tilden, who won the popular vote, charged his Republican opponent, Rutherford B. Hayes, with fraudulent vote counting. The decision went to a congressional committee which, acting strictly along party lines, gave the presidency to "Rutherfraud" B. Hayes, as he was dubbed by opponents. A similar question of legitimacy hung over the 2000 election. After Florida completed its machine recount of votes, the Democrats requested a hand tally in selected counties where the ballots were in dispute. The Republicans responded by suing in the Miami district court to prohibit the manual recounting. Meanwhile Florida election officials, mainly Republicans, set November 14 as the date to certify the election results, thereby disallowing the returns on overseas ballots which might favor Al Gore. In turn, Democrats sued to extend the deadline. Eventually, appeals by both parties reached the Florida Supreme Court and finally the U.S. Supreme Court, which voted five to four along partisan lines to halt the counting. Time had run out, and on December 12 Gore conceded defeat. With less fanfare than usual, George W. Bush took the oath of office in January 2001.

Global Warming

Bush took office without a clear agenda and for the first few months continued some of his predecessor's policies. For example, he ultimately relented on his campaign promise to prohibit federal spending on stem cell research. However, in managing the federal budget, Bush struck out on his own. Clinton, pressured by the rising deficit when he took office, did so well in curbing federal spending that he had produced a surplus. Bush immediately pushed for a new tax law that would reduce the budget surplus by $1.35 trillion over ten years with tax cuts allocated principally to wealthy Americans. With corporate profits and the economy slowing dramatically during the first months of the Bush administration, Congress approved substantial tax reductions with hope of stimulating the economy.

On policies concerning the environment, Bush acted quickly and aggressively to defer or to overturn several key programs established under Clinton. In July 2001, the Environmental Protection Agency announced a delay in asking states to draft plans to protect some 21,000 waterways severely impaired by agricultural runoff. Meanwhile, Bush's advisers reconsidered proposals that would have prohibited the development of nearly one-third of the national forests.

No issue was so important or so controversial as climate change, a challenge that most scientists and world leaders agreed required international solutions. During the late 1970s, scientists presented data indicating that the earth was warming, causing polar icecaps to melt, oceans to rise, and ultimately marine life to die, and they pointed to the emission of "greenhouse gases," the by-products of the fossil fuels burned to run factories and automobiles, as the main cause. To curb this dangerous trend, the United States, the European Economic Community, and twenty-eight other countries had ratified the Montreal Protocol on Substances that Deplete the Ozone Layer of 1987, which established a timetable for phasing out the production of greenhouse gases by the end of the century. However, a few years later, in June 1992, at the first Earth Summit sponsored by the United Nations, the U.S. delegates took a more cautious approach, demanding that limits on greenhouse gas emissions be voluntary rather than mandatory. Although responsible for the production of more greenhouse gases than any other nation, nearly 25 percent of the total worldwide, the United States now refused to make a firm commitment.

The controversy came to a head four years later at the world summit on global warming held in Kyoto, Japan. In advance of the meetings, the major U.S. automakers advised President Clinton against signing any treaty. Meanwhile Senate Republicans secured a nonbinding resolution that specified that the terms of any treaty require developing nations, including China, India, and Mexico, to control their emissions as well. Clinton sent Gore to Kyoto to find a middle ground. In the end, the Kyoto Protocol outlined targets and timetables for the reduction of greenhouse gases and required the richer, industrialized countries to take the lead, specifying an average 5.2 percent reduction from 1990s levels by 2012. Although the fifteen-member nations of the European Union endorsed the terms of the treaty, both Japan and the United States held out.

Shortly after taking office, President George W. Bush announced his opposition to the terms of the Kyoto Protocol, leaving 178 other countries to agree to mandatory reductions in greenhouse gases without the participation of the United States. Bush instead created a task force to conduct additional studies on the impact of human activity on climate change. Meanwhile, the U.S. Energy Information Administration released new data showing that carbon dioxide emissions had risen 3 percent in the United States during the previous year alone, one of the largest increases in recent times. In July 2001, 1,500 scientists affiliated with the UN Intergovernmental Panel on Climate Change, the leading authority on global warming, met in Amsterdam and confirmed, as a key member said, that "the problem of global change is real, and it is more serious than is currently perceived politically."

A Global Community?

The changing climate was only one issue tied to globalization, a term used to characterize the belief that worldwide processes were causing national economies, cultures, and borders to melt away. Beginning in the 1970s, social scientists began to study and debate the degree to which to which people throughout the world were affected by events happening far from their homelands. If nothing else, they pointed out, people in most parts of the world could keep up on these events by watching CNN or tapping into the Internet—and drink Coke while they were doing it. But the big questions concerning globalization centered on political economy. Now that communism has collapsed, they asked, would a steady expansion of free trade among nations create the basis for a global community?

There were many answers to this question. Some observers argued that the interpenetration of markets and cultural patterns—the enormous sales of Hollywood movies in China, for example—set the stage for other exchanges. President Clinton, for instance, contended that the expansion of the free market in China improved the prospects for democracy in that nation. Others argued that the global economy depended less on "interpenetration" than "domination" of the marketplace by the industrialized nations. Whereas physical occupation of territory defined the form of colonialism that prevailed before World War II, a new "colonialism" had come into existence since the 1960s that relied on a few multinational corporations controlling distant economies throughout the world. To back up this argument, they referred to a UN report that estimated that about 90 percent of the multinational corporations that did business worldwide were headquartered in the industrialized nations of North America, Europe, and Japan. Known collectively as the Triad, the consortium of these nations, home to only 15 percent of the world's population, produced nearly 75 percent of the world's goods by the late 1990s. One critic described this situation as not like a "global village" but more like "global pillage." Some traditional economists discounted the significance of these developments, insisting that trading activities date to the earliest civilizations and that well-organized transnational economies were the hallmark of the Industrial Age. The growth of international foreign trade in the last half of the twentieth century, they claimed, approximated that in the last half of the nineteenth century.

What made the current trend toward "globalization" distinctive was, therefore, not the rate of growth but the absolute volume and character of the exchange. Revenues from multinational corporations grew phenomenally at the end of the twentieth century. The 1998 total revenue of Wal-Mart Stores, Inc., with retail outlets in many parts of the world, surpassed the gross domestic product of Greece ($119.3 billion as compared to $119.1 billion). Because the member nations of the Triad were homes to the world's largest multinational corporations, they also reaped the largest share of the wealth. A UN annual human development report stated that "global inequalities in income and living standards have reached grotesque proportions." The report offered statistics showing that the gap in wealth between the upper 20 percent and the world's poorest people was at the end of the nineteenth century 30 to 1; by 1990 it reached 60 to 1; and by the end of the century it had widened to 74 to 1.

While many political observers and scholars predicted that globalization would bring both free markets and democracy to more and more of the world's people, others became increasingly skeptical. At the turn of the twenty-first century, an international protest movement emerged that targeted the most powerful organization in the global economy, the World Trade Organization (WTO) and the International Monetary Fund (IMF), or World Bank. In November 1999, thousands of protestors converged in Seattle, Washington, site of the annual meeting of the WTO, only to be pushed back by local police. In response, the WTO formulated new procedures for its meetings, secreting delegates behind walls and banning demonstrations from the area near future sites. Nevertheless, confrontations continued, the most dramatic occurring at a meeting of delegates from the eight leading industrial nations in Genoa, Italy, in 2001, which resulted in the death of one protestor.

Experts on globalization could not agree if the trend toward a single international market challenged traditional notions of national sovereignty and laid the foundation for global democracy or if the post–cold war world order was increasingly challenged by civil wars, ethnic and religious clashes, and the breakup of nation-states.

More than 5,000 activists gathered in Seattle in November 1999 to demonstrate against the meeting of the World Trade Organization. The event, which was marked by a violent clash with police and the arrest of dozens of protestors, marked the beginning of a movement for global economic justice.

SOURCE: © AFP/CORBIS (FT0022933).

Terrorist Attack on America

On September 11, 2001, hijackers, armed only with knives and box cutters, crashed two jetliners into each of New York's World Trade Center towers, while a third jetliner slammed into the Pentagon in Virginia. A fourth plane, diverted from its terrorist mission by courageous passengers, hurtled to the ground near Pittsburgh. In all, 246 people perished in the four planes. At the sites of the attack, the damage was devastating. At the Pentagon, which had been built to withstand terrorist attacks, a huge explosion followed by fierce fires destroyed a large section of the defense complex. The death toll soon reached 184, including 59 people who had been on board the hijacked airliner. In New York, the number of lives lost was, as Mayor Rudolph W.

The United States conducted air strikes on the village of Rahesh, near the capital city Kabul, in November 2001 in a military campaign to drive the Taliban from power in Afghanistan.

SOURCE: © AP/Wide World Photos (6051224).

Guilani said, "horrendous." The collapse of the twin towers, most likely caused by the intense fires propelled by the planes' jet fuel, brought death to thousands, including hundreds of police and rescue workers who had dashed into the buildings to help. At the end of the day, the New York City Fire Department had lost 350 firefighters, nearly thirty times the number ever lost by the department in a single incident. The nation watched in horror as the events vividly unfolded in live newscoverage on TV. The stark images of the second plane hitting the WTC, the dramatic collapse of the buildings, and the fear on the faces of thousands fleeing the sites were replayed over and over again on televisions throughout the world.

While the media recalled Pearl Harbor, President Bush declared the deadly attacks an act of war and vowed to hunt down those responsible for the "evil, despicable acts of terror." Congress, with only one dissenting vote, granted him power to take whatever steps necessary. The Department of Justice began what it described as the largest and most intensive investigation ever conducted, and the president issued a blanket warning to all nations who harbor terrorists. Secretary of State Colin Powell stated clearly, "You're either with us or against us." For the first time ever, NATO invoked the mutual defense clause in its founding treaty, which in effect supported any U.S. military response.

Observers described Bush's response as the defining moment of his presidency, as it was for the lives of many Americans. A patriotic surge found flags displayed on homes and cars—even painted on the faces of children. Millions of Americans rushed to donate blood, and thousands traveled to New York to assist rescue efforts. Prayer vigils were held in churches, synagogues, and mosques, as well as in public buildings and parks. Millions of dollars were soon raised for the relief effort and to assist the families of those who perished.

Many businesses, especially those in the travel, entertainment, or hazardous materials industries, were closed in the days following the attack. Major sports events, including baseball, football, and golf, were cancelled or postponed. As a precautionary measure, skyscrapers in the largest cities, such as the Sears Tower in Chicago, the building that had surpassed the WTC as the nation's tallest, were evacuated. The stock market, after a three-day pause, reopened to the worst week in the history of Wall Street since the Great Depression. Financial analysts declared that the already faltering economy had now certainly entered a recession.

Perhaps most dramatic was the unprecedented shutdown of all airports in the United States, stranding thousands around the world. Service returned several days later at greatly reduced levels and with enhanced security. Even plastic knives were banned in airport restaurants. President Bush created a new Cabinet-level agency, Homeland Security, charged with coordinating the efforts of more than forty other agencies to protect Americans against terrorists and to respond to any such attacks. He also allocated millions of dollars to boost the budgets of the Department of Defense, the CIA, and the FBI. But fear had chilled most Americans' spirit. In the face of a $15 billion bailout of the airline industry quickly passed by the Senate, they cancelled vacations and applied for refunds for airline tickets already purchased. Two-thirds of those polled believed the worst might still come.

The day following the highly coordinated terrorist attack, President Bush identified the Saudi Arabian Osama bin Laden as the prime suspect. Administration officials linked the airline hijackers, all presumed to be Islamic fundamentalists, to his Al-Qaeda network, which apparently had dispatched them to train at American flight schools. Although a communique from bin Laden denied involvement, U.S. intelligence sources insisted that only bin Laden had the resources to carry out such a sophisticated operation and sufficient motivation. In 1998, bin Laden had issued a decree that granted religious legitimacy to all efforts to expel the United States from the lands of Islam in the Middle East. His network of terrorist cells, which reportedly operated in sixty countries, had directed rage at what they believe to be the global arrogance of the

CHRONOLOGY

1981 MTV and CNN start broadcasting as cable channels

1986 Immigration Reform and Control Act addresses concerns about illegal aliens

1987 Allan Bloom publishes *The Closing of the American Mind*

1988 Indian Gaming Regulatory Act allows Indian tribes to operate gambling establishments

George Bush is elected president

Terrorist attack on Pam Am plane over Lockerbie, Scotland

1989 Tiananmen Square demonstration in China

Communist authority collapses in Eastern Europe

1990 August: Iraqi invasion of Kuwait leads to massive U.S. military presence in the Persian Gulf

1991 January–February: Operation Desert Storm forces Iraq out of Kuwait

Operation Rescue launched in Wichita, Kansas

Soviet Union dissolves into Commonwealth of Independent States

1992 Rodney King verdict sparks rioting in Los Angeles

UN holds first Earth Summit

Bill Clinton is elected president

1993 Terrorist bombing of World Trade Center kills six people

Federal agents conduct seige of Branch Davidian compound in Waco, Texas

Clinton administration introduces comprehensive health-care reform, but it fails to win passage in Congress

Congress approves the North American Free Trade Agreement

1994 Republicans win control of Senate and House for first time in forty years

Congress approves the General Agreement on Tariffs and Trade

Congress passes the Comprehensive AIDS Revenue Emergency Act

Congress passes "Defense of Marriage" Act

California voters approve Proposition 187

1995 Bombing of Alfred P. Murrah Federal Building in Oklahoma City kills 168 people

Clinton announces Dayton Accords to mediate civil war in Bosnia

1996 Congress passes Welfare Reform Act

Congress enacts the Antiterrorism and Effective Death Penalty Act

President Bill Clinton is reelected

1997 Kyoto Protocol endorsed by European Union but not United States

1998 U.S. embassies in Kenya and Tanzania bombed by terrorists

House of Representatives votes to impeach President Clinton, but vote fails in Senate

1999 U.S. joins NATO forces in Kosovo

Protesters disrupt meetings of the World Trade Organization in Seattle

2000 USS *Cole* bombed by terrorists

2001 George W. Bush becomes president after contested election

Terrorists attack World Trade Center and Pentagon

U.S. begins military campaign in Afghanistan

United States—its accumulation of unprecedented wealth when poverty and hopelessness extended across the Middle East.

With bin Laden presumed to be hiding in Afghanistan and supported by the ruling Taliban government, President Bush insisted that the Taliban regime hand over the terrorists "or they will share in their fate." He dispatched U.S. aircraft carriers to join the U.S. forces already assembled in the Persian Gulf region, and mobilized reservists for a possible invasion. On October

7, he ordered the first air strikes in Afghanistan, with the stated goal of destroying Al-Qaeda's terrorist training camps and bringing down the Taliban government that was shielding bin Laden.

CONCLUSION

Although the attack on the WTC and the Pentagon stunned and infuriated most Americans, it represented only the most destructive in the series of terrorist attacks that had been levied against the United States since the 1980s. In 1999, the U.S. Commission on National Security/Twenty-first Century, which has been established by Congress to evaluate the nation's defense systems, had concluded that "America will become increasingly vulnerable to hostile attack on our homeland" and that "Americans will likely die on American soil, possibly in large numbers." The security promised by the end of the cold war seemed more elusive than ever. By early 2002, the Taliban government had collapsed much sooner than anticipated by U.S. military advisors. However, the war continued. President Bush, who had asked Americans to be patient "in understanding that it will take time to achieve our goals," broadened the scope and declared a world-wide war on terrorism.

REVIEW QUESTIONS

1. Is the United States entering a "new era" in the twenty-first century? What effects have the globalized economy and the fall of the Soviet Union had on American political life?

2. How is the "new economy" different from the old economy? How has it reshaped American business and financial practices? Explain the relationship between the new economy and electronic media, such as the Internet and cable television.

3. Evaluate the presidency of Bill Clinton. Compare his domestic and foreign policies to those of the Republican presidents who preceded and followed him in office. What was the impact of the scandals that plagued his presidency?

4. Describe the major demographic trends revealed by the 2000 census. Identify the racial and ethnic groups with the greatest gains in population. How have various legislation acts since 1965 affected immigration to the United States? How have communities changed as a result of the influx of new immigrants?

5. The concept of globalization is highly controversial. Are borders between nations "melting away" as some scholars contend? How does this concept square with the description of the United States as the single superpower in the world? Does this concept apply primarily to economics, or is it useful for discussing issues related to culture, media, the environment, and population trends?

6. Earlier scholars predicted that the end of the cold war would bring peace and promote democracy throughout the world. Events, beginning with the Persian Gulf War, have instead suggested a new basis for international affairs. Describe the importance of regional and ethnic conflicts in the Middle East and Central Europe.

RECOMMENDED READING

Angus Kress Gillespie, *Twin Towers: The Life of New York City's World Trade Center* (1999). A detailed history of the buildings, including the political background and the process of design and construction. Gillespie traces the emergence of the World Trade Center as a popular symbol of New York City and center of international commerce.

Mark S. Hamm, *Apocalypse in Oklahoma: Waco and Ruby Ridge Revenge* (1997). Provides a succinct overview of the events leading to the bombing of the federal building in Oklahoma City in 1995, seeing it as an act of murderous revenge.

David Held, ed., *A Globalizing World? Culture, Economics, Politics* (2000). Four essays addressing various aspects of globalization. This slim volume offers a concise summary of the major theories of globalization and compares the contemporary situation with previous eras.

Neil Howe, *Millennials Rising: The Next Generation* (2000). An optimistic assessment of the generation of Americans who were born on or after 1982 and projections for their future. Howe surveys statistics as well as cultural trends and concludes that the rising generation shows a return to conservative family values and a respect for rules.

William G. Hyland, *Clinton's World: Remaking American Foreign Policy* (1999). Evaluates the first post–cold war president's decisions with regard to the major international events of the 1990s. Examines the developing policies toward Russia and Asia. Hyland offers a fairly negative assessment.

Robert K. Kaplan, *The Coming Anarchy: Shattering the Dreams of the Post–Cold War* (2000). Nine essays on international affairs that provide an often disturbing assessment of the prospects for peace. Kaplan discusses the rise of ethnic conflict in regions such as Sierra Leone, Russia, and India and weighs the signficance of increasing tribalistic warfare, the breakdown of central government authority in several nations, and the rise in crime in post-Communist countries.

Judith Millwer, Stephen Engelberg, and William Broad, *Germs: Biological Weapons and America's Secret War* (2001). Beginning with the use of salmonella to poison food in Oregon in 1984, this book narrates the history of biological warfare in the last half of the twentieth century. The authors, veteran reporters for the *New York Times*, argue that the United States is ill equipped to protect its citizens against a serious biological attack.

Jill Nelson, ed., *Police Brutality: An Anthology* (2000). Twelve essays written by scholars, activists, and writers that discuss, from a variety of perspectives, police presence in American communities. Several essays focus on the broad historical dimensions of this issue, tracing the roots back to the time of slavery.

New York Times staffwriters, *The Downsizing of America* (1996). A well-researched account detailing the devastating impact of corporate "downsizing" on American communities and families.

Howard Rheingold, *The Virtual Community* (1994). Very thoughtful examination of the promises and problems posed by the new computer-based technologies associated with "virtual communities."

Micah L. Sifry and Christopher Cerf, eds., *The Gulf War Reader* (1991). An excellent collection of historical essays, government documents, and political addresses that provides a comprehensive overview of the Persian Gulf War.

Janet Thomas, *The Battle in Seattle: The Story Behind and Beyond the WTO* (2000). An impassioned, eyewitness account by a participant in the 1999 demonstrations against the World Trade Organization, which the author describes as a "global tailspin at the end of the century."

ADDITIONAL BIBLIOGRAPHY

Foreign Policy and International Affairs

Stephen F. Cohen, *Failed Crusade: America and the Tragedy of Post-Communist Russia* (2000)

John L. Gaddis, *The United States and the End of the Cold War* (1992)

David Halberstam, *War in a Time of Peace: Bush, Clinton, and the Generals* (2001)

Avigdor Haselkorn, *The Continuing Storm: Iraq, Poisonous Weapons and Deterrence* (1999)

Richard Hallion, *Storm over Iraq* (1992)

Elaine Landau, *Osama Bin Laden: A War Against the West* (2002)

Tomas W. Lippman, *Madeleine Albright and the New American Diplomacy* (2000)

Robert Litwack, *Rogue States and U.S. Foreign Policy: Containment After the Cold War* (1999)

David Moslery and Bob Catley, *Global America: Imposing Liberalism on a Recalcitrant World* (2000)

Alvin A. Rubinstein, Albina Shayevich, and Boris Zlotnikov, eds., *The Clinton Foreign Policy Reader: Presidential Speeches with Commentary* (2000)

Jeff Wheelwright, *The Irritable Heart: The Medical Mystery of the Gulf War* (2001)

The New Economy

Paul Andrew, *How the Web Was Won* (1999)

Michael A. Bernstein and David A. Adler, eds., *Understanding American Economic Decline* (1994)

Michael Lewis, *The New New Thing: A Silicon Valley Story* (2000)

Ted G. Lewis, *Microsoft Rising and Other Tales of Silicon Valley* (1999)

Robert H. Reid, *Architects of the Web* (1997)

Bob Woodward, *Maestro: Greenspan's Fed and the American Boom* (2000)

Changing American Communities

David Brooks, *Bobos in Paradise: The New Upper Class and How They Got There* (2000)

Helen Hayes, *U.S. Immigration and the Undocumented: Ambivalent Lives, Furtive Lives* (2001)

Denis Lynn Daly Heyck, ed., *Barrios and Borderlands: Cultures of Latinos and Latinas in the United States* (1993)

Bill Ong Hing, *Making and Remaking Asian America through Immigration Policy, 1850–1990* (1993)

J. Eric Oliver, *Democracy in Suburbia* (2001)

Adam Ward Rome, *The Bulldozer in the Countryside: Suburban Sprawl and the Rise of American Environmentalism* (2001)

Reed Ueda, *Postwar Immigrant America* (1994)

New Age of Anxiety

Jewelle Taylor Gibbs, *Race and Justice: Rodney King and O. J. Simpson in a House Divided* (1996)

Chester Hartman, ed., *Double Exposure: Poverty and Race in America* (1997)

James D. Hunter, *Culture Wars: The Struggle to Define America* (1991)

Randall Kennedy, *Race, Crime, and the Law* (1997)

Lawrence Levine, *The Opening of the American Mind: Canons, Culture, and History* (1996)

Andrea McArdle and Tanya Erzen, eds., *Zero Tolerance: Quality of Life and the New Police Brutality in New York City* (2001)

Brigitte Nacos, *Terrorism and the Media* (1994)

Christian Parenti, *Lockdown America: Police and Prisons in the Age of Crisis* (1999)

David M. Reimers, *Unwelcome Strangers: American Identity and the Turn Against Immigration* (1998)

Roger Simon, *Divided We Stand: How Al Gore Beat George Bush and Lost the Presidency* (2001)

Robert C. Smith, *Racism in the Post-Civil Rights Era* (1995)

James D. Tabor and Eugene V. Gallagher, *Why Waco? Cults and the Battle for Religious Freedom in America* (1995)

The Clinton Presidency

Lauren Berlant and Lisa Duggan, eds., *Our Monica, Ourselves: The Clinton Affair and the National Interest* (2001)

Vincent Bugliosi, *The Betrayal of America: How the Supreme Court Undermined the Constitution and Chose Our President* (2001)

Colin Campbell and Bert A. Rockman, eds., *The Clinton Legacy* (1999)

James Carville, *Stickin': The Case for Loyalty* (2000)

Joe Conason and Gene Lyons, *The Hunting of the President: The Ten-Year Campaign to Destroy Bill and Hillary Clinton* (2000)

Richard A. Posner, *An Affair of State: The Investigation, Impeachment, and Trial of President Clinton* (1999)

Steven E. Schier, ed., *The Postmodern Presidency: Bill Clinton's Legacy in U.S. Politics* (2000)

Susan Schmidt and Micahel Weisskopf, *Truth at Any Cost: Ken Starr and the Unmaking of Bill Clinton* (2000)

Hanes Walton, Jr., *Reelection: William Jefferson Clinton as a Native-Son Presidential Candidate* (2000)

Bob Woodward, *The Agenda: Inside the Clinton White House* (1994)

Biography

John Robert Greene, *The Presidency of George Bush* (2000)

Harry Hurt, *The Lost Tycoon: The Many Lives of Donald J. Trump* (1993)

Molly Ivins and Lou Dubose, *Shrub: The Short But Happy Political Life of George W. Bush* (2000)

Faith Karlene, *Madonna, Bawdy & Soul* (1997)

David Maraniss, *First in His Class: A Biography of Bill Clinton* (1995)

Joyce Milton, *The First Partner: Hillary Rodham Clinton* (1999)

Roger Morris, *Partners in Power: The Clintons and Their America* (1996)

Gerald L. Posner, *Citizen Perot: His Life and Times* (1996)

Richard A. Serrano, *One of Ours: Timothy McVeigh and the Oklahoma City Bombing* (1998)

Mel Steely, *The Gentleman from Georgia: The Biography of Newt Gingrich* (2000)

Globalization

Walden Bello, *The Future in the Balance* (2001)

Jeremy Brecher, Tim Costello, and Brandan Smith, *Globalization From Below* (2000)

Alexander Cockburn, Jeffrey St. Clair, and Alan Sekula, *Five Days That Shook the World: The Battle for Seattle and Beyond* (2001)

Anthony Giddens, *Runaway World* (1999)

Edward S. Herman and Robert W. McChesney, *The Global Media: The New Missionaries of Corporate Capitalism* (1997)

Joshua Karliner, *The Corporate Planet: Ecology and Politics in the Age of Globalization* (1997)

Margaret Keck and Kathryn Sikkink, *Activists Beyond Borders: Advocacy Networks in International Politics* (1998)

Amory Starr, *Naming the Enemy: Anti-Corporate Movements Confront Globalization* (2001)

John D. Wirth, *Smelter Smoke in North America: The Politics of Transborder Pollution* (2000)

Michael Hardt and Antonio Negri, *Empire* (2000)

HISTORY ON THE INTERNET

http://oyez.nwu.edu/

The Oyez Project of Northwestern University provides information on Supreme Court decisions, especially the written Court opinions. The cases of *Bush v. Palm Beach County Canvassing Board* (2000) and *Bush v. Gore* (2000) were two key U.S. Supreme Court decisions in the presidential election crisis of 2000. Search this site for the written opinions of the justices on these two historical decisions of the Court.

http://www.nytimes.com/learning/general/specials/impeachment/

A New York Times site which explains the impeachment process not just in relationship to Clinton, but over the entire history of the United States with all presidents who were either threatened with impeachment, impeached, or censured.

http://jurist.law.pitt.edu/impeach.htm

An extremely large site consisting of links to other sites which explain just about any aspect of the Clinton impeachment which might interest the student of history.

http://www.bartleby.com/124/pres64.html

Bill Clinton's First Inaugural Address, January 21, 1993

http://www.bartleby.com/124/pres65.html

Bill Clinton's Second Inaugural Address, January 20, 1997

http://www.bartleby.com/124/pres66.html

George W. Bush's Inaugural Address, January 20, 2001

The World Trade Center and Ways of Remembering

The first plane hit the north tower of the World Trade Center at 8:48 am. The second plane struck the south tower at 9:03 am. The two massive, 110-story "twin towers" soon collapsed into a nightmarish rubble, as millions of disbelieving viewers watched the scene on television. By then, many Americans had already begun to speak of the event as the defining moment of their own lifetimes, declaring that they would forever remember where they were and what they were doing when reports of the tragedy reached them. While the events were still unfolding, Americans began to search for ways to place the terrorist attack on America in historical perspective. How would their memories make sense of the experience in the long run? How did the larger context of U.S. history frame the horrible events of September 11, 2001?

Newscasters, commentators, political figures, and ordinary citizens all struggled to find appropriate historical analogies for attacks on the World Trade Center and the Pentagon. They repeatedly invoked two twentieth century events that seemed to offer at least some parallels. One was the surprise Japanese attack on the American naval fleet anchored in Pearl Harbor, Hawai'i, on December 7, 1941. Both enemy attacks came from the air and lasted just over an hour. The death toll was high in both cases, with 2,403 Americans dead in Pearl Harbor. In his address the next day, President Franklin D. Roosevelt memorialized the date as one "which will live in infamy." "Always will our whole nation remember the character of the onslaught against us," he predicted while asking Congress for a declaration of war against Japan. On September 11, 2001, newscasters almost instantaneously revived President Roosevelt's descriptive phrase. This new "day of infamy," they suggested, carried as much historical weight as the event that brought the United States into World War II.

The second frequently cited historical parallel was the assassination of President John F. Kennedy on November 22, 1963. Kennedy's death and funeral underscored the new power of television to transform nation into a community witnessing momentous and shocking events as they unfolded. Indeed, millions of Americans had watched in disbelief as Kennedy's accused assassin, Lee Harvey Oswald, was gunned down in a Dallas police station the day after the President had been killed. And

People ran for safety following the collapse of the World Trade Center after the terrorist attack on the New York landmark on September 11, 2001.

SOURCE: Associated Press, AP.

just as Americans would never forget where they were and what they were doing when they heard the news about JFK, so it seemed that the WTC attack would also prove a life-long marker of memory.

These two historical analogies are far from perfect. Pearl Harbor was a military target, thousands of miles from the mainland; the attack had clearly come from a nation state that had a deep economic and diplomatic rivalry with the U.S. In contrast, the 9/11 assault came against a symbol of American economic power with no military significance, and it marked the first time that American civilians had ever suffered mass casualties at the hands of a foreign enemy. And that enemy appeared to be not a nation state but rather a shadowy international organization of radical Islamic terrorists. The JFK assassination had surely demonstrated the growing power of television to focus an entire nation's attention. But Americans would never really agree on the cause and meaning of Kennedy's tragic death. For decades, American citizens, abetted by a cottage industry of conspiracy theorists, film makers, historians, novelists, and journalists continued to argue about who was responsible, what motives were in play, and how history might have been different had Kennedy lived.

By the evening of September 11th, groups of people across the nation gathered in candlelight vigils to honor the victims of the terrorist attacks. President Bush declared September 14th a National Day of Prayer and Remembrance.

SOURCE: © Reuters New Media Inc./CORBIS.

What role did the media play in shaping our understanding of the events of 9/11/01? Unlike the bombing of U.S. naval ships in Pearl Harbor, the terrorist attack on the World Trade Center occurred, virtually, before the eyes of millions of Americans. Video cameras caught the image of the second plane hitting the south tower, the panic on the faces of those fleeing the scene, the smoke billowing from the towers, and their sudden collapse. Reporters were soon on the scene to interview eyewitnesses and to pull comments from traumatized survivors. The networks immediately pre-empted regular programming and allowed millions of Americans to watch in horror as the televised images played and replayed the attack. The newscasters narrated the events, drawing out the analogy with Pearl Harbor, and giving the unfolding story a title, such as "Attack on America" or "Day of Infamy." Within a few days, programmers had edited the videotapes to enhance the drama. They added scenes, such as images of cell phones to remind viewers of the final calls many of the victims made to their loved ones. They overlaid the images of towers collapsing with an unfurling American flag and added patriotic music. To enhance further the emotional impact, they borrowed cinematic techniques, slowing down the pace to draw out the action. They also used jump cuts, juxtaposing in fast time an image of the burning or collapsing towers with a close-up shot of an anguished face of an observer, putting the viewer emotionally into the picture.

But the shaping of historical memory took place on other levels as well. At hundreds of funerals and memorial services held in communities throughout the Greater New York area, many thousands of strangers joined families of the victims in paying respects and trying to make sense of it all. Makeshift memorials sprouted up in lower Manhattan with people leaving flowers, personal notes, and artwork. At the Massachusetts Institute of Technology in Cambridge, Massachusetts, faculty and students built a Reflecting Wall, consisting of a re-created fragment of the familiar World Trade Center façade.

For more long-term efforts at documenting collective memory, historians and museums looked to the Internet. Some 70 history oriented institutions came together to create a new Internet site, 911history.net, devoted to collecting oral histories and artifacts from the event. And the Library of Congress spearheaded another site, September11.archive.org, which by mid-October had already put on-line more than 500,000 pages related to the terrorist attacks, ranging from daily news reports to personal memorials. As Diane Kresh of the Library of Congress put it, "The Internet has become for many the public commons, a place where they can come together and talk." A more permanent memorial will no doubt be a part of the reconstruction of Lower Manhattan. Through all these projects, Americans will continue demonstrating how creating historical memory is an active and dynamic process. ■

APPENDIX

THE DECLARATION OF INDEPENDENCE

When in the course of human events it becomes necessary for one people to dissolve the political bands which have connected them with another and to assume, among the powers of the earth, the separate and equal station to which the laws of nature and of nature's God entitle them, a decent respect to the opinions of mankind requires that they should declare the causes which impel them to the separation.

We hold these truths to be self-evident, that all men are created equal; that they are endowed by their Creator with certain unalienable rights; that among these are life, liberty, and the pursuit of happiness. That, to secure these rights, governments are instituted among men, deriving their just powers from the consent of the governed; that, whenever any form of government becomes destructive of these ends, it is the right of the people to alter or to abolish it, and to institute a new government, laying its foundation on such principles, and organizing its powers in such form, as to them shall seem most likely to effect their safety and happiness. Prudence, indeed, will dictate that governments long established should not be changed for light and transient causes; and, accordingly, all experience hath shown that mankind are more disposed to suffer, while evils are sufferable, than to right themselves by abolishing the forms to which they are accustomed. But when a long train of abuses and usurpations, pursuing invariably the same object, evinces a design to reduce them under absolute despotism, it is their right, it is their duty, to throw off such government and to provide new guards for their future security. Such has been the patient sufferance of these colonies, and such is now the necessity which constrains them to alter their former systems of government. The history of the present King of Great Britain is a history of repeated injuries and usurpations, all having, in direct object, the establishment of an absolute tyranny over these States. To prove this, let facts be submitted to a candid world:

He has refused his assent to laws the most wholesome and necessary for the public good.

He has forbidden his governors to pass laws of immediate and pressing importance, unless suspended in their operation till his assent should be obtained; and, when so suspended, he has utterly neglected to attend to them.

He has refused to pass other laws for the accommodation of large districts of people, unless those people would relinquish the right of representation in the legislature, a right inestimable to them and formidable to tyrants only.

He has called together legislative bodies at places unusual, uncomfortable, and distant from the depository of their public records, for the sole purpose of fatiguing them into compliance with his measures.

He has dissolved representative houses, repeatedly for opposing, with manly firmness, his invasions on the rights of the people.

He has refused, for a long time after such dissolutions, to cause others to be elected; whereby the legislative powers, incapable of annihilation, have returned to the people at large for their exercise; the state remaining, in the meantime, exposed to all the danger of invasion from without and convulsions within.

He has endeavored to prevent the population of these States; for that purpose, obstructing the laws for naturalization of foreigners, refusing to pass others to encourage their migration hither, and raising the conditions of new appropriations of lands.

He has obstructed the administration of justice by refusing his assent to laws for establishing judiciary powers.

He has made judges dependent on his will alone for the tenure of their offices and the amount and payment of their salaries.

He has erected a multitude of new offices and sent hither swarms of officers to harass our people and eat out their substance.

He has kept among us, in time of peace, standing armies, without the consent of our legislatures.

He has affected to render the military independent of, and superior to, the civil power.

He has combined with others to subject us to a jurisdiction foreign to our Constitution and unacknowledged by our laws, giving his assent to their acts of pretended legislation—

For quartering large bodies of armed troops among us;

For protecting them, by mock trial, from punishment for any murders which they should commit on the inhabitants of these States;

For cutting off our trade with all parts of the world;

For imposing taxes on us without our consent;

For depriving us, in many cases, of the benefit of trial by jury;

For transporting us beyond seas to be tried for pretended offences;

For abolishing the free system of English laws in a neighboring province, establishing therein an arbitrary government, and enlarging its boundaries, so as to render it at once an example and fit instrument for introducing the same absolute rule into these colonies;

For taking away our charters, abolishing our most valuable laws, and altering, fundamentally, the powers of our governments.

For suspending our own legislatures and declaring themselves invested with power to legislate for us in all cases whatsoever.

He has abdicated government here by declaring us out of his protection and waging war against us.

He has plundered our seas, ravaged our coasts, burnt our towns, and destroyed the lives of our people.

He is, at this time, transporting large armies of foreign mercenaries to complete the works of death, desolation, and tyranny already begun with circumstances of cruelty and perfidy scarcely paralleled in the most barbarous ages, and totally unworthy the head of a civilized nation.

He has constrained our fellow citizens, taken captive on the high seas, to bear arms against their country, to become the executioners of their friends and brethren, or to fall themselves by their hands.

He has excited domestic insurrections amongst us and has endeavored to bring on the inhabitants of our frontiers, the merciless Indian savages, whose known rule of warfare is an undistinguished destruction of all ages, sexes, and conditions.

In every stage of these oppressions, we have petitioned for redress in the most humble terms; our repeated petitions have been answered only by repeated injury. A prince whose character is thus marked by every act which may define a tyrant is unfit to be the ruler of a free people.

Nor have we been wanting in attention to our British brethren. We have warned them, from time to time, of attempts made by their legislature to extend an unwarrantable jurisdiction over us. We have reminded them of the circumstances of our emigration and settlement here. We have appealed to their native justice and magnanimity, and we have conjured them, by the ties of our common kindred, to disavow these usurpations, which would inevitably interrupt our connections and correspondence. They, too, have been deaf to the voice of justice and consanguinity. We must, therefore, acquiesce in the necessity which denounces our separation, and hold them, as we hold the rest of mankind, enemies in war, in peace, friends.

We, therefore, the representatives of the United States of America, in general Congress assembled, appealing to the Supreme Judge of the world for the rectitude of our intentions, do, in the name and by the authority of the good people of these colonies, solemnly publish and declare, that these united colonies are, and of right ought to be, free and independent states: that they are absolved from all allegiance to the British Crown, and that all political connection between them and the state of Great Britain is, and ought to be, totally dissolved; and that, as free and independent states, they have full power to levy war, conclude peace, contract alliances, establish commerce, and to do all other acts and things which independent states may of right do. And, for the support of this declaration, with a firm reliance on the protection of Divine Providence, we mutually pledge to each other our lives, our fortunes, and our sacred honor.

THE CONSTITUTION OF THE UNITED STATES OF AMERICA

We the people of the United States, in order to form a more perfect union, establish justice, insure domestic tranquillity, provide for the common defense, promote the general welfare, and secure the blessings of liberty to ourselves and our posterity, do ordain and establish this Constitution for the United States of America.

Article I

Section 1. All legislative powers herein granted shall be vested in a Congress of the United States, which shall consist of a Senate and House of Representatives.

Section 2. 1. The House of Representatives shall be composed of members chosen every second year by the people of the several States, and the electors in each State shall have the qualifications requisite for electors of the most numerous branch of the State legislature.

2. No person shall be a representative who shall not have attained to the age of twenty-five years, and been seven years a citizen of the United States, and who shall not, when elected, be an inhabitant of that State in which he shall be chosen.

3. Representatives and direct taxes[1] shall be apportioned among the several States which may be included within this Union, according to their respective numbers, which shall be determined by adding to the whole number of free persons, including those bound to service for a term of years, and excluding Indians not taxed, three fifths of all other persons.[2] The actual enumeration shall be made within three years after the first meeting of the Congress of the United States, and within every subsequent term of ten years, in such manner as they shall by law direct. The number of representatives shall not exceed one for every thirty thousand, but each State shall have at least one representative; and until such enumeration shall be made, the State of New Hampshire shall be entitled to choose three, Massachusetts eight, Rhode Island and Providence Plantations one, Connecticut five, New York six, New Jersey four, Pennsylvania eight, Delaware one, Maryland six, Virginia ten, North Carolina five, South Carolina five, and Georgia three.

4. When vacancies happen in the representation from any State, the executive authority thereof shall issue writs of election to fill such vacancies.

5. The House of Representatives shall choose their speaker and other officers; and shall have the sole power of impeachment.

Section 3. 1. The Senate of the United States shall be composed of two senators from each State, chosen by the legislature thereof,[3] for six years; and each senator shall have one vote.

2. Immediately after they shall be assembled in consequence of the first election, they shall be divided as equally as may be into three classes. The seats of the senators of the first class shall be vacated at the expiration of the second year, of the second class at the expiration of the fourth year, and of the third class at the expiration of the sixth year, so that one third may be chosen every second year; and if vacancies happen by resignation, or otherwise, during the recess of the legislature of any State, the executive thereof may make temporary appointments until the next meeting of the legislature, which shall then fill such vacancies.[4]

3. No person shall be a senator who shall not have attained to the age of thirty years, and been nine years a citizen of the United States, and who shall not, when elected, be an inhabitant of that State for which he shall be chosen.

4. The Vice President of the United States shall be President of the Senate, but shall have no vote, unless they be equally divided.

5. The Senate shall choose their other officers, and also a president pro tempore, in the absence of the Vice President, or when he shall exercise the office of President of the United States.

6. The Senate shall have the sole power to try all impeachments. When sitting for that purpose, they shall be on oath or affirmation. When the President of the United States is tried, the chief justice shall preside: and no person shall be convicted without the concurrence of two thirds of the members present.

7. Judgment in cases of impeachment shall not extend further than to removal from office, and disqualification to hold and enjoy any office of honor, trust or profit under the United States: but the party convicted shall nevertheless be liable and subject to indictment, trial, judgment and punishment, according to law.

Section 4. 1. The times, places, and manner of holding elections for senators and representatives, shall be prescribed in each State by the legislature thereof; but the Congress may at any time by law make or alter such regulations, except as to the places of choosing senators.

2. The Congress shall assemble at least once in every year, and such meeting shall be on the first Monday in December, unless they shall by law appoint a different day.

Section 5. 1. Each House shall be the judge of the elections, returns and qualifications of its own members, and a majority of each shall constitute a quorum to do business; but a smaller number may adjourn from day to day, and may be authorized to compel the attendance of absent members, in such manner, and under such penalties as each House may provide.

2. Each House may determine the rules of its proceedings, punish its members for disorderly behavior, and, with the concurrence of two thirds, expel a member.

3. Each House shall keep a journal of its proceedings, and from time to time publish the same, excepting such parts as may in their judgment require secrecy; and the yeas and nays of the members of either House on any question

[1] See the Sixteenth Amendment.
[2] See the Fourteenth Amendment.
[3] See the Seventeenth Amendment.

[4] See the Seventeenth Amendment.

shall, at the desire of one fifth of those present, be entered on the journal.

4. Neither House, during the session of Congress, shall, without the consent of the other, adjourn for more than three days, nor to any other place than that in which the two Houses shall be sitting.

Section 6. 1. The senators and representatives shall receive a compensation for their services, to be ascertained by law, and paid out of the Treasury of the United States. They shall in all cases, except treason, felony, and breach of the peace, be privileged from arrest during their attendance at the session of their respective Houses, and in going to and returning from the same; and for any speech or debate in either House, they shall not be questioned in any other place.

2. No senator or representative shall, during the time for which he was elected, be appointed to any civil office under the authority of the United States, which shall have been created, or the emoluments whereof shall have been increased, during such time; and no person holding any office under the United States shall be a member of either House during his continuance in office.

Section 7. 1. All bills for raising revenue shall originate in the House of Representatives; but the Senate may propose or concur with amendments as on other bills.

2. Every bill which shall have passed the House of Representatives and the Senate, shall, before it become a law, be presented to the President of the United States; If he approves he shall sign it, but if not he shall return it, with his objections, to that House in which it shall have originated, who shall enter the objections at large on their journal, and proceed to reconsider it. If after such reconsideration two thirds of that House shall agree to pass the bill, it shall be sent, together with the objections, to the other House, by which it shall likewise be reconsidered, and if approved by two thirds of that House, it shall become a law. But in all such cases the votes of both Houses shall be determined by yeas and nays, and the names of the persons voting for and against the bill shall be entered on the journal of each House respectively. If any bill shall not be returned by the President within ten days (Sundays excepted) after it shall have been presented to him, the same shall be a law, in like manner as if he had signed it, unless the Congress by their adjournment prevent its return, in which case it shall not be a law.

3. Every order, resolution, or vote to which the concurrence of the Senate and the House of Representatives may be necessary (except on a question of adjournment) shall be presented to the President of the United States; and before the same shall take effect, shall be approved by him, or being disapproved by him, shall be repassed by two thirds of the Senate and House of Representatives, according to the rules and limitations prescribed in the case of a bill.

Section 8. The Congress shall have the power

1. To lay and collect taxes, duties, imposts, and excises, to pay the debts and provide for the common defense and general welfare of the United States; but all duties, imposts, and excises shall be uniform throughout the United States.

2. To borrow money on the credit of the United States;

3. To regulate commerce with foreign nations, and among the several States, and with the Indian tribes;

4. To establish a uniform rule of naturalization, and uniform laws on the subject of bankruptcies throughout the United States;

5. To coin money, regulate the value thereof, and of foreign coin, and fix the standard of weights and measures;

6. To provide for the punishment of counterfeiting the securities and current coin of the United States;

7. To establish post offices and post roads;

8. To promote the progress of science and useful arts, by securing for limited times to authors and inventors the exclusive right to their respective writings and discoveries;

9. To constitute tribunals inferior to the Supreme Court;

10. To define and punish piracies and felonies committed on the high seas, and offenses against the law of nations;

11. To declare war, grant letters of marque and reprisal, and make rules concerning captures on land and water;

12. To raise and support armies, but no appropriation of money to that use shall be for a longer term than two years;

13. To provide and maintain a navy;

14. To make rules for the government and regulation of the land and naval forces;

15. To provide for calling forth the militia to execute the laws of the Union, suppress insurrections and repel invasions;

16. To provide for organizing, arming, and disciplining the militia, and for governing such part of them as may be employed in the service of the United States, reserving to the States respectively, the appointment of the officers, and the authority of training the militia according to the discipline prescribed by Congress;

17. To exercise exclusive legislation in all cases whatsoever, over such district (not exceeding ten miles square) as may, by cession of particular States, and the acceptance of Congress, become the seat of the government of the United States, and to exercise like authority over all places purchased by the consent of the legislature of the State in which the same shall be, for the erection of forts, magazines, arsenals, dockyards, and other needful buildings; and

18. To make all laws which shall be necessary and proper for carrying into execution the foregoing powers, and all other powers vested by this Constitution in the government of the United States, or any department or officer thereof.

Section 9. 1. The migration or importation of such persons as any of the States now existing shall think proper to admit, shall not be prohibited by the Congress prior to the year one thousand eight hundred and eight, but a tax or duty may be imposed on such importation, not exceeding ten dollars for each person.

2. The privilege of the writ of habeas corpus shall not be suspended, unless when in cases of rebellion or invasion the public safety may require it.

3. No bill of attainder or ex post facto law shall be passed.

4. No capitation, or other direct, tax shall be laid, unless in proportion to the census or enumeration hereinbefore directed to be taken.[5]

5. No tax or duty shall be laid on articles exported from any State.

6. No preference shall be given by any regulation of commerce or revenue to the ports of one State over those of another: nor shall vessels bound to, or from, one State be obliged to enter, clear, or pay duties in another.

7. No money shall be drawn from the treasury, but in consequence of appropriations made by law; and a regular statement and account of the receipts and expenditures of all public money shall be published from time to time.

8. No title of nobility shall be granted by the United States: and no person holding any office of profit or trust under them, shall, without the consent of the Congress, accept of any present, emolument, office, or title, of any kind whatever, from any king, price, or foreign State.

Section 10. 1. No State shall enter into any treaty, alliance, or confederation; grant letters of marque and reprisal; coin money; emit bills of credit; make any thing but gold and silver coin a tender in payment of debts; pass any bill of attainder, ex post facto law, or law impairing the obligation of contracts, or grant, any title of nobility.

2. No State shall, without the consent of the Congress, lay any imposts or duties on imports or exports, except what may be absolutely necessary for executing its inspection laws: and the net produce of all duties and imposts laid by any State on imports or exports, shall be for the use of the treasury of the United States; and all such laws shall be subject to the revision and control of the Congress.

3. No State shall, without the consent of the Congress, lay any duty of tonnage, keep troops, or ships of war in time of peace, enter into any agreement or compact with another State, or with a foreign power, or engage in war, unless actually invaded, or in such imminent danger as will not admit of delay.

Article II

Section 1. 1. The executive power shall be vested in a President of the United States of America. He shall hold his office during the term of four years, and, together with the Vice President, chosen for the same term, be elected, as follows:

2. Each State shall appoint, in such manner as the legislature thereof may direct, a number of electors, equal to the whole number of senators and representatives to which the State may be entitled in the Congress: but no senator or representative, or person holding any office of trust or profit under the United States, shall be appointed an elector.

The electors shall meet in their respective States, and vote by ballot for two persons, of whom one at least shall not be an inhabitant of the same State with themselves. And they shall make a list of all the persons voted for, and of the number of votes for each; which list they shall sign and certify, and transmit sealed to the seat of the government of the United States, directed to the president of the Senate. The president of the Senate shall, in the presence of the Senate and House of Representatives, open all the certificates, and the votes shall then be counted. The person having the greatest number of votes shall be the President, if such number be a majority of the whole number of electors appointed; and if there be more than one who have such majority, and have an equal number of votes, then the House of Representatives shall immediately choose by ballot one of them for President; and if no person have a majority, then from the five highest on the list the said House shall in like manner choose the President. But in choosing the President, the votes shall be taken by States, the representation from each State having one vote; a quorum for this purpose shall consist of a member or members from two thirds of the States, and a majority of all the States shall be necessary to a choice. In every case after the choice of the President, the person having the greatest number of votes of the electors shall be the Vice President. But if there should remain two or more who have equal votes, the Senate shall choose from them by ballot the Vice President.[6]

3. The Congress may determine the time of choosing the electors, and the day on which they shall give their votes; which day shall be the same throughout the United States.

4. No person except a natural born citizen, or a citizen of the United States, at the time of the adoption of this Constitution, shall be eligible to the office of President; neither shall any person be eligible to the office who shall not have attained to the age of thirty-five years, and been fourteen years a resident within the United States.

5. In case of the removal of the President from office, or of his death, resignation, or inability to discharge the powers and duties of the said office, the same shall devolve on the Vice President, and the congress may by law provide for the case of removal, death, resignation or inability, both of the President and Vice President, declaring what officer shall then act as President, and such officer shall act accordingly until the disability be removed, or a President shall be elected.

6. The President shall, at stated times, receive for his services a compensation which shall neither be increased nor diminished during the period for which he shall have been elected, and he shall not receive within that period any other emolument from the United States, or any of them.

7. Before he enter on the execution of his office, he shall take the following oath or affirmation:—"I do

---

[5]See the Sixteenth Amendment.

[6]Superseded by the Twelfth Amendment.

solemnly swear (or affirm) that I will faithfully execute the office of President of the United States, and will to the best of my ability, preserve, protect and defend the Constitution of the United States."

Section 2. 1. The President shall be commander in chief of the army and navy of the United States, and of the militia of the several States, when called into the actual service of the United States; he may require the opinion in writing, of the principal officer in each of the executive departments, upon any subject relating to the duties of their respective offices, and he shall have power to grant reprieves and pardons for offenses against the United States, except in cases of impeachment.

2. He shall have power, by and with the advice and consent of the Senate, to make treaties, provided two thirds of the senators present concur; and he shall nominate, and by and with the advice and consent of the Senate, shall appoint ambassadors, other public ministers and consuls, judges of the Supreme Court, and all other officers of the United States, whose appointments are not herein otherwise provided for, and which shall be established by law; but the Congress may by law vest the appointment of such inferior officers, as they think proper, in the President alone, in the courts of laws, or in the heads of departments.

3. The President shall have power to fill up all vacancies that may happen during the recess of the Senate, by granting commissions which shall expire at the end of their next session.

Section 3. He shall from time to time give to the Congress information of the state of the Union, and recommend to their consideration such measures as he shall judge necessary and expedient; he may, on extraordinary occasions, convene both Houses, or either of them, and in case of disagreement between them with respect to the time of adjournment, he may adjourn them to such time as he shall think proper; he shall receive ambassadors and other public ministers; he shall take care that the laws be faithfully executed, and shall commission all the officers of the United States.

Section 4. The President, Vice President, and all civil officers of the United States, shall be removed from office on impeachment for, and conviction of, treason, bribery, or other high crimes and misdemeanors.

Article III

Section 1. The judicial power of the United States shall be vested in one Supreme Court, and in such inferior courts as the Congress may from time to time ordain and establish. The judges, both of the Supreme and inferior courts, shall hold their offices during good behavior, and shall, at stated times, receive for their services, a compensation, which shall not be diminished during their continuance in office.

Section 2. 1. The judicial power shall extend to all cases, in law and equity, arising under this Constitution, the laws of the United States, and treaties made, or which shall be made, under their authority;—to all cases of admiralty and maritime jurisdiction;—to controversies to which the United States shall be a party;[7]—to controversies between two or more States;—between a State and citizens of another State;—between citizens of different States;—between citizens of the same State claiming lands under grants of different States, and between a State, or the citizens thereof, and foreign States, citizens or subjects.

2. In all cases affecting ambassadors, other public ministers and consuls, and those in which a State shall be party, the Supreme Court shall have original jurisdiction. In all the other cases before mentioned, the Supreme Court shall have appellate jurisdiction, both as to law and fact, with such exceptions, and under such regulations as the Congress shall make.

3. The trial of all crimes, except in cases of impeachment, shall be by jury; and such trial shall be held in the State where the said crimes shall have been committed; but when not committed within any State, the trial shall be such place or places as the congress may by law have directed.

Section 3. 1. Treason against the United States shall consist only in levying war against them, or in adhering to their enemies, giving them aid and comfort. No person shall be convicted of treason unless on the testimony of two witnesses to the same overt act, or on confession in open court.

2. The Congress shall have power to declare the punishment of treason, but no attainder of treason shall work corruption of blood, or forfeiture except during the life of the person attained.

Article IV

Section 1. Full faith and credit shall be given in each State to the public acts, records, and judicial proceedings of every other State. And the Congress may by general laws prescribe the manner in which such acts, records and proceedings shall be proved, and the effect thereof.

Section 2. 1. The citizens of each State shall be entitled to all privileges and immunities of citizens in the several States.[8]

2. A person charged in any State with treason, felony, or other crime, who shall flee from justice, and be found in another State, shall on demand of the executive authority of the State from which he fled, be delivered up to be removed to the State having jurisdiction of the crime.

3. No person held to service or labor in one State under the laws thereof, escaping into another, shall, in consequence of any law or regulation therein, be discharged from such service or labor, but shall be delivered up on claim of the party to whom such service or labor may be due.[9]

Section 3. 1. New States may be admitted by the Congress into this Union; but no new State shall be formed or erected within the jurisdiction of any other State, nor any State be formed by the junction of two or more States, or parts of States, without the consent of the legislatures of the States concerned as well as of the Congress.

---

[7]See the Eleventh Amendment.
[8]See the Fourteenth Amendment, Sec. 1.
[9]See the Thirteenth Amendment.

2. The Congress shall have power to dispose of and make all needful rules and regulations respecting the territory or other property belonging to the United States; and nothing in this Constitution shall be so construed as to prejudice any claims of the United States, or of any particular State.

Section 4. The United States shall guarantee to every State in this Union a republican form of government, and shall protect each of them against invasion; and on application of the legislature, or of the executive (when the legislature cannot be convened) against domestic violence.

Article V

The Congress, whenever two thirds of both Houses shall deem it necessary, shall propose amendments to this Constitution, or, on the application of the legislatures of two thirds of the several States, shall call a convention for proposing amendments, which in either case shall be valid to all intents and purposes, as part of this Constitution, when ratified by the legislatures of three fourths of the several States, or by conventions in three fourths thereof, as the one or the other mode of ratification may be proposed by the Congress; Provided that no amendment which may be made prior to the year one thousand eight hundred and eight shall in any manner affect the first and fourth clauses in the ninth section of the first article; and that no State, without its consent, shall be deprived of its equal suffrage in the Senate.

Article VI

1. All debts contracted and engagements entered into, before the adoption of this Constitution, shall be as valid against the United States under this Constitution, as under the Confederation.[10]

2. This Constitution, and the laws of the United States which shall be made in pursuance thereof; and all treaties made, or which shall be made, under the authority of the United States, shall be the supreme law of the land; and the judges in every State shall be bound thereby, any thing in the Constitution or laws of any State to the contrary notwithstanding.

3. The senators and representatives before mentioned, and the members of the several State legislatures, and all executive and judicial officers, both of the United States and of the several States, shall be bound by oath or affirmation to support this Constitution; but no religious test shall ever be required as a qualification to any office or public trust under the United States.

Article VII

The ratification of the conventions of nine States shall be sufficient for the establishment of this Constitution between the States so ratifying the same.

Done in Convention by the unanimous consent of the States present the seventeenth day of September in the year of our Lord one thousand seven hundred and eighty-

seven, and of the independence of the United States of America the twelfth. In witness whereof we have hereunto subscribed our names.

[Names omitted]

* * *

Articles in addition to, and amendment of, the Constitution of the United States of America, proposed by Congress, and ratified by the legislatures of the several States, pursuant to the fifth article of the original Constitution.

Amendment I [First ten amendments ratified December 15, 1791]

Congress shall make no law respecting an establishment of religion, or prohibiting the free exercise thereof; or abridging the freedom of speech, or of the press; or the right of the people peaceably to assemble, and to petition the government for a redress of grievances.

Amendment II

A well regulated militia, being necessary to the security of a free State, the right of the people to keep and bear arms, shall not be infringed.

Amendment III

No soldier shall, in time of peace be quartered in any house, without the consent of the owner, nor in time of war, but in a manner to be prescribed by law.

Amendment IV

The right of the people to be secure in their persons, houses, papers, and effects, against unreasonable searches and seizures, shall not be violated, and no warrants shall issue, but upon probable cause, supported by oath or affirmation, and particularly describing the place to be searched, and the persons or things to be seized.

Amendment V

No person shall be held to answer for a capital or otherwise infamous crime, unless on a presentment or indictment of a grand jury, except in cases arising in the land or naval forces, or in the militia, when in actual service in time of war or public danger; nor shall any person be subject for the same offense to be twice put in jeopardy of life or limb; nor shall be compelled in any criminal case to be a witness against himself, nor be deprived of life, liberty, or property, without due process of law; nor shall private property be taken for public use, without just compensation.

Amendment VI

In all criminal prosecutions, the accused shall enjoy the right to a speedy and public trial, by an impartial jury of the State and district wherein the crime shall have been committed, which district shall have been previously ascertained by law, and to be informed of the nature and cause of the accusation; to be confronted with the witnesses against him; to have compulsory process for obtaining witnesses in his favor, and to have the assistance of counsel for his defense.

---

[10]See the Fourteenth Amendment, Sec. 4.

Amendment VII

In suits at common law, where the value in controversy shall exceed twenty dollars, the right of trial by jury shall be preserved, and no fact tried by a jury shall be otherwise reexamined in any court of the United States, than according to the rules of the common law.

Amendment VIII

Excessive bail shall not be required, nor excessive fines imposed, nor cruel and unusual punishments inflicted.

Amendment IX

The enumeration in the Constitution of certain rights shall not be construed to deny or disparage others retained by the people.

Amendment X

The powers not delegated to the United States by the Constitution, nor prohibited by it to the States, are reserved to the States respectively, or to the people.

Amendment XI [January 8, 1798]

The judicial power of the United States shall not be construed to extend to any suit in law or equity, commended or prosecuted against one of the United States by citizens of another State, or by citizens or subjects of any foreign State.

Amendment XII [September 25, 1804]

The electors shall meet in their respective States, and vote by ballot for President and Vice President, one of whom, at least, shall not be an inhabitant of the same State with themselves; they shall name in their ballots the person voted for as President, and in distinct ballots, the person voted for as Vice President, and they shall make distinct lists of all persons voted for as President and of all persons voted for as Vice President, and of the number of votes for each, which lists they shall sign and certify, and transmit sealed to the seat of the government of the United States, directed to the President of the Senate;—The President of the Senate shall, in the presence of the Senate and House of Representatives, open all the certificates and the votes shall then be counted;—The person having the greatest number of votes for President, shall be the President, if such number be a majority of the whole number of electors appointed; and if no person have such majority, then from the persons having the highest numbers not exceeding three on the list of those voted for as President, the House of Representatives shall choose immediately, by ballot, the President. But in choosing the President, the votes shall be taken by States, the representation from each State having one vote; a quorum for this purpose shall consist of a member or members from two thirds of the States, and a majority of all the States shall be necessary to a choice. And if the House of Representatives shall not choose a President whenever the right of choice shall devolve upon them, before the fourth day of March next following, then the Vice President shall act as President, as in the case of the death or other constitutional disability of the President.

The person having the greatest number of votes as Vice President shall be the Vice President, if such number be a majority of the whole number of electors appointed, and if no person have a majority, then from the two highest numbers on the list, the Senate shall choose the Vice President; a quorum for the purpose shall consist of two thirds of the whole number of Senators, and a majority of the whole number shall be necessary to a choice. But no person constitutionally ineligible to the office of President shall be eligible to that of Vice President of the United States.

Amendment XIII [December 18, 1865]

Section 1. Neither slavery nor involuntary servitude, except as a punishment for crime whereof the party shall have been duly convicted, shall exist within the United States, or any place subject to their jurisdiction.

Section 2. Congress shall have power to enforce this article by appropriate legislation.

Amendment XIV [July 28, 1868]

Section 1. All persons born or naturalized in the United States, and subject to the jurisdiction thereof, are citizens of the United States and of the State wherein they reside. No State shall make or enforce any law which shall abridge the privileges or immunities of citizens of the United States; nor shall any State deprive any person of life, liberty, or property, without due process of law; nor deny to any person within its jurisdiction the equal protection of the laws.

Section 2. Representatives shall be apportioned among the several States according to their respective numbers, counting the whole number of persons in each State, excluding Indians not taxed. But when the right to vote at any election for the choice of electors for President and Vice President of the United States, representatives in Congress, the executive and judicial officers of a State, or the members of the legislature thereof, is denied to any of the male inhabitants of such State, being twenty-one years of age, and citizens of the United States, or in any way abridged, except for participating in rebellion, or other crime, the basis of representation there shall be reduced in the proportion which the number of such male citizens shall bear to the whole number of male citizens twenty-one years of age in such State.

Section 3. No person shall be a senator or representative in Congress, or elector of President and Vice President, or hold any office, civil or military, under the United States, or under any State, who having previously taken an oath, as a member of Congress, or as an officer of the United States, or as a member of any State legislature, or as an executive or judicial officer of any State, to support the Constitution of the United States, shall have engaged in insurrection or rebellion against the same, or given aid or comfort to the enemies thereof. But Congress may by a vote of two thirds of each House, remove such disability.

Section 4. The validity of the public debt of the United States, authorized by law, including debts incurred for payment of pensions and bounties for services in suppressing insurrection or rebellion; shall not be questioned.

But neither the United States nor any State shall assume or pay any debt or obligation incurred in aid of insurrection or rebellion against the United States, or any claim for the loss or emancipation of any slave; but all such debts, obligations, and claims shall be held illegal and void.

Section 5. The Congress shall have the power to enforce, by appropriate legislation, the provisions of this article.

Amendment XV [March 30, 1870]

Section 1. The right of citizens of the United States to vote shall not be denied or abridged by the United States or by any State on account of race, color, or previous condition of servitude.

Section 2. The Congress shall have power to enforce this article by appropriate legislation.

Amendment XVI [February 25, 1913]

The Congress shall have power to lay and collect taxes on incomes, from whatever source derived, without apportionment among the several States, and without regard to any census or enumeration.

Amendment XVII [May 31, 1913]

The Senate of the United States shall be composed of two senators from each State, elected by the people thereof, for six years; and each senator shall have one vote. The electors in each State shall have the qualifications requisite for electors of the most numerous branch of the State legislature.

When vacancies happen in the representation of any State in the Senate, the executive authority of such State shall issue writs of election to fill such vacancies: Provided, That the legislature of any State may empower the executive thereof to make temporary appointments until the people fill the vacancies by election as the legislature may direct.

This amendment shall not be so construed as to affect the election or term of any senator chosen before it becomes valid as part of the Constitution.

Amendment XVIII'' [January 29, 1919]

After one year from the ratification of this article, the manufacture, sale, or transportation of intoxicating liquors within, the importation thereof into, or the exportation thereof from the United States and all territory subject to the jurisdiction thereof for beverage purposes is thereby prohibited.

The Congress and the several States shall have concurrent power to enforce this article by appropriate legislation.

This article shall be inoperative unless it shall have been ratified as an amendment to the Constitution by the legislatures of the several States, as provided in the constitution, within seven years from the date of the submission hereof to the States by Congress.

Amendment XIX [August 26, 1920]

The right of citizens of the United States to vote shall not be denied or abridged by the United States or by any State on account of sex.

Congress shall have the power to enforce this article by appropriate legislation.

Amendment XX [January 23, 1933]

Section 1. The terms of the President and Vice President shall end at noon on the 20th day of January and the terms of Senators and Representatives at noon on the 3d day of January, of the years in which such terms would have ended if this article had not been ratified; and the terms of their successors shall then begin.

Section 2. The Congress shall assemble at least once in every year, and such meeting shall begin at noon on the 3d day of January, unless they shall by law appoint a different day.

Section 3. If, at the time fixed for the beginning of the term of President, the President-elect shall have died, the Vice President-elect shall become President. If a President shall not have been chosen before the time fixed for the beginning of his term, or if the President-elect shall have failed to qualify, then the Vice President-elect shall act as President until a President shall have qualified; and the Congress may by law provide for the case wherein neither a President-elect nor a Vice President-elect shall have qualified, declaring who shall then act as President, or the manner in which one who is to act shall be selected, and such person shall act accordingly until a President or Vice President shall have qualified.

Section 4. The Congress may by law provide for the case of the death of any of the persons from whom, the House of Representatives may choose a President whenever the right of choice shall have devolved upon them, and for the case of the death of any of the persons from whom the Senate may choose a Vice President whenever the right of choice shall have devolved upon them.

Section 5. Sections 1 and 2 shall take effect on the 15th day of October following the ratification of this article.

Section 6. This article shall be inoperative unless it shall have been ratified as an amendment to the Constitution by the legislatures of three-fourths of the several States within seven years from the date of its submission.

Amendment XXI [December 5, 1933]

Section 1. The Eighteenth Article of amendment to the Constitution of the United States is hereby repealed.

Section 2. The transportation or importation into any State, Territory, or possession of the United States for delivery or use therein of intoxicating liquors in violation of the laws thereof, is hereby prohibited.

Section 3. This article shall be inoperative unless it shall have been ratified as an amendment to the Constitution by conventions in the several States, as provided in the Constitution, within seven years from the date of the submission thereof to the States by the Congress.

''Repealed by the Twenty-first Amendment.

Amendment XXII [March 1, 1951]

No person shall be elected to the office of the President more than twice, and no person who has held the office of President, or acted as President, for more than two years of a term to which some other person was elected President shall be elected to the office of the President more than once.

But this article shall not apply to any person holding the office of President when this article was proposed by the Congress, and shall not prevent any person who may be holding the office of President, or acting as President, during the term within which this article becomes operative from holding the office of President or acting as President during the remainder of such term.

This article shall be inoperative unless it shall have been ratified as an amendment to the Constitution by the legislatures of three-fourths of the several States within seven years from the date of its submission to the States by the Congress.

Amendment XXIII [March 29, 1961]

Section 1. The District constituting the seat of Government of the United States shall appoint in such manner as the Congress may direct.

A number of electors of President and Vice President equal to the whole number of Senators and Representatives in Congress to which the District would be entitled if it were a State, but in no event more than the least populous State; they shall be in addition to those appointed by the States, but they shall be considered, for the purposes of the election of President and Vice President, to be electors appointed by a State; and they shall meet in the District and perform such duties as provided by the twelfth article of amendment.

Section 2. The Congress shall have power to enforce this article by appropriate legislation.

Amendment XXIV [January 23, 1964]

Section 1. The right of citizens of the United States to vote in any primary or other election for President or Vice President, for electors for President or Vice President, or for Senator or Representative in Congress, shall not be denied or abridged by the United States or any State by reason of failure to pay any poll tax or other tax.

Section 2. The Congress shall have power to enforce this article by appropriate legislation.

Amendment XXV [February 10, 1967]

Section 1. In case of the removal of the President from office or of his death or resignation, the Vice President shall become President.

Section 2. Whenever there is a vacancy in the office of the Vice President, the President shall nominate a Vice President who shall take office upon confirmation by a majority of both Houses of Congress.

Section 3. Whenever the President transmits to the President pro tempore of the Senate and the Speaker of the House of Representatives his written declaration that he is unable to discharge the powers and duties of his office, and until he transmits to them a written declaration to the contrary, such powers and duties shall be discharged by the Vice President as Acting President.

Section 4. Whenever the Vice president and a majority of either the principal officers of the executive departments or of such other body as Congress may by law provide, transmit to the President pro tempore of the Senate and the Speaker of the House of Representatives their written declaration that the President is unable to discharge the powers and duties of his office, the Vice President shall immediately assume the powers and duties of the office as Acting President.

Thereafter, when the President transmits to the President pro tempore of the Senate and the Speaker of the House of Representatives his written declaration that no inability exists, he shall resume the powers and duties of his office unless the Vice President and a majority of either the principal officers of the executive departments or of such other body as Congress may by law provide, transmit within four days to the President pro tempore of the Senate and the Speaker of the House of Representatives their written declaration that the President is unable to discharge the powers and duties of his office. Thereupon Congress shall decide the issue, assembling within forty-eight hours for that purpose if not in session. If the Congress, within twenty-one days after receipt of the latter written declaration, or, if Congress is not in session, within twenty-one days after Congress is required to assemble, determines by two-thirds vote of both Houses that the President is unable to discharge the powers and duties of his office, the Vice President shall continue to discharge the same as Acting President; otherwise, the President shall resume the powers and duties of his office.

Amendment XXVI [June 30, 1971]

Section 1. The right of citizens of the United States who are eighteen years of age or older to vote shall not be denied or abridged by the United States or by any State on account of age.

Section 2. The Congress shall have power to enforce this article by appropriate legislation.

Amendment XXVII[12] [May 7, 1992]

No law, varying the compensation for services of the Senators and Representatives, shall take effect until an election of Representatives shall have intervened.

---

[12] James Madison proposed this amendment in 1789 together with the ten amendments that were adopted as the Bill of Rights, but it failed to win ratification at the time. Congress, however, had set no deadline for its ratification, and over the years—particularly in the 1980s and 1990s—many states voted to add it to the Constitution. With the ratification of Michigan in 1992 it passed the threshold of 3/4ths of the states required for adoption, but because the process took more than 200 years, its validity remains in doubt.

PRESIDENTS AND VICE PRESIDENTS

1. George Washington (1789)
   John Adams (1789)
2. John Adams (1797)
   Thomas Jefferson (1797)
3. Thomas Jefferson (1801)
   Aaron Burr (1801)
   George Clinton (1805)
4. James Madison (1809)
   George Clinton (1809)
   Elbridge Gerry (1813)
5. James Monroe (1817)
   Daniel D. Thompkins (1817)
6. John Quincy Adams (1825)
   John C. Calhoun (1825)
7. Andrew Jackson (1829)
   John C. Calhoun (1829)
   Martin Van Buren (1833)
8. Martin Van Buren (1837)
   Richard M. Johnson (1837)
9. William H. Harrison (1841)
   John Tyler (1841)
10. John Tyler (1841)
11. James K. Polk (1845)
    George M. Dallas (1845)
12. Zachary Taylor (1849)
    Millard Fillmore (1849)
13. Millard Fillmore (1850)
14. Franklin Pierce (1853)
    William R. King (1853)
15. James Buchanan (1857)
    John C. Breckinridge (1857)
16. Abraham Lincoln (1861)
    Hannibal Hamlin (1861)
    Andrew Johnson (1865)
17. Andrew Johnson (1865)
18. Ulysses S. Grant (1869)
    Schuyler Colfax (1869)
    Henry Wilson (1873)
19. Rutherford B. Hayes (1877)
    William A. Wheeler (1877)
20. James A. Garfield (1881)
    Chester A. Arthur (1881)
21. Chester A. Arthur (1881)
22. Grover Cleveland (1885)
    T. A. Hendricks (1885)
23. Benjamin Harrison (1889)
    Levi P. Morgan (1889)

24. Grover Cleveland (1893)
    Adlai E. Stevenson (1893)
25. William McKinley (1897)
    Garret A. Hobart (1897)
    Theodore Roosevelt (1901)
26. Theodore Roosevelt (1901)
    Charles Fairbanks (1905)
27. William H. Taft (1909)
    James S. Sherman (1909)
28. Woodrow Wilson (1913)
    Thomas R. Marshall (1913)
29. Warren G. Harding (1921)
    Calvin Coolidge (1921)
30. Calvin Coolidge (1923)
    Charles G. Dawes (1925)
31. Herbert C. Hoover (1929)
    Charles Curtis (1929)
32. Franklin D. Roosevelt (1933)
    John Nance Garner (1933)
    Henry A. Wallace (1941)
    Harry S. Truman (1945)
33. Harry S. Truman (1945)
    Alben W. Barkley (1949)
34. Dwight D. Eisenhower (1953)
    Richard M. Nixon (1953)
35. John F. Kennedy (1961)
    Lyndon B. Johnson (1961)
36. Lyndon B. Johnson (1963)
    Hubert H. Humphrey (1965)
37. Richard M. Nixon (1969)
    Spiro T. Agnew (1969)
    Gerald R. Ford (1973)
38. Gerald R. Ford (1974)
    Nelson A. Rockefeller (1974)
39. James E. Carter Jr. (1977)
    Walter F. Mondale (1977)
40. Ronald W. Reagan (1981)
    George H. Bush (1981)
41. George H. Bush (1989)
    James D. Quayle III (1989)
42. William J. Clinton (1993)
    Albert Gore (1993)
43. William J. Clinton (1997)
    Albert Gore (1997)
44. George W. Bush (2001)
    Richard Cheney (2001)

PRESIDENTIAL ELECTIONS

Year	Number of States	Candidates	Party	Popular Vote*	Electoral Vote[†]	Percentage of Popular Vote
1789	11	GEORGE WASHINGTON	No party designations		69	
		John Adams			34	
		Other Candidates			35	
1792	15	GEORGE WASHINGTON	No party designations		132	
		John Adams			77	
		George Clinton			50	
		Other Candidates			5	
1796	16	JOHN ADAMS	Federalist		71	
		Thomas Jefferson	Democratic-Republican		68	
		Thomas Pinckney	Federalist		59	
		Aaron Burr	Democratic-Republican		30	
		Other Candidates			48	
1800	16	THOMAS JEFFERSON	Democratic-Republican		73	
		Aaron Burr	Democratic-Republican		73	
		John Adams	Federalist		65	
		Charles C. Pinckney	Federalist		64	
		John Jay	Federalist		1	
1804	17	THOMAS JEFFERSON	Democratic-Republican		162	
		Charles C. Pinckney	Federalist		14	
1808	17	JAMES MADISON	Democratic-Republican		122	
		Charles C. Pinckney	Federalist		47	
		George Clinton	Democratic-Republican		6	
1812	18	JAMES MADISON	Democratic-Republican		128	
		DeWitt Clinton	Federalist		89	
1816	19	JAMES MONROE	Democratic-Republican		183	
		Rufus King	Federalist		34	
1820	24	JAMES MONROE	Democratic-Republican		231	
		John Quincy Adams	Democratic-Republican		1	
1824	24	JOHN QUINCY ADAMS	Democratic-Republican	108,740	84	30.5
		Andrew Jackson	Democratic-Republican	153,544	99	43.1
		William H. Crawford	Democratic-Republican	46,618	41	13.1
		Henry Clay	Democratic-Republican	47,136	37	13.2
1828	24	ANDREW JACKSON	Democrat	647,286	178	56.0
		John Quincy Adams	National-Republican	508,064	83	44.0
1832	24	ANDREW JACKSON	Democrat	687,502	219	55.0
		Henry Clay	National-Republican	530,189	49	42.4
		William Wirt	Anti-Masonic	} 33,108	7	2.6
		John Floyd	National-Republican		11	

*Percentage of popular vote given for any election year may not total 100 percent because candidates receiving less than 1 percent of the popular vote have been omitted.

[†]Prior to the passage of the Twelfth Amendment in 1904, the electoral college voted for two presidential candidates; the runner-up became Vice-President. Data from *Historical Statistics of the United States, Colonial Times to 1957* (1961), pp. 682–683, and *The World Almanac.*

PRESIDENTIAL ELECTIONS
(continued)

Year	Number of States	Candidates	Party	Popular Vote	Electoral Vote	Percentage of Popular Vote
1836	26	MARTIN VAN BUREN	Democrat	765,483	170	50.9
		William H. Harrison	Whig		73	
		Hugh L. White	Whig		26	
		Daniel Webster	Whig	739,795	14	49.1
		W. P. Mangum	Whig		11	
1840	26	WILLIAM H. HARRISON	Whig	1,274,624	234	53.1
		Martin Van Buren	Democrat	1,127,781	60	46.9
1844	26	JAMES K. POLK	Democrat	1,338,464	170	49.6
		Henry Clay	Whig	1,300,097	105	48.1
		James G. Birney	Liberty	62,300		2.3
1848	30	ZACHARY TAYLOR	Whig	1,360,967	163	47.4
		Lewis Cass	Democrat	1,222,342	127	42.5
		Martin Van Buren	Free-Soil	291,263		10.1
1852	31	FRANKLIN PIERCE	Democrat	1,601,117	254	50.9
		Winfield Scott	Whig	1,385,453	42	44.1
		John P. Hale	Free-Soil	155,825		5.0
1856	31	JAMES BUCHANAN	Democrat	1,832,955	174	45.3
		John C. Frémont	Republican	1,339,932	114	33.1
		Millard Fillmore	American ("Know Nothing")	871,731	8	21.6
1860	33	ABRAHAM LINCOLN	Republican	1,865,593	180	39.8
		Stephen A. Douglas	Democrat	1,382,713	12	29.5
		John C. Breckinridge	Democrat	848,356	72	18.1
		John Bell	Constitutional Union	592,906	39	12.6
1864	36	ABRAHAM LINCOLN	Republican	2,206,938	212	55.0
		George B. McClellan	Democrat	1,803,787	21	45.0
1868	37	ULYSSES S. GRANT	Republican	3,013,421	214	52.7
		Horatio Seymour	Democrat	2,706,829	80	47.3
1872	37	ULYSSES S. GRANT	Republican	3,596,745	286	55.6
		Horace Greeley	Democrat	2,843,446	*	43.9
1876	38	RUTHERFORD B. HAYES	Republican	4,036,572	185	48.0
		Samuel J. Tilden	Democrat	4,284,020	184	51.0
1880	38	JAMES A. GARFIELD	Republican	4,453,295	214	48.5
		Winfield S. Hancock	Democrat	4,414,082	155	48.1
		James B. Weaver	Greenback-Labor	308,578		3.4
1884	38	GROVER CLEVELAND	Democrat	4,879,507	219	48.5
		James G. Blaine	Republican	4,850,293	182	48.2
		Benjamin F. Butler	Greenback-Labor	175,370		1.8
		John P. St. John	Prohibition	150,369		1.5
1888	38	BENJAMIN HARRISON	Republican	5,447,129	233	47.9
		Grover Cleveland	Democrat	5,537,857	168	48.6
		Clinton B. Fisk	Prohibition	249,506		2.2
		Anson J. Streeter	Union Labor	146,935		1.3

*Because of the death of Greeley, Democratic electors scattered their votes.

PRESIDENTIAL ELECTIONS
(continued)

Year	Number of States	Candidates	Party	Popular Vote	Electoral Vote	Percentage of Popular Vote
1892	44	GROVER CLEVELAND	Democrat	5,555,426	277	46.1
		Benjamin Harrison	Republican	5,182,690	145	43.0
		James B. Weaver	People's	1,029,846	22	8.5
		John Bidwell	Prohibition	264,133		2.2
1896	45	WILLIAM MCKINLEY	Republican	7,102,246	271	51.1
		William J. Bryan	Democrat	6,492,559	176	47.7
1900	45	WILLIAM MCKINLEY	Republican	7,218,491	292	51.7
		William J. Bryan	Democrat; Populist	6,356,734	155	45.5
		John C. Woolley	Prohibition	208,914		1.5
1904	45	THEODORE ROOSEVELT	Republican	7,628,461	336	57.4
		Alton B. Parker	Democrat	5,084,223	140	37.6
		Eugene V. Debs	Socialist	402,283		3.0
		Silas C. Swallow	Prohibition	258,536		1.9
1908	46	WILLIAM H. TAFT	Republican	7,675,320	321	51.6
		William J. Bryan	Democrat	6,412,294	162	43.1
		Eugene V. Debs	Socialist	420,793		2.8
		Eugene W. Chafin	Prohibition	253,840		1.7
1912	48	WOODROW WILSON	Democrat	6,296,547	435	41.9
		Theodore Roosevelt	Progressive	4,118,571	88	27.4
		William H. Taft	Republican	3,486,720	8	23.2
		Eugene V. Debs	Socialist	900,672		6.0
		Eugene W. Chafin	Prohibition	206,275		1.4
1916	48	WOODROW WILSON	Democrat	9,127,695	277	49.4
		Charles E. Hughes	Republican	8,533,507	254	46.2
		A. L. Benson	Socialist	585,113		3.2
		J. Frank Hanly	Prohibition	220,506		1.2
1920	48	WARREN G. HARDING	Republican	16,143,407	404	60.4
		James M. Cox	Democrat	9,130,328	127	34.2
		Eugene V. Debs	Socialist	919,799		3.4
		P. P. Christensen	Farmer-Labor	265,411		1.0
1924	48	CALVIN COOLIDGE	Republican	15,718,211	382	54.0
		John W. Davis	Democrat	8,385,283	136	28.8
		Robert M. La Follette	Progressive	4,831,289	13	16.6
1928	48	HERBERT C. HOOVER	Republican	21,391,993	444	58.2
		Alfred E. Smith	Democrat	15,016,169	87	40.9
1932	48	FRANKLIN D. ROOSEVELT	Democrat	22,809,638	472	57.4
		Herbert C. Hoover	Republican	15,758,901	59	39.7
		Norman Thomas	Socialist	881,951		2.2
1936	48	FRANKLIN D. ROOSEVELT	Democrat	27,752,869	523	60.8
		Alfred M. Landon	Republican	16,674,665	8	36.5
		William Lemke	Union	882,479		1.9
1940	48	FRANKLIN D. ROOSEVELT	Democrat	27,307,819	449	54.8
		Wendell L. Willkie	Republican	22,321,018	82	44.8
1944	48	FRANKLIN D. ROOSEVELT	Democrat	25,606,585	432	53.5
		Thomas E. Dewey	Republican	22,014,745	99	46.0

PRESIDENTIAL ELECTIONS
(continued)

Year	Number of States	Candidates	Party	Popular Vote	Electoral Vote	Percentage of Popular Vote
1948	48	HARRY S. TRUMAN	Democrat	24,105,812	303	49.5
		Thomas E. Dewey	Republican	21,970,065	189	45.1
		J. Strom Thurmond	States' Rights	1,169,063	39	2.4
		Henry A. Wallace	Progressive	1,157,172		2.4
1952	48	DWIGHT D. EISENHOWER	Republican	33,936,234	442	55.1
		Adlai E. Stevenson	Democrat	27,314,992	89	44.4
1956	48	DWIGHT D. EISENHOWER	Republican	35,590,472	457[*]	57.6
		Adlai E. Stevenson	Democrat	26,022,752	73	42.1
1960	50	JOHN F. KENNEDY	Democrat	34,227,096	303[†]	49.9
		Richard M. Nixon	Republican	34,108,546	219	49.6
1964	50	LYNDON B. JOHNSON	Democrat	42,676,220	486	61.3
		Barry M. Goldwater	Republican	26,860,314	52	38.5
1968	50	RICHARD M. NIXON	Republican	31,785,480	301	43.4
		Hubert H. Humphrey	Democrat	31,275,165	191	42.7
		George C. Wallace	American Independent	9,906,473	46	13.5
1972	50	RICHARD M. NIXON[‡]	Republican	47,165,234	520	60.6
		George S. McGovern	Democrat	29,168,110	17	37.5
1976	50	JIMMY CARTER	Democrat	40,828,929	297	50.1
		Gerald R. Ford	Republican	39,148,940	240	47.9
		Eugene McCarthy	Independent	739,256		
1980	50	RONALD REAGAN	Republican	43,201,220	489	50.9
		Jimmy Carter	Democrat	34,913,332	49	41.2
		John B. Anderson	Independent	5,581,379		
1984	50	RONALD REAGAN	Republican	53,428,357	525	59.0
		Walter F. Mondale	Democrat	36,930,923	13	41.0
1988	50	GEORGE BUSH	Republican	48,901,046	426	53.4
		Michael Dukakis	Democrat	41,809,030	111	45.6
1992	50	BILL CLINTON	Democrat	43,728,275	370	43.2
		George H.W. Bush	Republican	38,167,416	168	37.7
		H. Ross Perot	United We Stand, America	19,237,247		19.0
1996	50	BILL CLINTON	Democrat	45,590,703	379	49.0
		Robert Dole	Republican	37,816,307	159	41.0
		H. Ross Perot	Reform	7,874,283		8.0
2000	50	GEORGE W. BUSH	Republican	50,456,169	271	48.0
		Albert Gore	Democrat	50,996,116	266	48.0
		Ralph Nader	Green	2,767,176	0	3.0

[*]Walter B. Jones received 1 electoral vote.

[†]Harry F. Byrd received 15 electoral votes.

[‡]Resigned August 9, 1974: Vice President Gerald R. Ford became President.

ADMISSION OF STATES INTO THE UNION

State	Date of Admission	State	Date of Admission
1. Delaware	December 7, 1787	26. Michigan	January 26, 1837
2. Pennsylvania	December 12, 1787	27. Florida	March 3, 1845
3. New Jersey	December 18, 1787	28. Texas	December 29, 1845
4. Georgia	January 2, 1788	29. Iowa	December 28, 1846
5. Connecticut	January 9, 1788	30. Wisconsin	May 29, 1848
6. Massachusetts	February 6, 1788	31. California	September 9, 1850
7. Maryland	April 28, 1788	32. Minnesota	May 11, 1858
8. South Carolina	May 23, 1788	33. Oregon	February 14, 1859
9. New Hampshire	June 21, 1788	34. Kansas	January 29, 1861
10. Virginia	June 25, 1788	35. West Virginia	June 20, 1863
11. New York	July 26, 1788	36. Nevada	October 31, 1864
12. North Carolina	November 21, 1789	37. Nebraska	March 1, 1867
13. Rhode Island	May 29, 1790	38. Colorado	August 1, 1876
14. Vermont	March 4, 1791	39. North Dakota	November 2, 1889
15. Kentucky	June 1, 1792	40. South Dakota	November 2, 1889
16. Tennessee	June 1, 1796	41. Montana	November 8, 1889
17. Ohio	March 1, 1803	42. Washington	November 11, 1889
18. Louisiana	April 30, 1812	43. Idaho	July 3, 1890
19. Indiana	December 11, 1816	44. Wyoming	July 10, 1890
20. Mississippi	December 10, 1817	45. Utah	January 4, 1896
21. Illinois	December 3, 1818	46. Oklahoma	November 16, 1907
22. Alabama	December 14, 1819	47. New Mexico	January 6, 1912
23. Maine	March 15, 1820	48. Arizona	February 14, 1912
24. Missouri	August 10, 1821	49. Alaska	January 3, 1959
25. Arkansas	June 15, 1836	50. Hawaii	August 21, 1959

DEMOGRAPHICS OF THE UNITED STATES

POPULATION GROWTH

Year	Population	Percent Increase
1630	4,600	
1640	26,600	478.3
1650	50,400	90.8
1660	75,100	49.0
1670	111,900	49.0
1680	151,500	35.4
1690	210,400	38.9
1700	250,900	19.2
1710	331,700	32.2
1720	466,200	40.5
1730	629,400	35.0
1740	905,600	43.9
1750	1,170,800	29.3
1760	1,593,600	36.1
1770	2,148,100	34.8
1780	2,780,400	29.4
1790	3,929,214	41.3
1800	5,308,483	35.1
1810	7,239,881	36.4
1820	9,638,453	33.1
1830	12,866,020	33.5
1840	17,069,453	32.7
1850	23,191,876	35.9
1860	31,443,321	35.6
1870	39,818,449	26.6
1880	50,155,783	26.0
1890	62,947,714	25.5
1900	75,994,575	20.7
1910	91,972,266	21.0
1920	105,710,620	14.9
1930	122,775,046	16.1
1940	131,669,275	7.2
1950	150,697,361	14.5
1960	179,323,175	19.0
1970	203,235,298	13.3
1980	226,545,805	11.5
1990	248,709,873	9.8
2000	281,421,906	9.0

Source: *Historical Statistics of the United States* (1975); *Statistical Abstract by the United States* (1991, 1997). Population Estimates Program, Population Division, U.S. Census Bureau, April 2001.

Note: Figures for 1630–1780 include British colonies within limits of present United States only; Native American population included only in 1930 and thereafter.

WORKFORCE

Year	Total Number Workers (1000s)	Farmers as % of Total	Women as % of Total	% Workers in Unions
1810	2,330	84	(NA)	(NA)
1840	5,660	75	(NA)	(NA)
1860	11,110	53	(NA)	(NA)
1870	12,506	53	15	(NA)
1880	17,392	52	15	(NA)
1890	23,318	43	17	(NA)
1900	29,073	40	18	3
1910	38,167	31	21	6
1920	41,614	26	21	12
1930	48,830	22	22	7
1940	53,011	17	24	27
1950	59,643	12	28	25
1960	69,877	8	32	26
1970	82,049	4	37	25
1980	108,544	3	42	23
1990	117,914	3	45	16
2000	140,900	5.5	47	18.6

Source: *Historical Statistics of the United States* (1975); *Statistical Abstract of the United States* (1991, 1996). Population Estimates Program, Population Division, U.S. Census Bureau, April 2001.

VITAL STATISTICS
(per thousands)

Year	Births	Deaths	Marriages	Divorces
1800	55	(NA)	(NA)	(NA)
1810	54.3	(NA)	(NA)	(NA)
1820	55.2	(NA)	(NA)	(NA)
1830	51.4	(NA)	(NA)	(NA)
1840	51.8	(NA)	(NA)	(NA)
1850	43.3	(NA)	(NA)	(NA)
1860	44.3	(NA)	(NA)	(NA)
1870	38.3	(NA)	9.6 (1867)	0.3 (1867)
1880	39.8	(NA)	9.1 (1875)	0.3 (1875)
1890	31.5	(NA)	9.0	0.5
1900	32.3	17.2	9.3	0.7
1910	30.1	14.7	10.3	0.9
1920	27.7	13.0	12.0	1.6
1930	21.3	11.3	9.2	1.6
1940	19.4	10.8	12.1	2.0
1950	24.1	9.6	11.1	2.6
1960	23.7	9.5	8.5	2.2
1970	18.4	9.5	10.6	3.5
1980	15.9	8.8	10.6	5.2
1990	16.7	8.6	9.8	4.7
2000	14.8	8.8	8.5	4.1

Source: *Historical Statistics of the United States* (1975); *Statistical Abstract of the United States* (1991, 1997). Population Estimates Program, Population Division, U.S. Census Bureau, January 2001.

RACIAL COMPOSITION OF THE POPULATION
(in thousands)

Year	White	Black	Indian	Hispanic	Asian
1790	3,172	757	(NA)	(NA)	(NA)
1800	4,306	1,002	(NA)	(NA)	(NA)
1820	7,867	1,772	(NA)	(NA)	(NA)
1840	14,196	2,874	(NA)	(NA)	(NA)
1860	26,923	4,442	(NA)	(NA)	(NA)
1880	43,403	6,581	(NA)	(NA)	(NA)
1900	66,809	8,834	(NA)	(NA)	(NA)
1910	81,732	9,828	(NA)	(NA)	(NA)
1920	94,821	10,463	(NA)	(NA)	(NA)
1930	110,287	11,891	(NA)	(NA)	(NA)
1940	118,215	12,866	(NA)	(NA)	(NA)
1950	134,942	15,042	(NA)	(NA)	(NA)
1960	158,832	18,872	(NA)	(NA)	(NA)
1970	178,098	22,581	(NA)	(NA)	(NA)
1980	194,713	26,683	1,420	14,609	3,729
1990	205,710	30,486	2,065	22,354	7,458
2000	226,861	35,470	2,448	31,387	11,279

Source: U.S. Bureau of the Census, *U.S. Census of Population: 1940*, vol. II, part 1, and vol. IV, part 1; *1950*, vol. II, part 1; *1960*, vol. I, part 1; *1970*, vol. I, part B; and *Current Population Reports*, P25-1095 and P25-1104; *Statistical Abstract of the United States* (1997); Population Estimates Program, Population Division, U.S. Census Bureau, January 2001.

IMMIGRATION, BY ORIGIN
(in thousands)

Period	Europe	Americas	Asia
1820–30	106	12	—
1831–40	496	33	—
1841–50	1,597	62	—
1851–60	2,453	75	42
1861–70	2,065	167	65
1871–80	2,272	404	70
1881–90	4,735	427	70
1891–1900	3,555	39	75
1901–10	8,065	362	324
1911–20	4,322	1,144	247
1921–30	2,463	1,517	112
1931–40	348	160	16
1941–50	621	355	32
1951–60	1,326	997	150
1961–70	1,123	1,716	590
1971–80	800	1,983	1,588
1981–90	762	3,616	2,738
1991–2000	1,100	3,800	2,200

Source: *Historical Statistics of the United States* (1975); *Statistical Abstract of the United States* (1991); Population Estimates Program, Population Division, U.S. Census Bureau, April 2001.

TEXT CREDITS

Chapter 18: Text: From John W. Morris, Charles R. Goins and Edwin C. McReynolds, *Historical Atlas of Oklahoma, 3rd Edition*. Copyright © 1965, 1976, 1986 by the University of Oklahoma Press. Reprinted with the permission of the publishers.

Chapter 19: Text: From Bailyn et. al., *The Great Republic: A History of the American People*, Third Edition, Volume One. Copyright © 1985 by D.C. Heath and Company. Reprinted with permission of Houghton Mifflin Company.

Chapter 20: Text: From Carville Earle, *Geographical Inquiry and American Historical Problems*. Copyright © 1992 by the Board of Trustees of the Leland Stanford Junior University. With the permission of Stanford University Press, www.sup.org.

Chapter 22: Text: From *Atlas of American Women* by Barbara C. Shortridge, Macmillan, Copyright 1987. Reprinted by permission of The Gale Group.

Chapter 27: Text: From Allen Ginsberg, "Howl," from *Collected Poems, 1947–1980*. Copyright © 1955 by Allen Ginsberg. Reprinted by permission of HarperCollins Publishers Inc.

Chapter 29: Text: "The Times They are a-Changin" by Bob Dylan. Copyright © 1963, 1964 by Warner Bros. Inc. Copyright renewed 1991 by Special Rider Music. All rights reserved. International copyright secured. Reprinted by permission.

Chapter 31: Text: From Robert Griffith, *Major Problems in American History Since 1945*. Copyright © 1992 by D.C. Heath and Company. Used by permission of Houghton Mifflin Company.

INDEX

SINGLE PC LICENSE AGREEMENT AND LIMITED WARRANTY

READ THIS LICENSE CAREFULLY BEFORE OPENING THIS PACKAGE. BY OPENING THIS PACKAGE, YOU ARE AGREEING TO THE TERMS AND CONDITIONS OF THIS LICENSE. IF YOU DO NOT AGREE, DO NOT OPEN THE PACKAGE. PROMPTLY RETURN THE UNOPENED PACKAGE AND ALL ACCOMPANYING ITEMS TO THE PLACE YOU OBTAINED THEM.

1. GRANT OF LICENSE and OWNERSHIP: The enclosed computer programs ("Software") are licensed, not sold, to you by Prentice-Hall, Inc. ("We" or the "Company") and in consideration of your purchase or adoption of the accompanying Company textbooks and/or other materials, and your agreement to these terms. We reserve any rights not granted to you. You own only the disk(s) but we and/or our licensors own the Software itself. This license allows you to use and display your copy of the Software on a single computer (i.e., with a single CPU) at a single location for academic use only, so long as you comply with the terms of this Agreement. You may make one copy for back up, or transfer your copy to another CPU, provided that the Software is usable on only one computer.

2. RESTRICTIONS: You may not transfer or distribute the Software or documentation to anyone else. Except for backup, you may not copy the documentation or the Software. You may not network the Software or otherwise use it on more than one computer or computer terminal at the same time. You may not reverse engineer, disassemble, decompile, modify, adapt, translate, or create derivative works based on the Software or the Documentation. You may be held legally responsible for any copying or copyright infringement which is caused by your failure to abide by the terms of these restrictions.

3. TERMINATION: This license is effective until terminated. This license will terminate automatically without notice from the Company if you fail to comply with any provisions or limitations of this license. Upon termination, you shall destroy the Documentation and all copies of the Software. All provisions of this Agreement as to limitation and disclaimer of warranties, limitation of liability, remedies or damages, and our ownership rights shall survive termination.

4. LIMITED WARRANTY AND DISCLAIMER OF WARRANTY: Company warrants that for a period of 60 days from the date you purchase this SOFTWARE (or purchase or adopt the accompanying textbook), the Software, when properly installed and used in accordance with the Documentation, will operate in substantial conformity with the description of the Software set forth in the Documentation, and that for a period of 30 days the disk(s) on which the Software is delivered shall be free from defects in materials and workmanship under normal use. The Company does not warrant that the Software will meet your requirements or that the operation of the Software will be uninterrupted or error-free. Your only remedy and the Company's only obligation under these limited warranties is, at the Company's option, return of the disk for a refund of any amounts paid for it by you or replacement of the disk. THIS LIMITED WARRANTY IS THE ONLY WARRANTY PROVIDED BY THE COMPANY AND ITS LICENSORS, AND THE COMPANY AND ITS LICENSORS DISCLAIM ALL OTHER WARRANTIES, EXPRESS OR IMPLIED, INCLUDING WITHOUT LIMITATION, THE IMPLIED WARRANTIES OF MERCHANTABILITY AND FITNESS FOR A PARTICULAR PURPOSE. THE COMPANY DOES NOT WARRANT, GUARANTEE OR MAKE ANY REPRESENTATION REGARDING THE ACCURACY, RELIABILITY, CURRENTNESS, USE, OR RESULTS OF USE, OF THE SOFTWARE.

5. LIMITATION OF REMEDIES AND DAMAGES: IN NO EVENT, SHALL THE COMPANY OR ITS EMPLOYEES, AGENTS, LICENSORS, OR CONTRACTORS BE LIABLE FOR ANY INCIDENTAL, INDIRECT, SPECIAL, OR CONSEQUENTIAL DAMAGES ARISING OUT OF OR IN CONNECTION WITH THIS LICENSE OR THE SOFTWARE, INCLUDING FOR LOSS OF USE, LOSS OF DATA, LOSS OF INCOME OR PROFIT, OR OTHER LOSSES, SUSTAINED AS A RESULT OF INJURY TO ANY PERSON, OR LOSS OF OR DAMAGE TO PROPERTY, OR CLAIMS OF THIRD PARTIES, EVEN IF THE COMPANY OR AN AUTHORIZED REPRESENTATIVE OF THE COMPANY HAS BEEN ADVISED OF THE POSSIBILITY OF SUCH DAMAGES. IN NO EVENT SHALL THE LIABILITY OF THE COMPANY FOR DAMAGES WITH RESPECT TO THE SOFTWARE EXCEED THE AMOUNTS ACTUALLY PAID BY YOU, IF ANY, FOR THE SOFTWARE OR THE ACCOMPANYING TEXTBOOK. BECAUSE SOME JURISDICTIONS DO NOT ALLOW THE LIMITATION OF LIABILITY IN CERTAIN CIRCUMSTANCES, THE ABOVE LIMITATIONS MAY NOT ALWAYS APPLY TO YOU.

6. GENERAL: THIS AGREEMENT SHALL BE CONSTRUED IN ACCORDANCE WITH THE LAWS OF THE UNITED STATES OF AMERICA AND THE STATE OF NEW YORK, APPLICABLE TO CONTRACTS MADE IN NEW YORK, AND SHALL BENEFIT THE COMPANY, ITS AFFILIATES AND ASSIGNEES. HIS AGREEMENT IS THE COMPLETE AND EXCLUSIVE STATEMENT OF THE AGREEMENT BETWEEN YOU AND THE COMPANY AND SUPERSEDES ALL PROPOSALS OR PRIOR AGREEMENTS, ORAL, OR WRITTEN, AND ANY OTHER COMMUNICATIONS BETWEEN YOU AND THE COMPANY OR ANY REPRESENTATIVE OF THE COMPANY RELATING TO THE SUBJECT MATTER OF THIS AGREEMENT. If you are a U.S. Government user, this Software is licensed with "restricted rights" as set forth in subparagraphs (a)-(d) of the Commercial Computer-Restricted Rights clause at FAR 52.227-19 or in subparagraphs (c)(1)(ii) of the Rights in Technical Data and Computer Software clause at DFARS 252.227-7013, and similar clauses, as applicable.

Should you have any questions concerning this agreement please contact in writing: Legal Department, Prentice Hall, One Lake Street, Upper Saddle River, NJ 07458. If you need assistance with technical difficulties, call: 1-800-677-6337. If you wish to contact the Company for any reason, please contact in writing: Deborah O'Connell, Media Editor for Humanities, Prentice Hall, One Lake Street, Upper Saddle River, NJ 07458.